T0210702

Preface

The 13th International Conference on Applied Cryptography and Network Security (ACNS 2015) was held during June 2–5, 2015, at Columbia University in New York City.

The conference received 157 submissions. They went through a double-anonymous review process, and 33 papers were selected. We were helped by 50 Program Committee members and 138 external reviewers.

We were honored to host Matthew Green and Vitaly Shmatikov as invited speakers.

This volume represents the revised version of the accepted papers, along with the abstracts of the invited talks.

The Program Committee selected two papers to receive the Best Student Paper Award. To be eligible, papers had to be co-authored by a full-time student who presented the paper at the conference. This year's co-winners of the award were:

Alberto Compagno, Mauro Conti, Paolo Gasti, Luigi V. Mancini, Gene Tsudik, "Violating Consumer Anonymity: Geo-locating Nodes in Named Data Networking"

Esha Ghosh, Olga Ohrimenko, Roberto Tamassia, "Zero-Knowledge Authenticated Order Queries and Order Statistics on a List"

This year's conference was the result of a collaborative effort by four of us: Tal Malkin served as the program chair, selecting the Program Committee and leading their efforts in the careful selection of the papers that you will find in this volume. Vladimir Kolesnikov, Allison Bishop Lewko, and Michalis Polychronakis served as general chairs, taking care of all logistic and organizational needs, from the website, registration, publicity, sponsors, and all local arrangements required for hosting the conference at Columbia University.

We would like to thank the Program Committee members as well as the external reviewers for their volunteered hard work invested in selecting the program. We thank the ACNS Steering Committee for their support; Shai Halevi for providing his Web-review and submission system to be used for the conference, and for providing technical support; Marios Pomonis and Suphannee Sivakorn for their help with the local arrangements. We gratefully acknowledge the generous financial support of our industrial sponsors: Facebook and Google as golden sponsors, and AT&T as a silver sponsor. Finally, big thanks are due to all authors of submitted papers.

June 2015

Tal Malkin
Vladimir Kolesnikov
Allison Bishop Lewko
Michalis Polychronakis

Organization

Program Committee

Shweta Agrawal	IIT Delhi, India
Nuttapong Attrapadung	AIST, Japan
Alex Biryukov	University of Luxembourg, Luxembourg
John Black	University of Colorado at Boulder, USA
Alexandra Boldyreva	Georgia Tech, USA
Christina Brzuska	MSR Cambridge, UK
Christian Cachin	IBM Research – Zurich, Switzerland
Dario Catalano	University of Catania, Italy
Melissa Chase	MSR Redmond, USA
Jie Chen	East China Normal University, China
Liqun Chen	HP Labs, UK
Seung Geol Choi	US Naval Academy, USA
Ivan Damgrd	Aarhus University, Denmark
Jean Paul Degabriele	Royal Holloway University of London, UK
Itai Dinur	ENS, France
Nelly Fazio	City College, CUNY, USA
Phillipa Gill	Stony Brook University, USA
Dov Gordon	ACS, USA
Shai Halevi	IBM T.J. Watson Research Center, USA
Goichiro Hanaoka	AIST, Japan
Aggelos Kiayias	University of Athens, Greece
Ranjit Kumaresan	MIT, USA
Kwangsu Lee	Korea University, Korea
Tancrède Lepoint	CryptoExperts, France
Adriana Lopez-Alt	Google, USA
Nasir Memon	NYU Poly, USA
Andrew Miller	University of Maryland, USA
Payman Mohassel	Yahoo Labs, USA
David Naccache	ENS, France
Kobbi Nissim	Harvard University, USA and Ben-Gurion University, Israel
Yossef Oren	Columbia University, USA
Periklis Papakonstantinou	Tsinghua University, China
Charalampos Papamanthou	University of Maryland, USA
Vasilis Pappas	Appthority Inc., USA
Mathias Payer	Purdue University, USA
Thomas Peyrin	Nanyang Technological University, Singapore
David Pointcheval	ENS, France

Michalis Polychronakis	Stony Brook University, USA
Elizabeth Quaglia	Huawei Technologies, France
Carla Ràfols	Ruhr University Bochum, Germany
Mike Rosulek	Oregon State University, USA
Emily Shen	MIT Lincoln Laboratory, USA
François-Xavier Standaert	UC Louvain, Belgium
Michael Steiner	IBM Research – Bangalore, India
Vanessa Teague	University of Melbourne, Australia
Isamu Teranishi	NEC, Japan
Stefano Tessaro	UC Santa Barbara, USA
Arkady Yerukhimovich	MIT Lincoln Laboratory, USA
Moti Yung	Google and Columbia, USA
Jianying Zhou	Institute for Infocomm Research, Singapore

External Reviewers

Divesh Aggarwal	Nils Fleischhacker	Daniel Kraschewski
Shashank Agrawal	Benjamin Fuller	Hugo Krawczyk
Saikrishna Badrinarayan	Chaya Ganesh	Wang Lei
Foteini Baldimtsi	Aijun Ge	Fu Li
Carsten Baum	Rémi Géraud	Yong Li
Iddo Bentov	Vincent Grosso	Joseph Liu
Shaoying Cai	Tzipora Halevi	Vadim Lyubashevsky
Nishanth Chandran	Yoshikazu Hanatani	Nadia El Mrabet
Suresh Chari	Gottfried Herold	Alex Malozemoff
Cheng Chen	Felix Heuer	Takahiro Matsuda
Yu Chen	Takato Hirano	Alexander May
Carlos Cid	Jung Yeon Hwang	Weizhi Meng
Yann Le Corre	William E. Skeith III	Arno Mittelbach
Craig Costello	Hkon Jacobsen	Pierrick Méaux
Yuanxi Dai	Aayush Jain	Napa Naja
Bernardo David	Christian Janson	Toan Nguyen
Gareth Davies	Jeremy Jean	Antonio Nicolosi
Rafael Del Pino	Anthony Journault	Jesper Buus Nielsen
Patrick Derbez	Charanjit Jutla	Ivica Nikolic
Daniel Dinu	Ali El Kaafarani	Jianting Ning
Maria Dubovitskaya	Pierre Karpman	Jared Nishikawa
François Durvaux	Akinori Kawachi	Koji Nuida
Nico Döttling	Khoongming Khoo	Kazuma Ohara
Keita Emura	Dmitry Khovratovich	Satsuya Ohata
Jieun Eom	Dakshita Khurana	Jiaxin Pan
Pooya Farshim	Yuichi Komano	Giorgos Panagiotakos
Sebastian Faust	Venkata Kopala	Dimitris Papadopoulos
Houda Ferradi	Venkata Koppula	Stefano Paris
Ben Fisch	Ahmed E. Kosba	Jong Hwan Park

Seunghwan Park
Anat Paskin-Cherniavsky
Milinda Perera
Leo Perrin
Thomas Peters
Santos Merino Del Pozo
Orazio Puglisi
Mario Di Raimondo
Samuel Ranelucci
Chester Rebeiro
Francesco Regazzoni
Aditi Roy
Napa Sae-Bae
Katerina Samari
Kai Samelin
Somitra Sanadhya
Yu Sasaki

Dvir Schirman
Dominique Schröder
Jacob Schuldt
Minhye Seo
Kyoji Shibutani
SeongHan Shin
Hossein Siadati
Dale Sibborn
Cassandra Sparks
Le Su
Tadanori Teruya
Miaomiao Tian
Yiannis Tselekounis
Aleksei Udovenko
Mayank Varia
Vesselin Velichkov
Daniele Venturi

Christian Wachsmann
Bogdan Warinschi
Yohei Watanabe
Hongjun Wu
Keita Xagawa
Jia Xu
Sophia Yakoubov
Shota Yamada
Guang Yang
Yanjiang Yang
Attila Yavuz
Kazuki Yoneyama
Yu Yu
Thomas Zacharias
Bingsheng Zhang
Yupeng Zhang
Zongyang Zhang

Program Chair

Tal Malkin   Columbia University

General Chairs

Vladimir Kolesnikov   Bell Labs, USA
Allison Bishop Lewko   Columbia University, USA
Michalis Polychronakis   Stony Brook University, USA

Invited Talks

All Your SSL Are Belong To Us

Vitaly Shmatikov

Cornell Tech

Abstract. SSL/TLS is the de facto standard for secure Internet communications. Deployed widely in Web browsers and non-browser software, it is intended to provide end-to-end security even against active, man-in-the-middle attacks. This security fundamentally depends on correct validation of X.509 certificates presented when the connection is established.

I will first demonstrate that many SSL/TLS deployments are completely insecure against man-in-the-middle attacks. Vulnerable software includes cloud computing clients, merchant SDKs responsible for transmitting payment information from e-commerce sites to payment processors, online shopping software, and many forms of middleware. Even worse, several popular SSL/TLS implementations do not validate certificates correctly and thus all software based on them is generically insecure. These bugs affect even common Web browsers, where minor validation errors such as recent certificate expiration can mask serious issues such as failure to authenticate the Web server's identity.

I will then analyze the root causes of these vulnerabilities and describe how we used "frankencerts," a new methodology for automatically testing SSL/TLS implementations, to uncover dozens of subtle certificate validation bugs in popular SSL/TLS implementations.

From Strong Mathematics to Weak Cryptography

Matthew Green

Johns Hopkins University

Abstract. The past three decades have been a remarkable time for the science of cryptography. From the first provably-secure protocols to the practice-oriented work of the 1990s, the research community has accumulated a wealth of knowledge about secure protocol design. However, the distribution of this wealth has not been even. Even in 2015 we continue to see routine 'breaks' of core cryptographic standards and software, often caused by the continued use of obsolete primitives and protocol design techniques. These failures have serious consequences – ranging from the immediate cost of remediation to a long-term potential loss of confidence in security protocols.

In this talk I will discuss the interaction between the cryptographic research community and cryptographic community responsible for bringing cryptography into practice. I will summarize some of the recent and important research results related to core cryptographic standards, and how cryptographers have both impacted – or failed to impact – standards development. I will also discuss the implications of this interaction, and the how poor communication between communities may have facilitated some decryption efforts revealed by recent NSA leaks.

Contents

Secure Computation I: Primitives and New Models

Universally Verifiable Multiparty Computation from Threshold Homomorphic Cryptosystems

Berry Schoenmakers and Meilof Veeningen[(✉)]

Department of Mathematics and Computer Science, TU Eindhoven,
Eindhoven, The Netherlands
berry@win.tue.nl, m.veeningen@tue.nl

Abstract. Multiparty computation can be used for privacy-friendly out-sourcing of computations on private inputs of multiple parties. A computation is outsourced to several computation parties; if not too many are corrupted (e.g., no more than half), then they cannot determine the inputs or produce an incorrect output. However, in many cases, these guarantees are not enough: we need correctness even if *all* computation parties may be corrupted; and we need that correctness can be verified even by parties that did not participate in the computation. Protocols satisfying these additional properties are called "universally verifiable". In this paper, we propose a new security model for universally verifiable multiparty computation, and we present a practical construction, based on a threshold homomorphic cryptosystem. We also develop a multiparty protocol for jointly producing non-interactive zero-knowledge proofs, which may be of independent interest.

1 Introduction

Multiparty computation (MPC) provides techniques for privacy-friendly out-sourcing of computations. Intuitively, MPC aims to provide a cryptographic "black box" which receives private inputs from multiple "input parties"; performs a computation on these inputs; and provides the result to a "result party" (an input party, any third party, or the public). This black box is implemented by distributing the computation between multiple "computation parties", with privacy and correctness being guaranteed in case of passive corruptions (e.g., [BCD+09]), active corruption of a minority of computation parties (e.g., [CDN01]), or active corruption of all-but-one computation parties (e.g., [DPSZ12]).

However, multiparty computation typically does *not* provide any guarantees in case all computation parties are corrupted. That is, the result party has to trust that at least some of the computation parties did their job, and has no way of independently verifying the result. In particular, the result party has no way of proving to an external party that his computation result is indeed correct. *Universally verifiable* multiparty computation addresses these issues by requiring that the correctness of the result can be verified by any party, even if all computation parties are corrupt [dH12]. It was originally introduced in the context of e-voting [CF85,SK95], but it is relevant whenever MPC is applied in a setting where not all of the parties that provide inputs or obtain outputs are

© Springer International Publishing Switzerland 2015
T. Malkin et al. (Eds.): ACNS 2015, LNCS 9092, pp. 3–22, 2015.
DOI: 10.1007/978-3-319-28166-7_1

participants in the computation. In particular, apart from contexts like e-voting where "the public" or an external watchdog wants to be sure of correctness, it is also useful in scenarios where (many) different input parties outsource a computation to the cloud and require a correctness guarantee.

Unfortunately, the state-of-the-art on universally verifiable MPC is unsatisfactory. The concept of universally verifiable MPC was first proposed in [dH12], where it was also suggested that it can be achieved for MPC based on threshold homomorphic cryptosystems. However, [dH12] does not provide a rigorous security model for universal verifiability or analysis of the proposed construction; and the construction has some technical disadvantages (e.g., a proof size depending on the number of computation parties). The scheme recently proposed in [BDO14] solves part of the problem. Their protocols provide "public auditability", meaning that anybody can verify the result of a computation, but *only* if that result is public. In particular, it is not possible for a result party to prove just that an encryption of the result is correct, which is important if this result is to be used in a later protocol without being revealed.

In this paper, we propose a new security model for universally verifiable multiparty computation, and a practical construction achieving it. As in [dH12], we adapt the well-known actively secure MPC protocols based on threshold homomorphic cryptosystems from [CDN01, DN03]. Essentially, these protocols perform computations on encrypted values; security against active adversaries is achieved by letting parties prove correctness of their actions using interactive zero-knowledge proofs. Such interactive proofs only convince parties present at the computation; but making them non-interactive makes them convincing also to external parties. Concretely, the result of a computation is a set of encryptions of the inputs, intermediate values, and outputs of the computation, along with non-interactive zero-knowledge proofs of their correctness. Correctness of the result depends just on the correct set-up of the cryptosystem. Privacy holds under the original conditions of [CDN01], i.e., if under half of the computation parties are corrupted; but as we discuss, this threshold can be raised to $n-1$ at the expense of sacrificing robustness. (Note that when computing with encryptions, we cannot hope to achieve privacy if all computation parties are corrupted: this would essentially require fully homomorphic encryption.)

We improve on [dH12] in two main ways. First, we provide a security model for universal verifiability (in the random oracle model), and security proofs for our protocols in that model. Second, we propose a new "multiparty" variant of the Fiat-Shamir heuristic to make the zero-knowledge proofs non-interactive, which may be of independent interest. Compared to [dH12], it eliminates the need for trapdoor commitments. Moreover, it makes the proof size independent of the number of parties performing the computation. We achieve this latter advantage by homomorphically combining contributions from the different parties.

As such, universally verifiable MPC provides a practical alternative to recent (single-party) techniques for verifiable outsourcing. Specifically, many papers on verifiable computation focus on efficient verification, but do not cover privacy [PHGR13, WB13]. Those works that do provide privacy, achieve this by combining costly primitives, e.g., fully homomorphic encryption with verifiable

$a \in_R S$	sample a uniformly at random from S
$\mathsf{send}(v; \mathcal{P}), \mathsf{recv}(\mathcal{P})$	send v to/receive from $\mathcal{P}$ over secure channel
$\mathsf{bcast}(v)$	exchange v over broadcast channel
party $\mathcal{P}$ **do** S	let party $\mathcal{P}$ perform S; other parties do nothing
parties $i \in \mathcal{Q}$ **do** S	let parties $i \in \mathcal{Q}$ perform S in parallel
$\mathcal{H} : \{0,1\}^* \to \{0,1\}^{2l}$	cryptographic hash function (l security parameter)
$F \subset \mathcal{I} \cup \mathcal{P} \cup \{\mathcal{R}, \mathcal{V}\}$	global variable: set of parties found to misbehave
$\mathsf{paillierdecode}(x)$	threshold Paillier decoding (p. 6):
	$((x-1) \div N)(4\Delta^2)^{-1} \bmod N$
$\mathsf{fsprove}(\Sigma; v; w; aux)$	Fiat-Shamir proof (p. 8): $(a,s) := \Sigma.\mathsf{ann}(v,w)$;
	$c := \mathcal{H}(v\|a\|aux); r := \Sigma.\mathsf{res}(v,w,a,s,c); \pi := (a,c,r)$
$\mathsf{fsver}(\Sigma; v; a, c, r; aux)$	verification of Fiat-Shamir Σ-proof (p. 8):
	$\mathcal{H}(v\|a\|aux) = c \wedge \Sigma.\mathsf{ver}(v; a; c; r)$

Fig. 1. Notation in algorithms, protocols, and processes

computation [FGP14]; or functional encryption with garbled circuits [GKP+13]. A recent work [ACG+14] also considers the possibility of achieving verifiable computation with privacy by distributing the computation; but it does not guarantee correctness if all computation parties are corrupted, nor does it allow third parties to be convinced of this fact. In contrast, our methods guarantee correctness even if all computation parties are corrupted, and even convince other parties than the input party. In particular, any third party can be convinced, and the computation may involve the inputs of multiple mutually distrusting input parties. Moreover, in contrast to the above works, our methods rely on basic cryptographic primitives such as Σ-protocols and the threshold homomorphic Paillier cryptosystem, readily available nowadays in cryptographic libraries like SCAPI [EFLL12].

Outline. First, we briefly recap the CDN scheme for secure computation in the presence of active adversaries from [CDN01,DN03], instantiated using Paillier encryption (Sect. 2). Then, we show how the proofs in this protocol can be made non-interactive using the Fiat-Shamir heuristic and our new multiparty variant (Sect. 3). Finally, we propose a security model for universally verifiable MPC, and show that CDN with non-interactive proofs is universally verifiable (Sect. 4). We conclude in Sect. 5. We list potentially non-obvious notation in our pseudocode in Fig. 1.

2   Secure Computation from Threshold Cryptography

We review the "CDN protocol" [CDN01] for secure computation in the presence of active adversaries based on a threshold homomorphic cryptosystem. The protocol involves m input parties $i \in \mathcal{I}$, n computation parties $i \in \mathcal{P}$, and a result party $\mathcal{R}$. The aim of the protocol is to compute a function $f(x_1, \ldots, x_m)$ (seen as an arithmetic circuit) on private inputs x_i of the input parties, such that the result party obtains the result.

2.1   Computation Using a Threshold Homomorphic Cryptosystem

The protocol uses a (t, n)-threshold homomorphic cryptosystem, with $t = \lceil n/2 \rceil$. In such a cryptosystem, anybody can encrypt a plaintext using the public key; add two ciphertexts to obtain a (uniquely determined) encryption of the sum of the corresponding plaintexts; and multiply a ciphertext by a constant to obtain a (uniquely determined) encryption of the product of the plaintext with the constant. Decryption is only possible if at least t out of the n decryption keys are known. A well-known homomorphic cryptosystem is the Paillier cryptosystem [Pai99]: here, the public key is an RSA modulus $N = pq$; $a \in \mathbb{Z}_N$ is encrypted with randomness $r \in \mathbb{Z}_N^*$ as $(1 + N)^a r^N \in \mathbb{Z}_{N^2}^*$; and the product of two ciphertexts is an encryption of the sum of the two corresponding plaintexts. (From now on, we suppress moduli for readability.) A threshold variant of this cryptosystem was presented in [DJ01]. The (threshold) decryption procedure is a bit involved; we postpone its discussion until Sect. 2.2. The CDN protocol can also be instantiated with other cryptosystems; but in this paper, we will focus on the Paillier instantiation.

Computation of $f(x_1, \ldots, x_m)$ is performed in three phases: the input phase, the computation phase, and the output phase. In the input phase, each input party encrypts its input x_i, and broadcasts the encryption X_i. In the computation phase, the function f is evaluated gate-by-gate. Addition and subtraction are performed using the homomorphic property of the encryption scheme. For multiplication[1] of X and Y, each computation party $i \in \mathcal{P}$ chooses a random value d_i, and broadcasts encryptions D_i of d_i and E_i of $d_i \cdot y$. The computation parties then compute $X \cdot D_1 \cdots D_n$, and threshold decrypt it to learn $x + d_1 + \ldots + d_n$. Observe that this allows them to compute an encryption of $(x + d_1 + \ldots + d_n) \cdot y$, and hence, using the E_i, also an encryption of $x \cdot y$. Finally, in the output phase, when the result of the computation has been computed as encryption X of x, the result party obtains x by broadcasting random encryption D of d and obtaining a threshold decryption $x - d$ of $X \cdot D^{-1}$.

Active security is achieved by letting the parties prove correctness of all information they exchange. Namely, the input parties prove knowledge of their inputs X_i (this prevents parties from choosing inputs depending on other inputs). The computation parties prove knowledge of D_i, and prove that E_i is indeed a correct multiplication of D_i and Y; and they prove the correctness of their contributions to the threshold decryption of $X \cdot D_1 \cdots D_n$ and $X \cdot D^{-1}$. Finally, the result party proves knowledge of D. We now discuss these proofs of correctness and their influence on the security of the overall protocol.

2.2   Proving Correctness of Results

The techniques in the CDN protocol for proving correctness are based on Σ-protocols. Recall that a Σ-protocol for a binary relation R is a three-move protocol in which a potentially malicious prover convinces a honest verifier that he

---

[1] Here, we use the improved multiplication protocol from [DN03]: the multiplication protocol from [CDN01] has a subtle problem, in which the subroutine for additively sharing an encrypted value requires unknown encryption randomness to be returned.

Σ-Protocol 1. Σ_{PK}: Proof of plaintext knowledge

[**Relation**] $R = \{(X; x, r) \mid X = (1 + N)^x r^N\}$

[**Announcement**] $\Sigma.\mathsf{ann}(X; x, r) :=$
$\quad a \in_R \mathbb{Z}_N; u \in_R \mathbb{Z}_N^*; A := (1 + N)^a u^N; \mathbf{return}\ (A; a, u)$

[**Response**] $\Sigma.\mathsf{res}(X; x, r; A; a, u; c) :=$
$\quad t := \lfloor (a + cx)/N \rfloor; d := a + cx; e := u r^c (1 + N)^t; \mathbf{return}\ (d, e)$

[**Verification**] $\Sigma.\mathsf{ver}(X; A; c; d, e) := (1 + N)^d e^N \overset{?}{=} A X^c$

[**Extractor**] $\Sigma.\mathsf{ext}(X; A; c; c'; d, e; d', e') :=$
$\quad \alpha, \beta := \text{"values such that } \alpha(c - c') + \beta N = 1\text{"};\ \mathbf{return}\ ((d - d')\alpha, (e/e')^\alpha X^\beta)$

[**Simulator**] $\Sigma.\mathsf{sim}(X; c) :=$
$\quad d \in_R \mathbb{Z}_N; e \in_R \mathbb{Z}_N^*; A := (1 + N)^d e^N X^{-c}; \mathbf{return}\ (A; c; d, e)$

---

knows a *witness* w for *statement* v such that $(v; w) \in R$. First, the prover sends an *announcement* (computed using algorithm $\Sigma.\mathsf{ann}$) to the verifier; the verifier responds with a uniformly random *challenge*; and the prover sends his *response* (computed using algorithm $\Sigma.\mathsf{res}$), which the verifier verifies (using predicate $\Sigma.\mathsf{ver}$). Σ-protocols satisfy the following properties:

Definition 1. *Let $R \subset V \times W$ be a binary relation and $L_R = \{v \in V \mid \exists w \in W : (v; w) \in R\}$ its language. Let Σ be a collection of p.p.t. algorithms $\Sigma.\mathsf{ann}$, $\Sigma.\mathsf{res}$, $\Sigma.\mathsf{sim}$, $\Sigma.\mathsf{ext}$, and polynomial time predicate $\Sigma.\mathsf{ver}$. Let C be a finite set called the* challenge space. *Then Σ is a Σ-protocol* for relation R *if:*

Completeness. *If $(a; s) \leftarrow \Sigma.\mathsf{ann}(v; w)$, $c \in C$, and $r \leftarrow \Sigma.\mathsf{res}(v; w; a; s; c)$, then $\Sigma.\mathsf{ver}(v; a; c; r)$.*

Special Soundness. *If $v \in V$, $c \neq c'$, $\Sigma.\mathsf{ver}(v; a; c; r)$, and $\Sigma.\mathsf{ver}(v; a; c'; r')$, then $w \leftarrow \Sigma.\mathsf{ext}(v; a; c; c'; r; r')$ satisfies $(v; w) \in R$.*

Special Honest-Verifier Zero-Knowledgeness. *If $v \in L_R$, $c \in C$, then $(a; r) \leftarrow \Sigma.\mathsf{sim}(v; c)$ has the same probability distribution as $(a; r)$ obtained by $(a; s) \leftarrow \Sigma.\mathsf{ann}(v; w)$, $r \leftarrow \Sigma.\mathsf{res}(v; w; a; s; c)$. If $v \notin L_R$, then $(a; r) \leftarrow \Sigma.\mathsf{sim}(v; c)$ satisfies $\Sigma.\mathsf{ver}(v; a; c; r)$.*

Completeness states that a protocol between a honest prover and verifier succeeds; special soundness states that there exists an extractor $\Sigma.\mathsf{ext}$ that can extract a witness from two conversations with the same announcement; and special honest-verifier zero-knowledgeness states that there exists a simulator $\Sigma.\mathsf{sim}$ that can generate conversations with the same distribution as full protocol runs without knowing the witness. While special honest-verifier zero-knowledgeness demands an identical distribution for the simulation, statistical indistinguishability is sufficient for our purposes; in this case, we speak of a "statistical Σ-protocol". In the remainder, we will need that our Σ-protocols have "non-trivial announcements", in the sense that when $(a; r)$ and $(a'; r')$ are both obtained from $\Sigma.\mathsf{sim}(v; c)$, then with overwhelming probability, $a \neq a'$. (Indeed, this will be the case for all Σ-protocols in this paper.) This property, which is required

---

Σ-Protocol 2. Σ_{CM}: Proof of correct multiplication

[Relation] $R = \{(X, Y, Z; y, r, s) \mid Y = (1 + N)^y r^N \wedge Z = X^y s^N\}$

[Announcement] $\Sigma.\mathsf{ann}(X, Y, Z; y, r, s) :=$

$a \in_R \mathbb{Z}_N; u, v \in_R \mathbb{Z}_N^*; A := (1 + N)^a u^N; B := X^a v^N;$ **return** $(A, B; a, u, v)$

[Response] $\Sigma.\mathsf{res}(X, Y, Z; y, r, s; A, B; a, u, v; c) :=$

$t := \lfloor (a + cy)/N \rfloor; d := a + cy; \; e := u r^c (1 + N)^t; f := v X^t s^c; $ **return** (d, e, f)

[Verification] $\Sigma.\mathsf{ver}(X, Y, Z; A, B; c; d, e, f) := (1 + N)^d e^N \overset{?}{=} AY^c \wedge X^d f^N \overset{?}{=} BZ^c$

[Extractor] $\Sigma.\mathsf{ext}(X, Y, Z; A, B; c; c'; d, e, f; d', e', f') :=$

$\alpha, \beta :=$ "values such that $\alpha(c - c') + \beta N = 1$"

return $((d - d')\alpha, (e/e')^\alpha Y^\beta, (f/f')^\alpha Z^\beta)$

[Simulator] $\Sigma.\mathsf{sim}(X, Y, Z; c) :=$

$d \in_R \mathbb{Z}_N; e, f \in_R \mathbb{Z}_N^*; A := (1 + N)^d e^N Y^{-c}; B := X^d f^N Z^{-c}$

return $(A, B; c; d, e, f)$

---

by the Fiat-Shamir heuristic [AABN08], essentially follows from the hardness of the relation; see [SV15] for details.

The CDN protocol uses a sub-protocol in which multiple parties simultaneously provide proofs based on the same challenge, called the "multiparty Σ-protocol". Namely, suppose each party from a set P wants to prove knowledge of a witness for a statement $v_i \in L_R$ with some Σ-protocol. To achieve this, each party in P broadcasts a commitment to its announcement; then, the computation parties jointly generate a challenge; and finally, all parties in P broadcast their response to this challenge, along with an opening of their commitment. The multiparty Σ-protocol is used as a building block in the CDN protocol by constructing a simulator that provides proofs on behalf of honest parties without knowing their witnesses ("zero-knowledgeness"), and extracts witnesses from corrupted parties that give correct proofs ("soundness").

The CDN protocol uses three Σ-protocols: Σ_{PK} proving plaintext knowledge, Σ_{CM} proving correct multiplication, and Σ_{CD} proving correct decryption. The first two are due to [CDN01] (which also proves that they are Σ-protocols). Σ_{PK} (Σ-Protocol 1) proves knowledge of x, r such that $X = (1+N)^x r^N$ is an encryption of x with randomness r. Σ_{CM} (Σ-Protocol 2) proves knowledge of (y, r, s) for (X, Y, Z) such that $Y = (1+N)^y r^N$ is an encryption of y with randomness r and $Z = X^y s^N$ is an encryption of the product of the plaintexts of X and Y randomised with s.

Proof Σ_{CD} of correct decryption (Σ-protocol 3) is due to [Jur03]. In the threshold variant of Paillier encryption due to Damgård and Jurik [DJ01, Jur03], safe primes $p = 2p' + 1, q = 2q' + 1$ are used for the RSA modulus $N = pq$. Key generation involves generating a secret value d such that, given $c' = c^{4\Delta^2 d}$, anybody can compute the plaintext of c by "decoding" c' as $\mathsf{paillierdecode}(c') := ((c' - 1) \div N)(4\Delta^2)^{-1} \bmod N$. Here, $\Delta = n!$ and $\div$ denotes division as integers (using $N | c' - 1$). The value d is then (t, n) Shamir-shared modulo $Np'q'$ between the computation parties as shares s_i. Threshold decryption is done by letting t

---

Σ-Protocol 3. Σ_{CD}: Proof of correct decryption (statistical)

[Relation] $R = \{(d, d_i, v, v_i; \Delta s_i) \mid d_i^2 = d^{4\Delta s_i} \wedge v_i = v^{\Delta s_i}\}$

[Announcement] $\Sigma.\mathsf{ann}(d, d_i, v, v_i; \Delta s_i) :=$ // $k = \log_2 N$; k_2 stat. sec. param
    $u \in_R [0, 2^{2k+2k_2}]$; $a := d^{4u}$; $b := v^u$; **return** $(a, b; u)$

[Response] $\Sigma.\mathsf{res}(d, d_i, v, v_i; \Delta s_i; a, b; u, c) :=$
    $r := u + c\Delta s_i$; **return** r

[Verification] $\Sigma.\mathsf{ver}(d, d_i, v, v_i; a, b; c; r) := d^{4r} \stackrel{?}{=} a(d_i)^{2c} \wedge v^r \stackrel{?}{=} b(v_i)^c$

[Extractor] $\Sigma.\mathsf{ext}(d, d_i, v, v_i; a, b; c; c'; r; r') := $ **return** $(r - r')/(c - c')$

[Simulator] $\Sigma.\mathsf{sim}(d, d_i, v, v_i; c) :=$
    $r \in_R [0, 2^{2k+2k_2}]$; **return** $(d^{4r}(d_i)^{-2c}, v^r(v_i)^{-e}; c; r)$

---

parties each compute $c_i = c^{2\Delta s_i}$; the value $c^{4\Delta^2 d}$ is obtained by applying Shamir reconstruction "in the exponent". Correct decryption is proven with respect to a public set of verification values. Namely, the public key includes values v, $v_0 = v^{\Delta^2 d}$, and $v_i = v^{\Delta s_i}$ for all computation parties $i \in \mathcal{P}$. Hence, in Σ_{CD}, parties prove correctness of their decryption shares c_i of c by proving knowledge of $\Delta s_i = \log_{c^4}(c_i^2) = \log_v(v_i)$ for (c, c_i, v, v_i). (In the same way, v_0 can be used to prove correctness of c' with respect to c using a single instance of Σ_{CD}.) Note that this is a statistical Σ-protocol: this is because witness Δs_i is a value modulo the secret value $Np'q'$, so modulo reduction is not possible.

2.3 Security of the CDN Protocol

In [CDN01], it is shown that the CDN protocol implements secure function evaluation in Canetti's non-concurrent model [Can98] if only a minority of computation parties are corrupted. Essentially, this means that in this case, the computation succeeds; the result is correct; and the honest parties' inputs remain private. This conclusion is true assuming honest set-up and security of the Paillier encryption scheme and the trapdoor commitment scheme used. If a majority of computation parties is corrupted, then because threshold $\lceil n/2 \rceil$ is used for the threshold cryptosystem, privacy is broken. As noted [ST06, IPS09], this can be remedied by raising the threshold, but in that case, the corrupted parties can make the computation break down at any point by refusing to cooperate. In Sect. 4.1, we present a variant of this model in which we prove the security of our protocols (using random oracles but no trapdoor commitments).

3 Multiparty Non-interactive Proofs

In this section, we show how to produce non-interactive zero-knowledge proofs in a multiparty way. At several points in the above CDN protocol, all parties from a set P prove knowledge of witnesses for certain statements; the computation parties are convinced that those parties that succeed, do indeed know a witness.

In CDN, these proofs are interactive; but for universal verifiability, we need non-interactive proofs that convince any third party. The traditional method to make proofs non-interactive is the Fiat-Shamir heuristic; in Sect. 3.1, we outline it, and show that it is problematic in a multiparty setting. In Sect. 3.2, we present a new, "multiparty" Fiat-Shamir heuristic that works in our setting, and has the advantage of achieving smaller proofs by "homomorphically combining" the proofs of individual parties. In the remainder, $C \subset \mathcal{I} \cup \mathcal{P} \cup \{\mathcal{R}, \mathcal{V}\}$ denotes the set of corrupted parties; and F denotes the set of parties who failed to provide a correct proof when needed; this only happens for corrupted parties, so $F \subset C$.

Our results are in the random oracle model [BR93, Wee09], an idealised model of hash functions. In this model, evaluations of the hash function $\mathcal{H}$ are modelled as queries to a "random oracle" $\mathcal{O}$ that evaluates a perfectly random function. When simulating an adversary, a simulator can intercept these oracle queries and answer them at will, as long as the answers look random to the adversary. Security in the random oracle model does not generally imply security in the standard model [GK03], but it is often used because it typically gives simple, efficient protocols, and its use does not seem to lead to security problems in practice [Wee09]. See [SV15] for a detailed description of our use of random oracles; and Sect. 5 for a discussion of the real-world implications of the particular flavour of random oracles we use.

3.1 The Fiat-Shamir Heuristic and Witness-Extended Emulation

The obvious way of making the proofs in the CDN protocol non-interactive, is to apply the Fiat-Shamir heuristic to all individual Σ-protocols. That is, party $i \in \mathcal{P}$ produces proof of knowledge π of a witness for statement v as follows[2]:

$$(a; s) := \Sigma.\mathsf{ann}(v; w); c := \mathcal{H}(v||a||aux); r := \Sigma.\mathsf{res}(v; w; a; s; c); \pi := (a; c; r).$$

Let us denote this procedure $\mathsf{fsprove}(\Sigma; v; w; aux)$. A verifier accepts those proofs $\pi = (a; c; r)$ for which $\mathsf{fsver}(\Sigma; v; \pi; aux)$ holds, where $\mathsf{fsver}(\Sigma; v; a, c, r; aux)$ is defined as $\mathcal{H}(v||a||aux) = c \wedge \Sigma.\mathsf{ver}(v; a; c; r)$.

Recall that security proofs require a simulator that simulates proofs of honest parties (zero-knowledgeness) and extracts witnesses of corrupted parties (soundness). In the random oracle model, Fiat-Shamir proofs for honest parties can be simulated by simulating a Σ-protocol conversation (a, c, r) and programming the random oracle so that $\mathcal{H}(v||a||aux) = c$. Witnesses of corrupted parties can be extracted by rewinding the adversary to the point where it made an oracle query for $v||a||aux$ and supplying a different value; but, as we discuss in [SV15], this extraction can make the simulator very inefficient. In fact, if Fiat-Shamir proofs take place in R different rounds, then extracting witnesses may increase the running time of the simulator by a factor $O(R!)$. The reason is that the oracle query

---

[2] Here, aux should contain at least the prover's identity. Otherwise, corrupted parties could replay proofs by honest parties, which breaks the soundness property below because witnesses for these proofs cannot be extracted by rewinding the adversary to the point of the oracle query and reprogramming the random oracle.

for a proof in one round may have in fact already been made in a previous round, in which case rewinding the adversary to extract one witness requires recursively extracting witnesses for all intermediate rounds. Hence, we can essentially only use the Fiat-Shamir heuristic in a constant number of rounds.

Moreover, in the CDN protocol, applying the Fiat-Shamir heuristic to each individual proof has the disadvantage that the verifier needs to check a number of proofs that depends linearly on the number of computation parties. In particular, for each multiplication gate, the verifier needs to check n proofs of correct multiplication and t proofs of correct decryption. Next, we show that we can avoid both the technical problems with witness extended emulation and the dependence on the number of computation parties by letting the computation parties collaboratively produce "combined proofs". (As discussed in [SV15], there are other ways of just solving the technical problems with witness extended emulation, but they are not easier than the method we propose.)

3.2 Combined Proofs with the Multiparty Fiat-Shamir Heuristic

The crucial observation (e.g., [Des93, KMR12]) allowing parties to produce non-interactive zero-knowledge proofs collaboratively is that, for many Σ-protocols, conversations of proofs with the same challenge can be "homomorphically combined". For instance, consider the classical Σ-protocol for proving knowledge of a discrete logarithm due to Schnorr [Sch89]. Suppose we have two Schnorr conversations proving knowledge of $x_1 = \log_g h_1$, $x_2 = \log_g h_2$, i.e., two tuples $(a_1; c; r_1)$ and $(a_2; c; r_2)$ such that $g^{r_1} = a_1(h_1)^c$ and $g^{r_2} = a_2(h_2)^c$. Then $g^{r_1+r_2} = (a_1 a_2)(h_1 h_2)^c$, so $(a_1 a_2; c; r_1 + r_2)$ is a Schnorr conversation proving knowledge of discrete logarithm $x_1 + x_2 = \log_g(h_1 h_2)$. For our purposes, we demand that such homomorphisms satisfy two properties. First, when conversations of at least $\lceil n/2 \rceil$ parties are combined, the result is a valid conversation (the requirement of having at least $\lceil n/2 \rceil$ conversations is needed for decryption proofs to ensure that there are enough decryption shares). Second, when fewer than $\lceil n/2 \rceil$ parties are corrupted, the combination of different honest announcements with the same corrupted announcements is likely to lead to a different combined announcement. This helps to eliminate the rewinding problems for Fiat-Shamir discussed above.

Definition 2. *Let Σ be a Σ-protocol for relation $R \subset V \times W$. Let Φ be a collection of partial functions Φ.stmt, Φ.ann, and Φ.resp. We call Φ a homomorphism of Σ if:*

Combination. *Let c be a challenge; I a set of parties such that $|I| \geq \lceil n/2 \rceil$; and $\{(v_i; a_i; r_i)\}_{i \in I}$ a collection of statements, announcements, and responses. If Φ.stmt$(\{v_i\}_{i \in I})$ is defined and for all i, Σ.ver$(v_i; a_i; c; r_i)$ holds, then also Σ.ver$(\Phi$.stmt$(\{v_i\}_{i \in I}); \Phi$.ann$(\{a_i\}_{i \in I}); c; \Phi$.resp$(\{r_i\}_{i \in I}))$.*

Randomness. *Let c be a challenge; $C \subset I$ sets of parties such that $|C| < \lceil n/2 \rceil \leq |I|$; $\{v_i\}_{i \in I}$ statements s.t. Φ.stmt$(\{v_i\}_{i \in I})$ is defined; and $\{a_i\}_{i \in I \cap C}$ announcements. If $(a_i; \cdot), (a_i'; \cdot) \leftarrow \Sigma$.sim$(v_i; c)$ $\forall i \in I \setminus C$, then with overwhelming probability, Φ.ann$(\{a_i\}_{i \in I}) \neq \Phi$.ann$(\{a_i\}_{i \in I \cap C} \cup \{a_i'\}_{i \in I \setminus C})$.*

Protocol 4. $M\Sigma$: The Multi-Party Fiat-Shamir Heuristic

1. // **pre:** Σ is a Σ-protocol with homomorphism Φ, P is a set of non-failed
2. //   parties $(P \cap F = \emptyset)$, $v_P = \{v_i\}_{i \in P}$ statements w/ witnesses $w_P = \{w_i\}_{i \in P}$
3. // **post:** if $|P \setminus F| \geq \lceil n/2 \rceil$, then $v_{P \setminus F}$ is the combined statement
4. // $\Phi.\mathsf{stmt}(\{v_i\}_{i \in P \setminus F})$, and $\pi_{P \setminus F}$ is a corresponding Fiat-Shamir proof
5. // **invariant:** $F \subset C$: set of failed parties only includes corrupted parties
6. $(v_{P \setminus F}, \pi_{P \setminus F}) \leftarrow M\Sigma(\Sigma, \Phi, P, v_P, w_P, aux) :=$
7. **repeat**
8.   **parties** $i \in P \setminus F$ **do**
9. $(a_i; s_i) := \Sigma.\mathsf{ann}(v_i; w_i); h_i := \mathcal{H}(a_i\|i); \mathsf{bcast}(h_i)$
10.   **parties** $i \in P \setminus F$ **do** $\mathsf{bcast}(a_i)$
11. $F' := F; F := F \cup \{i \in P \setminus F \mid h_i \neq \mathcal{H}(a_i\|i)\}$
12.   **if** $F = F'$ **then**   // all parties left provided correct hashes
13. $c := \mathcal{H}(\Phi.\mathsf{stmt}(\{v_i\}_{i \in P \setminus F})\|\Phi.\mathsf{ann}(\{a_i\}_{i \in P \setminus F})\|aux)$
14.   **parties** $i \in P \setminus F$ **do** $r_i := \Sigma.\mathsf{res}(v_i; w_i; a_i; s_i; c); \mathsf{bcast}(r_i)$
15. $F := F \cup \{i \in P \setminus F \mid \neg\Sigma.\mathsf{ver}(v_i; a_i; c; r_i)\}$
16.   **if** $F = F'$ **then**   // all parties left provided correct responses
17.   **return** $(\Phi.\mathsf{stmt}(\{v_i\}_{i \in P \setminus F}),$
18. $(\Phi.\mathsf{ann}(\{a_i\}_{i \in P \setminus F}); c; \Phi.\mathsf{resp}(\{r_i\}_{i \in P \setminus F})))$
19. **until** $|P \setminus F| < \lceil n/2 \rceil$ // until not enough parties left
20. **return** $(\bot, \bot)$

Given a Σ-protocol with homomorphism Φ, parties holding witnesses $\{w_i\}$ for statements $\{v_i\}$ can together generate a Fiat-Shamir proof $(a; \mathcal{H}(v\|a\|aux); r)$ of knowledge of a witness for the "combined statement" $v = \Phi.\mathsf{stmt}(\{v_i\})$. Namely, the parties each provide announcement a_i for their own witness; compute $a = \Phi.\mathsf{ann}(\{a_i\})$ and $\mathcal{H}(v\|a\|aux)$; and provide responses r_i. Taking $r = \Phi.\mathsf{resp}(\{r_i\})$, the combination property from the above definition guarantees that we indeed get a validating proof. However, we cannot simply let the parties broadcast their announcements in turn, because to prove security in that case, the simulator needs to provide the announcements for the honest parties without knowing the announcements of the corrupted parties, hence without being able to program the random oracle on the combined announcement. We solve this by starting with a round in which each party commits to its announcement (the same trick was used in a different setting in [NKDM03])[3].

The *multiparty Fiat-Shamir heuristic* (Protocol 4) let parties collaboratively produce Fiat-Shamir proofs based on the above ideas. Apart from the above procedure (lines 8, 9, 10, 13, and 14), the protocol also contains error handling. Namely, we throw out parties that provide incorrect hashes to their announcements (line 11) or incorrect responses (line 15). If we have correct responses for all correctly hashed announcements, then we apply the homomorphism (line 17–18); otherwise, we try again with the remaining parties. If the number of parties drops below $\lceil n/2 \rceil$, the homomorphism can no longer be applied, so we

---

[3] As in [NKDM03], it may be possible to remove the additional round under the non-standard known-target discrete log problem.

return with an error (line 20). Note that, as in the normal Fiat-Shamir heuristic, the announcements do not need to be stored if they can be computed from the challenge and response (as will be the case for the Σ-protocols we consider).

Concerning security, recall that we need a simulator that simulates proofs of honest parties without their witnesses (zero-knowledgeness) and extracts the witnesses of corrupted parties (soundness). In [SV15], we present such a simulator. Essentially, it "guesses" the announcements of the corrupted parties based on the provided hashes; then simulates the Σ-protocol for the honest parties; and programs the random oracle on the combined announcement. It obtains witnesses for the corrupted parties by rewinding to just before the honest parties provide their announcements: this way, the corrupted parties are forced to use the announcements that they provided the hashes of (hence special soundness can be invoked), whereas the honest parties can provide new simulated announcements by reprogramming the random oracle. The simulator requires that fewer than $\lceil n/2 \rceil$ provers are corrupted so that we can use the randomness property of the Σ-protocol homomorphism (Definition 2). (When more than $\lceil n/2 \rceil$ provers are corrupted, we use an alternative proof strategy that uses witness-extended emulation instead of this simulator.)

3.3   Homomorphisms for the CDN Protocol

In the CDN protocol, the multiparty Fiat-Shamir heuristic allows us to obtain a proof that multiplication was done correctly that is independent of the number of computation parties. Recall that, for multiplication of encryptions X of x and Y of y, each computation party provides encryptions D_i of d_i and E_i of $d_i \cdot y$, and proves that E_i encrypts the product of the plaintexts of Y and D_i; and each computation party provides decryption share S_i of encryption $XD_1 \cdots D_n$, and proves it correct. As we will show now, the multiplication proofs can be combined with homomorphism Φ_{CM} into one proof that $\prod E_i$ encrypts the product of the plaintexts of Y and $\prod D_i$; and the decryption proofs can be combined with homomorphism Φ_{CD} into one proof that a combination S_0 of the decryption shares is correct. In the CDN protocol, the individual D_i, E_i, and S_i are not relevant, so also the combined values convince a verifier of correct multiplication.

In more detail, the homomorphism Φ_{CM} for Σ_{CM} is defined on statements $\{(X, Y_i, Z_i)\}_{i \in I}$ which share encryption X, and it proves that the multiplication on plaintexts of X with $\prod Y_i$ is equal to $\prod Z_i$. We let $\Phi.\text{stmt}(\{(X, Y_i, Z_i)\}_{i \in I}) = (X, \prod_{i \in I} Y_i, \prod_{i \in I} Z_i)$ and $\Phi.\text{ann}(\{A_i, B_i\}_{i \in I}) = (\prod_{i \in I} A_i, \prod_{i \in I} B_i)$. For the response, we would like to define $d = \sum_{i \in I} d_i$, $e = \prod_{i \in I} e_i$, and $f = \prod_{i \in I} f_i$; but because $\sum_{i \in I} d_i$ is computed modulo N, we need to add correction factors to e and f: $e = (\prod_{i \in I} e_i)(1+N)^k$ and $f = (\prod_{i \in I} f_i)Y^k$ (where $k = \lfloor (\sum_{i \in I} d_i)/N \rfloor$).

The homomorphism Φ_{CD} for Σ_{CD} combines correctness proofs of decryption shares into a proof of correct decryption with respect to an overall verification value. Let $I \geq \lceil n/2 \rceil$ be sufficiently many parties to decrypt a ciphertext, let $\{\lambda_i\}_{i \in I}$ be Lagrange interpolation coefficients for these parties. (Note that λ_i are not always integral; but we will always use $\Delta\lambda_i$, which *are* integral.) Let s_i be their shares of the decryption key $d = \sum_{i \in I} \Delta\lambda_i s_i$. Recall that decryption works by letting each party $i \in I$ provide decryption share $c_i = c^{2\Delta s_i}$; computing $c' = \prod_{i \in I} c_i^{2\Delta \lambda_i}$; and from this determining the plaintext as paillierdecode(c'). Parties prove correctness of their decryption shares c_i by proving that $\log_{c^4} c_i^2 = \log_v v_i$, where v, v_i are publicly known verification values such that $v_i = v^{\Delta s_i}$. Now, if $\log_{c^4} c_i^2 = \log_v v_i$ for all i, then

$$\log_{c^4} c' = \log_{c^4} \prod_{i \in I} c_i^{2\Delta \lambda_i} = \log_v \prod_{i \in I} v_i^{\Delta \lambda_i} = \log_v \prod_{i \in I} (v^{\Delta s_i})^{\Delta \lambda_i} = \log_v v^{\Delta^2 d}.$$

Hence, decryption proofs for shares c_i with respect to verification values v_i can be combined into a decryption proof for c' with respect to verification value $v_0 := v^{\Delta^2 d}$. Formally, $\Phi.\mathsf{stmt}(\{(d, d_i, v, v_i)\}_{i \in I} = \left(d, \prod_{i \in I} c_i^{\Delta \lambda_i}, v, \prod_{i \in I} v_i^{\Delta \lambda_i}\right)$; $\Phi.\mathsf{ann}(\{(a_i, b_i)\}_{i \in I}) = \left(\prod_{i \in I} a_i^{\Delta \lambda_i}, \prod_{i \in I} b_i^{\Delta \lambda_i}\right)$; and $\Phi.\mathsf{resp}(\{r_i\}_{i \in I}) = \sum \Delta \lambda_i r_i$. For the combination property of Definition 2, note that we really need $I \geq \lceil n/2 \rceil$ in order to apply Lagrange interpolation. For the randomness property, note that if $|C| < \lceil n/2 \rceil$, then at least one party in $I \notin C$ has a non-zero interpolation coefficient, hence the contribution of this party to the announcement ensures that the two combined announcements are different.

4 Universally Verifiable MPC

In the previous section, we have shown how to produce non-interactive zero-knowledge proofs in a multiparty way. We now use this observation to obtain universally verifiable MPC. We first define security for universally verifiable MPC; and then obtain universally verifiable MPC by adapting the CDN protocol.

4.1 Security Model for Verifiable MPC

Our security model is an adaptation of the model of [Can98, CDN01] to the setting of universal verifiability in the random oracle model. We first explain the general execution model, which is as in [Can98, CDN01] but with a random oracle added; we then explain how to model verifiability in this execution model as the behaviour of the ideal-world trusted party. The general execution model compares protocol executions in the real and ideal world.

In the real world, a protocol π between m input parties $i \in \mathcal{I}$, n computation parties $i \in \mathcal{P}$, a result party $\mathcal{R}$ and a verifier $\mathcal{V}$ is executed on an open broadcast network with rushing in the presence of an active static adversary $\mathcal{A}$ corrupting parties $C \subset \mathcal{I} \cup \mathcal{P} \cup \{\mathcal{R}, \mathcal{V}\}$. The protocol execution starts by incorruptibly setting up the Paillier threshold cryptosystem, i.e., generating public key $\mathsf{pk} = (N, v, v_0, \{v_i\}_{i \in \mathcal{P}})$ with RSA modulus N and verification values v, v_0, v_i, and secret key shares $\{s_i\}_{i \in \mathcal{P}}$ (see Sect. 2.2). Each input party $i \in \mathcal{I}$ gets input (pk, x_i); each computation party $i \in \mathcal{P}$ gets input (pk, s_i); and the result party $\mathcal{R}$ gets input pk. The adversary gets the inputs $(\mathsf{pk}, \{x_i\}_{i \in \mathcal{I} \cap C}, \{s_i\}_{i \in \mathcal{P} \cap C})$ of the corrupted parties, and has an auxiliary input a. During the protocol, parties can query the random oracle; the oracle answers new queries randomly, and

---

Process 5. $\mathcal{T}_{\text{VSFE}}$: trusted party for verifiable secure function evaluation

1. // compute f on $\{x_i\}_{i \in \mathcal{I}}$ for $\mathcal{R}$ with corrupted parties C; $\mathcal{V}$ learns encryption
2. $\mathcal{T}_{\text{VSFE}}(C, (N, v, v_0, \{v_i\}_{i \in \mathcal{P}})) :=$
3.   // input phase
4.   **foreach** $i \in \mathcal{I} \setminus C$ **do** $x_i := \text{recv}(\mathcal{I}_i)$ // honest inputs
5. $\{x_i\}_{i \in \mathcal{I} \cap C} := \text{recv}(\mathcal{S})$ // corrupted inputs
6.   **if** $|\mathcal{P} \cap C| \geq \lceil n/2 \rceil$ **then** $\text{send}(\{x_i\}_{i \in \mathcal{I} \setminus C}, \mathcal{S})$ // send to corrupted majority
7.   // computation phase
8. $r := f(x_1, \ldots, x_m)$
9.   // output phase
10.   **if** $\mathcal{R} \notin C$ **then**   // honest $\mathcal{R}$: adversary learns encryption, may block result
11. $s \in_R \mathbb{Z}_N^*$; $R := (1 + N)^r s^N$; $res := (r, s)$; $\text{send}(R, \mathcal{S})$
12.   **if** $|\mathcal{P} \cap C| \geq \lceil n/2 \rceil$ **and** $\text{recv}(\mathcal{S}) = \bot$ **then** $res := \bot$; $R := \bot$
13. $\text{send}(res, \mathcal{R})$
14.   **else**   // corrupted $\mathcal{R}$: adversary learns output, may block result to $\mathcal{V}$
15. $\text{send}(r, \mathcal{S})$; $s := \text{recv}(\mathcal{S})$
16.   **if** $s = \bot$ **then** $R := \bot$ **else** $R := (1 + N)^r s^N$
17.   // proof phase
18.   **if** $\mathcal{V} \notin C$ **then** $\text{send}(R, \mathcal{V})$

---

repeated queries consistently. At the end of the protocol, each honest party outputs a value according to the protocol; the corrupted parties output $\bot$; and the adversary outputs a value at will. Define $\text{EXEC}_{\pi, \mathcal{A}}(k, (x_1, \ldots, x_m), C, a)$ to be the random variable, given security parameter k, consisting of the outputs of all parties (including the adversary) and the set $\mathcal{O}$ of oracle queries and responses.

The ideal-world execution similarly involves m input parties $i \in \mathcal{I}$, n computation parties $i \in \mathcal{P}$, result party $\mathcal{R}$, verifier $\mathcal{V}$, and an adversary $\mathcal{S}$ corrupting parties $C \subset \mathcal{I} \cup \mathcal{P} \cup \{\mathcal{R}, \mathcal{V}\}$; but now, there is also an incorruptible trusted party $\mathcal{T}$. As before, the execution starts by setting up the keys $(\text{pk}, \{s_i\}_{i \in \mathcal{P}})$ of the Paillier cryptosystem. The input parties receive x_i as input; the trusted party receives a list C of corrupted parties and the public key pk. Then, it runs the code $\mathcal{T}_{\text{VSFE}}$ shown in Process 5, which we explain later. The adversary gets inputs $(\text{pk}, C, \{x_i\}_{i \in \mathcal{I} \cap C}, \{s_i\}_{i \in \mathcal{P} \cap C})$, and outputs a value at will. In this model, there is no random oracle; instead, the adversary chooses the set $\mathcal{O}$ of oracle queries and responses (typically, those used to simulate a real-world adversary). As in the real-world case, $\text{IDEAL}_{\mathcal{T}_{\text{SFE}}, \mathcal{S}}(k, (x_1, \ldots, x_m), C, a)$ is the random variable, given security parameter k, consisting of all parties' outputs and $\mathcal{O}$.

Definition 3. *Protocol π implements verifiable secure function evaluation in the random oracle model if, for every probabilistic polynomial time real-world adversary $\mathcal{A}$, there exists a probabilistic polynomial time ideal-world adversary $\mathcal{S}_\mathcal{A}$ such that, for all inputs $x_1, \ldots, x_m$; all sets of corrupted parties C; and all auxiliary input a: $\text{EXEC}_{\pi, \mathcal{A}}(k; x_1, \ldots, x_m; C; a)$ and $\text{IDEAL}_{\mathcal{T}_{VSFE}, \mathcal{S}_\mathcal{A}}(k; x_1, \ldots, x_m; C; a)$ are computationally indistinguishable in security parameter k.*

We remark that, while security in non-random-oracle secure function evaluation [Can98, CDN01] is preserved under (subroutine) composition, this is not the case for our random oracle variant. The reason is that our model and protocols assume that the random oracle is not used outside of the protocol. Using the random oracle model with dependent auxiliary input [Unr07, Wee09] might be enough to obtain a composition property; but adaptations are needed to make our protocol provably secure in that model. See Sect. 5 for a discussion.

We now discuss the trusted party $\mathcal{T}_{\mathrm{VSFE}}$ for verifiable secure function evaluation. Whenever the computation succeeds, $\mathcal{T}_{\mathrm{VSFE}}$ guarantees that the results are correct. Namely, $\mathcal{T}_{\mathrm{VSFE}}$ sends the result r of the computation and randomness s to $\mathcal{R}$ (line 13), and it sends encryption $(1 + N)^r s^N$ of the result with randomness s to $\mathcal{V}$ (line 18); if the computation failed, $\mathcal{R}$ gets $(\perp, \perp)$ and $\mathcal{V}$ gets $\perp$.[4] Whether $\mathcal{T}_{\mathrm{VSFE}}$ guarantees privacy (i.e., only $\mathcal{R}$ can learn the result) and robustness (i.e., the computation does not fail) depends on which parties are corrupted. Privacy and robustness with respect to $\mathcal{R}$ are guaranteed as long as only a minority of computation parties are corrupted. If not, then in line 6, $\mathcal{T}_{\mathrm{VSFE}}$ sends the honest parties' inputs to the adversary; and in line 12, it gives the adversary the option to block the computation by sending $\perp$. Note that the adversary receives the inputs of the honest parties after it provides the inputs of the corrupted parties, so even if privacy is broken, the adversary cannot choose the corrupted parties' inputs based on the honest parties' inputs. For robustness with respect to $\mathcal{V}$, the result party needs to be honest. If not, then in line 15, $\mathcal{T}_{\mathrm{VSFE}}$ gives the adversary the option to block $\mathcal{V}$'s result by sending $\perp$; in any case, it can choose the randomness. (Note that these thresholds are specific to CDN's "honest majority" setting; e.g., other protocols may satisfy privacy if all computation parties except one are corrupted.)

Note that this model does not cover the "universality" aspect of universally verifiable MPC. This is because the security model for secure function evaluation only covers the input/output behaviour of protocols, not the fact that "the verifier can be anybody". Hence, we design universally verifiable protocols by proving that they are verifiable, and then arguing based on the characteristics of the protocol (e.g., the verifier does not have any secret values) that this verifiability is "universal".

4.2 Universally Verifiable CDN

We now present the UVCDN protocol (Protocol 6) for universally verifiable secure function evaluation. At a high level, this protocol consists of the input,

---

[4] Although we only guarantee computational indistinguishability and the verifier does not know what value is encrypted, this definition *does* guarantee that $\mathcal{V}$ receives the correct result. This is because the ideal-world output of the protocol execution contains $\mathcal{R}$'s r and s and $\mathcal{V}$'s $(1 + N)^r s^N$, so a distinguisher between the ideal and real world can check correctness of $\mathcal{V}$'s result. (If s were not in $\mathcal{R}$'s result, this would not be the case, and correctness of $\mathcal{V}$'s result would *not* be guaranteed.) Also, note that although privacy depends on the security of the encryption scheme, correctness *does not rely on any knowledge assumption*.

Protocol 6. UVCDN: universally verifiable CDN

---

1.   // **pre:** $\mathsf{pk}/\{s_i\}_{i\in\mathcal{P}}$ threshold Paillier public/secret keys, $\{x_i\}_{i\in\mathcal{I}}$ function input
2.   // **post:** output R according to ideal functionality ITM 5
3. $R \leftarrow \mathsf{UVCDN}(\mathsf{pk} = (N, v, v_0, \{v_i\}_{i\in\mathcal{P}}), \{s_i\}_{i\in\mathcal{P}}, \{x_i\}_{i\in\mathcal{I}}) :=$
4.   **parties** $i \in \mathcal{I}$ **do**   // input phase
5. $r_i \in_R \mathbb{Z}_N^*; X_i := (1 + N)^{x_i} r_i^N; \pi_{\mathrm{PK},i} := \mathsf{fsprove}(\Sigma_{\mathrm{PK}}; X_i; x_i, r_i; i)$
6. $h_i := \mathcal{H}(X_i || \pi_{\mathrm{PK},i} || i); \mathsf{bcast}(h_i); \mathsf{bcast}(X_i, \pi_{\mathrm{PK},i})$
7. $F := \{i \in \mathcal{I} \mid h_i \neq \mathcal{H}(X_i || \pi_{\mathrm{PK},i} || i) \vee \neg\mathsf{fsver}(\Sigma_{\mathrm{PK}}; X_i; \pi_{\mathrm{PK},i}; i)\}$
8.   **foreach** $i \in F$ **do** $X_i := 1$
9.   **foreach** gate **do**   // computation phase
10.   **if** $\langle$constant gate c with value $v\rangle$ **then** $X_c := (1 + N)^v$
11.   **if** $\langle$addition gate c with inputs $a, b\rangle$ **then** $X_c := X_a X_b$
12.   **if** $\langle$subtraction gate c with inputs $a, b\rangle$ **then** $X_c := X_a X_b^{-1}$
13.   **if** $\langle$multiplication gate c with inputs $a, b\rangle$ **then**   // [DN03] multiplication
14.   **parties** $i \in \mathcal{P} \setminus F$ **do**
15. $d_i \in_R \mathbb{Z}_N; r_i, t_i \in_R \mathbb{Z}_N^*; D_i := (1 + N)^{d_i} r_i^N; E_i := (X_b)^{d_i} t_i^N$
16. $\mathsf{bcast}(D_i, E_i)$
17. $(\cdot, D_c, E_c; \pi_{\mathrm{CM}c}) :=$
18. $\mathrm{M}\Sigma(\Sigma_{\mathrm{CM}}, \Phi_{\mathrm{CM}}, \mathcal{P} \setminus F, \{(X_b, D_i, E_i)\}_{i\in\mathcal{P}\setminus F}, \{(d_i, r_i, t_i)\}_{i\in\mathcal{P}\setminus F})$
19.   **if** $|\mathcal{P} \setminus F| < \lceil n/2\rceil$ **then break**
20. $S_c := X_a \cdot D_c$
21.   **parties** $i \in \mathcal{P} \setminus F$ **do** $S_i := (S_c)^{2\Delta s_i}; \mathsf{bcast}(S_i)$
22. $(\cdot, S_{0,c}, \cdot, \cdot; \pi_{\mathrm{CD}c}) :=$
23. $\mathrm{M}\Sigma(\Sigma_{\mathrm{CD}}, \Phi_{\mathrm{CD}}, \mathcal{P} \setminus F, \{(S_c, S_i, v, v_i)\}_{i\in\mathcal{P}\setminus F}, \{\Delta s_i\}_{i\in\mathcal{P}\setminus F})$
24.   **if** $|\mathcal{P} \setminus F| < \lceil n/2\rceil$ **then break**
25. $s := \mathsf{paillierdecode}(S_{0,c}); X_c := (X_b)^s \cdot E_c^{-1}$
26.   **if** $|\mathcal{P} \setminus F| < \lceil n/2\rceil$ **then parties** $i \in \mathcal{I} \cup \mathcal{P} \cup \{\mathcal{R}\}$ **do return** $\bot$
27.   **party** $\mathcal{R}$ **do** $d \in_R \mathbb{Z}_N; s \in_R \mathbb{Z}_N^*; D := (1 + N)^d s^N$ // output phase
28.   **party** $\mathcal{R}$ **do** $\pi_{\mathrm{PK}d} := \mathsf{fsprove}(\Sigma_{\mathrm{PK}}; D; d, s; \mathcal{R}); \mathsf{bcast}(D, \pi_{\mathrm{PK}d})$
29.   **if** $\neg\mathsf{fsver}(\Sigma_{\mathrm{PK}}; D; \pi_{\mathrm{PK}d}; \mathcal{R})$ **then parties** $i \in \mathcal{I} \cup \mathcal{P} \cup \{\mathcal{R}\}$ **do return** $\bot$
30. $Y := X_{\mathrm{outgate}} \cdot D^{-1}; $**parties** $i \in \mathcal{P} \setminus F$ **do** $Y_i := Y^{2\Delta s_i}; \mathsf{bcast}(Y_i)$
31. $(\cdot, Y_0, \cdot, \cdot; \pi_{\mathrm{CD}}; y) := \mathrm{M}\Sigma(\Sigma_{\mathrm{CD}}, \Phi_{\mathrm{CD}}, \mathcal{P} \setminus F, \{(Y, Y_i, v, v_i)\}_{i\in\mathcal{P}\setminus F}, \{\Delta s_i\}_{i\in\mathcal{P}\setminus F}, D)$
32.   **if** $|\mathcal{P} \setminus F| < \lceil n/2\rceil$ **then parties** $i \in \mathcal{I} \cup \mathcal{P} \cup \{\mathcal{R}\}$ **do return** $\bot$
33.   **party** $\mathcal{R}$ **do**
34. $y := \mathsf{paillierdecode}(Y_0); r := y + d$
35. $\mathsf{send}(\{(D_c, E_c, \Pi_{\mathrm{CM}c}, S_{0,c}, \Pi_{\mathrm{CD}c})\}_{c\in\mathrm{gates}}, (D, \pi_{\mathrm{PK}d}, Y_0, \pi_{\mathrm{CD}y}); \mathcal{V})$ // proof
36.   **return** (r, s) // phase
37.   **parties** $i \in \mathcal{I} \cup \mathcal{P}$ **do return** $\bot$
38.   **party** $\mathcal{V}$ **do** $\pi := \mathsf{recv}(\mathcal{R}); $**return** $\mathsf{vercomp}(\mathsf{pk}, \{X_i\}_{i\in\mathcal{I}}, \pi)$

---

computation, and multiplication phases of the CDN protocol, with all proofs made non-interactive, followed by a new *proof phase*. As discussed, we can use the normal Fiat-Shamir (FS) heuristic in only a constant number of rounds; and we can use the multiparty FS heuristic only when it gives a "combined statement" that makes sense. Hence, we choose to use the FS heuristic for the proofs by the input and result parties, and the multiparty FS heuristic for the proofs by the computation parties.

Algorithm 7. vercomp: verifier's gate-by-gate verification of the computation

1. // **pre**: pk public key, $\{X_i\}_{i\in\mathcal{I}}$ encryptions, $(\{\Pi_{\mathrm{mul}i}\}, \Pi_{\mathrm{result}})$ tuple
2. // **post**: if $(\{\Pi_{\mathrm{mul}i}\}, \Pi_{\mathrm{result}})$ proves correctness of Y, $X_o = Y$; otherwise, $X_o = \bot$
3. $X_o \leftarrow \mathsf{vercomp}(\mathsf{pk} = (N, v, v_0, \{v_i\}_{i\in\mathcal{P}}), \{X_i\}_{i\in\mathcal{I}}, (\{\Pi_{\mathrm{mul}i}\}, \Pi_{\mathrm{result}})) :=$
4.   // verification of input phase: see lines 6–8 of UVCDN
5.   // verification of computation phase
6.   **foreach** gate **do**
7.   **if** $\langle$constant gate c with value $v\rangle$ **then** $X_c := (1+N)^v$
8.   **if** $\langle$addition gate c with inputs $a, b\rangle$ **then** $X_c := X_a X_b$
9.   **if** $\langle$subtraction gate c with inputs $a, b\rangle$ **then** $X_c := X_a X_b^{-1}$
10.   **if** $\langle$multiplication gate c with inputs $a, b\rangle$ **then**
11. $(D; E; a, c, r; S_0; a', c', r') := \Pi_{\mathrm{mul}c}$; $S := X_a \cdot D^{-1}$
12.   **if** $\neg\mathsf{fsver}(\Sigma_{\mathrm{CM}}; X_b, D, E; a; c; r)$ **then return** $\bot$
13.   **if** $\neg\mathsf{fsver}(\Sigma_{\mathrm{CD}}; S, S_0, v, v_0; a'; c'; r')$ **then return** $\bot$
14. $s := \mathsf{paillierdecode}(S_0)$; $X_c := (X_b)^s E^{-1}$
15.   // verification of output phase
16. $(D; a_{\mathrm{out}}, c_{\mathrm{out}}, r_{\mathrm{out}}; Y_0; a_{\mathrm{dec}}, c_{\mathrm{dec}}, r_{\mathrm{dec}}) := \Pi_{\mathrm{result}}$
17.   **if** $\neg\mathsf{fsver}(\Sigma_{\mathrm{PK}}; D; a_{\mathrm{out}}, c_{\mathrm{out}}, r_{\mathrm{out}}; \mathcal{R})$ **then return** $\bot$
18. $Y := X_{\mathrm{outgate}} \cdot D^{-1}$
19.   **if** $\neg\mathsf{fsver}(\Sigma_{\mathrm{CD}}; Y, Y_0, v, v_0; a_{\mathrm{dec}}, c_{\mathrm{dec}}, r_{\mathrm{dec}}; D)$ **then return** $\bot$
20. $y := \mathsf{paillierdecode}(Y_0)$
21.   **return** $(1+N)^y D$ // encryption of $y + d = r$

In more detail, during the *input phase* of the protocol, the input parties provide their inputs (lines 4–8). As in the CDN protocol, each party encrypts its input and compiles a FS proof of knowledge (line 5). In the original CDN protocol, these encryptions and proofs would be broadcast directly; however, if a majority of computation parties are corrupted, then this allows corrupted parties to adapt their inputs based on the inputs of the honest parties. To prevent this, we let each party first broadcast a hash of its input and proof; only after all parties have committed to their inputs using this hash are the actual encrypted inputs and proofs revealed (line 6). All parties that provide an incorrect hash or proof have their inputs set to zero (line 7–8).

The remainder of the computation follows the CDN protocol. During the *computation phase*, the function is evaluated gate-by-gate; for multiplication gates, the multiplication protocol from [DN03] is used, with proofs of correct multiplication and decryption using the multiparty FS heuristic (lines 14–25). During the *output phase*, the result party obtains the result by broadcasting an encryption of a random d and proving knowledge using the normal FS heuristic (lines 27–28); the computation parties decrypt the result plus d, proving correctness using the multiparty FS heuristic (line 31). From this, the result party learns result r (line 34); and it knows the intermediate values from the protocol and the proofs showing they are correct.

Finally, we include a *proof phase* in the UVCDN protocol in which the result party sends these intermediate values and proofs to the verifier (line 35). The verifier runs procedure vercomp (Algorithm 7) to verify the correctness of the computation (line 38). The inputs to this verification procedure are the public key of the Paillier cryptosystem; the encrypted inputs $\{X_i\}_{i \in \mathcal{I}}$ by the input parties; and the proof π by the result party (which consists of proofs for each multiplication gate, and the two proofs from the output phase of the protocol). The verifier checks the proofs for each multiplication gate from the computation phase (lines 6–14); and the proofs from the output phase (lines 16–20), finally obtaining an encryption of the result (line 21). While not specified in vercomp, the verifier does also verify the proofs from the input phase: namely, in lines 7–8 of UVCDN, the verifier receives encrypted inputs and verifies their proofs to determine the encrypted inputs $\{X_i\}_{i \in \mathcal{I}}$ of the computation.

Apart from checking the inputs during the input phase, the verifier does not need to be present for the remainder of the computation until receiving π from $\mathcal{R}$. This is what makes verification "universal": in practice, we envision that a trusted party publicly announces the Paillier public keys, and the input parties publicly announce their encrypted inputs with associated proofs: then, anybody can use the verification procedure to verify if a given proof π is correct with respect to these inputs. In [SV15], we prove that:

Theorem 1. *Protocol UVCDN implements verifiable secure function evaluation in the random oracle model.*

The proof uses two simulators: one for a honest majority of computation parties; one for a corrupted majority. The former simulator extends the one from [CDN01], obtaining privacy with a reduction to semantic security of the threshold Paillier cryptosystem. The latter does not guarantee privacy, and so can simulate the adversary by running the real protocol, ensuring correctness by witness-extended emulation.

5   Concluding Remarks

Our security model is specific to the CDN setting in two respects. First, we explicitly model that the verifier receives a Paillier encryption of the result (as opposed to another kind of encryption or commitment). We chose this formulation for concreteness; but our model generalises easily to other representations of the result. Second, it is specific to the setting where a minority of parties may be actively corrupted; but it is possible to change the model to other corruption models. For instance, it is possible to model the setting from [BDO14] where privacy is guaranteed when there is at least one honest computation party (and our protocols can be adapted to that setting). The combination of passively secure multiparty computation with universal verifiability is another interesting possible adaptation.

Our protocols are secure in the random oracle model "without dependent auxiliary input" [Wee09]. This means our security proofs assume that the random oracle has not been used before the protocol starts. Moreover, our simulator can only simulate logarithmically many sequential runs of our protocol due to technical limits of witness-extended emulation. These technical issues reflect the real-life problem that a verifier cannot see if a set of computation parties have just performed a computation, or they have simply replayed an earlier computation transcript. As discussed in [Unr07], both problems can be solved in practice by instantiating the random oracle with a keyed hash function, with every computation using a fresh random key. Note that all existing constructions require the random oracle model; achieving universally verifiable (or publicly auditable) multiparty computation in the standard model is open.

Several interesting variants of our protocol are possible. First, it is easy to achieve publicly auditable multiparty computation [BDO14] by performing a public decryption of the result rather than a private decryption for the result party. Another variant is basic outsourcing of computation, in which the result party does not need to be present at the time of the computation, but afterwards gets a transcript from which it can derive the computation result. Finally, it is possible to achieve universal verifiability using other threshold cryptosystems than Paillier. In particular, while the threshold ElGamal cryptosystem is much more efficient than threshold Paillier, it cannot be used directly with our protocols because it does not have a general decryption operation; but universally verifiable multiparty using ElGamal should still be possible by instead adapting the "conditional gate" variant of the CDN protocol from [ST04].

Finally, to close the loop, we note that our techniques can also be applied to reduce the cost of verification in universally verifiable voting schemes. Namely, for voting schemes relying on homomorphic tallying, we note that the Σ-proofs for correct decryption of the election result by the respective talliers can be combined into a single Σ-proof of constant size (independent of the number of talliers). Similarly, for voting schemes relying on mix-based tallying, the Σ-proofs for correct decryption of each vote by the respective talliers is reduced to a constant size per vote.

Acknowledgements. The authors thank Sebastiaan de Hoogh, Thijs Laarhoven, and Niels de Vreede for useful discussions. This work was supported in part by the European Commission through the ICT program under contract INFSO-ICT-284833 (PUFFIN). The research leading to these results has received funding from the European Union Seventh Framework Programme (FP7/2007-2013) under grant agreement no 609611 (PRACTICE).

References

[AABN08] Abdalla, M., An, J.H., Bellare, M., Namprempre, C.: From Identification to signatures via the Fiat-Shamir transform: necessary and sufficient conditions for security and forward-security. IEEE Trans. Inf. theory **54**(8), 3631–3646 (2008)

[ACG+14] Ananth, P., Chandran, N., Goyal, V., Kanukurthi, B., Ostrovsky, R.: Achieving privacy in verifiable computation with multiple servers – without FHE and without pre-processing. In: Krawczyk, H. (ed.) PKC 2014. LNCS, vol. 8383, pp. 149–166. Springer, Heidelberg (2014)

[BCD+09] Bogetoft, P., Christensen, D.L., Damgård, I., Geisler, M., Jakobsen, T., Krøigaard, M., Nielsen, J.D., Nielsen, J.B., Nielsen, K., Pagter, J., Schwartzbach, M., Toft, T.: Secure multiparty computation goes live. In: Dingledine, R., Golle, P. (eds.) FC 2009. LNCS, vol. 5628, pp. 325–343. Springer, Heidelberg (2009)

[BDO14] Baum, C., Damgård, I., Orlandi, C.: Publicly auditable secure multi-party computation. In: Abdalla, M., De Prisco, R. (eds.) SCN 2014. LNCS, vol. 8642, pp. 175–196. Springer, Heidelberg (2014)

[BR93] Bellare, M., Rogaway, P.: Random oracles are practical: a paradigm for designing efficient protocols. In: Proceedings of CCS 1993, pp. 62–73. ACM (1993)

[Can98] Canetti, R.: Security and composition of multi-party cryptographic protocols. J. Cryptol. **13**, 2000 (1998)

[CDN01] Cramer, R., Damgård, I.B., Nielsen, J.B.: Multiparty computation from threshold homomorphic encryption. In: Pfitzmann, B. (ed.) EUROCRYPT 2001. LNCS, vol. 2045, pp. 280–300. Springer, Heidelberg (2001)

[CF85] Cohen, J., Fischer, M.: A robust and verifiable cryptographically secure election scheme. In: Proceedings of FOCS 1985, pp. 372–382. IEEE (1985)

[Des93] Desmedt, Y.: Threshold cryptosystems. In: Seberry, J., Zheng, Y. (eds.) AUSCRYPT 1992. LNCS, vol. 718, pp. 1–14. Springer, Heidelberg (1993)

[dH12] de Hoogh, S.: Design of large scale applications of secure multiparty computation: secure linear programming. Ph.D. thesis, Eindhoven University of Technology (2012)

[DJ01] Damgård, I., Jurik, M.: A generalisation, a simpli.cation and some applications of paillier's probabilistic public-key system. In: Kim, K. (ed.) PKC 2001. LNCS, vol. 1992, pp. 119–136. Springer, Heidelberg (2001)

[DN03] Damgård, I.B., Nielsen, J.B.: Universally composable efficient multiparty computation from threshold homomorphic encryption. In: Boneh, D. (ed.) CRYPTO 2003. LNCS, vol. 2729, pp. 247–264. Springer, Heidelberg (2003)

[DPSZ12] Damgård, I., Pastro, V., Smart, N., Zakarias, S.: Multiparty computation from somewhat homomorphic encryption. In: Safavi-Naini, R., Canetti, R. (eds.) CRYPTO 2012. LNCS, vol. 7417, pp. 643–662. Springer, Heidelberg (2012)

[EFLL12] Ejgenberg, Y., Farbstein, M., Levy, M., Lindell, Y.: SCAPI: The secure computation application programming interface. IACR Cryptology ePrint Archive 2012:629 (2012)

[FGP14] Fiore, D., Gennaro, R., Pastro, V.: Efficiently verifiable computation on encrypted data. In: Proceedings of CCS 2014, pp. 844–855. ACM (2014)

[GK03] Goldwasser, S., Kalai, Y.T.: On the (In)security of the Fiat-Shamir paradigm. In: Proceedings of FOCS 2003, pp. 102–113. IEEE Computer Society (2003)

[GKP+13] Goldwasser, S., Kalai, Y.T., Popa, R.A., Vaikuntanathan, V., Zeldovich, N.: Reusable garbled circuits and succinct functional encryption. In: Proceedings of STOC 2013, pp. 555–564. ACM (2013)

[IPS09] Ishai, Y., Prabhakaran, M., Sahai, A.: Secure arithmetic computation with no honest majority. In: Reingold, O. (ed.) TCC 2009. LNCS, vol. 5444, pp. 294–314. Springer, Heidelberg (2009)

[Jur03] Jurik, M.J.:. Extensions to the Paillier cryptosystem with applications to cryptological protocols. Ph.D. thesis, University of Aarhus (2003)

[KMR12]   Keller, M., Mikkelsen, G.L., Rupp, A.: Efficient threshold zero-knowledge
          with applications to user-centric protocols. In: Smith, A. (ed.) ICITS 2012.
          LNCS, vol. 7412, pp. 147–166. Springer, Heidelberg (2012)
[NKDM03] Nicolosi, A., Krohn, M.N., Dodis, Y., Mazières, D.: Proactive two-party
          signatures for user authentication. In: Proceedings of NDSS 2003. The
          Internet Society (2003)
[Pai99]   Paillier, P.: Public-key cryptosystems based on composite degree residuos-
          ity classes. In: Stern, J. (ed.) EUROCRYPT 1999. LNCS, vol. 1592, pp.
          223–238. Springer, Heidelberg (1999)
[PHGR13] Parno, B., Howell, J., Gentry, C., Raykova, M.: Pinocchio: nearly practical
          verifiable computation. In: Proceedings of S&P 2013, pp. 238–252. IEEE
          (2013)
[Sch89]   Schnorr, C.-P.: Efficient identification and signatures for smart cards. In:
          Brassard, G. (ed.) CRYPTO 1989. LNCS, vol. 435, pp. 239–252. Springer,
          Heidelberg (1990)
[SK95]   Sako, K., Kilian, J.: Receipt-free mix-type voting scheme. In: Guillou, L.C.,
          Quisquater, J.-J. (eds.) EUROCRYPT 1995. LNCS, vol. 921, pp. 393–403.
          Springer, Heidelberg (1995)
[ST04]   Schoenmakers, B., Tuyls, P.: Practical two-party computation based on the
          conditional gate. In: Lee, P.J. (ed.) ASIACRYPT 2004. LNCS, vol. 3329,
          pp. 119–136. Springer, Heidelberg (2004)
[ST06]   Schoenmakers, B., Tuyls, P.: Efficient binary conversion for Paillier
          encrypted values. In: Vaudenay, S. (ed.) EUROCRYPT 2006. LNCS, vol.
          4004, pp. 522–537. Springer, Heidelberg (2006)
[SV15]   Schoenmakers, B., Veeningen, M.: Universally verifiable multiparty com-
          putation from threshold homomorphic cryptosystems. Cryptology ePrint
          Archive, Report 2015/058 (full version of this paper) (2015). http://eprint.
          iacr.org/
[Unr07]   Unruh, D.: Random oracles and auxiliary input. In: Menezes, A. (ed.)
          CRYPTO 2007. LNCS, vol. 4622, pp. 205–223. Springer, Heidelberg (2007)
[WB13]   Walfish, M., Blumberg, A.J.: Verifying computations without reexecut-
          ing them: from theoretical possibility to near-practicality. Electron. Collo-
          quium Computat. Complex. 20, 165 (2013)
[Wee09]   Wee, H.: Zero knowledge in the random oracle model, revisited. In: Mat-
          sui, M. (ed.) ASIACRYPT 2009. LNCS, vol. 5912, pp. 417–434. Springer,
          Heidelberg (2009)

Communication-Optimal Proactive Secret Sharing for Dynamic Groups

Joshua Baron[4], Karim El Defrawy[1], Joshua Lampkins[1,3]($\boxtimes$),
and Rafail Ostrovsky[2,3]

[1] Information and Systems Sciences Laboratory (ISSL), HRL Laboratories,
Malibu, CA 90265, USA
kmeldefrawy@hrl.com
[2] Department of Computer Science, UCLA, Los Angeles, CA 90095, USA
rafail@cs.ucla.edu
[3] Department of Mathematics, UCLA, Los Angeles, CA 90095, USA
jlampkins@math.ucla.edu
[4] RAND Corporation, Santa Monica, CA 90401, USA
jbaron@rand.org

Abstract. *Proactive* secret sharing (PSS) schemes are designed for settings where long-term confidentiality of secrets is required, specifically, when *all participating parties may eventually be corrupted*. PSS schemes periodically refresh secrets and reset corrupted parties to an uncorrupted state; in PSS the corruption threshold of parties is replaced with a corruption *rate* which cannot be violated. In *dynamic proactive secret sharing* (DPSS) the group of participating parties can vary during the course of execution. Accordingly, DPSS is ideal when the set of participating parties changes over the lifetime of the secret or where removal of parties is necessary if they become severely corrupted. This paper presents the first DPSS scheme with optimal amortized per-secret communication in the number of parties, n: This paper requires $O(1)$ communication, as compared to $O(n^4)$ or $\exp(n)$ in previous work. We present perfectly and statistically secure schemes with near-optimal threshold in each case. We also describe how to construct a communication-efficient dynamic proactively-secure multiparty computation (DPMPC) protocol which achieves the same thresholds.

Keywords: Proactive security · Secret sharing · Mobile secret sharing · Dynamic groups · Secure multiparty computation

1 Introduction

Secret sharing [6,31] is a foundational primitive in cryptography, especially in secure computation. A secret sharing scheme typically consists of a protocol for sharing a secret (or multiple secrets) and a protocol for reconstructing the

---

J. Baron—Work performed while at HRL Laboratories.
J. Lampkins—Work performed while at HRL Laboratories.

© Springer International Publishing Switzerland 2015
T. Malkin et al. (Eds.): ACNS 2015, LNCS 9092, pp. 23–41, 2015.
DOI: 10.1007/978-3-319-28166-7_2

shared secret(s). The secret sharing protocol distributes shares of the secret among n parties in the presence of an adversary who may corrupt up to t parties; security of the secret sharing scheme ensures that such an adversary will learn no information about the secret.

However, traditional secret sharing may be insufficient in some real-world settings; specifically, settings that may require a secret to be secured for a long period of time, especially with respect to the ability of an adversary to *eventually corrupt all parties*. Traditional (threshold-based) secret sharing schemes are insecure once $t + 1$ parties have been corrupted. Of particular concern are distributed storage and computing settings in the presence of advanced persistent threats who, given sufficient time, will successfully corrupt enough parties to break the threshold that guarantees security. To address this issue, Ostrovsky and Yung [28] introduced the *proactive security* model. In this model, the execution of the protocol(s) is divided into phases. The adversary is allowed to corrupt and decorrupt parties at will, under the constraint that no more than a threshold number of parties are corrupt in any given phase. This means that every party may eventually become corrupt subject to the corruption rate constraint. Such an adversary is called a *mobile* adversary.[1]

While standard proactively-secure protocols are able to satisfy security requirements of long-term storage and computation, they lack the ability to change the number of parties during the course of the protocol. Such a restraint is particularly challenging in the case of long-term storage or computation, which was one of the reasons that the proactive security model was constructed in the first place. We refer to secret sharing schemes that are both proactively-secure and allow the set of parties to dynamically change as *dynamic proactive secret sharing* (DPSS) schemes. Such schemes have also been the subject of numerous papers [17,30,33,34] but none of them has satisfying (linear or constant) communication complexity. The dynamic setting allows for the reality that some parties (deployed as physical or virtual servers) may be attacked to the point of not being able to be reset to a pristine, uncorrupted state (e.g., they may become physically damaged). When the set of parties can be dynamically changed, this issue could be addressed by excluding the severely corrupted one(s) entirely (and, ideally, include new uncorrupted ones). In addition, DPSS within large distributed systems enables a truly "moving target defense", where the set of participating nodes is a smaller, dynamically changing subset of the whole distributed system that is therefore more difficult to target for attack.

We argue that adopting efficient DPSS schemes in the future may help prevent large-scale compromises of servers that store user data, often at financial institutions or large enterprises [27,32]. Such breaches show an increasing need for secure long-term storage solutions. Standard secret sharing can address this issue by distributing data to avoid single points of compromise or failure, but

---

[1] The term "mobile" is heavily used in the secure computation literature: "dynamic" secret sharing, as discussed in this paper, has historically been called "mobile" secret sharing (for instance, see [30]), which is a completely different concept than the mobile adversary definition.

given enough time, an adversary may be able to compromise all the servers that store the data. Proactive secret sharing partially addresses this issue by refreshing and recovering, yet still has no means of securing against a server that becomes "permanently" compromised (e.g., by compromising its boot system and/or firmware). Dynamic proactive secret sharing addresses this issue by allowing the set of servers to change dynamically in response to corruptions and removing permanently compromised servers. Furthermore, the total number of servers may change, thereby increasing the concrete number of servers that would have to be corrupted to exceed the threshold corruption rate. Thus in response to an attack, the threshold may be temporarily raised to increase security, and when the attack is resolved, the threshold may be reduced by reducing the number of participating servers to increase efficiency. Our goal is therefore to construct a communication-efficient DPSS scheme, particularly one that can be used as a building block in a system for storing large data files and where the proactive refresh and recovery of shares becomes a performance bottleneck when the number of parties (or servers) increases. While we acknowledge that several other layers of security must be developed for a complete data storage solution to be secure against a mobile adversary, we argue that constructing an efficient DPSS is an important step towards realizing this goal though.

1.1 Techniques

We first briefly outline the techniques utilized in the rest of the paper.

Batched Secret Sharing. One of the foundational techniques allowing us to achieve optimal amortized communication complexity is batched secret sharing [21]. Such sharings are used to encode a "batch" of multiple secrets as distinct points on a single polynomial, and then distribute shares to each party as in standard Shamir secret sharing [31]. The number of secrets stored in the polynomial (the "batch size") is chosen to be $O(n)$. This allows the parties to share $O(n)$ secrets with $O(n)$ total communication complexity so that the amortized complexity is $O(1)$ per secret.

Hyper-Invertible Matrices. A hyper-invertible matrix [5] satisfies the property that any square submatrix formed by removing rows and columns is invertible. Hyper-invertible matrices are used in our protocol for efficient error detection. If a vector of $n - 3t$ secret sharings is concatenated with t random sharings and then multiplied by a $n \times (n - 2t)$ hyper-invertible matrix, then each party can be given one of the sharings in the resultant vector of n sharings without revealing any information about the $n - 3t$ secrets. Furthermore, if any of the original $n - 2t$ sharings are malformed (meaning that the shares do not lie on a polynomial of correct degree), then at least $2t + 1$ of the resultant n sharings will be malformed. This allows the parties to verify that sharings are correct while preserving the privacy of the secrets. Since $n - 3t$ (which is $O(n)$) sharings are verified by sending n (also $O(n)$) sharings to n parties, this only requires constant amortized communication bandwidth.

Party Virtualization. Party virtualization [8] is a method for transforming a multiparty protocol by replacing each party in the protocol with a "virtual" party. The virtual party is a committee of parties that perform a multiparty protocol to emulate the actions of an individual party in the original (untransformed) protocol. The advantage of this technique is that it allows the corruption threshold to be raised from that of the untransformed protocol. In [15], the authors demonstrate how to raise the corruption threshold to near-optimal while only increasing the communication complexity by a constant factor, which is the approach we take in this paper.

1.2 Contributions

In this paper we present a new communication-optimal *dynamic proactive secret sharing (DPSS)* scheme. In addition to a protocol for distributing shares of a secret and a protocol for reconstructing the secret, a DPSS scheme must also contain a protocol for *refreshing* the shares and (in the case of a malicious adversary) for *recovering* the shares amongst a group of parties that may change from one refresh to the next. A refresh protocol changes the shares held by the parties such that old shares (before the refresh) cannot be combined with new shares (after the refresh) to gain any information about the secret. A recovery protocol allows decorrupted parties to recover shares that may have been destroyed or altered by the adversary. The communication complexity of the refresh and recovery protocols are often a bottleneck for proactive secret sharing schemes.

As will be defined in Sect. 4.1 (Definition 4), a DPSS scheme consists of three protocols: Share, Redistribute, and Open that distribute, redistribute, and reconstruct shares of a secret, respectively. For the protocols Share and Open, we use the protocols RobustShare and Reco (respectively) from [15].

Our main contribution is the construction of a new Redistribute protocol with the following properties: (1) *Optimal (Constant Amortized) Communication Bandwidth:* Out of currently published protocols for DPSS, ours has the lowest amortized communication complexity. We achieve $O(1)$ per-secret amortized communication complexity (measured as the number of field elements).[2] (2) *No Cryptographic Assumptions:* Ours is the first DPSS scheme that provides information-theoretic security without making any cryptographic assumptions. (3) *Eliminating Party Virtualization:* The most efficient DPSS protocol to date is that of [30] where "party virtualization" is utilized when the set of parties is decreased.[3] "Party virtualization" occurs when each real party holds internal data (i.e., shares) corresponding to some virtual party. That is, there are n

---

[2] We only claim that the amortized communication complexity is optimal. Reducing the non-amortized complexity is a possible area for future work.

[3] Note that the term "party virtualization" has a different meaning in [30] than is typically used, either in Sect. 1.1 or in other secure computation literature such as [15]; we use here the terminology of [30] in quotes and only in this paragraph.

parties, but there are $n + v$ virtual parties, and while each real party gets her own private share, each real party also gets all v shares of all the virtual parties. As stated in [30], this technique is "somewhat unsatisfying theoretically because using this method to reduce the threshold does not reduce the asymptotic computational overhead of the protocol." In this paper, we present a DPSS protocol that does not use party virtualization as in [30] and thus reduces the asymptotic computational and communication overhead of the protocol.

Finally, as an application of our DPSS scheme we briefly describe how to construct a dynamic proactively-secure multiparty computation (DPMPC) protocol.

1.3 Outline

The rest of the paper is organized as follows: In Sect. 2 we discuss related work. The roadblocks facing constructing an efficient DPSS scheme are described in Sect. 3. We give the necessary technical preliminaries in Sect. 4 and then give the details of our DPSS scheme in Sect. 5 (while some of the subprotocols are deferred to the full version of this paper [4]). In Sect. 6 we describe how the threshold may be raised in the statistical security setting. We show how our DPSS scheme can be applied to secure multiparty computation in Sect. 7. Security definitions and proofs are given in the full version of this paper [4].

2 Related Work

The same work [28] introducing the proactive security model also contained the first proactive secret sharing (PSS) scheme and proactively-secure multiparty computation (PMPC) protocol. PSS was the central tool introduced in [28], and there has been significant follow up work on PSS schemes, both in the synchronous and asynchronous network models (see Table 1 for a comparison). Currently the most efficient (non-dynamic) PSS scheme is [3], which has an optimal $O(1)$ amortized communication complexity per secret share, is UC-secure and achieves near-optimal thresholds for both perfect and statistical cases. Currently, the most efficient DPSS scheme is that of [30], which works in asynchronous networks, provides cryptographic security and achieves a corruption threshold of $t/n < 1/3$, but has prohibitive communication complexity in the number of parties, namely $O(n^4)$. Compared to [30], our DPSS protocols require only constant (amortized) communication are perfectly (resp. statistically) secure with near-optimal corruption thresholds of $t/n < 1/3 - \epsilon$ (resp. $t/n < 1/2 - \epsilon$) and work with synchronous networks. Extending our work to asynchronous networks and improving the threshold and communication bounds of [30] is still an open problem.

In addition to proactive secret sharing, proactive security has played a fundamental role in several areas, including proactively secure threshold encryption and signature schemes [7,10,18–20,25,26,29] (and in particular [1], which also sketches a definition of UC security in the proactive framework), intrusion-resilient signatures [24], eavesdropping games [22], pseudorandomness [11], and state-machine replication [12,13].

Table 1. Comparison of Non-Dynamic Proactive Secret Sharing (PSS) and Dynamic Proactive Secret Sharing (DPSS) Schemes. Threshold is for each reboot phase. Our communication complexity is amortized per bit.

Paper	Dynamic	Network	Security	Threshold	Communication complexity
[33]	Yes	synch.	Cryptographic	$t/n < 1/2$	$\exp(n)$
[34]	Yes	asynch.	Cryptographic	$t/n < 1/3$	$\exp(n)$
[9]	No	asynch.	Cryptographic	$t/n < 1/3$	$O(n^4)$
[30]	Yes	asynch.	Cryptographic	$t/n < 1/3$	$O(n^4)$
[23]	No	synch.	Cryptographic	$t/n < 1/2$	$O(n^2)$
[3]	No	synch.	Perfect	$t/n < 1/3 - \epsilon$	$O(1)$
[3]	No	synch.	Statistical	$t/n < 1/2 - \epsilon$	$O(1)$
This paper	Yes	synch.	Perfect	$t/n < 1/3 - \epsilon$	$O(1)$
This paper	Yes	synch	Statistical	$t/n < 1/2 - \epsilon$	$O(1)$

The only two known general PMPC protocols are [28] and [3]. The former protocol is proven secure in the stand-alone corruption model and requires at least $O(Cn^3)$ communication complexity (where C is the size of the circuit), while the latter is UC-secure and has near-linear communication complexity of $O(DC \log^2(C) \text{polylog}(n) + D \text{poly}(n) \log^2(C))$ (where D is the depth of the circuit). We provide a dynamic PMPC protocol in this paper, whereas neither of the above PMPC protocols is dynamic.

3   Roadblocks in Constructing Communication-Optimal DPSS

The most efficient DPSS scheme to date is that of [30], and the most efficient PSS scheme to date is that of [3]. In this section, we explain why straightforward modifications of either of these would not produce a DPSS scheme with optimal communication requirements.

In [3], the refresh is performed by having the parties generate new polynomials Q to mask the old polynomials H; then each party generates a share of the new polynomial by locally computing her share of $H + Q$ and relabeling $H \leftarrow H + Q$. Although this works in the non-dynamic proactive setting, in the dynamic proactive setting this would allow t corrupt parties in the old group and an additional t' corrupt parties in the new group to learn their shares on the new polynomial (where t' is the corruption threshold in the new group). This could be enough for the adversary to reconstruct the secret(s) rendering the scheme insecure.

In [30], this issue is prevented by constructing the polynomial Q such that no party in the old group knows her share of Q. More specifically, the parties in the old group construct a polynomial R_j for each P'_j in the new group such that $R_j(\beta_j) = 0$. Then the Q and the R_j are generated simultaneously so that each party in the old group only learns her share of $Q + R_j$ for each j. This technique preserves security but would not yield the optimal communication bandwidth that we aim for. Generating one polynomial for each party in the new group would result in a communication complexity of at least $O(n^2)$ for masking $O(n)$ secrets while our goal is $O(1)$ (amortized) communication per secret.

In this paper we provide a solution that generates the polynomials Q without revealing any share of Q to the parties in the old group, and maintains optimal communication efficiency. This technique is one of the main contributions of the paper and is described in detail in Sect. 5.2.

4   Preliminaries

In this section we provide some preliminaries required for the rest of the paper.

4.1   Definitions

We first provide definitions of secret sharing (SS), proactive secret sharing (PSS), and dynamic proactive secret sharing (DPSS) schemes. The definitions below are for perfectly secure protocols; the definitions for statistically secure protocols are the same, except that the termination, correctness, and secrecy properties are allowed to be violated with negligible probability. As our protocols are for sharings of multiple secrets, we write the protocols for a vector of secrets over a finite field $\mathbb{F}$, treating the case in which the vector is of length one as a special case.

Definition 1. *A* secret sharing scheme *consists of two protocols,* Share *and* Open, *which allows a dealer to share a vector of secrets* s *among a group of n parties such that the secrets remain secure against an adversary, and allows any group of $n - t$ uncorrupted parties to reconstruct the secrets.*

Assuming that no more than t parties are corrupt throughout the execution of the protocols, the following three properties hold:

- *Termination: All honest parties will complete the execution of* Share *and* Open.
- *Correctness: Upon completing* Share, *there is a fixed vector* $\mathbf{v} \in \mathbb{F}^W$ *(where W is the number of secrets to be shared) such that all honest parties will output* v *upon completion of* Open. *Furthermore, if the dealer was honest during the execution of* Share, *then* $\mathbf{v} = \mathbf{s}$.
- *Secrecy: If the dealer is uncorrupted, then the adversary gains no information on* s.

The definition of a PSS scheme is essentially the same as the definition of an SS scheme, with the addition of Refresh and Recovery protocols for securing against a mobile adversary. The Refresh protocol refreshes data to prevent a mobile adversary from learning secrets, and the Recovery protocols allows de-corrupted parties to recover their secrets, preventing the adversary from destroying data. Before defining a PSS scheme, we need to define refresh and recovery phases.

Definition 2. *A refresh phase (resp. recovery phase) is the period of time between two consecutive executions of the* Refresh *(resp.* Recovery*) protocol. Furthermore, the period between* Share *and the first* Refresh *(resp.* Recovery*) is a phase, and the period between the last* Refresh *(resp.* Recovery*) and* Open *is a phase. Any* Refresh *(resp.* Recovery*) protocol is considered to be in both adjacent phases.*

Definition 3. *A* proactive secret sharing scheme *consists of four protocols,* Share, Refresh, Recover, *and* Open, *which allows a dealer to share a vector of secrets* s *among a group of n parties such that the secrets remain secure against a mobile adversary, and allows any group of n−t uncorrupted parties to reconstruct the secrets. The* Refresh *protocol prevents the mobile adversary from discovering the secrets, and the* Recover *protocol prevents the adversary from destroying the secrets.*

Assuming that no more than t parties are corrupt during any recovery phase, the following two properties hold:

- *Termination: All honest parties will complete each execution of* Share, Refresh, Recover, *and* Open.
- *Correctness: Same as in Definition 1.*

Assuming that no more than t parties are corrupt during any refresh phase, the following property holds:

- *Secrecy: Same as in Definition 1.*

For the definition of a DPSS scheme, we combine the Refresh and Recover protocols into one protocol, Redistribute, which also allows transferring the set of secrets from one group of parties to another and change the threshold. Similarly, we combine *refresh phase* and *recovery phase*, and refer to it simply as a *phase*.

As the number of parties changes, the threshold must change as well. For any given number of parties, n, there is a corresponding threshold, t, which will depend on the particular security and network assumptions of the scheme. Let $\tau(n)$ denote the threshold corresponding to n, and let $n^{(i)}$ denote the number of parties during phase i.

Definition 4. *A* dynamic proactive secret sharing scheme *consists of three protocols,* Share, Redistribute, *and* Open, *which allows a dealer to share a vector of secrets* s *among a group of* $n^{(1)}$ *parties such that the secrets remain secure against a mobile adversary, and allows any group of* $n^{(L)} - t^{(L)}$ *uncorrupted parties to reconstruct the secrets (where L is the last phase). The* Redistribute *protocol prevents the mobile adversary from discovering or destroying the secrets, and allows the set of parties and the threshold to change.*

Assuming that for each i, no more than $t^{(i)} = \tau(n^{(i)})$ parties are corrupt during phase i, the following three properties hold:

- *Termination: All honest parties currently engaged in the protocol will complete each execution of* Share, Redistribute, *and* Open.
- *Correctness: Same as in Definition 1.*
- *Secrecy: Same as in Definition 1.*

4.2 Notation and Technical Details

We assume that there are W secrets in some finite field $\mathbb{F}$ stored among a party set $\mathcal{P}$ of size n. The secrets are stored as follows:

We fix some generator ζ of $\mathbb{F}^*$. Each batch of ℓ secrets is stored in a polynomial H of degree d (where the value of d depends on the security model as described below). The polynomial H is chosen such that $H(\zeta^j)$ is the jth secret for $j \in [\ell]$ and $H(\zeta^{\ell+j})$ is random for $j \in [d-\ell+1]$. (We use the notation $[X]$ to denote the set $\{1, \ldots, X\}$, and we let $[X] \times [Y]$ denote the Cartesian product of the two sets. We let $[A, B]$ denote the set of integers $[A, \ldots, B]$). Each party $P_i \in \mathcal{P}$ is given $H(\alpha_i)$ as her share of the secret. In our scheme we use the protocol RobustShare from [15] to perform the sharing. When the secrets are to be opened, all parties send their shares to some party, who interpolates the shares on the polynomials to reconstruct the secrets. We use the protocol Reco from [15] to perform secret opening.

Our new redistribution protocol given in Sect. 5 redistributes the secrets to a new set of parties $\mathcal{P}'$ of size n'. The parties in $\mathcal{P}'$ are denoted by P'_j for $j \in [n']$. The share of a party $P'_j \in \mathcal{P}'$ is $H(\beta_j)$. We require that $\alpha_i \neq \beta_j$ for each i, j (and that no α_i or β_j is equal to ζ^k for any $k \in [\ell]$). Since we use the labels t, ℓ, and d for $\mathcal{P}$, we use the labels t', ℓ', and d' for $\mathcal{P}'$.

For simplicity of notation, our redistribution protocol below assumes that W is a multiple of $4\ell^2(n - 3t)$. If W is not a multiple of $4\ell^2(n - 3t)$, we can generate random sharings of batches to make it so. Using RanDouSha from [15], this can be done with poly(n) communication complexity, and since it adds only a poly(n) amount of data to W, this does not affect the overall communication complexity of redistributing W secrets.

In this paper we provide a perfectly secure and a statistically secure version of the redistribution protocol required to construct our DPSS scheme. For the perfectly (statistically) secure protocol, the threshold can be made arbitrarily close to $n/3$ ($n/2$). We describe the threshold, batch size, and degree of polynomials for the two versions below.

In the perfectly secure protocol, we fix three nonzero constants η, θ, and ι that satisfy $\eta + \theta + \iota < 1/3$. The batch size, ℓ, is the highest power of 2 not greater than $\lfloor \eta n \rfloor$; the threshold is $t = \lfloor \theta n \rfloor$; and the degree of the polynomials that share the secrets are $d = \ell + t + \lfloor \iota n \rfloor - 1$. The number of parties may increase or decrease by no more than a factor of 2 at each redistribution. Furthermore, the number of parties cannot decrease so much that the corrupt parties in the old group can interpolate the new polynomials (i.e., $d' - \ell' \geq t$); and the number of parties cannot increase so much that the uncorrupted parties in the old group cannot interpolate the new polynomials in the presence of corrupt shares (i.e., $d' + 2t + 1 \leq n$).

In the statistically secure protocol, we initially pick a low threshold, and then later raise the threshold using the party virtualization[4] technique of [15]. The protocol in Sect. 5 is written as a perfectly secure protocol with a lower threshold, and then this is raised using statistically secure virtualization (see Sect. 6 for a discussion of this). For the initial, low threshold, we select the batch size, ℓ, to be the highest power of 2 not greater than $n/4$; the threshold is $t < n/16$; and the degree of the polynomials is $d = \ell + 2t - 1$. In the statistically secure version, we assume that t will increase or decrease by a factor of no more than 2 at each redistribution (i.e., $t/2 \leq t' \leq t$).

Note that while (theoretically) it may seem that there is no reason to raise n without raising t, in a real world setting one may increase n while fixing t precisely to increase the concrete number of additional servers that an adversary has to corrupt. To simplify demonstration in this paper we assume that n is minimal for a given t (i.e., we assume that n could not be decreased without decreasing t).

Our redistribution protocol requires the use of a hyper-invertible matrix. A *hyper-invertible* matrix is such that any square submatrix formed by removing rows and columns is invertible. It is shown in [5] that one can construct a hyper-invertible matrix as follows: Pick $2a$ distinct field elements $\theta_1, \ldots, \theta_a, \phi_1, \ldots, \phi_a \in \mathbb{F}$, and let M be the matrix be such that if $(y_1, \ldots, y_a)^T = M(x_1, \ldots, x_a)^T$, then the points $(\theta_1, y_1), \ldots, (\theta_a, y_a)$ lie on the polynomial of degree $\leq a - 1$ which evaluates to x_j at ϕ_j for each $j \in [a]$. (In other words, M interpolates the points with x-coordinates $\theta_1, \ldots, \theta_a$ on a polynomial given the points with x-coordinates $\phi_1, \ldots, \phi_a$ on that polynomial.) Then any submatrix of M is hyper-invertible. For our protocol, we let M be some (publicly known) hyper-invertible matrix with n rows and $n - 2t$ columns.

Throughout the protocol, the Berlekamp-Welch algorithm is used to interpolate polynomials in the presence of corrupt shares introduced by the adversary. As was noted in [16], if M is as above and $\boldsymbol{y} = M\boldsymbol{x}$, then we can also use Berlekamp-Welch to "interpolate" $\boldsymbol{x}$ from $\boldsymbol{y}$ if the adversary corrupts no more than t coordinates of $\boldsymbol{y}$.

5   The Redistribution Protocol

In this section, we provide the details of the protocol that redistributes sharings of secrets from one set of parties to another. The first portion of the protocol changes the threshold of the polynomials that share the secret (if the number of servers is changing). Recall that the batch size is the highest power of two not

---

[4] The term "party virtualization" has a different meaning in [30] than it has in [15].

greater than $\lfloor \eta n \rfloor$ (resp. $n/4$) in the perfectly (resp. statistically) secure protocol. This means that a change in the threshold/number of servers does not necessarily lead to a change in batch size. Thus there are four cases to consider: (1) The threshold is decreasing, and the batch size is not changing; (2) the threshold is decreasing, and the batch size is decreasing; (3) the threshold is increasing, and the batch size is not changing; and (4) the threshold is increasing, and the batch size is increasing. The second portion of the protocol refreshes the sharings and allows parties in the new group to learn their shares.

To simplify exposition, the protocol is broken into several sub-protocols. The four protocols Threshold_Change$_i$ for $i = 1, 2, 3, 4$ correspond to the four cases outlined in the previous paragraph. The protocol Refresh_Recovery performs refresh and recovery.

In order to change the set of parties, the current (honest) parties must agree on which parties to remove and which parties to add. This could be determined by the parties jointly invoking a voting algorithm, by a trusted administrator making the decision, or by following some pre-determined schedule. How exactly this is implemented is beyond the scope of this paper.

We now provide an overview and the intuition behind the operation of the protocol.

5.1 Overview of Threshold Change

To simplify the illustration of the operation of the protocol we will treat Threshold_Change$_2$ as an example. In this case we are decreasing the threshold and batch size. Since we restrict the batch size to be a power of 2, the batch size will be cut in half (that is, $\ell' = \ell/2$). If the parties had access to an uncorruptible trusted party, then the parties could have the trusted party change the threshold and batch size for a polynomial H as follows:

1. Each party sends all their shares of the degree d polynomial H to the trusted party.
2. The trusted party constructs two new polynomials h_1 and h_2 of degree d' such that $h_1(\zeta^j) = H(\zeta^j)$ and $h_2(\zeta^j) = H(\zeta^{\ell'+j})$ for each $j \in [\ell']$. Fresh randomness is used for to determine the points $h_i(\zeta^j)$ for $i = 1, 2$ and $j = [\ell' + 1, d' + 1]$.
3. The trusted party sends each party their shares of h_1 and h_2.

In the absence of a trusted party, the parties emulate this simplified protocol using hyper-invertible matrices. The parties will take a vector of $n - 3t$ sharings, add to this t extra random sharings, and then via local computations, multiply the vector by a $n \times n - 2t$ hyper-invertible matrix to get a vector of n sharings. Each party is assigned one of these n sharings and is sent all shares of this sharing from the other parties. Then each party acts as the trusted party in the steps above. The fact that the original vector of $n - 3t$ sharings was padded with an extra t sharings prevents the adversary from learning any information on the secrets.

Once each party is done acting as the trusted party, she then sends the shares of the results to the other parties. Each party, upon receiving the n (or fewer) shares, can apply the Berlekamp-Welch algorithm to interpolate the vector of n shares in the presence of errors to reconstruct the pre-image under multiplication by the hyper-invertible matrix, which is a vector of $n - 2t$ shares. The first $n - 3t$ of these are taken to be the party's shares of the new sharings.

In the case where the trusted party performs the operations, fresh randomness is generated by the trusted party to use in the new sharings. When the parties jointly perform this operation without a trusted party, they instead generate random sharings R, apply a hyper-invertible matrix to these sharings (as they did with the sharings of the actual secrets), and use the points on the resultant sharings as randomness for the new sharing polynomials.

5.2   Overview of Refresh and Recovery

The protocol Refresh_Recovery is a modification of the protocol Block-Redistribute from [3] that is still secure in the dynamic setting (recall that a straightforward adoption is insecure as discussed in Sect. 3). The recovery is performed in essentially the same way as in [3], with the exception that in our scheme the shares are transferred to a new group of parties instead of back to the same group. (The scheme in [3] is for PSS, not DPSS.)

In the dynamic setting, refresh cannot be performed as in [3]. As mentioned in Sect. 3, we need a way for the parties to mask the polynomials H with polynomials Q such that no party in the old group knows a share of $H + Q$ and no party in the new group knows a share of the original H.[5] In [3], the parties generate sharings U that share their shares, and then each party receives a linear combination of these shares that will allow her to recover her shares (if they were corrupted). In our protocol, the parties in the old group generate sharings U that share their shares (just as in [3]), and they additionally generate sharings V, some of which store random data and some of which store a batch of all zeros; then each party in the new group receives a linear combination of the U's and the V's such that this linear combination stores the party's share of $H + Q$ for some masking polynomial Q. Thus the parties in the new group see their shares of $H + Q$ without seeing their shares of H, while the parties in the old group—because the V were generated randomly—do not know any share of Q (and hence they do not know any share of $H + Q$).

---

[5] However, if there is overlap between the old and new groups of servers, such that $P_i = P'_j$ for some $P_i \in \mathcal{P}$ and some $P'_j \in \mathcal{P}'$, and if $\alpha_i = \beta_j$, then this party will know her share of both H and $H + Q$. Nevertheless, this does not cause a security problem, as it does not cause the threshold to be violated; even in this case, only t parties in the old group know shares of H, and only t' parties in the new group know shares of $H + Q$.

5.3   Protocol Specification

In this section we describe the specification of our redistribution protocol. As stated in Definition 4, a DPSS scheme consists of three protocols, Share, Redistribute (which we describe in this section), and Open. For the protocols Share and Open, we use the protocols RobustShare and Reco (respectively) from [15]. Our contribution is the construction of the redistribution protocol (Fig. 1).

The protocol RobustShare allows the parties to share $O(n^2)$ secrets with $O(n^2)$ communication complexity using batch sharing. This is accomplished with hyper-invertible matrices to ensure robustness. The protocol Reco opens a batch of secrets by sending each share to whichever party is supposed to learn the secret. That party then performs error detection/correction to interpolate the secrets in the presence of (possibly) corrupt shares. The protocol RanDouSha from [15] is also used as a subprotocol in our redistribution protocol. The protocol RanDouSha generates random sharings of degree d and additional sharings of the same secrets using degree $2d$ polynomials with constant amortized communication bandwidth. However, for our protocols we do not use the degree $2d$ sharings. There are some instances in which we require a variant of RanDouSha that generates sharings of batches of all zeros. Modifying the protocol to do this is straightforward, as is the modification of the security proof.

The input to the protocol is a $t, \mathcal{P}, Corr, t', \mathcal{P}'$ and a collection of polynomials $H_a^{(k,m)}$ for $(a, k, m) \in [\ell] \times [n - 3t] \times [B]$ that store the secrets.
1. If $t' \neq t$, then one of the following steps is executed:
    1.1 If $t' < t$ and $\ell' = \ell$, invoke Threshold_Change$_1$.
    1.2 If $t' < t$ and $\ell' < \ell$, invoke Threshold_Change$_2$.
    1.3 If $t' > t$ and $\ell' = \ell$, invoke Threshold_Change$_3$.
    1.4 If $t' > t$ and $\ell' > \ell$, invoke Threshold_Change$_4$.
2. Invoke Refresh_Recovery.

Fig. 1. Redistribute.

As seen in Fig. 1, there are four cases for threshold change. To simplify the treatment we only focus on case 2 (see Fig. 2), which is when the threshold is decreasing and the batch size is decreasing, and defer the other three cases to the full version of this paper [4].

The following subprotocol (Fig. 3) describes how refresh and recovery is performed. This subprotocol will be executed at each redistribution regardless of whether the threshold is changing.

After Refresh_Recovery is completed, the parties relabel the $H_a^{(k,m)}$ again so that k varies from 1 to $n' - 3t'$ instead of $n - 3t$. The relabeling is performed in such a way that it preserves lexicographical order as described in the last steps of protocols Threshold_Change$_2$ and Threshold_Change$_4$.

Lowering the Threshold, Batch Size Decreases

Since we assume that the number of parties decreases by no more than a factor of 2, we know that $\ell' = \ell/2$.

1. The parties invoke RanDouSha to generate masking polynomials $H_a^{(k,m)}$ of degree $\leq d$ for $k \in [n - 3t + 1, n - 2t]$ and $a \in [\ell]$, as well as random

   polynomials $R_a^{(k,m)}$ of degree $\leq d$ for $k \in [n - 2t]$ and $a \in [2\ell]$ (where $m \in [B]$).

2. Define $\widetilde{H}_a^{(k,m)}$ for $k \in [n]$ by

$$\left(\widetilde{H}_a^{(1,m)}, \ldots, \widetilde{H}_a^{(n,m)}\right)^T = M \left(H_a^{(1,m)}, \ldots, H_a^{(n-2t,m)}\right)^T,$$

   and similarly define $\widetilde{R}_a^{(k,m)}$ for $k \in [n]$. Each party locally computes their shares of these polynomials and sends his share of each $\widetilde{H}_a^{(j,m)}$ and $\widetilde{R}_a^{(j,m)}$ to party P_j.

3. Each P_i uses Berlekamp-Welch to interpolate the shares of $\widetilde{H}_a^{(i,m)}$ and $\widetilde{R}_a^{(i,m)}$ received in the previous step.

4. Each P_i computes (shares of) the unique polynomials $\widetilde{h}_{2a-1}^{(i,m)}, \widetilde{h}_{2a}^{(i,m)}$ of degree $\leq d'$ for $a \in [\ell]$ and $m \in [B]$ that satisfy the following:

   4.1 $\widetilde{h}_{2a-1}^{(i,m)}(\zeta^j) = \widetilde{H}_a^{(i,m)}(\zeta^j)$ for $j \in [\ell']$.

   4.2 $\widetilde{h}_{2a-1}^{(i,m)}(\zeta^{\ell'+j}) = \widetilde{R}_{2a-1}^{(i,m)}(\zeta^j)$ for $j \in [d' - \ell' + 1]$.

   4.3 $\widetilde{h}_{2a}^{(i,m)}(\zeta^j) = \widetilde{H}_a^{(i,m)}(\zeta^{\ell'+j})$ for $j \in [\ell']$.

   4.4 $\widetilde{h}_{2a}^{(i,m)}(\zeta^{\ell'+j}) = \widetilde{R}_{2a}^{(i,m)}(\zeta^j)$ for $j \in [d' - \ell' + 1]$.

5. Each P_i sends each $\widetilde{h}_a^{(i,m)}(\alpha_j)$ to each P_j.

6. If we define $h_a^{(k,m)}$ to be the unique polynomials of degree $\leq d'$ satisfying

   6.1 $h_{2a-1}^{(k,m)}(\zeta^j) = H_a^{(k,m)}(\zeta^j)$ for $j \in [\ell']$,

   6.2 $h_{2a-1}^{(k,m)}(\zeta^{\ell'+j}) = R_{2a-1}^{(k,m)}(\zeta^j)$ for $j \in [d' - \ell' + 1]$,

   6.3 $h_{2a}^{(k,m)}(\zeta^j) = H_a^{(k,m)}(\zeta^{\ell'+j})$ for $j \in [\ell']$,

   6.4 $h_{2a}^{(k,m)}(\zeta^{\ell'+j}) = R_{2a}^{(k,m)}(\zeta^j)$ for $j \in [d' - \ell' + 1]$,

   then it is clear that

$$\left(\widetilde{h}_a^{(1,m)}, \ldots, \widetilde{h}_a^{(n,m)}\right)^T = M \left(h_a^{(1,m)}, \ldots, h_a^{(n-2t,m)}\right)^T.$$

   So each party uses Berlekamp-Welch to interpolate their shares of the $h_a^{(k,m)}$ from the shares of the $\widetilde{h}_a^{(k,m)}$ received in the previous step.

7. We place a lexicographical order on the polynomials $H_a^{(k,m)}$ by assigning to the polynomial the vector (m, k, a) and using the lexicographical order on these 3-dimensional vectors to induce an ordering on the polynomials. We similarly place a lexicographical order on the polynomials $h_a^{(k,m)}$. To simplify notation throughout the rest of the protocol, we now relabel $\left\{H_a^{(k,m)}\right\}_{\substack{m = 1, \ldots, 4B \\ k = 1, \ldots, n - 3t \\ a = 1, \ldots, \ell'}} \leftarrow \left\{h_a^{(k,m)}\right\}_{\substack{m = 1, \ldots, B \\ k = 1, \ldots, n - 3t \\ a = 1, \ldots, 2\ell}}$ in such a way that this map preserves lexicographical order. We then re-label $B \leftarrow 4B$.

Fig. 2. Threshold_Change$_2$.

1. *Double Sharing Batched Secrets*

   1.1 The parties generate sharings of $\ell t B$ random sharings by invoking RanDouSha. We will denote these random secrets by $H_a^{(k,m)}$, where a and m range over the same values as before, but $k \in [n - 3t + 1, n - 2t]$.

   1.2 Each party batch-shares all of his shares of each $H_a^{(k,m)}$ using RobustShare. That is, P_i chooses polynomials $U^{(i,1,m)}, \ldots, U^{(i,(n-2t),m)}$ of degree $\leq d'$ such that $U^{(i,k,m)}(\zeta^j) = H_j^{(k,m)}(\alpha_i)$ for $j \in [\ell]$ and $U^{(i,k,m)}(\zeta^{\ell'+j})$ is random for $j \in [d' - \ell' + 1]$ and shares them via RobustShare.

2. *Verifying Correctness*

   2.1 Define $\widetilde{H}_a^{(k,m)}$ and $\widetilde{U}_a^{(k,m)}$ for $k \in [n]$ by

   $$\left(\widetilde{H}_a^{(1,m)}, \ldots, \widetilde{H}_a^{(n,m)} \right)^T = M \left(H_a^{(1,m)}, \ldots, H_a^{(n-2t,m)} \right)^T$$

   and

   $$\left(\widetilde{U}_a^{(1,m)}, \ldots, \widetilde{U}_a^{(n,m)} \right)^T = M \left(U_a^{(1,m)}, \ldots, U_a^{(n-2t,m)} \right)^T.$$

   Each party in $\mathcal{P}$ locally computes their shares of these polynomials.

   2.2 Each party in $\mathcal{P}$ sends *all* their shares of $\widetilde{H}_a^{(k,m)}$ and $\widetilde{U}^{(i,k,m)}$ to party P_k for each a, i, and m.

   2.3 Each P_k uses Berlekamp-Welch on the shares of each $\widetilde{U}^{(i,k,m)}$ to interpolate $\widetilde{U}^{(i,k,m)}(\zeta^j)$ for each $j \in [\ell']$.

   2.4 Each P_k uses Berlekamp-Welch on the shares of each $\widetilde{H}_a^{(k,m)}$. to interpolate $\widetilde{H}^{(i,k,m)}(\alpha_i)$ for each $i \in [n]$.

   2.5 Each P_k checks if the shares of $\widetilde{H}_a^{(k,m)}$ are consistent with the interpolation of the polynomial $\widetilde{U}^{(i,k,m)}$. That is, P_k checks if $\widetilde{U}^{(i,k,m)}(\zeta^j) = \widetilde{H}_j^{(k,m)}(\alpha_i)$ for each $j \in [\ell']$. If some $\widetilde{U}^{(i,k,m)}$ does not pass this check, then P_k sends $(P_k, \textbf{accuse}, P_i)$ to each party in $\mathcal{P}'$.

   2.6 Each $P_j' \in \mathcal{P}'$ uses the accusations sent in the previous step to determine a set $Corr_j'$ of parties in $\mathcal{P}$ that might be corrupt. More specifically, P_j' reads through the list of accusations, and adds parties to $Corr_j'$ according to the following rule: If neither of the parties in the current accusation are in $Corr_j'$, then add both of them to $Corr_j'$; otherwise, ignore the accusation.

3. *Share Transfer*

Fig. 3. Refresh_Recovery.

3.1   Each $P'_j \in \mathcal{P}'$ selects a set G_j of parties in $\mathcal{P} - Corr_j$ such that $|G_j| = n - 2t$. Then P'_j sends this set to each member of G_j.

3.2   For each $P'_j \in \mathcal{P}'$, let $\{z_1^{(j)}, \ldots, z_{n-2t}^{(j)}\}$ denote the set of indices of parties in G_j. Let $\lambda_{j,i}$ denote the Lagrange coefficients for interpolating P'_j's share of a secret from the shares of parties in G_j (i.e. for a polynomial f of degree $\leq d'$, $f(\beta_j) = \lambda_{j,1} f(\alpha_{z_1^{(j)}}) + \cdots + \lambda_{j,n-2t} f(\alpha_{z_{n-2t}^{(j)}}))$.

3.3   The parties in $\mathcal{P}$ execute RanDouSha to generate degree d' polynomials $V^{(j,k,m)}$ for $(j,k,m) \in [\ell' + 1, d' + 1] \times [n - 3t] \times [B]$. The parties in $\mathcal{P}$ also use RanDouSha to generate degree d' polynomials $V^{(j,k,m)}$ for $(j,k,m) \in [\ell'] \times [n - 3t] \times [B]$ that are random subject to the constraint that $V^{(j,k,m)}(\zeta^w) = 0$ for each $w \in [\ell']$.

3.4   Define degree d' polynomials $Q_a^{(k,m)}$ for $(a,k,m) \in [\ell'] \times [n-3t] \times [B]$ by $Q_a^{(k,m)}(\zeta^w) = 0$ for $w \in [\ell']$ and $Q_a^{(k,m)}(\zeta^w) = V^{(w,k,m)}(\zeta^a)$ for $w \in [\ell' + 1, d' + 1]$. Let $\mu_{j,i}$ denote the Lagrange coefficients for interpolating P'_j's share of a secret from the points at ζ^i for $i \in [d' + 1]$ (i.e. for a polynomial f of degree $\leq d'$, $f(\beta_j) = \mu_{j,1} f(\zeta^1) + \cdots + \mu_{j,d'+1} f(\zeta^{d'+1})$.)

3.5   For each $k \in [n - 3t]$, each $m \in [B]$, and each $j \in [n']$, each party in G_j sends his share of

$$\lambda_{j,1} U^{(z_1^{(j)}, k, m)} + \cdots + \lambda_{j,n-2t} U^{(z_{n-2t}^{(j)}, k, m)}$$
$$+ \mu_{j,1} V^{(1,k,m)} + \cdots + \mu_{j,d'+1} V^{(d'+1,k,m)}$$

to P'_j.

3.6   Each P'_j uses Berlekamp-Welch to interpolate the polynomials received in the previous step for each $k \in [n - 3t]$ and each $m \in [B]$. Since for each $a \in [\ell']$,

$$\lambda_{j,1} U^{(z_1^{(j)}, k, m)}(\zeta^a) + \cdots + \lambda_{j,n-2t} U^{(z_{n-2t}^{(j)}, k, m)}(\zeta^a)$$
$$+ \mu_{j,1} V^{(1,k,m)}(\zeta^a) + \cdots + \mu_{j,d'+1} V^{(d'+1,k,m)}(\zeta^a)$$
$$= \lambda_{j,1} H_a^{(k,m)}(\alpha_{z_1^{(j)}}) + \cdots + \lambda_{j,n-2t} H_a^{(k,m)}(\alpha_{z_{n-2t}^{(j)}})$$
$$+ \mu_{j,1} Q_a^{(k,m)}(\zeta^1) + \cdots + \mu_{j,d'+1} Q_a^{(k,m)}(\zeta^{d'+1})$$
$$= H_a^{(k,m)}(\beta_j) + Q_a^{(k,m)}(\beta_j).$$

P'_j has his share of each batch of refreshed data.

Fig. 3. (*continued*)

6   Party Virtualization

As stated in Sect. 1.2, we do not require "party virtualization" as defined in [30]. However for the statistical version of our protocol, we require the use of a party virtualization technique similar to that in [14] (note that these are different techniques as noted before in Sect. 1.2). The technique, initially introduced in [8], replaces an individual party with a committee of parties that emulates the actions of an individual party. This is done such that the number of corrupt committees is lower than the number of corrupt parties. This allows us to raise the threshold in *the statistical case* from the initial threshold of $t < n/16$ to $t < (1/2 - \epsilon)n$ for arbitrary $\epsilon > 0$. In [2], the authors show how to perform party virtualization such that there is a constant number of communication rounds. We refer the reader to [2, 14] for details.

Changing the threshold when party virtualization is used is fairly straightforward. The only requirement is that the threshold of the original (non-virtualized) protocol still satisfies $t < n/16$ when the threshold changes. During redistribution, the parties in the new group will be arranged into committees as in the old group, and shares will be transferred from the virtual parties in the old group to the virtual parties in the new group as specified in [2].

7   Dynamic Proactive Multiparty Computation

Our DPSS scheme can be used to construct a dynamic proactive secure multiparty computation (DPMPC) protocol. A secure multiparty computation (MPC) protocol allows a set of parties to compute a function of their private inputs remaining secure against an adversary who may corrupt some of the parties. A DPMPC protocol is an MPC protocol secure against a mobile adversary in which the set of parties performing the computation and the corruption threshold may change during the course of the protocol.[6]

In [3], the authors show how to proactivize the MPC scheme of [14] by executing a refresh and recovery protocol between each layer of circuit computation. To construct our DPMPC scheme, we execute our Redistribute protocol between each circuit layer as in [3].

Acknowledgements. The fourth author is supported in part by NSF grants 09165174, 1065276, 1118126 and 1136174, US-Israel BSF grant 2008411, OKAWA Foundation Research Award, IBM Faculty Research Award, Xerox Faculty Research Award, B. John Garrick Foundation Award, Teradata Research Award, and Lockheed-Martin Corporation Research Award. This material is based upon work supported by the Defense Advanced Research Projects Agency through the U.S. Office of Naval Research under Contract N00014-11-1-0392. The views expressed are those of the author and do not reflect the official policy or position of the Department of Defense or the U.S. Government.

---

[6] Although the set of parties may change throughout the course of the protocol, the inputs of the original set of parties are used to compute the circuit.

References

1. Almansa, J.F., Damgård, I., Nielsen, J.B.: Simplified threshold RSA with adaptive and proactive security. In: Vaudenay, S. (ed.) EUROCRYPT 2006. LNCS, pp. 593–611. Springer, Heidelberg (2006)
2. Baron, J., El Defrawy, K., Lampkins, J., Ostrovsky, R.: How to withstand mobile virus attacks, revisited (full version). Cryptology ePrint Archive, Report 2013/529 (2013). http://eprint.iacr.org/
3. Baron, J., El Defrawy, K., Lampkins, J., Ostrovsky, R.: How to withstand mobile virus attacks, revisited. In: Proceedings of the 2014 ACM Symposium on Principles of Distributed Computing, PODC 2014, pp. 293–302. ACM, New York (2014)
4. Baron, J., El Defrawy, K., Lampkins, J., Ostrovsky, R.: Communication-optimal proactive secret sharing for dynamic groups (full version). Cryptology ePrint Archive, Report 2015/304 (2015). http://eprint.iacr.org/
5. Beerliová-Trubíniová, Z., Hirt, M.: Perfectly-secure MPC with linear communication complexity. In: Canetti, R. (ed.) TCC 2008. LNCS, vol. 4948, pp. 213–230. Springer, Heidelberg (2008)
6. Blakley, G.R.: Safeguarding cryptographic keys. In: Proceedings of the AFIPS National Computer Conference, vol. 48, pp. 313–317 (1979)
7. Boldyreva, A.: Threshold Signatures, multisignatures and blind signatures based on the gap-diffie-hellman-group signature scheme. In: Desmedt, Y.G. (ed.) Public Key Cryptography — PKC 2003. LNCS, vol. 2567, pp. 31–46. Springer, Heidelberg (2002)
8. Bracha, G.: An O(log n) expected rounds randomized byzantine generals protocol. J. ACM **34**(4), 910–920 (1987)
9. Cachin, C., Kursawe, K., Lysyanskaya, A., Strobl, R.: Asynchronous verifiable secret sharing and proactive cryptosystems. In: ACM Conference on Computer and Communications Security, pp. 88–97 (2002)
10. Canetti, R., Gennaro, R., Jarecki, S., Krawczyk, H., Rabin, T.: Adaptive security for threshold cryptosystems. In: Wiener, M. (ed.) CRYPTO 1999. LNCS, vol. 1666, pp. 98–115. Springer, Heidelberg (1999)
11. Canetti, R., Herzberg, A.: Maintaining security in the presence of transient faults. In: Desmedt, Y.G. (ed.) CRYPTO 1994. LNCS, vol. 839, pp. 425–438. Springer, Heidelberg (1994)
12. Castro, M., Liskov, B.: Proactive recovery in a byzantine-fault-tolerant system. In: OSDI, pp. 273–288 (2000)
13. Castro, M., Liskov, B.: Practical byzantine fault tolerance and proactive recovery. ACM Trans. Comput. Syst. **20**(4), 398–461 (2002)
14. Damgård, I., Ishai, Y., Krøigaard, M.: Perfectly secure multiparty computation and the computational overhead of cryptography. In: Gilbert, H. (ed.) EUROCRYPT 2010. LNCS, vol. 6110, pp. 445–465. Springer, Heidelberg (2010)
15. Damgård, I., Ishai, Y., Krøigaard, M., Nielsen, J.B., Smith, A.: Scalable multiparty computation with nearly optimal work and resilience. In: Wagner, D. (ed.) CRYPTO 2008. LNCS, vol. 5157, pp. 241–261. Springer, Heidelberg (2008)
16. Damgård, I.B., Nielsen, J.B.: Scalable and unconditionally secure multiparty computation. In: Menezes, A. (ed.) CRYPTO 2007. LNCS, vol. 4622, pp. 572–590. Springer, Heidelberg (2007)
17. Desmedt, Y., Jajodia, S.: Redistributing secret shares to new access structures and its applications. Technical Report ISSE TR-97-01, George Mason University, July 1997

18. Frankel, Y., Gemmell, P., MacKenzie, P.D., Yung, M.: Optimal-resilience proactive public-key cryptosystems. In: Proceedings of the 38th Annual Symposium on Foundations of Computer Science, FOCS 1997, pp. 384, Washington, DC, USA. IEEE Computer Society (1997)
19. Frankel, Y., Gemmell, P.S., MacKenzie, P.D., Yung, M.: Proactive RSA. In: Kaliski Jr., B.S. (ed.) CRYPTO 1997. LNCS, vol. 1294, pp. 440–454. Springer, Heidelberg (1997)
20. Frankel, Y., MacKenzie, P.D., Yung, M.: Adaptive security for the additive-sharing based proactive RSA. In: Kim, K. (ed.) PKC 2001. LNCS, vol. 1992, pp. 240–263. Springer, Heidelberg (2001)
21. Franklin, M., Yung, M.: Communication complexity of secure computation (extended abstract). In: Proceedings of the Twenty-Fourth Annual ACM Symposium on Theory of Computing, STOC 1992, pp. 699–710, New York, NY, USA. ACM (1992)
22. Franklin, M.K., Galil, Z., Yung, M.: Eavesdropping games: a graph-theoretic approach to privacy in distributed systems. In: FOCS, pp. 670–679 (1993)
23. Herzberg, A., Jarecki, S., Krawczyk, H., Yung, M.: Proactive secret sharing or: how to cope with perpetual leakage. In: Coppersmith, D. (ed.) CRYPTO 1995. LNCS, vol. 963, pp. 339–352. Springer, Heidelberg (1995)
24. Itkis, G., Reyzin, L.: SiBIR: signer-base intrusion-resilient signatures. In: Yung, M. (ed.) CRYPTO 2002. LNCS, vol. 2442, p. 499. Springer, Heidelberg (2002)
25. Jarecki, S., Olsen, J.: Proactive RSA with non-interactive signing. In: Tsudik, G. (ed.) FC 2008. LNCS, vol. 5143, pp. 215–230. Springer, Heidelberg (2008)
26. Jarecki, S., Saxena, N.: Further simplifications in proactive RSA signatures. In: Kilian, J. (ed.) TCC 2005. LNCS, vol. 3378, pp. 510–528. Springer, Heidelberg (2005)
27. McMillan, R.: $1.2m hack shows why you should never store bitcoins on the internet (2013)
28. Ostrovsky, R., Yung, M.: How to withstand mobile virus attacks. In: Proceedings of the Tenth Annual ACM Symposium on Principles of Distributed Computing, pp. 51–59. ACM Press (1991)
29. Rabin, T.: A simplified approach to threshold and proactive RSA. In: Krawczyk, H. (ed.) CRYPTO 1998. LNCS, vol. 1462, pp. 89–104. Springer, Heidelberg (1998)
30. Schultz, D.: Mobile proactive secret sharing. Ph.D. thesis, Massachusetts Institute of Technology (2007)
31. Shamir, A.: How to share a secret. Commun. ACM **22**(11), 612–613 (1979)·
32. Silver-Greenberg, J., Goldstein, M., Perlroth, N.: JPMorgan Chase hacking affects 76 million households (2014). http://dealbook.nytimes.com/2014/10/02/jpmorgan-discovers-further-cyber-security-issues/
33. Wong, T.M., Wang, C., Wing, J.M.: Verifiable secret redistribution for archive system. In: IEEE Security in Storage Workshop, pp. 94–106 (2002)
34. Zhou, L., Schneider, F.B., van Renesse, R.: Apss: proactive secret sharing in asynchronous systems. ACM Trans. Inf. Syst. Secur. **8**(3), 259–286 (2005)

Round-Optimal Password-Based Group Key Exchange Protocols in the Standard Model

Jing Xu[1](✉), Xue-Xian Hu[1,2], and Zhen-Feng Zhang[1]

[1] Trusted Computing and Information Assurance Laboratory, Institute of Software, Chinese Academy of Sciences, Beijing 100190, China
{xujing,huxuexian,zfzhang}@tca.iscas.ac.cn
[2] State Key Laboratory of Mathematical Engineering and Advanced Computing, Information Engineering University, Zhengzhou 450002, China

Abstract. Password-based group key exchange protocols allow group users who share only a short, low entropy password to agree on a cryptographically strong session key. One fundamental complexity measure of such protocols is its *round complexity*. In this paper, we present the first *one-round* password-based group key exchange protocol in the common random string model. Furthermore, we propose a completely new approach to remove the need for the common random string and then construct a *two-round* password-based group key exchange protocol that does not require any setup assumption. This is - to the best of our knowledge - the first password-based group key exchange protocol without trusted setup. Using indistinguishability obfuscation as main tool, both protocols are provably secure in the standard model.

Keywords: Group key exchange protocol · Password based authentication · Round complexity · Indistinguishability obfuscation

1 Introduction

Password-based authenticated key exchange (PAKE) protocols [1] allow users who share only a short, low-entropy password to agree on a cryptographically strong session key. PAKE protocols are fascinating from a theoretical perspective, as they can be viewed as a means of "bootstrapping" a common cryptographic key from the (essentially) minimal setup assumption of a short, shared secret. PAKE protocols are also important in practice, since passwords are perhaps the most common and widely-used means of authentication. In this paper, we consider PAKE protocols in the group setting where the number of users involved in the computation of a common session key can be large.

This work was supported by the National Grand Fundamental Research (973) Program of China under Grant 2013CB338003, China Postdoctoral Science Foundation under Grant 2014M552524, and the National Natural Science Foundation of China (NSFC) under Grants 61170279, U1536205 and 61170278.

© Springer International Publishing Switzerland 2015
T. Malkin et al. (Eds.): ACNS 2015, LNCS 9092, pp. 42–61, 2015.
DOI: 10.1007/978-3-319-28166-7_3

The difficulty in designing password-based protocols is to prevent *off-line* dictionary attacks whereby an eavesdropping adversary exhaustively enumerates passwords, attempting to match the correct password to the eavesdropped session. However, the adversary can always correctly determine the correct password via an *on-line* dictionary attack in which the adversary tries to impersonate one of the parties using each possible password. Although an *on-line* dictionary attack is not avoidable, the damage it may cause can be mitigated by other means such as limiting the number of failed login attempts. Roughly, a secure password-based protocol guarantees that an exhaustive *on-line* dictionary attack is the "best" possible strategy for an adversary.

1.1 Related Work

Group Key Exchange Protocols. Bresson et al. [2] introduced a formal security model for group key exchange protocols and proposed the first provably secure protocol for this setting. Their protocol use a ring structure for the communication, in which each user has to wait for the message from his predecessor before producing his own. Unfortunately, the nature of their communication structure makes their protocols quite impractical for large groups due to the number of rounds of communication linear in the number of group users. Later, Burmester and Desmedt [3,4] proposed a more efficient and practical group key exchange protocol, in which the number of rounds of communication is constant. Their protocol has been formally analyzed by Katz and Yung [5], who also proposed the first constant round and fully scalable authenticated group key exchange protocol which is provably secure in the standard model. Recently, Boneh and Zhandry [6] constructed the first multiparty non-interactive key exchange protocol requiring no trusted setup, and gave the formal security proof in the static and semi-static models.

Password-Based Group Key Exchange Protocols. Adding password authentication services to a group key exchange protocol is not trivial since redundancy in the flows of the protocol can open the door to password dictionary attacks. Bresson et al. [7] proposed the first solution to the group Diffie-Hellman key exchange problem in the password-based scenario. However, their protocol has a total number of rounds which is linear in the number of group users and their security analysis requires ideal models, which is impractical for large groups. Later, two different password-based versions [8,9] of Burmester-Desmedt protocol were proposed, and unfortunately, both of them are not secure [10]. Also, Abdalla et al. [10] demonstrated the first password-based group key exchange protocol in a constant number of rounds. Their protocol is provably secure in the random oracle and ideal cipher models.

To date, there are only a few general approaches for constructing password-based group key exchange protocols in the standard model (i.e., without random oracles). Abdalla and Pointcheval [11] constructed the first such protocol with a proof of security in the standard model. Their protocol combines smooth projective hash function with the construction of Burmester and Desmedt [3,4] and includes only 5 rounds communication, but requires a common reference string model. Later, Abdalla et al. [12] presented a compiler, that transforms any provably secure (password-based) two-party key exchange protocol into a provably secure (password-based) group key exchange protocol with two more rounds of communication. Their compiler uses non-interactive and non-malleable commitment schemes as main technical tools, also requires a common reference string model.

1.2   Technical Contributions

Round complexity is a central measure of efficiency for any interactive protocol. In this paper, our main goal is to further improve bounds on the round complexity of password-based group key exchange protocol.

Towards this goal, we propose the first *one-round* password-based group key exchange protocol which is provably secure in the standard model. Our main tool is indistinguishability obfuscation, for which a candidate construction was recently proposed by Garg et al. [14]. The essential idea is the following: the public parameter consists an obfuscated program for a pseudorandom function PRF which requires knowledge of the password pw to operate, so that each user in the group can independently evaluate the obfuscated program to obtain the output session key. To prevent the *off-line* dictionary attack, we require the random value r_i used for generating the ciphertext c_i also as input of the obfuscated program.

Our second contribution is *two-round* password-based group key exchange protocol without any setup. The existing constructions require a trusted setup to publish public parameters, which means whoever generates the parameters can obtain all group users' passwords and compute the agreed session key. However, this may be less appealing than the "plain" model where there is no additional setup. Motivated by this observation, we propose a completely new approach to password-based group key exchange protocol with no trusted setup. The resulting scheme is the first secure password-based group key exchange protocol which does not rely on a random oracle or a setup, only requires two rounds of communication. Our central challenge is how to create a way to let each group user run setup for himself securely. In fact, at a first glance, it seems that letting each user publish an obfuscated program might fully resolve this problem. However, such an approach fails because a potentially malicious program can be replaced by an adversary. Specifically, an adversary may publish a malicious program that simply outputs the input password. To prevent such attacks, we extend the Burmester-Desmedt protocol framework [3,4] to the password setting, where the Diffie-Hellman key exchanges are replaced by indistinguishability obfuscation, and let each user generate two obfuscated programs. The first obfuscated program is used to obtain other users' random value, and the second program is used to generate the shared key with the user's neighbors, where the output of the first program is only as the input of the second program. Moreover, each user's partial message broadcasted for computing the session key is generated by his own program and cannot be replaced. Thus, even if the adversary replace some programs, any password information will not be disclosed.

1.3   Outline of the Paper

The rest of this paper is organized as follows. Section 2 recalls the security model usually used for password-based group key exchange protocol, and Sect. 3 recalls the definition of different cryptographic primitives essential for our study. We then propose two round-optimal constructions for password-based group key exchange protocol in Sects. 4 and 5, respectively. Sections 6 concludes.

2   Password-Based Group Key Exchange

In this section, we briefly recall the formal security model for password-based group key exchange protocols as presented in [10] (which is based on the model by Bresson [13]).

In a password-based group key exchange protocol, we assume for simplicity a fixed, polynomial-size set $\mathcal{U} = \{U_1, \ldots, U_l\}$ of potential users. Each user $U \in \mathcal{U}$ may belong to several subgroup $\mathcal{G} \subseteq \mathcal{U}$, each of which has a unique password $pw_\mathcal{G}$ associated to it. The password $pw_\mathcal{G}$ is known to all the users $U_i \in \mathcal{G}$ wishing to establish a common session key.

Let $U^{\langle i \rangle}$ denote the i-th instance of a participant U and b be a bit chosen uniformly at random. During the execution of the protocol, an adversary $\mathcal{A}$ could interact with protocol participants via several oracle queries, which model adversary's possible attacks in the real execution. All possible oracle queries are listed in the following:

- $Execute(U_1^{\langle i_1 \rangle}, \ldots, U_n^{\langle i_n \rangle})$: This query models passive attacks in which the attacker eavesdrops on honest executions among the user instances $U_1^{\langle i_1 \rangle}, \ldots, U_n^{\langle i_n \rangle}$. It returns the messages that were exchanged during an honest execution of the protocol.
- $Send(U^{\langle i \rangle}, m)$: This oracle query is used to simulate active attacks, in which the adversary may tamper with the message being sent over the public channel. It returns the message that the user instance $U^{\langle i \rangle}$ would generate upon receipt of message m.
- $Reveal(U^{\langle i \rangle})$: This query models the possibility that an adversary gets session keys. It returns to the adversary the session key of the user instance $U^{\langle i \rangle}$.
- $Test(U^{\langle i \rangle})$: This query tries to capture the adversary's ability to tell apart a real session key from a random one. It returns the session key for instance $U^{\langle i \rangle}$ if $b = 1$ or a random number of the same size if $b = 0$. This query is called only once.

Besides the above oracle queries, some terminologies are defined as follows.

- **Partnering:** Let the session identifier sid^i of a user instance $U^{\langle i \rangle}$ be a function of all the messages sent and received by $U^{\langle i \rangle}$ as specified by the protocol. Let the partner identifier pid^i of a user instance $U^{\langle i \rangle}$ be the set of all participants with whom $U^{\langle i \rangle}$ wishes to establish a common session key. Two instances $U_1^{\langle i_1 \rangle}$ and $U_2^{\langle i_2 \rangle}$ are said to be partnered if and only if $pid_1^{i_1} = pid_2^{i_2}$ and $sid_1^{i_1} = sid_2^{i_2}$.

– **Freshness:** We say an instance $U^{\langle i \rangle}$ is *fresh* if the following conditions hold: (1) $U^{\langle i \rangle}$ has accepted the protocol and generated a valid session key; (2) No *Reveal* queries have been made to $U^{\langle i \rangle}$ or to any of its partners.

Correctness. The correctness of password-based group key exchange protocol requires that, whenever two instances $U_1^{\langle i_1 \rangle}$ and $U_2^{\langle i_2 \rangle}$ are partnered and have accepted, both instances should hold the same non-null session key.

Security. For any adversary $\mathcal{A}$, let $Succ(\mathcal{A})$ be the event that $\mathcal{A}$ makes a single *Test* query directed to some fresh instance $U^{\langle i \rangle}$ at the end of a protocol P and correctly guesses the bit b used in the *Test* query. Let $\mathcal{D}$ be the user's password dictionary (i.e., the set of all possible candidate passwords). The advantage of $\mathcal{A}$ in violating the semantic security of the protocol P is defined as:

$$\mathrm{Adv}_{P,\mathcal{D}}(\mathcal{A}) = |2Pr[Succ(\mathcal{A})] - 1|.$$

Definition 1 (Security). A password-based group key exchange protocol P is said to be secure if for every dictionary $\mathcal{D}$ and every (non-uniform) polynomial-time adversary $\mathcal{A}$,

$$\mathrm{Adv}_{P,\mathcal{D}}(\mathcal{A}) < \mathcal{O}(q_s)/|\mathcal{D}| + negl(\lambda),$$

where q_s is the number of *Send* oracle queries made by the adversary to different protocol instances and λ is a security parameter.

3 Preliminaries

In this section we start by briefly recalling the definition of different cryptographic primitives essential for our study. Let $x \leftarrow S$ denote a uniformly random element drawn from the set S.

3.1 Indistinguishability Obfuscation

We will start by recalling the notion of indistinguishability obfuscation (iO) recently realized in [14] using candidate multilinear maps [15].

Definition 2 (Indistinguishability Obfuscation). An *indistinguishability obfuscator* iO for a circuit class $\mathcal{C}_\lambda$ is a PPT uniform algorithm satisfying the following conditions:

– iO(λ, C) preserves the functionality of C. That is, for any $C \in \mathcal{C}_\lambda$, if we compute $C' =$ iO(λ, C), then $C'(x) = C(x)$ for all inputs x.
– For any λ and any two circuits $C_0, C_1 \in \mathcal{C}_\lambda$ with the same functionality, the circuits iO(λ, C_0) and iO(λ, C_1) are indistinguishable. More precisely, for all pairs of PPT adversaries (Samp, D) there exists a negligible function α such that, if

$$\Pr[\forall x, C_0(x) = C_1(x) : (C_0, C_1, \tau) \leftarrow \mathrm{Samp}(\lambda)] > 1 - \alpha(\lambda)$$

then

$$|\Pr[D(\tau, \mathrm{iO}(\lambda, C_0)) = 1] - \Pr[D(\tau, \mathrm{iO}(\lambda, C_1)) = 1]| < \alpha(\lambda)$$

In this paper, we will make use of such indistinguishability obfuscators for all polynomial-size circuits:

Definition 3 (Indistinguishability Obfuscation for P/*poly*). A uniform PPT machine iO is called an indistinguishability obfuscator for P/*poly* if the following holds: Let $\mathcal{C}_\lambda$ be the class of circuits of size at most λ. Then iO is an indistinguishability obfuscator for the class $\{\mathcal{C}_\lambda\}$.

3.2   Constrained Pseudorandom Functions

A pseudorandom function (PRF) [16] is a function PRF: $\mathcal{K} \times \mathcal{X} \to \mathcal{Y}$ where PRF$(k, \cdot)$is indistinguishable from a random function for a randomly chosen key k. Following Boneh and Waters [17], we recall the definition of constrained pseudorandom function.

Definition 4 (Constrained Pseudorandom Function). A PRF F: $\mathcal{K} \times \mathcal{X} \to \mathcal{Y}$ is said to be *constrained* with respect to a set system $\mathcal{S} \subseteq 2^{\mathcal{X}}$ if there is an additional key space $\mathcal{K}_\mathcal{C}$ and two additional algorithms:

- F.constrain(k, S): On input a PRF key $k \in \mathcal{K}$ and the description of a set S$\in \mathcal{S}$ (so that S $\subseteq \mathcal{X}$), the algorithm outputs a constrained key $k_S \in \mathcal{K}_\mathcal{C}$.
- F.eval(k_S, x): On input $k_S \in \mathcal{K}_\mathcal{C}$ and $x \in \mathcal{X}$, the algorithm outputs

$$F.eval(k_S, x) = \begin{cases} F(k, x) & \text{if } x \in S \\ \bot & \text{otherwise} \end{cases}$$

For ease of notation, we write $F(k_S, x)$ to represent $F.eval(k_S, x)$.

Security. Intuitively, we require that even after obtaining several constrained keys, no polynomial time adversary can distinguish a truly random string from the PRF evaluation at a point not queried. This intuition can be formalized by the following security game between a challenger and an adversary $\mathcal{A}$.

Let F: $\mathcal{K} \times \mathcal{X} \to \mathcal{Y}$ be a constrained PRF with respect to a set system $\mathcal{S} \subseteq 2^{\mathcal{X}}$. The security game consists of three phases:

Setup Phase. The challenger chooses a random key $K \leftarrow \mathcal{K}$ and a random bit $b \leftarrow \{0, 1\}$.

Query Phase. In this phase, $\mathcal{A}$ is allowed to ask for the following queries:
- Evaluation Query: On input $x \in \mathcal{X}$, it returns $F(K, x)$.
- Key Query: On input $S \in \mathcal{S}$, it returns F.constrain(K, S).
- Challenge Query: $\mathcal{A}$ sends $x \in \mathcal{X}$ as a challenge query. If $b = 0$, the challenger outputs $F(K, x)$. Else, the challenger outputs a random element $y \leftarrow \mathcal{Y}$.

Guess Phase. $\mathcal{A}$ outputs a guess b' of b.

Let $E \subseteq \mathcal{X}$ be the set of evaluation queries, $C \subseteq \mathcal{S}$ be the set of constrained key queries and $Z \subseteq \mathcal{X}$ the set of challenge queries. $\mathcal{A}$ wins if $b = b'$ and $E \bigcap Z = \phi$ and $C \bigcap Z = \phi$. The advantage of $\mathcal{A}$ is defined to be $\text{Adv}_{\mathcal{A}}^F(\lambda) = |\Pr[\mathcal{A}\text{wins}] - 1/2|$.

Definition 5. The PRF F is a secure constrained PRF with respect to $\mathcal{S}$ if for all probabilistic polynomial time adversaries $\mathcal{A}$, $\text{Adv}_{\mathcal{A}}^F(\lambda)$ is negligible in λ.

3.3 CCA Secure Encryption

Definition 6 (Public-Key Encryption). A public-key encryption scheme Σ consist of three algorithms:

- Gen: (randomized) key generation algorithm. It outputs a pair (pk, sk) consisting of a public key and a secret key, respectively.
- Enc: (randomized) encryption algorithm. It outputs a ciphertext $c = Enc_{pk}(m)$ for any message m and a valid public key pk.
- Dec: deterministic decryption algorithm. It outputs $m = Dec_{sk}(c)$ or $\bot = Dec_{sk}(c)$ for a ciphertext c and a secret key sk.

In order to make the randomness used by Enc explicit, we write $Enc_{pk}(m; r)$ to highlight the fact that random coins r are used to encrypt the message m.

Perfect Correctness. We say that the encryption scheme has perfect correctness if for overwhelming fraction of the randomness used by the key generation algorithm, for all messages we have $\Pr[Dec_{sk}(Enc_{pk}(m)) = m] = 1$.

CCA Security [18]. The CCA security of the $\Sigma = $ (Gen; Enc; Dec) is defined via the following security game between a challenger and an adversary $\mathcal{A}$:

1. The challenger generates $(pk; sk) \leftarrow Gen(1^\lambda)$ and $b \leftarrow \{0, 1\}$, and gives pk to $\mathcal{A}$.
2. The adversary $\mathcal{A}$ asks decryption queries c, which are answered with the message $Dec_{sk}(c)$.
3. The adversary $\mathcal{A}$ inputs (m_0, m_1) with $|m_0| = |m_1|$ to the challenger, and receives a challenge ciphertext $c^* = Enc_{pk}(m_b)$.
4. The adversary $\mathcal{A}$ asks further decryption queries $c \neq c^*$, which are answered with the message $Dec_{sk}(c)$.
5. The adversary $\mathcal{A}$ outputs a bit b', and wins the game if $b' = b$.

We say that a PKE scheme Σ is CCA secure if for all (non-uniform) probabilistic polynomial time adversaries $\mathcal{A}$, $|\Pr[b' = b] - 1/2|$ is negligible.

4 One-Round Password-Based Group Key Exchange Protocol

In this section we present our construction of a one-round password-based group key exchange protocol. The idea is the following: each user broadcasts a ciphertext c_i of the password pw using random r_i. In the setup phase, a key K is chosen for a constrained pseudorandom function PRF. The shared session key will be the function PRF evaluated at the concatenation of the ciphertexts c_i and pw. To allow each user to compute the session key, the setup will publish an obfuscated program for PRF which requires knowledge of the password pw to operate. However, the adversary may obtain the obfuscated program for PRF and then mount an *off-line* dictionary attack, that is, the adversary guesses password pw^*

and inputs it to the obfuscated program. By observing whether the program outputs $\perp$, the adversary can find the correct password. Therefore, besides the password pw, the random r_i is also required as input of the obfuscated program. In this way, all users can compute the session key, but anyone else without the password, will therefore be unable to compute the session key.

A formal description appears in Fig. 1. The correctness is trivial by inspection. For security, we have the following theorem.

Protocol I

Consider an execution of the protocol among users $U_1, \cdots, U_n$ wishing to establish a common session key and let pw be their joint password chosen uniformly at random from a dictionary **Dict** of size N. Let $\Sigma = (\text{Gen}; \text{Enc}; \text{Dec})$ be a public-key encryption scheme and iO be a program indistinguishability obfuscator.

Setup: Run the key generation algorithm Gen on input 1^k, where $k \in \mathbb{N}$ is a security parameter, to obtain a pair (pk, sk) of public and secret keys (i.e., $(pk, sk) \leftarrow \textbf{Gen}(1^k)$). Choose a random key K to obtain an instance of a pseudorandom function PRF. Build the program P_{PGKE} in Figure 2, and then output pk and $P_{iO} = \text{iO}(P_{PGKE})$ as the public parameters.

Round 1: Each user U_i proceeds as:
1. Choose r_i randomly, encrypt the password pw using r_i with respect to the public key pk, and generate the ciphertext $c_i = \textbf{Enc}_{pk}(pw; r_i)$.
2. Broadcast c_i.

Key Generation: Each user U_i runs P_{iO} on $(c_1, c_2, \cdots, c_n, pw, i, r_i)$ to obtain the session key SK or $\perp$.

Fig. 1. An honest execution of the password-based group key exchange protocol

Theorem 1. *If Σ is a CCA-secure public-key encryption scheme, PRF a secure constrained PRF, and iO a secure indistinguishability obfuscator, then the protocol in Fig. 1 is a secure password-based group key exchange protocol.*

Proof. Fix a PPT adversary $\mathcal{A}$ attacking the password-based group key exchange protocol. We use a hybrid argument to bound the advantage of $\mathcal{A}$. Let $\textbf{Hyb}_0$ represent the initial experiment, in which $\mathcal{A}$ interacts with the real protocol as defined in Sect. 2. We define a sequence of experiments $\textbf{Hyb}_1, \ldots, \textbf{Hyb}_5$, and denote the advantage of adversary $\mathcal{A}$ in experiment $\textbf{Hyb}_i$ as:

$$\text{Adv}_i(\mathcal{A}) \stackrel{\text{def}}{=} 2 \cdot \Pr[\mathcal{A} \text{ succeeds in } \textbf{Hyb}_i] - 1.$$

We bound the difference between the adversary's advantage in successive experiments, and then bound the adversary's advantage in the final experiment.

Inputs: $c_1, c_2, \cdots, c_n$, password pw, i, r_i
Constants: PRF key K, the public key pk

    1. If $c_i \neq Enc_{pk}(pw; r_i)$, output $\bot$
    2. Otherwise, output $PRF(K, c_1, c_2, \cdots, c_n, pw)$

Fig. 2. The program P_{PGKE}

Finally, combining all the above results gives the desired bound on $\mathrm{Adv}_0(\mathcal{A})$, the adversary's advantage when attacking the real protocol.

Experiment Hyb$_1$. In this experiment, whenever a session key is needed to be computed by an honest simulated user instance $U^{\langle i \rangle}$, we directly compute it as $sk_U^{\langle i \rangle} = PRF(K, c_1, \cdots, c_n, pw_i)$ instead of by calling the obfuscated program $P_{iO}(c_1, \cdots, c_n, pw_i, i, r_i)$.

Lemma 1. $Adv_0(\mathcal{A}) = Adv_1(\mathcal{A})$.

Proof. Notice that, for an honest simulated instance, the verification procedure $c_i = \mathbf{Enc}_{pk}(pw; r_i)$ in program P_{PGKE} will always holds. Therefore, this verification step could be omitted without changing the adversary's view and advantage.

Experiment Hyb$_2$. For each honest simulated user instance $U_i^{\langle s \rangle}$, which is involved in either an **Execute** or a **Send** query, we compute $c_i = \mathbf{Enc}_{pk}(pw_0; r_i)$ instead of $c_i = \mathbf{Enc}_{pk}(pw_i; r_i)$, where pw_0 represents some *dummy password* not in the dictionary **Dict** but in the plaintext space of the encryption scheme Σ.

Lemma 2. $|Adv_1(\mathcal{A}) - Adv_2(\mathcal{A})| < negl(\lambda)$.

Proof. First note that, with respect to the honest simulated users, the verification procedure in program P_{PGKE} has been removed in the last experiment. Denote by $q_{es} = q_{exe} + q_{send}$. We define $\mathbf{Hyb}_1^{(\eta)}$ ($0 \leq \eta \leq n \cdot q_{es}$) to be a sequence of hybrid variants of experiment $\mathbf{Hyb}_1$ such that, for every $\eta = n \cdot \xi + \gamma, 0 \leq \xi < q_{es}, 0 \leq \gamma \leq n$, the first ξ **Execute** or **Send** queries are answered according to experiment $\mathbf{Hyb}_2$, the last $q_{es} - \xi - 1$ queries are replied the same as in experiment $\mathbf{Hyb}_1$; when the $(\xi + 1)$-th **Execute** or **Send** oracle is asked, the first γ ciphertexts of $(c_1, c_2, \cdots, c_n)$ are computed according to experiment $\mathbf{Hyb}_2$ and the rest $n - \gamma$ ciphertexts are treated the same as in experiment $\mathbf{Hyb}_1$. As one can easily verify, the hybrids $\mathbf{Hyb}_1^{(0)}$ and $\mathbf{Hyb}_1^{(n \cdot q_{es})}$ are equivalent to the experiments $\mathbf{Hyb}_1$ and $\mathbf{Hyb}_2$, respectively.

    In such case, if there is an adversary $\mathcal{A}$ whose advantage gap between $\mathbf{Hyb}_1$ and $\mathbf{Hyb}_2$ are non-negligible in security parameter, there would exist an η such that the adversary's advantage gap between $\mathbf{Hyb}_1^{(\eta-1)}$ and $\mathbf{Hyb}_1^{(\eta)}$ are non-negligible. Then, we would be able to build an adversary $\mathcal{B}$ violating the CPA security of the encryption scheme Σ with non-negligible advantage from the adversary $\mathcal{A}$ as follows.

Upon receiving the public key pk of the encryptions scheme Σ from his challenger, the adversary $\mathcal{B}$ initializes the public parameters for the group key exchange protocol. It selects a random $K \in \mathcal{K}$, chooses password pw_i for every users $U_i \in \mathbf{U}$, and picks a bit $b \in \{0,1\}$ for answering the **Test** oracle. Then, for $\eta = n \cdot \xi + \gamma$, it simulates the **Execute, Send, Reveal** and **Test** oracles exactly as in hybrid $\mathbf{Hyb}_1^{(\eta)}$ except for the γ-th ciphertext of $(c_1, c_2, \cdots, c_n)$ in the $(\xi + 1)$-th **Execute** or **Send** oracle. In this case, the adversary $\mathcal{B}$ gives pw and pw_0 to its challenger to obtain a challenging ciphertext c_i^* that is either $\mathbf{Enc}_{pk}(pw)$ or $\mathbf{Enc}_{pk}(pw_0)$, and it uses this ciphertext in place of c_i to answer the $(\xi + 1)$-th *Execute* query. At last, $\mathcal{B}$ checks whether $\mathcal{A}$ succeeds or not. If $\mathcal{A}$ succeeds in this hybrid game, then $\mathcal{B}$ outputs 1. Otherwise, it outputs 0.

The distinguishing advantage of $\mathcal{B}$ is exactly equal to the adversary $\mathcal{A}$'s advantage gap between $\mathbf{Hyb}_1^{(\eta-1)}$ and $\mathbf{Hyb}_1^{(\eta)}$. Then, the lemma follows by notice that the encryption scheme Σ is a CPA secure one.

Experiment $\mathbf{Hyb}_3$. In this experiment, we first let the simulator record the corresponding decryption key sk when generating the public key pk. Then, we define the following event:

PwdGuess : During the experiment, an honest user instance $U^{(i)}$ with password pw_i is activated by some input message $(c_1, \cdots, c_{i-1}, \perp, c_{i+1}, \cdots, c_n)$, such that there exists some index $j \in [n]$ and $j \neq i$ satisfying $Dec_{sk}(c_j) = pw_i$.
Whenever the event **PwdGuess** happens, the adversary is declared successful and the experiment ends; Otherwise, the experiment is simulated in the same way as in the last experiment.

Lemma 3. $Adv_2(\mathcal{A}) \leq Adv_3(\mathcal{A})$.

Proof. Even when the event **PwdGuess** happens in experiment $\mathbf{Hyb}_2$, the adversary would not necessarily succeed in this case. As a result, the modification made in experiment $\mathbf{Hyb}_3$ introduces a new way for the adversary to succeed.

Experiment $\mathbf{Hyb}_4$. Replace the $PRF(\cdot)$ in P_{PGKE} by an constrained pseudorandom function $PRF^C(\cdot)$, arriving at the program P'_{PGKE} given in Fig. 3. The constrained set C is defined as $C = \mathcal{M}^n \times \mathbf{Dict} \setminus \{(c_1, c_2, \cdots, c_n, pw) : pw \in \mathbf{Dict}, \forall i \in [n], c_i \notin Enc_{pk}(pw), \text{ and } \exists j \in [n], c_j \in Enc_{pk}(pw_0)\}$.

Lemma 4. $|Adv_3(\mathcal{A}) - Adv_4(\mathcal{A})| < negl(\lambda)$.

Proof. Because the dummy password pw_0 in experiment $\mathbf{Hyb}_2$ is derived from the plaintext space randomly, then with overwhelming probability (in fact, bigger than $(1 - n/|\mathbf{Dict}| \cdot 2^\lambda)$), the input to the pseudorandom function PRF in program P_{PGKE} will belong to the set C defined as above. Therefore, with overwhelming probability, the modified program P'_{PGKE} has the same functionality with the original program P_{PGKE}. The security of the indistinguishable obfuscator iO implies that the adversary's advantage gap between the experiment $\mathbf{Hyb}_4$ and $\mathbf{Hyb}_3$ is no more than the probability that P'_{PGKE} differs from P_{PGKE}, thus is negligible. The lemma's result follows.

Inputs: $c_1, c_2, \cdots, c_n$, password pw, i, r_i
Constants: Constrained PRF key K_C, the public key pk

1. If $c_i \neq Enc_{pk}(pw; r_i)$, output $\perp$
2. Otherwise, output $PRF^C(K_C, c_1, c_2, \cdots, c_n, pw)$

Fig. 3. The program P'_{PGKE}

Experiment Hyb$_5$. Recall that only the situation when event PwdGuess does not happen (i.e., $(c_1, c_2, \cdots, c_n, pw_i) \notin C$) is considered since **Hyb$_3$**. Then, when a session key is needed to be computed by an honest user instance, we evaluate it as $sk_U^{\langle i \rangle} \leftarrow_R \{0,1\}^\lambda$ instead of $sk_U^{\langle i \rangle} = PRF(K, c_1, c_2, \cdots, c_n, pw_i)$.

Lemma 5. $|Adv_4(\mathcal{A}) - Adv_5(\mathcal{A})| < negl(\lambda)$.

Proof. We reduce the problem of distinguishing the experiments **Hyb$_4$** and **Hyb$_5$** to the security of constrained PRF presented above. Assume that $\mathcal{A}$ is a protocol adversary that is defined as in **Hyb$_4$**. We construct a PRF adversary $\mathcal{B}$ against the security of the constrained pseudorandom function PRF as follows. When the adversary $\mathcal{B}$ receives the constrained key k_C of PRF with respected to the constrained set C, it simulates the protocol execution for $\mathcal{A}$ as in **Hyb$_4$**. Note that the program P'_{PGKE} is used in this experiment and all the queries asked by $\mathcal{A}$ could be answered with overwhelming probability by utilizing it. However, when a honest simulated user instance needs to generate a session key, $\mathcal{B}$ asks its own challenge query, getting back either a value computed from the function PRF or a value selected uniformly at random, and used it as the session key. Finally, $\mathcal{B}$ checks whether $\mathcal{A}$ succeeds or not. If $\mathcal{A}$ succeeds, then $\mathcal{B}$ outputs 1. Otherwise, it outputs 0.

It follows that the advantage of $\mathcal{B}$ is exactly equal to the adversary $\mathcal{A}$'s advantage gap between **Hyb$_4$** and **Hyb$_5$**.

Bounding the Advantage in Hyb$_5$. Consider the different ways for the adversary to succeed in Hyb$_5$:

1. The Event PwdGuess happens;
2. The adversary successfully guesses the bit used by the **Test** oracle.

Since all oracle instances are simulated using dummy passwords, the adversary's view is independent of the passwords that are chosen for each group of users. Then we have $\Pr[\text{PwdGuess}] \leq Q(\lambda)/D_\lambda$, where $Q(\lambda)$ denotes the number of *Send* oracle queries and D_λ denotes the dictionary size. Conditioned on PwdGuess not occurring, the adversary can succeed only in case 2. But since all session keys defined throughout the experiment are chosen uniformly and independently at random, the probability of success in this case is exactly $1/2$. Then, we have

$$Pr[Success] \leq Pr[\texttt{PwdGuess}] + Pr[Success|\overline{\texttt{PwdGuess}}] \cdot (1 - Pr[\texttt{PwdGuess}])$$

$$= \frac{1}{2} + \frac{1}{2} \cdot Pr[\texttt{PwdGuess}]$$

$$\leq \frac{1}{2} + \frac{Q(\lambda)}{2 \cdot D_\lambda}$$

and so $Adv_5(\mathcal{A}) \leq \frac{Q(\lambda)}{D_\lambda}$. Taken together, Lemmas 1–5 imply that $Adv_0(\mathcal{A}) \leq \frac{Q(\lambda)}{D_\lambda} + negl(\lambda)$ as desired. $\qquad\square$

5 Two-Round Password-Based Group Key Exchange Protocol with No Setup

In this section, we show how to remove the trusted setup and common reference string (CRS) from the password-based group key exchange protocol in the previous section. Intuitively, letting each user publish an obfuscated program and run setup for himself might fully resolve this problem. However, unlike the protocol I in the previous section, the obfuscated programs generated by group users are susceptible to a "replace" attack - i.e., the adversary may replace the program with a malicious program that simply outputs the input password. Then, the message broadcasted by an honest user may disclose the information about password. With this message, the adversary can mount an *off-line* dictionary attack and obtain the password, thus breaking the security of protocol. We believe that such attacks are the principle reason that the existing constructions require a trusted setup to publish public parameters.

To overcome the above difficulties, we present a new methodology for constructing password-based group key exchange protocol with no setup. The basic idea of our construction follows the Burmester-Desmedt [3, 4] construction where the Diffie-Hellman key exchanges are replaced by indistinguishability obfuscation. As in the Burmester-Desmedt protocol, our protocol assumes a ring structure for the users so that we can refer to the predecessor and successor of a user. Each user in the group will run setup for himself and his neighbors (predecessor and successor), and generate two obfuscated programs.

- The first obfuscated program P^{iO-dec} is used to obtain other users' random value s. This program takes as input "ciphertext" c and user password pw, and outputs the corresponding "plaintext" s.
- The second obfuscated program P^{iO} is used to generate the shared key with the user's neighbors. This program takes as input two random value s_i and s_{i+1} generated by the user U_i and its neighbor U_{i+1} respectively, and outputs the shared K_i. However, to make the key K_i shared only between U_i and its neighbor U_{i+1} (i.e., other users cannot obtain the key K_i), an obfuscated program P^{iO} for PRF will be required the knowledge of a seed r to operate. More precisely, each user generates a seed r_i and computes $s_i = PRG(r_i)$, where PRG is a pseudorandom generator.

Protocol II

Consider an execution of the protocol among users $U_1, \cdots, U_n$ wishing to establish a common session key and let pw be their joint password chosen uniformly at random from a dictionary **Dict** of size N. Let F_1 and F_2 be two pseudorandom functions (PRF), PRG_1 and PRG_2 be two pseudorandom generators, and iO be a program indistinguishability obfuscator.

Round 1: Each user U_i proceeds as:
1. Choose r_i^L and r_i^R randomly, compute $s_i^L = PRG_1(r_i^L)$ and $s_i^R = PRG_1(r_i^R)$.
2. Choose a PRF key K_{i-enc} for PRF F_1 and a PRF key K_i for PRF F_2.
3. Compute $c_i^L = s_i^L + F_1(K_{i-enc}, pw, U_i, U_{i-1})$ and $c_i^R = s_i^R + F_1(K_{i-enc}, pw, U_{i+1}, U_i)$.
4. Build the program P_i^{dec} in Figure 5, and the program P_i in Figure 6.
5. Broadcast c_i^L, c_i^R, $P_i^{iO-dec} = $ iO (P_i^{dec}) and $P_i^{iO} = $ iO (P_i).

Round 2: Each user U_i proceeds as:
1. Run P_{i+1}^{iO-dec} on $(c_{i+1}^L, pw, U_{i+1}, U_i)$ to obtain s_{i+1}^L.
2. Run P_{i-1}^{iO-dec} on $(c_{i-1}^R, pw, U_i, U_{i-1})$ to obtain s_{i-1}^R.
3. Run P_i^{iO} on $(s_{i+1}^L, s_i^R, r_i^R, U_{i+1}, U_i)$ to obtain K_i.
4. Run P_{i-1}^{iO} on $(s_i^L, s_{i-1}^R, r_i^L, U_i, U_{i-1})$ to obtain K_{i-1}.
5. Compute $X_i = K_i / K_{i-1}$ and broadcast X_i.

Key Generation: Each user U_i computes the MSK $= K_i^n \cdot \prod_{j=1}^{n-1} X_{i+j}^{n-j}$ and the session key SK $= PRG_2(MSK)$.

Fig. 4. An honest execution of No-Setup password-based group key exchange protocol

In our protocol, each group user U_i executes two correlated instances to obtain K_{i-1} and K_i, one with his predecessor and one with his successor so each user can authenticate his neighbors, and then computes and broadcasts $X_i = K_i / K_{i-1}$. After this round, each user is capable of computing the group session key SK. For the message $X_i = K_i / K_{i-1}$ broadcasted by U_i in the second round, K_i is generated by U_i's own program P_i, which cannot be replaced. Moreover, the output of the first program P^{iO-dec} is only as the input of the second program P^{iO}. Thus, even if the adversary replace P^{iO-dec} and P^{iO} into malicious programs, from the messages broadcasted, he cannot obtain any information about the password or the session key.

A formal description appears in Fig. 4. In an honest execution of the protocol, it is easy to verify that all honest users in the protocol will terminate by accepting and computing the same $MSK = \prod_{j=1}^n K_j$ and the same session key SK. Therefore, the correctness of the protocol follows directly. For the security, we have the following theorem.

Theorem 2. If PRG is a secure pseudorandom generator, PRF a secure constrained PRF, and iO a secure indistinguishability obfuscator, then the protocol in Fig. 4 is a secure password-based group key exchange protocol with no setup.

Inputs: c, password pw, U_1, U_2
Constants: PRF F_1 key K_{i-enc}
Outputs: $c - F_1(K_{i-enc}, pw, U_1, U_2)$

Fig. 5. The program P_i^{dec}

Inputs: s_1, s_2, r, U_1, U_2
Constants: PRF F_2 key K_i
1. If $PRG(r) = s_1$ or $PRG(r) = s_2$, output $F_2(K_i, s_1, s_2, U_1, U_2)$
2. Otherwise, output $\bot$

Fig. 6. The program P_i

Proof. Fix a PPT adversary $\mathcal{A}$ attacking the password-based group key exchange protocol. We construct a sequence of experiments $\mathbf{Hyb_0}, \ldots, \mathbf{Hyb_{13}}$, with the original experiment corresponding to $\mathbf{Hyb_0}$. Let $Adv_i(\mathcal{A})$ denote the advantage of $\mathcal{A}$ in experiment $\mathbf{Hyb_i}$. To prove the desired bound on $Adv(\mathcal{A}) = Adv_0(\mathcal{A})$, we bound the effect of each change in the experiment one the advantage of $\mathcal{A}$, and then show that $Adv_{13}(\mathcal{A}) \leq \frac{Q(\lambda)}{D(\lambda)}$ (where, recall, $Q(\lambda)$ denotes the number of on-line attacks made by $\mathcal{A}$, and $D(\lambda)$ denotes the dictionary size).

Experiment $\mathbf{Hyb_1}$. Here we change the way **Execute** queries are answered. Specifically, for $i = 1, \ldots, n$, we will choose random $s_i^L, s_i^R \in \{0, 1\}^{2\lambda}$ instead of generating them from PRG. Let the set $\widehat{S} = \{s_i^L, s_i^R | i = 1, \ldots, n\}$. The security of PRG yields the Lemma 6.

Lemma 6. $| Adv_0(\mathcal{A}) - Adv_1(\mathcal{A}) | \leq negl(\lambda)$.

Experiment $\mathbf{Hyb_2}$. In this experiment, We constrain the PRF F_2 so that it can only be evaluated at points (s_1, s_2, U_1, U_2) where $s_1 \notin \widehat{S}$ or $s_2 \notin \widehat{S}$. Then we replace F_2 with F_2^C in the program P_i, arriving at the program P_i' given in Fig. 7. In respond to a query **Execute**, output $P_i^{iO} = \text{iO}(P_i')$.

Lemma 7. $| Adv_1(\mathcal{A}) - Adv_2(\mathcal{A}) | \leq negl(\lambda)$.

Proof. Note that with overwhelming probability, none of $s \in S$ in **Experiment** Hyb$_1$ has a pre-image under PRG. Therefore, with overwhelming probability, there is no input to P_i^{iO} that will cause PRF F_2 to be evaluated on points of the form (s_1, s_2, U_1, U_2) where $s_1 \in \widehat{S}$ and $s_2 \in \widehat{S}$. We can conclude that the programs P_i and P_i' are functionally equivalent. Then based on the indistinguishability obfuscation property, it is easy to see that the hybrids Hyb$_1$ and Hyb$_2$ are computationally indistinguishable. Thus, security of iO yields the lemma.

Inputs: s_1, s_2, r, U_1, U_2
Constants: Constrained PRF F_2 key K_i^C
    1. If $PRG(r) = s_1$ or $PRG(r) = s_2$, output $F_2^C(K_i^C, s_1, s_2, U_1, U_2)$
    2. Otherwise, output $\perp$

Fig. 7. The program P_i'

Experiment Hyb$_3$. In this experiment, we change once again the simulation of the **Execute** queries so that the value K_i for $i = 1, \ldots, n$ are chosen as a random string of the appropriate length.

Lemma 8. $\mid Adv_2(\mathcal{A}) - Adv_3(\mathcal{A}) \mid \leq negl(\lambda)$.

Proof. This follows from the security of PRF as a constrained PRF (as in Definition 4). We construct a PRF adversary $\mathcal{B}$ that breaks the security of PRF as a constrained PRF as follows: adversary $\mathcal{B}$ simulates the entire experiment for $\mathcal{A}$. In response to **Execute**$(U_1^{\langle i_1 \rangle}, \ldots, U_n^{\langle i_n \rangle})$ query, $\mathcal{B}$ computes c_i^L, c_i^R with correct password pw exactly as in experiment Hyb$_2$. $\mathcal{B}$ also asks its PRF F_2 oracle and thus always reveals the correct key. At the end of the experiment, $\mathcal{B}$ makes a real-or-random challenge query for the constrained function PRF^C as defined above. One can easily see that, $\mathcal{B}$ is given a real PRF or a random value, then its simulation is performed exactly as in experiment Hyb$_2$ or experiment Hyb$_3$, respectively. Thus, the distinguishing advantage of $\mathcal{B}$ is exactly $\mid Adv_2(\mathcal{A}) - Adv_3(\mathcal{A}) \mid$.

Experiment Hyb$_4$. In this experiment, we change once again the simulation of the **Execute** queries so that the value MSK is chosen as a random string of the appropriate length.

Lemma 9. $Adv_3(\mathcal{A}) = Adv_4(\mathcal{A})$.

Proof. Note that in the simulation of **Execute** oracle in experiment Hyb$_3$, the values K_i for $i = 1, \ldots, n$ are chosen at random. Then, from the transcript $T = \{X_1, \ldots, X_n\}$ that the adversary receives as output for an **Execute** query, the values K_i are constrained by the following n equations.

$$X_1 = K_1 / K_n$$

$$\vdots$$

$$X_n = K_n / K_{n-1}$$

Of these equations, only $n - 1$ are linearly independent. Furthermore, we have

$$MSK = \prod_{i=1}^{n} K_i.$$

Since the last equation is linearly independent of the previous ones, MSK that each user computes in an **Execute** query is independent of the transcript T that the adversary sees. Thus, no computationally unbounded adversary can tell the experiment Hyb_3 apart from Hyb_4, i.e. $\text{Adv}_3(\mathcal{A}) = \text{Adv}_4(\mathcal{A})$.

Experiment Hyb$_5$. In this experiment, we change once more the simulation of the **Execute** queries so that the session key SK is chosen uniformly at random. The security of PRG guarantees that its output is statistically close to be uniform when given a random value as input, which yields the Lemma 10.

Lemma 10. $\mid Adv_4(\mathcal{A}) - Adv_5(\mathcal{A}) \mid \leq negl(\lambda)$.

Experiment Hyb$_6$. In this experiment, we change last time the simulation of the **Execute** queries. Specifically, in response to a query **Execute**$(U_1^{\langle i_1 \rangle}, \ldots, U_n^{\langle i_n \rangle})$ we now compute $c_i^L = s_i^L + F_1(pw_0, U_i, U_{i-1})$ and $c_i^R = s_i^R + F_1(pw_0, U_{i+1}, U_i)$ for $i = 1, \ldots, n$, where pw_0 represents some dummy password not in the dictionary **Dict**. We note that in the simulation of **Execute** oracle in experiment Hyb_1, the values s_i^L, s_i^R for $i = 1, \ldots, n$ are chosen at random, and the function F_1 is pseudorandom. So the Lemma 11 holds.

Lemma 11. $\mid Adv_5(\mathcal{A}) - Adv_6(\mathcal{A}) \mid \leq negl(\lambda)$.

Experiment Hyb$_7$. In this experiment we begin to modify the **Send** oracle. Let **Send**$_0(\Pi_{U_i}^j, U_1, \cdots, U_n)$ denote a "prompt" message that causes the user instance $\Pi_{U_i}^j$ to initiate the protocol in a group $\mathcal{G} = \{U_1, \cdots, U_n\}$ that contains user U_i; let **Send**$_1(\Pi_{U_i}^j, \{(c_1^L, c_1^R, P_1^{iO-dec}, P_1^{iO}), \ldots, (c_n^L, c_n^R, P_n^{iO-dec}, P_n^{iO})\})$ denote sending the message $\{(c_1^L, c_1^R, P_1^{iO-dec}, P_1^{iO}), \ldots, (c_n^L, c_n^R, P_n^{iO-dec}, P_n^{iO})\}$ to user instance $\Pi_{U_i}^j$; let **Send**$_2(\Pi_{U_i}^j, \{X_1, \ldots, X_n\})$ denote sending the message $\{X_1, \ldots, X_n\}$ to user instance $\Pi_{U_i}^j$.

In experiment Hyb_7 we modify the way **Send**$_0$ query is handled. In response to a query **Send**$_0(\Pi_{U_i}^j, U_1, \cdots, U_n)$, $\Pi_{U_i}^j$ chooses random $s_i^L, s_i^R \in \{0, 1\}^{2\lambda}$ instead of generating them from PRG and computes the $c_i^L = s_i^L + F_1(pw_0, U_i, U_{i-1})$ and $c_i^R = s_i^R + F_1(pw_0, U_{i+1}, U_i)$, where pw_0 represents some dummy password not in the dictionary **Dict**.

Lemma 12. $\mid Adv_6(\mathcal{A}) - Adv_7(\mathcal{A}) \mid \leq negl(\lambda)$.

Proof. The proof is similar to those of Lemmas 6 and 11, and follows easily from the security of PRG and PRF.

Experiment Hyb$_8$. In this experiment, we change again the simulation of the **Send**$_0$ query. We constrain the PRF F_1 so that it can only be evaluated at points (pw, U_1, U_2) where pw is contained in the dictionary **Dict**. Then we replace F_1 with F_1^C in the program P_i^{dec}, arriving at the program $\hat{P}_i^{dec}$ given in Fig. 8. In respond to a query **Send**$_0$, output $P_i^{iO-dec} = \text{iO} \ (\hat{P}_i^{dec})$.

Lemma 13. $\mid Adv_7(\mathcal{A}) - Adv_8(\mathcal{A}) \mid \leq negl(\lambda)$.

Inputs: c, password pw, U_1, U_2
Constants: Constrained PRF F_1 key K^C_{i-enc}
Outputs: $c - F^C_1(K^C_{i-enc}, pw, U_1, U_2)$

Fig. 8. The program $\hat{P}^{dec}_i$

Proof. Since the group users share a password chosen uniformly at random from the dictionary **Dict**, we can conclude that the programs P^{dec}_i and $\hat{P}^{dec}_i$ are functionally equivalent. Then based on the indistinguishability obfuscation property, it is easy to see that the hybrids Hyb_7 and Hyb_8 are computationally indistinguishable. Thus, security of iO yields the lemma.

Experiment Hyb_9. In this experiment, we change the simulation of the $Send_1$ query. In response to a query $Send_1$, if $\{(c^L_1, c^R_1, P^{iO-dec}_1, P^{iO}_1), \ldots, (c^L_n, c^R_n, P^{iO-dec}_n, P^{iO}_n)\}$ was output by a previous query of the form $Send_0$, the values K_i and K_{i-1} are chosen uniformly at random. As the lemma below shows, the difference in the advantage between Hyb_8 and Hyb_9 is negligible. The proof of Lemma 14 is omitted here since it follows easily from the security of PRF F_1 as a constrained PRF, where the outputs of $Send_0$ are always using dummy password.

Lemma 14. $| Adv_8(\mathcal{A}) - Adv_9(\mathcal{A}) | \leq negl(\lambda)$.

Experiment Hyb_{10}. In this experiment, we change again the simulation of the $Send_1$ query. In response to a query $Send_1$, if $\{(c^L_1, c^R_1, P^{iO-dec}_1, P^{iO}_1), \ldots, (c^L_n, c^R_n, P^{iO-dec}_n, P^{iO}_n)\}$ was generated by the adversary using correct password pw, the experiment ends.

Lemma 15. $Adv_9(\mathcal{A}) \leq Adv_{10}(\mathcal{A})$.

Proof. The only situation in which Hyb_{10} proceeds differently from Hyb_9 occurs when the adversary correctly guess the password. All this does is introduce a new way for the adversary to succeed, so $Adv_9(\mathcal{A}) \leq Adv_{10}(\mathcal{A})$.

Experiment Hyb_{11}. In this experiment, we change once more the simulation of the $Send_1$ query. In response to a query $Send_1$, if $\{(c^L_1, c^R_1, P^{iO-dec}_1, P^{iO}_1), \ldots, (c^L_n, c^R_n, P^{iO-dec}_n, P^{iO}_n)\}$ was generated by the adversary using incorrect password, the values K_i is chosen uniformly at random.

Lemma 16. $| Adv_{10}(\mathcal{A}) - Adv_{11}(\mathcal{A}) | \leq negl(\lambda)$.

Proof. Note that, for user instance $\Pi^j_{U_i}$, the program P^{iO}_i can not be altered by the adversary. Moreover, since s^R_i as one of inputs of P^{iO}_i is generated, the adversary can not get it or change it. Then the proof follows easily from the security of PRF F_2 as a constrained PRF. We construct a PRF adversary $\mathcal{B}$

that breaks the security of PRF as a constrained PRF as follows: adversary $\mathcal{B}$ simulates the entire experiment for $\mathcal{A}$. In response to **Send** query, $\mathcal{B}$ responds with correct password pw exactly as in experiment Hyb_{10}. $\mathcal{B}$ also asks its PRF F_2 oracle and thus always reveals the correct key. At the end of the experiment, $\mathcal{B}$ makes a real-or-random challenge query for the constrained function PRF^C as defined above. One can easily see that, $\mathcal{B}$ is given a real PRF or a random value, then its simulation is performed exactly as in experiment Hyb_{10} or experiment Hyb_{11}, respectively. Thus, the distinguishing advantage of $\mathcal{B}$ is exactly $|\text{Adv}_{10}(\mathcal{A}) - \text{Adv}_{11}(\mathcal{A})|$.

Experiment Hyb_{12}. In this experiment, we change once more the simulation of the **Send$_2$** query. In response to a query $\textbf{Send}_2(\Pi_{U_i}^j, \{X_1, \ldots, X_n\})$, the value MSK is chosen uniformly at random.

Lemma 17. $Adv_{11}(\mathcal{A}) = Adv_{12}(\mathcal{A})$.

Proof. The proof of Lemma 17 uses arguments similar to those in the proof of Lemma 9, omitted.

Experiment Hyb_{13}. In this experiment, we change again the simulation of the **Send$_2$** query so that the session key SK is chosen uniformly at random. The security of PRG guarantees that its output is statistically close to be uniform when given a random value as input, which yields the Lemma 18.

Lemma 18. $|Adv_{12}(\mathcal{A}) - Adv_{13}(\mathcal{A})| \leq negl(\lambda)$.

Bounding the Advantage in Hyb_{13}. We now conclude the experiment Hyb_{13}. First, the session keys of all accepting instances are chosen at random. Second, all oracle instances simulated using dummy passwords, so the adversary's view of the protocol is independent of the passwords that are chosen for each group of users. Finally, the probability that an adversary guesses the correct password is at most $\frac{Q(\lambda)}{D_\lambda}$. Similar to the proof of Theorem 1, we have $\text{Adv}_{13}(\mathcal{A}) \leq \frac{Q(\lambda)}{D_\lambda}$. Taken together, Lemmas 6–18 imply that $\text{Adv}_0(\mathcal{A}) \leq \frac{Q(\lambda)}{D_\lambda} + negl(\lambda)$ as desired.   □

6 Conclusion

In this paper, we proposed two round-optimal constructions for password-based group key exchange protocol. In particular we obtain a *one-round* protocol in the common reference string model and a *two-round* protocol in the "plain" model where there is no additional setup. Both protocols are provably secure in the standard model. It remains an interesting open problem to further reduce the computational costs of group users, whilst maintaining its optimal communication rounds.

References

1. Pointcheval, D.: Password-based authenticated key exchange. In: Fischlin, M., Buchmann, J., Manulis, M. (eds.) PKC 2012. LNCS, vol. 7293, pp. 390–397. Springer, Heidelberg (2012)
2. Bresson, E., Chevassut, O., Pointcheval, D., Quisquater, J.-J.: Provably authenticated group Diffie-Hellman key exchange. In: Proceedings of the 8th Annual ACM Conference on Computer and Communications Security, pp. 255–264. ACM (2001)
3. Burmester, M., Desmedt, Y.G.: A secure and efficient conference key distribution system. In: De Santis, A. (ed.) EUROCRYPT 1994. LNCS, vol. 950, pp. 275–286. Springer, Heidelberg (1995)
4. Burmester, M., Desmedt, Y.: A secure and scalable group key exchange system. Inf. Process. Lett. **94**(3), 137–143 (2005)
5. Katz, J., Yung, M.: Scalable protocols for authenticated group key exchange. In: Boneh, D. (ed.) CRYPTO 2003. LNCS, vol. 2729, pp. 110–125. Springer, Heidelberg (2003)
6. Boneh, D., Zhandry, M.: Multiparty key exchange, efficient traitor tracing, and more from indistinguishability obfuscation. In: Garay, J.A., Gennaro, R. (eds.) CRYPTO 2014, Part I. LNCS, vol. 8616, pp. 480–499. Springer, Heidelberg (2014)
7. Bresson, E., Chevassut, O., Pointcheval, D.: Group Diffie-Hellman key exchange secure against dictionary attacks. In: Zheng, Y. (ed.) ASIACRYPT 2002. LNCS, vol. 2501, pp. 497–514. Springer, Heidelberg (2002)
8. Dutta, R., Barua, R.: Password-based encrypted group key agreement. Int. J. Netw. Secur. **3**(1), 30–41 (2006)
9. Lee, S.M., Hwang, J.Y., Lee, D.-H.: Efficient password-based group key exchange. In: Katsikas, S.K., López, J., Pernul, G. (eds.) TrustBus 2004. LNCS, vol. 3184, pp. 191–199. Springer, Heidelberg (2004)
10. Abdalla, M., Bresson, E., Chevassut, O., Pointcheval, D.: Password-based group key exchange in a constant number of rounds. In: Yung, M., Dodis, Y., Kiayias, A., Malkin, T. (eds.) PKC 2006. LNCS, vol. 3958, pp. 427–442. Springer, Heidelberg (2006)
11. Abdalla, M., Pointcheval, D.: A scalable password-based group key exchange protocol in the standard model. In: Lai, X., Chen, K. (eds.) ASIACRYPT 2006. LNCS, vol. 4284, pp. 332–347. Springer, Heidelberg (2006)
12. Abdalla, M., Chevalier, C., Granboulan, L., Pointcheval, D.: Contributory password-authenticated group key exchange with join capability. In: Kiayias, A. (ed.) CT-RSA 2011. LNCS, vol. 6558, pp. 142–160. Springer, Heidelberg (2011)
13. Bresson, E., Chevassut, O., Pointcheval, D.: A security solution for IEEE 802.11s Ad-Hoc mode: password authentication and group Diffie-Hellman key exchange. Int. J. Wirel. Mob. Comput. **2**(1), 4–13 (2007)
14. Garg, S., Gentry, C., Halevi, S., Raykova, M., Sahai, A., Waters, B.: Candidate indistinguishability obfuscation and functional encryption for all circuits. In: FOCS 2013, pp. 40–49. IEEE (2013)
15. Gentry, C., Sahai, A., Waters, B.: Homomorphic encryption from learning with errors: conceptually-simpler, asymptotically-faster, attribute-based. In: Canetti, R., Garay, J.A. (eds.) CRYPTO 2013, Part I. LNCS, vol. 8042, pp. 75–92. Springer, Heidelberg (2013)
16. Goldreich, O., Goldwasser, S., Micali, S.: How to construct random functions. J. ACM **34**(4), 792–807 (1986)

17. Boneh, D., Waters, B.: Constrained pseudorandom functions and their applications. In: Sako, K., Sarkar, P. (eds.) ASIACRYPT 2013, Part II. LNCS, vol. 8270, pp. 280–300. Springer, Heidelberg (2013)
18. Naor, M., Yung, M.: Pulbic-key cryptosystems provably secure against chosen ciphertext attacks. In 22nd Annual ACM Symposium on Theory of Computing, pp. 427–437 (1990)

Public Key Cryptographic Primitives

Generic Construction of UC-Secure Oblivious Transfer

Olivier Blazy[1] and Céline Chevalier[2]($\boxtimes$)

[1] XLim, Université de Limoges, Limoges, France
[2] Université Panthéon-Assas, Paris, France
celine.chevalier@ens.fr

Abstract. We show how to construct a completely generic UC-secure oblivious transfer scheme from a collision-resistant chameleon hash scheme (CH) and a CCA encryption scheme accepting a smooth projective hash function (SPHF).

Our work is based on the work of Abdalla *et al.* at Asiacrypt 2013, where the authors formalize the notion of *SPHF-friendly* commitments, *i.e.* accepting an SPHF on the language of valid commitments (to allow *implicit* decommitment), and show how to construct from them a UC-secure oblivious transfer in a generic way. But Abdalla *et al.* only gave a DDH-based construction of SPHF-friendly commitment schemes, furthermore highly relying on pairings. In this work, we show how to generically construct an SPHF-friendly commitment scheme from a collision-resistant CH scheme and an SPHF-friendly CCA encryption scheme. This allows us to propose an instanciation of our schemes based on the DDH, as efficient as that of Abdalla *et al.*, but without requiring any pairing. Interestingly, our generic framework also allows us to propose an instanciation based on the learning with errors (LWE) assumption. For the record, we finally propose a last instanciation based on the decisional composite residuosity (DCR) assumption.

Keywords: Commitments · Smooth Projective Hash Functions · CCA encryption · Oblivious Transfer · UC framework

1 Introduction

Oblivious Transfer (OT) was introduced in 1981 by Rabin [Rab81] as a way to allow a receiver to get exactly one out of k messages sent by another party, the sender. In these schemes, the receiver should be oblivious to the other values, and the sender should be oblivious to which value was received. This primitive has been widely used and studied in the community, and recently, the authors of [ABB+13] propose a generic way to obtain a UC-secure oblivious transfer scheme from an SPHF-friendly commitment scheme, and an instanciation based on DDH. In this paper, our goal is to strengthen their result to obtain a truly generic way to obtain a UC-secure oblivious transfer scheme, so we follow their path of construction from commitment schemes.

© Springer International Publishing Switzerland 2015
T. Malkin et al. (Eds.): ACNS 2015, LNCS 9092, pp. 65–86, 2015.
DOI: 10.1007/978-3-319-28166-7_4

Commitment schemes have become a very useful tool used in cryptographic protocols. These two-party primitives (between a committer and a receiver) are divided into two phases. In a first *commit* phase, the committer gives the receiver an analogue of a sealed envelope containing a value m, while in the second *opening* phase, the committer reveals m in such a way that the receiver can verify it was indeed m that was contained in the envelope. It is required that a committer cannot change the committed value (*i.e.*, he should not be able to open to a value different from the one he committed to), this is called the *binding* property. It is also required that the receiver cannot learn anything about m before the opening phase, this is called the *hiding* property. El Gamal [ElG84] or Cramer-Shoup [CS02] encryptions are famous examples of perfectly binding commitments, and Pedersen encryption [Ped91] is the most known example of perfectly hiding commitments.

In many applications, for example password-based authenticated key-exchange in which the committed value is a password, one wants the decommitment to be implicit, which means that the committer does not really open its commitment, but rather convinces the receiver that it actually committed to the value it pretended to. In [ACP09], the authors achieved this property thanks to the notion of *Smooth Projective Hash Functions* [CS02, GL03], which has been widely used since then (see [KV11, BBC+13b, ABB+13] for instance). These hash functions are defined such as their value can be computed in two different ways if the input belongs to a particular subset (the *language*), either using a private hashing key or a public projection key along with a private witness ensuring that the input belongs to the language. The hash value obtained is indistinguishable from random in case the input does not belong to the language (property of *smoothness*) and in case the input does belong to the language but no witness is known (property of *pseudo-randomness*).

An additional difficulty arises when one wants to prove the protocols in the universal composability framework proposed in [Can01]. In a nutshell, security in the UC framework is captured by an ideal functionality (in an ideal world) and a protocol is proven secure if, given any adversary to the protocol in the real world, one can construct a simulator of this adversary such that no environment can distinguish between the execution in the ideal world (between dummy players, the ideal functionality and the simulator of the adversary) and the execution in the real world (between the real players executing the real protocol and interacting between themselves and the adversary) in a non-negligible way. Skipping the details, when the protocol makes use of commitments, this usually forces those commitments to be both *extractable* (meaning that a simulator can recover the value m committed to thanks to a trapdoor) and *equivocable* (meaning that a simulator can open a commitment to a value m' different from the value m it committed to thanks to a trapdoor), which is quite a difficult goal to achieve.

The now classical way [CF01, ACP09, ABB+13] to achieve both extractability and equivocability is to combine an equivocable CPA encryption scheme (such as Pedersen [Ped91]) and an extractable CCA encryption scheme (such as Cramer-Shoup [CS02]) and to link them with an SPHF in order to obtain an implicit decommitment. What we show in this paper is that we can broaden the class of primitives that can be used for the equivocable part, by using chameleon hashes (introduced in [KR00]), which can be seen as conceptually easier building blocks to understand and to construct.

Related Work. The first UC-secure commitment schemes were given by [CF01] and [DN02] and the former were the first to formalize the methodology described in the previous section (combining an equivocable primitive and an extractable primitive). Building on their idea, the authors of [ACP09] add the notion of smooth projective hash function to obtain implicit decommitment and obtain the first UC-secure password-authenticated key-exchange in the standard model as an application. Many works have been done in the same field since then, for instance [Lin11, FLM11, BCPV13] for the UC-commitment schemes and [KV11, BBC+13b] for the UC PAKE schemes, in which the relations between commitments and SPHF have proven being very useful. This relation was formalized in [ABB+13] by the notion of SPHF-*friendly commitments*, expliciting the properties to be fulfilled by the commitment in order to accept an SPHF (and thus to be very useful for all kinds of applications). The authors also prove that their new notion of SPHF-friendly commitments is strictly stronger than the notion of UC commitments and give an example of such a commitment scheme based on Haralambiev commitment [Har11, Sect. 4.1.4] and Cramer-Shoup encryption, in a pairing-friendly setting. They also propose a generic way to construct UC one-round PAKE and oblivious transfer scheme from this primitive.

Many oblivious transfer schemes have been proposed since [Rab81], including some in the UC framework [NP01, CLOS02]. Recently, some instantiations have tried to reach round-optimality [HK07], or low communication costs [PVW08]. As already explained, the authors of [ABB+13] propose a generic way to obtain a UC-secure oblivious transfer scheme from an SPHF-friendly commitment scheme, and an instantiation based on DDH. Choi *et al.* [CKWZ13] also propose a generic method and an efficient instantiation secure against adaptive corruptions in the CRS model with erasures, based on DDH, but it is only 1-out-of-2 and it does not scale to 1-out-of-k OT, for $k > 2$.

Contributions.[1] Our first contribution is to give a generic construction of SPHF-friendly commitments, which have proven since [ABB+13] to be an extremely useful primitive, from two simple blocks: a collision-resistant chameleon hash (CH) function which is verifiable (either publicly or for the receiver only) and an SPHF-friendly CCA encryption scheme. The extra requirement on the CH function is simple to achieve as soon as only classical algebraic operations are applied to the randomness, and SPHF-friendly encryption is now well-known since [CS02], with several instances (contrary to SPHF-friendly commitments, which is a difficult task). We then give three instantiations of this SPHF-friendly scheme, respectively based on DDH, LWE and DCR.

---

[1] This is an extended abstract. The full paper [BC15] is available at the Cryptology Eprint Archive, http://eprint.iacr.org.

Our construction thus allows us to provide, as a second and main contribution, a generic way to obtain a UC-secure OT scheme from the same building blocks (CH and CCA encryption) and three concrete instantiations from DDH, LWE and DCR. While the construction in [ABB+13] is an ad hoc solution with pairings, ours is generic and does not specifically induce pairings. Furthermore, our 3 instantiations come straightforward from our generic framework (and [ABB+13] can be derived from it).

Concerning complexity comparisons, the most studied assumptions in the literature are variants of DDH. Our version of 1-out-of-t oblivious transfer is apparently almost equivalent to that given in [ABB+13] in raw number of elements because we need a communication complexity of $9m+6$ elements in $\mathbb{G}$ and a scalar, compared to $8m + 4^2$ in $\mathbb{G}_1$, m in $\mathbb{G}_2$ and a scalar (with $t = 2^m$), but since we do not need a pairing-friendly setting, none of our elements have to be bigger, hence the comparison is in favor of our new proposal (by an equivalent of $m/2 - 1$ elements). (Those numbers do not take into account in both cases the last message that transmits the database, adding an additional m elements in both cases).

To compare with existing protocols in the case of 1-out-of-2 under SXDH, [ABB+13] needs 12 elements in $\mathbb{G}_1$, and 1 in $\mathbb{G}_2$ during 3 rounds (some elements previously in $\mathbb{G}_2$ can be transferred into $\mathbb{G}_1$ in this case, and one can be skipped), [CKWZ13] requires 26 group elements and 7 scalars in 4 rounds ; and using [GWZ09] to achieve a constant-size CRS, [PVW08] requires 8 rounds and 51 elements. Using plain DDH, we need 15 group elements (but because [ABB+13] requires one in $\mathbb{G}_2$ we have strictly the same communication cost with a better scaling and no pairing computation) hence under classical instantiation both schemes require to transmit roughly 3200 bits of data.

Communication cost comparisons of various Elliptic Curve based OT schemes			
Paper	Assumption	# Group elements	# Rounds
Static Security			
[PVW08] + [GWZ09]	SXDH	51	8
[CKWZ13]	SXDH	26 + 7s	4
Adaptive security			
[ABB+13]	SXDH	12 $\mathbb{G}_1$ + 1 $\mathbb{G}_2$	3
This paper	DDH	15	3

Considering classical instantiations on Barreto-Naehrig Curves [BN05], elements on a DDH curve are at least twice smaller than the big ones on a SXDH one, making our scheme have a better scaling for 1-out-of-m OT. With recent attacks exploiting the existence of a pairing, managing to maintain the efficiency

---

[2] It should be noted that their original computation was off by one scalar, probably half the projection key was missing.

while removing the need for a pairing structure is a strong asset of elliptic curve based cryptography. For constructions based on generic hypothesis, the construction of [PVW08] leads to a non constant size CRS (in the number of user), while ours achieve constant (and small) CRS size.

2   Definitions

In this section we recall classical definitions and tools that are going to be useful in the rest of the paper.

Commitments. Formal definitions and results from [ABB+13] are given in the full version but we give here an informal overview to help the unfamiliar reader with the following. A *non-interactive labelled commitment scheme* $\mathcal{C}$ is defined by three algorithms:

- SetupCom($1^{\mathfrak{K}}$) takes as input the security parameter $\mathfrak{K}$ and outputs the global parameters, passed through the CRS ρ to all other algorithms;
- Com$^{\ell}(x)$ takes as input a label ℓ and a message x, and outputs a pair (C, δ), where C is the commitment of x for the label ℓ, and δ is the corresponding opening data (a.k.a. decommitment information). This is a probabilistic algorithm.
- VerCom$^{\ell}(C, x, \delta)$ takes as input a commitment C, a label ℓ, a message x, and the opening data δ and outputs 1 (true) if δ is a valid opening data for C, x and ℓ. It always outputs 0 (false) on $x = \bot$.

The basic properties required for commitments are *correctness* (for all correctly generated CRS ρ, all commitments and opening data honestly generated pass the verification VerCom test), the *hiding property* (the commitment does not leak any information about the committed value) and the *binding property* (no adversary can open a commitment in two different ways).

A commitment scheme is said *equivocable* if it has a second setup SetupComT($1^{\mathfrak{K}}$) that additionally outputs a trapdoor τ, and two algorithms

- SimCom$^{\ell}(\tau)$ that takes as input the trapdoor τ and a label ℓ and outputs a pair (C, eqk), where C is a commitment and eqk an equivocation key;
- OpenCom$^{\ell}(\mathsf{eqk}, C, x)$ that takes as input a commitment C, a label ℓ, a message x, an equivocation key eqk, and outputs an opening data δ for C and ℓ on x.

such as the following properties are satisfied: *trapdoor correctness* (all simulated commitments can be opened on any message), *setup indistinguishability* (one cannot distinguish the CRS ρ generated by SetupCom from the one generated by SetupComT) and *simulation indistinguishability* (one cannot distinguish a real commitment (generated by Com) from a fake commitment (generated by SCom), even with oracle access to fake commitments), denoting by SCom the algorithm that takes as input the trapdoor τ, a label ℓ and a message x and which outputs $(C, \delta) \xleftarrow{\$} \mathsf{SCom}^{\ell}(\tau, x)$, computed as $(C, \mathsf{eqk}) \xleftarrow{\$} \mathsf{SimCom}^{\ell}(\tau)$ and $\delta \leftarrow \mathsf{OpenCom}^{\ell}(\mathsf{eqk}, C, x)$.

A commitment scheme $\mathcal{C}$ is said *extractable* if it has a second setup SetupComT($1^{\mathfrak{K}}$) that additionally outputs a trapdoor τ, and a new algorithm

– ExtCom$^\ell(\tau, C)$ which takes as input the trapdoor τ, a commitment C, and a label ℓ, and outputs the committed message x, or $\perp$ if the commitment is invalid.

such as the following properties are satisfied: *trapdoor correctness* (all commitments honestly generated can be correctly extracted: for all ℓ, x, if $(C, \delta) \xleftarrow{\$}$ Com$^\ell(x)$ then ExtCom$^\ell(C, \tau) = x$), *setup indistinguishability* (as above) and *binding extractability* (one cannot fool the extractor, *i.e.*, produce a commitment and a valid opening data to an input x while the commitment does not extract to x).

We recall in Sect. 3 the difficulties implied by a commitment being both equivocable and extractable and give a construction of such a commitment.

Smooth Projective Hash Function. Smooth projective hash functions (SPHF) were introduced by Cramer and Shoup in [CS02] for constructing encryption schemes. A projective hashing family is a family of hash functions that can be evaluated in two ways: using the (secret) hashing key, one can compute the function on every point in its domain, whereas using the (public) *projected* key one can only compute the function on a special subset of its domain. Such a family is deemed *smooth* if the value of the hash function on any point outside the special subset is independent of the projected key. The notion of SPHF has already found applications in various contexts in cryptography (*e.g.* [GL03, Kal05, ACP09]). A Smooth Projective Hash Function over a language $\mathfrak{L} \subset X$, onto a set $\mathcal{G}$, is defined by five algorithms (Setup, HashKG, ProjKG, Hash, ProjHash):

– Setup($1^\mathfrak{K}$) where $\mathfrak{K}$ is the security parameter, generates the global parameters param of the scheme, and the description of an $\mathcal{NP}$ language $\mathfrak{L}$;
– HashKG($\mathfrak{L}$, param), outputs a hashing key hk for the language $\mathfrak{L}$;
– ProjKG(hk, $(\mathfrak{L}, \text{param}), W$), derives the projection key hp from the hashing key hk.
– Hash(hk, $(\mathfrak{L}, \text{param}), W$), outputs a hash value $v \in \mathcal{G}$, thanks to the hashing key hk and W.
– ProjHash(hp, $(\mathfrak{L}, \text{param}), W, w$), outputs the hash value $v' \in \mathcal{G}$, thanks to the projection key hp and the witness w that $W \in \mathfrak{L}$.

In the following, we consider $\mathfrak{L}$ as a hard-partitioned subset of X, *i.e.* it is computationally hard to distinguish a random element in $\mathfrak{L}$ from a random element in $X \setminus \mathfrak{L}$.

A Smooth Projective Hash Function SPHF should satisfy the following properties:

– *Correctness*: Let $W \in \mathfrak{L}$ and w a witness of this membership. Then, for all hashing keys hk and associated projection keys hp we have Hash(hk, $(\mathfrak{L}, \text{param}), W$) = ProjHash(hp, $(\mathfrak{L}, \text{param}), W, w$).
– *Smoothness*: For all $W \in X \setminus \mathfrak{L}$ the following distributions are statistically indistinguishable:

$$\Delta_0 = \left\{ (\mathfrak{L}, \mathsf{param}, W, \mathsf{hp}, v) \;\middle|\; \begin{array}{l} \mathsf{param} = \mathsf{Setup}(1^{\mathfrak{K}}), \mathsf{hk} = \mathsf{HashKG}(\mathfrak{L}, \mathsf{param}), \\ \mathsf{hp} = \mathsf{ProjKG}(\mathsf{hk}, (\mathfrak{L}, \mathsf{param}), W), \\ v = \mathsf{Hash}(\mathsf{hk}, (\mathfrak{L}, \mathsf{param}), W) \end{array} \right\}$$

$$\Delta_1 = \left\{ (\mathfrak{L}, \mathsf{param}, W, \mathsf{hp}, v) \;\middle|\; \begin{array}{l} \mathsf{param} = \mathsf{Setup}(1^{\mathfrak{K}}), \mathsf{hk} = \mathsf{HashKG}(\mathfrak{L}, \mathsf{param}), \\ \mathsf{hp} = \mathsf{ProjKG}(\mathsf{hk}, (\mathfrak{L}, \mathsf{param}), W), v \xleftarrow{\$} \mathcal{G} \end{array} \right\}.$$

Labelled Encryption Scheme. A labelled public-key encryption scheme $\mathcal{E}$ is defined by four algorithms:

- $\mathsf{Setup}(1^{\mathfrak{K}})$, where $\mathfrak{K}$ is the security parameter, generates the global parameters param of the scheme;
- $\mathsf{KeyGen}(\mathsf{param})$ generates a pair of keys, the public encryption key pk and the private decryption key sk;
- $\mathsf{Encrypt}^{\ell}(\mathsf{pk}, m; r)$ produces a ciphertext c on the input message $m \in \mathcal{M}$ under the label ℓ and encryption key pk, using the random coins r;
- $\mathsf{Decrypt}^{\ell}(\mathsf{sk}, c)$ outputs the plaintext m encrypted in c under the label ℓ, or $\perp$ for an invalid ciphertext.

An encryption scheme $\mathcal{E}$ should satisfy the following properties

- *Correctness*: for all key pair $(\mathsf{pk}, \mathsf{sk})$, any label ℓ, all random coins r and all messages m, $\mathsf{Decrypt}^{\ell}(\mathsf{sk}, \mathsf{Encrypt}^{\ell}(\mathsf{pk}, m; r)) = m$.

- *Indistinguishability under chosen-ciphertext attacks*: this security notion IND-CCA can be formalized by the following experiments $\mathsf{Exp}_{\mathcal{A}}^{\mathsf{ind\text{-}cca\text{-}b}}(\mathfrak{K})$, where the adversary $\mathcal{A}$ transfers some internal state state between the various calls FIND and GUESS, and makes use of the oracle ODecrypt:

> $\mathsf{Exp}_{\mathcal{A}}^{\mathsf{ind\text{-}cca\text{-}b}}(\mathfrak{K})$
> $\quad \mathsf{param} \xleftarrow{\$} \mathsf{Setup}(1^{\mathfrak{K}})$
> $\quad (\mathsf{pk}, \mathsf{sk}) \xleftarrow{\$} \mathsf{KeyGen}(\mathsf{param})$
> $\quad (\ell^{*}, m_0, m_1, \mathsf{state}) \leftarrow \mathcal{A}^{\mathsf{ODecrypt}(\cdot)}(\mathsf{FIND} : \mathsf{pk})$
> $\quad c^{*} \leftarrow \mathsf{Encrypt}^{\ell^{*}}(\mathsf{pk}, m_b)$
> $\quad b' \leftarrow \mathcal{A}^{\mathsf{ODecrypt}(\cdot)}(\mathsf{state}, \mathsf{GUESS} : c^{*})$
> $\quad \mathsf{If}\ ((\ell^{*}, c^{*}) \in \mathcal{CT}) \quad \mathsf{Return}\ 0$
> $\quad \mathsf{Else} \quad \mathsf{Return}\ b'$

- $\mathsf{ODecrypt}^{\ell}(c)$: This oracle outputs the decryption of c under the label ℓ and the challenge decryption key sk. The input queries (ℓ, c) are added to the list $\mathcal{CT}$.

These experiments implicitly define the advantages $\mathsf{Adv}_{\mathcal{E}}^{\mathsf{ind\text{-}cca}}(\mathcal{A}, \mathfrak{K})$ and $\mathsf{Adv}_{\mathcal{E}}^{\mathsf{ind\text{-}cca}}(t)$. One sometimes uses the notation $\mathsf{Adv}_{\mathcal{E}}^{\mathsf{ind\text{-}cca}}(q_d, t)$ to bound the number of decryption queries.

In the following we also want two additional properties. First we want an additional functionality, we want to be able to supersede the decryption, by an implicit decommitment. So we require the encryption to admit an efficient implicit decommitment. We will call an SPHF-friendly encryption, an encryption where there exists an SPHF for the Language of valid ciphertexts of a message m using as sole witness the randomness used in the encryption.

We then are going to want to strengthen the idea of ind-cca encryption. In the sense that we are going to encrypt vector of messages, and when the challenges vectors shares some component we want to provide the randomness used specifically for those components to the adversary. (Intuitively this would be done to allow an honest computation of the SPHF on this part). In [ABB+13], they call such property VIND-PO-CCA for Partial Opening, and show that Cramer-Shoup encryption obeys such property. We recall this security notion in the full version for the sake of completeness. We denote by $\mathsf{nEncrypt}^{\ell}(\mathsf{pk}, m; r)$ and $\mathsf{nDecrypt}^{\ell}(\mathsf{sk}, c)$ the corresponding algorithms for encryption or decryption of vectors of n bits.

Chameleon Hash. A Chameleon Hash Function is traditionally defined by three algorithms $\mathsf{CH} = (\mathsf{KeyGen}, \mathsf{CH}, \mathsf{Coll})$:

- $\mathsf{KeyGen}(\mathfrak{K})$: Outputs the chameleon hash key ck and the trapdoor tk;
- $\mathsf{CH}(\mathsf{ck}, m; r)$: Picks a random r, and outputs the chameleon hash a.
- $\mathsf{Coll}(\mathsf{ck}, m, r, m', \mathsf{tk})$: Takes as input the trapdoor tk, a start message and randomness pair (m, r) and a target message m' and outputs a target randomness r' such that $\mathsf{CH}(\mathsf{ck}, m; r) = \mathsf{CH}(\mathsf{ck}, m'; r')$.

The standard security notion for CH is collision resistance, which means it is infeasible to find $(m_1, r_1), (m_2, r_2)$ such that $\mathsf{CH}(\mathsf{ck}, m_1, r_1) = \mathsf{CH}(\mathsf{ck}, m_2, r_2)$ and $m_1 \neq m_2$ given only the Chameleon hash key ck. Formally, CH is $(t, \varepsilon) - \mathsf{coll}$ if for the adversary $\mathcal{A}$ running in time at most t we have:

$$\Pr\left[\begin{array}{l} (\mathsf{ck}, \mathsf{tk}) \xleftarrow{\$} \mathsf{KeyGen}(\mathfrak{K}); ((m_1, r_1), (m_2, r_2)) \xleftarrow{\$} \mathcal{A}(\mathsf{ck}) \\ \wedge \quad \mathsf{CH}(\mathsf{ck}, m_1; r_1) = \mathsf{CH}(\mathsf{ck}, m_2; r_2) \wedge m_1 \neq m_2 \end{array} \right] \leq \varepsilon.$$

However, any user in possession of the trapdoor tk is able to find a collision using Coll. Additionally, Chameleon Hash functions have the uniformity property, which means the hash value leaks nothing about the message input. Formally, for all pair of messages m_1 and m_2 and the randomly chosen r, the probability distributions of the random variables $\mathsf{CH}(\mathsf{ck}, m_1, r)$ and $\mathsf{CH}(\mathsf{ck}, m_2, r)$ are computationally indistinguishable.

We need here the hash value to be verifiable, so that we add two VKeyGen and Valid algorithms (executed by the receiver) and we modify the existing algorithms as follows:

- $\mathsf{VKeyGen}(\mathsf{ck})$: Outputs the chameleon designated verification key vk and the trapdoor vtk. This trapdoor can be empty or public if the chameleon hash is publicly verifiable.
- $\mathsf{CH}(\mathsf{ck}, \mathsf{vk}, m; r)$: Picks a random r, and outputs the chameleon hash a as well as the *witness* d, *i.e.* the corresponding data needed to verify a.
- $\mathsf{Valid}(\mathsf{ck}, \mathsf{vk}, m, a, d, \mathsf{vtk})$: Allows to check that the sender knows how to open a Chameleon Hash a to a specific value m for the witness d. The verification can be public if vtk is empty or public, or specific to the receiver otherwise.

– Coll(ck, vk, m, r, m', tk): Takes as input the public keys, the trapdoor tk, a start message m and randomness r and a target message m' and outputs a target randomness r' such that if CH(ck, vk, $m; r$) = (a, d), then CH(ck, vk, $m'; r'$) = (a, d').

Once again, we expect the chameleon hash to be collision resistant on the first part of the output, which means it is infeasible to find $(m_1, r_1), (m_2, r_2)$ such that CH(ck, vk, m_1, r_1) = (a, d_1) and CH(ck, m_2, r_2) = (a, d_2) and $m_1 \neq m_2$ given only the Chameleon public keys ck and vk.

We expect the verification to be sound, which means that, given a tuple (m, a, d) satisfying Valid(ck, vk, m, a, d, vtk), there always exists at least one tuple (r, d') such that CH(ck, vk, $m; r$) = (a, d').

Protocols in the UC Framework. The goal of the UC framework is to ensure that UC-secure protocols will continue to behave in the ideal way even if executed in a concurrent way in arbitrary environments. It is a simulation-based model, relying on the indistinguishability between the real world and the ideal world. In the ideal world, the security is provided by an ideal functionality $\mathcal{F}$, capturing all the properties required for the protocol and all the means of the adversary. In order to prove that a protocol Π emulates $\mathcal{F}$, one has to construct, for any polynomial adversary $\mathcal{A}$ (which controls the communication between the players), a simulator $\mathcal{S}$ such that no polynomial environment $\mathcal{Z}$ (the distinguisher) can distinguish between the real world (with the real players interacting with themselves and $\mathcal{A}$ and executing the protocol π) and the ideal world (with dummy players interacting with $\mathcal{S}$ and $\mathcal{F}$) with a significant advantage. The adversary can be either *adaptive*, *i.e.* allowed to corrupt users whenever it likes to, or *static*, *i.e.* required to choose which users to corrupt prior to the execution of the session sid of the protocol. After corrupting a player, $\mathcal{A}$ has complete access to the internal state and private values of the player, takes its entire control, and plays on its behalf.

UC-Secure Oblivious Transfer. The ideal functionality of an Oblivious Transfer (OT) protocol is depicted in Fig. 1. It is inspired from [CKWZ13, ABB+13].

3   Generic Construction of UC-Secure Oblivious Transfer

In this section, we show how to construct in a generic way a UC-secure oblivious transfer from any collision-resistant chameleon hash and CCA-2 encryption scheme.

In [ABB+13], the authors give a way to construct such a UC-secure oblivious transfer protocol from an SPHF-friendly commitment, but they only give an instantiation of such an SPHF-friendly commitment in a DDH-based setting, using Haralambiev commitment scheme [Har11] and Cramer-Shoup encryption scheme [CS02].

Our goal is thus to strengthen the generic part of the construction, by showing how to construct, in a generic way, a UC-secure SPHF-friendly commitment

The functionality $\mathcal{F}_{(1,k)\text{-OT}}$ is parametrized by a security parameter $\mathfrak{K}$. It interacts with an adversary $\mathcal{S}$ and a set of parties $P_1,\ldots,P_n$ via the following queries:

- **Upon receiving an input (Send, sid, ssid, $P_i, P_j, (m_1,\ldots,m_k)$) from party P_i,** with $m_i \in \{0,1\}^{\mathfrak{K}}$: record the tuple (sid, ssid, $P_i, P_j, (m_1,\ldots,m_k)$) and reveal (Send, sid, ssid, P_i, P_j) to the adversary $\mathcal{S}$. Ignore further Send-message with the same ssid from P_i.
- **Upon receiving an input (Receive, sid, ssid, P_i, P_j, s) from party P_j,** with $s \in \{1,\ldots,k\}$: record the tuple (sid, ssid, P_i, P_j, s), and reveal (Receive, sid, ssid, P_i, P_j) to the adversary $\mathcal{S}$. Ignore further Receive-message with the same ssid from P_j.
- **Upon receiving a message (Sent, sid, ssid, P_i, P_j) from the adversary $\mathcal{S}$:** ignore the message if (sid, ssid, $P_i, P_j, (m_1,\ldots,m_k)$) or (sid, ssid, P_i, P_j, s) is not recorded; otherwise send (Sent, sid, ssid, P_i, P_j) to P_i and ignore further Sent-message with the same ssid from the adversary.
- **Upon receiving a message (Received, sid, ssid, P_i, P_j) from the adversary $\mathcal{S}$:** ignore the message if (sid, ssid, $P_i, P_j, (m_1,\ldots,m_k)$) or (sid, ssid, P_i, P_j, s) is not recorded; otherwise send (Received, sid, ssid, P_i, P_j, m_s) to P_j and ignore further Received-message with the same ssid from the adversary.

Fig. 1. Ideal Functionality for 1-out-of-k Oblivious Transfer $\mathcal{F}_{(1,k)\text{-OT}}$

scheme in any setting, from a collision-resistant chameleon hash and a CCA-2 encryption scheme.

3.1 From Commitment to Oblivious Transfer

Introduction. In an oblivious transfer scheme, we consider the interaction between a server, possessing a database called DB containing $t = 2^m$ lines, and a user, willing to request the line j of the database in an oblivious way. Informally, this implies that the user will gain no information about the other lines of the database, and also that the server will obtain no information about the specific line the user wants to obtain.

In the protocol described in [ABB+13], from a high point of view[3], the user sends to the server a commitment of the number j of the line it is willing to obtain. The server then computes a pair of keys for a smooth projective hash function (SPHF) adapted to the commitment. It keeps secret the hash key and sends the projection key to the user, along with the hash value of all the lines of the database. Thanks to the properties of the SPHF, the user will then be able to recover the particular line it wants, using the public projection key and the secret random coins it used to create its committed value in the first place. The properties of the SPHF also ensure that the server has no idea about the line the user is requiring, and that the user cannot obtain any information from the hash values of the other lines of DB, which are exactly the requirements of a secure OT.

---
[3] Note that we omit here for the sake of simplicity the creation of a secure channel between the user and the server (this is only needed in the adaptive version of the protocol).

The authors of this protocol prove its security in the UC framework, which implies the use of a commitment with strong security properties. Indeed, the simulator of a user needs to be able to change its mind about the line required, hence an *equivocable* commitment; and the simulator of a server also needs to be able to extract the line required by the user, hence an *extractable* commitment. Unfortunately, combining both equivocability and extractability on the same commitment scheme, especially if we require this commitment scheme to admit an SPHF, is a difficult task and requires more security properties, as we recall in the following.

Properties for Commitments. We informally recall these specific properties, defined in [ABB+13] and formally stated in the full version. We call a commitment scheme E^2 (for *extractable and equivocable* and the necessary properties) if the indistinguishable setup algorithm outputs a common trapdoor that allows both equivocability and extractability, and the two following properties are satisfied: *strong simulation indistinguishability* (one cannot distinguish a real commitment (generated by Com) from a fake commitment (generated by SCom), even with oracle access to the extraction oracle (ExtCom) and to fake commitments (using SCom)) and *strong binding extractability* (one cannot fool the extractor, *i.e.*, produce a commitment and a valid opening data (not given by SCom) to an input x while the commitment does not extract to x, even with oracle access to the extraction oracle (ExtCom) and to fake commitments (using SCom)).

A commitment is said to be *robust* if one cannot produce a commitment and a label that extracts to x' (possibly $x' = \perp$) such that there exists a valid opening data to a different input x, even with oracle access to the extraction oracle (ExtCom) and to fake commitments (using SCom).

Finally, a commitment is said to be SPHF-*friendly* if it is an E^2 commitment that admits an SPHF on the languages $L_x = \{(\ell, C) | \exists \delta, \mathsf{VerCom}^\ell(C, x, \delta) = 1\}$, and that is both strongly-simulation-indistinguishable and robust.

3.2   Generic Construction of SPHF-Friendly Commitment

Introduction. We start by a high-level description of the (Cramer-Shoup-based) commitment given in [ABB+13] in the pairing-friendly setting $(\mathcal{G}_1, g_1, h_1, \mathcal{G}_2, g_2, \mathcal{G}_T, p, e)$. They set $T = g_2{}^t$, t being a value chosen at random in $\mathcal{Z}_p$. We omit the labels for the sake of simplicity. First, they cut the message M to be committed into bits, denoted here as $M = (M_i)_i \in \{0,1\}^m$. They then compute a TC4 Haralambiev [Har11] equivocable commitment of each bit M_i: $a = (a_i)_i$ with $a_i = g_2{}^{r_{i,M_i}} T^{M_i}$ with r_{i,M_i} chosen at random in $\mathcal{Z}_p$ and $r_{i,\overline{M_i}} = 0$. The opening values (for decommitment) are the values $d_{i,j} = g_1{}^{r_{i,j}}$. They then compute a multi-Cramer-Shoup encryption $b = (b_{i,j})_{i,j}$ of $d = (d_{i,j})_{i,j}$ with randomness $s = (s_{i,j})_{i,j}$. The commitment is (a, b), the opening information being s. To open the commitment, the receiver checks the validity of the ciphertexts b_{i,M_i}, extracts each value d_{i,M_i} from b_{i,M_i} and s_{i,M_i} and finally checks whether the equality $e(g_1, a_i/T^{M_i}) = e(d_{i,M_i}, g_2)$ holds.

The equivocability of the commitment is ensured by the knowledge of t, enabling the sender to set $r_{i,\overline{M_i}} = r_{i,M_i} \pm t$ rather than $r_{i,\overline{M_i}} = 0$. The extractability is ensured by the knowledge of the decryption keys of the Cramer-Shoup encryption.

Our first goal, in this concrete instantiation, is to get rid of the pairing setting, and in particular of the pairing verification, in order to be able to propose constructions in other settings. To this aim, we change the TC4 commitment of M_i for a *verifiable* chameleon hash of M_i. Making this change enables us to get a generic version of this commitment, requiring only "compatible" chameleon hash (playing the role of the TC4 scheme above) and CCA encryption schemes (playing the role of the Cramer-Shoup above). The chameleon hash can either be publicly verifiable (which gives us a non-interactive commitment), or verifiable by the receiver, which requires a pre-flow, in which the server generates a verification key and its trapdoor and sends the verification key to the sender.

Building Blocks. We assume the existence of compatible CCA-encryption (Setup, KeyGen, Encrypt, Decrypt) and chameleon hash (KeyGen, VKeyGen, CH, Coll, Valid), in the sense that is feasible to compute a CCA-encryption of the opening value of the chameleon hash. For example, a Pedersen Chameleon Hash is not compatible with Cramer Shoup encryption, as we would need to encrypt the randomness as a scalar, while the decryption algorithm only allows us to recover group elements.

In order for our commitment to accept an SPHF, we require the CCA-encryption to accept an SPHF on the language of valid ciphertexts. The precise language needed will depend on the way the chameleon hash is verified, but will be easily constructed by combining several simple languages as described in [BBC+13a].

We require the chameleon hash to be verifiable by the receiver. For the sake of concision, we describe here the case where the chameleon hash is only verifiable by the server. In this case, we need a pre-flow, in which the server is assumed to execute the algorithm VKeyGen to generate a verification key and its trapdoor and send the verification key to the sender. This makes the commitment not completely non-interactive anymore but it should be noted that if the global protocol is not one-round, these values can be sent by the receiver during the first round of the protocol. In the case where the chameleon hash is publicly verifiable, one simply has to consider the keys vk and vtk empty, and ignore the pre-flow.

Construction. We now describe the different algorithms of our chameleon-hashed targeted commitment protocol CHCS from player P to Q (see Sect. 2 for the notations of the algorithms).

– **Setup and simulated setup algorithms:** SetupComT($1^{\mathfrak{K}}$) (the algorithm for setup with trapdoors) generates the various parameters param, for the setting of the SPHF-friendly labelled CCA-encryption scheme and the chameleon hash scheme. It then generates the corresponding keys and trapdoors: (ck, tk) for the chameleon hash scheme and (ek, dk) for the encryption scheme.

For $\mathsf{SetupCom}(1^{\mathfrak{K}})$ (the algorithm for setup without trapdoors), the setting and the keys are generated the same way, but forgetting the way the keys were constructed (such as the scalars, in a DDH-based setting), thus without any trapdoor.

The algorithms both output the CRS $\rho = (\mathsf{ek}, \mathsf{ck}, \mathsf{param})$. In the first case, τ denotes the trapdoors $(\mathsf{dk}, \mathsf{tk})$.

- **Pre-flow (verification key generation algorithm):** player Q executes $\mathsf{VKeyGen}(\mathsf{ck})$ to generate the chameleon designated verification key vk and the trapdoor vtk and sends vk to the sender P.
- **Targeted commitment algorithm:** $\mathsf{Com}^{\ell}(M; Q)$ from player P to player Q, for $M = (M_i)_i \in \{0,1\}^m$ and a label ℓ, works as follows:
  - For $i \in [\![1, m]\!]$, it chooses r_{i,M_i} at random and computes $\mathsf{CH}(\mathsf{ck}, \mathsf{vk}, M_i; r_{i,M_i})$ to obtain the hash value a_i and the corresponding opening value d_{i,M_i}. It samples at random the values $r_{i,1-M_i}$ and $d_{i,1-M_i}$. We denote as $a = (a_1, \ldots, a_m)$ the tuple of commitments and $d = (d_{i,j})_{i,j}$.
  - For $i \in [\![1, m]\!]$ and $j = 0, 1$, it gets $b = (b_{i,j})_{i,j} = 2\mathsf{mEncrypt}_{\mathsf{pk}}^{\ell'}(d; s)$, where s is taken at random and $\ell' = (\ell, a)$.

  The commitment is $C = (a, b)$, and the opening information is the m-tuple $\delta = (s_{1,M_1}, \ldots, s_{m,M_m})$.
- **Verification algorithm:** $\mathsf{VerCom}^{\ell}(\mathsf{vtk}, C, M, \delta)$ first checks the validity of the ciphertexts b_{i,M_i} with randomness s_{i,M_i}, then extracts d_{i,M_i} from b_{i,M_i} and s_{i,M_i}, and finally checks the chameleon hash a_i with opening value d_{i,M_i}, for $i \in [\![1, m]\!]$, via the algorithm $\mathsf{Valid}(\mathsf{ck}, \mathsf{vk}, M_i, a_i, d_{i,M_i}, \mathsf{vtk})$.
- **Simulated targeted commitment algorithm:** $\mathsf{SimCom}^{\ell}(\tau; Q)$ from the simulator to player Q, takes as input the equivocation trapdoor, namely tk, from $\tau = (\mathsf{dk}, \mathsf{tk})$, and outputs the commitment $C = (a, b)$ and equivocation key $\mathsf{eqk} = s$, where
  - For $i \in [\![1, m]\!]$, it chooses $r_{i,0}$ at random, computes $(a_i, d_{i,0}) = \mathsf{CH}(\mathsf{ck}, \mathsf{vk}, 0; r_{i,0})$, and uses the equivocation trapdoor tk to compute $r_{i,1}$ used to open the chameleon hash to 1 such that $\mathsf{CH}(\mathsf{ck}, \mathsf{vk}, 1; r_{i,1})$ is equal to $(a_i, d_{i,1})$. This leads to a and d, making $d_{i,j}$ the opening value for $a_{i,j}$ for all $i \in [\![1, m]\!]$ and $j = 0, 1$.
  - b is built as above: $b = (b_{i,j})_{i,j} = 2\mathsf{mEncrypt}_{\mathsf{pk}}^{\ell'}(d; s)$, where $\mathsf{eqk} = s$ is taken at random and $\ell' = (\ell, a)$.
- **Equivocation algorithm:** $\mathsf{OpenCom}^{\ell}(\mathsf{eqk}, C, M)$ simply uses part of the equivocation key eqk (computed by the SimCom algorithm) to obtain the opening information $\delta = (s_{1,M_1}, \ldots, s_{m,M_m})$ in order to open to $M = (M_i)_i$.
- **Extraction algorithm:** $\mathsf{ExtCom}^{\ell}(\tau, \mathsf{vtk}, C)$ takes as input the extraction trapdoor, namely the decryption key dk, from $\tau = (\mathsf{dk}, \mathsf{tk})$, the verification trapdoor vtk and a commitment $C = (a, b)$. For $i \in [\![1, m]\!]$ and $j = 0, 1$, it first extracts the value $d_{i,j}$ from the ciphertext $b_{i,j}$, using the decryption key dk. Then, for $i \in [\![1, m]\!]$, it checks the chameleon hash a_i with opening values $d_{i,0}$ and $d_{i,1}$ with the help of the algorithm $\mathsf{Valid}(\mathsf{ck}, \mathsf{vk}, j, a_i, d_{i,j}, \mathsf{vtk})$ for $j = 0, 1$. If only one opening value $d_{i,j}$ satisfies the verification equality of

the chameleon hash, then $j = M_i$. If this condition holds for each $i \in [\![1, m]\!]$, then the extraction algorithm outputs $(M_i)_i$. Otherwise (either if b could not be correctly decrypted, or there was an ambiguity while checking a, with at least one chameleon hash a_i with two possible opening values $d_{i,0}$ and $d_{i,1}$), it outputs $\bot$.

Security Result. Given a publicly verifiable collision-resistant chameleon hash and a secure CCA-encryption accepting an SPHF on the language of valid ciphertexts, the above construction provides a commitment scheme which is SPHF-friendly.

Proof. According to the results recalled at the beginning of this section, page 10, we first need to prove that this $\mathbf{E}^2$ commitment is *strongly-simulation-indistinguishable* and *robust*. Due to lack of space, the proof of this result is postponed to the full version.

One then additionally needs to construct an SPHF on the languages $\mathsf{L}_M = \{(\ell, C) |\, \exists \delta \text{ such that } \mathsf{VerCom}^\ell(\mathsf{vtk}, C, M, \delta) = 1\}$. Recall that the CCA-encryption admits an SPHF on the languages $\mathsf{L}_M^{\mathsf{enc}} = \{(\ell, C) |\, \exists r \text{ such that } \mathsf{Encrypt}^\ell(\mathsf{pk}, M; r)) = C\}$, directly giving us the required SPHF since the algorithm VerCom, on input $C = (a, b)$, first checks the CCA-encryptions b_{i, M_i} and then verifies the chameleon hashes a_i for all i. More precisely, the required language is as follows: $\mathsf{L}_M = \{(\ell, C) | \forall i \in \{1, \dots, m\} \ \exists r_{i, M_i}, s_{i, M_i}, d_{i, M_i} \text{ such that } \mathsf{mEncrypt}^{*, \ell}(\mathsf{pk}, (d_{i, M_i})_i; (s_{i, M_i})_i) = (b_{i, M_i})_i \text{ and that } \mathsf{CH}(\mathsf{ck}, \mathsf{vk}, M_i; r_{i, M_i}) = (a_i, d_{i, M_i})\}$, on which one can easily construct an SPHF by disjunction using the method described in [ACP09, BBC+13a][4].

3.3   Generic Construction of UC-Secure Oblivious Transfer

Introduction. We denote by DB the database of the server containing $t = 2^m$ lines, and j the line requested by the user in an oblivious way. We assume the existence of a Pseudo-Random Generator (PRG) F with input size equal to the plaintext size, and output size equal to the size of the messages in the database and a IND-CPA encryption scheme $\mathcal{E} = (\mathsf{Setup}_{\mathrm{cpa}}, \mathsf{KeyGen}_{\mathrm{cpa}}, \mathsf{Encrypt}_{\mathrm{cpa}}, \mathsf{Decrypt}_{\mathrm{cpa}})$ with plaintext size at least equal to the security parameter. We also assume the existence of compatible CCA-encryption and chameleon hash with the properties described in the former section, and we generically obtain from them the SPHF-friendly commitment scheme given above.

Protocol. We exactly follow the construction given in [ABB+13], giving the protocol presented on Fig. 2. The only difference is that we take advantage of the pre-flow to ask the server to generate the CH verification keys $(\mathsf{vk}, \mathsf{vtk})$. For the sake of simplicity, we only give the version for adaptive security, in which

---

[4] The notation $\mathsf{mEncrypt}^{*, \ell}(\mathsf{pk}, (d_{i, M_i})_i; (s_{i, M_i})_i)$ simply means that we compute $\mathsf{2mEncrypt}^\ell(\mathsf{pk}, (d_{i,j})_{i,j}; (s_{i,j})_{i,j})$ and take the m components corresponding to $j = M_i$ for every i.

the server generates pk and c to create a somewhat secure channel (they would not be used in the static version).

CRS: $\rho = (\mathsf{ek}, \mathsf{ck}, \mathsf{param}) \overset{\$}{\leftarrow} \mathsf{SetupCom}(1^{\mathfrak{K}})$, $\mathsf{param}_{\mathsf{cpa}} \overset{\$}{\leftarrow} \mathsf{Setup}_{\mathsf{cpa}}(1^{\mathfrak{K}})$.

Pre-flow:
1. Server generates a key pair $(\mathsf{pk}, \mathsf{sk}) \overset{\$}{\leftarrow} \mathsf{KeyGen}_{\mathsf{cpa}}(\mathsf{param}_{\mathsf{cpa}})$ for $\mathcal{E}$, stores sk and completely erases the random coins used by KeyGen
2. Server generates a verification key pair $(\mathsf{vk}, \mathsf{vtk}) \overset{\$}{\leftarrow} \mathsf{VKeyGen}(\mathsf{ck})$ for CH, stores vtk and completely erases the random coins used by VKeyGen
3. Server sends pk and vk to User

Index query on j:
1. User chooses a random value J, computes $R \leftarrow F(J)$ and encrypts J under pk:
   $c \overset{\$}{\leftarrow} \mathsf{Encrypt}_{\mathsf{cpa}}(\mathsf{pk}, J)$
2. User computes $(C, \delta) \overset{\$}{\leftarrow} \mathsf{Com}^{\ell}(j)$ with $\ell = (\mathsf{sid}, \mathsf{ssid}, P_i, P_j)$
3. User stores δ and completely erases J, R and the random coins used by Com and $\mathsf{Encrypt}_{\mathsf{cpa}}$ and sends C and c to Server

Database input $(n_1, \ldots, n_t)$:
1. Server decrypts $J \leftarrow \mathsf{Decrypt}_{\mathsf{cpa}}(\mathsf{sk}, c)$ and then $R \leftarrow F(J)$
2. For $s = 1, \ldots, t$: Server computes $\mathsf{hk}_s \overset{\$}{\leftarrow} \mathsf{HashKG}(L_s, \mathsf{param})$,
   $\mathsf{hp}_s \leftarrow \mathsf{ProjKG}(\mathsf{hk}_s, (L_s, \mathsf{param}), (\ell, C))$, $K_s \leftarrow \mathsf{Hash}(\mathsf{hk}_s, (L_s, \mathsf{param}), (\ell, C))$,
   and $N_s \leftarrow R \oplus K_s \oplus n_s$
3. Server erases everything except $(\mathsf{hp}_s, N_s)_{s=1,\ldots,t}$ and sends them over a secure channel

Data recovery:
Upon receiving $(\mathsf{hp}_s, N_s)_{s=1,\ldots,t}$, User computes
$K_j \leftarrow \mathsf{ProjHash}(\mathsf{hp}_j, (L_j, \mathsf{param}), (\ell, C), \delta)$ and gets $n_j \leftarrow R \oplus K_j \oplus N_j$.

Fig. 2. UC-Secure 1-out-of-t OT from an SPHF-Friendly Commitment (for Adaptive Security

Security Result. The oblivious transfer scheme described in Fig. 2 is UC-secure in the presence of adaptive adversaries, assuming reliable erasures and authenticated channels, as soon as the commitment scheme is constructed from a secure publicly-verifiable chameleon hash and a secure CCA encryption scheme admitting an SPHF on the language of valid ciphertexts, as described in the former section.

The proof remains the same; It is given in the full version for completeness.

4   Instantiation Based on Cramer-Shoup Encryption (DDH)

Let us now show how to build SPHF-friendly commitment schemes from various assumptions. While it may seem to be a tremendously far-fetched idea for a construction, we are going to show throughout the following sections that in fact such schemes can be easily built on any of the main modern fields of cryptographic hypotheses.

We start with the construction based on DDH: Since it is easier to understand, it will help to underline the key points. This commitment revisits the one used in [ABB+13] but we remove the pairing used in it thanks to the methods described in the previous section, by generating vtk on the fly. For the chameleon hash, we are going to use a CDH-based Pedersen encryption scheme. However as such CH is not designated verifier, we are going to transform it in an Haralambiev way [Har11, Sect. 4.1.4]. For the CCA encryption we will rely on an extended version of Cramer-Shoup encryption.

4.1   Building Blocks

CDH-based Chameleon Hash[5]

- KeyGen($\mathfrak{K}$): Outputs the chameleon hash key $\mathsf{ck} = (g, h)$ and the trapdoor $\mathsf{tk} = \alpha$, where $g^\alpha = h$;
- VKeyGen(ck): Generates $\mathsf{vk} = f$ and $\mathsf{vtk} = \log_g(f)$
- CH($\mathsf{ck}, \mathsf{vk}, m; r$): Picks a random $r \in \mathbb{Z}_p$, and outputs the chameleon hash $a = h^r g^m$. Sets $d = f^r$.
- Coll(m, r, m', tk): outputs $r' = r + (m - m')/\alpha$.
- Valid($\mathsf{ck}, \mathsf{vk}, m, a, d, \mathsf{vtk}$): The user outputs d, so that one can check if $a = h^m \cdot d^{1/\mathsf{vtk}}$.

The trivial way to check this CH requires a pairing instead of knowing vtk. Note that this trivial verification indeed leads to the protocol described in [ABB+13]. Instead, we let the verifier (the server in latter use) picks a new f and its discrete logarithm.

$2m$-labelled multi twisted Cramer-Shoup Encryption Scheme. We first recall the Cramer-Shoup encryption scheme, which is IND-CCA under the DDH assumption.

- KeyGen($\mathfrak{K}$): Assuming two independent generators g and h, for random scalars $x_1, x_2, y_1, y_2, z \xleftarrow{\$} \mathbb{Z}_p$, we set $\mathsf{sk} = (x_1, x_2, y_1, y_2, z)$ to be the private decryption key and $\mathsf{ek} = (g_1, g_2, c = g_1^{x_1} g_2^{x_2}, d = g_1^{y_1} g_2^{y_2}, h_1 = g_1^z, \mathcal{H})$ to be the public encryption key, where $\mathcal{H}$ is a random collision-resistant hash function from $\mathcal{H}$.

---

[5] As there is no pairing in our construction, we do not really need the linear based version of both schemes, but similar variants can be imagined based on the linear assumption or even on any matrix assumption [EHK+13].

- If $M \in \mathbb{G}$, the Cramer-Shoup encryption is defined as $\mathsf{CS}^\ell(\mathsf{pk}, M; r) = (u = g_1^r, v = g_2^r, e = h^r \cdot M, w = (cd^\theta)^r)$, where $\theta = H(\ell, u, v, e)$.
- Such a ciphertext is decrypted by $M = e/u^z$, after having checked the validity of the ciphertext: $w \stackrel{?}{=} u^{x_1 + \theta y_1} v^{x_2 + \theta y_2}$.

The above scheme can be extended naturally to encrypt vectors of group elements $\boldsymbol{D} = (D_1, \ldots, D_{2m}) \in \mathbb{G}^{2m}$, by having $2m$ tuples of random scalars in the secret key, and a global value θ for the encryption. The authors of [ABB+13] proved that this scheme is $\mathsf{VIND\text{-}PO\text{-}CCA}$ under the DDH assumption.

4.2 Diffie-Hellman Based Commitment Scheme

We simply apply the construction described in Sect. 3 to obtain the commitment scheme from these blocks.

- $\mathsf{SetupComT}(1^\mathfrak{K})$ generates a multiplicative group $\mathsf{param} = (p, \mathbb{G}, g)$; $\mathsf{ek} = (g_1, g_2, c, d, h_1, \mathcal{H})$ and the decryption key dk corresponding to the various discrete log in basis g, $\mathsf{ck} = (g, h)$, tk the respective discrete logarithm.
  For $\mathsf{SetupCom}(1^\mathfrak{K})$, the CRS is generated the same way, but forgetting the scalars, and thus without any trapdoor.
  The algorithms both output $\rho = (\mathsf{ek}, \mathsf{ck}, \mathsf{param})$.
- Pre-flow: During the preflow, the server Q runs $\mathsf{VKeyGen}(\mathsf{ck})$ and outputs $\mathsf{vk} = f$ and keeps its discrete logarithm vtk.
- $\mathsf{Com}^\ell(M; Q)$ from player P to player Q, for $\boldsymbol{M} = (M_i)_i \in \{0,1\}^m$ and a label ℓ, works as follows:
  - For $i \in [\![1, m]\!]$, it chooses a random $r_{i, M_i} \in \mathbb{Z}_p$, a random $r_{i, 1 - M_i}$, and computes $a_i = g^{M_i} h^{r_{i, M_i}}$ and sets $d_{i,j} = f^{r_{i,j}}$ for $j = 0, 1$, which makes d_{i, M_i} part of the opening value for a_i to M_i. Let us write $\boldsymbol{a} = (a_1, \ldots, a_m)$, the tuple of commitments.
  - For $i \in [\![1, m]\!]$ and $j = 0, 1$, it gets $\boldsymbol{b} = (b_{i,j})_{i,j} = \mathsf{2mEncrypt}^{\ell'}(\mathsf{pk}, \boldsymbol{d}; \boldsymbol{s})$, where $\boldsymbol{s}$ is from the random string and $\ell' = (\ell, \boldsymbol{a})$.

  The commitment is $C = (\boldsymbol{a}, \boldsymbol{b})$, and the opening information is the m-tuple $\delta = (s_{M_1}, \ldots, s_{M_m})$.
- $\mathsf{VerCom}^\ell(C, \boldsymbol{M}, \delta)$ checks the validity of the ciphertexts b_{i, M_i} with s_{M_i}, extracts d_{i, M_i} from b_{i, M_i} and s_{i, M_i}, and checks whether $(a_i / g^{M_i})^{\mathsf{vtk}} = d_{i, M_i}$.
- $\mathsf{SimCom}^\ell(\tau)$ takes as input the equivocation trapdoor, namely tk, and outputs $C = (\boldsymbol{a}, \boldsymbol{b})$ and $\mathsf{eqk} = \boldsymbol{s}$, where
  - For $i \in [\![1, m]\!]$, it chooses a random $r_{i,0}$, sets $a_i = g^{r_{i,0}}$, and uses the equivocation trapdoor to computes the randomness $r_{i,1} = r_{i,0} - 1/\mathsf{tk}$. This leads to $\boldsymbol{a}$ and $\boldsymbol{d}$;
  - $\boldsymbol{b}$ is built as above: $\boldsymbol{b} = (b_{i,j})_{i,j} = \mathsf{2mEncrypt}^{\ell'}(\mathsf{pk}, \boldsymbol{d}; \boldsymbol{s})$, with random scalars $\mathsf{eqk} = (s_{*,i,j})_{i,j}$.
- $\mathsf{OpenCom}^\ell(\mathsf{eqk}, C, \boldsymbol{M})$ simply uses eqk to set the opening value $\delta = (s_{M_1}, \ldots, s_{M_m})$ in order to open to $\boldsymbol{M} = (M_i)_i$.

– $\mathsf{ExtCom}^\ell(\tau, C)$ takes as input the extraction trapdoor, namely the decryption key dk and the chameleon verification trapdoor vtk. Given $\boldsymbol{b}$, it can decrypt all the $b_{i,j}$ into $d_{i,j}$ and checks consistency with $(a_i/g^j)^{\mathsf{vtk}} \stackrel{?}{=} d_{i,j}$ or not. If, for each i, exactly one $j = M_i$ satisfies the equality, then the extraction algorithm outputs $(M_i)_i$, otherwise (no correct decryption or ambiguity with several possibilities) it outputs $\bot$.

4.3 The SPHF Associated with the Commitment Scheme

For the sake of simplicity, we first give an explicit writing of the said SPHF when the strings are of length one.

This SPHF is defined on Cramer-Shoup encryption (see for instance [BBC+13b]), except that it is done on an encryption of "an encryption of M, such that the projected hash value of this encryption is the value sent in the commitment of M", rather than simply on an encryption of M. But the internal language is easily verifiable, making this SPHF having the good properties simply applying the methodology described in [BBC+13b].

– $\mathsf{Com}^\ell(b; Q)$: A commitment to a bit m_i, can now be written as $C = h^{r_{m_i}} g^{m_i}, b_{1,0} = (h_1^{s_0} g^{r_0}, g_1^{s_0}, g_2^{s_0}, (cd^\beta)^{s_0}), b_{1,1} = (h_1^{s_1} g^{r_1}, g_1^{s_1}, g_2^{s_1}, (cd^\beta)^{s_1})$. where $\beta = \mathcal{H}(h^{r_b} g^{m_i}, (h_1^{s_j} g^{r_j}, g_1^{s_j}, g_2^{s_j})_{j \in [\![0,1]\!]})$ and the session id.
– $\mathsf{VerCom}^\ell(C, b, \delta)$:
  • $\mathsf{ProjKG}(C, b; Q)$: To implicitly check if the commitment is a valid commitment to b, one simply has to compute projection keys $\mathsf{hp} = h^\lambda f^\mu, \mathsf{hp}_{m_i} = h_1^\mu g_1^{\mu m_i} g_2^{\nu m_i} (cd^\beta)^{\theta m_i}$, where all new Greek letters are random scalars. And the hash value $H_{m_i} = (C/g^{m_i})^\lambda \cdot \boldsymbol{b}_{m_i}^{\mathsf{hk}_{m_i}}$.)
  • $\mathsf{ProjHash}(C, b, \mathsf{hp}_{m_i}; P)$: The prover will compute $H'_{m_i} = \mathsf{hp}_{m_i}^{s_{m_i}} \mathsf{hp}^{r_{m_i}}$.

If everything was done honestly, those two values are equal, otherwise they are seemingly random. To see why this is smooth, considering the number of free variables in the system of equations generated by the public view of the projection key hp guarantees that not enough information leaks about the hashing keys in order to weaken the smoothness.

In the real protocol where the string is cut into bits, one simply has to do an AND of all those languages, where $H = \prod H_{i,m_i}$, and where one uses a vector of projections keys hp_{i,m_i}. To optimize the construction on bit strings, one can simply use the polynomial trick from [BBC+13a], where they provide hp_1, a random scalar ϵ and assume that $\mathsf{hp}_i = \mathsf{hp}_1^{\epsilon(i-i)}$, a classical inversion argument on the matrices of discrete logarithm of the given exponents will show that the SPHF remains smooth.

Efficiency consideration shows that the pre-flow requires 2 group elements (1 for pk, 1 for vk), for each bit we need 9 elements (1 for a_i and 2*4 for $b_{i,\{0,1\}}$, we also have the additional encryption for the verification linked to the pre-flow (so 2 elements). We now need to give two elements for the hp, and in case of more that one bit, a random scalar ϵ. Overall this leads to $9m + 6$ group elements and a scalar.

5 Instantiation Based on Dual Regev Encryption (LWE)

Lattices present an interesting challenge, since because of the noise many properties are harder to achieve. However, our construction requires only two simple blocks to work.

Chameleon Hash. We present here a Chameleon Hash constructed from the SIS assumption, following the chameleon hash given in [CHKP10] but using the Micciancio-Peikert trapdoor generation [MP12]. We here only present the scheme, since the security proof comes directly following the proof of Lemma 4.1 in [CHKP10].

Let $k = \lceil \log q \rceil = O(\log \mathfrak{K})$ and $m = O(\mathfrak{K}k)$. Let $\mathcal{D} = D_{\mathbb{Z}^{\bar{m} \times \mathfrak{K}k}, \omega(\sqrt{\log \mathfrak{K}})}$ be the Gaussian distribution over $\mathbb{Z}^{\bar{m} \times \mathfrak{K}k}$ with parameter $\omega(\sqrt{\log \mathfrak{K}})$ and let $s = O(\sqrt{\mathfrak{K}k})$ be a Gaussian parameter. Let the randomness space be defined as $\mathcal{R} := D_{\mathbb{Z}^m, s \cdot \omega(\sqrt{\log \mathfrak{K}})}$. Then, the Chameleon Hash is defined as follows:

- KeyGen($\mathfrak{K}$): choose a random matrix $\mathbf{A}_0 \xleftarrow{\$} \mathbb{Z}_q^{\mathfrak{K} \times \ell}$. Sample $(\mathbf{A}_1, \mathbf{R}_1) \xleftarrow{\$}$ GenTrap$^{\mathcal{D}}(1^{\mathfrak{K}}, 1^m, q)$. Define ck $:= (\mathbf{A}_0, \mathbf{A}_1)$ and tk $:= \mathbf{R}_1$.
- VKeyGen(ck): Outputs vk $= \perp$, vtk $= \perp$
- CH(ck, vk, m; r): choose a vector $\mathbf{r}$ from the Gaussian distribution $D_{\mathbb{Z}^m, s \cdot \omega(\sqrt{\log \mathfrak{K}})}$, $\mathbf{r} \leftarrow D_{\mathbb{Z}^m, s \cdot \omega(\sqrt{\log \mathfrak{K}})}$. Compute the chameleon hash value $\mathbf{c} = \mathbf{A}_0 \mathbf{m} + \mathbf{A}_1 \mathbf{r}$. Return the chameleon hash $\mathbf{c}$ and the opening information $\mathbf{r}$. (which we will later commit using the CCA2 scheme)
- Coll(tk, $(\mathbf{m}_0, \mathbf{r}_0), \mathbf{m}_1$): compute $\mathbf{u} = (\mathbf{A}_0 \mathbf{m}_0 + \mathbf{A}_1 \mathbf{r}_0) - \mathbf{A}_0 \mathbf{m}_1$ and sample $\mathbf{r}_1 \in \mathbb{Z}^m$ according to $D_{\Lambda_{\mathbf{u}}^{\perp}(\mathbf{A}_1), s \cdot \omega(\sqrt{\log \mathfrak{K}})}$, $\mathbf{r}_1 \xleftarrow{\$}$ SampleD($\mathbf{R}_1, \mathbf{A}_1, \mathbf{u}, s$).
- Verify(ck, vtk, m, c, r): accept if $\|\mathbf{r}\| \leq s \cdot \omega(\sqrt{\log \mathfrak{K}}) \cdot \sqrt{m}$ and $\mathbf{c} = \mathbf{A}_0 \mathbf{m} + \mathbf{A}_1 \mathbf{r}$; otherwise, reject.

It should be noted, that the trapdoor allows to recover not only a collision, but also a preimage if need be.

Naive $2m$-labelled multi LWE-based Encryption Scheme. Katz and Vaikuntanathan proposed in [KV09] a labelled CCA-Encryption with an approximate SPHF. In order to achieve the $2m$-labelled, one simply has to use the same label in all the encryptions, and then add a one-time signature, built for example by using the previous chameleon hash.

Oblivious Transfer using an Approximate SPHF. The approximate SPHF presented in [KV09] is sufficient for our application with a small modification to our generic framework. Indeed, instead of obtaining two identical values for Hash and ProjHash, the correctness only guarantees that for a well-formed ciphertext, those two values have a small Hamming distance, hence xoring the two values together leads to a string with low Hamming weight. Assuming the line in the database is first encoded using an Error Correcting Code, and then masked by the server using the Hash value, the user can then use his projective hash value to recover a word near a valid encoding for the required entry, and then decoding using the Error Correcting Code as the remaining nose is small, he will recover the valid string. On invalid lines, the noise is seemingly random, hence beyond the decoding limit of any possible code.

6   Instantiation Based on Paillier Encryption (Composite Residuosity)

The solution is pretty straightforward on how to instantiate the previous scheme while relying on a DCR assumption. This simply requires the generic transformation from any native DDH scheme into a DCR based one presented in [HO09].

It is interesting to note that this boils down to using the Paillier-based CCA encryption presented in [CS02], in addition to a DCR-based Chameleon Hash encryption. (Operations are done modulo N^2 except if indicated otherwise)

For lack of space, we only present here the two needed building blocks and postpone the description of the commitment scheme and the associated smooth projective hash function to the full version.

DCR-based Chameleon Hash. We simply use a direct transposition of the Chameleon Hash described in Sect. 4 in a group of order Z_{N^2}. While this may be improved, the description remain simple.

$2m$-labelled multi DCR-based Encryption Scheme. We use the variant of the CCA-2 encryption introduced in [CS02]. The encryption key ek is now a tuple $(g, s, \tilde{s})$, where $g = N + 1$, $s = g^{k_0}$ and $\tilde{s}_i = g^{k_i}$ where $\boldsymbol{k} \xleftarrow{\$} [\![0, \lfloor N^2/2 \rfloor]\!]^{\beta+2}$, and the encryption process becomes:

Encrypt(pk, $M; w$): pick $w \xleftarrow{\$} [\![0, N/2]\!]$ and compute $\gamma = \mathcal{H}(\ell', g^w, Ms^w, \tilde{s}_1^w)$, and $b = (g^w, Ms^w, \tilde{s}_1^w \prod_{j=2}^{\beta+1} s_j^{w\gamma_j})$.

Once again, knowing the respective discrete logarithms in the encryption keys allows to decrypt the ciphertext.

Acknowledgements. This work was supported in part by the French ANR-14-CE28-0003 EnBiD Project.

References

[ABB+13] Abdalla, M., Benhamouda, F., Blazy, O., Chevalier, C., Pointcheval, D.: SPHF-friendly non-interactive commitments. In: Sako, K., Sarkar, P. (eds.) ASIACRYPT 2013, Part I. LNCS, vol. 8269, pp. 214–234. Springer, Heidelberg (2013)

[ACP09] Abdalla, M., Chevalier, C., Pointcheval, D.: Smooth projective hashing for conditionally extractable commitments. In: Halevi, S. (ed.) CRYPTO 2009. LNCS, vol. 5677, pp. 671–689. Springer, Heidelberg (2009)

[BBC+13a] Ben Hamouda, F., Blazy, O., Chevalier, C., Pointcheval, D., Vergnaud, D.: Efficient UC-secure authenticated key-exchange for algebraic languages. In: Kurosawa, K., Hanaoka, G. (eds.) PKC 2013. LNCS, vol. 7778, pp. 272–291. Springer, Heidelberg (2013)

[BBC+13b] Benhamouda, F., Blazy, O., Chevalier, C., Pointcheval, D., Vergnaud, D.: New techniques for SPHFs and efficient one-round PAKE protocols. In: Canetti, R., Garay, J.A. (eds.) CRYPTO 2013, Part I. LNCS, vol. 8042, pp. 449–475. Springer, Heidelberg (2013)

[BC15] Blazy, O., Chevalier, C.: Generic Construction of UC-Secure Oblivious Transfer. Cryptology ePrint Archive, 2015. Full version of the present paper

[BCPV13] Blazy, O., Chevalier, C., Pointcheval, D., Vergnaud, D.: Analysis and improvement of lindell's UC-secure commitment schemes. In: Jacobson, M., Locasto, M., Mohassel, P., Safavi-Naini, R. (eds.) ACNS 2013. LNCS, vol. 7954, pp. 534–551. Springer, Heidelberg (2013)

[BN05] Barreto, P.S.L.M., Naehrig, M.: Pairing-friendly elliptic curves of prime order. In: Preneel, B., Tavares, S. (eds.) SAC 2005. LNCS, vol. 3897, pp. 319–331. Springer, Heidelberg (2006)

[Can01] Canetti, R.: Universally composable security: A new paradigm for cryptographic protocols. In: 42nd FOCS, pp. 136–145. IEEE Computer Society Press (2001)

[CF01] Canetti, R., Fischlin, M.: Universally composable commitments. In: Kilian, J. (ed.) CRYPTO 2001. LNCS, vol. 2139, p. 19. Springer, Heidelberg (2001)

[CHKP10] Cash, D., Hofheinz, D., Kiltz, E., Peikert, C.: Bonsai trees, or how to delegate a lattice basis. In: Gilbert, H. (ed.) EUROCRYPT 2010. LNCS, vol. 6110, pp. 523–552. Springer, Heidelberg (2010)

[CKWZ13] Choi, S.G., Katz, J., Wee, H., Zhou, H.-S.: Efficient, adaptively secure, and composable oblivious transfer with a single, global CRS. In: Kurosawa, K., Hanaoka, G. (eds.) PKC 2013. LNCS, vol. 7778, pp. 73–88. Springer, Heidelberg (2013)

[CLOS02] Canetti, R., Lindell, Y., Ostrovsky, R., Sahai, A.: Universally composable two-party and multi-party secure computation. In: 34th ACM STOC, pp. 494–503. ACM Press, New York (2002)

[CS02] Cramer, R., Shoup, V.: Universal hash proofs and a paradigm for adaptive chosen ciphertext secure public-key encryption. In: Knudsen, L.R. (ed.) EUROCRYPT 2002. LNCS, vol. 2332, p. 45. Springer, Heidelberg (2002)

[DN02] Damgård, I.B., Nielsen, J.B.: Perfect hiding and perfect binding universally composable commitment schemes with constant expansion factor. In: Yung, M. (ed.) CRYPTO 2002. LNCS, vol. 2442, p. 581. Springer, Heidelberg (2002)

[EHK+13] Escala, A., Herold, G., Kiltz, E., Ràfols, C., Villar, J.: An algebraic framework for Diffie-Hellman assumptions. In: Canetti, R., Garay, J.A. (eds.) CRYPTO 2013, Part II. LNCS, vol. 8043, pp. 129–147. Springer, Heidelberg (2013)

[ElG84] El Gamal, T.: A public key cryptosystem and a signature scheme based on discrete logarithms. In: Blakely, G.R., Chaum, D. (eds.) CRYPTO 1984. LNCS, vol. 196, pp. 10–18. Springer, Heidelberg (1985)

[FLM11] Fischlin, M., Libert, B., Manulis, M.: Non-interactive and re-usable universally composable string commitments with adaptive security. In: Lee, D.H., Wang, X. (eds.) ASIACRYPT 2011. LNCS, vol. 7073, pp. 468–485. Springer, Heidelberg (2011)

[GL03] Gennaro, R., Lindell, Y.: A framework for password-based authenticated key exchange. In: Biham, E. (ed.) EUROCRYPT 2003. LNCS, vol. 2656, pp. 524–543. Springer, Heidelberg (2003)

[GWZ09] Garay, J.A., Wichs, D., Zhou, H.-S.: Somewhat non-committing encryption and efficient adaptively secure oblivious transfer. In: Halevi, S. (ed.) CRYPTO 2009. LNCS, vol. 5677, pp. 505–523. Springer, Heidelberg (2009)

[Har11] Haralambiev, K.: Efficient cryptographic primitives for non-interactive zero-knowledge proofs and applications. Ph.D. Thesis, New York University (2011)

[HK07] Horvitz, O., Katz, J.: Universally-composable two-party computation in two rounds. In: Menezes, A. (ed.) CRYPTO 2007. LNCS, vol. 4622, pp. 111–129. Springer, Heidelberg (2007)

[HO09] Hemenway, B., Ostrovsky, R.: Lossy trapdoor functions from smooth homomorphic hash proof systems. In: Electronic Colloquium on Computational Complexity (ECCC), vol. 16, p. 127 (2009)

[Kal05] Kalai, Y.T.: Smooth projective hashing and two-message oblivious transfer. In: Cramer, R. (ed.) EUROCRYPT 2005. LNCS, vol. 3494, pp. 78–95. Springer, Heidelberg (2005)

[KR00] Krawczyk, H., Rabin, T.: Chameleon signatures. In: NDSS 2000. The Internet Society (2000)

[KV09] Katz, J., Vaikuntanathan, V.: Smooth projective hashing and password-based authenticated key exchange from lattices. In: Matsui, M. (ed.) ASIACRYPT 2009. LNCS, vol. 5912, pp. 636–652. Springer, Heidelberg (2009)

[KV11] Katz, J., Vaikuntanathan, V.: Round-optimal password-based authenticated key exchange. In: Ishai, Y. (ed.) TCC 2011. LNCS, vol. 6597, pp. 293–310. Springer, Heidelberg (2011)

[Lin11] Lindell, Y.: Highly-efficient universally-composable commitments based on the DDH assumption. In: Paterson, K.G. (ed.) EUROCRYPT 2011. LNCS, vol. 6632, pp. 446–466. Springer, Heidelberg (2011)

[MP12] Micciancio, D., Peikert, C.: Trapdoors for lattices: simpler, tighter, faster, smaller. In: Pointcheval, D., Johansson, T. (eds.) EUROCRYPT 2012. LNCS, vol. 7237, pp. 700–718. Springer, Heidelberg (2012)

[NP01] Naor, M., Pinkas, B.: Efficient oblivious transfer protocols. In: 12th SODA, pp. 448–457. ACM-SIAM (2001)

[Ped91] Pedersen, T.P.: Non-interactive and information-theoretic secure verifiable secret sharing. In: Feigenbaum, J. (ed.) CRYPTO 1991. LNCS, vol. 576, pp. 129–140. Springer, Heidelberg (1992)

[PVW08] Peikert, C., Vaikuntanathan, V., Waters, B.: A framework for efficient and composable oblivious transfer. In: Wagner, D. (ed.) CRYPTO 2008. LNCS, vol. 5157, pp. 554–571. Springer, Heidelberg (2008)

[Rab81] Rabin, M.O.: How to exchange secrets with oblivious transfer. Technical Report TR81, Harvard University (1981)

Non-malleability Under Selective Opening Attacks: Implication and Separation

Zhengan Huang[1], Shengli Liu[1(✉)], Xianping Mao[1], and Kefei Chen[2,3]

[1] Department of Computer Science and Engineering, Shanghai Jiao Tong University,
Shanghai 200240, China
zhahuang.sjtu@gmail.com, {slliu,maoxp}@sjtu.edu.cn
[2] School of Science, Hangzhou Normal University, Hangzhou 310036, China
kfchen@sjtu.edu.cn
[3] State Key Laboratory of Mathematical Engineering and Advanced Computing,
Wuxi 214000, China

Abstract. We formalize the security notions of non-malleability under selective opening attacks (NM-SO security) in two approaches: the indistinguishability-based approach and the simulation-based approach. We explore the relations between NM-SO security notions and the known selective opening security notions, and the relations between NM-SO security notions and the standard non-malleability notions.

Keywords: Public-key encryption · Non-malleability · Selective opening attack

1 Introduction

Non-malleability. The basic goal of public-key encryption (PKE) schemes is to guarantee the privacy of messages. The universally accepted formalization for this is semantic security proposed in [9], which requires that it be infeasible to learn any useful information of the message from the ciphertext. However, some cryptographic applications in a complex setting suggest that non-malleability is necessary. Non-malleability (NM), introduced by Dolev, Dwork and Naor [8] in 1991, requires that given a challenge ciphertext, it be infeasible to generate ciphertexts whose decryptions are related to the decryption of the challenge ciphertext. Nowadays, two main kinds of formalizations (indistinguishability-based [5] and simulation-based [8]) of non-malleability are widely accepted, especially the first one. (Actually, there is another formalization of non-malleability, comparison-based non-malleability [1,5]). Similar to semantic security, the formal security definitions of indistinguishability-based non-malleability (IND-NM) and simulation-based non-malleability (SIM-NM) consider all the three kinds of standard attacks: chosen-plaintext attacks (CPA), non-adaptive chosen-ciphertext attacks (CCA1) [16] and adaptive chosen-ciphertext attacks (CCA2) [8,18]. The combination of SIM-NM, IND-NM and CPA, CCA1, CCA2 gives six specific security notions (e.g., IND-NM-CPA security). The relations among these six security notions were figured out in [5,17].

© Springer International Publishing Switzerland 2015
T. Malkin et al. (Eds.): ACNS 2015, LNCS 9092, pp. 87–104, 2015.
DOI: 10.1007/978-3-319-28166-7_5

Selective Opening Security (Under Sender Corruptions). In Eurocrypt 2009, Bellare et al. [4] introduced the notion of selective opening security (SOA security) under sender corruptions. Roughly speaking, selective opening attack (for sender corruptions) is as follows: n senders encrypt their own messages with the public key of a single receiver. The adversary can corrupt some of these senders, by opening their ciphertexts, i.e., obtaining their messages and the random coins which were used during the encryption. The goal of SOA security is to guarantee the privacy of the unopened messages. In [4], Bellare et al. presented two SOA security notions, the indistinguishability-based one (IND-SO) and the simulation-based one (SIM-SO). Later, Hemenway et al. [12] introduced the notions of IND-SO-CCA1/CCA2 security and SIM-SO-CCA1/CCA2 security. Over the years, several PKE schemes were proposed and proved to possess SOA security [10–13]. The relations between IND-SO-CPA security and SIM-SO-CPA security were clarified by Böhl et al. [3]. Bellare et al. [2] separated IND-CPA (even IND-CCA2) and SIM-SO-CPA security. Recently, Hofheinz and Rupp [15] showed a separation between IND-CCA2 and IND-SO-CCA2 security, and a "partial" equivalence between IND-CPA and IND-SO-CPA security.

To the best of our knowledge, how to formalize non-malleability under selective opening attacks remains elusive. Very recently, Hofheinz and Rupp referred to "NM-SO-CPA security" in [15]. But they did not present any formal definition.

Our Contributions. This paper focuses on security notions and their relations. We first formalize the notion of simulation-based non-malleability under selective opening attacks (SIM-NM-SO), and the notion of indistinguishability-based non-malleability under selective opening attacks (IND-NM-SO). We figure out the relations among SIM-NM-SO-CPA(/CCA1/CCA2) security, IND-NM-SO-CPA(/CCA1/CCA2) security, SIM/IND-SO-CPA(/CCA1/CCA2) security and non-malleability security SIM/IND-NM-CPA(/CCA1/CCA2). Specifically, our results are as follows (see Fig. 1). Below, we use SEC1 $\Rightarrow$ SEC2 to indicate that SEC1 implies SEC2, and SEC1 $\nRightarrow$ SEC2 to indicate the existence of some PKE scheme achieving SEC1 but not SEC2, for any two security notions SEC1 and SEC2.

1. *NM-SO versus SO*:
   (a) *Simulation-based* (Sect. 4):
      i. "SIM-NM-SO-ATK $\underset{\nLeftarrow}{\Rightarrow}$ SIM-SO-ATK", for any ATK $\in$ {CPA, CCA1, CCA2}.
      ii. For those PKE schemes having an invertible decryption algorithm (Definition 8), if the range of its decryption algorithm is recognizable, "SIM-SO-CCA2 $\Leftrightarrow$ SIM-NM-SO-CCA2".
   (b) *Indistinguishability-based* (Sect. 5):
      i. "IND-NM-SO-CPA $\underset{\nRightarrow}{\nLeftarrow}$ IND-SO-CCA1".
      ii. "IND-NM-SO-CCA1/CPA $\underset{\nLeftarrow}{\Rightarrow}$ IND-SO-CCA1/CPA", but "IND-NM-SO-CCA2 $\Leftrightarrow$ IND-SO-CCA2".
2. *NM-SO versus NM*:
   (a) *Simulation-based* (Sect. 6):

    i. "SIM-NM-SO-ATK $\overset{\Rightarrow}{\not\Leftarrow}$ SIM-NM-ATK", for any ATK $\in$ {CPA, CCA1, CCA2}. In fact, we have a stronger result: "SIM-NM-CCA2 $\nRightarrow$ SIM-NM-SO-CPA", which suggests "SIM-NM-ATK$'$ $\nRightarrow$ SIM-NM-SO-ATK$''$", for any ATK$'$, ATK$'' \in$ {CPA, CCA1, CCA2}.

(b) *Indistinguishability-based* (Sect. 7):

    i. "IND-NM-SO-ATK $\Rightarrow$ IND-NM-ATK", for any ATK $\in$ {CPA, CCA1, CCA2}.

    ii. "IND-NM-CCA2 $\nRightarrow$ IND-NM-SO-CCA2", and "IND-NM-SO-CPA $\nRightarrow$ IND-NM-CCA1".

3. *SIM-NM-SO versus IND-NM-SO* (Sect. 8):

"IND-NM-SO-ATK $\nRightarrow$ SIM-NM-SO-ATK", for any ATK $\in$ {CCA1, CCA2}. In fact, we have a stronger result: "IND-NM-SO-CCA2 $\nRightarrow$ SIM-NM-SO-CCA1".

Based on the relations that we obtained, (in Sect. 9) we conclude that some known PKE schemes have already obtained SIM-NM-SO-CCA2 or IND-NM-SO-CCA2 security. More specifically, the NC-CCA2 secure encryption scheme proposed by Fehr et al. [10] is SIM-NM-SO-CCA2 secure; Any IND-SO-CCA2 secure encryption scheme (e.g., [11,12]) is IND-NM-SO-CCA2 secure.

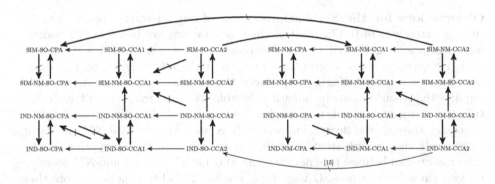

Fig. 1. Relations among SO-NM securities, SO securities and NM securities.

Techniques for the Implications. For two main non-trivial implication results, we provide their high-level descriptions of the reasonings here.

– For our contribution 1. (a).ii., the key point is how to construct a SIM-NM-SO-CCA2 simulator S_{NS} from a SIM-SO-CCA2 simulator S. Given S's output out_S, if it is a valid message, S_{NS} can simply generate a ciphertext by encrypting it, such that the decryption of S_{NS}'s output equals out_S. The barrier is that when out_S is not a valid message, this method doesn't work. To overcome this issue, we apply the idea from [17], assuming that there is an algorithm F recovering ciphertexts from decrypted messages. Under this assumption, S_{NS} can use F to recover a ciphertext from out_S, if out_S falls into the range of decrypted messages. However, this method fails if out_S does not belong to the range of the decryption algorithm Dec. This problem can be solved by assuming that the range of the decryption algorithm Dec is recognizable. With the recognizable property of Dec, SIM-SO-CCA2 security ensures that S's output out_S is almost always in the range of Dec as long as the SIM-SO-CCA2 adversary's final output is in the range.

- For our contribution 2. (a).i., the key point is constructing a SIM-NM-ATK simulator S_N from a SIM-NM-SO-ATK simulator S_{NS}. Note that S_{NS} has the ability, which S_N doesn't, to ask an opening query. To overcome this issue, we consider a special "half-uniform" message distribution, which consists of two independent distributions and the second is a uniform one. Correspondingly, the challenge message vector generated from this specific distribution also consists of two parts. If S_{NS} outputs a "half-uniform" distribution and asks to open the uniform part, S_N can always answer it on its own by returning a uniformly chosen message vector. However, S_N still cannot deal with a misbehaved S_{NS} which outputs other distributions or it does not open the uniform part. To solve this problem, we construct a behaved SIM-NM-SO-ATK adversary A_{NS}, which always outputs a half-uniform distribution and asks to open the uniform part, and then SIM-NM-SO-ATK security guarantees S_{NS} is behaved, except with negligible probability.

Observations for the Separations. Some of our separation results can be seen as extensions of [1,17]. Most of these separations are based on the following observations. Let's look at the SIM-based notions first. A SIM-NM security notion requires that the decryptions of both of the adversary's and the simulator's outputs be indistinguishable. Note that a non-NM security notion only requires that their outputs be indistinguishable. We can provide a uniformly distributed string, which leads to a special ciphertext (e.g., decrypted to sk), to the adversary through the decryption oracle. It is hard for any SIM-NM simulator to generate such a ciphertext, since it has no access to the decryption oracle. This feature can be used to separate some SIM-based NM and non-NM security notions (in a SOA or non-SOA setting). For the IND-based notions, note that even under CPA attacks, an IND-NM adversary can make a *one-time* parallel decryption query *after* receiving the challenge ciphertext. This feature can be used to separate some IND-based NM and non-NM security notions (in a SOA or non-SOA setting).

Open Question. The primary open question is to figure out the relations between SIM-NM-SO and IND-NM-SO security notions. The barriers we encounter are as follows. For NM security notions, there is always a parallel decryption process *after* the adversary receiving the challenge ciphertext. This fact makes the relation between these two notions (even under CPA attacks) similar to that between SIM-SO-CCA2 and IND-SO-CCA2 security. Besides that, we also need to deal with the aforementioned issue, i.e., the SIM-NM-SO simulator's output always contains a ciphertext vector.

2 Preliminaries

Notations. Throughout this paper, we use κ as the security parameter, and ϵ as the empty string. For $n \in \mathbb{N}^+$, let $[n]$ denote the set $\{1, 2, \cdots, n\}$. For a finite set $\mathcal{S}$, let $s \leftarrow \mathcal{S}$ denote the process of sampling an element s uniformly at random from $\mathcal{S}$. For a probabilistic algorithm A, let $\mathcal{R}_A$ denote the randomness space of A. We let $y \leftarrow A(x; R)$ denote the process of running A on input x and inner randomness $R \in \mathcal{R}_A$, and outputting y. We write $y \leftarrow A(x)$ for $y \leftarrow A(x; R)$ with uniformly chosen $R \in \mathcal{R}_A$. If A's running time is polynomial in κ, we say that A is a probabilistic polynomial-time (PPT) algorithm. For two sequences of random variables $X = \{X_\kappa\}_{\kappa \in \mathbb{N}}$ and $Y = \{Y_\kappa\}_{\kappa \in \mathbb{N}}$, if for any PPT algorithm D, $|\Pr[D(X_\kappa, 1^\kappa) = 1] - \Pr[D(Y_\kappa, 1^\kappa) = 1]|$ is negligible in κ, we say that X and Y are computationally indistinguishable (denoted by $X \stackrel{c}{\approx} Y$).

We use boldface letters for vectors. For a vector $\mathbf{m}$ (resp. a finite set $\mathcal{S}$), we let $|\mathbf{m}|$ (resp. $|\mathcal{S}|$) denote the length of the vector (resp. the size of the set). For a set $I = \{i_1, i_2, \cdots, i_{|I|}\} \subseteq [|\mathbf{m}|]$, let $\mathbf{m}[I] = (\mathbf{m}[i_1], \mathbf{m}[i_2], \cdots, \mathbf{m}[i_{|I|}])$. We write $m \in \mathbf{m}$ to denote $m \in \{\mathbf{m}[i] | i \in [|\mathbf{m}|]\}$, extending the set membership notation to vectors.

Decryption Oracles. For simplicity, we will use the notations $\mathcal{O}_1(\cdot)$ and $\mathcal{O}_2(\cdot)$ in all the security notions throughout the paper. In a chosen-plaintext attack (CPA), both the oracles $\mathcal{O}_1(\cdot)$ and $\mathcal{O}_2(\cdot)$ always return ϵ. In a non-adaptive chosen-ciphertext attack (CCA1), $\mathcal{O}_1(\cdot) = \mathsf{Dec}(sk, \cdot)$, and $\mathcal{O}_2(\cdot)$ still returns ϵ whatever it is queried. In an adaptive chosen-ciphertext attack (CCA2), both $\mathcal{O}_1(\cdot)$ and $\mathcal{O}_2(\cdot)$ are $\mathsf{Dec}(sk, \cdot)$, with the only exception that $\mathcal{O}_2(\cdot)$ returns ϵ when queried on a ciphertext appeared in the challenge ciphertext vector.

Non-malleability for Encryption. The first definition of non-malleability for encryption was proposed by Dolev, Dwork and Naor [8] in 1991. Their definition is simulation-based. Several years later, comparison-based and indistinguishability-based definitions of non-malleability were proposed [1,5], and their relations were explored in [5,17]. We recall the simulation/indistinguishability-based definitions in [17] as follows.

Definition 1 (SIM-NM Security). *A public-key encryption scheme* $\mathsf{PKE} = (\mathsf{Gen}, \mathsf{Enc}, \mathsf{Dec})$ *is SIM-NM-ATK secure, if for any stateful PPT adversary* $A = (A_1, A_2)$*, there is a stateful PPT simulator* $S = (S_1, S_2)$*, such that*

$$\mathsf{Exp}^{\text{SIM-NM-ATK-Real}}_{\mathsf{PKE}, A}(\kappa) \stackrel{c}{\approx} \mathsf{Exp}^{\text{SIM-NM-ATK-Ideal}}_{\mathsf{PKE}, S}(\kappa),$$

where $ATK \in \{CPA, CCA1, CCA2\}$*, experiments* $\mathsf{Exp}^{\text{SIM-NM-ATK-Real}}_{\mathsf{PKE}, A}(\kappa)$ *and* $\mathsf{Exp}^{\text{SIM-NM-ATK-Ideal}}_{\mathsf{PKE}, S}(\kappa)$ *are defined in Table 1.*

Definition 2 (IND-NM Security). *A public-key encryption scheme* $\mathsf{PKE} = (\mathsf{Gen}, \mathsf{Enc}, \mathsf{Dec})$ *is IND-NM-ATK secure, if for any stateful PPT adversary*

$A = (A_1, A_2, A_3)$, its advantage $\mathbf{Adv}_{\mathsf{PKE},A}^{\mathrm{IND\text{-}NM\text{-}ATK}}(\kappa)$ is negligible, where $ATK \in \{CPA,\ CCA1,\ CCA2\}$. Here

$$\mathbf{Adv}_{\mathsf{PKE},A}^{\mathrm{IND\text{-}NM\text{-}ATK}}(\kappa) := |\Pr[\mathsf{Exp}_{\mathsf{PKE},A}^{\mathrm{IND\text{-}NM\text{-}ATK\text{-}1}}(\kappa) = 1]$$
$$- \Pr[\mathsf{Exp}_{\mathsf{PKE},A}^{\mathrm{IND\text{-}NM\text{-}ATK\text{-}0}}(\kappa) = 1]|,$$

where experiment $\mathsf{Exp}_{\mathsf{PKE},A}^{\mathrm{IND\text{-}NM\text{-}ATK\text{-}b}}(\kappa)$ $(b \in \{0,1\})$ is defined in Table 1, and we require that in the experiment, $|\mathbf{m}_0| = |\mathbf{m}_1|$, and $|\mathbf{m}_0[i]| = |\mathbf{m}_1[i]|$ for any $i \in [|\mathbf{m}_0|]$.

Remark 1. Note that in Definitions 1 and 2, the ciphertexts contained in $\mathbf{y}$ may be invalid (i.e., $\perp \in \mathbf{x}$). According to [17], these two definitions are stronger than the versions which require that $\mathbf{y}$ must be valid ciphertexts.

Selective Opening Security for Encryption. Selective opening security notions were presented by Bellare et al. [4] in Eurocrypt 2009. We follow [3, 4, 12] for the definitions.

Definition 3 (SIM-SO Security [3]). *A public-key encryption scheme* $\mathsf{PKE} = (\mathsf{Gen}, \mathsf{Enc}, \mathsf{Dec})$ *is SIM-SO-ATK secure, if for any stateful PPT adversary* $A = (A_1, A_2, A_3)$, *there is a stateful PPT simulator* $S = (S_1, S_2, S_3)$, *such that*

$$\mathsf{Exp}_{\mathsf{PKE},A}^{\mathrm{SIM\text{-}SO\text{-}ATK\text{-}Real}}(\kappa) \overset{c}{\approx} \mathsf{Exp}_{\mathsf{PKE},S}^{\mathrm{SIM\text{-}SO\text{-}ATK\text{-}Ideal}}(\kappa),$$

where $ATK \in \{CPA,\ CCA1,\ CCA2\}$, experiments $\mathsf{Exp}_{\mathsf{PKE},A}^{\mathrm{SIM\text{-}SO\text{-}ATK\text{-}Real}}(\kappa)$ and $\mathsf{Exp}_{\mathsf{PKE},S}^{\mathrm{SIM\text{-}SO\text{-}ATK\text{-}Ideal}}(\kappa)$ are defined in Table 1.

Table 1. SIM-NM, SIM-SO, IND-NM and IND-SO experiments

SIM-NM experiment:		SIM-SO experiment:	
$\mathsf{Exp}_{\mathsf{PKE},A}^{\mathrm{SIM\text{-}NM\text{-}ATK\text{-}Real}}(\kappa)$:	$\mathsf{Exp}_{\mathsf{PKE},S}^{\mathrm{SIM\text{-}NM\text{-}ATK\text{-}Ideal}}(\kappa)$:	$\mathsf{Exp}_{\mathsf{PKE},A}^{\mathrm{SIM\text{-}SO\text{-}ATK\text{-}Real}}(\kappa)$:	$\mathsf{Exp}_{\mathsf{PKE},S}^{\mathrm{SIM\text{-}SO\text{-}ATK\text{-}Ideal}}(\kappa)$:
$(pk, sk) \leftarrow \mathsf{Gen}(1^\kappa)$	$(pk, sk) \leftarrow \mathsf{Gen}(1^\kappa)$	$(pk, sk) \leftarrow \mathsf{Gen}(1^\kappa)$	$(\mathcal{M}, s_1) \leftarrow S_1(1^\kappa)$
$(\mathcal{M}, s) \leftarrow A_1^{\mathcal{O}_1(\cdot)}(pk)$	$(\mathcal{M}, s) \leftarrow S_1(pk)$	$(\mathcal{M}, s_1) \leftarrow A_1^{\mathcal{O}_1(\cdot)}(pk)$	$\mathbf{m} \leftarrow \mathcal{M}$
$\mathbf{m} \leftarrow \mathcal{M}$	$\mathbf{m} \leftarrow \mathcal{M}$	$\mathbf{m} \leftarrow \mathcal{M}$	$(I, s_2) \leftarrow S_2(s_1)$
$\mathbf{c} \leftarrow \mathsf{Enc}(pk, \mathbf{m})$	$(\mathbf{y}, \sigma) \leftarrow S_2(s)$	$\mathbf{r} \leftarrow (\mathcal{R}_{\mathsf{Enc}})^{|\mathbf{m}|}$	$out_s \leftarrow S_3(\mathbf{m}[I], s_2)$
$(\mathbf{y}, \sigma) \leftarrow A_2^{\mathcal{O}_2(\cdot)}(\mathbf{c}, s)$	For $i \in [|\mathbf{y}|]$,	$\mathbf{c} \leftarrow \mathsf{Enc}(pk, \mathbf{m}; \mathbf{r})$	return $(\mathcal{M}, \mathbf{m}, I, out_s)$
For $i \in [|\mathbf{y}|]$,	If $\mathbf{y}[i] = \mathrm{COPY}$,	$(I, s_2) \leftarrow A_2^{\mathcal{O}_2(\cdot)}(\mathbf{c}, s_1)$	
If $\mathbf{y}[i] \in \mathbf{c}$,	then $\mathbf{x}[i] := \mathrm{COPY}$	$out_A \leftarrow A_3^{\mathcal{O}_2(\cdot)}(\mathbf{m}[I], \mathbf{r}[I], s_2)$	
then $\mathbf{x}[i] := \mathrm{COPY}$	else, $\mathbf{x}[i] := \mathsf{Dec}(sk, \mathbf{y}[i])$	return $(\mathcal{M}, \mathbf{m}, I, out_A)$	
else, $\mathbf{x}[i] := \mathsf{Dec}(sk, \mathbf{y}[i])$	return $(\mathcal{M}, \mathbf{m}, \mathbf{x}, \sigma)$		
return $(\mathcal{M}, \mathbf{m}, \mathbf{x}, \sigma)$			
IND-NM experiment:		**IND-SO experiment:**	
$\mathsf{Exp}_{\mathsf{PKE},A}^{\mathrm{IND\text{-}NM\text{-}ATK\text{-}b}}(\kappa)$:		$\mathsf{Exp}_{\mathsf{PKE},A}^{\mathrm{IND\text{-}SO\text{-}ATK\text{-}b}}(\kappa)$:	
$(pk, sk) \leftarrow \mathsf{Gen}(1^\kappa)$		$(pk, sk) \leftarrow \mathsf{Gen}(1^\kappa)$	
$(\mathbf{m}_0, \mathbf{m}_1, s) \leftarrow A_1^{\mathcal{O}_1(\cdot)}(pk)$		$(\mathcal{M}, \mathsf{Resamp}_{\mathcal{M}}, s_1) \leftarrow A_1^{\mathcal{O}_1(\cdot)}(pk)$	
$\mathbf{c} \leftarrow \mathsf{Enc}(pk, \mathbf{m}_b)$		$\mathbf{m}_0 \leftarrow \mathcal{M}$	
$(\mathbf{y}, \sigma) \leftarrow A_2^{\mathcal{O}_2(\cdot)}(\mathbf{c}, s)$		$\mathbf{r} \leftarrow (\mathcal{R}_{\mathsf{Enc}})^{|\mathbf{m}_0|}$	
For $i \in [|\mathbf{y}|]$,		$\mathbf{c} \leftarrow \mathsf{Enc}(pk, \mathbf{m}_0; \mathbf{r})$	
If $\mathbf{y}[i] \in \mathbf{c}$, then $\mathbf{x}[i] := \mathrm{COPY}$		$(I, s_2) \leftarrow A_2^{\mathcal{O}_2(\cdot)}(\mathbf{c}, s_1)$	
else $\mathbf{x}[i] := \mathsf{Dec}(sk, \mathbf{y}[i])$		$\mathbf{m}_1 \leftarrow \mathsf{Resamp}_{\mathcal{M}}(I, \mathbf{m}_0[I])$	
$b' \leftarrow A_3^{\mathcal{O}_2(\cdot)}(\mathbf{x}, \sigma)$		$b' \leftarrow A_3^{\mathcal{O}_2(\cdot)}(\mathbf{m}_b, \mathbf{r}[I], s_2)$	
return b'		return b'	

For indistinguishability-based selective opening (IND-SO) security notion, we restrict message distributions to be *efficiently re-samplable*. In [3], this kind of security notion is called "weak" IND-SO security.

Definition 4 (Efficiently Re-samplable). *A message distribution $\mathcal{M}$ is efficiently re-samplable, if there is a PPT algorithm $\mathsf{Resamp}_{\mathcal{M}}$, such that for any $\mathbf{m}$ sampled from $\mathcal{M}$ and any subset $I \subseteq [|\mathbf{m}|]$, $\mathsf{Resamp}_{\mathcal{M}}(I, \mathbf{m}[I])$ samples from $\mathcal{M}|_{I, \mathbf{m}[I]}$, i.e., $\mathbf{m}' \leftarrow \mathsf{Resamp}_{\mathcal{M}}(I, \mathbf{m}[I])$ is sampled from the distribution $\mathcal{M}$, conditioned on $\mathbf{m}'[I] = \mathbf{m}[I]$.*

Definition 5 (IND-SO Security). *A public-key encryption scheme $\mathsf{PKE} = (\mathsf{Gen}, \mathsf{Enc}, \mathsf{Dec})$ is IND-SO-ATK secure, if for any stateful PPT adversary $A = (A_1, A_2, A_3)$, its advantage $\mathbf{Adv}_{\mathsf{PKE},A}^{\text{IND-SO-ATK}}(\kappa)$ is negligible, where $ATK \in \{CPA,\ CCA1,\ CCA2\}$. Here*

$$\mathbf{Adv}_{\mathsf{PKE},A}^{\text{IND-SO-ATK}}(\kappa) := |\Pr\,[\mathsf{Exp}_{\mathsf{PKE},A}^{\text{IND-SO-ATK-1}}(\kappa) = 1]$$
$$-\ \Pr[\mathsf{Exp}_{\mathsf{PKE},A}^{\text{IND-SO-ATK-0}}(\kappa) = 1]|,$$

where experiment $\mathsf{Exp}_{\mathsf{PKE},A}^{\text{IND-SO-ATK-}b}(\kappa)$ ($b \in \{0,1\}$) is defined in Table 1.

3   Non-malleability Under Selective Opening Attack

In this section, we formalize non-malleability under selective opening attacks for PKE. We consider simulation-based and indistinguishability-based formalizations of this security, which we call SIM-NM-SO security and IND-NM-SO security, respectively.

Simulation-Based Selective Opening Non-malleability. The simulation-based notion of non-malleability under selective opening attacks combines SIM-NM security and SIM-SO security. Informally, a SIM-NM-SO-ATK adversary is a SIM-NM-ATK adversary being allowed to make an additional selective opening query. Similarly, the related simulator is also allowed to make an opening query. The formal definition is as follows.

Definition 6 (SIM-NM-SO Security). *A public-key encryption scheme $\mathsf{PKE} = (\mathsf{Gen}, \mathsf{Enc}, \mathsf{Dec})$ is SIM-NM-SO-ATK secure, if for any stateful PPT adversary $A = (A_1, A_2, A_3)$, there is a stateful PPT simulator $S = (S_1, S_2, S_3)$, such that*

$$\mathsf{Exp}_{\mathsf{PKE},A}^{\text{SIM-NM-SO-ATK-Real}}(\kappa) \overset{c}{\approx} \mathsf{Exp}_{\mathsf{PKE},S}^{\text{SIM-NM-SO-ATK-Ideal}}(\kappa),$$

where $ATK \in \{CPA,\ CCA1,\ CCA2\}$, experiments $\mathsf{Exp}_{\mathsf{PKE},A}^{\text{SIM-NM-SO-ATK-Real}}(\kappa)$ and $\mathsf{Exp}_{\mathsf{PKE},S}^{\text{SIM-NM-SO-ATK-Ideal}}(\kappa)$ are defined as follows:

$\mathsf{Exp}_{\mathsf{PKE},A}^{\mathsf{SIM\text{-}NM\text{-}SO\text{-}ATK\text{-}Real}}(\kappa):$

    $(pk, sk) \leftarrow \mathsf{Gen}(1^\kappa)$

    $(\mathcal{M}, s_1) \leftarrow A_1^{\mathcal{O}_1(\cdot)}(pk)$

    $\mathbf{m} \leftarrow \mathcal{M}$

    $\mathbf{r} \leftarrow (\mathcal{R}_{\mathsf{Enc}})^{|\mathbf{m}|}$

    $\mathbf{c} \leftarrow \mathsf{Enc}(pk, \mathbf{m}; \mathbf{r})$

    $(I, s_2) \leftarrow A_2^{\mathcal{O}_2(\cdot)}(\mathbf{c}, s_1)$

    $(\mathbf{y}, \sigma) \leftarrow A_3^{\mathcal{O}_2(\cdot)}(\mathbf{m}[I], \mathbf{r}[I], s_2)$

    For $i \in [|\mathbf{y}|]$,

        If $\mathbf{y}[i] \in \mathbf{c}$, then $\mathbf{x}[i] := \mathrm{COPY}$

        else, $\mathbf{x}[i] := \mathsf{Dec}(sk, \mathbf{y}[i])$

    return $(\mathcal{M}, \mathbf{m}, I, \mathbf{x}, \sigma)$

$\mathsf{Exp}_{\mathsf{PKE},S}^{\mathsf{SIM\text{-}NM\text{-}SO\text{-}ATK\text{-}Ideal}}(\kappa):$

    $(pk, sk) \leftarrow \mathsf{Gen}(1^\kappa)$

    $(\mathcal{M}, s_1) \leftarrow S_1(pk)$

    $\mathbf{m} \leftarrow \mathcal{M}$

    $(I, s_2) \leftarrow S_2(s_1)$

    $(\mathbf{y}, \sigma) \leftarrow S_3(\mathbf{m}[I], s_2)$

    For $i \in [|\mathbf{y}|]$,

        If $\mathbf{y}[i] = \mathrm{COPY}$, then $\mathbf{x}[i] := \mathrm{COPY}$

        else, $\mathbf{x}[i] := \mathsf{Dec}(sk, \mathbf{y}[i])$

    return $(\mathcal{M}, \mathbf{m}, I, \mathbf{x}, \sigma)$

Indistinguishability-Based Selective Opening Non-malleability. The indistinguishability-based notion of non-malleability under selective opening attacks is also a combination of IND-NM security and IND-SO security. However, there are some subtleties in this combination. First, as the notion of IND-SO security, we require that every message distribution outputted by the adversary should be *efficiently re-samplable*. Second, in this combination, an adversary should be allowed to make two special oracle queries, a selective opening query and a parallel decryption query. In the following formal definition, we allow the adversary to decide the order of these two oracle queries. More specifically, the adversary can make these two queries at any time after receiving the vector of challenge ciphertexts, but only once for each oracle. Note that we require the adversary *has to* make these two oracle queries, since the "challenge bit" b is given through the opening oracle $\mathsf{Open}_{b,\mathcal{M},\mathbf{m}_0,\mathbf{r}}(\cdot)$. The formal definition is as follows.

Definition 7 (IND-NM-SO Security). *A public-key encryption scheme* $\mathsf{PKE} = (\mathsf{Gen}, \mathsf{Enc}, \mathsf{Dec})$ *is IND-NM-SO-ATK secure, if for any stateful PPT adversary* $A = (A_1, A_2)$*, its advantage* $\mathbf{Adv}_{\mathsf{PKE},A}^{\mathrm{IND\text{-}NM\text{-}SO\text{-}ATK}}(\kappa)$ *is negligible, where* $ATK \in \{CPA, \ CCA1, \ CCA2\}$*. Here*

$$\mathbf{Adv}_{\mathsf{PKE},A}^{\mathrm{IND\text{-}NM\text{-}SO\text{-}ATK}}(\kappa) := |\Pr[\mathsf{Exp}_{\mathsf{PKE},A}^{\mathrm{IND\text{-}NM\text{-}SO\text{-}ATK\text{-}1}}(\kappa) = 1]$$
$$- \Pr[\mathsf{Exp}_{\mathsf{PKE},A}^{\mathrm{IND\text{-}NM\text{-}SO\text{-}ATK\text{-}0}}(\kappa) = 1]|,$$

where experiment $\mathsf{Exp}_{\mathsf{PKE},A}^{\mathrm{IND\text{-}NM\text{-}SO\text{-}ATK\text{-}b}}(\kappa)$ *($b \in \{0, 1\}$) and the related oracles are defined as follows. In experiment* $\mathsf{Exp}_{\mathsf{PKE},A}^{\mathrm{IND\text{-}NM\text{-}SO\text{-}ATK\text{-}b}}(\kappa)$*, we require that adversary* A_2 *access to both oracles* $\mathsf{Open}_{b,\mathcal{M},\mathbf{m}_0,\mathbf{r}}(\cdot)$ *and* $P_{sk,\mathbf{c}}(\cdot)$ *just once respectively.*

$\mathsf{Exp}_{\mathsf{PKE},A}^{\mathsf{IND\text{-}NM\text{-}SO\text{-}ATK\text{-}}b}(\kappa)$:

  $(pk, sk) \leftarrow \mathsf{Gen}(1^{\kappa})$

  $(\mathcal{M}, \mathsf{Resamp}_{\mathcal{M}}, s_1) \leftarrow A_1^{\mathcal{O}_1(\cdot)}(pk)$

  $\mathbf{m}_0 \leftarrow \mathcal{M}$

  $\mathbf{r} \leftarrow (\mathcal{R}_{\mathsf{Enc}})^{|\mathbf{m}_0|}$

  $\mathbf{c} \leftarrow \mathsf{Enc}(pk, \mathbf{m}_0; \mathbf{r})$

  $b' \leftarrow A_2^{\mathsf{Open}_{b,\mathcal{M},\mathbf{m}_0,\mathbf{r}}(\cdot), P_{sk,\mathbf{c}}(\cdot), \mathcal{O}_2(\cdot)}(\mathbf{c}, s_1)$

  return b'

Oracle $\mathsf{Open}_{b,\mathcal{M},\mathbf{m}_0,\mathbf{r}}(I)$:

  $\mathbf{m}_1 \leftarrow \mathsf{Resamp}_{\mathcal{M}}(I, \mathbf{m}_0[I])$

  return $(\mathbf{m}_b, \mathbf{r}[I])$

Oracle $P_{sk,\mathbf{c}}(\mathbf{y})$:

  For $i \in [|\mathbf{y}|]$,

    If $\mathbf{y}[i] \in \mathbf{c}$, then $\mathbf{x}[i] := \mathsf{COPY}$

    else, $\mathbf{x}[i] := \mathsf{Dec}(sk, \mathbf{y}[i])$

  return $\mathbf{x}$

Remark 2. In [3,10], the notions of traditional selective opening security were generalized to a new version, where the adversary is allowed to make multiple opening queries adaptively. SIM-NM-SO security and IND-NM-SO security can also be naturally generalized to the similar notions. In this paper, for simplicity, when we talk about selective opening attack (i.e., SIM/IND-SO security or SIM/IND-NM-SO security), we just consider the adversaries making one round of opening query. However, all the results investigated in this paper can be extended to the generalized notions.

4 Relations Between SIM-NM-SO Securities and SIM-SO Securities

In this section, we explore the relations between SIM-NM-SO securities and SIM-SO securities.

SIM-NM-SO-ATK $\Rightarrow$ SIM-SO-ATK. We provide a high-level description of the reasoning here.

Given any SIM-SO-ATK adversary $A = (A_1, A_2, A_3)$ for an encryption scheme PKE, we construct a SIM-NM-SO-ATK adversary A' (in Table 2). If $\mathsf{Exp}_{\mathsf{PKE},A'}^{\mathsf{SIM\text{-}NM\text{-}SO\text{-}ATK\text{-}Real}}(\kappa) := (\mathcal{M}, \mathbf{m}, I, \mathbf{x}, \sigma)$, then $\mathsf{Exp}_{\mathsf{PKE},A}^{\mathsf{SIM\text{-}SO\text{-}ATK\text{-}Real}}(\kappa) = (\mathcal{M}, \mathbf{m}, I, \sigma)$. SIM-NM-SO-ATK security guarantees that there is a simulator S' with respect to A', such that $\mathsf{Exp}_{\mathsf{PKE},S'}^{\mathsf{SIM\text{-}NM\text{-}SO\text{-}ATK\text{-}Ideal}}(\kappa) \overset{c}{\approx} \mathsf{Exp}_{\mathsf{PKE},A'}^{\mathsf{SIM\text{-}NM\text{-}SO\text{-}ATK\text{-}Real}}(\kappa)$, i.e., $(\mathcal{M}_{S'}, \mathbf{m}_{S'}, I_{S'}, \mathbf{x}_{S'}, \sigma_{S'}) \overset{c}{\approx} (\mathcal{M}, \mathbf{m}, I, \mathbf{x}, \sigma)$. Hence, $(\mathcal{M}_{S'}, \mathbf{m}_{S'}, I_{S'}, \sigma_{S'}) \overset{c}{\approx} (\mathcal{M}, \mathbf{m}, I, \sigma)$. Based on S', we can construct a SIM-SO-ATK simulator S (in Table 2), such that $\mathsf{Exp}_{\mathsf{PKE},S}^{\mathsf{SIM\text{-}SO\text{-}ATK\text{-}Ideal}}(\kappa) := (\mathcal{M}_{S'}, \mathbf{m}_{S'}, I_{S'}, \sigma_{S'})$. Hence, we have the following theorem.

Theorem 1 (SIM-NM-SO-ATK $\Rightarrow$ SIM-SO-ATK). *For any ATK $\in$ {CPA, CCA1, CCA2}, SIM-NM-SO-ATK security implies SIM-SO-ATK security.*

SIM-SO-ATK $\not\Rightarrow$ SIM-NM-SO-ATK. Now we show that SIM-SO security is strictly weaker than SIM-NM-SO-ATK security. Formally, we have the following theorem.

Table 2. Constructions of adversary $A' = (A_1', A_2', A_3')$ and simulator $S = (S_1, S_2, S_3)$

$A_1'^{\mathcal{O}_1(\cdot)}(pk)$:	$A_2'^{\mathcal{O}_2(\cdot)}(\mathbf{c}, s_1)$:	$A_3'^{\mathcal{O}_2(\cdot)}(\mathbf{m}[I], \mathbf{r}[I], s_2)$:
$(\mathcal{M}, s_1) \leftarrow A_1'^{\mathcal{O}_1(\cdot)}(pk)$	$(I, s_2) \leftarrow A_2'^{\mathcal{O}_2(\cdot)}(\mathbf{c}, s_1)$	$out_A \leftarrow A_3'^{\mathcal{O}_2(\cdot)}(\mathbf{m}[I], \mathbf{r}[I], s_2)$
return $(\mathcal{M}, s_1)$	return (I, s_2)	$\mathbf{y} := \mathbf{c}$, $\sigma := out_A$
		return $(\mathbf{y}, \sigma)$
$S_1(1^\kappa)$:	$S_2(s_1)$:	$S_3(\mathbf{m}[I], s_2)$:
$(pk, sk) \leftarrow \mathsf{Gen}(1^\kappa)$	$(I, s_2) \leftarrow S_2'(s_1)$	$(\mathbf{y}, \sigma) \leftarrow S_3'(\mathbf{m}[I], s_2)$
$(\mathcal{M}, s_1) \leftarrow S_1'(pk)$	return (I, s_2)	$out_S := \sigma$
return $(\mathcal{M}, s_1)$		return out_S

Theorem 2 (SIM-SO-ATK $\nRightarrow$ SIM-NM-SO-ATK). *For any ATK $\in$ {CPA, CCA1, CCA2}, there is a SIM-SO-ATK secure PKE scheme, which is not SIM-NM-SO-ATK secure.*

We prove this theorem with two counterexamples.

In the case of ATK = CPA, we consider the Goldwasser-Micali probabilistic encryption scheme (the GM scheme) [9]. In [4], Bellare et al. pointed out that the GM scheme is SIM-SO-CPA secure. We claim that the GM scheme is not SIM-NM-SO-CPA secure because of its homomorphic property. Roughly speaking, let the challenge ciphertext vector $\mathbf{c}$ be generated from a random message vector $\mathbf{m}$. We can construct an adversary A who encrypts bit 0 to obtain a ciphertext y', and then outputs$\mathbf{y} := (y' \cdot \mathbf{c}[i])_{i \in [n]} \neq \mathbf{c}$. Obviously, the decryption of $\mathbf{y}$ is $\mathbf{x} := (0 \oplus \mathbf{m}[i])_{i \in [n]} = \mathbf{m}$. However, no PPT simulator S can output a ciphertext vector $\mathbf{y}$ satisfying $\mathbf{x} = \mathbf{m}$, since $\mathbf{m}$ was uniformly chosen and no information about $\mathbf{m}$ is leaked to S except the opened messages.

In the case of ATK $\in$ {CCA1, CCA2}, we show a counterexample as follows. The main idea of our counterexample is similar to that in [17]. Let $\mathsf{PKE} = (\mathsf{Gen}, \mathsf{Enc}, \mathsf{Dec})$ be an encryption scheme. We construct a new scheme $\widetilde{\mathsf{PKE}} = (\widetilde{\mathsf{Gen}}, \widetilde{\mathsf{Enc}}, \widetilde{\mathsf{Dec}})$ in Table 3.

Table 3. $\widetilde{\mathsf{PKE}} = (\widetilde{\mathsf{Gen}}, \widetilde{\mathsf{Enc}}, \widetilde{\mathsf{Dec}})$

$\widetilde{\mathsf{Gen}}(1^\kappa)$:	$\widetilde{\mathsf{Enc}}(\widetilde{pk}, m)$:	$\widetilde{\mathsf{Dec}}(\widetilde{sk}, \widetilde{c})$:
$(pk, sk) \leftarrow \mathsf{Gen}(1^\kappa)$	$c \leftarrow \mathsf{Enc}(pk, m)$	Parse $\widetilde{c} = (c, b, \vartheta)$
$\theta \leftarrow \{0, 1\}^\kappa$	return $\widetilde{c} := (c, 1, 0^\kappa)$	If $b = 0$ and $\vartheta = 1^\kappa$, then return θ
$\widetilde{pk} := pk$		If $b = 0$ and $\vartheta = \theta$, then return $\bot$
$\widetilde{sk} := (sk, \theta)$		If $b = 1$ and $\vartheta = 0^\kappa$, set $m = \mathsf{Dec}(sk, c)$
return $(\widetilde{pk}, \widetilde{sk})$		$\quad$ If $m = \bot$, then return 0;
		$\quad$ else, return m
		Otherwise, return 0

To prove that $\widetilde{\mathsf{PKE}}$ is not SIM-NM-SO-CCA1/CCA2 secure, consider the adversary A: A obtains θ by querying the decryption oracle on input $(c, 0, 1^\kappa)$, and outputs a ciphertext whose decryption is $\bot$. Notice that any PPT simulator S has no information about the uniformly chosen θ, since it cannot access to the decryption oracle. So the probability that the simulator outputs a ciphertext whose decryption is $\bot$ is negligible. Consider the distinguisher D: On input $(\mathcal{M}, \mathbf{m}, I, \mathbf{x}, \sigma)$, return 1 if and only if $\bot \in \mathbf{x}$. Then D can distinguish $\mathsf{Exp}^{\text{SIM-NM-SO-CCA1/CCA2-Real}}_{\widetilde{\mathsf{PKE}}, A}(\kappa)$ and $\mathsf{Exp}^{\text{SIM-NM-SO-CCA1/CCA2-Ideal}}_{\widetilde{\mathsf{PKE}}, S}(\kappa)$. Hence, $\widetilde{\mathsf{PKE}}$ is not SIM-NM-SO-CCA1/CCA2 secure. Now, what remains is to prove the SIM-SO-CCA1/CCA2 security of $\widetilde{\mathsf{PKE}}$, which is guaranteed by PKE's SIM-SO-CCA1/CCA2 security. Due to space limitations, the formal proof will be given in the full version of this paper.

Remark 3. The aforementioned analysis actually shows that $\widetilde{\mathsf{PKE}}$ is not SIM-NM-SO-CCA1 secure, *even if* PKE *is SIM-SO-CCA2 secure*. So we have a stronger conclusion: "SIM-SO-CCA2 $\not\Rightarrow$ SIM-NM-SO-CCA1", and a similar analysis gives "SIM-SO-CCA2 $\not\Rightarrow$ SIM-NM-CCA1".

A Note on SIM-NM-SO-CCA2. In [17], Pass et al. specified a special condition (i.e., the message space and the range of the decryption algorithm are identical), under which IND-NM-CCA1/CCA2 security and SIM-NM-CCA1/CCA2 security are equivalent. Interestingly, we find that under this condition, if the range of the decryption algorithm is recognizable (i.e., roughly speaking, there is a polynomial-time algorithm, which can determine whether an element is in the range of the decryption algorithm), then SIM-SO-CCA2 security implies SIM-NM-SO-CCA2 security (i.e., these two security notions are equivalent). Below we recall the special condition proposed in [17], which we name "invertible decryption".

Definition 8 (Invertible Decryption). *Let* $\mathsf{PKE} = (\mathsf{Gen}, \mathsf{Enc}, \mathsf{Dec})$ *be a PKE scheme.* Dec *is invertible if there exists a PPT algorithm* F*, such that for any ciphertext* c*,* $\mathsf{Dec}(sk, \mathsf{F}(pk, \mathsf{Dec}(sk, c))) = \mathsf{Dec}(sk, c)$*, where* $(pk, sk) \leftarrow \mathsf{Gen}(1^\kappa)$*.*

Theorem 3. *If a SIM-SO-CCA2 secure PKE scheme has an invertible decryption algorithm, and the range of the decryption algorithm is recognizable in polynomial time, then the scheme is also SIM-NM-SO-CCA2 secure.*

Proof. Let $\mathsf{PKE} = (\mathsf{Gen}, \mathsf{Enc}, \mathsf{Dec})$ be a SIM-SO-CCA2 secure encryption scheme, such that it has an inverting algorithm F, and the range of Dec is recognizable. Now we prove PKE is SIM-NM-SO-CCA2 secure.

For any PPT adversary $A = (A_1, A_2, A_3)$ attacking PKE in the sense of SIM-NM-SO-CCA2, we construct a PPT adversary $A' = (A_1', A_2', A_3')$ attacking PKE in the sense of SIM-SO-CCA2 as follows.

Receiving a public key pk, A_1' runs A_1 on the input of pk. For any decryption query c' asked by A_1, A_1' sends c' to its own decryption oracle, and then returns the answer to A_1. At some point, A_1 returns a message distribution $\mathcal{M}$. Then, A_1' outputs $\mathcal{M}$ to the challenger.

On the other side, the challenger samples $\mathbf{m} \leftarrow \mathcal{M}$ and $\mathbf{r} \leftarrow (\mathcal{R}_{\mathsf{Enc}})^{|\mathbf{m}|}$, and generates $\mathbf{c}^* \leftarrow \mathsf{Enc}(pk, \mathbf{m}; \mathbf{r})$.

Receiving $\mathbf{c}^*$ from the challenger, A'_2 runs A_2 on the input of $\mathbf{c}^*$. For any decryption query c' asked by A_2, A'_2 answers it with its own decryption oracle as before (of course, both A_2 and A'_2 are not allowed to query $c' \in \mathbf{c}^*$). At some point, A_2 returns a subset $I \subset [|\mathbf{c}^*|]$. Then, A'_2 outputs I to the challenger.

Receiving $\mathbf{m}[I]$ and $\mathbf{r}[I]$, A'_3 runs A_3 on the input of $\mathbf{m}[I]$ and $\mathbf{r}[I]$. For any decryption query c' asked by A_3, A'_3 answers it as before. At last, A_3 returns its final output $(\mathbf{y}, \sigma)$. Then, A'_3 generates $\mathbf{x}$ (where $|\mathbf{x}| = |\mathbf{y}|$) as follows: For $i = 1, 2, \cdots, |\mathbf{y}|$, if $\mathbf{y}[i] \notin \mathbf{c}^*$, submit $\mathbf{y}[i]$ to A''s decryption oracle and denote the decryption by $\mathbf{x}[i]$; if $\mathbf{y}[i] \in \mathbf{c}^*$, set that $\mathbf{x}[i] := \mathsf{COPY}$. Finally, A'_3 outputs $out_{A'} := (\mathbf{x}, \sigma)$.

Notice that A' perfectly simulates experiment $\mathsf{Exp}_{\mathsf{PKE}, A}^{\mathsf{SIM}\text{-}\mathsf{NM}\text{-}\mathsf{SO}\text{-}\mathsf{ATK}\text{-}\mathsf{Real}}(\kappa)$ for A. Hence,

$$\mathsf{Exp}_{\mathsf{PKE}, A'}^{\mathsf{SIM}\text{-}\mathsf{SO}\text{-}\mathsf{CCA2}\text{-}\mathsf{Real}}(\kappa) = (\mathcal{M}, \mathbf{m}, I, out_{A'}) = (\mathcal{M}, \mathbf{m}, I, \mathbf{x}, \sigma)$$
$$= \mathsf{Exp}_{\mathsf{PKE}, A}^{\mathsf{SIM}\text{-}\mathsf{NM}\text{-}\mathsf{SO}\text{-}\mathsf{CCA2}\text{-}\mathsf{Real}}(\kappa). \tag{1}$$

Since PKE is $\mathsf{SIM}\text{-}\mathsf{SO}\text{-}\mathsf{CCA2}$ secure, there is a PPT simulator $S' = (S'_1, S'_2, S'_3)$ such that

$$\mathsf{Exp}_{\mathsf{PKE}, S'}^{\mathsf{SIM}\text{-}\mathsf{SO}\text{-}\mathsf{CCA2}\text{-}\mathsf{Ideal}}(\kappa) \stackrel{c}{\approx} \mathsf{Exp}_{\mathsf{PKE}, A'}^{\mathsf{SIM}\text{-}\mathsf{SO}\text{-}\mathsf{CCA2}\text{-}\mathsf{Real}}(\kappa). \tag{2}$$

Now, based on S', we construct a simulator $S = (S_1, S_2, S_3)$ in the sense of $\mathsf{SIM}\text{-}\mathsf{NM}\text{-}\mathsf{SO}\text{-}\mathsf{CCA2}$.

Receiving a public key pk, S_1 runs S'_1 on the input of 1^κ. Then S_1 outputs the $\mathcal{M}_{S'}$ returned by S'_1.

On the other side, the challenger samples $\mathbf{m}_{S'} \leftarrow \mathcal{M}_{S'}$, without returning anything to S.

Later, S'_2 outputs a subset $I_{S'}$. S_2 outputs $I_{S'}$ to the challenger.

Upon receiving $\mathbf{m}_{S'}[I_{S'}]$, S_3 runs S'_3 on the input of $\mathbf{m}_{S'}[I_{S'}]$, obtaining S'_3's final output $out_{S'}$. After parsing $out_{S'} = (\mathbf{x}_{S'}, \sigma_{S'})$, S_3 checks whether there is some $i_0 \in [|\mathbf{x}_{S'}|]$ such that $\mathbf{x}_{S'}[i_0] \neq \mathsf{COPY}$ and meanwhile $\mathbf{x}_{S'}[i_0]$ is not in the range of Dec. It is feasible to check that in polynomial time since the range of Dec is recognizable. If there is such an i_0, then S_3 aborts by outputting a random string. Otherwise, S_3 generates $\mathbf{y}_S$ (where $|\mathbf{y}_S| = |\mathbf{x}_{S'}|$) as follows: For $i = 1, 2, \cdots, |\mathbf{y}_S|$, if $\mathbf{x}_{S'}[i] = \mathsf{COPY}$, then set $\mathbf{y}_S[i] = \mathsf{COPY}$; otherwise, generate $\mathbf{y}_S[i] \leftarrow \mathsf{F}(pk, \mathbf{x}_{S'}[i])$. Finally, S_3 outputs $(\mathbf{y}_S, \sigma_{S'})$.

Let bad denote the event that S aborts. If bad does not occur, then for any $j \in [|\mathbf{x}_{S'}|]$ such that $\mathbf{x}_{S'}[j] \neq \mathsf{COPY}$, there is some ciphertext $\hat{c}_j$ (not has to be valid), such that $\mathsf{Dec}(sk, \hat{c}_j) = \mathbf{x}_{S'}[j]$. We have $\mathsf{Dec}(sk, \mathbf{y}_S[j]) = \mathsf{Dec}(sk, \mathsf{F}(pk, \mathsf{Dec}(sk, \hat{c}_j))) = \mathsf{Dec}(sk, \hat{c}_j) = \mathbf{x}_{S'}[j]$. In this case,

$$\mathsf{Exp}_{\mathsf{PKE}, S}^{\mathsf{SIM}\text{-}\mathsf{NM}\text{-}\mathsf{SO}\text{-}\mathsf{CCA2}\text{-}\mathsf{Ideal}}(\kappa) = (\mathcal{M}_{S'}, \mathbf{m}_{S'}, I_{S'}, \mathbf{x}_{S'}, \sigma_{S'})$$
$$= (\mathcal{M}_{S'}, \mathbf{m}_{S'}, I_{S'}, out_{S'})$$
$$= \mathsf{Exp}_{\mathsf{PKE}, S'}^{\mathsf{SIM}\text{-}\mathsf{SO}\text{-}\mathsf{CCA2}\text{-}\mathsf{Ideal}}(\kappa).$$

So for any PPT algorithm D,

$$|\Pr[D(\mathsf{Exp}_{\mathsf{PKE},S}^{\text{SIM-NM-SO-CCA2-Ideal}}(\kappa)) = 1]$$
$$- \ \Pr[D(\mathsf{Exp}_{\mathsf{PKE},S'}^{\text{SIM-SO-CCA2-Ideal}}(\kappa)) = 1]| \le \Pr[\mathsf{bad}].$$

Notice that if $\Pr[\mathsf{bad}]$ is negligible, then we have

$$\mathsf{Exp}_{\mathsf{PKE},S}^{\text{SIM-NM-SO-CCA2-Ideal}}(\kappa) \stackrel{c}{\approx} \mathsf{Exp}_{\mathsf{PKE},S'}^{\text{SIM-SO-CCA2-Ideal}}(\kappa). \qquad (3)$$

Combining Eqs. (1), (2) and (3) gives

$$\mathsf{Exp}_{\mathsf{PKE},A}^{\text{SIM-NM-SO-CCA2-Real}}(\kappa) \stackrel{c}{\approx} \mathsf{Exp}_{\mathsf{PKE},S}^{\text{SIM-NM-SO-CCA2-Ideal}}(\kappa).$$

Hence, what remains is to prove that $\Pr[\mathsf{bad}]$ is negligible. We consider the following distinguisher D':

Algorithm $D'(\mathcal{M}, \mathbf{m}, I, out)$:
  Parse $out = (\mathbf{x}, \sigma)$
  For $i \in [|\mathbf{x}|]$,
    If $\mathbf{x}[i] \ne \mathrm{COPY}$ and $\mathbf{x}[i]$ is not in the range of Dec, then return 1
  Return 0

It is obvious that $\Pr[D'(\mathsf{Exp}_{\mathsf{PKE},A'}^{\text{SIM-SO-CCA2-Real}}(\kappa)) = 1] = 0$, and that $\Pr[D'(\mathsf{Exp}_{\mathsf{PKE},S'}^{\text{SIM-SO-CCA2-Ideal}}(\kappa)) = 1] = \Pr[\mathsf{bad}]$. In other words,

$$\Pr[\mathsf{bad}] = |\Pr[D'(\mathsf{Exp}_{\mathsf{PKE},A'}^{\text{SIM-SO-CCA2-Real}}(\kappa)) = 1]$$
$$- \ \Pr[D'(\mathsf{Exp}_{\mathsf{PKE},S'}^{\text{SIM-SO-CCA2-Ideal}}(\kappa)) = 1]|.$$

Hence, Eq. (2) guarantees that $\Pr[\mathsf{bad}]$ is negligible. $\qquad\square$

5 Relations Between IND-NM-SO Securities and IND-SO Securities

In this section, we explore the relations between IND-NM-SO securities and IND-SO securities. First of all, for any ATK $\in$ {CPA, CCA1, CCA2}, an IND-NM-SO-ATK adversary is more powerful than an IND-SO-ATK adversary in that it can make an additional query to oracle $P_{sk}(\cdot)$. Intuitively, IND-NM-SO-ATK security implies IND-SO-ATK security. Further more, any IND-SO-CCA2 adversary A is able to access to the decryption oracle after receiving the challenge ciphertext vector. So providing A the ability to make a parallel decryption query yields no additional power. The above analysis results in the following theorem.

Theorem 4 (IND-NM-SO-ATK⇒IND-SO-ATK, IND-NM-SO-CCA2 ⇔ IND-SO-CCA2). *For any ATK $\in$ {CPA, CCA1, CCA2}, IND-NM-SO-ATK security implies IND-SO-ATK security. Further more, if ATK = CCA2, these two securities are equivalent.*

IND-NM-SO-CPA $\not\Leftarrow\atop\not\Rightarrow$ IND-SO-CCA1. Formally, we have the following theorem. This is an direct extension of the conclusion in [1]. So we just provide a high-level description of the reasoning here.

Theorem 5 (IND-NM-SO-CPA $\not\Leftarrow\atop\not\Rightarrow$ IND-SO-CCA1). *There is an IND-SO-CCA1 secure PKE scheme, which is not IND-NM-SO-CPA secure; vice verse.*

The Direction $\not\Leftarrow$. Note that after receiving the challenge ciphertext, the IND-SO-CCA1 adversary cannot access to the decryption oracle, but the IND-NM-SO-CPA adversary still can make a parallel decryption query. Based on this observation, any PKE scheme, achieving IND-SO-CCA1 but not IND-SO-CCA2 security, might be used as a counterexample. The following scheme PKE′ (in Table 4), with message space $\{0,1\}^\kappa$, is from [1]. If the basic scheme PKE = (Gen, Enc, Dec) is IND-SO-CCA1 secure, then we can prove that PKE′ is IND-SO-CCA1 secure but not IND-NM-SO-CPA secure. The formal proof will be given in the full version of this paper.

Table 4. PKE′ = (Gen′, Enc′, Dec′)

Gen′(1^κ):	Enc′(pk', m):	Dec′(sk', c):
$(pk, sk) \leftarrow$ Gen(1^κ)	$c_1 \leftarrow$ Enc(pk, m)	Parse $c = (c_1, c_2)$
$pk' := pk$	$c_2 \leftarrow$ Enc($pk, \overline{m}$)	$m = $ Dec(sk, c_1)
$sk' := sk$	(Note: $\overline{m}$ is the bitwise	return m
return (pk', sk')	complement of m)	
	return $c := (c_1, c_2)$	

The Direction $\not\Rightarrow$. Note that an IND-NM-SO-CPA adversary can make just a one-time decryption query (although it is parallel), but an IND-SO-CCA1 adversary can query the decryption oracle polynomial times. Based on this observation, we provide a PKE scheme PKE″, which is identical to the scheme $\widetilde{\text{PKE}}$ in Sect. 4, except that during the decryption, roughly, the decryption algorithm returns the original secret key sk instead of the special symbol $\bot$, in the case of "$b = 0$ and $\vartheta = \theta$". The analysis is similar to that in Sect. 4. The IND-SO-CCA1 adversary can obtain θ by querying the decryption oracle on input $(c, 0, 1^\kappa)$, so it can obtain the original sk by querying on $(c, 0, \theta)$. Hence, PKE″ is not IND-SO-CCA1 secure. However, the IND-NM-SO-CPA adversary cannot make any other decryption query after the parallel decryption query. Notice that θ is uniformly chosen, so PKE″ can be proved IND-NM-SO-CPA secure. The formal proof will be given in the full version of this paper.

Remark 4. Since IND-SO-CCA1 (resp. IND-NM-SO-CCA1) security implies IND-SO-CPA (resp. IND-NM-SO-CPA) security, we have the following corollary.

Corollary 1 (IND-SO-CPA/CCA1 $\not\Rightarrow$ IND-NM-SO-CPA/CCA1).
IND-SO-CPA/CCA1 security is strictly weaker than IND-NM-SO-CPA/ CCA1 security.

6 Relations Between SIM-NM-SO Securities and SIM-NM Securities

SIM-NM-SO-ATK $\Rightarrow$ SIM-NM-ATK. Compared with the conclusion that "SIM-NM-SO-ATK $\Rightarrow$ SIM-SO-ATK", this conclusion is not that obvious. That is because, compared with the SIM-NM-SO-ATK adversary, although the SIM-NM-ATK adversary is less powerful (i.e., not allowed to make any opening query), the corresponding simulator also has less information (i.e., not allowed to make any opening query) about the message vector. Formally, we have the following theorem. Due to space limitations, its formal proof will be given in the full version of this paper.

Theorem 6 (SIM-NM-SO-ATK $\Rightarrow$ SIM-NM-ATK). *For any ATK $\in$ {CPA, CCA1, CCA2}, SIM-NM-SO-ATK security implies SIM-NM-ATK security.*

Remark 5. We can also prove Theorem 6 by simply constructing a "non-opening" SIM-NM-SO-ATK adversary, which is a copy of the SIM-NM-ATK adversary. Hence, our proof, the overview of which has been provided in the Introduction, actually shows that even considering constrained SIM-NM-SO-ATK adversary (i.e., "opening" adversary), Theorem 6 still holds.

SIM-NM-ATK $\not\Rightarrow$ SIM-NM-SO-ATK. We will show that the IND-CCA2 secure Cramer-Shoup scheme [6,7] (the CS scheme) is SIM-NM-CCA2 secure. But the CS scheme is not SIM-SO-CPA secure [2]. According to Theorem 1, it is not SIM-NM-SO-CPA secure either. Consequently, "SIM-NM-ATK' $\not\Rightarrow$ SIM-NM-SO-ATK''", for any ATK', ATK'' $\in$ {CPA, CCA1, CCA2}.

To show that the CS scheme is SIM-NM-CCA2 secure, we use the following two facts: (1) For any PKE scheme having an invertible decryption algorithm, it is IND-NM-CCA2 secure iff it is SIM-NM-CCA2 secure [17, Theorem 6]. (2) IND-CCA2 security is equivalent to IND-NM-CCA2 security, since the parallel decryption query provides no additional ability to the adversary in the case of CCA2. So what remains is to show that the CS scheme has an invertible decryption algorithm. Let (Enc, Dec) denote the corresponding encryption/decryption algorithms. Following the notations of [7], any valid ciphertext ψ of the CS scheme has the form $\psi := (a, \hat{a}, c, d) \in G^4$, the message space is G, and the range of Dec is $G \bigcup \{\text{reject}\}$, where G is a group of prime order q (see [7]). We construct an inverting algorithm F as follows: On input $(pk, \text{Dec}(sk, \psi))$, if $\text{Dec}(sk, \psi) \in G$, then F runs $\text{Enc}(pk, \text{Dec}(sk, \psi))$ and returns the generated ciphertext; If $\text{Dec}(sk, \psi) = \text{reject}$, then F returns an arbitrary ciphertext not in G^4.

7 Relations Between IND-NM-SO Securities and IND-NM Securities

Theorem 7 (IND-NM-CCA2 $\not\Rightarrow$ IND-NM-SO-CCA2). *There is an IND-NM-CCA2 secure PKE scheme, which is not IND-NM-SO-CCA2 secure.*

Theorem 8 (IND-NM-SO-ATK $\Rightarrow$ IND-NM-ATK). *For any ATK $\in \{CPA, CCA1, CCA2\}$, IND-NM-SO-ATK security implies IND-NM-ATK security.*

Notice that IND-NM-CCA2 (resp. IND-NM-SO-CCA2) security is equivalent to IND-CCA2 (resp. IND-SO-CCA2) security, so Theorem 7 is directly from [15], which separated IND-CCA2 security and IND-SO-CCA2 security. The conclusion of Theorem 8 is not surprising at all. One subtlety here is that the ways that message vectors are sampled in these two notions are different. Due to space limitations, the proof of Theorem 8 will be given in the full version of this paper.

Remark 6. In Sect. 5, we have showed that scheme PKE″ is IND-NM-SO-CPA secure. It is easy to see that PKE″ is not IND-NM-CCA1 secure. So we conclude that "IND-NM-SO-CPA $\not\Rightarrow$ IND-NM-CCA1".

8 Relations Between SIM-NM-SO Securities and IND-NM-SO Securities

For the relations between SIM-NM-SO securities and IND-NM-SO securities, we have the following conclusion. Its proof is similar to that of Theorem 2 and [17, Theorem 4], so we just provide a sketch here.

Theorem 9 (IND-NM-SO-CCA1/CCA2 $\not\Rightarrow$ SIM-NM-SO-CCA1/CCA2). *For any ATK $\in \{CCA1, CCA2\}$, there is an IND-NM-SO-ATK secure PKE scheme, which is not SIM-NM-SO-ATK secure.*

Proof. (Sketch) Let PKE $=$ (Gen, Enc, Dec) be an IND-NM-SO-CCA1/CCA2 secure encryption scheme. We construct the scheme $\widetilde{\mathsf{PKE}} = (\widetilde{\mathsf{Gen}}, \widetilde{\mathsf{Enc}}, \widetilde{\mathsf{Dec}})$ described in Table 3. Note that in Sect. 4, we have shown that $\widetilde{\mathsf{PKE}}$ is not SIM-NM-SO-CCA1/CCA2 secure, and the reasoning there does not involve the security of the basic scheme PKE. So here we just need to prove that $\widetilde{\mathsf{PKE}}$ achieves IND-NM-SO-CCA1/CCA2 security.

For any PPT adversary $\widetilde{A}$ attacking $\widetilde{\mathsf{PKE}}$ in the sense of IND-NM-SO-CCA1/CCA2 with non-negligible advantage, roughly speaking, we construct a PPT adversary A attacking PKE (in the sense of IND-NM-SO-CCA1/CCA2) as follows: Receiving the public key, A chooses $\theta \leftarrow \{0,1\}^\kappa$, and uses this θ and its own decryption oracle to answer $\widetilde{A}$'s decryption queries. A outputs the same message distribution $\mathcal{M}$ as $\widetilde{A}$ does, transforms any component $\mathbf{c}[i]$ of its own challenge ciphertext vector into $(\mathbf{c}[i], 1, 0^\kappa)$ to get a modified challenge ciphertext vector and passes the modified one to $\widetilde{A}$. A uses its own opening oracle to answer $\widetilde{A}$'s opening query. Finally, A returns $\widetilde{A}$'s final output. Notice that A perfectly simulates the IND-NM-SO-CCA1/CCA2 experiment (about $\widetilde{PKE}$) for $\widetilde{A}$. So A's advantage is also non-negligible, contradicting the assumption.   □

Remark 7. Note that $\widetilde{PKE}$ is not SIM-NM-SO-CCA1 secure, *even if* PKE *is IND-NM-SO-CCA2 secure*. So we actually have a stronger conclusion: "IND-NM-SO-CCA2 $\not\Rightarrow$ SIM-NM-SO-CCA1".

9 Constructions

Fortunately, there are some known selective opening secure PKE schemes achieving SIM/IND-NM-SO securities. Details are as follows.

SIM-NM-SO-CCA2 Secure Construction. The Fehr-Hofheinz-Kiltz-Wee encryption scheme (the FHKW scheme) is SIM-SO-CCA2 secure [10,13,14]. We claim that the decryption algorithm of the FHKW scheme is invertible, and the range of the decryption algorithm is recognizable. Hence, according to Theorem 3, the FHKW scheme is SIM-NM-SO-CCA2 secure. Our claim is justified as follows.

According to [10], any valid ciphertext of the FHKW scheme has the form $(X_1, \cdots, X_L, T)$, and the message space is $\{0,1\}^L$. For any ciphertext of the form $(X_1, \cdots, X_L, T)$, where $X_i \in \mathcal{X}$ and $T \in \mathcal{XT}$, its decryption is an L-bit string. Since $\mathcal{X}$ and $\mathcal{XT}$ are both efficiently recognizable, any invalid ciphertext $(X_1, \cdots, X_L, T)$ (i.e., $X_i \notin \mathcal{X}$ for some i, or $T \notin \mathcal{XT}$) will be decrypted to $\bot$. In other words, the range of the decryption algorithm is $\{0,1\}^L \bigcup \{\bot\}$, which is recognizable. As to the special inverting algorithm F, we construct it as follows: Let (Enc, Dec) denote the encryption/decryption algorithms of the FHKW scheme. For any ciphertext c, we have that $\mathsf{Dec}(sk, c) \in \{0,1\}^L \bigcup \{\bot\}$. If $\mathsf{Dec}(sk, c) \in \{0,1\}^L$, F runs $\mathsf{Enc}(pk, \mathsf{Dec}(sk, c))$ and returns the generated ciphertext; If $\mathsf{Dec}(sk, c) = \bot$, F returns an arbitrary ciphertext $(X_1, \cdots, X_L, T)$ where $X_i \notin \mathcal{X}$ or $T \notin \mathcal{XT}$.

IND-NM-SO-CCA2 Secure Construction. According to Theorem 4, IND-NM-SO-CCA2 security is equivalent to IND-SO-CCA2 security. So any IND-SO-CCA2 secure encryption scheme (e.g. the PKE scheme constructed from all-but-many lossy trapdoor functions [11]) meets IND-NM-SO-CCA2 security.

Acknowledgments. We would like to thank the anonymous reviewers for their helpful comments. This work is funded by the Specialized Research Fund for the Doctoral Program of Higher Education under Grant 20110073110016, the Scientific Innovation Projects of Shanghai Education Committee under Grant 12ZZ021, and the National Natural Science Foundation of China under Grants 61170229, 61373153, 61133014 and 61472114.

References

1. Bellare, M., Desai, A., Pointcheval, D., Rogaway, P.: Relations among notions of security for public-key encryption schemes. In: Krawczyk, H. (ed.) CRYPTO 1998. LNCS, vol. 1462, pp. 26–45. Springer, Heidelberg (1998)

2. Bellare, M., Dowsley, R., Waters, B., Yilek, S.: Standard security does not imply security against selective-opening. In: Pointcheval, D., Johansson, T. (eds.) EURO-CRYPT 2012. LNCS, vol. 7237, pp. 645–662. Springer, Heidelberg (2012)
3. Böhl, F., Hofheinz, D., Kraschewski, D.: On definitions of selective opening security. In: Fischlin, M., Buchmann, J., Manulis, M. (eds.) PKC 2012. LNCS, vol. 7293, pp. 522–539. Springer, Heidelberg (2012)
4. Bellare, M., Hofheinz, D., Yilek, S.: Possibility and impossibility results for encryption and commitment secure under selective opening. In: Joux, A. (ed.) EURO-CRYPT 2009. LNCS, vol. 5479, pp. 1–35. Springer, Heidelberg (2009)
5. Bellare, M., Sahai, A.: Non-malleable encryption: equivalence between two notions, and an indistinguishability-based characterization. In: Wiener, M. (ed.) CRYPTO 1999. LNCS, vol. 1666, pp. 519–536. Springer, Heidelberg (1999)
6. Cramer, R., Shoup, V.: A practical public key cryptosystem provably secure against adaptive chosen ciphertext attack. In: Krawczyk, H. (ed.) CRYPTO 1998. LNCS, vol. 1462, pp. 13–25. Springer, Heidelberg (1998)
7. Cramer, R., Shoup, V.: Design and analysis of practical public-key encryption schemes secure against adaptive chosen ciphertext attack. SIAM J. Comput. 33(1), 167–226 (2003)
8. Dolev, D., Dwork, C., Naor, M.: Non-malleable cryptography. SIAM J. Comput. 30(2), 391–437 (2000)
9. Goldwasser, S., Micali, S.: Probabilistic encryption. J. Comput. Syst. Sci. 28(2), 270–299 (1984)
10. Fehr, S., Hofheinz, D., Kiltz, E., Wee, H.: Encryption schemes secure against chosen-ciphertext selective opening attacks. In: Gilbert, H. (ed.) EUROCRYPT 2010. LNCS, vol. 6110, pp. 381–402. Springer, Heidelberg (2010)
11. Hofheinz, D.: All-but-many lossy trapdoor functions. In: Pointcheval, D., Johansson, T. (eds.) EUROCRYPT 2012. LNCS, vol. 7237, pp. 209–227. Springer, Heidelberg (2012)
12. Hemenway, B., Libert, B., Ostrovsky, R., Vergnaud, D.: Lossy Encryption: constructions from general assumptions and efficient selective opening chosen ciphertext security. In: Wang, X., Lee, D.H. (eds.) ASIACRYPT 2011. LNCS, vol. 7073, pp. 70–88. Springer, Heidelberg (2011)
13. Huang, Z., Liu, S., Qin, B.: Sender-equivocable encryption schemes secure against chosen-ciphertext attacks revisited. In: Kurosawa, K., Hanaoka, G. (eds.) PKC 2013. LNCS, vol. 7778, pp. 369–385. Springer, Heidelberg (2013)
14. Huang, Z., Liu, S., Qin, B., Chen, K.: Fixing the sender-equivocable encryption scheme in eurocrypt 2010. In: 2013 5th International Conference on Intelligent Networking and Collaborative Systems (INCoS), pp. 366–372. IEEE (2013)
15. Hofheinz, D., Rupp, A.: Standard versus selective opening security: separation and equivalence results. In: Lindell, Y. (ed.) TCC 2014. LNCS, vol. 8349, pp. 591–615. Springer, Heidelberg (2014)
16. Naor, M., Yung, M.: Public-key cryptosystems provably secure against chosen ciphertext attacks. In: Proceedings of the Twenty-Second Annual ACM Symposium on Theory of Computing, pp. 427–437. ACM (1990)
17. Pass, R., Shelat, A., Vaikuntanathan, V.: Relations among notions of non-malleability for encryption. In: Kurosawa, K. (ed.) ASIACRYPT 2007. LNCS, vol. 4833, pp. 519–535. Springer, Heidelberg (2007)
18. Rackoff, C., Simon, D.R.: Non-interactive zero-knowledge proof of knowledge and chosen ciphertext attack. In: Feigenbaum, J. (ed.) CRYPTO 1991. LNCS, vol. 576, pp. 433–444. Springer, Heidelberg (1992)

A Signature Scheme with a Fuzzy Private Key

Kenta Takahashi[1]([✉]), Takahiro Matsuda[2], Takao Murakami[2],
Goichiro Hanaoka[2], and Masakatsu Nishigaki[3]

[1] Hitachi, Ltd., Yokohama, Japan
kenta.takahashi.bw@hitachi.com
[2] National Institute of Advanced Industrial Science and Technology (AIST),
Tokyo, Japan
{t-matsuda,takao-murakami,hanaoka-goichiro}@aist.go.jp
[3] Shizuoka University, Hamamatsu, Japan
nisigaki@inf.shizuoka.ac.jp

Abstract. In this paper, we introduce a new concept that we call *fuzzy signature*, which is a signature scheme that uses a noisy string such as biometric data as a private key, but *does not require auxiliary data* (which is also called helper string in the context of fuzzy extractors), for generating a signature. Our technical contributions are three-fold: (1) We first give the formal definition of fuzzy signature, together with a formal definition of a "setting" that specifies some necessary information for fuzzy data. (2) We give a generic construction of a fuzzy signature scheme based on a signature scheme with certain homomorphic properties regarding keys and signatures, and a new tool that we call *linear sketch*. (3) We specify a certain setting for fuzzy data, and then give concrete instantiations of these building blocks for our generic construction, leading to our proposed fuzzy signature scheme.

We also discuss how fuzzy signature schemes can be used to realize a biometric-based PKI that uses biometric data itself as a cryptographic key, which we call the *public biometric infrastructure (PBI)*.

Keywords: Fuzzy signature · Public biometric infrastructure

1 Introduction

1.1 Background and Motivation

The public key infrastructure (PKI), which enables authentication and cryptographic communication, plays a significant role as an infrastructure for information security, and is expected to be used for personal use (e.g. national ID, e-government service) more and more widely. In the PKI, private and public keys are generated for each user at the time of registration, and a certificate authority (CA) guarantees the link between the public key and the user's identity by issuing a public key certificate. The user can publish his/her digital signature by using the private signing key. However, since the user has to manage his/her

© Springer International Publishing Switzerland 2015
T. Malkin et al. (Eds.): ACNS 2015, LNCS 9092, pp. 105–126, 2015.
DOI: 10.1007/978-3-319-28166-7_6

private key in a highly secure manner [6], it is not very convenient in some situations. For example, the user is required to possess a hardware token (e.g. smart card, USB token) that contains his/her private key, and memorize a password to activate the key. Such limitations reduce usability, and especially, carrying a dedicated device can be a burden to users. This becomes more serious for elderly people in an aging society.

A feasible approach for solving this problem fundamentally is to use *biometric data* (e.g. fingerprint, iris, and finger-vein) as a cryptographic key. Namely, since biometric data is a part of human body, it can offer a more usable way to link the private key and the individual. Moreover, a multibiometric sensor that simultaneously acquires multiple biometric information (e.g. iris and face [1]; fingerprint and finger-vein [15]) has been recently developed to obtain enough entropy at one time, and we can also expect that longer strings will be produced from various biometric data in the near future.

However, since biometric data is noisy and fluctuates each time it is captured, it cannot be used directly as a key. Intuitively, it seems that this issue can be immediately solved by using a *fuzzy extractor* [4], but this is not always the case. More specifically, for extracting a string by a fuzzy extractor, an auxiliary data called a helper string is necessary, and therefore, the user is still enforced to carry a dedicated device that stores it. (We discuss the limitations of the approaches with helper data (i.e. the fuzzy-extractor-based approaches) in more detail in Appendix A.) Hence, it is considered that the above problem cannot be straightforwardly solved by using the fuzzy extractor, and another cryptographic technique by which noisy data can be used as a cryptographic private key without relying on any auxiliary data, is necessary.

Fuzzy Signature: A Signature Scheme with a Fuzzy Private Key. In this paper, we introduce a new concept of digital signature that we call *fuzzy signature*. Consider an ordinary digital signature scheme. The signing algorithm Sign is defined as a function that takes a signing key sk and a message m as input, and outputs a signature $\sigma \leftarrow \mathsf{Sign}(sk, m)$[1]. Thus, it is natural to consider that its "fuzzy" version Sign should be defined as a function that takes a noisy string x and a message m as input, and outputs $\sigma \leftarrow \mathsf{Sign}(x, m)$. In this paper, we refer to such digital signature (i.e. digital signature that allows to use a noisy string itself as a signing key) as *fuzzy signature*. It should be noted that some studies proposed a fuzzy identity based signature (FIBS) scheme [7,20,21,23,24], which uses a noisy string as a verification key. However, fuzzy signature is a totally different concept since it does not allow a fuzzy verification key, but allows a *fuzzy signing key* (i.e. *fuzzy private key*).

Figure 1 shows the architecture of fuzzy signature in the left, and that of digital signature using a fuzzy extractor in the right. In fuzzy signature, the key generation algorithm $\mathsf{KG_{FS}}$ takes a noisy string (e.g. biometric feature) x as input, and outputs a verification key vk.; The signing algorithm $\mathsf{Sign_{FS}}$ takes

---

[1] Strictly speaking, in this paper we adopt the syntax in which Sign also takes a public parameter as input (see Sect. 2.2). In this section, we omit it for simplicity.

another noisy string x' and a message m as input, and outputs a signature σ.; The verification algorithm $\mathsf{Ver_{FS}}$ takes vk, m, and σ as input, and verifies whether σ is valid or not. If x' is close to x, σ is verified as valid (the formal definitions of these algorithms are given in Sect. 3). We emphasize that a fuzzy signature scheme cannot be constructed based on a fuzzy extractor, since it requires a helper string P along with a noisy string x' to make a signature σ on a message m. Hence, to date, the realization of fuzzy signature has been an open problem.

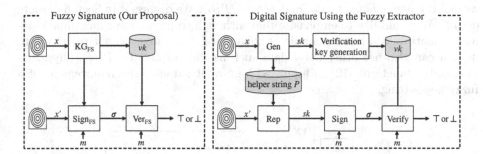

Fig. 1. Architecture of fuzzy signature (our proposal) (left), and that of digital signature using a fuzzy extractor (right) (x, x': noisy string, sk: signing key, vk: verification key, σ: signature, m: message, $\top$: valid, $\bot$: invalid).

1.2   Our Contributions

In this paper, we show that under the assumption that a noisy string is uniform and has enough entropy, a secure fuzzy signature scheme can be indeed realized. More specifically, our technical contributions are three-fold:

1. **Formal Definition of Fuzzy Signature (Sect. 3):** We first formalize a *fuzzy key setting* that specifies some necessary information for fuzzy data (e.g. a metric space to which fuzzy data belongs, and a distribution of fuzzy data over it, etc.). We then give a formal definition of a fuzzy signature scheme that is associated with a fuzzy key setting.
2. **Generic Construction (Sect. 4):** In order to better understand our ideas and the security arguments for our proposed scheme clearly and in a modular manner, we give a generic construction of a fuzzy signature from an ordinary signature scheme with certain homomorphic properties regarding keys and signatures (which is formally defined in Sect. 2.2), and a new technical tool that we call *linear sketch* that incorporates a kind of encoding and error correction processes. (We explain how it works and is used informally in Sect. 1.3, and give a formal definition in Sect. 4.1.)
3. **Concrete Instantiation (Sect. 5):** We specify a concrete fuzzy key setting in which fuzzy data is distributed uniformly over some metric space, and then show how to realize the underlying signature scheme and a linear sketch scheme that can be used in the generic construction for this fuzzy key setting.

Our signature scheme is based on the Waters signature scheme [22], which we modify so that it satisfies the homomorphic property required in our generic construction. Our linear sketch scheme is based on the Chinese reminder theorem and some form of linear coding and error correction.

In Sect. 1.3, we give an overview of how our proposed fuzzy signature scheme is constructed.

It is expected that our fuzzy signature scheme can be used to realize a biometric-based PKI that uses biometric data itself as a cryptographic key, which we call the *public biometric infrastructure (PBI)*. We discuss it in Sect. 6 in more detail. We would like to emphasize that although so far we have mentioned biometric feature as a main example of noisy data, our scheme is not restricted to it, and can also use other noisy data such as the output of a PUF (physically unclonable function) [12] as input, as long as it satisfies the requirement of a fuzzy key setting.

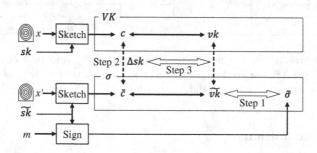

Fig. 2. An overview of our generic construction of a fuzzy signature scheme. The box "Sketch" indicates one of the algorithms of a primitive that we call "linear sketch," which is formalized in Sect. 4.1.

1.3   Overview of Our Fuzzy Signature Scheme

Our proposed fuzzy signature scheme Σ_{FS} is constructed based on an ordinary signature scheme (let us call it the "underlying scheme" Σ for the explanation here). In Fig. 2, we illustrate an overview of our construction of a fuzzy signature scheme. Our basic strategy is as follows: In the signing algorithm $\mathsf{Sign}_{\mathsf{FS}}(x', m)$ (where x' is a noisy string and m is a message to be signed), we do not extract a signing key sk (for the underlying scheme Σ) directly from x' (which is the idea of the fuzzy-extractor-based approach), but use a randomly generated key pair $(\widetilde{vk}, \widetilde{sk})$ of Σ, generate a signature $\widetilde{\sigma}$ using $\widetilde{sk}$, and also create a "sketch" $\widetilde{c}$ (via the algorithm denoted by "Sketch" in Fig. 2), which is a kind of "one-time pad" ciphertext of the signing key $\widetilde{sk}$ using x' as a "one-time pad key"[2], and let

---

[2] The procedure "Sketch" is actually not the one-time pad encryption, but more like a (one-way) "encoding," because we do not need to decrypt $\widetilde{c}$ to recover $\widetilde{sk}$. This is the main reason why we call $\widetilde{c}$ "sketch" (something that contains the information of $\widetilde{sk}$), not "ciphertext".

a signature σ consist of $(\widetilde{vk}, \widetilde{\sigma}, \widetilde{c})$. This enables us to generate a fresh signature $\widetilde{\sigma}$ without being worried about the fuzziness of x'. Here, however, since $\widetilde{\sigma}$ is a valid signature only under $\widetilde{vk}$, in order to generate a signature next time, we need to somehow carry the "encrypted" signing key $\widetilde{c}$. To avoid it, in the key generation algorithm $\mathsf{KG_{FS}}(x)$ (where x is also a noisy string measured at the key generation), we also generate a "sketch" c of another fresh signing key sk using x as the "one-time pad key", and put it as a part of a verification key of our fuzzy signature scheme. Hence, a verification key VK in our fuzzy signature scheme Σ_{FS} consists of a verification key vk (corresponding to the signing key sk generated at the key generation) of the underlying scheme Σ, and the sketch c generated from sk and x. Here, by using some kind of error correction method with which we can remove "noise" from c and $\widetilde{c}$, and comparing them, we can calculate the "difference" Δsk between sk and $\widetilde{sk}$, similarly to what we can do for one-time pad ciphertexts.[3] Thus, if the underlying scheme Σ has the property that "given two verification keys $(vk, \widetilde{vk})$ and a (candidate) difference Δsk, one can verify that the difference between the secret keys sk and $\widetilde{sk}$ (corresponding to vk and $\widetilde{vk}$, respectively) is indeed Δsk", we can verify the signature $\sigma = (\widetilde{vk}, \widetilde{\sigma}, \widetilde{c})$ of Σ_{FS} under the verification key $VK = (vk, c)$ by first checking the validity of $\widetilde{\sigma}$ under $\widetilde{vk}$ (Step 1), then recovering Δsk from c and $\widetilde{c}$ (Step 2), and finally checking whether the difference between vk and $\widetilde{vk}$ indeed corresponds to Δsk (Step 3). The explanation so far is exactly what we do in our generic construction in Sect. 4.

To concretely realize the above strategy, we propose a variant of the Waters signature scheme [22] (which we call *modified Waters signature* (MWS)) that satisfies all our requirements. We also formalize the methods for "one-time padding secret keys (sk and $\widetilde{sk}$) by noisy strings" and "reconstructing the difference between two secret keys", as a tool that we call *linear sketch*, and show how to realize a linear sketch scheme that can be used together with the MWS scheme to realize our fuzzy signature scheme Σ_{FS}.

2 Preliminaries

In this section, we review the basic notation and the definitions of primitives.

Basic Notation. $\mathbb{N}$, $\mathbb{Z}$, and $\mathbb{R}$ denote the sets of all natural numbers, all integers, and all real numbers, respectively. If $n \in \mathbb{N}$, then we define $[n] := \{1, \dots, n\}$. If $a, b \in \mathbb{N}$, then "$\mathrm{GCD}(a, b)$" denotes the greatest common divisor of a and b, and if $a \in \mathbb{R}$, then "$\lfloor a \rfloor$" denotes the maximum integer which does not exceed a.

---

[3] Recall that the original one-time pad encryption $c = m \oplus K$ (where c, m, and K are a ciphertext, a message, and a key, respectively) has "linearity" in the sense that given two ciphertexts $c_1 = m \oplus K_1$ and $c_2 = m \oplus K_2$ of the same message m under different keys K_1 and K_2, we can calculate the difference $\Delta K = K_1 \oplus K_2$ by computing $c_1 \oplus c_2$.

If S is a finite set, then "$|S|$" denotes its size, and "$x \leftarrow_R S$" denotes that x is chosen uniformly at random from S. If Φ is a distribution (over some set), then $x \leftarrow_R \Phi$ denotes that x is chosen according to the distribution Φ. "$x \leftarrow y$" denotes that y is (deterministically) assigned to x. If x and y are bit-strings, then $|x|$ denotes the bit-length of x, and "$(x||y)$" denotes the concatenation of x and y. "(P)PTA" denotes a *(probabilistic) polynomial time algorithm*.

If $\mathcal{A}$ is a probabilistic algorithm, then "$y \leftarrow_R \mathcal{A}(x)$" denote that $\mathcal{A}$ computes y by taking x as input and using an internal randomness that is chosen uniformly at random, and if we need to specify the randomness, we denote by "$y \leftarrow \mathcal{A}(x; r)$" (in which case the computation of $\mathcal{A}$ is deterministic that takes x and r as input). If furthermore $\mathcal{O}$ is a (possibly probabilistic) algorithm or a function, then "$\mathcal{A}^{\mathcal{O}}$" denotes that $\mathcal{A}$ has oracle access to $\mathcal{O}$. Throughout the paper, "k" denotes a security parameter. A function $f(\cdot) : \mathbb{N} \to [0, 1]$ is said to be *negligible* if for all positive polynomials $p(\cdot)$ and all sufficiently large k, we have $f(k) < 1/p(k)$.

2.1 Bilinear Groups and Computational Problems

We say that $\mathcal{BG} = (p, \mathbb{G}, \mathbb{G}_T, g, e)$ constitutes (symmetric) bilinear groups if p is a prime, $\mathbb{G}$ and $\mathbb{G}_T$ are cyclic groups with order p, g is a generator of $\mathbb{G}$, and $e : \mathbb{G} \times \mathbb{G} \to \mathbb{G}_T$ is an efficiently (in $|p|$) computable mapping satisfying the following two properties: (*Bilinearity:*) For all $g' \in \mathbb{G}$ and $a, b \in \mathbb{Z}_p$, it holds that $e(g'^a, g'^b) = e(g', g')^{ab}$, and (*Non-degeneracy:*) for all generators g' of $\mathbb{G}$, $e(g', g')$ is not the identity element of $\mathbb{G}_T$.

For convenience, we denote by BGGen an algorithm (referred to as a bilinear group generator) that, on input 1^k, outputs a description of bilinear groups $\mathcal{BG}$.

Definition 1. *We say that the computational Diffie-Hellman (CDH) assumption holds with respect to* BGGen *if for all PPTAs* $\mathcal{A}$, $\mathsf{Adv}^{\mathrm{CDH}}_{\mathsf{BGGen}, \mathcal{A}}(k) := \Pr[\mathcal{BG} \leftarrow \mathsf{BGGen}(1^k); a, b \leftarrow_R \mathbb{Z}_p : \mathcal{A}(\mathcal{BG}, g^a, g^b) = g^{ab}]$ *is negligible.*

2.2 Signature

Syntax and Correctness. We model a signature scheme Σ as a quadruple of the PPTAs (Setup, KG, Sign, Ver) that are defined as follows: The setup algorithm Setup takes 1^k as input, and outputs a public parameter pp.; The key generation algorithm KG takes pp as input, and output a verification/signing key pair (vk, sk).; The signing algorithm Sign takes pp, sk, and a message m as input, and outputs a signature σ.; The verification algorithm Ver takes pp, vk, m, and σ as input, and outputs either $\top$ or $\bot$. Here, "$\top$" (resp. "$\bot$") indicates that σ is a valid (resp. invalid) signature of the message m under the key vk.

We require for all $k \in \mathbb{N}$, all pp output by $\mathsf{Setup}(1^k)$, all (vk, sk) output by $\mathsf{KG}(pp)$, and all messages m, we have $\mathsf{Ver}(pp, vk, m, \mathsf{Sign}(pp, sk, m)) = \top$.

EUF-CMA Security. Here, we recall the definition of *existential unforgeability against chosen message attacks* (**EUF-CMA** security).

For a signature scheme $\Sigma = (\mathsf{Setup}, \mathsf{KG}, \mathsf{Sign}, \mathsf{Ver})$ and an adversary $\mathcal{A}$, consider the following EUF-CMA experiment $\mathsf{Expt}_{\Sigma,\mathcal{A}}^{\text{EUF-CMA}}(k)$:

$$\mathsf{Expt}_{\Sigma,\mathcal{A}}^{\text{EUF-CMA}}(k) : [\ pp \leftarrow_{\mathsf{R}} \mathsf{Setup}(1^k);\ (vk, sk) \leftarrow_{\mathsf{R}} \mathsf{KG}(pp);$$
$$\mathcal{Q} \leftarrow \emptyset;\ (m', \sigma') \leftarrow_{\mathsf{R}} \mathcal{A}^{\mathcal{O}_{\mathsf{Sign}}(\cdot)}(pp, vk);$$
$$\text{If } m' \notin \mathcal{Q} \wedge \mathsf{Ver}(pp, vk, m', \sigma') = \top \text{ then return 1 else return 0 }],$$

where $\mathcal{O}_{\mathsf{Sign}}$ is the signing oracle which takes a message m as input, updates $\mathcal{Q}$ by $\mathcal{Q} \leftarrow \mathcal{Q} \cup \{m\}$, and returns a signature $\sigma \leftarrow_{\mathsf{R}} \mathsf{Sign}(pp, sk, m)$.

Definition 2. *We say that a signature scheme Σ is* EUF-CMA *secure if for all PPTA adversaries $\mathcal{A}$, $\mathsf{Adv}_{\Sigma,\mathcal{A}}^{\text{EUF-CMA}}(k) := \Pr[\mathsf{Expt}_{\Sigma,\mathcal{A}}^{\text{EUF-CMA}}(k) = 1]$ is negligible.*

Homomorphic Properties of Keys and Signatures. For our fuzzy signature scheme, we will utilize a signature scheme that has certain homomorphic properties regarding keys and signatures, and thus we formalize the properties here.

Definition 3. *Let $\Sigma = (\mathsf{Setup}, \mathsf{KG}, \mathsf{Sign}, \mathsf{Ver})$ be a signature scheme. We say that Σ is* homomorphic *if it satisfies the following properties:*

- *For all parameters pp output by Setup, the signing key space constitutes a cyclic abelian group $(\mathcal{K}_{pp}, +)$, and the key generation algorithm KG can be described by using the deterministic PTA KG' as follows:*

$$\mathsf{KG}(pp) : [sk \leftarrow_{\mathsf{R}} \mathcal{K}_{pp};\ vk \leftarrow \mathsf{KG}'(pp, sk);\ Return\ (vk, sk).]. \tag{1}$$

- *There exists a deterministic PTA M_{vk} that takes a public parameter pp (output by Setup), a verification key vk (output by $\mathsf{KG}(pp)$), and a "shift" $\Delta sk \in \mathcal{K}_{pp}$ as input, and outputs the "shifted" verification key vk'.*
  We require that for all pp output by Setup and all $sk, \Delta sk \in \mathcal{K}_{pp}$, it holds that

$$\mathsf{KG}'(pp, sk + \Delta sk) = \mathsf{M}_{\mathsf{vk}}(pp, \mathsf{KG}'(pp, sk), \Delta sk). \tag{2}$$

- *There exists a deterministic PTA $\mathsf{M}_{\mathsf{sig}}$ that takes a public parameter pp (output by Setup), a verification key vk (output by $\mathsf{KG}(pp)$), a message m, a signature σ, and a "shift" $\Delta sk \in \mathcal{K}_{pp}$ as input, and outputs a "shifted" signature σ'.*
  We require that for all pp output by Setup, all messages m, all $sk, \Delta sk \in \mathcal{K}_{pp}$, the following two distributions are identical:

$$\{\sigma' \leftarrow_{\mathsf{R}} \mathsf{Sign}(pp, sk + \Delta sk, m) : \sigma'\}, \quad and$$
$$\{\sigma \leftarrow_{\mathsf{R}} \mathsf{Sign}(pp, sk, m);\ \sigma' \leftarrow \mathsf{M}_{\mathsf{sig}}(pp, \mathsf{KG}'(pp, sk), m, \sigma, \Delta sk) : \sigma'\}. \tag{3}$$

Furthermore, we require that for all pp output by Setup, all $sk, \Delta sk \in \mathcal{K}_{pp}$, and all (m, σ) satisfying $vk = \mathsf{KG}'(pp, sk)$ and $\mathsf{Ver}(pp, vk, m, \sigma) = \top$, it holds that

$$\mathsf{Ver}(pp, \mathsf{M}_{\mathsf{vk}}(pp, vk, \Delta sk), m, \mathsf{M}_{\mathsf{sig}}(pp, vk, m, \sigma, \Delta sk)) = \top. \tag{4}$$

On "Weak" Distributions of Signing Keys. Let $\Sigma = (\mathsf{Setup}, \mathsf{KG}, \mathsf{Sign}, \mathsf{Ver})$ be a signature scheme with the homomorphic property (as per Definition 3) with secret key space $\mathcal{K}_{pp}$ for a public parameter pp, and thus there exists the algorithm KG' such that KG can be written as in Eq. (1). Let $u : \mathbb{N} \to \mathbb{N}$ be any function. For an EUF-CMA adversary $\mathcal{A}$ attacking Σ, let $\widetilde{\mathsf{Adv}}_{\Sigma,\mathcal{A}}^{\text{EUF-CMA}}(k)$ be the advantange of $\mathcal{A}$ in the experiment that is the same as $\mathsf{Expt}_{\Sigma,\mathcal{A}}^{\text{EUF-CMA}}(k)$, except that a secret key sk is chosen by $sk \leftarrow_{\mathsf{R}} \widetilde{\mathcal{K}}_{pp}$ (instead of $sk \leftarrow_{\mathsf{R}} \mathcal{K}_{pp}$) where $\widetilde{\mathcal{K}}_{pp}$ denotes an arbitrary (non-empty) subset of $\mathcal{K}_{pp}$ satisfying $|\mathcal{K}_{pp}|/|\widetilde{\mathcal{K}}_{pp}| \leq u(k)$.

We will use the following fact, which is obtained as a corollary of the lemma shown by Dodis and Yu [5, Lemma 1].

Lemma 1. *(Corollary of* [5, Lemma 1]*)* *Under the above setting, for any PPTA adversary $\mathcal{A}$, it holds that* $\widetilde{\mathsf{Adv}}_{\Sigma,\mathcal{A}}^{\text{EUF-CMA}}(k) \leq u(k) \cdot \mathsf{Adv}_{\Sigma,\mathcal{A}}^{\text{EUF-CMA}}(k)$.

Waters Signature Scheme. Our fuzzy signature scheme is based on the Waters signature scheme [22], and thus we recall it here. (We consider the version where the setup and the key generation (for each user) is separated.)

Let $\ell = \ell(k)$ be a positive polynomial, and let BGGen be a bilinear group generator (as defined in Sect. 2.1). Then, the Waters signature scheme Σ_{Wat} for ℓ-bit messages are constructed as in Fig. 3. Σ_{Wat} is known to be EUF-CMA secure if the CDH assumption holds with respect to BGGen [22].

$\mathsf{Setup}_{\mathsf{Wat}}(1^k)$: $\qquad \mathcal{BG} := (p, \mathbb{G}, \mathbb{G}_T, g, e) \leftarrow \mathsf{BGGen}(1^k)$ $\qquad h, u', u_1, \ldots, u_\ell \leftarrow_{\mathsf{R}} \mathbb{G}$ $\qquad pp \leftarrow (\mathcal{BG}, h, u', (u_i)_{i \in [\ell]})$ $\qquad$ Return pp.	$\mathsf{Sign}_{\mathsf{Wat}}(pp, sk, m)$: $\qquad$ Parse m as $(m_1 \| \ldots \| m_\ell) \in \{0,1\}^\ell$. $\qquad r \leftarrow_{\mathsf{R}} \mathbb{Z}_p$ $\qquad \sigma_1 \leftarrow h^{sk} \cdot (u' \prod_{i \in [\ell]} u_i^{m_i})^r$; $\quad \sigma_2 \leftarrow g^r$ $\qquad$ Return $\sigma \leftarrow (\sigma_1, \sigma_2)$.
$\mathsf{KG}_{\mathsf{Wat}}(pp)$: $\qquad sk \leftarrow_{\mathsf{R}} \mathbb{Z}_p$ $\qquad vk \leftarrow g^{sk}$ $\qquad$ Return (vk, sk).	$\mathsf{Ver}_{\mathsf{Wat}}(pp, vk, m, \sigma)$: $\qquad (\sigma_1, \sigma_2) \leftarrow \sigma$ $\qquad$ Parse m as $(m_1 \| \ldots \| m_\ell) \in \{0,1\}^\ell$. $\qquad$ If $e(\sigma_2, u' \cdot \prod_{i \in [\ell]} u_i^{m_i}) \cdot e(vk, h) = e(\sigma_1, g)$ $\qquad\qquad\qquad\qquad\quad$ then return $\top$ else return $\bot$.

Fig. 3. The Waters signature scheme Σ_{Wat} [22].

3   Definitions for Fuzzy Signature

In this section, we introduce the definitions of Fuzzy Signature (FS).

As mentioned in Sect. 1, to define FS, we need to define some "setting" that models a space to which a fuzzy data (used as a signing key of FS) belongs, a distribution from which fuzzy data is sampled, etc. We therefore first formalize it as a *fuzzy key setting* in Sect. 3.1, and then define FS that is associated with a fuzzy key setting in Sect. 3.2.

3.1   Formalization of Fuzzy Key Setting

Consider a typical biometric authentication scheme, in which a "fuzzy" biometric feature $x \in X$ (where X is some metric space) is measured and extracted from a user at the registration phase.; At the authentication phase, a biometric feature x' is measured and extracted from a (possibly different) user, and this user is considered the user who generated the biometric data x and thus authentic if x and x' are sufficiently "close" according to some metric.

We abstract out this typical setting for "identifying fuzzy objects" as a "fuzzy key setting", and formalize it here. Roughly, a fuzzy key setting specifies (1) the metric space to which fuzzy data (such as biometric data) belongs (X in the above example), (2) the distribution of fuzzy data sampled at the "registration phase" (x in the above example), and (3) the error distribution that models "fuzziness" of the fuzzy data (the relationship between x and x' in the above example).

We adopt what we call the "universal error model", which assumes that for all objects U that produce fuzzy data that we are interested in, if U produces a data x at the first measurement (say, at the registration phase), if the same object is measured next time, then the measured data x' follows the distribution $\{e \leftarrow_R \Phi; x' \leftarrow x + e : x'\}$. That is, the error distribution Φ is independent of individual U. (We also assume that the metric space constitutes an abelian group so that addition is well-defined.)

Formally, a fuzzy key setting $\mathcal{F}$ consists of $((\mathsf{d}, X), t, \mathcal{X}, \Phi, \epsilon)$, each of which is defined as follows:

(d, X): This is a metric space, where X is a space to which a possible fuzzy data x belongs, and $\mathsf{d} : X^2 \to \mathbb{R}$ is the corresponding distance function. We furthermore assume that X constitutes an abelian group.

t: ($\in \mathbb{R}$) This is the threshold value, determined by a security parameter k. Based on t, the false acceptance rate (FAR) and the false rejection rate (FRR) are determined. We require that the $\mathsf{FAR} := \Pr[x, x' \leftarrow_R \mathcal{X} : \mathsf{d}(x, x') < t]$ is negligible in k.

$\mathcal{X}$: This is a distribution of fuzzy data over X.

Φ: This is an error distribution (see the above explanation).

ϵ: ($\in [0, 1]$) This is an error parameter that represents FRR. We require that for all $x \in X$, $\mathsf{FRR} := \Pr[e \leftarrow_R \Phi : \mathsf{d}(x, x + e) \geq t] \leq \epsilon$.

3.2   Fuzzy Signature

A fuzzy signature scheme Σ_{FS} for a fuzzy key setting $\mathcal{F} = ((\mathsf{d}, X), t, \mathcal{X}, \Phi, \epsilon)$ consists of the four algorithms $(\mathsf{Setup}_{\mathsf{FS}}, \mathsf{KG}_{\mathsf{FS}}, \mathsf{Sign}_{\mathsf{FS}}, \mathsf{Ver}_{\mathsf{FS}})$:

$\mathsf{Setup}_{\mathsf{FS}}$: This is the setup algorithm that takes the description of the fuzzy key setting $\mathcal{F}$ and 1^k as input (where k determines the threshold value t of $\mathcal{F}$), and outputs a public parameter pp.

$\mathsf{KG}_{\mathsf{FS}}$: This is the key generation algorithm that takes pp and a fuzzy data $x \in X$ as input, and outputs a verification key vk.

$\mathsf{Sign_{FS}}$: This is the signing algorithm that takes pp, a fuzzy data $x' \in X$, and a message m as input, and outputs a signature σ.

$\mathsf{Ver_{FS}}$: This is the (deterministic) verification algorithm that takes pp, vk, m, and σ as input, and outputs either $\top$ ("accept") or $\bot$ ("reject").

Correctness. We require a natural correctness requirement: For all $k \in \mathbb{N}$, all pp output by $\mathsf{Setup_{FS}}(\mathcal{F}, 1^k)$, all $x, x' \in X$ such that $\mathsf{d}(x, x') < t$, and all messages m, it holds that $\mathsf{Ver_{FS}}(pp, \mathsf{KG_{FS}}(pp, x), m, \mathsf{Sign_{FS}}(pp, x', m)) = \top$.

EUF-CMA *Security.* For a fuzzy signature scheme, we consider EUF-CMA security in a similar manner to that for an ordinary signature scheme, reflecting the universal error model of a fuzzy key setting.

For a fuzzy signature scheme Σ_{FS} for a fuzzy key setting $\mathcal{F} = ((\mathsf{d}, X), t, \mathcal{X}, \Phi, \epsilon)$ and an adversary $\mathcal{A}$, consider the following experiment $\mathsf{Expt}^{\text{EUF-CMA}}_{\Sigma_{\mathsf{FS}}, \mathcal{F}, \mathcal{A}}(k)$:

$$\mathsf{Expt}^{\text{EUF-CMA}}_{\Sigma_{\mathsf{FS}}, \mathcal{F}, \mathcal{A}}(k) : [\ pp \leftarrow_{\mathsf{R}} \mathsf{Setup_{FS}}(\mathcal{F}, 1^k);\ x \leftarrow_{\mathsf{R}} \mathcal{X};\ vk \leftarrow \mathsf{KG_{FS}}(pp, x);$$
$$\mathcal{Q} \leftarrow \emptyset;\ (m', \sigma') \leftarrow_{\mathsf{R}} \mathcal{A}^{\mathcal{O}_{\mathsf{Sign_{FS}}}(\cdot)}(pp, vk):$$
$$\text{If } m' \notin \mathcal{Q} \wedge \mathsf{Ver_{FS}}(pp, vk, m', \sigma') = \top \text{ then return 1 else return 0 }],$$

where $\mathcal{O}_{\mathsf{Sign_{FS}}}$ is the signing oracle that takes a message m as input, and operates as follows: It updates $\mathcal{Q}$ by $\mathcal{Q} \leftarrow \mathcal{Q} \cup \{m\}$, samples $e \leftarrow_{\mathsf{R}} \Phi$, computes a signature $\sigma \leftarrow_{\mathsf{R}} \mathsf{Sign_{FS}}(pp, x + e, m)$, and returns σ.

Definition 4. *We say that a fuzzy signature scheme Σ_{FS} is* EUF-CMA *secure if for all PPTA adversaries $\mathcal{A}$,* $\mathsf{Adv}^{\text{EUF-CMA}}_{\Sigma_{\mathsf{FS}}, \mathcal{F}, \mathcal{A}}(k) := \Pr[\mathsf{Expt}^{\text{EUF-CMA}}_{\Sigma_{\mathsf{FS}}, \mathcal{F}, \mathcal{A}}(k) = 1]$ *is negligible.*

4   Generic Construction

In this section, we show a generic construction for a fuzzy signature scheme. This construction is based on a new tool that we call *linear sketch* and a signature scheme with the homomorphic property (as per Definition 3). We introduce a *linear sketch* scheme in Sect. 4.1, and then in Sect. 4.2, we show the generic construction.

4.1   Linear Sketch

Definition 5. *Let $\mathcal{F} = ((\mathsf{d}, X), t, \mathcal{X}, \Phi, \epsilon)$ be a fuzzy key setting. We say that a pair of deterministic PTAs $\mathcal{S} = (\mathsf{Sketch}, \mathsf{DiffRec})$ is a* linear sketch *scheme for $\mathcal{F}$, if it satisfies the following three properties:*

Syntax and Correctness: *Sketch is the "sketching" algorithm that takes the description Λ of an abelian group $(\mathcal{K}, +)$, an element $s \in \mathcal{K}$, and a fuzzy data $x \in X$ as input, and outputs a "sketch" c.; DiffRec is the "difference reconstruction" algorithm that takes Λ and two values c, c' (supposedly output by Sketch) as input, and outputs the "difference" $\Delta s \in \mathcal{K}$.*
It is required that for all $x, x' \in X$ such that $\mathsf{d}(x, x') < t$, and for all $s, \Delta s \in \mathcal{K}$, it holds that

$$\mathsf{DiffRec}(\Lambda, \mathsf{Sketch}(\Lambda, s, x), \mathsf{Sketch}(\Lambda, s + \Delta s, x')) = \Delta s. \tag{5}$$

Linearity: *There exists a deterministic PTA* M_c *satisfying the following: For all* $x, e \in X$ *such that* $d(x, x + e) < t$, *and for all* $s, \Delta s \in \mathcal{K}$, *it holds that*

$$\text{Sketch}(\Lambda, s + \Delta s, x + e) = M_c(\Lambda, \text{Sketch}(\Lambda, s, x), \Delta s, e). \quad (6)$$

Simulatability: *There exists a PPTA* Sim *such that for all* $s \in \mathcal{K}$, *the following two distributions are statistically indistinguishable (in the security parameter* k *that is associated with* t *in* $\mathcal{F}$ *):*

$$\{x \leftarrow_R \mathcal{X}; \ c \leftarrow \text{Sketch}(\Lambda, s, x) : c\} \quad and \quad \{c \leftarrow_R \text{Sim}(\Lambda) : c\}. \quad (7)$$

4.2 Generic Construction

Let $\mathcal{F} = ((d, X), t, \mathcal{X}, \Phi, \epsilon)$ be a fuzzy key setting, and let $\Sigma = (\text{Setup}, \text{KG}, \text{Sign}, \text{Ver})$ be a signature scheme. We assume that Σ has the homomorphic property (Definition 3), namely, its secret key space (given pp) is a cyclic abelian group $(\mathcal{K}_{pp}, +)$, and has the additional algorithms KG', M_{vk}, and M_{sig}. Let $\mathcal{S} = (\text{Sketch}, \text{DiffRec})$ be a linear sketch scheme for $\mathcal{F}$. Using Σ and $\mathcal{S}$, we construct a fuzzy signature scheme $\Sigma_{FS} = (\text{Setup}_{FS}, \text{KG}_{FS}, \text{Sign}_{FS}, \text{Ver}_{FS})$ for the fuzzy key setting $\mathcal{F}$ as in Fig. 4.

$\text{Setup}_{FS}(\mathcal{F}, 1^k)$:	$\text{Sign}_{FS}(pp, x', m)$:	$\text{Ver}_{FS}(pp, VK, m, \sigma)$:
$pp_s \leftarrow_R \text{Setup}(1^k)$	$(pp_s, \Lambda) \leftarrow pp$	$(pp_s, \Lambda) \leftarrow pp$
Let $\Lambda := (\mathcal{K}_{pp_s}, +)$.	$\widetilde{sk} \leftarrow_R \mathcal{K}_{pp_s}$	$(vk, c) \leftarrow VK$
Return $pp \leftarrow (pp_s, \Lambda)$.	$\widetilde{vk} \leftarrow \text{KG}'(pp_s, \widetilde{sk})$	$(\widetilde{vk}, \widetilde{\sigma}, \widetilde{c}) \leftarrow \sigma$
$\text{KG}_{FS}(pp, x)$:	$\widetilde{\sigma} \leftarrow_R \text{Sign}(pp_s, \widetilde{sk}, m)$	If $\text{Ver}(pp_s, \widetilde{vk}, m, \widetilde{\sigma}) = \bot$
$(pp_s, \Lambda) \leftarrow pp$	$\widetilde{c} \leftarrow \text{Sketch}(\Lambda, \widetilde{sk}, x')$	then return $\bot$.
$sk \leftarrow_R \mathcal{K}_{pp_s}$	Return $\sigma \leftarrow (\widetilde{vk}, \widetilde{\sigma}, \widetilde{c})$.	$\Delta sk \leftarrow \text{DiffRec}(\Lambda, c, \widetilde{c})$
$vk \leftarrow \text{KG}'(pp_s, sk)$		If $M_{vk}(pp_s, vk, \Delta sk) = \widetilde{vk}$
$c \leftarrow \text{Sketch}(\Lambda, sk, x)$		then return $\top$ else return $\bot$.
Return $VK \leftarrow (vk, c)$.		

Fig. 4. A generic construction of a fuzzy signature scheme Σ_{FS} for a fuzzy key setting $\mathcal{F}$ based on a signature scheme Σ with the homomorphic property and a linear sketch scheme $\mathcal{S}$ for $\mathcal{F}$.

The security of the fuzzy signature scheme Σ_{FS} is guaranteed as follows.

Theorem 1. *If* Σ *is* EUF-CMA *secure and* $\mathcal{S}$ *is a linear sketch scheme, then the fuzzy signature scheme* Σ_{FS} *is* EUF-CMA *secure.*

Proof Sketch of Theorem 1. The formal proof of Theorem 1 is given in the full version due to the lack of space, and here we give an overview of the proof.

Let $\mathcal{A}$ be any PPTA adversary that attacks the EUF-CMA security of the fuzzy signature scheme Σ_{FS}. Note that in the original EUF-CMA experiment $\text{Expt}_{\Sigma_{FS}, \mathcal{F}, \mathcal{A}}^{\text{EUF-CMA}}(k)$, the verification key VK is generated as follows:

$$[x \leftarrow_R \mathcal{X}; \ sk \leftarrow_R \mathcal{K}_{pp_s}; \ vk \leftarrow \text{KG}'(pp_s, sk); \ c \leftarrow \text{Sketch}(\Lambda, sk, x); \ VK \leftarrow (vk, c)].$$

Then, consider a "simulated process" for generating VK, which is the same as above except that the step with the underline is replaced with "$c \leftarrow_R \mathsf{Sim}(\Lambda)$". Then, by the simulatability of the linear sketch scheme $\mathcal{S}$, the distribution of VK generated in the original process and that of the simulated process are statistically indistinguishable.

Furthermore, note also that the signing oracle $\mathcal{O}_{\mathsf{Sign}_{\mathsf{FS}}}(m)$ in the original EUF-CMA experiment $\mathsf{Expt}^{\mathsf{EUF\text{-}CMA}}_{\Sigma_{\mathsf{FS}}, \mathcal{F}, \mathcal{A}}$ generates a signature σ as follows:

$$[e \leftarrow_R \Phi; \; \widetilde{sk} \leftarrow_R \mathcal{K}_{pp_s}; \; \widetilde{vk} \leftarrow \mathsf{KG}'(pp_s, \widetilde{sk}); \; \widetilde{\sigma} \leftarrow_R \mathsf{Sign}(pp_s, \widetilde{sk}, m);$$
$$\widetilde{c} \leftarrow \mathsf{Sketch}(\Lambda, \widetilde{sk}, x + e); \; \sigma \leftarrow (\widetilde{vk}, \widetilde{\sigma}, \widetilde{c})].$$

By the homomorphic property of the underlying signature scheme Σ, and the linearity property of the linear sketch scheme $\mathcal{S}$, the following process generates a signature σ whose distribution is exactly the same as σ generated as above.

$$[e \leftarrow_R \Phi; \Delta sk \leftarrow_R \mathcal{K}_{pp_s}; \; \widetilde{sk} \leftarrow sk + \Delta sk; \; \widetilde{vk} \leftarrow \mathsf{M}_{\mathsf{vk}}(pp_s, vk, \Delta sk);$$
$$\widehat{\sigma} \leftarrow_R \mathsf{Sign}(pp_s, sk, m); \; \widetilde{\sigma} \leftarrow \mathsf{M}_{\mathsf{sig}}(pp_s, vk, m, \widehat{\sigma}, \Delta sk);$$
$$\widetilde{c} \leftarrow \mathsf{M}_{\mathsf{c}}(\Lambda, c, \Delta sk, e); \; \sigma \leftarrow (\widetilde{vk}, \widetilde{\sigma}, \widetilde{c})]. \qquad (8)$$

Now, notice that an EUF-CMA adversary $\mathcal{B}$ for the underlying signature scheme Σ, who is given (pp_s, vk) and has access to the signing oracle $\mathcal{O}_{\mathsf{Sign}}(\cdot) := \mathsf{Sign}(pp_s, sk, \cdot)$, can perform the simulated process for generating VK (as explained above) and also simulate the process in Eq. (8) for $\mathcal{A}$. Furthermore, in the full proof, we show that if $\mathcal{A}$ outputs a successful forgery pair $(m', \sigma' = (\widetilde{vk}', \widetilde{\sigma}', \widetilde{c}'))$ such that $\mathsf{Ver}_{\mathsf{FS}}(pp, VK, m', \sigma') = \top$, then we can "extract" a successful forgery pair $(m', \widehat{\sigma}')$ such that $\mathsf{Ver}(pp_s, vk, m', \widehat{\sigma}') = \top$ by using the algorithms $\mathsf{DiffRec}$ and $\mathsf{M}_{\mathsf{sig}}$. (Roughly speaking, we can calculate the difference $\Delta sk'$ that corresponds to the difference between vk and $\widetilde{vk}'$ from c and $\widetilde{c}'$ via $\mathsf{DiffRec}$, and use $\Delta sk'$ to calculate $\widehat{\sigma}'$ via $\mathsf{M}_{\mathsf{sig}}$.) This enables us to turn $\mathcal{A}$ into an adversary (reduction algorithm) $\mathcal{B}$ attacking the EUF-CMA security of Σ. □

5   Instantiation

In this section, we first specify a concrete fuzzy key setting $\mathcal{F}$ for which our proposed fuzzy signature scheme is constructed in Sect. 5.1. Next, in Sect. 5.2, we provide some mathematical preliminaries used for our concrete linear sketch scheme and signature scheme. Armed with them, in Sects. 5.3 and 5.4, we show the concrete linear sketch scheme $\mathcal{S}$ for $\mathcal{F}$ and the signature scheme Σ_{MWS}, respectively, that can be used in our generic construction given in Sect. 4, which results in our proposed fuzzy signature scheme.

Our proposed fuzzy signature scheme for the fuzzy setting $\mathcal{F}$ (introduced in Sect. 5.1) is obtained straightforwardly from our generic construction in which $\mathcal{S}$ and Σ_{MWS} shown in this section are used. Though somewhat redundant, for the reader's convenience, we give a full description of the scheme in Appendix B.

On the Treatment of Real Numbers. Below, we use real numbers to represent and process fuzzy data. We assume that a suitable representation with sufficient accuracy is chosen to encode the real numbers whenever they need to be treated by the algorithms considered below. (If an algorithm takes a real number as input, its running time is according to the encoded version of input.)

5.1   Fuzzy Key Setting

Here, we specify a concrete fuzzy key setting $\mathcal{F} = ((\mathsf{d}, X), t, \mathcal{X}, \varPhi, \epsilon)$ for which our FS scheme is constructed.

Metric space (d, X): We define the space X by $X := [0, 1)^n \subset \mathbb{R}^n$, where n is a parameter specified by the context (e.g. an object from which we measure fuzzy data). We use the L_∞-norm as the distance function $\mathsf{d} : X \times X \to \mathbb{R}$. Namely, for $\mathbf{x} = (x_1, \ldots, x_n) \in X$ and $\mathbf{x}' = (x_1', \ldots, x_n') \in X$, we define $\mathsf{d}(\mathbf{x}, \mathbf{x}') := \|\mathbf{x} - \mathbf{x}'\|_\infty := \max_{i \in [n]} |x_i - x_i'|$. Note that X forms an abelian group with respect to coordinate-wise addition (modulo 1).

Threshold t: For a security parameter k, we define the threshold $t \in \mathbb{R}$ so that

$$k = \lfloor -n \log_2(2t) \rfloor. \tag{9}$$

Looking ahead, this guarantees that the algorithm "WGen" that we introduce in the next subsection, is a PTA in k. We do not show that FAR is negligible here, because it is indirectly implied by the EUF-CMA security of our proposed fuzzy signature scheme.

Distribution $\mathcal{X}$: The uniform distribution over $[0, 1)^n$. (Regarding how to relax this requirement, see the discussion in Sect. 6.)

Error distribution $\varPhi$ and Error parameter ϵ: $\varPhi$ is any efficiently samplable (according to k) distribution over X such that FRR $\leq \epsilon$ for all $x \in X$.

5.2   Mathematical Preliminaries

Group Isomorphism Based on Chinese Remainder Theorem. Let $n \in \mathbb{N}$. Let $w_1, \ldots, w_n \in \mathbb{N}$ be positive integers with the same bit length (i.e. $\lceil \log_2 w_1 \rceil = \cdots = \lceil \log_2 w_n \rceil$), such that

$$\forall i \in [n] : w_i \leq 1/(2t), \qquad \text{and} \qquad \forall i \neq j \in [n] : \mathsf{GCD}(w_i, w_j) = 1, \tag{10}$$

and $W = \prod_{i \in [n]} w_i = \varTheta(2^k)$, where k is defined as in Eq. (9).

We assume that there exists a deterministic algorithm WGen that on input (t, n) outputs $\mathbf{w} = (w_1, \ldots, w_n)$ satisfying the above.

For vectors $\mathbf{v} = (v_1, \ldots, v_n) \in \mathbb{Z}^n$ and $\mathbf{w} = (w_1, \ldots w_n) \in \mathbb{Z}^n$, we define

$$\mathbf{v} \bmod \mathbf{w} := (v_1 \bmod w_1, \ldots, v_n \bmod w_n). \tag{11}$$

For vectors $\mathbf{v}_1, \mathbf{v}_2 \in \mathbb{Z}^n$, we define the equivalence relation "$\sim$" by $\mathbf{v}_1 \sim \mathbf{v}_2 \overset{\text{def}}{\Leftrightarrow} \mathbf{v}_1 \bmod \mathbf{w} = \mathbf{v}_2 \bmod \mathbf{w}$, and let $\mathbb{Z}_\mathbf{w}^n := \mathbb{Z}^n / \sim$ be the quotient set of $\mathbb{Z}^n$ by $\sim$.

(Note that $(\mathbb{Z}_{\mathbf{w}}^n, +)$ constitutes an abelian group, where the addition is modulo $\mathbf{w}$ as defined in Eq. (11).)

Consider the following system of equations: given $\mathbf{v}, \mathbf{w} \in \mathbb{Z}^n$, find V such that $V \bmod w_i = v_i$ ($i \in [n]$). According to the Chinese remainder theorem (CRT), the solutoin V is determined uniquely modulo W. Thus, for a fixed $\mathbf{w} \in \mathbb{Z}^n$, we can define a mapping $\mathsf{CRT}_{\mathbf{w}} : \mathbb{Z}_{\mathbf{w}}^n \to \mathbb{Z}_W$ such that $\mathsf{CRT}_{\mathbf{w}}(\mathbf{v}) = V \in \mathbb{Z}_W$. We denote by $\mathsf{CRT}_{\mathbf{w}}^{-1}$ the "inverse" procedure of $\mathsf{CRT}_{\mathbf{w}}$.

Note that $\mathsf{CRT}_{\mathbf{w}}$ satisfies the following homomorphism: For all $\mathbf{v}_1, \mathbf{v}_2 \in \mathbb{Z}_{\mathbf{w}}^n$, it holds that $\mathsf{CRT}_{\mathbf{w}}(\mathbf{v}_1 + \mathbf{v}_2) = \mathsf{CRT}_{\mathbf{w}}(\mathbf{v}_1) + \mathsf{CRT}_{\mathbf{w}}(\mathbf{v}_2) \bmod W$. Since $\mathsf{CRT}_{\mathbf{w}}$ is bijective between $\mathbb{Z}_{\mathbf{w}}^n$ and $\mathbb{Z}_W$, $\mathsf{CRT}_{\mathbf{w}}$ is an isomorphism.

Coding and Error Correction. Let $\mathbf{w} = (w_1, \ldots, w_n) \in \mathbb{N}^n$ be the n-dimensional vector satisfying the requirements in Eq. (10). Similarly to $\mathbb{Z}_{\mathbf{w}}^n$, we define $\mathbb{R}_{\mathbf{w}}^n := \mathbb{R}^n / \sim$ be the quotient set of real vector space $\mathbb{R}^n$ by the equivalence relation $\sim$, where for a real number $y \in \mathbb{R}$, we define $r = y \bmod w_i$ by the number such that $\exists n \in \mathbb{Z} : y = n w_i + r$ and $0 \le r < w_i$.

Let $\mathsf{E}_{\mathbf{w}} : \mathbb{R}^n \to \mathbb{R}_{\mathbf{w}}^n$ be the following function:

$$\mathsf{E}_{\mathbf{w}}(\mathbf{x}) := (w_1 x_1, \ldots, w_n x_n) \in \mathbb{R}_{\mathbf{w}}^n. \tag{12}$$

Note that $\mathsf{E}_{\mathbf{w}}(\mathbf{x} + \mathbf{e}) = \mathsf{E}_{\mathbf{w}}(\mathbf{x}) + \mathsf{E}_{\mathbf{w}}(\mathbf{e})$ (mod $\mathbf{w}$) holds. Therefore, $\mathsf{E}_{\mathbf{w}}$ can be viewed as a kind of linear coding.

Let $\mathsf{C}_{\mathbf{w}} : \mathbb{R}_{\mathbf{w}}^n \to \mathbb{Z}_{\mathbf{w}}^n$ be the following function:

$$\mathsf{C}_{\mathbf{w}}((y_1, \ldots, y_n)) := (\lfloor y_1 + 0.5 \rfloor, \ldots, \lfloor y_n + 0,5 \rfloor). \tag{13}$$

We note that the round-off operation $\lfloor y_i + 0.5 \rfloor$ in $\mathsf{C}_{\mathbf{w}}$ can be regarded as a kind of error correction. Specifically, by the conditions in Eq. (10), the following properties are satisfied: For any $\mathbf{x}, \mathbf{x}' \in X$, if $\|\mathbf{x} - \mathbf{x}'\|_\infty < t$, then we have

$$\|\mathsf{E}_{\mathbf{w}}(\mathbf{x}) - \mathsf{E}_{\mathbf{w}}(\mathbf{x}')\|_\infty < t \cdot \max_{i \in [n]}\{w_i\} \le 0.5.$$

Therefore, for such $\mathbf{x}, \mathbf{x}'$, it always holds that

$$\mathsf{C}_{\mathbf{w}}\Big(\mathsf{E}_{\mathbf{w}}(\mathbf{x}) - \mathsf{E}_{\mathbf{w}}(\mathbf{x}')\Big) = \mathbf{0}. \tag{14}$$

Additionally, for any $\mathbf{x} \in \mathbb{R}^n$ and $\mathbf{s} \in \mathbb{Z}_{\mathbf{w}}^n$, the following holds:

$$\mathsf{C}_{\mathbf{w}}(\mathbf{x} + \mathbf{s}) = \mathsf{C}_{\mathbf{w}}(\mathbf{x}) + \mathbf{s} \quad (\bmod \ \mathbf{w}). \tag{15}$$

5.3   Linear Sketch

Let $\mathcal{F} = ((\mathsf{d}, X), t, \mathcal{X}, \Phi, \epsilon)$ be the fuzzy key setting defined in Sect. 5.1, and let $\mathbf{w} = (w_1, \ldots, w_n) = \mathsf{WGen}(t, n)$, where n is the dimension of X, and let $W = \prod_{i \in [n]} w_i$. We consider the linear sketch scheme $\mathcal{S} = (\mathsf{Sketch}, \mathsf{DiffRec})$ for $\mathcal{F}$ and the additive group $(\mathbb{Z}_W, +)$ ($=: \Lambda$), as described in Fig. 5 (left).

$\mathsf{Sketch}(\Lambda, s \in \mathbb{Z}_W, \mathbf{x} \in [0,1)^n)$:	$\mathsf{M_c}(\Lambda, \mathbf{c}, \Delta s, \mathbf{e})$:
$\quad \mathbf{c} \leftarrow (\mathsf{CRT_w^{-1}}(s) + \mathsf{E_w}(\mathbf{x})) \bmod \mathbf{w}$	$\quad \mathbf{c'} \leftarrow (\mathbf{c} + \mathsf{CRT_w^{-1}}(\Delta s) + \mathsf{E_w}(\mathbf{e})) \bmod \mathbf{w}$
$\quad$ Return $\mathbf{c}$.	$\quad$ Return $\mathbf{c'}$.
$\mathsf{DiffRec}(\Lambda, \mathbf{c}, \mathbf{c'})$:	$\mathsf{Sim}(\Lambda)$:
$\quad \Delta \mathbf{s} \leftarrow \mathsf{C_w}(\mathbf{c} - \mathbf{c'}); \quad \Delta s \leftarrow \mathsf{CRT_w}(\Delta \mathbf{s})$	$\quad \mathbf{c} \leftarrow_R \mathbb{R}_\mathbf{w}^n$
$\quad$ Return Δs.	$\quad$ Return $\mathbf{c}$.

Fig. 5. The linear sketch scheme $\mathcal{S} = (\mathsf{Sketch}, \mathsf{DiffRec})$ for the fuzzy key setting $\mathcal{F}$ (left), and the auxiliary algorithms $\mathsf{M_c}$ and Sim for showing the linearity property and the simulatability property, respectively (right).

We remark that although a sketch $\mathbf{c} = \mathsf{Sketch}(\Lambda, s, \mathbf{x})$ leaks some information of $\mathbf{x}$ (in particular, it leaks $w_i x_i \bmod 1$ for every $i \in [n]$) even if $s \in \mathbb{Z}_W$ is chosen uniformly at random, it does not affect the EUF-CMA security of our fuzzy signature scheme.

Lemma 2. *The linear sketch scheme $\mathcal{S}$ in Fig. 5 (left) satisfies Definition 5.*

Proof of Lemma 2. Correctness follows from the properties of the functions $\mathsf{CRT_w}$, $\mathsf{E_w}$, and $\mathsf{C_w}$. Specifically, let $\mathbf{x}, \mathbf{x'} \in X$ be such that $d(\mathbf{x}, \mathbf{x'}) = \|\mathbf{x} - \mathbf{x'}\|_\infty < t$. Let $s, \Delta s \in \mathbb{Z}_W$, and let $\mathbf{s} = \mathsf{CRT_w^{-1}}(s)$ and $\Delta \mathbf{s} = \mathsf{CRT_w^{-1}}(\Delta s)$. Furthermore, let $\mathbf{c} = \mathsf{Sketch}(\Lambda, s, \mathbf{x}) = (\mathbf{s} + \mathsf{E_w}(\mathbf{x})) \bmod \mathbf{w}$ and $\mathbf{c'} = \mathsf{Sketch}(\Lambda, s + \Delta s, \mathbf{x'}) = (\mathbf{s} + \Delta \mathbf{s} + \mathsf{E_w}(\mathbf{x'})) \bmod \mathbf{w}$. Then, we have

$$\mathsf{C_w}(\mathbf{c} - \mathbf{c'}) = \mathsf{C_w}\Big(\mathbf{s} + \mathsf{E_w}(\mathbf{x}) - (\mathbf{s} + \Delta \mathbf{s} + \mathsf{E_w}(\mathbf{x'}))\Big)$$
$$\overset{(*)}{=} \Delta \mathbf{s} + \mathsf{C_w}\Big(\mathsf{E_w}(\mathbf{x}) - \mathsf{E_w}(\mathbf{x'})\Big) \overset{(\dagger)}{=} \Delta \mathbf{s},$$

where $(*)$ is due to Eq. (15) (we omit to write "mod $\mathbf{w}$"), and $(\dagger)$ is due to Eq. (14) and $\|\mathbf{x} - \mathbf{x'}\|_\infty < t$. Thus, $\mathsf{DiffRec}(\Lambda, \mathsf{Sketch}(\Lambda, s, \mathbf{x}), \mathsf{Sketch}(\Lambda, s + \Delta s, \mathbf{x'})) = \mathsf{CRT_w}(\mathsf{C_w}(\mathbf{c} - \mathbf{c'})) = \mathsf{CRT_w}(\Delta \mathbf{s}) = \Delta s$, satisfying Eq. (5).

Regarding linearity, we consider the algorithm $\mathsf{M_c}$ as described in Fig. 5 (upper-right). To see that $\mathsf{M_c}$ satisfies linearity, let $\mathbf{x}, \mathbf{e} \in \mathbb{R}_\mathbf{w}^n$ and $s, \Delta s \in \mathbb{Z}_W$, and let $\mathbf{s} = \mathsf{CRT_w^{-1}}(s)$ and $\Delta \mathbf{s} = \mathsf{CRT_w^{-1}}(\Delta s)$. Then, note that $\mathsf{Sketch}(\Lambda, s, \mathbf{x}) = (\mathbf{s} + \mathsf{E_w}(\mathbf{x})) \bmod \mathbf{w}$ and $\mathsf{CRT_w^{-1}}(s + \Delta s) = (\mathbf{s} + \Delta \mathbf{s}) \bmod \mathbf{w}$. Thus, it holds that

$$\mathsf{M_c}(\Lambda, \mathsf{Sketch}(\Lambda, s, \mathbf{x}), \Delta s, \mathbf{e}) = \Big(\mathbf{s} + \mathsf{E_w}(\mathbf{x}) + \Delta \mathbf{s} + \mathsf{E_w}(\mathbf{e})\Big) \bmod \mathbf{w}$$
$$= \Big(\mathbf{s} + \Delta \mathbf{s} + \mathsf{E_w}(\mathbf{x} + \mathbf{e})\Big) \bmod \mathbf{w} = \mathsf{Sketch}(\Lambda, s + \Delta s, \mathbf{x} + \mathbf{e}),$$

satisfying Eq. (6).

Regarding simulatability, note that by our requirement that $\mathcal{X}$ is the uniform distribution over $[0,1)^n$, if $\mathbf{x} \leftarrow_R \mathcal{X}$, then the output of $\mathsf{Sketch}(\Lambda, s, \mathbf{x})$ is uniformly distributed over $\mathbb{R}_\mathbf{w}^n$, no matter what $s \in \mathbb{Z}_W$ is. Therefore, the probabilistic algorithm $\mathsf{Sim}(\Lambda)$ described in Fig. 5 (bottom-right) that outputs a uniformly distributed value $\mathbf{c}$ over $\mathbb{R}_\mathbf{w}^n$ satisfies the simulatability. This completes the proof of Lemma 2. $\qquad\square$

5.4   Modified Waters Signature Scheme

Here, we show a variant of the Waters signature [22], which we call the *modified Waters signature* (MWS) scheme Σ_{MWS}.

Specific Bilinear Group Generator $\mathsf{BGGen_{MWS}}$. In the MWS scheme, we use a (slightly) non-standard way for specifying bilinear groups, namely, the order p of (symmetric) bilinear groups is generated based on an integer $W = \prod_{i \in [n]} w_i$, where $\mathbf{w} = (w_1, \ldots, w_n) \in \mathbb{Z}^n$ satisfies the conditions in Eq. (10), so that p is the smallest prime satisfying $W | p - 1$. More concretely, we consider the following algorithm PGen for choosing p from W: On input $W \in \mathbb{N}$, for $i = 1, 2, \ldots$ check if $p = iW + 1$ is a prime and return p if this is the case. Otherwise, increment $i \leftarrow i + 1$ and go to the next iteration.

According to the prime number theorem, the density of primes among the natural numbers that are less than N is roughly $1/\ln N$, and thus, for i's that are exponentially smaller than W, the probability that $iW + 1$ is a prime can be roughly estimated as $1/\ln W$. Therefore, by using the above algorithm PGen, one can find a prime p satisfying $W | p - 1$ by performing the primality testing for $O(\ln W) = O(k)$ times on average (recall that $W = \Theta(2^k)$). Furthermore, if $\mathsf{PGen}(W)$ outputs p, then it is guaranteed that $p/W = O(k)$. (This fact is used for security).

Let $\mathsf{BGGen_{MWS}}$ denote an algorithm that, given 1^k, runs $\mathbf{w} \leftarrow \mathsf{WGen}(t, n)$ where t and n are the parameters from the fuzzy data setting $\mathcal{F}$ corresponding the security parameter k, computes $W \leftarrow \prod_{i \in [n]} w_i$, $p \leftarrow \mathsf{PGen}(W)$, and outputs a description of bilinear groups $\mathcal{BG} = (p, \mathbb{G}, \mathbb{G}_T, g, e)$, where $\mathbb{G}$ and $\mathbb{G}_T$ are cyclic groups with order p and $e : \mathbb{G} \times \mathbb{G} \to \mathbb{G}_T$ is a bilinear map.

Construction. Using $\mathsf{BGGen_{MWS}}$ and the algorithms in the original Waters signature scheme Σ_{Wat} (see Fig. 3), the MWS scheme $\Sigma_{\mathsf{MWS}} = (\mathsf{Setup_{MWS}}, \mathsf{KG_{MWS}}, \mathsf{Sign_{MWS}}, \mathsf{Ver_{MWS}})$ is constructed as in Fig. 6 (left). Note that the component pp_{Wat} in a public parameter pp (generated by $\mathsf{Setup_{MWS}}$) is distributed identically to that generated in the original Waters scheme Σ_{Wat} in which the bilinear group generator $\mathsf{BGGen_{MWS}}$ is used. Therefore, Σ_{MWS} can be viewed as the original Waters scheme Σ_{Wat}, except that (1) we specify how to generate the parameter of bilinear groups by $\mathsf{BGGen_{MWS}}$, and (2) we use a secret key sk' (for the Waters scheme) of the form $sk' = z^{sk} \bmod p$, thereby we change the signing key space from $\mathbb{Z}_p$ to $\mathbb{Z}_W$.

In the following, we show that Σ_{MWS} satisfies EUF-CMA security (based on the CDH assumption with respect to $\mathsf{BGGen_{MWS}}$) and the homomorphic property (Definition 3), and thus can be used as the underlying signature scheme for our generic construction of a fuzzy signature scheme. (One might suspect the plausibility of the CDH assumption with respect to $\mathsf{BGGen_{MWS}}$ due to our specific choice of p. We discuss it in Appendix C.)

Lemma 3. *If the CDH assumption holds with respect to* $\mathsf{BGGen_{MWS}}$, *then the MWS scheme* Σ_{MWS} *is* EUF-CMA *secure.*

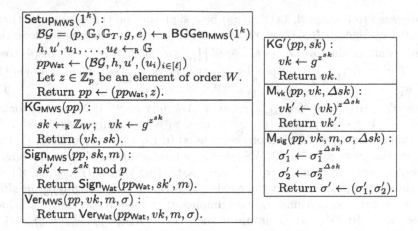

Fig. 6. The modified Waters signature (MWS) scheme Σ_{MWS} (left), and the auxiliary algorithms (KG', $\mathsf{M_{vk}}$, $\mathsf{M_{sig}}$) for showing the homomorphic property (right).

Proof of Lemma 3.   Let $pp = (pp_{\mathsf{Wat}}, z)$ be a public parameter output by $\mathsf{Setup_{MWS}}$, let $D_{pp}^{(1)} = \{sk \leftarrow_{\mathsf{R}} \mathbb{Z}_W; sk' \leftarrow z^{sk} \bmod p : sk'\}$ and $D_{pp}^{(2)} = \{sk' \leftarrow_{\mathsf{R}} \mathbb{Z}_p : sk'\}$. Note that the support of $D_{pp}^{(1)}$ is a strict subset of that of $D_{pp}^{(2)}$.

Now, let $\mathcal{A}$ be any PPTA that attacks the EUF-CMA security of the MWS scheme. Let Expt_1 be the original EUF-CMA experiment, i.e. $\mathsf{Expt}_{\Sigma_{\mathsf{MWS}}, \mathcal{A}}^{\mathsf{EUF\text{-}CMA}}(k)$, and let Expt_2 be the experiment that is defined in the same manner as Expt_1, except that sk' is sampled according to the distribution $D_{pp}^{(2)}$. For both $i \in \{1, 2\}$, let Adv_i be the advantage of $\mathcal{A}$ (i.e. the probability of $\mathcal{A}$ outputting a successful forgery) in Expt_i. Then, by Lemma 1, we have $\mathsf{Adv}_1 \leq (p/W) \cdot \mathsf{Adv}_2 = O(k) \cdot \mathsf{Adv}_2$. Furthermore, it is straightforward to see that succeeding in forging in Expt_2 is as difficult as succeeding in breaking the EUF-CMA security of the original Waters scheme Σ_{Wat} (in which the bilinear group generator $\mathsf{BGGen_{MWS}}$ is used), and thus Adv_2 is negligible if Σ_{Wat} is EUF-CMA secure.

Finally, due to Waters [22], if the CDH assumption holds with respect to $\mathsf{BGGen_{MWS}}$, then the Waters scheme Σ_{Wat} (in which $\mathsf{BGGen_{MWS}}$ is used,) is EUF-CMA secure. Combining all the explanations proves the lemma.   □

Lemma 4. *The MWS scheme Σ_{MWS} is homomorphic (as per Definition 3).*

Proof of Lemma 4.   Consider the algorithms (KG', $\mathsf{M_{vk}}$, $\mathsf{M_{sig}}$) that are described in Fig. 6 (right). It is easy to see that using KG', $\mathsf{KG_{MWS}}$ can be rewritten with the process in Eq. (1), where the secret key space is $\mathbb{Z}_W$.

Moreover, it should also be easy to see that $\mathsf{M_{vk}}$ satisfies the requirement in Eq. (2). Indeed, let $pp = (pp_{\mathsf{Wat}}, z)$ be a public parameter, and let $sk, \Delta sk \in \mathbb{Z}_W$. Then, it holds that $\mathsf{M_{vk}}(pp, \mathsf{KG}'(pp, sk), \Delta sk) = (g^{z^{sk}})^{z^{\Delta sk}} = g^{z^{sk + \Delta sk}} = \mathsf{KG}'(pp, sk + \Delta sk)$, satisfying Eq. (2).

Finally, we observe that $\mathsf{M_{sig}}$ satisfies the requirements in Eqs. (3) and (4). Let $pp = (pp_{\mathsf{Wat}}, z)$ and $sk, \Delta sk \in \mathbb{Z}_W$ as above, and $m = (m_1 \| \ldots \| m_\ell) \in \{0, 1\}^\ell$

be a message to be signed. Let (σ_1, σ_2) be a signature on the message m that is generated by $\mathsf{Sign}_{\mathsf{MWS}}(pp, sk, m; r)$, where $r \in \mathbb{Z}_p$ is a randomness. By definition, σ_1 and σ_2 are of the form $\sigma_1 = h^{z^{sk}} \cdot (u' \prod_{i \in [\ell]} u_i^{m_i})^r$ and $\sigma_2 = g^r$, respectively. Thus, if $\sigma' = (\sigma_1', \sigma_2')$ is output by $\mathsf{M}_{\mathsf{sig}}(pp, vk, m, \sigma, \Delta sk)$, then it holds that $\sigma_1' = \sigma_1^{z^{\Delta sk}} = h^{z^{sk + \Delta sk}} \cdot (u' \prod_{i \in [\ell]} u_i^{m_i})^{r \cdot z^{\Delta sk}}$, and $\sigma_2' = \sigma_2^{z^{\Delta sk}} = g^{r \cdot z^{\Delta sk}}$. This implies $\sigma' = (\sigma_1', \sigma_2') = \mathsf{Sign}_{\mathsf{MWS}}(pp, sk + \Delta sk, m; r \cdot z^{\Delta sk})$. Note that for any $\Delta sk \in \mathbb{Z}_W$, if $r \leftarrow_{\mathsf{R}} \mathbb{Z}_p$, then $((r \cdot z^{\Delta sk}) \bmod p)$ is uniformly distributed in $\mathbb{Z}_p$. This implies that the distributions considered in Eq. (3) are identical. Furthermore, by the property of the MWS scheme (which is inherited from the original Waters scheme), any signature $\sigma' = (\sigma_1', \sigma_2')$ satisfying $\mathsf{Ver}_{\mathsf{MWS}}(pp, vk, m, \sigma') = \top$ must satisfy the property that there exists $r' \in \mathbb{Z}_p$ such that $\mathsf{Sign}_{\mathsf{MWS}}(pp, sk, m; r') = \sigma'$. Putting everything together implies that for any $sk, \Delta sk \in \mathbb{Z}_W$, any message $m \in \{0,1\}^\ell$, any signature σ such that $\mathsf{Ver}_{\mathsf{MWS}}(pp, vk, m, \sigma) = \top$, if $vk = \mathsf{KG}'(pp, sk)$, $vk' = \mathsf{M}_{\mathsf{vk}}(pp, vk, \Delta sk)$, and $\sigma' = \mathsf{M}_{\mathsf{sig}}(pp, vk, m, \sigma, \Delta sk)$, then it holds that $\mathsf{Ver}_{\mathsf{MWS}}(pp, vk', m, \sigma') = \top$. Therefore, the requirement regarding Eq. (4) is satisfied as well. This completes the proof of Lemma 4.   □

6   Towards Public Biometric Infrastructure

As one of the promising applications of our fuzzy signature scheme Σ_{FS}, we discuss how it can be used to realize a biometric-based PKI that we call the *public biometric infrastructure (PBI)*.

The PBI is a biometric-based PKI that allows to use biometric data itself as a private key. Since it does not require a helper string to extract a private key, it does not require users to carry a dedicated device that stores it. Like the PKI, it provides the following functionalities: (1) registration, (2) digital signature, (3) authentication, and (4) cryptographic communication. At the time of registration, a user presents his/her biometric data x, from which the public key pk is generated. A certificate authority (CA) issues a public key certificate to ensure the link between pk and the user's identify (in the same way as the PKI). It must be sufficiently hard to restore x or estimate any "acceptable" biometric feature (i.e. biometric feature $\tilde{x}$ that is sufficiently close to x) from pk. This requirement is often referred to as *irreversibility* [8,19]. Note that the irreversibility is clearly included in the unforgeability, since the adversary who obtains x or $\tilde{x}$ can forge a signature σ for any message m. Since our fuzzy signature scheme Σ_{FS} is EUF-CMA secure, it also satisfies the irreversibility.

It is well-known that a digital signature scheme can be used to realize authentication and cryptographic communication, as standardized in [9]. Firstly, a challenge-response authentication protocol can be constructed based on a digital signature scheme (refer to [18] for details). Secondly, an authenticated key exchange (AKE) protocol can also be constructed based on a digital signature scheme and Diffie-Hellman Key Exchange protocol. In the same way, we can construct an authentication protocol and a cryptographic communication protocol in the PBI using our fuzzy signature scheme Σ_{FS}.

Remaining Challenges and Future Work. In Sect. 5, we showed an EUF-CMA secure FS scheme Σ_{FS}. However, we proved this under the assumption that a noisy string is uniform and has enough entropy. Thus, when using a biometric feature as a noisy string in Σ_{FS}, its EUF-CMA security is, for now, guaranteed only in the case where a biometric feature is uniform and has enough entropy.

A well-known approach to measure the biometric entropy is Daugman's *discrimination entropy* [2]. He considered a distribution of a Hamming distance m between two iriscodes (well-known iris features [3]) that are extracted from two different irises, and showed that it can be quite well approximated using the binomial distribution $B(n, p)$, where $n = 249$ and $p = 0.5$. He referred to the parameter n (= 249) as a discrimination entropy. The probability that two different iriscodes exactly match can be approximated to be 2^{-249}. However, it does not mean that a fuzzy signature scheme using the iriscode x is as secure as an ordinary signature scheme with a 249-bit private key, since the adversary does not have to estimate the original iriscode x, but only has to estimate an iriscode $\tilde{x}$ that is sufficiently close to x.

If a single biometric feature does not have enough entropy, we can use a multibiometric fusion scheme [16] that combines multiple sources of biometric information (e.g. fingerprint, face, and iris; left iris and right iris) to increase entropy. A multibiometric sensor that simultaneously acquires multiple biometrics (e.g. iris and face [1]; fingerprint and finger-vein [15]) has also been widely developed in recent years. Thus, we consider that using multiple biometrics is one possible direction to increase entropy without affecting usability.

Also, a biometric feature is non-uniform in general. The relation between the security in the uniform key setting (ideal model) and the one in the non-uniform key setting (real model) has been studied in several works in cryptography, e.g. [5]. As future work, we plan to prove the security of our fuzzy signature scheme in the non-uniform case, by applying (or extending) the techniques from them.

Acknowledgement. The authors would like to thank the anonymous reviewers of ACNS 2015 for their invaluable comments and suggestions.

A   More on the Limitations of Fuzzy-Extractor-Based Approaches

The right of Fig. 1 shows an example of a digital signature system using the fuzzy extractor. Assume that the client generates a signature on a message, and the server verifies it. At the time of registration, a signing key sk and a helper string P are generated from a noisy string (e.g. biometric feature) x, and a verification key vk corresponding to sk is generated and stored in a server-side DB. At the time of signing, the client generates a signature σ on a message m using P and another noisy string x', and sends σ to the server. The server verifies whether σ is a valid signature on m under vk. If x' is close to x, it outputs "⊤" (valid). Otherwise, it outputs "⊥" (invalid). The important point here is that the helper string P has to be stored in some place so that the client can retrieve it at the time of signing.

There are three possible models for storing the helper string: Store-on-Token (SOT), Store-on-Client (SOC), and Store-on-Server (SOS). In the SOT, the helper string is stored in a hardware token (e.g. smart card, USB token). Since this model requires each user to possess a token, it reduces usability. In the SOC, the helper string is stored in a client device. Although this model can be applied to the applications where each user has his/her own client device, it cannot be employed if the client device is shared by general public (e.g. bank ATM, POS, and kiosk terminal). In the SOS, the helper string is stored in a server-side DB, and the client queries for the helper string to the server at the time of signing. However, it cannot be used in an offline environment (i.e. a user generates a signature, which is sent to the server later, offline).

To sum up, the SOT reduces usability, and the SOC/SOS limit the client environment. Although a digital signature scheme using biometrics is proposed in [10,11] and an extended version of the PKI based on biometrics is discussed in [17], all of them require additional data like the helper string and suffer from this kind of problem.

B   Full Description of the Proposed Fuzzy Signature Scheme

Let $\ell = \ell(k)$ be a positive polynomial that denotes the length of messages. Let $\mathcal{F} = ((\mathsf{d}, X), t, \mathcal{X}, \Phi, \epsilon)$ be the fuzzy key setting defined in Sect. 5.1, where t (and n) are determined according to the security patameter k. Let $\mathsf{BGGen_{MWS}}$ be the bilinear group generator defined in Sect. 5.4. Then, our proposed fuzzy signature scheme $\Sigma_{\mathsf{FS}} = (\mathsf{Setup_{FS}}, \mathsf{KG_{FS}}, \mathsf{Sign_{FS}}, \mathsf{Ver_{FS}})$ for the fuzzy key setting $\mathcal{F}$ is constructed as in Fig. 7.

It should be straightforward to see that Σ_{FS} is a straightforward combination of the linear sketch scheme $\mathcal{S}$ for $\mathcal{F}$ shown in Sect. 5.3 and the MWS scheme Σ_{MWS} shown in Sect. 5.4.

C   On the Plausibility of the CDH Assumption with Respect to $\mathsf{BGGen_{MWS}}$

For the security of the MWS scheme Σ_{MWS} constructed in Sect. 5.4, we need to assume that the CDH assumption holds with respect to $\mathsf{BGGen_{MWS}}$. One might suspect the plausibility of this assumption because of our specific choice of the order p. However, to the best of our knowledge, there is no effective attack on the discrete logarithm assumption in the groups $\mathbb{G}$ and $\mathbb{G}_T$, let alone the CDH assumption.

Actually, the discrete logarithm problem for the multiplicative group $(\mathbb{Z}_p^*, \cdot)$ is easy because $W | p - 1$ and $W = \prod_{i \in [n]} w_i$, and thus we can apply the Pohlig-Hellman algorithm [13] to reduce an instance of the discrete logarithm problem

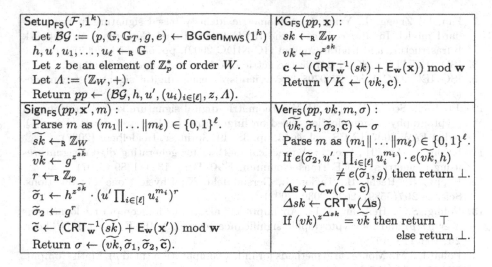

Fig. 7. The full description of the proposed fuzzy signature scheme Σ_{FS}.

in $\mathbb{Z}_p^*$ to instances of the discrete logarithm problems in $\mathbb{Z}_{w_i}$. *However, it does not mean that the Pohlig-Hellman algorithm is applicable to the discrete logarithm problem in* $\mathbb{G}$ *or* $\mathbb{G}_T$, *whose order is a prime.*

Note that a verification/signing key pair (vk, sk) of the MWS scheme Σ_{MWS} is of the following form $(vk, sk) = (g^{z^{sk}}, sk)$, where $sk \leftarrow_{\mathsf{R}} \mathbb{Z}_W$, and z and W are in a public parameter pp. In fact, due to the existence of the bilinear map $e : \mathbb{G} \times \mathbb{G} \to \mathbb{G}_T$, a variant of Pollard' ρ-algorithm [14] is applicable, and one can recover sk from vk (and pp) with $O(\sqrt{W})$ steps. However, this is exponential time in a security parameter k. (Recall that $W = \Theta(2^k)$.) This also does not contradict the EUF-CMA security of the MWS scheme shown in Lemma 3.

References

1. Connaughton, R., Bowyer, K.W., Flynn, P.J.: Fusion of face and iris biometrics. In: Burge, M.J., Bowyer, K.W. (eds.) Handbook of Iris Recognition, pp. 219–237. Springer, London (2013). Chap. 12
2. Daugman, J.: The importance of being random: statistical principles of iris recognition. Pattern Recogn. **36**(2), 279–291 (2003)
3. Daugman, J.: How iris recognition works. IEEE Trans. Circuits Syst. Video Technol. **14**, 21–30 (2004)
4. Dodis, Y., Reyzin, L., Smith, A.: Fuzzy extractors: how to generate strong keys from biometrics and other noisy data. In: Cachin, C., Camenisch, J.L. (eds.) EUROCRYPT 2004. LNCS, vol. 3027, pp. 523–540. Springer, Heidelberg (2004)
5. Dodis, Y., Yu, Y.: Overcoming weak expectations. In: Sahai, A. (ed.) TCC 2013. LNCS, vol. 7785, pp. 1–22. Springer, Heidelberg (2013)
6. Ellison, C., Schneier, B.: Ten risks of PKI: what you're not being told about public key infrastructure. Comput. Secur. J. **16**(1), 1–7 (2000)

7. Fan, L., Zheng, J., Yang, J.: A biometric identity based signature in the standard model. In: Proceedings of the IEEE International Conference on Network Infrastructure and Digital Content (IC-NIDC 2009). pp. 552–556 (2009)
8. ISO/IEC JTC 1/SC 27 24745: Biometric information protection (2011)
9. ISO/IEC JTC 1/SC 27 9798-3: Mechanisms using digital signature techniques (1998)
10. Jo, J.-G., Seo, J.-W., Lee, H.-W.: Biometric digital signature key generation and cryptography communication based on fingerprint. In: Preparata, F.P., Fang, Q. (eds.) FAW 2007. LNCS, vol. 4613, pp. 38–49. Springer, Heidelberg (2007)
11. Kwon, T., Lee, H., Lee, J.: A practical method for generating digital signatures using biometrics. IEICE Trans. Commun. **E90–B**(6), 1381–1389 (2007)
12. Pappu, R., Recht, B., Taylor, J., Gershenfeld, N.: Physical one-way functions. Science **297**(5589), 2026–2030 (2002)
13. Pohlig, S.C., Hellman, M.E.: An improved algorithm for computing logarithms over $gf(p)$ and its cryptographic significance (corresp.). IEEE Trans. Inf. Theor. **24**, 106–110 (1978)
14. Pollard, J.M.: Monte carlo methods for index computation (mod p). Math.Comput. **32**, 918–924 (1978)
15. Raghavendra, R., Raja, K.B., Surbiryala, J., Busch, C.: A low-cost multimodal biometric sensor to capture finger vein and fingerprint. In: Proceedings of 2014 IEEE the International Joint Conference on Biometrics (IJCB 2014), pp. 1–7 (2014)
16. Ross, A., Nandakumar, K., Jain, A.K.: Handbook of Multibiometrics. Springer, Heidelberg (2006)
17. Scheirer, W.J., Bishop, B., Boult, T.E.: Beyond pki: the biocryptographic key infrastructure. In: Proceedings of the 2010 IEEE International Workshop on Information Forensics and Security (WIFS 2010), pp. 1–6 (2010)
18. Schneier, B.: Applied Cryptography. Wiley, New York (1995)
19. Simoens, K., Yang, B., Zhou, X., Beato, F., Busch, C., Newton, E., Preneel, B.: Criteria towards metrics for benchmarking template protection algorithms. In: Proceedings of the 5th IAPR International Conference on Biometrics (ICB 2012) (2012)
20. Wang, C., Chen, W., Liu, Y.: A fuzzy identity based signature scheme. In: Proceedings of the International Conference on E-Business and Information System Security (EBISS 2009), pp. 1–5 (2009)
21. Wang, C., Kim, J.-H.: Two constructions of fuzzy identity based signature. In: Proceedings of the 2nd International Conference on Biomedical Engineering and Informatics (BMEI 2009), pp. 1–5 (2009)
22. Waters, B.: Efficient identity-based encryption without random oracles. In: Cramer, R. (ed.) EUROCRYPT 2005. LNCS, vol. 3494, pp. 114–127. Springer, Heidelberg (2005)
23. Wu, Q.: Fuzzy biometric identity-based signature in the standard model. J. Comput. Inf. Syst. **8**(20), 8405–8412 (2012)
24. Yang, P., Cao, Z., Dong, X.: Fuzzy identity based signature with applications to biometric authentication. Comput. Electr. Eng. **37**(4), 532–540 (2011)

Practical Ciphertext-Policy Attribute-Based Encryption: Traitor Tracing, Revocation, and Large Universe

Zhen Liu[1]([✉]) and Duncan S. Wong[2]

[1] City University of Hong Kong, Hong Kong SAR, China
zhenliu7-c@my.cityu.edu.hk
[2] Security and Data Sciences, ASTRI, Hong Kong SAR, China
duncanwong@astri.org

Abstract. In Ciphertext-Policy Attribute-Based Encryption (CP-ABE), a user's decryption key is associated with attributes which in general are not related to the user's identity, and the same set of attributes could be shared between multiple users. From the decryption key, if the user created a decryption blackbox for sale, this malicious user could be difficult to identify from the blackbox. Hence in practice, a useful CP-ABE scheme should have some tracing mechanism to identify this 'traitor' from the blackbox. In addition, being able to revoke compromised keys is also an important step towards practicality, and for scalability, the scheme should support an exponentially large number of attributes. However, none of the existing traceable CP-ABE schemes simultaneously supports revocation and large attribute universe. In this paper, we construct the first practical CP-ABE which possesses these three important properties: (1) blackbox traceability, (2) revocation, and (3) supporting large universe. This new scheme achieves the fully collusion-resistant blackbox traceability, and when compared with the latest fully collusion-resistant blackbox traceable CP-ABE schemes, this new scheme achieves the same efficiency level, enjoying the sub-linear overhead of $O(\sqrt{N})$, where N is the number of users in the system, and attains the same security level, namely, the fully collusion-resistant traceability against policy-specific decryption blackbox, which is proven in the standard model with selective adversaries. The scheme supports large attribute universe, and attributes do not need to be pre-specified during the system setup. In addition, the scheme supports revocation while keeping the appealing capability of conventional CP-ABE, i.e. it is highly expressive and can take any monotonic access structures as ciphertext policies.

Keywords: Attribute-based encryption · Ciphertext-policy · Traitor tracing · Revocation · Large attribute universe

1 Introduction

In some emerging applications such as user-side encrypted cloud storage, users may store encrypted data on a public untrusted cloud and let other users who

© Springer International Publishing Switzerland 2015
T. Malkin et al. (Eds.): ACNS 2015, LNCS 9092, pp. 127–146, 2015.
DOI: 10.1007/978-3-319-28166-7_7

have eligible credentials decrypt and access the data. The decryption credentials could be based on the users' roles and do not have to be their identities. For example, a user Alice wants to encrypt some documents, upload to the cloud, and let all PhD students and alumni in the Department of Mathematics download and decrypt. *Attribute-Based Encryption* (ABE), introduced by Sahai and Waters [25], provides a solution to this type of applications. In a Ciphertext-Policy ABE (CP-ABE) [2,10] scheme[1], each user possesses a set of attributes and a decryption key, the encrypting party can encrypt the documents using an access policy (e.g. a Boolean formula) on attributes, and a user can decrypt if and only if the user's attributes satisfy the policy. Hence in this example, Alice can encrypt the documents under "(Mathematics AND (PhD Student OR Alumni))", which is an access policy defined over descriptive *attributes*, so that only those receivers whose attributes satisfy this policy can decrypt.

Among the recently proposed CP-ABE schemes [2,6,9,11,14,15,21,26], one of the latest works is due to Lewko and Waters [15]. Their scheme achieves high expressivity (i.e. can take any monotonic access structures as ciphertext policies), and is provably secure against adaptive adversaries in the standard model. The scheme is also efficient and removes the one-use restriction that other comparable schemes have [14,21]. As of the current Public Key Infrastructure which mandates the capabilities of key generation, revocation, and certified binding between identities and public keys, before the CP-ABE being able to deploy in practice, we should provision a practical CP-ABE scheme with three important features: (1) traceability, (2) revocation, and (3) large universe. Very recently, a handful of research works have been done on each one of these while the fundamental open problem remains is the existence of an efficient scheme which supports these three features at once.

Traceability / Traitor Tracing. Access policies in CP-ABE do not have to contain any receivers' identities, and more commonly, a CP-ABE policy is role-based and attributes are *shared* between multiple users. In practice, a malicious user, with attributes shared with multiple other users, might leak a decryption blackbox/device, which is made of the user's decryption key, for the purpose of financial gain or some other forms of incentives, as the malicious user has little risk of being identified out of all the users who can build a decryption blackbox with identical decryption capability. Being able to identify this malicious user is crucial towards the practicality of a CP-ABE system.

Given a well-formed decryption key, if the *tracing algorithm* of a CP-ABE scheme can identify the malicious user who created the key, the scheme is called Whitebox Traceable CP-ABE [17]. Given a decryption blackbox, while the decryption key and even the decryption algorithm could be hidden inside the blackbox, if the *tracing algorithm* can still find out the traitor whose key has been used in constructing the blackbox, the scheme is called Blackbox Traceable CP-ABE [16]. In this stronger notion, there are two types of blackboxes: key-like decryption blackbox and policy-specific decryption blackbox. A key-like

---

[1] Due to page limitation, here we focus on CP-ABE, while skipping discussions about Key-Policy ABE.

decryption blackbox has an attribute set associated and can decrypt encrypted messages with policies being satisfied by the attribute set. A policy-specific decryption blackbox has a policy associated and can decrypt encrypted messages with the same policy. Liu et al. [18] formally proved that if a CP-ABE scheme is traceable against policy-specific decryption blackbox then it is also traceable against key-like decryption blackbox, and proved that the CP-ABE scheme in [16] is *fully collusion-resistant traceable* against policy-specific decryption blackbox in the standard model with selective adversaries. The scheme in [16] is highly expressive, and as a fully collusion-resistant blackbox traceable CP-ABE scheme, it achieves the most efficient level to date, i.e. the overhead for the fully collusion-resistant traceability is in $O(\sqrt{N})$, where N is the number of users in the system. Note that fully collusion-resistant traceability means that the number of colluding users in constructing a decryption blackbox is not limited and can be arbitrary. Another recent blackbox traceable CP-ABE scheme is due to Deng et al. [7], but the scheme is only *t-collusion-resistant* traceable, where the number of colluding users is limited, i.e., less than a parameter t, and the scheme's security is proven in the random oracle model.

Revocation. For any encryption systems that involve many users, private keys might get compromised, users might leave or be removed from the systems. When any of these happens, the corresponding user keys should be revoked. In the literature, several revocation mechanisms have been proposed in the context of CP-ABE. In [24][2], Sahai et al. proposed an *indirect* revocation mechanism, which requires an authority to periodically broadcast a key update information so that only the non-revoked users can update their keys and continue to decrypt messages. In [1], Attrapadung and Imai proposed a *direct* revocation mechanism, which allows a revocation list to be specified directly during encryption so that the resulting ciphertext cannot be decrypted by any decryption key which is in the revocation list even though the associated attribute set of the key satisfies the ciphertext policy. The direct revocation mechanism does not need any periodic key updates that an indirect revocation mechanism requires. It does not affect any non-revoked users either. In direct revocation, a system-wide revocation list could be made public and revocation could be taken into effect promptly as the revocation list could be updated immediately once a key is revoked. In this paper, we focus on achieving direct revocation in CP-ABE.

Large Attribute Universe. In most CP-ABE schemes, the size of the attribute universe is polynomially bounded in the security parameter, and the attributes have to be fixed during the system setup. In a large universe CP-ABE, the attribute universe can be exponentially large, any string can be used as an attribute, and attributes do not need to be pre-specified during setup. Although "somewhat" large universe CP-ABE schemes have been proposed or discussed previously [1,14,22,26], as explained by Rouselakis and Waters [23], limitations

---

[2] Note that in this paper we focus on the conventional revocation, which is to prevent a compromised or revoked user from decrypting newly encrypted messages. In [24], revoking access on previously encrypted data is also considered.

exist. The first "truly" large universe CP-ABE construction, in which there is no restriction on ciphertext policies or attributes associated with the decryption keys, was proposed in [23].

1.1 Our Results

We propose the first practical CP-ABE scheme that simultaneously supports (1) traceability against policy-specific decryption blackbox, (2) (direct) revocation and (3) "truly" large attribute universe. The scheme's traceability is fully collusion-resistant, that is, the number of colluding users in constructing a decryption blackbox is not limited and can be arbitrary. Furthermore, the traceability is public, that is, anyone can run the tracing algorithm. The scheme is also highly expressive that allows any monotonic access structures to be the ciphertext policies.

The scheme is proven selectively secure and traceable in the standard model. This is comparable to the policy-specific blackbox traceability of the fully collusion-resistant traceable CP-ABE [18] and also to the security of the "truly" large universe CP-ABE [23]. The selective security is indeed a weakness when compared with the full security of [15,16], but as discussed in [23], selective security is still a meaningful notion and can be a reasonable trade off for performance in some circumstances. Furthermore, in light of the proof method of [15] that achieves full security through selective techniques, we can see that developing selectively secure schemes could be an important stepping stone towards building fully secure ones.

Table 1 compares this new scheme with the representative results in conventional CP-ABE [15], blackbox traceable CP-ABE [16], and large universe CP-ABE [23], all of which are provably secure in the standard model and highly expressive. The scheme's overhead is in $O(\sqrt{N})$, where N is the number of users in a system, and for fully collusion-resistant blackbox traceable CP-ABE, this is the most efficient one to date. Furthermore, when compared with the existing fully collusion-resistant blackbox traceable CP-ABE scheme in [16], at the cost of $\sqrt{N}$ additional elements in private key, our construction achieves revocation and "truly" large universe. For achieving better performance, this new scheme is constructed on prime order groups, rather than composite order groups, as it has been showed (e.g. in [8,13]) that constructions on composite order groups will result in significant loss of efficiency.

Paper Outline. In Sect. 2, we propose a definition for CP-ABE supporting policy-specific blackbox traceability, direct revocation and large attribute universe. As of [16], the definition is 'functional', namely each decryption key is uniquely indexed by $k \in \{1, \ldots, N\}$ (N is the number of users in the system) and given a policy-specific decryption blackbox, the tracing algorithm Trace can return the index k of a decryption key which has been used for building the decryption blackbox. On direct revocation, in our definition, the Encrypt algorithm takes a revocation list $R \subseteq \{1, \ldots, N\}$ as an additional input so that a message encrypted under the (revocation list, access policy) pair $(R, \mathbb{A})$ would only allow

Table 1. Features and efficiency comparison

a / b	Blackbox traceability	Revocation	Large universe	Public key size	Ciphertext size	Private key size	Pairings in decryption
[15][c]	×	×	×	$14 + 6\|\mathcal{U}\|$	$7 + 6l$	$6 + 6\|S\|$	$9 + 6\|I\|$
[23]	×	×	$\checkmark$	6	$2 + 3l$	$2 + 2\|S\|$	$1 + 3\|I\|$
[16,18][d]	$\checkmark$	×	×	$3 + 4\sqrt{N} + \|\mathcal{U}\|$	$17\sqrt{N} + 2l$	$4 + \|S\|$	$10 + 2\|I\|$
this work	$\checkmark$	$\checkmark$	$\checkmark$	$5 + 5\sqrt{N}$	$16\sqrt{N} + 3l$	$2 + 2\|S\| + \sqrt{N}$	$9 + 3\|I\|$

[a] All the four schemes are provably secure in the standard model and highly expressive.
[b] Let N be the number of users in the system, $|\mathcal{U}|$ the size of the attribute universe, l the number of rows of the LSSS matrix for an access policy, $|S|$ the size of the attribute set of a decryption key, and $|I|$ the number of attributes for a decryption key to satisfy a ciphertext policy.
[c] The efficiency evaluation here is based on the prime order construction in the full version.
[d] The construction in [16,18] is on composite order groups where the group order is the product of three large primes, and the efficiency evaluation is based on the composite order groups.

users whose (index, attribute set) pair (k, S) satisfies $(k \notin R) \wedge (S \; satisfies \; \mathbb{A})$ to decrypt.

On the construction, we refer to the 'functional' CP-ABE in Sect. 2 as Revocable CP-ABE (R-CP-ABE), then extend the R-CP-ABE to a primitive called Augmented R-CP-ABE (AugR-CP-ABE), which will lastly be transformed to a policy-specific blackbox *traceable* R-CP-ABE. More specifically, in Sect. 3, we define the encryption algorithm of AugR-CP-ABE as $\mathsf{Encrypt}_A(\mathsf{PP}, M, R, \mathbb{A}, \bar{k})$ which takes one more parameter $\bar{k} \in \{1, \ldots, N+1\}$ than the original one in R-CP-ABE. This also changes the decryption criteria in AugR-CP-ABE in such a way that an encrypted message can be recovered using a decryption key $\mathsf{SK}_{k,S}$, which is identified by index $k \in \{1, \ldots, N\}$ and associated with an attribute set S, only if $(k \notin R) \wedge (S \; satisfies \; \mathbb{A}) \wedge (k \geq \bar{k})$. On the security, we formalize and show that a message-hiding and index-hiding AugR-CP-ABE can be transformed to a secure R-CP-ABE with policy-specific blackbox traceability.

In Sect. 4, we propose a *large universe* AugR-CP-ABE construction, and prove its message-hiding and index-hiding properties in the standard model. Combining it with the results in Sect. 3, we obtain a large universe R-CP-ABE construction, which is efficient (with overhead size in $O(\sqrt{N})$), highly expressive, and provably secure and traceable in the standard model.

To construct the AugR-CP-ABE, we borrow ideas from the CP-ABE constructions in [16,23] and Trace & Revoke scheme in [8]. However, the combination is not trivial and may result in inefficient or insecure systems. In particular, besides achieving the important features for practicality, such as traitor tracing, revocation, large universe, high expressivity and efficiency, we achieve provable security and traceability in the standard model. As we will discuss later in Sect. 4, proving the blackbox traceability while supporting the large attribute universe is one of the most challenging tasks in this work. As we can see, the proof techniques for blackbox traceability in [16] are no longer applicable for large universe, while that for large universe in [23] are only for confidentiality rather than for blackbox traceability.

2   Revocable CP-ABE and Blackbox Traceability

In this section, we define Revocable CP-ABE (or R-CP-ABE for short) and its security, which are based on conventional (non-traceable, non-revocable) CP-ABE (e.g. [15,23]). Similar to the traceable CP-ABE in [16], in our 'functional' definition, we explicitly assign and identify users using unique indices. Then we formalize traceability against policy-specific decryption blackbox on R-CP-ABE.

2.1   Revocable CP-ABE

Given a positive integer n, let $[n]$ be the set $\{1, 2, \ldots, n\}$. A Revocable CP-ABE (R-CP-ABE) scheme consists of four algorithms:

Setup(λ, N) $\to$ (PP, MSK). The algorithm takes as input a security parameter λ and the number of users in the system N, runs in polynomial time in λ, and outputs a public parameter PP and a master secret key MSK. We assume that PP contains the description of the attribute universe $\mathcal{U}^3$.

KeyGen(PP, MSK, S) $\to$ SK$_{k,S}$. The algorithm takes as input PP, MSK, and an attribute set S, and outputs a secret key SK$_{k,S}$ corresponding to S. The secret key is assigned and identified by a unique index $k \in [N]$.

Encrypt(PP, $M, R, \mathbb{A}$) $\to CT_{R,\mathbb{A}}$. The algorithm takes as input PP, a message M, a revocation list $R \subseteq [N]$, and an access policy $\mathbb{A}$ over $\mathcal{U}$, and outputs a ciphertext $CT_{R,\mathbb{A}}$. $(R, \mathbb{A})$ is included in $CT_{R,\mathbb{A}}$.

Decrypt(PP, $CT_{R,\mathbb{A}}$, SK$_{k,S}$) $\to M$ or $\perp$. The algorithm takes as input PP, a ciphertext $CT_{R,\mathbb{A}}$, and a secret key SK$_{k,S}$. If $(k \in [N] \setminus R)$ AND (S satisfies $\mathbb{A}$), the algorithm outputs a message M, otherwise it outputs $\perp$ indicating the failure of decryption.

Correctness. For any attribute set $S \subseteq \mathcal{U}$, index $k \in [N]$, revocation list $R \subseteq [N]$, access policy $\mathbb{A}$, and message M, suppose (PP, MSK) $\leftarrow$ Setup(λ, N), SK$_{k,S}$ $\leftarrow$ KeyGen(PP, MSK, S), $CT_{R,\mathbb{A}} \leftarrow$ Encrypt(PP, $M, R, \mathbb{A}$). If $(k \in [N] \setminus R) \wedge$ (S satisfies $\mathbb{A}$) then Decrypt(PP, $CT_{R,\mathbb{A}}$, SK$_{k,S}$) $= M$.

Security. The security of the R-CP-ABE is defined using the following message-hiding game, which is a typical semantic security game and is similar to that for conventional CP-ABE [15,23] security.

Game$_{MH}$. The message-hiding game is defined between a challenger and an adversary $\mathcal{A}$ as follows:

Setup. The challenger runs Setup(λ, N) and gives the public parameter PP to $\mathcal{A}$.

---

[3] For large universe and also in our work, the attribute universe depends only on the size of the underlying group $\mathbb{G}$, which depends on λ and the group generation algorithm.

Phase 1. For $i = 1$ to Q_1, $\mathcal{A}$ adaptively submits (index, attribute set) pair (k_i, S_{k_i}) to ask for secret key for attribute set S_{k_i}. For each (k_i, S_{k_i}) pair, the challenger responds with a secret key $\mathsf{SK}_{k_i, S_{k_i}}$, which corresponds to attribute set S_{k_i} and has index k_i.

Challenge. $\mathcal{A}$ submits two equal-length messages M_0, M_1 and a (revocation list, access policy) pair $(R^*, \mathbb{A}^*)$. The challenger flips a random coin $b \in \{0, 1\}$, and sends $CT_{R^*, \mathbb{A}^*} \leftarrow \mathsf{Encrypt}(\mathsf{PP}, M_b, R^*, \mathbb{A}^*)$ to $\mathcal{A}$.

Phase 2. For $i = Q_1 + 1$ to Q, $\mathcal{A}$ adaptively submits (index, attribute set) pair (k_i, S_{k_i}) to ask for secret key for attribute set S_{k_i}. For each (k_i, S_{k_i}) pair, the challenger responds with a secret key $\mathsf{SK}_{k_i, S_{k_i}}$, which corresponds to attribute set S_{k_i} and has index k_i.

Guess. $\mathcal{A}$ outputs a guess $b' \in \{0, 1\}$ for b.

$\mathcal{A}$ wins the game if $b' = b$ under the **restriction** that none of the queried $\{(k_i, S_{k_i})\}_{i=1}^{Q}$ can satisfy $(k_i \in [N] \setminus R^*)$ AND $(S_{k_i} \; satisfies \; \mathbb{A}^*)$. The advantage of $\mathcal{A}$ is defined as $\mathsf{MHAdv}_{\mathcal{A}} = |\Pr[b' = b] - \frac{1}{2}|$.

Definition 1. *An N-user R-CP-ABE scheme is secure if for all probabilistic polynomial time (PPT) adversaries $\mathcal{A}$, $\mathsf{MHAdv}_{\mathcal{A}}$ is negligible in λ.*

We say that an N-user R-CP-ABE scheme is *selectively* secure if we add an **Init** stage before **Setup** where the adversary commits to the access policy $\mathbb{A}^*$.

Remark: (1) Although the KeyGen algorithm is responsible for determining/assigning the index of each user's secret key, to capture the security that an adversary can adaptively choose secret keys to corrupt, the above model allows $\mathcal{A}$ to specify the index when querying for a key, i.e., for $i = 1$ to Q, $\mathcal{A}$ submits pairs of (k_i, S_{k_i}) for secret keys with attribute sets corresponding to S_{k_i}, and the challenger will assign k_i to be the index of the corresponding secret key, where $Q \leq N$, $k_i \in [N]$, and $k_i \neq k_j \; \forall 1 \leq i \neq j \leq Q$ (this is to guarantee that each user/key can be *uniquely* identified by an index). (2) For $k_i \neq k_j$ we do not require $S_{k_i} \neq S_{k_j}$, i.e., different users/keys may have the same attribute set.

Remark: (1) The R-CP-ABE defined above extends the conventional definition for non-revocable CP-ABE [15,16,23], where the revocation list R is always empty. (2) When the revocation list R needs an update due to, for example, some secret keys being compromised or some users leaving the system, the updated R needs to be disseminated to encrypting parties. In practice, this can be done in a similar way to the certificate revocation list distribution in the existing Public Key Infrastructure, namely an authority may update R, and publish it together with the authority's signature generated on it. (3) From the view of the public, R is just a set of numbers (in $[N]$). These numbers (or indices) do not have to provide any information on the corresponding users, in fact, besides the authority who runs KeyGen, each user only knows his/her own index. Also, encrypting parties do not need to know the indices of any users in order to encrypt but only the access policies. Although associating a revocation list with a ciphertext might make the resulting CP-ABE look less purely attribute-based, it does not undermine the capability of CP-ABE, that is, enabling fine-grained access control on encrypted messages.

2.2 Blackbox Traceability

A policy-specific decryption blackbox $\mathcal{D}$ is described by a (revocation list, access policy) pair $(R_{\mathcal{D}}, \mathbb{A}_{\mathcal{D}})$ and a non-negligible probability value ϵ (i.e. $\epsilon = 1/f(\lambda)$ for some polynomial f), and this blackbox $\mathcal{D}$ can decrypt ciphertexts generated under $(R_{\mathcal{D}}, \mathbb{A}_{\mathcal{D}})$ with probability at least ϵ. Such a blackbox can reflect most practical scenarios, which include the key-like decryption blackbox for sale and decryption blackbox "found in the wild", which are discussed in [16,18]. In particular, once a blackbox is found being able to decrypt ciphertexts (regardless of how this is found, for example, an explicit description of the blackbox's decryption ability is given, or the law enforcement agency finds some clue), we can regard it as a policy-specific decryption blackbox with the corresponding (revocation list, access policy) pair (which is associated to the ciphertext).

We now define the tracing algorithm and traceability against policy-specific decryption blackbox.

$\mathsf{Trace}^{\mathcal{D}}(\mathsf{PP}, R_{\mathcal{D}}, \mathbb{A}_{\mathcal{D}}, \epsilon) \rightarrow \mathbb{K}_T \subseteq [N]$. Trace *is an oracle algorithm that interacts with a policy-specific decryption blackbox $\mathcal{D}$. By given the public parameter* PP, *a revocation list* $R_{\mathcal{D}}$, *an access policy* $\mathbb{A}_{\mathcal{D}}$, *and a probability value* ϵ, *the algorithm runs in time polynomial in* λ *and* $1/\epsilon$, *and outputs an index set* $\mathbb{K}_T \subseteq [N]$ *which identifies the set of malicious users. Note that* ϵ *has to be polynomially related to* λ, *i.e.* $\epsilon = 1/f(\lambda)$ *for some polynomial* f.

Traceability. The following tracing game captures the notion of **fully collusion-resistant traceability** against policy-specific decryption blackbox. In the game, the adversary targets to build a decryption blackbox $\mathcal{D}$ that can decrypt ciphertexts under some (revocation list, access policy) pair $(R_{\mathcal{D}}, \mathbb{A}_{\mathcal{D}})$.

$\mathsf{Game_{TR}}$. The tracing game is defined between a challenger and an adversary $\mathcal{A}$ as follows:

Setup. The challenger runs $\mathsf{Setup}(\lambda, N)$ and gives the public parameter PP to $\mathcal{A}$.

Key Query. For $i = 1$ to Q, $\mathcal{A}$ adaptively submits (index, attribute set) pair (k_i, S_{k_i}) to ask for secret key for attribute set S_{k_i}. For each (k_i, S_{k_i}) pair, the challenger responds with a secret key $\mathsf{SK}_{k_i, S_{k_i}}$, which corresponds to attribute set S_{k_i} and has index k_i.

Decryption Blackbox Generation. $\mathcal{A}$ outputs a decryption blackbox $\mathcal{D}$ associated with a (revocation list, access policy) pair $(R_{\mathcal{D}}, \mathbb{A}_{\mathcal{D}})$ and a non-negligible probability value ϵ.

Tracing. The challenger runs $\mathsf{Trace}^{\mathcal{D}}(\mathsf{PP}, R_{\mathcal{D}}, \mathbb{A}_{\mathcal{D}}, \epsilon)$ to obtain an index set $\mathbb{K}_T \subseteq [N]$.

Let $\mathbb{K}_{\mathcal{D}} = \{k_i | 1 \leq i \leq Q\}$ be the index set of secret keys corrupted by the adversary. We say that $\mathcal{A}$ wins the game if the following two conditions hold:

1. $\Pr[\mathcal{D}(\mathsf{Encrypt}(\mathsf{PP}, M, R_\mathcal{D}, \mathbb{A}_\mathcal{D})) = M] \geq \epsilon$, where the probability is taken over the random choices of message M and the random coins of $\mathcal{D}$. A decryption blackbox satisfying this condition is said to be a *useful policy-specific decryption blackbox*.
2. $\mathbb{K}_T = \emptyset$, or $\mathbb{K}_T \not\subseteq \mathbb{K}_\mathcal{D}$, or $((k_t \in R_\mathcal{D})$ OR $(S_{k_t}$ *does not satisfy* $\mathbb{A}_\mathcal{D}) \forall k_t \in \mathbb{K}_T)$.

We denote by $\mathsf{TRAdv}_\mathcal{A}$ the probability that $\mathcal{A}$ wins.

Remark: For a useful policy-specific decryption blackbox $\mathcal{D}$, the traced $\mathbb{K}_T$ must satisfy $(\mathbb{K}_T \neq \emptyset) \wedge (\mathbb{K}_T \subseteq \mathbb{K}_\mathcal{D}) \wedge (\exists k_t \in \mathbb{K}_T \; s.t. \; (k_t \in [N]\backslash R_\mathcal{D})$ AND $(S_{k_t}$ *satisfies* $\mathbb{A}_\mathcal{D}))$ for traceability. (1) $(\mathbb{K}_T \neq \emptyset) \wedge (\mathbb{K}_T \subseteq \mathbb{K}_\mathcal{D})$ captures the preliminary traceability that the tracing algorithm can extract at least one malicious user and the coalition of malicious users cannot frame any innocent user. (2) $(\exists k_t \in \mathbb{K}_T \; s.t. \; (k_t \in [N] \backslash R_\mathcal{D})$ AND $(S_{k_t} \; satisfies \; \mathbb{A}_\mathcal{D}))$ captures the *strong traceability* that the tracing algorithm can extract at least one malicious user whose secret key enables $\mathcal{D}$ to have the decryption ability corresponding to $(R_\mathcal{D}, \mathbb{A}_\mathcal{D})$, i.e. whose index is not in $R_\mathcal{D}$ and whose attribute set satisfies $\mathbb{A}_\mathcal{D}$. We refer to [12,16] on why strong traceability is desirable.

Note that, as of [4,5,8,12,16], we are modeling a stateless (resettable) decryption blackbox – such a blackbox is just an oracle and maintains no state between activations. Also note that we are modeling public traceability, namely, the Trace algorithm does not need any secrets and anyone can perform the tracing.

Definition 2. *An N-user R-CP-ABE scheme is traceable against policy-specific decryption blackbox if for all PPT adversaries $\mathcal{A}$, $\mathsf{TRAdv}_\mathcal{A}$ is negligible in λ.*

We say that an N-user R-CP-ABE is *selectively* traceable against policy-specific decryption blackbox if we add an **Init** stage before **Setup** where the adversary commits to the access policy $\mathbb{A}_\mathcal{D}$.

In the traceable CP-ABE of [16], given a decryption blackbox, it is guaranteed that at least one secret key in the blackbox will be traced. But in the traceable R-CP-ABE above, it is possible to trace *all the active secret keys* in the blackbox. In particular, given a decryption blackbox $\mathcal{D}$ described by $(R_\mathcal{D}, \mathbb{A}_\mathcal{D})$ and non-negligible probability ϵ, we can run Trace to obtain an index set $\mathbb{K}_T$ so that $(\mathbb{K}_T \neq \emptyset) \wedge (\mathbb{K}_T \subseteq \mathbb{K}_\mathcal{D}) \wedge (\exists k_t \in \mathbb{K}_T \; s.t. \; (k_t \in [N]\backslash R_\mathcal{D})$ AND $(S_{k_t} \; satisfies \; \mathbb{A}_\mathcal{D}))$. Then, we can set a new revocation list $R'_\mathcal{D} = R_\mathcal{D} \cup \{k_t \in \mathbb{K}_T \mid (k_t \in [N] \backslash R_\mathcal{D})$ AND $(S_{k_t} \; satisfies \; \mathbb{A}_\mathcal{D})\}$ and test whether $\mathcal{D}$ can decrypt ciphertexts under $(R'_\mathcal{D}, \mathbb{A}_\mathcal{D})$. If $\mathcal{D}$ can still decrypt the ciphertexts with non-negligible probability ϵ', we can run Trace on $(R'_\mathcal{D}, \mathbb{A}_\mathcal{D}, \epsilon')$ and obtain a new index set $\mathbb{K}'_T$, where $(\mathbb{K}'_T \neq \emptyset) \wedge (\mathbb{K}'_T \subseteq \mathbb{K}_\mathcal{D}) \wedge (\exists k_t \in \mathbb{K}'_T \; s.t. \; (k_t \in [N]\backslash R'_\mathcal{D})$ AND $(S_{k_t} \; satisfies \; \mathbb{A}_\mathcal{D}))$. By repeating this process, iteratively expanding the revocation list, until $\mathcal{D}$ can no longer decrypt the corresponding ciphertexts, we have finished finding out *all the active* malicious users of $\mathcal{D}$.

3 Augmented R-CP-ABE

As outlined in Sect. 1.1, we now define Augmented R-CP-ABE (AugR-CP-ABE) from the R-CP-ABE above, and formalize its security notions, then show that a secure AugR-CP-ABE can be transformed to a secure R-CP-ABE with blackbox traceability. In Sect. 4, we propose a concrete construction of AugR-CP-ABE.

3.1 Definitions

An AugR-CP-ABE scheme has four algorithms: $\mathsf{Setup_A}$, $\mathsf{KeyGen_A}$, $\mathsf{Encrypt_A}$, and $\mathsf{Decrypt_A}$. The setup and key generation algorithms are the same as that of R-CP-ABE. For the encryption algorithm, it takes one more parameter $\bar{k} \in [N+1]$ as input, and is defined as follows.

$\mathsf{Encrypt_A}(\mathsf{PP}, M, R, \mathbb{A}, \bar{k}) \rightarrow CT_{R,\mathbb{A}}$. The algorithm takes as input PP, a message M, a revocation list $R \subseteq [N]$, an access policy $\mathbb{A}$, and an index $\bar{k} \in [N+1]$, and outputs a ciphertext $CT_{R,\mathbb{A}}$. $(R, \mathbb{A})$ **is included in** $CT_{R,\mathbb{A}}$, **but the value of** $\bar{k}$ **is not.**

The decryption algorithm is also defined in the same way as that of R-CP-ABE. However, the correctness definition is changed to the following.

Correctness. For any attribute set $S \subseteq \mathcal{U}$, index $k \in [N]$, revocation list $R \subseteq [N]$, access policy $\mathbb{A}$ over $\mathcal{U}$, encryption index $\bar{k} \in [N+1]$, and message M, suppose $(\mathsf{PP}, \mathsf{MSK}) \leftarrow \mathsf{Setup_A}(\lambda, N)$, $\mathsf{SK}_{k,S} \leftarrow \mathsf{KeyGen_A}(\mathsf{PP}, \mathsf{MSK}, S)$, $CT_{R,\mathbb{A}} \leftarrow \mathsf{Encrypt_A}(\mathsf{PP}, M, R, \mathbb{A}, \bar{k})$. If $(k \in [N] \setminus R) \wedge (S$ satisfies $\mathbb{A}) \wedge (k \geq \bar{k})$ then $\mathsf{Decrypt_A}(\mathsf{PP}, CT_{R,\mathbb{A}}, \mathsf{SK}_{k,S}) = M$.

Note that during decryption, as long as $(k \in [N] \setminus R) \wedge (S$ satisfies $\mathbb{A})$, the decryption algorithm outputs a message, but only when $k \geq \bar{k}$, the output message is equal to the correct message, that is, if and only if $(k \in [N] \setminus R) \wedge (S$ satisfies $\mathbb{A}) \wedge (k \geq \bar{k})$, can $\mathsf{SK}_{k,S}$ correctly decrypt a ciphertext under $(R, \mathbb{A}, \bar{k})$. If we always set $\bar{k} = 1$, the functions of AugR-CP-ABE are identical to that of R-CP-ABE. In fact, the idea behind transforming an AugR-CP-ABE to a traceable R-CP-ABE, that we will show shortly, is to construct an AugR-CP-ABE with index-hiding property, and then always sets $\bar{k} = 1$ in normal encryption, while using $\bar{k} \in [N+1]$ to generate ciphertexts for tracing.

Security. We define the security of AugR-CP-ABE in two games. The first game is a **message-hiding game** and says that a ciphertext created using index $N + 1$ is unreadable by anyone. The second game is an **index-hiding game** and captures the intuition that a ciphertext created using index $\bar{k}$ reveals no non-trivial information about $\bar{k}$.

$\mathsf{Game}_{\mathsf{MH}}^{\mathsf{A}}$. The **message-hiding game** $\mathsf{Game}_{\mathsf{MH}}^{\mathsf{A}}$ is similar to $\mathsf{Game}_{\mathsf{MH}}$ except that the **Challenge** phase is

Challenge. $\mathcal{A}$ submits two equal-length messages M_0, M_1 and a (revocation list, access policy) pair $(R^*, \mathbb{A}^*)$. The challenger flips a random coin $b \in \{0,1\}$, and sends $CT_{R^*, \mathbb{A}^*} \leftarrow \mathsf{Encrypt_A}(\mathsf{PP}, M_b, R^*, \mathbb{A}^*, N+1)$ to $\mathcal{A}$.

$\mathcal{A}$ wins the game if $b' = b$. The advantage of $\mathcal{A}$ is defined as $\mathsf{MH}^{\mathsf{A}}\mathsf{Adv}_{\mathcal{A}} = |\Pr[b' = b] - \frac{1}{2}|$.

Definition 3. *An N-user Augmented R-CP-ABE scheme is message-hiding if for all PPT adversaries $\mathcal{A}$ the advantage $\mathsf{MH^AAdv}_\mathcal{A}$ is negligible in λ.*

$\mathsf{Game}_{\mathsf{IH}}^{\mathsf{A}}$. In the **index-hiding game**, we require that, for any (revocation list, access policy) pair $(R^*, \mathbb{A}^*)$, an adversary cannot distinguish between a ciphertext under $(R^*, \mathbb{A}^*, \bar{k})$ and $(R^*, \mathbb{A}^*, \bar{k} + 1)$ without a secret key $\mathsf{SK}_{\bar{k}, S_{\bar{k}}}$ such that $(\bar{k} \in [N] \setminus R^*) \wedge (S_{\bar{k}} \text{ satisfies } \mathbb{A}^*)$. The game takes as input a parameter $\bar{k} \in [N]$ which is given to both the challenger and the adversary. The game is similar to $\mathsf{Game}_{\mathsf{MH}}$ except that the **Challenge** phase is

Challenge. $\mathcal{A}$ submits a message M and a (revocation list, access policy) pair $(R^*, \mathbb{A}^*)$. The challenger flips a random coin $b \in \{0, 1\}$, and sends $CT_{R^*, \mathbb{A}^*} \leftarrow \mathsf{Encrypt}_\mathsf{A}(\mathsf{PP}, M, R^*, \mathbb{A}^*, \bar{k} + b)$ to $\mathcal{A}$.

$\mathcal{A}$ wins the game if $b' = b$ under the **restriction** that none of the queried pairs $\{(k_i, S_{k_i})\}_{i=1}^Q$ can satisfy $(k_i = \bar{k}) \wedge (k_i \in [N] \setminus R^*) \wedge (S_{k_i} \text{ satisfies } \mathbb{A}^*)$. The advantage of $\mathcal{A}$ is defined as $\mathsf{IH^AAdv}_\mathcal{A}[\bar{k}] = |\Pr[b' = b] - \frac{1}{2}|$.

Definition 4. *An N-user Augmented R-CP-ABE scheme is index-hiding if for all PPT adversaries $\mathcal{A}$ the advantages $\mathsf{IH^AAdv}_\mathcal{A}[\bar{k}]$ for $\bar{k} = 1, \ldots, N$ are negligible in λ.*

We say that an Augmented R-CP-ABE scheme is *selectively* index-hiding if we add an **Init** stage before **Setup** where the adversary commits to the challenge access policy $\mathbb{A}^*$.

3.2 The Reduction of Traceable R-CP-ABE to Augmented R-CP-ABE

Let $\Sigma_\mathsf{A} = (\mathsf{Setup}_\mathsf{A}, \mathsf{KeyGen}_\mathsf{A}, \mathsf{Encrypt}_\mathsf{A}, \mathsf{Decrypt}_\mathsf{A})$ be an AugR-CP-ABE, define $\mathsf{Encrypt}(\mathsf{PP}, M, R, \mathbb{A}) = \mathsf{Encrypt}_\mathsf{A}(\mathsf{PP}, M, R, \mathbb{A}, 1)$, then $\Sigma = (\mathsf{Setup}_\mathsf{A}, \mathsf{KeyGen}_\mathsf{A}, \mathsf{Encrypt}, \mathsf{Decrypt}_\mathsf{A})$ is a R-CP-ABE derived from Σ_A. In the following, we show that if Σ_A is message-hiding and index-hiding, then Σ is secure (w.r.t. Definition 1). Furthermore, we propose a tracing algorithm Trace for Σ and show that if Σ_A is message-hiding and index-hiding, then Σ (equipped with Trace) is traceable (w.r.t. Definition 2).

Theorem 1. *If Σ_A is message-hiding and index-hiding (resp. selectively index-hiding), then Σ is secure (resp. selectively secure).*

Proof. Due to page limitation, the proof details are omitted here and can be found in the full version [19].

We now propose a tracing algorithm Trace, which uses a general tracing method previously used in [3–5,8,16,20], and show that equipped with Trace, Σ is traceable (w.r.t. Def. 2).

$\mathsf{Trace}^\mathcal{D}(\mathsf{PP}, R_\mathcal{D}, \mathbb{A}_\mathcal{D}, \epsilon) \to \mathbb{K}_T \subseteq [N]$: Given a policy-specific decryption blackbox $\mathcal{D}$ associated with a (revocation list, access policy) pair $(R_\mathcal{D}, \mathbb{A}_\mathcal{D})$ and probability $\epsilon > 0$, the tracing algorithm works as follows:

1. For $k = 1$ to $N + 1$, do the following:
    (a) Repeat the following $8\lambda(N/\epsilon)^2$ times:
        i Sample M from the message space at random.
        ii Let $CT_{R_{\mathcal{D}}, \mathbb{A}_{\mathcal{D}}} \leftarrow \mathsf{Encrypt}_{\mathsf{A}}(PP, M, R_{\mathcal{D}}, \mathbb{A}_{\mathcal{D}}, k)$.
        iii Query oracle $\mathcal{D}$ on input $CT_{R_{\mathcal{D}}, \mathbb{A}_{\mathcal{D}}}$, and compare the output of $\mathcal{D}$ with M.
    (b) Let $\hat{p}_k$ be the fraction of times that $\mathcal{D}$ decrypted the ciphertexts correctly.
2. Let $\mathbb{K}_T$ be the set of all $k \in [N]$ for which $\hat{p}_k - \hat{p}_{k+1} \geq \epsilon/(4N)$. Output $\mathbb{K}_T$.

Theorem 2. *If Σ_{A} is message-hiding and index-hiding (resp. selectively index-hiding), then Σ is traceable (resp. selectively traceable).*

Proof. Due to page limitation, the proof details are omitted here and can be found in the full version [19].

4   An Efficient Augmented R-CP-ABE

We propose an AugR-CP-ABE scheme which is highly expressive and efficient with sub-linear overhead in the number of users in the system. It is also *large universe*, where attributes do not need to be enumerated during setup, and the public parameter size is independent of the attribute universe size. We prove that this AugR-CP-ABE scheme is message-hiding and selectively index-hiding in the standard model.

Combining this AugR-CP-ABE with the results in Sect. 3.2, we obtain a large universe R-CP-ABE which is selectively secure and traceable, and for a fully collusion-resistant blackbox traceable CP-ABE, the resulting R-CP-ABE achieves the most efficient level to date, with sub-linear overhead.

To obtain this practical CP-ABE scheme supporting traitor tracing, revocation and large universe, we borrow ideas from the Blackbox Traceable CP-ABE of [16], the Trace and Revoke scheme of [8] and the Large Universe CP-ABE of [23], but the work is not trivial as a straightforward combination of the ideas would result in a scheme which is inefficient, insecure, or is not able to achieve strong traceability. Specifically, by incorporating the ideas from [8,23] into the Augmented CP-ABE of [16], we can obtain a large universe AugR-CP-ABE which is message-hiding, but proving the index-hiding property is a challenging task. The proof techniques for index-hiding in [16] only work if the attribute universe size is polynomial in the security parameter and the parameters of attributes have to be enumerated during setup. They are not applicable to large universe. The proof techniques in [23] are applicable to large universe, but work only for message-hiding, while not applicable to index-hiding. To prove index-hiding in the large universe setting, we introduce a new assumption that the index-hiding of our large universe AugR-CP-ABE can be based on. In particular, in the underlying q-1 assumption of [23] on bilinear groups $(p, \mathbb{G}, \mathbb{G}_T, e)$, the challenge term $T \in \mathbb{G}_T$ is $e(g, g)^{ca^{q+1}}$ or a random element, and such a term in the target group could be used to prove the message-hiding as the message space is $\mathbb{G}_T$. To prove the index-hiding, which is based on the ciphertext components in the source group $\mathbb{G}$, we need the challenge term to be in the source group $\mathbb{G}$ so that the simulator can embed the challenge term into these ciphertext components. Inspired by the Source Group q-Parallel BDHE Assumption in [15], which is a close relative to the (target group) Decisional Parallel BDHE Assumption in [26], we modify the q-1 assumption to its source group version where the challenge term is $g^{ca^{q+1}}$ or a random element in $\mathbb{G}$. Based on this new assumption and with a new crucial proof idea, we prove the index-hiding property for our large universe AugR-CP-ABE. We prove that this new assumption holds in the generic group model.

4.1 Preliminaries

Linear Secret-Sharing Schemes (LSSS). An LSSS is a share-generating matrix A whose rows labeled by attributes via a function ρ. An attribute set S satisfies the LSSS access matrix (A, ρ) if the rows labeled by the attributes in S have the *linear reconstruction* property, namely, there exist constants $\{\omega_i\}$ such that, for any valid shares $\{\lambda_i\}$ of a secret s, we have $\sum_i \omega_i \lambda_i = s$. The formal definitions of access structures and LSSS can be found in the full version [19].

Bilinear Groups. Let $\mathcal{G}$ be a group generator, which takes a security parameter λ and outputs $(p, \mathbb{G}, \mathbb{G}_T, e)$ where p is a prime, $\mathbb{G}$ and $\mathbb{G}_T$ are cyclic groups of order p, and $e : \mathbb{G} \times \mathbb{G} \to \mathbb{G}_T$ is a map such that: (1) (Bilinear) $\forall g, h \in \mathbb{G}, a, b \in \mathbb{Z}_p, e(g^a, h^b) = e(g, h)^{ab}$, (2) (Non-Degenerate) $\exists g \in \mathbb{G}$ such that $e(g, g)$ has order p in $\mathbb{G}_T$. We refer to $\mathbb{G}$ as the *source group* and $\mathbb{G}_T$ as the *target group*. We assume that group operations in $\mathbb{G}$ and $\mathbb{G}_T$ as well as the bilinear map e are efficiently computable, and the description of $\mathbb{G}$ and $\mathbb{G}_T$ includes a generator of $\mathbb{G}$ and $\mathbb{G}_T$ respectively.

Complexity Assumptions. Besides the Decision 3-Party Diffie-Hellman s Assumption (D3DH) and the Decisional Linear Assumption (DLIN) that are used in [8] to achieve traceability in broadcast encryption, the index-hiding property of our AugR-CP-ABE construction will rely on a new assumption, which is similar to the Source Group q-Parallel BDHE Assumption [15] and is closely related to the q-1 assumption in [23]. We refer to it as the Extended Source Group q-Parallel BDHE Assumption. Here we only review this new assumption, and refer to the full version [19] for the details of the D3DH and DLIN.

The Extended Source Group q-Parallel BDHE Assumption *Given a group generator $\mathcal{G}$ and a positive integer q, define the following distribution:*

$$(p, \mathbb{G}, \mathbb{G}_T, e) \xleftarrow{R} \mathcal{G}(\lambda), \quad g \xleftarrow{R} \mathbb{G}, \ a, c, d, b_1, \ldots, b_q \xleftarrow{R} \mathbb{Z}_p,$$

$$D = ((p, \mathbb{G}, \mathbb{G}_T, e), \ g, g^{cd}, g^d, g^{da^q},$$

$$g^{a^i}, \ g^{b_j}, \ g^{a^i b_j}, \ g^{a^i/b_j^2}, \ g^{cdb_j} \quad \forall i, j \in [q],$$

$$g^{a^i/b_j} \qquad \forall i \in [2q] \setminus \{q+1\}, j \in [q],$$

$$g^{a^i b_{j'}/b_j^2} \qquad \forall i \in [2q], j, j' \in [q] \ s.t. \ j' \neq j,$$

$$g^{cda^i b_{j'}/b_j}, g^{cda^i b_{j'}/b_j^2} \qquad \forall i \in [q], j, j' \in [q] \ s.t. \ j \neq j'),$$

$$T_0 = g^{ca^{q+1}}, T_1 \xleftarrow{R} \mathbb{G}.$$

The advantage of an algorithm $\mathcal{A}$ in breaking the Extended Source Group q-Parallel BDHE Assumption is $Adv_{\mathcal{G},\mathcal{A}}^{q}(\lambda) := |\Pr[\mathcal{A}(D, T_0) = 1] - \Pr[\mathcal{A}(D, T_1) = 1]|$.

Definition 5. $\mathcal{G}$ *satisfies the Extended Source Group q-Parallel BDHE Assumption if $Adv_{\mathcal{G},\mathcal{A}}^{q}(\lambda)$ is a negligible function of λ for any PPT algorithm $\mathcal{A}$.*

This new assumption is closely related to the q-1 assumption in [23], except that the challenge term $g^{ca^{q+1}}$ remains in the source group, all the input terms (in D) replace c with cd, and additional input terms g^d and g^{da^q} are given to the adversary. The relation between this assumption and the q-1 assumption is analogous to that between the Source Group q-Parallel BDHE Assumption [15] and the Decisional Parallel BDHE Assumption [26], i.e. the challenge term changes from a term in the target group (i.e. $e(g, g)^{ca^{q+1}}$) to a term in the source group (i.e. $g^{ca^{q+1}}$), and the input terms are modified accordingly (i.e. replacing c with cd, and adding g^d). The main difference is that in this new assumption, there is an additional input term g^{da^q}. Note that giving the term g^{da^q} does not pose any problem in the generic group model. Intuitively, there are two ways that the adversary may make use of the term g^{da^q}: (1) pairing g^{da^q} with the challenge term: since the pairing result of any two input terms would not be $e(g, g)^{cda^{2q+1}}$, the adversary cannot break this new assumption in this way; (2) pairing the challenge term with another input term whose exponent contains d: however, the result could be a random element or one of $\{ e(g, g)^{c^2 da^{q+1}}, e(g, g)^{cda^{q+1}}, e(g, g)^{c^2 db_j a^{q+1}}, e(g, g)^{c^2 da^{q+1+i} b_{j'}/b_j}, e(g, g)^{c^2 da^{q+1+i} b_{j'}/b_j^2}\}$, and as there is no input term which can be paired with g^{da^q} to obtain any of these terms, the adversary cannot break this new assumption by this way either. In the full version [19] we prove that this assumption holds in the generic group model. It is worth mentioning that Liu et al. [18] modified the Source Group q-Parallel BDHE Assumption [15] by adding g^{da^q} to and removing $g^{a^{q+2}}, \ldots, g^{a^{2q}}$ from the input terms.

Notations. Suppose that the number of users N in the system equals to m^2 for some m. In practice, if N is not a square, we can add some "dummy" users until it pads to the next square. We arrange the users in an $m \times m$ matrix and uniquely assign a tuple (i, j), where $i, j \in [m]$, to each user. A user at position (i, j) of the matrix has index $k = (i - 1) * m + j$. For simplicity, we directly use (i, j) as the index where $(i, j) \geq (\bar{i}, \bar{j})$ means that $((i > \bar{i}) \vee (i = \bar{i} \wedge j \geq \bar{j}))$. Let $[m, m]$ be the set $\{(i, j) | i, j \in [m]\}$. The use of pairwise notation (i, j) is purely a notational convenience, as $k = (i-1) * m + j$ defines a bijection between $\{(i, j) | i, j \in [m]\}$ and $[N]$. For a given vector $\boldsymbol{v} = (v_1, \ldots, v_d)$, by $g^{\boldsymbol{v}}$ we mean the vector $(g^{v_1}, \ldots, g^{v_d})$. Furthermore, for $g^{\boldsymbol{v}} = (g^{v_1}, \ldots, g^{v_d})$ and $g^{\boldsymbol{w}} = (g^{w_1}, \ldots, g^{w_d})$, by $g^{\boldsymbol{v}} \cdot g^{\boldsymbol{w}}$ we mean the vector $(g^{v_1 + w_1}, \ldots, g^{v_d + w_d})$, i.e. $g^{\boldsymbol{v}} \cdot g^{\boldsymbol{w}} = g^{\boldsymbol{v} + \boldsymbol{w}}$, and by $e_d(g^{\boldsymbol{v}}, g^{\boldsymbol{w}})$ we mean $\prod_{k=1}^{d} e(g^{v_k}, g^{w_k})$, i.e. $e_d(g^{\boldsymbol{v}}, g^{\boldsymbol{w}}) = e(g, g)^{(\boldsymbol{v} \cdot \boldsymbol{w})}$, where $(\boldsymbol{v} \cdot \boldsymbol{w})$ is the inner product of $\boldsymbol{v}$ and $\boldsymbol{w}$. Given a prime p, one can randomly choose $r_x, r_y, r_z \in \mathbb{Z}_p$, and set $\chi_1 = (r_x, 0, r_z)$, $\chi_2 = (0, r_y, r_z)$, $\chi_3 = \chi_1 \times \chi_2 = (-r_y r_z, -r_x r_z, r_x r_y)$. Let $span\{\chi_1, \chi_2\} = \{\nu_1 \chi_1 + \nu_2 \chi_2 | \nu_1, \nu_2 \in \mathbb{Z}_p\}$ be the subspace spanned by χ_1 and χ_2. We can see that χ_3 is orthogonal to the subspace $span\{\chi_1, \chi_2\}$

and $\mathbb{Z}_p^3 = span\{\boldsymbol{\chi}_1, \boldsymbol{\chi}_2, \boldsymbol{\chi}_3\} = \{\nu_1\boldsymbol{\chi}_1 + \nu_2\boldsymbol{\chi}_2 + \nu_3\boldsymbol{\chi}_3 | \nu_1, \nu_2, \nu_3 \in \mathbb{Z}_p\}$. For any $\boldsymbol{v} \in span\{\boldsymbol{\chi}_1, \boldsymbol{\chi}_2\}$, $(\boldsymbol{\chi}_3 \cdot \boldsymbol{v}) = 0$, and for random $\boldsymbol{v} \in \mathbb{Z}_p^3$, $(\boldsymbol{\chi}_3 \cdot \boldsymbol{v}) \neq 0$ happens with overwhelming probability.

4.2 Augmented R-CP-ABE Construction

Now we propose a large universe Augmented R-CP-ABE, where the attribute universe is $\mathcal{U} = \mathbb{Z}_p$.

$\mathsf{Setup}_A(\lambda, N = m^2) \rightarrow (\mathsf{PP}, \mathsf{MSK})$. The algorithm calls the group generator $\mathcal{G}(\lambda)$ to get $(p, \mathbb{G}, \mathbb{G}_T, e)$, and sets the attribute universe to $\mathcal{U} = \mathbb{Z}_p$. It then randomly picks $g, h, f, f_1, \ldots, f_m, G, H \in \mathbb{G}$, $\{\alpha_i, r_i, z_i \in \mathbb{Z}_p\}_{i \in [m]}$, $\{c_j \in \mathbb{Z}_p\}_{j \in [m]}$, and outputs the public parameter PP and master secret key MSK

$$\mathsf{PP} = \Big((p, \mathbb{G}, \mathbb{G}_T, e),\ g,\ h,\ f,\ f_1, \ldots, f_m,\ G,\ H,$$
$$\{E_i = e(g,g)^{\alpha_i}, G_i = g^{r_i}, Z_i = g^{z_i}\}_{i \in [m]},\ \{H_j = g^{c_j}\}_{j \in [m]} \Big),$$
$$\mathsf{MSK} = \Big(\alpha_1, \ldots, \alpha_m,\ r_1, \ldots, r_m,\ c_1, \ldots, c_m \Big).$$

A counter $ctr = 0$ is implicitly included in MSK.

$\mathsf{KeyGen}_A(\mathsf{PP}, \mathsf{MSK}, S \subseteq \mathbb{Z}_p) \rightarrow \mathsf{SK}_{(i,j),S}$. The algorithm first sets $ctr = ctr + 1$ and computes the corresponding index in the form of (i,j) where $1 \leq i, j \leq m$ and $(i-1)*m+j = ctr$. Then it picks random exponents $\sigma_{i,j} \in \mathbb{Z}_p$, $\{\delta_{i,j,x} \in \mathbb{Z}_p\}_{\forall x \in S}$, and outputs a secret key $\mathsf{SK}_{(i,j),S} = \big((i,j), S, K_{i,j}, K'_{i,j}, K''_{i,j}, \{\bar{K}_{i,j,j'}\}_{j' \in [m] \setminus \{j\}}, \{K_{i,j,x}, K'_{i,j,x}\}_{x \in S}\big)$ where

$$K_{i,j} = g^{\alpha_i} g^{r_i c_j} (ff_j)^{\sigma_{i,j}},\ K'_{i,j} = g^{\sigma_{i,j}},\ K''_{i,j} = Z_i^{\sigma_{i,j}},$$
$$\{\bar{K}_{i,j,j'} = f_{j'}^{\sigma_{i,j}}\}_{j' \in [m] \setminus \{j\}},\ \{K_{i,j,x} = g^{\delta_{i,j,x}},\ K'_{i,j,x} = (H^x h)^{\delta_{i,j,x}} G^{-\sigma_{i,j}}\}_{x \in S}.$$

$\mathsf{Encrypt}_A(\mathsf{PP}, M, R, \mathbb{A} = (A, \rho), (\bar{i}, \bar{j})) \rightarrow CT_{R,(A,\rho)}$. $R \subseteq [m,m]$ is a revocation list. $\mathbb{A} = (A, \rho)$ is an LSSS matrix where A is an $l \times n$ matrix and ρ maps each row A_k of A to an attribute $\rho(k) \in \mathcal{U} = \mathbb{Z}_p$. The encryption is for recipients whose (index, attribute set) pairs $((i,j), S_{(i,j)})$ satisfy $((i,j) \in [m,m] \setminus R) \wedge (S_{(i,j)}\ satisfies\ (A, \rho)) \wedge ((i,j) \geq (\bar{i}, \bar{j}))$. Let $\bar{R} = [m,m] \setminus R$ and for $i \in [m]$, $\bar{R}_i = \{j' | (i,j') \in \bar{R}\}$, that is, $\bar{R}$ is the non-revoked index list, and $\bar{R}_i$ is the set of non-revoked column index on the i-th row. The algorithm randomly chooses $\kappa, \tau, s_1, \ldots, s_m, t_1, \ldots, t_m \in \mathbb{Z}_p$, $\boldsymbol{v}_c, \boldsymbol{w}_1, \ldots, \boldsymbol{w}_m \in \mathbb{Z}_p^3$, $\xi_1, \ldots, \xi_l \in \mathbb{Z}_p$, and $\boldsymbol{u} = (\pi, u_2, \ldots, u_n) \in \mathbb{Z}_p^n$. In addition, it randomly chooses $r_x, r_y, r_z \in \mathbb{Z}_p$, and sets $\boldsymbol{\chi}_1 = (r_x, 0, r_z)$, $\boldsymbol{\chi}_2 = (0, r_y, r_z)$, $\boldsymbol{\chi}_3 = \boldsymbol{\chi}_1 \times \boldsymbol{\chi}_2 = (-r_y r_z, -r_x r_z, r_x r_y)$. Then it randomly chooses $\boldsymbol{v}_i \in \mathbb{Z}_p^3\ \forall i \in \{1, \ldots, \bar{i}\}$, $\boldsymbol{v}_i \in span\{\boldsymbol{\chi}_1, \boldsymbol{\chi}_2\}\ \forall i \in \{\bar{i}+1, \ldots, m\}$, and computes a ciphertext $\langle R, (A, \rho), (\boldsymbol{R}_i, \boldsymbol{R}'_i, Q_i, Q'_i, Q''_i, T_i)_{i=1}^m, (\boldsymbol{C}_j, \boldsymbol{C}'_j)_{j=1}^m, (P_k, P'_k, P''_k)_{k=1}^l \rangle$ as follows:

1. For each row $i \in [m]$:
   - if $i < \bar{i}$: randomly chooses $\hat{s}_i \in \mathbb{Z}_p$, and sets
   $$R_i = g^{v_i}, \quad R_i' = g^{\kappa v_i},$$
   $$Q_i = g^{s_i}, \quad Q_i' = (f \prod_{j' \in \bar{R}_i} f_{j'})^{s_i} Z_i^{t_i} f^{\pi}, \quad Q_i'' = g^{t_i}, \quad T_i = E_i^{\hat{s}_i}.$$
   - if $i \geq \bar{i}$: sets
   $$R_i = G_i^{s_i v_i}, \quad R_i' = G_i^{\kappa s_i v_i}, Q_i = g^{\tau s_i (v_i \cdot v_c)},$$
   $$Q_i' = (f \prod_{j' \in \bar{R}_i} f_{j'})^{\tau s_i (v_i \cdot v_c)} Z_i^{t_i} f^{\pi}, Q_i'' = g^{t_i}, \quad T_i = M \cdot E_i^{\tau s_i (v_i \cdot v_c)}.$$

2. For each column $j \in [m]$:
   - if $j < \bar{j}$: randomly chooses $\mu_j \in \mathbb{Z}_p$, and sets
   $$C_j = H_j^{\tau(v_c + \mu_j \chi_3)} \cdot g^{\kappa w_j}, C_j' = g^{w_j}.$$
   - if $j \geq \bar{j}$: sets $C_j = H_j^{\tau v_c} \cdot g^{\kappa w_j}, C_j' = g^{w_j}.$
3. For each $k \in [l]$: sets $P_k = f^{A_k \cdot u} G^{\xi_k}, \quad P_k' = (H^{\rho(k)} h)^{-\xi_k}, \quad P_k'' = g^{\xi_k}.$

$\text{Decrypt}_A(PP, CT_{R,(A,\rho)}, SK_{(i,j),S}) \to M$ or $\perp$. If $(i,j) \in R$ or S does not satisfy (A, ρ), the algorithm outputs $\perp$, otherwise:
1. Since S satisfies (A, ρ), the algorithm can efficiently compute constants $\{\omega_k \in \mathbb{Z}_p\}$ such that $\sum_{\rho(k) \in S} \omega_k A_k = (1, 0, \ldots, 0)$, then compute

$$D_P = \prod_{\rho(k) \in S} \left(e(K_{i,j}', P_k) \cdot e(K_{i,j,\rho(k)}, P_k') \cdot e(K_{i,j,\rho(k)}', P_k'') \right)^{\omega_k}$$

$$= \prod_{\rho(k) \in S} \left(e(g^{\sigma_{i,j}}, f^{A_k \cdot u}) \right)^{\omega_k} = e(g^{\sigma_{i,j}}, f)^{\sum_{\rho(k) \in S} \omega_k (A_k \cdot u)} = e(g^{\sigma_{i,j}}, f)^{\pi}.$$

Note that if S does not satisfy (A, ρ), no such constants $\{\omega_k\}$ would exist.
2. Since $(i,j) \in \bar{R}(= [m,m] \setminus R)$ implies $j \in \bar{R}_i$, the algorithm can compute

$$\bar{K}_{i,j} = K_{i,j} \cdot (\prod_{j' \in \bar{R}_i \setminus \{j\}} \bar{K}_{i,j,j'}) = g^{\alpha_i} g^{r_i c_j} (f f_j)^{\sigma_{i,j}} \cdot (\prod_{j' \in \bar{R}_i \setminus \{j\}} f_{j'}^{\sigma_{i,j}})$$

$$= g^{\alpha_i} g^{r_i c_j} \cdot (f \prod_{j' \in \bar{R}_i} f_{j'})^{\sigma_{i,j}}.$$

Note that if $(i,j) \in R$ (implying $j \notin \bar{R}_i$), the algorithm cannot produce such a $\bar{K}_{i,j}$. The algorithm then computes

$$D_I = \frac{e(\bar{K}_{i,j}, Q_i) \cdot e(K_{i,j}'', Q_i'')}{e(K_{i,j}', Q_i')} \cdot \frac{e_3(R_i', C_j')}{e_3(R_i, C_j)}.$$

3. Computes $M = T_i/(D_P \cdot D_I)$ as the output message. Suppose that the ciphertext is generated from message M' and encryption index $(\bar{i}, \bar{j})$, it can be verified that only when $(i > \bar{i})$ or $(i = \bar{i} \wedge j \geq \bar{j})$, $M = M'$. This is because for $i > \bar{i}$, we have $(v_i \cdot \chi_3) = 0$ (since $v_i \in span\{\chi_1, \chi_2\}$), and for $i = \bar{i}$, we have that $(v_i \cdot \chi_3) \neq 0$ happens with overwhelming probability (since v_i is randomly chosen from $\mathbb{Z}_p^3$). The correctness details can be found in the full version [19].

4.3 Augmented R-CP-ABE Security

The following theorem states that the AugR-CP-ABE proposed above is message-hiding. Then in Theorem 4, we state that the AugR-CP-ABE is also selectively index-hiding.

Theorem 3. *No PPT adversary can win* $\mathsf{Game}^{\mathsf{A}}_{\mathsf{MH}}$ *with non-negligible advantage.*

Proof. The argument for message-hiding in $\mathsf{Game}^{\mathsf{A}}_{\mathsf{MH}}$ is straightforward since an encryption to index $N + 1$ (i.e. $(m + 1, 1)$) contains no information about the message. The simulator simply runs $\mathsf{Setup}_{\mathsf{A}}$ and $\mathsf{KeyGen}_{\mathsf{A}}$ and encrypts M_b under the challenge (revocation list, access policy) pair $(R^*, \mathbb{A}^*)$ and index $(m + 1, 1)$. Since for all $i = 1$ to m, $T_i = E_i^{s_i}$ contains no information about the message, the bit b is perfectly hidden and $\mathsf{MH}^{\mathsf{A}}\mathsf{Adv}_{\mathcal{A}} = 0$.

Theorem 4. *Suppose that the D3DH, the DLIN and the Extended Source Group q-Parallel BDHE Assumption hold. Then no PPT adversary can selectively win* $\mathsf{Game}^{\mathsf{A}}_{\mathsf{IH}}$ *with non-negligible advantage, provided that the challenge LSSS matrix's size $l \times n$ satisfies $l, n \le q$.*

Proof. It follows Lemmas 1 and 2 below.

Lemma 1. *If the D3DH and the Extended Source Group q-Parallel BDHE Assumption hold, then for $\bar{j} < m$, no PPT adversary can selectively distinguish between an encryption to $(\bar{i}, \bar{j})$ and $(\bar{i}, \bar{j} + 1)$ in* $\mathsf{Game}^{\mathsf{A}}_{\mathsf{IH}}$ *with non-negligible advantage, provided that the challenge LSSS matrix's size $l \times n$ satisfies $l, n \le q$.*

Proof. In $\mathsf{Game}^{\mathsf{A}}_{\mathsf{IH}}$ with index $(\bar{i}, \bar{j})$, let $(R^*, (A^*, \rho^*))$ be the challenge (revocation list, access policy) pair, the restriction is that the adversary $\mathcal{A}$ does not query a secret key for (index, attribute set) pair $((i, j), S_{(i,j)})$ such that $((i, j) = (\bar{i}, \bar{j})) \wedge ((i, j) \in [m, m] \setminus R^*) \wedge (S_{(i,j)} \; satisfies \; (A^*, \rho^*))$. Under this restriction, there are two ways for $\mathcal{A}$ to take:

Case I: In Phase 1 and Phase 2, $\mathcal{A}$ does not query a secret key with index $(\bar{i}, \bar{j})$.

Case II: In Phase 1 or Phase 2, $\mathcal{A}$ queries a secret key with index $(\bar{i}, \bar{j})$. Let $S_{(\bar{i}, \bar{j})}$ be the corresponding attribute set. **Case II** has the following sub-cases:

1. $(\bar{i}, \bar{j}) \notin [m, m] \setminus R^*$, $S_{(\bar{i}, \bar{j})}$ satisfies (A^*, ρ^*).
2. $(\bar{i}, \bar{j}) \notin [m, m] \setminus R^*$, $S_{(\bar{i}, \bar{j})}$ does not satisfy (A^*, ρ^*).
3. $(\bar{i}, \bar{j}) \in [m, m] \setminus R^*$, $S_{(\bar{i}, \bar{j})}$ does not satisfy (A^*, ρ^*).

If $\mathcal{A}$ is in **Case I, Case II.1** or **Case II.2**, it follows the restrictions in the index-hiding game for Augmented Broadcast Encryption (AugBE) in [8], where the adversary does not query the key with index $(\bar{i}, \bar{j})$ or $(\bar{i}, \bar{j})$ is not in the receiver list $[m, m] \setminus R^*$. **Case II.3** captures the index-hiding requirement of Augmented R-CP-ABE in that even if a user has a key with index $(\bar{i}, \bar{j})$ and $(\bar{i}, \bar{j}) \notin R^*$, the user cannot distinguish between an encryption to $(R^*, (A^*, \rho^*), (\bar{i}, \bar{j}))$ and

$(R^*, (A^*, \rho^*), (\bar{i}, \bar{j}+1))$ if $S_{(\bar{i}, \bar{j})}$ does not satisfy (A^*, ρ^*). This is the most challenging part of proving the index-hiding when we attempt to *securely intertwine* the tracing techniques of broadcast encryption (e.g. [8]) into the large universe CP-ABE (e.g. [23]). Compared to the proof of [16], the challenge here is to prove the index-hiding in the large universe setting, as discussed previously.

To prove this lemma, we flip a random coin $c \in \{0, 1\}$ as our guess on which case that $\mathcal{A}$ is in. In particular, if $c = 0$, we guess that $\mathcal{A}$ is in **Case I**, **Case II.1** or **Case II.2**, and make a reduction that uses $\mathcal{A}$ to solve a D3DH problem instance, using a proof technique similar to that of [8]. Actually, in this proof, we reduce from our AugR-CP-ABE to the AugBE in [8]. If $c = 1$, we guess that $\mathcal{A}$ is in **Case I**, **Case II.2** or **Case II.3**, and use $\mathcal{A}$ to solve an Extended Source Group q-Parallel BDHE problem instance, which is where the main novelty resides among all the proofs in this work. The proof details are provided in the full version [19].

Lemma 2. *If the D3DH, the DLIN and the Extended Source Group q-Parallel BDHE Assumption hold, then for $1 \leq \bar{i} \leq m$, no PPT adversary can selectively distinguish between an encryption to $(\bar{i}, m)$ and $(\bar{i}+1, 1)$ in Game_{IH}^{A} with non-negligible advantage, provided that the challenge LSSS matrix's size $l \times n$ satisfies $l, n \leq q$.*

Proof. Similar to the proof of Lemma 6.3 in [8], to prove this lemma we define the following hybrid experiment: H_1: encrypt to $(\bar{i}, \bar{j} = m)$; H_2: encrypt to $(\bar{i}, \bar{j} = m+1)$; and H_3: encrypt to $(\bar{i}+1, 1)$. This lemma follows Claims 1 and 2 below.

Claim 1. *If the D3DH and the Extended Source Group q-Parallel BDHE Assumption hold, then no PPT adversary can selectively distinguish between experiment H_1 and H_2 with non-negligible advantage, provided that the challenge LSSS matrix's size $l \times n$ satisfies $l, n \leq q$.*

Proof. The proof is identical to that for Lemma 1.

Claim 2. *If the D3DH and the DLIN hold, then no PPT adversary can distinguish between experiment H_2 and H_3 with non-negligible advantage.*

Proof. Note that $(\bar{i}, m+1) \notin [m, m]$ implies that for any revocation list $R^* \subseteq [m, m]$, we have $(\bar{i}, m+1) \notin \bar{R}^*(= [m, m] \setminus R^*)$, i.e., the adversaries for distinguishing H_2 and H_3 will not be in **Case II.3**. Thus, similar to that of case $c = 0$ in the proof of Lemma 1, in this proof we reduce from our AugR-CP-ABE to the AugBE in [8]. In the proof of index-hiding for an AugBE scheme Σ_{AugBE} in [8, Lemma 6.3], two hybrid experiments were defined and proven indistinguishable via a sequence of hybrid sub-experiments.

– H_2^{AugBE}: Encrypt to $(\bar{i}, m+1)$, (i.e. H_2 in [8])
– H_3^{AugBE}: Encrypt to $(\bar{i}+1, 1)$, (i.e. H_5 in [8])

By following [8, Lemma 6.3], *if the D3DH and the DLIN hold, no PPT adversary can distinguish between H_2^{AugBE} and H_3^{AugBE} for Σ_{AugBE} with non-negligible advantage.* Suppose there is a PPT adversary $\mathcal{A}$ that can distinguish between H_2 and H_3 for our AugR-CP-ABE scheme with non-negligible advantage. We can build a reduction, which is similar to that of case $c = 0$ in the proof of Lemma 1, to use $\mathcal{A}$ to distinguish between H_2^{AugBE} and H_3^{AugBE} for Σ_{AugBE} with non-negligible advantage.

5 Conclusion

In this paper, we proposed the first practical CP-ABE that simultaneously supports (1) traitor tracing, (2) revocation and (3) large universe. The scheme is highly expressive in supporting any monotonic access structures. Besides achieving fully collusion-resistant blackbox traceability and direct revocation, it is also efficient with the overhead in $O(\sqrt{N})$ only. Furthermore, it supports large attribute universe and does not need to fix the values of attributes during the system setup. The scheme was proven selectively secure and traceable in the standard model.

References

1. Attrapadung, N., Imai, H.: Conjunctive broadcast and attribute-based encryption. In: Shacham, H., Waters, B. (eds.) Pairing 2009. LNCS, vol. 5671, pp. 248–265. Springer, Heidelberg (2009)
2. Bethencourt, J., Sahai, A., Waters, B.: Ciphertext-policy attribute-based encryption. In: IEEE Symposium on Security and Privacy, pp. 321–334 (2007)
3. Boneh, D., Franklin, M.K.: An efficient public key traitor tracing scheme. In: Wiener, M. (ed.) Advances in Cryptology – CRYPTO 1999. LNCS, vol. 1666, pp. 338–353. Springer, Heidelberg (1999)
4. Boneh, D., Sahai, A., Waters, B.: Fully collusion resistant traitor tracing with short ciphertexts and private keys. In: Vaudenay, S. (ed.) EUROCRYPT 2006. LNCS, vol. 4004, pp. 573–592. Springer, Heidelberg (2006)
5. Boneh, D., Waters, B.: A fully collusion resistant broadcast, trace, and revoke system. In: ACM Conference on Computer and Communications Security, pp. 211–220 (2006)
6. Cheung, L., Newport, C.C.: Provably secure ciphertext policy ABE. In: ACM Conference on Computer and Communications Security, pp. 456–465 (2007)
7. Deng, H., Wu, Q., Qin, B., Mao, J., Liu, X., Zhang, L., Shi, W.: Who is touching my cloud. In: Kutyłowski, M., Vaidya, J. (eds.) ESORICS 2014, Part I. LNCS, vol. 8712, pp. 362–379. Springer, Heidelberg (2014)
8. Garg, S., Kumarasubramanian, A., Sahai, A., Waters, B.: Building efficient fully collusion-resilient traitor tracing and revocation schemes. In: ACM Conference on Computer and Communications Security, pp. 121–130 (2010)
9. Goyal, V., Jain, A., Pandey, O., Sahai, A.: Bounded ciphertext policy attribute based encryption. In: Aceto, L., Damgård, I., Goldberg, L.A., Halldórsson, M.M., Ingólfsdóttir, A., Walukiewicz, I. (eds.) ICALP 2008, Part II. LNCS, vol. 5126, pp. 579–591. Springer, Heidelberg (2008)

10. Goyal, V., Pandey, O., Sahai, A., Waters, B.: Attribute-based encryption for fine-grained access control of encrypted data. In: ACM Conference on Computer and Communications Security, pp. 89–98 (2006)
11. Herranz, J., Laguillaumie, F., Ràfols, C.: Constant size ciphertexts in threshold attribute-based encryption. In: Nguyen, P.Q., Pointcheval, D. (eds.) PKC 2010. LNCS, vol. 6056, pp. 19–34. Springer, Heidelberg (2010)
12. Katz, J., Schröder, D.: Tracing insider attacks in the context of predicate encryption schemes. In: ACITA (2011). https://www.usukita.org/node/1779
13. Lewko, A.: Tools for simulating features of composite order bilinear groups in the prime order setting. In: Pointcheval, D., Johansson, T. (eds.) EUROCRYPT 2012. LNCS, vol. 7237, pp. 318–335. Springer, Heidelberg (2012)
14. Lewko, A., Okamoto, T., Sahai, A., Takashima, K., Waters, B.: Fully secure functional encryption: attribute-based encryption and (hierarchical) inner product encryption. In: Gilbert, H. (ed.) EUROCRYPT 2010. LNCS, vol. 6110, pp. 62–91. Springer, Heidelberg (2010)
15. Lewko, A., Waters, B.: New proof methods for attribute-based encryption: achieving full security through selective techniques. In: Safavi-Naini, R., Canetti, R. (eds.) CRYPTO 2012. LNCS, vol. 7417, pp. 180–198. Springer, Heidelberg (2012)
16. Liu, Z., Cao, Z., Wong, D.S.: Blackbox traceable CP-ABE: how to catch people leaking their keys by selling decryption devices on ebay. In: ACM Conference on Computer and Communications Security, pp. 475–486 (2013)
17. Liu, Z., Cao, Z., Wong, D.S.: White-box traceable ciphertext-policy attribute-based encryption supporting any monotone access structures. IEEE Trans. Inf. Forensics Secur. 8(1), 76–88 (2013)
18. Liu, Z., Cao, Z., Wong, D.S.: Traceable CP-ABE: how to trace decryption devices found in the wild. IEEE Trans. Inf. Forensics Secur. 10(1), 55–68 (2015)
19. Liu, Z., Wong, D.S.: Practical attribute-based encryption: Traitor tracing, revocation, and large universe. IACR Cryptology ePrint Archive 2014, 616 (2014). http://eprint.iacr.org/2014/616
20. Naor, D., Naor, M., Lotspiech, J.: Revocation and tracing schemes for stateless receivers. In: Kilian, J. (ed.) CRYPTO 2001. LNCS, vol. 2139, pp. 41–62. Springer, Heidelberg (2001)
21. Okamoto, T., Takashima, K.: Fully secure functional encryption with general relations from the decisional linear assumption. In: Rabin, T. (ed.) CRYPTO 2010. LNCS, vol. 6223, pp. 191–208. Springer, Heidelberg (2010)
22. Okamoto, T., Takashima, K.: Fully secure unbounded inner-product and attribute-based encryption. In: Wang, X., Sako, K. (eds.) ASIACRYPT 2012. LNCS, vol. 7658, pp. 349–366. Springer, Heidelberg (2012)
23. Rouselakis, Y., Waters, B.: Practical constructions and new proof methods for large universe attribute-based encryption. In: ACM Conference on Computer and Communications Security, pp. 463–474 (2013)
24. Sahai, A., Seyalioglu, H., Waters, B.: Dynamic credentials and ciphertext delegation for attribute-based encryption. In: Safavi-Naini, R., Canetti, R. (eds.) CRYPTO 2012. LNCS, vol. 7417, pp. 199–217. Springer, Heidelberg (2012)
25. Sahai, A., Waters, B.: Fuzzy identity-based encryption. In: Cramer, R. (ed.) EUROCRYPT 2005. LNCS, vol. 3494, pp. 457–473. Springer, Heidelberg (2005)
26. Waters, B.: Ciphertext-policy attribute-based encryption: an expressive, efficient, and provably secure realization. In: Catalano, D., Fazio, N., Gennaro, R., Nicolosi, A. (eds.) PKC 2011. LNCS, vol. 6571, pp. 53–70. Springer, Heidelberg (2011)

Secure Computation II: Applications

Zero-Knowledge Authenticated Order Queries and Order Statistics on a List

Esha Ghosh[1][✉], Olga Ohrimenko[2], and Roberto Tamassia[1]

[1] Department of Computer Science, Brown University, Providence, USA
{esha_ghosh,roberto_tamassia}@brown.edu
[2] Microsoft Research, Cambridge, UK
oohrim@microsoft.com

Abstract. An order query takes as input a set of elements from a list (ordered sequence) $\mathcal{L}$, and asks for this set to be ordered using the total order induced by $\mathcal{L}$. We introduce two formal models for answering order queries on a list in a verifiable and private manner. Our first model, called *zero-knowledge list* (ZKL), generalizes the standard two-party model of membership queries on a set to order queries on a list in zero-knowledge. We present a construction of ZKL based on zero-knowledge sets and a homomorphic integer commitment. Our second model, *privacy-preserving authenticated list* (PPAL), extends authenticated data structures by adding a zero-knowledge privacy requirement. This is a three-party model, where a list is outsourced by a trusted owner to an untrusted cloud server, which answers order queries issued by clients and returns proofs of the answers. PPAL supports data integrity against a malicious server and privacy protection against a malicious client. Though PPAL can be implemented using our ZKL construction, this construction is not as efficient as desired in cloud applications. We present an *efficient* PPAL construction based on our novel technique of blinded bilinear accumulators and bilinear maps. Both our models are provably secure in the Random Oracle model and are zero-knowledge (e.g., hiding even the size of the list). We also show that the ZKL and PPAL frameworks can be extended to support fundamental statistical queries efficiently and in zero-knowledge.

1 Introduction

Releasing verifiable partial information while maintaining privacy is a requirement in many practical scenarios where the data being dealt with is sensitive. A basic case is releasing a subset of a set and proving its authenticity in a privacy-preserving way (referred to as zero-knowledge property) [10,12,26,29]. However, in many other cases, the information is stored in data structures to support richer type of queries. In this paper, we consider *order queries* on two or more elements of a list, where the answer to the query returns the elements rearranged according to their order in the list. Order queries lie at the heart of many practical applications where the order between queried elements is revealed and proved but the rank of the queried elements in the list and information about other elements in the list should be protected.

© Springer International Publishing Switzerland 2015
T. Malkin et al. (Eds.): ACNS 2015, LNCS 9092, pp. 149–171, 2015.
DOI: 10.1007/978-3-319-28166-7_8

In an auction with a single winner (e.g., online ad auction for a single ad spot) every participant submits her secret bid to the auction organizer. After the top bidder is announced, a participant wishes to verify that her bid was inferior. The organizer would then provide a proof without revealing the amount of the top bid, the rank of the participant's bid, or any information about other bids.

Lenders often require an individual or a couple to prove eligibility for a loan by providing a bank statement and a pay stub. Such documents contain sensitive information beyond what the lender is looking for: whether the bank account balance and salary are above given thresholds. A desirable alternative would be to provide a proof from the bank and employer that these thresholds are met without revealing exact figures and even hiding who of the two spouses earns more.

The above examples can be generalized using order queries on an ordered set, aka list, that return the order of the queried elements as well as a proof of this order but without revealing anything more than the answer itself. We address this problem by introducing two different models: *zero knowledge lists* (ZKL) and *privacy-preserving authenticated lists* (PPAL).

ZKL considers two party model and extends zero knowledge sets [12,29] to lists. In ZKL a prover commits to a list and a verifier queries the prover to learn the order of a subset of list elements. The verifier should be able to verify the answer but learn no information about the rest of the list, e.g., the size of the list, the order of other elements of the list or the rank of the queried element(s). Here both the prover and the verifier can act as malicious adversaries. While the prover may want to give answers inconsistent with the initial list he committed to, the verifier may try to learn information beyond the query answer or arbitrarily deviate from the protocol.

PPAL considers three parties: the owner of the list, the server who answers list queries on behalf of the owner, and the client who queries the server. The privacy guarantee of PPAL is the same as in ZKL. For authenticity, PPAL assumes that the owner is trusted while the server and the client could be malicious. This trust model allows for a much more efficient construction than ZKL, as we will see later in the paper. PPAL has direct applications to outsourced services where the server is modeling the cloud service that the owner uses to interact with her clients.

We note that PPAL can be viewed as a privacy-preserving extension of authenticated data structures (ADS) (see, e.g., [19,20,28,36]), which also operate in a three party model: the server stores the owner's data and proves to the client the answer to a query. However, privacy properties have not been studied in this model and as a consequence, known ADS constructions leak information about the rest of the data through their proofs of authenticity. For example, the classic Merkle hash tree [28] on a set of n elements proves membership of an element via a proof of size $\log n$, thus leaking information about the size of the set. Also, if the elements are stored at the leaves in sorted order, the proof of *membership* of an element reveals its rank.

In this paper, we define the security properties for ZKL and PPAL and provide efficient constructions for them. The privacy property against the verifier in ZKL and the client in PPAL is *zero knowledge*. That is, the answers and the proofs are indistinguishable from those that are generated by a simulator that knows nothing except the previous and current queries and answers and, hence, cannot possibly leak any information beyond that. While we show that PPAL can be implemented using our ZKL construction, we also provide a direct PPAL construction that is considerably more efficient thanks to the trust that clients put in the list owner. Let n be the size of the list and m be the size of the query, i.e., the number of list elements whose order is sought. Our PPAL construction uses proofs of $O(m)$ size and allows the client to verify a proof in $O(m)$ time. The owner executes the setup in $O(n)$ time and space. The server uses $O(n)$ space to store the list and related authentication information, and takes $O(\min(m \log n, n))$ time to answer a query and generate a proof. In contrast, in the ZKL construction, the time and storage requirements have an overhead that linearly depends on the security parameter. Note that ZKL also supports (non-) membership queries. The client in PPAL and the verifier in ZKL require only one round of communication for each query. Our ZKL construction is based on zero knowledge sets and homomorphic integer commitments. Our PPAL construction uses a novel technique of blinding of accumulators along with bilinear aggregate signatures. Both are secure in the random oracle model.

2   Problem Statement, Models, Related Work, and Contributions

In this section, we state our problem, outline our models, review related work, and summarize our contributions. Formal definitions and constructions are in the rest of the paper. Detailed proofs and construction that are omitted due to space restrictions are available in the full version [17].

2.1   Problem Statement and Models

Let $\mathcal{L}$ be a totally ordered list of distinct elements. An *order query* on $\mathcal{L}$ is defined as follows: given a set of elements of $\mathcal{L}$, return these elements rearranged according to their order in $\mathcal{L}$ and a proof of this order. Both models we introduce, PPAL and ZKL, support this query. ZKL, in addition to order queries, supports provable membership and non-membership queries. Beside providing authenticity, the proofs are required not to leak any information beyond the answer.

ZKL: This model has two parties: prover and verifier. The prover initially computes a commitment to a list $\mathcal{L}$ and reveals the commitment to the verifier. Later the verifier asks membership and order queries on $\mathcal{L}$ and the prover responds with a proof. Both the prover and the verifier can be malicious:

- The prover may try to give answers inconsistent with the initial commitment.
- The verifier may try to learn from the proofs additional information about $\mathcal{L}$ beyond what he has inferred from the answers. E.g., if the verifier has performed two order queries with answers $x < y$ and $x < z$, he may want to find out whether $y < z$ or $z < y$.

The security properties of ZKL, *completeness, soundness* and *zero-knowledge*, guarantee security against malicious prover and verifier. Completeness mandates that honestly generated proofs always satisfy the verification test. Soundness states that the prover should not be able to come up with a query, and corresponding inconsistent (with the initial commitment) answers and convincing proofs. Finally, zero-knowledge means that each proof reveals the answer and nothing else. In other words, there must exist a simulator, that given only oracle access to $\mathcal{L}$, can simulate proofs for membership and order queries that are indistinguishable from real proofs.

PPAL: This model has three parties: owner, server and client. The owner generates list $\mathcal{L}$ and outsources it to the server. The owner also sends (possibly different) digest information with respect to $\mathcal{L}$ to the server and the client. Given an order query from the client, the server, using the server digest, builds and returns to the client the answer and its proof, which is verified by the client using the client digest. Both the server and the client can be malicious:

- The server may try to forge proofs for incorrect answers to (order) queries, e.g., prove an incorrect ordering of a pair of elements of $\mathcal{L}$.
- The client, similar to the verifier in ZKL, may try to learn from the proofs additional information about list $\mathcal{L}$ beyond what he has inferred from the answers.

Note that in typical cloud database applications, the client is allowed to have only a restricted view of the data structure and the server enforces an access control policy that prevents the client from getting answers to unauthorized queries. This motivates the curious, possibly malicious, behavior from the client where he tries to ask ill-formed queries or queries violating the access control policy. However, we assume that the server enforces client's legitimate behavior by refusing to answer illegal queries. Hence, the security model for PPAL is defined as follows.

The properties of PPAL, *Completeness, Soundness* and *Zero-Knowledge*, guarantee security against malicious server and client. They are close to the ones of ZKL except for soundness. For PPAL it enforces that the client does not accept proofs forged by the server for incorrect answers w.r.t. owner's list. PPAL's owner and server together can be thought of as a single party in ZKL, the prover. Hence, ZKL soundness protects against the prover who tries to give answers inconsistent with her own initial commitment. In the PPAL model, the owner and the server are separate parties where the owner is trusted and soundness protects against a malicious server only.

To understand the strength of the zero-knowledge property, let us illustrate to what extent the proofs are non-revealing. This property guarantees that a client, who adaptively queries a static list, does not learn anything about ranks of the queried elements, the distance between them or even the size of $\mathcal{L}$. The client is not able to infer any relative order information that is not inferable by the rule of transitivity from the previously queried orders. It is worth noting that in the context of leakage-free redactable signature schemes, privacy property has been defined using game-based definitions in *transparency* [6,34] and *privacy* [11,23]. However, our definition of simulatability of the query responses, or the zero-knowledge property, is a simpler and more intuitive way to capture the property of leakage-freeness.

Efficiency: We characterize the ideal efficiency goals of our models as follows, where $\mathcal{L}$ is a list of n items and m is the query size. The space for storing list $\mathcal{L}$ and the auxiliary information for generating proofs should be $O(n)$. As in related work, a multiplicative factor for element size of $O(\mathsf{poly(k)})$, where k is the security parameter, is not shown in $O(\cdot)$. The setup to preprocess list $\mathcal{L}$ should take $O(n)$ time. The proof of the answer to a query should have $O(m)$ size. Processing a query to generate the answer and its proof should take $O(m)$ time. Verifying the proof of an answer should take $O(m)$ time.

Applications of Order Queries to Order Statistics: Our PPAL order queries can be used as a building block to answer efficiently and in zero knowledge (i.e., the returned proofs should be simulatable) many interesting statistical queries about a list $\mathcal{L}$ with n elements. Let a *pair order proof* denote the proof of the order of two elements from $\mathcal{L}$. Then a PPAL client can send the server a subset S of m list elements and request the server to return the *maximum, minimum,* or the *median* element of S w.r.t. the order of the elements in the list. This can be done by providing m pair order proofs. Order queries also can be extended to return the *top t* elements of S by means of $t(m - t)$ pair order proofs, or only $m - 1$ pair order proofs if the order between the top t elements can be revealed, where $t < m$. Finally, given an element a in $\mathcal{L}$, the server can return the elements of S that are above (or below) the *threshold* value a by means of m pair order proofs. It is important to note that neither of these queries reveal anything more than the answer itself. Moreover, the size of the proof returned for each query is proportional to the query size and is optimal for the threshold query where the proof size is proportional to the answer size. We note that these statistical queries are also supported by ZKL.

2.2   Related Work

First, we discuss work on data structures that answer queries in zero knowledge. Our ZKL is the first extension of this work to lists and order queries. We then mention signature schemes that can be used to instantiate outsourced data structures that require privacy and integrity to be maintained. However, such instantiations are not efficient since they are based on different models of usage and underlying data. Finally, we outline leakage-free redactable signature schemes for ordered lists and other structured data. These signature schemes are not as efficient as our construction and their definitions are game-based as opposed to our intuitive zero-knowledge definition. Finally we discuss follow-up work on PPAL.

Zero Knowledge Data Structures: Zero-knowledge dictionary and range queries have received considerable attention in literature [10,12,26,29,32]. Our proposed ZKL model is the first generalization of this line of work that supports order queries.

The model of *zero knowledge set* (ZKS) was introduced by Micali *et al.* [29] where a prover commits to a finite set S in such a way that, later on, she will be able to efficiently (and non-interactively) prove statements of the form $x \in S$ or $x \notin S$ without leaking any information about S beyond what has been queried for, not even the size of S. The prover should not be able to prove contradictory statements about an element. Chase *et al.* [12] abstracted the above solution and described it in terms of a *mercurial commitment*, which was later generalized to q-trapdoor mercurial commitments in [10,26] and a closely related notion of *vector commitments* was proposed in [9]. Kate *et al.* [22] suggested a weaker primitive called *nearly-zero knowledge set* where the set size is not private. Ostrovsky *et al.* [32] generalized (non-)membership queries to orthogonal range queries on multidimensional dataset and considered adding privacy to their protocol. However, the use of NP-reductions and probabilistically checkable proofs makes their generic construction expensive.

We note that a recent work on DNSSEC zone enumeration by Goldberg *et al.* [18] uses a model related to our PPAL model and is independently developed. The framework supports only set (non-)membership queries and answers them in f-zero knowledge. This property ensures that the information leaked to the verifier is in terms of a function f on the set, e.g., f is the set size in [18].

Signature Schemes: A three party model where the owner digitally signs a data document and outsources it to the server and the server discloses to the client only part of the signed document along with a legitimately derived signature on it (without the owner's involvement), can be instantiated with a collection of signature schemes, namely, *content extraction, quotable, arithmetic, redactable, homomorphic, sanitizable and transitive signatures* [7,21,30,31,35,38]. Additionally, if the signatures reveal no information about the parent document, then this approach can be used to add privacy. However the generic instantiation, with signature schemes that do not specifically address structured data, is inefficient for most practical purposes.

Ahn *et al.* [1] present a unified framework for computing on authenticated data where a third party can derive a signature on an object x' from a signature on a parent object x as long as $P(x, x') = 1$ for some predicate P that captures the *authenticatable relationship* between x and x'. Additionally, a derived signature reveals no extra information about the parent x. This line of work was later refined in [2,37]. The authors in [1] propose a computationally expensive scheme based on the RSA accumulator and predicates for specific data structures are not considered. A related notion of malleable signature scheme was proposed in [13], where given a signature σ on a message x, it is possible to efficiently derive a signature σ' on a message x' such that $x' = T(x)$ for an *allowable* transformation T without access to the secret key. The privacy definition of [13] (simulation context hiding) is stronger than that of [1] as it allows for adversarially-generated keys and signatures. However, the owner is a trusted party in our PPAL setting and therefore the stronger notion of simulation context hiding is not relevant in this framework. Moreover, in our PPAL model, given a quote from a document and a proof of the quote, the client *should* be able to verify that the quote is indeed in the document, this is inverse of the notion of unlinkability in [13].

Leakage-Free Signature Schemes for Structural Data: A *leakage-free redactable signature scheme (LRSS)* allows a third party to remove, or *redact*, parts of a signed document without signer's involvement. The verifier only sees the remaining redacted document and is able to verify that it is valid and authentic. Leakage-freeness property ensures that the redacted document and its signature do not reveal anything about the content or position of the removed parts. We discuss LRSSs that specifically look at structural data and ordered lists. In Table 1 we show that PPAL outperforms known LRSS constructions. Another significant difference of our work is the definition of privacy. The zero-knowledge property is more intuitive and simple in capturing the leakage-freeness property compared to the game based definitions in the LRSS literature [6,34].

Kundu and Bertino [24] introduced the idea of structural signatures for ordered trees (subsuming ordered lists) that support public redaction of subtrees by third-parties. This work was later extended to undirected graphs and DAGs [25]. The notion was later formalized as *LRSS* for ordered trees in [6] and subsequently several attacks on [24] were also proposed in [6,33]. The basic idea of the LRSS scheme presented in [6] is to sign *all possible ordered pairs* of elements of an ordered list. So both the computation cost and the storage space are quadratic in the number of elements of the list.

Building on the work of [6,34] proposed a LRSS for lists that has quadratic time and space complexity. Poehls *et al.* [33] presented a LRSS scheme for a list that has linear time and space complexity but assumes an associative non-abelian hash function, whose existence has not been formally proved. Kundu *et al.* [23], presented a construction that uses quadratic space at the server. Chang *et al.* [11] presented a leakage-free redactable signature scheme for a string (which can be viewed as a list) that hides the location of the redacted or deleted portions of the string at the expense of quadratic verification cost. None of the constructions of [11,23,24] satisfy our definition of zero-knowledge.

Follow-up Work: Finally we note that in recent work [16], Ghosh *et al.* have generalized the models introduced in this paper to general abstract data types that support both query and update operations. Also, they have presented efficient constructions for dynamic lists and partially-ordered sets of bounded dimension.

2.3   Contributions and Organization of the Paper

Our contributions are novel models and efficient constructions. After reviewing preliminary concepts and cryptographic primitives, in Sect. 3, we introduce the zero-knowledge list (ZKL) model. We describe our ZKL construction, its security

Table 1. Comparison of our ZKL and PPAL constructions with previous work. All the time and space complexities are asymptotic. Notation: n is the list size, m is the query size, k is the security parameter. WLOG we assume list elements are k bit long. Following the standard convention, we omit a multiplicative factor of $O(k)$ for element size in every cell. Assumptions: Strong RSA Assumption (SRSA); Existential Unforgeability under Chosen Message Attack (EUCMA) of the underlying signature scheme; Random Oracle Model (ROM); n-Element Aggregate Extraction Assumption (nEAE); Associative non-abelian hash function (AnAHF) [**non-standard**]; Collision Resistant Hash Function (CRHF); Discrete Log Assumption (DL); Factoring a composite (FC); n-Bilinear Diffie Hellman Inversion Assumption (nBDHI).

	[35]	[21]	[11]	[6]	[34]	[33]	[23]	[12]	ZKL	PPAL
Zero-knowledge				✓	✓	✓		✓	✓	✓
Setup time	$n\log n$	n	n	n^2	n^2	n	n	nk	nk	n
Storage space	n	n	n	n^2	n^2	n	n^2	nk	nk	n
Order query time	m	$n\log n$	n	mn	m	n	n		mk	$\min(m\log n, n)$
(Non)-Member query time								mk	mk	
Order verification time	$m\log n\log m$	$m\log n$	n^2	m^2	m^2	m	m	mk	mk	m
(Non)-Member verification time								mk	mk	
Proof size	m	$m\log n$	n	m^2	m^2	m	n	mk	mk	m
Assumption	RSA	RSA	SRSA, Division	EUCMA, nEAE	ROM, nEAE	**AnAHF**	ROM, RSA	CRHF, DL	ROM, CRHF, SRSA, FC	ROM, nBDHI

and efficiency in Sect. 4. In Sect. 5, we introduce the privacy-preserving authenticated list (PPAL) model. An efficient PPAL construction based on bilinear maps, its performance and security properties are given in Sect. 6. In Table 1, we compare our ZKL and PPAL construction with previous work in terms of performance and assumptions. We specifically indicate which constructions satisfy the zero-knowledge property. Our PPAL construction outperforms all previous work based on widely accepted assumptions [6,34] (the construction of [33] is based on a non-standard assumption).

3   Preliminaries

3.1   Data Type

We consider a *linearly ordered list* $\mathcal{L}$ as a data structure that the owner wishes to store with the server. A list is an ordered set of elements $\mathcal{L} = \{x_1, x_2, \ldots, x_n\}$, where each $x_i \in \{0,1\}^*, \forall x_1, x_2 \in \mathcal{L}, x_1 \neq x_2$ and either $x_1 < x_2$ or $x_2 < x_1$. Hence, $<$ is a strict order on elements of $\mathcal{L}$ that is irreflexive, asymmetric and transitive.

We denote the set of elements of the list $\mathcal{L}$ as $\mathsf{Elements}(\mathcal{L})$. A sublist of $\mathcal{L}$, δ, is defined as: $\delta = \{x \mid x \in \mathsf{Elements}(\mathcal{L})\}$. Note that the order of elements in δ may not follow the order of $\mathcal{L}$. We denote with $\pi_{\mathcal{L}}(\delta)$ the permutation of the elements of δ under the order of $\mathcal{L}$. $\mathcal{L}(x_i)$ denotes the membership of element x_i in $\mathcal{L}$, i.e., $\mathcal{L}(x_i) = \mathsf{true}$ if $x_i \in \mathcal{L}$ and $\mathcal{L}(x_i) = \mathsf{false}$ if $x_i \notin \mathcal{L}$. For all x_i such that $\mathcal{L}(x_i) = \mathsf{true}$, $\mathsf{rank}(\mathcal{L}, x_i)$ denotes the rank of element x_i in the list, $\mathcal{L}$.

3.2   Cryptographic Primitives

We now describe the cryptographic primitives that are used in our construction and cryptographic assumptions that underlie the security of our method. In particular, our zero knowledge list construction relies on homomorphic integer commitments, zero knowledge protocol to prove a number is non-negative and zero knowledge sets, while the construction for privacy preserving lists relies on bilinear aggregate signatures and n-Bilinear Diffie Hellman Inversion assumption.

Homomorphic Integer Commitment Scheme: We use a homomorphic integer commitment scheme HomIntCom that is statistically hiding and computationally binding [5,14]. The latter implies the existence of a trapdoor and, hence, can be used to "equivocate" a commitment (i.e., open the commitment to any message using the trapdoor). We denote a commitment to x as $C(x; r)$ where r is the randomness used for the commitment. For simplicity, we sometimes drop r from the notation and use $C(x)$ to denote the commitment to x. The *homomorphism* of the scheme is defined as $C(x + y) = C(x) \times C(y)$.

Proving an Integer is Non-negative in Zero-Knowledge: We use the following (interactive) protocol between a prover and a verifier: the prover sends a commitment c to an integer $x \geq 0$ to the verifier and proves in zero-knowledge that the committed integer is non-negative, without opening c. We denote this protocol as $\mathsf{P} \leftrightarrow \mathsf{V}(x, r : c = C(x; r) \wedge x \geq 0)$. As a concrete construction we use the protocol of [27] which is a Σ protocol, i.e., *honest verifier zero knowledge* and can be made non-interactive zero-knowledge (NIZK) in the random oracle model using Fiat-Shamir heuristic [15].

Zero Knowledge Set Scheme: Let D be a set of key value pairs. If (x, v) is a key, value pair of D, then we write $D(x) = v$ to denote v is the value corresponding to the key x. For the keys that are not present in D, $x \notin D$, we write $D(x) = \bot$. A Zero Knowledge Set scheme (ZKS) [29] consists of three probabilistic polynomial time algorithms, $\mathsf{ZKS} = (\mathsf{ZKSSetup}, \mathsf{ZKSProver} = (\mathsf{ZKSP}_1, \mathsf{ZKSP}_2), \mathsf{ZKSVerifier})$, and queries are of the form "is key x in D?". The $\mathsf{ZKSSetup}$ algorithm takes the security parameter as input and produces a public key for the scheme that both the prover ($\mathsf{ZKSProver}$) and the verifier ($\mathsf{ZKSVerifier}$) take as input. The prover, Prover, is a tuple of two algorithms: ZKSP_1 takes the security parameter, the public key, and the set D and produces a short digest commitment com for D. ZKSP_2 takes a query x and produces the value $v = D(x)$, and the corresponding proof of (non-)membership, proof_x. The verifier, $\mathsf{ZKSVerifier}$, takes the security parameter, the public key, com, a query x, an answer $D(x)$, and proof_x and returns a bit b, where $b = \mathsf{ACCEPT}/\mathsf{REJECT}$. For our construction of zero knowledge lists we pick a ZKS construction of [12] that is based on mercurial commitments.

Bilinear Aggregate Signature Scheme: Our PPAL scheme relies on bilinear aggregate signature scheme of Boneh *et al.* [4]. Given signatures $\sigma_1, \ldots, \sigma_n$ on *distinct* messages $M_1, \ldots, M_n$ from n distinct users $u_1, \ldots, u_n$, it is possible to aggregate these signatures into a single short signature σ such that it (and the n messages) convince the verifier that the n users indeed signed the n original messages (i.e., user i signed message M_i). We use the special case where a single user signs n *distinct* messages $M_1, \ldots, M_n$. The security requirement of an aggregate signature scheme guarantees that the aggregate signature σ is valid if and only if the aggregator used all σ_i's to construct it.

3.3 Hardness Assumption

Let p be a large k-bit prime where $k \in \mathbb{N}$ is a security parameter. Let $n \in \mathbb{N}$ be polynomial in k, $n = \mathsf{poly}(k)$. Let $e : G \times G \to G_1$ be a bilinear map where G and G_1 are groups of prime order p and g be a random generator of G. We denote a probabilistic polynomial time (PPT) adversary $\mathcal{A}$ as an adversary who is running in time $\mathsf{poly}(k)$. We use $\mathcal{A}^{\mathsf{alg}(\mathsf{input}, \cdots)}$ to show that an adversary $\mathcal{A}$ has an oracle access to an instantiation of an algorithm alg with first argument set to input and $\ldots$ denoting that $\mathcal{A}$ can give arbitrary input for the rest of the arguments.

Definition 1 (n-Bilinear Diffie Hellman Inversion (n-BDHI) [3]). *Let s be a random element of $\mathbb{Z}_p^*$ and n be a positive integer. Then, for every PPT adversary $\mathcal{A}$ there exists a negligible function $\nu(.)$ such that:*

$$Pr[s \xleftarrow{\$} \mathbb{Z}_p^*; y \leftarrow \mathcal{A}(\langle g, g^s, g^{s^2}, \ldots, g^{s^n} \rangle) : y = e(g,g)^{\frac{1}{s}}] \leq \nu(k).$$

4   Zero Knowledge List (ZKL)

We generalize the idea of consistent set membership queries [12,29] to support membership and order queries in *zero-knowledge* on a list with *no repeated elements*. More specifically, given a totally ordered list of unique elements $\mathcal{L} = \{y_1, y_2, \ldots, y_n\}$, we want to support non-interactively and in zero-knowledge, (proofs reveal nothing beyond the query answer, not even the size of the list) queries of the following form:

- Is $y_i \in \mathcal{L}$ or $y_i \notin \mathcal{L}$, i.e., $\mathcal{L}(y_i) = \mathsf{true}$ or $\mathcal{L}(y_i) = \mathsf{false}$?
- For two elements $y_i, y_j \in \mathcal{L}$, what is their relative order, i.e., $y_i < y_j$ or $y_j < y_i$ in $\mathcal{L}$?

We adopt the same adversarial model as in [12,29,32]. There are two parties: the *prover* and the *verifier*. The *prover* initially commits to a list of elements and makes the commitment public. We now formally describe the model and the security properties.

4.1   Model

A Zero Knowledge List scheme (ZKL) consists of three probabilistic polynomial time algorithms: (Setup, Prover = $(\mathsf{P}_1, \mathsf{P}_2)$, Verifier). The queries are of the form (δ, flag) where $\delta = \{z_1, \ldots, z_m\}$, $z_i \in \{0,1\}^*$, is a collection of elements, $\mathsf{flag} = 0$ denotes a (non-)membership query and $\mathsf{flag} = 1$ denotes an order query. In the following sections, we will use state to represent a variable that saves the current state of the algorithm (when it finishes execution).

PK $\leftarrow$ Setup(1^k) The Setup algorithm takes the security parameter as input and produces a public key PK for the scheme. The prover and the verifier both take as input the string PK that can be a random string (in which case, the protocol is in the common random string model) or have a specific structure (in which case the protocol is in the trusted parameters model).

(com, state) $\leftarrow \mathsf{P}_1(1^k, \mathsf{PK}, \mathcal{L})$ P_1 takes the security parameter, the public key PK and the list $\mathcal{L}$, and produces a short digest commitment com for the list.

(member, proof_M, order, proof_O) $\leftarrow \mathsf{P}_2(\mathsf{PK}, \mathsf{state}, \delta, \mathsf{flag})$ where $\delta = \{z_1, \ldots, z_m\}$ and flag denotes the type of query. P_2 produces the membership information of the queried elements, member $= \{\mathcal{L}(z_1), \ldots, \mathcal{L}(z_m)\}$ and the proof of membership (and non-membership), proof_M. proof_O is set depending on flag:
  flag $= 0$: P_2 sets order and proof_O to $\perp$ and returns (member, $\mathsf{proof}_M, \perp, \perp$).
  flag $= 1$: Let $\tilde{\delta} = \{z_i \mid i \in [1, m] \wedge \mathcal{L}(z_i) = \mathsf{true}\}$. P_2 produces the correct list order among the elements of $\tilde{\delta}$, order $= \pi_\mathcal{L}(\tilde{\delta})$, and the proof of the order, proof_O.

$b \leftarrow$ Verifier(1^k, PK, com, δ, flag, member, proof$_M$, order, proof$_O$) Verifier takes the security parameter, the public key PK, the commitment com and a query (δ, flag) and member, proof$_M$, order, proof$_O$ and returns a bit b, where $b =$ ACCEPT/REJECT.

Example: Let us illustrate the above functionality with a small example. Let $\mathcal{L} = \{A, B, C\}$ and (δ, flag) = ($\{B, D, A\}$, 1) be the query. Given this query P$_2$ returns member = $\{\mathcal{L}(B), \mathcal{L}(D), \mathcal{L}(A)\}$ = $\{$true, false, true$\}$, the corresponding proofs of membership and non-membership in proof$_M$, order = $\{A, B\}$ and the corresponding proof of order between A and B in proof$_O$.

4.2 Security Properties

Recall that the security properties of ZKL, *Completeness, Soundness* and *Zero-Knowledge*, guarantee security against malicious prover and verifier. Completeness mandates that honestly generated proofs always satisfy the verification test. Soundness states that the prover should not be able to come up with a query, and corresponding inconsistent (with the initial commitment) answers and convincing proofs. Finally, zero-knowledge ensures that each proof reveals the answer and nothing else.

Definition 2 (Completeness). *For every list $\mathcal{L}$, every query δ and every* flag,

$\Pr[$PK $\leftarrow$ Setup(1^k);

(com, state) $\leftarrow$ P$_1$(1^k, PK, $\mathcal{L}$);

(member, proof$_M$, order, proof$_O$) $\leftarrow$ P$_2$(PK, state, δ, flag) :

Verifier(1^k, PK, com, δ, flag, member, proof$_M$, order, proof$_O$) = ACCEPT] = 1

Definition 3 (Soundness). *For every PPT malicious prover algorithm,* Adv, *for every query δ and for every* flag *there exists a negligible function* $\nu(.)$ *such that:*

$\Pr[$PK $\leftarrow$ Setup(1^k);

(com, member^1, proof$_M^1$, order^1, proof$_O^1$, member^2,

proof$_M^2$, order^2, proof$_O^2$) $\leftarrow$ Adv(1^k, PK) :

Verifier(1^k, PK, com, δ, flag, member^1, proof$_M^1$, order^1, proof$_O^1$) = ACCEPT$\wedge$

Verifier(1^k, PK, com, δ, flag, member^2, proof$_M^2$, order^2, proof$_O^2$) = ACCEPT$\wedge$

((member$^1 \neq$ member^2) $\vee$ (order$^1 \neq$ order^2))] $\leq \nu(k)$

Definition 4 (Zero-Knowledge). *There exists a PPT simulator* Sim = (Sim$_1$, Sim$_2$, Sim$_3$) *such that for every PPT malicious verifier* Adv =

$(\mathsf{Adv}_1, \mathsf{Adv}_2)$, *there exists a negligible function* $\nu(.)$ *such that:*

$$| \Pr[\mathsf{PK} \leftarrow \mathsf{Setup}(1^k); (\mathcal{L}, \mathsf{state}_A) \leftarrow \mathsf{Adv}_1(1^k, \mathsf{PK});$$

$$(\mathsf{com}, \mathsf{state}_P) \leftarrow \mathsf{P}_1(1^k, \mathsf{PK}, \mathcal{L}) :$$

$$\mathsf{Adv}_2^{\mathsf{P}_2(\mathsf{PK}, \mathsf{state}_P, \cdot)}(\mathsf{com}, \mathsf{state}_A) = 1] -$$

$$\Pr[(\mathsf{PK}, \mathsf{state}_S) \leftarrow \mathsf{Sim}_1(1^k); (\mathcal{L}, \mathsf{state}_A) \leftarrow \mathsf{Adv}_1(1^k, \mathsf{PK});$$

$$(\mathsf{com}, \mathsf{state}_S) \leftarrow \mathsf{Sim}_2(1^k, \mathsf{state}_S) :$$

$$\mathsf{Adv}_2^{\mathsf{Sim}_3^{\mathcal{L}}(1^k, \mathsf{state}_S)}(\mathsf{com}, \mathsf{state}_A) = 1]| \leq \nu(k),$$

where Sim_3 *has oracle access to* $\mathcal{L}$, *that is, given a query* (δ, flag), Sim_3 *can query the list* $\mathcal{L}$ *to learn only the membership/non-membership of elements in* δ *and, if* $\mathsf{flag} = 1$, *learn the list order of the elements of* δ *in* $\mathcal{L}$.

4.3 ZKL Construction

The construction uses zero knowledge set scheme, homomorphic integer commitment scheme, zero-knowledge protocol to prove non-negativity of an integer and a collision resistant hash function $\mathbb{H} : \{0,1\}^* \rightarrow \{0,1\}^l$, if the elements of the list $\mathcal{L}$ are larger that l bits. In particular, given an input list $\mathcal{L}$ the prover P_1 creates a set D where for every element $y_j \in \mathcal{L}$ it adds a (key,value) pair $(\mathbb{H}(y_j), C(j))$. $\mathbb{H}(y_j)$ is a hash of y_j and $C(j)$ is a homomorphic integer commitment of $\mathsf{rank}(\mathcal{L}, y_j)$ (assuming $\mathsf{rank}(\mathcal{L}, y_j) = j$, wlog). P_1 sets up a zero knowledge set on D using ZKSP_1 from a zero-knowledge set scheme $\mathsf{ZKS} = (\mathsf{ZKSSetup}, \mathsf{ZKSProver} = (\mathsf{ZKSP}_1, \mathsf{ZKSP}_2), \mathsf{ZKSVerifier})$ [12]. The output of ZKSP_1 is a commitment to D, com, that P_1 sends to the verifier.

P_2 operates as follows. Membership and non-membership queries of the form $(\delta, 0)$ are replied in the same fashion as in zero knowledge set, by invoking ZKSP_2 on the hash of every element of sublist δ. Recall that as a response to a membership query for a key, ZKSP_2 returns the value corresponding to this key. In our case, the queried key is $\mathbb{H}(y_j)$ and the value returned by ZKSP_2, $D(\mathbb{H}(y_j))$, is the commitment $C(j)$ where j is the rank of element y_j in the list $\mathcal{L}$, if $y_j \in \mathcal{L}$. If $y_j \notin \mathcal{L}$, the value returned is $\perp$. Hence, the verifier receives the commitments to ranks for queried member elements. These commitments are never opened but are used as part of order proofs.

For a given order query $(\delta, 1)$, for every adjacent pair of elements in the returned order, order, P_2 gives a proof of order. Recall that order contains the member elements of δ, arranged according to their order in the list $\mathcal{L}$. P_2 proves the order between two elements y_i and y_j as follows. Let $\mathsf{rank}(\mathcal{L}, y_i) = i, \mathsf{rank}(\mathcal{L}, y_j) = j$, and $C(i), C(j)$ be the corresponding commitments and, wlog, let $i < j$. As noted above, $C(i)$ and $C(j)$ are already returned by P_2 as part of the membership proof. Additionally, P_2 returns a commitment to 1, $C(1)$, and its opening information ρ. Note that, the verifier can compute $C(1)$ himself, but then the prover needs $C(1)$ computed by the verifier, to be able to generate proof for non-negativity of $C(j - i - 1)$. To avoid this interaction, we make the prover send $C(1)$ and its opening.

The verification of the query answer proceeds as follows. Verifier computes $C(j - i - 1) := C(j)/(C(i)C(1))$ using the homomorphic property of the integer commitment scheme. P_2 uses the zero knowledge protocol $P \leftrightarrow V(x, r : c = C(x; r) \land x \geq 0)$ to convince Verifier that $C(j - i - 1)$ is a commitment to value ≥ 0. Note that we use the non-interactive general zero-knowledge version of the protocol as discussed in Sect. 3. Hence, the query phase proceeds in a single round.

We note that we require Verifier to verify that $j - i - 1 \geq 0$ and not $j - i \geq 0$ since otherwise a cheating prover Adv can do the following: store the same arbitrary non-negative integer as a rank for every element in the list, hence, $C(j - i)$ and $C(i - j)$ are commitments to 0, and Adv can always succeed in proving an arbitrary order. However, an honest prover can always prove the non-negativity of $C(j - i - 1)$ as $|j - i| \geq 1$ for any rank i, j of the list.

Also, we note that the commitments to ranks can be replaced by commitments to a strictly monotonic sequence as long as there is a 1:1 correspondence with the rank sequence. In this case, the distance between two elements will also be positive and, hence, the above protocol still holds.

Theorem 1. *The zero-knowledge list (ZKL) construction of Sect. 4.3 is a non-interactive two-party protocol that satisfies the security properties of completeness (Definition 2), soundness (Definition 3) and zero-knowledge (Definition 4) in the random oracle model (inherited from NIZK). The construction has the following performance, where n is the list size, m is the query size, each element of the list is a k-bit (if not, we can use a hash function to reduce every element to a k-bit string, as shown in the construction).*

- *The prover executes the commitment phase in $O(nk)$ time and space, where the multiplicative factor k is inherited from the height of the tree.*
- *In the query phase, the prover computes the proof of the answer in $O(mk)$ time.*
- *The verifier verifies the proof in $O(mk)$ time and space.*

The soundness of the ZKL scheme follows from the soundness of the ZKS scheme, the binding property of the commitment scheme, and the correctness of protocol $P \leftrightarrow V(x, r : c = C(x; r) \land x \geq 0)$ (see Sect. 3.2). For the zero-knowledge property, we write a simulator that uses the ZKS simulator and the trapdoor of the commitment scheme to equivocate commitments. The formal proof of Theorem 1 is omitted due to space restrictions and is presented in [17].

5   Privacy Preserving Authenticated List (PPAL)

In the previous section we presented a model and a construction for a new primitive called zero knowledge lists. As we noticed earlier, ZKL model gives the desired functionality to verify order queries on lists. However, the corresponding construction does not provide the efficiency one may desire in cloud computing setting where the verifier (client) has limited memory resources as we discuss in Sect. 5.3. In this section we address this setting and define a model for privacy preserving authenticated lists, PPAL, that is executed between three parties. This model, arguably, fits cloud scenario better and, as we will see, our construction is also more efficient.

5.1   Model

PPAL is a tuple of three probabilistic polynomial time algorithms (Setup, Query, Verify) executed between the owner of the data list $\mathcal{L}$, the server who stores $\mathcal{L}$ and answers queries from the client and the client who issues queries on the elements of the list and verifies corresponding answers. We note that this model assumes that the query is on the member elements of the list, i.e., for any query, δ, Elements(δ) $\subseteq$ Elements($\mathcal{L}$). In other words, this model does not support proofs of non-membership, similar to other data structures that support only positive membership proofs, e.g., [6,8,9,11,23,24,33].

(digest$_C$, digest$_S$) $\leftarrow$ Setup($1^k, \mathcal{L}$) This algorithm takes the security parameter and the source list $\mathcal{L}$ as input and produces two digests digest$_C$ and digest$_S$ for the list. This algorithm is run by the owner. digest$_C$ is sent to the client and digest$_S$ is sent to the server.

(order, proof) $\leftarrow$ Query(digest$_S, \mathcal{L}, \delta$) This algorithm takes the server digest generated by the owner, digest$_S$, the source list, $\mathcal{L}$, and a queried sublist, δ, as input, where a sublist of a list $\mathcal{L}$ is defined as: Elements(δ) $\subseteq$ Elements($\mathcal{L}$). The algorithm produces the list order of the elements of $\mathcal{L}$, order $= \pi_{\mathcal{L}}(\delta)$, and a proof, proof, of the answer. This algorithm is run by the server. Wlog, we assume $|\delta| > 1$. In the trivial case of $|\delta| = 1$, the server returns an empty proof, i.e., (order $= \delta$, proof $= \bot$).

$b \leftarrow$ Verify(digest$_C, \delta$, order, proof) This algorithm takes digest$_C$, a queried sublist δ, order and proof and returns a bit b, where $b = $ ACCEPT iff Elements(δ) $\subseteq$ Elements($\mathcal{L}$) and order $= \pi_{\mathcal{L}}(\delta)$. Otherwise, $b = $ REJECT. This algorithm is run by the client.

5.2   Security Properties

A PPAL has three important security properties. Recall that the properties of PPAL, *Completeness*, *Soundness* and *Zero-Knowledge*, guarantee security against malicious server and client. They are close to the ones of ZKL except for soundness. For PPAL it enforces that the client does not accept proofs forged by the server for incorrect answers w.r.t. owner's list. We describe each security definition formally below.

The first property is *Completeness*. This property ensures that for any list $\mathcal{L}$ and for any sublist δ of $\mathcal{L}$, if digest$_C$, digest$_S$, order, proof are generated honestly, i.e., the owner and the server honestly execute the protocol, then the client will be always convinced about the correct list order of δ.

Definition 5 (Completeness). *For all lists* $\mathcal{L}$ *and all sublists* δ *of* $\mathcal{L}$

$$\Pr[(\text{digest}_C, \text{digest}_S) \leftarrow \text{Setup}(1^k, \mathcal{L}); (\text{order}, \text{proof}) \leftarrow \text{Query}(\text{digest}_S, \mathcal{L}, \delta) :$$
$$\text{Verify}(\text{digest}_C, \delta, \text{order}, \text{proof}) = \text{ACCEPT} \wedge \text{order} = \pi_{\mathcal{L}}(\delta)] = 1$$

The second security property is *Soundness*. This property ensures that once an honest owner generates a pair ($\text{digest}_C, \text{digest}_S$) for a list $\mathcal{L}$, even a malicious server will not be able to convince the client of an incorrect order of elements belonging to the list $\mathcal{L}$. This property ensures integrity of the scheme.

Definition 6 (Soundness). *For all PPT malicious query algorithms* Adv, *for all lists* $\mathcal{L}$ *and all query sublists* δ *of* $\mathcal{L}$, *there exists a negligible function* $\nu(.)$ *such that:*

$$\Pr[(\text{digest}_C, \text{digest}_S) \leftarrow \text{Setup}(1^k, \mathcal{L}); (\text{order}, \text{proof}) \leftarrow \text{Adv}(\text{digest}_S, \mathcal{L}) :$$
$$\text{Verify}(\text{digest}_C, \delta, \text{order}, \text{proof}) = \text{ACCEPT} \wedge \text{order} \neq \pi_{\mathcal{L}}(\delta)] \leq \nu(k)$$

The last property is *Zero-Knowledge*. This property captures that even a malicious client cannot learn anything about the list (and its size) beyond what the client has queried for. Informally, this property involves showing that there exists a simulator such that even for adversarially chosen list $\mathcal{L}$, no adversarial client (verifier) can tell if it is talking to a honest owner and honest server who know $\mathcal{L}$ and answer w.r.t. $\mathcal{L}$, or to the simulator that only has oracle access to the list $\mathcal{L}$.

Definition 7 (Zero-Knowledge). *There exists a PPT simulator* Sim $=$ $(\text{Sim}_1, \text{Sim}_2)$ *such that for all PPT malicious verifiers* Adv $= (\text{Adv}_1, \text{Adv}_2)$, *there exists a negligible function* $\nu(.)$ *such that:*

$$| \Pr[(\mathcal{L}, \text{state}_A) \leftarrow \text{Adv}_1(1^k); (\text{digest}_C, \text{digest}_S) \leftarrow \text{Setup}(1^k, \mathcal{L}) :$$
$$\text{Adv}_2^{\text{Query}(\text{digest}_S, \mathcal{L}, .)}(\text{digest}_C, \text{state}_A) = 1]-$$
$$\Pr[(\mathcal{L}, \text{state}_A) \leftarrow \text{Adv}_1(1^k); (\text{digest}_C, \text{state}_S) \leftarrow \text{Sim}_1(1^k) :$$
$$\text{Adv}_2^{\text{Sim}_2^{\mathcal{L}}(1^k, \text{state}_S)}(\text{digest}_C, \text{state}_A) = 1]| \leq \nu(k)$$

Here Sim_2 has oracle access to $\mathcal{L}$, that is given a sublist δ of $\mathcal{L}$, Sim_2 can query the list $\mathcal{L}$ to learn only the correct list order of the sublist δ and cannot look at $\mathcal{L}$.

5.3 Construction of PPAL via ZKL

We show how a PPAL can be instantiated via a ZKL in Theorems 2 and 3 and then discuss that the resulting construction does not yield the desired efficiency.

Theorem 2. *Given a non-interactive ZKL scheme* ZKL $=$ (Setup, Prover $=$ (P_1, P_2), Verifier), *which supports queries of the form* (δ, flag) *on a list* $\mathcal{L}$, *we can instantiate a PPAL scheme for the list* $\mathcal{L}$, PPAL $=$ (Setup, Query, Verify), *which supports queries of the form* δ, *where* δ *is a sublist of* $\mathcal{L}$, *as follows:*

PPAL.Setup($1^k, \mathcal{L}$): *Invoke* PK $\leftarrow$ ZKL.Setup(1^k) *and* (com, state) $\leftarrow$ ZKL.
    $P_1(1^k, PK, \mathcal{L})$. *Return* (digest$_C$ = (PK, com), digest$_S$ = (PK, com, state)).
PPAL.Query(digest$_S$, $\mathcal{L}$, δ): *Invoke* (member, proof$_M$, order, proof$_O$) $\leftarrow$ ZKL.
    $P_2(PK, state, \delta, 1)$. *Return* (order, proof = (proof$_M$, proof$_O$)).
PPAL.Verify(digest$_C$, δ, order, proof$_M$, proof$_O$): *Set* member = $\{1, 1, \ldots, 1\}$
    such that |member| = |δ| = |order|. *Return bit b where b* $\leftarrow$
    ZKL.Verifier(1^k, PK, com, δ, 1, member, proof$_M$, order, proof$_O$).

Theorem 3. *A PPAL scheme instantiated using a ZKL scheme,* ZKL =
(Setup, Prover = (P_1, P_2), Verifier) *has the following performance:*

- *The owner's runtime and space are proportional to the runtime and space of*
  ZKL.Setup *and* ZKL.P_1, *respectively.*
- *The server's runtime and space are proportional to the runtime and space of*
  ZKL.P_2.
- *The client's runtime and space are proportional to the runtime and space of*
  ZKL.Verifier.

The correctness of Theorems 2 and 3 follow from the definition of PPAL and
ZKL models. In a PPAL instantiated with the ZKL construction of Sect. 4, the
owner runs in time and space $O(kn)$ and the server requires space $O(kn)$, where
n is the list size and each element of the list is k-bits long. To answer a query of
size m, the server runs in time $O(km)$ and the verification time of the client is
$O(km)$.

As we see, this generic construction is not very efficient due to the multiplicative factor $O(k)$ and heavy cryptographic primitives. In Sect. 6, we present
a direct PPAL construction which is a factor of $O(k)$ more efficient in space and
computation requirements as compared to an adaptation of our ZKL construction from Sect. 4.

6   PPAL Construction

We start by presenting the intuition behind our construction of a privacy preserving authenticated list (PPAL). Next, we give more details on the algorithms
and analyze the security and efficiency of the construction.

Intuition: Every element of the list is associated with a member witness where
a member witness is a blinded component of the bilinear accumulator public
key. This allows us to encode the rank of the element in the member witness and
then "blind" rank information with randomness. Every pair of (element, member
witness) is signed by the owner and the signatures are aggregated using bilinear
aggregate signature scheme [4], to compute the list digest signature. Signatures
and digest are sent to the server, who can use them to prove authenticity when
answering client queries. The owner also sends the list digest signature and the
public key of the bilinear aggregate signature scheme to the client. The advantage
of using an aggregate signature is for the server to be able to compute a valid

digest signature for any sublist of the source list by exploiting the homomorphic nature of aggregate signatures, that is without owner's involvement. Moreover, the client can verify the individual signatures in a single invocation to aggregate signature verification.

The owner also sends to the server linear (in the list size) number of random elements used in the encoding of member witnesses. These random elements allow the server to compute the order witnesses on queried elements, without the owner's involvement. The order witness encodes the distance between two elements, i.e., the difference between element ranks, without revealing anything about it. Together with member witnesses, the client can later use bilinear map to verify the order of the elements.

Construction: Our construction for PPAL is presented in Fig. 1. We denote *member witness* for $x_i \in \mathcal{L}$ as $t_{x_i \in \mathcal{L}}$. For two elements $x_i, x_j \in \mathcal{L}$, such that $x_i < x_j$ in $\mathcal{L}$, $t_{x_i < x_j}$ is an *order witness* for the order between x_i and x_j. The construction works as follows.

In the Setup phase, the owner generates secret key (v, s) and public key g^v, where v is used for signatures. The owner picks a distinct random element r_i from the group $\mathbb{Z}_p^*$ for each element x_i in the list $\mathcal{L}$, $i \in [1, n]$. The element r_i is used to compute the member witness $t_{x_i \in \mathcal{L}}$. Later in the protocol, together with r_j, it is also used by the server to compute the order witness $t_{x_i < x_j}$. The owner also computes individual signatures, σ_i's, for each element and aggregates them into a digest signature $\sigma_{\mathcal{L}}$ for the list. It returns the signatures and member witnesses for every element of $\mathcal{L}$ in $\Sigma_{\mathcal{L}}$ and the set of random numbers picked for each index to be used in order witnesses in $\Omega_{\mathcal{L}}$. The owner sends $\mathsf{digest}_C = (g^v, \sigma_{\mathcal{L}})$ to the client and $\mathsf{digest}_S = (g^v, \sigma_{\mathcal{L}}, \langle g, g^s, g^{s^2}, \ldots, g^{s^n} \rangle, \Sigma_{\mathcal{L}}, \Omega_{\mathcal{L}})$ and $\mathcal{L}$ to the server.

Given a query δ, the server returns a response list order that contains elements of δ in the order they appear in $\mathcal{L}$. The server uses information in $\Sigma_{\mathcal{L}}$ to compute the digest signature for the sublist, σ_{order}, and its membership verification unit $\lambda_{\mathcal{L}'}$ which are part of the Σ_{order} component of the proof. To compute the Ω_{order} component of the proof, the server uses corresponding blinding values in $\Omega_{\mathcal{L}}$ and elements g^{s^d} where d's correspond to distances between ranks of queried elements.

The client first checks that all the returned elements are signed by the owner using Σ_{order} and then verifies the order of the returned elements using Ω_{order}. Hence, the client uses bilinear map for two purposes: first for member verification and then to verify the order. The query phase has a single round of communication between client and server.

We now describe the preprocessing step at the server that reduces the query time for a query of size m on a list of size n from $O(n)$ to $O(\min\{m \log n, n\})$. Let $\psi_i = \mathcal{H}(t_{x_i \in \mathcal{L}} || x_i)$ for $x_i \in \mathcal{L}$. The server computes and stores a balanced binary tree over n leaves, where the ith leaf corresponds to x_i and stores ψ_i. Each internal node of the tree stores the product of the values at its children. When answering a query of size m, the server can compute $\lambda_{\mathcal{L}'}$ by using partial products that correspond to intervals between elements in the query. There are $m + 1$ such partial products. Since each partial product can be computed using

Notation: $k \in \mathbb{N}$ is the security parameter of the scheme; G, G_1 multiplicative cyclic groups of prime order p where p is large k-bit prime; g: a random generator of G; e: computable bilinear nondegenerate map $e : G \times G \to G_1$; $\mathcal{H} : \{0,1\}^* \to G$: full domain hash function (instantiated with a cryptographic hash function); all arithmetic operations are performed using $\mod p$. $\mathcal{L}$ is the input list of size $n = \text{poly}(k)$, where x_i's are distinct and $\text{rank}(\mathcal{L}, x_i) = i$. System parameters are $(p, G, G_1, e, g, \mathcal{H})$.

$(\text{digest}_C, \text{digest}_S) \leftarrow \text{Setup}(1^k, \mathcal{L})$, where

$\mathcal{L}$ is the input list of length n;

$\text{digest}_C = (g^v, \sigma_\mathcal{L})$;

$\text{digest}_S = (g^v, \sigma_\mathcal{L}, \langle g, g^s, g^{s^2}, \ldots, g^{s^n}\rangle, \Sigma_\mathcal{L}, \Omega_\mathcal{L})$ and

$\langle s \overset{\$}{\leftarrow} \mathbb{Z}_p^*, v \overset{\$}{\leftarrow} \mathbb{Z}_p^* \rangle$ is the secret key of the owner;

$\Sigma_\mathcal{L} = \langle \{t_{x_i \in \mathcal{L}}, \sigma_i\}_{1 \le i \le n}, \mathcal{H}(\omega)\rangle$ is member authentication information and ω is the list nonce;

$\Omega_\mathcal{L} = \langle r_1, r_2, \ldots, r_n\rangle, r_i \ne r_j$ for $i \ne j$, is order authentication information;

$\sigma_\mathcal{L}$ is the digest signature of the list $\mathcal{L}$.

These elements are computed as follows:

For every element x_i in $\mathcal{L} = \{x_1, \ldots, x_n\}$: Pick $r_i \overset{\$}{\leftarrow} \mathbb{Z}_p^*$. Compute member witness for index i as $t_{x_i \in \mathcal{L}} \leftarrow (g^{s^i})^{r_i}$ and signature for element x_i as $\sigma_i \leftarrow \mathcal{H}(t_{x_i \in \mathcal{L}} || x_i)^v$.

Pick the nonce, $\omega \overset{\$}{\leftarrow} \{0,1\}^*$, which should be unique for each list.

Set salt $\leftarrow (\mathcal{H}(\omega))^v$. salt is treated as a list identifier which protects against mix-and-match attack and also protects from the leakage that the queried result is the complete list.

The list digest signature is computed as: $\sigma_\mathcal{L} \leftarrow \text{salt} \times \prod_{1 \le i \le n} \sigma_i$.

$(\text{order}, \text{proof}) \leftarrow \text{Query}(\text{digest}_S, \mathcal{L}, \delta)$, where

$\delta = \{z_1, \ldots, z_m\}$ s.t. $z_i \in \mathcal{L}, \forall i \in [1, m]$, is the queried sublist;

$\text{order} = \pi_\mathcal{L}(\delta) = \{y_1, \ldots, y_m\}$;

$\text{proof} = (\Sigma_{\text{order}}, \Omega_{\text{order}})$:

$\Sigma_{\text{order}} = (\sigma_{\text{order}}, T, \lambda_{\mathcal{L}'})$ where $\mathcal{L}' = \mathcal{L} \setminus \delta$;

$T = \{t_{y_1 \in \mathcal{L}}, \ldots, t_{y_m \in \mathcal{L}}\}$;

$\Omega_{\text{order}} = \{t_{y_1 < y_2}, t_{y_2 < y_3}, \ldots, t_{y_{m-1} < y_m}\}$.

These elements are computed as follows:

The digest signature for the sublist: $\sigma_{\text{order}} \leftarrow \prod_{y_j \in \text{order}} \sigma_{\text{rank}(\mathcal{L}, y_j)}$.

The member verification unit: $\lambda_{\mathcal{L}'} \leftarrow \mathcal{H}(\omega) \times \prod_{x \in \mathcal{L}'} \mathcal{H}(t_{x_{\text{rank}(\mathcal{L}, x)} \in \mathcal{L}} || x)$.

For every $j \in [1, m-1]$: Let $i' = \text{rank}(\mathcal{L}, y_j)$ and $i'' = \text{rank}(\mathcal{L}, y_{j+1})$, and $r' = \Omega_\mathcal{L}[i']^{-1}$ and $r'' = \Omega_\mathcal{L}[i'']$. Compute $t_{y_j < y_{j+1}} \leftarrow (g^{s^d})^{r' r''}$ where $d = |i' - i''|$.

$b \leftarrow \text{Verify}(\text{digest}_C, \delta, \text{order}, \text{proof})$ where $\text{digest}_C, \delta, \text{order}, \text{proof}$ are defined as above. The algorithm checks the following:

- Compute $\xi \leftarrow \prod_{y_j \in \delta} \mathcal{H}(t_{y_j \in \mathcal{L}} || y_j)$ and check if $e(\sigma_{\text{order}}, g) \overset{?}{=} e(\xi, g^v)$.

- Check if $e(\sigma_\mathcal{L}, g) \overset{?}{=} e(\sigma_{\text{order}}, g) \times e(\lambda_{\mathcal{L}'}, g^v)$.

- For every $j \in [1, m-1]$, $e(t_{y_j \in \mathcal{L}}, t_{y_j < y_{j+1}}) \overset{?}{=} e(t_{y_{j+1} \in \mathcal{L}}, g)$.

Return ACCEPT iff all the equalities of the three steps verify, and REJECT, otherwise.

Fig. 1. Privacy-preserving authenticated list (PPAL) construction

$O(\log n)$ precomputed products in the tree, it takes $O(m \log n)$ time to compute the product of $m + 1$ of them. The server takes $O(n)$ for preprocessing and the query time is reduced to $O(\min\{m \log n, n\})$.

We summarize the properties and efficiency of our PPAL construction in Theorem 4.

Theorem 4. *The privacy-preserving authenticated list (PPAL) construction of Fig. 1 satisfies the security properties of completeness (Definition 5), soundness (Definition 6) and zero-knowledge (Definition 7) in the random oracle model (inherited from [4]) and under the n-BDHI assumption (Definition 1). Also, the construction has the following performance, where n denotes the list size and m denotes the query size.*

- *The owner and the server use $O(n)$ space.*
- *The owner performs the setup phase in $O(n)$ time and goes offline.*
- *The server performs the preprocessing phase in $O(n)$ time.*
- *Query phase is a single-round protocol between the server and the client.*
- *The server computes the answer to a query and its proof in $O(\min\{m \log n, n\})$ time.*
- *The client verifies the proof in $O(m)$ time and space.*

The formal proof is omitted due to space restrictions and is available in [17]. Here we highlight the proof of soundness and zero knowledge. To prove soundness, we assume that there exists a malicious server Adv, which forges the order on a non-trivial sublist $\delta = \{x_1, \ldots, x_m\}$, where $m \geq 2$, for a list $\mathcal{L}$. Then there exists at least one inversion pair (x_i, x_j) whose order is flipped in Adv's forgery. Wlog assume that $u < v$ where $u = \mathsf{rank}(\mathcal{L}, x_i)$ and $v = \mathsf{rank}(\mathcal{L}, x_j)$. Then Adv must have forged the witness $t_{x_j < x_i} = \left(g^{s^{(u-v)}}\right)^{r_1 r_2^{-1}}$ that passes the verification, where $r_1, r_2 \in \mathbb{Z}_p^*$ are the blinded components of elements x_i and x_j, respectively. We show that by invoking Adv and using its forged witness $t_{x_j < x_i}$, we can construct a PPT adversary that successfully breaks the n-BDHI hardness assumption [3] by outputting $e\left(t_{x_j < x_i}, (g^{s^{v-u-1}})^{r_1^{-1} r_2}\right) = e(g, g)^{\frac{1}{s}}$, where $g^{s^{v-u-1}}$ is part of the input to the n-BDHI problem.

For the zero knowledge property, we write a simulator that can produce witnesses identically distributed to real witnesses by giving it only oracle access to the list, and using the fact that our PPAL construction uses witnesses blinded in their exponents.

Acknowledgment. This research was supported in part by the National Science Foundation under grant CNS–1228485. Olga Ohrimenko worked on this project in part while at Brown University. We are grateful to Melissa Chase, Markulf Kohlweiss, Anna Lysyanskaya, and Claire Mathieu for useful discussions and for their feedback on early drafts of this work. We would also like to thank Ashish Kundu for introducing us to his work on structural signatures and Jia Xu for sharing a paper through personal communication.

References

1. Ahn, J.H., Boneh, D., Camenisch, J., Hohenberger, S., Shelat, A., Waters, B.: Computing on authenticated data. In: Cramer, R. (ed.) TCC 2012. LNCS, vol. 7194, pp. 1–20. Springer, Heidelberg (2012)
2. Attrapadung, N., Libert, B., Peters, T.: Computing on authenticated data: new privacy definitions and constructions. In: Wang, X., Sako, K. (eds.) ASIACRYPT 2012. LNCS, vol. 7658, pp. 367–385. Springer, Heidelberg (2012)
3. Boneh, D., Boyen, X.: Efficient selective-ID secure identity-based encryption without random oracles. In: Cachin, C., Camenisch, J.L. (eds.) EUROCRYPT 2004. LNCS, vol. 3027, pp. 223–238. Springer, Heidelberg (2004)
4. Boneh, D., Gentry, C., Lynn, B., Shacham, H.: Aggregate and verifiably encrypted signatures from bilinear maps. In: Biham, E. (ed.) EUROCRYPT 2003. LNCS, vol. 2656, pp. 416–432. Springer, Heidelberg (2003)
5. Boudot, F.: Efficient proofs that a committed number lies in an interval. In: Preneel, B. (ed.) EUROCRYPT 2000. LNCS, vol. 1807, pp. 431–444. Springer, Heidelberg (2000)
6. Brzuska, C., et al.: Redactable signatures for tree-structured data: definitions and constructions. In: Zhou, J., Yung, M. (eds.) ACNS 2010. LNCS, vol. 6123, pp. 87–104. Springer, Heidelberg (2010)
7. Camacho, P., Hevia, A.: Short transitive signatures for directed trees. In: Dunkelman, O. (ed.) CT-RSA 2012. LNCS, vol. 7178, pp. 35–50. Springer, Heidelberg (2012)
8. Camenisch, J., Kohlweiss, M., Soriente, C.: An accumulator based on bilinear maps and efficient revocation for anonymous credentials. In: Jarecki, S., Tsudik, G. (eds.) PKC 2009. LNCS, vol. 5443, pp. 481–500. Springer, Heidelberg (2009)
9. Catalano, D., Fiore, D.: Vector commitments and their applications. In: Hanaoka, G., Kurosawa, K. (eds.) PKC 2013. LNCS, vol. 7778, pp. 55–72. Springer, Heidelberg (2013)
10. Catalano, D., Fiore, D., Messina, M.: Zero-knowledge sets with short proofs. In: Smart, N.P. (ed.) EUROCRYPT 2008. LNCS, vol. 4965, pp. 433–450. Springer, Heidelberg (2008)
11. Chang, E.-C., Lim, C.L., Xu, J.: Short redactable signatures using random trees. In: Fischlin, M. (ed.) CT-RSA 2009. LNCS, vol. 5473, pp. 133–147. Springer, Heidelberg (2009)
12. Chase, M., Healy, A., Lysyanskaya, A., Malkin, T., Reyzin, L.: Mercurial commitments with applications to zero-knowledge sets. In: Cramer, R. (ed.) EUROCRYPT 2005. LNCS, vol. 3494, pp. 422–439. Springer, Heidelberg (2005)
13. Chase, M., Kohlweiss, M., Lysyanskaya, A., Meiklejohn, S.: Malleable signatures: complex unary transformations and delegatable anonymous credentials. IACR Cryptology ePrint Archive 2013/179 (2013)
14. Damgård, I.B., Fujisaki, E.: A statistically-hiding integer commitment scheme based on groups with hidden order. In: Zheng, Y. (ed.) ASIACRYPT 2002. LNCS, vol. 2501, pp. 125–142. Springer, Heidelberg (2002)
15. Fiat, A., Shamir, A.: How to prove yourself: practical solutions to identification and signature problems. In: Odlyzko, A.M. (ed.) CRYPTO 1986. LNCS, vol. 263, pp. 186–194. Springer, Heidelberg (1987)
16. Ghosh, E., Goodrich, M.T., Ohrimenko, O., Tamassia, R.: Fully-dynamic verifiable zero-knowledge order queries for network data. IACR Cryptology ePrint Archive 2015/283 (2015)

17. Ghosh, E., Ohrimenko, O., Tamassia, R.: Verifiable member and order queries on a list in zero-knowledge. IACR Cryptology ePrint Archive 2014/632 (2014)
18. Goldberg, S., Naor, M., Papadopoulos, D., Reyzin, L., Vasant, S., Ziv, A.: NSEC5: provably preventing DNSSEC zone enumeration. Cryptology ePrint Archive, Report 2014/582 (2014)
19. Goodrich, M.T., Nguyen, D., Ohrimenko, O., Papamanthou, C., Tamassia, R., Triandopoulos, N., Lopes, C.V.: Efficient verification of web-content searching through authenticated web crawlers. PVLDB 5(10), 920–931 (2012)
20. Goodrich, M.T., Tamassia, R., Schwerin, A.: Implementation of an authenticated dictionary with skip lists and commutative hashing. In: Proceedings of the DARPA Information Survivability Conference and Exposition II (2001)
21. Johnson, R., Molnar, D., Song, D., Wagner, D.: Homomorphic signature schemes. In: Preneel, B. (ed.) CT-RSA 2002. LNCS, vol. 2271, pp. 244–262. Springer, Heidelberg (2002)
22. Kate, A., Zaverucha, G.M., Goldberg, I.: Constant-size commitments to polynomials and their applications. In: Abe, M. (ed.) ASIACRYPT 2010. LNCS, vol. 6477, pp. 177–194. Springer, Heidelberg (2010)
23. Kundu, A., Atallah, M.J., Bertino, E.: Leakage-free redactable signatures. In: Proceedings of the CODASPY (2012)
24. Kundu, A., Bertino, E.: Structural signatures for tree data structures. PVLDB 1(1), 138–150 (2008)
25. Kundu, A., Bertino, E.: Privacy-preserving authentication of trees and graphs. Int. J. Inf. Sec. 12(6), 467–494 (2013)
26. Libert, B., Yung, M.: Concise mercurial vector commitments and independent zero-knowledge sets with short proofs. In: Micciancio, D. (ed.) TCC 2010. LNCS, vol. 5978, pp. 499–517. Springer, Heidelberg (2010)
27. Lipmaa, H.: On diophantine complexity and statistical zero-knowledge arguments. In: Laih, C.-S. (ed.) ASIACRYPT 2003. LNCS, vol. 2894, pp. 398–415. Springer, Heidelberg (2003)
28. Merkle, R.C.: Protocols for public key cryptosystems. In: Proceedings of the IEEE Symposium on Security and Privacy (1980)
29. Micali, S., Rabin, M.O., Kilian, J.: Zero-knowledge sets. In: Proceedings of the FOCS (2003)
30. Micali, S., Rivest, R.L.: Transitive signature schemes. In: Preneel, B. (ed.) CT-RSA 2002. LNCS, vol. 2271, pp. 236–243. Springer, Heidelberg (2002)
31. Miyazaki, K., Hanaoka, G., Imai, H.: Digitally signed document sanitizing scheme based on bilinear maps. In: Proceedings of the ASIACCS (2006)
32. Ostrovsky, R., Rackoff, C., Smith, A.: Efficient consistency proofs for generalized queries on a committed database. In: Díaz, J., Karhumäki, J., Lepistö, A., Sannella, D. (eds.) ICALP 2004. LNCS, vol. 3142, pp. 1041–1053. Springer, Heidelberg (2004)
33. Poehls, H.C., Samelin, K., Posegga, J., De Meer, H.: Length-hiding redactable signatures from one-way accumulators in $O(n)$. Technical report MIP-1201, Faculty of Computer Science and Mathematics (FIM), University of Passau (2012)
34. Samelin, K., Pöhls, H.C., Bilzhause, A., Posegga, J., de Meer, H.: Redactable signatures for independent removal of structure and content. In: Ryan, M.D., Smyth, B., Wang, G. (eds.) ISPEC 2012. LNCS, vol. 7232, pp. 17–33. Springer, Heidelberg (2012)

35. Steinfeld, R., Bull, L., Zheng, Y.: Content extraction signatures. In: Kim, K. (ed.) ICISC 2001. LNCS, vol. 2288, pp. 285–304. Springer, Heidelberg (2002)
36. Tamassia, R.: Authenticated data structures. In: Di Battista, G., Zwick, U. (eds.) ESA 2003. LNCS, vol. 2832, pp. 2–5. Springer, Heidelberg (2003)
37. Wang, Z.: Improvement on Ahn et al.'s RSA P-homomorphic signature scheme. In: Keromytis, A.D., Di Pietro, R. (eds.) SecureComm 2012. LNICST, vol. 106, pp. 19–28. Springer, Heidelberg (2013)
38. Yi, X.: Directed transitive signature scheme. In: Abe, M. (ed.) CT-RSA 2007. LNCS, vol. 4377, pp. 129–144. Springer, Heidelberg (2006)

Private Database Access with HE-over-ORAM Architecture

Craig Gentry[1], Shai Halevi[1], Charanjit Jutla[1]([✉]), and Mariana Raykova[2]

[1] IBM T.J. Watson Research Center, Yorktown Heights, USA
csjutla.@us.ibm.com
[2] SRI International, Menlo Park, USA

Abstract. Enabling private database queries is an important and challenging research problem with many real-world applications. The goal is such that the client obtains the results of its queries without learning anything else about the database, while the outsourced server learns nothing about the queries or data, including access patterns. The secure-computation-over-ORAM architecture offers a promising approach to this problem, permitting sub-linear time processing of the queries (after pre-processing) without compromising security.

In this work we examine the feasibility of this approach, focusing specifically on secure-computation protocols based on somewhat-homomorphic encryption (SWHE). We devised and implemented secure two-party protocols in the semi-honest model for the path-ORAM protocol of Stefanov et al. This provides access by index or keyword, which we extend (via pre-processing) to limited conjunction queries and range queries. The SWHE schemes we consider allow easy batching or "SIMD" operations, and also let us vary the plaintext space in use. These capabilities let us devise many sub-protocols that are interesting in their own right, for tasks such as encrypted comparisons, blinded permutations, and the really expensive ORAM eviction step.

We implemented our protocols on top of the `HElib` homomorphic encryption library. Our basic single-threaded implementation takes about 30 min to process a query on a database with 2^{22} records and 120-bit long keywords, providing a cause for optimism about the viability of this direction, and we expect a better optimized implementation to be much faster.

Keywords: Comparison protocols · Homomorphic encryption · ORAM · PIR · Private queries · Secure computation

1 Introduction

The recent explosive growth of data outsourcing raises the issue of privacy guarantees for the outsourced data. While encryption can protect the *content* of the outsourced data, it remains a challenging problem to *access* the data privately.

This research was done as part of IARPA SPAR Program Contract No. D11PC20202.

© Springer International Publishing Switzerland 2015
T. Malkin et al. (Eds.): ACNS 2015, LNCS 9092, pp. 172–191, 2015.
DOI: 10.1007/978-3-319-28166-7_9

Since it is often possible to deduce important information from the access pattern alone (see e.g., [17] for some examples), it is important to even hide the access pattern from the server.

Solutions for hiding the access pattern include the oblivious RAM (ORAM) of Goldreich and Ostrovsky [12] and private information retrieval (PIR) of Chor et al. [4]. Recent years saw a surge in the level of interest and volume of new work in this area, addressing better efficiency, increased functionality, new threat models, and more. Roughly speaking, solutions can be categorized as either PIR-like protocols that inherently work in linear time in the size of the database, or ORAM-based solutions that have linear-time pre-processing but sub-linear access time (at the price of keeping some secret storage at the client). The current work is of the latter type.

The problem of private queries becomes even harder in situations where the client is not the data-owner and we need to ensure that the client also does not learn too much. Below we sometimes refer to this setting as *symmetric* private queries (borrowing the terminology from symmetric-PIR). For example, consider an organization that wants to maintain its internal access-control policy for the data that it outsourced to the cloud. In this case it is not enough to require that the cloud provider does not learn anything about the data. We must also ensure that an individual client from the organization who queries the database only gets the data that it asked for (and was authorized to obtain[1]), and the access protocol does not inadvertently leak anything else about the data. Similar concerns arise for a government organization setting up an encrypted server with need-based access for its clients[2].

1.1   Previous and Concurrent Work

A promising direction for addressing (symmetric) private-query is the secure-computation-over-ORAM architecture of Ostrovsky and Shoup [22] and Gordon et al. [13]. Here the client and server use secure two-party protocols to simulate the actions of an underlying ORAM protocol. This way we can keep the sub-linear access time of the underlying ORAM, while ensuring that the parties do not learn anything beyond the output of the original protocol, i.e., the server learns nothing and the client only learns the answer to its query.

In [13,22], this architecture was proposed as a solution for generic multi-party computation in RAM complexity, i.e., without having to transform the original insecure RAM computation into a binary circuit. The first implementation of a system along this line was due to Gordon et al. [13], using Yao-circuit-type two party protocols over the tree-ORAM of Shi et al. [25]. Gentry et al. later proposed a few optimizations for the underlying ORAM scheme [8], and also suggested to utilize low-degree homomorphic encryption for the two-party protocols over this ORAM, but did not implement any of these protocols.

---

[1] This report only covers the implementation of the private query protocols themselves, we briefly comment on the related authorization issue in Appendix B of the full version [9].

[2] Such was the requirement of a recent IARPA SPAR program [16].

Very recently, Liu et al. [21] developed an automated compiler for secure two-party computation, using the Gordon et al. architecture of Yao-based protocols over tree-ORAM (with many optimizations). Also, Keller and Scholl [19] extended the secure-computation-over-ORAM architecture to handle any number $n \geq 2$ of parties. They use the SPDZ framework [7] (with protocols based on algebraic-black-box approach with preprocessing) and use both tree-ORAM and path-ORAM as the underlying ORAM schemes. (Path-ORAM was recently proposed by Stefanov et al. [26] and is a variant of tree-ORAM with better asymptotic efficiency. As we will see later, our work utilizes Path-ORAM. The work of Keller and Scholl is concurrent to ours.)

Along a different direction, many recent works have aimed at achieving extremely high speed by somewhat compromising privacy, leaking a small amount of information about the access pattern. Some notable examples of work along this direction is the CryptDB system of Popa et al. [24], and recent works on searchable symmetric encryption due to Pappas et al. [23] Cash et al. [3], and Jarecki et al. [18].

1.2 This Work

In this work we designed and implemented a system for symmetric private queries in the semi-honest adversary model, supporting private database access by either index or keyword. We focus on exploring the feasibility of the direction advocated by Gentry et al. [8], of using secure-computation protocols based on low-degree homomorphic encryption over the tree-ORAM scheme. Specifically, we used for the underlying ORAM a slight modification of the Path-ORAM protocol of Stefanov et al. [26], and implemented our two-party computation protocols based on the HElib homomorphic-encryption library [15].

Our results show cause for optimism regarding the feasibility of this direction: Our single-threaded implementation can query a moderate-size database with 2^{22} records on a 120-bit keyword in just over 30 min. This indicates that SWHE-based protocols are not as slow as commonly believed. Moreover there is a wide range of further optimizations that can be applied (both algorithmic and implementation-level), and we expect a better optimized system to be one to three orders of magnitude faster (see discussion in Sect. 5). In this report we describe all the sub-protocols that went into our implementation, and also describe some extensions of the basic system to support range queries, authorization, and even provide limited support for conjunctions via pre-processing.

Our work is similar in many ways to the concurrent work of Keller and Scholl [19]. In particular they also developed secure-computation-over-ORAM protocols for arrays (access-by-index) and dictionaries (access-by-keyword). Some important differences between our work and [19] include the following:

- Keller and Scholl target generic multiparty secure computation rather than data outsourcing. In particular in their system all the parties need to keep state as large as all of the data (since they use secret-sharing to share the entire state).

Also the current work includes extensions that are more specific for data out-sourcing such as range queries, conjunctive queries, and authorization.

- The protocols in [19] are all in the "algebraic black-box model" (using the SPDZ framework) while ours use SWHE as the basic tool. As we discuss below, introducing new SWHE-based secure protocols is one of the contributions of the current work.

We also note that our performance numbers cannot be directly compared to those from [19], since they only report the online numbers and not the "expensive" offline computations that are done by the SPDZ framework.

SWHE-Based Secure Computation. Beyond the specific application of private queries, another contribution of the current work is in developing several new SWHE-based secure computation protocols that are interesting on their own. In particular, the SWHE schemes we consider allow ciphertext packing and agility in the choice of the underlying plaintext space, which leads to surprisingly efficient sub-protocols for important tasks.

Encrypted Equal-to-Zero and Comparisons. Comparing encrypted numbers is a common low-level task in many cryptographic protocols, and significant effort was invested in optimizing it, see e.g., [5, 20, 27, 28]. In our context, we need the result to be encrypted, i.e. we want the end result to be an encryption of the answer bit, zero or one.

In the simplest setting, we would like to transform an encryption of an n-bit value x into an encryption of a bit b such that $b = 0$ if $x = 0$ and $b = 1$ if $x \neq 0$. Computing b homomorphically from x without any interaction requires homomorphic degree roughly 2^n, or we can use a single communication round to get an encryption of the individual bits of x, and then can use degree-n homomorphism to compute the answer. But we can actually do much better. In Sect. 3.1 we describe a protocol that *uses only additive homomorphism*, works in $\log^* n$ communicating rounds, and requires $O(n)$ homomorphic addition operations. Moreover using batching techniques, this protocol can be implemented with only $O(\log n)$ additions and shifts. The end result has complexity $\tilde{O}(n + k)$ (with k the security parameter), which is asymptotically more efficient than previous protocols in the literature.

Our protocol relies on the flexibility of contemporary lattice-based encryption schemes that enable additive homomorphism relative to arbitrary moduli. The core of our new equal-to-zero protocol is a one-message sub-protocol that transforms the encryption of the n-bit x into an encryption of a $\log n$-bit y such that $y = 0$ if and only if $x = 0$. This size-reduction protocol uses the fact that an n-bit value is equal to zero if and only if the sum of its bits is zero, when using homomorphism modulo $m > n$. Applying the size-reduction protocol $\log^* n$ times reduces the problem to a constant-size instance, which we can solve using any of the existing techniques.

We also describe in Sect. 3.2 a protocol for comparing encrypted numbers, where on inputs x, y we obtain an encryption of a bit b such that $b = 1$ if $y > x$

and $b = 0$ otherwise. This protocol uses n parallel executions of the equal-to-zero protocol on $\log n$-bit values, and some local computation using additive homomorphism. Hence, it too takes $\log^* n$ rounds, and using ciphertext-packing can be made to run in complexity quasi-linear in $n + k$ (with k the security parameter).

The basic comparison protocol from Sect. 3.2 requires that we have encryptions of the separate bits of the numbers that we compare, but in our application one of these numbers comes from long-term storage and storing its encrypted bits would entail a somewhat large plaintext-to-ciphertext expansion ratio. Hence, we also describe in Sect. 3.2 another optimization that allows us to encrypt this number as a single integer (or a sequence of integer digits), so long as the integer(s) are stored in *reverse bit order* (this is not to be confused with big-endian format, as we actually do integer operations on this reversed integer).

Blinded Permutation. This protocol, described in Sect. 3.3, allows two parties to shuffle obliviously an array. The input to this protocol is an encrypted array a and an encrypted permutation p, and the output is the encryption of the permuted array, namely a' such that $a'[p[i]] = a[i]$. The main idea of this protocol is that the server can "blind" the permutation p by permuting it randomly with another random permutation q that it knows, then send it to the client for decryption. The client decrypts and gets $q \circ p$, uses it to permute the array a and returns it to server, who now permutes by q^{-1} to get the final result. (Of course, more blinding is needed also to hide a from the client.)

Homomorphic Path-ORAM Eviction. While the homomorphic ORAM eviction protocol which is central to secure-computation-over-ORAM may not be considered interesting in its own right, the linear time protocol we design using the batching feature of SWHE (as opposed to a quadratic-time naive approach) displays the rich capabilities of SWHE based approach to secure computation. This particular protocol may be considered the highlight of this work, and we describe it in detail in Sect. 4.2.

Security. The security property of all these protocols (in the semi-honest model) asserts that neither party learns anything during the execution of these protocols. That is, the view of each party consists only of ciphertexts under the other party's key and of random plaintext elements that are encrypted under its own key. (Hence the entire view can be simulated without knowledge of the encrypted values.)

Different Flavor of Protocols. Our equal-to-zero and comparison protocols are in some ways quite different than existing protocols in the literature: almost all HE-based protocols in the literature can be described in the arithmetic black-box model [6]. In that model there is an algebraic ring which is shared among parties, and sub-protocols for operations in the ring as used as the basis for everything else. (Usually the overriding complexity measure is the number of invocations of the ring operations.)

Our equal-to-zero protocol is different: while only using additive homomorphism, it does not fit in the algebraic black-box model since it relies on an interplay between different algebraic rings to get better efficiency. This approach, coupled with the ability to compute locally low-degree functions (not just linear), makes SWHE a very useful tool for designing efficient protocols.

Building secure-computation protocols based on SWHE is a new research direction, whereas protocols based on Yao circuits or additive-HE schemes have been investigated and optimized for over two decades. This work helps lay the groundwork for SWHE-based protocols, which are sure to find more uses.

Our Implementation. We implemented our private query solution with all its sub-protocols over the HElib software library [15]. We built our implementation to handle a moderate-size database of a few million entries. Specifically, our choice of parameters for this implementation can handle a database of up to 2^{24} records, with keywords of up to 120 bits.[3]

We tested it on the equivalent of a 2^{22}-record database with 120-bit keywords, running on a five-year-old IBM BladeCenter HS22/7870, with two Intel X5570 (4-core) processors, running at 2.93 GHz. However, one consequence of using HElib is that our implementation is inherently single-threaded (since HElib is not thread-safe), so we only utilized one of the eight cores available on that machine. Processing a single access-by-keyword request took over 32 min, of which just under three minutes were devoted to obtaining the information itself, and the rest for maintenance operations (i.e., updating the ORAM trees and running the eviction protocol). As we said above, we expect that a better-optimized implementation would be able to do much better (even if we don't count the 8× speedup that one could get from just using all eight cores). We describe some possible optimizations in Appendix E of the full version [9].

2   Background

2.1   The Path-ORAM Protocol

In the basic path-ORAM protocol [26], the server keeps an N-element database in a complete binary tree of height $h = \log N$, where each node in the tree contains a bucket large enough to store a small constant number Z of data elements. In addition there is also a moderate-size stash of S entries to keep elements that do not fit elsewhere (we think of the stash as being kept at the root of the tree). The content of all the buckets is encrypted under the client's key, in particular the server does not know how many elements are actually stored in each bucket.

Each database element with logical address $v \in [N]$ is associated with a random leaf L_v, and the client keeps an N-entry table of the mapping $v \mapsto L_v$. (I.e., entry v in the table contains the leaf number L_v.)

Denote by d_v the data corresponding to logical address v. The protocol maintains the invariant that the triple (L_v, v, d_v) is stored in one of the buckets on the path from the root to the leaf L_v. Access to logical address v consists of two

---

[3] Both of these restrictions eventually stem from working with packed ciphertexts over the 6361'st cyclotomic field, which have 120 plaintext slots.

subroutines, one for doing the actual access and another one to clean up after the access.

Access. To access the data in logical address v, the client looks up L_v in its table and asks the server for the entire path from the root to leaf L_v. Upon receiving all the buckets in this path, the client decrypts them, finds a triple of the form (L_v, v, d_v) in one of the buckets, and this value d_v is the requested data.

The client either leaves the data unchanged (if the operation is a read) or overwrites it with a new value (if it is a write). We denote the resulting data by d'_v. In either case, it chooses a new random leaf $L'_v \in [N]$ and updates its table with the new L'_v value. The client then removes the triple (L_v, v, d_v) from the bucket where it was found, and puts the triple (L'_v, v, d'_v) in the root bucket. Finally it re-encrypts all the buckets and send them back to the server, who replaces all the buckets on the path to L_v by the new encrypted buckets. Since the new triple is placed at the root, this operation maintains the tree invariant of the scheme.

Eviction. To prevent the root bucket from overflowing, the client and server run a "maintenance" subroutine whose goal is to evict triples from their current buckets and push them lower down the tree: The client and server agree on some "eviction path" (in [26] this is the same as the read path), and each entry in that path $e_i = (L_i, v_i, d_i)$ is pushed as far down that path as it can go toward its target leaf L_i. The stash is used to avoid over-filling the buckets (with conflicts resolved greedily).

It is easy to see that as long as the stash does not overflow, the view of the server is computationally independent of the access pattern (assuming the security of the encryption scheme). Stefanov et al. proved in [25] that when using the read path for eviction and setting $S = O(\log N)$, the probability of the stash overflowing is negligible. In our implementation we instead use the deterministic eviction strategy that was proposed by Gentry et al. in [8]. We ran experiments and found that this deterministic strategy allows us to use smaller buckets, namely only $Z = 2$ as opposed to $Z = 4$ which is needed when evicting along the read-path.

Putting it Together. In the complete construction, the ORAM also stores the mapping $v \mapsto L_v$. Specifically, the server keeps $\ell = \lceil \log(N) \rceil$ complete binary trees as above, with the level-i tree having $2^{\ell-i}$ leaves. In the largest tree ($i = 0$), each entry corresponds to one logical address $v \in \{0, \dots, N-1\}$, and it contains the user data for that logical address. For the next tree ($i = 1$), each entry corresponds to two consecutive logical addresses, and it contains the two leaf-numbers in the largest tree that are currently assigned to those logical addresses. More generally, each entry in the tree at level $i + 1$ corresponds to the union of two level-i intervals (which is altogether a size-2^{i+1} interval of logical addresses), and that entry contains two leaf-numbers of the level-i tree, namely the leaves that are currently assigned to the entries of those two level-i intervals. With each entry in every tree we store also the first logical address of the interval of that entry, as well as the leaf that is currently assigned to that entry (in the current tree). Thus each entry is of the form

$$\text{level } 0: \quad (L^*, v, \text{user-data})$$
$$\text{level} > 0: \quad (L^*, v, L_1, L_2)$$

where L^* is the leaf currently assigned to that entry, $[v, v + 2^i)$ is its interval, and (L_1, L_2) are the leafs in the next tree that are currently assigned to the two sub-intervals $[v, v + 2^{i-1})$, $[v + 2^{i-1}, v + 2^i)$. Of course, all of the buckets in all of the trees are encrypted under a key known to the client.

The "tree at the last level ℓ", which has a single node, is kept by the client. That tree has just a single entry, corresponding to the interval $[0, 2^\ell)$, and containing two leaf-numbers of the tree at level $\ell - 1$ that are currently assigned to the entries of the sub-intervals $[0, 2^{\ell-1}), [2^{\ell-1}, 2^\ell)$.

ORAM Access Query. To access the logical address v, the client looks in its level-ℓ "tree" and determines the level-$(\ell - 1)$ sub-interval containing v, namely j such that $(j - 1)2^{\ell-1} \le v < j2^{\ell-1}$. The client sets $v_{\ell-1} = (j - 1)2^{\ell-1}$ and $L^{(\ell-1)} = L_j^{(\ell-1)}$, chooses at random a new leaf $\hat{L}^{(\ell-1)}$ and replaces $L_j^{(\ell-1)}$ by this new value in the list. Then the client proceeds iteratively for $i = \ell - 1$ down to 0:

1. Request from the server all the buckets on the path from the root of the level-i tree down to the leaf $L^{(i)}$. Decrypt them and find in them an entry of the form $(L^{(i)}, v_i, \text{data})$.
2. If $i > 0$ do the following:
   (a) Parse data $= (L_1^{(i-1)}, L_2^{(i-1)})$, choose a new random leaf in the next tree, $\hat{L}^{(i-1)}$.
   (b) Determine the level-$(i - 1)$ sub-interval containing v, namely $j = 1$ if $v < v_i + 2^{i-1}$ and $j = 2$ otherwise. If $j = 1$ then set $v_{i-1} = v_i + 2^{i-1}$ and otherwise $v_{i-1} = v_i$, and also set $L^{(i-1)} = L_j^{(i-1)}$.
   (c) Replace $L_j^{(i-1)}$ by $\hat{L}^{(i-1)}$ inside data, denoting the result by data$'$.
   Else ($i = 0$), if this is a write operation then set data$'$ to be the new value. Otherwise (read), set data$' = $ data.
3. Remove the entry $(L^{(i)}, v_i, \text{data})$ from the bucket where it was found, and place in the root bucket the entry $(\hat{L}^{(i)}, v_i, \text{data}')$. Re-encrypt all the buckets and send to the server.

Finally, the client and server run the Eviction subroutine for each of the trees $i = 0, 1, \ldots, \ell - 1$. If this was a read operation then the return value is the data value from the last level $i = 0$.

Access by Keyword. Gentry et al. described in [8] how to extend this protocol to access elements by keyword rather than by index, when the database itself is sorted by that keyword: In an entry corresponding to an interval $[v, v + 2^i)$ we keep not only the two leaf values L_1, L_2 for the next tree, but also the keyword value K of the database record at the middle of this interval (i.e., at index $v + 2^{i-1}$). The access procedure is then modified so that in Step 2b above we choose the sub-interval by comparing the keyword K^* that we seek to the value K that is stored with the current entry, setting $j = 1$ if $K^* < K$ and $j = 2$ otherwise.

Note that even if the keyword K^* that we search for is not in the ORAM, we will still return some data at the end of the access protocol, Namely the data corresponding to the smallest keyword $K' \geq K^*$ in the ORAM. Jumping ahead, in our private-query protocol we handle this matter by multiplying the data with the indicator bit $\chi(K = K^*)$.

2.2 Somewhat Homomorphic Encryption (SWHE)

Our implementation of the private database search protocol relies on the HElib library for implementing homomorphic encryption [14,15]. One of the features of this library that we utilize is the ability to choose freely the plaintext space. In particular, we often mix homomorphic operations modulo different moduli (e.g., 2,16,128) in the same protocol. We denote homomorphic addition and multiplication by $\boxplus$ and $\boxtimes$, respectively.

Another feature of HElib that we rely on is the ability to "pack" many plaintext elements in a single ciphertext and apply to them operations in a SIMD manner. We refer to the different plaintext values in a single ciphertext as the "plaintext slots" of that ciphertext. (For the specific parameters that we chose for our implementation we get 120 plaintext slots per ciphertext.) Our protocols use in particular the HElib procedures for computing total sums and partial sums of the plaintext slots, and the efficient implementation of permuting the slots as described in [14]. We also use the ability to homomorphically extract the bits in the binary representation of the plaintext elements when the plaintext space is a power of two, as described in [11] and [1, Appendix B].

3 Main Building Blocks

Below we describe the main low-level protocols that we use in our implementation, for things like comparing numbers, permuting arrays, etc. These protocols could be useful in many other settings as well.

In all the protocols below we use encryption schemes that support at least additive homomorphism with function privacy (in the honest-but-curious model). Below we assume for simplicity that they all operate over plaintext space $R = Z_m$ for some integer m.[4] We assume that we can instantiate the cryptosystem relative to an arbitrary plaintext space $R = Z_m$, and we use several different instances with different plaintext spaces. As mentioned in Sect. 2, contemporary

---

[4] Essentially the same protocols apply also to more complex plaintext spaces, such as vectors over rings and polynomial rings.

lattice-based cryptosystems indeed support additive homomorphism (and more) with a free choice of the plaintext space.

In terms of security, all the sub-protocols below have the property that the view of each player consists only of ciphertexts relative to keys of the other player, and ciphertext under its own keys that encrypt uniformly random plaintext elements (independent of the input and output of the protocol). Although we do not argue here the security of the sub-protocols in isolation, we use that property when proving that the high-level protocol that uses them is secure (in the honest-but-curious model).

3.1 Equal-to-Zero Protocol

The server has an input ciphertext $c = HE_C(x)$, encrypting some $x \in R$ under the client key. The goal of the protocol is for the server to obtain an encryption of a single bit b under the client key, such that $b = 0$ if $x = 0$, and $b = 1$ otherwise. Let n be the number of bits that it takes to represent an element in R, so $|R| \leq 2^n$.

The protocol consists of multiple rounds, where in each round we transform an equal-to-zero instance with plaintext space of some size S into another equal-to-zero instance with plaintext space of size $O(\log S)$. After $\log^* n$ such rounds we arrive at an instance relative to a small constant plaintext-space, and then use standard protocols (e.g., a secure computation of the AND function) to compute the final bit encryption. The plaintext-space reduction protocol consists of only a single message flow (i.e., half a round) and it is described next.

Plaintext-Space Reduction. We begin by turning the encryption of x into encryption of (roughly) the bits of x. Namely, the server proceeds as follows:

S1. Choose a random $a \in R$ and use homomorphism to compute $c' \leftarrow c \boxplus a = HE_C(x + a)$.

S2. Denote the bit representation of a by $a_{n-1} \ldots a_1 a_0$. Encrypt the bits a_i under the server's key, but *relative to plaintext space* Z_{n+1}, getting $c_i = HE_S(a_i)$ for $i = 0, \ldots, n-1$.

The server sends to the client both c' and all the c_i's. The client then proceeds as follows:

C3. Decrypt c' to obtain the value $x' = x + a \in R$, and let $x'_{n-1} \ldots x'_0$ be the bit representation of this value. Note that $x' = a$ iff $x = 0$.

C4. Use the homomorphism to XOR the bit x'_i into a new ciphertext c'_i for all i, by setting $c'_i = c_i$ if $x'_i = 0$ and $c'_i = 1 \boxminus c_i$ if $x'_i = 1$.
Let $y_i = a_i \oplus x'_i$ be the value encrypted in the ciphertext c'_i, and observe that the y_i's are all zero if and only if $x = 0$.

C5. Use homomorphism to sum up all the c'_i's, thus getting a ciphertext $c'' \leftarrow \boxplus_i c'_i = HE_S(\sum_i y_i)$.

The crux of the protocol is that since the scheme HE_S is homomorphic relative to the plaintext space Z_{n+1}, and since c'' is the sum of n bits, then it encrypts zero if and only if all the y_i's are zeros, namely if and only if $x = 0$. Thus we reduced the original ciphertext c (which was relative to the plaintext space R of size up to 2^n), to a ciphertext c'' relative to the plaintext space Z_{n+1}, so that c'' encrypts a zero if and only if the original c encrypts a zero.

Equal-to-Zero. Our equal-to-zero protocol repeats the above plaintext-space reduction protocol for $\log^* n$ rounds, switching the client and server roles for each round, until we arrive at a plaintext space of constant size (which can be made as small as Z_3, but no smaller).

In the last step of the protocol, however, we replace the step C5 by a secure encrypted-AND protocol. (If the cryptosystem supports multiplicative homomorphism then we can use it directly. Otherwise, we can use any standard secure-computation protocol, e.g., based on OT.) In our implementation we stop at plaintext space Z_8, and then use multiplicative homomorphism to complete the protocol.

Once we have an encryption of the target bit relative to some small plaintext space, we can convert it to an encryption relative to the original plaintext space R (or any other desirable plaintext space), e.g., by a one-round protocol of blind/encrypt/re-encrypt/unblind.

We note that the original scheme (that determines the input and output to the protocol) need not even support full additive homomorphism: it is enough for it to be *blindable*, and indeed in our implementation we sometime apply this protocol to AES in counter mode. The intermediate schemes with smaller plaintext space, however, must be (at least) additively homomorphic, and for those we use lattice-based encryption schemes.

We also note that we can use essentially the same protocol to compute an encrypted bit b which is zero if *the lowest ℓ bits of x are zero* and one otherwise (for any value of $\ell \leq n$ known to the client). The only difference is that in the first invocation of the plaintext reduction sub-protocol the client only computes the c_i''s for $i = 0, \ldots \ell-1$ in step C4 (rather than all of them). We use this variant in our sub-protocol for computing the encrypted permutation during eviction, see Sect. 4.2.

3.2   Comparison Protocol

This protocol builds on the equal-to-zero protocol from above. For our basic protocol, we have the client holding an n-bit number y in the clear, and also holding the bit-wise encryption of another number x under the server's key. The goal of the protocol is for the client to obtain an encryption of a single bit b under the client key, such that $b = 0$ if $x \geq y$ and $b = 1$ if $y > x$. Later in this subsection we discuss some optimizations that we use when transforming our actual setting that we have in our implementation to the one needed for this protocol.

Input. The client holds a plaintext element $y \in Z_{2^n}$ and n ciphertexts $c_i = HE_S(x_i)$ under the server key that encrypt the bits of the integer $x = \sum_{i=0}^{n-1} x_i 2^i$, relative to plaintext space Z_{n+1}.

C1. The client XORs the bits of y into the c_i's, setting $c_i' = c_i$ if $y_i = 0$ and $c_i' = 1 \boxminus c_i$ if $y_i = 1$. Denote by $b_i = y_i \oplus x_i$ the bits that are encrypted in the c_i''s.

At this point we note that if $x = y$ then all the b_i's are zero, and if $x \neq y$ then some of the b_i's are ones. Moreover, the largest index i^* for which $b_i = 1$ corresponds to the top bit where x, y differ.

C2. The client uses additive homomorphism to compute the *partial sums*, i.e. for all i its sets $c_i'' \leftarrow \boxplus_{i' \geq i} c_i' = HE_S(s_i)$, where $s_i = \sum_{j=i}^{b} b_i$.

Note that if $x = y$ then all the s_i's are zero, and if the top bit in which x, y disagree has index i^* then we have $s_i = 0$ for all $i > i^*$ and $s_i \neq 0$ for all $i \leq i^*$ (since each of the latter s_i's is a sum of $\leq n$ bits, not all of them zero).

EQ.3. The client and server apply the equal-to-zero protocol from Sect. 3.1 to each of the ciphertexts c_i''. At the conclusion of these protocols the client holds $\hat{c}_i$, $i = 0, \ldots, n-1$, where $\hat{c}_i = HE_S(0)$ for $i > i^*$ and $\hat{c}_i = HE_S(1)$ for $i \leq i^*$.

C4. Subtracting $\hat{c}_{i+1}$ from $\hat{c}_i$ for all $i < n$ yield ciphertexts $\tilde{c}_i$, all of which encrypt the bit 0 except $\tilde{c}_{i^*} = HE_C(1)$. (If $x = y$ then all the $\tilde{c}_i$'s encrypt zeros.)

C5. The client multiplies $c_i^* = y_i \boxdot \tilde{c}_i$.

Clearly we still have $c_i^* = HE_S(0)$ for $i \neq i^*$, but for $i = i^*$ we now have $c_{i^*}^* = HE_S(1)$ if $y_{i^*} = 1$ and $c_{i^*}^* = Enc_S(0)$ if $y_{i^*} = 0$. Recalling that i^* is the top bit where x, y disagree (if any), we have that $y > x$ if and only if $y_{i^*} = 1$. Hence all the c_i^*'s are encryption of 0's if $c \geq y$, and one of them is an encryption of 1 if $y > x$.

C6. Summing up the c_i^*'s yields $c^* = HE_S(b)$ where $b = 1$ if $y > x$ and $b = 0$ if $x \geq y$, as needed.

Encrypting Integers in Reverse Bit-Order. In our implementation, we use the encrypted comparison protocol to compare the keyword held by the client to the pivots that are stored encrypted on disk as part of the path-ORAM structure. This means that at the beginning of the protocol the server has the value x (pivot) encrypted under the client key, and the client has the value y (keyword) in the clear.

If the pivot value x is encrypted bitwise in the ORAM structure then transforming it to the starting state needed for the protocol above would be a straightforward one-flow blind-decrypt-unblind protocol. However, to save on bandwidth in other parts of the protocol we would prefer to encrypt the pivot as either a single integer or a sequence of integer digits, which makes it harder to extract the bits. To handle this issue without resorting to higher-degree homomorphism we note that if we encrypt the integer x in *reverse bit order* then a much simpler comparison protocol can be obtained. Due to space limitations, this protocol is described only in the full version (see [9]).

3.3   Blinded Permutations

As input to this protocol, the server has an encryption under the client key of a size-ℓ array a and another size-ℓ array p containing a permutation of the index set $\{1, 2, \ldots, \ell\}$ (over some plaintext space $\mathbb{Z}_m$ with $m \geq \ell$). The output of the server is an encrypted array a' which is obtained by permuting a according to p. Namely, $a'[p[i]] = a[i]$ for all i.

The basic idea of the protocol is the following: The server blinds the encrypted permutation p by permuting it with a new random permutation q; the net effect of this is that when the client receives this (packed) ciphertext and decrypts it, then it comprises of the permutation $p \circ q^{-1}$. The server also blinds the array a with a random vector r. It further encrypts r under its own HE key to obtain R. Next, it permutes both the blinded a and R using q, and sends these two ciphertexts along with the blinded permutation. As mentioned earlier, the client obtains $p \circ q^{-1}$, and applies this permutation to the other two ciphertexts, (homomorphically) blinds them both using a same fresh random array, and sends them back to the client. The client now only needs to decrypt the permuted blinding array r, and subtract it (homomorphically) from the permuted (and still encrypted) a.

The protocol is described in Fig. 1 in the full version [9].

4   Protocols for Private Queries

Below we describe at a high level the main protocols in our implementation. More detailed description is available in the full version [9]. At a high-level, every database access proceeds tree by tree, and processing each tree is done in two phases. First the server reads the root-leaf "read-path" from the tree and the client and server engage in a *Read-and-Update* protocol. Then the server reads a (potentially different) root-leaf "evict path" from the tree, and the client and server engage in an *Eviction* protocol.

We logically use additive two-out-of-two secret sharing to share the ORAM state between the client and server, but rely on an optimization that allows the client to hold just a single AES key instead of a long share. Namely, the ORAM trees themselves are stored at the server, encrypted using AES-CTR under the client's key.

4.1   ORAM Read and Update

The read-phase protocols are used to read a path from one tree in the encrypted ORAM structure, extract from it the information that we need in order to read the next tree, and update the read path. At the beginning of the read phase, the server is holding a single root-leaf path, with each entry encrypted separately using AES-CTR under the client's key. In addition the server is also holding an AES-CTR encryption of a tag t^*, identifying the entry to extract from this path, and the client is holding in the clear the keyword that it is looking for (which should be compared to the pivot in that entry).

This phase consists of four parts:

Extract. Extract a single entry from the path containing the information that we seek. More details on this step are given in Appendix D.1 of the full version [9].

Compare. Compare the pivot in the extracted entry against the keyword that we are searching for. Compute a single encrypted bit that contains the result of that comparison. This is done using the comparison protocol from Sect. 3.2. The low-level details are described in Appendix D.2 of the full version [9].

Oblivious-Transfer. Extract one of the two data-items in the entry, depending on the value of the encrypted bit, getting in the clear the path to read in the next tree, and also an encryption of the identifier tag to seek in that path. This is a fairly standard 1-of-2 OT protocol, details are provided in Appendix D.3 of the full version [9].

Update. Update the path in the current tree, marking the entry that was extracted as "empty", and copying its content to an available empty slot in the root bucket. Also update the leaf value for that entry to a new random leaf. This protocol is fairly standard on a high level, but uses some HE-specific optimizations to speed up low-level operations, see details in Appendix D.4 of the full version [9].

When processing the largest tree (that contains the data itself), then in the OT step we also execute an equality protocol to check that the keyword matches the one that we search for, and multiply the returned data by the resulting bit, thus zero-ing it out if the keyword does not exist in the database.

4.2   ORAM Eviction

Eviction consists of first computing (an encryption of) the permutation to apply to the entries along the eviction path, and then applying it using the protocol from Sect. 3.3. At the beginning of the eviction phase, the client and server agree on the eviction path, and the server has the content of all the buckets along that path, which are all encrypted under the client AES key. Each entry of every bucket contains a target-leaf field, we begin the protocol with one round of blind/decrypt/re-encrypt/unblind that converts these AES ciphertexts to HE ciphertexts and also packs them in the slots of a single HE ciphertext.

For a height-h tree with Z-size buckets and S-size stash, we therefore have $hZ + S$ plaintext elements packed in one HE ciphertext, each of them an h-bit string. In our implementation we use $Z = 2$, $h \leq 22$ and $S = 24$, and use 120-slot ciphertexts, so a single ciphertext can hold (more than) $2hZ + S$ target-leaf fields. We will need the extra hZ slots to hold "dummy entries" in the protocol below. The eviction phase consists of several sub-protocols, as described below.

Sub-protocol 1: Position Bits. Denote the target leaf of the i'th entry in the path by $l[i]$, and denote the leaf at the bottom of the eviction path by l^*. For every level $j = 1 \ldots h$ in the tree (with $j = 0$ the root and $j = h$ the leaves), we first want to compute ciphertexts $C_j[i]$ under the client key that encrypt one if $l[i]$

and l^* agree on the first (lowest) j bits, and zero otherwise. This means that entry i wants to get evicted at least as far down as level j. These bits should be encrypted w.r.t. plaintext space Z_m for $m \geq 2hZ + S$, in our implementation we use $m = 128$.

To compute the $C_j[i]$'s, we use additive homomorphism to subtract l^* from the $l[i]$'s, getting encryption of $\delta[i] = l[i] - l^*$, and then apply our equal-to-zero protocol from Sect. 3.1 h times to each $\delta[i]$, each time computing whether the bottom j bits of $\delta[i]$ are zero (for $j = 0 \ldots h - 1$). Note that if the $\delta[i]$'s are all packed in a single ciphertext then we just need to perform h executions of the protocol, one per j, and we get packed ciphertexts $C_j[0 \ldots 119]$. Also we can perform most of the first plaintext-reduction step in the equal-to-zero sub-protocol only once (rather than for every j separately).

Position Indexes. Once we have the encrypted bits $C_j[i]$, we can sum them up to get an encryption of the level to which this entry wants to be evicted. Denote this index by $v[i]$. Although the protocol below does not use the encryption of $v[i]$, it is nonetheless convenient to use the $v[i]$'s to explain the working of this protocol. Roughly, in this protocol we would want to sort the entries by their position index.

Sub-protocol 2: Adding Dummy Ciphertexts. Next we add encryption of some dummy entries, to ensure that for any level below the root $j > 0$ we have at least $(h - j + 1)Z$ entries with position indexed $v[i] \geq j$. The reason is that we must ensure that once the entries are sorted by their position index, no entry is sent further down the path below the level that that it wants to get to. Hence if we have less than $(h - j + 1)Z$ entries that want to get to level j or below, we need to fill these levels with dummy entries so that entries that want to go to higher levels will not get sorted into the lower ones.

We begin by computing encrypted counts E_j of how many entries want to be evicted to levels j and below, simply by summing $E_j = \boxplus_i C_j[i]$ (each E_j can be computed in $\log{(2hZ + S)}$ steps by appropriate shifts and additions). Similarly the number of entries that want to go exactly to level j is $E'_j = E_j \boxminus E_{j+1}$. Let e_j denote the number encrypted in the ciphertext E_j, and e'_j denote the number encrypted in the ciphertext E'_j.

Next we use the E_j's to compute for each level j how many dummy entries (between 0 and Z) are needed at that level. I.e., for all $j = 1 \ldots h$ and $k = 1 \ldots Z$ we compute an encryption of the bit $\sigma_{j,k}$ which is one if we need to add k or more dummies to level j and zero otherwise. It can be verified that the condition we need is

$$\sigma_{j,k} = 0 \text{ iff } \exists j' \geq j \text{ s.t. } \left(\sum_{t=j}^{j'} e'_t\right) > (j' - j)Z + k. \tag{1}$$

That is, if there are more than $(j' - j)Z + k$ entries that want to be evicted to levels between j and j' (for some j'), then we need to add less than k dummies to level j.

Unfortunately we cannot use the comparison protocol from Sect. 3.2 to compute the bits $\sigma_{j,k}$ from the E'_i's, since the e'_i's are sum of bits, so they are integers which are not encoded in reverse bit order. However, the e_i''s are relatively small (at most $2hZ + S = 112$) hence even the naive protocol is reasonably efficient. Specifically for each j' we subtract $(\boxplus_{t=j}^{j'} E_t') \boxminus ((j' - j)Z + k)$, over plaintext space Z_{128}, and then use homomorphic bit extraction to get the MSB of the result, which is the indicator bit $\chi(\sum_t e_t' \leq (j' - j)Z + k)$. Computing the AND of these indicator bits gives us the bit $\sigma_{j,k}$ that we seek. We can actually pack these comparisons and run them in a SIMD manner, so that the protocol runs in linear time instead of quadratic time. Specifically, for each value of j' we can compute a ciphertext such that in the j-th slot is the encryption of the value $\sum_{t=j}^{j'} e_t'$. We note that this sub-protocol is the most time-consuming part of the entire ORAM-access procedure. In our implementation it accounts for roughly 35% of the total running time. However, a naive protocol which pushes entries as far down as possible (limited by $C_j[i]$), iteratively and starting from level h upto 0, would have quadratic complexity. Thus, our sub-protocol is already a major improvement.

Once we have the $\sigma_{j,k}$'s, we prepare encryption of Zh dummy entries, where the position index of the (j, k) entry is set as $\sigma_{j,k} \cdot j$. This means that we get exactly the right number of dummies with position index $v[i] = j$, and the rest of the dummies have position index $v[i] = 0$. More specifically, we compute the encrypted bits $C_j[i]$ for these dummies: if we put the (j, k) dummy in some index i, then for any $j' = 1 \ldots h$, the bit encrypted in $C_{j'}[i]$ is zero if $j' > j$, and it is $\sigma_{j,k}$ if $j' \leq j$.

Sub-protocol 3: Sorting by Position Indexes. All that is left now is to sort by position indexes. Note that because we added the dummies, then an entry that wants to go to level j will not be moved to a deeper level $j' > j$ in the sorted order, because there are at least $(h-j)Z$ entries that want to go to levels below j.

We update the counts E_j and E_j', counting the $C_j[i]$'s of the dummies too. Also we compute $C_j'[i] = C_j[i] \boxminus C_{j+1}[i]$ for all i, j, which is 1 if entry i wants to go exactly to level j. Then for every entry i we compute its position in the sorted order as

$$P[i] = \boxplus_j \left(C_j'[i] \boxtimes \left((\boxplus_{i' < i} C_j'[i']) \boxplus E_{j+1} \right) \right).$$

That is, if entry i wants to be at level j, then before it in the order will come all the entries that want to go to $j' > j$ (there are e_{j+1} such entries) and all the entries that want to go to level j and have index smaller than i in the current array.

Sub-protocol 4: Applying the Permutation. Now that we have an encryption of the permutation that we need to apply to the entries, we use our blinded permutation protocol from Sect. 3.3 to effect this permutation. This means that we pack all the data of the entries in a HE ciphertext, then apply the protocol from Sect. 3.3 to this ciphertext, and then convert these ciphertexts back to AES-encrypted ciphertext. In our implementation we need two HE ciphertexts to pack all the data from all the entries in the path so we apply the blinded-permutation protocol twice.

Note that, since we initially put the dummy entries at the end of the packed ciphertext, the last Zh entries after sorting must be dummies, so we can just ignore them when converting back to AES encryption.

5   Implementation

We implemented our protocols over the `HElib` implementation [15] of the BGV scheme [2], which is currently the only publicly available implementation of SWHE that supports most of the functionality that we need.

For our target setting, we used a database with 2^{22} records with 120-bit keywords and only a few bytes worth of data. As explained in Appendix B of the full version [9], we can handle large records by using a two-tier system, using a database as above just to get the index of the target record and then use standard ORAM without the secure-computation layer to get the records themselves.

In retrospect, the size of the records and keywords does not have much impact on the performance, indeed over 95 % of the time is spent on sub-protocols which are not affected by the record/keyword sizes, and the ones that are affected only have complexity linear in that size. (For example, extrapolating from our timing results we could have handled keywords of size over 6000 bits with a moderate change of the implementation and without changing any of the parameters, and it would have added perhaps two minutes to the query time.)

Parameters and Design Choices. Since the analysis of the parameters for the bucket size in the path-ORAM constructions is not tight, for the implementation of our system we ran experiments to find the number of entries needed in the root (the parameter S from Sect. 2.1) and intermediate nodes (the parameter Z). We tested two eviction strategies, the one from [26] that uses the read path also as eviction path, and the one from [8] that deterministically covers all the paths in reverse-bit order. For each of these two strategies we tried several different sizes for the non-root nodes, and for each of those we run the ORAM for 2^{24} accesses and recorded the largest size that the stash at the root ever grows to.

Our experiments show that for the eviction strategy from [26] we need $Z = 4$ entries in the non-root nodes before the stash size stabilizes, whereas $Z = 2$ entries were enough for the deterministic strategy from [8]. Moreover for the latter strategy with $Z = 2$, the stash never grew beyond $S = 5$ entries, so we expect that setting $S = 24$ gives a reasonable security margin. This means that the entire root-to-leaf path in our largest tree needs to hold $hZ + S = 22 \cdot 2 + 24 = 68$ entries. However, our sub-protocol 2 from Sect. 4.2 for computing permutations requires that we add Z more dummy entries per non-root node, thus for that sub-protocol we need to handle $2hZ + S = 112$ entries.

At this point, our design choices were dictated by the interfaces that are available (or not) in `HElib`. `HElib` is built to provide an effective use of ciphertext-packing techniques [10], and in particular it provides the ability to view the multiple plaintext elements encrypted in a single ciphertext as an array and arbitrarily permute that array.

The largest circuit depth that we need to handle in our protocols is $\lceil \log 112 \rceil = 7$ (in Sub-protocol 2 from Sect. 4.2), and the heuristic estimate provided by HElib indicates that for this depth we have a lower-bound of $\phi(m) \geq 6157$ on the m-th cyclotomic ring that we need to use (for security parameter $\lambda = 80$). Adding the constraint that the number of plaintext slots (which is the order of the quotient group $Z_m^*/(2)$) must be at least 112, we chose to work with $m = 6361$, for which $\phi(m) = 6360$, we have $|Z_m^*/(2)| = 120$ slots, and each slot can hold an element of the field $GF(2^{53})$.

Finally, a modulo-2 ciphertext space would have let us pack at most 6360 plaintext bits per ciphertext, but to fit all the relevant information of an entire root-to-leaf path in the deepest tree into a single ciphertext, we needed to use plaintext space somewhat larger than that. Hence we chose to encrypt some of the data relative to plaintext space modulo $2^4 = 16$, which lets us pack four times more bits in each ciphertext. We also make use of a modulo-128 plaintext space for some of our sub-protocols.

Performance. With these parameters, a native homomorphic multiplication in HElib takes roughly 50ms, and permuting the 120-slot arrays takes just under one second. Our implementation of the entire protocol with these parameters runs in about 32 min per access (1904 s). Table 1 summarizes the breakout of this time into the different sub-protocols from Sect. 4. In that table, Extract, Compare, OT, and Update are the four sub-protocols of the read phase, and Evict1-4 are the four sub-protocol of the eviction phase.

Table 1. Running times of different sub-protocols in our implementation.

Extract	Compare	OT	Update	Total read
38 s	92 s	41 s	70 s	=241 s

Evict1	Evict2	Evict3	Evict4	Total evict
91 s	757 s	487 s	331 s	=1663 s

As seen in Table 1, the most expensive are Sub-protocols 2 and 3 in the eviction phase. In particular, computing the bits $\sigma_{j,k}$ from the e_j''s as in Eq. (1) takes 669 s (35 % of the total).

We note that only the first three sub-protocols in the read phase are on the critical path for obtaining the information, all other sub-protocols can be executed "off line" after the information was obtained. Hence our current implementation features a latency of about three minutes per query, but throughput limitation of 32 min per query.

In terms of the time to process the separate trees, the read-and-update phase takes roughly 11 s per tree, regardless of the height of that tree (since this implementation manipulates a single packed ciphertext for any tree up to height 24). The current implementation of the eviction phase takes about $5h + 18$ seconds to process a height-h tree, so the first tree takes 25 s, and the last (height-22) tree takes 130 s. Overall, the running time of this implementation on a size-2^h database ($h \leq 24$) would be

$$\text{Time}(2^h) \approx 2.5h^2 + 31.5h \text{ seconds,}$$

of which only about $8h$ seconds are on the critical path. As we mentioned above, the keyword size does not make a big difference in our implementation: shorter keywords will not save us any time, and longer keywords will not cost us much (but would require some change in the implementation).

We view these numbers as encouraging; they indicate that SWHE-based protocols are not as slow as commonly believed. Moreover, this is only a first-step implementation and there is much room for improvement. In the full version [9] we list a few promising avenues.

References

1. Alperin-Sheriff, J., Peikert, C.: Practical bootstrapping in quasilinear time. In: Canetti, R., Garay, J.A. (eds.) CRYPTO 2013, Part I. LNCS, vol. 8042, pp. 1–20. Springer, Heidelberg (2013)
2. Brakerski, Z., Gentry, C., Vaikuntanathan, V.: (Leveled) fully homomorphic encryption without bootstrapping. In: ITCS, pp. 309–325 (2012)
3. Cash, D., Jarecki, S., Jutla, C., Krawczyk, H., Roşu, M.-C., Steiner, M.: Highly-scalable searchable symmetric encryption with support for boolean queries. In: Canetti, R., Garay, J.A. (eds.) CRYPTO 2013. LNCS, vol. 8042, pp. 353–373. Springer, Heidelberg (2013)
4. Chor, B., Kushilevitz, E., Goldreich, O., Sudan, M.: Private information retrieval. J. ACM **45**(6), 965–981 (1998)
5. Damgård, I.B., Fitzi, M., Kiltz, E., Nielsen, J.B., Toft, T.: Unconditionally secure constant-rounds multi-party computation for equality, comparison, bits and exponentiation. In: Halevi, S., Rabin, T. (eds.) TCC 2006. LNCS, vol. 3876, pp. 285–304. Springer, Heidelberg (2006)
6. Damgård, I.B., Nielsen, J.B.: Universally composable efficient multiparty computation from threshold homomorphic encryption. In: Boneh, D. (ed.) CRYPTO 2003. LNCS, vol. 2729, pp. 247–264. Springer, Heidelberg (2003)
7. Damgård, I., Pastro, V., Smart, N., Zakarias, S.: Multiparty computation from somewhat homomorphic encryption. In: Safavi-Naini, R., Canetti, R. (eds.) CRYPTO 2012. LNCS, vol. 7417, pp. 643–662. Springer, Heidelberg (2012)
8. Gentry, C., Goldman, K.A., Halevi, S., Julta, C., Raykova, M., Wichs, D.: Optimizing ORAM and using it efficiently for secure computation. In: De Cristofaro, E., Wright, M. (eds.) PETS 2013. LNCS, vol. 7981, pp. 1–18. Springer, Heidelberg (2013)
9. Gentry, C., Halevi, S., Jutla, C., Raykova, M.: Private database access with he-over-oram architecture. Cryptology ePrint Archive, Report 2014/345 (2014). http://eprint.iacr.org/2014/345
10. Gentry, C., Halevi, S., Smart, N.P.: Fully homomorphic encryption with polylog overhead. In: Pointcheval, D., Johansson, T. (eds.) EUROCRYPT 2012. LNCS, vol. 7237, pp. 465–482. Springer, Heidelberg (2012)

11. Gentry, C., Halevi, S., Smart, N.P.: Better bootstrapping in fully homomorphic encryption. In: Fischlin, M., Buchmann, J., Manulis, M. (eds.) PKC 2012. LNCS, vol. 7293, pp. 1–16. Springer, Heidelberg (2012)
12. Goldreich, O., Ostrovsky, R.: Software protection and simulation on oblivious RAMs. J. ACM **43**(3), 431–473 (1996)
13. Dov Gordon, S., Katz, J., Kolesnikov, V., Krell, F., Malkin, T., Raykova, M., Vahlis, Y.: Secure two-party computation in sublinear (amortized) time. In: CCS (2012)
14. Halevi, S., Shoup, V.: Algorithms in HElib. Cryptology ePrint Archive, Report 2014/106 (2014). http://eprint.iacr.org/
15. Halevi, S., Shoup, V.: HElib - An Implementation of homomorphic encryption (2014). https://github.com/shaih/HElib/
16. IARPA. Security and privacy assurance research (spar) program (2011). http://www.iarpa.gov/index.php/research-programs/spar/baa
17. Islam, M.S., Kuzu, M., Kantarcioglu, M.: Access pattern disclosure on searchable encryption: ramification, attack and mitigation. In: 19th Annual Network and Distributed System Security Symposium, NDSS 2012. The Internet Society (2012)
18. Jarecki, S., Jutla, C.S., Krawczyk, H., Rosu, M.-C., Steiner, M.: Outsourced symmetric private information retrieval. In: ACM Conference on Computer and Communications Security - ACM-CCS 2013, pp. 875–888. ACM (2013)
19. Keller, M., Scholl, P.: Efficient, oblivious data structures for MPC. Cryptology ePrint Archive, Report 2014/137 (2014). http://eprint.iacr.org/
20. Lipmaa, H., Toft, T.: Secure equality and greater-than tests with sublinear online complexity. In: Fomin, F.V., Freivalds, R., Kwiatkowska, M., Peleg, D. (eds.) ICALP 2013. LNCS, vol. 7966, pp. 645–656. Springer, Heidelberg (2013)
21. Liu, C., Huang, Y., Shi, E., Hicks, M., Katz, J.: Automating efficient ram-model secure computation. In: Proceedings of 35th IEEE Symposium on Security and Privacy (2014)
22. Ostrovsky, R., Shoup, V.: Private information storage. In: STOC (1997)
23. Pappas, V., Raykova, M., Vo, B., Bellovin, S.M., Malkin, T.: Private search in the real world. In: Proceedings of the 27th Annual Computer Security Applications Conference, ACSAC 2011, pp. 83–92 (2011)
24. Popa, R.A., Redfield, C.M.S., Zeldovich, N., Balakrishnan, H.: CryptDB: processing queries on an encrypted database. Commun. ACM **55**(9), 103–111 (2012)
25. Shi, E., Hubert Chan, T.-H., Stefanov, E., Li, M.: Oblivious RAM with $O((logN)^3)$ worst-case cost. In: Lee, D.H., Wang, X. (eds.) ASIACRYPT 2011. LNCS, vol. 7073, pp. 197–214. Springer, Heidelberg (2011)
26. Stefanov, E., van Dijk, M., Shi, E., Fletcher, C.W., Ren, L., Yu, X., Devadas, S.: Path ORAM: an extremely simple oblivious RAM protocol. In: Sadeghi, A.-R., Gligor, V.D., Yung, M. (eds.) ACM Conference on Computer and Communications Security, pp. 299–310. ACM (2013)
27. Toft, T.: Sub-linear, secure comparison with two non-colluding parties. In: Catalano, D., Fazio, N., Gennaro, R., Nicolosi, A. (eds.) PKC 2011. LNCS, vol. 6571, pp. 174–191. Springer, Heidelberg (2011)
28. Yu, C.-H.: Sign modules in secure arithmetic circuits. Cryptology ePrint Archive, Report 2011/539 (2011). http://eprint.iacr.org/

Accumulable Optimistic Fair Exchange from Verifiably Encrypted Homomorphic Signatures

Jae Hong Seo[1]([⊠]), Keita Emura[2], Keita Xagawa[3], and Kazuki Yoneyama[4]

[1] Myongji University, Seoul, South Korea
jaehongseo@mju.ac.kr
[2] NICT, Tokyo, Japan
k-emura@nict.go.jp
[3] NTT Secure Platform Laboratories, Tokyo, Japan
xagawa.keita@lab.ntt.co.jp
[4] Ibaraki University, Ibaraki, Japan
kazuki.yoneyama.sec@ibaraki.ac.jp

Abstract. Let us consider a situation where a client (Alice) frequently buys a certain kind of product from a shop (Bob) (e.g., an online music service sells individual songs at the same price, and a client buys songs multiple times in a month). In this situation, Alice and Bob would like to aggregate the total transactions and pay once per month because individual payments are troublesome. Though optimistic fair exchange (OFE) has been considered in order to swap electronic items simultaneously, known OFE protocols cannot provide such aggregate function efficiently because various costs are bounded by the number of transactions in the period. In order to run this aggregation procedure efficiently, we introduce a new kind of OFE called Accumulable OFE (AOFE) that allows clients to efficiently accumulate payments in each period. In AOFE, any memory costs, computational costs, and communication complexity of the payment round must be constant in terms of the number of transactions. Since a client usually has just a low power and poor memory device, these efficiency are desirable in practice. Currently known approaches (e.g., based on verifiably encrypted signature scheme) are not very successful for constructing AOFE. Thus, we consider a new approach based on a new cryptographic primitive called verifiably encrypted homomorphic signature scheme (VEHS). In this paper, we propose a generic construction of AOFE from VEHS, and also present a concrete VEHS scheme over a composite-order bilinear group by using the dual-form signature techniques. This VEHS scheme is also of independent interest. Since we can prove the security of VEHS without random oracles, our AOFE protocol is also secure without random oracles. Finally, we implemented our AOFE protocol, and it is efficient enough for practical use.

Keywords: Optimistic fair exchange · Homomorphic signatures · Verifiably encrypted signatures

© Springer International Publishing Switzerland 2015
T. Malkin et al. (Eds.): ACNS 2015, LNCS 9092, pp. 192–214, 2015.
DOI: 10.1007/978-3-319-28166-7_10

1   Introduction

In a real trade, a buyer and a seller can exchange goods and money simultaneously in a physical way. Conversely, it is difficult to swap electronic items simultaneously because exchange is usually done through an asynchronous network such as the Internet. Then, a client, Alice, must send her e-cash before receiving an item from a shop, Bob. If Bob is malicious, Bob can abscond with the e-cash without sending the item. Thus, to prevent such a malicious Bob, the fairness is considered as one of the most important requirements for electronic commerce.

Protocols that provide the fair exchange of electronic items are called fair exchange (FE) protocols. FE protocols are roughly classified into two types: those with or without a trusted third party (TTP). An FE protocol without TTP, for example, a gradual release protocol [1–3], is far from practical in terms of communication complexity because the secret must be divided and sent gradually. FE with TTP can be achieved efficiently, but in-line [4,5] or on-line [6,7] TTP protocols are also not practical in a sense because TTP must be involved in all sessions in order to relay transactions between parties. Optimistic FE (OFE) [8–14] is the best of both worlds. Most OFE protocols have the following form; first, Alice sends a partial signature, which is a kind of a contract; that is, a valid partial signature itself is not evidence of payment. Next, Bob sends an item or a signature. Finally, Alice sends a full signature, which is like a check; that is, Bob can cash a valid full signature. When Bob does not receive the full signature from Alice after he sends the item, Bob can obtain the full signature from a TTP, called an adjudicator. The adjudicator has the power to convert the valid partial signature into a valid full signature. That is, the adjudicator does not need to participate in a session as long as the protocol is executed as usual.

1.1   Motivation

Let us consider a situation where Alice frequently buys a certain kind of product from Bob. For example, an online music service sells individual songs at the same price, and a client buys songs multiple times in a month. Another example is an online game; that is, exchanging in-game currency or virtual goods for real money. In these situations, it would be much desirable to allow Alice and Bob to aggregate the total transactions and pay once per month than individual payments if possible.

For the above application, Alice and Bob can perform OFE; both would repeatedly run $k \leq n$ sessions to exchange k partial signatures and k items, and Alice finally sends k full signatures in parallel at the end of a period, where k denotes the number of transactions between Alice and Bob and n be the maximum number of transactions. Although the ordinary OFE could be successful (for fairness) in several applications including the above, we point out that the OFE would be suffered from its linear complexity in k; that is, it is not well scalable in terms of k. More precisely,

- *In terms of memory (RAM) for full signatures:* Alice needs to keep k full signatures if she finally sends k full signatures at the end of the period; Of course, Alice can use an external storage unit to store intermediate state information (e.g., messages, signatures, and public keys) for each transaction, but she must send all k full signatures to Bob at the end of the period; that is, the required RAM size depends on k. In particular, clients may only have a device with an insufficient RAM, so that small memory requirement is desirable.

  For Bob, since he is required to receive and verify all full signatures at the end of the period, the required RAM size also depends on k.

- *In terms of computation for verification:* Since k full signatures are sent by Alice, Bob needs to perform verification algorithm k times individually at the end of the period. Furthermore, Bob (shop) has many clients besides Alice, and so he will be very busy to verify all full signatures given by several clients at the end of the period.

- *In terms of communication for sending signatures:* At the end of the period, Alice and Bob exchange all k full signatures. The network bandwidth of Bob will be stringent at the end of the period since all clients send all their full signatures at the almost same time.

The more frequent the transactions become (i.e., k and n become larger), the more these costs cause the protocol to be impractical. Thus, it is desirable to reduce these costs by accumulating full signatures, and we need an OFE protocol to achieve it. Here, we call this special OFE *accumulable OFE* (AOFE).

Küpçü and Lysyanskaya [15] introduced an OFE protocol (called useful OFE) as a partial solution. In their protocol, exchange of k items is solved by k times repetition of cheap computations, and heavy computations are executed only once within a period. However, if the resolution by the adjudicator is done at the end of the period, Alice and Bob must send all unresolved signatures; and thus, the memory problem remains.

1.2   This Work

We propose the first AOFE protocol. The main building block is a new primitive called *verifiably encrypted homomorphic signature scheme* (VEHS). This paper pioneers a new application of a homomorphic signature scheme (HS), that differs from known applications involving network coding [16] and public computation on authenticated data [17]. Our AOFE protocol is categorized as *setup-free*[1] and *stand-alone,*[2] which are desirable properties [18].

Verifiably Encrypted Signatures. A typical construction of OFE is based on a verifiably encrypted signature (VES) scheme such as [19–23]. The structure of

---

[1] We say an OFE protocol is *setup-free* if the client does not need to contact the adjudicator except when receiving and verifying the public key certificate of the adjudicator.

[2] We say an OFE protocol is *stand-alone* if the full signature is an ordinary signature.

a VES scheme is such that a signer generates an encrypted signature ω, a verifier can check the validity of ω but not decrypt it, and the adjudicator can decrypt ω and output an ordinary signature σ.[3] Thus, it is compatible with OFE when replacing the signer with the client, the verifier with the shop, the encrypted signature with the partial signature, and the ordinary signature with the full signature. Dodis et al. [12] showed a generic construction of OFE from a VES scheme.[4] We basically follow this paradigm. However, if we simply apply this paradigm, it seems not easy to achieve AOFE because ordinary VES schemes do not support a mechanism to accumulate k full signatures. We solve the problem by using a special type of VES which has an accumulation functionality of signatures.

Why Homomorphic Signatures? In order to construct a VES scheme with such an accumulation functionality, a naive idea is to use aggregate signature (AS) or multi-signature (MS). Originally, these signatures do not match the situation of AOFE (i.e., accumulating full signatures of a signer) because AS and MS are used to accumulate signatures of different signers. Thus, we need a special AS or MS that works correctly and is still secure even if all signatures are generated by the same signer. Though some sequential AS schemes [20, 21,25,26] can match this purpose, however, it is not clear whether such the sequential aggregating property can be implemented over encrypted signatures. Since Bellare et al. [27] showed that the BGLS AS [20] can be used without any restriction when the signer's public key is appended to each signed message, and the aggregating property is preserved for encrypted signatures in the BGLS AS. Also, history-free AS [28] can preserve the aggregating property due to history-freeness. However, the BGLS AS and all known constructions of history-free AS rely on random oracle (RO) heuristics, and therefore we may also require a RO even if we can construct a VES based on such schemes. Although RO model schemes have better performance in many cryptographic areas, there are evidences to show the riskiness of schemes with security proofs only in the RO model [29]. Though, Hohenberger et al. [30] propose a technique to remove ROs with multi-linear maps and the technique could be used for the above ASs, there is no known practical construction of multi-linear maps. From the above reasons, we do not select AS or MS schemes to create (verifiably) encrypted signatures according to the VES setting.

---

[3] As an example, let us consider the Waters signature scheme [24] with public key $x = g^\alpha$ and secret key h^α and the corresponding VES scheme [21]. Let $\sigma = (\sigma_1, \sigma_2) = (h^\alpha \cdot H(m)^r, g^r)$ for random r be an ordinary signature. Let $\mathsf{apk} = y = g^\beta$ be the adjudicator's public key. Then, we define $\omega = (\omega_1, \omega_2, \omega_3) = (\sigma_1 \cdot y^t, \sigma_2, g^t)$ for random t. The verfication of an encrypted signature checks if $e(\omega_1, g) = e(h, x) \cdot e(H(m), \omega_2) \cdot e(y, \omega_3)$ or not.

[4] Correctly speaking, they constructed OFE from EUF-CMA secure signature, IND-CCA secure public-key encryption, and simulation-sound non-interactive zero-knowledge proof system, which yield a VES scheme.

We consider HS as a candidate for accumulating signatures. HS allows one to compute linear combinations of given signatures with only public information. The key observation here is that it is possible to accumulate homomorphic signatures by linearly combining them, where messages are of special form so that one can recover each message from a linear combination of them. Also, Alice can accumulate signatures during the period so that she needs only small RAM to compute an accumulated signature. Moreover, we can achieve homomorphic property over encrypted signatures thanks to a homomorphic encryption such as the ElGamal encryption. Therefore, HS could be a good candidate to attain scalability for VES (and OFE also) in terms of the number of transactions k.

Our Contribution. In this paper, we propose a generic method to construct an AOFE protocol based on a VEHS scheme, and also propose a concrete VEHS scheme based on composite-order bilinear groups by using the dual-form signature technique [31,32]. By applying our AOFE protocol, we can achieve that any computational costs of parties and communication complexity of the payment round are constant in terms of k. Moreover, the required RAM space is also constant in terms of k. We describe some technical details of this work.

Security Model of AOFE. We extend the model of OFE in the multi-user setting [12] by introducing algorithms for accumulation of signatures and partial signatures, Acc and PAcc, respectively. We consider three security requirements for clients, shops, and the adjudicator, respectively. The security against clients means that a client cannot produce valid partial signatures such that the verification of the full signature (derived from partial signatures) is not valid. The security against shops means that a shop cannot produce a valid full signature that the adjudicator does not give all ordinary signatures to the shop. The security against the adjudicator means that the adjudicator cannot produce a valid full signature for which the client has not given all partial signatures to the adjudicator.

Security Model of VEHS. Formulating a reasonable security model for VEHS is not a trivial matter, and there exists a subtle issue which is not captured by just simply combining security models of VES and HS. Secure VEHS must satisfy *unforgeability* and *opacity*: Unforgeability guarantees that no adversary can produce a valid encrypted signature which is not generated by the signer. Opacity guarantees that no adversary can produce a valid ordinary signature which is not generated by the adjudicator or the signer. Note that both unforgeability and opacity must be relaxed in the VEHS setting because linear combinations of valid signatures are not regarded as a forgery as they are in the HS setting. Such a complicated situation does not occur with VES and HS. See Sect. 3 for details.

Construction of VEHS. Several types of HS have been studied in the pioneering works [33,34], for example, pairing-based constructions [16,17,35–38], lattice-

based constructions [39,40], an RSA-based construction [41], a multi-source setting [42], and a homomorphic message authentication code [43]. In this paper,
we use the composite-order pairing groups for the following technical reason; in
the security proof, we must construct a simulator (which solves a hard problem)
from an adversary of VEHS. As mentioned above, opacity captures the case
where the adversary might forge an ordinary signature of a linear combination
of the messages of which the adversary already obtains the encrypted signatures
and ordinary signatures. If we use known HS schemes in the prime-order pairing
groups, the simulator must guess which messages the adversary uses to forge.
However, there are exponentially many combinations of messages; thus, the simulator cannot work. (We will discuss this point in detail in the full version.)
On the other hand, if we use HS schemes in the composite-order pairing groups
such as the ALP12 signature [17], the simulator does not need to guess messages
thanks to the dual-form signature technique [31,32]. This technique allows the
simulator to proceed with the simulation while keeping the signing key as long
as possible. Fortunately, we can avoid the guessing problem by exploiting this
simulation.

According to the classical design principle of VES on the pairing groups,
we extend the ALP12 signature to the VES setting; that is, an encrypted signature ω is obtained by encrypting an ordinary signature σ with the ElGamal
encryption. We prove that our VEHS scheme is secure in the proposed model
under assumptions in [17,44] without ROs. Though the original security proof
of the ALP12 signature does not consider opacity, we show that the special situation of opacity is also solved by applying the dual-form signature technique.
We finally note that encrypted signatures can also be accumulated thanks to the
homomorphism of the ElGamal encryption.

AOFE from VEHS. The design is more complicated than constructing OFE
from VES. There are two challenging problems; one is how to encode messages,
and the other is how to handle sessions.

For simplicity, we begin with a slightly restricted setting that *a single kind
of items is sold with a single rate in a period* (e.g., the on-line music store which
sells singles). This setting helps to understand the essential design principle of
our construction. After that, we show an extension to the general setting (i.e.,
items and rates are variable).

For the first problem, we use a vector-representation of the transaction flag
as a message. For example, unit vectors $(1, 0, \ldots, 0)$ and $(0, 1, 0, \ldots, 0) \in \mathbb{Z}_N^n$ are
signed for the first and second transactions in a period, respectively, and the
accumulated signature corresponds to $(1, 1, 0, \ldots, 0)$, where n is the maximum
number of transactions in a period and N is an integer. Such an encoded vector
is called a *properly augmented vector* [37,45]. Bob can cash the accumulated
signature as the full signature according to the Hamming weight of the corresponding message: For example, Alice's signature on $(1, 1, 0, \ldots, 0)$ indicates
that Alice buys two items in the period.) This prevents reuse of a valid signature
because reuses can be detected by checking if the message vector contains values
other than 0 and 1. Attacks except for reuse attacks are prevented thanks to

the unforgeability and opacity of the underlying VEHS. Note that such a message representation does not contain information of items because the amount of money of the item is fixed, and such information is contained in a file identifier.

For the second problem, we use a file identifier τ which is contained in the models of HS and VEHS inherently. τ is used to control the range of linear combination operations that are allowed. If τ is the same for two signatures, signatures can be accumulated. Otherwise, signatures cannot be accumulated. In our AOFE protocol, τ contains identities of a client and a shop (e.g., Alice and Bob), the name and amount of money of an item, and a period of time. Hence, accumulation is possible only for transactions between Alice and Bob for the item in the period, and is prevented for other cases. This ensures security in the multi-user setting, as in [12]. Since a shop does transactions with multiple clients in the same period, security in the multi-user setting is a realistic situation. Note that it is known that security in the single-user setting does not imply security in the multi-user setting [12]. Additionally, we consider more general settings such as when Alice can choose an item from multiple items with a specific amount of money for each transaction, and show a concrete construction.

Our VEHS scheme has $O(n)$ size of public parameters where n is the maximum number of transactions in a period. Hence, Alice and Bob need $O(n)$ size of storages to store public parameters. As mentioned in Sect. 1.1, Alice uses her RAM space by taking necessary information out from the storage. In our instantiation, computation of Alice in each transaction and the end of a period only needs a constant number of contents of public parameters (i.e., each signing needs one of $\{h_i\}_{i\in[n]}$). For example, a message $(1, 1, \ldots, 0) \in \mathbb{Z}_N^n$ will be mapped to a single group element $h_1 h_2$. Thus, our instantiation certainly solves the memory problem. We show an implementation result of our AOFE protocol based on our VEHS scheme in the full version. Though schemes in the composite-order pairing groups usually require a high computational cost, our implementation result shows that our VEHS scheme is efficient enough for practical use.

We also give a way to extend the restricted setting to more general setting such that Alice can choose an item from multiple items with distinct amount of money for each transaction. To deal with distinct values we add a message m_i (for the i-th transaction) representing an amount of money and name of an item to the message vector. We extend the properly augmented vector to $(0, \ldots, 1, \ldots, 0, 0, \ldots, m_i, \ldots, 0)$ where the last half elements are added for containing m_i. The first half elements guarantee secure accumulation as our construction with the restricted setting. In the general setting, file identifier τ just contains identities of a client and a shop (e.g., Alice and Bob), and a period of time because the name and the amount of money may change for each period.

Organization. We define AOFE and VEHS in Sects. 2 and 3, respectively. We construct AOFE from VEHS in Sect. 4. We finally construct VEHS in the composite-order pairing groups in Sect. 5.

2   Definitions of Accumulable Optimistic Fair Exchange

In this section, we define the syntax of AOFE and its security requirements.

An AOFE protocol involves four kinds of parties, clients, shops, an adjudicator, and a trusted party. (We here divide a TTP into an adjudicator and a trusted party that generates only a public parameter.) Roughly, an AOFE protocol is executed as follows: A trusted party generates a public parameter which will be used in every participants in the protocol. Clients and the adjudicator generate their/its key pairs. A client and a shop run the protocol as follows: First, for i-th session of a period, the client generates a partial signature $\omega^{(i)}$ and an ordinary signature $\sigma^{(i)}$ on a message m_i and sends $(\omega^{(i)}, m_i)$ to the shop. The client can also accumulate messages and ordinary signatures to an accumulated message and an accumulated ordinary signature in order to reduce the memory cost. Then, the shop verifies $\omega^{(i)}$ and sends an item corresponding to m_i to the client. The shop can also accumulate messages and partial signatures to an accumulated message and an accumulated partial signature in order to reduce the memory cost. In the end of the period, the client sends the accumulated ordinary signature as the full signature to the shop. The shop verifies the full signature, and he can cash a check if the full signature is correct. Otherwise, the shop asks the resolution to the adjudicator by sending the accumulated message and the accumulated partial signature. The adjudicator verifies them and produces the full signature from the accumulated partial signature.

We note that we formulate a model of AOFE by extending the model of OFE *in the multi-user setting* [12].

First, we define the syntax of AOFE.

Definition 2.1 (Syntax of AOFE)

OFE.Setup(1^κ): *This probabilistic algorithm is run by the trusted third party. It takes security parameter 1^κ as input and outputs public parameters* pp. *Hereafter, we omit the public parameter* pp *from the arity of algorithms.*

OFE.AdjGen(1^κ): *This probabilistic algorithm takes as input security parameter 1^κ and outputs a pair of keys for an adjudicator* (apk, ask).

OFE.Gen(1^κ): *This probabilistic algorithm takes as input security parameter 1^κ, and outputs a verification/signing key pair* (vk_j, sk_j) *for a user j.*

OFE.Sign(sk_j, apk, m, aux): *This probabilistic algorithm takes as input signing key sk_j,* apk,[5] *message m to be signed and some session information* aux,[6] *and outputs an ordinary signature σ.*

OFE.Vrfy(vk_j, apk, m, σ, aux): *This deterministic algorithm takes as input vk_j,* apk, *m, σ and* aux, *and outputs 1 if σ is valid, and 0 otherwise.*

PSign(sk_j, apk, m, aux): *This probabilistic algorithm takes as input sk_j,* apk, *m and* aux, *and outputs a partial signature ω.*

PVrfy(vk_j, apk, m, ω, aux): *This deterministic algorithm takes as input vk_j,* apk, *m, ω and* aux, *and outputs 1 if ω is valid, and 0 otherwise.*

---

[5] apk is not always used. However, since the definition of OFE.Sign in OFE [12] contains apk, we adopt the same formulation.

[6] For example, session information contain the current period, and identities of parties.

$\mathsf{Acc}(\mathsf{vk}_j, \mathsf{apk}, \{m_i, \sigma^{(i)}\}_{i=1}^\ell, \mathsf{aux})$: *This probabilistic algorithm takes as input* vk_j, apk, $\{m_i, \sigma^{(i)}\}$ *and* aux, *where* $\sigma^{(i)}$ *is an ordinary signature on* m_i *under* vk_j *and* apk, *and outputs an ordinary signature* σ *on* $\sum_{i=1}^\ell m_i$ *under* vk_j *and* apk.

$\mathsf{PAcc}(\mathsf{vk}_j, \mathsf{apk}, \{m_i, \omega^{(i)}\}_{i=1}^\ell, \mathsf{aux})$: *This probabilistic algorithm takes as input* vk, apk, $\{m_i, \omega^{(i)}\}$ *and* aux, *where* $\omega^{(i)}$ *is a partial signature on* m_i *under* vk_j *and* apk, *and outputs a partial signature* ω *on* $\sum_{i=1}^\ell m_i$ *under* vk_j *and* apk.

$\mathsf{Res}(\mathsf{ask}, \mathsf{apk}, \mathsf{vk}_j, m, \omega, \mathsf{aux})$: *This (possibly) probabilistic algorithm takes as input* ask, apk, vk_j, m, ω *and* aux, *and outputs an ordinary signature* σ *on* m *under* vk_j *if* $\mathsf{PVrfy}(\mathsf{vk}_j, \mathsf{apk}, m, \omega, \mathsf{aux}) = 1$.

Correctness of AOFE must guarantee that an accumulated signature from valid partial signatures is always acceptable as well as correctness of ordinary OFE.

Definition 2.2 (Correctness). *We say that AOFE satisfies correctness if the following conditions are satisfied: For all* $\kappa \in \mathbb{N}$, *all* $\mathsf{pp} \leftarrow \mathsf{OFE.Setup}(1^\kappa)$, *all* $(\mathsf{apk}, \mathsf{ask}) \leftarrow \mathsf{OFE.AdjGen}(1^\kappa)$, *all* $(\mathsf{vk}_j, \mathsf{sk}_j) \leftarrow \mathsf{OFE.Gen}(1^\kappa)$, *all* $\ell \in \mathbb{N}$, *all* $m, m_i \in \mathcal{M}$ *for* $i = 1, \ldots, \ell$, *and all* $\mathsf{aux} \in \{0,1\}^*$,

1. $\mathsf{OFE.Vrfy}\big(\mathsf{vk}_j, \mathsf{apk}, m, \mathsf{OFE.Sign}(\mathsf{sk}_j, \mathsf{apk}, m, \mathsf{aux}), \mathsf{aux}\big) = 1$,
2. $\mathsf{OFE.Vrfy}\big(\mathsf{vk}_j, \mathsf{apk}, \sum_{i=1}^\ell m_i, \mathsf{Acc}(\mathsf{vk}_j, \mathsf{apk}, \{m_i, \mathsf{OFE.Sign}(\mathsf{sk}_j, \mathsf{apk}, m_i, \mathsf{aux})\}_{i=1}^\ell, \mathsf{aux}), \mathsf{aux}\big) = 1$,
3. $\mathsf{PVrfy}\big(\mathsf{vk}_j, \mathsf{apk}, m, \mathsf{PSign}(\mathsf{sk}_j, \mathsf{apk}, m, \mathsf{aux}), \mathsf{aux}\big) = 1$,
4. $\mathsf{PVrfy}\big(\mathsf{vk}_j, \mathsf{apk}, \sum_{i=1}^\ell m_i, \mathsf{PAcc}(\mathsf{vk}_j, \mathsf{apk}, \{m_i, \mathsf{PSign}(\mathsf{sk}_j, \mathsf{apk}, m_i, \mathsf{aux})\}_{i=1}^\ell, \mathsf{aux}), \mathsf{aux}\big) = 1$,
5. $\mathsf{OFE.Vrfy}\big(\mathsf{vk}_j, \mathsf{apk}, m, \mathsf{Res}(\mathsf{ask}, \mathsf{apk}, \mathsf{vk}_j, m, \mathsf{PSign}(\mathsf{sk}_j, \mathsf{apk}, m, \mathsf{aux}), \mathsf{aux}), \mathsf{aux}\big) = 1$,
6. *and* $\mathsf{OFE.Vrfy}\big(\mathsf{vk}_j, \mathsf{apk}, \sum_{i=1}^\ell m_i, \mathsf{Res}(\mathsf{ask}, \mathsf{apk}, \mathsf{vk}_j, \sum_{i=1}^\ell m_i, \mathsf{PAcc}(\mathsf{vk}_j, \mathsf{apk}, \{m_i, \mathsf{PSign}(\mathsf{sk}_j, \mathsf{apk}, m_i, \mathsf{aux})\}_{i=1}^\ell, \mathsf{aux}), \mathsf{aux}), \mathsf{aux}\big) = 1$.

The ambiguity property guarantees that the resolved signature from a partial signature is indistinguishable from the real signature corresponding to the partial signature. In practice, the ambiguity property is necessary to hide if the transaction has some trouble between a client and a shop. We note that the client who causes a trouble in a transaction with a shop should still keep to participate with a transaction with other shops as in the real world and the shop will hope to avoid that the bank knows if the ordinary signature is obtained from the adjudicator, on cashing a check.

Definition 2.3 (Ambiguity [46]). *We say that AOFE satisfies ambiguity if any resolved signature* $\mathsf{Res}(\mathsf{ask}, \mathsf{apk}, \mathsf{vk}_j, m, \mathsf{PSign}(\mathsf{sk}_j, \mathsf{apk}, m, \mathsf{aux}), \mathsf{aux})$ *(resp.* $\mathsf{Res}(\mathsf{ask}, \mathsf{apk}, \mathsf{vk}_j, \sum_{i=1}^\ell m_i, \mathsf{PAcc}(\mathsf{vk}_j, \mathsf{apk}, \{m_i, \mathsf{PSign}(\mathsf{sk}_j, \mathsf{apk}, m_i, \mathsf{aux})\}_{i=1}^\ell, \mathsf{aux}), \mathsf{aux})$) *is computationally indistinguishable from the real signature* $\mathsf{OFE.Sign}(\mathsf{sk}_j, \mathsf{apk}, m, \mathsf{aux})$ *(resp.* $\mathsf{Acc}(\mathsf{vk}_j, \mathsf{apk}, \{m_i, \mathsf{OFE.Sign}(\mathsf{sk}_j, \mathsf{apk}, m_i, \mathsf{aux})\}_{i=1}^\ell, \mathsf{aux})$).

Next, we consider the security model for AOFE. The model contains three requirements: *security against clients*, *security against shops*, and *security against the adjudicator*.

The security against clients means that a client cannot produce valid partial signatures from which the verification of the full signature derived is not valid.

Definition 2.4 (Security against Clients). *We say that an AOFE scheme satisfies security against clients if no PPT adversary $\mathcal{E}$ has a non-negligible advantage (as a function of κ) in the following game:*

1. *Adversary $\mathcal{E}$ is given* pp *and* apk, *where* pp $\leftarrow$ OFE.Setup(1^κ) *and* (apk, ask) $\leftarrow$ OFE.AdjGen(1^κ).
2. *$\mathcal{E}$ is allowed to issue queries to the following oracle:*
   Resolution oracle: *This oracle receives verification key* vk_j, *message* m, *partial signature* ω *and* aux. *It verifies* PVrfy(vk_j, apk, m, ω, aux) $= 1$, *and returns ordinary signature* $\sigma \leftarrow$ Res(ask, apk, vk_j, m, ω, aux) *to the adversary.*
3. *Finally, $\mathcal{E}$ outputs* ($\{m_i^*, \omega^{(i)*}\}_{i=1}^\ell$, $vk_\mathcal{E}$, aux*). *We say that $\mathcal{E}$ wins if for $i = 1$ to ℓ,* PVrfy($vk_\mathcal{E}$, apk, $m_i^*, \omega^{(i)*}$, aux*) $= 1$, $\sigma^{(i)*} \leftarrow$ Res(ask, apk, $vk_\mathcal{E}$, $m_i^*, \omega^{(i)*}$, aux*) *and* OFE.Vrfy($vk_\mathcal{E}$, apk, $\sum_{i=1}^\ell m_i^*$, Acc($vk_\mathcal{E}$, apk, $\{m_i^*, \sigma^{(i)*}\}_{i=1}^\ell$, aux*), aux*) $= 0$.

The advantage of $\mathcal{E}$ is defined as $\mathsf{Adv}_\mathcal{E}^{OFE.Client}(\kappa) := \Pr[\mathcal{E}\ wins]$.

$\mathcal{E}$ can select arbitrary verification key $vk_\mathcal{E}$ for a client to attack. Thus, this definition is for the multi-user setting as [12], and captures the situation that $\mathcal{E}$ generates $vk_\mathcal{E}$ without obeying OFE.Gen (i.e., there exists no corresponding signing key $sk_\mathcal{E}$).

The security against shops means that no shop can produce a valid full signature unless the shop obtains all ordinary signatures corresponding to the full signature.

Definition 2.5 (Security against Shops). *We say that an AOFE scheme satisfies security against shops if no PPT adversary $\mathcal{E}$ has a non-negligible advantage (as a function of κ) in the following game:*

1. *Adversary $\mathcal{E}$ is given* pp, apk *and* vk_A, *where* pp $\leftarrow$ OFE.Setup(1^κ), (apk, ask) $\leftarrow$ OFE.AdjGen(1^κ) *and* (vk_A, sk_A) $\leftarrow$ OFE.Gen(1^κ) *for the target client A. Tables T_{psig} and T_{res} are initialized as $\emptyset$.*
2. *$\mathcal{E}$ is allowed to issue queries to the following oracles:*
   Partial signing oracle: *This oracle receives message m and* aux. *It returns partial signature* $\omega \leftarrow$ PSign(sk_A, apk, m, aux) *to the adversary, and stores* ((m, aux), ω) *in table T_{psig}.*
   Resolution oracle: *This oracle receives verification key* vk_j, *message* m, *partial signature* ω *and* aux. *It verifies* PVrfy(vk_j, apk, m, ω, aux) $= 1$, *returns ordinary signature* $\sigma \leftarrow$ Res(ask, apk, vk_j, m, ω, aux) *to the adversary, and stores* ((vk_j, m, ω, aux), σ) *in table T_{res}.*
3. *Finally, $\mathcal{E}$ outputs* (m^*, σ^*, aux*). *We say that $\mathcal{E}$ wins if* OFE.Vrfy(vk_A, apk, m^*, σ^*, aux*) $= 1$, *and either of the following holds:*
   - aux* $\neq$ aux *for any entry* (($\cdot$, aux), $\cdot$) $\in T_{psig}$ *and* (($\cdot, \cdot, \cdot$, aux), $\cdot$) $\in T_{res}$.

- $m^* \neq \sum_{i=1}^{\ell} m_i^*$ *for all sets* $\{((m_i^*, \mathsf{aux}^*), \cdot)\}_{i=1}^{\ell} \subseteq T_{psig}$.
- $m^* \neq \sum_{i=1}^{\ell} m_i^*$ *for all sets* $\{((vk_A, m_i^*, \cdot, \mathsf{aux}^*), \cdot)\}_{i=1}^{\ell} \subseteq T_{res}$.

The advantage of $\mathcal{E}$ is defined as $\mathsf{Adv}_{\mathcal{E}}^{OFE.Shop}(\kappa) := \Pr[\mathcal{E} \ wins]$.

As in the definition of OFE [12], the target client A is chosen at the beginning of the game. $\mathcal{E}$ can pose the target message for arbitrary verification key vk_j except vk_A to the resolution oracle. Thus, this definition is for the multi-user setting as [12]. That means, $\mathcal{E}$ can arbitrarily interact with all clients and establish sessions with them except the target session. Note that $\mathcal{E}$ does not need the ordinary signing oracle because it can be simulated by the combination of the partial signing oracle and the resolution oracle.

The security against the adjudicator means that no adjudicator can produce a valid full signature unless the adjudicator can generate its public key malignly and obtain all partial signatures corresponding to the full signature.

Definition 2.6 (Security against Adjudicator). *We say that an AOFE scheme satisfies security against the adjudicator if no PPT adversary $\mathcal{E}$ has a non-negligible advantage (as a function of κ) in the following game:*

1. *Adversary $\mathcal{E}$ is given* pp, *and* vk_A, *where* pp $\leftarrow$ OFE.Setup(1^κ) *and* $(vk_A, sk_A) \leftarrow$ OFE.Gen(1^κ) *for the target client A. $\mathcal{E}$ outputs* apk*. *A table T_{psig} is initialized as $\emptyset$.*
2. *$\mathcal{E}$ is allowed to issue queries to the following oracle:*
   Partial signing oracle: *This oracle receives message m and* aux. *It returns partial signature $\omega \leftarrow$ PSign$(sk_A, \mathsf{apk}^*, m, \mathsf{aux})$ to the adversary, and stores $((m, \mathsf{aux}), \omega)$ in table T_{psig}.*
3. *Finally, $\mathcal{E}$ outputs $(m^*, \sigma^*, \mathsf{aux}^*)$. We say that $\mathcal{E}$ wins if* OFE.Vrfy$(vk_A, \mathsf{apk}^*, m^*, \sigma^*, \mathsf{aux}^*) = 1$, *and either of the following holds:*
   - $\mathsf{aux}^* \neq \mathsf{aux}$ *for any entry* $((\cdot, \mathsf{aux}), \cdot) \in T_{psig}$.
   - $m^* \neq \sum_{i=1}^{\ell} m_i^*$ *for all sets* $\{((m_i^*, \mathsf{aux}^*), \cdot)\}_{i=1}^{\ell} \subseteq T_{psig}$.

The advantage of $\mathcal{E}$ is defined as $\mathsf{Adv}_{\mathcal{E}}^{OFE.Adj}(\kappa) := \Pr[\mathcal{E} \ wins]$.

As in the definition of OFE [12], the target client A is chosen at the beginning of the game. Note that $\mathcal{E}$ does not need the resolution oracle because $\mathcal{E}$ can have ask* corresponding to apk*.

We additionally note that if the trusted party, who generates pp $\leftarrow$ OFE.Setup (1^κ), colluded with an adjudicator, the adjudicator could forge a signature. Indeed, our AOFE scheme built upon a VEHS scheme in Sect. 5 is vulnerable to this attack.[7]

In this paper, we focus on the basic security properties as in [12]. However, additional properties such as abuse-freeness [47], non-repudiation [48], and timely termination [9] can be also considered by the same way as previous works.

---

[7] Consider the malicious adjudicator knowing the discrete logarithm of h_i, $\log_{g_1}(h_i)$.

3 Definitions of Verifiably Encrypted Homomorphic Signature

In this section, we explain the syntax of VEHS and its security definitions. A VEHS scheme VEHS consists of the following ten algorithms. Let the underlying message space $\mathcal{M}$ be represented as $\mathcal{M} := R^n$ for some integer n and ring R, and let $\mathcal{T}$ be a file-identifier space.

Definition 3.1 (Syntax of VEHS). *We here describe the syntax of VEHS.*

Setup($1^\kappa, 1^n$): *This probabilistic algorithm is run by the trusted third party. It takes security parameter 1^κ and the length of vectors to be signed 1^n as input and outputs public parameters pp. Hereafter, we omit the public parameter pp from the arity of algorithms.*

AdjGen(1^κ): *This probabilistic algorithm takes as input security parameter 1^κ and outputs a pair of keys for an adjudicator* (apk, ask).

Gen(1^κ): *This probabilistic algorithm takes as input security parameter 1^κ, and outputs a verification/signing key pair for a signer* (vk, sk).

Sign(sk, τ, $\boldsymbol{v}$): *This probabilistic algorithm takes as input a signing key* sk, *a file identifier $\tau \in \mathcal{T}$, and a vector $\boldsymbol{v} \in \mathbb{Z}_p^n$ to be signed, and outputs a signature σ.*

Vrfy(vk, τ, $\boldsymbol{v}$, σ): *This deterministic algorithm takes as input* vk, τ, $\boldsymbol{v}$, *and σ, and outputs 1 if σ is valid, and 0 otherwise.*

Create(sk, apk, τ, $\boldsymbol{v}$): *This probabilistic algorithm takes as input* sk, apk, τ, *and $\boldsymbol{v}$, and outputs a VES ω.*

VesVrfy(apk, vk, τ, $\boldsymbol{v}$, ω): *This deterministic algorithm takes as input* apk, vk, τ, $\boldsymbol{v}$, *and ω, and outputs 1 if ω is valid, and 0 otherwise.*

Derive(vk, τ, $\{\gamma_i, \boldsymbol{v}_i, \sigma^{(i)}\}_{i=1}^\ell$): *This probabilistic algorithm takes as input* vk, τ, *and $\{\gamma_i, \boldsymbol{v}_i, \sigma^{(i)}\}$, where γ_i is a weight and $\sigma^{(i)}$ is a signature on $\boldsymbol{v}_i$ with τ under* vk, *and outputs a signature σ on $\sum_{i=1}^\ell \gamma_i \boldsymbol{v}_i$ with τ under* vk.

VesDerive(vk, apk, τ, $\{\gamma_i, \boldsymbol{v}_i, \omega^{(i)}\}_{i=1}^\ell$): *This probabilistic algorithm takes as input* vk, τ, *and $\{\gamma_i, \boldsymbol{v}_i, \omega^{(i)}\}$, where γ_i is a weight and $\omega^{(i)}$ is a VES on $\boldsymbol{v}_i$ with τ under* vk and apk, *and outputs a VES ω on $\sum_{i=1}^\ell \gamma_i \boldsymbol{v}_i$ with τ under* vk and apk.

Adj(ask, apk, vk, ω, τ, $\boldsymbol{v}$): *This (possibly) probabilistic algorithm takes as input* (ask, apk, vk, ω, τ, $\boldsymbol{v}$), *and outputs an ordinary signature σ on $\boldsymbol{v}$ with τ under* vk *if* VesVrfy(apk, vk, ω, τ, $\boldsymbol{v}$) = 1.

Let us define correctness of VEHS.

Definition 3.2 (Correctness). *We say a VEHS scheme VEHS is correct if the following conditions are satisfied: For all $\kappa, n \in \mathbb{N}$, all* (apk, ask) $\leftarrow$ AdjGen(1^κ), *all* (vk, sk) $\leftarrow$ Gen(1^κ), *all $\tau \in \mathcal{T}$ and $\boldsymbol{v} \in \mathcal{M}$, and all $\ell \in \mathbb{N}$, we require the following conditions:*

1. Vrfy$\big($vk, τ, $\boldsymbol{v}$, Sign(sk, τ, $\boldsymbol{v}$)$\big)$ = 1.
2. Vrfy$\big($vk, τ, $\sum_{i=1}^\ell \gamma_i \boldsymbol{v}_i$, Derive(vk, τ, $\{\gamma_i, \boldsymbol{v}_i, \sigma^{(i)}\}_{i=1}^\ell$)$\big)$ = 1 *if all* Vrfy(vk, τ, $\boldsymbol{v}_i$, $\sigma^{(i)}$) = 1.

3. $\mathsf{VesVrfy}\big(\mathsf{apk}, \mathsf{vk}, \tau, \boldsymbol{v}, \mathsf{Create}(\mathsf{sk}, \mathsf{apk}, \tau, \boldsymbol{v})\big) = 1$.
4. $\mathsf{VesVrfy}\big(\mathsf{apk}, \mathsf{vk}, \tau, \sum_{i=1}^{\ell} \gamma_i \boldsymbol{v}_i, \mathsf{VesDerive}(\mathsf{vk}, \mathsf{apk}, \tau, \{\gamma_i, \boldsymbol{v}_i, \omega^{(i)}\}_{i=1}^{\ell})\big) = 1$
   if all $\mathsf{VesVrfy}(\mathsf{apk}, \mathsf{vk}, \tau, \boldsymbol{v}_i, \omega^{(i)}) = 1$.

We can define additional property *resolution independence* of VEHS as that in the context of VES [49]. Roughly speaking, resolution independence implies that an ordinal signature and resolved signature have the same distribution. Since we omit the detail of proofs, we defer the definition of resolution independence to the full version.

We next extend *extractability* of VES [22] to that of VEHS. Roughly speaking, extractability implies that a signature extracted from a valid VES via the Adj algorithm is always valid. Again, we omit the formal defintion of extractability due to page limit.

We define the two security notions *unforgeability* and *opacity*. We consult the security definitions of [17] (Definition 12: unforgeability of a linearly homomorphic signature scheme) and [23] (Definition 4: unforgeability and opacity of a VES scheme). Since VEHS inherits both properties of homomorphic signatures and VESs, we need to keep in mind the security requirements in both contexts.

Before giving definitions, we briefly review unforgeability and opacity of a VES scheme. In the unforgeability game defined in [23], an adversary $\mathcal{A}$ is allowed to obtain VESs from the creation oracle which returns a VES for a queried message, and is also allowed to access the adjudication oracle which extracts and returns a signature for a queried message/VES pair. We strengthen the adversary by allowing it to be a malicious adjudicator. By this strengthening, unforgeability guarantees that even malicious adjudicator cannot produce a valid VES ω^* which is not generated by the creation oracle. Opacity is also defined under the same design principle, where no adversary can produce a valid ordinary signature σ^* which is not generated by the adjudication oracle.

In both definitions, we need to modify the winning condition of $\mathcal{A}$ in the VEHS context because of the homomorphic property. Therefore, we adopt the winning condition of the unforgeability game of [17]. In their unforgeability game, we say that $\mathcal{A}$ wins if $\mathcal{A}$ can produce a valid signature on a message, where the message does not belong to the subspace spanned by all queried messages, or they have a different file identifier from those previously obtained.

Definition 3.3 (Unforgeability). *A VEHS scheme* VEHS *is said to be unforgeable if no PPT adversary* $\mathcal{A}$ *has a non-negligible advantage (as a function of κ and n) in the following game:*

1. $\mathcal{C}$ *runs* $\mathsf{pp} \leftarrow \mathsf{Setup}(1^\kappa)$, *initializes a table* $T_{ves} \leftarrow \emptyset$, *and gives* pp *to the adversary.* $\mathcal{A}$ *chooses* apk^*, *and sends it to the challenger* $\mathcal{C}$. $\mathcal{C}$ *runs* $(\mathsf{vk}, \mathsf{sk}) \leftarrow \mathsf{Gen}(1^\kappa)$, *and sends* vk *to* $\mathcal{A}$.
2. $\mathcal{A}$ *is allowed to issue queries to the following oracle:*
   Creation oracle: *This oracle receives a file identifier* $\tau \in \mathcal{T}$ *and an n-dimensional vector* $\boldsymbol{v} \in R^n$. *It computes* $\omega \leftarrow \mathsf{Create}(\mathsf{sk}, \mathsf{apk}^*, \tau, \boldsymbol{v})$, *stores* $((\tau, \boldsymbol{v}), \omega)$ *in the table* T_{ves}, *and returns* ω *to the adversary.*

3. *Finally, $\mathcal{A}$ outputs a file identifier τ^*, a vector v^*, and a signature σ^*. We say that $\mathcal{A}$ wins if $(\tau^*, v^*) \in \mathcal{M}$ and $\mathsf{Vrfy}(\mathsf{vk}, \tau^*, v^*, \sigma^*) = 1$ hold, and either of the following holds:*

    Class I: *$\tau^* \neq \tau$ for any entry $((\tau, \cdot), \cdot) \in T_{ves}$ and $v^* \neq \mathbf{0}$.*

    Class II: *There exists τ such that $\tau^* = \tau$ and $((\tau, \cdot), \cdot) \in T_{ves}$, and $v^* \notin \mathrm{span}(v_1, \ldots, v_k)$, where $v_1, \ldots, v_k$ are vectors which appeared in T_{ves} such that $((\tau^*, v_j), \cdot) \in T_{ves}$ for all $j \in [k]$.*

The advantage of $\mathcal{A}$ is defined as $\mathsf{Adv}_{\mathcal{A}}^{Forge}(\kappa, n) := \Pr[\mathcal{A} \ wins]$.

Definition 3.4 (Opacity). *A VEHS scheme VEHS is said to be* opaque *if no PPT adversary $\mathcal{A}$ has a non-negligible advantage (as a function of κ and n) in the following game:*

1. *C runs $\mathsf{pp} \leftarrow \mathsf{Setup}(1^\kappa)$, initializes two tables $T_{ves}, T_{sig} \leftarrow \emptyset$, and gives pp to the adversary. C runs $(\mathsf{apk}, \mathsf{ask}) \leftarrow \mathsf{AdjGen}(1^\kappa)$ and $(\mathsf{vk}, \mathsf{sk}) \leftarrow \mathsf{Gen}(1^\kappa)$, and sends apk and vk to $\mathcal{A}$.*

2. *$\mathcal{A}$ is allowed to issue queries to the following two oracles:*

    Creation oracle: *This oracle is the same as that of the unforgeability game.*

    Adjudication oracle: *This oracle receives a file identifier $\tau \in \mathcal{T}$, an n-dimensional vector $y \in R^n$, and a VES ω. If $\mathsf{VesVrfy}(\mathsf{vk}, \mathsf{apk}, \tau, y, \omega) \rightarrow 0$, then it returns $\perp$. Otherwise, it computes $\sigma \leftarrow \mathsf{Adj}(\mathsf{ask}, \mathsf{apk}, \mathsf{vk}, \omega, \tau, y)$, stores $((\tau, y), \sigma)$ in the table T_{sig}, and returns σ to the adversary.*

3. *Finally, $\mathcal{A}$ outputs an identifier τ^*, a vector y^*, and a signature σ^*. We say that $\mathcal{A}$ wins if $(\tau^*, y^*) \in \mathcal{M}$, $y^* \neq \mathbf{0}$, and $\mathsf{Vrfy}(\mathsf{vk}, \tau^*, y^*, \sigma^*) = 1$ hold, and either of the following holds:*

    Class I: *$\tau^* \neq \tau$ for any entry $((\tau, \cdot), \cdot) \in T_{ves} \cup T_{sig}$.*

    Class II: *There exists τ such that $\tau^* = \tau$ and $((\tau, \cdot), \cdot) \in T_{ves} \cup T_{sig}$, and $y^* \notin \mathrm{span}(v_1, \ldots, v_k)$, where $v_1, \ldots, v_k$ are vectors which appeared in T_{ves} with τ^*; that is, $((\tau^*, v_j), \cdot) \in T_{ves}$ for all $j \in [k]$.*

    Class III: *There exists τ such that $\tau^* = \tau$ and $((\tau, \cdot), \cdot) \in T_{ves} \cup T_{sig}$, $y^* \in \mathrm{span}(v_1, \ldots, v_k)$, and $y^* \notin \mathrm{span}(y_1, \ldots, y_l)$, where $v_1, \ldots, v_k$ are vectors which appeared in T_{ves} such that $((\tau^*, v_j), \cdot) \in T_{ves}$ for all $j \in [k]$ and $y_1, \ldots, y_l$ are vectors which appeared in T_{sig} with τ^*, that is, $((\tau^*, y_j), \cdot) \in T_{sig}$ for all $j \in [l]$.*

The advantage of $\mathcal{A}$ is defined as $\mathsf{Adv}_{\mathcal{A}}^{Opac}(\kappa, n) := \Pr[\mathcal{A} \ wins]$.

4 Constructions of Accumulable Optimistic Fair Exchange

4.1 Simple Construction and Its Limitation

First, we consider a simple solution toward our goal, and explain its limitations. Let Alice be a client and Bob be a shop. We suppose that Alice and Bob do transactions k times in a period. The simple construction is based on the conventional VES with simple message aggregation (whereas AOFE is based on the

VES aggregation). That is, in the i-th transaction, Alice computes a VES on a message $m_1|| \cdots ||m_i$, say $\omega^{(i)}$, and sends $(m_i, \omega^{(i)})$ to Bob as a contract. Then, at the finish, Alice sends a full signature on the message $m_1|| \cdots ||m_k$, which is used as the check for all transactions in this period. The adjudicator verifies a transcript, decrypts a VES $\omega^{(k)}$, and returns $\sigma^{(k)}$, Alice's full signature on the message $m_1|| \cdots ||m_k$, to Bob.

The weak point of this solution is that it does not support *history-free accumulation*. This property is desirable for a network with out-of-order delivery: Even Alice sends $(m_1, \omega^{(1)})$ and $(m_2, \omega^{(2)})$, Bob may receive $(m_2, \omega^{(2)})$ at first, and later he receives $(m_1, \omega^{(1)})$. Then, Bob cannot verify the validity of the VES $(m_2, \omega^{(2)})$, because he does not know m_1. Therefore, Bob cannot return goods and Alice will be annoyed. That is, the simple construction requires that Bob sequentially verifies encrypted signatures.

As another example, if Alice sends $(m_i, \omega^{(i)})$, where $\omega^{(i)}$ is a VES on m_i, then this problem seems to be solved. However, such a construction is inefficient as we already discussed in the introduction.

Therefore, the approach based on ordinary VES does not fully satisfy our definition of security; and thus, we must consider another approach (i.e., an approach based on VEHS).

4.2   Generic Construction of AOFE from VEHS

Here, we show our generic construction of AOFE (OFE.Setup, OFE.AdjGen, OFE.Gen, OFE.Sign, OFE.Vrfy, PSign, PVrfy, Acc, PAcc, Res) from VEHS (Setup, AdjGen, Gen, Sign, Vrfy, Create, VesVrfy, Derive, VesDerive, Adj) in the restricted setting (i.e., the name and the cost of an item is fixed in a period). Compared to the simple construction, our generic construction satisfies the ambiguity property, and allows Bob to verify VESs in parallel (or regardless of the order).

Recall that a file identifier τ can be an arbitrary string in VEHS due to our security definitions for VEHS in Sect. 3. We use it to designate identities of a client and a shop, the name and amount of money of an item, and a certain period, e.g., $\tau := H(\text{Alice}||\text{Bob}||\text{Music}||\$10||\text{May})$, where H is a collision resistance hash function. τ is set as session information aux. We suppose that Alice and Bob do transactions k times in a period, where transactions occur at most n times, i.e., $k \leq n$. Let $\mathcal{M} = R^n$ be a message space of VEHS with ring R and integer n. Let $v_i \in R^n$ be a unit vector whose i-th element is 1 and the other elements are 0, that is, $v_i = (0, \ldots, 0, 1, 0, \ldots, 0)$. In the i-th phase, a message is defined as a properly augmented vector v_i.

Setup Phase

1. OFE.Setup(1^κ): pp $\leftarrow$ Setup($1^\kappa, 1^n$) is provided to all users and the adjudicator.
2. OFE.AdjGen(1^κ): The adjudicator generates (apk, ask) $\leftarrow$ AdjGen(1^κ).
3. OFE.Gen(1^κ): User i generates (vk$_i$, sk$_i$) $\leftarrow$ Gen(1^κ).[8]

---

[8] Because key generation algorithms for a signer and the adjudicator are independent in VEHS, our AOFE protocol is setup-free.

Transaction Phase (For $i = 1$ to k). Alice's key is $(\mathsf{vk}_A, \mathsf{sk}_A)$. Identities of Alice and Bob, the name and amount of money of the item, and the period of the transaction are specified by τ. Initially, Alice sets $\boldsymbol{v} = (0, \ldots, 0)$ and $\sigma = \bot$, and Bob sets $\boldsymbol{v} = (0, \ldots, 0)$ and $\omega = \bot$.

1. $\mathsf{OFE.Sign}(\mathsf{sk}_A, \mathsf{apk}, \boldsymbol{v}_i, \tau)$: Alice generates signature $\sigma^{(i)} \leftarrow \mathsf{Sign}(\mathsf{sk}_A, \tau, \boldsymbol{v}_i)$ as the ordinary signature.
2. $\mathsf{Acc}(\mathsf{vk}_A, \mathsf{apk}, \{(\boldsymbol{v}, \sigma), (\boldsymbol{v}_i, \sigma^{(i)})\}, \tau)$: If $i = 1$, then Alice sets $\boldsymbol{v} := \boldsymbol{v}_1$ and $\sigma := \sigma^{(1)}$. Otherwise, Alice updates $\boldsymbol{v} \leftarrow \boldsymbol{v} + \boldsymbol{v}_i$, and $\sigma \leftarrow \mathsf{Derive}(\mathsf{vk}_A, \tau, \{(1, \boldsymbol{v}, \sigma), (1, \boldsymbol{v}_i, \sigma^{(i)})\})$.[9]
3. $\mathsf{PSign}(\mathsf{sk}_A, \mathsf{apk}, \boldsymbol{v}_i, \tau)$: Alice generates VES $\omega^{(i)} \leftarrow \mathsf{Create}(\mathsf{sk}_A, \mathsf{apk}, \tau, \boldsymbol{v}_i)$ as the partial signature. Alice sends $(\omega^{(i)}, \boldsymbol{v}_i)$ to Bob as a contract.
4. $\mathsf{PVrfy}(\mathsf{vk}_A, \mathsf{apk}, \boldsymbol{v}_i, \omega^{(i)}, \tau)$: Bob verifies that $\boldsymbol{v}_i$ is a unit vector $(\overbrace{0, \ldots, 0}^{i-1}, 1, 0, \ldots, 0)$, and $\mathsf{VesVrfy}(\mathsf{apk}, \mathsf{vk}_A, \tau, \boldsymbol{v}_i, \omega^{(i)}) = 1$. If so, Bob sends the item to Alice.
5. $\mathsf{PAcc}(\mathsf{vk}_A, \mathsf{apk}, \{(\boldsymbol{v}, \omega), (\boldsymbol{v}_i, \omega^{(i)})\}, \tau)$: If $i = 1$, then Bob sets $\boldsymbol{v} := \boldsymbol{v}_1$ and $\omega := \omega^{(1)}$. Otherwise, Bob updates $\boldsymbol{v} \leftarrow \boldsymbol{v} + \boldsymbol{v}_i$, and $\omega \leftarrow \mathsf{VesDerive}(\mathsf{vk}_A, \mathsf{apk}, \tau, \{(1, \boldsymbol{v}, \omega), (1, \boldsymbol{v}_i, \omega^{(i)})\})$.[10]

Check Phase (The end of the period)

1. Alice sends σ as the full signature as a check.[11]
2. $\mathsf{OFE.Vrfy}(\mathsf{vk}_A, \mathsf{apk}, \boldsymbol{v}, \sigma, \tau)$: Bob verifies that $\boldsymbol{v}$ has the form $(\overbrace{1, \ldots, 1}^{k}, 0, \ldots, 0)$, and $\mathsf{Vrfy}(\mathsf{vk}_A, \tau, \boldsymbol{v}, \sigma) = 1$. If so, Bob can cash a check with σ.
3. $\mathsf{Res}(\mathsf{ask}, \mathsf{apk}, \mathsf{vk}_A, \boldsymbol{v}, \omega, \tau)$: If $\mathsf{OFE.Vrfy}(\mathsf{vk}_A, \mathsf{apk}, \boldsymbol{v}, \sigma, \tau) = 0$ or Bob has not received the full signature by the end of the period, Bob sends $(\boldsymbol{v}, \omega)$ to the adjudicator. The adjudicator verifies that both $\boldsymbol{v}$ has the form $(\overbrace{1, \ldots, 1}^{k}, 0, \ldots, 0)$, and $\mathsf{VesVrfy}(\mathsf{apk}, \mathsf{vk}_A, \tau, \boldsymbol{v}, \omega) = 1$. Then, the adjudicator runs $\sigma \leftarrow \mathsf{Adj}(\mathsf{ask}, \mathsf{apk}, \mathsf{vk}_A, \omega, \tau, \boldsymbol{v})$, and sends σ to Bob.

Correctness and ambiguity of our AOFE protocol are trivially derived from correctness and resolution independence of VEHS; and thus, we omit to prove it.

Note that Bob seems to be able to choose the weight values, and can get a weighted signature from the adjudicator that might not be agreed by Alice. However, this problem does not occur by syntax of messages: the adjudicator verifies the validity of the received sum of VESs by checking the form of $\boldsymbol{v}$ in the step 3 of the Check phase. The adjudicator refuses the malformed weight even if Bob chooses the invalid ones: for example, the adjudicator rejects a message

---

[9] Then, Alice needs to store just one message and one ordinary signature in her memory during a transaction period.
[10] Then, Bob also needs to store just one message and one partial signature in his memory during a transaction period.
[11] Since the full signature is also an ordinary signature, our protocol is stand-alone.

$v = (2, 1, 1, 0, \ldots, 0)$. Moreover, unforgeability of VEHS guarantees that Bob cannot forge any partial signature of a message vector that the i-th value is 1 when the i-th transaction between Alice and Bob does not occur.

4.3 Security

Due to page limits, we defer the proofs of Theorems 4.1, 4.2, and 4.3 to the full version. We only comment intuition.

Theorem 4.1 (Security against Clients). *Our AOFE protocol is secure against clients if the underlying VEHS scheme is extractable.*

Since the client cannot forge a valid encrypted signature such that the corresponding ordinary signature is not valid because of extractability of the underlying VEHS, this property is guaranteed.

Theorem 4.2 (Security against Shops). *Our AOFE protocol is secure against shops if the underlying VEHS scheme is opaque and resolution independent.*

Since the shop cannot forge a valid full signature without knowing one of corresponding ordinary signatures because of opacity of the underlying VEHS, this property is guaranteed. Also, we need resolution independence to simulate the resolution oracle.

Theorem 4.3 (Security against Adjudicator). *Our AOFE protocol is secure against the adjudicator if the underlying VEHS scheme is unforgeable.*

Since the adjudicator cannot forge both a valid encrypted signature and the corresponding valid ordinary signature without knowing the signing key of the client because of unforgeability of the underlying VEHS, this property is guaranteed.

4.4 Extension to General Setting

The above AOFE protocol only supports the case in which the name and cost of an item in a period are fixed. This protocol covers a situation where Alice frequently buys a certain kind of product from Bob at a flat rate (e.g., an online music service sells individual songs at the same price, and a client buys songs multiple times in a month). Here, we consider the general setting where each item has a distinct amount of money, and Alice can choose an arbitrary item in each transaction. We provide a key idea to extend our basic AOFE protocol into general setting, and the details of the extended AOFE protocol and its security analysis appear in the full version of this paper.

On choosing an item, Alice must include the name and cost of the item in the message field instead of in the file identifier. That is, we add a message m_i (e.g., $H(\text{Music}||\$10)$) to the message vector v_i as $(v_i||m_i v_i) = (0, \ldots, 0, 1, 0, \ldots, 0, m_i, 0, \ldots, 0) \in R^{2n}$, and the file identifier just designates the identities of a client and a shop, and a period (e.g., $\tau := H(\text{Alice}||\text{Bob}||\text{May})$), where H is a collision resistance hash function. Thus, at the end of the period, the accumulated message vector v is $(1, \ldots, 1, 0, \ldots, 0, m_1, \ldots, m_k, 0, \ldots, 0)$. As the restricted setting, if Bob tries to choose the weight values, and to get a weighted signature from the adjudicator that might not be agreed by Alice, it is prevented by checking the form of the first k elements of v. Thus, the security of the construction in the general setting can be proved in the same way as the restricted setting.

5 Construction of Verifiably Encrypted Homomorphic Signature

We first give the definition of bilinear groups. We then propose our VEHS scheme.

5.1 Bilinear Groups with Composite Order

For a set X and an element $x \in X$, $x \leftarrow_\$ X$ denotes x is chosen uniformly at random from X.

Let us recall the property of composite-order pairing groups. Let $(\mathbb{G}, \mathbb{G}_T)$ be a bilinear group of composite order $N = p_1 p_2 p_3$, let $e : \mathbb{G} \times \mathbb{G} \to \mathbb{G}_T$ be a bilinear map, and let $\mathcal{G}$ be a group generator, where $\mathcal{G}$ with the security parameter κ outputs $(\mathbb{G}, \mathbb{G}_T, e, N = p_1 p_2 p_3)$. For $i, j \in \{1, 2, 3\}$, let $\mathbb{G}_i$ denote the subgroup of $\mathbb{G}$ of the order p_i, and $\mathbb{G}_{i,j}$ $(i \neq j)$ denote the subgroup $\mathbb{G}$ of the order $p_i p_j$. We note that "orthogonality" of subgroups is as follows. For all $g_i \in \mathbb{G}_i$ and $h_j \in \mathbb{G}_j$ where $i, j \in \{1, 2, 3\}$ and $i \neq j$, $e(g_i, h_j) = 1_T$ holds. Here, 1_T is the unit of $\mathbb{G}_T$. This property is applied in our verification algorithms such that elements of $\mathbb{G}_3$ contained in signatures/VESs are canceled out by pairing computations.

In the proposed scheme, we require that algorithms except for Setup randomly choose an element from the subgroups of $\mathbb{G}$ without knowing the corresponding orders. To do so, generators of subgroups ($g \in \mathbb{G}_1$ and $X_{p_3} \in \mathbb{G}_3$ in the scheme) are included in pp. That is, algorithms just choose a random value $r \in \mathbb{Z}_N$, and compute its exponentiation, e.g., $u := g^r$ and $R_3 = X_{p_3}^r$, and so on. We simply denote these procedures as $u \leftarrow_\$ \mathbb{G}_1$ and $R_3 \leftarrow_\$ \mathbb{G}_3$, respectively.

Assumptions. We will employ the following assumptions in the literature in order to prove the security. Due to the space limit, we informally introduce the assumptions. For strict definitions, see the papers [17,44] or the full version of this paper. We note that they are hard in the generic group model.

Assumption LW1' [44]: Let $g \leftarrow_\$ \mathbb{G}_1$, $X_3 \leftarrow_\$ \mathbb{G}_3$, $T_b \leftarrow_\$ \mathbb{G}_{1,2}$, and $T_{1-b} \leftarrow_\$ \mathbb{G}_1$ for $b \leftarrow_\$ \{0, 1\}$. Given (g, X_3, T_0, T_1), it is infeasible to decide b.[12]

Assumption LW2 [44]: Let $g, X_1 \leftarrow_\$ \mathbb{G}_1$, $X_2, Y_2 \leftarrow_\$ \mathbb{G}_2$, $Y_3, Z_3 \leftarrow_\$ \mathbb{G}_3$, and $T \leftarrow_\$ \mathbb{G}$. Given $(g, X_1 X_2, Z_3, Y_2 Y_3)$ and T, it is infeasible to decide if $T \leftarrow_\$ \mathbb{G}$ or $T \leftarrow_\$ \mathbb{G}_{1,3}$.

---

[12] In the original assumption LW1 [44], given $g \leftarrow_\$ \mathbb{G}_1$, $X_3 \leftarrow_\$ \mathbb{G}_3$, and $T \in \mathbb{G}$, it is infeasible to decide if $T \leftarrow_\$ \mathbb{G}_1$ or $T \leftarrow_\$ \mathbb{G}_{1,2}$.

Assumption ALP3 [17]: Let $g, f, g^\xi, X_1 \leftarrow_\$ \mathbb{G}_1$ where $\xi \leftarrow_\$ \mathbb{Z}_N, X_2, Y_2, Z_2 \leftarrow_\$$ $\mathbb{G}_2$, and $X_3, Y_3, Z_3 \leftarrow_\$ \mathbb{G}_3$. Given $(g, f, g^\xi, X_1 X_2, X_3, Y_2 Y_3)$ and T, it is infeasible to decide if $T = f^\xi Z_3$ or $f^\xi Z_2 Z_3$.

Assumption ALP4 [17]: Let $g \leftarrow_\$ \mathbb{G}_1$, $X_2, Y_2, Z_2 \leftarrow_\$ \mathbb{G}_2$, $X_3 \leftarrow_\$ \mathbb{G}_3$, and $a, b, c \leftarrow_\$ \mathbb{Z}_N$. Given $(g, g^a, g^b, g^{ab} X_2, X_3, g^c Y_2, Z_2)$, it is infeasible to compute $e(g, g)^{abc}$.

5.2 VEHS in Composite-Order Pairing Groups

Our scheme is based on the Attrapadung-Libert-Peters linearly-homomorphic signature scheme [17], the ALP12 scheme in short, which is based on the Lewko-Waters signature scheme [44] in the composite-order pairing groups, and the ElGamal encryption scheme [50]. Thanks to the pairing, we can verify a VES, i.e., an encrypted signature.

One might wonder why we employ the composite-order setting because we already have VES schemes and HS schemes in the prime-order setting. The reason is that there are technical hurdles we cannot solve by our best efforts, although we can simply construct VEHSs from HS schemes in the prime-order setting and the ElGamal encryption scheme. Let $\sigma = (\sigma_1, \sigma_{\text{rest}})$ be an ordinary signature. Let $\mathsf{apk} = y = g^\beta$ be the adjudicator's public key. Then, we let a VES $\omega = (\omega_1, \omega_2, \omega_3)$ as $\omega_1 \leftarrow \sigma_1 \cdot y^t$, $\omega_2 \leftarrow \sigma_{\text{rest}}$, and $\omega_3 \leftarrow g^t$. The main hurdle is the security proof on class-III opacity in Definition 3.4. Roughly speaking, we have to solve the problem in an assumption by using the adversary's power to strip y^t off ω_1. With VES schemes, one can guess which VES will be stripped out and thus embed the problem into ω. We fail to adopt this technique in the HS setting: it is hard to guess which vector $\boldsymbol{v}_i$ on τ^* the adversary will use to forge $\boldsymbol{y}^*$. Fortunately, we can prove class-III opacity in the composite-order setting by using the dual-form signature technique as we discuss in the introduction.

Our VEHS Scheme

- Setup($1^\kappa, 1^n$): Choose bilinear groups $(\mathbb{G}, \mathbb{G}_T)$ of order $N = p_1 p_2 p_3$ such that $(\mathbb{G}, \mathbb{G}_T, e, N) \leftarrow_\$ \mathcal{G}$. Choose $g, u, v, h_1, \ldots, h_n \leftarrow_\$ \mathbb{G}_1$ and $X_{p_3} \leftarrow_\$ \mathbb{G}_3$. $\mathsf{pp} = (\mathbb{G}, \mathbb{G}_T, e, N, g, X_{p_3}, u, v, \{h_i\}_{i \in [n]})$. Here, we let $H_{\mathsf{hom}}(\boldsymbol{v}) := \prod_{i \in [n]} h_i^{v_i}$, where $\boldsymbol{v} = (v_1, \ldots, v_n) \in \mathbb{Z}_N^n$. Note that $\prod_{i \in [\ell]} H_{\mathsf{hom}}(\boldsymbol{v}_i)^{\gamma_i} = H_{\mathsf{hom}}(\sum_{i \in [\ell]} \gamma_i \boldsymbol{v}_i)$ holds. We omit the public parameter pp from inputs of following algorithms.
- AdjGen(1^κ): Choose $\beta \leftarrow_\$ \mathbb{Z}_N$ and compute $y \leftarrow g^\beta$. Output $(\mathsf{apk}, \mathsf{ask}) = (y, \beta)$.
- Gen(1^κ): Choose $\alpha \leftarrow_\$ \mathbb{Z}_N$ and compute g^α. Output $\mathsf{vk} = g^\alpha$ and $\mathsf{sk} = \alpha$.
- Sign($\mathsf{sk}, \tau, \boldsymbol{v}$): Return $\bot$ if $\boldsymbol{v} = \boldsymbol{0}$. Choose $r \leftarrow_\$ \mathbb{Z}_N$ and $R_3, R_3' \leftarrow_\$ \mathbb{G}_3$. Compute $\sigma_1 \leftarrow H_{\mathsf{hom}}(\boldsymbol{v})^\alpha \cdot (u^\tau v)^r \cdot R_3$ and $\sigma_2 \leftarrow g^r \cdot R_3'$. Output $\sigma = (\sigma_1, \sigma_2)$.[13]
- Vrfy($\mathsf{vk}, \tau, \boldsymbol{v}, \sigma$): Parse $\sigma = (\sigma_1, \sigma_2)$. Return 1 iff $e(\sigma_1, g) = e(H_{\mathsf{hom}}(\boldsymbol{v}), g^\alpha) \cdot e(u^\tau v, \sigma_2)$ holds. Otherwise, return 0.

---

[13] As a remark, a client Alice needs to compute H_{hom} for a vector $\boldsymbol{v} = (0, 0, \ldots, 0, 1, 0, \ldots, 0)$ in the AOFE protocol based on our VEHS scheme. Therefore, no n-dependent computation is required for Alice in our AOFE protocol.

- Create(sk, apk, τ, $\boldsymbol{v}$): Run $\sigma := (\sigma_1, \sigma_2) \leftarrow$ Sign(sk, τ, $\boldsymbol{v}$). Choose $t \leftarrow_\$ \mathbb{Z}_N$ and $R_3'' \leftarrow_\$ \mathbb{G}_3$, compute $\omega_1 \leftarrow \sigma_1 \cdot y^t$, $\omega_2 \leftarrow \sigma_2$, and $\omega_3 \leftarrow g^t \cdot R_3''$. Output $\omega = (\omega_1, \omega_2, \omega_3)$.
- VesVrfy(apk, vk, τ, $\boldsymbol{v}$, ω): Parse $\omega = (\omega_1, \omega_2, \omega_3)$. Return 1 iff $e(\omega_1, g) = e(H_{\mathsf{hom}}(\boldsymbol{v}), g^\alpha) \cdot e(u^\tau v, \omega_2) \cdot e(y, \omega_3)$ holds. Otherwise, return 0.
- Derive(vk, τ, $\{\gamma_i, \boldsymbol{v}_i, \sigma^{(i)}\}_{i=1}^{\ell}$): Parse $\sigma^{(i)} = (\sigma_{i,1}, \sigma_{i,2})$. Choose $\tilde{r} \leftarrow_\$ \mathbb{Z}_N$ and $\tilde{R}_3, \tilde{R}_3' \leftarrow_\$ \mathbb{G}_3$. Compute $\sigma_1 \leftarrow \left(\prod_{i \in [\ell]} \sigma_{i,1}^{\gamma_i} \right) \cdot (u^\tau v)^{\tilde{r}} \cdot \tilde{R}_3$ and $\sigma_2 \leftarrow \left(\prod_{i \in [\ell]} \sigma_{i,2}^{\gamma_i} \right) \cdot g^{\tilde{r}} \cdot \tilde{R}_3'$. Output $\sigma = (\sigma_1, \sigma_2)$.
- VesDerive(vk, apk, τ, $\{\gamma_i, \boldsymbol{v}_i, \omega^{(i)}\}_{i=1}^{\ell}$): Parse $\omega^{(i)} = (\omega_{i,1}, \omega_{i,2}, \omega_{i,3})$. Choose $\tilde{r}$, $\tilde{t} \leftarrow_\$ \mathbb{Z}_N$ and $\tilde{R}_3, \tilde{R}_3', \tilde{R}_3'' \leftarrow \mathbb{G}_3$. Compute $\omega_1 \leftarrow \left(\prod_{i \in [\ell]} \omega_{i,1}^{\gamma_i} \right) \cdot (u^\tau v)^{\tilde{r}} \cdot y^{\tilde{t}} \cdot \tilde{R}_3$, $\omega_2 \leftarrow \left(\prod_{i \in [\ell]} \omega_{i,2}^{\gamma_i} \right) \cdot g^{\tilde{r}} \cdot \tilde{R}_3'$, and $\omega_3 \leftarrow \left(\prod_{i \in [\ell]} \omega_{i,3}^{\gamma_i} \right) \cdot g^{\tilde{t}} \cdot \tilde{R}_3''$. Output $\omega = (\omega_1, \omega_2, \omega_3)$.
- Adj(ask, apk, vk, ω, τ, $\boldsymbol{v}$): Parse $\omega = (\omega_1, \omega_2, \omega_3)$. Return $\perp$ if VesVrfy(apk, vk, τ, $\boldsymbol{v}$, ω) $\rightarrow 0$. Choose $\tilde{r} \leftarrow_\$ \mathbb{Z}_N$ and $\tilde{R}_3, \tilde{R}_3' \leftarrow_\$ \mathbb{G}_3$. Compute $\sigma_1 \leftarrow (\omega_1 / \omega_3^\beta) \cdot (u^\tau v)^{\tilde{r}} \cdot \tilde{R}_3$ and $\sigma_2 \leftarrow \omega_2 \cdot g^{\tilde{r}} \cdot \tilde{R}_3'$. Output $\sigma = (\sigma_1, \sigma_2)$.

Remark 5.1. We note that a HS scheme $HS =$ (Setup, Gen, Sign, Vrfy, Derive) is the ALP12 scheme [17, Sect. 4]. We build our VEHS scheme upon them by introducing AdjGen, Create, VesVrfy, VesDerive, and Adj.

Security. We show correctness and security of our VEHS scheme.

Theorem 5.1 (Informal). **VEHS** *is correct, resolution-independent, and extractable unconditionally.* **VEHS** *is unforgeable and opaque under the assumptions* **LW1′**, **LW2**, **ALP3**, *and* **ALP4**.

Due to space limit, we defer the proofs of correctness and security to the full version.

References

1. Even, S., Goldreich, O., Lempel, A.: A randomized protocol for signing contracts. Commun. ACM **28**(6), 637–647 (1985)
2. Ben-Or, M., Goldreich, O., Micali, S., Rivest, R.L.: A fair protocol for signing contracts. IEEE Trans. IT **36**(1), 40–46 (1990)
3. Boneh, D., Naor, M.: Timed commitments. In: Bellare, M. (ed.) CRYPTO 2000. LNCS, vol. 1880, pp. 236–254. Springer, Heidelberg (2000)
4. Bahreman, A., Tygar, J.D.: Certified electronic mail. In: NDSS 1994, pp. 3–19 (1994)
5. Coffey, T., Saidha, P.: Non-repudiation with mandatory proof of receipt. ACM SIGCOMM Comput. Commun. Rev. **26**(1), 6–17 (1996)
6. Cox, B., Tygar, J.D., Sirbu, M.: NetBill security and transaction protocol. USENIX Workshop on Electronic Commerce 1995, 77–88 (1995)
7. Deng, R.H., Gong, L., Lazar, A.A., Wang, W.: Practical protocols for certified electronic mail. J. Netw. Syst. Manage. **4**(3), 279–297 (1996)

8. Asokan, N., Schunter, M., Waidner, M.: Optimistic protocols for fair exchange. In: ACM CCS 1997, pp. 7–17 (1997)
9. Asokan, N., Shoup, V., Waidner, M.: Optimistic fair exchange of digital signatures. In: Nyberg, K. (ed.) EUROCRYPT 1998. LNCS, vol. 1403, pp. 591–606. Springer, Heidelberg (1998)
10. Asokan, N., Shoup, V., Waidner, M.: Asynchronous protocols for optimistic fair exchange. In: IEEE Symposium on S&P 1998, pp. 86–99 (1998)
11. Dodis, Y., Reyzin, L.: Breaking and repairing optimistic fair exchange from PODC 2003. In: Digital Rights Management Workshop 2003, pp. 47–54 (2003)
12. Dodis, Y., Lee, P.J., Yum, D.H.: Optimistic fair exchange in a multi-user setting. In: Okamoto, T., Wang, X. (eds.) PKC 2007. LNCS, vol. 4450, pp. 118–133. Springer, Heidelberg (2007)
13. Huang, X., Mu, Y., Susilo, W., Wu, W., Xiang, Y.: Further observations on optimistic fair exchange protocols in the multi-user setting. In: Nguyen, P.Q., Pointcheval, D. (eds.) PKC 2010. LNCS, vol. 6056, pp. 124–141. Springer, Heidelberg (2010)
14. Micali, S.: Simple and fast optimistic protocols for fair electronic exchange. In: PODC, pp. 12–19 (2003)
15. Küpçü, A., Lysyanskaya, A.: Usable optimistic fair exchange. Comput. Netw. 56(1), 50–63 (2012)
16. Freeman, D., Katz, J., Waters, B., Boneh, D.: Signing a linear subspace: signature schemes for network coding. In: Jarecki, S., Tsudik, G. (eds.) PKC 2009. LNCS, vol. 5443, pp. 68–87. Springer, Heidelberg (2009)
17. Attrapadung, N., Libert, B., Peters, T.: Computing on authenticated data: new privacy definitions and constructions. In: Wang, X., Sako, K. (eds.) ASIACRYPT 2012. LNCS, vol. 7658, pp. 367–385. Springer, Heidelberg (2012)
18. Zhu, H., Bao, F.: Stand-alone and setup-free verifiably committed signatures. In: Pointcheval, D. (ed.) CT-RSA 2006. LNCS, vol. 3860, pp. 159–173. Springer, Heidelberg (2006)
19. Camenisch, J., Damgård, I.: Verifiable encryption, group encryption, and their applications to separable group signatures and signature sharing schemes. In: Okamoto, T. (ed.) ASIACRYPT 2000. LNCS, vol. 1976, p. 331. Springer, Heidelberg (2000)
20. Boneh, D., Gentry, C., Lynn, B., Shacham, H.: Aggregate and verifiably encrypted signatures from bilinear maps. In: Biham, E. (ed.) EUROCRYPT 2003, vol. 2656, pp. 416–432. Springer, Heidelberg (2003)
21. Lu, S., Ostrovsky, R., Sahai, A., Shacham, H., Waters, B.: Sequential aggregate signatures and multisignatures without random oracles. In: Vaudenay, S. (ed.) EUROCRYPT 2006. LNCS, vol. 4004, pp. 465–485. Springer, Heidelberg (2006)
22. Rückert, M., Schröder, D.: Security of verifiably encrypted signatures and a construction without random oracles. In: Shacham, H., Waters, B. (eds.) Pairing 2009. LNCS, vol. 5671, pp. 17–34. Springer, Heidelberg (2009)
23. Nishimaki, R., Xagawa, K.: Verifiably Encrypted Signatures with Short Keys Based on the Decisional Linear Problem and Obfuscation for Encrypted VES. In: Kurosawa, K., Hanaoka, G. (eds.) PKC 2013. LNCS, vol. 7778, pp. 405–422. Springer, Heidelberg (2013)
24. Waters, B.: Efficient identity-based encryption without random oracles. In: Cramer, R. (ed.) EUROCRYPT 2005. LNCS, vol. 3494, pp. 114–127. Springer, Heidelberg (2005)

25. Lee, K., Lee, D.H., Yung, M.: Sequential aggregate signatures with short public keys: design, analysis and implementation studies. In: Kurosawa, K., Hanaoka, G. (eds.) PKC 2013. LNCS, vol. 7778, pp. 423–442. Springer, Heidelberg (2013)

26. Lee, K., Lee, D.H., Yung, M.: Aggregating CL-Signatures revisited: extended functionality and better efficiency. In: Sadeghi, A.-R. (ed.) FC 2013. LNCS, vol. 7859, pp. 171–188. Springer, Heidelberg (2013)

27. Bellare, M., Namprempre, C., Neven, G.: Unrestricted aggregate signatures. In: Arge, L., Cachin, C., Jurdziński, T., Tarlecki, A. (eds.) ICALP 2007. LNCS, vol. 4596, pp. 411–422. Springer, Heidelberg (2007)

28. Fischlin, M., Lehmann, A., Schröder, D.: History-free sequential aggregate signatures. In: Visconti, I., De Prisco, R. (eds.) SCN 2012. LNCS, vol. 7485, pp. 113–130. Springer, Heidelberg (2012)

29. Canetti, R., Goldreich, O., Halevi, S.: The random oracle methodology, revisited. J. ACM **51**(4), 557–594 (2004)

30. Hohenberger, S., Sahai, A., Waters, B.: Replacing a random oracle: full domain hash from indistinguishability obfuscation. In: Nguyen, P.Q., Oswald, E. (eds.) EUROCRYPT 2014. LNCS, vol. 8441, pp. 201–220. Springer, Heidelberg (2014)

31. Waters, B.: Dual system encryption: realizing fully secure IBE and HIBE under simple assumptions. In: Halevi, S. (ed.) CRYPTO 2009. LNCS, vol. 5677, pp. 619–636. Springer, Heidelberg (2009)

32. Gerbush, M., Lewko, A., O'Neill, A., Waters, B.: Dual form signatures: an approach for proving security from static assumptions. In: Wang, X., Sako, K. (eds.) ASIACRYPT 2012. LNCS, vol. 7658, pp. 25–42. Springer, Heidelberg (2012)

33. Desmedt, Y.: Computer security by redefining what a computer is. In: NSPW 1993, pp. 160–166 (1993)

34. Johnson, R., Molnar, D., Song, D., Wagner, D.: Homomorphic signature schemes. In: Preneel, B. (ed.) CT-RSA 2002. LNCS, vol. 2271, pp. 244–262. Springer, Heidelberg (2002)

35. Attrapadung, N., Libert, B.: Homomorphic network coding signatures in the standard model. In: Catalano, D., Fazio, N., Gennaro, R., Nicolosi, A. (eds.) PKC 2011. LNCS, vol. 6571, pp. 17–34. Springer, Heidelberg (2011)

36. Catalano, D., Fiore, D., Warinschi, B.: Adaptive pseudo-free groups and applications. In: Paterson, K.G. (ed.) EUROCRYPT 2011. LNCS, vol. 6632, pp. 207–223. Springer, Heidelberg (2011)

37. Catalano, D., Fiore, D., Warinschi, B.: Efficient network coding signatures in the standard model. In: Fischlin, M., Buchmann, J., Manulis, M. (eds.) PKC 2012. LNCS, vol. 7293, pp. 680–696. Springer, Heidelberg (2012)

38. Attrapadung, N., Libert, B., Peters, T.: Efficient completely context-hiding quotable and linearly homomorphic signatures. In: Kurosawa, K., Hanaoka, G. (eds.) PKC 2013. LNCS, vol. 7778, pp. 386–404. Springer, Heidelberg (2013)

39. Boneh, D., Freeman, D.M.: Homomorphic signatures for polynomial functions. In: Paterson, K.G. (ed.) EUROCRYPT 2011. LNCS, vol. 6632, pp. 149–168. Springer, Heidelberg (2011)

40. Boneh, D., Freeman, D.M.: Linearly homomorphic signatures over binary fields and new tools for lattice-based signatures. In: Catalano, D., Fazio, N., Gennaro, R., Nicolosi, A. (eds.) Public-Key Cryptography – PKC 2011, vol. 6571, pp. 1–16. Springer, Heidelberg (2011)

41. Gennaro, R., Katz, J., Krawczyk, H., Rabin, T.: Secure network coding over the integers. In: Nguyen, P.Q., Pointcheval, D. (eds.) PKC 2010. LNCS, vol. 6056, pp. 142–160. Springer, Heidelberg (2010)

42. Agrawal, S., Boneh, D., Boyen, X., Freeman, D.M.: Preventing pollution attacks in multi-source network coding. In: Nguyen, P.Q., Pointcheval, D. (eds.) PKC 2010. LNCS, vol. 6056, pp. 161–176. Springer, Heidelberg (2010)
43. Agrawal, S., Boneh, D.: Homomorphic MACs: MAC-based integrity for network coding. In: Abdalla, M., Pointcheval, D., Fouque, P.-A., Vergnaud, D. (eds.) ACNS 2009. LNCS, vol. 5536, pp. 292–305. Springer, Heidelberg (2009)
44. Lewko, A., Waters, B.: New techniques for dual system encryption and fully secure HIBE with short ciphertexts. In: Micciancio, D. (ed.) TCC 2010. LNCS, vol. 5978, pp. 455–479. Springer, Heidelberg (2010)
45. Freeman, D.M.: Improved security for linearly homomorphic signatures: a generic framework. In: Fischlin, M., Buchmann, J., Manulis, M. (eds.) PKC 2012. LNCS, vol. 7293, pp. 697–714. Springer, Heidelberg (2012)
46. Huang, Q., Yang, G., Wong, D.S., Susilo, W.: Ambiguous optimistic fair exchange. In: Pieprzyk, J. (ed.) ASIACRYPT 2008. LNCS, vol. 5350, pp. 74–89. Springer, Heidelberg (2008)
47. Garay, J.A., Jakobsson, M., MacKenzie, P.D.: Abuse-free optimistic contract signing. In: Wiener, M. (ed.) CRYPTO 1999. LNCS, vol. 1666, pp. 449–466. Springer, Heidelberg (1999)
48. Zhou, J., Gollmann, D.: A fair non-repudiation protocol. In: IEEE Symposium on S&P 1996, pp. 55–61 (1996)
49. Calderon, T., Meiklejohn, S., Shacham, H., Waters, B.: Rethinking verifiably encrypted signatures: a gap in functionality and potential solutions. In: Benaloh, J. (ed.) CT-RSA 2014. LNCS, vol. 8366, pp. 349–366. Springer, Heidelberg (2014)
50. ElGamal, T.: A public key cryptosystem and a signature scheme based on discrete logarithms. IEEE Trans. IT **31**(4), 469–472 (1985)

LightCore: Lightweight Collaborative Editing Cloud Services for Sensitive Data

Weiyu Jiang[1,2,3], Jingqiang Lin[1,2], Zhan Wang[1,2(✉)], Huorong Li[1,2,3], and Lei Wang[1,2]

[1] State Key Laboratory of Information Security, Institute of Information Engineering, Chinese Academy of Sciences, Beijing, China
{jiangweiyu,linjingqiang,wangzhan,lihuorong,wanglei}@iie.ac.cn
[2] Data Assurance and Communication Security Research Center, Chinese Academy of Sciences, Beijing, China
[3] University of Chinese Academy of Sciences, Beijing, China

Abstract. Collaborative editing cloud servers allow a group of online users to concurrently edit a document. Every user achieves consistent views of the document by applying others' modifications, which are pushed by the cloud servers. The cloud servers repeatedly transform, order, broadcast modifications,and merge them into a joint version in a real-time manner (typically, less than one second). However, in existing solutions such as Google Docs and Cloud9, the servers employ operational transformation to resolve edit conflicts and achieve consistent views for each online user, so all inputs (and the document) are processed as plaintext by the cloud servers. In this paper, we propose LightCore, a collaborative editing cloud service for sensitive data against *honest-but-curious* cloud servers. A LightCore client applies stream cipher algorithms to encrypt input characters that compose the text of the document before the user sends them to servers, while the keys are shared by all authorized users and unknown to the servers. The *byte-by-byte* encryption feature of stream cipher enables the servers to finish all heavy processing and provide collaborative editing cloud services as the existing solutions without the protections against curious servers. Therefore, the lightweight load of clients is kept while the users' sensitive data are protected. We implement LightCore supporting two different methods to generate keystreams, i.e., the "pure" stream cipher and the CTR mode of block cipher. Note that the document is usually modified by collaborative users for many times, and the sequence of text segments is not input and encrypted in chronological order. So, different from the stateless CTR mode of block cipher, the overall performance of high-speed but stateful stream cipher varies significantly with different key update rules and use scenarios. The analysis and evaluation results on the prototype system show that, LightCore provides secure collaborative editing services for resource-limited clients. Finally, we suggest the suitable keystream policy for different use scenarios according to these results.

Keywords: Collaborative editing cloud service · Operational transformation · Stream cipher · Key management · Block cipher mode of operation

© Springer International Publishing Switzerland 2015
T. Malkin et al. (Eds.): ACNS 2015, LNCS 9092, pp. 215–239, 2015.
DOI: 10.1007/978-3-319-28166-7_11

1   Introduction

With the progress of cloud computing, the collaborative editing service (e.g., Google Docs, Office Online and Cloud9) becomes a popular and convenient choice for online users. With such a service, a group of users can cooperatively edit documents through networks; in particular, they can *concurrently* modify a same document, even write on a same line. Meanwhile, the collaborative editing cloud service provides consistent views to all clients in a timely manner; for example, if each of two independent users concurrently inserts one character into a same line that are displayed identically on their own screens, all users will immediately see both these two characters appear in the expected positions.

The servers of collaborative editing cloud services carry out heavy processing to coordinate all online users' operations. Firstly, the cloud servers are responsible for receiving operation inputs from clients, transforming operations by operational transformation (OT) [1] to resolve conflicts, modifying the stored documents into a joint version based on these transformed operations, and then broadcasting modifications to all online clients. To transform operations, the server revises the position of a modification based on all the other concurrent operations. For example, when Alice and Bob respectively insert 'a' and 'b' in the ith and j^{th} positions, Bob's operation is transformed to be executed in the $(j+1)^{th}$ if Alice's operation is executed firstly and $i < j$. Secondly, during the editing phase, the above steps are repeated continuously in a real-time manner, to enable instant reading and writing on clients. Finally, the servers have to maintain a history of joint versions, because users' operations may be done on different versions due to the uncertain network delays. In a word, this centralized architecture takes full advantages of the cloud servers' powerful computing, elasticity and scalability, and brings convenience to resource-limited clients.

In order to enable the cloud servers to coordinate the operations and resolve possible conflicts by OT, existing online collaborative editing systems process only plaintext (or unencrypted) inputs. Therefore, the cloud service provider is always able to read all clients' documents. This unfriendly feature might disclose users' sensitive data, for example, to a curious internal operator in the cloud system. Although the SSL/TLS protocols are adopted to protect data in transit against external attackers on the network, the input data are always decrypted before being processed by the cloud servers.

In this paper, we propose LightCore, a collaborative editing cloud service for sensitive data. In LightCore, before being sent to the cloud, all input characters are encrypted by a stream cipher algorithm, which encrypts the plaintext byte by byte. These characters compose the content of the document. The texts are always transmitted, processed and stored in ciphertext. The cryptographic keys are shared by authorized users, and the encryption algorithms are assumed to be secure. The other operation parameters except the input texts are still sent and processed as plaintext, so the cloud servers can employ OT to coordinate all operations into a joint version but not understand the document.

LightCore assumes honest-but-curious cloud servers. On one hand, the honest cloud servers always follow their specification to execute the requested operations; on the other hand, a curious server tries to read or infer the sensitive texts in the users' documents. Note that the honesty feature is assumed to ensure service availability and data integrity; but not for the confidentiality of sensitive data. A malicious cloud server that arbitrarily deviates from its protocol, might break service availability or data integrity, but could not harm confidentiality, because the keys are held by clients only and every input character never appears as plaintext outside the clients.

By adopting stream cipher algorithms, LightCore keeps the lightweight load of clients, and takes advantage of the powerful resources of cloud servers as the existing collaborative editing cloud solutions. Because the stream cipher algorithm encrypts only the text byte by byte and the length of each input text is unchanged after being encrypted, the servers can conduct OT and other processing without understanding the ciphertext. On the contrary, the block cipher algorithms encrypt texts block by block (typically, 128 bits or 16 bytes), so the OT processing in ciphertext by servers is extremely difficult because users modify the text (i.e., insert or delete) in characters. That is, each character would have to be encrypted into one block with padding, to support the user operations in characters, which leads to an enormous waste in storage and transmission; otherwise, the workload of resolving edit conflicts would be transferred to the clients, which is unsuitable for resource-limited devices.

In fact, the "byte-by-byte" encryption feature can be implemented by stream cipher, or the CTR mode of block cipher.[1] In LightCore (and other collaborative editing systems), the text of a document is composed of a sequence of text segments with unfixed lengths. Because the document is a result of collaborative editing by several users, these text segments are not input and encrypted in chronological order, e.g., the sequence of {'Collaborative', 'Editing', 'Cloud'} is the result of {'Collaborative Document Cloud'} after deleting 'Document' and then inserting 'Editing' by different users. Each text segment is associated with an attribute[2] called keystream_info, containing the parameters to decrypt it. For the CTR mode of block cipher, keystream_info contains a key identifier, a random string $nonceIV$, an initial counter and an offset in a block; for stream cipher, it contains a key identifier and an initial position offset of the keystream. Note that all users share a static $master key$, and each $data key$ to initialize cipher is derived from the master key and the key identifier.

The efficiency of LightCore varies as the $keystream policy$ changes, that is, (a) different methods are used to generate keystreams, and (b) different key update rules of stream cipher are used in certain use scenarios (if stream cipher is used). In general, stream cipher has higher encryption speed and smaller delay than block cipher [2], but with a relative heavy initialization phase before generating keystreams. Moreover, different from the stateless CTR mode, stream cipher is stateful: given a key, to generate the jth byte of keystream, all k^{th} bytes ($k < j$) must be generated firstly. Therefore, insertion operations in

---

[1] Other block cipher modes of operation such as OFB and CFB, also generate the keystream in bytes, but are less efficient.

[2] Other typical attributes include font, color, size, etc..

random positions (e.g., an insertion in Line 1 after another in Line 2) require the decrypters to cache bytes of keystream to use later; and deletion operations cause the decrypters to generate lots of obsoleted bytes of keystream. This performance degradation is mitigated by updating the data keys of stream cipher in LightCore: the user (or encrypter) generates a new data key, re-initializes the encryptor and then generates keystreams by bytes to encrypt texts. The key update rules are designed by balancing (a) the cost of initialization and keystream generation, and (b) the distribution and order of the deletion and insertion operations.

We implement LightCore based on Etherpad, an open-source collaborative editing cloud system. The LightCore prototype supports the RC4 stream cipher algorithm and the AES CTR mode. Two principles of stream cipher key update rules are adopted, that is, a user (or encrypter) updates the key of stream cipher, if (a) the generated bytes of the keystream come to a predetermined length, or (b) the user moves to another position previous to the line of the current cursor to insert texts. Then, the evaluation and analysis on the prototype suggest the suitable keystream policy with detailed parameters for different typical use scenarios.

LightCore provides collaborative editing cloud services for online users, with the following properties:

- *Reasonable confidentiality against honest-but-curious cloud servers.* All input characters are encrypted at the client side before being sent to the cloud servers, either these texts are kept in the document or deleted finally. The content of the document is kept secret to servers, but the format information such as length, paragraph, font and color is known, which enables the servers to coordinate users' operations.
- *Lightweight workload on clients.* The cloud servers of LightCore are responsible for receiving users' edit inputs, resolving edit conflicts, maintaining the documents, and distributing the current freshest versions to online clients. Compared with those of existing collaborative editing solutions, a LightCore user only needs to additionally generate keystreams to protect input texts as an encrypter and decrypt texts from servers as a decrypter.
- *Real-time and full functionality.* The byte-by-byte lightweight encryption is fully compatible with uncrypted real-time collaborative editing services, no editing function is impeded or disabled. Even for a new user that logins to the system to access a very long and repeatedly-edited document, the keystream policy facilitates the user to decrypt it in real time.

The rest of the paper is organized as follows. Section 2 introduces the background and related work on collaborative systems and edit conflict solutions. Section 3 describes the assumptions and threat model. The system design, including the basic model, key management and keystream policy, is given in the Sect. 4. Section 5 describes the implementation of LightCore, and security analysis is presented in Sect. 6. In Sect. 7, we illustrates performance evaluation, and present keystream polices suggestions. Finally, we conclude this paper and analyze our future work in Sect. 8.

2 Background and Related Work

2.1 Real-Time Collaborative Editing Systems

Collaborative editing is the practice of groups producing works together through individual contributions. In current collaborative editing systems, modifications (e.g., insertions, deletions, font format or color setting) marked with their authors, are propagated from one collaborator to the other collaborators in a timely manner (less than 500 ms). Applying collaborative editing in textual documents, programmatic source code [3,4] or video has been a mainstream.

Distributed systems techniques for ordering [5] and storing have been applied in most real-time collaborative editing systems [6–8], including collaborative editor softwares and browser-based collaborative editors. Most of these have adopted decentralized settings, but some well-known systems use central cloud resources to simplify synchronization between clients (e.g., Google Docs [9] and Microsoft Office Online [10]). In a collaborative editing system with decentralized settings, the clients take more burden on broadcasting, ordering modifications and resolving conflicts. However, in a cloud-based collaborative systems, cloud servers help to order and merge modifications, resolve conflicts, broadcast operations and store documents. It not only saves the deployment and maintenance cost but also reduces the burden on clients by using cloud resources.

However, the cloud may not be completely trusted by users. In order to protect sensitive data from unauthorized disclosure, data of users are encrypted before being sent to the cloud [11–14]. SPORC [15] encrypts modifications with block cipher AES at the client side, but the cloud server can only order, broadcast and store operations, so it takes much burden for the clients to resolve conflicts and restore the documents from series of operations when accessing the documents. In our scheme, data are encrypted with stream cipher, and no functionalities of cloud servers are impeded or disabled.

There are four main features in real-time collaborative editing systems: (a) highly interactive clients are responded instantly via the network, (b) volatile participants are free to join or leave during a session, (c) modifications are not pre-planned by the participants, and (d) edit conflicts on the same data are required to be well resolved to achieve the consistent views at all the clients. As the modifications are collected and sent every less than 500 ms, the size of the input text is relatively small (about 2 to 4 characters) in spite of the copy and paste operations. In this case, edit conflicts happen very frequently.

2.2 Operational Transformation

The edit conflict due to concurrent operations is one of the main challenges in collaborative editing systems. Without an efficient solution to edit conflicts, it may result in inconsistent text in different clients when collaborators concurrently edit the same document. There are many methods to resolve conflicts such as the lock mechanism [16,17] and differ-patch [18–20]. Among these methods, operational transformation (OT) [1] adopted in our system is an efficient technology for consistency maintenance when concurrent operations frequently happen. OT was pioneered by C. Ellis and S. Gibbs [21] in the GROVE system. In more than 20 years, OT has evolved to acquire new capabilities in new applications [22–24]. In 2009, OT was adopted as a core technique behind the collaboration features in Apache Wave and Google Docs.

In OT, modifications from clients may be defined as a series of operations. OT ensures consistency by synchronizing shared state, even if concurrent operations arrive at different time points. For example, a string "preotty", called S, is shared on the clients C_1 and C_2, C_1 modifies S into "pretty" by deleting the character at the 3th position and C_2 modifies S into "preottily" by inserting "il" after the 5th position concurrently, the consistent result should be "prettily". However, without appropriate solutions, it may cause inconsistency at client C_1: shift from "pretty" as the result of deletion to "prettyil" as the result of insertion.

OT preserves consistency by transforming the position of an operation based on the previously applied concurrent operations. By adopting OT, for each two concurrent operations: op_i and op_j irrelevant of the execution sequence, the OT function $T(\cdot)$ satisfies : $op_i \circ T(op_j, op_i) \equiv op_j \circ T(op_i, op_j)$, where $op_i \circ op_j$ denotes the sequence of operations containing op_i followed by op_j and $\equiv$ denotes equivalence of the two sequences of operations. In the above example, the consistent result "prettily" can be achieved at client C_1 by transforming the operation "insert 'il' after the 5th position" into "insert 'il' after the 4th position" based on the operation "delete the character at the 3th position".

In a collaborative editing cloud service, the cloud servers can be responsible for receiving and caching editing operations in its queue, imposing order on each editing operation, executing OT on concurrent operations based on the order iteratively, broadcasting these editing operations to other clients and applying them in its local copy to maintain a latest version of the document. When receiving an operation op_{r_c} from the client, the cloud server execute OT as follows:

- Notes that the operation op_{r_c} is generated from the client's latest revision r_c.

$$S_0 \to S_1 \to \dots S_{r_c} \to S_{r_c+1} \to \dots \to S_{r_H}$$

  denotes the operation series stored in cloud. op_c is relative to S_{r_c}.
- The cloud server needs to compute new op_{r_c}' relative to S_{r_H}. The cloud server firstly computes a new op_{r_c}' relative to S_{r_c+1} by computing $T(S_{r_c+1}, op_{r_c})$. Similarly the cloud server can repeat for S_{r_c+2} and so forth until op_{r_c}' represented relative to S_{r_H} is achieved.

Edit conflicts are also required to be resolved by OT at the client. Considering network delay and the requirement of non-block editing at the client, the local editing operations may not be processed by the server timely. Therefore, the client should cache its local operations in its queue, and execute OT on the concurrent operations based on these cached operations.

3   Assumptions and Threat Model

LightCore functionally allows multiple collaborators to edit the shared documents and view changes from other collaborators using cloud resources. We assume that all the authorized collaborators mutually trust each other and strive together to complete the same task (e.g., drafting a report or programming a system). That is, all the changes committed by the client of any collaborator are well-intentioned, and respectable by other collaborators.

The collaborative privileges are granted and managed by a special collaborator, called the *initiator*, who is in charge of creating the target document for future collaborative editing, generating the shared secret passcode and distributing it among all authorized collaborators through out-of-band channels. The passcode is used for deriving the master encryption key to protect the shared contents and updates. We assume that the passcode is strong enough to resist guessing attacks and brute force attacks. The master key with a random string is used to generate the data key, which initializes cryptographic algorithms to generate keystreams. We assume that the cryptographic algorithms to encrypt data are secure. Meanwhile, we assume that the random string will not be repeatedly generated by the clients.

We assume that the client of each collaborator runs in a secure environment which guarantees that

- the generation and distribution of shared secret and privilege management on the client of the initiator are appropriately maintained;
- the secret passcode and keys that appear in the clients, are not stolen by any attacker;
- the communication channel between the client and the cloud is enough to transmit all necessary data in real time and protected by existing techniques such as SSL/TLS.

In LightCore, the cloud server is responsible for storing and maintaining the latest content, executing operations (delete, insert, etc.) on the content, resolving operational conflicts, and broadcasting the updates among multiple clients. The cloud server is considered to be honest-but-curious. In case of risking its reputation, the honest cloud server will timely and correctly disseminate modifications committed by all the authorized clients without maliciously attempting to add, drop, alter, or delay operation requests. However, motivated by economic benefits or curiosity, the cloud provider or its internal employees may spy or probe into the shared content, determine the document type (e.g., a letter) by observing the format and layout, and discover the pivot part of the documents by analyzing the frequency and quantity of access.

Additionally, we assume that the cloud servers will protect the content from unauthorized users access and other traditional network attacks (such as DoS attacks), and keep the availability of share documents, for example, by redundancy.

4   System Design

This section describes the system design of LightCore. We firstly give the basic model, including the specifications of clients and servers, and the encryption scheme. Then, the key management of LightCore is presented, and we analyze two different ways to generate keystreams.

4.1   Basic Model

Similar to existing collaborative editing systems, LightCore involves a group of collaborative users and a cloud server. Each client communicates with the server over the Internet, to send its operations and receive modifications from others in real time. For each document, the server maintains a history of versions. That is, it keeps receiving operations from users, and these modifications make the document shift from a version to another one. When applying modifications on a version, the server may need OT to transform some operations. The server also keeps sending the current freshest version to users, that is, all transformed operations since the last version is sent. Because a user is still editing on the stale version when the freshest one is being sent, the OT processing may also be required to update its view at the client side. The above procedure is shown in Fig. 1.

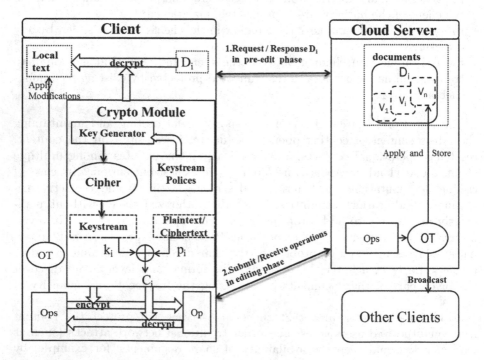

Fig. 1. System model

In LightCore, we design the crypto module for protecting the documents at the client side. The input characters of insertion operation (not deletion operation without inputs) are encrypted with keystreams byte by byte, but the position of each operation is sent in plaintext. When receiving the operation from one client, the cloud server may transform the operation by OT and apply it in the latest version based on the position. That is, no functionalities of the cloud server are impeded or disabled in ciphertext. After receiving the operation from other users through the cloud servers, the input characters of the operation will be firstly decrypted, so that it can be presented at the screen in plaintext.

Client. At the client side, users are authenticated by the cloud before entering the system. The collaborative privileges are granted and managed by the initiator, who is in charge of creating the target document. Therefore, only authorized users can download or edit the document. Meanwhile, the master key to generate keystreams, which are to encrypt the text of the document, is only delivered to the authorized users by the initiator. Without the master key, both the cloud server and attackers from the network cannot read or understand the document.

There are two main phases at the client side to edit a document in Light-Core: the *pre-edit* phase and the *editing* phase. In this pre-edit phase, the client requests a document to maintain a local copy, and the server will respond with the current freshest version of the document to the client. Before generating the local copy, the user is required to input a passcode, and the document is decrypted with the master key derived from the passcode. This decryption time depends on the length of the document, different from that of decrypting the small text of each operation (Op) in the editing phase. Then, the local copy is used for user's edit operations, so that edit operations will not be interrupted by network delay or congestion. In the editing phase, the client encrypts its input characters of each operation before sending it to the cloud server. Meanwhile, the operation is cached in a queue (Ops) so that its concurrent operations can be transformed by OT, when it is not successfully received and processed by the server. In the system, every operation is associated with a revision number of the document, which denotes the version that the operation is generated from. When receiving an operation of other clients from the cloud server, the input characters of the operation are firstly decrypted. Then, the client may execute OT on the operation based on the revision number, and applies the modification in its local copy.

Server. First of all, to follow users' requirements and the specification, access control is enforced by the cloud server. The server maintains a history of versions for each document. In the pre-edit phase, the server sends the freshest encrypted document to the client, and holds an ordered list of modification records for the document (Ops). Every modification record contains an operation, its revision number and its author information. In the editing phase, the server keeps receiving operations from the clients, transforming them by executing OT functions based on the modification records, ordering each operation by imposing a global revision number on it and broadcasting these updated operations with new revision numbers to other collaborative clients. Meanwhile, the cloud server merges these operations into a freshest version of the document in ciphertext, and adds them to the modification records.

Encrypted Operations. We preserve confidentiality for users' data by adopting symmetric cryptographic algorithms with the "byte-by-byte" encryption feature at the client side. In our system, each modification at the client is called an operation. There are two types of edit operations: *insertion* and *deletion*. The other operations including copy and paste can also be represented by these two types of operations. An insertion is comprised of the position of the insertion in the document and the inserted text. And a deletion is comprised of the position of the deletion and the length of deleted text. Each inserted text segment of the operation is associated with an attribute called keystream_info, containing the parameters to encrypt and decrypt it. The other operations related to setting font or color are also supported by taking font or color value as attributes.

By applying the byte-by-byte encryption algorithms, the length of each input text is kept unchanged after being encrypted. The cloud server can conduct OT and other processing without understanding the ciphertext. Compared with block cipher, applying stream cipher (including the CTR mode of block cipher) in the system has the following advantages:

- It is impervious for the cloud server to help to resolve conflicts. To satisfy real-time view presentation, the operations are submitted every 500 ms, so the input text of the operation is generally very small (about 2 to 4 characters). Applying block cipher to encrypt characters block by block makes it difficult for the server to conduct OT functions because users modify the text in characters. That is, the position of the operation related to OT would be extremely difficult to be determined, when modifying a character in a block with an unfixed length of padding. In this case, the OT processing overhead of the server would be transferred to the clients.
- It is feasible for the cloud server to hold a freshest well-organized document. Without understanding the content of the text encrypted by stream cipher, the server can merge operations and apply operations in the latest version of the document based on the position and unchanged length of the text. So, a freshest well-organized document in ciphertext is kept at the server. However, it is costly for the server to apply operations encrypted by block cipher in the latest version of the document. That is, each character would have to be encrypted into one block with fixed-length padding, to support operations in characters, which leads to an enormous waste in storage and transmission; otherwise, a series of operations would be processed at the client side when a user requests the document in the pre-edit phase. Although clients can actively submit a well-organized document to the cloud periodically, the transmission cost may also increase the burden on clients.

4.2 Key Management

We construct a crypto module at the client to encrypt and decrypt the text of the document. In the crypto module, both stream cipher and the CTR mode of block cipher are supported. Each document is assigned a *master key* (denoted as mk), derived from a passcode. When users access the document, the passcode is required to be input. The passcode may be transmitted through out-of-band channels. We assume that the delivery of the passcode among users is secure.

The text segment of the document is encrypted with the *data key* (denoted as DK), which initializes the cryptographic algorithm to generate keystreams. The *data key* is generated by computing $DK = H(mk, userId \parallel keyId)$, where H is a secure keyed-hash mac function (e.g., SHA-256-HMAC), mk is the *master key*, *userId* is the identity of the collaborator, and *keyId* is a random key identifier. The *userId* with a unique value in the system is attached to each operation as the attribute `author` to distinguish different writers. The *keyId* generated by the client is a parameter contained in the attribute `keystream_info`. For the CTR mode of block cipher, `keystream_info` contains a key identifier, a random string *nonceIV*, an initial counter and an offset in a block; the string *nonceIV* $\parallel$ *counter* is the input of the block cipher, to generate keystreams, and the counter is increased by one after each block. For stream cipher, it contains a key identifier and an initial position offset of the keystream; the initial position offset locates the bytes of the keystream to decrypt the first character of the text segment. The *keyId* and *nonceIV* generated randomly ensure that the keystreams will not be resued. Therefore, different collaborators with different *data key* generate non-overlapping keystreams, and bytes of keystreams are not reused to encrypt data.

After encrypting the input texts, the client will send the operation with the attributes `author` and `keystream_info`. Therefore, authorized readers and writers with the same master key can compute the *data key* and generate the same keystreams, based on the attributes when decrypting the texts.

4.3 Keystream Policies

Both stream cipher and block cipher CTR mode are applied in our system. In general, stream cipher has higher encryption speed and smaller delay than block cipher [2], but the performance of the stateful stream cipher may be degraded when decrypting a document generated from random insertions and deletions. In order to achieve an efficient cryptographic scheme, we design two key update rules for stream cipher, which take full advantage of stream cipher while match the features of collaborative editing cloud services.

Comparison of Two Types of Cipher. In both stream cipher and the CTR mode of block cipher, each byte of the plaintext is encrypted one at a time with the corresponding byte of the keystream, to give a byte of the cipher-text. During the execution of the two types of cipher, it involves initialization phase and keystream generation phase. We test the initialization latency and

Table 1. Comparison of stream cipher and CTR mode of block cipher

Algorithms / Performance	Stream Cipher			Block Cipher CTR
	ISSAC [25]	Rabbit [26]	RC4 [27]	AES-CTR
Initialization latency	41.73 us	41.31 us	35.53 us	56.79 us
Keystream generation speed	24.07 MB/s	15.45 MB/s	21.86 MB/s	3.30 MB/s

keystream generation speed of ISSAC, Rabbit, RC4 and AES-CTR by JavaScript on browsers. The results in Table 1 illustrate that the speed of these stream cipher algorithms is much faster than AES, but all of them are with a relatively heavy initialization phase before generating keystreams. For example, the time of executing 1000 times of initialization of RC4 is approximately equal to that of generating 0.38 MB bytes of a keystream. For the CTR mode of stateless block cipher, keystream generation is only related to the counter as the input of block cipher. Given the counter and cryptographic key, the CTR mode of block cipher outputs the corresponding bytes of the keystream.

It generally requires only one initialization (round key schedule) for the CTR mode of block cipher, for multiple block encryption or decryption. Unlike the CTR mode of block cipher, stream cipher is stateful: given a key, to generate the jth byte of keystream, all k^{th} bytes ($k < j$) must be generated firstly. Therefore, when decrypting documents by stream cipher, insertion operations in random positions (e.g., an insertion in Line 1 after another in Line 2) require the decrypters to cache bytes of keystreams to use later; and deletion operations cause the decrypters to generate lots of obsoleted bytes of keystreams. Examples of the impact from random insertions and deletions are shown in Fig. 2.

When decrypting a document generated from random insertions, it may require repeatedly initializing the stream cipher and generating obsoleted bytes of keystreams, for the resource-limited clients without enough cache. If all collaborative clients input characters in sequential positions of the document, the position of the inserted texts in a document will be consistent with the position of the used bytes in the keystream. In this case, decrypting the document only requires one initialization and the sequentially generated keystream will be in full use. However, the text segments of the document are not input and encrypted in chronological order due to random insertions. In this case, it may cause inconsistent positions of the text segments and their used bytes of keystreams. For example: a character c_1 is inserted in the position previous to the character c_2 encrypted with the ith byte of the keystream; as the keystream cannot be reused for security consideration, c_1 is encrypted with the jth byte where $i < j$; to decrypt c_1, the bytes from 0th to j^{th} should be firstly generated; if the ith byte is not cached, the client shall re-initialize the stream cipher to generate bytes from 0th to i^{th} when decrypting c_2; therefore, the bytes from 0th to i^{th} called *obsoleted bytes* are repeatedly generated; otherwise, bytes from 0th to i^{th} shall be preserved until they are reused. In fact, it is difficult to determine whether and when the generated bytes of the keystream will be reused. In this case, the

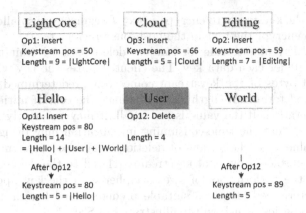

Fig. 2. Examples of random insertions and deletions

size of cached bytes may be larger than that of the document. It is not advisable to cache so large bytes of keystreams when the document is of large size.

Random deletions also cause the decrypter to generate lots of obsoleted bytes with stream cipher. For example, a text segment $T = <c_1, c_2, ..., c_n>$ is firstly inserted by a client, and characters $<c_2, ..., c_{n-1}>$ are deleted by another client; if all the characters of T are encrypted with the bytes of the keystream initialized by the same key, the bytes of the keystream related to $<c_2, ..., c_{n-1}>$ are required to be generated to decrypt c_n. In this example, $n-2$ obsoleted bytes of the keystream are generated. However, if c_n is encrypted with the bytes of another keystream, which is initialized by a updated key, the $n-2$ obsoleted bytes would not be generated. In this case, only one additional initialization with the new data key is required. Note that, it is efficient only when the time to generate the continuous deleted bytes of the keystream is longer than that of the additional initialization. If the size of deleted characters is small, it may less efficient for frequently initializing the stream cipher.

Key Update Rules for Stream Cipher. If a stable performance is expected, adopting the stateless CTR mode of block cipher is suggested. However, to take full advantage of fast stream cipher in LightCore, we design two key update rules to mitigate the performance degradation for stream cipher: the user (or encrypter) generates a new data key, re-initializes the stream cipher algorithm and then generates keystreams by bytes to encrypt texts. The key update rules are designed by balancing (a) the cost of initialization and keystream generation, and (b) the distribution and order of the insertion and deletion operations.

One key update rule for random insertions is to keep the consistency between the positions of the used bytes in the keystream with the positions of inserted characters in the document. In LightCore, we update the data key to initialize the stream cipher when the user moves to another position previous to the line of the current cursor to insert texts. Therefore, we can ensure that the positions of the bytes in the keystream to encrypt a text T segment are smaller than those of the bytes to encrypt the text in the positions previous to T.

The second key update rule for random deletions is to limit the length of the keystream under each data key. The client updates the key when the generated or used bytes of the keystream come to a predetermined length. The value of the predetermined length should balance the cost of initialization and keystream generation. If the value is too small, it may frequently initialize the stream cipher so that the time-consuming initialization may bring much overhead. If the value is too large, lots of deletions may also cause much overhead for generating obsoleted bytes of keystreams related to the deleted characters. By evaluating the performance of stream cipher with the key update rules of different predetermined length, a suitable predetermined length can be set in different use scenarios, which will be illustrated in Sect. 7.

5   Implementation

We built the LightCore prototype on top of Etherpad, a Google open-source real-time collaborative system. The client-side code implemented by JavaScript can be executed on different browsers (IE, Chrome, Firefox, Safari, etc.). The cloud server of the system is implemented on Node.js, a platform built on Chrome's JavaScript runtime. Based on the implementation of Etherpad, there are some issues to be addressed as follows, when we implement the prototype system.

5.1   Client Improvement

In the pre-edit phase, the decrypter shall decrypt the whole document from the beginning to the end. If stream cipher is used and the data keys are updated, the decrypter may find multiple data keys are used alternatively; for example, a text segment encrypted with the data key DK_1, may be cut into two text segments by inserting another text segment encrypted with another data key DK_2; then it results in an alternatively-used data key list DK_1, DK_2, DK_1. Therefore, in the pre-edit phase, the decrypter shall keep the statuses of multiple stream ciphers initialized with different data keys; otherwise, it may need to initialize a same data key and generate a same keystream for more than one time. To balance the memory requirement and the efficiency, in the prototype, the client maintains the status of two stream ciphers initialized with different data key for each author of the document. One is called the *current decryptor*, and the other is to back up the current one called the *backup decryptor*. When decrypting a text segment encrypted by a new decryptor, the clients back up the current decryptor and update the current decryptor by re-initializing it with a new data key. If a text segment is required to be decrypted by the backup decryptor, the clients will exchange the current decryptor with the backup one. The generated bytes of the keystream by each decryptor are cached, until a predetermined length (1 KB in the prototype system) is reached or the decryptor is updated.

In the editing phase, the input characters of each insertion is encrypted before being sent to the cloud; so, the user (as a decrypter) receives and decrypts texts as the same order that the encrypter encrypt the texts. The client maintains the status of only one decryptor for each client to decrypt the operations from other clients. The bytes of the keystream are sequentially generated to be used, but the generated keystream is not cached since they will not be reused.

Attributes Update. In order to decrypt the text correctly, the attribute `keystream_info`, including the position information of used bytes of the keystream, is attached to each insertion operation. The position information is expressed by the offset of the byte in the keystream related to the first character of the insertion. However, random insertions will change the value of `keystream_info`. For example: a text segment $T = < c_1, c_2, ..., c_n >$ is encrypted by the bytes from k^{th} to $(k+n)^{th}$ of one keystream, and the offset k is regarded as the value of attribute `keystream_info` A; then, a new text is inserted between c_i and c_{i+1} of T; finally, T is cut into two text segments $T_1 = < c_1, c_2, .., c_i >$ and $T_2 = < c_{i+1}, c_{i+2}, .., c_n >$ with the same value of A. In fact, the value of A of T_2 should be revised into $k+i$ when decrypting the full document. Fortunately, this attribute value is easily revised by the client in the pre-edit phase. Instead of maintaining attributes `keystream_info` of all the old operations, and revising them for each random insertion in the editing phase, it is efficient for the client to calculate the correct attribute value of the latter text segment based on the length of the previous text segments with the same `keystream_info`, because all the texts and the attributes are downloaded from the server during the decryption process in the pre-edit phase.

5.2 Sever Improvement

Attributes Update. The correct value of attribute `keystream_info` can be also changed by random deletions. For example: a text segment $T = < c_1, c_2, ..., c_n >$ is encrypted by the bytes from k^{th} to $(k+n)^{th}$ of one keystream, and the offset k is regarded as the value of attribute `keystream_info` A; then, a substring $< c_{i+1}, c_{i+2}, .., c_j > (i > 0, j < n)$ of T is deleted; finally, T is cut into two text segments $T_1 = < c_1, c_2, .., c_i >$ and $T_2 = < c_{j+1}, c_{j+2}, .., c_n >$ with the same value of A. In fact, the value of A of T_2 should be updated into $k+j$ when decrypting the full document. This problem is perfectly solved at the server side, and it cannot be done at the client side.

As all the text segments with the related attributes are stored at the cloud, and the servers apply each operation in the latest version of the document, a small embedded code to update the value of `keystream_info` is executed at the cloud server, when the cloud server is processing the received operations. Instead of revising it at the client which does not maintain the attributes of deleted texts, it is more reasonable for the server to revise it and store the updated attributes with the text.

5.3   Character Set and Special Character

The client is implemented by JavaScript in Browsers that use the UTF-16 character set, so the encrypted texts may contain illegal characters. In the UTF-16 character set, each character in BMP plane-0 (including ASCII characters, East Asian languages characters, etc.) [28] will be presented as 2 bytes, and 0xDF80 to 0xDFFF in hexadecimal is reserved. Therefore, in the LightCore client, if the encrypted result is in the zone from 0xDF80 to 0xDFFF (i.e., an illegal characters in UTF-16), it will be XORed with 0×0080 to make it a legal UTF-16 character. In the prototype, LightCore supports ASCII characters, which are in the zone from 0×0000 to $0 \times 007F$. At the same time, the above XORing may make the decrypted character be an illegal ASCII character; for example, the input 'a' (0×0061 in hexadecimal) will result in $0 \times 00e1$, an illegal ASCII character. So, in this case, the decrypter will XOR it with 0×0080 again if it finds the decrypted result is in the zone from 0×0080 to $0 \times 00FF$. We plan to support other languages characters in the future, and one more general technique is to map the encrypted result in the zone from 0xDF80 to 0xDFFF, into a 4-bytes legal UTF-16 character.

In our system, the newline character ($0 \times 000A$ in hexadecimal) is a special character that is not encrypted. As mentioned above, the cloud servers need the position information of user operations to finish processing. In Etherpad and LightCore, the position is represented as (a) the line number and (b) the index at that line. So, the unencrypted newline characters enable the servers to locate the correct positions of user operations. This method discloses some information to the curious servers, as well as other format attributes; see Sect. 6 for the detailed analysis.

6   Security Analysis

In LightCore, all user data including all operations and every version of the documents are processed in the cloud. Attackers from inside or outside might attempt to alter or delete the user data, or disrupt the cloud services. However, for the reputation and benefits of the cloud service provider, the honest-but-curious cloud servers are supposed to preserve integrity, availability and consistency for the data of users. The cloud service provider will deploy adequate protections to prevent such external attacks, including access control mechanisms to prevent malicious operations on a document by other unauthorized users.

Preserving the confidentiality of users' documents is the main target of Light-Core. Firstly, in our system, only the authorized users with the shared *master key* can read the texts of the documents. LightCore adopts stream cipher and the CTR mode of block cipher to encrypt data at the client side. In the editing phase, the input texts of each operation is encrypted before being sent to the cloud. Therefore, the input texts is transmitted in ciphertext and documents in the cloud are also stored in ciphertext. Secondly, the algorithms are assumed to be secure and the keys only appears on the clients. So, these keys could only be leaked by the collaborative users or the clients, which are also assumed to be trusted. Finally, data keys are generated in a random way by each user, and LightCore uses each byte of the keystreams generated by data keys for only one time. Any text is encrypted by the keystreams generated specially for it. So, the curious servers cannot infer the contents by analyzing the difference of two decrypted texts.

In order to maintain the functionalities of the cloud servers, we only encrypt the input texts of each operation but not the position of the operation. The position of each operation and the length of the operated text are disclosed to the cloud servers, which may leak a certain of indirect sensitive information (including the number of lines, the distribution of paragraphs and other structure information). We assume these data can only be access by the authorized clients and the cloud servers, and they are not disclosed to external attackers by adopting the SSL protocol. In this case, the related data are limited to the cloud and the clients. Additionally, the attributes attached to the text segments, including font, color, author identity, keystream_info, might also be used to infer the underline information of the documents. For example, a text segment with the "bold" attribute may disclose its importance; A text segment with "list" attribute may also leak some related information. However, some of the attributes can be easily protected by encrypting them at the client in LightCore, because the cloud servers are not required to process all of them (for example, font, size, color, etc.). Therefore, encrypting these attributes will not impede the basic functionalities of the cloud servers. To protect these attributes will be included in our future work. Anyway, attributes author and keystream_info cannot be encrypted, because these attributes related to the basic functionalities of the cloud servers.

Another threat from the cloud, is to infer sensitive data by collecting and analyzing data access patterns from careful observations on the inputs of clients. Even if all data are transmitted and stored in an encrypted format, traffic analysis techniques can reveal sensitive information about the documents. For example, analysis on the frequency of modifications on a certain position could reveal certain properties of the data; the access history to multiple documents could disclose access habits of a user and the relationship of the documents; access to the same document even the same line from multiple users could suggest a common interest. We do not resolve the attacks resulted from such traffic analysis and access pattern analysis. However, in a high interactive collaborative editing system, modifications are submitted and sent about every 500 ms, which generates a large amount of information flow in the editing phase. Therefore, it is very costly for curious cloud servers to collect and analyze traffic information and access patterns, which do not directly leak sensitive information.

7 Performance Evaluation

The basic requirement of LightCore is that the highly interactive client can view the modifications of other clients in real time. During the editing process, each operation is processed by the sending client, the cloud server and the receiving clients. The whole process shall be very short and the latency of transmission shall be low. Therefore, the added cryptographic computation shall make no difference on real time. The feature of quick joining to edit is also expected to be satisfied. Therefore, the time of decrypting the document should be short when new clients join. In this section, we present the results of the experiments, to show that a high performance of LightCore is achieved, and we also suggest the suitable keystream policies for different use scenarios.

We installed the cloud server on a Ubuntu system machine with 3.4 GHZ Inter(R) Core(TM) i7-2600 and 4 GB of RAM. We evaluated the performance of the crypto module on FireFox Browser of version 34.0.5. The algorithms of stream cipher or block cipher (CTR mode) are configurable in LightCore. In our experiments, we test the performance of the crypto module at the client that implements the stream cipher RC4 or the CTR mode of block cipher AES.

Table 2. Performance of Concurrent modifications from 20 Clients

	Queuing time	Applying time	Transmission time	Decryption time (RC4)	Total time
Original System	0.04 ms	5.91 ms	22.58 ms	–	1209 ms
LightCore	0.04 ms	5.91 ms	22.58 ms	0.38 ms	1236 ms

7.1 Real Time

We evaluate the performance at the client of both the original collaborative system without crypto module and LightCore with crypto module. At the client side, the input texts of each insertion are encrypted before being sent to the cloud servers. When receiving the operation, the client will firstly decrypt it, transform it based on the operations in the local queue and apply it in its local copy. In order to evaluate the time of these main procedures, we make an experiment that 20 collaborators from different clients quickly input texts in the same document concurrently. The time of transforming an operation (called the queuing time), the time of applying an operation in its local copy (called the applying time) and the transmission time of each operation are given in Table 2. In fact, the main difference lies in the added encryption/decryption process, and the other processes are not affected. The decryption time less than 500 ms has no influence on real time. In order to test the concurrent capability, in the experiment, we set a client C only responsible for receiving operations from the 20 clients. The total time from the start time to applying 20 operations in its local copy at the client C is also given in Table 2. We can see that the total time 1236 ms of LightCore is only 27 ms longer than that of the original system, which has no difference on human sensory perception.

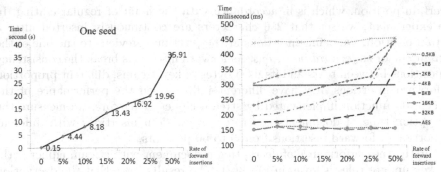

(a) One cryptographic key without key up- (b) Multiple cryptographic keys with key update
date

Fig. 3. Time of decrypting documents of 1 MB generated from random insertions

7.2   Decryption Time of Pre-edit Phase

In LightCore, the cloud servers maintain the freshest well-organized document, by modifying the stored document into a joint version based on OT. When join to edit, the clients download the freshest document, decrypt it, and then apply (or present) it on the editor. For resource-limited clients with the decryption function, a short time to join (i.e., pre-edit phase) is expected. In this part, we evaluate the performance of the decryption functionality implemented by the CTR mode of block cipher (AES) and stream cipher (RC4). Unlike stateless block cipher, the performance of stateful stream cipher varies in decrypting documents generated from different insertions and deletions. For the resource-limited clients, the size of buffer to cache bytes of keystreams is limited to less than 1 KB in LightCore. Without enough buffer to cache bytes of keystreams to use latter, insertion operations in random positions require re-initialization and generating obsoleted bytes of keystreams. And deletion operations may also cause obsoleted bytes of keystreams.

For the two types of operations, we implement two stream cipher key update rules in LightCore, that is, the client updates the key of stream cipher, if (a) the generated bytes of the keystream comes to a predetermined length or (b) the user moves to another line previous to its current line to insert some texts. We make two experiments, one is to evaluate the performance when decrypting documents generated by random insertions and the other is to measure the performance when decrypting documents generated by random deletions.

Experiment of Random Insertions. In this experiment, documents of 1 MB are firstly generated by inserting texts in random positions of the documents. We suppose that users generally edit the document in the field of view, so we limit the distance of the positions between two continuous insertions less than 50 lines. Although texts of small size may be inserted in random positions when users are modifying the document, we suppose that users input texts continuously after a certain position, which is in accordance with the habit of regular editing. In the experiment, we set that 256 characters are continuously inserted after a certain position. We define insertions at the positions previous to the line of the current cursor as *forward insertions*. As forward insertions break the consistency of positions between texts and its used bytes of keystreams, different proportion of forward insertions may have different influence on the performance of the decryption function implemented by stream cipher. Therefore, we measure the decryption time of documents generated by random insertions with different proportion of forward insertions from 0 to 50 percents.

Firstly, the performance of decrypting a document with stream cipher without key update rules is given in Fig. 3(a). The results show that the decryption time increases with the proportions of forward insertions. When the proportion of forward insertions comes to 15 percents, the decryption time, longer than 8 s, may be still intolerable for users. We evaluate the performance of LightCore implemented by stream cipher of different predetermined lengths of keystreams from 0.5 KB to 32 KB. The results in Fig. 3(b) show that the time of decrypting the documents with stream cipher is less than 500 ms. Although the decryption time of adopting AES CTR maintains about 300 ms, the performance of stream cipher of the predetermined length 16 KB or 32 KB is better than AES CTR. The main differences lie in the different number of initialization and that of obsoleted bytes of keystreams, which are given in Table 3 of Appendix A.

Experiment of Random Deletions. In this experiment, we generate documents of 1 MB by sequentially appending 2 MB text and subsequently deleting 1 MB text in random positions. The documents are encrypted with stream cipher of different predetermined lengths of keystreams from 0.5 KB to 32 KB or AES CTR. We suppose that the length of each deleted text may have influence on the decryption time of stream cipher. For example, a long text segment $T =< c_1, c_2, ..., c_n >$ is encrypted with the bytes in the position from 0th to n^{th} of one keystream, and the predetermined length of the keystream is n. If each deleted text is longer than n, T may be deleted and this keystream has not to be generated when decrypting the document. If each deleted text is short, the character c_n may not be deleted. In order to decrypt c_n, the obsoleted bytes from 1th to $(n-1)^{th}$ of this keystream are required to be generated. We test the decryption time of documents with different length of deleted text from 32 to 8192 characters. The results in Fig. 4 show that the decryption time of stream cipher RC4 is linearly decreasing with the length of each deletion text. Although the decryption time of AES CTR maintains about 300 ms, the performance of RC4 is more efficient for the predetermined length of keystreams longer than 16 KB. When the deleted text is longer than 2048 characters, the value of the 8 KB curve is approximately equal to that of 16 KB curve. When the deleted text is longer than 4096 characters, the value at 4096 of 8 KB curve (219 ms) and that of 16KB curve (229 ms) is smaller than that of 32 KB curve. In fact, it will not be better for adopting stream cipher of the predetermined length of keystreams longer than 32 KB. The main difference lies in the number of ini-

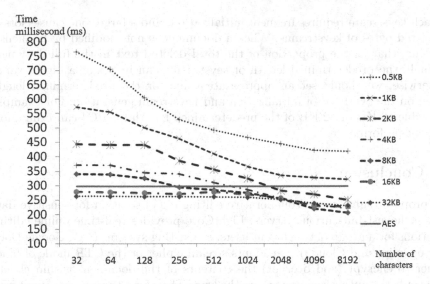

Fig. 4. Time of decrypting documents of 1 MB generated from firstly appending 2 MB text and then deleting 1MB in random positions

tialization and that of obsoleted bytes of keystreams, which is given in Table 4 of Appendix A. If the value of predetermined length is larger than 32 KB, the more obsoleted bytes of keystreams bring more overhead even if the number of initialization decreases.

Suggestions for Keystream Polices. The results of the experiments above illustrate that the efficiency of LightCore varies as the keystream policy changes. Therefore, users can determine different keystream polices based on their requirements in different use scenarios. If a stable decryption time is expected, adopting the CTR mode of block cipher may be more suitable. If a shorter decryption time is expected, especially for documents of large size, a faster stream cipher of different key update rules is suggested to be adopted. If a large size of texts are input sequentially after the position of each forward insertion, it can achieve an efficient performance of stream cipher by re-initializing the stream cipher with a new data key and setting a large value of the predetermined length. However, when a document is corrected by frequently inserting small text each time (e.g., 2 to 10 characters), we suggest combining stream cipher with block cipher CTR mode in LightCore, that is, (a) the clients encrypt data with stream cipher when users are sequentially appending text at some positions; and (b) encrypt data with block cipher CTR mode when forward insertions happen. In this case, it will not result in heavy overhead for frequent initialization of stream cipher. Note that block CTR mode and stream cipher can be used simultaneously in LightCore.

Efficient key update rules should balance the overhead of initialization and that of generating obsoleted bytes of keystreams. A small predetermined length of each keystream requires frequent initialization, and a larger one causes lots of obsoleted bytes of keystreams. When a document is not modified by frequently deleting, that is, the proportion of the total deleted text in the full document is small, the predetermined length of keystreams can be set at a bigger value. Otherwise, we should set an appropriate value for the predetermined length based on the overhead of initialization and keystream generation. For example, the value 16 KB or 32 KB of the predetermined length for RC4 can bring more efficient performance.

8 Conclusion

We propose LightCore, a collaborative editing cloud solution for sensitive data against honest-but-curious servers. LightCore provides real-time online editing functions for a group of concurrent users, as existing systems (e.g., Google Docs, Office Online and Cloud9). We adopts stream cipher or the CTR mode of block cipher to encrypt (and decrypt) the contents of the document within clients, while only the authorized users share the keys. Therefore, the servers cannot read the contents, but the byte-by-byte encryption feature enables the cloud servers to process user operations in the same way as existing collaborative editing cloud systems. In order to optimize the decryption time in the pre-edit phase under certain use scenarios, we analyze different keystream policies, including the method to generate keystreams and the key update rules. Experiments on the prototype system show that LightCore provides efficient online collaborative editing services for resource-limited clients.

We plan to extend LightCore in the following aspects. Firstly, in the current design and implementation, only the texts of the document are protected and then the servers may infer a limited number of information about the document from the formats. We will analyze the possibility of encrypting more attributes (e.g., font, color and list) while the servers' processing is not impeded or disabled. Secondly, for a given document, the client can dynamically switch among different keystream policies in an intelligent way, according to the editing operations that happened and the prediction. Finally, more languages characters will be supported in LigthCore.

Acknowledgement. This work was partially supported by National 973 Program under award No. 2014CB340603, National 863 Program under award No. 2013AA01A214, and Strategy Pilot Project of Chinese Academy of Sciences under award No. XDA06010702.

A   Appendix

Table 3 shows the detailed size of obsoleted bytes of keystreams to be generated and the number of initialization, when decrypting a document of 1 MB generated from random insertions. The first row of Table 3 denotes the rate of forward insertions (or inserting text at the position previous to the line of the current

Table 3. Obsoleted bytes of keystreams and initialization resulted from random insertions

Rate	0		0.05		0.1		0.15		0.2		0.25		0.5	
	Obsol	Init	Obsol	Init	Obsol	Init	Obsol	Init	Obsol	Init	Obsol	Init	Obsol	Init
0.5 KB	0	2048	30	2045	25	2044	25	2056	35	2068	37	2076	57	2161
1 KB	0	1024	51	1095	104	1197	144	1275	207	1401	252	1481	428	1838
2 KB	0	512	77	577	166	662	274	753	382	848	420	901	994	1402
4 KB	0	256	73	293	190	350	316	407	491	479	628	525	1672	983
8 KB	0	128	10	132	52	148	79	155	174	170	152	166	1282	399
16 KB	0	64	1	65	0	64	1	64	0	64	0	64	0	64
32 KB	0	32	2	34	0	32	6	3	0	33	0	33	0	32
one seed	0	1	3419	98	7159	179	12406	287	15897	387	198557	447	34881	808

cursor) from 0 to 0.5 (50 percents). The first column denotes the predetermined length of keystreams. We give the related obsoleted bytes of keystreams in the column titled "Obsol" and the size of obsoleted bytes is given in KB. The related number of initialization is shown in the column titled "Init". The number of initialization and the size of obsoleted bytes is increasing with the rate of forward insertions when the predetermined length is given. The results show that it results in much initialization and lots of obsoleted bytes of the keystream, if the key to initialize the stream cipher is not updated during the whole encryption process (one seed). When the two principles of stream cipher key update rules are adopted in LightCore, the stream cipher of a longer predetermined length of keystreams may cause less initialization and more obsoleted bytes of keystreams.

Table 4. Obsoleted bytes of keystreams and initialization resulted from random deletions

Length	128		256		512		1024		2048		4096		random	
	Obsol	Init	Obsol	Init	Obsol	Init	Obsol	Init	Obsol	Init	Obsol	Init	Obsol	Init
0.5 KB	319	3094	182	2615	123	2396	79	2224	49	2121	11	2050	77	2200
1 KB	572	1914	433	1762	258	1489	147	1275	72	1143	47	1087	136	1242
2 KB	935	1022	677	1000	525	922	318	809	170	662	85	594	276	760
4 KB	947	512	815	511	733	509	553	475	318	413	165	336	461	475
8 KB	970	253	967	251	868	248	779	243	559	242	269	208	817	253
16 KB	996	128	968	128	932	128	899	128	807	126	551	125	1023	128
32 KB	1002	64	974	64	966	64	951	64	914	64	705	62	1024	64

Table 4 shows the detailed size of obsoleted bytes of keys streams to be generated and the number of initialization, when decrypting a document of 1 MB generated by sequentially appending text to 2 MB and then deleting text at random positions to 1 MB. The first row of Table 4 denotes the length of each deleted text. The first column denotes the predetermined length of keystreams. We give the related obsoleted bytes of keystreams in the column titled "Obsol" and the size of obsoleted bytes is given in KB. The related number of initialization is shown in the column titled "Init". The column titled "random" denotes that the length of each deleted text is randomly determined. The number of initialization and the size of obsoleted bytes is decreasing with the length of each deleted text when the predetermined length is given. Given a smaller predetermined length of keystreams (0.5 KB or 1 KB, e.g.), initialization may bring more overhead than obsoleted bytes of keystreams. The results show that it causes less initialization and more obsoleted bytes of keystreams when a larger predetermined length of keystreams is given for stream cipher key update rules.

References

1. Sun, D., Sun, C.: Context-based operational transformation in distributed collaborative editing systems. IEEE Trans. Parallel Distrib. Syst. **20**(10), 1454–1470 (2009)
2. Shamir, A.: Stream ciphers: dead or alive? In: Lee, P.J. (ed.) ASIACRYPT 2004. LNCS, vol. 3329, pp. 78–78. Springer, Heidelberg (2004)
3. Lautamäki, J., Nieminen, A., Koskinen, J., Aho, T., Mikkonen, T., Englund, M.: Cored: browser-based collaborative real-time editor for Java web applications. In: 12 Computer Supported Cooperative Work (CSCW), pp. 1307–1316 (2012)
4. Fan, H., Sun, C.: Supporting semantic conflict prevention in real-time collaborative programming environments. ACM SIGAPP Appl. Comput. Rev. **12**(2), 39–52 (2012)
5. Lamport, L.: Time, clocks, and the ordering of events in a distributed system. Commun. ACM **21**(7), 558–565 (1978)
6. Nédelec, B., Molli, P., Mostéfaoui, A., Desmontils, E.: LSEQ: an adaptive structure for sequences in distributed collaborative editing. In: Proceedings of the 2013 ACM symposium on Document engineering, pp. 37–46 (2013)
7. Nédelec, B., Molli, P., Mostéfaoui, A., Desmontils, E.: Concurrency effects over variable-size identifiers in distributed collaborative editing. In: Proceedings of the International workshop on Document Changes: Modeling, Detection, Storage and Visualization (2013)
8. Vidot, N., Cart, M., Ferrié, J., Suleiman, M.: Copies convergence in a distributed real-time collaborative environment. In: Proceeding on the ACM 2000 Conference on Computer Supported Cooperative Work (CSCW), pp. 171–180 (2000)
9. Google Docs (2014). http://docs.google.com/
10. Office Online (2014). http://office.microsoft.com/zh-cn/online/FX100996074.aspx
11. Raykova, M., Zhao, H., Bellovin, S.M.: Privacy enhanced access control for outsourced data sharing. In: 16th International Conference on Financial Cryptography and Data Security (FC), pp. 223–238 (2012)
12. di Vimercati, S.D.C., Foresti, S., Jajodia, S., Livraga, G., Paraboschi, S., Samarati, P.: Enforcing dynamic write privileges in data outsourcing. Comput. Secur. **39**, 47–63 (2013)
13. Zhou, L., Varadharajan, V., Hitchens, M.: Secure administration of cryptographic role-based access control for large-scale cloud storage systems. J. Comput. Syst. Sci. **80**(8), 1518–1533 (2014)

14. Li, M., Yu, S., Ren, K., Lou, W.: Securing personal health records in cloud computing: patient-centric and fine-grained data access control in multi-owner settings. In: Jajodia, S., Zhou, J. (eds.) SecureComm 2010. LNICST, vol. 50, pp. 89–106. Springer, Heidelberg (2010)
15. Feldman, A.J., Zeller, W.P., Freedman, M.J., Felten, E.W.: SPORC: group collaboration using untrusted cloud resources. In: 9th USENIX Symposium on Operating Systems Design and Implementation, pp. 337–350 (2010)
16. Sang, C., Li, Q., Kong, L.: Tenant oriented lock concurrency control in the shared storage multi-tenant database. In: 16th IEEE International Enterprise Distributed Object Computing Conference Workshops (EDOC), pp. 179–189 (2012)
17. Sun, C.: Optional and responsive fine-grain locking in internet-based collaborative systems. IEEE Trans. Parallel Distrib. Syst. $13(9)$, 994–1008 (2002)
18. Fraser, N.: Differential synchronization. In: Proceedings of the 2009 ACM Symposium on Document Engineering, New York, USA, pp. 13–20 (2009)
19. Fuzzy patch April 2009. http://neil.fraser.name/writing/patch/
20. Myers, E.W.: An O(ND) difference algorithm and its variations. Algorithmica $1(2)$, 251–266 (1986)
21. Bernstein, P.A., Hadzilacos, V., Goodman, N.: Concurrency Control and Recovery in Database Systems. Addison Wesley, Reading (1987)
22. Ressel, M., Nitsche-Ruhland, D., Gunzenhäuser, R.: An integrating, transformation-oriented approach to concurrency control and undo in group editors. In: Proceedings of the ACM 1996 Conference on Computer Supported Cooperative Work (CSCW), pp. 288–297 (1996)
23. Ressel, M., Gunzenhäuser, R.: Reducing the problems of group undo. In: Proceedings of the International ACM SIGGROUP Conference on Supporting Group Work, pp. 131–139 (1999)
24. Sun, C.: Undo as concurrent inverse in group editors. Interactions $10(2)$, 7–8 (2003)
25. Schneier, B.: Fast software encryption. In: 7th International Workshop (FSE 2000), vol. 1978, pp. 182–184 (1994)
26. Boesgaard, M., Vesterager, M., Pedersen, T., Christiansen, J., Scavenius, O.: Rabbit: a new high-performance stream cipher. In: Johansson, T. (ed.) FSE 2003. LNCS, vol. 2887, pp. 307–329. Springer, Heidelberg (2003)
27. Mousa, A., Hamad, A.: Evaluation of the RC4 algorithm for data encryption. IJCSA $3(2)$, 44–56 (2006)
28. Hoffman, P., Yergeau, F.: Utf-16, an encoding of iso 10646, Technical report RFC 2781, February 2000

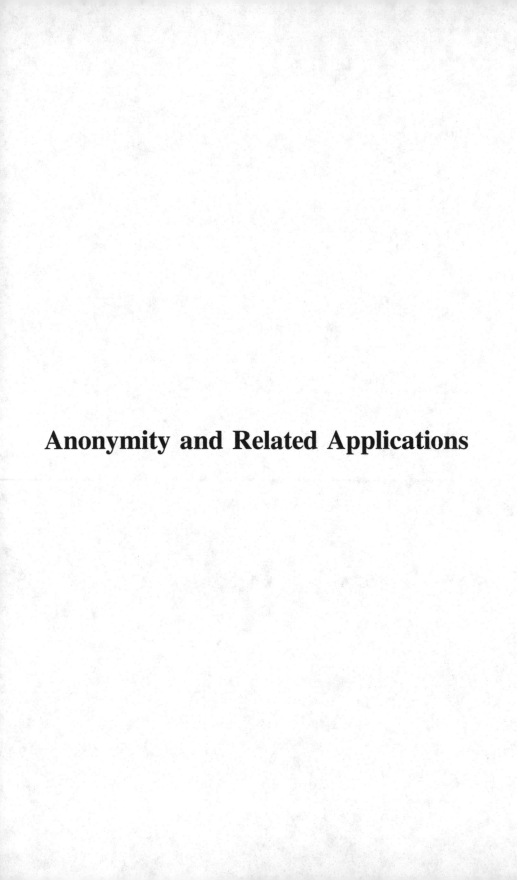

Anonymity and Related Applications

Violating Consumer Anonymity: Geo-Locating Nodes in Named Data Networking

Alberto Compagno[1]([⊠]), Mauro Conti[2], Paolo Gasti[3],
Luigi Vincenzo Mancini[1], and Gene Tsudik[4]

[1] Sapienza University of Rome, Rome, Italy
{compagno,mancini}@di.uniroma1.it
[2] University of Padua, Padua, Italy
conti@math.unipd.it
[3] New York Institute of Technology, New York, NY, USA
pgasti@nyit.edu
[4] University of California, Irvine, CA, USA
gts@ics.uci.edu

Abstract. Named Data Networking (NDN) is an instance of information-centric network architecture designed as a candidate replacement for the current IP-based Internet. It emphasizes efficient content distribution, achieved via in-network caching and collapsing of closely-spaced content requests. NDN also offers strong security and explicitly decouples content from entities that distribute it. NDN is widely assumed to provide better privacy than IP, mainly because NDN packets lack source and destination addresses. In this paper, we show that this assumption does not hold in practice. In particular, we present several algorithms that help locate consumers by taking advantage of NDN router-side content caching. We use simulations to evaluate these algorithms on a large and realistic topology, and validate the results on the official NDN testbed. Beyond locating consumers, proposed techniques can also be used to detect eavesdroppers.

Keywords: Name data networking · Geolocation · Privacy

1 Introduction

Despite its impressive longevity, popularity and overall success, the Internet is starting to suffer from limitations of its original early 1980-s design. Current protocols (in particular, IP) were conceived when remote login, email and resource sharing were the most prominent Internet use-cases. However, a significant fraction of today's Internet traffic corresponds to content distribution. Recognizing this paradigm shift in the nature of Internet traffic, multiple large-scale research efforts [5,19,20,22,32] have been trying – in the last 5–6 years – to address the shortcomings of the current Internet, with the long-term goal of replacing it with a next-generation Internet architecture. One such effort is Named Data Networking (NDN) [15].

© Springer International Publishing Switzerland 2015
T. Malkin et al. (Eds.): ACNS 2015, LNCS 9092, pp. 243–262, 2015.
DOI: 10.1007/978-3-319-28166-7_12

NDN is an example of Content-Centric Networking (CCN), where content – rather than a host or an interface – plays the central role in the architecture. NDN is primarily oriented towards efficient large-scale data distribution. Rather than contacting a host at some IP address in order to request data, an NDN *consumer* directly requests desired content by name by issuing an *interest packet*. The network takes care of finding and returning the nearest copy of requested content that "satisfies" the consumer's interest. To this end, NDN features *ubiquitous content caching*, i.e., any host or router can store a copy of the content it receives or forwards, and use it to satisfy subsequent interests. NDN also provides *interest collapsing*, i.e., only the first of multiple *closely spaced* interests for the same content is forwarded by each router. Unlike IP datagrams, NDN interests and content packets do not carry source or destination addresses. One of the alleged consequences of this feature is *consumer location privacy*. In this paper we show that two fundamental NDN features (ubiquitous caching and interest collapsing) can be used to violate consumer location privacy. Specifically, we show how information leaked by caching and interest collapsing can be used to identify and locate consumers.

Assuming that the adversary can associate NDN routers with their physical location using existing methods, we focus on designing techniques that identify the router closest to the targeted consumer. We then show that proposed techniques can be used to determine consumers' location, as well as detect "eavesdroppers" that are surreptitiously requesting content for a particular set of users, e.g., in audio/video conferencing applications [14,33]. We validate our results via experiments on the official NDN testbed [21]. Finally, we propose some countermeasure that mitigate these attacks.

We believe that this topic is both timely and important, since one of the key design goals of NDN is *security by design*. This is in contrast with today's Internet where security and privacy problems were (and are still being) identified and patched along the way. Therefore, assessing *if* and *how* geo-location and eavesdroppers identification can be implemented must be done *before* NDN is fully deployed. Furthermore, even though the research community has made significant efforts in geo-locating hosts in the current Internet [9,13,16,17,23, 24,29–31], none of these techniques apply to locating consumers in NDN. (See Sect. 3.) In fact, to the best of our knowledge, all prior techniques rely on the ability to directly address the victim host. This is not possible in NDN since consumers cannot be contacted directly.

Organization: We start by overviewing the NDN architecture in Sect. 2. Related work is discussed in Sect. 3. Section 4 introduces our system and adversary models. Proposed techniques are presented in Sect. 5 and evaluated in Sect. 6. Detection of eavesdroppers is addressed in Sect. 7. Finally, geo-location countermeasures are presented in Sect. 8. We conclude in Sect. 9.

2   NDN Overview

NDN supports two types of packets: *interest* and *content* [4]. Notable fields in content packets are: (1) content name, (2) payload, and (3) digital signature computed by the producer. Names are intended to be human-readable, consisting of one or more components with a hierarchical structure. In NDN notation, "/" separates name components, e.g., /ndn/cnn/politics.

Consumers request desired content by name, via interests. NDN routers forward interests towards the content producer responsible for the requested name, using longest name-prefix matching for routing. If the requested content is not encountered in caches of any intervening routers, the interest eventually arrives to the producer. Upon receipt of the interest, the producer injects the content into the network, thus *satisfying* the interest. The requested content packet is then forwarded towards the consumer, traversing – in reverse – the path of the preceding interest.

Each NDN router maintains three data structures: (1) Pending Interest Table (PIT) storing interests that are not yet satisfied, (2) Forwarding Interest Base (FIB) containing routing information, and (3) Content Store (CS) where forwarded content is cached. When an NDN router receives an interest, it first looks up its PIT to check whether another interest for the same name is currently pending. There are two possible outcomes:

1. The PIT look-up succeeds, i.e., PIT entry for the same name exists and:
   - The incoming interface of the present interest is new, the router updates the PIT entry by adding the new interface to *arrival-interfaces* set. The interest is not forwarded further. This feature is called *interest collapsing*.
   - The present interest's incoming interface is already in the set of that entry's *arrival-interfaces*. In this case, the interest is simply discarded.
2. The PIT look-up fails. The router performs local cache look for the content name referenced in the interest, and:
   - The cache look-up succeeds. The content is returned on the arriving interface of the interest and no further actions are taken.
   - Otherwise, the router creates a new PIT entry and forwards the present interest out on one or more interfaces, according to its FIB.

However, note that caching of content in routers is not mandatory. Although each NDN router is expected to cache content, it is not required to do so. A router can choose whether to cache a given content based on local criteria, such as: size and occupancy rate of its cache, content name, as well as consumer or producer wishes, i.e., the interest might request caching or no caching, or the content itself might convey caching preferences.

3   Related Work

The goal of current geo-location techniques is to associate a physical location with a particular IP address. There are many studies that investigate geo-location in today's Internet [9, 13, 16, 17, 23, 24, 30, 31].

Prior work can be divided in two classes: *measurement-based* and *database-driven* techniques. The former involve a set of geographically distributed *landmark* hosts with known locations. Their purpose is to determine the position of the target IP address using round-trip time (RTT) information as the basis for triangulation. An algorithm estimates the location of the target IP using historical data constructed using ground truth [13]. Multiple techniques can then be used to improve accuracy. For example, Wong et al. [30,31] combine delay measurements with locations of cities. [31] uses Bézier curves to represent a region containing the target IP, while [30] leverage a three-tier approach, where every tier refines results of the previous one. Finally, Eriksson et al. [9] propose a learning-based approach, where population density is used to construct a Naïve Bayes estimator.

All these techniques assume that, packets sent to a particular IP address and echoed back (e.g., via `ping`) are guaranteed to come from the same physical host. Therefore, multiple RTT measurements correspond to the same target. In contrast, requesting multiple NDN content packets created by the same producer does not guarantee that requested content will be found at the same place. Because of in-network caching, different content packets might be served by distinct entities. Thus, RTT measurements obtained by the landmarks can refer to different nodes, and cannot be immediately used to locate a single target.

Database-driven approaches determine the target IP's location using DNS LOC records, `WhoIs` lookups, Border Gateway Protocol (BGP) router tables, and/or other public databases (e.g., ARIN [3], RIPE [25], GeoTrace [12] and MaxMind GeoIP [11]). These resources either provide direct geographic information, as in DNS LOC, or reveal indirect clues, such as the organization or Autonomous System (AS) number that owns a particular IP address. For example, techniques like GTrace [24], GeoTrack and GeoCluster [23] use these public resources to locate the target IP, and then further refine the findings using RTT measurements. Recent work by Liu et al. [17] utilizes location data that users willingly disclose via location-sharing services. This technique can locate a host with a median estimation error of 799 m – an order of magnitude better than other approaches.

Because NDN consumers have no network-layer addresses, current geo-location techniques are not directly applicable. However, it is possible to use current techniques to locate content producers. Although there are no addresses that can identify hosts in NDN, name-spaces can serve the same purpose. In fact, all producers publishing within specific namespaces (e.g., `/cnn/`, or `/microsoft/`) might be naturally located within the same Autonomous System (AS). Name prefixes could thus reveal location information. Similarly, routing tables can reveal location information for name-spaces. Although, at this stage, there are no location databases for NDN, it is not hard to anticipate these resources becoming available if and when NDN becomes wider deployed.

4   System and Adversary Model

In the rest of the paper we consider the scenario illustrated in Fig. 1. A consumer (C) retrieves content, composed of multiple packets, from a producer (P).

We focus on the case where C requests *non-popular* content, i.e., content that is unlikely to have been recently requested by others. Thus, it is not cached in relevant routers. Each interest traverses multiple routers before being satisfied by P. The adversary (Adv) controls a set of hosts (hereafter called *landmarks*), connected to NDN routers. These hosts controlled by Adv have no special privileges and cannot eavesdrop on links between routers. We denote router i as R_i and landmark j as L_j. Adv's goal is to determine C's location in the network, i.e., identify the router closest to C.

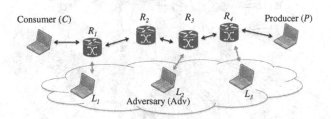

Fig. 1. Scenario considered throughout the paper.

4.1   System Model

We represent network topology as a undirected graph $G = \langle V, E \rangle$, where V is the set of vertices (routers) and E is the set of edges (links between routers). Our experiments on the official NDN testbed (see Sect. 6) show that NDN links are largely symmetric, i.e., bandwidth and delay are the same in either direction. For this reason, our system model also considers all links to be symmetric.

We performed experiments on the AT&T topology from Rocketfuel [26], depicted in Fig. 2. It contains 625 vertexes and 2101 edges. In the experiments we assume that every router caches content packets, which is the default NDN setting. However, because NDN does not mandate a specific caching policy, we also discuss how to apply geolocation techniques when some (or all) routers do not cache content packets (see Sect. 5).

4.2   Adversary Model

We assume that C requests – and Adv can exploit – a large number of data packets, possibly corresponding to a single piece of content, e.g., a high-resolution video. We consider two distinct classes of adversaries: *outsiders* and *insiders*. The former cannot directly (passively) monitor packets exchanged between P and C. We assume that an outsider knows what type of applications C and P are using. Therefore it might infer the structure and naming of content packets. However, if unique/secret naming is negotiated between P and C, outsiders cannot guess content names. Insiders can observe packets exchanged by P and C. For example, an insider could be a compromised WiFi access point to which

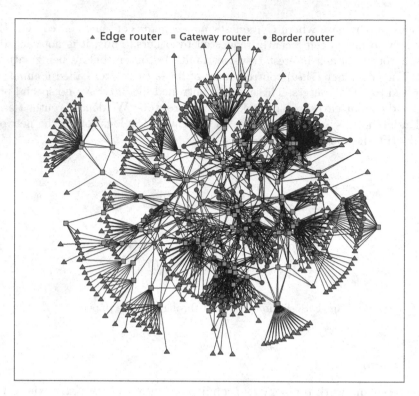

Fig. 2. AT&T topology

C is directly connected, or a malicious P. Thus, countermeasures such as content name randomization are not effective.

Our analysis makes the following assumptions:

1. **Topology Information:** Adv knows the topology and geographic distribution of routers. Today, some AS-s already publish this information [26]. Moreover, it has been shown that it is possible to reconstruct topology even if this information is not publicly available [7].
2. **Routing Information:** Adv is aware of how interests are routed. Given the sheer number of routers and AS-s involved in today's Internet routing, it is unlikely that routing information can be kept secret.
3. **Distance from Sources:** Adv can determine the distance of a content packet (expressed in terms of number of hops) from its closest source (e.g., a cache) using Content Fetch Time (CFT) information, i.e., the time between sending an interest and receiving the related content. Our experiments on the official NDN testbed [21], reported in Sect. 6, confirm that this is indeed currently possible.
4. **Naming Information:** Adv can predict the name of content packets requested by C. As mentioned earlier, insiders and outsiders have different capabilities.

5. **Arbitrary Landmark Location:** *Adv* can connect landmarks to arbitrary routers in the network. For example, it can use a geographically distributed botnet, or purchase resources from (multiple) cloud services with machines located in different parts of the world. We allow *Adv* to select landmarks *adaptively* (i.e., the next landmark is selected after gathering information from all current landmarks) or *non-adaptively*, meaning that all landmarks are chosen at once.

6. **Upper-bound on Landmarks:** *Adv* can compromise (or purchase) up to a fixed subset of nodes in a given topology, in order to turn them into landmarks.

We refer to *Adv* with all aforementioned capabilities as *routing-aware*. As an extension, we later consider a variant *Adv* that has no knowledge of routing information. We call it *non-routing-aware Adv*.

5   Locating Consumers in NDN

To locate C, *Adv* requests cached content previously requested by C from multiple landmarks L_i. Each landmark measures CFT for each content. Since content is cached (and therefore served) by some router on the return path between C to P ($P{\rightarrow}C$ from here on), landmarks might learn some information about $P{\rightarrow}C$. Hence, *Adv* can use this information to infer the location of C.

If no intervening router caches content, *Adv* can use NDN interest collapsing feature to locate C. For the sake of simplicity, and without loss of generality, we describe *Adv*'s steps to locate a specific R_i.

Recall that, as an interest traverses routers on the path from C to P, it creates state in the form of a PIT entry. After receiving the interest, P injects requested content into the network. As the content travels back towards C, each router that forwards it flushes the corresponding PIT entry for that content. However, if an interest from a landmark reaches R_i before the corresponding PIT entry is flushed, (i.e., before the content packet requested by C arrives), the CFT measured by the landmark will be lower than the CFT for content fetched from P. This is due to interest collapsing: the landmark's interest is not forwarded by R_i since an entry for previously pending interest (for the same content) already exists in R_i's PIT. As shown in [2], this CFT difference can be easily identified by the landmark. In practice, different routers will adhere to different caching strategies. Thus, while some routers might cache all packets, others will not. Therefore, each landmark might have to probe either PIT-s, or CS-s, or both.

Regardless of caching, *Adv* can only retrieve content reviously requested by C from routers, and not from C itself. *Adv*'s interests are routed toward P, and can reach C only if C is on a path $Adv{\rightarrow}P$. However, because C is a host and not a router, it is never part of $Adv{\rightarrow}P$. For this reason, we define *Adv*'s goal as identifying C's first-hop router. This allows *Adv* to accurately pinpoint the C's location, e.g., possibly within a few blocks in a densely populated city. Moreover, compared to expected errors in current geo-location techniques (on the order of 10km using state-of-the-art [17]), identifying an edge router instead of an end-host introduces only negligible errors. For this reason, in the rest of the paper, we use C to indicate the edge router closest to the actual consumer.

Routing-Aware Adversary. Knowledge of network topology and all routing tables allows landmarks to identify the source of content packets via CFT measurements. This information reveals how far the content travels in the network to reach the landmark. Given this distance, as well as topology and routing information, Adv can determine which router served the content. Listing 1.1 describes the steps Adv performs to identify C. For each L_i, Adv calculates path $L_i \rightarrow P$ and measures the number of hops (i.e., $hops_{L_i}$) between L_i and the cache serving the content (see lines 6–10, Listing 1.1). Then, Adv identifies the router at position $hops_{L_i}$ in the path $L_i \rightarrow P$ as a router on $P \rightarrow C$. N_C represents the set of candidate nodes for C (lines 11–15).

Intuitively, location of landmarks with respect to routers on $P \rightarrow C$ path affects the precision of locating C. In non-adaptive selection, Adv randomly selects all landmarks at once. In the adaptive case, landmark selection is performed as follows. Let R_g be a router identified by Adv as part of the path $P \rightarrow C$. To find the next router on the path, Adv selects a L_i that is far away from P, such that the path from L_i to P contains R_g (i.e., $L_i \rightarrow P = L_i \rightarrow R_g \rightarrow P$). Thus, if L_i retrieves content cached by router $R_i \neq R_g$, then R_i must (1) be on $P \rightarrow C$, and (2) be $n \geq 1$ hops closer to C compared to R_g. The larger n, the fewer landmarks are required to identify C. This process is repeated until no new landmarks are able to discover routers closer to C, or if Adv reached its maximum number of landmarks.

Listing 1.1. GuessPath - Routing Aware Adversary.

```
1   Input: G; P; landmarks L; gateway routers; edge routers
2   Output: N_Path (nodes believed to be part of the path P→C);
3          N_C (nodes believed to include C)
4   N_Path ← P
5   N_C ← ∅
6   for each available landmark L_i {
7        path_{L_i} ← calculate path L_i→P, ordered from L_i to P
8        hops_{L_i} ← number of hops measured when retrieving from L_i
9        N_Path ← N_Path ∪ {element at position hops_{Li} in path_{Li}}
10  }
11  for each n, s.t. n in N_Path, and n is a gateway router {
12       for each n̄, s.t. n̄ is an edge router, and n̄ is connected to n {
13            N_C ← n̄
14       }
15  }
```

Non-Routing-Aware Adversary. The non-routing-aware adversary has no knowledge of the content of routing tables. Without this knowledge, measuring distances between the caches satisfying the landmarks' interests and the landmarks does not provide as much information as in the case of routing-aware adversaries. In fact, given a distance, Adv can identify a *set* of caching routers that contains the one serving her requests, instead of a single router. In this case the Adv's strategy includes three phases: *Phase 1*: collecting information from landmarks to assign a *score* to each node, *Phase 2*: using scores to determine routers that are likely in the path; and *Phase 3*: further refining the selection. Pseudocode for the three phases is reported in Listing 1.2.

Listing 1.2. GuessPath - Non-Routing Aware Adversary.

```
1
2   Input: G; P; landmarks L; threshold; numberOfComp;
3          gateway routers; edge routers
4   Output: N_Path (nodes believed to be part of the path
5          P→C); N_C (nodes believed to include C)
6   N_Path ← P, N_C ← ∅
7   for each landmark L_i {
8       R_i ← router at one hop from L_i
9   }
10  PHASE 1
11  for i = 1 to size(L) {
12      hops_{L_i} ← number of hops measured when retrieving from L_i
13      hops_{R_i} ← hops_{L_i} − 1
14      suspectNodes_{L_i} ← all nodes n_{L_i} at distance hops_{L_i} from L_i
15      suspectPaths_{L_i} ← all possible paths to reach nodes
16          suspectNodes_{L_i} from L_i
17      for each landmark L_j ≠ L_i {
18          if ∃ spath in suspectPaths_{L_i}, s.t. R_j is in spath {
19              hops_{L_j} ← number of hops measured when
20                  retrieving from L_j
21              if ((hops_{R_j}) ≠ hops_{L_i} − (position of R_j in spath)){
22                  remove spath from suspectPaths_{L_i}
23              }
24          }
25      }
26      for each spath in suspectPaths_{L_i} {
27          n = node at position hops_{L_i} in spath
28          Score_n = Score_n + 1/(hops_{L_i})^2
29      }
30  }
31  PHASE 2
32  for each n in V {
33      if (Score_n > threshold) {
34          N'_Path ← n
35      }
36  }
37  PHASE 3
38  N_Path ← getConnComp(N'_Path, numberOfComp)
39  for each n in N_Path and n is a gateway router {
40      for each n̄ is an edge router and n̄ connected to n {
41          N_C ← n̄
42      }
43  }
```

Phase 1 is based on two observations. First, estimation done independently by each landmark L_i (i.e., suspect nodes computed in line 13 in Listing 1.2) could be partially incorrect. Because L_i does not have access to routing information, it might include routers that are not on $P \rightarrow C$. However, estimates from different landmarks can be checked against each other for consistency: nodes that are not consistently considered as potential routers in the path from C to P will be assigned a zero score. This consistency check (lines 16–24 in Listing 1.2) is motivated as follows. Because each landmark L_i is connected to just one router R_i, learning the number of hops from L_i to the source also implies learning the distance from R_i to the source of the content. Moreover, because routing information is not available to *Adv*, every path from L_i to a "suspect" node is a candidate (suspect) path. Let us consider the situation in Fig. 3(b) where R_j, one hop away from L_j, belongs to a suspect path for L_i. In this case, distance measured by L_i and L_j for R_j must be the same. If two distances differ, the suspect path for L_i is considered incorrect and no score is added to the suspect node, as shown in Fig. 3(c).

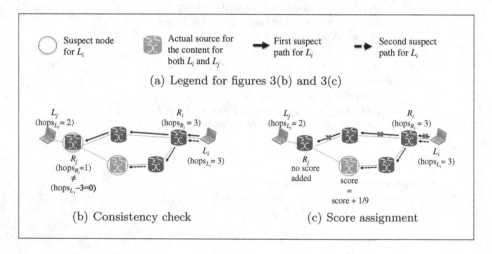

(a) Legend for figures 3(b) and 3(c)

(b) Consistency check

(c) Score assignment

Fig. 3. Non-routing aware – Phase 1.

The second observation is used to add a score to the nodes selected as possible candidates to be on the $P \rightarrow C$ path (denoted hereafter by N_{Path}). In this case, the closer L_i is to N_{Path}, the more specific is the information provided by L_i. For example, if we connect L_i to a node in this path, L_i could identify the source without error – the content will be retrieved in zero hops, i.e., from the same router to which L_i is connected. Instead, if we connect L_i at a certain distance (denoted as $hops_{L_i}$) from a node on N_{Path}, L_i will consider any node that is $hops_{L_i}$-hops away from itself as a possible node in N_{Path}. As a consequence, the greater $hops_{L_i}$, the higher is the number of candidate nodes; thus, errors are more likely. In Listing 1.2, this observation is reflected in line 27 where $1/(hops_{L_i})^2$ is used to assign a score to the nodes. The intuition behind this assignment has a geometric explanation. Considering the selected node L_i as the center of a sphere and the distance $hops_{L_i}$ as the radius, the area of the sphere is a good estimator of the number of candidate nodes.

Phase 2 uses the scores provided in Phase 1 to select a number of nodes as sources of content packets. In this case, we select the nodes that exceed a predefined threshold as possible sources.

Phase 3 further refines node selection. We use the set of selected nodes from Phase 2 to create a subgraph of G. Then, we compute connected components in this new graph and we order them from the closest to the farthest from the producer. We consider the distance from a component $ConnComp[i]$ to the producer as the distance, computed in graph G, from the closest node of $ConnComp[i]$ to the producer. Therefore, Adv assumes that the nodes from $ConnComp[0]$ to $ConnComp[k-1]$ are in the path $P{\rightarrow}C$. Finally, we consider all edge nodes connected to gateway nodes in N_{Path} as the nodes that include C.

Landmarks are selected to minimize the difference between: (i) the score assigned to the new landmark by the previous selection step, and (ii) the average score.

6   Evaluation

In the current Internet, the relationship between RTT and distance measured in hops is subject to variation of the triangle inequality. Such variations make RTT-based distance estimation unreliable [18]. We studied this phenomenon on the NDN tested, and we evaluate how it affects the attacks discussed in this paper. To this end, we used Amazon Elastic Compute Cloud (EC2) [8] virtual machine instances. Each EC2 instance was connected to the testbed at a different router, and was used to either publish or request content. We performed exhaustive tests, including producer/consumer combinations. Figure 4(b) summarizes our findings. It also shows approximate physical straight-line distance between NDN nodes. Reported CFT is obtained after subtracting the CFT between the EC2 instance acting as C and the first-hop router. Our experiments confirm that: (1) links between routers are symmetric in terms of bandwidth and delay, except as discussed below; (2) triangle inequality violations only add a small amount of noise to distance estimation. CFT is symmetric for every link except for UA-REMAP, PKU-UCLA and PKU-NEU. In the first case, asymmetry is due to the paths UA→REMAP vs REMAP→CSU→UA. We consider asymmetry in PKU-NEU and PKU-UCLA links to be an artifact of the current NDN testbed, since it is deployed as an IP overlay, and not a property of NDN.

We ran multiple experiments in which we connected P and C to different nodes. For every experiment we measure CFT connecting landmarks to all nodes in the testbed. Our measurements reveal that 8% of landmarks provided an incorrect distance, likely due to violation of triangle inequality. Therefore, actual distance measurements on the testbed would be affected by "random noise" with probability 8 %.

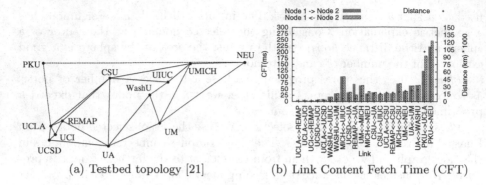

(a) Testbed topology [21]   (b) Link Content Fetch Time (CFT)

Fig. 4. The NDN Testbed.

6.1 Performance of Our Algorithms

To evaluate the effectiveness of our strategies, we defined three metrics, which can be informally summarized as: (a) how effective are our strategies in identifying nodes in the path? (b)Of the selected nodes, how far from C is the closest? (c) How often do our strategies correctly identify C? Although (c) is arguably the most "natural" metric, it is also the one that provides the least amount of information, representing a simple binary outcome (identified/not identified). Therefore, we believe that (a) and (b) complement this metric by providing further details on *how close Adv* is to identifying C.

We express (a) as two quantities: *true positive* (i.e., nodes that have been correctly identified) and *false positives* (nodes that have been erroneously flagged as part of the path):

$$\text{True positive} = \frac{\#\text{ of output nodes in the path}}{\#\text{ of total nodes in the path}}$$

$$\text{False positive} = \frac{\#\text{ of output nodes not in the path}}{\#\text{ of total nodes not in the path}}$$

We compared our strategy with random guessing. This represents the best adversarial strategy if NDN truly provides consumer anonymity, i.e., if the adversary can gather no information at all about consumers. We model random guessing using the urn model without replacement [10] where the number of draws q is the number of nodes identified by our strategy in the same setting. Let N be the number of nodes in the topology, and m the length of the path $P{\rightarrow}C$. The probability of choosing j nodes from the path is:

$$\mathbb{P}(j) = \frac{\binom{m}{j}\binom{N-m}{q-j}}{\binom{N}{q}} \tag{1}$$

We calculate *true_pos* for our random strategy as the expected number of nodes chosen from the path, divided by the number of nodes:

$$true\_pos = \frac{\left(\sum_{j=1}^{\min(m,q)} j \cdot \mathbb{P}(j)\right)}{m} \qquad (2)$$

Analogously, false positive are calculated as the expected number of incorrectly selected nodes $(q - j)$ divided by the number of nodes:

$$false\_pos = \frac{\left(\sum_{j=0}^{\min(m,q)} (q - j) \cdot \mathbb{P}(j)\right)}{(N - m)} \qquad (3)$$

With respect to (b), we select as baseline the average distance to the consumer in the network. In particular, we calculate the average of the distance from every node in the network to the consumer as:

$$avg = \frac{\left(\sum_{i=0}^{N} d(i)\right)}{N} \qquad (4)$$

where $d(i)$ is the distance of node i from the consumer.

We report results for paths of length 6. This length was selected since it is the most likely distance in several topologies (see Fig. 5.)

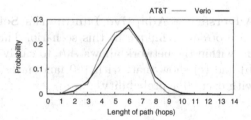

Fig. 5. Probability distribution of path lengths in the AT&T (see Fig. 2) and Verio [26] topologies.

Routing-Aware Adversary – Non-Adaptive Landmarks Selection. Results in this configuration for AT&T are reported in Fig. 6(a). Our technique is able to keep false positive very low due to the availability of routing information. It is interesting to note that the algorithm is not always able to guess all the nodes in the path, regardless of the number of landmarks used. The reason for this is that, sometimes, a router in the path cannot satisfy any interest from the landmarks because these interests can always be satisfied by other routers.

Figure 6(b) compares our strategy with random guessing. In this case, our guess for C is almost always at most two hops away from C, compared to five hops for random guessing.

Figure 6(c) shows how often our algorithm identifies the consumer. When our strategy is able to identify at least one node one hop away from the consumer node, it always identifies the consumer node. This is the case with 200 and 350 landmarks, where our strategy identifies C in the vast majority of our simulations.

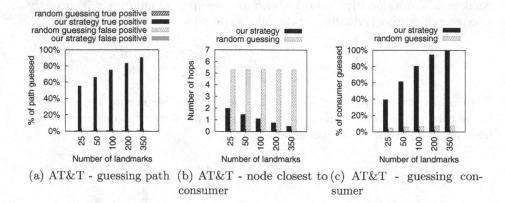

(a) AT&T - guessing path   (b) AT&T - node closest to   (c) AT&T - guessing consumer   consumer   sumer

Fig. 6. Routing aware adversary - Non-adaptive landmarks selection.

Routing-Aware-Adversary – Adaptive Landmarks Selection. Figure 7 shows the performance of our technique in this scenario. The ability to adaptively select locations within the network allows Adv to easily identify C in our topology. Figure 7(b) and (c) show that, with 100 landmarks, our algorithm is able to identify C with over 90 % probability.

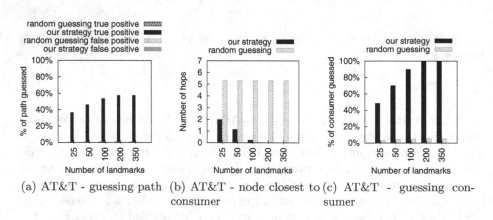

(a) AT&T - guessing path   (b) AT&T - node closest to   (c) AT&T - guessing consumer   consumer   sumer

Fig. 7. Routing aware adversary - Adaptive landmarks selection.

Non-Routing-Aware Adversary – Non-Adaptive Landmarks Selection.
Figure 8 shows performance of Listing 1.2 on AT&T with respect to false positives
and false negatives. Our experiments were performed with *threshold* and k set
respectively to 1.5 and 2. Compared to *routing aware* adversary, the number
of false positives is higher. However, overall performance is still good: Fig. 8(a)
shows that false positives are below 20 %. Similarly to the routing-aware case,
we are not able to always guess the entire path $P{\rightarrow}C$, as reported in Fig. 8(b).
A similar behavior is shown in Fig. 8(c).

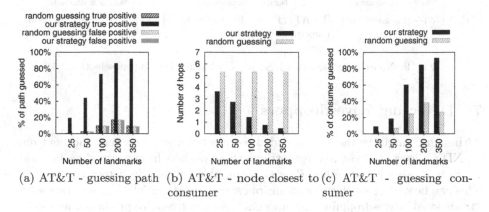

(a) AT&T - guessing path (b) AT&T - node closest to (c) AT&T - guessing con-
                              consumer   sumer

Fig. 8. Non-routing aware adversary - Non-adaptive landmarks selection.

Non-Routing-Aware Adversary – Adaptive Landmarks Selection. Performance of this scenario are reported in Fig. 9. Figure 9(a) shows that our algorithm reduces the number of false positives in the AT&T topology. This strategy
is able to significantly outperform random guessing strategy (Fig. 9(b) and (c)).

Table 1 summarizes the performance of all our strategies. We report performance of random guessing obtained under the same conditions.

Table 1. Performance of our strategies.

		Number of	% of consumer guessed	
		landmarks	Our strategy	Random guessing
Non-routing aware	Non-adaptive	350	99,3 %	7,4 %
	Adaptive	200	100 %	0,5 %
Routing aware	Non-adaptive	350	93,0 %	25,4 %
	Adaptive	350	77,1 %	19,3 %

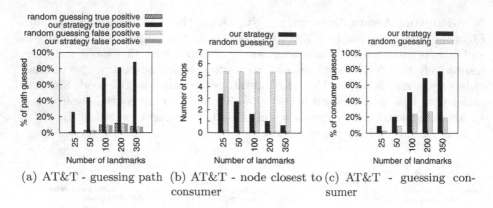

(a) AT&T - guessing path (b) AT&T - node closest to (c) AT&T - guessing con-
                              consumer   sumer

Fig. 9. Non-routing aware adversary - Adaptive landmarks selection.

7 Detecting Eavesdroppers

Although C might be the only intended recipient of a set of content packets from
P, NDN allows any host to later retrieve these packets from routers' caches and
possibly do so without either P or C being able to directly detect this action.
This can be seen as an effective means of eavesdropping in NDN: in contrast with
"traditional" eavesdropping, this approach does not require privileged access to
the networking infrastructure and can be performed independent of the geographic location of Adv with respect to P and C.

One way to detect this type of eavesdropping is by using techniques presented in this paper. For example, P and C could "rent" a set of geographically
distributed hosts while they are exchanging content packets. These rented hosts
would implement the algorithms discussed in the paper. Eavesdroppers will then
be consistently identified as extraneous consumers (other than C), and possibly
located. We envision that such a service could be easily offered by companies
such as Amazon, Microsoft, or other geographically distributed cloud providers.

8 Discussion of How to Mitigate Geo-Location Attacks

One natural approach to prevent aforementioned attacks is to simply disable
router content caching. Besides negating one of the main benefits on NDN, efficacy of this countermeasure is limited. In fact, an insider Adv that knows exact
timing of interest packets emitted by C can implement PIT-based techniques
outlined in [2]. Under normal conditions, Adv has a very small window (a few
ms to a few hundreds ms) to extract information from PIT-s on a single packet.
However, it is safe to assume that P and C exchange a large number of content
packets. This significantly simplifies the attack. Moreover, an insider Adv could
delay injecting content packets into the network upon receiving an interest. This
would force interests from C to be stored in all PITs along the path $P{\rightarrow}C$ for
longer, thus further simplifying the attack.

A better approach involves using unpredictable names [1]: P and C can initially agree on a secret seed (e.g., via authenticated Diffie-Hellman key exchange) and use it to generate pseudo-random content names. Since the seed would be known only to the two communicating parties, no outsider can guess content names. Adv therefore cannot request content, which is necessary to locate C. Unfortunately, this solution requires both P and C to be actively engaged in the secret agreement procedure. This could generate a significant (additional) load on P, and will negating the benefit of caching and interest collapsing. Furthermore, this approach is ineffective against insider Adv who knows the seed.

Another approach is to "confuse" Adv by requesting content packets from multiple geographic locations at the same time. Intuitively, since in this case there are multiple consumers, geo-location algorithms would identify many of them with roughly the same probability, offering a weak form of privacy (i.e., k-anonymity [27]) and deniability to C.

To the best of our knowledge, the only approach completely effective against attacks discussed in this paper is the anonymizing network ANDaNA [6]. ANDaNA is an NDN equivalent of Tor [28]. It allows end host to join an anonymizing network as "onion routers", which anonymize consumers' requests. Unfortunately, the additional overhead and latency might be prohibitive for many applications.

9   Conclusion

In-network content caching, a key feature of NDN, has been shown to have unexpected privacy implications [1]. In this paper, we provided another example of how abuse of network state can lead to loss of privacy in NDN. We designed several techniques geared for adversaries with varying capabilities and evaluated proposed techniques via simulations on a realistic network topology. We then used the actual NDN testbed to validate our results.

Experiments show that plausible adversaries can locate consumers with high probability, i.e., over 90% in many scenarios. Furthermore, even adversaries with relatively little knowledge of the network can successfully locate consumers with high probability, albeit, using more resources.

We then discussed several countermeasures, showing that even disabling caches on all routers does not completely prevent this attack. Moreover, the only effective countermeasure we are aware of (ANDaNA) imposes significant overhead on the communicating parties. Finally, we sketched out how the proposed techniques can help identify eavesdroppers in NDN, which is a rather unexpected outcome of router state.

We believe that the impact of our results goes beyond geo-location. NDN has been widely assumed to provide better consumer privacy than the current IP-based Internet due to lack of source/destination addresses. However, this paper casts serious doubt on this belief. Further, we argue that our geo-location techniques apply, to some extent, not only to NDN, but to any network architecture that supports ubiquitous caching.

Acknowledgments. Alberto Compagno and Luigi Vincenzo Mancini have been partially supported by the European Commission Directorate General Home Affairs, under the GAINS project, HOME/2013/CIPS/AG/4000005057, and by the European Commission H2020 SUNFISH project, N. 644666. Mauro Conti is supported by a Marie Curie Fellowship funded by the European Commission under the agreement No. PCIG11-GA-2012-321980. This work is also partially supported by the TENACE PRIN Project 20103P34XC funded by the Italian MIUR, and by the Project "Tackling Mobile Malware with Innovative Machine Learning Techniques" funded by the University of Padua. Gene Tsudik's work was supported by United States National Science Foundation (NSF) under award: CNS-1040802: FIA: Collaborative Research: Named Data Networking (NDN).

Appendix A: Testbed Measurements

Figure 10(a) and (b) show that CFT can be used to accurately estimate distance. In Fig. 10(a), we connected P to University of California, Irvine (UCI) and C to University of Arizona (UA), while in Fig. 10(b) we connect C to the University of Memphis node. Landmarks were connected to all nodes in the testbed. In both cases, 8 % of landmarks provided an incorrect distance, likely due to violation of triangle inequality. Therefore, we added "random noise" with probability 8 % in the experiments presented in this paper.

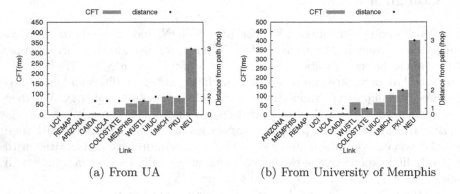

(a) From UA   (b) From University of Memphis

Fig. 10. CFT vs. distance for content published at UCI.

References

1. Acs, G., Conti, M., Gasti, P., Ghali, C., Tsudik, G.: Cache privacy in named-data networking. In: ICDCS, pp. 41–51. IEEE Computer Society (2013)
2. Ambrosin, M., Conti, M., Gasti, P., Tsudik, G.: Covert ephemeral communication in named data networking. In: AsiaCCS, pp. 15–26. ACM (2014)
3. American Registry for Internet Numbers (ARIN). https://www.arin.net/

4. CCNx protocol. http://www.ccnx.org/releases/latest/doc/technical/CCNxProto col.html
5. ChoiceNet. https://code.renci.org/gf/project/choicenet/
6. DiBenedetto, S., Gasti, P., Tsudik, G., Uzun, E.: Andana: anonymous named data networking application. In: NDSS. IEEE Computer Society (2012)
7. Donnet, B., Friedman, T.: Internet topology discovery: a survey. Commun. Surv. Tutorials 9(4), 56–69 (2007)
8. Amazon Elastic Computing Cloud (EC2). http://aws.amazon.com/ec2
9. Eriksson, B., Barford, P., Sommers, J., Nowak, R.: A learning-based approach for IP geolocation. In: Krishnamurthy, A., Plattner, B. (eds.) PAM 2010. LNCS, vol. 6032, pp. 171–180. Springer, Heidelberg (2010)
10. Friedman, B.: A simple urn model. Commun. Pure Appl. Math. 2(1), 59–70 (1949)
11. MaxMind GeoIP database. https://www.maxmind.com/
12. GeoTrace. http://www.nabber.org/projects/geotrace/
13. Gueye, B., Ziviani, A., Crovella, M., Fdida, S.: Constraint-based geolocation of internet hosts. Trans. Network. 14(6), 1219–1232 (2006)
14. Jacobson, V., Smetters, D.K., Briggs, N.H., Plass, M.F., Thornton, P.S.J.D., Braynard, R.L.: Voccn: voice-over content centric networks. In: ReArch. ACM (2009)
15. Jacobson, V., Smetters, D.K., Thornton, J.D., Plass, M.F., Briggs, N.H., Braynard, R.L.: Networking named content. In: CoNEXT, pp. 1–12. ACM (2009)
16. Katz-Bassett, E., John, J.P., Krishnamurthy, A., Wetherall, D., Anderson, T., Chawathe, Y.: Towards IP geolocation using delay and topology measurements. In: SIGCOMM IMC, pp. 71–84. ACM (2006)
17. Liu, H., Zhang, Y., Zhou, Y., Zhang, D., Fu, X., Ramakrishnan, K.: Mining check-ins from location-sharing services for client-independent ip geolocation. In: INFO-COM, pp. 619–627. IEEE (2014)
18. Lumezanu, C., Baden, R., Spring, N., Bhattacharjee, B.: Triangle inequality and routing policy violations in the internet. In: Moon, S.B., Teixeira, R., Uhlig, S. (eds.) PAM 2009. LNCS, vol. 5448, pp. 45–54. Springer, Heidelberg (2009)
19. MobilityFirst FIA Overview. http://mobilityfirst.winlab.rutgers.edu
20. Named data networking project (NDN). http://named-data.org
21. NDN testbed. http://named-data.net/ndn-testbed/
22. Nebula. http://nebula.cis.upenn.edu
23. Padmanabhan, V.N., Subramanian, L.: An investigation of geographic mapping techniques for internet hosts. SIGCOMM Comput. Comm. Rev. 31(4), 173–185 (2001)
24. Periakaruppan, R., Nemeth, E.: Gtrace - a graphical traceroute tool. In: USENIX LISA, pp. 69–78. ACM (1999)
25. Réseaux IP Européens (RIPE). http://www.ripe.net/
26. Rocketfuel. http://research.cs.washington.edu/networking/rocketfuel/
27. Sweeney, L.: k-anonymity: A model for protecting privacy. Int. J. Uncertainty Fuzziness Knowl. Based Syst. 10(5), 557–570 (2002)
28. Tor Project: Anonymity Online. https://www.torproject.org
29. Verde, N.V., Ateniese, G., Gabrielli, E., Mancini, L.V., Spognardi, A.: No nat'd user left behind: Fingerprinting users behind NAT from netflow records alone. In: ICDCS, pp. 218–227. IEEE Computer Society (2014)
30. Wang, Y., Burgener, D., Flores, M., Kuzmanovic, A., Huang, C.: Towards street-level client-independent ip geolocation. In: USENIX NSDI, pp. 365–379. USENIX Association (2011)

31. Wong, B., Stoyanov, I., Sirer, E.G.: Octant: A comprehensive framework for the geolocalization of internet hosts. In: USENIX NSDI, pp. 313–326. USENIX Association (2007)
32. XIA - eXpressive Internet Architecture. http://www.cs.cmu.edu/~xia/
33. Zhu, Z., Burke, J., Zhang, L., Gasti, P., Lu, Y., Jacobson, V.: A new approach to securing audio conference tools. In: AINTEC, pp. 120–123. ACM (2011)

Post-Quantum Forward-Secure Onion Routing
(Future Anonymity in Today's Budget)

Satrajit Ghosh[1](✉) and Aniket Kate[2]

[1] Indian Statistical Institute (ISI), Kolkata, India
satneo@gmail.com
[2] CISPA, Saarland University, Saarbrücken, Germany
aniket@mmci.uni-saarland.de

Abstract. The onion routing (OR) network Tor provides anonymity to its users by routing their encrypted traffic through three proxies (or nodes). The key cryptographic challenge, here, is to establish symmetric session keys using a secure key exchange between the anonymous user and the selected nodes. The Tor network currently employs a one-way authenticated key exchange (1W-AKE) protocol ntor for this purpose. Nevertheless, ntor as well as other known 1W-AKE protocols rely solely on some classical Diffie-Hellman (DH) type assumptions for their (forward) security, and privacy of today's anonymous communication cannot be ensured once quantum computers arrive.

In this paper, we demonstrate utility of lattice-based cryptography towards solving this problem for onion routing. In particular, we present a novel hybrid 1W-AKE protocol (HybridOR) that is secure under the lattice-based ring learning with error (ring-LWE) assumption or the gap DH assumption. Due to its hybrid design, HybridOR is not only resilient against quantum attacks but also allows the OR nodes to use the current DH public keys and subsequently requires no modification to the current Tor public key infrastructure. Moreover, thanks to the recent progress in lattice-based cryptography in the form of efficient ring-based constructions, our protocol is also computationally more efficient than the currently employed 1W-AKE protocol ntor, and it only introduces manageable communication overhead to the Tor protocol.

Keywords: Tor · Onion routing · Forward anonymity · Learning with errors · Compatibility

1 Introduction

Lattice-based cryptographic constructions have drawn an overwhelming amount of research attention in the last decade [7,35,37,40,44]. Their strong provable worst case security guarantee, apparent resistance to quantum attacks, high asymptotic efficiency and flexibility towards realizing powerful primitives (e.g., fully homomorphic encryption [21]) have been the vital reasons behind their popularity. Although the powerful primitives such as fully homomorphic encryption

© Springer International Publishing Switzerland 2015
T. Malkin et al. (Eds.): ACNS 2015, LNCS 9092, pp. 263–286, 2015.
DOI: 10.1007/978-3-319-28166-7_13

are still very far from being ideal for practical use, several recent efforts have demonstrated that performance of lattice-based constructions for basic encryption and authentication primitives is comparable with (and sometimes even better than) performance of corresponding primitives in the classical RSA or DLog settings [26,33,35]. As a result, some work has started to appear towards developing lattice-based version of real-world cryptographic protocols [6,41,49]. In this work, we explore the utility of plausibly quantum-secure yet highly efficient lattice-based cryptography to anonymous communication networks (ACNs).

Over the last three decades, several ACNs have been proposed and few implemented [11,12,16,24,42,45]. Among these, with its more than two million users and six thousand onion routing (OR) proxies spread all across the world, the OR network Tor [16,48] has turned out to be a huge success. Today, along with anonymous web browsing and service hosting, Tor is also extensively used for censorship-resistant communication [14].

A typical realization of an OR network (such as Tor) consists of an overlay network of proxies (or nodes) that routes their users' traffic to their Internet-based destinations. A user chooses an ordered sequence of OR nodes (i.e., a path) through the OR network using a path selection strategy, and constructs a cryptographic *circuit* using a public-key infrastructure (PKI) such that every node in the path shares a symmetric session key with the anonymous user. While employing the circuit to send a message anonymously to a destination, the user forms an *onion* by wrapping the message in multiple layers of symmetric encryption such that upon receiving the onion every node can decrypt (or remove) one of the layers and then forward it to the next node in the circuit.

From the cryptographic point of view, the key challenge with an OR protocol is to securely agree upon the required session keys so that a user can individually authenticate the nodes in her circuits while maintaining her anonymity (except from the first node). Since its inception, Tor employed an interactive forward-secret key-exchange protocol called the Tor authentication protocol (TAP) to agree upon those session keys in a *telescoping (or multi-pass)* construction [16]. Due to its atypical use of CPA-secure RSA encryption, TAP was considered weaker in terms of performance as well as security [23]. Recently, Goldberg, Stebila and Ustaoglu [25] formalized the OR key agreement security by introducing the concept of one-way authenticated key exchange (1W-AKE), and designed a provably secure 1W-AKE protocol called ntor. With its significantly better computation and communication efficiency, ntor has since replaced TAP in the real-world Tor implementation [15].

Security of ntor and other 1W-AKE protocols [3,10,28–30] requires some variant of Diffie–Hellman (DH) assumption in the classical discrete logarithm (DLog) setting. As the DLog problem and all of its weaker DH variants can be solved in polynomial time (in the security parameter) using quantum computers, the security of these 1W-AKE constructions and subsequently the confidentially and anonymity of the OR communications will be broken in the post-quantum world. Importantly, the current 1W-AKE protocols are also *not* forward-secure against the quantum attacks; the confidentially and anonymity of even *today's* OR communications can be violated once quantum computers arrive.

Although this raises concern regarding the privacy of today's anonymous communication in the future, making drastic modifications to the current OR infrastructure by replacing the current 1W-AKE construction with a lattice-based construction may be injudicious; e.g., in Tor, this will require completely changing the public key infrastructure (PKI). As a result, it presents an interesting challenge to define a lattice-based 1W-AKE protocol that offers forward security in the post-quantum world without significantly affecting the current cryptographic infrastructure and performance.

Our Contribution. In this paper, we resolve this challenge by presenting a novel hybrid 1W-AKE protocol (HybridOR) that combines lattice-based key exchange with the standard DH key exchange. The channel security of HybridOR relies on the (standard) ring variant of learning with error (ring-LWE) assumption or the gap Diffie–Hellman (GDH) assumption, while its forward secrecy and the security against an man-in-the-middle impersonator rely respectively on the ring-LWE assumption and the GDH assumption. Moreover, while achieving this enhanced security properties, HybridOR does not require any modifications to the current Tor public keys or directory infrastructure.

We observe that HybridOR is computationally more efficient than the currently employed ntor protocol; in particular, the efficiency improvement on both the client and the node sides is nearly 33 %. Although this improved security and efficiency comes at the cost of increased communication, both the client and the node will have to communicate three Tor cells each, which we find to be manageable for the Tor network today. Finally, along with apparent resistance to quantum attacks and the worst case security guarantee, as our HybridOR protocol is a 1W-AKE, it can also be used to realize a universally composable OR protocol [2].

2   Background

In this section, we present a brief overview of the OR protocol, the GDH assumption in the DLog setting, and describe the lattice-based learning with errors problem.

2.1   Onion Routing

In the original OR protocol [42] circuits were constructed in a non-interactive manner. In particular, a user created an onion where each layer contained a symmetric session key for an OR node and the IP address of the successor OR node in the circuit, all encrypted with the original node's public key such that each node can decrypt a layer, determine the symmetric session key and forward the rest of the onion along to the next OR node. Unless public keys are rotated frequently, this approach cannot guarantee forward security for the anonymous communication; thus, in the second generation OR network [16] (i.e., Tor), circuits are constructed incrementally and interactively, where symmetric session keys are established using a forward-secure authenticated Diffie–Hellman (DH) key exchange involving the OR node's public key. In the second generation Tor protocol, circuits are constructed using the Tor authentication protocol (TAP) involving a CPA-secure RSA encryption and a DH key exchange. Currently, the third generation Tor network employs the provably secure (against the GDH assumption [38]) and significantly more efficient ntor protocol [25].

In related efforts, Backes et al. [2] observe that, with minor modifications, universally composable (UC) security [8] is possible for the existing Tor protocol, if the employed key agreement protocol is a one-way authenticated key exchange [25].

One-Way Authenticated Key Exchange—1W-AKE. Goldberg et al. introduce a security definition of (one-way anonymous) one-way authenticated key exchanges (1W-AKE) to facilitate design of provably secure session key agreement protocols for onion routing [25]. (See Sect. 3 for a complete 1W-AKE definition.)

They also fixed a key agreement protocol proposed in [39] to obtain a provably secure construction called the ntor protocol, which has replaced the TAP protocol in the current Tor network. In ntor, the client sends a fresh ephemeral key g^x to the node. The node computes and sends a fresh ephemeral key g^y to the client and calculates the session key as $H((g^x)^y, (g^x)^b)$, where b is the long term secret key of the node.

Recently, Backes, Kate, and Mohammadi [3] introduced a 1W-AKE protocol Ace that improves upon the computational efficiency of ntor. In Ace the client sends two fresh ephemeral keys g^{x_1} and g^{x_2} to the node. The node sends one fresh ephemeral key g^y to the client. The client and node compute the shared secret as $g^{x_1 b + x_2 y} = (g^b)^{x_1}(g^y)^{x_2} = (g^{x_1})^b(g^{x_2})^y$. The source of efficiency in Ace comes from the fact that one can do two exponentiations at the same time using a multi-exponentiation trick. (See Fig. 3 in Appendix A for a pictorial illustration of ntor and Ace.)

In contrast to the above interactive 1W-AKE protocol, a single-pass construction using a non-interactive key exchange is possible as well. However, achieving forward secrecy without regularly rotating the PKI keys for all Tor nodes is not possible [30], and periodic public key rotation should be avoided for scalability reasons. There have been attempts to solve this problem in the identity-based cryptography setting [30] or the certificate-less cryptography setting [10]. Nevertheless, as discussed in [2], key authorities required in these constructions can be difficult to implement in practice.

2.2 Gap Diffie-Hellman—GDH

Let $\mathbb{G}$ be a multiplicative group with large prime order p and $g \in \mathbb{G}$ be the generator of the group. Given a triple (g, g^a, g^b) for $a, b \in_r \mathbb{Z}_p^*$, the gap version of Diffie-Hellman (GDH) problem is to find the element g^{ab} with the help of a Decision Diffie-Hellman (DDH) oracle [38]. The DDH oracle $\mathcal{O}^{ddh}$ takes input as (G, g, g^a, g^b, z) for some $z \in \mathbb{G}$ and tells whether $z = g^{ab}$ or not, that is whether the tuple is a DH tuple or not. For the security parameter λ, solving GDH problem in $\mathbb{G}$ is assumed to be a hard problem. More formally,

Definition 1 (GDH Assumption). *For all algorithm A, the advantage of solving GDH in the group G is defined as,*

$$Adv_A^{gdh} = \Pr[A^{\mathcal{O}^{ddh}}(p, g, g^a, g^b) = g^{ab}, (a, b) \in_r \mathbb{Z}_p^{*2}].$$

The GDH assumption states that Adv_A^{gdh} is a negligible function of the security parameter λ for all PPT algorithms A.

2.3 Learning with Errors—LWE

Learning with errors (LWE) is a problem of distinguishing noisy random linear equations from truly random ones, for a small amount of noise. It has been shown to be as hard as some worst case lattice problems [44], and its different variants have been employed in designing lattice-based cryptosystems [34,36,43, 44]. The main drawback of schemes based on LWE [44] is that they are based on matrix operations, which are quite inefficient and result in large key sizes. To overcome these problems, in last few years, special lattices with additional algebraic structures are used to construct cryptographic protocols.

LWE for Polynomial Ring. To reduce computation, communication and storage complexity, Lyubashevsky [35] propose an algebraic variant of LWE, *ring-LWE*, the problem is defined over a polynomial ring.

Let $\mathbb{Z}_q$ be the set of integers from $\lfloor -q/2 \rfloor$ to $\lfloor q/2 \rfloor$, and let $\mathbb{Z}[x]$ be the set of polynomials with coefficients in $\mathbb{Z}$. Consider $f(x) = x^n + 1 \in \mathbb{Z}[x]$, where the degree of the polynomial $n \geq 1$ is a power of 2, which makes $f(x)$ irreducible over the $\mathbb{Z}$. Let $R = \mathbb{Z}[x]/\langle f(x) \rangle$ be the ring of integer polynomials modulo $f(x)$ such that elements of R can be represented by integer polynomials of degree less than n. Let $q \equiv 1 \mod 2n$ be a sufficiently large public prime modulus (bounded by a polynomial in n), and let $R_q = \mathbb{Z}_q[x]/\langle f(x) \rangle$ be the ring of integer polynomials modulo both $f(x)$ and q. The ring R_q contains all the polynomials of degree less than n with coefficient in $\mathbb{Z}_q$, along with two operations, polynomial addition and multiplication modulo $f(x)$.

Let χ be the error distribution over R, which is concentrated on *small* elements of R. See [35] for details of the error distribution for the security and the correctness of the system. We denote $\mathbb{D}_{s,\chi}$ as the ring-LWE distribution over R_q^2, obtained by choosing uniformly random $a \leftarrow R_q$ and $e \leftarrow \chi$, and outputs $(a, a \cdot r + e)$ for some $r \leftarrow R_q$.

Decision ring-LWE Problem. The decision version of ring-LWE is to distinguish between two distributions, $\mathbb{D}_{s,\chi}$, for uniformly random $s \leftarrow R_q$ and a uniformly random distribution in $R_q \times R_q$ (denoted by $U_{R_q \times R_q}$), given a $poly(n)$ number of independent samples. More formally,

Definition 2 (Decision ring-LWE Assumption). *The decision ring-LWE problem for n, q, χ is to distinguish the output of $\mathcal{O}^{\mathbb{D}_{s,\chi}}$ oracle from the output*

of an oracle $U_{R_q \times R_q}$ that returns uniform random samples from $R_q \times R_q$. If A is an algorithm, the advantage of A is defined as

$$Adv_A^{drlwe} = |\Pr[A^{\mathcal{O}^{\mathbb{D}_{s,\chi}}}(\cdot)] - \Pr[A^{\mathcal{O}^{U_{R_q \times R_q}}}(\cdot)]|.$$

The decision ring-LWE assumption states that for given values of n, q, and χ, for every PPT adversary A, Adv_A^{drlwe} is negligible in the security parameter λ.

The hardness results for the LWE problem are described in [35,40,44]. Brakerski et al. [7] show the classical hardness of the LWE problem. Ding et al. [13] mention that for any $t \in \mathbb{Z}^+$, such that $gcd(t, q) = 1$, the LWE assumption still holds if we choose $b = \langle \mathbf{a}, \mathbf{r} \rangle + te$. We use $t = 2$ for our construction.

It is important to note that ring-LWE samples are pseudorandom even when the secret r is chosen from the error distribution [1,37]. Ducas et al. [17] show that the ring-LWE problem is hard in any ring $\mathbb{Z}[x]/\langle \Phi_m \rangle$, for any cyclotomic polynomial $\Phi_m(x)$.

Robust Extractors. One of the important problems with the lattice-based key exchange protocols is the error correction (or reconciliation) of the shared secret. In literature, there are different methods [13,20] to agree on a shared secret from noisy shared secret values. For our construction we adopt the method due to Ding et al. [13] and recall the corresponding concept of robust extractors and the signal functions below.

Definition 3 (Robust Extractors). *An algorithm $f(\cdot)$ is a robust extractor on $\mathbb{Z}_q$ with error tolerance δ with respect to a hint function $h(\cdot)$ if:*

- *$f(\cdot)$ takes an input $x \in \mathbb{Z}_q$ and a signal $\alpha \in \{0, 1\}$, and outputs $k = f(x, \alpha) \in \{0, 1\}$.*
- *$h(\cdot)$ takes an input $y \in \mathbb{Z}_q$ and outputs a signal value $\alpha = h(y) \in \{0, 1\}$.*
- *$f(x, \alpha) = f(y, \alpha)$, for any $x, y \in \mathbb{Z}_q$, such that $(x - y)$ is even and $|x - y| \leq \delta$, where $\alpha = h(y)$.*

We use the robust extractor as described in [13]. For $q > 2$ define $\alpha_0 : \mathbb{Z}_q \to \{0, 1\}$ and $\alpha_1 : \mathbb{Z}_q \to \{0, 1\}$ as follows:

$$\alpha_0(x) = \begin{cases} 0, & \text{if } x \in [-\lfloor \frac{q}{4} \rfloor, \lfloor \frac{q}{4} \rfloor]; \\ 1, & \text{otherwise.} \end{cases} \quad \alpha_1(x) = \begin{cases} 0, & \text{if } x \in [-\lfloor \frac{q}{4} \rfloor + 1, \lfloor \frac{q}{4} \rfloor + 1]; \\ 1, & \text{otherwise.} \end{cases}$$

The hint algorithm $h(\cdot)$ generates the signal α for some $y \in \mathbb{Z}_q$ by tossing a random coin $b \leftarrow \{0, 1\}$ and computing $\alpha = h(y) = \alpha_b(y)$. Finally the robust extractor computes the common value as:

$$f(x, \alpha) = (x + \alpha \cdot \frac{q-1}{2} \mod q) \mod 2,$$

where $x \in \mathbb{Z}_q, |x - y| \leq \delta$ and $x - y$ is even. In [13], the authors prove that $f(\cdot)$ is a randomness extractor with respect to $h(\cdot)$ for an odd integer $q > 8$ with error tolerance $\delta = \frac{q}{4} - 2$. Also if x is uniformly random in $\mathbb{Z}_q$, then $f(x, \alpha)$ is uniform in $\{0, 1\}$, where $\alpha = h(x)$.

It is easy to extend this notion for ring settings. Any element in R_q can be represented by a degree $n-1$ polynomial. For example any $a \in R_q$ can be written in the form $a_0 + a_1 x + \cdots + a_{n-1} x^{n-1}$. In that case the extractor can extract n bits from an element of R_q. We extend $\alpha_0^R(a), \alpha_1^R(a) : R_q \rightarrow R_2$ as follows:

$$\alpha_0^R(a) = \sum_{i=0}^{n-1} \alpha_0(a_i) x^i; \quad \alpha_1^R(a) = \sum_{i=0}^{n-1} \alpha_1(a_i) x^i.$$

The algorithm $h^R(\cdot)$ can be defined in the same manner as $h^R(a) = \alpha_b^R(a)$, for $b \leftarrow \{0, 1\}$. Similarly define the extractor in the ring settings $f^R(a, \alpha) : R_q \rightarrow R_2$ as:

$$f^R(a, \alpha) = (a + \alpha \cdot \frac{q-1}{2} \mod q) \mod 2.$$

Authenticated Key Exchange in the Lattice Setting. Fujioka et al. [19] provide the first CK^+ secure [9,19,31] authenticated key exchange (AKE) protocol from a key-encapsulation mechanism (KEM) based on ring-LWE problem in the standard model. However due to the huge communication cost (≈ 139625 bytes) their lattice-based AKE is not suitable for real-world applications. In [20], Fujioka et al. propose a generic construction for AKE from OW-CCA KEMs in random oracle model. When instantiated with ring-LWE settings, their AKE protocol gives a much more efficient solution to the problem. Still, communication cost for [20] reaches about 10075 bytes. Peikert [41] proposes a new low-bandwidth error correction technique for ring-LWE based key exchange, and provides practical lattice based protocols for key transport and AKE. Ding et al. [13] propose another method for error correction and design a passively secure DH-like key exchange scheme based on both the LWE and the ring-LWE problem. Zhang et al. [49] extend the above AKE protocol to ideal lattice settings, and their lattice-based AKE protocol gives weak perfect forward secrecy in the Bellare-Rogaway model [4]. Recently Bos et al. [6] demonstrate the practicality of using ring-LWE based key exchange protocols in real life systems. They employ lattice-based key exchange in TLS protocol. Their implementation reveals that the performance price for switching from pre-quantum-safe to post-quantum-safe key exchange is not too high and can already be considered practical, which further motivates our efforts towards defining a 1W-AKE protocol in the lattice setting.

3   1W-AKE Security Definition

Goldberg et al. [25] define the security requirements for a one-way authenticated key exchange (1W-AKE) protocol, which are refined in [3]. In this section we recall the security requirements for a 1W-AKE protocol between an anonymous client and an authenticated node.

A 1W-AKE protocol is a tuple of ppt algorithms (SetUp, Init, Resp, CompKey), where SetUp generates the system parameters and the static long-term keys for the node. The client calls Init to initiate the 1W-AKE protocol and the node uses Resp to respond to an Init. Finally, the client uses CompKey to verify the key-confirmation message and compute the key. We assume that a PKI is given, that means for a node N all parties $\{P_1, \ldots, P_m\}$ can obtain a certified public key pk_N.

Along with protocol correctness, a secure 1W-AKE protocol should respect the following properties:

1W-AKE Security. An attacker should not learn anything about the session key of an uncompromised session, even if it completely compromises several other sessions, introduces fake identities or even learn some uncompromised session secret.

1W-anonymity. A node should not be distinguish between communicating with two different clients.

3.1   Correctness

In a 1W-AKE protocol an anonymous client (denoted by ⊛) tries to establish a shared secret key with a node N. The client calls Init(N, pk_N, cs), which returns

---

upon send^P($params, N$):
  $(m, st, \Psi) \leftarrow$ Init$(N, params, cs)$
  $ake\_st^P(\Psi) \leftarrow (N, st)$; send (m, Ψ)

upon send$^P(\Psi, m)$ and $ake\_st^P(\Psi) = \perp$:
  $(m', (k, \star, st), \Psi) \leftarrow$ Resp(sk_P, P, m, cs);

  $result\_st^P(\Psi) \leftarrow (k, st, \star)$; send m'

upon send$^P(\Psi, m)$ and $ake\_st^P(\Psi) \neq \perp$:
  $(N, st) \leftarrow ake\_st^P(\Psi)$; check for a valid pk_N
  $(k, N, st) \leftarrow$ CompKey$(pk_N, m, \Psi, (N, st))$

  erase $ake\_st^P(\Psi)$; $result\_st^P(\Psi) \leftarrow (k, N, st)$

upon reveal_next^P:
  $(x, X) \leftarrow$ Gen(1^λ); append (x, X) to cs; send X

upon partner$^P(X)$:
  if a key pair (x, X) is in the memory then send x

upon sk_reveal$^P(\Psi)$:
  if $result\_st^P(\Psi) = (k, N, st)$ then send k

upon establish_certificate(N, pk_N):
  register the public key pk_N for the party N

upon test$^P(\Psi)$: (one time query)
  $(k, N, st) \leftarrow result\_st^P(\Psi)$
  if $k \neq \perp$ and $N \neq \star$ and Ψ is 1W-AKE fresh then
    if $b = 1$ then send k else send $k' \leftarrow_R \{0, 1\}^{|k|}$

Fig. 1. W-AKE Security Challenger: $\mathsf{Ch}_b^{\text{KE}}(1^\lambda)$, where λ is the security parameter. If any invocation outputs $\perp$, the challenger erases all session-specific information for that session and aborts that session. [3]

an output message m, session id Ψ and session state st. The client sends m to N. Init takes a queue cs as input, where cs stores already chosen keys. If cs is empty then Init generates a fresh output message m. In response, N runs $\mathsf{Resp}(sk_N, N, m, cs)$ and outputs $(m', (k, \circledast, \overrightarrow{v}), \Psi_N)$, where m' is the response message to the client, k is the session key computed by N, and $\overrightarrow{v}$ contains ephemeral public keys for the session Ψ_N. On receiving m', the client computes $(k', N, \overrightarrow{v}')$ by calling $\mathsf{CompKey}(pk_N, m', \Psi, st)$, where k' is the session key computed by the client and $\overrightarrow{v}'$ is the list of ephemeral public keys. An 1W-AKE protocol is correct if for every party N:

$$\Pr[(m, st, \Psi) \leftarrow \mathsf{Init}(N, pk_N, cs), (m', (k, \circledast, \overrightarrow{v}), \Psi_N) \leftarrow \mathsf{Resp}(sk_N, N, m, cs),$$
$$(k', N, \overrightarrow{v}') \leftarrow \mathsf{CompKey}(pk_N, m', \Psi, st) : k = k' \wedge \overrightarrow{v} = \overrightarrow{v}')] = 1.$$

3.2   1W-AKE Security

The goal of the adversary in the 1W-AKE security experiment is to distinguish the session key of an uncompromised session from a random key. It requires an active attacker to not learn anything about the key or be able to impersonate an honest node.

In the security game, a challenger $\mathsf{Ch}^{\mathrm{KE}}$ represents honest parties $(P_1, \ldots, P_m)$ and allows the attacker a fixed set of queries described in Fig. 1. The challenger internally runs the 1W-AKE algorithm, and simulates each party. For the challenge, the adversary asks $\mathsf{Ch}^{\mathrm{KE}}$ for the session key of an uncompromised session Ψ for a party P by querying $test^P(\Psi)$ (one time query). $\mathsf{Ch}^{\mathrm{KE}}$ sends the correct session key or a randomly chosen session key to the attacker with equal probability. The attacker's task is to determine whether the given key corresponds to the real session Ψ or is random.

For triggering the initiation session, triggering the response to a key exchange, and for completing a key exchange, the challenger allows the adversary to query $send^P(\cdot, m)$. For the compromising parties, the attacker can ask the following queries:

- $\mathsf{reveal\_next}^P$: ask the party P to reveal the next public key that will be chosen.
- $\mathsf{partner}^P(X)$: ask for the secret key for a public key X.
- $\mathsf{sk\_reveal}^P(\Psi)$: ask for the session key of a session Ψ.
- $\mathsf{establish\_certificate}(N, pk_N)$: register new long-term public keys pk_N for an unused identity N.

The challenger maintains several variables for each party P:

- $params$ stores public parameters for the AKE protocol.
- $ake\_st^P(\Psi)$ stores the key exchange state for the party P in the session Ψ. It contains ephemeral keys that will be deleted after the completion of the key exchange.
- $result\_st^P(\Psi)$ stores the resulting state for the party P for a completed session Ψ. This result state contains the established session key k, the identity of the peer party, which is $\circledast$ if the peer is anonymous, otherwise the identity of the peer.

A state st that typically contains two vectors $\vec{v_0}, \vec{v_1}$ that contain the ephemeral and the long-term public keys used for establishing the session key of Ψ.

The attacker is a **partner** of a public key X if one of the following conditions hold:

- X has not been used yet.
- X is the public key that the attacker registered using a `establish_certificate`(N,X) query.
- X was the response of a `send`^{P} or `reveal_next`^{P} query and there is a successive query `partner`$^P(X)$.

In order to prevent the attacker from trivially winning the game, Goldberg et al. [25] propose the *freshness* notion for the challenge session. A challenge session is *1W-AKE fresh* if the following conditions hold:

1. Let $(k, N, st) = result\_st^P(\Psi)$. For every vector $\vec{v_i}$ in st there is at least one element X in $\vec{v_i}$ such that the attacker is not a **partner** of X.
2. If $ake\_st^P(\Psi) = (\vec{v}, N)$ for the challenge session Ψ, the adversary did not issue `sk_reveal`$^N(\Psi')$, for any Ψ' such that $ake\_st^N(\Psi') = (\vec{v}, \circledast)$.

After a successful key exchange with a party N, an anonymous client outputs a tuple $(k, N, \vec{v_0}, \vec{v_1})$, where k is the session key. $\vec{v_0}, \vec{v_1}$ is the transcript of the protocol. The node N outputs $(k, \circledast, \vec{v_0}, \vec{v_1})$ to denote that the peer party is anonymous.

Definition 4 (1W-AKE Security). *Let λ be a security parameter and let the number of parties $m \geq 1$. A protocol π is said to be 1W-AKE secure if, for all probabilistic polynomial time (ppt) adversaries A, the advantage $Adv_A^{1w\text{-}ake}(\pi, \lambda, m)$ that A distinguishes a session of a 1W-AKE fresh session from a randomly chosen session key is negligible in λ, where $Adv_A^{1w\text{-}ake}(\pi, \lambda, m)$ is defined as:*

$$Adv_A^{1w\text{-}ake}(\pi, \lambda, m) = |Pr(A(trans(\pi), k) = 1) - Pr(A(trans(\pi), k') = 1|,$$

where $trans(\pi)$ is the transcript of the protocol, k is the real session key and k' is the random session key.

Forward Secrecy. In key exchange forward secrecy ensures that a session key derived from long-term keys remains secret even if the long-term keys are compromised in the future. A 1W-AKE secure protocol provides forward secrecy if the long-term public keys of the participating parties appear in the output vector of the protocol [25]. In that case the adversary can be **partner** with a long-term public key, ensuring forward secrecy in the security game.

3.3   One-Way Anonymity

The purpose of one-way anonymity is that an adversary (even a node) cannot guess which client is participating in the key exchange. The client always knows that it is participating in a key exchange protocol with the node, but from the node's point of view (or from the point of view of other nodes), the participating client must be anonymous. The proof for the 1W-anonymity property of our protocol is exactly the same as the proof of the 1W-anonymity of ntor [25], and we refer the reader to [25] for the security definition and 1W-anonymity proof.

4   Our Protocol

In this section we describe the HybridOR protocol, a hybrid lattice-based onion routing protocol. We call this protocol hybrid as the long-term part of the key comes from a DH key exchange, whereas the ephemeral part of the key comes from a lattice based key exchange. Hence the security of the protocol essentially depends on the hard problems in either setting, namely the hardness of the GDH problem from the DLog setting or the hardness of the ring-LWE problem from the lattice-based setting.

In our HybridOR protocol, The client generates fresh ephemeral keys $p_C \in R_q$ and $g^x \in \mathbb{G}$ and sends them to the node. The node generates a fresh ephemeral key $p_N \in R_q$ and computes $k_{1N} = p_C r_N + t e'_N \approx a r_C r_N$, a signal value $\alpha = h^R(k_{1N})$. The node sends p_N and α to the client. The client computes $k_{1C} = p_N r_C + t r'_C \approx a r_C r_N$. Recall that $t = 2$. The client and node *approximately agree* on the shared secret value k_{1C} and k_{1N}. To achieve *exact agreement* on the shared secret from the approximate shared secret, the robust extractor $f^R(\cdot)$ is used. The client and node compute the shared secret k_1, k_2, and sk as follows:

$$k_1 = f^R(k_{1N}, \alpha), \ \ k_2 = (g^x)^s, \ \ sk = H_1(k_1) \oplus H_2(k_2) \ \text{(node-side)}$$
$$k_1 = f^R(k_{1C}, \alpha), \ \ k_2 = (g^s)^x, \ \ sk = H_1(k_1) \oplus H_2(k_2) \ \text{(client-side)}$$

4.1   Construction

Figure 2 provides a detailed description of the HybridOR protocol. The node N runs the SetUp algorithm (see Sect. 2.1) to generate the system parameters. In HybridOR the SetUp algorithm can be seen as a combination of two separate SetUp algorithms. One part generates the system parameters for the DH-like key exchange (as in [3,25]) and the other part generates the parameters for the lattice based settings (as in [13]).

The SetUp algorithm generates a group $\mathbb{G}$ with large prime order p, where the GDH [38] problem is hard. Let $g \in \mathbb{G}$ be the generator of the group. The *Setup* algorithm further generates the public parameters for the lattice based settings as described in Sect. 2.3. It publishes the dimension n, the prime modulus q, the description of the ring R and the error distribution χ in the public parameter.

The node samples $a \leftarrow R_q$ and $s \leftarrow \mathbb{Z}_p^*$, computes g^s, and publishes $(R, n, q, t, \chi, a, G, g, g^s)$ as the public parameter of the protocol. where g^s is the long term public key of the node with s as the secret key. The node also publishes $H_{st}(\cdot), H_1(\cdot), H_2(\cdot)$ and a $PRF(\cdot)$ in the public parameter, where $H_{st}(\cdot)$ is a collision-resistant hash function, $H_1(\cdot)$ is a randomness extractor and $H_2(\cdot)$ is

---

SetUp(N, λ):

1. For the security parameter λ, generate system parameters (R, n, q, t, χ) and $(\mathbb{G}, g, p)$.
2. Sample $a \leftarrow R_q$.
3. Sample $s \leftarrow \mathbb{Z}_p^*$ and compute g^s.
4. Output (a, g^s) as public key, and s as secret key.

Init($(a, g^s), N$):

1. Sample $(r_C, e_C) \in \chi$ and $x \leftarrow \mathbb{Z}_p^*$.
2. Generate ephemeral key pairs $(r_C, p_C = ar_C + te_C)$ and (x, g^x).
3. Set session id $\Psi_C \leftarrow H_{st}(p_C, g^x)$.
4. Update $st(\Psi_C) \leftarrow (\text{HybOR}, N, r_C, p_C, x, g^x)$.
5. Set $m_C \leftarrow (\text{HybOR}, N, p_C, g^x)$.
6. Output m_C, Ψ_C.

Resp($(a, g^s), s, p_C, g^x$):

1. Sample $(r_N, e_N, e_N') \in \chi$.
2. Generate an ephemeral key pair $(r_N, p_N = ar_N + te_N)$.
3. Compute $k_{1N} = p_C r_N + te_N'$ and $\alpha = h^R(k_{1N})$.
4. Set session id $\Psi_N \leftarrow H_{st}(p_N, \alpha)$.
5. Compute $k_1 = f^R(k_{1N}, \alpha)$ and $k_2 = (g^x)^s$.
6. Compute $(sk_m, sk) \leftarrow H_1(k_1, p_C, p_N, N, \text{HybOR}) \oplus H_2(k_2, g^x, g^s, N, \text{HybOR})$.
7. Compute $t_N = PRF(sk_m, N, p_N, \alpha, p_C, g^x, \text{HybOR}, \text{node})$.
8. Set $m_N \leftarrow (\text{HybOR}, p_N, \alpha, t_N)$.
9. Erase r_N and output m_N.

CompKey($(a, g^s), \Psi_C, t_N, p_N, \alpha$):

1. Retrieve N, r_C, p_C, x, g^x from $st(\Psi_C)$ if it exists.
2. Compute $k_{1C} = p_N r_C + te_C$.
3. Compute $k_1 = f^R(k_{1C}, \alpha)$ and $k_2 = (g^s)^x$.
4. Compute $(sk_m, sk) \leftarrow H_1(k_1, p_C, p_N, N, \text{HybOR}) \oplus H_2(k_2, g^x, g^s, N, \text{HybOR})$.
5. Verify $t_N = PRF(sk_m, N, p_N, \alpha, p_C, g^x, \text{HybOR}, \text{node})$.
6. Erase $st(\Psi_C)$ and output sk.

If any verification fails, the party erases all session-specific information and aborts.

Fig. 2. A detailed description of the HybridOR protocol

a random oracle. The $PRF(\cdot)$ is a pseudorandom function that is used to generate the key confirmation message. Note that according to [18], we instantiate a randomness extractor with HMAC. However, we can also use the key derivation function HKDF [32] to instantiate H_1.

To initiate a new key exchange session the anonymous client C calls the Init algorithm. Init randomly samples r_C and e_C from the error distribution χ and x from $\mathbb{Z}_p^*$. It computes the ephemeral key pair as $pk_C = (p_C, g^x)$ and $sk_C = (r_C, x)$, where $p_C = ar_C + te_C \mod q$. Init sets the local session identifier as $\psi_C = H_{st}(p_C, g^x)$, where H_{st} is a collision-resistant hash function. The session information of the client is stored in the variable $st(\psi)$ as $st(\psi_C) = (\text{HybOR}, N, r_C, p_C, x, g^x)$. Init generates the outgoing message $m_C = (\text{HybOR}, N, p_C, g^x)$, and sends (ψ_C, m_C) to the node N over the network.

In response to the message the node runs Resp, which verifies whether $p_C \in R_q$ and $g^x \in \mathbb{G}$. On successful verification it randomly samples r_N and e_N from the error distribution χ and computes $p_N = ar_N + te_N \mod q$. Resp outputs the ephemeral key pair (p_N, r_N), where p_N is the public part and r_N remains secret to the node. Resp further samples $e'_N \leftarrow \chi$ and computes $k_{1N} = p_C r_N + te'_N \mod q$ and $\alpha = h^R(k_{1N})$. $h^R(\cdot)$ is a randomized algorithm used to generate the signal value α, as described in Sect. 2.3. To ensure the correctness of the shared secret computation, N sends α to the client [13]. The node computes the short-term shared secret (k_1) and the long-term shared secret (k_2) as:

$$k_1 = f^R(k_{1N}, \alpha), \quad k_2 = (g^x)^s = g^{xs},$$

where $f^R(\cdot)$ is the robust extractor as defined in Sect. 2.3. By short-term shared secret we mean the shared secret computed using the client's ephemeral key and node's ephemeral key. By long-term shared secret we mean the shared secret computed by using the client's ephemeral key and node's long-term or static key.

The node computes the session key sk, the PRF key sk_m and the key confirmation message t_N as:

$$(sk_m, sk) = H_1(k_1, p_C, p_N, N, \mathsf{HybOR}) \oplus H_2(k_2, g^x, g^s, N, \mathsf{HybOR})$$
$$t_N = PRF(sk_m, N, p_N, \alpha, p_C, g^x, \mathsf{HybOR}, \mathsf{node}).$$

The tag t_N provides only a means for the key confirmation. Resp returns the session identifier $\psi_N = H_{st}(p_N, \alpha)$ and a message $m_N = (\mathsf{HybOR}, p_N, \alpha, t_N)$. The node sends (ψ_N, m_N) to the client. The node completes the session by deleting (r_N, e_N, e'_N) and outputting $(sk, \circledast, (\overrightarrow{v_0}, \overrightarrow{v_1}))$, where $\overrightarrow{v_0} = \{p_C, g^x\}$ and $\overrightarrow{v_1} = \{p_N, g^s\}$. $\circledast$ denotes that the identity of the client is not known to the node.

On receiving the message (ψ_N, m_N) for the session ψ_C, the client C calls the algorithm CompKey to compute the session key. CompKey first checks whether the session ψ_C is active; if so, it retrieves the required session information, namely r_C, p_C, x, g^x from $st(\psi_C)$. Then it checks whether $p_N \in R_q$. After successful verification CompKey computes the shared secrets k_1, k_2 as follows:

$$k_{1C} = p_N r_C + te_C \mod q,$$
$$k_1 = f^R(k_{1C}, \alpha), \quad k_2 = (g^s)^x = g^{xs}.$$

The client computes $(sk_m, sk) = H_1(k_1, p_C, p_N, N, \mathsf{HybOR}) \oplus H_2(k_2, g^x, g^s, N, \mathsf{HybOR})$, where sk is the session key and sk_m is the PRF key. It verifies the key-confirmation message t_N using the key sk_m. After that the client completes the session ψ_C by deleting $st(\psi_C)$ and outputting $(sk, N, (\overrightarrow{v_0}, \overrightarrow{v_1}))$, where $\overrightarrow{v_0} = \{p_C, g^x\}$ and $\overrightarrow{v_1} = \{p_N, g^s\}$. If any verification fails during the session execution, the party erases all session-specific information and aborts the session.

In Fig. 3 in Appendix A, we compare HybridOR with the ntor and Ace protocols in the literature.

Correctness. To analyze the correctness of HybridOR, we can see HybridOR as a combination of two key exchange protocols, namely the Diffie-Hellman key exchange protocol and the lattice-based protocol by Ding et al. [13]. Hence the correctness of HybridOR directly follows from the correctness of DH key exchange and the correctness of the lattice-based protocol [13].

For the DH part, the node computes $(g^x)^s = g^{xs}$ and the client computes $(g^s)^x = g^{xs}$. Further, both client and node computes $H_2(g^{xs}, g^x, g^s, N, \text{HybOR})$. For the lattice part the node computes $k_{1N} = p_C r_N + t e'_N \approx a r_C r_N$ and the client computes $k_{1C} = p_N r_C + t e_C \approx a r_C r_N$. The node also computes $\alpha = h^R(k_{1N})$ and sends it to the client. The client and node use α to make sure that the shared secret k_1 computed from k_{1N} (for the node) and k_{1C} (for the client) do not produce different results in modulo operation. They use the robust extractor $f^R(\cdot)$ (see Sect. 2.3) and compute $k_1 = f^R(k_{1N}, \alpha) = f^R(k_{1C}, \alpha)$. More details of the robust extractor can be found in [13]. After computing the shared secret k_1 the client and node both computes $H_1(k_1, p_C, p_N, N, \text{HybOR})$. Further, from both parts of the shared secret they compute the session key and PRF key for the protocol as $(sk_m, sk) = H_1(k_1, p_C, p_N, N, \text{HybOR}) \oplus H_2(g^{xs}, g^x, g^s, N, \text{HybOR})$.

5   Security Analysis

5.1   Type of Adversary

To analyze the 1W-AKE security of our protocol, we consider three types of 1W-AKE adversaries. We classify the type of adversary depending on the power of the adversary in the test session. For all other sessions the adversary can be partner to any public values, after respecting the freshness condition of the 1W-AKE security game.

Type-I Adversary. The first type of adversary cannot be partner to any of the public values in the test session. By proving security against this kind of adversary we show that an active adversary without the knowledge of any secret values used in the test session cannot learn anything about the session key.

Type-II Adversary. The second type of adversary can be the partner with only the ephemeral public key from a node N in the test session. By proving the security against this kind of adversary we give the security guarantee of the protocol against a man-in-the-middle adversary trying to impersonate the node N to the client.

Type-III Adversary. The third type of adversary can be partner with only the long term public key in the test session. This gives the guarantee of forward security of the protocol; i.e., even if some information about the long-term private key is known to the adversary, the adversary cannot learn any information about the already created session key.

5.2   Security Against Type-I Adversary

We show that HybridOR is secure against Type-I adversary under either the GDH or the ring-LWE assumption. The motivation of this security theorem is to show that even if the ring-LWE assumption or the GDH assumption (but not both) is broken, HybridOR remains secure against Type-I adversary.

Theorem 1. *The protocol* HybridOR *is 1W-AKE secure against a PPT Type-I adversary under the GDH or the ring-LWE assumption, considering H_1 as randomness extractor and H_2 as random oracle. More precisely, for any PPT Type-I adversary A,*

$$Adv_A^{1w\text{-}ake} \leq \min(Adv_{A \circ B_{0,1}}^{drlwe} + Adv_{A \circ B_{1,2}}^{drlwe}, Adv_{A \circ B'}^{GDH}),$$

where $B_{0,1}$, $B_{1,2}$ and B' are the reduction algorithms as described in the proof.

Proof. To prove the security against a Type-I adversary, first we define a sequence of three games G_0 to G_2. Let E_i be the event that the adversary guesses bit b^* in game G_i.

G_0: This is the original 1W-AKE security game, where the reduction algorithm B generates all the public values honestly in all the sessions.

G_1: This game is identical to G_0, except here p_C is generated uniformly at random in the *test* session.

G_2: This game is similar to G_1, except here p_N is generated uniformly at random in the *test* session and also the *test* session secret k_1 is generated uniformly at random.

As G_0 is the real 1W-AKE game, we can bound $\Pr(E_0)$ as

$$Adv_A^{1w\text{-}ake} = |\Pr(E_0) - 1/2|. \tag{1}$$

Lemma 1. *No PPT Type-I adversary can distinguish between G_0 and G_1 under the decision ring-LWE assumption, if H_1 is a randomness extractor and H_2 is a random oracle.*

Proof. If there exists a PPT Type-I adversary A that can distinguish between G_0 and G_1, then we can construct a PPT reduction algorithm $B_{0,1}$ that can efficiently distinguish between tuples from a ring-LWE distribution and a uniform distribution.

In G_0, (a, p_C) are samples from a ring-LWE distribution, such that $p_C = ar_C + te_C$. In G_1, (a, p_C) are samples from a uniform distribution over $R_q \times R_q$. Under the decisional ring-LWE assumption these two distributions are indistinguishable.

Solving Decision ring-LWE. To simulate the 1W-AKE challenger for A the reduction algorithm $B_{0,1}$ guesses ψ_i to be the *test* session. In the *test* session it honestly generates $(\mathbb{G}, g, g^x, g^s)$. $B_{0,1}$ also takes a pair (a_0, u_0) from the ring-LWE challenger and sets $a = a_0$ and $p_C = u_0$. Now if (a_0, u_0) is a ring-LWE sample, then there exists an $r_C, e_C \in \chi$ such that $p_C = ar_C + te_C$ and in that case the output of $B_{0,1}$ is distributed exactly as in G_0. Whereas if (a_0, u_0) is sample from a uniform distribution over R_q^2, $B_{0,1}$ simulates G_1 for A. Thus, if A can distinguish G_0 from G_1, then $A \circ B_{0,1}$ can distinguish ring-LWE samples from samples from a uniform distribution over R_q^2. Thus if A can distinguish G_0 from G_1, $A \circ B_{0,1}$ can solve the decision ring-LWE problem. Hence,

$$|\Pr(E_0) - \Pr(E_1)| \leq Adv_{A \circ B_{0,1}}^{drlwe}. \qquad (2)$$

$\square$

Lemma 2. *No PPT Type-I adversary can distinguish between G_1 and G_2 under the decision ring-LWE assumption, if H_1 is a randomness extractor and H_2 is a random oracle.*

Proof. If there exists a PPT Type-I adversary A that can distinguish between G_1 and G_2, then we can construct an PPT reduction algorithm $B_{1,2}$ that can efficiently distinguish between tuples from a ring-LWE distribution and a uniform distribution.

In G_1, (a, p_N) are samples from a ring-LWE distribution, such that $p_N = ar_N + te_N$. In G_2, (a, p_N) are samples from a uniform distribution over $R_q \times R_q$. Under the decisional ring-LWE assumption these two distributions are indistinguishable. In G_2, k_1 is also distributed as a random element from R_q. In both the cases p_C is uniformly distributed over R_q.

Solving Decision ring-LWE. To simulate the 1W-AKE challenger for A the reduction algorithm $B_{1,2}$ guesses ψ_i to be the *test* session. In the *test* session it honestly generates $(\mathbb{G}, g, g^u, g^v)$. $B_{1,2}$ also takes $\{(a_0, u_0), (a_1, u_1)\}$ from the ring-LWE challenger and sets $a = a_0$, $p_C = a_1$, $p_N = u_0$ and $k_1 = u_1$. Now if $\{(a_0, u_0), (a_1, u_1)\}$ are ring-LWE samples, then there exist $r_N, e_N, e_N' \in \chi$ such that $p_N = ar_N + te_N$ and $k_1 = p_C r_N + te_N'$. In that case the output of $B_{1,2}$ is distributed exactly as in G_1. Whereas if $\{(a_0, u_0), (a_1, u_1)\}$ are samples from uniform distribution over R_q^2, $B_{1,2}$ simulates G_2 for A. Thus, if A can distinguish G_1 from G_2, then $A \circ B_{1,2}$ can distinguish ring-LWE samples from samples from uniform distribution over R_q^2.

Thus if a PPT Type-I adversary A can distinguish between G_1 and G_2, then we can construct a reduction $B_{1,2}$ which can efficiently solve the ring-LWE problem. As a result we can write,

$$|\Pr(E_1) - \Pr(E_2)| \leq Adv_{A \circ B_{1,2}}^{drlwe}. \qquad (3)$$

$\square$

Analysis of G_2. In G_2 the adversary has to guess a b^* in the 1W-AKE game to distinguish between the real session key sk and randomly chosen session key sk'. As p_C, p_N and k_1 are chosen uniformly at random from R_q, and $H_1(\cdot)$ is a randomness extractor, the resulting session key sk is uniformly distributed over the key space. On the other hand, sk' is also chosen uniformly from the key space. As a result, the adversary has no information about b^*, and hence

$$\Pr(E_2) = 1/2. \qquad (4)$$

By combining Eqs. (1)–(4), we can write:

$$Adv_A^{1w\text{-}ake} \leq Adv_{A \circ B_{0,1}}^{drlwe} + Adv_{A \circ B_{1,2}}^{drlwe}. \qquad (5)$$

Lemma 3. *The protocol* HybridOR *is 1W-AKE secure against a PPT Type-I adversary under the GDH assumption in the random oracle model.*

Proof. If there exists a PPT Type-I adversary A that can break the 1W-AKE security of the protocol, then we can construct a PPT reduction algorithm B' against the GDH challenger. A is allowed to make a polynomial number ($poly(\lambda)$) of session queries. B' also simulates the random oracle H_2. Let $\{\mathbb{G}, g, g^u, g^v\}$ be the GDH challenge. B' has to compute g^{uv} in order to win the game.

The algorithm B' guesses ψ_i to be a *test* session. To simulate the ψ_i, C runs the SetUp and generates (R, n, q, t, χ). It uses the group G and generator g from the GDH challenger in the public parameters. B' samples $a \leftarrow R$ sets (a, g^u) as the static key pair of the server and simulates ψ_i session by setting:

$$g^x = g^v, \ (p_C)_i = ar_C + te_C, \ (p_N)_i = ar_N + te_N,$$
$$(K_1)_i = (p_C)_i r_N + te'_N, (\alpha)_i = Signal((k_1)_i),$$

where, $r_C, r_N, e_C, e_N, e'_N \in_r \chi$. B' tosses a coin and chooses $b \in_r \{0,1\}$. If $b = 0$ then B' computes the session key by computing $H_1((k_1)_i, (p_C)_i, (p_N)_i, N,$ HybOR$) \oplus H_2(\cdot, g^x, g^u, N,$ HybOR$)$, where $H_1(\cdot)$ is a randomness extractor and B programs $H_2(\cdot)$ as a random oracle. B sends the session key to A. If $b = 1$ then B sends a random session key to A.

But in order to compute the correct test session key and to win the game, A has to query the random oracle $H_2(\cdot)$ with the same input. Otherwise A cannot distinguish a real session key from a random one, as $H_2(\cdot)$ is modeled as a random oracle. Whenever A makes a query $H_2(Z, g^x, g^u, N,$ HybOR$)$ for some $Z \in \mathbb{G}$, B' asks the DDH oracle whether (g^x, g^v, Z) is a valid *DDH* tuple. If that is the case, then $Z = g^{uv}$ and B' sends the answer to the GDH challenger. Clearly the reduction B' is efficient. B' has to guess the test session with probability $1/poly(\lambda)$, so if A breaks the 1W-AKE protocol with non-negligible probability then B' will be able to solve the GDH problem with significant probability. Hence we can write,

$$Adv_A^{1w\text{-}ake} \leq Adv_{A \circ B'}^{GDH}. \tag{6}$$

Note that for all other sessions with the same server, the reduction B' has to simulate the protocol correctly without the knowledge of the private key u. If not managed properly, simulation may fail due to inconsistent H_2 queries. B' uses the DDH oracle to respond consistently to the H_2 queries and the sk_reveal queries for the sessions that involve g^u. In particular for H_2 queries that involve g^s, B' first verifies using the DDH oracle that the shared secret are computed honestly before responding with the session key. $\quad\square$

Conclusion. By combining Eqs. (5) and (6), we prove the result.

Note that the Type-I adversary A cannot be partner to any of the public values in the test session only. For all other sessions it can be a partner to almost all values after respecting the freshness criterion. So in order to simulate a 1W-AKE challenger for the adversary A, the reduction perfectly simulates all other sessions. As a result the challenger can satisfy any kind of queries (see Sect. 3.2) from the A during the simulation. $\quad\square$

5.3 Security Against Type-II Adversary

In this section we show that in the pre-quantum computing era (today) HybridOR is secure against PPT Type-II adversary. Here we consider an active adversary which can actually become a partner with the ephemeral key of the server. We show that even in that case the adversary will not be able to win the 1W-AKE game.

Theorem 2. *The protocol* HybridOR *is 1W-AKE secure against a PPT Type-II adversary under the GDH assumption in the random oracle model.*

The proof of Theorem 2 is shifted to the full version of the paper [22]. Notice that this theorem directly imply that a Type-II adversary can break the 1W-AKE security of HybridOR in a quantum world. As in the quantum world the Type-II adversary can compute the discrete log of the long term secret g^s and it is already partner to the ephemeral secret p_N in the *test* session. Hence the adversary can compute the session key and wins the 1W-AKE game.

In order to make this protocol secure against Type-II adversary in a quantum world we need replace the long term key with a quantum secure component. But in that case we cannot use our current DH public keys and subsequently requires modification to the current Tor public key infrastructure. So, in today's scenario it is sufficient to follow the HybridOR design in the current form. As we can deploy this easily in the current Tor network.

5.4 Security Against Type-III Adversary

A more important question to ask now is whether HybridOR provides forward security in the post-quantum world. If not, then the privacy of today's anonymous communication cannot be ensured once quantum computers arrive. We prove that HybridOR is forward secure if the ring-LWE problem is hard. The motive of this theorem is to show that by using HybridOR in Tor we can aim at the privacy of today's anonymous communication even after quantum computers arrive.

Theorem 3. HybridOR *is 1W-AKE secure against a PPT Type-III adversary under the ring-LWE assumption. More precisely, for any PPT Type-III adversary A,*

$$Adv_A^{1w\text{-}ake} \leq Adv_{A \circ B_{0,1}}^{drlwe} + Adv_{A \circ B_{1,2}}^{drlwe},$$

where $B_{0,1}$ and $B_{1,2}$ are the reduction algorithms as described in the proof.

The proof intuition of Theorem 3 is discussed in the full version [22].

Quantum Safe Reduction. In [47] Song pointed out that a post-quantum secure scheme against a classical adversary does not immediately guarantee that the scheme is also secure against a quantum adversary. Song gives conditions under which a classical proof can be lifted to provide quantum security. One of the condition is that the classical reduction is a *straight-line* reduction. That means that the reduction runs the adversary from start to end without any rewinding or restarting. Our reductions against Type-III adversary are straight-line, hence they satisfy Song's criterion for security against a quantum adversary.

6   Performance Analysis

We analyze the performance of HybridOR, and compare it with the ntor protocol.

Parameters. To achieve computational efficiency and to reduce the size of the public parameters, in HybridOR we use an algebraic variant of LWE called ring-LWE [35]. Similar to other ring-LWE based protocols [6,41,49], the security and performance of HybridOR essentially depend on the three factors: n, q, and β. Here, n is the degree of the irreducible polynomial $f(x)$, q is the prime modulus and $\beta = \sqrt{2\pi}\sigma$ for the standard deviation σ of the error distribution χ.

Lindner and Peikert [33] show how the parameters (n, q, β) affect the security and performance of lattice based systems. They choose parameter set $(256, 4093, 8.35)$ for *medium security* level and claimed that to be comparable with 128-bit AES security. Nevertheless, several implementations of lattice-based cryptographic primitives [20,46] use $n = 512$ to achieve *high security*. To be on the safer side, we also choose a *high security* level, and use parameter set $(512, 1051649, 8.00)$ (as used in [46]) in our implementation for R_q.

For the DLog group $\mathbb{G}$, we use the elliptic curve cryptographic (ECC) setting with points (compressed form) of size $p = 256$ bits, such as provided by Curve25519 [5].

Computation Cost. We assume that the elements r_C, e_C, p_C and g^x are precomputed on the client side, and the elements r_N, e_N, e'_N, and p_N are precomputed on the node side, e.g. in idle cycles. In our analysis, they are received by the code as an input. In that case, to compute the session secret $\{k_1, k_2\}$, the client and the node each have to perform 1 multiplication and 1 addition in R_q and 1 exponentiation in $\mathbb{G}$.

Multiplications over R_q can be performed efficiently using an FFT-based algorithm [35], which takes $O(n \log n)$ for a serial implementation and $O(\log n)$ time for a parallel implementation [26]. It is important to observe that these multiplications are more efficient than exponentiation in $\mathbb{G}$ (even in ECC settings). As a result the total computation cost of the node (with precomputation) is mainly dominated by exponentiation in $\mathbb{G}$.

As a proof of concept, we implement our protocol in a machine with a 6-core Intel Xeon (W3690) processor, each core running at 3.47 GHz. We use the GMP [27] library and the Tor library to implement the protocol. The code is compiled with -O3 optimizations using gcc 4.6.3.

For our choice of parameter set $(512, 1051649, 8.00)$ and ECC Curve25519, both the client and the node require $\approx 150\mu s$ to compute the shared secret. The multiplication along with one addition in R_q only requires $\approx 50\mu s$, and the exponentiation in $\mathbb{G}$ requires $\approx 100\mu s$.

The ntor protocol in Tor requires two exponentiations in $\mathbb{G}$ on both sides, and correspondingly requires $\approx 200\mu s$ to compute the shared secret. As a result, our unoptimized proof-of-concept HybridOR implementation is nearly 1.5 times faster than the ntor protocol used in Tor. Note that, for ntor, using some parallelization technique both the node and the client can reduce the computation cost to 1.33

exponentiations (for $\lambda = 128$) [3]; however, the current Tor implementation does not employ these.

Communication Cost. In the HybridOR protocol the client has to send an element $g^x \in \mathbb{G}$ and an element $p_C \in R_q$ to the node. We require 32 bytes to represent an element on Curve25519. On the other hand, for an element in R_q, we require at most $1/8(n \lg q)$ bytes, which is around 1280 bytes for the chosen parameter set $(512, 1051649, 8.0)$. Therefore, the client communicates 1312 bytes to the server.

On the other hand, the node has to send an element $p_N \in R_q$, an n-bit signal α, and the key confirmation message of 32 bytes to the client. That requires a total of $1/8(n \lg q + n) + 32$ bytes. For the chosen parameter set $(512, 1051649, 8.0)$, the node has to send about 1376 bytes to the client.

The current Tor implementation employs 512-byte cells; thus, for HybridOR, the client and the node each will have to communicate three cells. In comparison, for the currently employed ntor protocol, a single cell from the client and the server suffices. However, it is possible to use smaller value for q without affecting the security, which can reduce the communication overhead of the protocol.

7   Conclusion

Lattice-based cryptographic protocols are supposed to offer resilience against attacks by quantum computers, and the recent efficient ring-based constructions also put them in the realm of the practical use. In this paper, we demonstrated their utility to onion routing. In particular, we have presented a novel lattice-based 1W-AKE protocol HybridOR, which extracts its security from both the classically secure GDH assumption and the quantum-secure ring-LWE assumption. On one hand, we based its security against man-in-the-middle imperson-ation attacks only on the GDH assumption as we do not expect an adversary to have quantum capabilities today, and it allows us to leverage the current Tor PKI in its current form. On the other hand, we base its forward secrecy on the arguably quantum-secure ring-LWE assumption, which allows us to make HybridOR more efficient compared to the currently employed ntor protocol.

We also analyzed performance of our protocol in terms of its computation and communication cost for the 128-bit security setting. Our performance analysis demonstrates that post-quantum 1W-AKE can already be considered practical for use today.

Finally, we view our efficient HybridOR construction to be of independent interest to other authenticated key exchange protocols as well as anonymous communication scenarios over the Internet, and we plan to explore some those scenarios in the future.

Acknowledgements. We would like to thank Sujoy Sinha Roy for his suggestions regarding the ring-LWE implementation. This work was supported by the German Universities Excellence Initiative, and was partially supported by CoEC and R.C. Bose Centre for Cryptology and Security, ISI Kolkata.

A   Comparison Between the ntor, Ace, and HybridOR Protocols

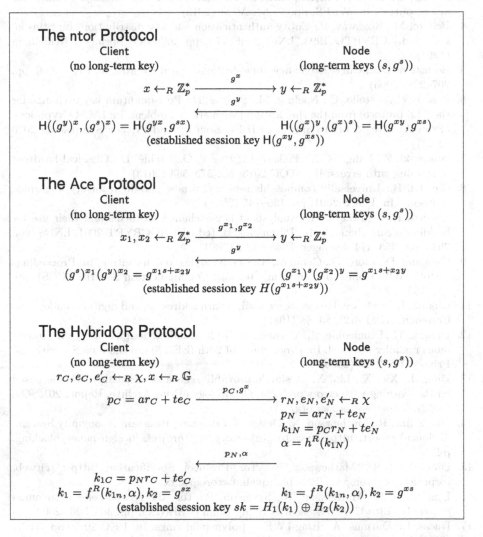

The ntor Protocol

Client
(no long-term key)

Node
(long-term keys (s, g^s))

$$x \leftarrow_R \mathbb{Z}_p^* \xrightarrow{\quad g^x \quad} y \leftarrow_R \mathbb{Z}_p^*$$
$$\xleftarrow{\quad g^y \quad}$$

$$\mathsf{H}((g^y)^x, (g^s)^x) = \mathsf{H}(g^{yx}, g^{sx}) \qquad \mathsf{H}((g^x)^y, (g^x)^s) = \mathsf{H}(g^{xy}, g^{xs})$$

(established session key $\mathsf{H}(g^{xy}, g^{xs})$)

The Ace Protocol

Client
(no long-term key)

Node
(long-term keys (s, g^s))

$$x_1, x_2 \leftarrow_R \mathbb{Z}_p^* \xrightarrow{\quad g^{x_1}, g^{x_2} \quad} y \leftarrow_R \mathbb{Z}_p^*$$
$$\xleftarrow{\quad g^y \quad}$$

$$(g^s)^{x_1}(g^y)^{x_2} = g^{x_1 s + x_2 y} \qquad (g^{x_1})^s (g^{x_2})^y = g^{x_1 s + x_2 y}$$

(established session key $H(g^{x_1 s + x_2 y})$)

The HybridOR Protocol

Client
(no long-term key)

Node
(long-term keys (s, g^s))

$$r_C, e_C, e_C' \leftarrow_R \chi, x \leftarrow_R \mathbb{G}$$
$$p_C = ar_C + te_C \xrightarrow{\quad p_C, g^x \quad} r_N, e_N, e_N' \leftarrow_R \chi$$
$$p_N = ar_N + te_N$$
$$k_{1N} = p_C r_N + te_N'$$
$$\alpha = h^R(k_{1N})$$
$$\xleftarrow{\quad p_N, \alpha \quad}$$

$$k_{1C} = p_N r_C + te_C'$$
$$k_1 = f^R(k_{1n}, \alpha), k_2 = g^{sx} \qquad k_1 = f^R(k_{1n}, \alpha), k_2 = g^{xs}$$

(established session key $sk = H_1(k_1) \oplus H_2(k_2)$)

Fig. 3. A comparative overview of the ntor, Ace, and HybridOR protocols: For readability, we neglect the information used for the key derivation and confirmation messages.

References

1. Applebaum, B., Cash, D., Peikert, C., Sahai, A.: Fast cryptographic primitives and circular-secure encryption based on hard learning problems. In: Halevi, S. (ed.) CRYPTO 2009. LNCS, vol. 5677, pp. 595–618. Springer, Heidelberg (2009)

2. Backes, M., Goldberg, I., Kate, A., Mohammadi, E.: Provably secure and practical onion routing. In: Proceedings of 25th IEEE Computer Security Foundations Symposium (CSF) (2012)
3. Backes, M., Kate, A., Mohammadi, E.: Ace: an efficient key-exchange protocol for onion routing. In: WPES, pp. 55–64. ACM (2013)
4. Bellare, M., Rogaway, P.: Entity authentication and key distribution. In: Stinson, D.R. (ed.) CRYPTO 1993. LNCS, vol. 773, pp. 232–249. Springer, Heidelberg (1994)
5. Bernstein, D.J.: Curve25519: new diffie-hellman speed records. In: PKC 2006, pp. 207–228 (2006)
6. Bos, J.W., Costello, C., Naehrig, M., Stebila, D.: Post-quantum key exchange for the TLS protocol from the ring learning with errors problem. In: IACR Cryptology ePrint Archive, 2014. To appear at IEEE Security and Privacy Symposium 2015 (2014)
7. Brakerski, Z., Langlois, A., Peikert, C., Regev, O., Stehlé, D.: Classical hardness of learning with errors. In: STOC 2013, pp. 575–584 (2013)
8. Canetti, R.: Universally composable security: a new paradigm for cryptographic protocols. In: FOCS 2001, pp. 136–145 (2001)
9. Canetti, R., Krawczyk, H.: Analysis of key-exchange protocols and their use for building secure channels. In: Pfitzmann, B. (ed.) EUROCRYPT 2001. LNCS, vol. 2045, pp. 453–474. Springer, Heidelberg (2001)
10. Catalano, D., Fiore, D., Gennaro, R.: Certificateless onion routing. In: Proceedings of 16th ACM Conference on Computer and Communication Security (CCS), pp. 151–160 (2009)
11. Chaum, D.: Untraceable electronic mail, return addresses, and digital pseudonyms. Commun. ACM **4**(2), 84–88 (1981)
12. Danezis, G., Dingledine, R., Mathewson, N.: Mixminion: design of a type III anonymous remailer protocol. In: Proceedings of 24th IEEE Symposium on Security and Privacy, pp. 2–15 (2003)
13. Ding, J., Xie, X., Lin, X.: A simple provably secure key exchange scheme based on the learning with errors problem. Cryptology ePrint Archive, Report 2012/688 (2012). http://eprint.iacr.org/
14. Dingledine, R., Mathewson, N.: Design of a Blocking-Resistant Anonymity System. Technical report. https://svn.torproject.org/svn/projects/design-paper/blocking.pdf
15. Dingledine, R., Mathewson, N.: Tor Protocol Specification. https://gitweb.torproject.org/torspec.git?a=blob_plain;f=tor-spec.txt
16. Dingledine, R., Mathewson, N., Syverson, P.: Tor: the second-generation onion router. In: 13th USENIX Security Symposium (USENIX), pp. 303–320 (2004)
17. Ducas, L., Durmus, A.: Ring-LWE in polynomial rings. In: PKC 2012, pp. 34–51 (2012)
18. Fouque, P.-A., Pointcheval, D., Zimmer, S.: HMAC is a randomness extractor and applications to TLS. In: ACM ASIACCS 2008, pp. 21–32 (2008)
19. Fujioka, A., Suzuki, K., Xagawa, K., Yoneyama, K.: Strongly secure authenticated key exchange from factoring, codes, and lattices. In: PKC 2012, pp. 467–484 (2012)
20. Fujioka, A., Suzuki, K., Xagawa, K., Yoneyama, K.: Practical and post-quantum authenticated key exchange from one-way secure key encapsulation mechanism. In: ACM ASIACCS 2013, pp. 83–94 (2013)
21. Gentry, C.: Fully homomorphic encryption using ideal lattices. In: STOC 2009, pp. 169–178 (2009)

22. Ghosh, S., Kate, A.: Post-quantum forward-secure onion routing. Cryptology ePrint Archive, Report 2015/008 (2015). http://eprint.iacr.org/
23. Goldberg, I.: On the security of the tor authentication protocol. In: Danezis, G., Golle, P. (eds.) PET 2006. LNCS, vol. 4258, pp. 316–331. Springer, Heidelberg (2006)
24. Goldberg, I.: Privacy enhancing technologies for the internet III: ten years later. In: Digital Privacy: Theory, Technologies and Practices, pp. 3–18 (2007)
25. Goldberg, I., Stebila, D., Ustaoglu, B.: Anonymity and one-way authentication in key exchange protocols. Des. Codes Crypt. 67(2), 245–269 (2013)
26. Göttert, N., Feller, T., Schneider, M., Buchmann, J., Huss, S.: On the design of hardware building blocks for modern lattice-based encryption schemes. In: Prouff, E., Schaumont, P. (eds.) CHES 2012. LNCS, vol. 7428, pp. 512–529. Springer, Heidelberg (2012)
27. Granlund, T., The GMP Development Team.: GMP: the GNU Multiple Precision Arithmetic Library, 6.0 edn (2014). http://gmplib.org/
28. Kate, A., Goldberg, I.: Using sphinx to improve onion routing circuit construction. In: FC 2010, pp. 359–366 (2010)
29. Kate, A., Zaverucha, G.M., Goldberg, I.: Pairing-based onion routing. In: PETS 2007, pp. 95–112 (2007)
30. Kate, A., Zaverucha, G.M., Goldberg, I.: Pairing-based onion routing with improved forward secrecy. ACM Trans. Inf. Syst. Secur. 13(4), 29 (2010)
31. Krawczyk, H.: HMQV: a high-performance secure diffie-hellman protocol. In: Shoup, V. (ed.) CRYPTO 2005. LNCS, vol. 3621, pp. 546–566. Springer, Heidelberg (2005)
32. Krawczyk, H.: Cryptographic extraction and key derivation: the HKDF scheme. In: Rabin, T. (ed.) CRYPTO 2010. LNCS, vol. 6223, pp. 631–648. Springer, Heidelberg (2010)
33. Lindner, R., Peikert, C.: Better key sizes (and attacks) for LWE-based encryption. In: Kiayias, A. (ed.) CT-RSA 2011. LNCS, vol. 6558, pp. 319–339. Springer, Heidelberg (2011)
34. Lyubashevsky, V., Micciancio, D.: Asymptotically efficient lattice-based digital signatures. In: Canetti, R. (ed.) TCC 2008. LNCS, vol. 4948, pp. 37–54. Springer, Heidelberg (2008)
35. Lyubashevsky, V., Peikert, C., Regev, O.: On ideal lattices and learning with errors over rings. J. ACM 60(6), 43:1–43:35 (2013)
36. Micciancio, D.: Improving lattice based cryptosystems using the hermite normal form. In: Silverman, J.H. (ed.) CaLC 2001. LNCS, vol. 2146, pp. 126–145. Springer, Heidelberg (2001)
37. Micciancio, D., Regev, O.: Lattice-based cryptography. In: Post-Quantum Cryptography, pp. 147–191 (2009)
38. Okamoto, T., Pointcheval, D.: The gap-problems: a new class of problems for the security of cryptographic schemes. In: PKC 2001, pp. 104–118 (2001)
39. Øverlier, L., Syverson, P.: Improving efficiency and simplicity of tor circuit establishment and hidden services. In: PETS 2007, pp. 134–152 (2007)
40. Peikert, C.: Public-key cryptosystems from the worst-case shortest vector problem: extended abstract. In: STOC 2009, pp. 333–342 (2009)
41. Peikert, C.: Lattice Cryptography for the Internet. Cryptology ePrint Archive, Report 2014/070 (2014). http://eprint.iacr.org/
42. Reed, M., Syverson, P., Goldschlag, D.: Anonymous connections and onion routing. IEEE J-SAC 16(4), 482–494 (1998)

43. Regev, O.: New lattice-based cryptographic constructions. J. ACM **51**(6), 899–942 (2004)
44. Regev, O.: On lattices, learning with errors, random linear codes, and cryptography. In: STOC 2005, pp. 84–93 (2005)
45. Rennhard, M., Plattner, B.: Introducing MorphMix: peer-to-peer based anonymous internet usage with collusion detection. In: ACM WPES 2002, pp. 91–102 (2002)
46. Roy, S.S., Vercauteren, F., Mentens, N., Chen, D.D., Verbauwhede, I.: Compact Ring-LWE based Cryptoprocessor. Cryptology ePrint Archive, Report 2013/866 (2013). http://eprint.iacr.org/
47. Song, F.: A note on quantum security for post-quantum cryptography. In: Mosca, M. (ed.) PQCrypto 2014. LNCS, vol. 8772, pp. 246–265. Springer, Heidelberg (2014)
48. The Tor Project. https://www.torproject.org/ (2003). Accessed November 2014
49. Zhang, J., Zhang, Z., Ding, J., Snook, M., Dagdelen, O.: Authenticated Key Exchange from Ideal Lattices. Cryptology ePrint Archive, Report 2014/589 (2014). http://eprint.iacr.org/. To appear at Eurocrypt 2015

Scalable Divisible E-cash

Sébastien Canard[1], David Pointcheval[2], Olivier Sanders[1,2](✉),
and Jacques Traoré[1]

[1] Orange Labs, Applied Crypto Group, Caen, France
olivier.sanders@orange.com
[2] CNRS, ENS, INRIA, and PSL, Paris, France

Abstract. Divisible E-cash has been introduced twenty years ago but no construction is both fully secure in the standard model and efficiently scalable. In this paper, we fill this gap by providing an anonymous divisible E-cash construction with constant-time withdrawal and spending protocols. Moreover, the deposit protocol is constant-time for the merchant, whatever the spent value is. It just has to compute and store 2^l serial numbers when a value 2^l is deposited, compared to 2^n serial numbers whatever the spent amount (where 2^n is the global value of the coin) in the recent state-of-the-art paper. This makes a very huge difference when coins are spent in several times.

Our approach follows the classical tree representation for the divisible coin. However we manage to build the values on the nodes in such a way that the elements necessary to recover the serial numbers are common to all the nodes of the same level: this leads to strong unlinkability and anonymity, the strongest security level for divisible E-cash.

1 Introduction

Compared to regular cash, electronic payment systems offer greater convenience for end-users, but usually at the cost of a loss in terms of privacy. Introduced in 1982 by Chaum [12], electronic cash (E-cash) is one solution to reconcile the benefits of both solutions. As with regular cash, users of such systems can withdraw coins from a bank and then spend them to different merchants, while remaining anonymous, with unlinkable transactions. There is however one major difference: if a banknote or a coin can hardly be duplicated, this is on the contrary very easy to copy the series of bits constituting an electronic coin, as for any electronic data. It is therefore necessary, when designing an E-cash system, to provide a way of detecting double-spendings (*i.e.* two spendings using the same coin) and then to allow identification of the underlying defrauder. The challenge is to ensure such features without weakening the anonymity, or the efficiency, of the resulting scheme.

1.1 Related Work

Designing an E-cash system which can handle any amount for a payment (as it is the case for regular cash) is not a trivial task and several kinds of solutions exist in the literature.

© Springer International Publishing Switzerland 2015
T. Malkin et al. (Eds.): ACNS 2015, LNCS 9092, pp. 287–306, 2015.
DOI: 10.1007/978-3-319-28166-7_14

One of them is to make use of coins of the smallest possible denomination (*e.g.* one cent), but this raises the problem of storing and spending the thousands of coins which become necessary to handle any amount. In [5], the authors partially address this latter problem by providing a compact E-cash system where users can withdraw wallets of N coins at once and store them efficiently. Unfortunately, each coin must be spent one by one which is unsuitable for practical use.

Another solution is to manage several denominations but, in practice, a user can be unable to make a payment if his wallet does not contain the kind of denomination he needs, since giving change back is not easy. For example, a user may have a wallet which only contains coins of $10 while having to pay $8. Such solution does not permit the user to make such payment, while he has enough money! This can be solved by using transferable e-cash systems, which in particular permits money change by the merchant, but at the cost of a larger coin [13].

The last solution to our initial problem has been proposed by Okamoto and Ohta [20] under the name of *divisible E-cash*. Such a system enables users to withdraw a coin C of a large value V, and then to spend it in several transactions, but in such a way that the sum of the amount of these transactions v_i is at most the global amount: $V \geq \sum v_i$. Typically, the coin is of value $V = 2^n$, and one can spend it with transactions of values $v_i = 2^{\ell_i}$, with $\ell_i \in \{0, \ldots, n\}$. This is currently the most relevant solution to solve the above problem and we now focus on this type of E-cash.

Since their introduction, many divisible E-cash schemes have been proposed (*e.g.* [6–8,18,19]), most of them sharing the same following idea. Every coin of global value 2^n is associated with a binary tree with 2^n leaves, each leaf being associated with a unique serial number. When a user spends a value of 2^ℓ, he reveals some information related to an unspent node s of depth $n - \ell$ (and so with 2^ℓ descendant leaves). This allows the bank to recover the 2^ℓ serial numbers associated to the transaction. Such serial numbers, that the bank cannot link to a withdraw, are very convenient to detect defrauders. Indeed, a double-spending implies two transactions involving two nodes with a common subtree and so with common descendant leaves. Therefore, there will be a collision in the list of serial numbers stored by the bank, meaning that there is a double-spending.

Again, the main difficulty is to reconcile this double-spending technique with users' anonymity. The first constructions [10,19,20] only offered a weak level of anonymity since several spendings involving the same divisible coin could be linked one to each other. In [18], the first unlinkable system was proposed but the transaction still revealed which part of the coin was spent. Moreover, a trusted authority was necessary to recover defrauders' identity.

The first *truly* anonymous construction was provided in [6] but is rather inefficient. Indeed, this scheme makes use of several groups of different orders, whose generation is very expensive. Moreover, the spending phase requires complex non-interactive zero-knowledge (NIZK) proofs, which make it impractical. An improvement was later proposed in [7], with a much more efficient spending, but the resulting tree construction still suffers from similar downsides. In [2], the authors chose a different approach to construct their binary tree, using cryptographic hash functions. Unfortunately, such functions are not compatible with efficient NIZK proofs so that the authors relied on cut-and-choose protocols to prove the validity of the trees (and so of the coins). The resulting scheme was therefore proved secure under an unconventional security model where the bank is only ensured that it will not loose money on average. The security of all these constructions necessitate the use of the random oracle model (ROM) and the constructions are most of the time incompatible with Groth-Sahai proof methodology [16], and so the ROM cannot be avoided.

A first attempt to construct a divisible E-cash system secure in the standard model is due to Izabachène and Libert [17], but the resulting scheme is impractical, because of no efficient double-spending detection. Indeed, each time a coin is deposited to the bank, the latter has to compare it (by performing several costly computations) with all already deposited coins. This is due to the lack of serial numbers which was identified by the authors as the main cause of the inefficiency of their scheme.

Recently, the first practical E-cash system secure in the standard model was proposed in [8], with constant-time withdrawal and spending protocols. Unlike the previous schemes, where a new tree was generated by the users each time they withdrew coins, this new construction considers only one tree provided in the public parameters. This significantly alleviates the withdrawal and spending protocols since proving the validity of the tree is no longer necessary. However the scheme has two drawbacks, as identified by its authors: First, the public parameters must contain many elements allowing to recover the serial numbers (for double-spending detection), they are thus large; Second, while the deposit protocol is constant-time for the merchant, even for a one-cent deposit, the bank must perform 2^n pairing computations and store the results in a database. This obviously affects the scalability of the proposed scheme.

1.2   Our Contribution

In this paper, we improve the latter solution by fixing these two drawbacks. Although our scheme shares similarities with the one of [8], it differs on the binary tree generation. Indeed, in [8], the elements g_s associated with each node s were randomly and independently generated. This implies that the elements $\tilde{g}_{s \mapsto f}$, provided to the bank to recover the serial numbers of leaf f from node s, differ according to each node s, leading to the above two issues.

Indeed, an anonymous scheme must reveal no information on the coin used in the transaction. So the bank does not know the involved node s but only its level $|s|$ (since it corresponds to the amount of the transaction). It follows that the bank does not know which elements $\tilde{g}_{s \mapsto f}$ it should use to compute the underlying serial numbers. It has no other choice than performing the computations with all possible nodes s' of level $|s|$. This ensures that the valid serial numbers will be recovered but at the cost of many useless computations. This also increases the risk of false double-spending detections, since additional (fake) serial numbers will be stored.

To prevent this problem, we design our tree differently: The nodes are now related in such a way that the elements needed to recover the serial numbers are common to every node at the same level. This reduces the size of the public parameters while avoiding useless computations. Indeed, with our solution, the bank only computes and stores 2^ℓ serial numbers when a value 2^ℓ is deposited, compared to 2^n in [8], whatever the value of the transaction (even for 1 cent).

However, these relations between nodes could also be used to break the strong unlinkability expected from an anonymous divisible E-cash system. To address this problem, we first require that the users encrypt some of the elements they send to the merchant. Unfortunately, the randomness used during the encryption is a problem to recover the deterministic serial numbers. We therefore add some elements in the public parameters which will allow the bank to efficiently cancel the randomness, without endangering the security of our scheme.

These modifications will slightly increase the complexity of the spending protocol but will lead to a much more efficient deposit one. Our solution can then be seen as a way to make the practical divisible E-cash system from [8] highly scalable.

1.3 Organization

In Sect. 2, we recall some definitions and present the computational assumption our protocol will rely on. Section 3 reviews the syntax of a divisible E-cash system along with informal definitions of the security properties. Section 4 provides a high level description of our construction, while Sect. 5 goes into the details. An improved fair variant is proposed in Sect. 6. Because of lack of space, the security analysis is postponed to the full version [9].

2   Preliminaries

2.1 Bilinear Groups

Bilinear groups are a set of three cyclic groups, $\mathbb{G}_1$, $\mathbb{G}_2$, and $\mathbb{G}_T$, of prime order p, along with a bilinear map $e : \mathbb{G}_1 \times \mathbb{G}_2 \to \mathbb{G}_T$ with the following properties:

1. for all $g \in \mathbb{G}_1, \widetilde{g} \in \mathbb{G}_2$ and $a, b \in \mathbb{Z}_p$, $e(g^a, \widetilde{g}^b) = e(g, \widetilde{g})^{a \cdot b}$;
2. for any $g \neq 1_{\mathbb{G}_1}$ and $\widetilde{g} \neq 1_{\mathbb{G}_2}$, $e(g, \widetilde{g}) \neq 1_{\mathbb{G}_T}$;
3. the map e is efficiently computable.

Galbraith, Paterson, and Smart [14] defined three types of pairings: in type 1, $\mathbb{G}_1 = \mathbb{G}_2$; in type 2, $\mathbb{G}_1 \neq \mathbb{G}_2$ but there exists an efficient homomorphism $\phi : \mathbb{G}_2 \to \mathbb{G}_1$, while no efficient one exists in the other direction; in type 3, $\mathbb{G}_1 \neq \mathbb{G}_2$ and no efficiently computable homomorphism exist between $\mathbb{G}_1$ and $\mathbb{G}_2$, in either direction.

Our construction, as well as the one of [8], requires the use of asymmetric pairings (*i.e.* of type 2 or type 3). For simplicity, we will only consider pairings of type 3 in this work, which is not a strong restriction (see [11]) since these pairings offer the best efficiency.

2.2   Computational Assumption

Besides the classical SXDH and $q - $ SDH [4] assumptions in bilinear groups, our construction relies on a new computational assumption, we call EMXDH, since this is an extension of the multi-cross-Diffie-Hellman assumption.

Definition 1 (SXDH Assumption). *For $k \in \{1, 2\}$, the* DDH *assumption is hard in $\mathbb{G}_k$ if, given $(g, g^x, g^y, g^z) \in \mathbb{G}_k^4$, it is hard to distinguish whether $z = x \cdot y$ or z is random. The* SXDH *assumption holds if* DDH *is hard in both $\mathbb{G}_1$ and $\mathbb{G}_2$*

Definition 2 ($q - $ SDH Assumption). *Given $(g, g^x, g^{x^2}, ..., g^{x^q}) \in \mathbb{G}_1$, it is hard to output a pair $(m, g^{\frac{1}{x+m}})$.*

Definition 3 (EMXDH Assumption). *Given $(g, g^a, g^x, g^t, \widetilde{g}, \widetilde{g}^a) \in \mathbb{G}_1^4 \times \mathbb{G}_2^2$, $(\{g^{y^i}\}_{i=1}^{i=n}, \{g^{t \cdot y^i}\}_{i=1}^{i=n}, \{g^{x \cdot y^i}\}_{i=1}^{i=n-1}, \{g^{x \cdot t \cdot y^i}\}_{i=1}^{i=n-1}, \{\widetilde{g}^{1/y^i}\}_{i=1}^{i=n}) \in \mathbb{G}_1^{4n-2} \times \mathbb{G}_2^n$, as well as $(g^{z_1}, g^{z_2}) \in \mathbb{G}_1$, it is hard to distinguish whether $(z_1, z_2) = (x \cdot y^n / a, x \cdot t \cdot y^n / a)$ or (z_1, z_2) is random.*

We discuss the hardness of the problem related to this assumption in Appendix A. We stress however that this assumption, as the SXDH one, would clearly be wrong with a symmetric pairing since the test $e(g^{z_1}, g^a) = e(g^x, g^{y^n})$ would allow distinguishing a random z_1 from a valid one.

This assumption will underlie the anonymity of our construction. However, as explained in Sect. 6, one can rely on a weaker assumption if a weaker level of anonymity is enough.

2.3   Digital Signature Scheme

A digital signature scheme Σ is defined by three algorithms:

- the key generation algorithm Σ.Keygen which outputs a pair of signing and verification keys (sk, pk) – we assume that sk always contains pk;
- the signing algorithm Σ.Sign which, on input the signing key sk and a message m, outputs a signature σ;
- and the verification algorithm Σ.Verify which, on input m, σ and pk, outputs 1 if σ is a valid signature on m under pk, and 0 otherwise.

The standard security notion for a signature scheme is *existential unforgeability under chosen message attacks* (EUF-CMA) [15] which means that it is hard, even given access to a signing oracle, to output a valid pair (m, σ) for a message m never asked to the oracle. In this paper we will also use two variants. The first one is the security against *selective chosen message attacks* (SCMA), which limits the oracle queries to be asked before having seen the key pk. The second one is a *strong unforgeability* (SUF) where the adversary must now output a valid pair (m, σ) which was not returned by the signing oracle (a new signature for an already signed message is a valid forgery) but can only ask one query to the signing oracle (OTS, for One-Time Signature).

2.4   Groth-Sahai Proof Systems

In [16], Groth and Sahai propose a non-interactive proofs system, in the common reference string (CRS) model, which captures most of the relations for bilinear groups. There are two types of CRS that yields either perfect soundness or perfect witness indistinguishability. These two types of CRS are computationally indistinguishable (under the SXDH assumption in our setting).

To prove that some variables satisfy a set of relations, the prover first commits to them (by using the elements from the CRS) and then computes one proof element per relation. Efficient non-interactive witness undistinguishable proofs are available for pairing-product equations or multi-exponentiation equations. The former are of the type:

$$\prod_{i=1}^{n} e(A_i, \widetilde{X}_i) \prod_{i=1}^{n} \prod_{j=1}^{n} e(X_i, \widetilde{X}_j)^{a_{i,j}} = t_T$$

for variables $\{X_i\}_{i=1}^{n} \in \mathbb{G}_1$, $\{\widetilde{X}_i\}_{i=1}^{n} \in \mathbb{G}_2$ and constant $t_T \in \mathbb{G}_T$, $\{A_i\}_{i=1}^{n} \in \mathbb{G}_1$, $\{a_{i,j}\}_{i,j=1}^{n} \in \mathbb{Z}_p$.
   The latter are of the type:

$$\prod_{i=1}^{n} A_i^{y_i} \prod_{j=1}^{n} X_j^{b_j} \prod_{i=1}^{n} \prod_{j=1}^{n} X_j^{y_i \cdot a_{i,j}} = T$$

for variables $\{X_i\}_{i=1}^{n} \in \mathbb{G}_k$, $\{y_i\}_{i=1}^{n} \in \mathbb{Z}_p$ and constant $T \in \mathbb{G}_k$, $\{A_i\}_{i=1}^{n} \in \mathbb{G}_k$, $\{b_i\}_{i=1}^{n} \in \mathbb{Z}_p$, $\{a_{i,j}\}_{i,j=1}^{n} \in \mathbb{Z}_p$ for $k \in \{1, 2\}$.
   Multi-exponentiation equations also admit non-interactive zero-knowledge (NIZK) proofs at no additional cost.

3   Divisible E-cash System

For consistency, we recall the syntax of a divisible E-cash system described in [8]. For simplicity, we borrow their notations.

Syntax. A divisible e-cash system is defined by the following algorithms, that involve at least three entities: the bank $\mathcal{B}$, a user $\mathcal{U}$ and a merchant $\mathcal{M}$.

- Setup($1^k, V$): On inputs a security parameter k and an integer V, this probabilistic algorithm outputs the public parameters $p.p.$ for divisible coins of global value V. We assume that $p.p.$ are implicit to the other algorithms, and that they include k and V. They are also an implicit input to the adversary, we will then omit them.
- BKeygen(): This probabilistic algorithm executed by the bank $\mathcal{B}$ outputs a key pair (bsk, bpk). It also sets L as an empty list, that will store all deposited coins. We assume that bsk contains bpk.

- Keygen(): This probabilistic algorithm executed by a user $\mathcal{U}$ (resp. a merchant $\mathcal{M}$) outputs a key pair (usk, upk) (resp. (msk, mpk)). We assume that usk (resp. msk) contains upk (resp. mpk).
- Withdraw($\mathcal{B}$(bsk, upk), $\mathcal{U}$(usk, bpk)): This is an interactive protocol between the bank $\mathcal{B}$ and a user $\mathcal{U}$. At the end of this protocol, the user gets a divisible coin C of value V or outputs $\perp$ (in case of failure) while the bank stores the transcript Tr of the protocol execution or outputs $\perp$.
- Spend($\mathcal{U}$(usk, C, bpk, mpk, v), $\mathcal{M}$(msk, bpk, v)): This is an interactive protocol between a user $\mathcal{U}$ and a merchant $\mathcal{M}$. At the end of the protocol the merchant gets a master serial number Z of value v (the amount of the transaction they previously agreed on) along with a proof of validity Π or outputs $\perp$. $\mathcal{U}$ either updates C or outputs $\perp$.
- Deposit($\mathcal{M}$(msk, bpk, (v, Z, Π)), $\mathcal{B}$(bsk, L, mpk)): This is an interactive protocol between a merchant $\mathcal{M}$ and the bank $\mathcal{B}$. $\mathcal{B}$ checks that Π is valid on v and Z and that (v, z, Π) has never been deposited (corresponding to the case of a cheating merchant). $\mathcal{B}$ then recovers the m (for some $m \geq v$) serial numbers $z_1, \ldots, z_m$ corresponding to this transaction and checks whether, for some $1 \leq i \leq m$, $z_i \in L$. If none of the serial numbers is in L, then the bank credits $\mathcal{M}$'s account of v, stores (v, Z, Π) and appends $\{z_1, \ldots, z_m\}$ to L. Else, there is at least an index $i \in \{1, \ldots, m\}$ and a serial number z' in L such that $z' = z_i$. The bank then recovers the tuple (v', Z', Π') corresponding to z' and publishes $[(v, Z, \Pi), (v', Z', \Pi')]$.
- Identify((v_1, Z_1, Π_1), (v_2, Z_2, Π_2), bpk): On inputs two different valid transcripts (v_1, Z_1, Π_1) and (v_2, Z_2, Π_2), this deterministic algorithm outputs a user's public key upk if there is a collision between the serial numbers derived from Z_1 and from Z_2, and $\perp$ otherwise.

Security Model. Besides correctness, the authors of [8] formally defined 3 security properties that a secure divisible e-cash system must achieve. The first one is *traceability* which requires that no coalition of users can spend more than they have withdrawn without revealing one of their identities. The second one is *exculpability* which requires that no user can be falsely accused of double-spending, even by a coalition of the bank, users and merchants. Eventually, the last property expected by such schemes is *anonymity* which means that no one can learn anything about a spending except the information already available from the environment (such as the date, the value of the spending,...).

However, they also describe two variants of anonymity that they called *unlinkability* and *strong unlinkability*. The former requires that two spendings from the same coin cannot be linked except by revealing which part of the coin is spent. The latter strengthens the level of anonymity by forbidding this additional leakage of information. A divisible, strongly unlinkable, e-cash system can be made anonymous by providing a way to identify double-spenders using only public information and so without the help of a trusted entity.

As explained in [8], a divisible e-cash system which is just unlinkable cannot achieve the anonymity property. In this paper, we improve on [8] by reducing the storage and computation of the anonymous version (strongly unlinkable).

$\text{Exp}_{\mathcal{A}}^{tra}(1^k, V)$

1. $p.p. \leftarrow \text{Setup}(1^k, V)$
2. $(\text{bsk}, \text{bpk}) \leftarrow \text{BKeygen}()$
3. $[(v_1, Z_1, \Pi_1), \ldots, (v_u, Z_u, \Pi_u)] \xleftarrow{\$} \mathcal{A}^{\mathcal{O}\text{Add}, \mathcal{O}\text{Corrupt}, \mathcal{O}\text{AddCorrupt}, \mathcal{O}\text{Withdraw}_\mathcal{B}, \mathcal{O}\text{Spend}}(\text{bpk})$
4. If $\sum_{i=1}^{u} v_i > m \cdot V$ and $\forall i \neq j$, $\text{Identify}((v_i, Z_i, \Pi_i), (v_j, Z_j, \Pi_j)) = \perp$,
   then return 1
5. Return 0

Fig. 1. Traceability security game

$\text{Exp}_{\mathcal{A}}^{excu}(1^k, V)$

1. $p.p. \leftarrow \text{Setup}(1^k, V)$
2. $\text{bpk} \leftarrow \mathcal{A}()$
3. $[(v_1, Z_1, \Pi_1), (v_2, Z_2, \Pi_2)] \leftarrow \mathcal{A}^{\mathcal{O}\text{Add}, \mathcal{O}\text{Corrupt}, \mathcal{O}\text{AddCorrupt}, \mathcal{O}\text{Withdraw}_\mathcal{U}, \mathcal{O}\text{Spend}}()$
4. If $\text{Identify}((v_1, Z_1, \Pi_1), (v_2, Z_2, \Pi_2), \text{bpk}) = \text{upk}$ and upk not corrupted,
   then return 1
5. Return 0

Fig. 2. Exculpability security game

$\text{Exp}_{\mathcal{A}}^{anon-b}(1^k, V)$

1. $p.p. \leftarrow \text{Setup}(1^k, V)$
2. $\text{bpk} \leftarrow \mathcal{A}()$
3. $(v, \text{upk}_0, \text{upk}_1, \text{mpk}) \leftarrow \mathcal{A}^{\mathcal{O}\text{Add}, \mathcal{O}\text{Corrupt}, \mathcal{O}\text{AddCorrupt}, \mathcal{O}\text{Withdraw}_\mathcal{U}, \mathcal{O}\text{Spend}}()$
4. If upk_0 or upk_1 is not registered, then return 0
5. If $c_{\text{upk}_i} > m_{\text{upk}_i} \cdot V - v$ for $i \in \{0, 1\}$, then return 0
6. $(v, Z, \Pi) \leftarrow \text{Spend}(C(\text{usk}_b, C, \text{mpk}, v), \mathcal{A}())$
7. $b^* \leftarrow \mathcal{A}^{\mathcal{O}\text{Add}, \mathcal{O}\text{Corrupt}, \mathcal{O}\text{AddCorrupt}, \mathcal{O}\text{Withdraw}_\mathcal{U}, \mathcal{O}\text{Spend}^*}()$
8. If upk_0 or upk_1 has been corrupted, then return 0
9. Return $(b = b^*)$

Fig. 3. Anonymity security game

We recall the security games in Figs. 1, 2, and 3. The adversary $\mathcal{A}$ can add new users (either corrupted or honest) to the system, corrupt existing ones or ask them to spend any value. This is modelled by queries to $\mathcal{O}\text{Add}$, $\mathcal{O}\text{AddCorrupt}$, $\mathcal{O}\text{Corrupt}$ and $\mathcal{O}\text{Spend}$ oracles. Moreover, according to each game, it may have access to the $\mathcal{O}\text{Withdraw}_\mathcal{B}$ (resp. $\mathcal{O}\text{Withdraw}_\mathcal{U}$) oracle which executes the bank's side (resp. user's side) of the Withdraw protocol. A divisible E-cash system is:

- *traceable* if $\Pr[\text{Exp}_{\mathcal{A}}^{tra}(1^k, V) = 1]$ is negligible for any $\mathcal{A}$;
- *exculpable* if $\Pr[\text{Exp}_{\mathcal{A}}^{excu}(1^k, V) = 1]$ is negligible for any $\mathcal{A}$;
- *anonymous* if $\Pr[\text{Exp}_{\mathcal{A}}^{anon-1}(1^k, V)]$ - $\Pr[\text{Exp}_{\mathcal{A}}^{anon-0}(1^k, V)]$ is negligible for any $\mathcal{A}$.

4 Our Construction

Notation. Let $\mathcal{S}_n$ be the set of bitstrings of size smaller than n and $\mathcal{F}_n$ be the set of bitstrings of size exactly n. For every $s \in \mathcal{S}_n$, $|s|$ denotes the length of s, and we define the set $\mathcal{F}_n(s)$ as $\{f \in \mathcal{F}_n : s$ is a prefix of $f\}$. For any $i \in \{0, \ldots, n\}$, we set $\mathcal{L}(i)$ as $\{b_{i+1}...b_n : b_j \in \{0,1\}\}$, *i.e.* the set of bitstrings of size $n - i$, indexed by $i + 1, \ldots, n$. Therefore, $\mathcal{L}(n)$ only contains the empty string, while $\mathcal{L}(0) = \mathcal{F}_n$.

In the following, each node s of a tree of depth n (defining a coin of value 2^n) will refer to an element of $\mathcal{S}_n$. The root will then be associated with the empty string ϵ and a leaf with an element of $\mathcal{F}_n$. For all $s \in \mathcal{S}_n \setminus \mathcal{F}_n$, the left child (resp. the right child) of s will refer to $s||0$ (resp. $s||1$).

4.1 High Level Description

The initial construction [8] works in a bilinear group $(p, \mathbb{G}_1, \mathbb{G}_2, \mathbb{G}_T, e)$, where g (resp. $\widetilde{g}$) is a generator of $\mathbb{G}_1$ (resp. $\mathbb{G}_2$) and $G = e(g, \widetilde{g})$. The core idea of their construction is to define one single tree in the public parameters which is common to all the coins. Each node s (resp. leaf f) of this tree is associated with an element $g_s \leftarrow g^{r_s} \in \mathbb{G}_1$ (resp. $\chi_f \leftarrow G^{y_f}$) for some random scalar r_s (resp. y_f). Each (divisible) coin is associated to a secret scalar x which implicitly defines its serial numbers as $\{G^{x \cdot y_f}\}_{f \in \mathcal{F}_n}$. To allow the bank to detect double-spendings, the public parameters contain, for each $s \in \mathcal{S}_n$ and each $f \in \mathcal{F}_n(s)$, the element $\widetilde{g}_{s \mapsto f} \leftarrow \widetilde{g}^{y_f/r_s} \in \mathbb{G}_2$. Indeed, by using them and the element $t_s = g_s^x$ provided by the user during the spending, the bank is able to recover the serial numbers $\{G^{x \cdot y_f}\}_{f \in \mathcal{F}_n(s)}$ since $e(t_s, \widetilde{g}_{s \mapsto f}) = G^{x \cdot y_f}$.

Limitations. However, this solution has two drawbacks. First, it implies public parameters of significant size since they must contain $(n+1) \cdot 2^n$ elements $\widetilde{g}_{s \mapsto f}$. Second, each of these elements depends on a node s, so that the bank needs to know the spent node s^* to select the correct $\widetilde{g}_{s^* \mapsto f}$ and compute the associated serial numbers. Unfortunately, to achieve the strong unlinkability or the anonymity properties, a divisible E-cash must not reveal this node s^*. Therefore, the only way for the bank to detect double-spendings is to compute, for every node s of the same level than s^* and for every $f \in \mathcal{F}_n(s)$, the pairings $e(t_{s^*}, \widetilde{g}_{s \mapsto f})$. For a deposit of one cent, the bank must then perform 2^n pairings to get the 2^n potential serial numbers, only one of them being valid. This additionally increases the risk of false positive.

Our Approach. In this work, we construct our parameters in such a way that the elements used to compute the serial numbers do no longer depend on the specific nodes, but only on the levels of the nodes in the tree (and so only on the spent values, which are publicly known). More precisely, for each level i, we provide 2^{n-i} pairs of elements of $\mathbb{G}_2$ which will be used by the bank each time a node of this level is deposited. Therefore, the bank will no longer need to perform useless computations and so will only have to compute V serial numbers when a value V will be deposited. Moreover, it decreases the size of the public parameters since only $2^{n+2} - 2$ elements (instead of $(n+1) \cdot 2^n$) of $\mathbb{G}_2$ are necessary.

Description. Informally, we associate the root ϵ of our tree with an element $g_\epsilon \in \mathbb{G}_1$, and each level i, from 1 to n, with two random scalars $y_{i,0}, y_{i,1} \xleftarrow{\$} \mathbb{Z}_p$. Given a node s associated with an element $g_s \in \mathbb{G}_1$ we can compute the element $g_{s||0} \leftarrow g_s^{y_{|s|+1,0}}$ associated with its left child and the element $g_{s||1} \leftarrow g_s^{y_{|s|+1,1}}$ associated with its right child. Therefore, as illustrated on Fig. 4, each node $s = b_1 \ldots b_{|s|}$ is associated with an element $g_s \leftarrow g^{y_\epsilon \prod_{i=1}^{|s|} y_{i,b_i}}$.

To allow the bank to compute the serial numbers associated to this node, we provide, for all $i = 0, \ldots, n$, and for each $f = b_{i+1} \ldots b_n \in \mathcal{L}(i)$, the value $\widetilde{g}_{i,f} \leftarrow \widetilde{g}^{\prod_{j=i+1}^{n} y_{j,b_j}}$. The point here is that $\widetilde{g}_{i,f}$ is common to every node of level i and so will be used by the bank each time a deposit of value 2^{n-i} is made. As illustrated on Fig. 5 (which shows the generic tree without the secret value x), the serial numbers of a coin associated with the secret x are then implicitly defined as $\{G^{x \cdot y_\epsilon \prod_{i=1}^{n} y_{i,b_i}}\}_{b_1 \ldots b_n \in \mathcal{F}_n}$.

Unfortunately, we cannot provide $t_s = g_s^x$ during a spending as in [8]. Revealing this element indeed breaks the anonymity of our new scheme. For example, if s is a node of level $n-1$, then a spending involving its left child $s||0$ and a spending involving its right child $s||1$ should be unlinkable. However, this is not true when we reveal $g_{s||0}^x$ and $g_{s||1}^x$, since one can simply check whether the equality $e(g_{s||0}^x, \widetilde{g}_{n-1,1}) = e(g_{s||1}^x, \widetilde{g}_{n-1,0})$ holds. Indeed:

$$e(g_{s||0}^x, \widetilde{g}_{n-1,1}) = e(g_s^x, \widetilde{g})^{y_{n,0} \cdot y_{n,1}} = e(g_{s||1}^x, \widetilde{g}_{n-1,0}).$$

To overcome this problem, at the spending time, the user will just send an ElGamal encryption of $t_s = g_s^x$ under the public key $k_{|s|}$, i.e. a pair $(g^{r_1}, t_s \cdot k_{|s|}^{r_1})$

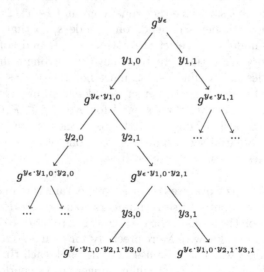

Fig. 4. Divisible coin

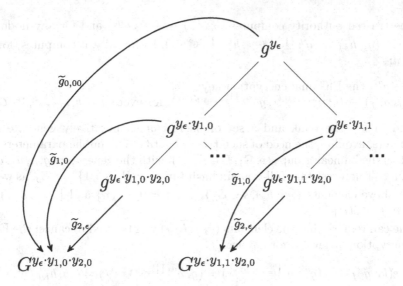

Fig. 5. Computing serial numbers

for some random $r_1 \xleftarrow{\$} \mathbb{Z}_p$. This will slightly increase the number of elements and the complexity of the proof that the user must produce during a spending, but it will ensure the strong unlinkability of our scheme. For the same reasons, we cannot reveal the security tag $\mathsf{upk}^R \cdot h_s^x$ (where R is obtained by hashing some public information related to the transaction), which is used in [8] to identify a double-spender. We will just provide an ElGamal encryption of it under the same public key.

Despite the randomness used in the ciphertexts, the bank must remain able to compute the deterministic serial numbers. We will then provide some additional elements $\widetilde{h}_{i,f}$ (see Sect. 4.2) in the public parameters to cancel this randomness without endangering the anonymity of our scheme.

Security Analysis. All the differences between our solution and the one of [8] lead to a new proof of anonymity. Indeed, in the latter, the elements g_s are chosen randomly which enables the reduction $\mathcal{R}$ to embed a DDH challenge in one node s^* without affecting the other ones, but with a few additional inputs. Therefore, $\mathcal{R}$ can handle any query involving the other nodes as long as its guess on s^* is correct. This is no longer the case with our solution since the elements g_s are now related, hence the stronger EMXDH assumption described in Sect. 2.2.

4.2 Setup

Public Parameters. Let $(p, \mathbb{G}_1, \mathbb{G}_2, \mathbb{G}_T, e)$ be the description of bilinear groups of prime order p, elements g, h, u_1, u_2, w be generators of $\mathbb{G}_1$, and $\widetilde{g}$ be a generator of $\mathbb{G}_2$. We denote $G = e(g, \widetilde{g})$. A trusted authority generates $(y_\epsilon, a_0) \xleftarrow{\$} \mathbb{Z}_p^2$ and, for $i = 1, \ldots, n$, $(y_{i,0}, y_{i,1}, a_i) \xleftarrow{\$} \mathbb{Z}_p^3$.

The trusted authority computes $(g_\epsilon, h_\epsilon) \leftarrow (g^{y_\epsilon}, h^{y_\epsilon})$ and for any node $s = b_1 \ldots b_{|s|}$, $(g_s, h_s) \leftarrow (g^{y_\epsilon \prod_{i=1}^{|s|} y_{i,b_i}}, h^{y_\epsilon \prod_{i=1}^{|s|} y_{i,b_i}})$. Eventually, it computes, for $i = 0, \ldots, n$:

- $k_i \leftarrow g^{a_i}$, the ElGamal encryption key;
- $(\widetilde{g}_{i,f}, \widetilde{h}_{i,f}) \leftarrow (\widetilde{g}^{\prod_{j=i+1}^{n} y_{j,b_j}}, \widetilde{g}^{-a_i \prod_{j=i+1}^{n} y_{j,b_j}})$, for every $f = b_{i+1} \ldots b_n \in \mathcal{L}(i)$.

As said in [8], the bank and a set of users can cooperatively generate such parameters, avoiding the need of such trusted entity. The public parameters $p.p.$ are set as the bilinear groups $(p, \mathbb{G}_1, \mathbb{G}_2, \mathbb{G}_T, e)$, with the generators g, h, u_1, u_2, w and $\widetilde{g}$, a collision-resistant full-domain hash function $H : \{0,1\}^* \to \mathbb{Z}_p$, as well as all the above elements $\{(g_s, h_s), s \in \mathcal{S}_n\}$, $\{k_i, i = 0, \ldots, n\}$ and $\{(\widetilde{g}_{i,f}, \widetilde{h}_{i,f}), i = 0, \ldots, n, f \in \mathcal{L}(i)\}$.

One can remark that the elements $(\widetilde{g}_{i,f}, \widetilde{h}_{i,f})$ will be used to cancel the ElGamal encryption at level i, for any leaf f:

$$e(k_i, \widetilde{g}_{i,f}) = e(g^{a_i}, \widetilde{g}^{\prod_{j=i+1}^{n} y_{j,b_j}}) = (g, \widetilde{g}^{a_i \prod_{j=i+1}^{n} y_{j,b_j}}) = e(g, \widetilde{h}_{i,f})^{-1}.$$

As a consequence, it is important to note that ElGamal encryptions under k_i are not semantically secure because of these elements, but the one-wayness will be enough for our purpose.

Although our construction is compatible with both the random oracle and the standard models, we will only describe, for the sake of clarity, a protocol with provable security in the standard model. We must therefore add to the public parameters the description of a common reference string (CRS) for the perfect soundness setting of the Groth-Sahai [16] proofs system and a one-time signature scheme Σ_{ots} (e.g. the one of [4]).

5   Our Divisible E-cash System

In this section, we provide an extended description of our new protocol. Then, we discuss its efficiency.

5.1   The Protocol

- BKeygen(): The bank has to sign two different kinds of messages and so selects two signature schemes denoted Σ_0 and Σ_1.
  - The former will be used to compute signatures τ_s on pairs (g_s, h_s) for every node s of the tree. Such signatures will allow users to prove during a spending that they use a valid pair (g_s, h_s) without revealing it.
  - The latter will be used by the bank during the Withdraw protocol to certify the secret values associated with the withdrawn coin.

  Both schemes has to allow signatures on elements of $\mathbb{G}_1^2$ while being compatible with Groth-Sahai [16] proofs. We will therefore instantiate them with the structure preserving signature scheme proposed in [1], since it was proven to be optimal for type 3 pairings.

The bank generates the pair $(\mathsf{sk}_1, \mathsf{pk}_1) \leftarrow \Sigma_1.\mathsf{Keygen}(p.p.)$ and the pairs $(\mathsf{sk}_0^{(i)}, \mathsf{pk}_0^{(i)}) \leftarrow \Sigma_0.\mathsf{Keygen}(p.p.)$, for each level $i = 0, \ldots, n$ of the tree, and computes, for every node $s \in \mathcal{S}_n$, $\tau_s \leftarrow \Sigma_0.\mathsf{Sign}(\mathsf{sk}_0^{(|s|)}, (g_s, h_s))$. Eventually, it will set bsk as sk_1 and bpk as $(\{\mathsf{pk}_0^{(i)}\}_i, \mathsf{pk}_1, \{\tau_s\}_{s \in \mathcal{S}_n})$. A way to reduce the size of this public key is described in Remark 5.

- $\mathsf{Keygen}()$: Each user (resp. merchant) selects a random usk $\leftarrow \mathbb{Z}_p$ (resp. msk) and gets upk $\leftarrow g^{\mathsf{usk}}$ (resp. mpk $\leftarrow g^{\mathsf{msk}}$). In the following we assume that upk (resp. mpk) is public, meaning that anyone can get an authentic copy of it.
- $\mathsf{Withdraw}(\mathcal{B}(\mathsf{bsk}, \mathsf{upk}), \mathcal{U}(\mathsf{usk}, \mathsf{bpk}))$: To withdraw a divisible coin, the user must jointly compute with the bank a random scalar x (thus without control on it), and then get a certificate. In practice, the scalar x is computed as $x = x_1 + x_2$ where x_1 is chosen and kept secret by the user and x_2 is chosen by the bank and given to the user. It is also necessary to bind this secret value to the user's identity to allow identification of double-spenders.
  The user then computes u_1^{usk} and $u_2^{x_1}$, sends them along with upk to the bank, and proves knowledge of x_1 and usk (in a zero-knowledge way, such as the Schnorr's interactive protocol [21]). If the proof is valid, the bank chooses a random x_2, and checks that $u = u_2^{x_1} \cdot u_2^{x_2}$ was not previously used, the bank computes $\sigma \leftarrow \Sigma_1.\mathsf{Sign}(\mathsf{sk}_1, (u_1^{\mathsf{usk}}, u))$ and sends it to the user, together with x_2. The user computes $x = x_1 + x_2$, and sets $C \leftarrow (x, \sigma)$. σ is thus a signature on the pair $(u_1^{\mathsf{usk}}, u_2^x)$, which strongly binds the user to the randomly chosen x.
- $\mathsf{Spend}(\mathcal{U}(\mathsf{usk}, C, \mathsf{bpk}, \mathsf{mpk}, 2^\ell), \mathcal{M}(\mathsf{msk}, \mathsf{bpk}, 2^\ell))$: To spend a value 2^ℓ, the user selects an unspent node s of level $n-\ell$ and two random scalars $r_1, r_2 \leftarrow \mathbb{Z}_p$ and computes $R \leftarrow H(info)$, $t_s \leftarrow (g^{r_1}, g_s^x \cdot k_{n-\ell}^{r_1})$ and $v_s \leftarrow (g^{r_2}, \mathsf{upk}^R \cdot h_s^x \cdot k_{n-\ell}^{r_2})$, where $info$ is some information related to the transaction (date, amount, merchant's public key, $\ldots$). Actually, t_s and v_s are ElGamal encryptions of g_s^x, the identifier of the node, and of $\mathsf{upk}^R \cdot h_s^x$, the security tag used to identify double-spenders. But of course, he must additionally prove that the plaintexts in t_s and v_s are valid, i.e. they are related to the values certified during a withdrawal. To do so, he will provide Groth-Sahai proof of knowledge of σ, and proof of existence of τ_s to attest the validity of the pair (g_s, h_s).
  However, Groth-Sahai [16] proofs can be re-randomized. This can be a problem in our case, since a dishonest merchant could re-randomize a valid transcript and to deposit it again. This would lead an honest user to be accused of double-spending, and so would break the exculpability property.
  To prevent this bad behavior, the user first generates a one-time signature key pair $(\mathsf{sk}_{ots}, \mathsf{pk}_{ots}) \leftarrow \Sigma_{ots}.\mathsf{Keygen}(1^k)$ and certifies the public key into $\mu \leftarrow w^{\frac{1}{\mathsf{usk} + H(\mathsf{pk}_{ots})}}$. This key pair will then be used to sign the transcript (including the proofs).
  Next, the user computes Groth-Sahai commitments to $\mathsf{usk}, x, r_1, r_2, g_s, h_s$, τ_s, σ, μ, $U_1 = u_1^{\mathsf{usk}}$, and $U_2 = u_2^x$, and provides a NIZK proof π that the committed values satisfy:

$$t_s = (g^{r_1}, g_s^x \cdot k_{n-\ell}^{r_1}) \quad \wedge \quad v_s = (g^{r_2}, (g^R)^{\mathsf{usk}} \cdot h_s^x \cdot k_{n-\ell}^{r_2})$$

$$U_2 = u_2^x \quad \wedge \quad U_1 = u_1^{\mathsf{usk}} \quad \wedge \quad \mu^{(\mathsf{usk} + H(\mathsf{pk}_{ots}))} = w$$

along with a NIWI proof π' that the committed values satisfy:

$$1 = \Sigma_0.\texttt{Verify}(\texttt{pk}_0^{(n-\ell)}, (g_s, h_s), \tau_s) \quad \wedge \quad 1 = \Sigma_1.\texttt{Verify}(\texttt{pk}_1, (U_1, U_2), \sigma).$$

Finally, the user computes $\eta \leftarrow \Sigma_{ots}.\texttt{Sign}(\texttt{sk}_{ots}, H(R\|t_s\|v_s\|\pi\|\pi'))$ and sends it to $\mathcal{M}$ along with $\texttt{pk}_{ots}, t_s, v_s, \pi, \pi'$.

The merchant then checks the validity of the proofs and of the signatures, and accepts the transaction if everything is correct. In such a case, he stores $(2^\ell, Z, \Pi)$ where $Z \leftarrow (t_s, v_s)$ and $\Pi \leftarrow (\pi, \pi', \texttt{pk}_{ots}, \eta)$.

- $\texttt{Deposit}(\mathcal{M}(\texttt{msk}, \texttt{bpk}, (2^\ell, Z, \Pi)), \mathcal{B}(\texttt{bsk}, L, \texttt{mpk}))$: Upon receiving the tuple $(2^\ell, Z = (t_s, v_s), \Pi = (\pi, \pi', \texttt{pk}_{ots}, \eta))$, the bank first checks the validity of the proofs and signatures. Then, it checks that it was not previously deposited. To this aim, it parses t_s as $(t_s[1], t_s[2])$, and for each $f \in \mathcal{L}(n-\ell)$, it computes the serial numbers $z_f \leftarrow e(t_s[2], \widetilde{g}_{n-\ell,f}) \cdot e(t_s[1], \widetilde{h}_{n-\ell,f})$ and checks whether $z_f \in L$. If none of them is in L, which means that none was already spent, the bank adds these elements to this list L and associates them with the transcript $(2^\ell, Z, \Pi)$. Else, there is an element $z' \in L$ such that for some f, $z_f = z'$. The bank recovers the corresponding transcript $(2^{\ell'}, Z', \Pi')$ and outputs $[(2^\ell, Z, \Pi), (2^{\ell'}, Z', \Pi')]$.

As remarked above, $e(k_i, \widetilde{g}_{i,f}) \cdot e(g, \widetilde{h}_{i,f}) = 1$, for any level i and any leaf f, and so $z_f = e(g_s^x, \widetilde{g}_{n-\ell,f})$, and is thus independent of r_1.

As noticed in [8], the bank does not actually have to store and compare the elements $z_i \in \mathbb{G}_T$ but only their fingerprints, that can be small hash values for some collision-resistant hash function.

- $\texttt{Identify}((2^{\ell_1}, Z_1, \Pi_1), (2^{\ell_2}, Z_2, \Pi_2), \texttt{bpk})$: To recover the identity of a double-spender from such a pair of transcripts, one first checks the validity of both transcripts and returns $\bot$ if one of them is not correct. One then parses Z_i as (t_{s_i}, v_{s_i}) and computes the lists $S_i \leftarrow \{e(t_{s_i}[2], \widetilde{g}_{n-\ell_i,f}) \cdot e(t_{s_i}[1], \widetilde{h}_{n-\ell_i,f}), \forall f \in \mathcal{L}(n - \ell_i)\}$, for $i = 1, 2$. One returns $\bot$ if there is no collision between S_1 and S_2. In case of collision, there are $f_1 \in \mathcal{L}(n - \ell_1)$ and $f_2 \in \mathcal{L}(n - \ell_2)$ such that

$$e(g_{s_1}^{x_1}, \widetilde{g}_{n-\ell_1,f_1}) = e(t_{s_1}[2], \widetilde{g}_{n-\ell_1,f_1}) \cdot e(t_{s_1}[1], \widetilde{h}_{n-\ell_1,f_1})$$
$$= e(t_{s_2}[2], \widetilde{g}_{n-\ell_2,f_2}) \cdot e(t_{s_2}[1], \widetilde{h}_{n-\ell_2,f_2}) = e(g_{s_2}^{x_2}, \widetilde{g}_{n-\ell_2,f_2}).$$

But then, since the x's values are mutually chosen by the user and the bank, they are random, while all the other elements are fixed from the setup. This is thus quite unlikely this equality holds for different random x and different paths in the tree: such a collision is a double-spending of a leaf $f \in \mathcal{L}(0) = \mathcal{F}_n$ in the tree parametrized by $x = x_1 = x_2$.

In addition, because of the signature σ, and the soundness of the NIWI in the transcript, the same user is necessarily associated to the two coins: it is quite unlikely two users come up with the same x. Then, if one lets T_i be $e(v_{s_i}[2], \widetilde{g}_{n-\ell_i,f_i}) \cdot e(v_{s_i}[1], \widetilde{h}_{n-\ell_i,f_i})$, for $i = 1, 2$, since we also have $e(h_{s_1}^{x_1}, \widetilde{g}_{n-\ell_1,f_1}) = e(h_{s_2}^{x_2}, \widetilde{g}_{n-\ell_2,f_2})$, as above, we have the simplification $T_i = e(\texttt{upk}_i^{R_i} \cdot h_{s_i}^{x_i}, \widetilde{g}_{n-\ell_i,f_i})$, and even:

$$T_1/T_2 = e(\texttt{upk}^{R_1}, \widetilde{g}_{n-\ell_1,f_1})/e(\texttt{upk}^{R_2}, \widetilde{g}_{n-\ell_2,f_2}) = e(\texttt{upk}, \widetilde{g}_{n-\ell_1,f_1}^{R_1}/\widetilde{g}_{n-\ell_2,f_2}^{R_2}).$$

In order to trace the double-spender, one has to compute, for each public key upk_i, the value $e(\mathsf{upk}_i, \widetilde{g}_{n-\ell_1,f_1}^{R_1}/\widetilde{g}_{n-\ell_2,f_2}^{R_2})$ until one gets a match with T_1/T_2, in which case the algorithm outputs upk_i.

Remark 4. We stress that a collision on the serial numbers (or on their finger-prints) means that for the secret values x_1, x_2, and for the secret nodes s_1, s_2 at public levels ℓ_1, ℓ_2, there are $f_1 \in \mathcal{L}(n - \ell_1)$ and $f_2 \in \mathcal{L}(n - \ell_2)$ verifying:

$$x_1 \cdot y_\epsilon \prod_{i=1}^{n-\ell_1} y_{i,b_{1,i}} \prod_{j=n-\ell_1+1}^{n} y_{j,b_{1,j}} = x_2 \cdot y_\epsilon \prod_{i=1}^{n-\ell_2} y_{i,b_{2,i}} \prod_{j=n-\ell_2+1}^{n} y_{j,b_{2,j}}$$

Since the secret x_1 and x_2 are randomly chosen after the values $y_{i,b}$ have been randomly fixed, the collision is quite unlikely if $x_1 \neq x_2$. Similarly, because of the random choice of the values $y_{i,b}$, it is quite unlikely there exist two disctint sequences $(b_{1,i}) \neq (b_{2,i})$ such that $\prod_{i=1}^{n} y_{i,b_{1,i}} = \prod_{i=1}^{n} y_{i,b_{2,i}}$. As a consequence, the two sequences are equal, which means that $s_1 \| f_1 = s_2 \| f_2$: a collision corre-sponds to two spendings involving the same path $s_1 \| f_1$ in the tree parametrized by $x = x_1 = x_2$, with overwhelming probability.

On the other hand, one can easily check that a double-spending automatically leads to a collision.

Remark 5. The appropriate combination of the node s and the final path f into $s \| f$ from the root to the leaf in all the serial number computations comes from the signature τ_s that involves the key at the appropriate public level (since this is related to the value of the coin). Our approach consists in generating $(n + 1)$ public keys $\mathsf{pk}_0^{(i)}$ (one for each level i) and a signature τ_s for every node $s \in \mathcal{S}_n$, all in the public key bpk of the bank. Proving that (g_s, h_s) is valid for a spending of 2^ℓ can then be achieved by proving knowledge of a signature τ_s such that $\Sigma_0.\mathsf{Verify}(\mathsf{pk}_0^{(n-\ell)}, (g_s, h_s), \tau_s) = 1$.

Unfortunately, this solution implies a bank public key of significant size since it must contain $(n + 1)$ public keys (one for each level) and $2^{n+1} - 1$ structure preserving signatures (one for each node).

Another way of proving the validity of the pair (g_s, h_s) is to notice that, for every $f \in \mathcal{L}(|s|)$, there is a leaf $\ell \in \mathcal{F}_n$ such that $s \| f = \ell$. Therefore, $e(g_s, \widetilde{g}_{|s|,f}) = e(g_\ell, \widetilde{g})$ and $e(h_s, \widetilde{g}_{|s|,f}) = e(h_\ell, \widetilde{g})$. Since the element $\widetilde{g}_{|s|,f}$ is com-mon to every node of level $|s|$, it can be revealed by the user so only the validity of the pair (g_ℓ, h_ℓ) remains to be proved. Therefore, the bank can generate only one key pair $(\mathsf{sk}_0, \mathsf{pk}_0)$ (instead of $n + 1$ such key pairs) and provide 2^n signa-tures $\tau_\ell \leftarrow \Sigma_0.\mathsf{Sign}(\mathsf{sk}_0, (g_\ell, h_\ell))$ for all the leaves (instead of $2^{n+1} - 1$, for all the nodes). This slightly increases the size of the proof since the user will have to commit to (g_ℓ, h_ℓ) and prove statements on them, but this allows to significantly reduce the size of bpk.

The security of our divisible e-cash system is stated by the following theorem, proved in the full version [9].

Theorem 6. *In the standard model, assuming that the hash function H is collision-resistant, our divisible e-cash system is anonymous under the SXDH and the EMXDH assumptions, traceable if Σ_0 is an EUF-SCMA secure signature scheme and Σ_1 is an EUF-CMA secure signature scheme, and achieves the exculpability property under the $q-$ SDH assumption if Σ_{ots} is a SUF-secure one-time signature scheme.*

5.2 Efficiency

We compare in Fig. 6 the efficiency of our construction (including the Remark 5) with the one of [8], which is the most efficient scheme regarding the `Withdraw` and the `Spend` protocols, and with the one from [7], whose `Deposit` protocol is less expensive but which is only compatible with the random oracle model.

For proper comparison, we add the elements $\tilde{g}_{s \mapsto f}$ (see Sect. 4.1) to the public parameters of [8].

Schemes	Canard-Gouget [7]	Canard *et al* [8]	Our work
Standard Model	no	yes	yes
Public Parameters	$2^{n+3}|q| + 1\ pk$	$(n+2)\ pk$ $+ (1 + (n+1)2^n)\ \mathbb{G}_2$ $+ (2^{n+2} + 3)\ \mathbb{G}_1$ $+ (2^{n+1} - 1)\ |\text{Sign}|$	$2\ pk$ $+ (2^{n+2} - 1)\ \mathbb{G}_2$ $+ (2^{n+2} + n + 4)\ \mathbb{G}_1$ $+ 2^n\ |\text{Sign}|$
Withdraw Computations	$(2^{n+3} + 2^{n+2} - 5)\text{exp}$ $+ (n+2)\ \text{Sign}$	1 Sign	1 Sign
Coin Size	$(2^{n+2} + n + 1)\ |q|$ $+ (n+2)\ |\text{Sign}|$	$2\ |p| + |\text{Sign}|$	$2\ |p| + |\text{Sign}|$
Spend Computations	$NIZK\{\ 3\ \text{exp}^*$ $+ 2\ \text{Sign} + 2\ \text{Pair}\ \}$ $+ 1\ \text{exp}$	$NIZK\{\ 2\ \text{exp}$ $+ 2\ \text{Sign}\ \} + 3\ \text{exp}$ $+ 1\ \text{Sign}$	$NIZK\{\ 4\ \text{exp}$ $+ 2\ \text{Sign} + 2\ \text{Pair}\ \}$ $+ 7\ \text{exp} + 1\ \text{Sign}$
Transfer size of Spend	$3\ |q| + |NIZK|$	$2\ \mathbb{G}_1 + 1\ |\text{Sign}|$ $+ |NIZK|$	$4\ \mathbb{G}_1 + 1\ |\text{Sign}|$ $+ 1\ \mathbb{G}_2 + |NIZK|$
Deposit Computations	2^{l+1}exp	$2^n\ \text{Pair}$	$2^{l+1}\ \text{Pair}$
Deposit size	$2^l\ |q| + |\text{Spend}|$	$2^n\ \mathbb{G}_T + |\text{Spend}|$	$2^l\ \mathbb{G}_T + |\text{Spend}|$

Fig. 6. Efficiency comparison between related works and our construction for coins of value 2^n and `Spend` and `Deposit` of value 2^l ($l \le n$). The space and times complexities are given from the user's point of view. `exp` refers to an exponentiation, `pair` to a pairing computation, `Sign` to the cost of the signature issuing protocol whose public key is pk. $NIZK\{\text{exp}\}$ denotes the cost of a $NIZK$ proof of a multi-exponentiation equation, $NIZK\{\text{pair}\}$ the one of a pairing product equation and $NIZK\{\text{Sign}\}$ the one of a valid signature. $NIZK\{\text{exp}^*\}$ refers to the cost of a proof of equality of discrete logarithms in groups of different orders.

For a 128-bits security level, we have (see [14]) $|q| = |\mathbb{G}_T| = 3072$, $|p| = |\mathbb{G}_1| = 256$ and $|\mathbb{G}_2| = 512$ by using Barreto-Naehrig curves [3]. Therefore, for

$n = 10$ (allowing to divide the coin in 1024 parts), the public parameters of [7] require 3.1 MB of storage space, those of [8] require 1.1 MB while ours only require 525 KB.

Compared to [8], the main advantage of our solution lies in the Deposit protocol. Indeed, in the former solution, the bank has to compute and store 2^n serial numbers z_i (most of them being invalid) for each transaction, no matter which value was spent. Considering the number of transactions that a payment system may have to handle, this may become cumbersome. Our solution significantly alleviates the computing and storage needs of the bank since the number of z_i that it must recover is exactly the same as the spent value. However, this improvement implies a slight increase of the complexity of the Spend protocol but we argue that the trade-off remains reasonable. Moreover, it is possible to get rid of the 2 Pair in the $NIZK$ proof, at the cost of increasing the public parameters, by not taking into account the Remark 5.

6   Fair Divisible E-cash System

The protocol described above achieves the strongest level of anonymity where users cannot be identified as long as they remain honest. However, it may be necessary for legal reasons to allow some entity (*e.g.* the police) to identify any spender. Our construction can be modified to add such an entity, that we will call an *opener*, leading to a *fair* divisible E-cash system. The point is that these modifications will decrease the complexity of our construction and weaken the assumption underlying its anonymity.

Let us consider the Setup algorithm defined in Sect. 4.2. A trusted authority was needed to generate the scalars $(a_0, y_\epsilon, \{a_i, y_{i,0}, y_{i,1}\}_{i=1}^{i=n})$ involved in the construction of the tree. Indeed, an entity knowing them can easily break the anonymity of the scheme (but not its exculpability or its traceability).

Let us assume that the Setup algorithm is run by the opener. Since every transcript of a Spend protocol contains a pair $t_s = (g^r, g_s^x \cdot k_{n-|s|}^r)$ for some coin secret x and some random scalar r, the opener can recover:

$$g^x \leftarrow (g_s^x \cdot k_{n-|s|}^r \cdot (g^r)^{-a_{|s|}})^{(y_\epsilon \prod_{i=1}^{|s|} y_{i,b_i})^{-1}}$$

which only depends on the coin secret x. It then only remains to link this value with the user's identity. One way to achieve this is to slightly modify the Withdraw protocol by requiring that users also send g^x, prove that it is well formed and send a signature on it under upk. These elements will then be stored by the bank in a public register that will be used by the opener to identify spenders (the signature will ensure the exculpability property).

This new way of identifying spenders allows to alleviate our construction. Regarding the Spend protocol, computing the pair v_s (and proving statement about it) is no longer necessary since it was only useful to identify double-spenders. Regarding the public parameters, the elements h_s can be discarded since they were only involved in the computation of v_s. Finally, the Identify algorithm which suffers from a linear cost in the number of users is replaced by the constant-time computation of g^x described above.

Another benefit of this fair divisible E-cash system is that its anonymity now relies on the following assumption, which is clearly weaker than the EMXDH assumption (see Definition 3):

Definition 7 (Weak EMXDH Assumption). *Given* $(g, g^a, g^x, \widetilde{g}, \widetilde{g}^a) \in \mathbb{G}_1^3 \times \mathbb{G}_2^2$, $(\{g^{y^i}\}_{i=1}^{i=n}, \{g^{x \cdot y^i}\}_{i=1}^{i=n-1}, \{\widetilde{g}^{1/y^i}\}_{i=1}^{i=n}) \in \mathbb{G}_1^{2n-1} \times \mathbb{G}_2^n$, *as well as* $g^z \in \mathbb{G}_1$, *it is hard to distinguish whether* $z = x \cdot y^n/a$ *or* z *is random.*

7 Conclusion

In this work we have proposed a new divisible E-cash system which improves the state-of-the art paper [8] by addressing its two downsides, namely the storage and computational costs of the deposit protocol and the size of the public parameters. Our solution relies on a new way of constructing the binary tree which induces several modifications compared to [8] leading to the first efficient and scalable divisible E-cash system secure in the standard model.

Acknowledgments. This work was supported in part by the French ANR Projects ANR-12-INSE-0014 SIMPATIC and ANR-11-INS-0013 LYRICS, and in part by the European Research Council under the European Community's Seventh Framework Programme (FP7/2007–2013 Grant Agreement no. 339563 – CryptoCloud).

A   Security of the EMXDH Assumption

First, let us consider the weak-EMXDH assumption defined in Sect. 6. Informally, this assumption relies on the fact that, since $g^z \in \mathbb{G}_1$, we can combine it with every element of $\mathbb{G}_2$ (but not $\mathbb{G}_1$ since we use an asymmetric bilinear map) provided by the challenge. Therefore, the assumption holds if $e(g^z, \widetilde{g}^a)$ and $e(g^z, \widetilde{g}^{1/y^j})$, for $0 \leq j \leq n$, are undistinguishable from random elements of $\mathbb{G}_T$, given all the inputs from the challenge.

If $z = x \cdot y^n/a$ then $e(g^z, \widetilde{g}^a) = G^{x \cdot y^n}$ and $e(g^z, \widetilde{g}^{y^{-j}}) = G^{x \cdot y^{n-j}/a}$, for $G = e(g, \widetilde{g})$. While all the other combinations lead to G, G^{a^2}, G^x, $\{G^{y^i}\}_{i=-n}^{i=n}$, $\{G^{ay^i}\}_{i=-n}^{i=n}$, $\{G^{xy^i}\}_{i=-n}^{i=n-1}$, $\{G^{axy^i}\}_{i=0}^{i=n-1}$. No linear combination of the latter can help to distinguish the former.

The elements provided in the challenge allow (see the full version [9]) to generate the public parameters g_s for each node $s \in \mathcal{S}_n$ as well as the pairs $(\widetilde{g}_{i,f}, \widetilde{h}_{i,f})$ for every $0 \leq i \leq n$ and $f \in \mathcal{F}_n$ but also to compute the element g_s^x involved in the pair t_s sent during the Spend protocol. This is enough for the fair divisible E-cash system sketched in Sect. 6. Unfortunately, the anonymous version described in Sect. 5 also requires to provide, for each $s \in \mathcal{S}_n$, the elements $h_s = g_s^t$ for some $t \in \mathbb{Z}_p$. Such elements are used during a spending to compute the element $h_s^x = (g_s^x)^t$ involved in the pair v_s necessary to identify double-spenders without the help of an opener.

The problem is that a reduction cannot know the value t. Therefore, it is necessary to provide for most elements w of $\mathbb{G}_1$ of the challenge, the associated ones w^t, hence the EMXDH assumption.

References

1. Abe, M., Groth, J., Haralambiev, K., Ohkubo, M.: Optimal structure-preserving signatures in asymmetric bilinear groups. In: Rogaway, P. (ed.) CRYPTO 2011. LNCS, vol. 6841, pp. 649–666. Springer, Heidelberg (2011)
2. Au, M.H., Susilo, W., Mu, Y.: Practical anonymous divisible e-cash from bounded accumulators. In: Tsudik, G. (ed.) FC 2008. LNCS, vol. 5143, pp. 287–301. Springer, Heidelberg (2008)
3. Barreto, P.S.L.M., Naehrig, M.: Pairing-friendly elliptic curves of prime order. In: Preneel, B., Tavares, S. (eds.) SAC 2005. LNCS, vol. 3897, pp. 319–331. Springer, Heidelberg (2006)
4. Boneh, D., Boyen, X.: Short signatures without random oracles and the SDH assumption in bilinear groups. J. Crypt. 21(2), 149–177 (2008)
5. Camenisch, J.L., Hohenberger, S., Lysyanskaya, A.: Compact e-cash. In: Cramer, R. (ed.) EUROCRYPT 2005. LNCS, vol. 3494, pp. 302–321. Springer, Heidelberg (2005)
6. Canard, S., Gouget, A.: Divisible e-cash systems can be truly anonymous. In: Naor, M. (ed.) EUROCRYPT 2007. LNCS, vol. 4515, pp. 482–497. Springer, Heidelberg (2007)
7. Canard, S., Gouget, A.: Multiple denominations in e-cash with compact transaction data. In: Sion, R. (ed.) FC 2010. LNCS, vol. 6052, pp. 82–97. Springer, Heidelberg (2010)
8. Canard, S., Pointcheval, D., Sanders, O., Traoré, J.: Divisible e-cash made practical. In: Katz, J. (ed.) PKC 2015. LNCS, vol. 9020, pp. 77–100. Springer, Heidelberg (2015)
9. Canard, S., Pointcheval, D., Sanders, O., Traoré, J.: Scalable divisible e-cash. In: Malkin, T., Kolesnikov, V., Lewko, A.B., Polychronakis, M. (eds.) ACNS 2015. LNCS, vol. 9092, pp. 287–306. Springer, Heidelberg (2015). Full version available on Cryptology ePrint Archive, http://eprint.iacr.org/
10. Chan, A.H., Frankel, Y., Tsiounis, Y.: Easy come - easy go divisible cash. In: Nyberg, K. (ed.) EUROCRYPT 1998. LNCS, vol. 1403, pp. 561–575. Springer, Heidelberg (1998)
11. Chatterjee, S., Menezes, A.: On cryptographic protocols employing asymmetric pairings - the role of Ψ revisited. Discrete Appl. Math. 159(13), 1311–1322 (2011)
12. Chaum, D.: Blind signatures for untraceable payments. In: Chaum, D., Rivest, R.L., Sherman, A.T. (eds.) CRYPTO 1982, pp. 199–203. Springer, New York (1982)
13. Chaum, D., Pedersen, T.P.: Transferred cash grows in size. In: Rueppel, R.A. (ed.) EUROCRYPT 1992. LNCS, vol. 658, pp. 390–407. Springer, Heidelberg (1993)
14. Galbraith, S.D., Paterson, K.G., Smart, N.P.: Pairings for cryptographers. Discrete Appl. Math. 156(16), 3113–3121 (2008)
15. Goldwasser, S., Micali, S., Rivest, R.L.: A digital signature scheme secure against adaptive chosen-message attacks. SIAM J. Comput. 17(2), 281–308 (1988)
16. Groth, J., Sahai, A.: Efficient non-interactive proof systems for bilinear groups. In: Smart, N.P. (ed.) EUROCRYPT 2008. LNCS, vol. 4965, pp. 415–432. Springer, Heidelberg (2008)

17. Izabachène, M., Libert, B.: Divisible e-cash in the standard model. In: Abdalla, M., Lange, T. (eds.) Pairing 2012. LNCS, vol. 7708, pp. 314–332. Springer, Heidelberg (2013)
18. Nakanishi, T., Sugiyama, Y.: Unlinkable divisible electronic cash. In: Okamoto, E., Pieprzyk, J.P., Seberry, J. (eds.) ISW 2000. LNCS, vol. 1975, pp. 121–134. Springer, Heidelberg (2000)
19. Okamoto, T.: An efficient divisible electronic cash scheme. In: Coppersmith, D. (ed.) CRYPTO 1995. LNCS, vol. 963, pp. 438–451. Springer, Heidelberg (1995)
20. Okamoto, T., Ohta, K.: Universal electronic cash. In: Feigenbaum, J. (ed.) CRYPTO 1991. LNCS, vol. 576, pp. 324–337. Springer, Heidelberg (1992)
21. Schnorr, C.-P.: Efficient identification and signatures for smart cards. In: Brassard, G. (ed.) CRYPTO 1989. LNCS, vol. 435, pp. 239–252. Springer, Heidelberg (1990)

Recovering Lost Device-Bound Credentials

Foteini Baldimtsi[1], Jan Camenisch[2], Lucjan Hanzlik[3]([✉]), Stephan Krenn[4], Anja Lehmann[2], and Gregory Neven[2]

[1] Boston University, Boston, USA
foteini@bu.edu
[2] IBM Research – Zurich, Rüschlikon, Switzerland
{jca,anj,nev}@zurich.ibm.com
[3] Wrocław University of Technology, Wrocław, Poland
lucjan.hanzlik@pwr.wroc.pl
[4] AIT Austrian Institute of Technology GmbH, Vienna, Austria
stephan.krenn@ait.ac.at

Abstract. Anonymous credential systems allow users to authenticate in a secure and private fashion. To protect credentials from theft as well as from being shared among multiple users, credentials can be bound to physical devices such as smart cards or tablets. However, device-bound credentials cannot be exported and backed up for the case that the device breaks down or is stolen. Restoring the credentials one by one and re-enabling the legitimate owner to use them may require significant efforts from the user. We present a mechanism that allows users to store some partial backup information of their credentials that will allow them to restore them through a single interaction with a device registration authority, while security and privacy are maintained. We therefore define anonymous credentials *with backup* and provide a generic construction that can be built on top of many existing credential systems.

Keywords: Anonymous credentials · Backup · Restore credentials

1 Introduction

Digital credentials are used to certify a set of attributes for a user (i.e., birth date, sex, clearances, access rights, or qualifications), similar to traditional paper-based credentials such as identity cards or driving licenses. However, their electronic nature makes them easy to duplicate and share. This is particularly problematic when users have an incentive to share their credentials, e.g., when they give access to payed subscription services such as music or video streaming. The problem becomes even worse when *anonymous* credentials are used, since a service provider cannot determine whether two *presentations* (i.e., authentications) were performed using the same or different credentials.

This work was supported by the European Community through the Seventh Framework Programme (FP7) under grant agreement number 318424 (*FutureID*) and by project S40012/K1102 at Wrocław University of Technology.

© Springer International Publishing Switzerland 2015
T. Malkin et al. (Eds.): ACNS 2015, LNCS 9092, pp. 307–327, 2015.
DOI: 10.1007/978-3-319-28166-7_15

Service providers therefore often protect credentials by "binding" them to an uncloneable hardware device that can perform authentications, but from which the credentials are not easily extracted. The main idea is that physical access to the device is required to be able to present the credential. A high-security way of doing so is by embedding the credentials on tamperproof smart cards or secure elements; while for lower-security use cases, storing the credentials in obfuscated form on the user's phone or tablet PC may suffice.

Unfortunately, both those techniques do not allow users to make backups of their credentials in order to recover if the device breaks down, or is lost or stolen. Instead, they will have to re-issue all the credentials and possibly also revoke the old ones. However, a single device may store many such credentials and replacing all of them is often costly and impracticable since it might require off-line authentication steps such as appearing in person at an office, receiving a letter by paper mail, or answering secondary security questions. Although efficient backup mechanisms for credentials—and in particular, anonymous credentials—seem essential, no such construction has been proposed so far in the literature.

Our Contributions. In this paper, we describe a scheme for efficient backup and restoration of device-bound credentials. Rather than binding the credentials to the device directly, we propose binding credentials to the user, while devices are registered to users as well. To perform a correct authentication, the user must prove that the credential is bound to the same user to which the device is registered. Credentials can then be exported and backed up in the traditional way, while a device registration authority prevents credential sharing and theft by ensuring that users can only register a limited number of devices and cannot register devices in other users' names.

We consider very strong security features for users as well as service providers. We assume that users store their backups on untrusted media that could fall into the wrong hands of malicious users, or even of malicious device manufacturers. In spite of having access to the backup and being able to register new devices to any user, the attacker should not be able to impersonate the user. We do so by requiring the user to keep a strong secret in an offline vault, e.g., on a piece of paper stored in a safe place. To maintain an acceptable level of usability, however, the vault secret is solely needed for device registration but not for everyday use.

We first give a high level description of an anonymous credential system with backup (BPABC) in Sect. 2, where we also define the syntax of BPABC and give an overview of the related security requirements. Besides the basic functionalities and backup, our framework covers advanced issuance (i.e., attributes can be carried over into new credentials without revealing them to the issuer), scope-exclusive pseudonyms (i.e., pseudonyms that are linkable for a fixed scope string, but unlinkable across scopes), revocation, and equality predicates (i.e., users can prove equality of hidden attributes, potentially across multiple credentials). In Sect. 3 we give a high-level description of the generic construction of a BPABC scheme together with a sketch of its security proof.

Related Work. Anonymous credentials were originally envisioned by Chaum [Cha81, Cha85], and subsequently a large number of schemes have been proposed, e.g., [BL13, BCC+09, CH02, CL01, CL02, CL04, Bra99, PZ13, CMZ14, GGM14]. Various formalizations of basic credential schemes have been proposed in the literature, typically only considering a limited set of features, e.g., Camenisch and Lysyanskaya [CL01] or Garman et al. [GGM14]. Recently, Camenisch et al. [CKL+14] presented the so far most holistic definitional framework for attribute-based credential systems, covering the same features as our framework, except that theirs was limited to software credentials only and thus there was no need for backup. Following their approach of a unified definitional framework, we extend their syntax, definitions, and generic construction to additionally support device-bound credentials.

2 Device-Bound Credentials with Backup

A privacy-enhancing attribute-based credential system (PABC) consists of *users* $\mathcal{U}$ that can request credentials on their attributes from *issuers*, $\mathcal{I}$, and *verifiers*, $\mathcal{V}$, to whom users can present (i.e., prove possession of) an arbitrary set of their credentials. Additionally, in a PABC system *with backup* (BPABC), *device manufacturers* $\mathcal{DM}$ generate hardware tokens, and *device credential issuers* $\mathcal{DI}$ can issue device credentials that can only be used if the device is physically present. The idea is that software credentials certify the users' attributes, whereas device credentials only guarantee that a user has physical access to a valid device. Then, upon presentation, the user shows that he possesses a valid device, and an arbitrary set of software credentials that also belong to the same user.

When joining the system, every user computes a user secret key *usk*, which is used to bind credentials to the user and allows him to derive unique *pseudonyms* for different *scopes*, where a scope may be an arbitrary bit string. Pseudonyms are linkable if computed twice for the same scope, but are completely unlinkable across scopes. Furthermore, a user computes a *vault user secret/public key* pair (*vusk, vupk*). Upon presentation, the user needs to know *vupk*, whereas the vault user secret key *vusk* can be stored in a secure vault (e.g., it could be written on paper and stored in a safe), and is only needed to "authenticate" the user every time he obtains a new device or in order to restore a lost device.

Note here that any method to legitimately re-obtaining credentials (anonymous or not) requires some secret data to be stored outside the used hardware tokens, e.g., on paper or an offline data stick. This is, because otherwise the honest owner of a credential could not prove legitimate ownership of a credential once the adversary got access to his device, as the adversary would know exactly the same information and could thus perfectly imitate the user. In traditional settings, this data may be the correct response to a security question for a given service. For a backup mechanism to be practical, it is important that the amount of secret data, as well as the number of modifications and look-ups of this data are kept small. In our construction, the secret data consists of only a single long-term signing key, independent of the number of credentials, and needs to only be accessed when setting up a new device.

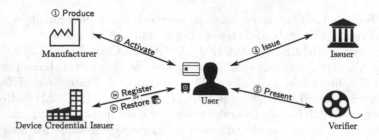

Fig. 1. All steps of a BPABC system are user-centric, and no two actions taken by the user can be linked unintentionally.

In Fig. 1 we describe the main steps of BPABC. Every user may possess several devices, and store an arbitrary set of his software credentials on any of these devices. Users can obtain software credentials from issuers as in a traditional credential system using ④ Issue, i.e., no device is required to obtain a credential. However, we assume that presenting credentials to verifiers using ⑤ Present always requires possession of a device.[1] Furthermore, certain credentials may be bound to specific devices, i.e., they only can be used with this specific device, by binding it to a device binding identifier *dbid* that is unique for every device.

The device manufacturer first generates a device containing a certificate of genuineness using the algorithm ① Produce. When buying a device, the user first has to activate it in interaction with the manufacturer by running the protocol ② Activate, at the end of which the device contains an initial device credential. Now, the user has two possibilities to personalize his device. If the user wants to register a new device, he runs ③ₐ Register in interaction with the device credential issuer. If, on the other hand, the user wants to restore a lost device, he runs ③ᵦ Restore with $\mathcal{DI}$. In both cases, the user uses his vault secret key *vusk* for this personalization; in the latter case, he further uses some backup token that was computed prior to losing the device. Restoring a device can be seen as a special way of registering a device: while for a plain registration, the device receives a fresh *dbid*, restoring allows the user to register the new device with the *dbid of the lost device*. Doing so allows the user to use all his software credentials (including those that were bound to the lost device) with the new device. However, the security requirements of the system guarantee that no user can abuse this restoring procedure to clone or duplicate devices, i.e., it is ensured that at any point in time at most one device with a certain *dbid* is valid in the system.

We chose a multi-step approach for personalizing the device to ensure maximum security to all involved parties, and to model reality more accurately. For instance, requiring to first activate the device with the manufacturer gives him the chance to deny this activation, e.g., if the vendor reported the given device to be stolen. However, as no personal information is involved in the Activate

---

[1] Note that this is without loss of generality, as the system parameters could simply contain a dummy issuer key for which a user can compute a dummy device credential whenever the verifier's policy does not require possession of a physical device.

protocol on the user side, the manufacturer does not learn any information about the user, but only that a given device is now activated. Splitting the activation and personalization steps allows us to distinguish the device credential issuer (e.g., a public authority) and the manufacturer (e.g., a smart card producer).

2.1 Syntax of Anonymous Credentials with Backup

In the following we formally specify the syntax and interfaces of an anonymous credential system with backup (BPABC). We kept the syntax as close as possible to that of PABC schemes without backup [CKL+14].

We denote algorithms by sans serif font, e.g., A, B. Drawing s uniformly at random from a set S is denoted by $s \xleftarrow{\$} S$. Similarly, $a \xleftarrow{\$} A$ denotes that a is the output of a randomized algorithm A. For a two party protocol (A, B), we write $(out_A; out_B) \xleftarrow{\$} \langle (A(in_A); B(in_B) \rangle$ to denote that A obtained output out_A on input in_A (accordingly for B). For sets $\mathcal{P} \subseteq \mathcal{S}$, we write $\mathcal{P}^c$ for the complement of $\mathcal{P}$, i.e., $\mathcal{P}^c = \mathcal{S} \setminus \mathcal{P}$. We write $(x_i)_{i=1}^n$ to denote the vector $(x_1, \ldots, x_n)$. Finally, for $n \in \mathbb{N}$, we write $[n] := \{1, \ldots, n\}$.

A BPABC scheme consists of a specification of an attribute space $\mathcal{AS} \subseteq \pm\{0,1\}^\ell$, algorithms SPGen, UKGen, VKGen, IKGen, DMKGen, Produce, ITGen, ITVf, Present, Verify, Revoke, BTGen, and protocols $\langle \mathcal{U}.\text{Issue}, \mathcal{I}.\text{Issue} \rangle$, $\langle \mathcal{U}.\text{Register}, \mathcal{DI}.\text{Register} \rangle$, $\langle \mathcal{U}.\text{Restore}, \mathcal{DI}.\text{Restore} \rangle$, $\langle \mathcal{U}.\text{Activate}, \mathcal{DM}.\text{Activate} \rangle$ defined as:

SPGen $\xrightarrow{\$}$ $\boldsymbol{spar}$. On input 1^κ, this *system parameter generation* algorithm generates system parameters *spar*.

UKGen $\xrightarrow{\$}$ $\boldsymbol{usk}$. On input system parameters *spar*, the *user key generation* algorithm outputs a user secret key *usk*.

VKGen $\xrightarrow{\$}$ $(\boldsymbol{vusk}, \boldsymbol{vupk})$. On input system parameters *spar*, the *vault user key generation* algorithm outputs a vault user secret/public key pair.

IKGen $\xrightarrow{\$}$ $(\boldsymbol{isk}, \boldsymbol{ipk}, \boldsymbol{RI})$. On input *spar*, the *(device) issuer key generation* algorithm outputs a public/private issuer key pair and some initial public revocation information, *RI*. Formally, our construction does not require to distinguish software and device credential issuers. However, to ease presentation, we will write $(disk, dipk, RI_{\mathcal{DI}})$ whenever an issuer is currently in the role of a device credential issuer.

DMKGen $\xrightarrow{\$}$ $(\boldsymbol{dmsk}, \boldsymbol{dmpk})$. On input *spar*, the *device manufacturer key generation* algorithm outputs a public/secret manufacturer key pair.

Produce $\xrightarrow{\$}$ cert. On input a secret manufacturer key *dmsk*, the *device production* algorithm outputs a genuineness certificate.

$\langle \mathcal{U}.\text{Activate}; \mathcal{DM}.\text{Activate} \rangle$ $\xrightarrow{\$}$ $((\boldsymbol{dsk}, \boldsymbol{dbid}, \boldsymbol{dcred}_{init}), \varepsilon)$. In this interactive *device activation* protocol, the user takes inputs $(dmpk, \text{cert})$, whereas the device manufacturer takes input *dmsk*. At the end of the protocol, the user obtains a device secret key *dsk*, a device binding identifier *dbid* and the initial device credential $dcred_{init}$.

$\langle \mathcal{U}.\text{Register}; \mathcal{DI}.\text{Register} \rangle$ $\xrightarrow{\$}$ $(\boldsymbol{dcred}, \boldsymbol{RI'}_{\boldsymbol{DI}})$. In this *device registration* protocol, the user takes inputs $(dipk, dmpk, vusk, vupk, dsk, dbid, dcred_{init}, drh)$, while the device credential issuer takes inputs $(disk, dmpk, RI_{\mathcal{DI}}, drh)$, where the inputs and outputs are defined as before. Moreover, drh is the revocation handle for the new device. As the result of this protocol, the user obtains the device credential $dcred$, while the issuer receives an updated revocation information $RI'_{\mathcal{DI}}$.

ITGen $\overset{\$}{\rightarrow} (nym, pit, sit)$. To issue a software credential, a user needs to generate an *issuance token* that defines the attributes of the credentials to be issued, where (some of) the attributes and the secret key can be hidden from the issuer and can be blindly "carried over" from credentials that the user already possesses (so that the issuer is guaranteed that hidden attributes were vouched for by another issuer).

Taking inputs $\left(usk, scope_{\mathcal{U}}, rh, \left(ipk_i, RI_i, cred_i, (a_{i,j})_{j=1}^{n_i}, R_i\right)_{i=1}^{k+1}, E, M, vupk, dbid\right)$, the *issuance token generation* algorithm outputs a user pseudonym nym and a public/secret issuance token (pit, sit). The inputs are defined as follows:

- usk is the user's secret key;
- $scope_{\mathcal{U}}$ is the scope of the generated user pseudonym nym, where $scope = \varepsilon$ if no pseudonym is to be generated (in which case $nym = \varepsilon$);
- rh is the revocation handle for $cred_{k+1}$ (e.g., chosen by the issuer before);
- $(ipk_i, RI_i)_{i=1}^{k}$ are the issuers' public keys and current revocation information for $(cred_i)_{i=1}^{k}$; (ipk_{k+1}, RI_{k+1}) correspond to the issuer of the new credential;
- $(cred_i)_{i=1}^{k}$ are credentials owned by the user and involved in this issuance and $cred_{k+1} = \varepsilon$ is a placeholder for the new credential to be issued;
- $R_i \subseteq [n_i]$ is the set of attribute indices for which the value is revealed;
- for $i \in [k]$, $(a_{i,j})_{j=1}^{n_i}$ is the list of attribute values certified in $cred_i$; $(a_{k+1,j})_{j \in R_{k+1}}$ are the attributes of $cred_{k+1}$ that are revealed to the issuer;
- $(a_{k+1,j})_{j \notin R_{k+1}}$ are the attributes of $cred_{k+1}$ that remain hidden;
- $((k+1, j), (i', j')) \in E$ means that the jth attribute of the new credential will have the same value as the j'th attribute of the i'th credential;
- $M \in \{0,1\}^*$ is a message to which the issuance token is to be bound;
- $vupk$ is the user's vault public key;
- $dbid$ is the device's binding identifier which can be set to ε if the new credential should not be device bound.

ITVf $\overset{\$}{\rightarrow}$ accept/reject. On inputs $\left(nym, pit, scope_{\mathcal{U}}, rh, (ipk_i, RI_i, (a_{i,j})_{j \in R_i})_{i=1}^{k+1}, E, M\right)$, this *issuance token verification* algorithm outputs whether to accept or to reject the issuance token. For $j = 1, \ldots, k$ all inputs are as before, but for $k+1$ they are for the new credential to be issued based on pit.

$\langle \mathcal{U}.\text{Issue}; \mathcal{I}.\text{Issue} \rangle \overset{\$}{\rightarrow} (cred, RI')$. In the interactive *issuance* protocol, the user takes input sit, whereas the issuer takes inputs (isk, pit, RI), where pit has been verified by the issuer before. At the end of the protocol, the user obtains a credential $cred$ as an output, while the issuer receives an updated revocation information RI'.

Present $\overset{\$}{\rightarrow} (pt, nym, dnym)$. On input $\left(usk, scope_{\mathcal{U}}, \left(ipk_i, RI_i, cred_i, (a_{i,j})_{j=1}^{n_i}, R_i\right)_{i=1}^{k}, E, M, dsk, scope_{\mathcal{D}}, (dipk, RI_{\mathcal{DI}}, dcred), \mathcal{BD}, vupk\right)$, the *presentation* algorithm outputs a presentation token *pt*, a user pseudonym *nym*, and a device pseudonym *dnym*. Most of the inputs are as before, but:

- $E \subseteq \{(i,j) : i \in [k], j \in [n_i]\}$, where $((i,j),(i',j')) \in E$ means that the presentation token proves that $a_{i,j} = a_{i',j'}$ without revealing the actual attribute values. That is, E enables one to prove equality predicates;
- M is a message to which the presentation is bound. This might, e.g., be a nonce chosen by $\mathcal{V}$ to prevent replay attacks, where $\mathcal{V}$ uses a presentation token to impersonate a user towards another verifier;
- *dsk* is the user's device secret key stored in the secure element of the device;
- $scope_{\mathcal{D}}$ is the scope of the generated device pseudonym *dnym*;
- *dipk* and $RI_{\mathcal{DI}}$ are the public key and current revocation information of the issuer of the device credential *dcred*;
- $\mathcal{BD} \subseteq [k]$ is a set of indices specifying which credentials are device-bound;
- *vupk* is the user's vault public key;

Verify $\xrightarrow{\$}$ accept/reject. The *presentation verification* algorithm takes $\big(pt, nym, scope_{\mathcal{U}}, (ipk_i, RI_i, (a_{i,j})_{j \in R_i})_{i=1}^{k}, E, M, dnym, scope_{\mathcal{D}}, dipk, RI_{\mathcal{DI}}, \mathcal{BD}\big)$ defined as before as inputs, and outputs whether to accept or to reject a presentation token. For notational convenience, we assume that a term like $(a_{i,j})_{j \in R_i}$ implicitly also describes the set R_i.

Revoke $\xrightarrow{\$}$ RI'. The *revocation* algorithm takes as inputs (isk, RI, rh), where *isk* is the issuer's secret key, RI is the current revocation information, and rh is the revocation handle to be revoked. It outputs an updated revocation information RI'.

BTGen $\xrightarrow{\$}$ (*dnym*, *pbt*, *sbt*). The *backup token generation* algorithm takes as input $\big(dsk, vupk, dipk, RI_{\mathcal{DI}}, dcred, dbid\big)$, where all the values are as before. It outputs a device pseudonym *dnym* and a public/secret backup token (*pbt*, *sbt*), which will allow the user to carry over the current *dbid* into a new device upon restoring. In theory, the entire backup token may be stored in a public cloud, as no adversary would be able to use it to get a new device credential re-issued. However, as *sbt* may contain personally identifying information, it is recommended to store *sbt* privately or only in an encrypted form.

$\langle \mathcal{U}.\text{Restore}; \mathcal{DI}.\text{Restore} \rangle \xrightarrow{\$} (dcred, RI'_{\mathcal{DI}})$. In the *device restoring* protocol, the user takes as input $(sbt, dipk, dmpk, vusk, dsk, dcred_{init}, drh)$, whereas the device issuer takes as input $(dnym, pbt, disk, dmpk, RI_{\mathcal{DI}}, drh)$. At the end of the protocol, the user outputs a fresh device credential *dcred*, while the issuer receives an updated revocation information $RI'_{\mathcal{DI}}$.

2.2 Security Definitions (Informal)

We now next describe the security properties of an attribute-based credential system with backup. Our definitions extend that of Camenisch et al. [CKL+14], who gave a comprehensive formal definitional framework for traditional credential schemes. As our system involves more types of parties and offers more interfaces, the formal definitions are quite complex, thus we only sketch the intuition here and refer to the full version for the formal definitions.

Oracles. In our definitions, the adversary is granted access to three oracles: a device manufacturer oracle $\mathcal{O}^{\text{producer}}$, an issuer oracle $\mathcal{O}^{\text{issuer}}$, and a user oracle $\mathcal{O}^{\text{user}}$, allowing the adversary to interact with honest device manufacturers, issuers, and users, respectively. While most of the interfaces of the oracles are natural, $\mathcal{O}^{\text{user}}$ has additional interfaces that allow the adversary to "steal" a device with a specific set of credentials from an honest user. Furthermore, the adversary is given interfaces to use such a device. His available options depend on the assumed security guarantees of the devices. We explicitly distinguish the following three types of devices, but our definitions are flexible enough to be easily adopted for other settings as well. First, if the devices are assumed to have secure memory and are protected by strong PINs, then the adversary essentially cannot profit from the stolen device at all. Second, if the memory is assumed to be secure but no strong PINs are used, then the adversary can use (i.e., backup, present, etc.) the stolen device and the credentials on them, but he does not learn the precise values of the user secret key or the credentials. Finally, if no assumption on the device are made, the adversary learns all the information stored on the device, including the user secret key and the credentials.

We believe that parameterizing our security definitions by the assumed security of the devices is useful to realistically model a broad range of real world scenarios, as, for instance, the security guarantees of eID cards, smart phones, or public transport tickets might drastically differ in practice. Clearly, making no assumptions on the devices results in the strongest definitions; however, as the computational capacity of embedded devices is often limited, our approach of considering additional properties is essential to obtain practical protocols.

Completeness. If all parties behave honestly, all protocols can be run successfully. In particular, honest users interacting with an honest counterpart can always activate, register, and restore devices, as well as obtain and present credentials.

Unforgeability. We define unforgeability as a game between an adversary and the $\mathcal{O}^{\text{producer}}$, $\mathcal{O}^{\text{issuer}}$, $\mathcal{O}^{\text{user}}$ oracles. The adversary can produce new devices, obtain and revoke credentials from honest issuers, instruct honest users to obtain credentials on inputs of his choice, request presentation tokens and receive backup tokens for given device credentials. Moreover, as mentioned above, he can "steal" devices and receive the device credential together with the software credentials and secret keys. At the end of the game the adversary outputs a number of presentation tokens and pseudonyms and wins if at least one of the presentation tokens is a forgery, or an issuance token successfully submitted to the honest issuer oracle was a forgery. A token is a forgery if it is *inconsistent* with the world the adversary interacts with using oracles $\mathcal{O}^{\text{producer}}$, $\mathcal{O}^{\text{issuer}}$, and $\mathcal{O}^{\text{user}}$. Informally, being consistent here means that for each token returned by the adversary, all software credentials are bound to the same use secret key, the pseudonym *nym* is sound for the given scope $scope_{\mathcal{U}}$, values of revealed attributes are correct, the equality relation E is satisfied, all credentials presented in the token are either bound to the same device binding identifier *dbid* or to ε and bound to the same vault public key. Moreover, presentation tokens must have been created using a valid device credential (issued for a genuine device using restore or register), the device pseudonym *dnym* is sound for the given scope $scope_D$ and the device credential must be signed such that the signature is verifiable with the vault public key.

Privacy. Similar to Camenisch et al. [CKL+14], we define privacy via a simulation based approach. We consider a set of honest users and let the adversary control all other parties in the system (device manufacturers, issuers, and verifiers). It should be computational infeasible for the adversary to distinguish whether he is communicating with the real set of honest users, or with a simulator, S, that only has access to the public information of the respective protocol (e.g., revealed attributes, scopes, public keys). For this, we define a filter $\mathcal{F}$ that has the same interfaces as the user oracle $\mathcal{O}^{user}$, but sanitizes the inputs beforeforwarding them to the S. For instance, unlinkability of presentation is ensured by not forwarding the credential identifiers *cid* (that the adversary gives to $\mathcal{O}^{user}$) to S. Furthermore, the filter performs comprehensive book keeping to exclude trivial distinguishing attacks that would result from requesting presentation tokens from invalid credentials which would be answered by the S but not by $\mathcal{O}^{user}$.

3   A Generic Construction and Its Security

One possible way to realize recoverable device-bound credentials would be to choose a unique "recovery secret" a for each device-bound credential and embed its image through a one-way function $f(a)$ as an additional attribute in the credential. This attribute is not revealed during presentation, but to backup a credential *cred*, he stores a presentation token *pt* revealing $f(a)$ on insecure backup media, and stores a in a secure offline vault. To restore *cred* upon loss, the user sends *pt* and a to the issuer, who checks if *pt* and $f(a)$ are correct, and then participates in an advanced issuance protocol that allows the user to blindly carry over all attributes from *cred* into a new credential that will be bound to freshly chosen recovery secret a'.[2]

One drawback of this construction is that a malicious device issuer getting access to a user's device carrying some software credentials could simply reissue himself a new device credential, as he would then just omit the proof of knowledge for a. The device issuer could then use the user's software credentials with the new device, and the user would have no option to revoke the malicious device credential as it would contain a fresh revocation handle.

This problem could be mitigated by encrypting credentials before loading them onto the device. The decryption key could be stored inside the secure element of the device, and the credentials would only be decrypted in this secure environment. So a malicious device issuer finding a user's device would not learn

---

[2] Alternatively, one could also use the same a for all device-bound credentials, and then only prove in zero-knowledge that one knows the trapdoor a to the attribute $f(a)$.

the user's software credentials and thus could not impersonate him. However, reality shows that virtually any tamperproof device can be broken by a sufficiently powerful adversary. In this case a user could again be impersonated.

One solution to this problem is to let the verifier not only check that the user owns a valid device credential, but also that the user "accepted" this credential. On a very high level, this can be done by letting the user sign his device credential, and embed the verification key of this signature into all his credentials as an attribute. Then, at presentation, the user shows that he owns a device credential and a signature thereon, and that the public verification key is also contained in all the other credentials. As a malicious device issuer may never learn the signing key of this user (as it is stored in a secure vault), he may not impersonate the user with a fresh device credential any more, as this would require forging a signature on this credential.

A bit more precisely, each user computes a signature key pair $(vusk, vupk)$ and stores $vusk$ in a bank vault as his *vault user secret key*, and only needs to access $vusk$ when (re-)obtaining device credentials. After buying and activating a device, the user requests a device credential $dcred$, that certifies the validity of the device and a unique device binding identifier $dbid$. The device credential $dcred$ is bound to $vupk$. All software credentials also get bound to $vupk$, and optionally to $dbid$ if the credential is to be bound to a specific device; if no $dbid$ is given, the credential can be used with any device. Upon loss of a device, the user now only needs to get $dcred$ re-issued, but all the software credentials can be left unchanged. To ensure that only the legitimate user can re-obtain and later prove possession of a device credential, we let the user sign the (unique) revocation handle rh of $dcred$ using $vusk$. Upon presentation, the user now not only shows that he possesses a device credential, but also that he knows a signature under $vupk$ on rh. This signature protects against malicious credential issuers, which cannot create such proof of signature knowledge on a non-revoked token rh. Unfortunately, binding the credentials to $vupk$ by adding it as an attribute does not work here generically, as this would require that the attribute space of the credential scheme subsumes the key (message) space of the signature scheme. Furthermore, standard signatures would require the verifier to learn the signature verification key $vupk$, which must not be revealed to maintain unlinkability. Therefore, upon device registration, the user commits to $vupk$ and lets the issuer additionally sign this commitment. Using commuting signatures [Fuc11] additionally allows us to perform the required proofs with only publishing a commitment to $vupk$, but not $vupk$ itself, therefore achieving the required privacy goals.

What is left, is to bind this signature to the specific credential. To do so, the issuer, instead of only signing the vault public key, signs a combination of $vupk$ and the revocation handle, rh, for the credential issued. Thus, once the credential gets revoked, the signature of the issuer becomes useless. Since revocation handles do not necessarily belong to the message (key) space of commuting signatures, we sign the value $\phi(rh)$ instead of signing the actual revocation handle rh, for some appropriate mapping function ϕ. Finally, we also use a proof system that allows to verify that commitments to rh and $\phi(rh)$ are consistent.

3.1   Building Blocks

In the following, we briefly recap the non-standard building blocks required for the generic construction presented in this section.

Privacy-Enhancing Attribute-Based Credentials. Because of space limitations and to avoid redundancy, we refrain from giving formal definitions for PABC systems, but refer to Camenisch et al. [CKL+14].

Informally, anonymous credentials (without backup) have the same interfaces as introduced in Sect. 2.1, except for all the backup-related parts. That is, they consist of the following algorithms and protocols: SPGen, UKGen, IKGen, ITGen, ITVf, $\langle \mathcal{U}.\mathsf{Issue}; \mathcal{I}.\mathsf{Issue}\rangle$, Present, Verify, Revoke. The input/output behavior and the required security properties are again similar to Sects. 2.1 and 2.2, respectively.

Commuting Signatures and Verifiable Encryption. On a high level, commuting signatures combine digital signatures, encryption, and proof systems, such that one can commit to (any subset of) signature verification key, message, and signature, and still be able to prove that the three values are a valid key/message/signature tuple. In the following we give a slightly simplified version of the interfaces introduced by Fuchsbauer [Fuc11].

$\mathsf{SPGen}_{\mathsf{CS}}$. On input global system parameters $spar_{\mathsf{g}}$, this *system parameter generation* algorithms outputs signature parameters $spar_{\mathsf{CS}}$. These system parameters are input to all algorithms in the following, but we will sometimes omit this for notational convenience.

$\mathsf{KeyGen}_{\mathsf{CS}}$. On input $spar_{\mathsf{CS}}$, this *key generation* algorithm outputs a signature key pair (sk, pk).

$\mathsf{Com}_{\mathsf{CS}}$. On input a message m in the signature or the key space, this *commitment* algorithm outputs a commitment $cs_{\mathcal{M}}$ and opening information $ocs_{\mathcal{M}}$.

$\mathsf{Com}_{\mathcal{M}}$. On input a message m from the message space, this *commitment* algorithm extends $\mathsf{Com}_{\mathsf{CS}}$ by, among others, proofs of consistency. Note that the key space is consistent with the message space and therefore one can also use this algorithm to commit to verification keys.

$\mathsf{DCom}_{\mathsf{CS}}$. On input a commitment $cs_{\mathcal{M}}$ and opening $ocs_{\mathcal{M}}$, this *decommitment* algorithm outputs the committed message m.

$\mathsf{CombCom}_{\mathsf{CS}}$. On input two commitment/opening pairs $(cs_1, ocs_1), (cs_2, ocs_2)$ to m_1, m_2 in the message or key space, this *commitment combining* algorithm outputs a commitment/opening pair (cs_3, ocs_3) of type $\mathsf{Com}_{\mathcal{M}}$ to $m_1 \otimes m_2$.

$\mathsf{VerCombCom}_{\mathsf{CS}}$. On input three commitments cs_i, $i = 1, 2, 3$, this *combined commitment verification* algorithm outputs 1, if and only if cs_3 is the output of $\mathsf{CombCom}_{\mathsf{CS}}$ on input cs_1, cs_2.

$\mathsf{SigCom}_{\mathsf{CS}}$. On input a secret key sk and a commitment $cs_{\mathcal{M}}$, this *commitment signing* algorithm outputs a signature σ, a commitment/opening pair (cs_σ, ocs_σ) to σ, and a proof π_σ of the validity of the signature.

$$\pi'_\sigma \xleftarrow{\$} \mathsf{AdPrC}_\mathcal{M}(pk, (cs_\mathcal{M}, ocs_\mathcal{M}), (cs_\sigma), \pi_\sigma)$$
$$\pi'_\sigma \xleftarrow{\$} \mathsf{AdPrDC}(pk, (cs_\mathcal{M}), (cs_\sigma, ocs_\sigma), \pi'_\sigma)$$
$$(cs'_\sigma, ocs'_\sigma) \xleftarrow{\$} \mathsf{Com}_\mathcal{M}(\sigma)$$
$$\pi'_\sigma \xleftarrow{\$} \mathsf{AdPrC}(pk, (cs_\mathcal{M}), (cs'_\sigma, ocs'_\sigma), \pi'_\sigma)$$
$$\text{if } cs_{pk} \neq \varepsilon \text{ and } ocs_{pk} \neq \varepsilon:$$
$$\qquad \pi'_\sigma \xleftarrow{\$} \mathsf{AdPrC}_\mathcal{K}((cs_{pk}, ocs_{pk}), (cs_\mathcal{M}), (cs_{\sigma, new}), \pi'_\sigma)$$
$$\text{Output } ((cs'_\sigma, ocs'_\sigma), \pi'_\sigma)$$

Fig. 2. $\mathsf{RandSign}((pk, cs_{pk}, ocs_{pk}), (cs_\mathcal{M}, ocs_\mathcal{M}), (\sigma, cs_\sigma, ocs_\sigma, \pi_\sigma))$

$\mathsf{Verify}_{\mathsf{CS}}$. On input a public key pk, a message m, a signature σ (or commitments to (some of) these values), and a proof π, this *verification* algorithm outputs accept if and only if π is a valid proof that σ is a signature on m for the public key pk.

AdPrC. On input pk, $cs_\mathcal{M}$, (cs_σ, ocs_σ), and π such that $\mathsf{Verify}_{\mathsf{CS}}(pk, cs_\mathcal{M}, \sigma, \pi) = $ accept (where σ is obtained using $\mathsf{DCom}_{\mathsf{CS}}$), this *committing proof adaption* algorithm outputs a proof π' such that $\mathsf{Verify}_{\mathsf{CS}}(pk, cs_\mathcal{M}, cs_\sigma, \pi') = $ accept; to decommit in a proof, AdPrDC works the other way round (i.e., adapts π such that it verifies for σ and not for cs_σ).

$\mathsf{AdPrC}_\mathcal{M}$. On input pk, $(cs_\mathcal{M}, ocs_\mathcal{M})$, cs_σ, and π such that $\mathsf{Verify}_{\mathsf{CS}}(pk, m, cs_\sigma, \pi) = $ accept, this *committing proof adaption* algorithm outputs π' such that $\mathsf{Verify}_{\mathsf{CS}}(pk, cs_\mathcal{M}, cs_\sigma, \pi') = $ accept; again, $\mathsf{AdPrDC}_\mathcal{M}$ works the other way round,

$\mathsf{AdPrC}_\mathcal{K}$. On input (cs_{pk}, ocs_{pk}), $cs_\mathcal{M}$, cs_σ, and π such that $\mathsf{Verify}_{\mathsf{CS}}(pk, cs_\mathcal{M}, cs_\sigma, \pi) = $ accept, the *committing proof adaption* algorithm outputs π' such that $\mathsf{Verify}_{\mathsf{CS}}(cs_{pk}, cs_\mathcal{M}, cs_\sigma, \pi') = $ accept; $\mathsf{AdPrDC}_\mathcal{K}(cs_{pk}, cs_\mathcal{M}, cs_\sigma, \pi)$ works the other way round.

We require that $(\mathsf{Com}_{\mathsf{CS}}, \mathsf{DCom}_{\mathsf{CS}})$ is a secure extractable commitment scheme. We also require **strong unforgeability** (under chosen message attack), i.e., the adversary cannot output a new pair message/signature (m, σ). Moreover, all the proofs must be simulatable using an appropriate trapdoor, for details we refer to Fuchsbauer [Fuc11].

In addition to the above algorithms, Fig. 2 specifies the algorithm $\mathsf{RandSign}$ that we will use in our construction. The procedure takes as input a commuting signature for which the signature is given as commitment and adapts it to a commuting signature for which the signature, the message and optionally the public key are given as commitments (the commitment to signature is re-randomized), such that the inputs cs_σ and π_σ cannot be linked to cs'_σ and π'_σ.

3.2 The Construction

In the following we show how to build a BPABC system from a PABC system and a commuting signature scheme $(\mathsf{Com}_\mathcal{M}, \dots)$. In the construction, let $\mathsf{H}_{\mathcal{AS}} : \{0,1\}^* \to \mathcal{AS}$ and $\mathsf{H}_{\mathcal{MS}} : \{0,1\}^* \to \mathcal{MS}$ be collision-resistant hash functions, where $\mathcal{AS}$ is the attribute space of the PABC system, and $\mathcal{MS}$ is the message space of presentation tokens used in the PABC system. Let $(\mathsf{Com}_\mathsf{c}, \ldots)$ be a standard commitment scheme. Furthermore, let ϕ be a homomorphism from the message space of Com_c to the message space of $\mathsf{Com}_\mathcal{M}$, that additionally has the property that $\phi(m_1) \otimes \phi(m_2) = \phi(m_1 \oplus m_2)$, where $m_1, m_2, m_1 \oplus m_2$ are in the message space of Com_c. Finally, let $(\mathsf{Prove}_\phi, \mathsf{Verify}_\phi)$ be a zero-knowledge proof system for statements:

$$\mathsf{ZKP}\left[(\alpha) : c_1 = \mathsf{Com}_\mathcal{M}(\phi(\alpha)) \ \wedge \ c_2 = \mathsf{Com}_\mathsf{c}(\alpha)\right].$$

Below we give a simplified generic construction of our BPABC scheme, based on the PABC credential scheme [CKL+14] and commuting signatures. The complete construction is given in the full version and actually does not build upon PABC's, but rather extends the generic PABC-construction, as we require access to the commitment values produced and consumed by the building blocks of the PABC scheme. In the description below, we assume, for the sake of simplicity, that we can extract the commitments from PABC presentation and issuance tokens, which allows us to focus on the extensions needed to obtain the BPABC.

Setup and Key Generation

SPGen: The system parameters $spar$ consist of the parameters $spar_{\mathsf{PABC}}$ of the PABC system, $spar_{\mathsf{CS}}$ of the commuting signature scheme, and two attributes $\{\mathsf{initial}, \mathsf{activated}\} \in \mathcal{AS}$. These parameters in particular specify all required domains, e.g., of revocation handles, etc.

UKGen: As in PABC, i.e., compute the user key as $usk \xleftarrow{\$} \mathsf{UKGen}(spar_{\mathsf{PABC}})$.

VKGen: Compute the vault keys as $(vusk, vupk) \xleftarrow{\$} \mathsf{KeyGen}_{\mathsf{CS}}(spar_{\mathsf{CS}})$, e.g., being keys for the commuting signature scheme.

IKGen: The issuer key consists of an issuer's key for the PABC system and a key for the commuting signature scheme. For device credential issuers the key also comprises two scopes and list to keep track of used pseudonyms:

- Compute $(isk_{\mathsf{PABC}}, ipk_{\mathsf{PABC}}, RI_{\mathsf{PABC}}) \xleftarrow{\$} \mathsf{IKGen}_{\mathsf{PABC}}(spar_{\mathsf{PABC}})$.
- Compute $(isk_{\mathsf{CS}}, ipk_{\mathsf{CS}}) \xleftarrow{\$} \mathsf{KeyGen}_{\mathsf{CS}}(spar_{\mathsf{CS}})$.
- Set $ipk = (ipk_{\mathsf{PABC}}, ipk_{\mathsf{CS}})$, $isk = (isk_{\mathsf{PABC}}, isk_{\mathsf{CS}}, ipk)$, and $RI = RI_{\mathsf{PABC}}$.
- For *device credential issuers* further generate two scopes $scope_{bup}, scope_{reg}$ $\xleftarrow{\$} \mathcal{SCP}$ (for backup pseudonyms and for registration pseudonyms) and an empty list $\mathcal{L}_{dnym}$ to store used pseudonyms.
  Set $dipk = (ipk, scope_{bup}, scope_{reg})$, $disk = isk$, and $RI_{\mathcal{DI}} = (RI, \mathcal{L}_{dnym})$.

DMKGen: The device manufacturer's key consists of an issuer's key for the PABC system, a scope for activation pseudonyms and an empty list $\mathcal{L}_{\mathsf{cert}}$ to store used pseudonyms:

- Compute $(dmsk_{\mathsf{PABC}}, dmpk_{\mathsf{PABC}}, RI_{\mathsf{PABC}}) \xleftarrow{\$} \mathsf{IKGen}_{\mathsf{PABC}}(spar_{\mathsf{PABC}})$.
- Generate empty list $\mathcal{L}_{\mathsf{cert}}$ and $scope_{act} \xleftarrow{\$} \mathcal{SCP}$.

- Set $dmpk = (dmpk_{PABC}, RI_{PABC}, \mathcal{L}_{cert}, scope_{act})$, and the secret key to $dmsk = (dmsk_{PABC}, dmpk_{PABC})$.

Produce: Generate an initial device secret key dsk_{cert} and issue a device credential under $dmsk$.

- Compute device secret key $dsk_{cert} \xleftarrow{\$} \mathsf{UKGen}_{PABC}(spar_{PABC})$.
- Choose a random revocation handle drh.
- Issue (locally) a PABC credential $cred_{cert}$ for the attribute initial, device key dsk_{cert} and revocation handle drh under the device manufacturer's issuance key $dmsk_{PABC}$.
- Set $\mathsf{cert} = (cred_{cert}, dsk_{cert})$.

Device Activation and Registration

Activate: To activate a device, the user runs a protocol with the device manufacturer where $\mathcal{U}$ derives a new device secret key dsk as $dsk = dsk' \oplus dsk_{cert}$ for a randomly chosen dsk'. The user also obtains a credential on dsk from $\mathcal{DM}$. Thereby, $\mathcal{DM}$ can verify that dsk is correctly derived from a previously certified dsk_{cert} but does not learn the new device key. A simplified version of the activation protocol is depicted in Fig. 3. For the sake of simplicity, we therein omit the openings from the in- and outputs of the commitment algorithms.

Register: To register a device with a device credential issuer $\mathcal{DI}$, the user (assisted by his device) runs a protocol with $\mathcal{DI}$. Therein, $\mathcal{U}$ shows that he has an activation credential $dcred_{init}$ from $\mathcal{DM}$ on some (secret) device key dsk and identifier $dbid$. The device credential issuer then blindly carries over $dsk, dbid$ into a

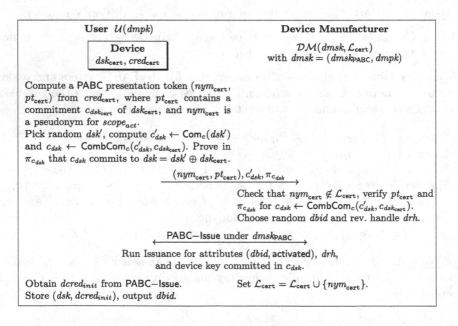

Fig. 3. Device activation

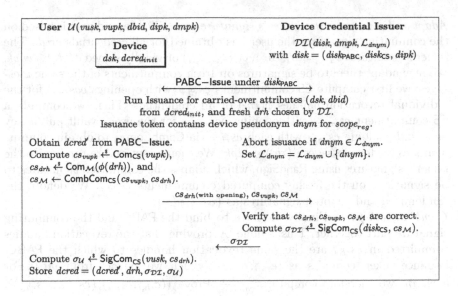

Fig. 4. Device registration

new credential that also includes a revocation handle drh. In addition, $\mathcal{DI}$ also signs a commitment on a combination of drh and the user's vault public key $vupk$, and the user signs a commitment of $\phi(drh)$, both using the commuting signature scheme. The registration information then consists of the credential and both signatures. The simplified registration protocol is given in Fig. 4. For simplicity, we again omit the openings from the in- and outputs of the commitment algorithms.

Credential Issuance and Presentation

ITGen: This algorithm produces an issuance token for input $(usk, scope_{\mathcal{U}}, rh, (ipk_i, RI_i, cred_i, (a_{i,j})_{j=1}^{n_i}, R_i)_{i=1}^{k+1}, E, M, vupk, dbid_{\mathcal{D}})$ and combines an PABC issuance token with a commuting signature as follows:

1. *Compute* PABC *issuance token.* First, the input to ITGen$_{\mathsf{PABC}}$ needs to be prepared such that is also captures the device-binding property, i.e., the relation E gets extended to express which credentials are device-bound, and that they are all bound to the same device. More precisely, given k credentials $cred_i = (cred_i', dbid_i, rh_i, (\sigma_{\mathcal{I},i}, cs_{\sigma,i}, ocs_{\sigma,i}, \pi_{\sigma,i}))$, one first verifies whether all device-bound credentials with $dbid_i \neq \varepsilon$ contain the same device identifier $dbid^*$. We denote $\mathcal{BD}$ for the set of all device-bound credentials. If at least one credential is device-bound, then the new credential should be also device-bound as well, i.e., verify that $dbid_{\mathcal{D}} = dbid^*$ and set $dbid_{k+1} = dbid_{\mathcal{D}}$. Abort with output $\bot$ if any of the checks fails. Update the relation expression to $E' = E \cup \{((i, n_i + 1), (j, n_j + 1)) : i, j \in \mathcal{BD} \cup \{k+1\}\}$ and use E' to obtain the PABC issuance token. That is, we run ITGen$_{\mathsf{PABC}}(usk, scope_{\mathcal{U}}, rh, (ipk_i, RI_i, cred_i', ((a_{i,j})_{j=1}^{n_i}, dbid_i), R_i)_{i=1}^{k+1}, E', M)$ receiving (nym', pit', sit').

2. *Adapt and randomize the Issuer's signatures $\sigma_{\mathcal{I},i}$.* The second part is based on the commuting signatures the user has obtained for all credentials $cred_i$. The issuer's signatures $\sigma_{\mathcal{I},i} = (\sigma_i, cs_{\sigma,i}, ocs_{\sigma,i}, \pi_{\sigma,i})$ originally signed $\phi(rh_i) \otimes vupk$. We now adapt them to be signatures on fresh commitments of the same messages: we first compute CS commitments $cs_{rh,i}$ (with openings $ocs_{rh,i}$) for the individual revocation handles $\phi(rh_i)$ of all credentials. Then, we compute a CS commitment cs_{vupk} (with opening ocs_{vupk}) for the user's vault public key $vupk$ and combine cs_{vupk} with each $cs_{rh,i}$ via CombCom$_{CS}$ to obtain commitments $cs_{\mathcal{M},i}$ for messages $\phi(rh_i) \otimes vupk$. We then adopt and re-randomize the issuer's signatures using RandSign, which adapts the committed signatures to be signatures on the freshly computed commitments $cs_{\mathcal{M},i}$. We denote the randomized and adapted signatures as $(cs'_{\sigma,i}, \pi'_{\sigma,i})$.

3. *Combine both parts.* Finally, we have to bind the PABC and the commuting signature part together. This is done by proving that the revocation handles committed in $cs_{rh,i}$ are the same revocation handles to which the PABC-issuance token commits as $(c_{rh,i}, o_{rh,i})$ (which we extract from pit'). For each rh_i we therefore compute $\pi^{\phi}_{rh,i} \xleftarrow{\$} \mathsf{Prove}_{\phi}((c_{rh,i}, o_{rh,i}), (cs_{rh,i}, ocs_{rh,i}))$. We set $pit = (pit', \mathcal{BD}, cs_{vupk}, (cs_{\mathcal{M},i}, cs_{rh,i}, \pi^{\phi}_{rh,i}, cs'_{\sigma,i}, \pi'_{\sigma,i})^{k}_{i=1})$, $sit = (sit', dbid_{\mathcal{D}}, cs_{vupk}, ocs_{vupk})$ and $nym = nym'$.

<u>ITVf:</u> Verify the PABC issuance token pit', proofs $\pi^{\phi}_{rh,i}$, that $(cs'_{\sigma,i}, \pi'_{\sigma,i})$ are valid issuer signatures on $cs_{\mathcal{M},i}$, and that VerCombCom$_{CS}(cs_{rh_i}, cs_{vupk}, cs_{\mathcal{M},i}) = 1$ for $i = 1, \ldots, k$. Output reject if any of the check fails, and accept otherwise.

<u>Issue:</u> Issuance of a software credential (possibly bound to a device if $dbid_{\mathcal{D}} \neq \varepsilon$) consists of a PABC issuance protocol, and a commuting signature generated by the issuer as depicted in Fig. 5.

<u>Present:</u> A presentation token for $(usk, scope_{\mathcal{U}}, (ipk_i, RI_i, cred_i, (a_{i,j})^{n_i}_{j=1}, R_i)^{k}_{i=1}, E, M, dsk, scope_{\mathcal{D}}, (dipk, RI_{\mathcal{DI}}, dcred), \mathcal{BD}, vupk)$ consists of two PABC presentation tokens (one for the software credentials, and one for the device credential) and randomized commuting signatures:

1. *Compute PABC presentation token pt' for the software credentials.* Parse each credential as $cred_i = (cred'_i, dbid_i, rh_i, \sigma_{\mathcal{I},i})$. Adapt the relation E to include the device-binding relations, i.e., use the indices in set $\mathcal{BD}$ to compute $E' = E \cup \{((i, n_i+1), (j, n_j+1)) : i, j \in \mathcal{BD}\}$. Compute (nym, pt') for all software credentials $cred_1, \ldots, cred_k$ by running Present$_{PABC}(usk, scope_{\mathcal{U}}, (ipk_i, RI_i, cred'_i, ((a_{i,j})^{n_i}_{j=1}, dbid_i), R_i)^{k}_{i=1}, E', M)$.

2. *Compute PABC presentation token pt'' for the device credential.* If $dcred \neq \varepsilon$, parse $dcred = (dcred', drh, \sigma_{\mathcal{DI}}, \sigma_{\mathcal{U}})$, and compute presentation token $(dnym, pt'')$ as Present$_{PABC}(dsk, scope_{\mathcal{D}}, (ipk_{\mathcal{DI}}, RI_{\mathcal{DI}}, dcred', (dbid_{\mathcal{D}})), \emptyset, M)$. If $dcred = \varepsilon$ abort with output $\perp$.

3. *Bind pt' and pt'' together.* Extract $(c_{dbid,\mathcal{D}}, o_{dbid,\mathcal{D}})$ from pt'' and, for some $i \in \mathcal{BD}$, $(c_{dbid,i}, o_{dbid,i})$ from pt'. Prove that both commit to the same value in π_{dbid}.

User $\mathcal{U}(ipk, sit)$ **Issuer** $\mathcal{I}(isk, RI, pit)$
with $sit = (sit', dbid_\mathcal{D}, cs_{vupk}, ocs_{vupk})$ with $isk = (isk_{PABC}, isk_{CS})$

$\xleftarrow{\quad\text{PABC}-\text{Issue under } isk_{PABC}\quad}$

Run PABC Issuance for new software credential as
defined in sit', pit' (incl. revocation handle rh_{k+1}).

Obtain $cred'$ from PABC$-$Issue.
$(cs_{rh}, ocs_{rh}) \xleftarrow{\$} \mathsf{Com}_\mathcal{M}(\phi(rh_{k+1}))$,
$(cs_\mathcal{M}, ocs_\mathcal{M}) \leftarrow \mathsf{CombCom}_{CS}((cs_{vupk}, ocs_{vupk}), (cs_{rh}, ocs_{rh}))$.

$\xrightarrow{\quad cs_{rh}, ocs_{rh}, cs_\mathcal{M} \quad}$

Verify that cs_{rh} and $cs_\mathcal{M}$ are correct.
Compute $\sigma_\mathcal{I} \xleftarrow{\$} \mathsf{SigCom}_{CS}(isk_{CS}, cs_\mathcal{M})$.

$\xleftarrow{\quad \sigma_\mathcal{I} = (\sigma, cs_\sigma, ocs_\sigma, \pi_\sigma) \quad}$

Update $\sigma_\mathcal{I}$ to be a signature on the message
$(\phi(rh_{k+1}) \otimes vupk) \leftarrow \mathsf{DCom}_{CS}(cs_\mathcal{M}, ocs_\mathcal{M})$, set
$\pi_\sigma \xleftarrow{\$} \mathsf{AdPrDC}_\mathcal{M}(ipk_{CS}, (cs_\mathcal{M}, ocs_\mathcal{M}), (cs_\sigma, ocs_\sigma), \pi_\sigma)$.
Output $cred = (cred', dbid_\mathcal{D}, rh_{k+1}, \sigma_\mathcal{I})$.

Fig. 5. Credential issuance

4. *Adapt and randomize the Issuer's signatures $\sigma_{\mathcal{I},i}$ and $\sigma_{\mathcal{DI}}$.* Similarly as in the ITGen algorithm we adapt the issuer's signatures $\sigma_{\mathcal{I},i} = (\sigma_i, cs_{\sigma,i}, ocs_{\sigma,i}, \pi_{\sigma,i})$ on $\phi(rh_i) \otimes vupk$ to be signatures on fresh commitments of the same messages. To this end, we first compute CS commitments $cs_{rh,i}$ (with openings $ocs_{rh,i}$) for the individual revocation handles $\phi(rh_i)$ for all $i = 1, \ldots, k, \mathcal{D}$. Then, we compute a CS commitment cs_{vupk} (with opening ocs_{vupk}) for the user's vault public key $vupk$ and combine cs_{vupk} with each $cs_{rh,i}$ via $\mathsf{CombCom}_{CS}$ to obtain commitments $cs_{\mathcal{M},i}$ for messages $\phi(rh_i) \otimes vupk$. We then adopt and re-randomize the issuer's signatures using $\mathsf{RandSign}$, which adapts the committed signatures to be signatures on the freshly computed commitments $cs_{\mathcal{M},i}$. We denote the randomized and adapted signatures for all $i = 1, \ldots, k, \mathcal{D}$ as $(cs'_{\sigma,i}, \pi'_{\sigma,i})$, where $(cs'_{\sigma,\mathcal{D}}, \pi'_{\sigma,\mathcal{D}})$ stands for the adapted signature of the device credential issuer.

5. *Adapt and randomize the User's signature $\sigma_\mathcal{U}$ (contained in dcred).* In a similar vein, we adapt the user's signature $\sigma_\mathcal{U} = (\sigma, cs_{\sigma,\mathcal{U}}, ocs_{\sigma,\mathcal{U}}, \pi_{\sigma,\mathcal{U}})$ on the revocation handle of the device credential $\phi(drh)$ using procedure $\mathsf{RandSign}$. However, here we also adapt the proof using a commitment to $vupk$. Note that this ensures that the final signature proof is not only for a committed signature on a committed message, but that also the public key is given as a commitment. This is required here, as the user's public key would serve as a unique identifier otherwise. We denote the randomized user signature on message $cs_{rh,\mathcal{D}}$ and under key cs_{vupk} (computed in the step above) as $(cs'_{\sigma,\mathcal{U}}, \pi'_{\sigma,\mathcal{U}})$.

6. *Bind the PABC part and CS part together.* This is again similar to the ITGen algorithm: we bind both parts together by extracting the commitments for all revocation handles from the PABC tokens and proving that they contain the

same values as the CS commitments used in the commuting signatures part. That is, for all $i = 1, \ldots, k$ we extract $(c_{rh,i}, o_{rh,i})$ from pt' and $(c_{rh,\mathcal{D}}, o_{rh,\mathcal{D}})$ from pt'' and compute $\pi_{rh,i}^{\phi} \xleftarrow{\$} \mathsf{Prove}_\phi((c_{rh,i}, o_{rh,i}), (cs_{rh,i}, ocs_{rh,i}))$.

Finally, we compose the presentation token as $pt = ((pt', pt'', \pi_{dbid}, cs_{vupk}, (cs_{\mathcal{M},i}, cs_{rh,i}, \pi_{rh,i}^{\phi}, cs'_{\sigma,i}, \pi'_{\sigma,i})_{i=1}^{k,\mathcal{D}}, cs'_{\sigma,\mathcal{U}}, \pi'_{\sigma,\mathcal{U}}), nym, dnym)$.

<u>Verify</u>: Verify both presentation tokens (nym, pt'), $(dnym, pt'')$, proofs π_{dbid}, $\pi_{rh,i}^{\phi}$ and that all $cs_{\mathcal{M},i}$ are valid combinations of commitments $cs_{rh,i}$ and cs_{vupk} (for $i = 1, \ldots, k, \mathcal{D}$). Moreover, verify the credential issuer's signatures under $cs_{\mathcal{M},i}$ and the user's signature under $cs_{rh,\mathcal{D}}$ and for key cs_{vupk}. Output reject if any of the checks fails, and accept otherwise.

<u>Revoke</u>: On input (isk, RI, rh) parse isk as $(isk_{\mathsf{PABC}}, isk_{\mathsf{CS}}, ipk)$ and run the PABC revocation algorithm $\mathsf{Revoke}_{\mathsf{PABC}}(isk_{\mathsf{PABC}}, RI_{\mathsf{PABC}}, rh)$.

Backup and Restore

<u>BTGen</u>: Upon input $(dsk, vupk, dipk, RI_{\mathcal{DI}}, dcred, dbid_{\mathcal{D}})$ parse $dcred = (dcred', drh, \sigma_{\mathcal{DI}}, \sigma_{\mathcal{U}})$ and compute the presentation token $(dnym, pt) \leftarrow \mathsf{Present}_{\mathsf{PABC}}(dsk, scope_{bup}, (ipk_{\mathcal{DI}}, RI_{\mathcal{DI}}, dcred', (dbid_{\mathcal{D}})), \emptyset, M)$ for the device credential. Extract the commitment and opening (c_{dbid}, o_{dbid}) to the device identifier $dbid_{\mathcal{D}}$ and commitment and opening (c_{drh}, o_{drh}) to the device revocation handle. Set the public part to $pbt = (pt, drh, o_{drh})$, $sbt = (dbid, c_{dbid}, o_{dbid})$ and output $(dnym, pbt, sbt)$.

<u>Restore</u>: The restore procedure is initiated by the user when he obtained his new (and activated) device including a new device key dsk' and activation credential $dcred'_{init}$. The user then runs the restore protocol with the device credential issuer $\mathcal{DI}$ where he obtains a new device credential $cred'$ that contains the device identifier $dbid$ from the backup token. The simplified protocol is given in Fig. 6.

Theorem 1 (Informal). *The BPABC-system constructed above is unforgeable for all types of devices, if the underlying PABC- and the CS-schemes are unforgeable and* Prove_ϕ *is extractable and sound. It is further private for devices with secure memory without PINs, if the PABC-scheme is private,* Prove_ϕ *is zero-knowledge, and the CS scheme can be simulated given commitments to messages or/and verification keys.*

3.3 Intuition Underlying the Security Proofs

Due to space limitations, we only give the intuition of our security proofs.

Privacy. Our generic construction can be shown to be private, if one assumes secure memory without strong PINs, cf. Sect. 2.2. Note that without assuming secure memory, the adversary could in particular learn the user's secret key from which it could (deterministically) derive pseudonyms for arbitrary scopes, and could thus easily link arbitrary presentations to the user; achieving privacy

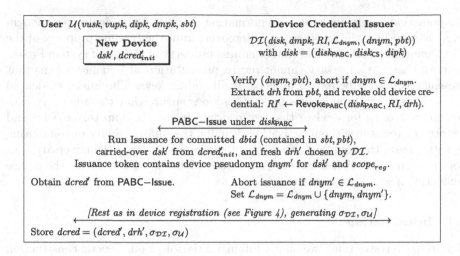

Fig. 6. Restore protocol

with insecure memory would therefore require to update *usk* upon re-issuance if scope-exclusive pseudonyms are required.

To prove the above statement we essentially need to show that the commuting signature part, the PABC scheme and the Prove$_\phi$ prove system can be simulated. As our privacy definitions extend those given by Camenisch et al. [CKL+14], it can be shown that the parts related to the classic PABC system used in our construction can be simulated using their simulator. Simulating the Prove$_\phi$ system that is used to bind revocation handles in PABC and CS commitments can be done by the zero-knowledge property of the used proof system. Finally we have to show that commuting signatures can be simulated. First note that in all used commuting signatures, the messages and the signatures are given as commitments. Moreover, the verification keys for those commuting signatures are either the publicly known keys of issuers or the users vault public key given also as commitment. Therefore, we can use the results from [Fuc11], that there exists a simulator, that given commitments to messages and verification keys can compute commitments to signatures and valid proofs of correctness.

Unforgeability. Our generic construction satisfies the unforgeability property for all types of devices. This means that there exists no forgery among the issuance and presentation tokens returned by the adversary in the unforgeability game.

First note that credentials in our generic construction are classic PABC system credentials with an additional commuting signature under $\phi(rh) \otimes vupk$. From the unforgeability property of the PABC system, it follows that all presentation or issuance tokens returned by the adversary satisfy that all software credentials are bound to the same user secret key, the pseudonym *nym* is sound for the given *scope$_\mathcal{U}$*, the revealed attribute values are correct, the equality relation E for blinded attributes is satisfied, the committed device binding identifier are the same in all presented credentials (this is also ensured by the E relation) except the ones that are given opening information to ε, and the device pseudonym *dnym* is sound for the given $scope_{\mathcal{U}}$. Moreover, from the binding property of the CS commitments scheme and the soundness property of the proof system Prove_ϕ we have that the adversary cannot return presentation or issuance tokens that present credentials bound to different vault public keys. The initial credential and scope specific pseudonyms for static scopes ensure that the adversary cannot create tokens for devices that are restored from a backup token twice and restored or register without activation. Finally, the unforgeability of commuting signatures and the soundness property of Prove_ϕ ensure that the adversary cannot create presentation tokens for software credentials with a device the device credential of which was revoked.

3.4 Instantiation

Due to space restrictions, we omit a full instantiation of our generic construction here. Similar to Camenisch et al. [CKL+14], it can be instantiated using Pedersen commitments [Ped91, DF02], CL-signatures [CL02], a variant of the Nakanishi et al. revocation scheme [NFHF09], and the pseudonym scheme used in the IBM identity mixer [IBM10]. The new parts of the construction based on commuting signatures can be instantiated using the scheme proposed by Fuchsbauer [Fuc11], and the proof system Prove_ϕ can be obtained using standard techniques.

References

[BCC+09] Belenkiy, M., Camenisch, J., Chase, M., Kohlweiss, M., Lysyanskaya, A., Shacham, H.: Randomizable proofs and delegatable anonymous credentials. In: Halevi, S. (ed.) CRYPTO 2009. LNCS, vol. 5677, pp. 108–125. Springer, Heidelberg (2009)

[BL13] Baldimtsi, F., Lysyanskaya, A.: Anonymous credentials light. In: ACM CCS 2013, pp. 1087–1098. ACM (2013)

[Bra99] Brands, S.: Rethinking public key infrastructure and digital certificates - building in privacy. Ph.D. thesis, Eindhoven Institute of Technology, Eindhoven, The Netherlands (1999)

[CH02] Camenisch, J., Van Herreweghen, E.: Design and implementation of the idemix anonymous credential system. In: Atluri, V. (ed.) ACM CCS 2002, pp. 21–30. ACM (2002)

[Cha81] Chaum, D.: Untraceable electronic mail, return addresses, and digital pseudonyms. Commun. ACM **24**(2), 84–88 (1981)

[Cha85] Chaum, D.: Security without identification: transaction systems to make big brother obsolete. Commun. ACM **28**(10), 1030–1044 (1985)

[CKL+14] Camenisch, J., Krenn, S., Lehmann, A., Mikkelsen, G.L., Neven, G., Pedersen, M.Ø.: Formal treatment of privacy-enhancing credential systems. Cryptology ePrint Archive, Report 2014/708 (2014). http://eprint.iacr.org/

[CL01] Camenisch, J.L., Lysyanskaya, A.: An efficient system for non-transferable anonymous credentials with optional anonymity revocation. In: Pfitzmann, B. (ed.) EUROCRYPT 2001. LNCS, vol. 2045, pp. 93–118. Springer, Heidelberg (2001)

[CL02] Camenisch, J.L., Lysyanskaya, A.: A signature scheme with efficient proto-
        cols. In: Cimato, S., Galdi, C., Persiano, G. (eds.) SCN 2002. LNCS, vol.
        2576, pp. 268–289. Springer, Heidelberg (2003)
[CL04] Camenisch, J.L., Lysyanskaya, A.: Signature schemes and anonymous cre-
        dentials from bilinear maps. In: Franklin, M. (ed.) CRYPTO 2004. LNCS,
        vol. 3152, pp. 56–72. Springer, Heidelberg (2004)
[CMZ14] Chase, M., Meiklejohn, S., Zaverucha, G.: Algebraic MACs and keyed-
        verification anonymous credentials. In: ACM CCS 2014, pp. 1205–1216.
        ACM (2014)
[DF02] Damgård, I.B., Fujisaki, E.: A statistically-hiding integer commitment
        scheme based on groups with hidden order. In: Zheng, Y. (ed.) ASI-
        ACRYPT 2002. LNCS, vol. 2501, pp. 125–142. Springer, Heidelberg (2002)
[Fuc11] Fuchsbauer, G.: Commuting signatures and verifiable encryption. In:
        Paterson, K.G. (ed.) EUROCRYPT 2011. LNCS, vol. 6632, pp. 224–245.
        Springer, Heidelberg (2011)
[GGM14] Garman, C., Green, M., Miers, I.: Decentralized anonymous credentials. In:
        NDSS 2013. The Internet Society (2014)
[IBM10] IBM Research Zurich - Security Team. Specification of the identity mixer
        cryptographic library. IBM Technical report RZ 3730 (99740) (2010)
[NFHF09] Nakanishi, T., Fujii, H., Hira, Y., Funabiki, N.: Revocable group signa-
        ture schemes with constant costs for signing and verifying. In: Jarecki,
        S., Tsudik, G. (eds.) PKC 2009. LNCS, vol. 5443, pp. 463–480. Springer,
        Heidelberg (2009)
[Ped91] Pedersen, T.P.: Non-interactive and information-theoretic secure verifiable
        secret sharing. In: Feigenbaum, J. (ed.) CRYPTO 1991. LNCS, vol. 576,
        pp. 129–140. Springer, Heidelberg (1992)
[PZ13] Paquin, C., Zaverucha, G.: U-prove Cryptographic specification v1.1
        (revision 2). Technical report, Microsoft Corporation, April 2013

Cryptanalysis and Attacks
(Symmetric Crypto)

Analysis of Boomerang Differential Trails via a SAT-Based Constraint Solver URSA

Aleksandar Kircanski[✉]

Matasano Security, Part of NCC Group, 48 West 25th Street, 4th Floor,
New York, NY 10010, USA
aleks@matasano.com

Abstract. Obtaining differential patterns over many rounds of a cryptographic primitive often requires working on local differential trail analysis. In the case of boomerang and rectangle attacks, merging two short differential trails into one long differential pattern is required. It was previously shown by Murphy that caution should be exercised as there is increased chance of running into contradictions in the middle rounds of the primitive.

In this paper, we propose the use of a SAT-based constraint solver URSA as aid in analysis of differential trails and find that previous rectangle/boomerang attacks on XTEA, SHACAL-1 and SM3 primitives are based on incompatible trails. Given the C specification of the cryptographic primitive, verifying differential trail portions requires minimal work on the side of the cryptanalyst.

1 Introduction

Differential cryptanalysis [6, 53] is a technique used to break cryptographic primitives such as block ciphers or hash functions. It rests on the existence of high-probability differential trails. A differential trail for an iterative cryptographic primitive can be seen as a sequence of constraints modeling the relations between inner states of primitive executions [25, 29]. Differential trails are built either manually [52, 53, 55], or, with the help of automated tools [9, 30, 38]. To estimate the overall probability of a given differential trail, certain independence assumptions between the constraints need to be introduced.

The validity of such independence assumptions may not always be justified as the constraints may interact and such interactions may severely influence the overall probability calculation. This is especially the case when differential analysis is used to model quartets of primitive executions as opposed to pairs. For example, in the context of boomerang or rectangle attacks, two short high-probability differential trails are connected in one differential pattern over many rounds of the primitive [4, 49].

In 2011, Murphy provided examples of boomerang differential trails that impose dependent constraints on the AES and DES S-boxes [42]. When the dependencies are taken into account, the probability of the overall probabilistic pattern drops to 0. Subsequently, several previously used boomerang trails for

© Springer International Publishing Switzerland 2015
T. Malkin et al. (Eds.): ACNS 2015, LNCS 9092, pp. 331–349, 2015.
DOI: 10.1007/978-3-319-28166-7_16

primitives based on the Addition, Rotation and Xor (ARX) [46] operations were found to be *incompatible*, i.e., have the probability equal to 0. For example, this was the case for boomerang differential attacks against BLAKE [8] and Skein [10], which invalidated the corresponding attacks [30]. The discussion related to Murphy's initial doubts [42] was continued by Kim *et al.* in [26]. It was argued that the only reliable way to estimate the boomerang/rectangle attack probability is to attempt to perform the attack itself. Since this is often impossible due to the high computational complexity requirements, estimating the probabilities or their lower bounds via independence assumptions often remains the only way to assess the attack success rate (see, e.g., [3]).

In general, the compatibility or incompatibility of a set of differential constraints can be established as follows. Given a set of constraints, one can simply attempt to find particular inputs for the cryptographic primitive that will conform to such a constraint set in the given round/step span, using techniques such as such as message modification [53]. The main drawback of this approach is that it requires custom implementations and potentially tedious work, e.g., when attempting to prove that some particular boomerang trails are incompatible. Another way to establish (in)compatibility is to apply differential constraint reasoning, where one abstracts away from particular inner state bit-values and deduces consequences from the current differential knowledge base. In case of ARX primitives, one-bit and also multi-bit constraints have been proposed for such reasoning [9,30,36]. In 2012, a tool for reasoning on arbitrary ARX primitives using multi-bit constraints has been proposed by Leurent [30]. Although very powerful, ARXtools also has some limits when it comes to constraint compatibility verification. Namely, the primitive specification may be somewhat cumbersome and also the analysis of primitives with non-ARX components is not possible.

In 2012, a SAT-based constraint solver URSA (Uniform Reduction to SAT) was proposed [20]. It simplifies using SAT solvers in tasks such as cryptanalysis problems. Namely, instead of encoding a problem directly in terms of propositional formulae, the user has to specify the problem in a custom, C-like specification language. In many situations, this means that the C implementation of cryptographic algorithms can be directly used by the URSA system.

Previous work in logical cryptanalysis includes direct translation of crypto-primtives into SAT formulas. This was done for, e.g., DES, MD4/5, Trivium, AES, Keccak and GLUON-64. [13,21,23,35,40,44]. One of the tools used in this area is CryptoMiniSat [48]. More powerful theories (than predicate logic) and solvers were also tested in cryptanalysis, including a constraint solver STP [14]. A non-direct application of SAT/SMT in cryptanalysis includes establishing probability upper bounds for differential trails in the case of Salsa20 stream cipher and NORX scheme for authenticated encryption scheme [22,41]. Closely related to our work are [39,45], while [45] was developed parallel to our work.

Our Contribution: We show that URSA system in conjunction with SAT solvers can be used for detecting contradictions in differential and rectangle differential trails. As the tool allows almost direct translation from the crypto primitive C-code to the URSA language, verifying trail portions requires little setup time. We analyze best previous rectangle attacks on the XTEA and SHACAL-1 block ciphers [12,31,50] and locate contradictions in these trails. In addition, we detect contradictions in previous boomerang distinguishers [3] for the SM3 hash function. This shows that the probability estimations for these attacks are invalid and that it remains unknown whether the attacks will work or not. Next, we provide examples of *unaligned* rectangle trails in the context of XTEA block cipher (end of Sect. 3.1). The existence of such trails has been mentioned previously in [4] and it is interesting to note an actual example of such trails. Finally, we point out a type of contradiction that occurs in primitives with linear key/message expansions which, to the best of our knowledge, was not discussed in previous literature.

This paper is organized as follows. In Sect. 2 we review the rectangle attack, reasoning on bit-constraints, the URSA system, and also present the notation used throughout the paper. The incompatibilities found in the rectangle trails for XTEA and SHACAL-1 are discussed in Sects. 3.1 and 3.2. Finally, the analysis of boomerang trails used in the SM3 distinguisher is given in Sect. 3.3. The conclusion is provided in Sect. 4.

2 Background and Notation

In this section, a brief description of the rectangle attacks on block ciphers and boomerang distinguishers on hash functions is provided, followed by an introduction to 1-bit conditions and reasoning about differential trails. Finally, an overview of the URSA system is provided along with the notation used throughout the paper.

2.1 The Rectangle Attack

In 1999, Wagner introduced a chosen-ciphertext cryptanalytic technique against block ciphers and named it the boomerang attack [49]. The technique exploits non-random behavior of carefully crafted encryption quartets. It works well against ciphers for which there exist short differentials with very high probability. The amplified boomerang attack [24], also known as the rectangle attack [4], is a chosen-plaintext variant of the boomerang attack.

Below, a rectangle attack against a cryptographic function such as a block cipher is summarized. Denote the generic permutation in question by E and it's input by x. The quartet structure that the adversary is interested in is shown in Fig. 1. The function is decomposed as $E = E_1 \circ E_0$ and two differential trails are assumed to exist: $\delta \xrightarrow{E_0} \Delta$ and $\gamma \xrightarrow{E_1} \Gamma$ with probabilities p and q, respectively. Here, δ and γ are the input differences for E_0 and E_1, respectively and Δ and Γ are the output differences. If the differentials propagate as specified in Fig. 1, the quartet is called a *right* quartet.

The main idea in the rectangle attack is to compute pairs of the form $(E(x_A), E(x_A \oplus \delta))$ for many randomly chosen x_A inputs and to count how many

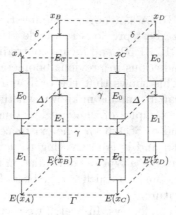

Fig. 1. The rectangle attack

pairs of such of pairs will constitute right quartets. The probabilistic analysis of such an event is as follows. Out of N encrypted pairs with input difference δ, about $p \cdot N$ will conform to the $\delta \xrightarrow{E_0} \Delta$ trail. Now, out of $p \cdot N$ such pairs, one can have about $\frac{(p \cdot N)^2}{2}$ candidate quartets. The probability that $E_0(x_A) \oplus E_0(x_C) = \gamma$ within a randomly chosen candidate quartet is 2^{-n}, where n is the E_0 output bit-length. This event always coincides with $E_0(x_B) \oplus E_0(x_D) = \gamma$ since $E_0(x_B) \oplus E_0(x_D) = E_0(x_A) \oplus \delta \oplus E_0(x_C) \oplus \delta = \delta \oplus \delta \oplus \gamma = \gamma$ and thus the probability of both $E_0(x_A) \oplus E_0(x_C) = E_0(x_B) \oplus E_0(x_D) = \gamma$ is in fact 2^{-n}. As a result, the expect number of quartets satisfying $E(x_A) \oplus E(x_C) = E(x_A) \oplus E(x_C) = \Gamma$ is $\frac{(p \cdot N)^2}{2} \cdot 2^{-n} \cdot q^2 = N^2 \cdot 2^{-n-1} \cdot p^2 \cdot q^2$.

The expected number of right quartets is augmented further by allowing the two differential trails to vary, i.e., by considering $\delta \xrightarrow{E_0} \Delta'$ and $\gamma' \xrightarrow{E_1} \Gamma$ for all possible valid pair choices for (Δ', γ'), that is

$$N^2 \cdot 2^{-n-1} \cdot \sum_{(\Delta', \gamma')} p_{\delta \to \Delta'}^2 \cdot q_{\gamma' \to \Gamma}^2 \qquad (1)$$

On the other hand, for a random permutation, the expected number of right quartets is $\frac{N^2}{2} \cdot 2^{-2n} = N^2 \cdot 2^{-2n-1}$. Comparing this estimate to (1) yields that if $\sum_{(\Delta', \gamma')} p_{\delta \to \Delta'}^2 \cdot q_{\gamma' \to \Gamma}^2 \gg 2^{-n}$, E can be distinguished from a random permutation.

In the literature [4, 32–34], the estimate (1) is further simplified as

$$N^2 \cdot 2^{-n-1} \cdot \sum_{\Delta'} p_{\delta \to \Delta'}^2 \cdot \sum_{\gamma'} q_{\gamma' \to \Gamma}^2$$

which is a sound estimate if one assumes the pairwise independence of all E_0 and E_1 trails.

As for the boomerang distinguisher for hash functions, the goal is to find a quartet (x_0, x_1, x_2, x_3) for function f such that

$$x_0 \oplus x_1 \oplus x_2 \oplus x_3 = 0$$
$$f(x_0) \oplus f(x_1) \oplus f(x_2) \oplus f(x_3) = 0 \tag{2}$$

which is called a *zero-sum* or equivalently, a *second-order collision*. This is done by a technique similar to the above described distinguisher, taking into account the message freedom that is available in the context of compression functions. For a more detailed introduction to boomerang distinguishers on hash functions, the reader is referred to [7].

2.2 Reasoning on 1-Bit Constraints

Searching for differential trails is facilitated by a constraints language introduced in [9]. Instead of working with *bit-values*, reasoning is performed on *bit-constraints*. The symbols used for expressing bit-constraints are provided in Table 1. For example, when we write -x-u, we mean a set of 4-bit pairs

$$\text{-x-u} = \{T, T' \in F_2^4 | T_3 = T_3', T_2 \neq T_2', T_1 = T_1', T_0 = 0, T_0' = 1\}$$

where T_i denotes i-th bit in word T.

Next, small examples of (a) a differential trail (b) a boomerang trail and (c) a boomerang trail incompatibility are provided. As for the differential trail, consider the following constraint specification over one 4-bit modular addition

$$\text{----} + \text{---x} = \text{---x} \tag{3}$$

The trail models a pair of additions $x_A + y_A = z_A$ and $x_B + y_B = z_B$ and specifies that $x_A = x_B$ and also that y_A and y_B, as well as z_A and z_B are different only on the least significant bit. It can be observed that the necessary condition for the trail to realize is $lsb(x_A) = lsb(x_B) = 0$.

As for the boomerang trail, in that context, one works with quartets instead of pairs. Consider a quartet of modular additions $x_\omega + y_\omega = z_\omega$, for $\omega \in \{A, B, C, D\}$. To specify a boomerang trail, two differential trails are required, labeled as the *top* trail and the *bottom* trail. This terminology comes from the fact that the two trails are specified on the bottom and the top round portions

Table 1. Symbols used to express 1-bit conditions [9]

$\delta(x,x')$	meaning	(0,0)	(0,1)	(1,0)	(1,1)		$\delta(x,x')$	meaning	(0,0)	(0,1)	(1,0)	(1,1)
?	anything	✓	✓	✓	✓		3	$x = 0$	✓	✓	-	-
-	$x = x'$	✓	-	-	✓		5	$x' = 0$	✓	-	✓	-
x	$x \neq x'$	-	✓	✓	-		7		✓	✓	✓	-
0	$x = x' = 0$	✓	-	-	-		A	$x' = 1$	-	✓	-	✓
u	$(x,x') = (0,1)$	-	✓	-	-		B		-	✓	✓	✓
n	$(x,x') = (1,0)$	-	-	✓	-		C	$x = 1$	-	-	✓	✓
1	$x = x' = 1$	-	-	-	✓		D		✓	-	✓	✓
#		-	-	-	-		E		-	✓	✓	✓

of the cryptographic primitive, respectively. For the purpose of this example, let (3) be the bottom trail and let the top trail be specified by

$$---- + ---x = --xx \qquad (4)$$

The bottom trail is imposed on $x_\omega + y_\omega = z_\omega$ for $\omega \in \{A, B\}$ and $\omega \in \{C, D\}$, whereas the top trail is imposed on $\omega \in \{A, C\}$ and $\omega \in \{B, D\}$. As shown below, taking the four sets of constraints on $x_\omega + y_\omega = z_\omega$ for $\omega \in \{A, B, C, D\}$ yields a contradiction, i.e., the boomerang trail incompatibility. The incompatibility of (3) and (4) follows from the fact that the necessary condition to have (4) is that the rightmost bit of x is 1, i.e., that $lsb(x_A) = lsb(x_C) = 1$ (and also $lsb(x_B) = lsb(x_D) = 1$). However, as shown above, the necessary condition for (3) is that $lsb(x_A) = lsb(x_B) = 0$ and thus no quartet of additions satisfies both trails.

2.3   The URSA System

The system was proposed in 2012 [20] and represents a high-level front-end to efficient SAT solvers. It translates constraint sets specified in a C-like language into SAT formulas, after which a SAT solver of user's preference is executed on the derived equations. The following example of URSA usage was provided in [20]. Let $x_{n+1} = (1664525x_n + 1013904223) \bmod 2^{32}$ for $n \geq 0$. To find x_0 given $x_{100} = 3998113695$, URSA is executed on the following code

```
nx=nseed;
for (ni=1; ni<=100; ni++)
    nx = nx*1664525+1013904223;
bc = (nx == 3998113695);
assert(bc);
```

which produces logical equations that can be solved by a SAT solver of user's preference.

2.4   Notation

The following notation is used throughout the paper:

x^b: The bth bit of a word x. For example x^0 is the least significant bit of x.

A, B, C, D: four branches of primitive executions, following Fig. 1.

$\Delta r_j^i[A, B]$: bit-constraint (a symbol from Table 1) at bit-position i in word r_j constraining branches A and B.

$\oplus, +$: bit-wise XOR and addition mod 2^{32}, respectively

$\ll, \gg$: left and right shift, defined on 32-bit values.

$\lll, \ggg$: left and right rotation, defined on 32-bit values.

3   Detecting Rectangle/Boomerang Trail Contradictions

In this section, we detect contradictions in the trails used in attacks on XTEA [31], SHACAL-1 [12,50] block ciphers and the SM3 [3] hash function. The first two attacks are rectangle related-key key recovery attacks and the latter attack is a distinguishing attack against a reduced-round SM3 compression function.

The general approach is to represent the primitive and the corresponding step constraints in the URSA language, run a SAT solver over the sequence of steps where a contradiction is suspected, i.e., typically around the middle steps where the rectangle trail switch [4,24,49] occurs. If the SAT solver reports no solutions, the next step is to locate where the contradiction is located, i.e., to find the minimal or close to minimal constraint set that yields a contradiction. This was done using a manual trial-and-error approach, i.e., by removing constraints as long as the system does not have solutions. Finally, the proof for the contradiction is built based on the reduced constraint set.

3.1   On the Incompatibility of XTEA Trails [31]

The key-recovery attack on 36-reduced-round XTEA [31] is a related-key attack since it requires differences in the key bits (as well as in plaintexts). It works with quartets of encryptions and falls into the category of rectangle attacks. Below, a brief specification of the cipher is provided. For a more detailed description, the reader is referred to [31,54].

XTEA takes as input a 64-bit plaintext and a 128-bit key. The encryption and decryption functions consist of 64 Feistel-network rounds. Two equivalent representations of one encryption round are schematically presented in Fig. 2, where on the right-hand side a shift-register based representation is provided. Feistel networks have been previously studied in the form of shift registers in the context of the DES block cipher [15], where the cipher was presented as a Non-Linear Feedback Shift Register with input. We use the shift-register based representations since such representations are elegant when it comes to working with differential trails [9,38].

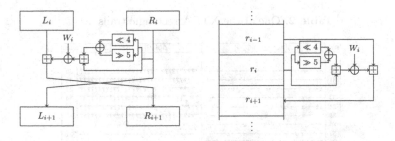

Fig. 2. Two equivalent representations of the XTEA round function

The 128-bit key is represented by four 32-bit words as $K = (K_0, K_1, K_2, K_3)$ and then, for $i = 1, \ldots 64$ expanded to 64 32-bit words, as specified by

$$W_i = \begin{cases} \lfloor \frac{i}{2} \rfloor \times \delta + K_{(\lfloor \frac{i}{2} \rfloor \times \delta)\&3} & \text{if } i \text{ is odd} \\ \lfloor \frac{i}{2} \rfloor \times \delta + K_{(\lfloor \frac{i}{2} \rfloor \times \delta \gg 11)\&3} & \text{if } i \text{ is even} \end{cases} \quad (5)$$

Here, $\delta = \lfloor (\sqrt{5}-1) \times 2^{31}) \rfloor =$ 0x9e3779b9. The subscripts to K in the expression above simply define an expansion of $K_0, \ldots K_3$ words over the XTEA rounds. The expression $\lfloor \frac{i}{2} \rfloor \times \delta$ specifies round constants.

The round function is specified next (see right-hand picture in Fig. 2). Denote the 64-bit plaintext in the form of two 32-bit words (A_0, A_1). Then, the encryption is done by calculating

$$r_{i+1} = r_{i-1} + (L(r_i) + r_i) \oplus W_i \quad (6)$$

for $i = 1, \ldots 64$, where $L(x) = (x \ll 4) \oplus (x \gg 5)$. The ciphertext is taken to be (r_{63}, r_{64}).

In [31], a related-key rectangle attack aiming to break 36 rounds of XTEA (rounds 16–51) and not requiring any weak-key assumptions is provided. The starting point for each rectangle attack is a family of top and bottom differential trails [4]. In [31], a family of trails is provided for E_0 (rounds 16–37) and one constant trail with probability 1 is provided for the bottom family (rounds 37–45). Then, each of the E_0 trails are connected to the fixed E_1 trail.

We used the URSA system to verify that the bottom trail cannot be connected to any of the trails in the top trail family. A particular high-probability representative pair of top-bottom trails (Table 3 in [31]) is shown in Table 2. The step numbers are given in the first and the last column, along with the active message words. Only the steps around the middle of the primitive are shown. Steps 35–37, where the contradiction can be localized, are marked in gray.

The bit-constraints provided by the top and the bottom trail in Table 2 are not fully propagated. Based only on the constraints given in the bottom trail in steps 36 and 37 and (6) for $i = 36$, one can conclude that $\Delta r_{35}^i[A, C] = \Delta r_{35}^i[B, D] = `-`$ for $i = 0, \ldots, 25$ and $\Delta r_{35}^{26}[A, C] = \Delta r_{35}^{26}[B, D] = `\text{x}`$. Taking

Table 2. One of the XTEA rectangle trails [31]

step	$\Delta[A,B] = \Delta[C,D]$	$\Delta[A,C] = \Delta[B,D]$	step
	$\vdots$	$\vdots$	
30	-------------------------------------	????????????????????????????????????	30
31	-------------------------------------	????????????????????????????????????	31
32	x------------------------------------	????????????????????????????????????	32
33	-----x-------------------------------	????????????????????????????????????	33
34	xx---x----x--------------------------	????????????????????????????????????	34
35	-----x----------x--------------------	????????????????????????????????????	35
36	----------x---x---x------------------	x------------------------------------	36
37	-----x-x----------------x------------	-------------------------------------	37
38	????????????????????????????????????	-------------------------------------	38
39	????????????????????????????????????	-------------------------------------	39
	$\vdots$	$\vdots$	

Table 3. A detailed view of (contradictory) steps 35–37

step	$\Delta[A,B] = \Delta[C,D]$	$\Delta[A,C] = \Delta[B,D]$
Δr_{35}	`------x--------x----------------`	`?????x-------------------------`
Δr_{36}	`---------x---x---x--------------`	`x-------------------------------`
$\Delta L(r_{36})$	`------x--x--x--------x---x------`	`------x-------------------------`
$\Delta s(r_{36}) = \Delta(r_{36} + L(r_{36})) \oplus W_{36}$	`?????????????????????????????x------`	`?????x--------------------------`
$\Delta r_{37} = \Delta(r_{35} + s(r_{36}))$	`------x-x-----------------x-----`	`--------------------------------`

into account these propagations, a detailed view of the relevant trail portion [31] is provided in Table 3.

In the proof below, let C_ω^i denote a carry bit at position $0 \le i \le 31$ on branch $\omega \in \{A, B, C, D\}$ in $r_{35} + (r_{36} + L(r_{36})) \oplus W_{36}$. We recall that in a 32-bit modular addition $z = x + y$, for $0 \le i \le 30$

$$z^{i+1} = x^{i+1} \oplus y^{i+1} \oplus c^i, \quad \text{where } c^i = maj(x^i, y^i, c^{i-1}) \tag{7}$$

while $c^{-1} = 0$.

Observation 1. *Constraints specified in Table 3 are contradictory.*

Proof: The argument about the contradiction is split in two cases:

(i) Let the bit $s^{26}(r_{36})$ for both $\Delta[A, B]$ and $\Delta[C, D]$ be inactive. In Table 3, this bit constraint is shown in the $\Delta s(r_{36})$ row (bit 26 from right-to-left in the $\Delta[A, B] = \Delta[C, D]$ column). This part of the proof replaces the '?' at this position by a '-'. As a consequence, $\Delta s^{27}(r_{36}) =$ '-' in the $\Delta[A, B] = \Delta[C, D]$ column of Table 3, since r_{36}, $L(r_{36})$ and W_{36} are inactive past bit-position 26.

It can be observed that $C_A^{25} = C_B^{25} = C_C^{25} = C_D^{25}$ and this carry value will be denoted by C. Namely, $C_A^{25} = C_C^{25}$ and $C_B^{25} = C_D^{25}$ since $\Delta s^i(r_{36}) = \Delta r_{35}^i =$ '-' for $0 \le i \le 25$ in the $\Delta[A, C] = \Delta[B, D]$ column. Furthermore, in the $\Delta[A, B] = \Delta[C, D]$ column, $\Delta s^{26}(r_{36}) =$ '-' due to the assumption and $\Delta r_{35}^{26} = \Delta r_{37}^{26} =$ 'x'. Thus, there is no carry disturbance from bit-position $i \le 25$ and $C_A^{25} = C_B^{25}$.

We show that both in the case $C = 0$ and the case $C = 1$, a contradiction is reached. According to the assumption of this part of the proof, the bit-value $s^{26}(r_{36})$ is equal to some fixed $b \in \{0, 1\}$ in both A and B branches. If $C = 0$, then $b = 0$ is a necessary condition, since if $b = 1$, the Δr_{37}^{27} constraint would be 'x' and this is not the case. However, since the $\Delta s^{26}(r_{36})$ is specified as 'x' for $\Delta[A, C]$ and $\Delta[B, D]$, the necessary condition $b = 0$ cannot be fulfilled in $\Delta[C, D]$ and therefore this path cannot behave according to the $\Delta[A, B] = \Delta[C, D]$ column of Table 3. In the case $C = 1$, a necessary condition $b = 1$ is derived and the contradiction argument proceeds analogously.

(ii) Let the negation of the assumption used in (i) hold. In other words, let $s^{26}(r_{36})$ be active in $\Delta[A, B]$ or, let the same bit be active in $\Delta[C, D]$. This disjunction implies that both bits are active simultaneously, since $s^{26}(r_{36})$ is active in both $\Delta[A, C]$ and $\Delta[B, D]$. Next, we have that $s^{25}(r_{36})$ is active in both $\Delta[A, B]$ and $\Delta[C, D]$, since otherwise there would not be a carry difference coming from bit position 25 and causing the two active bits to sum to an active bit in r_{37}^{26}. Finally, it follows that bits r_{37}^{27} in $\Delta[A, B]$ and $\Delta[C, D]$ are also active. This is true since $C_A^{26} \neq C_B^{26}$ and $C_C^{26} \neq C_D^{26}$. The first of the two equalities is true since both input bits and the output bit at position 26 are active when r_{37} is calculated. Independently, the second inequality is valid for the same reason on $\Delta[C, D]$.

The 'x' constraints on bit positions 25 and 26 in $\Delta s(r_{36})$ have the same sign (both 'u' or both 'n'), since they are caused by the carry propagation from bit position $i \leq 24$ in the r_{36} and $L(r_{36})$ summation. This is true both in $\Delta[A, B]$ and $\Delta[C, D]$. On the other hand, this cannot hold, since the constraint at bit position 26 in $\Delta s(r_{36})$ at $[A, C]$ corrupts this sign and thus we have a contradiction.   □

As already mentioned, we verified that the other top-bottom trail variants [31] are incompatible. It should be noted that all of the trails are induced by a difference at the most significant bit (MSB) positions in the key words. Previously, it was speculated [47] that if the top and the bottom trails start from the same bit position, contradictions are more likely to occur as the trails are likely to involve the same bit-positions. Our analysis confirms this intuition.

In this regard, one can also ask whether there exist *any* pair of compatible trails such that both top and the bottom trail are due to MSB disturbances in the round span discussed in [31] (31–37). Using URSA, this question can be answered by simply removing all of the trail constraints from the constraint representation and leave only those that enforce the top and the bottom trail expanded key disturbances. It should be noted that the task given to the SAT solver in this case is more difficult, since the solver has to effectively search for valid compatible differential trails. Increasing the number of rounds in the middle may result in impractical SAT solver execution times.

The following discussion is relevant at this point. To provide a lower bound for the probability of the distinguishing property used in the attack, most of the trails used in the previous literature on rectangle or boomerang attacks are *aligned* in the sense that the trails enforced on the opposite faces of the quartet structure share the same active bit positions. This allows having only two trails to model all four faces in the quartet of primitive execution. However, previously, *unaligned* trails have also been attributed to add to the overall attack probability [4]. In such a case, the primitive follows four different trails and results in the desired output difference.

We verified whether there exist both aligned and unaligned solutions to the round span discussed in [31]. The SAT solving phase for an aligned solution above took less than 30 min running as one process on 8-core 2.67 Ghz Intel i7 CPU before returning a negative answer. In other words, there exists no trails starting from the MSB positions in the 31–37 round span. However, interestingly enough, if the alignment constraints are removed, the solution does exist. The solution returned by the SAT solver follows four different (unaligned) trails and, as such, is different from the trails studied in the majority of previous literature (for rectangle attacks on block ciphers, see, e.g., [11,32,50] and as for boomerang distinguishers on hash functions see, e.g., [7,8]). As we are not aware of previous examples of unaligned trails in the literature, the extracted trails are presented in Table 7 in the Appendix, along with the corresponding plaintext and key values in Table 8.

The analysis above shows that contradictions that occur because both top and bottom trails start from the most significant bit may be resolved if one allows unaligned trails. This is relevant in the context of building compression function distinguishers, since having boomerang trails induced by MSB disturbances reduces the complexity of the final phase of the second order collision search [7,47].

3.2   On the Incompatibility of SHACAL-1 Trails [12,50]

In 2001, Handschuh and Naccache [16,17] proposed the SHACAL-1 block cipher and submitted it to the NESSIE (New European Schemes for Signatures, Integrity and Encryption) project [1]. SHACAL-1 is in fact the internal block cipher used within the SHA-1 hash function [43]. When applied in the Davies-Meyer mode, SHACAL-1 represents the SHA-1 compression function. Reduced-step SHACAL-1 was scrutinized both in the single-key and the related-key cryptanalytic models [5,18,27,33]. As for the full-round SHACAL-1, it was shown to be susceptible to a rectangle related-key attack with complexity better than exhaustive search in [12] in 2006.

However, Wang et al. [50] found multiple problems in previous attacks on SHACAL-1. In particular, it was observed that the previous attacks [5,18,27,33] do not work due to flaws in the provided differential trails. The trails turn out to be contradictory when regarded as single trails, i.e., independently of the quartet/rectangle context. Problems in these attacks are mostly related to the sign of active bits. In case only XOR differences are considered, these types of problems remain unnoticed [50].

Apart from finding flaws in previous attacks, [50] finds that the related-key rectangle attack [12] remains valid although it works against only a subset of the key space (2^{496} out of 2^{512} keys). In addition, [50] proposed a new related-key rectangle attack that works for 2^{504} out of 2^{512} keys. To the best of our knowledge, these are the best attacks against SHACAL-1.

In this section, we show that the two attacks above are in fact also flawed. Although the trails are non-contradictory when regarded independently, once connected as specified by the rectangle setting, incompatible constraints are placed on the inner state bits. Moreover, below, we point out a particular type of contradiction that is likely to occur in rectangle attacks on ciphers with linear key schedule with good diffusion such as SHACAL-1. To the best of our knowledge, this type of rectangle/boomerang attack contradiction has not been discussed in the previous literature.

Below, a specification of the SHACAL-1 encryption function based on recurrence relations is provided. To encrypt, the 160-bit plaintext and the 512-bit key are copied to $(r_0, r_{-1}, r_{-2}, r_{-3}, r_{-4})$ and $(W_0, W_1, \ldots W_{15})$, respectively. The block cipher key is expanded according to the SHA-1 message expansion

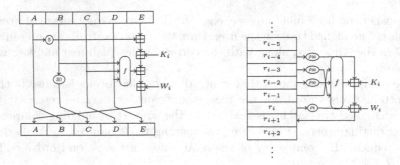

Fig. 3. Two equivalent representations of the SHA-1 state update step

$$W_i = (W_{i-3} \oplus W_{i-8} \oplus W_{i-14} \oplus W_{i-16}) \lll 1$$

for $i = 16, \ldots 79$. Next, 80 iterations of the function schematically represented in Fig. 3 are applied. Explicitly, for $i = 0, \ldots 79$, we have

$$r_{i+1} = r_{i-4} \lll \rho_{30}^i + K_i + f_i(r_{i-1}, r_{i-2} \lll \rho_{30}^i, r_{i-3} \lll \rho_{30}^i) + W_i + r_i \lll \rho_5^i$$

where K_i are the round constants, $\rho_{30}^i = 30$ and $\rho_5^i = 5$ for $4 \le i \le 79$ and for $0 \le i \le 3$, the rotational constants are properly adjusted. The bit-wise logical functions are defined as:

$$f(x, y, z) = \begin{cases} IF(x,y,z) = (x \wedge y) \vee (\neg x \wedge z) & 0 \le i \le 19 \\ XOR(x,y,z) = x \oplus y \oplus z & 20 \le i \le 39 \ or \ 60 \le i \le 79 \\ MAJ(x,y,z) = (x \wedge y) \vee (x \wedge z) \vee (y \wedge z) & 40 \le i \le 59 \end{cases}$$

The SHACAL-1 ciphertext is defined to be $(r_{80}, r_{79}, r_{78}, r_{77}, r_{76})$.

In Table 4, contradictory portions of the SHACAL-1 trails are given (extracted from Tables 7 and 8 in [50]).

Table 4. Incompatible SHACAL-1 trails [50]

step	$\Delta[A, B] = \Delta[C, D]$	$\Delta W[A, B] = \Delta W[C, D]$	$\Delta[A, C] = \Delta[B, D]$	$\Delta W[A, C] = \Delta W[B, D]$
29	--------------------------------------	----------------------------------	-----------------------------------x-	x-
30	--------------------------------------	----------------------------------	-----------------------------------xx	xx-
31	--------------------------------------x	----------------------------------	-----------------------------------	
32	-----------------------------------x---	----------------------------------	-----------------------------------x-	
33	------------------x-----------x	----------------------------------x-	-----------------------------------x- -x-	x---x-
34	?????????????????????????????????????		---------------------------------------	

Observation 2. *Constraints specified in Table 4 are contradictory.*

Proof: As shown by gray bits in the third column of Table 4, only one input bit to f_{33} for $[A, C]$ is active. Since f_{33} is in fact the XOR function, the output f_{33} bit at this position is active as well. The $\Delta W_{33}^1[A, C] = $ 'x' constraint cancels out this active bit since no bits are active in $\Delta r_{34}[A, C]$. This is possible only if the corresponding f_{33} output bit and $\Delta W_{33}^1[A, C]$ have opposite signs. The same should hold for $[B, D]$ and this yields a contradiction since $\Delta W_{33}^1[A, B] = \Delta W_{33}^1[C, D] =$ 'x'. ☐

As for the rectangle trails used in [12], we analyze the constraints in steps 57–63 in detail and show that these steps contain a contradiction. It should be noted that the top trail and the bottom trail for this attack cover steps 0–34 and 34–69, respectively. The contradictions are likely to occur in the region where both top and the bottom trails are specified, i.e., where the bottom and the top trails meet [30,42,47]. However, in this case, due to the message expansion linearity, the contradiction occurs in the late steps of the bottom trail as well.

In Table 5, trails for steps 57–63 are presented (Tables 2 and 3 in [12]). As can be observed, the $\Delta[A, B] = \Delta[C, D]$ column contains only '?' constraints since the top trail in late steps 57–63 is unspecified, as expected in the rectangle attack setting. However, since the message expansion in SHACAL-1 is linear, the $\Delta W[A, B] = \Delta W[C, D]$ is fully specified by the message expansion. The observation below shows that the linearly expanded constraints in the $\Delta W[A, B] = \Delta W[C, D]$ column do not allow the $\Delta[A, C] = \Delta[B, D]$ column to be satisfied.

Table 5. Incompatible SHACAL-1 trails [12]

step	$\Delta[A,B] = \Delta[C,D]$	$\Delta W[A,B] = \Delta W[C,D]$	$\Delta[A,C] = \Delta[B,D]$	$\Delta W[A,C] = \Delta W[B,D]$
57	??????????????????????????????	-x-----x-xxx--x-	---------------------------	
58	??????????????????????????????	-x-xxx--xx-x-	---------------------------	
59	??????????????????????????????	-x-x--x---xx-	---------------------------	
60	??????????????????????????????	-x----xx--xxx-	---------------------------	
61	??????????????????????????????	----xx--xx-x-xxxx-	---------------------------	----x--
62	??????????????????????????????	-x-xxxx-x-xx-x-	--------x--	--x-------
63	??????????????????????????????	-x--xxx-x-xxx-	---------------------------	

Observation 3. *Constraints specified in Table 5 are contradictory.*

Proof: According to Table 5, $\Delta W_{61}^2[A, C] =$ 'x'. The sign of this constraint is equal to that of $\Delta r_{62}^2[A, C] =$ 'x', since all other input bits in the step 62 modular addition are inactive. The sign of $\Delta r_{62}^2[A, C] =$ 'x' is opposite to the sign of $\Delta W_{62}^7[A, C]$ since these two constraints cancel out in step 63. Therefore, the sign of $\Delta W_{62}^7[A, C]$ is opposite to the sign of $\Delta W_{61}^2[A, C]$. The same holds for the $[B, D]$ face of the quartet. This yields a contradiction since $\Delta W_{61}^2[A, B] = W_{61}^2[C, D] =$ 'x' and $\Delta W_{62}^7[A, B] = W_{62}^7[C, D] =$ '-'. ☐

It follows that constraints in steps even outside the switch region should be carefully verified for primitives with linear message expansions, such as SHA-1, SHACAL-1 and SM3.

3.3   On the Incompatibility of SM3 Trails [2,3]

The SM3 hash function [19] is a cryptographic hashing standard in China adopted for use within the Trusted Computing framework in 2007 by the Chinese National Cryptographic Administration Bureau. It was designed by Xiaoyun Wang *et al.* and its design resembles the design of SHA-2 but includes additional fortifying features such as feeding two message-derived words into each step, as opposed to only one in the case of SHA-2.

SM3 is a Merkle-Damgård construction that processes 512-bit input message blocks and returns a 256-bit hash value. Since the attacks that we analyze below are attacks on the compression function, the specification of compression function is provided below. For more details, the reader is referred to [19].

Let the P_0 and P_1 functions, both operating on 32-bit words, be defined by:

$$P_0(X) = X \oplus (X \lll 9) \oplus (X \lll 17)$$
$$P_1(X) = X \oplus (X \lll 15) \oplus (X \lll 23).$$

The message block to be hashed is first represented as 16 32-bit words $M_0, \ldots, M_{15}$. Then, it is expanded to 68 32-bit words by letting $W_i = M_i$ for $0 \le i < 16$ and

$$W_i = P_1(W_{j-16} \oplus W_{j-9} \oplus (W_{j-3} \lll 15)) \oplus (W_{j-13} \lll 7) \oplus W_{j-6} \qquad (8)$$

for $16 \le i < 68$. We provide the specification of the step function using recurrence relations, similarly to the one used in [37]. The pre-fixed IV [19] is copied to $(l_0, l_{-1}, l_{-2}, l_{-3}, r_0, r_{-1}, r_{-2}, r_{-3})$ and the chaining values are computed over 64 steps as follows:

$$l_{i+1} = FF_i(l_i, l_{i-1}, l_{t-2} \lll \rho_9) + l_{i-3} \lll \rho_9 + W_i \oplus W_{i+4} + SS1_i \oplus (l_i \lll 12)$$
$$r_{i+1} = P_0(GG_i(r_i, r_{i-1}, r_{i-2} \lll \rho_{19}) + r_{i-3} \lll \rho_{19} + W_i + SS1_i)$$

where $SS1_i = (l_i \lll 12 + r_i + T_i) \lll 7$. The functions FF_i and GG_i are defined by

$$FF_i(X,Y,Z) = \begin{cases} X \oplus Y \oplus Z, & 0 \le i \le 15 \\ (X \wedge Y) \vee (Y \wedge Z) \vee (X \wedge Z) & 16 \le i < 64 \end{cases}$$

$$GG_i(X,Y,Z) = \begin{cases} X \oplus Y \oplus Z, & 0 \le i \le 15 \\ (X \wedge Y) \vee (\neg X \wedge Z) & 16 \le i < 64 \end{cases}$$

The round constants are $T_i = 0x79cc4519 \lll i$ for $i \in \{0, \ldots, 15\}$ and $T_i = 0x7a879d8a \lll i$, for $i \in \{16, \ldots, 63\}$. As for the rotation constants, $\rho_9^i = 9$ and $\rho_{19}^i = 19$ for $2 \le i \le 63$ and for $0 \le i < 2$, the rotational constants are properly adjusted.

Previous analysis of the reduced-step SM3 hash function includes preimage attacks [51,56], collision attacks [37] and boomerang distinguishing attacks [2,3, 28]. In [2], an example of a boomerang quartet is provided for the 35-step reduced SM3 and attacks against 36, 37 and 38 step-reduced SM3 with complexities $2^{73.4}$, 2^{94} and 2^{192} are provided.

Below, we show that the 37 and 38-step distinguishers [3] are based on incompatible differentials. In Table 6, the incompatible portion of the trails is presented (based on Tables 6 and 7 in [3]). The fact that the message expansion in SM3 is linear allows extracting all the message bit-constraints. In the top part of the table, the message constraints both for $W_i' = W_i \oplus W_{i+4}$ and W_i for $i = 15, \ldots 19$ are provided and in the bottom part the chaining values constraints are given. The bits relevant for the analysis are shaded in gray.

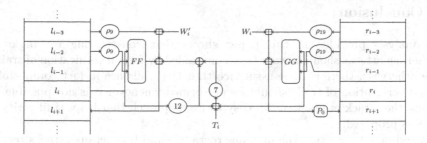

Fig. 4. The SM3 state update step

Observation 4. *Constraints specified in Table 6 are contradictory.*

Proof: Recall that

$$l_{19} = FF_{18}(l_{18}, l_{17}, l_{16} \lll 9) + l_{15} \lll 9 + W'_{18} + SS1_{18} \oplus (l_{18} \lll 12) \quad (9)$$

where $SS1_{18} = (l_{18} \lll 12 + r_{18} + T_{18}) \lll 7$. Since according to Table 6, $\Delta W'_{18}[A, C]$, $\Delta l_{18}[A, C]$, $\Delta r_{18}[A, C]$ and $\Delta l_{15}[A, C]$ contain no active bits and the same is true for $\Delta l_{19}[A, C]$, we have that $\Delta FF_{18}(l_{18}, l_{17}, l_{16} \lll 9)[A, C]$ cannot have any active bits either. The same statement holds for $\Delta FF_{18}(l_{18}, l_{17}, l_{16} \lll < 9)[B, D]$.

Consider the FF_{18} input bits for bit-position 10 in the modular addition (9). The FF_{18} input bit-constraints participating at this position are shaded in gray in Table 6. As can be observed, one of the input bits is active and, as established above, the function output bit is inactive. Since FF_{18} is the majority logical function MAJ, it follows that $l_{18}^{10} = l_{16}^{1}$ in both branches A and C. Again, the same statement holds for branches B and D. However, this is impossible since $\Delta l_{18}^{10}[A, B] = l_{18}^{10}[C, D] = $ 'x' and this is the only active input bit to FF_{18} at branches $[A, B]$ and $[C, D]$. This shows that the constraints are incompatible. $\square$

It is interesting to note that adding more freedom to the constraint set by removing the $\Delta l_{15}[A, C]$ and $\Delta l_{15}[B, D]$ constraints does not remove the contradiction.

Table 6. Incompatible SM3 boomerang trails [3]

step	$\Delta W'[A, B] = \Delta W'[C, D]$	$\Delta W[A, B] = \Delta W[C, D]$	$\Delta W'[A, C] = \Delta W'[B, D]$	$\Delta W[A, C] = \Delta W[B, D]$
15	x--------x------x---------------			
16	--------------------------------			
17	--------------------------------		-x-xx---x-x-x---xxx----x---	----x--------------------------
18	---x-----------x-x--------------		-----x---------------x-----	-----------x-----------x-x-x---
19	x--------x------x---------------		-----------x------x----x---	
step	$\Delta l[A, B] = \Delta l[C, D]$	$\Delta r[A, B] = \Delta r[C, D]$	$\Delta l[A, C] = \Delta l[B, D]$	$\Delta r[A, C] = \Delta r[B, D]$
15	--------------------------------	--------------------------------		
16	x--------x-----x--------------x	--------------------------------	-----------------xx----x---x	x-x-x-----xx-x---x-------xx---
17	-----x--------x--------x--x-xx	---xx--------x--------x-x-----	-xx--xx-x---x-x------xx-----	-------x---------x-x-x-x----x-x
18	---x-x-x-x--x-xx-----x-x-xx---	-xxx-x-x--xxx--xxx--xx-xxxx--xx-	--------------------------------	-------x---------x-x-x-x----x-x
19	???????????????????????????????	???????????????????????????????	--------------------------------	--------------------------------

4 Conclusion

The analysis provided in this paper shows that constructing rectangle or boomerang attacks should always be accompanied by formal verification of trails, since otherwise, there is little assurance that the trails are in fact compatible. Formal verification of trails should be performed whenever it is not possible to execute the attack in practice. An easy to use approach that helps trail verification was proposed.

Based on our analysis, the previous rectangle and boomerang attacks reaching the highest number of rounds against XTEA, SHACAL-1 and SM3 are shown to be based on incompatible differential trails. In addition, it was noted that contradictions in boomerang trails may appear not only in the middle of the primitive, but also in the bottom and the top rounds if the primitive has linear message expansion (as illustrated by one of the contradictions for SHACAL-1). Finally, in the context of the XTEA block cipher, we provided examples of unaligned boomerang trails that contribute to the overall rectangle attack probability and are relevant in the area of boomerang distinguishers on hash functions.

A Appendix

See Tables 7 and 8.

Table 7. XTEA boomerang trails with unaligned constraints (marked in gray)

step	$\Delta[A,B]$	$\Delta[C,D]$	$\Delta[A,C]$	$\Delta W[B,D]$
30	------------------------------	------------------------------	nnun--u-----u-----nn-un---nun-n-	nnun--u-----u-----nn-un---nun-n-
31	------------------------------	------------------------------	-----nu--u-uu---nn---nunuu------	-----nu--u-uu---nn---nunuu------
32	u-----------------------------	u------------------------------	-n-n-n------nnnnu--nnuu---------	-n-n-n------nnnnu--nnuu---------
33	------n------------------------	------n------------------------	n-u-u-u-nuu-u--n----------------	n-u-u-u-nuu-u--n----------------
34	-uu--uunnuu--------------------	un-unn----n--------------------	nnu-uu-nnuu--------------------	-n-u-u-nn--n-------------------
35	-nu-nn---u-uu-nnn--------------	u---nu--u-uu-nnn---------------	-n-u-n-------------------------	u-nu-u-------------------------
36	u--un---u---nu-nnnu-n----------	n--un---u---nu-nnnu-n----------	u------------------------------	n------------------------------
37	--nnu------uun-nun-----unu-----	--nnu------uun-nun-----unu-----		
38	-n-n----u-uun-u--u---unuu-nnu-n-	-n-n----u-uun-u--u---unuu-nnu-n-		

Table 8. XTEA unaligned quartet example

Key quartet			
K_A	0x4c266470 0x616feff	0x98254f67	0x6a6714
K_B	0x4c266470 0x616feff	0x98254f67	0x806a6714
K_C	0x4c266470 0x616feff	0x18254f67	0x6a6714
K_D	0x4c266470 0x616feff	0x18254f67	0x806a6714
Plaintext quartet			
P_A	0x259f4198 0xfb5aa217		
P_B	0x27ed0f0c 0xe49bdb36		
P_C	0xe8422de 0xfc22d87a		
P_D	0x7fa55484 0x8b285daf		

References

1. NESSIE - New European Schemes for Signatures, Integrity and Encryption. https://www.cosic.esat.kuleuven.be/nessie/
2. Bai, D., Yu, H., Wang, G., Wang, X.: Improved Boomerang Attacks on Round-Reduced SM3 and BLAKE-256. Cryptology ePrint Archive, Report 2013/852. http://eprint.iacr.org/
3. Bai, D., Yu, H., Wang, G., Wang, X.: Improved boomerang attacks on SM3. In: Boyd, C., Simpson, L. (eds.) ACISP 2013. LNCS, vol. 7959, pp. 251–266. Springer, Heidelberg (2013)
4. Biham, E., Dunkelman, O., Keller, N.: The rectangle attack - rectangling the serpent. In: Pfitzmann, B. (ed.) EUROCRYPT 2001. LNCS, vol. 2045, pp. 340–357. Springer, Heidelberg (2001)
5. Biham, E., Dunkelman, O., Keller, N.: Rectangle attacks on 49-round SHACAL-1. In: Johansson, T. (ed.) FSE 2003. LNCS, vol. 2887, pp. 22–35. Springer, Heidelberg (2003)
6. Biham, E., Shamir, A.: Differential cryptanalysis of DES-like cryptosystems. In: Menezes, A., Vanstone, S.A. (eds.) CRYPTO 1990. LNCS, vol. 537, pp. 2–21. Springer, Heidelberg (1991)
7. Biryukov, A., Lamberger, M., Mendel, F., Nikolić, I.: Second-order differential collisions for reduced SHA-256. In: Lee, D.H., Wang, X. (eds.) ASIACRYPT 2011. LNCS, vol. 7073, pp. 270–287. Springer, Heidelberg (2011)
8. Biryukov, A., Nikolić, I., Roy, A.: Boomerang attacks on BLAKE-32. In: Joux, A. (ed.) FSE 2011. LNCS, vol. 6733, pp. 218–237. Springer, Heidelberg (2011)
9. De Cannière, C., Rechberger, C.: Finding SHA-1 characteristics: general results and applications. In: Lai, X., Chen, K. (eds.) ASIACRYPT 2006. LNCS, vol. 4284, pp. 1–20. Springer, Heidelberg (2006)
10. Chen, J., Jia, K.: Improved related-key boomerang attacks on round-reduced threefish-512. In: Kwak, J., Deng, R.H., Won, Y., Wang, G. (eds.) ISPEC 2010. LNCS, vol. 6047, pp. 1–18. Springer, Heidelberg (2010)
11. Dunkelman, O., Fleischmann, E., Gorski, M., Lucks, S.: Related-key rectangle attack of the full HAS-160 encryption mode. In: Roy, B., Sendrier, N. (eds.) INDOCRYPT 2009. LNCS, vol. 5922, pp. 157–168. Springer, Heidelberg (2009)
12. Dunkelman, O., Keller, N., Kim, J.-S.: Related-key rectangle attack on the full SHACAL-1. In: Biham, E., Youssef, A.M. (eds.) SAC 2006. LNCS, vol. 4356, pp. 28–44. Springer, Heidelberg (2007)
13. Eibach, T., Pilz, E., Völkel, G.: Attacking bivium using SAT solvers. In: Kleine Büning, H., Zhao, X. (eds.) SAT 2008. LNCS, vol. 4996, pp. 63–76. Springer, Heidelberg (2008)
14. Ganesh, V., Govostes, R., Phang, K., Soos, M., Schwartz, E.: STP - A Simple Theorem Prover (2006–2013). http://stp.githubio/stp
15. Gong, G., Golomb, S.W.: Transform domain analysis of DES. IEEE Trans. Inf. Theory 45(6), 2065–2073 (1999)
16. Handschuh, H., Knudsen, L.R., Robshaw, M.: Analysis of SHA-1 in encryption mode. In: Naccache, D. (ed.) CT-RSA 2001. LNCS, vol. 2020, pp. 70–83. Springer, Heidelberg (2001)
17. Handschuh, H., Naccache, D.: SHACAL. NESSIE (2001)
18. Hong, S.H., Kim, J.-S., Lee, S.-J., Preneel, B.: Related-key rectangle attacks on reduced versions of SHACAL-1 and AES-192. In: Gilbert, H., Handschuh, H. (eds.) FSE 2005. LNCS, vol. 3557, pp. 368–383. Springer, Heidelberg (2005)

19. Internet Engineering Task Force. RFC: SM3 Hash Function, October 2011. https://tools.ietf.org/html/shen-sm3-hash-00
20. Janičić, P.: Uniform reduction to SAT. Log. Meth. Comput. Sci. **8**(3), 30 (2010)
21. Jovanović, D., Janičić, P.: Logical analysis of hash functions. In: Gramlich, B. (ed.) FroCos 2005. LNCS (LNAI), vol. 3717, pp. 200–215. Springer, Heidelberg (2005)
22. Jovanovic, P., Neves, S., Aumasson, J.-P.: Analysis of NORX. IACR Cryptology ePrint Archive 2014, p. 317 (2014)
23. Kamal, A.A., Youssef, A.M.: Applications of SAT solvers to AES key recovery from decayed key schedule images. In: 2010 Fourth International Conference on Emerging Security Information Systems and Technologies (SECURWARE), pp. 216–220. IEEE (2010)
24. Kelsey, J., Kohno, T., Schneier, B.: Amplified boomerang attacks against reduced-round MARS and Serpent. In: Schneier, B. (ed.) FSE 2000. LNCS, vol. 1978, pp. 75–93. Springer, Heidelberg (2001)
25. Khovratovich, D.: Methods of Symmetric Key Cryptanalysis (2011). http://research.microsoft.com/pubs/151070/state.pdf
26. Kim, J., Hong, S., Preneel, B., Biham, E., Dunkelman, O., Keller, N.: Related-key boomerang and rectangle attacks: theory and experimental analysis. IEEE Trans. Inf. Theory **58**(7), 4948–4966 (2012)
27. Kim, J.-S., Kim, G., Hong, S.H., Lee, S.-J., Hong, D.: The related-key rectangle attack – application to SHACAL-1. In: Wang, H., Pieprzyk, J., Varadharajan, V. (eds.) ACISP 2004. LNCS, vol. 3108, pp. 123–136. Springer, Heidelberg (2004)
28. Kircanski, A., Shen, Y., Wang, G., Youssef, A.M.: Boomerang and slide-rotational analysis of the SM3 hash function. In: Knudsen, L.R., Wu, H. (eds.) SAC 2012. LNCS, vol. 7707, pp. 304–320. Springer, Heidelberg (2013)
29. Knudsen, L.R., Robshaw, M.: The Block Cipher Companion. Information Security and Cryptography. Springer, Heidelberg (2011)
30. Leurent, G.: Analysis of differential attacks in ARX constructions. In: Wang, X., Sako, K. (eds.) ASIACRYPT 2012. LNCS, vol. 7658, pp. 226–243. Springer, Heidelberg (2012)
31. Lu, J.: Related-key rectangle attack on 36 rounds of the XTEA block cipher. Int. J. Inf. Sec. **8**(1), 1–11 (2009)
32. Lu, J., Kim, J.: Attacking 44 rounds of the SHACAL-2 block cipher using related-key rectangle cryptanalysis. IEICE Trans. **91–A**(9), 2588–2596 (2008)
33. Lu, J., Kim, J.-S., Keller, N., Dunkelman, O.: Differential and rectangle attacks on reduced-round SHACAL-1. In: Barua, R., Lange, T. (eds.) INDOCRYPT 2006. LNCS, vol. 4329, pp. 17–31. Springer, Heidelberg (2006)
34. Lu, J., Kim, J.-S., Keller, N., Dunkelman, O.: Related-key rectangle attack on 42-round SHACAL-2. In: Katsikas, S.K., López, J., Backes, M., Gritzalis, S., Preneel, B. (eds.) ISC 2006. LNCS, vol. 4176, pp. 85–100. Springer, Heidelberg (2006)
35. Massacci, F., Marraro, L.: Logical cryptanalysis as a SAT problem. J. Autom. Reasoning **24**(1–2), 165–203 (2000)
36. Mendel, F., Nad, T., Schläffer, M.: Finding SHA-2 characteristics: searching through a minefield of contradictions. In: Lee, D.H., Wang, X. (eds.) ASIACRYPT 2011. LNCS, vol. 7073, pp. 288–307. Springer, Heidelberg (2011)
37. Mendel, F., Nad, T., Schläffer, M.: Finding collisions for round-reduced SM3. In: Dawson, E. (ed.) CT-RSA 2013. LNCS, vol. 7779, pp. 174–188. Springer, Heidelberg (2013)
38. Mendel, F., Nad, T., Schläffer, M.: Improving local collisions: new attacks on reduced SHA-256. In: Johansson, T., Nguyen, P.Q. (eds.) EUROCRYPT 2013. LNCS, vol. 7881, pp. 262–278. Springer, Heidelberg (2013)

39. Mironov, I., Zhang, L.: Applications of SAT solvers to cryptanalysis of hash functions. In: Biere, A., Gomes, C.P. (eds.) SAT 2006. LNCS, vol. 4121, pp. 102–115. Springer, Heidelberg (2006)
40. Morawiecki, P., Srebrny, M.: A SAT-based preimage analysis of reduced KECCAK hash functions. Inf. Process. Lett. **113**(10), 392–397 (2013)
41. Mouha, N., Preneel, B.: Towards Finding Optimal Differential Characteristics for ARX: Application to Salsa20. http://eprint.iacr.org/
42. Murphy, S.: The return of the cryptographic boomerang. IEEE Trans. Inf. Theory **57**(4), 2517–2521 (2011)
43. National Institute of Standards and Technology. USA, Secure Hash Standard FIPS 180–2 (2002)
44. Perrin, L., Khovratovich, D.: Collision spectrum, entropy loss, t-sponges, and cryptanalysis of GLUON-64. In: Cid, C., Rechberger, C. (eds.) FSE 2014. LNCS, vol. 8540, pp. 82–103. Springer, Heidelberg (2015)
45. Prokop, L.: Using SAT Solvers to Detect Contradictions in Differential Characteristics. Advisors: F. Mendel, M. Schläffer, April 2014. http://lukas-prokop.at/proj/bakk_iaik/thesis.pdf
46. Weinmann, R.-P.: The ARX Challenge. In: Fast Software Encryption (FSE) (2009). Rump Session
47. Sasaki, Y.: Boomerang distinguishers on MD4-family: first practical results on full 5-pass HAVAL. In: Miri, A., Vaudenay, S. (eds.) SAC 2011. LNCS, vol. 7118, pp. 1–18. Springer, Heidelberg (2012)
48. Soos, M., Nohl, K., Castelluccia, C.: Extending SAT solvers to cryptographic problems. In: Kullmann, O. (ed.) SAT 2009. LNCS, vol. 5584, pp. 244–257. Springer, Heidelberg (2009)
49. Wagner, D.: The boomerang attack. In: Knudsen, L.R. (ed.) FSE 1999. LNCS, vol. 1636, pp. 156–170. Springer, Heidelberg (1999)
50. Wang, G., Keller, N., Dunkelman, O.: The delicate issues of addition with respect to XOR differences. In: Adams, C., Miri, A., Wiener, M. (eds.) SAC 2007. LNCS, vol. 4876, pp. 212–231. Springer, Heidelberg (2007)
51. Wang, G., Shen, Y.: Preimage and pseudo-collision attacks on step-reduced SM3 hash function. Inf. Process. Lett. **113**(8), 301–306 (2013)
52. Wang, X., Yin, Y.L., Yu, H.: Finding collisions in the full SHA-1. In: Shoup, V. (ed.) CRYPTO 2005. LNCS, vol. 3621, pp. 17–36. Springer, Heidelberg (2005)
53. Wang, X., Yu, H.: How to break MD5 and other hash functions. In: Cramer, R. (ed.) EUROCRYPT 2005. LNCS, vol. 3494, pp. 19–35. Springer, Heidelberg (2005)
54. Wheeler, D.J., Needham, R.M.: TEA Extensions. Technical Report, Computer Laboratory, University of Cambridge (1997)
55. Yun, A., Sung, S.H., Park, S., Chang, D., Hong, S.H., Cho, H.-S.: Finding collision on 45-Step HAS-160. In: Won, D.H., Kim, S. (eds.) ICISC 2005. LNCS, vol. 3935, pp. 146–155. Springer, Heidelberg (2006)
56. Zou, J., Wu, W., Wu, S., Su, B., Dong, L.: Preimage attacks on step-reduced SM3 hash function. In: Kim, H. (ed.) ICISC 2011. LNCS, vol. 7259, pp. 375–390. Springer, Heidelberg (2012)

Time–Memory Trade-Off Attack on the GSM A5/1 Stream Cipher Using Commodity GPGPU

(Extended Abstract)

Jiqiang Lu$^{(\boxtimes)}$, Zhen Li, and Matt Henricksen

Infocomm Security Department, Institute for Infocomm Research,
Agency for Science, Technology and Research,
1 Fusionopolis Way, #11-01 Connexis, Singapore 138632, Singapore
{jlu,liz,mhenricksen}@i2r.a-star.edu.sg

Abstract. Time–memory trade-off (TMTO) cryptanalysis is a powerful technique for practically breaking a variety of security systems in reality. There are mainly four general TMTO cryptanalysis methods, namely Hellman table cryptanalysis, rainbow table cryptanalysis, thin rainbow table cryptanalysis and thick rainbow table cryptanalysis, plus a few supplementary techniques that can be combined with a general method to produce possibly distinct TMTOs, like distinguished points. In this paper, we present a unified TMTO cryptanalysis, which we call unified rainbow table cryptanalysis, basing it on a unified rainbow table, then we describe its general combination with distinguished points, and finally we apply unified rainbow table cryptanalysis to the A5/1 stream cipher being used in the Global System for Mobile Communications (GSM). On a general-purpose graphics processing unit (GPGPU) computer with 3 NVIDIA GeForce GTX690 cards that cost about 15,000 United States dollars in total, we made a unified rainbow table of 984 GB in about 55 days, and implemented a unified rainbow table attack that had an online attack time of 9 s with a success probability of 34 % (or 56 %) when using 4 (respectively, 8) known keystreams (of 114 bits long each). If two such tables of 984 GB were generated, the attack would have an online attack time of 9 s with a success probability of 81 % when using 8 known keystreams. The practical results show again that nowadays A5/1 is rather insecure in reality and GSM should no longer use it.

Keywords: Time–memory trade-off · Hellman table cryptanalysis · Rainbow table cryptanalysis · Stream cipher · A5/1 · GPGPU

1 Introduction

Generally, there are two elementary cryptanalysis techniques that can be applicable to any cryptosystem from a theoretical perspective, namely exhaustive key search and the dictionary attack, which require a negligible number of data but represent two extreme cases in terms of time and memory complexities: exhaustive key search requires a negligible memory, but has a time complexity of the

© Springer International Publishing Switzerland 2015
T. Malkin et al. (Eds.): ACNS 2015, LNCS 9092, pp. 350–369, 2015.
DOI: 10.1007/978-3-319-28166-7_17

same order as the key size of the concerned cryptosystem, while the dictionary attack has a negligible time complexity, but requires a memory of the same order as the key size of the concerned cryptosystem. As the two elementary cryptanalysis techniques have a time or memory complexity of the same order as the key size of the concerned cryptosystem, it is usually impossible to apply them in reality to break a real-world cryptosystem during its lifetime, since the key size of a cryptosystem is usually set to be larger than that required for the designed lifetime of the cryptosystem.

In 1980, Hellman [24] introduced a cryptanalytic time–memory trade-off (TMTO), known as Hellman table cryptanalysis; it requires a memory less than that for the dictionary attack to store some precomputation tables, called Hellman tables, and has an online attack time smaller than that for exhaustive key search. If the required memory is small enough to be realistic, Hellman table cryptanalysis may allow an attacker to break a cryptosystem within a reasonable time. In 2003, Oechslin [31] described a refinement of Hellman table cryptanalysis, called rainbow table cryptanalysis, which is based on a rainbow table that has a different structure with a Hellman table; in a straightforward way, rainbow table cryptanalysis can be twice as fast as Hellman table cryptanalysis under the same precomputation complexity. By combining rainbow table cryptanalysis with Hellman table cryptanalysis, in 2006 Barkan, Biham and Shamir [10] gave two variants of rainbow table cryptanalysis, called thin and thick rainbow table cryptanalyses, that are based on thin and thick rainbow tables respectively. Except the four general TMTO cryptanalysis methods, there are several complicated variants [17,21] with merely theoretical interest, plus a few supplementary techniques that aim to improve a general TMTO method from certain aspect(s) but usually at the sacrifice of other aspects more or less, for example, distinguished points [18] and checkpoints [6]. A general TMTO method can be used alone, however, a supplementary technique has to be used together with a general TMTO method. When applied to particular areas, TMTO has been extended to time–memory–data trade-off (TMDTO) [14], time–memory–processor trade-off [3], time–memory–key trade-off [11,13], etc.

The A5/1 stream cipher was designed in 1987 for use in the Global System for Mobile Communications (GSM) to provide data confidentiality in Europe and the U.S.A. It was reported that by 2011, about 4 billion GSM users relied on A5/1 to protect their communications [1]. Since A5/1 was reverse-engineered partially in 1994 and completely in 1999 [4,16], many cryptanalytic results have been published on it, including guess-and-determine attacks [12,19,22], correlation attacks [8,20,27] and TMTO attacks [9,15,19,30]. From a realistic viewpoint, almost all these attacks are somewhat academic in the sense of their impact on the real-world security of GSM, for they either require a large data complexity, ranging usually from 1,500 to 70,000 known keystreams, or have a long attack time, typically from several minutes to hours. The only exception is Nohl's recent attack [30] using thick rainbow table cryptanalysis with distinguished points (i.e., fuzzy-rainbow table cryptanalysis [10]), which uses 8 known keystreams and has an online attack time of about 10 s on a general-purpose graphics processing unit (GPGPU) and a success probability of 87 %, plus 30 precomputation tables with a total of about 1.7 Terabytes, (Note that there were predecessors to this work with an inferior performance, say much larger precomputational workload). Nohl described mainly the details related to the structure of the precomputation tables, but did not disclose the online attack details (maybe because of his company's need for confidentiality). After an investigation, we find that Nohl's online attack on A5/1 is actually not so straightforward as a general TMTO attack from a theoretical viewpoint, and it seems that a crucial technique associated with the attack's precomputational workload and success probability is not disclosed.

In this paper, we make a few theoretical contributions to TMTO cryptanalysis and a practical contribution to the cryptanalysis of the GSM A5/1 stream cipher. First, inspired by thin and thick rainbow table cryptanalyses, we present a unified TMTO cryptanalysis, which we call unified rainbow table cryptanalysis, that is built on a unified rainbow table. Then, we discuss its general combination with distinguished points, as well as the resulting TMDTOs. On one hand the unified rainbow table itself represents a novel type of rainbow tables, and on the other hand it can be regarded as a unified model for rainbow-type tables, from which Hellman table, rainbow table, thin rainbow table and thick rainbow table can be easily obtained as special cases. Unified rainbow table cryptanalysis offers a trivially more comprehensive TMTO curve than the above four general methods, and its combination with distinguished points can offer a better TMDTO curve than any other general method except fuzzy-rainbow table cryptanalysis, but nevertheless it does not provide a better TMTO (or TMDTO) curve than the best previously known, thus it is merely of theoretical significance as a unified TMTO cryptanalysis. In particular, from its success probability formula, we can have success probability formulas for rainbow table, thin rainbow table and thick rainbow table cryptanalyses, which take into account some possible redundancy among different columns and the distinctions among different function variants. At last, we apply unified rainbow table cryptanalysis to A5/1, by working out a crucial theoretical technique. On a GPGPU computer with 3 NVIDIA GeForce GTX690 cards that cost about 15,000 United States dollars in total, we generated a unified rainbow table of 984 GB in about 55 days, and finally implemented a unified rainbow table attack that had an online attack time of 9 s with a success probability of 34 % (or 56 %) when using 4 (respectively, 8) known keystreams (of 114 bits long each). If two such tables of 984 GB were generated, the attack would have an online attack time of 9 s with a success probability of 81 % when using 8 known keystreams. Our attack on A5/1 is the first rainbow-type TMTO attack on A5/1 that reveals crucial theoretical techniques and implementation details, and the practical experimental results sufficiently show again that A5/1 is rather weak in terms of its realistic security.

The remainder of the paper is organised as follows. In the next section, we give the abbreviations and notation used throughout this paper and describe the A5/1 stream cipher. We present our unified rainbow table cryptanalysis in Sect. 3, describe its combination with distinguished points in Sect. 4, and discuss the resulting TMDTOs in Sect. 5. In Sect. 6, we describe our application of unified rainbow table cryptanalysis to A5/1 and give our experimental results. Section 7 concludes this paper. Because of page constraints, we leave many other theoretical and implementation materials in the full version of this paper.

2 Preliminaries

In this section we describe the abbreviations and notation and the A5/1 cipher.

2.1 Abbreviations and Notation

The bits of a value are numbered from left to right, starting with 1. In the description below and throughout this paper, we assume $f : \{1, 2, \ldots, N\} \rightarrow \{1, 2, \ldots, N\}$ is a one-way function, where N is a positive integer. We use the following abbreviations and notation.

CPU	Central Processing Unit
(GP)GPU	(General-Purpose) Graphics Processing Unit
GSM	the Global System for Mobile Communications
LFSR	Linear Feedback Shift Register
TM(D)TO	Time–Memory(–Data) Trade-Off
XOR/$\oplus$	bitwise logical exclusive OR
XNOR	the inverse of bitwise logical exclusive OR (XOR)
$\circ$	functional composition. When composing functions X and Y, Y$\circ$ X denotes the function obtained by first applying X and then applying Y. Sometimes we simply write X^i to denote $\overbrace{X \circ \cdots \circ X}^{i\ times}$, where i is a non-negative integer
e	the base of the natural logarithm, (e $= 2.71828\ldots$)
$\lfloor X \rfloor$	the largest integer that is less than or equal to X
$\mathcal{O}(X)$	a value that is of the same order as a value X
$X[i_1, \ldots, i_j]$	the j-bit string of bits $(i_1, \ldots, i_j)$ of a bit string X

2.2 The A5/1 Stream Cipher

A5/1 is a synchronous stream cipher, specifically a binary additive stream cipher. Its core part is a keystream generator, which is depicted in Fig. 1. The keystream generator is built on three Fibonacci linear feedback shift registers [5] (LFSRs) of 19, 22 and 23 bits long, which we denote by $R1, R2, R3$, respectively. As an LFSR with a primitive feedback polynomial can generate a maximum-length binary sequence, the three LFSRs have been set to have a primitive feedback polynomial each: The taps for $R1$ are at the 19th, 18th, 17th and 14th bits; the taps for $R2$ are at the 22th and 21th bits; and the taps for $R3$ are at the 23th, 22th, 21th and 8th bits. The three LFSRs are mutually clocked in a stop/go fashion under a majority function Maj of three bits from the three LFSRs, respectively. The majority function Maj takes as input the 9-th bit of $R1$, the 11-th bit of $R2$ and

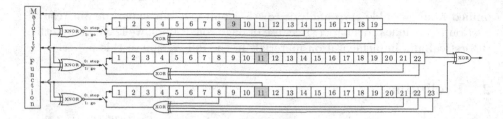

Fig. 1. The A5/1 keystream generator

the 11-th bit of $R3$, that is, $R1[9], R2[11], R3[11]$, and outputs the majority of the three input bits, more formally, it is defined to be $\mathtt{Maj}(R1[9], R2[11], R3[11]) = (R1[9] \times R2[11]) \oplus (R1[9] \times R3[11]) \oplus (R2[11] \times R3[11])$.

In a clocking cycle, for each LFSR, if the input bit to the $\mathtt{Maj}$ function is equal to the output of the $\mathtt{Maj}$ function, then the LFSR is clocked, outputting the rightmost bit as the output bit, and the feedback value is given by its feedback polynomial and is fed into the leftmost bit of the LFSR; otherwise, the LFSR remains invariant, but still outputs the rightmost bit as the output bit. Then, the keystream generator outputs the XOR of the output bits of the three LFSRs. The $\mathtt{Maj}$ function guarantees that at least two of the three LFSRs are clocked every clocking cycle.

A GSM conversation is represented as a series of frames of 114 bits long each, and it is classified into two categories: downlink (base station to mobile) conversation and uplink (mobile to base station) conversation; the number of frames can be at most 22 bits long, that is from 0 to $2^{22} - 1$. GSM sends a frame of conversation every $4.615\,\mathrm{ms}$, and thus a GSM conversation can usually be at most several hours unceasingly. For a conversation, GSM generates a 64-bit secret session key K from a master key, and uses the A5/1 stream cipher to encrypt every frame, with the frame number IV starting with a particular value generated by the system and being increased sequentially $(0 < IV < 2^{22})$.

When encrypting a frame of conversation, the A5/1 stream cipher first generates a 228-bit pseudorandom keystream through the keystream generator. The keystream generator takes as input the 64-bit secret session key K and the 22-bit publicly known frame number IV, and generates a 228-bit pseudorandom keystream in the following steps:

1. Initialization phase that involves: (a) setting the 64 bits of the three LFSRs to zero; (b) key setup that loads the 64-bit key into the LFSRs, with the $\mathtt{Maj}$ function ineffective; and (c) IV setup that loads the 22-bit IV into the LFSRs, with the $\mathtt{Maj}$ function ineffective.
2. 100 clockings on the three LFSRs with the $\mathtt{Maj}$ function effective and without outputting the output of the keystream generator.
3. 228 clockings on the three LFSRs with the $\mathtt{Maj}$ function effective and outputting the output of the keystream generator.

A 228-bit pseudorandom keystream is generated after Step 3. The first 114 bits of a 228-bit keystream are used for downlink conversation and the last 114 bits are used for uplink conversation. The A5/1 stream cipher encrypts a frame of conversation by XORing it with a 114-bit keystream, and produces a frame of ciphertext. Decryption is identical to encryption.

We refer to the internal state of the three LFSRs immediately after Step 1 (i.e., at the end of the initialization phase) as the initial state of a keystream.

3   The Unified Rainbow Table Cryptanalysis

In this section we present unified rainbow table cryptanalysis. Like the dictionary attack and the four general TMTO methods, unified rainbow table cryptanalysis also consists of two phases: offline precomputation phase to build one or more tables, and online attack phase to search the correct solution. We start with generating a unified rainbow table.

3.1   A Unified Rainbow Table

We define five parameters m, s, v, r, t, and each parameter is a positive integer.

- m: the number of starting points in a unified rainbow table.
- s: the number of the f variants used, namely $f_1, f_2, \ldots, f_s$, each constructed usually by a functional composition of the f function with a simple operation (called a color sometimes [10]), say an XOR with a unique number [32] or a rotation of a unique number of bits [24].
- v: the number of the f_i variant in each sector of the adjacent columns $(f_i, f_i, \ldots, f_i)$ with the same f_i variant.
- r: the number of the sector $(f_s)^v \circ \cdots \circ (f_2)^v \circ (f_1)^v$.
- t: the total number of appearances of the f variants, that is equal to rsv.

The attacker builds a unified rainbow table of size $m \times t$ by applying the following procedure:

1. Choose m starting points uniformly at random from the domain $\{1, 2, \ldots, N\}$, and we denote them by $SP_1, SP_2, \ldots, SP_m$.
2. For $1 \le i \le m$:
   (a) Let $x_{i,0} = SP_i$.
   (b) For $q = 1, 2, \ldots, r$:
       For $j = 1, 2, \ldots, s$:
           For $l = 1, 2, \ldots, v$:
               – Compute $x_{i,(q-1)\cdot sv+(j-1)\cdot v+l} = f_j(x_{i,(q-1)\cdot sv+(j-1)\cdot v+l-1})$.
               – If $(q = r)$ and $(j = s)$ and $(l = v)$, the value $x_{i,rsv}$ is termed the endpoint corresponding to SP_i; and we denote it by EP_i, that is $EP_i = x_{i,rsv}$.

3. Store the m pairs $(\mathrm{SP}_i, \mathrm{EP}_i)$ into a table sorted by the values of the endpoints, (and discard the intermediate values $x_{i,1}, x_{i,2}, \ldots, x_{i,rsv-1}$). The resulting table is called a unified rainbow table. This completes the construction of a unified rainbow table.

In short, the series of $\mathtt{f}$ variants used to generate a chain is $[(\mathtt{f}_s)^v \circ \cdots \circ (\mathtt{f}_2)^v \circ (\mathtt{f}_1)^v]^r$, or more intuitively

$$\underbrace{\overbrace{\underbrace{\mathtt{f}_1 \ldots \mathtt{f}_1}_{v\ times} \underbrace{\mathtt{f}_2 \ldots \mathtt{f}_2}_{v\ times} \ldots \underbrace{\mathtt{f}_s \ldots \mathtt{f}_s}_{v\ times}}^{1} \overbrace{\underbrace{\mathtt{f}_1 \ldots \mathtt{f}_1}_{v\ times} \underbrace{\mathtt{f}_2 \ldots \mathtt{f}_2}_{v\ times} \ldots \underbrace{\mathtt{f}_s \ldots \mathtt{f}_s}_{v\ times}}^{2} \ldots \overbrace{\underbrace{\mathtt{f}_1 \ldots \mathtt{f}_1}_{v\ times} \underbrace{\mathtt{f}_2 \ldots \mathtt{f}_2}_{v\ times} \ldots \underbrace{\mathtt{f}_s \ldots \mathtt{f}_s}_{v\ times}}^{r}}.$$

The unified rainbow table requires a memory of m units, and has a time complexity of $m \times r \times s \times v = mt$ computations of the $\mathtt{f}$ function, where we assume a computation of a variant $\mathtt{f}_j$ of the $\mathtt{f}$ function is approximately equal to a computation of the $\mathtt{f}$ function in terms of computational complexity, as in previous work [10, 24, 31].

3.2   Online Attack Procedure

Given an inversion target $y = \mathtt{f}(x)$, below we will describe an online attack procedure based on a unified rainbow table of Sect. 3.1. The online attack procedure is devised according to the structure of the unified rainbow table, so that certain previously computed values can be reused to save time.

The attacker tries to find the correct solution x by checking the unified rainbow table column by column in the following procedure. Recall that $t = rsv$.

1. For $j = s, s - 1, \ldots, 1$:
   (a) Apply the simple operation concatenated with $\mathtt{f}$ for constructing $\mathtt{f}_j$ to the given output y, and we denote the resulting value by $\widehat{y}_0$.
   (b) For $l = 1, 2, \ldots, v$:

   i. Set $y_0 = \widehat{y}_0$ if $j = s$; otherwise, compute $y_0 = \overbrace{(\mathtt{f}_s)^v \circ \cdots \circ (\mathtt{f}_{j+1})^v}^{from\ (\mathtt{f}_{j+1})^v\ until\ (\mathtt{f}_s)^v}(\widehat{y}_0)$.
   ii. For $q = 1, 2, \ldots, r$:
      A. Check whether y_{q-1} is an endpoint in the unified rainbow table. If y_{q-1} does not match any endpoint, we execute the next sub-step. However, if y_{q-1} atches an endpoint, EP_i say, then re-generate $x_{i,(r-q)\cdot sv+jv-l}$ from the corresponding starting point SP_i as $(\mathtt{f}_1)^{v-l} \circ [(\mathtt{f}_s)^v \circ \cdots \circ (\mathtt{f}_2)^v \circ (\mathtt{f}_1)^v]^{r-q}(\mathrm{SP}_i)$ if $j = 1$, or $(\mathtt{f}_j)^{v-l} \circ (\mathtt{f}_{j-1})^v \circ \cdots \circ (\mathtt{f}_2)^v \circ (\mathtt{f}_1)^v \circ [(\mathtt{f}_s)^v \circ \cdots \circ (\mathtt{f}_2)^v \circ (\mathtt{f}_1)^v]^{r-q}(\mathrm{SP}_i)$ if $j \neq 1$. Finally, $x_{i,(r-q)\cdot sv+jv-l}$ is likely to be the correct solution x, (Note that $x_{i,(r-q)\cdot sv+jv-l}$ may be a false alarm, and under this situation we need do extra work to test whether the recovered $x_{i,(r-q)\cdot sv+jv-l}$ is a false solution). If $x_{i,(r-q)\cdot sv+jv-l}$ is the correct solution, terminate the procedure.
      B. If $q \neq r$, compute $y_q = (\mathtt{f}_s)^v \circ \cdots \circ (\mathtt{f}_2)^v \circ (\mathtt{f}_1)^v(y_{q-1})$.
   iii. If $l \neq v$, compute $\widehat{y}_0 = \mathtt{f}_j(\widehat{y}_0)$.
2. The attack fails if the correct solution is not found after the above steps.

3.3 Online Time Complexity

Before further proceeding, we emphasize two points that are throughout this paper. As in previously published TMTO or TMDTO methods [7,10,13,14,24, 31]: first, we consider the online time complexity of the unified rainbow table attack as well as other TMTO attack methods in the worst scenario where the correct solution to the inversion target is found from the very first column of a precomputation table and no false alarm is taken into account; second, we consider the memory complexity in the unit of the number of starting-endpoint pairs, rather than the optimised memory complexity with certain sophisticated techniques like endpoint truncation [10,15]. Anyway, a recently emerging direction is to study the expected online time complexities and the optimised memory complexity, as done in [6,25,26]; we leave such studies as future work.

From the equations $y_q = (\mathtt{f}_s)^v \circ \cdots \circ (\mathtt{f}_2)^v \circ (\mathtt{f}_1)^v (y_{q-1})$ and $\widehat{y}_0 = \mathtt{f}_j(\widehat{y}_0)$ in Steps 1(b)(ii)(B) and 1(b)(iii), we can see that some previously computed values (i.e. y_{q-1} and $\widehat{y}_0$) are re-used during the next iteration, which enables us to save online attack time.

A detailed analysis reveals that the unified rainbow table attack has a total time complexity of approximately $\sum_{j=1}^{s-1}\sum_{l=1}^{v}[(s-j)\cdot v]+\sum_{j=1}^{s}\sum_{l=1}^{v}\sum_{q=1}^{r-1}sv+$ $\sum_{j=1}^{s}\sum_{l=1}^{v-1}1 = \frac{t^2}{r} - \frac{t^2}{2r^2} - \frac{t^2}{2sr^2} + \frac{t}{r} - s$ computations of the $\mathtt{f}$ function and $\sum_{j=1}^{s}\sum_{l=1}^{v}\sum_{q=1}^{r}1 = vrs = t$ table look-ups.

3.4 Success Probability

The success probability of the unified rainbow table attack is determined by the coverage rate of the unified rainbow table, that is defined to be the proportion of the number of distinct values for both starting points and intermediate values associated with the generation of the table to the size N of the domain.

As in previous work, we assume that the $\mathtt{f}$ function as well as its variants $\mathtt{f}_i$'s is a random function. Besides, in order to obtain an as accurate as possible formula, we need to consider the difference between two different function variants $\mathtt{f}_i$ and $\mathtt{f}_j$, which depends on how these function variants are constructed from the $\mathtt{f}$ function. If the function composed with $\mathtt{f}$ to construct a function variant is like an XOR operation with a unique integer, then we definitely have $\mathtt{f}_i(x) \neq \mathtt{f}_j(x)$ for any x when $1 \leq j \neq i \leq s$; however, if it is like a rotation of a unique number of bits, we may have $\mathtt{f}_i(x) = \mathtt{f}_j(x)$ for an x, and if there are many such x's then the function variants are unwanted. Thus, below we assume the first case for constructing the function variants. As a result, we obtain the following approximate formula on the expected success probability of the unified rainbow table attack.

Theorem 1. *If f, as well as its variants $f_1, f_2, \ldots, f_s$ constructed each by composing f with a simple function such that $f_i(x) \neq f_j(x)$ for any x when $1 \leq j \neq i \leq s$, is modeled as a random function mapping the set $\{1, 2, \ldots, N\}$ into itself, and the correct solution to the inversion target is chosen uniformly* *from the same set, then a unified rainbow table attack based on one unified rainbow table with parameters m, s, v, t has a success probability of approximately $\frac{\sum_{k=0}^{t-1} m_k}{N}$, where m, s, v, t are defined in Sect. 3.1 and m_k is computed as follows:*

$$\overline{m}_0 = \widehat{m}_0 = m_0 = N \cdot (1 - e^{-\frac{m}{N}}); \overline{m}_{k+1} = N \cdot (1 - e^{-\frac{\overline{m}_k}{N}});$$

$$\alpha = \lfloor \frac{k+1}{s \cdot v} \rfloor, \beta = \lfloor \frac{k+1-\alpha \cdot s \cdot v}{v} \rfloor, \delta = k+1-\alpha \cdot s \cdot v - \beta \cdot v = (k+1) \mod v,$$

$$\widehat{m}_{k+1} = \begin{cases} \overline{m}_{k+1} \cdot (1 - \frac{\sum_{i=0}^{\alpha-1} \sum_{j=0}^{v-1} \widehat{m}_{i \cdot s \cdot v + \beta \cdot v + j}}{N}), & \text{if } \delta = 0; \\ N \cdot (1 - e^{-\frac{\widehat{m}_k}{N}}) \cdot (1 - \frac{\sum_{i=0}^{\alpha-1} \sum_{j=0}^{v-1} \widehat{m}_{i \cdot s \cdot v + \beta \cdot v + j} + \sum_{j=0}^{\delta-1} \widehat{m}_{\alpha \cdot s \cdot v + \beta \cdot v + j}}{N}), & \text{if } \delta \neq 0. \end{cases}$$

$$m_{k+1} = N \cdot (1 - e^{-\frac{\widehat{m}_k}{N}}) \cdot (1 - \frac{\sum_{j=0}^{k} m_j}{N}).$$

3.5   TMTO Curve

Above we have described a unified rainbow table attack based on a unified rainbow table as well as its success probability. However, because of possible duplication of values associated with a precomputation table, the gain on its coverage rate is not as much as before when the number of starting points goes beyond a threshold value specified by a matrix stopping rule [14] theoretically. Alternatively, an attack may need more than one precomputation tables to reach a large success probability. This results in the following TMTO curve of unified rainbow table cryptanalysis.

Theorem 2. *Suppose P represents computational complexity for (offline) precomputation, T represents online time complexity, M represents memory complexity (for offline precomputation, since the memory complexity of online attack is negligible generally), s and r are those parameters used for unified rainbow table cryptanalysis. Then, unified rainbow table cryptanalysis approximately meets a time–memory trade-off $T \cdot M^3 = \frac{N^3}{s \cdot r} - \frac{N^3}{2s \cdot r^2} - \frac{N^3}{2s^2 \cdot r^2} + \frac{M \cdot N^2}{s \cdot r} - M^2 \cdot N$, where $P = N$, $M \leq N$ and $1 \leq s \cdot r \leq \frac{N}{M}$, plus $\frac{N^2}{s \cdot M^2}$ table look-ups.*

Furthermore, a simple analysis reveals the following result:

Corollary 1. *Hellman table, rainbow table, thin rainbow table, thick rainbow table and unified rainbow table cryptanalyses (can) have a TMTO curve $T \cdot M^2 = \mathcal{O}(N^2)$. Generally, rainbow table cryptanalysis has the best TMTO curve $2T \cdot M^2 \approx N^2$ among the five general TMTO methods.*

4   Unified Rainbow Table Cryptanalysis with Distinguished Points

When attacking a practical cryptosystem in reality, a huge precomputation table is usually required and stored in a hard disk, which makes a table look-up much more costly than a computation of the f function in terms of time, thus the supplementary technique of distinguished points is often used to speed up an online attack. Considering this, we briefly discuss a combination of unified rainbow table cryptanalysis with distinguished points in this section.

4.1   A Combination

Unified rainbow table cryptanalysis can be combined with distinguished points in the following way, where DP represents a distinguished point and two values represented by DP may be different, ($1 \leq i \leq m$, here m is the number of starting points).

$$\mathrm{SP}_i \overbrace{\underbrace{\xrightarrow{f_1 \cdots f_1} \mathrm{DP} \cdots \xrightarrow{f_1 \cdots f_1} \mathrm{DP}}_{v\,\mathrm{DP}s} \underbrace{\xrightarrow{f_2 \cdots f_2} \mathrm{DP} \cdots \xrightarrow{f_2 \cdots f_2} \mathrm{DP}}_{v\,\mathrm{DP}s} \cdots \underbrace{\xrightarrow{f_s \cdots f_s} \mathrm{DP} \cdots \xrightarrow{f_s \cdots f_s} \mathrm{DP}}_{v\,\mathrm{DP}s}}^{r\ times} = \mathrm{EP}_i.$$

Its online attack procedure is similar to the one for unified rainbow table cryptanalysis given in Sect. 3.2, in that we treat the series of functions $f_j \circ \cdots f_j$ for generating a distinguished point at here as a single function f_j in the attack procedure from Sect. 3.2. Suppose q is the expected average length of each sector with the same f_j variant, (i.e. the chain length is expected to be $t = r \cdot s \cdot v \cdot q$), then we can similarly obtain that such unified rainbow table cryptanalysis with distinguished points has an online time complexity of $\sum_{j=1}^{s}[q + (j-1) \cdot q \cdot v + (r-1) \cdot q \cdot s \cdot v] \cdot v = tsv + \frac{t}{r} - \frac{tsv}{2r} - \frac{tv}{2r}$ computations of the f function, plus rsv table look-ups.

4.2   TMTO Curve

Below is the TMTO curve of the combination described in Sect. 4.1.

Theorem 3. *Suppose P represents computational complexity for precomputation, T represents online time complexity, M represents memory complexity, plus those parameters v, s, r used for unified rainbow table cryptanalysis with distinguished points. Then, unified rainbow table cryptanalysis with distinguished points approximately meets a time–memory trade-off $T \cdot M^2 = (v - \frac{v}{2r} - \frac{v}{2rs} + \frac{1}{rs}) \cdot N^2$, where $P = N$, $M \leq N$ and $1 \leq r \cdot s \cdot v \leq \frac{N}{M}$, plus $\frac{r \cdot v \cdot N}{M}$ table look-ups.*

5   Time–Memory–Data Trade-Off Curves

In this section, we briefly discuss the time–memory–data trade-off (TMDTO) curves when unified rainbow table cryptanalysis and its combination with distinguished points are applied in certain situations where multiple data can be helpful, for example, cryptanalysis of some stream ciphers. We have the following result.

Theorem 4. *Suppose P represents computational complexity for precomputation, T represents online time complexity, M represents memory complexity, $D(\geq 2)$ represents the number of available data, v, s, r are those parameters used in unified rainbow table cryptanalysis without/with distinguished points. Then, unified rainbow table cryptanalysis approximately meets a time–memory–data trade-off $T \cdot M^2 \cdot D = \frac{N^2}{r} - \frac{N^2}{2r^2} - \frac{M \cdot D^2 \cdot N}{2r^2} + \frac{M \cdot D \cdot N}{r} - M \cdot N$, with $P = \frac{N}{D}$, $M \cdot D^2 \leq N$, $T \geq \frac{D^3}{r} - \frac{D^3}{r^2} + \frac{D^2}{r} - D$ and $1 \leq r \leq D$, plus $\frac{N}{M}$ table look-ups; and unified rainbow table cryptanalysis with distinguished points approximately meets a time–memory–data trade-off $2T \cdot M^2 \cdot D^2 = (2v - \frac{v}{r}) \cdot N^2 - \frac{(v-2) \cdot M \cdot D^2 \cdot N}{2r}$, with $P = \frac{N}{D}$, $M \cdot D^2 \leq N$, $T \geq (v + \frac{1}{r} - \frac{v}{r}) \cdot D^2$ and $1 \leq r \cdot v \leq D$, plus $\frac{r \cdot v \cdot N}{M \cdot D}$ table look-ups.*

At last, a detailed analysis gives the following result:

Corollary 2. *Hellman table, thin rainbow table and unified rainbow table cryptanalyses (can) have a TMDTO curve $T \cdot M^2 \cdot D^2 = \mathcal{O}(N^2)$, while rainbow table and thick rainbow table cryptanalyses have a TMDTO curve $T \cdot M^2 \cdot D = \mathcal{O}(N^2)$. Generally, among all the aforementioned TMDTO methods, fuzzy-rainbow table cryptanalysis is the best TMDTO method, and unified rainbow table cryptanalysis with distinguished points is the second best TMDTO method.*

6   Application to the GSM A5/1 Stream Cipher

In this section, we apply the TMDTO version of unified rainbow table cryptanalysis with distinguishing points to the A5/1 stream cipher, since its design allows us to conduct a TMDTO attack. We first describe the f function with respect to A5/1 and the structure of a unified rainbow table, then describe two crucial theoretical techniques and some implementation issues, and finally describe an experimental attack and its results on A5/1.

6.1   The f Function with Respect to A5/1

Since our goal is to recover a secret session key, clearly we should choose a suitable f function from the A5/1 keystream generator, so that we can have an efficient attack. A detailed analysis on A5/1 reveals the following result:

Proposition 1. *The state (of the three LFSRs) immediately after the key setup of the A5/1 keystream generator is a system of 64 linear functions of the 64 bits of the secret session key. The 64 secret key bits can be easily obtained by solving the system of 64 linear functions of the 64 secret key bits. Given the 64-bit state immediately after the IV setup of the A5/1 keystream generator, we can recover the state immediately before the IV setup (i.e., the state immediately after the key setup) with a time complexity of 22 clockings.*

Finally, after a further investigation we define the f function as follows.

Proposition 2. *With respect to A5/1, the f function starts with the initial state (that is immediately after the IV setup), and ends with the first 64 keystream bits. It takes the initial state as input, and outputs a 64-bit sequence. The 64-bit sequence is then input to the next f function as an initial state, and so on.*

6.2   The Structure of a Unified Rainbow Table

We targeted to build a reasonably large unified rainbow table with distinguished points. We set $m = 2^{37}, t = 2^{16}, r = 2^2, s = 2^6, v = 1, q = 2^8$; see Sect. 4.1 for the meaning of the parameters.

The starting points are of 64 bits long; every time we generate a 64-bit random from a particular sub-space as a starting point; and the used sub-spaces guarantee that the generated starting points are distinct one another. A variant f_i of the f function is a functional composition of f and an XOR operation with an integer i, $(i \in [0, s - 1]$, i.e., $i = 0, 1, \ldots, 63)$, that is, $f_i = f \oplus i$; the XOR operation works on the rightmost 6 bits of an output of f, which correspond to positions 1–6 of the first LFSR (i.e. $R1$) of the keystream generator. The distinguished points used here have zeros in eight bit positions 41–48 of a 64-bit value, which correspond to positions 17–19 of $R1$ and positions 1–5 of $R2$. Thus, on average it takes $q = 2^8$ computations to have a distinguished point. By the definitions of the f function and distinguished points, the endpoints are distinguished points that have zeros in the above-mentioned eight bits, and thus only 56 bits are effective for each endpoint. That is, a starting-endpoint pair takes a memory of 120 bits.

We do not use any other supplementary technique for the table, such as sequential starting points [24], index tables [15], endpoint truncation [15], or checkpoints [6].

6.3   Two Crucial Theoretical Techniques

We used two crucial theoretical techniques in our online attack on A5/1; the first one aims to reduce an attack's data complexity by using the sliding property [19] of the A5/1 keystream generator, and the second one aims to increase an attack's success probability by using the state convergence property [19,30] of the A5/1 keystream generator. In other words, the two techniques allow us to reach a certain success probability with much smaller precomputational workload. Since the first technique has been described and used in previous work like [19], below we only describe the second technique, which can be similarly applied to any stream cipher with a similar property. Note that Dj. Golić [19] also mentioned the state convergence property of A5/1, however, he used the property in a direct way — simply reducing the concerned searching space from the ideal 2^{64} to the convergent $2^{63.32}$ (upper bound), which (is not sufficient and should be followed by) is quite different from the technique we describe below. It seems that Nohl [30] used the state convergence property in some way comparable to the second technique described below, but he did not describe or even mention it (maybe because of his company's need for confidentiality), thus we are not sure

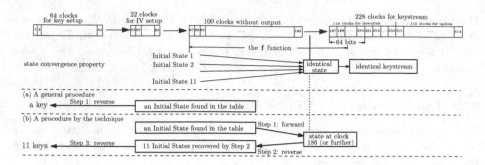

Fig. 2. The second technique compared with a general procedure

whether the second technique was used in [30]. To the best of our knowledge, the straightforward way that Dj. Golić used is the popular way to use the state convergence property, and none has explicitly described the second technique before.

The second technique relies on the fact that usually a few initial states of A5/1 will converge to the same internal state after the 100 clockings without output, known as the state convergence problem of A5/1 [19]. A theoretical analysis from [19] reveals that there are only $2^{63.32}$ possible states after the first clocking, and experimental results [15, 30] show that only about 15 % of the 2^{64} states is possible after the 100 clockings without output; and our experiments show that on average about $2^{3.5} \approx 11$ initial states can be obtained from a state just after the 100 clockings without output. Below we describe an approach to make use of this state convergence property, which is illustrated in Fig. 2.

Suppose $y = \mathtt{f}(x)$ is our inversion target. Let's consider the case with the first keystream segment, that is a preimage is also an initial state. When we find a preimage x^* to y from our (unified) rainbow table, we compute the internal state immediately after 100 (or 164, that is immediately after generating the first 64-bit keystream segment) clockings from x^*, and then we reverse this internal state at Clock 100 (respectively 164) to obtain all possible initial state(s) that can produce this internal state at Clock 100 (respectively 164), and finally we recover the corresponding session key for every obtained initial state and check whether one of them is the correct session key. (By contrast, a general procedure after finding a preimage x^* to y is to reverse x^* through the key and IV setups to check whether it could lead to the correct session key)

As mentioned earlier, on average about 11 initial states can be obtained from a state immediately after the 100 clockings without output; for some initial states, there are a large number of other initial states that converge to the same internal state at Clock 100, while for others there are a small number of other initial states that converge to the same internal state at Clock 100. For session keys such that there are a large number of other initial states that converge to the same internal state after 100 (or 164) clocks, there is a larger success rate to find it, because there is a larger probability that one of the many initial states converging to the same internal state is covered in the (unified) rainbow table, and as long as one of the convergent initial states is found with our rainbow table, then we can definitely recover the correct initial state and then find the correct session key; for session keys such that there are a small number of other initial states that converge to the same internal state after 100 (or 164) clocks, there is a smaller success rate to find it, for there is a smaller probability to cover one of the few convergent initial states in our table. This explains the existence of preferred session keys and non-preferred session keys for our attack.

The second technique also indicates why we did not define the f function to be from the state after the 100 clocks (without output) to the first 64-bit keystream segment. In this case, roughly 85 % of the points covered in a rainbow table would not have a corresponding initial state and thus is wasteful, and we cannot use the above technique to increase success probability.

The approach holds similarly for the cases with other keystream segments, where a preimage x^* to y obtained from our rainbow table is not an initial state, and we first compute forward to get the internal state immediately after 100 or 164 clockings, and then reverse this internal state to obtain all possible initial states that converge to the same internal state at Clock 100 or 164.

Note that we can compute the internal state after more than 100 (or 164) clockings from x^*, and then we reverse this state to obtain all the possible initial state(s). This could increase success probability slightly further, although our experiment shows that the gain is not much.

Thus, given a (unified) rainbow table, the second technique enables us to achieve a success probability of about 11 times as much as that for a naive attack (at the expense of negligible extra work). In other words, it enables us to reduce the precomputational workload by about 90 % to have a certain success probability. Notice that this technique is also owing partially to the fact that it is easy to reverse an internal state to the initial state position.

6.4   Implementation Issues

Below we briefly describe some implementation issues associated with our attack.

6.4.1   Implementations on A5/1

An efficient implementation of A5/1 is essential to our work, for it could save a lot of time during both precomputational and online phases. We have implemented three versions of A5/1 in C language:

1. A basic version that generates a keystream bit by bit under a session key;
2. A bit-slicing version that generates 64 keystreams in parallel under 64 different session keys; and
3. A multiple-bit version that generates a keystream block by block under a session key, by using several small precomputation tables, here a block consists of i bits generated simultaneously ($i \in [2, 8]$). (We did not consider $i > 8$, for the corresponding precomputation tables would take a large memory)

We have checked the performance of the three versions on a HP Z600 workstation with Intel Xeon Processor E5630 (2.53 GHz, 12 MB cache) and Ubuntu 12.04 operating system under the following three cases:

* Case A — the session key is fixed and, each time a large number of keystreams with only the first 64 bits are generated (10^6 in our test).
* Case B — each time the session key is updated and only the first 64 keystream bits are generated.
* Case C — only the part of the f function is considered.

For the three cases, the basic version has a throughput of approximately 202, 636 and 406 cycles/byte, respectively; the bit-slicing version has a throughput of approximately 29, 130 and 57 cycles/byte, respectively; and among the multiple-bit versions the four-bit version has a best throughput of approximately 89, 195 and 154 cycles/byte, respectively. We use the bit-slicing version (with further optimisation for using distinguished points) during offline precomputation phase, and use the four-bit version during online attack phase.

6.4.2 Computing a (Unified) Rainbow Table with GPGPU

We used the TMDTO version of unified rainbow table cryptanalysis with distinguishing points in our attack, and used a GPGPU workstation in both the offline precomputation and online attack phases.

The workstation used for our attack consists of a host system based on one dual XEON CPU (2 CPUs of Intel Xeon Processor E5-2620, 2 GHz, 15 MB cache and 32 GB ECC RAM each), one Quadro 600 GPU for display, 3 NVIDIA GeForce GTX690 graphics cards (which are actually 6 GTX680 cards roughly) for parallel computation, and 10 solid state disks (SSDs) of 480G SATA3 each. The total price was about 15,000 United States dollars. A GTX690 contains 8 graphic processing clusters (GPCs) and 16 streaming multiprocessors (SMXs); a streaming multiprocessor contains 192 streaming processors (SPs). In total, a GTX690 has 3072 cores with processor clock of 915MHz, and the on-chip memory is 2×2 GB GDDR5 with 2×256 bit width.

In the offline precomputation phase, the startpoints were processed by the 6 GTX680s in parallel; and 6 CPU threads were needed to control the 6 GPUs, respectively. The startpoints and endpoints were all located in host memory, and all of them can be accessed and modified by GPUs via direct memory access (DMA). Startpoints were randomly generated with no collisions, which were made by dividing the whole 2^{64} space into many small sections of equal length and then selecting a random number in each small section, (thus avoiding collisions). An additional thread was used to store the starting-endpoint pairs into a table. Whenever an endpoint was generated by a GPU, the additional thread put it into the input/output (I/O) buffer, and a fast I/O was achieved by writing out the buffer at one time. The additional thread was in parallel with the 6 threads controlling the 6 GPUs.

In the online attack phase, only one GPU (i.e. GTX680) was used, (which makes the attack feasible on laptops). Distinguishing points were computed on the GPUs, in a procedure similar to the offline phase; and the only difference was that the intermediate distinguishing points before reaching the endpoint were also recorded. We look up the 256 distinguishing points generated typically in an online chain by the optimized binary search, which took less than 1 s normally. Since GPU can modify the host memory via DMA, the host can check the generated distinguishing points in real time before the whole task on computing distinguishing points in GPU is finished. It is advisable to use an additional thread to check the calculated distinguishing point and perform table lookup of these distinguishing points. Therefore, table lookups are actually parallel with online computations on distinguishing points. Since a table lookup takes a shorter time than a computation on distinguishing points, virtually it does not need any time. The total online attack time is approximately the sum of the online computation time of distinguishing points and the online regeneration time of false alarms.

6.4.3   Configuration on SSDs

We used SSDs instead of general hard disks (HDDs), because SSD access is faster than CPU RAM access. Redundant Array of Independent Disks (RAID) is a data storage virtualization technology that combines multiple disk drive components into a logical unit for the purposes of data redundancy and performance improvement. The most common RAID configurations are RAID 0 (striping), RAID 1 and variants (mirroring), RAID 5 (distributed parity) and RAID 6 (dual parity). We have tested and compared RAID0 and RAID5. The stripe size is defaulted to be 128 KB, and the 10 SSDs of about 480 GB each used in our attack are viewed as a single virtual huge disk to users by being connected to an Intel SSD controller RS2WG160 which can control up to 16 SSDs. A RAID 0 splits data evenly across two or more disks (striped) without parity information for speed. RAID 0 is not resistant to any error or failure in disk, since it does not provide data redundancy. In most situations RAID 0 yielded the highest read and write performance, and its read and write speeds were tested to be approximately 3.2 GB/s and 1.8 GB/s, respectively.

6.4.4   Table Sorting for Fast Lookup

A unified rainbow table is sorted by the endpoints. In practice, there is a constraint on the maximum size of a file, so a dramatically large table has to be divided into a number of reasonably large parts to store. In our attack, we divide a unified rainbow table into 512 parts by dividing the space of the endpoints into 512 intervals equally, with each part of the table corresponding to a unique interval. During offline precomputation phase, after generating a starting-endpoint pair we simply store it into the part corresponding to the interval that the endpoint locates in; and during online attack phase, we can readily identify which part of the table the endpoint of an online chain is from, without searching it over all the parts of the table; then, binary search is performed in the identified part of the table.

6.4.5 Software Speedup of Table Access

A straightforward binary search (i.e. lookup) on an endpoint in the unified rainbow table with the 512 parts described in Sect. 6.4.4 takes 0.0073 s on SSD on average, (and 0.1400 s on HDD, thus the speedup is $\frac{0.1400}{0.0073} \approx 19$ times). Generally, given an A5/1 keystream in our attack, for an online chain we need to compute $r \times s \times v = 256$ distinguishing points and thus need to search 256 times in the unified rainbow table. Thus, the table lookups on all the 51 segments of a 114-bit keystream generally take $0.0073 \times 256 \times 51 \approx 96$ s on SSD (and $0.1400 \times 256 \times 51 \approx 1828$ s on HDD), regardless of the online computational time on f and its variants. We optimised the straightforward binary search with several software techniques on disk access: (1) Cached binary search with multithreading, which is $\frac{96}{31.1} \approx 3.09$ times of the standard binary search; (2) Endpoint indexing, which achieves a speedup of $\frac{31.1}{4.0} \approx 7.78$ times on the cached binary search; and (3) Multithreading with thread pool, which achieves a speedup of $\frac{4.0}{0.43} \approx 9.31$ times on the indexed and cached binary search. Taking all the three techniques into consideration, the final speedup is $3.09 \times 7.78 \times 9.31 \approx 223$ times compared to the straightforward binary search, that is, the table lookup time on all the 51 segments of a 114-bit keystream is reduced from the original 96 s to $\frac{96}{223} \approx 0.43$ s finally for our unified rainbow table. Our table lookup speed (on our SSD) is now $\frac{256 \times 51}{0.43} \approx 30,363$ searches per second, which is higher than the table lookup speed of 20,000 searches per second (i.e. 100,000 searches in 5 s) reported in Nohl's work.

6.4.6 Design Criteria on Compute Unified Device Architecture (CUDA)

NVIDIA's Compute Unified Device Architecture (CUDA) [28] is a programming model that integrates host code and GPU code in the same C/C++ source files. CUDA provides convenient lightweight programming abstractions of the actual parallelism implemented by the hardware architecture. Our attack used several key criteria introduced in [2,23,29] for optimising GPU, namely thread packing, arithmetic intensity and resource usage, warp divergence, the communication between host and device, the on-chip memory for storing lookup tables, and GPU error rate estimation.

6.5 Experimental Results

With the f function and parameters defined in Sect. 6.1, we first generated a unified rainbow table of about 1.6 TB on the workstation under the computing framework described in Sect. 6.4, which took about 54 days and involved about $2^{52.68}$ computations of the f function. The table became 984 GB (≈ 0.96 TB) after we sorted and removed starting-endpoint pairs with already existing endpoints, which took less than one day. That is, it took a total of about 55 days to make the 984 GB table on our GPGPU. The 984 GB table covered a total of about $2^{51.94}$ initial states (with possible duplication).

Then, we implemented and optimised a unified rainbow table attack based on the 984 GB table and downlink keystreams (of 114 bits long each). Based on four thousand tests, on average the attack had an online attack time of 9 s (of which: 5 s for computing online chains with one GPU, in parallel with table look-ups; and 4 s on false alarms with this GPU) with a success probability of 34 % when using 4 keystreams (204 segments); or an online attack time of 9 s with a success probability of 56 % when using 8 keystreams (408 segments), where two GPUs were used in parallel (i.e. one GTX690), and each of the two GPUs dealt with 4 keystreams for online chains (in parallel with table lookups) with 5 s and spent 4 s on false alarms.

At last, we targeted to generate three more tables of 984 GB with three different sets of the f variants, but at the moment the three other precomputation tables only had a size of 0.140 TB, 0.093 TB and 0.093 TB, respectively, (after sorting and removing degenerate starting-endpoint pairs). Using the four tables with a total size of $0.96 + 0.140 + 0.093 + 0.093 \approx 1.29$ TB, we got an experimental attack that used 4 keystreams (204 segments) and had an online attack time of 9 s (of which: 5 s for computing online chains with one GPU, in parallel with table look-ups of about 2 s; and 4 s on false alarms) with a success probability of 43 %. The attacks indicate that unified rainbow table cryptanalysis has a good performance as well.

Note that more cryptanalytic results can be extrapolated from the above experimental results, for example: If one more table of 984 GB was generated (i.e., a total of 1.92 TB), we could expect an attack that had an online attack time of $5 + 4 = 9$ s with a success probability $1 - (1 - 34\%)^2 \approx 56\%$ when using 4 keystreams, where two of the six GPUs were used in parallel (i.e. one GTX690), and each of the two GPUs dealt with a table for online chains (in parallel with table lookups) and false alarms; or an online attack time of $5 + 4 = 9$ s with a success probability $1 - (1 - 56\%)^2 \approx 81\%$ when using 8 keystreams, where two GTX690s (i.e. four GPUs) were used in parallel, and each of the two GTX690s dealt with a table for online chains (in parallel with table lookups) and false alarms.

7 Conclusions

In this paper, we have presented a unified TMTO cryptanalysis, called unified rainbow table cryptanalysis, have described its general combination with distinguished points, and have discussed their TMTO as well as TMDTO curves under the worst scenario. Finally, we applied unified rainbow table cryptanalysis to the A5/1 stream cipher, by working out a crucial technique that made the precomputational workload feasible to have an acceptable success probability. We made a unified rainbow table of 984 GB in about 55 days on a GPGPU computer with 3 NVIDIA GeForce GTX690 cards at a total cost of about 15,000 United States dollars, and implemented a unified rainbow table attack on A5/1, that had an online attack time of 9 s with a success probability of 34 % (or 56 %) when using 4 (respectively 8) keystreams.

Unified rainbow table cryptanalysis is of theoretical significance as a unified TMTO cryptanalysis framework, although it offers a trivially more comprehensive TMTO curve than the previously published four general TMTO methods and can offer the second best TMDTO curve when combined with distinguished points. From its success probability formula, we can have success probability formulas for rainbow table, thin rainbow table and thick rainbow table cryptanalyses, which take into account some possible redundancy among different columns and the distinctions among different function variants. The presented unified rainbow table attack on A5/1 is the first rainbow-type TMTO attack on A5/1 that reveals crucial techniques and implementation details, and is of practical significance, for the practical experimental results show again that A5/1 is rather insecure in reality.

Acknowledgments. This work resulted from an industry project on rainbow table cryptanalysis of the A5/1 stream cipher. The authors are very grateful to Wun-She Yap and Chee Hoo Yian for their participation in the early stage of the project, in particular, in the implementation of the A5/1 stream cipher.

References

1. http://en.wikipedia.org/wiki/A5/1
2. http://www.cs.virginia.edu/~mwb7w/cuda_support/optimization_techniques. html
3. Amirazizi, H.R., Hellman, M.E.: Time-memory-processor trade-offs. IEEE Trans. Inf. Theory **34**(3), 505–512 (1988)
4. Anderson, R.: A5, Newgroup Communication (1994)
5. Anderson, R.: On Fibonacci keystream generators. In: Preneel, B. (ed.) FSE 1994. LNCS, vol. 1008, pp. 346–352. Springer, Heidelberg (1995)
6. Avoine, G., Junod, P., Oechslin, P.: Characterization and improvement of time-memory trade-off based on perfect tables. ACM Trans. Inf. Syst. Secur. **11**(4), 17:1–17:22 (2008)
7. Barkan, E.: Cryptanalysis of ciphers and protocols. Ph.D. thesis, Technion – Israel Institute of Technology, Israel (2006)
8. Barkan, E., Biham, E.: Conditional estimators: an effective attack on A5/1. In: Preneel, B., Tavares, S. (eds.) SAC 2005. LNCS, vol. 3897, pp. 1–19. Springer, Heidelberg (2006)
9. Barkan, E., Biham, E., Keller, N.: Instant ciphertext-only cryptanalysis of GSM encrypted communication. J. Cryptology **21**(3), 392–429 (2008)
10. Barkan, E., Biham, E., Shamir, A.: Rigorous bounds on cryptanalytic time/memory tradeoffs. In: Dwork, C. (ed.) CRYPTO 2006. LNCS, vol. 4117, pp. 1–21. Springer, Heidelberg (2006)
11. Biham, E.: How to decrypt or even substitute DES-encrypted messages in 2^{28} steps. Inf. Process. Lett. **84**(3), 117–124 (2002)
12. Biham, E., Dunkelman, O.: Cryptanalysis of the A5/1 GSM stream cipher. In: Roy, B., Okamoto, E. (eds.) INDOCRYPT 2000. LNCS, vol. 1977, pp. 43–51. Springer, Heidelberg (2000)

13. Biryukov, A., Mukhopadhyay, S., Sarkar, P.: Improved time-memory trade-offs with multiple data. In: Preneel, B., Tavares, S. (eds.) SAC 2005. LNCS, vol. 3897, pp. 110–127. Springer, Heidelberg (2006)
14. Biryukov, A., Shamir, A.: Cryptanalytic time/memory/data tradeoffs for stream ciphers. In: Okamoto, T. (ed.) ASIACRYPT 2000. LNCS, vol. 1976, pp. 1–13. Springer, Heidelberg (2000)
15. Biryukov, A., Shamir, A., Wagner, D.: Real time cryptanalysis of A5/1 on a PC. In: Schneier, B. (ed.) FSE 2000. LNCS, vol. 1978, pp. 1–18. Springer, Heidelberg (2001)
16. Briceno, M., Goldberg, I., Wagner, D.: A pedagogical implementation of the GSM A5/1 (1999)
17. De, A., Trevisan, L., Tulsiani, M.: Time space tradeoffs for attacks against one-way functions and PRGs. In: Rabin, T. (ed.) CRYPTO 2010. LNCS, vol. 6223, pp. 649–665. Springer, Heidelberg (2010)
18. Denning, D.E.: Cryptography and Data Security. Addison-Wesley, Boston (1982)
19. Golić, J.D.: Cryptanalysis of alleged A5 stream cipher. In: Fumy, W. (ed.) EURO-CRYPT 1997. LNCS, vol. 1233, pp. 239–255. Springer, Heidelberg (1997)
20. Ekdahl, P., Johansson, T.: Another attack on A5/1. IEEE Trans. Inf. Theory 49(1), 284–289 (2003)
21. Fiat, A., Naor, M.: Rigorous time/space trade-offs for inverting functions. SIAM J. Comput. 29(3), 790–803 (1999)
22. Gendrullis, T., Novotný, M., Rupp, A.: A real-world attack breaking A5/1 within hours. In: Oswald, E., Rohatgi, P. (eds.) CHES 2008. LNCS, vol. 5154, pp. 266–282. Springer, Heidelberg (2008)
23. Harris, M.: Optimizing cuda. SC07: High Performance Computing With CUDA (2007)
24. Hellman, M.E.: A cryptanalytic time-memory trade-off. IEEE Trans. Inf. Theory 26(4), 401–406 (1980)
25. Hong, J.: The cost of false alarms in Hellman and rainbow tradeoffs. Des. Codes Crypt. 57(3), 293–327 (2010)
26. Hong, J., Moon, S.: A comparison of cryptanalytic tradeoff algorithms. J. Crypt. 26(4), 559–637 (2013)
27. Maximov, A., Johansson, T., Babbage, S.: An improved correlation attack on A5/1. In: Handschuh, H., Hasan, M.A. (eds.) SAC 2004. LNCS, vol. 3357, pp. 1–18. Springer, Heidelberg (2004)
28. Nickolls, J., Buck, I., Garland, M., Skadron, K.: Scalable parallel programming with cuda. Queue 6(2), 40–53 (2008)
29. Nvidia, C.: Compute unified device architecture programming guide (2007)
30. Nohl, K.: Attacking phone privacy. In: Black Hat USA 2010 Lecture Notes (2010). https://srlabs.de/decrypting-gsm/
31. Oechslin, P.: Making a faster cryptanalytic time-memory trade-off. In: Boneh, D. (ed.) CRYPTO 2003. LNCS, vol. 2729, pp. 617–630. Springer, Heidelberg (2003)
32. Standaert, F.X., Rouvroy, G., Quisquater, J.J., Legat, J.D.: A time-memory trade-off using distinguished points: new analysis & FPGA results. In: Kaliski Jr., B.S., Koç, Ç.K., Paar, C. (eds.) CHES 2002. LNCS, vol. 2523, pp. 593–609. Springer, Heidelberg (2003)

Evaluation and Cryptanalysis
of the Pandaka Lightweight Cipher

Yuval Yarom$^{(\boxtimes)}$, Gefei Li, and Damith C. Ranasinghe

The University of Adelaide, Adelaide, Australia
{yval,damith}@cs.adelaide.edu.au, gefei.li@student.adelaide.edu.au

Abstract. There is a growing need to develop lightweight cryptographic primitives suitable for resource-constrained devices permeating
in increasing numbers into the fabric of life. Such devices are exemplified
none more so than by batteryless radio frequency identification (RFID)
tags in applications ranging from automatic identification and monitoring to anti-counterfeiting. Pandaka is a lightweight cipher together
with a protocol proposed in INFOCOM 2014 for extremely resource
limited RFID tags. It is designed to reduce the hardware cost (area
of silicon) required for implementing the cipher by shifting the computationally intensive task of cryptographically secure random number
generation to the reader. In this paper we evaluate Pandaka and demonstrate that the communication protocol contains flaws which completely
undermine the security of the cipher and make Pandaka susceptible to
de-synchronisation. Furthermore, we show that, even without the protocol flaws, we can use a guess and determine method to mount an attack
on the cipher for the more challenging scenario of a known-plaintext
attack with an expected complexity of only 2^{55}. We conclude that Pandaka needs to be amended and highlight simple measures to prevent the
above attacks.

1 Introduction

Lightweight cryptography has received extensive coverage in recent years due to
the growth in low cost pervasive computing technologies such as Radio Frequency
Identification (RFID) propelled by significant progress in low power microelec-
tronics and lower manufacturing costs. Batteryless RFID tags are extremely
cheap, typically less than 50 cents, and enable remote and precise identification
of objects or people using wireless communication between *readers* connected to
back-end servers and *tags* attached to the objects or people [17]. The growing
ubiquity of RFID systems and their deployment in sensitive and in high-value
environments, such as their use in national passports, continue to stimulate
research into the security of these low cost computing devices. However, the limited resources available at the tags, as a consequence of the desire to drive tag
costs down [30], present new challenges to the provision of security mechanisms
for RFID systems [9,10].

Multiple lightweight ciphers have been proposed for such resource limited
environments in the recent literature [4,11–13,18,20,22,23,31,32], since exiting

© Springer International Publishing Switzerland 2015
T. Malkin et al. (Eds.): ACNS 2015, LNCS 9092, pp. 370–385, 2015.
DOI: 10.1007/978-3-319-28166-7_18

standard cryptographic primitives, such as AES (Advanced Encryption Standard), are much too area and power intensive to be practicable for implementation on low cost batteryless RFID tags [10,19,29]. However, since these ciphers are designed at the limits imposed by technology such as the number of gate equivalents (GEs) and available harvested power on batteryless tags, they are incapable of incorporating considerable security margins built into standard cryptographic mechanisms. Therefore, it is unsurprising that attacks that successfully break lightweight ciphers are frequently reported [2,7].

Recently, Chen et al. [8] suggested Pandaka—a stream cipher together with a communication protocol that exploit the resource imbalance between the tags and the back-end server, based on the concept of secure server-aided computations [1,21], to develop a lightweight cryptographic mechanism. Essentially, Pandaka shifts the bulk of the cryptographic operations to the reader, thereby reducing the implementation footprint at the tag.

At its core, Pandaka is a stream cipher that combines a secret state with a random seed generated by the reader to create a pseudo-random *derived key* which is subsequently XORed with a message block to encrypt it. The random seed, *indicators* in the Pandaka nomenclature, is also used for perturbing the state prior to the next round of encryption. For block integrity, Pandaka uses the 16 bit Cyclic Redundancy Check (CRC) generator, already available on a typical RFID tag [15]. The cipher has two suggested configurations, a 16 bit version, Pandaka(16,6), that has 96 bits of state, and a 32 bit version, Pandaka(32,6), with 192 bits of state.

We analyse the Pandaka cipher and protocol and make the following contributions:

- Describe a known-indicators attack on Pandaka, which exposes a weakness in the linear relationship between the state and the derived key (Sect. 3).
- Present an effective known-plaintext only attack on Pandaka, demonstrating that the security of the cipher depends on the size of the indicators rather than on the size of the reported internal state (Sect. 4).
- Highlight two weaknesses in the protocol's integrity mechanism: information disclosure; and a potential for de-synchronisation even in the absence of an active attacker. In the case of the Pandaka(16,6) configuration, the former completely reveals the plaintext in each block (Sect. 5).
- Analyse the weaknesses of the cipher and suggest directions for addressing them (Sect. 6).

2   Pandaka

Pandaka is a stream cipher that uses a shared secret between a tag and a reader, which we refer to as the *base keys*, and a random seed called *indicators* to generate a pseudorandom *derived key*. Subsequently, the derived key is XORed with the plaintext to produce the ciphertext. After generating the derived key, Pandaka updates the base keys based on the contents of the indicators. This update creates new base-key material for the encryption of the next block.

Following Chen et al. [8], we use Pandaka(L,N) to denote an instance of Pandaka with a block size of L bits and N base keys. Each base key has a length of L bits, hence the size of the state of Pandaka(L,N) is $L \times N$. The length of the indicators is $N + 2$.

The rest of this section describes the derived-key generation and the base-key update (or in other words state update) procedure. We also describe the protocol Pandaka uses for transferring the indicators from the reader at the heart of the base-key update procedure.

2.1   Derived-Key Generation

Pandaka uses N bits of the $N + 2$ indicator bits to select base keys. Each of these base-key selection bits corresponds to one of the base keys. As illustrated in Fig. 1, Pandaka computes the bitwise XOR of the base keys whose corresponding bits in the indicators are set to generate the derived key.

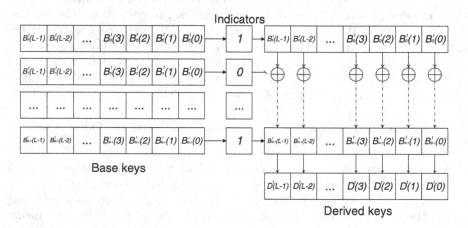

Fig. 1. Generating the derived key

More formally, let $B_k^t(i)$ denote bit $i \bmod L$ of the value of the kth base key, where $k = \{0, 1, ..., N - 1\}$, used for the tth encryption and let $I^t(k)$ denote the kth bit of the indicator used for the tth encryption. The derived key for the encryption $D^t(i)$ is calculated using

$$D^t(i) = B_0^t(i) \cdot I^t(0) \oplus B_1^t(i) \cdot I^t(1) \oplus \ldots \oplus B_{N-1}^t(i) \cdot I^t(N - 1) \qquad (1)$$

where $\oplus$ and $\cdot$ are the XOR and the AND operations. We recall that these are also the addition and multiplication operations in $GF(2)$.

2.2   Base-Key Update Procedure

In order to avoid using the same base keys for multiple encryptions, Pandaka perturbs the base keys after generating the derived key. The base-key update procedure only modifies the base keys used for the current encryption, i.e. those selected by the N base-key selection bits of the indicators. Subsequently, each of the selected base keys is rotated one bit to the left.

Following a rotation operation, Pandaka flips a select set of base key bits. The decision on which bits to flip is based on the values of the additional two bits, i.e. bits N and $N + 1$, of the indicators. If the value of these two bits is 00, no bits in the base keys are flipped, otherwise, for bit patterns 01, 10 and 11, Pandaka flips the base key bits whose position i modulo 3 is 0, 1, and 2, respectively.

Thus,

$$B_k^{t+1}(i) = \begin{cases} B_k^t(i) & \text{if } I^t(k) = 0 \\ B_k^t(i-1) \oplus FL(i, I^t) & \text{if } I^t(k) = 1 \end{cases} \tag{2}$$

where FL is the flip function defined as:

$$FL(i, I) = \begin{cases} 1 & \text{if } I(N) = 1, I(N+1) = 0 \text{ and } i \mod 3 = 0 \\ 1 & \text{if } I(N) = 0, I(N+1) = 1 \text{ and } i \mod 3 = 1 \\ 1 & \text{if } I(N) = 1, I(N+1) = 1 \text{ and } i \mod 3 = 2 \\ 0 & \text{otherwise} \end{cases} \tag{3}$$

2.3 Communication Protocol

The indicators used for encryption and decryption are generated by the reader. We assume that these are generated by a cryptographically secure random number generator. These indicators need to be communicated securely to the tag. The Pandaka protocol relies on a pre-agreed initial secret key between a tag and a reader to initiate communication. The Pandaka protocol is designed such that after each communication round the tag and the reader both share a secret derived key they can use to continue the communication.

The protocol uses three data block formats. F_1 blocks are used for transferring data from the reader to the tag. F_2 and F_3 blocks are used for transferring data from the tag to the reader. The protocol also includes protection against communication error.

F_1 **Blocks.** The F_1 blocks consist of two sections. The $N+2$ least significant bits (LSBs) of the block contain the indicators used for encrypting and decrypting the next block. The other $L - N - 2$ bits are for data. To send a message, the reader splits it into groups of $L - N - 2$ bits, and sends each of these groups in the data section of an F_1 block.

F_2 **Blocks.** The reader sends F_2 blocks to provide the tag with indicators for the blocks the tag sends. Each F_2 block contains $\left\lfloor \frac{L}{N+2} \right\rfloor$ sets of indicators. Of these, $\left\lfloor \frac{L}{N+2} \right\rfloor - 1$ are used for encrypting F_3 blocks sent from the tag to the reader, and the last set of indicators is used for encrypting the next F_2 or F_1 block sent by the reader. If $(N + 2) \nmid L$, then $L \mod (N + 2)$ most significant bits (MSBs) of the F_2 block are set to zero.

F_3 **Blocks.** Data is sent from the tag to the reader in F_3 blocks. Each block contains L data bits encrypted using indicators previously sent to the tag in an F_2 block. The Pandaka protocol does not specify how the reader and the tag agree on the number of F_3 blocks needed for a tag message.

Message Integrity. To ensure message integrity, each block is transmitted with a 16-bit cyclic redundancy check (CRC) code, using the specification outlined in the air interface protocol used by RFID tags, as specified in [15]. The CRC code is calculated on the block before the block is encrypted. On receipt, the block is decrypted and the CRC code is calculated again and matched against the transmitted code to help detect bit errors.

3   Known-Indicators Attack

First we analyse the cipher under a known-plaintext attack scenario where the corresponding indicators for a number of consecutive F_1 messages are also known. This is a simple extension of the common known-plaintext threat model to Pandaka. We show how an adversary can successfully use this information to recover the base keys of the tag. Successfully obtaining the base keys will allow an attacker to completely decipher all future communications. This attack exploits the weakness that the cipher relies completely on linear operations to generate the derived key.

We use $P^t(i)$ to denote the ith bit of the tth decrypted message and $C^t(i)$ to denote the ith bit of the corresponding encrypted message. We note that the derived key, D^t, used for encrypting the message can be calculated using $D^t = P^t \oplus C^t$ where $\oplus$ is a bitwise XOR operation.

For each base key we compute two values: (i) Q_k^t — the number of times that the kth base key has been used for generating the derived key; and (ii) $\mathscr{F}_k^t(i)$ — the flips applied to the ith bit of base key k since the first messages, i.e. when $t = 0$. More formally,

$$\begin{aligned} Q_k^0 &= 0 \\ Q_k^{t+1} &= Q_k^t + I^t(k) \end{aligned} \tag{4}$$

and

$$\begin{aligned} \mathscr{F}_k^0(i) &= 0 \\ \mathscr{F}_k^{t+1}(i) &= \begin{cases} \mathscr{F}_k^t(i)) & \text{if } I^t(k) = 0 \\ \mathscr{F}_k^t(i-1) \oplus FL(i, I^t) & \text{if } I^t(k) = 1 \end{cases} \end{aligned} \tag{5}$$

We note that $B_k^t(i) = B_k^0(i - Q_k^t) \oplus \mathscr{F}_k^t(i - Q_k^t)$. Hence,

$$P^t(i) \oplus C^t(i) = D^t(i) = \bigoplus_{k=0}^{N-1} (B_k^0(i - Q_k^t) \oplus \mathscr{F}_k^t(i - Q_k^t)) \cdot I^t(l) \tag{6}$$

or equivalently,

$$\bigoplus_{k=0}^{N-1} B_k^0(i - Q_k^t) \cdot I^t(l) = P^t(i) \oplus C^t(i) \oplus \bigoplus_{k=0}^{N-1} \mathscr{F}_k t(i - Q_k^t) \cdot I^t(l) \tag{7}$$

Recall that in F_1 blocks, for $0 \leq i < N+2$ we have $P^t(i) = I^{t+1}(i)$. Hence, given plaintext, ciphertext and indicators of T consecutive F_1 blocks, an attacker can construct $TL - N - 2$ linear equations in $B_k^0(i)$ over $GF(2)$. Solving this linear system reveals the values of the base keys.

The resultant linear system has a very distinctive and sparse structure which can be exploited to rapidly evaluate a solution to the system of equations. Figure 2 shows the matrix representation of a system of equations created for a choice of six sets of indicators for Pandaka(16,6), where shaded blocks indicate the value 1 and clear blocks indicate the value 0. The base-key selection bits of these indicators are 110100, 110010, 011100, 110100, 100100 and 001000.

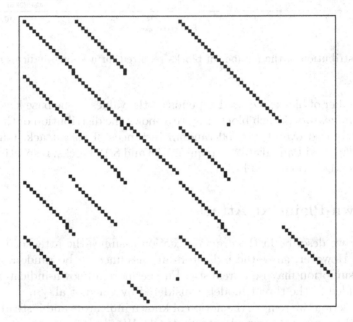

Fig. 2. Structure of a linear system

As Fig. 2 demonstrates, the matrix is divided into N groups of L columns, each group corresponding to a base key. The rows are also divided into groups of L, each group corresponding to a set of indicators. An $L \times L$ block is empty if the corresponding indicator bit is 0, otherwise, the block contains a possibly rotated $L \times L$ identity matrix. The magnitude of the rotation is determined by the number of instances the corresponding base key has been selected by previous indicators.

For $T \leq N$, the number of equations in the system is less than the size of the base-key bits NL, hence at least $N + 1$ blocks are required to solve the system. However, having $N + 1$ blocks does not guarantee a solution, to solve the system its rank must be equal to NL. In other words, the system should have NL independent equations.

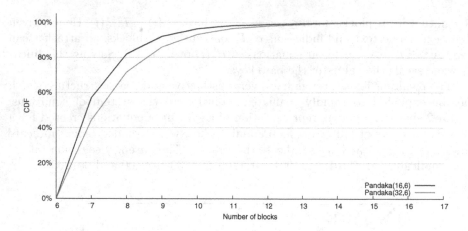

Fig. 3. Distribution of the number of blocks required for a known-indicators attack

The number of blocks required depends on the values of the base key selection bits in the indicators in each block. Figure 3 shows the distribution of the number of blocks required over 1,000,000 random instances of the attack. On average Pandaka(16,6) and Pandaka(32,6) require 7.76 and 8.12 blocks, respectively, with a worst-case scenario of 27 blocks.

4 Known-Plaintext Attack

The attack we describe in the previous section assumes the attacker knows the indicators. However, since the indicators are assumed to be randomly chosen, such an assumption may be unrealistic. Furthermore a known-indicators attack is not included in the threat models considered by Chen et al. [8].

In this section, we remove the notion of known indicators and instead consider the more challenging known-plaintext attack. We describe a known-plaintext attack which allows an adversary to completely recover the base keys using the plaintext (excluding the indicators) and the corresponding ciphertext of only a handful of consecutive F_1 blocks. By breaking the base keys, such an attacker can successfully decrypt further message blocks exchanged between the tag and the reader.

Here we use a guess and determine [3,16,27] approach where we guess the values of the indicators of some of the blocks and subsequently apply the procedure from the known-indicators attack in Sect. 3 to determine the values of the base keys.

The attack uses the recursive algorithm shown in Algorithm 1. It scans all possible values of the indicator sets, starting with I^0. For each value, the attack builds a system of linear equations using the technique discussed in Sect. 3 and, based on the properties of the linear system, decides on one of three options to proceed. If the linear system is inconsistent, it is clear that the current guess is wrong and the attack moves to the next guess. If the system is consistent, there

input : I: guessed indicators for the first T rounds
        P: plaintexts of the first n rounds
        C: ciphertexts of the first n rounds
output: Initial base-keys and indicators for the first round, if found

if $T > 0$ **then**
    Use Equation 7 with I, P, and C to create a system of $TL - N - 2$ linear equations ;
    if *the system is not consistent* **then**
        return *false*;
    if *the rank of the system is* NL **then**
        Solve the linear system;
        if *the solution matches all* n *known rounds* **then**
            Output solution;
            return *true*;
        else
            return *false*;
        end
    end
end
foreach *possible indicators value* i **do**
    $I' = $ add i to I;
    Recursively call this algorithm with I', P and N;
    if *result found* **then**
        return *true*;
end
return *false*

Algorithm 1. Known-Plaintext Attack

are two possibilities: (i) the rank of the system is NL, in which case we can solve the system, find the initial value of the base keys and verify the solution; or (ii) the rank of the system is less than NL where we do not have a solution and need to recursively guess the next set of indicators.

We use Gauss elimination with implicit row pivoting to test for consistency and to calculate the rank of the linear system. We note that the $(T-1)L - N - 2$ first equations in the system do not depend on the value of the indicators of the Tth round. Consequently, we do not need to apply the Gauss elimination process to the entire matrix for each guess. Instead, we can pre-compute the result of the elimination on the first $(T - 1)L - N - 2$ equations once. We can then use the pre-computed value to complete the elimination process on the L rows that are affected through the recursive process of guessing the indicators.

It is important to note that the value of the flipped bits (see Eq. 3) of the selected base keys does not affect the structure of the system of equations. That is, bit flips only affect the right-hand side of Eq. 7. Therefore, we can reuse the results of one Gauss elimination to all four indicator values that share the base-key selection bits and only differ in the value of the two flip bits. (I.e. indicator bits that define the four possible bit flips given in Eq. 3.)

Furthermore, we can optimise the guess and determine approach by halting the guessing of indicators when the rank of the system is greater than $NL - N$ and instead adding an adequate number of equations of the form $B_k^0(i) = x_j$ to obtain a full-ranked system and evaluate its solution. The number of equations we add is smaller than the number of base-key selection bits in an indicator; hence, this approach reduces the number of cases we need to evaluate.

In order to calculate the expected number of guesses to completely recover the base keys of Pandaka(16,6) and Pandaka(32,6) we first examine the structure of the linear system of equations created by the guesses of the first four rounds. At this stage, the linear system has $4L - N - 2$ equations, or 56 equations for Pandaka(16,6) and 120 for Pandaka(32,6). The rank of the system is not necessarily the same as the number of equations. Table 1 summarises the distribution of ranks over all possible combinations of indicators for the first four rounds.

As discussed above, the values of the base-key selection bits in the indicators determine the structure of the linear system. Using the same sequence of base-key selection bits in Pandaka(16,6) and Pandaka(32,6) produces similar systems of equations. Consequently, the distribution of the ranks of the linear system of equations indicated by the probability in Table 1 are the same in both versions of Pandaka where the only difference is the numeric value of the ranks.

Table 1. Rank distribution after four rounds of guesses

Pandaka(16,6)	Pandaka(32,6)	Probability
16	32	.000004
24	56	.0002
32	64	.0016
40	88	.0440
47	95	.0008
48	96	.0532
55	119	.0149
56	120	.8852

We now estimate the number of guesses required for completely scanning all possible values of the indicators given the indicator bits of the first four rounds. Summing the estimate over all possible combinations of the first four indicators gives an estimate of the size of the search space for the attack. There are 252 possible indicator values (there are 256 possible 8 bits combinations, of which the four with no base-key selection are illegal). Consequently, there are 252^4 possible combinations of four indicators.

We first look at the case where the indicators result in a system with a maximal rank, i.e. 56 for Pandaka(16,6) and 120 for Pandaka(32,6) and estimate the number of indicator guesses required to completely scan all of the combinations of indicator bits that result in a consistent non-full ranked system.

For that, we generate 1,000 random instances of Pandaka and evaluate the number of guesses required for solving each. For Pandaka(16,6), we require an average of 9.21 million guesses, with a 99 % confidence interval of 0.20 million. For Pandaka(32,6), the average is 9.23 million and the 99 % confidence interval is 0.18 million. We note that, due to the overlap of the confidence intervals, the estimates for Pandaka(16,6) and for Pandaka(32,6) are statistically indistinguishable. Hence, we conclude that the number of cases required does not depend on the block length L.

We argue that using the higher estimate above (9.23 million) for the case of a system with a lower rank is an overestimate of the number of guesses required for covering the whole search space. In a nutshell, when the rank of the system is lower, more iterations are required for solving the system and thus increasing the number of guesses, in contrast, when the rank of the system is lower, the probability of the attack ignoring the case due to linear-system inconsistencies is higher. We argue that the latter grows faster than the former, so that the expected number of guesses is lower than for a case of a fully-ranked system.

More specifically, we postulate that for each L dependent equations in the system we need to guess another round of indicators to get a system of degree NL. For simplicity we assume that because we have $N+2$ indicator bits, adding another round increases the number of guesses by a factor of 2^{N+2}, or 256 for the two Pandaka configurations.

We validate this assumption by counting the number of guesses required for solving consistent systems of rank $3L - N - 2$, i.e. systems in which L equations are dependent. The results are 2,039 million and 2,085 million for Pandaka(16,6) and Pandaka(32,6), respectively. These numbers are about 225 times larger than our estimate of the number of guesses required for solving the case of fully-ranked systems. Hence the assumption we used, increasing the guesses by a factor of 256, is an overestimate of the number of guesses required.

Chen et al. [8] demonstrates that each bit of the derived key is equally likely to be 0 or 1. Consequently, each dependent equation in the linear system we produce has a $1/2$ probability of resulting in an inconsistency. Thus, for a given guess of four indicators, if the difference between the rank of the system and the number of equations is r, the probability of the attack proceeding beyond these four indicators is 2^{-r}. Thus, the expected factor is in the order of $2^{\frac{(N+2)r}{L}} \cdot 2^{-r} = 2^{\frac{(N+2-L)r}{L}}$ and because $N+2 < L$ using the estimate of the fully-ranked system is an overestimate of the number of guesses required for non-fully-ranked systems.

Thus, we have 252^4 possible combinations of indicators for the first four rounds, and an estimate of 9.23 million guesses required for each combination. (9.23 million guesses is the higher estimate we have for a fully ranked system and, Hence, the estimated size of the search space is bounded by $252^4 \cdot 9.23 \cdot 10^6 \approx 2^{55}$. It is important to highlight that the same attack complexity applies to both Pandaka(16,6) and Pandaka(32,6). More significantly, the complexity we have evaluated is significantly lower than that postulated by Chen et al. [8] where they claim an attacker will need to guess all the values of the base keys, or 2^{96} and 2^{192} for Pandaka(16,6) and Pandaka(32,6), respectively.

For each of these 2^{55} guesses, the attacker needs to evaluate a linear system. As discussed above, parts of the system can be pre-computed, reducing the complexity of the evaluation. Furthermore, because we compute a system over $GF(2)$, we can use bitwise operations to calculate multiple field operations in parallel. Both these optimisations reduce the times required for solving the system.

An attacker can also pre-compute the reverse matrices a large number of combinations of indicator bits. By using these pre-computed matrices, the attacker avoids the computationally-intensive Gauss elimination, trading storage for speed.

The amount of plaintext required depends on the number of blocks required for solving the system. In Sect. 3 we see that up to 27 blocks may be required, with a typical number of 7 (Pandaka(16,6)) or 8 (Pandaka(32,6)) blocks. (See Fig. 3.) Additionally, because we are trying a large number of guesses, we need further plaintext bits to have a sufficiently high confidence that we have found the right key. Each additional bit halves the probability of accepting a wrong guess. Hence, with 2^{55} guesses and 55 additional bits, we have a probability of $1/e$ of accepting a wrong guess. With 74 additional bits the probability drops to below one attack in a million. Hence, for the typical case, we require 130 and 266 bits of plaintext for Pandaka(16,6) and Pandaka(32,6), respectively. For the worst case we require 290 and 722 bits.

5   Targeting the Protocol Flaws

Analysis of the communication protocol in Pandaka reveals a key design flaw related to the integrity check employed using CRCs [28]. The CRC code used for checking the integrity of messages reveals excessive amounts of information on the contents of the encrypted message.

CRC is a standard method of ensuring message integrity in network communication. RFID tags already include the circuity for calculating the proposed 16 bit CRC [15] and the CRC is used to identify bit erroneous communications as a result of bit errors. Pandaka reuses this circuity to ensure its messages' integrity, avoiding the cost of a dedicated circuity for evaluating the CRC.

5.1   Ciphertext-Only Attack

While the 16 bit CRC offers a high probability of error detection, for example it detects any single error burst less than 16 bits, it is designed to protect against unintentional errors and is not cryptographically secure. As described earlier, Pandaka calculates the CRC on the message before the encryption and transmits it together with the encrypted message. Thus, the CRC in Pandaka reveals 16 bits of information on the plaintext. For Pandaka(16,6), the 16 bit version of the protocol, the CRC effectively discloses the whole plaintext, negating the protection of the encryption. Therefore the current description of Pandaka(16,6) is completely broken.

For Pandaka(32,6), the CRC could be used to elevate a known-plaintext attack to a known-indicators attack. (See Sect. 3.) It is also possible that the CRC could be used as a source of information of the plaintext and subsequently facilitating a ciphertext only attack on Pandaka(32,6). One possibility for implementing the attack is to guess the 8 indicators bit in F_1 blocks. From this information and from the CRC, the attacker can create a set of 24 linear equations and subsequently use the attack in Sect. 4 to break the cipher. This attack has the potential of reducing the complexity of a ciphertext-only attack on Pandaka(32,6) from 2^{192} to approximately 2^{72}.

5.2 Active Attacks

Not being cryptographically secure also means that the CRC does not protect against malicious modifications of messages. The CRC code is linear, that is, given two messages A and B, $CRC(A \oplus B) = CRC(A) \oplus CRC(B)$. Thus, an active attacker can modify transmitted messages by flipping bits in the encrypted message and then calculate the correct CRC for the modified message even without knowing the contents of the message. However, it should be noted that such an attacker is beyond the threat model considered by Chen et al. [8].

The weakness of the CRC also results in a vulnerability to de-synchronisation attacks. With a 16 bit CRC, there is a probability of 2^{-16} of an arbitrary message having the correct CRC. If an attacker generates enough random messages, one of them is likely to have the correct CRC. When a tag receives such a message, it is accepted and Pandaka updates the cipher base keys. At this stage, the base keys at the tag diverge from those at the reader, preventing any further communication between the two. The de-synchronisation attack, Like the message modification vulnerability described above, is outside the threat model of Chen et al. [8].

6   Discussion

Pandaka aims to reduce the complexity of the tag by shifting the random number generation logic to the reader. While the idea is appealing and is worth further investigation, the implementation fails to meet the desired security level. In this section we review the main weaknesses of the implementation and suggest measures for addressing them.

Confusing Randomness with Security. For a stream cipher to be secure its random number generator must have good statistical properties. The converse, however, does not hold. A "good" random number generator that passes many standard tests for randomness is not necessarily cryptographically secure.

We recommend that, in addition to statistical tests, Pandaka is subjected to known and successful cryptanalysis techniques employed with stream and block ciphers such as linear cryptanalysis [24–26], differential cryptanalysis [5,6], and guess and determine [3,16,27].

Linearity. Linear systems are easy to reverse because they can be efficiently solved. More significantly, sparse systems of equations can be stored using less memory and solved extremely rapidly. Consequently, cipher designs aim to avoid linearity by including non-linear state update functions. Pandaka, however, only uses linear operations to update the state of the cipher.

The introduction of non-linear state update functions, both for generating the derived key and for perturbing the base-keys while increasing diffusion, would significantly increase the security of the cipher and provide protection against our attacks.

Limited Base-Key Perturbation. The purpose of the base-keys (or state) update is to provide new key material for following rounds. Pandaka uses a simple base-key update algorithm whose implementation only requires a small number of gates. However, the key material is hardly mixed, in fact mixing between base keys are non-existent. In Pandaka, key material of a base key is only used within the base key and the update (bit flip and rotation) of a given base key bit depends only on the state of a single indicator bit and all base keys are updated using the same algorithm.

Unfortunately, despite the simplicity in the hardware implementation, the algorithm is extremely easy to analyse and break. By combining the values of multiple key bits from multiple base keys to determine each updated base-key bit will increase the security of the procedure.

Synchronisation. Pandaka is a synchronous cipher with no mechanism for re-synchronisation of the sender (e.g. tag) and receiver (e.g. reader) in the event of lost messages. While the problem of bit errors have been addressed with the CRC, the cipher will easily self de-synchronise during: i) packet loss that often occurs in RFID communication networks due to packet collisions resulting from basing the air interface protocol of RFID system on the Slotted ALOHA protocol for facilitating simultaneous communications with multiple other tags [15]; ii) packet corruption and packet loss due to interferences from other readers communicating nearby that interfere and increase the noise in the communication channel between a reader and a tag referred to as the reader collision problem [14]; and iii) more rarely, a CRC collision (bit errors producing a message block with an identical CRC to the original value calculated by the sender)[28].

Thus Pandaka is vulnerable to self de-synchronisation even without the presence of an active attacker simply from corrupt messages and packet loss due to the wireless propagation environment and the nature of the communication protocol between RFID readers and tags.

7   Conclusions

Pandaka is designed for resource limited RFID tags. In order to reduce the hardware (area) cost of implementing the cipher in silicon chips Pandaka has used short shift registers and linear operations. The computationally intensive task of generating random numbers is allocated to the more resourceful RFID readers and overcomes the need to implement such a generator on the tag. Therefore Pandaka manages to significantly reduce the cost of implementing the cipher on a tag. Together with three message types and reader generated random numbers, Pandaka develops a state update mechanism that requires minimal hardware at the tag.

In this article we discuss several practical breaks of the Pandaka lightweight stream cipher. In particular, we show that in the more challenging known-plaintext scenario, using a guess and determine attack approach, Pandaka can be broken with an attack complexity of 2^{55} guesses using a known plaintext length of approximately 170 bits for Pandaka(16,6) and approximately 270 bits for Pandaka(32,6). Furthermore, we show that the information leak in the protocol by way of the CRC completely removes any protection provided by Pandaka(16,6) and dramatically reduces the attack complexity of a ciphertext-only attack on Pandaka(32,6).

We conclude our analysis by pointing out some of the most severe weaknesses of the cipher. The most obvious weakness is that the CRC value computed to improve message integrity exposes information on unencrypted blocks. Then, secondly, the lack of non-linearity in the design of the state update function. Although we suggest avenues for improving the cipher, any new design may be vulnerable to different attacks from those we have analysed and therefore a full analysis of the cipher would need to be performed in order to assess the strengths of any potential changes.

Acknowledgements. The authors wish to thank Dr Sylvan Elhay for the useful advice and productive discussions and A/Prof Orr Dunkelman for his suggestions. This research was supported by a grant from the Australian Research Council (DP140103448).

References

1. Abadi, M., Feigenbaum, J., Kilian, J.: On hiding information from an oracle. In: Proceedings of the 19th Annual ACM Symposium on Theory of Computing, pp. 195–203, New York, NY, US (1987)
2. Abdelraheem, M.A., Borghoff, J., Zenner, E., David, M.: Cryptanalysis of the light-weight cipher A2U2. In: Chen, L. (ed.) IMACC 2011. LNCS, vol. 7089, pp. 375–390. Springer, Heidelberg (2011)
3. Ahmadi, H., Eghlidos, T.: Heuristic guess-and-determine attacks on stream ciphers. IET Inf. Secur. **3**(2), 66–73 (2009)
4. Beaulieu, R., Shors, D., Smith, J., Treatman-Clark, S., Weeks, B., Wingers, L.: The SIMON and SPECK families of lightweight block ciphers. IACR Cryptology ePrint Archive 2013:404 (2013)
5. Biham, E., Shamir, A.: Differential cryptanalysis of DES-like cryptosystems. J. Cryptology **4**(1), 3–72 (1991)
6. Biham, E., Shamir, A.: Differential Cryptanalysis of the Data Encryption Standard. Springer, New York (1993)

7. Bogdanov, A., Rechberger, C.: A 3-subset meet-in-the-middle attack: cryptanalysis of the lightweight block cipher KTANTAN. In: Biryukov, A., Gong, G., Stinson, D.R. (eds.) SAC 2010. LNCS, vol. 6544, pp. 229–240. Springer, Heidelberg (2011)
8. Chen, M., Chen, S., Xiao, Q.: Pandaka: a lightweight cipher for RFID systems. In: Proceedings of IEEE INFOCOM 2014, pp. 172–180, Toronto, Ontario, Canada, April 2014
9. Cole, P.H., Ranasinghe, D.C.: Networked RFID Systems and Lightweight Cryptography: Raising Barriers to Counterfeiting. Springer, London (2008). doi:10.1007/978-3-540-71641-9
10. Cole, P.H., Turner, L.H., Hu, Z., Ranasinghe, D.C.: The next generation of RFID technology. In: Ranasinghe, D.C., Sheng, Q.Z., Zeadally, S. (eds.) Unique Radio Innovation for the 21st Century: Building Scalable and Global RFID Networks, pp. 3–23. Springer, Berlin (2011). ISBN 978-3-642-03461-9
11. David, M., Ranasinghe, D.C., Larsen, T.: A2U2: a stream cipher for printed electronics RFID tags. In: IEEE International Conference on RFID, pp. 176–183, Orlando, FL, US, April 2011
12. De Cannière, C., Dunkelman, O., Knežević, M.: KATAN and KTANTAN — a family of small and efficient hardware-oriented block ciphers. In: Clavier, C., Gaj, K. (eds.) CHES 2009. LNCS, vol. 5747, pp. 272–288. Springer, Heidelberg (2009)
13. Engels, D., Saarinen, M.-J.O., Schweitzer, P., Smith, E.M.: The hummingbird-2 lightweight authenticated encryption algorithm. In: Juels, A., Paar, C. (eds.) RFIDSec 2011. LNCS, vol. 7055, pp. 19–31. Springer, Heidelberg (2012)
14. Engels, D.W., Sarma, S.E.: The reader collision problem. In: 2002 IEEE International Conference on Systems, Man and Cybernetics, vol. 3, pp. 6–13. IEEE (2002)
15. EPC^{TM} Radio-Frequuency Identity Protocols Generation-2 UHF RFID Version 2.0.0 Ratified. EPCGLOBAL, November 2013
16. Feng, X., Liu, J., Zhou, Z., Wu, C., Feng, D.: A byte-based guess and determine attack on SOSEMANUK. In: Abe, M. (ed.) ASIACRYPT 2010. LNCS, vol. 6477, pp. 146–157. Springer, Heidelberg (2010)
17. Finkenzeller, K.: RFID Handbook. Wiley Online Library, Hoboken (2003)
18. Gong, Z., Nikova, S., Law, Y.W.: KLEIN: a new family of lightweight block ciphers. In: Juels, A., Paar, C. (eds.) RFIDSec 2011. LNCS, vol. 7055, pp. 1–18. Springer, Heidelberg (2012)
19. Juels, A., Weis, S.A.: Authenticating pervasive devices with human protocols. In: Shoup, V. (ed.) CRYPTO 2005. LNCS, vol. 3621, pp. 293–308. Springer, Heidelberg (2005)
20. Karakoç, F., Demirci, H., Harmancı, A.E.: AKF: a key alternating Feistel scheme for lightweight cipher designs. Inf. Process. Lett. **115**(2), 359–367 (2015)
21. Kawamura, S., Shimbo, A.: Fast server-aided secret computation protocols for modular exponentiation. IEEE J. Sel. Areas Commun. **11**(5), 778–784 (1993)
22. Knudsen, L., Leander, G., Poschmann, A., Robshaw, M.J.B.: PRINTCIPHER: a block cipher for IC-printing. In: Mangard, S., Standaert, F.-X. (eds.) CHES 2010. LNCS, vol. 6225, pp. 16–32. Springer, Heidelberg (2010)
23. Luo, Y., Chai, Q., Gong, G., Lai, X.: A lightweight stream cipher WG-7 for RFID encryption and authentication. In: GLOBECOM 2010, pp. 1–6, Miami, FL, US, December 2010
24. Matsui, M.: Linear cryptanalysis method for DES cipher. In: Helleseth, T. (ed.) EUROCRYPT 1993. LNCS, vol. 765, pp. 386–397. Springer, Heidelberg (1994)

25. Matsui, M., Yamagishi, A.: A new cryptanalytic method for FEAL cipher. IEICE Trans. Fundam. Electron. Commun. Comput. Sci. **E77**(1), 2–7 (1994)
26. Nyberg, K.: Linear approximation of block ciphers. In: De Santis, A. (ed.) EURO-CRYPT 1994. LNCS, vol. 950, pp. 439–444. Springer, Heidelberg (1995)
27. Pasalic, E.: On guess and determine cryptanalysis of LFSR-based stream ciphers. IEEE Trans. Inf. Theory **55**(7), 3398–3406 (2009)
28. Peterson, W.W., Brown, D.T.: Cyclic codes for error detection. Proc. IRE **49**(1), 228–235 (1961). doi:10.1109/JRPROC.1961.287814. ISSN 0096-8390
29. Ranasinghe, D.C., Engels, D.W., Cole, P.H.: Low cost RFID systems: confronting security and privacy. In: Paper Auto-ID Labs White Paper Journal, vol. 1 (2005)
30. Sarma, S.E.: Towards the 5 cent tag. White Paper-MIT Auto-ID Center (2001)
31. Shibutani, K., Isobe, T., Hiwatari, H., Mitsuda, A., Akishita, T., Shirai, T.: *Piccolo*: an ultra-lightweight blockcipher. In: Preneel, B., Takagi, T. (eds.) CHES 2011. LNCS, vol. 6917, pp. 342–357. Springer, Heidelberg (2011)
32. Wu, W., Zhang, L.: LBlock: a lightweight block cipher. In: Lopez, J., Tsudik, G. (eds.) ACNS 2011. LNCS, vol. 6715, pp. 327–344. Springer, Heidelberg (2011)

Privacy and Policy Enforcement

Cryptographic Enforcement of Information Flow Policies Without Public Information

Jason Crampton[1]([✉]), Naomi Farley[1], Gregory Gutin[1], Mark Jones[1],
and Bertram Poettering[2]

[1] Royal Holloway, University of London, Egham, UK
jason.crampton@rhul.ac.uk
[2] Ruhr University Bochum, Bochum, Germany

Abstract. The enforcement of access control policies using cryptographic primitives has been studied for over 30 years. When symmetric cryptographic primitives are used, each protected resource is encrypted and only authorized users are given the decryption key. Hence, users may require many keys. In most schemes in the literature, keys are derived from a single key explicitly assigned to the user and publicly available information. Recent work has challenged this design by developing schemes that do not require public information, the trade-off being that a user may require more than one key. However, these new schemes, which require a chain partition of the partially ordered set on which the access control policy is based, generally require more keys than necessary. Moreover, no algorithm is known for determining the best chain partition to use. In this paper we define the notion of a tree-based cryptographic enforcement scheme, which, like chain-based schemes, requires no public information but simultaneously has lower storage requirements. We formally establish that the strong security properties of recent chain-based schemes are preserved by tree-based schemes, and provide an efficient construction for deriving a tree-based enforcement scheme from a given policy that minimizes the number of keys required.

1 Introduction

Access control is a fundamental security service in modern computing systems. Informally, an access control system filters attempts by users to interact with protected resources, only allowing those interactions that are *authorized* by a *policy*, which is configured by the resource owner(s). Implementations of access control in software are vulnerable to compromise of the machine hosting the software. Moreover, such enforcement mechanisms do not work when protected resources are stored by an untrusted or semi-trusted third party, as is increasingly common.

In some situations, therefore, we may wish to use cryptographic techniques to enforce some form of access control. Such an approach is useful when data objects have the following characteristics: read often, by many users; written once, or rarely, by the owner of the data; and transmitted over unprotected networks. In such circumstances, protected data (objects) are encrypted and authorized users are given

© Springer International Publishing Switzerland 2015
T. Malkin et al. (Eds.): ACNS 2015, LNCS 9092, pp. 389–408, 2015.
DOI: 10.1007/978-3-319-28166-7_19

the appropriate cryptographic keys. When cryptographic enforcement is used, the problem we must address is the efficient and accurate distribution of encryption keys to authorized users.

In recent years, there has been a considerable amount of interest in *key encrypting* or *key assignment* schemes. In such schemes, a user is given a secret value – typically a single key – which enables the user to derive some collection of encryption keys which decrypt the objects for which she is authorized. Key derivation is performed using the secret value and some information made publicly available by the scheme administrator. These schemes are particularly suitable for policies that can be represented in terms of information flow.

Ideally, such a scheme should minimize the amount of public information and the time required to derive a key. Unsurprisingly, it is not possible to realize both objectives simultaneously, so trade-offs have been sought. Most schemes in the literature assume that each user is supplied with a single key from which other keys are derived with the help of some information published by the scheme administrator (see [10] for a survey of such schemes). In 2010, Crampton *et al.* [9] introduced a new type of scheme in which users may receive several keys. The significant advantage of this scheme is that no public information is required. Moreover, the simplicity of the underlying structure of the scheme makes it possible to prove the scheme possesses very strong security properties [12].

An information flow policy is defined by a partially ordered set X and a function mapping users and resources to elements in X. Most key assignment schemes are derived directly from X. The innovation introduced by Crampton *et al.* was to consider a partition of X into chains (or total orders). It is particularly easy to work with chains, but the partition breaks some of the "connectivity" of the partial ordering. These breaks are "repaired" by issuing more than one key to some users. However, one question that remains open is how best to choose the chain partition of a partially ordered set: there may be many such partitions and different choices may lead to chain partition schemes with different characteristics.

In this paper, we show that it is possible to work with trees, rather than chains, without reintroducing the need for public information, resulting in much more space-efficient key assignment. We define a tree-based, cryptographic enforcement scheme and provide a rigorous construction for such schemes from a given partially ordered set. We identify a number of different parameters that may be important in the context of a tree-based enforcement scheme. In particular, we consider the total number of keys that may be required in such a scheme and prove that a tree-based enforcement scheme with a minimal number of keys can be constructed in time $O(|X|^2)$. We show that a tree-based enforcement scheme for a given X will typically require fewer keys than a chain-based scheme. Moreover, we present an efficient algorithm for computing the best choice of tree from the information flow policy, in contrast to chain-based methods (which assume that a chain partition is given).

Our approach is based on constructing a weighted directed acyclic graph from X and then constructing a minimum weight spanning out-tree from the graph.

We establish a number of results about this out-tree that are likely to provide the foundation for further study of tree-based enforcement schemes.

In the next section, we introduce notation, relevant background material and related work. Then, in Sect. 3, we define a tree-based enforcement scheme, provide a method for constructing such schemes for a given information flow policy, and prove that all the resulting schemes have the property of strong key indistinguishability. In Sect. 4, we address the problem of finding a tree-based enforcement scheme that minimizes the total number of keys required to enforce a given policy, culminating in a polynomial-time algorithm for computing such a scheme. We conclude the paper with a summary of our contributions and some suggestions for future work. Those proofs that are useful in understanding our constructions are given in the body of the paper. The remainder, including the security proof for our construction (which extends an earlier proof by Freire *et al.* [12]), are in the appendix.

2 Background and Related Work

In this paper, we consider the cryptographic enforcement of access control policies. In particular, we focus on the enforcement of information flow policies using symmetric cryptographic primitives.[1]

2.1 Definitions and Notation

A *directed graph* (or *digraph*) $G = (V(G), E(G))$ is defined by a *vertex set* $V(G)$ and an *arc set* $E(G) \subseteq V(G) \times V(G)$. An arc in $E(G)$ is written in the form xy, where $x, y \in V(G)$. A *directed path* is a sequence of arcs $v_1v_2, v_2v_3, \ldots, v_{p-2}v_{p-1}, v_{p-1}v_p$, which we may also write as the sequence of vertices $v_1v_2 \ldots v_p$ through which the path passes. We write $x \leadsto_G y$ if there exists a directed path from x to y in G. For all $x \in V(G)$, we define $x \leadsto_G x$.

The *in-degree* of a vertex $v \in V(G)$ is defined to be the number of arcs of the form uv in $E(G)$. Given an undirected rooted tree, we may orient each edge in such a way that the root has in-degree 0 and all other vertices have in-degree 1; the resulting (acyclic) digraph is called an *out-tree*. Thus if a directed path exists between a pair of two vertices in an out-tree then it is unique. H is a *spanning subgraph* of a graph G if $V(H) = V(G)$. A *spanning out-tree* is a spanning subgraph that is an out-tree.

A *partially ordered set* or *poset* is a pair $(X, \leqslant)$, where $\leqslant$ is a binary, reflexive, anti-symmetric, transitive relation. Given a poset $(X, \leqslant)$, we write $x < y$ if $x \leqslant y$ and $x \neq y$; and we may write $x \geqslant y$ if $y \leqslant x$. We write $x \lessdot y$ and say y *covers* x if $x < y$ and there does not exist $z \in X$ such that $x < z < y$. We say x is *incomparable* to y, denoted $x \parallel y$, if $x \not\leqslant y$ and $y \not\leqslant x$. We say $Y \subseteq X$ is an *antichain* if for all $x, y \in Y$, either $x = y$ or $x \parallel y$: Y is a *maximum* antichain if $|Y| \geqslant |Z|$ for every other antichain $Z \subseteq X$; the *width* of X is the cardinality of a maximum antichain.

---

[1] There exists a large body of work on the enforcement of attribute-based policies using asymmetric cryptographic primitives, notably attribute-based encryption [6,13].

Given a poset $(X, \leqslant)$, we define the graph $H = (X, E_0)$, where $xy \in E_0$ if and only if $x > y$. H is called the *Hasse diagram* of $(X, \leqslant)$ and is a directed acyclic graph. A Hasse diagram of a simple poset is shown in Fig. 1 (on p. 393). We may also define the graph $H^* = (X, E_0^*)$, where $xy \in E_0^*$ if and only if $x > y$. The graph H^* is obtained by taking the transitive closure of H.

An *information flow policy* is defined by a partially ordered set of security labels $(X, \leqslant)$, a set of users U, a set of (protected) objects O, and a security function $\lambda : U \cup O \rightarrow X$. We say $u \in U$ is *authorized* to read $o \in O$ if $\lambda(u) \geqslant \lambda(o)$ [5].

2.2 Basic Methods of Cryptographic Enforcement

A natural way to enforce an information flow policy is to define a cryptographic key $\kappa(x)$ for each $x \in X$, encrypt object o with $\kappa(\lambda(o))$ and give u (or enable u to derive) all keys $\kappa(x)$ such that $x \leqslant \lambda(u)$. More specifically, let $G = (X, E(G))$ be an acyclic directed graph such that $E_0 \subseteq E(G) \subseteq E_0^*$. Then the transitive closure of G is equal to H^* and $x \leadsto_H y$ if and only if $x \leadsto_G y$. By publishing key derivation information for each arc in $E(G)$, it is possible to derive $\kappa(y)$ from $\kappa(x)$ if $x \leadsto_G y$. Thus, the total amount of key derivation information required is proportional to $|E(G)|$, while the number of key derivations will depend on the lengths of the directed paths in G. We provide a more formal account of the functionality required of a cryptographic enforcement scheme in Sect. 2.4.

Typically, key derivation information is generated using an appropriate symmetric cryptographic algorithm [1]: for arc $xy \in E(G)$, the inputs to the cryptographic algorithm will include $\kappa(x)$ and $\kappa(y)$. We write $Enc(m, \kappa)$ to denote the encryption of message m with key κ. There are three very well known ways to implement cryptographic enforcement of information flow policies [10]:

Basic – give u the set of keys $\{\kappa(x) : x \leqslant \lambda(u)\}$;
Iterative – give u a single key $\kappa(\lambda(u))$ and publish $\{Enc(\kappa(x), \kappa(y)) : x \lessdot y\}$;
Direct – give u a single key $\kappa(\lambda(u))$ and publish $\{Enc(\kappa(x), \kappa(y)) : x < y\}$.

We may evaluate different implementations by considering a number of parameters. Let $k(x)$ be the number of keys required by a user associated with x. Then we write k to denote the maximum value of $k(x)$ taken over all x and K to denote $\sum_{x \in X} k(x)$. We write p to denote the number of items of public information,[2] and d to denote the number of key derivation operations a user may be required to perform to derive a key. Let n denote the cardinality of X. Then the characteristics of the three schemes described above are summarized in Table 1.

Naturally, there is a trade-off between the amount of public information we need to compute and store centrally, and the number of key derivation operations that are required. The direct scheme, for example, minimizes the cost of key derivation at the expense of an increase in public information. Consider the

---

[2] It is assumed that the structure of the poset $(X, \leqslant)$ is known to all participants of a cryptographic enforcement scheme.

Table 1. How the parameters of various key assignment schemes vary

Scheme	Keys for u	K	k	p	d
Basic	$\{\kappa(x) : x \leqslant \lambda(u)\}$	$n + \lvert E_0^* \rvert$	$O(n)$	0	0
Iterative	$\{\kappa(\lambda(u))\}$	n	1	$\lvert E_0 \rvert$	$O(n)$
Direct	$\{\kappa(\lambda(u))\}$	n	1	$\lvert E_0^* \rvert$	1

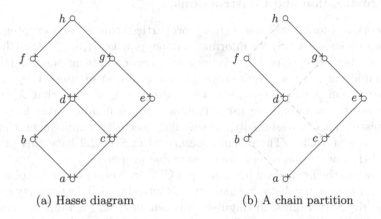

(a) Hasse diagram   (b) A chain partition

Fig. 1. The Hasse diagram of a simple poset $(X, \leqslant)$ and a chain partition

example in Fig. 1: the Hasse diagram of the poset has 8 vertices and 10 arcs, and
the width of the poset is 2; the graph of the transitive closure has 23 arcs.

More complex schemes have been devised to reduce the number of derivation
operations by increasing $\lvert E(G) \rvert$ [2,8,11]. In particular, Atallah *et al.* introduced
a scheme for policies where X is a total order, in which the number of derivation
operations was no greater than 2 and $\lvert E(G) \rvert = O(\lvert X \rvert \log \lvert X \rvert)$ [2]. Crampton
extended these ideas to arbitrary interval-based access control policies [8].

2.3   Chain Partition Techniques

We may consider other ways of enforcing an information flow policy. Crampton
et al. observed that one possibility is to decompose a partially ordered set $(X, \leqslant)$
into disjoint chains and then use one-way functions to derive keys [9]. In this case,
the arc set $E(G) \subseteq E_0$ and the transitive closure of G (the graph representing
the chain partition) is not necessarily equal to H^* (as illustrated in Fig. 1b, in
which deleted arcs are shown as gray dashed lines).

The advantage of such a scheme is that no public information is required. We
simply select a key for the top element in each chain and then use a (public)
one-way function F to iteratively compute the keys for the remaining elements
in each chain. In particular, if $x \lessdot y$ in a chain, then $\kappa(x) = F(\kappa(y))$.[3] Thus a

---

[3] This method is not appropriate for arbitrary posets because we may have $y \lessdot x$ and
$y \lessdot z$ [10].

user can simply derive keys by repeated applications of the one-way function. The trade-off in this case is that the user may need as many as w keys, one for each of w chains. In Fig. 1b, for example, a user assigned to vertex d will require $\kappa(d)$ and $\kappa(c)$. In short, it may be advantageous to eliminate public information, in which case each user may require multiple keys to support key derivation.

2.4   Formalization and Constructions

Recent work has formalized the security properties required of a cryptographic enforcement scheme (CES) for information flow policies [1,3,12]. Atallah et al. introduced the concepts of *key recovery* and *key indistinguishability* [1]. The former, informally, is the requirement that a coalition of users $V \subseteq U$ (the "adversary") can derive $\kappa(x)$ only if there exists $v \in V$ such that $\lambda(v) \geqslant x$. In other words, compromising users cannot lead to non-derivable keys being compromised. This is, essentially, the weakest security requirement that one might require of a CES. The schemes described in Sect. 2.2 have this property (provided the encryption scheme has reasonable properties).

However, in the interests of integrating a CES with other cryptographic tools, the stronger notion of indistinguishability was introduced. This property requires that the adversary cannot distinguish between $\kappa(x)$ and a random string (of the same length). The schemes discussed in Sect. 2.2 do not have this property (see [1], for example).

Informally, treating encryption keys as "just another encrypted data object" cannot be the basis for a robust cryptographic enforcement scheme. Specifically, the derivation of keys has to be separated from the decryption of data objects. We achieve this by introducing a secret value $\sigma(x)$ for each $x \in X$ from which $\kappa(x)$ may be derived. More formally, a CES for $(X, \leqslant)$ comprises the SetUp and Derive algorithms, the first being used to generate keys and the data used to derive keys, and the second to derive keys. Let $\mathcal{K}$ denote an arbitrary key space (typically $\mathcal{K} = \{0,1\}^l$ for some $l \in \mathbb{N}$).

- SetUp takes as input a security parameter ρ and a poset $(X, \leqslant)$ associated with an information flow policy. It outputs, for each element $x \in X$, a pair $(\sigma(x), \kappa(x))$: $\sigma(x)$ is used to derive keys $\kappa(y) \in \mathcal{K}$, where $y \leqslant x$; and $\kappa(x)$ is used to encrypt data objects associated with security label x. The SetUp algorithm also outputs a set of public information Pub, which is used to support key derivation.[4]
- Derive takes as input $(X, \leqslant)$, Pub, start and end points $x, y \in X$ and $\sigma(x)$. It outputs $\kappa(y) \in \mathcal{K}$ if and only if $y \leqslant x$. (In particular, $\kappa(x)$ can be derived from $\sigma(x)$.)

Atallah et al. described a CES in which two keys $\tau(x)$ and $\kappa(x)$ are derived from $\sigma(x)$ using a pseudorandom function and $(\tau(y), \kappa(y))$ is directly derivable from $\tau(x)$ only if $y \lessdot x$. (Thus, $\kappa(y)$ is iteratively derivable from $\sigma(x)$ if $x \rightsquigarrow y$.)

---

[4] In some schemes, it may be the case that $\kappa(y) = \sigma(y)$ for all $y \in X$; and in some schemes, it may be that the set of public information is empty.

The main innovation here is to separate the derivation and encryption functions of $\kappa(x)$, meaning that knowledge of the object decryption key $\kappa(x)$ does not help in deriving $\kappa(y)$. (Of course, exposure of $\tau(x)$ will allow for the derivation of $\tau(y)$ and hence $\kappa(y)$.)

Freire *et al.* introduce a security property called *strong key indistinguishability* [12], which we define formally in Fig. 4 and Definition 5 (on p. 401). The adversary selects a vertex x to attack and may then learn $\{\sigma(y) : y \ngeq x\}$ (as in the security model for key indistinguishability) and $\{\kappa(y) : y \neq x\}$; the adversary's task is to distinguish $\kappa(x)$ from random. They then define a CES for total orders that has the property of strong key indistinguishability, in which a key $\kappa(x)$ is derived from $\sigma(x)$ using a pseudorandom function and $\sigma(y)$ is directly derivable from $\sigma(x)$ only if $y \lessdot x$. Finally, they demonstrate how this CES can be extended to arbitrary posets using the chain partition construction described in Sect. 2.3.

3   Tree-Based Enforcement Schemes

In this work, we are interested in enforcing an information flow policy, defined in terms of the Hasse diagram of a partially ordered set $(X, \leqslant)$, using cryptographic primitives. We may enforce the policy in any way we see fit. We may, for example, increase the number of arcs (by including some subset of the transitive arcs), thereby decreasing the lengths of the directed paths in the graph and the number of key derivations that are required. Thus there is a trade-off between (increasing) the number of arcs and (decreasing) the amount of storage required for public information. In particular, we could include all transitive arcs, so that all paths are of length 1 (as in the direct scheme). Alternatively, we may increase the number of keys given to each user and reduce the derivation time (keeping the number of arcs constant). This corresponds to allowing the user to start from multiple points in the graph.

In practice, there may be constraints that will dictate what kind of cryptographic enforcement schemes will be appropriate. There may be constraints, for example, on the computational power and/or storage of the end-user devices; or it may not be possible to provide an on-line server to store public information. As noted in Table 1, there are four parameters that are likely to be of interest: k, K, p, and d. We may wish to minimize or impose an upper bound on one or more of these parameters. Certain choices have been well studied, particularly those for which $k = 1$ (when each user is given exactly one key and $E_0 \subseteq E(G) \subseteq E_0^*$). Alternatively, we can eliminate public information (by ensuring that every node has at most one in-arc), at the expense of an increase in the number of keys assigned to each vertex. It is these types of schemes that we consider in the remainder of this paper. In particular, we consider the problem of minimizing K, the total number of keys required.

In the special case that the Hasse diagram $H = (X, E_0)$ is a spanning out-tree, we may use simpler cryptographic primitives to enforce an information flow policy. Specifically, we know there is a unique directed path from x to y

whenever $y < x$. Hence, for all $x, y \in X$ such that $y \lessdot x$, we define $\kappa(y)$ to be $F(\kappa(x) \parallel y)$, where F is an appropriate one-way function [16] and $\parallel$ denotes string concatenation. In other words, keys are determined by the vertices, rather than the arcs, through which a directed path passes. In this case, we require no public information (apart from a description of the poset), because keys are derived only from a (secret) key and a (public) vertex label.

In general, of course, H is not an out-tree. We may assume without loss of generality, however, that our poset has a maximum element. If $(X, \leqslant)$ has more than one maximal element then we add a new element to X which is defined to be greater than all elements in X. (In this case, no user or object would be assigned to such an element.) Thus, we may assume that H^* has only one vertex of in-degree zero and so has a spanning out-tree [4, Prop. 1.7.1].

3.1   Constructing an Enforcement Scheme

In this paper, then, we investigate ways of constructing a spanning out-tree from $H^* = (G, E_0^*)$ (in order to eliminate the need for public information) by selecting an arc set that is a subset of E_0^*. However, we have to "repair" the Hasse diagram by allocating some users more than one key (because some of the paths will have been "broken" by the deletion of arcs). Thus it is interesting to consider how to select the arcs for deletion in such a way that the increase in the number of keys is minimized (either on a per-vertex basis or in total).

Figure 2 illustrates three out-trees derived from the poset in Fig. 1a. Removing arcs to create an out-tree inevitably means that certain paths are broken. The out-tree in Fig. 2a, for example, means that a user associated with vertex h only requires a single key and derivation requires no more than one hop. However, every other vertex (except a) requires additional keys in order to bridge the gaps. The above observations motivate the following definition.

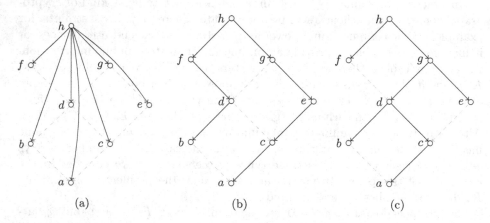

(a)   (b)   (c)

Fig. 2. Spanning out-trees derived from the poset in Fig. 1 by arc deletion

Definition 1. *Given an information flow policy* $(X, \leqslant)$, $E(T) \subseteq X \times X$ *defines a derivation out-tree* $T = (X, E(T))$ *if (i) T is a spanning out-tree; (ii) $xy \in E(T)$ implies $y < x$.*

Lemma 1. *Let $D = (V, E)$ be an acyclic digraph with only one vertex r of in-degree zero. Then by selecting one in-bound arc for each vertex $x \neq r$ we obtain a spanning out-tree of D. Furthermore, any spanning out-tree of D can be constructed in this way.*

Proof. First, let us prove that T is a spanning out-tree. Clearly, T has no directed cycle and every vertex of $x \neq r$ has in-degree 1. It remains to show that T is connected and contains r. Consider a vertex $y_1 \neq r$ and a longest directed path of T terminating at y_1: $P = y_t y_{t-1} \cdots y_1$. Since T has no directed cycle all vertices of P are distinct and since P is longest, $y_t = r$. Thus, every vertex of T is reachable from r showing that T is connected and contains r.

Now let T be a spanning out-tree. Note that for every vertex $x \neq r$ there is exactly one arc to x. Thus, T can be constructed by the procedure of the lemma. $\square$

If $T = (X, E)$ is a derivation out-tree and $x \not\geqslant u$, then $x \not\rightsquigarrow_T u$. However, we may have $u < x$ but $x \not\rightsquigarrow_T u$. Thus, the problem with a derivation out-tree, in the context of cryptographic enforcement schemes, is that some authorized labels will no longer be reachable. Accordingly, we extend the notion of a derivation out-tree to a tree-based enforcement scheme.

Definition 2. *Given an information flow policy* $(X, \leqslant)$, *a tree-based enforcement scheme is a pair (T, ϕ), where T is a derivation out-tree and $\phi : X \to 2^X$ is a key allocation function such that:*

- $x \in \phi(x)$;
- *if $u \leqslant x$ then there exists $z \in \phi(x)$ such that $z \rightsquigarrow_T u$;*
- *if $u \not\leqslant x$ then for all $z \in \phi(x)$, $z \not\rightsquigarrow_T u$.*

In a tree-based enforcement scheme (T, ϕ), directed paths in T are used to derive secrets (and hence keys): $E(T)$ determines the paths and ϕ determines the starting points of those paths (and hence the set of secrets that should be given to each user). In particular, $\phi(x) \setminus \{x\}$ is a set of vertices that were reachable from x in H^* that are no longer reachable in T. Thus, informally, $\phi(x)$ identifies a set of starting places in T from which all (and only those) nodes that were accessible in $(X, \leqslant)$ from x remain accessible in T, and $|\phi(x)| - 1$ is the number of *additional* secrets that will be required by a user with security label x.

Given a poset $(X, \leqslant)$ with maximum element r and a derivation out-tree $T = (X, E)$, define $\phi_E : X \to 2^X$, where

$$\phi_E(x) = \begin{cases} \{x\} & \text{if } x = r, \\ \{z \in X : \exists y \in X \text{ such that } yz \in E, x \geqslant z, x \not\geqslant y\} & \text{otherwise.} \end{cases}$$

We now establish that ϕ_E is the "best" tree-based enforcement scheme. First, we show that (T, ϕ_E) is indeed a tree-based enforcement scheme. We then show that for a given tree $T = (X, E)$, any tree-based enforcement scheme (T, ϕ), and any $x \in X$, $\phi(x) \supseteq \phi_E(x)$.

Lemma 2. *For any poset $(X, \leqslant)$ and any derivation out-tree $T = (X, E)$, (T, ϕ_E) is a tree-based enforcement scheme.*

Proof. We first show that $x \in \phi_E(x)$. This is trivially the case for $x = r$. If x is not the root vertex, there exists $y \in X$ such that $yx \in E$ (since T is a derivation out-tree). Moreover, $x \geqslant x$ and $x \not\geqslant y$ (since $yx \in E$ implies $x < y$). Hence, by definition, $x \in \phi_E(x)$.

Now consider the case $u < x$. Since T is a derivation out-tree, there exists a path $z_\ell z_{\ell-1} \ldots z_0$ in T, with $r = z_\ell$, $u = z_0$ and $\ell > 0$. If $z_i = x$ for some i then we are done (since $x \in \phi_E(x)$). Hence, we may assume that $z_i \neq x$ for all i. However, there exists a smallest integer $m < \ell$ such that $x \geqslant z_m$ and $x \not\geqslant z_{m+1}$. (If no such integer existed, we would have to conclude $r > x$.) By definition, $z_m \in \phi_E(x)$ and also $z_m \leadsto_T u$.

Finally, consider the case $u \not\leqslant x$ and suppose (in order to obtain a contradiction) there exists $z \in \phi_E(x)$ such that $z \leadsto_T u$. Then $u \leqslant z$ (by definition of a derivation out-tree and $\leadsto_T$) and $z \leqslant x$ (by definition of $\phi_E(x)$). By transitivity, $u \leqslant x$, the desired contradiction. □

Lemma 3. *For any tree-based enforcement scheme $(T = (X, E), \phi)$ and every vertex $x \in X$, $\phi(x) \supseteq \phi_E(x)$.*

Proof. Clearly $\phi(r) \supseteq \phi_E(r)$, by definition. Given $x \neq r$, suppose (in order to obtain a contradiction) that $z \in \phi_E(x)$ and $z \notin \phi(x)$. Then, by definition of ϕ_E, there exists $y \in X$ such that $yz \in E$, $x \geqslant z$ and $x \not\geqslant y$. Now, since $z \leqslant x$ and (T, ϕ) is an enforcement scheme, there exists $t \in \phi(x)$ such that $t \leadsto_T z$. Hence $t \leadsto_T y$ (since T is a tree and $yz \in E$). Therefore, $y \leqslant t$ and $t \leqslant x$, since (T, ϕ) is an enforcement scheme and $t \leadsto_T t$. By transitivity, $x \geqslant y$ (the desired contradiction). □

Thus, for a given tree T, (T, ϕ_E) is the enforcement scheme that minimizes, for each $x \in X$, the number of secrets required by a user assigned to x. Hence, for a given derivation out-tree $T = (X, E)$, it is reasonable to assume that we will always use the enforcement scheme (T, ϕ_E). Accordingly, we define

$$K(T) = \sum_{x \in X} |\phi_E(x)|.$$

That is $K(T)$ represents the total number of secrets required by a tree-based enforcement scheme based on the derivation out-tree T. Note also that $|\phi_E(x)|$ denotes the number of secrets required by a user assigned to security label x. Henceforth, given a derivation out-tree $T = (X, E)$, we will assume we will use the enforcement scheme (T, ϕ_E). Accordingly, we will write ϕ in preference to ϕ_E.

Let $T = (X, E)$ be a derivation out-tree. Then, for $y, z \in X$ such that $yz \in E$, define

$$\gamma(yz) = \{x \in X : x \geqslant z, x \not\geqslant y\}.$$

As we will see in Lemma 4 and Sect. 4, there is a strong connection between ϕ and γ, which we can use to compute a tree-based enforcement scheme efficiently.

Lemma 4. *Let $(X, \leqslant)$ be an information flow policy and let $T = (X, E)$ be a derivation out-tree. Then ϕ can be computed in time $O(|X|^2)$.*

Proof. By definition, $\phi(x) = \{z \in X : \exists y \in X \text{ such that } yz \in E, x \geqslant z, x \not\geqslant y\}$, for any x not equal to r in X. Moreover, there is a single arc in E of the form yz, for any $z \in X$, since T is a derivation out-tree. Thus, an algorithm to compute ϕ comprises an outer loop which iterates through the elements of X and an inner loop that iterates through the elements of E, where each iteration of the inner loop for arc yz tests whether $x \geqslant z$ and $x \not\geqslant y$. We can compute the adjacency matrix of H^* in time $O(|X|^2)$, which we can use to test whether $x \geqslant z$ (and $x \not\geqslant y$) in constant time. Moreover, $|E| = |X| - 1$ (since every vertex except the root has in-degree 1). Thus our algorithm runs in time $O(|X|^2)$.   □

3.2   Generating Keys

We now describe how to instantiate a tree-based enforcement scheme for $(X, \leqslant)$, given a derivation out-tree $T = (X, E)$, using a pseudorandom function (PRF). The scheme is a natural extension of the one used by Freire *et al.* for total orders [12].[5] Let ρ be a security parameter and $F \colon \{0,1\}^\rho \times \{0,1\}^* \to \{0,1\}^\rho$ be a PRF (as formally introduced in Sect. 3.3).

SetUp: The inputs to the algorithm are ρ and a derivation out-tree $T = (X, E)$ for $(X, \leqslant)$, with root vertex r.
Select secret value $s(r)$ uniformly at random from $\{0,1\}^\rho$. Set

$$\kappa(r) \stackrel{\text{def}}{=} F(s(r), r) \tag{1}$$

and, recursively, if y is a child of vertex x (in T), set

$$s(y) \stackrel{\text{def}}{=} F(s(x), y) \tag{2}$$

$$\kappa(y) \stackrel{\text{def}}{=} F(s(y), y) \tag{3}$$

Thus, for $xy \in E$, $s(y)$ is derived from $s(x)$ and the label of y, while $\kappa(y)$ is derived from $s(y)$ and the label of y.
Finally, define $\sigma(x) = \{s(y) : y \in \phi(x)\}$.
Derive: Given y, x and $\sigma(x)$, with $y \leqslant x$, there (uniquely) exists $z \in \phi(x)$ such that $z \rightsquigarrow_T y$.
If $z = y$, then (since $s(z) \in \sigma(x)$), compute $\kappa(z) = F(s(z), z)$. If $z \neq y$, then for each intermediate vertex t_i on the path $t_1 \ldots t_m$ between $t_1 = z$ and $t_m = y$, compute $s(t_i) = F(s(t_{i-1}), t_i)$. Finally, compute $\kappa(y) = F(s(y), y)$.

Our method for generating secrets is illustrated in Fig. 3.

---

[5] In the special case of a total order, we obtain the scheme of Freire *et al.*, modulo some differences in the choice of the second input to the PRF.

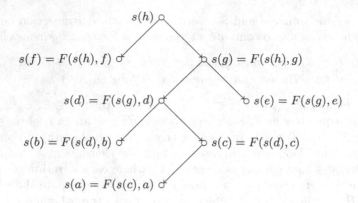

Fig. 3. The secrets generated for the spanning-out-tree in Fig. 2c

3.3   Security Analysis

We start by specifying what we understand by a PRF. Our definition is not the most general possible and is tailored to the requirements of our construction (as described in Sect. 3.2); specifically, we assume that the keyspace and range of the PRF are the same set.

Definition 3. *A* pseudorandom function $(F_\rho)_{\rho \in \mathbb{N}}$ *is a family of efficient functions* $F_\rho \colon \mathcal{K} \times \{0,1\}^* \to \mathcal{K}$, *where we understand ρ as a security parameter and* $\mathcal{K} = \{0,1\}^\rho$ *as the keyspace.*

We will usually write $F_{\rho,K}(x)$ to denote $F_\rho(K, x)$ for any $K \in \mathcal{K}$. To further simplify the notation, we will omit ρ when no confusion can arise. We write $\mathcal{D}^O \Rightarrow 1$ to denote a configuration where $\mathcal{D}$ is a probabilistic poly-time Turing machine that has oracle access to a function O and outputs a bit with value 1.

Definition 4. *Given a pseudorandom function F, we define the* advantage *of a distinguisher $\mathcal{D}$ to be*

$$\mathrm{Adv}_{\mathcal{D}}^F(\rho) = \left| \Pr[K \leftarrow_R \mathcal{K}; \mathcal{D}^{F_K(\cdot)} \Rightarrow 1] - \Pr[\varphi \leftarrow_R \langle\{0,1\}^* \to \mathcal{K}\rangle; \mathcal{D}^{\varphi(\cdot)} \Rightarrow 1] \right|,$$

where $\langle\{0,1\}^* \to \mathcal{K}\rangle$ denotes the universe of all functions mapping $\{0,1\}^*$ to $\mathcal{K}$. We say F is indistinguishable *from a random function if the advantage of any efficient distinguisher $\mathcal{D}$ is negligible.*

We next make precise the level of security that we target. We refer to [1,12] for recent discussions and comparisons of security models that are specific enough to allow the analysis of CESs using the formalisms of provable security. We reproduce here the strongest model from [12]; that is, the one formalising the highest level of security, which is based on the security experiment $\mathrm{Expt}_{X,x,\mathcal{A}}^{\mathrm{kist},b}(1^\rho)$ defined in Fig. 4. We write $\bar{\sigma}$ and $\bar{\kappa}$ to denote, respectively, vectors that list the values $\sigma(x)$ and $\kappa(x)$ for all $x \in X$.

$\mathrm{Expt}_{X,x,\mathcal{A}}^{\mathsf{kist},b}(1^\rho):$

1 $(\mathsf{Pub}, \bar{\sigma}, \bar{\kappa}) \leftarrow_R \mathsf{SetUp}(1^\rho, (X, \leqslant))$
2 $K_0 \leftarrow_R \mathcal{K}$
3 $K_1 \leftarrow \kappa(x)$
4 $b' \leftarrow_R \mathcal{A}((X, \leqslant), x, \mathsf{Pub}, \mathit{Corrupt}_{X,x}, \mathit{Keys}_{X,x}, K_b)$
5 Return b'

Fig. 4. Security experiment for strong key indistinguishability

Definition 5. *Let $(X, \leqslant)$ be an arbitrary poset. A CES for $(X, \leqslant)$ is strongly key indistinguishable with respect to static adversaries if, for all $x \in X$, the advantage of all efficient adversaries $\mathcal{A}$ that interact in experiment $\mathrm{Expt}_{X,x,\mathcal{A}}^{\mathsf{kist}}$ is negligible, where we define*

$$\mathrm{Adv}_{X,x,\mathcal{A}}^{\mathsf{kist}}(\rho) = \left| \Pr\left[\mathrm{Expt}_{X,x,\mathcal{A}}^{\mathsf{kist},1}(1^\rho) \Rightarrow 1 \right] - \Pr\left[\mathrm{Expt}_{X,x,\mathcal{A}}^{\mathsf{kist},0}(1^\rho) \Rightarrow 1 \right] \right|$$

and set $\mathit{Corrupt}_{X,x} = \{\sigma(v) : v \in X, x \nleqslant v\}$ and $\mathit{Keys}_{X,x} = \{\kappa(v) : v \in X \backslash \{x\}\}$.

Observe that in this definition, and in contrast to other models discussed in [1,12], the adversary obtains, in principle, *all* secrets embedded in the system (that is, all $\sigma(x)$ and $\kappa(x)$ values), excluding only those that would allow distinguishing the target key by trivial means (e.g., by invoking the Derive algorithm).[6]

The final step of our analysis is to prove that our tree-based enforcement scheme from Sect. 3.2 is strongly key indistinguishable. Observe that this implies that our scheme is secure in all the models considered in [1,12]. More formally, we have the following result.

Theorem 1. *Our tree-based enforcement scheme is strongly key indistinguishable in the sense of Definition 5. More precisely, for any poset $(X, \leqslant)$, $x \in X$, and efficient adversary $\mathcal{A}$, there exists a constant $0 \leqslant c \leqslant |X|$ and efficient distinguishers $\mathcal{D}_1^0, \ldots, \mathcal{D}_c^0, \mathcal{D}_1^1, \ldots, \mathcal{D}_c^1$ against the underlying PRF such that*

$$\mathrm{Adv}_{X,x,\mathcal{A}}^{\mathsf{kist}} \leqslant \mathrm{Adv}_{\mathcal{D}_1^0}^F + \cdots + \mathrm{Adv}_{\mathcal{D}_c^0}^F + \mathrm{Adv}_{\mathcal{D}_1^1}^F + \cdots + \mathrm{Adv}_{\mathcal{D}_c^1}^F .$$

4   Minimizing K in a Tree-Based Enforcement Scheme

So far, we have shown that it is possible to construct a tree-based enforcement scheme for an information flow policy $(X, \leqslant)$ that is strongly key indistinguishable. As we observed before, we will usually require our tree-based enforcement scheme to have some particular properties, such as minimizing the total number

---

[6] A variant of Definition 5 would consider dynamic adversaries: such an adversary is able to choose the challenge label x *during* the experiment, rather than having it fixed as one of the experiment's parameters. However, it has been shown that static and dynamic definitions of key indistinguishability are polynomially equivalent [12]. To simplify the exposition, therefore, we restrict our attention to the static case.

of keys or ensuring that all derivation paths are no longer than some threshold value. Hence, we require an algorithm to compute a derivation out-tree that satisfies the desired requirements, since, by Lemma 4, we can then compute the associated key allocation function ϕ in polynomial time.

In this section, we consider two questions: how to minimize K, the total number of keys allocated to vertices (by the key allocation function ϕ); and how to minimize $\widehat{K}$, the total number of keys distributed to users. The second question is interesting because, in practice, we might want to reduce the exposure of keys by ensuring that very few keys are associated with vertices to which many users are assigned. We solve both questions, demonstrating that it is surprisingly efficient to compute the required tree-based enforcement schemes in polynomial time. This is possible because of the connection between ϕ and γ, which leads to Theorem 2. We then state and prove Theorem 3, the main result of this section.

Our basic approach is to define a weight for each arc in E_0^* and construct a minimum weight spanning out-tree. Accordingly, given an information flow policy $((X, \leqslant), \lambda, U, O)$, where $\lambda : U \cup O \to X$, let $U(x) = \{u \in U : \lambda(u) = x\}$, and let $H = (X, E_0)$ be the Hasse diagram of X. Then we define the *weight function* $\omega : E_0^* \to \mathbb{N}$, where

$$\omega(yz) \overset{\text{def}}{=} \sum_{x \in \gamma(yz)} |U(x)|.$$

Theorem 2. *Let $(T = (X, E), \phi)$ be any tree-based enforcement scheme for $(X, \leqslant)$. Then*

$$\sum_{\substack{x \in X \\ x \neq r}} |U(x)| \cdot |\phi(x)| = \sum_{e \in E} \omega(e).$$

Proof. By definition, we have, for every $x \neq r$,

$$|\phi(x)| = |\{yz \in E : x \in \gamma(yz)\}|$$

and so

$$|U(x)| \cdot |\phi(x)| = |U(x)| \cdot |\{yz \in E : x \in \gamma(yz)\}|.$$

Hence

$$\sum_{\substack{x \in X \\ x \neq r}} |U(x)| \cdot |\phi(x)| = \sum_{\substack{x \in X \\ x \neq r}} |U(x)| \cdot |yz \in E : x \in \gamma(yz)|$$

and, since $r \notin \gamma(yz)$ for any $yz \in E$, we have

$$\sum_{\substack{x \in X \\ x \neq r}} |U(x)| \cdot |\phi(x)| = \sum_{yz \in E} \sum_{x \in \gamma(yz)} |U(x)| = \sum_{yz \in E} \omega(yz).$$

$\square$

Theorem 3. *Given an information flow policy $((X, \leqslant), U, O, \lambda)$, we can compute a tree-based enforcement scheme (T, ϕ) such that $\widehat{K}$ is minimized in time $O(|E_0^*| + |X|^2)$.*

Proof. For brevity, we write E for $E(T)$. By Theorem 2,

$$\widehat{K} = |U(r)| + \sum_{e \in E} \omega(e).$$

An algorithm to compute the weight function ω iterates through the arcs in E_0^* and, for a given arc yz, iterates through all x in X testing whether $x \geqslant z$ and $x \not\geqslant y$. In other words, we swap the inner and outer loops in the algorithm used in the proof of Lemma 4. Thus, we can compute ω in time $O(|X|^2)$.

Since $|U(r)|$ is fixed, we minimize $\widehat{K}$ by computing a derivation out-tree that minimizes $\sum_{e \in E} \omega(e)$. By Lemma 1, we can achieve this by selecting, for each non-root vertex $x \in X$, the minimum weight arc to x, where the weights are given by ω. We need only consider each arc (in E_0^*) once, which takes time $O(|E_0^*|)$. The resulting set of arcs forms a spanning out-tree of minimum weight and the number of additional keys required is $\sum_{e \in E} \omega(e)$. We can derive the associated key allocation function in time $O(|X|^2)$, by Lemma 4; the result follows. $\qquad\square$

Corollary 1. *Given an information flow policy $((X, \leqslant), U, O, \lambda)$, we can compute a tree-based enforcement scheme such that K is minimized in time $O(|E_0^*| + |X|^2)$.*

Corollary 2. *We can find, in time $O(|E_0^*| + |X|^{3/2} |E_0^*|^{1/2})$, a minimum weight spanning out-tree that has the minimum number of leaves among such trees.*

It is useful to find a minimum weight spanning out-tree with a minimum number of leaves because the number of leaves will impose an upper bound on $|\phi(x)|$. Note, however, that $|\phi(x)|$ may be greater than the width of X (and it is not difficult to construct such an example). This is because the set of arcs in the graph that is input to MINLEAF – the algorithm used to construct the spanning out-tree – will, in general, be a strict subset of E_0^*. Thus, the size of the maximal independent set in the graph that is input to MINLEAF can exceed the width of the poset (which is the equal to the size of the maximal independent set in $G = (X, E_0^*)$).

We now prove some further properties of γ. This enables us to reduce the running time of our algorithm because we show it is sufficient to consider only arcs in E_0 (rather than E_0^*) when constructing the minimum weight spanning out-tree.

Lemma 5. *Let $(X, \leqslant)$ be a partially ordered set. Then for all $x, y, z \in X$ such that $z < y < x$,*

$$\gamma(xy) \cap \gamma(yz) = \emptyset \quad and \quad \gamma(xz) \supseteq \gamma(yz) \cup \gamma(xy)$$

Corollary 3. *Let $(X, \leqslant)$ be a partially ordered set with Hasse diagram $H = (X, E_0)$. Then, for any path $x_1 x_2 \ldots x_p$ in H^*, $p > 2$, we have*

$$\omega(x_1 x_p) \geqslant \sum_{i=1}^{p-1} \omega(x_i x_{i+1}).$$

Corollary 4. *Let $(X, \leqslant)$ be a partially ordered set with Hasse diagram $H = (X, E_0)$. Then there exists a minimum weight spanning out-tree $T = (X, E)$ with $E \subseteq E_0$.*

Corollary 5. *We can compute a tree-based enforcement scheme for information flow policy $(X, \leqslant)$ in time $O(|E_0| + |X|^2)$.*

Remark 1. In practice, we expect that $|U(x)| > 0$, although our proofs do not make this assumption. If we do make this assumption, it is possible to strengthen the statement in Corollary 4 and assert that a minimum weight spanning out-tree can *only* contain arcs from the Hasse diagram.

Figure 5 illustrates the construction of the minimum weight spanning out-tree for the poset in Fig. 1 (assuming there is a single user for each vertex). The weight on arc ec is 3, for example, because $\gamma(ec) = \{c, d, f\}$. (The effect of retaining arc ec would be that $\kappa(c)$ would be required for each of c, d and f. Equivalently, $c \in \phi(d)$ and $c \in \phi(f)$ if we were to choose ec to belong to our derivation out-tree.) To construct a minimum weight spanning out-tree, we must select arcs ca and dc (and we select one or other of fd and gd). One possible scheme, when gd is retained rather than fd is illustrated in Fig. 5b; the scheme requires a total of 11 keys, being the sum of the weights on the retained arcs plus an extra one for the root vertex.

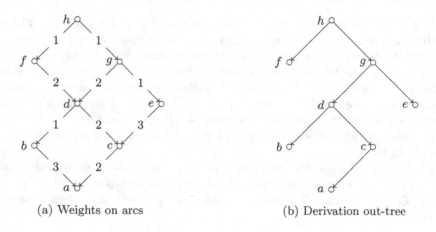

(a) Weights on arcs   (b) Derivation out-tree

Fig. 5. The minimum weight derivation tree for Fig. 1

Remark 2. Our construction will almost always require fewer keys than a scheme based on chain partitions. This follows by noting that any vertex x, such that $x > y$, $x > z$ and $\{y, z\}$ is an antichain, necessarily requires (at least) two keys in a chain partition scheme, but this is not necessarily true of our construction (since the derivation tree may include many antichains). Consider the chain partition in Fig. 1b and the derivation tree in Fig. 5b. The former would require 13 keys, while the latter only 11.

5   Conclusion

In this paper, we have introduced a new form of cryptographic scheme for the enforcement of information flow policies. Our scheme has the advantage that no public information is required for the derivation of decryption keys. Moreover, our tree-based scheme requires fewer keys (when X is not a total order), compared to existing chain-based approaches, to enforce a given policy. Nevertheless, our scheme retains the strong security properties that have recently been established for chain-based schemes [12]. From a practical perspective, we provide an efficient algorithm for computing an optimal derivation tree, in the sense that it requires the smallest number of keys. This is in sharp contrast to chain-based approaches, which provide no guidance on how best to select a chain partition of the poset (of which there may be many) nor provide a way of computing the number of keys required for a given partition. Thus, there are particular practical advantages to using a tree-based approach.

There are several interesting opportunities for future work. From a mathematical perspective, it would be interesting to establish the minimum total number of keys required by a chain-based scheme and, if possible, to quantify the benefits offered by a tree-based scheme. This is, however, likely to be non-trivial, as it is not clear that there exists a weight function for chain-based schemes that can be used to formulate a result analogous to Theorem 2. From a more practical perspective, it would be interesting to find an algorithm that can compute a derivation tree such that (i) no user requires more than w keys, where w is the width of the poset (ii) the total number of keys is as small as possible. In particular, such a construction may be useful in scenarios where the user devices have limited secure storage for keys. Our preliminary work on this problem suggests that no efficient algorithm exists, but whether it is an NP-hard problem remains open. We also intend to investigate whether a forest-based enforcement scheme, which would share some of the characteristics of tree- and chain-based schemes, would offer advantages in terms of reducing (i) the maximum number of steps required for key derivation (ii) the administrative effort required following key revocation (since we can limit key updates to those vertices within a tree in the forest). In Fig. 5b, for example, we could delete arc gd to yield a forest of two trees: each user assigned to vertex h or g would require an additional key ($\kappa(d)$) but worst-case key derivation would require two, rather than four, hops.

Acknowledgments. BP was supported by EPSRC Leadership Fellowship EP/H005455/1, a Sofja Kovalevskaja Award of the Alexander von Humboldt Foundation, and the German Federal Ministry for Education and Research.

A   Proofs

Proof (of Theorem 1). The argument proceeds using sequences of $|X| = n$ hybrid games that interpolate between experiments $\mathrm{Expt}^{kist,0}$ and $\mathrm{Expt}^{kist,1}$. In each hybrid step, if specific conditions are met, we replace one PRF instance by a random function; from the point of view of the adversary, the distance between each two consecutive hybrids is not greater than Adv^F, for an appropriate PRF distinguisher.

Fix a poset $(X, \leqslant)$, a derivation out-tree $T = (X, E(T))$ for X, a label $x \in X$, and an efficient adversary $\mathcal{A}$. Let $x_n \prec x_{n-1} \prec \cdots \prec x_2 \prec x_1 = r$ be any (reverse) linear extension of X; that is x_n is a smallest element in X and x_1 is the root.[7] For $b \in \{0,1\}$, we set $G_0^b = \mathrm{Expt}_{X,x,\mathcal{A}}^{\mathsf{kist},b}$ and define games $G_1^b, \ldots, G_n^b$ such that, if $x \not\leqslant x_k$ then G_k^b and G_{k-1}^b are identical, and if $x \leqslant x_k$ then the difference between games G_k^b and G_{k-1}^b is precisely that all PRF invocations with key $\sigma(x_k)$ are replaced by assignments with values in $\mathcal{K}$ drawn uniformly at random. Let S_k^b denote $\Pr[G_k^b \Rightarrow 1]$ for all b, k.

Observe that we replace PRF invocations by random assignments for precisely those labels x that do not have a corresponding entry in $\mathit{Corrupt}_{X,x}$. Observe also that, as we consider labels $x \in X$ in a suitable order, for all switchings from a PRF to a random function we have that the corresponding PRF key $\sigma(x)$ was replaced with a uniform random value before. Hence, by a standard reductionist argument, in the cases $x \leqslant x_k$ we have

$$|S_k^b - S_{k-1}^b| = |\Pr[G_k^b \Rightarrow 1] - \Pr[G_{k-1}^b \Rightarrow 1]| \leqslant \mathrm{Adv}_{\mathcal{D}}^F, \qquad (4)$$

for a specific (efficient) distinguisher $\mathcal{D}$; in addition, whenever $x \not\leqslant x_k$ we have $G_k^b = G_{k-1}^b$ and hence $|S_k^b - S_{k-1}^b| = 0$. Now, by repeated application of the triangle inequality and (4), we have

$$\left| S_0^b - S_n^b \right| \leqslant \sum_{i=1}^n \left| S_{i-1}^b - S_i^b \right| \leqslant \sum_{i=1}^c \mathrm{Adv}_{\mathcal{D}_i^b}^F,$$

where $c = |\{x' \in X : x \leqslant x'\}|$ and distinguishers $\mathcal{D}_i^b$ are constructed as specified. We now consider games G_n^0 and G_n^1. In both cases $\kappa(x)$ is picked uniformly at random, thus lines 2 and 3 in the experiment implement the same operation. Hence G_n^0 is identical to G_n^1 and $|S_n^0 - S_n^1| = 0$. Thus, we obtain

$$\mathrm{Adv}_{X,x,\mathcal{A}}^{\mathsf{kist}} = |S_0^1 - S_0^0| \leqslant |S_0^1 - S_n^1| + |S_n^1 - S_n^0| + |S_n^0 - S_0^0|$$

$$\leqslant \mathrm{Adv}_{\mathcal{D}_1^1}^F + \ldots + \mathrm{Adv}_{\mathcal{D}_c^1}^F + 0 + \mathrm{Adv}_{\mathcal{D}_1^0}^F + \ldots + \mathrm{Adv}_{\mathcal{D}_c^0}^F$$

as required.   □

Proof (of Corollary 1). We simply set $|U(x)| = 1$ and apply Theorems 2 and 3.   □

Proof (of Corollary 2). Replace H^* by its subgraph $D = (X, E)$ obtained as follows: for each vertex $x \neq r$ delete all arcs to x apart from those of minimum

---

[7] That is, if $x \leqslant y$ (in X) then $x \prec y$ (in the linear extension). Every (finite) partial order has at least one linear extension, which may be computed, in linear time, by representing the partial order as a directed acyclic graph and using a topological sort [7, §22.3].

weight (among arcs to x). Observe that D can be constructed in time $O(|E_0^*|)$. Find an out-tree with minimum number of leaves using algorithm MINLEAF [14]. It remains to observe that MINLEAF's runtime is $O(|E| + |X|^{3/2}|E|^{1/2})$.   □

Proof (of Lemma 5). Suppose $t \in \gamma(xy) \cap \gamma(yz)$. Since $t \in \gamma(yz)$, we have $t \geqslant z$ and $t \not\geqslant y$; since $t \in \gamma(xy)$, we have $t \geqslant y$, immediately leading to the desired contradiction.

Now suppose $t \in \gamma(xy)$. Then $t \geqslant y$ and $t \not\geqslant x$. Hence, we have $t > z$, by transitivity; thus $t \in \gamma(xz)$ and $\gamma(xy) \subseteq \gamma(xz)$. Finally, suppose $t \in \gamma(yz)$. Then $t \geqslant z$ and $t \not\geqslant y$. Now $t \not\geqslant x$ (otherwise, we would have $t > y$ by transitivity) and hence $t \in \gamma(xz)$; thus $\gamma(yz) \subseteq \gamma(xz)$.   □

Proof (of Corollary 3). Consider the case $p = 3$, with $x > y > z$. Using Lemma 5 and the fact that $|U(t)| \geqslant 0$ for all t, we have

$$\omega(xz) = \sum_{t \in \gamma(xz)} |U(t)|$$

$$\geqslant \sum_{t \in \gamma(xy)} |U(t)| + \sum_{t \in \gamma(yz)} |U(t)|$$

$$= \omega(xy) + \omega(yz).$$

Now suppose the result holds for all $p < P$ and consider a path $x_1 \ldots x_P$ containing P vertices. Then $x_1 x_{P-1} \in E_0^*$ and, by Lemma 5 and the inductive hypothesis, respectively, we have

$$\omega(x_1 x_P) \geqslant \omega(x_1 x_{P-1}) + \omega(x_{P-1} x_P)$$

$$\geqslant \omega(x_1 x_2) + \cdots + \omega(x_{P-2} x_{P-1}) + \omega(x_{P-1} x_P)$$

$$= \sum_{i=1}^{P-1} \omega(x_i x_{i+1})$$

Thus the result holds by induction.   □

Proof (of Corollary 4). Let $T' = (X, E')$ be a minimum weight spanning out-tree for $(X, \leqslant)$, and suppose arc xy is in E' but not in E_0. Then $x \leadsto_H y$ and let zy be the last arc in this path. Since $\omega(uv) \geqslant 0$ for each arc uv and by Corollary 3, $\omega(zy) \leqslant \omega(xy)$. Therefore by removing xy from E' and adding zy, we have a spanning out-tree with weight at most that of T'. By replacing every arc in $E' \setminus E_0$ in this way, we have a spanning out-tree $T = (X, E)$ of weight at most that of T', and therefore of minimum weight.   □

Proof (of Corollary 5). By Corollary 4, we may restrict our attention to arcs in the Hasse diagram. Thus we can compute the minimum weight derivation tree in time $O(|E_0|)$ and we can compute ϕ in time $O(|E_0| + |X|^2)$.   □

References

1. Atallah, M.J., Blanton, M., Fazio, N., Frikken, K.B.: Dynamic and efficient key management for access hierarchies. ACM Trans. Inf. Syst. Secur. **12**(3), 18 (2009)
2. Frikken, K.B., Atallah, M.J., Blanton, M.: Incorporating temporal capabilities in existing key management schemes. In: Biskup, J., López, J. (eds.) ESORICS 2007. LNCS, vol. 4734, pp. 515–530. Springer, Heidelberg (2007)
3. Ateniese, G., De Santis, A., Ferrara, A.L., Masucci, B.: Provably-secure time-bound hierarchical key assignment schemes. In: Juels et al. [15], pp. 288–297
4. Bang-Jensen, J., Gutin, G.: Digraphs: Theory, Algorithms and Applications, 2nd edn. Springer, London (2009)
5. Bell, D., LaPadula, L.: Secure computer systems: Unified exposition and Multicsinterpretation. Technical report MTR-2997, Mitre Corporation, Bedford, Massachusetts (1976)
6. Bethencourt, J., Sahai, A., Waters, B.: Ciphertext-policy attribute-based encryption. In: IEEE Symposium on Security and Privacy, pp. 321–334. IEEE Computer Society (2007)
7. Cormen, T.H., Leiserson, C.E., Rivest, R.L., Stein, C.: Introduction to Algorithms, 3rd edn. MIT Press (2009)
8. Crampton, J.: Practical and efficient cryptographic enforcement of interval-based access control policies. ACM Trans. Inf. Syst. Secur. **14**(1), 14 (2011)
9. Martin, K.M., Crampton, J., Daud, R.: Constructing key assignment schemes from chain partitions. In: Foresti, S., Jajodia, S. (eds.) Data and Applications Security and Privacy XXIV. LNCS, vol. 6166, pp. 130–145. Springer, Heidelberg (2010)
10. Crampton, J., Martin, K.M., Wild, P.R.: On key assignment for hierarchical access control. In: CSFW, pp. 98–111. IEEE Computer Society (2006)
11. De Santis, A., Ferrara, A.L., Masucci, B.: New constructions for provably-secure time-bound hierarchical key assignment schemes. Theor. Comput. Sci. **407**(1–3), 213–230 (2008)
12. Freire, E.S.V., Poettering, B., Paterson, K.G.: Simple, efficient and strongly ki-secure hierarchical key assignment schemes. In: Dawson, E. (ed.) CT-RSA 2013. LNCS, vol. 7779, pp. 101–114. Springer, Heidelberg (2013)
13. Goyal, V., Pandey, O., Sahai, A., Waters, B.: Attribute-based encryption for fine-grained access control of encrypted data. In: Juels et al. [15], pp. 89–98
14. Gutin, G., Razgon, I., Kim, E.J.: Minimum leaf out-branching and related problems. Theor. Comput. Sci. **410**(45), 4571–4579 (2009)
15. Juels, A., Wright, R.N., di Vimercati, S.D.C., (eds.) Proceedings of the 13th ACM Conference on Computer and Communications Security, CCS 2006, Alexandria, VA, USA, October 30 - November 3, 2006. ACM (2006)
16. Sandhu, R.S.: Cryptographic implementation of a tree hierarchy for access control. Inf. Process. Lett. **27**(2), 95–98 (1988)

A Fully Decentralized Data Usage Control Enforcement Infrastructure

Florian Kelbert[✉] and Alexander Pretschner

Technische Universität München, Munich, Germany
{kelbert,pretschn}@cs.tum.edu

Abstract. Distributed data usage control enables data owners to constrain how their data is used by remote entities. However, many data usage policies refer to events happening within several distributed systems, e.g. "at each point in time at most two clerks might have a local copy of this contract", or "a contract must be approved by at least two clerks before it is sent to the customer". While such policies can intuitively be enforced using a centralized infrastructure, major drawbacks are that such solutions constitute a single point of failure and that they are expected to cause heavy communication and performance overhead. Hence, we present the first fully decentralized infrastructure for the preventive enforcement of data usage policies. We provide a thorough evaluation of our infrastructure and show in which scenarios it is superior to a centralized approach.

1 Introduction

Due to the ever increasing value of data, the continuous protection of sensitive data throughout its entire lifetime has drawn much attention in recent years. Corresponding solutions are applicable in many contexts: businesses, military and governments aim at protecting their internal procedures, research reports, financial reports, and the like; individuals want to constrain businesses from using or releasing their private data, e.g. for advertisement or market research; copyright owners want their licenses to be respected.

Usage control [1,2] tackles such challenges by proposing different models and enforcement infrastructures [3–6]. Generally, policies describe how data may or may not be used once initial access has been granted. Additionally, policies might specify obligations that must be fulfilled before, upon, or after usage. Corresponding solutions [7–10] inject reference monitors, or Policy Enforcement Points (PEP), into different layers of the computing system. These PEPs intercept events within the system and enforce the Policy Decision Point's (PDP) decision such as allowing, modifying, inhibiting or delaying the event. By tracking *data flows*, such as when copying files or loading content from a database into a process, aforementioned solutions allow to enforce data usage policies on all representations of some data rather than on particular files or database entries. Hence, data usage policies are enforced independently of the data's concrete *representations* at runtime. Enforcement may be *preventive* or *detective* [1,6],

© Springer International Publishing Switzerland 2015
T. Malkin et al. (Eds.): ACNS 2015, LNCS 9092, pp. 409–430, 2015.
DOI: 10.1007/978-3-319-28166-7_20

meaning that policy violations never occur, or that they can be detected in hindsight, respectively.

This work tackles the problem of enforcing data usage policies on data that has been disseminated to remote systems. In this respect, solutions that track data flows across systems and attach the corresponding policies have been proposed [11,12]. Further, these solutions enable the enforcement of policies that can be independently evaluated on every single system, such as "do not open this document with editor X", or "do not print this document after 5pm". However, the preventive enforcement of more sophisticated *global policies* pertaining to events and/or the states of multiple systems, such as "not more than five instances of this software might be executed simultaneously", or "all copies of this document must be deleted upon the owner's demand", still poses challenges [6,13,14]. We are not aware of solutions that achieve preventive policy enforcement (i) without the need for any central components, (ii) on all copies and derivations of the original data, and (iii) which are deployable on commodity networks.

While Digital Rights Management solutions handle such challenges by deploying central license servers [15], such a solution comes with the drawbacks of being a single point of failure, privacy concerns, and the necessity that the central component must be always reachable by all PEPs. Moreover, a centralized solution is expected to impose significant performance and communication overhead [13,16]. The main reason is that the PEP is stateless. Hence, whenever a potentially relevant system event is observed by the PEP, it is unknown whether it is of actual importance for evaluation by the PDP. Consequently, all observed events would need to be signaled to the central PDP. While recent works addressed this problem by decentralizing some aspects of policy evaluation, data flow tracking, and/or information retrieval [6,8,17,18], some of them do not allow for preventive policy enforcement [6,18], while others effectively make use of central components [8,17], or do not integrate data flow tracking [8,17,18].

Problem. We tackle the problem of *enforcing global data usage control policies* if (i) the data to be protected resides, (ii) the data usage events occur, and (iii) the data flow events occur within and across multiple distributed systems. While a solution could naively be implemented in a centralized fashion, such a solution imposes drawbacks such as being a single point of failure. Intuitively, a centralized solution is also expected to impose significant performance and network communication overhead [13,16].

Solution. We design and implement a fully decentralized enforcement infrastructure with the goal to minimize aforementioned drawbacks and overheads. This infrastructure deploys one PDP at each site which takes all decisions pertaining to all local PEPs. Global policies are enforced by synchronizing the PDPs using a distributed database. We optimize the information being exchanged according to theoretical results [13].

Contribution. To the best of our knowledge, our contributions are:

1. The first fully decentralized architecture and implementation for the preventive enforcement of global data usage control policies (Sect. 3).
2. A thorough evaluation of the proposed and implemented architecture, showing in which scenarios its adoption is beneficial (Sect. 4).

Further, we provide the source code of our implementation as open source[1].

Attacker Model and Assumptions. Our infrastructure prevents users from using data in a way that does not comply with the corresponding policy—be the attempt intentional or unintentional. Foremost, we consider users without administrative privileges. Such a scenario is pervasive in business environments, where employees are given ready-to-use computing systems. To defend against stronger attackers, the trust anchor must be embedded at a lower layer, e.g. by using TPMs or SmartCards. Since our infrastructure runs as a process within the operating system, we assume both to be free of vulnerabilities. Otherwise, an attacker might be able to gain administrative privileges and switch off our infrastructure and/or tamper with it. Moreover, we assume state-of-the-art access control mechanisms to be in place.

Running Example. We illustrate our work along a running example, in which an insurance company provides potential customers the ability to request contract offers via a web interface. After internal processing of the request, the customer retrieves a contract offer via email, which may be accepted or declined via a web link. The entire scenario, including the insurance provider's internal data processing, is depicted in Fig. 1.

First, the customer fills a web form on the insurance provider's website. By submitting the form (1), a new ContractRequest (CR) object is created (2) and the web server sends the CR to a set of clerks via the mail server (3,4). One of the clerks will then review the attached CR (5) and start an analysis job on the internal data analysis server (6), thereby creating a new AnalysisResult (AR) object (7). Once the analysis is performed, the clerk retrieves the AR (8) and performs a manual review on her workstation (9). The clerk then creates a Contract (C) object using a collaborative word processor (10,11). Once created, C might be retrieved (12), reviewed (13) and revised (14) by several clerks. After C has been approved by a predefined number of clerks (15), one of the clerks retrieves its final version (16) and sends it to the customer via the mail server (17,18). Once the customer receives the offer, he might decline (19a) or accept (19b) the Contract. Alternatively, he might delete his initial ContractRequest altogether (19c).

Besides the application-specific events mentioned above, we also consider events originating at the operating system layer, i.e. system calls [10]. Using such an approach, we are able to detect data flows that happen outside the

---

[1] https://github.com/fkelbert/uc/ and https://github.com/fkelbert/uc4linux/.

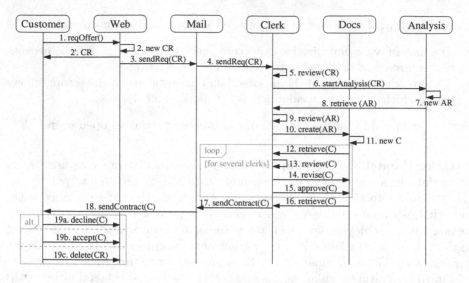

Fig. 1. Sequence of events in the running example.

application context or that have not been anticipated within the application context, e.g. if a clerk creates a copy of a Contract using a file manager or a shared file system.

Clearly, the customer's data flows through many different systems in many different formats. Further, the AnalysisResult and the Contract are data items that have been derived from the original ContractRequest and must as such be treated as containing the customer's personal data. All of these data items are stored and processed by many different systems and users, all of which must enforce data usage policies such as:

Policy 1: 'Exactly one contract offer must be sent to the customer not later than 30 days after a request has been received.'
Policy 2: 'If the customer declines an offer, all derived data items must not be used anymore.'
Policy 3: 'Each contract must be reviewed and approved by at least two clerks.'
Policy 4: 'At no point in time might two clerks have a copy of the same analysis result.'

Note, that all of those policies are *global policies*, meaning that they refer to data and events that are distributed across several systems.

2 Background

2.1 Existing Data Usage Control Infrastructures

Data usage control infrastructures have been built for various system layers and scenarios [4,6–10,12], and policy enforcement is usually performed using a PEP, a PDP, and a Policy Information Point (PIP). Once the PEP observes an attempt of using an object, this attempt is signaled to the PDP which is configured with the policies to be enforced. Depending on these policies, its internal state, and additional information from the PIP, the PDP decides whether to allow, inhibit, modify, or delay the usage attempt. The PEP is then in charge of enforcing the decision. The information provided by the PIP differs slightly in different models and includes subject and object attributes, environmental information, and details about which data takes which representations within the system, i.e. the system's *data flow state*.

The set of events intercepted by the PEP is categorized into two, possibly overlapping, subsets: *data usage events* and *data flow events*. Informally, data usage events are events whose occurrence is obliged or constrained by data usage policies. As such, all data usage events must be signaled to the PDP. Data flow events, in contrast, must be signaled to the PIP. According to an event's predefined semantics and its actual parameters, the PIP will update its data flow state. For example, if a ContractRequest data item is known to be stored as a database entry, then all result sets of database queries selecting this entry will also be associated with the same ContractRequest data item, and hence with the same data usage policies.

Using such a combination of policy enforcement and data flow tracking technology, data usage control infrastructures allow to not only protect one single data representation, such as a file or database entry, but rather all representations of the same data.

To differentiate between *detective* and *preventive* enforcement, the distinction between *desired events* and *actual events* is needed. Desired events are intercepted by PEPs *before* their execution and they may be inhibited or modified in correspondence with the PDP's decision. Actual events are intercepted by the PEP *after* their execution. They can not be inhibited or modified, but only be compensated for. Thus, desired events must be intercepted and evaluated for preventive enforcement, while actual events must be monitored because they cause state changes within the PDP and PIP.

2.2 Data Usage Control Policies: Syntax, Semantics, Evaluation

Building upon previous works [5,7,13,19], we assume policies to be specified as Event-Condition-Action (ECA) rules: once a triggering Event is observed and if the execution of this event would make the Condition true, then additional Actions might be performed. Notably, the triggering event might also be an artificial event, e.g. to indicate that a certain amount of time has passed. We will use the terms 'policy' and 'ECA rule' interchangeably. ECA conditions (Φ) are specified in terms of past linear temporal logics and their syntax is specified as:

$$\Psi = \underline{true} \mid \underline{false} \mid \mathcal{E}$$
$$\Sigma = \underline{isNotIn}(\mathcal{D}, \mathbb{P}(\mathcal{C})) \mid \underline{isCombined}(\mathcal{D}, \mathcal{D}, \mathbb{P}(\mathcal{C})) \mid \underline{isMaxIn}(\mathcal{D}, \mathbb{N}, \mathbb{P}(\mathcal{C}))$$
$$\Phi = (\Phi) \mid \Psi \mid \Sigma \mid \underline{not}(\Phi) \mid \Phi \underline{\ and\ } \Phi \mid \Phi \underline{\ or\ } \Phi \mid \Phi \underline{\ since\ } \Phi \mid \Phi \underline{\ before\ } \mathbb{N} \mid \underline{repmin}(\mathbb{N}, \mathbb{N}, \mathcal{E})$$

While the formal semantics of Φ are detailed in [13], we recap the intuitive semantics: $\mathcal{E}$ denotes the set of all data usage events (cf. Sect. 2.1); $\mathcal{D}$ denotes the set of data items to be protected; $\mathcal{C}$ denotes the set of all possible representations, or *containers*, for data, such as files and database entries. Ψ refers to boolean constants (*true*, *false*) and data usage events $\mathcal{E}$. Σ refers to so-called state-based operators, allowing to express constraints over the system's data flow state as computed and maintained by the PIP: *isNotIn*(d, C) is true iff data d is not in any of the containers C; *isCombined*(d_1, d_2, C) is true iff there is at least one container in C that contains both data d_1 and d_2; *isMaxIn*(d, m, C) is true iff data d is contained in at most m containers in C. For Φ, the semantics of *not*, *and* and *or* are intuitive; α *since* β is true iff β was true some time earlier and α was true ever since, or if α was always true; α *before* j is true iff α was true exactly j timesteps ago; *repmin*(j, m, e) is true iff event e happened at least m times in the last j timesteps. Further, we define *repmax*$(j, m, e) \equiv$ *not*(*repmin*$(j, m+1, e)$) and *always*$(\alpha) \equiv \alpha$ *since* *false*.

Fixing one data item d, Table 1 shows the example policies from Sect. 1 as ECA rules. Rule 1a expresses that the CEO must be notified via mail if no contract offer has been sent to the customer 30 days after a corresponding request. Note that this rule does have a wildcard trigger event, implying that the rule is evaluated upon every event. Further, this rule is detective only: satisfaction of the condition results in a compensating action; actual violation of the policy is not prevented. Rule 1b expresses that a contract offer must not be sent if there was no corresponding contract request, or if a contract offer was already sent. Rule 2 expresses that any attempt to use data item d is inhibited if the corresponding contract offer was declined in the past. Note, that we have used event *use* to refer to a set of events. This set might include events such as Analysis-Server.start, Docs.create and Mail.sendContract. Rule 3 expresses that sending of a contract is inhibited if this contract was not reviewed or approved by at least two clerks in the last 30 days. Rule 4 expresses that any event must be

Table 1. Example policies as ECA rules.

Policy 1	Event: *\<any\>*
(a)	Condition: (*Web.reqOffer(d)* *before* *30*) *and* *repmax(30, 0, Mail.sendContract(d))*
	Action: *Mail.notifyCEO(d)*
	Event: *Mail.sendContract(d)*
(b)	Condition: *repmax(30, 0, Web.reqOffer(d))* *or* *repmin(30, 1, Mail.sendContract(d))*
	Action: *inhibit*

Policy 2	Event: *use(d)*
	Condition: *not(always(not(Web.decline(d))))*
	Action: *inhibit*

Policy 3	Event: *Mail.sendContract(d)*
	Condition: *repmax(30, 1, Workstation.review(d))* *or* *repmax(30, 1, Docs.approve(d))*
	Action: *inhibit*

Policy 4	Event: *\<any\>(d)*
	Condition: *not(isMaxIn(d, 1, C_{\text{Workstation}}))*
	Action: *inhibit*

inhibited if its execution would lead to a state in which data d is in more than one of the clerk's workstations.

Policy Evaluation. A policy is evaluated whenever a trigger event occurs or if a predefined amount of time has passed. The amount of time is configurable per policy and the interval between two subsequent time-based policy evaluations is called a *timestep*. The introduction of timesteps is necessary for practical reasons: If an ECA condition such as $\varphi = (Web.reqOffer(d)\ \underline{before}\ 30[days])$ is to be evaluated, then it is unlikely that event $Web.reqOffer(d)$ has happened *exactly* 30 days (i.e. 2592000 s) ago. What is more likely and practical, however, is that $Web.reqOffer(d)$ has happened 'approximately' 30 days ago, e.g. 30 days ± 12 h. Similarly, consider the conjunction and disjunction of operators, *and* and *or*. While it is unlikely that two events happen at *exactly* the same point in time, what is more likely and practical is that two events happen within a specified time interval, i.e. within the same timestep.

For policy evaluation purposes, we consider conditions $\varphi \in \Phi$ as expression trees. Leaves represent the constants *true* and *false*, events $\mathcal{E}$, and state-based operators Σ; internal nodes are operators such as *before*, *since*, *and*, etc. Figure 2 depicts ECA rule 1a as expression tree. Leaves are stateful by storing whether the represented operand has become *true* or *false*, depending on the actual operand, during the current timestep. Whenever a PEP signals an event to the PDP, it is evaluated against all of φ's leaves, potentially changing their states. E.g., if a leaf represents the event Mail.sendContract, then this leaf's state changes to *true* once the PEP signals event Mail.sendContract. If a leaf corresponds to a state-based operator Σ, then its state is examined with the help of the PIP under consideration of the signaled event's data flow semantics. In a nutshell, the expression trees' leaves track which events have happened and which state-based operators have changed their state during the ongoing timestep.

Only if the event signaled by the PEP matches the ECA rule's trigger event, then the entire condition φ is evaluated, denoted $eval(\varphi)$. For this, the expression tree's internal nodes recursively query their child nodes for their current state. Subsequently, the internal nodes are evaluated using this information. Internal nodes also maintain a state, capturing historical values of child nodes. E.g. if $\varphi = (Web.reqOffer(d)\ \underline{before}\ 30[days])$, then *before* will keep a history of occurrences of $Web.reqOffer(d)$ for 30 days.

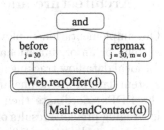

Fig. 2. Expression tree of ECA rule 1a.

If $eval(\varphi) = true$, then the ECA's actions will be triggered. Notably, evaluation of a condition $\varphi \in \Phi$ at the end of a timestep is different in that the leaves' evaluation results correspond to the truth values that have been 'accumulated' during the elapsed timestep: an event's truth value is *true* iff the event happened at least once during the elapsed timestep, while a state-based operator's truth value is *true* iff the operator was *true* at least once during the elapsed timestep. Note that cardinality operators such as _repmin_ count _all_ occurrences of an event during a timestep. Once $eval(\varphi)$ has been computed, the leaves' truth values are reset for the next timestep.

2.3   Distributed Policy Decisions

As motivated in Sect. 2.1, all data usage events and data flow events must be signaled to the PDP and PIP for decision making and data flow tracking purposes. Moreover, both the PDP and the PIP maintain an internal state necessary to perform those tasks. As discussed in [13], this leads to new challenges if the data to be protected, as well as the data usage and data flow events are distributed. One naive solution to enforce global policies is to deploy one central PDP/PIP. However, such an approach is expected to be poorly performing in terms of runtime and communication overhead [13,16].

The remaining challenge is to build an enforcement infrastructure that enforces global policies without the need for central components [14]. As such, it has been proposed to deploy PDPs and PIPs locally and consequently to keep all communication between PEP and PDP/PIP local [13]. However, consistent enforcement of global policies across all PDPs then necessitates their coordination. While naively each PDP/PIP could notify all internal state changes to all other PDPs/PIPs, we optimize our implementation according to formal results presented in [13]. In a nutshell, the paper analyzes for which policies and event traces coordination between PDPs may or may not be omitted. E.g., if $\varphi = e_1$ _or_ e_2 with $e_1, e_2 \in \mathcal{E}$, then if e_1 happens within system A while e_2 happens within system B, then two decentrally deployed PDPs on systems A and B can both _locally_ conclude $eval_A(\varphi) = eval_B(\varphi) = true$ without contacting the other PDP.

3   Architecture and Implementation

Our implementation deploys a PDP and a PIP at each site, such as a single system, or an organizational unit, cf. Fig. 3. Those components are responsible for local data flow tracking and policy evaluation (Sects. 2.1–2.2), as well as cross-system data flow tracking and policy shipment [12]. For deciding global policies, the PDPs coordinate their decisions using a distributed database (Sect. 3.2), leveraging previous results on how to efficiently enforce global data usage policies in distributed systems [13].

3.1   Distributed Policy Evaluation

Once a policy has been deployed at multiple PDPs, their decisions are expected to be consistent at all times. To explain how we achieve such consistency, we take the view of the PDP within system A, PDP_A, enforcing policy p_1 with trigger event $e_{p_1} \in \mathcal{E}$, condition $\varphi_{p_1} \in \Phi$, and action a_{p_1}. As described in Sect. 2.2, any event signaled to PDP_A potentially changes the state of leaves within φ_{p_1}.

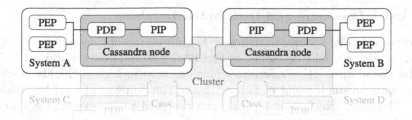

Fig. 3. High-level architecture view.

Since such state changes are of importance for other PDPs enforcing p_1, PDP_A publishes any such state changes via the distributed database. We assume this database to be always available and strongly consistent; Sect. 3.4 explains how this is achieved in practice.

As described in Sect. 2.2, φ_{p_1} must be evaluated whenever a timestep has passed or whenever a signaled event matches p_1's trigger event e_{p_1}. In any of those cases, PDP_A first evaluates φ_{p_1} locally. If this local evaluation yields $eval(\varphi_{p_1}) = true$, no further coordination with other PDPs is necessary: action a_{p_1} will be executed. However, if $eval(\varphi_{p_1}) = false$, then it might still be the case that φ_{p_1} is true globally, $eval^g(\varphi_{p_1}) = true$, i.e. when considering other PDPs' state changes. Hence, φ_{p_1} is re-evaluated: For each leaf of φ_{p_1} whose local state was $false$, a lookup within the distributed database is performed. If the lookup yields $true$, implying that the operator was satisfied at some other PDP, the parent nodes are recursively re-evaluated up to the root node.[2] For example, consider condition $\varphi_{p_1} = ev_1$ _and isCombined_(d_1, d_2, C), where at system A ev_1 is happening, while system B combines data items d_1 and d_2. Locally, both PDP_A and PDP_B evaluate φ_{p_1} to false, $eval_A(\varphi_{p_1}) = eval_B(\varphi_{p_1}) = false$. Subsequently, PDP_A looks up _isCombined_(d_1, d_2, C) in the distributed database, while PDP_B looks up whether ev_1 happened. Hence, distributed evaluation of φ_{p_1} results in $eval^g_A(\varphi_{p_1}) = eval^g_B(\varphi_{p_1}) = true$.

It is important to note that time-based policy evaluations must consistently happen at the same time across all PDPs. Otherwise, the PDPs might come to different conclusions when evaluating the same policy. Consider once again φ_{p_1}, a point in time t, a timestep interval of 10 min, and the fact that PDP_A evaluates at times $t, t + 10, t + 20, \ldots$, while PDP_B evaluates at times $t + 5, t + 15, \ldots$. Further, assume ev_1 happens at time $t + 2$, while _isCombined_(d_1, d_2, C) is only true at time $t + 7$. Then, PDP_A's evaluation at time $t + 10$ yields $true$, while PDP_B's evaluation yields $false$ at times $t + 5$ and $t + 15$. For this reason, our decentral PDPs always evaluate at the same time. While we are aware that such synchronization is subject to scheduling and clock synchronization issues, our experiments (cf. Sect. 4) did not reveal evaluation inconsistencies.

---

[2] In fact, for operators _isNotIn_ and _isMaxIn_ a lookup is performed if their local evaluation result is $true$ rather than $false$. This reflects that local satisfaction of those operators never implies their global satisfaction, while their local violation always implies their global violation [13].

3.2   Using Cassandra as a Distributed Database

As indicated in Fig. 3, our infrastructure is built on top of Cassandra—a distributed database originally developed at Facebook [20] and now maintained by The Apache Foundation [21]. Cassandra's purpose is to provide a "highly available service with no single point of failure" being run "on top of [...] hundreds of nodes" [20]. As such, Cassandra has been designed to achieve high scalability, availability, and performance.

Data Replication. In Cassandra, the entire set of nodes forming the distributed database is called a *cluster*. The cluster's data is organized via *keyspaces*, and each *table* is associated with exactly one keyspace. Keyspaces take a central role, since each keyspace's *replication strategy* defines among which nodes of the cluster its associated tables are replicated. Hence, data with the same replication requirements should be organized within the same keyspace. In our context, each PDP might need to enforce several policies at the same time and for each the set of remote PDPs with which coordination is required might differ. Hence, we represent each policy by exactly one keyspace. Consider policy p_1 constraining the usage of data d_1 which has representations in systems A and B. Then, in our implementation there exists keyspace k_{p_1} with replication strategy $k_{p_1}^{rep} = \{A, B\}$. Thus, if PDP_A shares a state change of φ_{p_1} within keyspace k_{p_1}, this information is replicated to exactly those PDPs for which it is of interest, i.e. PDP_B.

Data Consistency. With the CAP theorem [22] stating that consistency, availability, and partition-tolerance can not all be achieved at the same time, many eventually consistent databases have emerged. In this respect, Cassandra is flexible by allowing to trade consistency with performance. For the time being, we assume strong data consistency; Sect. 3.4 shows how this is efficiently achieved in practice. In case strong consistency is not sufficient, Cassandra provides linearizable consistency (compare-and-set transactions) on the basis of the Paxos consensus protocol [23].

As described in Sect. 4, our architecture can be flexibly deployed: While in Fig. 3 PDP, PIP, and Cassandra are local to the PEPs, it is possible to deploy those components remotely, allowing to set up a centralized infrastructure. We also assume all Cassandra nodes to know at least one seed node that is already part of the cluster; this is discussed in Sect. 3.5.

3.3   Bootstrapping and Cross-System Data Flows

Consider a set of PDPs/PIPs with their corresponding Cassandra nodes and assume that no data usage policy has yet been deployed. Then, at some point in time the first policy p_1 is deployed at PDP_A. While deploying, one or more containers are marked to contain data d_1 whose usage is constrained by p_1. This initial classification is performed by PIP_A. Since p_1 and d_1 are only known to PDP_A, PDP_A can independently take all decisions about p_1 as described in Sect. 2.2.

Now, consider that system A shares data d_1 with system B, e.g. via network transfer. From then on, also system B might influence the evaluation of p_1. Our implementation reflects this first cross-system data transfer of d_1 by creating keyspace k_{p_1} with $k_{p_1}^{rep} = \{A, B\}$. Consequently, all data written to k_{p_1} is immediately replicated to nodes A and B. As Cassandra's database triggers are experimental, actual data flow tracking and policy transfer to system B is performed via remote procedure calls using Apache Thrift [24].

Now, system B might further share data d_1 with system C. Since keyspace k_{p_1} exists already, our implementation adapts the existing keyspace to incorporate node C, $k_{p_1}^{rep} \leftarrow k_{p_1}^{rep} \cup \{C\} = \{A, B, C\}$. Notably, the keyspace's adaption is immediately perceived by node A, such that from now on all data written to k_{p_1} will be replicated to nodes A, B and C. In order to prevent conflicts and lost updates, this adaption of a keyspace's replication strategy must be atomic; we implemented corresponding locking mechanisms on top of the keyspace being updated. For atomic acquiring of the lock, we use Cassandra's *lightweight transactions*, which provide linearizable consistency.

3.4 Cassandra Consistency

In Cassandra, each single read and write operation can be configured with a *consistency level* (CL), which defines how many nodes of the corresponding keyspace must acknowledge the operation. Among others, Cassandra provides the self-explanatory consistency levels *One*, *Two*, *Three* and *All*. While using CL=*All* guarantees strong data consistency, as assumed in this paper up to now, it comes at the cost of performance and the requirement that all of the keyspace's nodes must be always online and reachable by all other nodes. By providing consistency level *Quorum*, Cassandra allows to achieve strong consistency without such drawbacks: If CL=*Quorum*, then operations must be acknowledged by at least half of the nodes. Consequently, strong consistency can be achieved by using CL=*Quorum* for all reads and writes. Note that strong consistency can also be achieved by using CL=*All* for all writes and CL=*One* for all reads.

Whenever a consistency level different from *One* is used, reads and writes to a keyspace might fail. If CL=*All*, then it is sufficient that only one of the keyspace's nodes is not available in order to make queries to the keyspace fail. Since failing of a node or some network link is not unlikely in practice, a consistency level of *All* can be considered impractical. If CL=*Quorum*, read and write operations might fail if half of the nodes of a keyspace are not available. While such situations are not impossible, e.g. if network partitions occur, they are much more unlikely in practice. Considering the Cassandra cluster from the point of view of a single node, any query to a keyspace with CL≠*One* fails in case the considered node is offline. While configurable, by default our implementation uses CL=*Quorum* for all reads and writes.

Our implementation tackles the aforementioned problems by two means: First, it is configurable how often and in which intervals failed queries are retried.

Second, if queries still fail after the predefined amount of tries, the PDP takes a fallback decision. Clearly, such a fallback decision depends on the policy being enforced, the scenario, and the attacker model. Hence, our policies can be configured accordingly.

3.5   Connecting Cassandra Nodes

When starting up, new Cassandra nodes need some way to discover the cluster they ought to participate in. Cassandra achieves this by defining a fixed set of seed nodes, through which new nodes can learn about the cluster. Since our original goal was to develop a fully decentral infrastructure, we provide solutions to the problem of integrating new nodes into an existing cluster without any well-known seed nodes. Unfortunately, Cassandra does not provide an API to explicitly command a running Cassandra node to further explore the cluster via some specific node. Having in mind that such a functionality would simplify the following solutions, we provide the following workarounds.

Recap the scenario described in Sect. 3.3, in which the very first policy p_1, protecting data d_1, is deployed at PDP_A, while PDP_B is not yet enforcing any policies. At some point in time, d_1, and subsequently policy p_1, is transferred to system B. In Sect. 3.3 we assumed system B's Cassandra node to participate in the cluster. Our solution is to not start the Cassandra node together with the PDP/PIP, but only once the first global policy ought to be enforced: Once PDP_B receives policy p_1 via remote procedure call from PDP_A, this call includes the address of system A's Cassandra node. Knowing this address, system B will start its Cassandra node, using the given address as a seed node.

Now, consider an extended scenario in which systems PDP_A and PDP_B enforce policy p_1, while PDP_C enforces policy p_2 which protects data d_2. Since the sets of systems enforcing p_1 and p_2 are disjoint, the overall cluster can be considered to be partitioned, while the single partitions are not aware of any other partitions. Once d_1 is transferred to system C, these two partitions must be merged. Since an explicit 'explore'-command as described above is missing, we solve this problem as follows: Once d_1 is transferred, we start a temporary Cassandra node which uses both A's Cassandra node as well as C's Cassandra node as seed nodes. Exploring the cluster through this temporary node, the previously autonomous parts of the cluster will get to know about each other. Once this has happened, the temporary node can be taken down again.

4   Evaluation

Since our goal was to improve over the communication and performance overhead imposed by a centralized approach, we conducted case studies to understand which approach causes which overheads in which situations. After detailing our experiment setup, we elaborate on the results obtained by enforcing ECA rules 1a, 1b and 2.

System Setup. Our virtual environment was based on VMware ESXi 5.1.0 with a host capacity of a $8 \times 2.6\,\text{GHz}$ CPU and $128\,\text{GB}$ RAM. All machines, s0..s7, were configured with a $4 \times 2.6\,\text{GHz}$ CPU. Further, s0 was configured with $16\,\text{GB}$ RAM, s1..s7 with $4\,\text{GB}$ RAM each. All machines run Linux Mint 17.1 64 bit, kernel 3.13.0; Cassandra was used in version 2.1.2; the infrastructure of PDP/PIP and its connection to Cassandra was written in Java 8; PEP and PDP communicated via Thrift 0.9.2. For the central system setup, s0 was hosting the central PDP/PIP instance, which was responsible for policy evaluation and data flow tracking for several PEPs being run on systems s1..s7. In this case, no Cassandra instance was run. For the decentral setup, systems s1..s7 all run exactly one instance of PEP, PDP, PIP, and Cassandra; s0 was not used. All cross-system communication was encrypted using SSL; Cassandra used CL=*Quorum*.

Parameters. We identified and experimented with the following parameters: (i) the policy being enforced, (ii) the total number of systems being usage controlled, (iii) the number of systems actually enforcing the policy, (iv) the event frequency, (v) the percentage of events relevant for data flow tracking and/or policy evaluation. Although those parameters impose a huge complexity on the performed experiments, we are confident that our results provide a good understanding of their influence on any overheads.

Experiment Execution. For each measurement we fixed all of the above parameters and randomly generated an event trace that matched the given (global) event frequency; each event was randomly assigned to one of the participating usage controlled systems. We then let the experiment run for 30 s, whereby the policy was evaluated upon every trigger event as well as for a timestep interval of one second. After each run, we reset the entire infrastructure. Note, that our PEPs intercepted the system events both before and after their execution, resulting in a *desired event* and an *actual event* being sent to the PDP. The data was gathered using `tcpdump` and standard datetime utilities.

We present the results that we obtained by enforcing ECA rules 1a, 1b and 2. For ECA rules 1a and 1b we fixed the total number of systems being usage controlled to three, and all of those systems where actually enforcing the policy. For ECA rule 2, a total number of seven usage controlled systems were monitored and enforcing the policy.

Communication Overhead. Figures 4 and 5 show the global communication overhead when enforcing ECA rules 1a and 1b, respectively. We experimented with the event frequency and the percentage of events relevant for data flow tracking and policy evaluation. Trends are visualized using linear regression.

The results produced by the central system setup (Figs. 4 and 5, ▲) where of little surprise: For each event being observed by a PEP, around 1070 Bytes were exchanged between the PEP and the PDP. The percentage of relevant events did not have any influence on the communication overhead. This is of no surprise when recapping that the PEP is stateless and that *every* event must be signaled to the PDP.

Running our decentralized infrastructure, our first observation is that Cassandra causes some base 'noise' of around 1050 Bytes/sec/node—independent of any operations being performed. This implies that the centralized approach will inexorably perform better in case of very low event frequencies as can be seen in Figs. 4 and 5. However, depending on the event frequency as well as the percent-

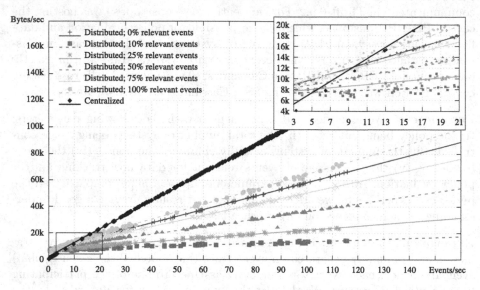

Fig. 4. Communication overhead when enforcing Policy 1a on three systems.

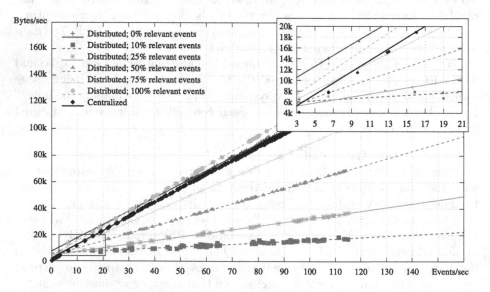

Fig. 5. Communication overhead when enforcing Policy 1b on three systems.

age of relevant events, our decentralized approach is capable of outperforming the centralized approach.

While in general event traces with a low percentage of relevant events perform particularly well (Figs. 4 and 5, _■_ (10 % relevant events), _＊_ (25 %)), we also observe some remarkable exceptions. First of all, aforementioned traces perform good for two reasons: (i) policies can in many cases be conclusively evaluated locally, avoiding costly lookups within the distributed database; (ii) a low percentage of relevant events implies a small amount of state changes that must be notified to other PDPs and thus written to the database. Secondly, traces with 0 % of relevant events perform badly (_＋_), since our infrastructure must perform database lookups for each event and timestep. Thirdly, traces with a high percentage of relevant events also perform badly (_＊_ (75 %), _●_ (100 %)). While in the latter case the PDPs can almost always decide locally, a high amount of state changes must be notified to other PDPs. Thus, the lion's share of the communication overhead is due to state changes being written to the database.

As depicted in Figs. 4 and 5, ECA rule 1a can be evaluated more efficiently than ECA rule 1b. The main reason is that evaluation of operator *before* in ECA rule 1a necessitates at most one database lookup per PDP per timestep, while in the worst case each *repmin* operator, which occurs twice in ECA rule 1b, necessitates one lookup upon every event.

Fixing several event frequencies, Figs. 6 and 7 show how the percentage of relevant events influences the total amount of Bytes being exchanged between all involved systems. To compare those numbers, we normalize the measurements by dividing the total amount of Bytes by the number of observed events. Again, for the centralized approach (_---_) the communication overhead is constant (1070 Bytes per event) and percentage of relevant events does not influence the amount of Bytes being exchanged.

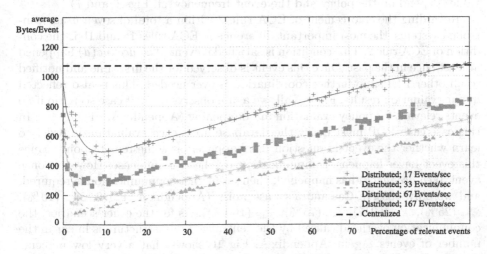

Fig. 6. Communication overhead when enforcing Policy 1a on three systems.

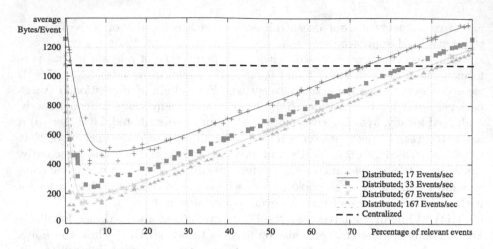

Fig. 7. Communication overhead when enforcing Policy 1b on three systems.

We observe that the decentralized approach performs best for high event frequencies (Figs. 6 and 7, $\_\ast\_$ (67 Events/sec), $\_\triangle\_$ (167 Events/sec)) and if the percentage of relevant events is around 3 % to 60 %. Firstly, this is because higher event frequencies exploit better Cassandra's base noise, which keeps the database consistent. Secondly, a low percentage of relevant events results in many situations in which the local PDPs can decide conclusively, while a low amount of state changes must be signaled to other PDPs. However, if the amount of relevant events is too low, then many lookups within the database are required, while the presence of many relevant events results in many writes to the database. Hence, the centralized approach outperforms the decentralized approach if the percentage of relevant events is very low or very high ($\lesssim 2$ %, $\gtrsim 85$ %; concrete values depend on the policy and the event frequency, cf. Figs. 6 and 7).

Regarding the enforcement of ECA rule 2 within a total of seven usage controlled systems, the most important difference to ECA rules 1a and 1b is the condition of ECA rule 2. This condition is satisfied if event $Web.decline(d)$ happened at least once in the past. Once this event is observed for the first time and notified to all other PDPs, no further coordination is ever needed. This is also reflected in our evaluation results. First of all, we again observe a worst case scenario if no events relevant for policy evaluation are happening (Appendix A, Fig. 9, $\_+\_$). In this case each PDP must query the database upon each evaluation in order to learn whether the event in question has happened at some remote point. Since this event never happens, communication overhead is immense. However, once event $Web.decline(d)$ has happened, then no further communication is required, and we only observe Cassandra's base noise (Appendix A, Fig. 9, $\_\blacksquare\_$ (10 %), $\_\ast\_$ (25 %), $\_\triangle\_$ (50 %), $\_\times\_$ (75 %), $\_\bullet\_$ (100 %)). As for the other scenarios, the communication overhead caused by the centralized infrastructure is linear in the number of events. Again, Appendix A, Fig. 10 shows that a very low percentage of relevant events (i.e. $\lesssim 2$ %) causes very high communication overheads.

However, different to the previous policies, Appendix A, Fig. 10 reveals that for ECA rule 2 the communication overhead for higher percentages of relevant events is constant; the decentralized approach outperforms the centralized approach if the global event frequency is higher than approximately 20 Events/sec.

In addition, we enforced ECA rule 1a within a total of seven usage controlled systems, only three of them being 'aware' of the protected data and thus enforcing the policy. While the communication overhead in the centralized approach was the same as in the scenarios described above, in the decentral approach it dropped to approximately 60 % of the above values for ECA rule 1a: While in the central approach still *every* event must be signaled to the central PDP, in our decentralized approach four out of three PDPs are not aware of any copy of the protected data and thus they neither enforce the policy nor participate in the corresponding Cassandra keyspace.

PDP Evaluation Times. Figure 8 shows how many milliseconds it takes for an event to be decided upon by the PDP for different event frequencies and percentages of relevant events. For each event, this includes (i) the time to send the event from the PEP to the PDP, (ii) the PDP's evaluation process, and (iii) the time to send the decision to the PEP.

For the *centralized infrastructure*, we observe that the evaluation times increase as the event frequency increases. Clearly, higher event frequencies push the central PDP towards its limits, since more events must be processed by the single component. Also, more events cause more load on the network an thus slightly higher network latency. For the same reasons as discussed above, the percentage of relevant events is irrelevant. Overall, the PEP usually gets responses from the PDP after 3 to 10 ms.

For the *distributed infrastructure*, we observed that the event frequency does *not* influence the PDP's evaluation times. However, we observe an anomaly when enforcing traces with 0 % relevant events. This is in correspondence with the communication overhead and can be explained by the fact that in this case the PDPs can never conclusively evaluate locally. Hence, for each event lookups within the database are required. By using the *Quorum* consistency level, this results in remote requests to other nodes of the cluster, decreasing performance of the evaluation process. In these cases, the PEP may need to wait up to 16 ms for the PDP's response. In contrast, if an event trace contains at least some relevant events, then the distributed decision process is capable of outperforming the centralized approach by providing responses between 2 to 9 ms.

Wrap-Up. Considering the bare numbers, we realize that a fully enforcement infrastructure is not unconditionally superior to a centralized one. According to our case studies, the adoption of a decentralized approach is particularly beneficial if (i) event frequencies are high, (ii) the percentage of events relevant for policy evaluation and/or data flow tracking is within a range of approximately 3 % to 60 %, and/or if (iii) the policy being enforced allows for many locally conclusive evaluations.

Instead of bluntly deploying either of those infrastructures, experiments as the ones above should be performed, considering the concrete parameters, i.e. the policies, the amount of systems, and the expected event traces, of a given application scenario. We also envision that such experiments can be performed at runtime, and that the technology in use (i.e. central or decentral) may be switched dynamically in correspondence with those live observations. While Cassandra simplified the implementation of our infrastructure, it comes at the cost of performance and communication overhead. It stands to reason that a tailored solution would improve upon those overheads.

5   Related Work

Service Automata [17] address the problem of enforcing policies that cannot be decided locally. For this, local "service automatons", roughly equivalent to PEP, PDP and PIP, monitor the execution of programs within a distributed system. If an automaton's knowledge is insufficient to take a policy decision, it delegates the decision to some other automaton. For this, each security-relevant event is statically mapped to one single responsible automaton; possibly conflicting events must be mapped to the same automaton. In contrast, our approach does not rely on such a static mapping, but allows each PDP to take the corresponding decisions. Further, Service Automata do not cater to the fact that the data to be protected might be copied both within and across systems.

Lazouski et al. [8] provide a framework that enforces usage control policies if data copies are distributed. Besides access and usage control rules, so-called PDP/PIP allocation policies are embedded into the protected data, specifying

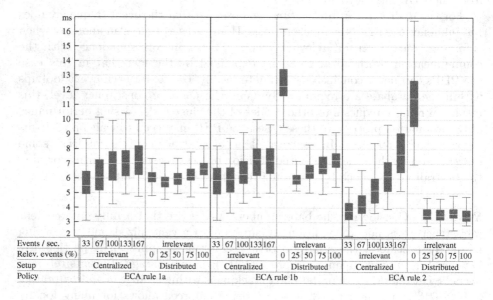

Fig. 8. PDP evaluation times when enforcing ECA rules 1a, 1b, and 2.

which PDPs and PIPs are involved in the decision process. Subject and object attributes required by the PDP are stored at different PIP locations. Different to our approach, the proposed allocation policies effectively introduce central components: for each protected data, the responsible PDP is fixed. Also, each attribute is under the responsibility of one single PIP. Failure of any of those components will break policy enforcement.

Bauer et al. [18] monitor LTL formulas in distributed systems using rewriting techniques. Whenever a local monitor observes an event that influences policy evaluation, the policy is rewritten according to predefined rules and then exchanged with the other local monitors. Hence, the local monitors are capable of detecting violation or satisfaction of the formula. The approach is different from ours in that it requires a synchronous system bus. Further, our approach is more expressive by also considering state-based usage control policies and by integrating data flow tracking.

Basin et al. [6, 25] are capable of detectively enforcing data usage policies in distributed systems. For this, log files are decentrally collected and a-posteriori (i.e. offline) merged and evaluated against data usage policies. In contrast, our approach also allows for the preventive enforcement of data usage policies.

6   Conclusions

We presented the first fully decentralized infrastructure for the preventive enforcement of global data usage policies if the data to be protected, as well as the corresponding data usage events, happen within multiple distributed systems.

We based the implementation of our infrastructure onto the distributed database Cassandra. Local monitors, PEPs, observe data usage events within the distributed system, and signal those events to local decision points, PDPs, which decide whether the event complies with the data usage policies. Since remote PDPs might also observe events that influence the local PDP's decision, the PDPs exchange relevant information via Cassandra. This way, we achieve consistent policy enforcement across multiple PDPs without any central components. To minimize the amount of database queries, we optimized our implementation using formal results from the literature.

We evaluated our infrastructure by comparing it with a centralized approach, in which one single PDP is responsible for taking all policy decisions for all events being observed by all distributed PEPs. Our case studies revealed that the adoption of a decentralized infrastructure is particularly beneficial in case the frequency of the observed system events is high and if approximately 3 % to 60 % of all events are of relevance for policy evaluation and/or data flow tracking. In terms of PDP evaluation times, our results revealed that the centralized and the decentralized approach perform similarly. For our decentralized infrastructure, the PEP usually gets policy evaluation results from the PDP within 2 to 9 ms. While performing our experiments, we also realized that all of the above evaluation results highly dependent on the policy being enforced. Notably, there also exist policies (cf. ECA rule 2) for which the decentralized approach performs tremendously better than the centralized one for most situations.

In any case, a decentralized infrastructure overcomes many problems omnipresent in a centralized approach. By deploying all components locally and by replicating data to different locations, there is no single point of failure and no need for a central component to be always available for all clients.

In terms of future work, we plan to experiment with the different consistency levels provided by Cassandra, which allow to trade consistency with performance. While we will likely be able to improve performance and communication overhead, it would be interesting to understand to which extent a non-strongly consistent database influences the consistency of the distributed policy evaluations. Clearly, it would depend on the considered scenario whether any such inconsistencies are acceptable. Depending on those results, a further option is to abandon off-the-shelf databases and to implement mechanisms specifically tailored to usage control requirements.

Acknowledgements. This work was supported by the DFG Priority Programme 1496 "Reliably Secure Software Systems - RS3", grant PR-1266/3.

A   Further Evaluation Results

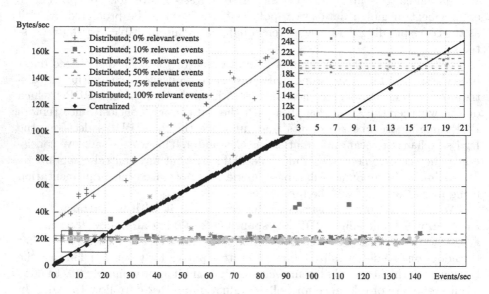

Fig. 9. Communication overhead when enforcing Policy 2 on seven systems.

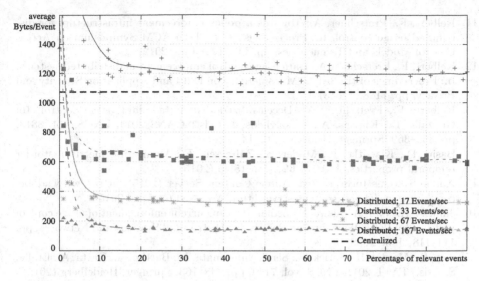

Fig. 10. Communication overhead when enforcing Policy 2 on seven systems.

References

1. Pretschner, P., Alexander, A., Hilty, H., Manuel, M., Basin, B., David, D.: Distributed usage control. Commun. ACM **49**(9), 39–44 (2006)
2. Park, J., Sandhu, R.: Towards usage control models: beyond traditional access control. In: Proceedings of the 7th ACM Symposium on Access Control Models and Technologies, pp. 57–64 (2002)
3. Park, J., Sandhu, R.: The UCONABC usage control model. ACM Trans. Inf. Syst. Secur. **7**(1), 128–174 (2004)
4. Zhang, X., Parisi-Presicce, F., Sandhu, R., Park, J.: Formal model and policy specification of usage control. ACM Trans. Inf. Syst. Secur. **8**(4), 351–387 (2005)
5. Hilty, M., Pretschner, A., Basin, D., Schaefer, C., Walter, T.: A policy language for distributed usage control. In: Biskup, J., López, J. (eds.) ESORICS 2007. LNCS, vol. 4734, pp. 531–546. Springer, Heidelberg (2007)
6. Basin, D., Harvan, M., Klaedtke, F., Zălinescu, E.: Monitoring data usage in distributed systems. IEEE Trans. Softw. Eng. **39**(10), 1403–1426 (2013)
7. Pretschner, A., Lovat, E., Büchler, M.: Representation-independent data usage control. In: Garcia-Alfaro, J., Navarro-Arribas, G., Cuppens-Boulahia, N., de Capitani di Vimercati, S. (eds.) DPM 2011 and SETOP 2011. LNCS, vol. 7122, pp. 122–140. Springer, Heidelberg (2012)
8. Lazouski, A., Mancini, G., Martinelli, F., Mori, P.: Architecture, workflows, and prototype for stateful data usage control in cloud. In: IEEE Security and Privacy Workshops, pp. 23–30, May 2014
9. Fromm, A., Kelbert, F., Pretschner, A.: Data protection in a cloud-enabled smart grid. In: Cuellar, J. (ed.) SmartGridSec 2012. LNCS, vol. 7823, pp. 96–107. Springer, Heidelberg (2013)
10. Harvan, M., Pretschner, A.: State-based usage control enforcement with data flow tracking using system call interposition. In: 3rd International Conference on Network and System Security, pp. 373–380, October 2009

11. Kelbert, F., Pretschner, A.: Towards a policy enforcement infrastructure for distributed usage control. In: Proceedings of the 17th ACM Symposium on Access Control Models and Technologies, pp. 119–122, June 2012

12. Kelbert, F., Pretschner, A.: Data usage control enforcement in distributed systems. In: Proceedings of the 3rd ACM Conference on Data and Application Security and Privacy, pp. 71–82 (2013)

13. Kelbert, F., Pretschner, A.: Decentralized distributed data usage control. In: Gritzalis, D., Kiayias, A., Askoxylakis, I. (eds.) CANS 2014. LNCS, vol. 8813, pp. 353–369. Springer, Heidelberg (2014)

14. Basin, D., Klaedtke, F., Müller, S., Zălinescu, E.: Monitoring metric firstorder temporal properties. J. ACM **62**, 15:1–15:45 (2015)

15. Adobe Systems Incorporated. Adobe Content Server (2015). http://www.adobe.com/solutions/ebook/content-server.html. Accessed 02 April 2015

16. Janicke, H., Cau, A., Siewe, F., Zedan, H.: Concurrent enforcement of usage control policies. In: IEEE Workshop on Policies for Distributed Systems and Networks, pp. 111–118, June 2008

17. Gay, R., Mantel, H., Sprick, B.: Service automata. In: Barthe, G., Datta, A., Etalle, S. (eds.) FAST 2011. LNCS, vol. 7140, pp. 148–163. Springer, Heidelberg (2012)

18. Bauer, A., Falcone, Y.: Decentralised LTL monitoring. In: Giannakopoulou, D., Méry, D. (eds.) FM 2012. LNCS, vol. 7436, pp. 85–100. Springer, Heidelberg (2012)

19. Kumari, P., Pretschner, A.: Deriving implementation-level policies for usage control enforcement. In: Proceedings of the 2nd ACM Conference on Data and Application Security and Privacy, pp. 83–94 (2012)

20. Lakshman, A., Malik, P.: Cassandra: a decentralized structured storage system. ACM SIGOPS Operating Syst. Rev. **44**(2), 35–40 (2010)

21. The Apache Software Foundation. The Apache Cassandra Project (2014). http://cassandra.apache.org/. Accessed 02 April 2015

22. Brewer, E.A.: Towards robust distributed systems. In: Proceedings of the 19th Annual ACM Symposium on Principles of Distributed Computing. Keynote (2000)

23. Lamport, L.: The part-time parliament. ACM Trans. Comput. Syst. **16**(2), 133–169 (1998)

24. The Apache Software Foundation. Apache Thrift (2014). https://thrift.apache.org/. Accessed 02 April 2015

25. Basin, D., Caronni, G., Ereth, S., Harvan, M., Klaedtke, F., Mantel, H.: Scalable offline monitoring. In: Bonakdarpour, B., Smolka, S.A. (eds.) RV 2014. LNCS, vol. 8734, pp. 31–47. Springer, Heidelberg (2014)

Oblivion: Mitigating Privacy Leaks by Controlling the Discoverability of Online Information

Milivoj Simeonovski[1]([✉]), Fabian Bendun[1], Muhammad Rizwan Asghar[2],
Michael Backes[1,3], Ninja Marnau[1], and Peter Druschel[3]

[1] CISPA, Saarland University, Saarbrucken, Germany
simeonovski@cs.uni-saarland.de
[2] The University of Auckland, Auckland, New Zealand
[3] Max Planck Institute for Software Systems (MPI-SWS), Saarbrucken, Germany

Abstract. Search engines are the prevalently used tools to collect information about individuals on the Internet. Search results typically comprise a variety of sources that contain personal information — either intentionally released by the person herself, or unintentionally leaked or published by third parties without being noticed, often with detrimental effects on the individual's privacy. To grant individuals the ability to regain control over their disseminated personal information, the European Court of Justice recently ruled that EU citizens have a *right to be forgotten* in the sense that indexing systems, such as Google, must offer them technical means to request removal of links from search results that point to sources violating their data protection rights. As of now, these technical means consist of a web form that requires a user to manually identify all relevant links herself upfront and to insert them into the web form, followed by a manual evaluation by employees of the indexing system to assess if the request to remove those links is eligible and lawful.

In this work, we propose a universal framework *Oblivion* to support the automation of the *right to be forgotten* in a scalable, provable and privacy-preserving manner. First, *Oblivion* enables a user to automatically find and tag her disseminated personal information using natural language processing (NLP) and image recognition techniques and file a request in a privacy-preserving manner. Second, *Oblivion* provides indexing systems with an automated and provable eligibility mechanism, asserting that the author of a request is indeed affected by an online resource. The automated eligibility proof ensures censorship-resistance so that only legitimately affected individuals can request the removal of corresponding links from search results. We have conducted comprehensive evaluations of *Oblivion*, showing that the framework is capable of handling 278 removal requests per second on a standard notebook (2.5 GHz dual core), and is hence suitable for large-scale deployment.

Keywords: Right to be forgotten · Privacy · EU legislation · Data protection · Information discoverability · Search engines

M.R. Asghar—This work was done when the author was at CISPA, Saarland University, Germany.

© Springer International Publishing Switzerland 2015
T. Malkin et al. (Eds.): ACNS 2015, LNCS 9092, pp. 431–453, 2015.
DOI: 10.1007/978-3-319-28166-7_21

1   Introduction

The Internet has undergone dramatic changes in the last two decades, evolving from a mere communication network to a global multimedia platform in which billions of users not only actively exchange information, but also increasingly carry out their daily personal activities. While this transformation has brought tremendous benefits to society, it has also created new threats to online privacy that existing technology is failing to keep pace with. In fact, protecting privacy on the Internet remains a widely unsolved challenge for users, providers, and legislators alike. Users tend to reveal personal information without considering the widespread, easy accessibility, potential linkage and permanent nature of online data. Many cases reported in the press indicate the resulting risks, which range from public embarrassment and loss of prospective opportunities (*e.g.,* when applying for jobs or insurance), to personal safety and property risks (*e.g.,* when stalkers, sexual offenders or burglars learn users' whereabouts).

Legislators have responded by tightening privacy regulations. The European Court of Justice recently ruled in Google Spain v. Mario Costeja González [9] that EU citizens have a fundamental *right to be forgotten* for digital content on the Internet, in the sense that indexing systems such as Google (or other search engines, as well as systems that make data easily discoverable, such as Facebook and Twitter) must offer users technical means to request removal of links in search results that point to sources containing their personal information and violating their data protection rights[1]. While a comprehensive expiration mechanism for digital data has often been postulated by privacy advocates in the past, this court decision, for the first time, imposes a legal constraint for indexing systems that operate in the EU to develop and deploy suitable enforcement techniques. As of now, the solution deployed by leading search engines, such as Google, Microsoft and Yahoo, consists of a simple web form that requires a user to manually identify all relevant links herself upfront and to insert them into the web form, followed by a manual evaluation by the search engine's employees to assess whether the author of the request is eligible and the request itself is lawful, *i.e.,* the data subject's right to privacy overrides the interests of the indexing operator and the freedom of speech and information.

According to the Google transparency report [16], the number of removal requests that have been submitted to Google since the court decision in May 2014 has already exceeded 1/5 of a million and the number of URLs that Google has evaluated for removal are approximately 3/4 of a million. Clearly, in order to enable efficient enforcement, it is essential to develop techniques that at least partly automate this process and are scalable to Internet size, while being

---

[1] In the court's case, the plaintiff requested the removal of the link to a 12-year old news article that listed his real-estate auction connected with social security debts from the Google search results about him. The court ruled that the indexing by a search engine of the plaintiff's personal data is "prejudicial to him and his fundamental rights to the protection of those data and to privacy — which encompass the *right to be forgotten* — [and overrides] the legitimate interests of the operator of the search engine and the general interest in freedom of information."

censorship-resistant by ensuring that malicious users cannot effectively blacklist links to Internet sources that do not affect them.

Our Contribution. We propose a universal framework, called *Oblivion*, providing the foundation to support the enforcement of the *right to be forgotten* in a scalable and automated manner. Technically, *Oblivion* provides means for a user to prove her eligibility[2] to request the removal of a link from search results based on trusted third party-issued digital credentials, such as her passport or electronic ID card.

Oblivion then leverages the trust imposed by these credentials to generate eligible removal requests. More specifically, the officially-generated signatures contained in such credentials comprise personally-identifiable information of the card owner, such as her signed passport picture, address, *etc*. These so-called signed *attributes* are subsequently automatically compared with publicly available data whose removal should be requested, in order to determine if a source indeed contains information about a given entity. In *Oblivion*, we use state-of-the-art natural language processing (NLP) and image recognition techniques, in order to cover textual and visually identifiable information about a user, respectively. Further modalities can be seamlessly integrated into *Oblivion*. These techniques in particular automate the task for a user to determine if she is actually affected by an online source in the first place. The outcome of these comparisons, based on the signed attributes, is then used to provide proof to the indexing system that a user is eligibly affected by a source. To avoid creating further privacy concerns, *Oblivion* lets the user prove her eligibility to request data removal without disclosing any further personal information beyond what is already available at the link. This approach applies to a variety of different indexing systems, and in particular goes beyond the concept of search engines that we refer to throughout the paper for reasons of concreteness. Moreover, *Oblivion* exploits the homomorphic properties of RSA [29] in order to verify the eligibility of an arbitrarily large set of user credentials using only a single exponentiation, and is thus capable of handling 278 requests per second on a standard notebook (2.5 GHz dual core and 8 GB RAM). We consider this suitable for large-scale deployment.

Outline. This paper is structured as follows. We review related work in Sect. 2. The conceptual overview of *Oblivion* and its detailed realization are presented in Sects. 3 and 4, respectively. Section 5 provides performance analysis of *Oblivion*. Section 6 discusses various aspects of *Oblivion*. Next, we conclude and outline

---

[2] With our framework we allow for the automation of the eligibility proof of the user. Eligibility in our framework describes the user being personally affected by an online source, or in legal terms being the *data subject*. The *right to be forgotten* additionally requires that the user's data protection rights override the legitimate interests of the search engine operator and the freedom of information. This assessment of the *lawfulness* of the request is a purely legal task, which is in the domain of courts. Hence the technical assessment of lawfulness is out of scope for our framework. If courts and regulators agree on guidelines for this assessment, *Oblivion* could be extended to a partly automated assessment of these guidelines in future work.

future work in Sect. 7. Appendix A formally states and proves the security properties of *Oblivion*.

2   Related Work

The most common way to prevent *web robots* (or *web crawlers*) [24] from indexing web content is *the Robots Exclusion Protocol* (*a.k.a.* robots.txt protocol) [2], a standard for controlling how web pages are indexed. Basically, robots.txt is a simple text file that allows site owners to specify and define whether and how indexing services access their web sites. The use of this protocol for privacy enforcement is limited, since the file that defines the protocol can only be placed and modified by the administrator of the web site. The individual whose personal data is being published is hardly capable of contacting and persuading all administrators of these sources to remove the data or modify the robots.txt file. There are many attempts to approach this privacy enforcement problem in an orthogonal fashion, by adding an expiration date to information at the time of its first dissemination [5,7,15,22,27,28]. The basic idea is to encrypt images and make the corresponding decryption key unavailable after a certain period of time. This requires the decryption key to be stored on a trusted server, which takes care of deleting the key after the expiration date has been reached. Although some of the approaches utilize CAPTCHAs to prevent crawling the images easily, there is no fundamental protection against archiving images and corresponding keys while they are still openly available, even though first successes using trusted hardware to mitigate this data duplication problem have been achieved [5]. Another approach in this direction is the concept of sticky policies [6,8,21,26]. The concept was originally introduced by Mont *et al.* [21] and requires a machine-readable access policy to be bound to the data before it is disseminated. The policy then ensures that the recipient of the data acts in accordance with the policy definition. However, enforcement of such policies has to be backed by additional underlying hardware and software infrastructure. In addition to these shortcomings, a user needs to take care to augment data with expiration dates before the data is disseminated in all these approaches. Thus these approaches are inherently unsuited to cope with data that is already openly available on the Internet or gets published by third parties. Finally, to implement the European Court of Justice's decision, Google, Microsoft and Yahoo recently launched dedicated web forms [17,20,34] for submitting removal requests. Users have to manually identify all relevant links and insert them into this form. Subsequently, the request is evaluated manually by the employees of the indexing system to assess first, weather the author is eligible to file that request and second, whether the link to the source needs to be deleted for a specific search. To this end, users have to additionally hand over a legible copy of an ID document. The necessity of handing over a user's full identity to use the service comes with additional privacy implications that one would like to avoid. *Oblivion* constitutes a technical follow-up to this solution, with a dedicated focus on censorship-resistance, while additionally avoiding the detrimental effect of having to disseminate further personal information.

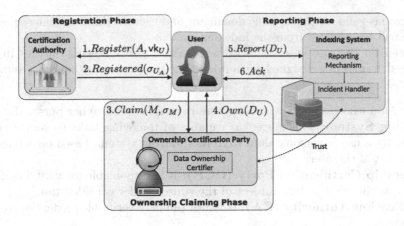

Fig. 1. Conceptual Overview of *Oblivion*.

3   Conceptual Overview of Oblivion

In this paper, we propose a framework laying the foundation for a privacy-preserving automation of the *right to be forgotten* in a scalable manner. The basic idea is that users automatically identify online sources that contain their personal data and can automatically request its removal from indexing systems, if it violates their data protection rights. Upon receiving the request, we enable the indexing service to automatically verify if the author of the request is provably affected by the source in question. Our framework is sufficiently generic to incorporate any type of data, such as text, pictures, voice and video. For brevity reasons, in this paper, we mainly focus on two data types: text and pictures.

3.1   Motivating Scenario and System Model

We start with a motivating scenario to explain the required functionality of the framework and the different parties involved. We assume that a user, Alice, discovers that an indexing service, say Google, returns certain query requests with links pointing to a document that contains her personal information and violates her privacy. In the next step, Alice contacts an Ownership Certification Party (OCP) in order to receive validation that this source indeed contains her personal information. Such an OCP could be a third party or the Google helpdesk. Along with the relevant links, she hands over publicly verifiable ID documents such as driver's license, passport or national ID card to the OCP. If the provided documents and the content of the article in question indeed match (which will be automatically checked by *Oblivion*), the OCP hands back a corresponding certificate. Alice then contacts Google to request removal of these links, providing an additional explanation, and proves her eligibility to do so based on the certificate of the OCP. Upon receiving this information, Google checks if the considered document is indeed indexed by Google, and if the OCP certificate is valid for this specific document and user. In this case, the requested article will be removed from the indexing system.

Based on this use case scenario, we consider the following entities in our proposed framework designed for automating the process of handling removal requests.

User: An authorized user who issues the request to remove her personal data.

Indexing System: This system is capable of removing links to sources containing a user's personal data from its indexing system, based on a removal request of the user.

Ownership Certification Party (OCP): It is responsible for verifying if the user is the eligible data subject of the source under consideration[3].

Certification Authority (CA): It issues publicly verifiable credentials to the users.

3.2 Threat Model and Security Objectives

We assume that all entities in the system fully trust the CA. However, a CA does not need to be online because the issuance of credentials to the users takes place out of band, typically for a longer period of time, say a couple of years.

Unlike the CA, the OCP is an entity that is not fully trusted from the user's perspective because it can try to learn the user's keying material and additional user credentials not required for the ownership verification; moreover, it might want to forge removal requests. The OCP is the only entity that is not part of the traditional system. The OCP can be run by the organization (*e.g.,* Google) that manages the indexing system, or it can be a third-party service. The OCP is assumed to be online during the execution of a request.

The indexing system is an entity inherently present in the traditional system. The indexing system and the OCP mutually trust each other; in practice, this is often trivially the case since the OCP and the indexing system are often managed by the same organization. If the OCP is an independent third party, this trust would typically be established via the CA using appropriate certificates.

We assume that users protect their private keys or at least, if their private keys are lost or stolen, a key revocation mechanism is installed and the user generates new keys. During the ownership verification, we do not assume any interaction between the users and the OCP. A user can present the OCP-signed proof to remove links to the data from multiple indexing systems, such as Google and Yahoo. We also consider an external adversary that could harm credibility of the user through replay attacks with the intention to make the service unavailable. For providing confidentiality over the communication network, we assume the presence of secure channels (such as SSL/TLS [11]) between a user, the OCP and the indexing system.

---

[3] Ownership in this context should not be confused with the legal term. Legally, the OCP can only assess and certify the individual's eligibility since, at least in EU context, legal ownership is not applicable to the right to be forgotten.

Based on these assumptions, we intend to achieve the following security objectives:

- *Minimal Disclosure:* An indexing system should not learn anything beyond what is required for eligibility checking and assessment of lawfulness. The court decision ruled that the right has to be judged on a case-by-case decision. Hereby, the right of the individual has to be balanced with the public right of information. Our system handles removal requests that prove eligibility but do not reveal any further information beyond what can be found in the online source in question[4].
- *Request Unforgeability:* The system should be designed such that an indexing system can only verify user requests without any possibility of forging existing or generating new requests on behalf of the user.
- *Censorship-Resistance:* The system should prevent censorship in the sense that only requests from provably affected users should be taken into account.

In addition to ensuring these security properties, the system should satisfy the following system properties in order to be suitable for large-scale deployment. It should be *scalable* in order to be able to process a large amount of queries simultaneously, while at the same time ensuring a thorough treatment of each individual query. It should *blend seamlessly into existing infrastructures*, to enable adoption by current indexing systems and certification authorities; moreover, the solution should be conceptually independent of the device and the operating system used. Finally, it should be *easy to understand and use* even for the general public.

3.3   Key Ideas of the Protocol

Oblivion is built on top of already available infrastructure (as explained in Sect. 3.1) that includes users, an indexing system and a CA. For the automatic verification of ownership, we introduce only a single new entity, the OCP, thus making our framework deployable in practice. In the framework, we distinguish three main phases: registration, ownership claim and reporting phases. Figure 1 presents the overall architecture for achieving the goals defined in Sect. 3.2.

Registration Phase. During the registration phase, each user registers with the CA as shown in Fig. 1. For the registration, a user presents (in Step 1) her attributes (along with evidence) and her verification key. The verification key should, for privacy reasons, be generated by the user herself before contacting the CA, but the generation of the key is orthogonal to our framework. The CA checks the validity of the attributes presented, certifies them and returns (in Step 2) a list of signed attributes, where each signed attribute is bound with

---

[4] Although *Oblivion* provides for minimal disclosure, the indexing system might request additional information, such as an author's name, for liability reasons in a real-world deployment of *Oblivion*. Moreover, the assessment of lawfulness could in some cases also require additional personal information.

the user's verification key. Typical examples of attributes are the date of birth, name or a user's profile picture.

Ownership Claim Phase. Once a registered user finds leakage of her personal data through the indexing system, she can contact the OCP claiming eligibility (in Step 3). This is the core phase in which the OCP expects justification of why the given piece of data affects the user. To make such a justification, the user can put tags on the given data that consist of her attributes which were signed by the CA. In order to improve usability, we automate the tagging and verification. One trivial automation method is to simply check if any user attribute appears anywhere in the article; if this happens, the matched item could be tagged with that attribute. The name attribute, say Alice, could be matched in this way.

The exact matching can semi-automate the tagging process but it cannot work in general because it may not return the correct results for all user attributes. Let us consider a user attribute in the form of a tuple: ⟨**Nationality, German**⟩ (as explained in Sect. 4.1). In order to match this attribute, the OCP has to check if the user attribute or its synonym has appeared in the article. This includes semantically linkable formulations, such as *being a citizen of Germany* and *having German nationality*.

Letting the user manually deploy this solution, *i.e.,* forcing the user to find synonyms of each possible word in the article, is an exhaustive task. Therefore, we employ an NLP-based technique — the named entity recognizer (NER) [14] in our case — for efficiently collecting all possible candidates in the article. The NER detects and classifies the data into various categories, such as person, organization, location, date and time, and it thus helps to identify if a user has attributes belonging to the category identified by the NER. If yes, we can perform exact matching or run a synonym checker [23] on identified categories. Articles containing a user's picture are tagged in a corresponding manner.

After the attributes are matched, the user has to generate a proof by preparing a message that contains a list of signed attributes that are required for the verification, the tagged article and her verification key. The user signs this message and sends it to the OCP (in Step 3) as an eligibility claim.

The OCP first verifies the message signature and the signed attributes used in the tagging. If the claim relates to text attributes, the OCP runs an entity disambiguator to identify whether the article is about the user. If the claim includes a picture, the OCP runs a corresponding face recognition algorithm. Upon successful evaluations of all steps, the OCP presents to the user an ownership token (in Step 4).

Reporting Phase. After receiving the ownership token from the OCP, the user sends a request for removal to the indexing system (in Step 5). The indexing system automatically validates the ownership token and then assesses whether to remove the links pointing to the user's personal information from its system. Finally, it sends (in Step 6) an acknowledgment to the user, which could be a *success* or *failure* message.

4   Realization Details of Oblivion

In this section, we provide details of each phase of our framework and explain the communication protocol to show interaction between different components. An indexing system and a user are denoted with IS and U, respectively. The communication protocol steps, described in this section, correspond to the flow illustrated in Fig. 1. After that, we provide details on how to securely and efficiently realize the proposed protocols using cryptographic primitives.

4.1   Registration Phase

As we can see in the communication protocol, a user sends (in Step 1) her attributes, $A = \{a_1, a_2, \ldots, a_n\}$, which characterize her, with supporting proofs and the verification key vk_U to the CA. Each user attribute $a_i \in A$ is a name and value key pair $\langle NAME, VALUE \rangle$, representing name of the attribute and value specific to each user, respectively. For instance, an attribute name could be *National*, and if say, a user is national of Germany, then the value will be *German*. Some general user attribute names include, but are not limited to, *Full Name*, *Date of Birth*, *Place of Birth*, *Current Residence* and *ID Picture*.

Upon a successful verification of the provided data, the CA issues a list of signed attributes $\sigma_{U_A} = \{\sigma_{U_{a_1}}, \sigma_{U_{a_2}}, \ldots, \sigma_{U_{a_n}}\}$ and sends it back to the user (in Step 2). Our attribute signing scheme binds every user's attribute with her verification key. Note that one of the attributes a_i is a profile picture that uniquely identifies the user.

Steps 1 and 2 constitute the registration phase that takes place securely and out of the band. The concept of digital signature together with user attributes (signed by the government) is already present in some EU countries [12,13,32].

4.2   Ownership Claim Phase

In order to make an ownership claim to the OCP, we consider a user client, say a browser plugin. The plugin sends the claim to the OCP and receives an ownership token from the OCP in the case the claim can be verified, cf. Figure 1. In order to do so, the first step is that the user client has to formulate the claim, then it has to identify personal information and finally the actual removal request has to be generated. In the next step, the OCP has to verify the request. This is done by first verifying the authenticity of the request and second verifying the relationship to the data. The latter verification depends on the type of data, *e.g.*, face recognition can be used for pictures. The last step is to generate the ownership token that is then transferred from the OCP to the user. In the following, we present the details of all these tasks.

Identifying Personal Information. For identifying user's personal information in an article (as illustrated in Fig. 2), a user client may run the NER algorithm locally (assuming it is delivered as a part of the user client) to extract all possible candidates. The NER algorithm could also be run as a third-party

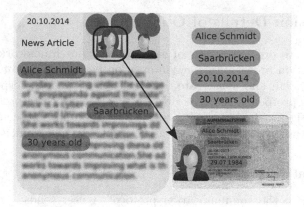

Fig. 2. An article illustrating personal information of Alice Schmidt who has an ID card with digital credentials issued by the German government.

service (*e.g.,* a web service), called by the user client. After running the NER algorithm, a user client picks each of the candidates and matches them with the user attributes (see Fig. 2).

If the match is not successful, a user client runs a synonym checker. If both words are synonyms then they are considered matched; otherwise, the next candidate is picked from the queue for the comparison. The synonym checker could be delivered as a part of the user client. To make the user client lightweight, we can assume a third party service (*e.g.,* a web service). In either case, the synonym checker should be very specific to the attributes issued by the CA[5].

Face Detection. Besides the textual description, an article could also contain a user's picture, either as a solo or a group picture. Like textual attributes, the user client can run the face detection algorithm to automatically detect the user's face. On successful detection, a user client can automatically include the CA-signed user picture in the removal request, which is explained next.

Generating Removal Request. After identifying personal information, a user client prepares a removal request. During the preparation, it chooses all signed attributes required for the ownership claim. Next, it packs them as $P_{\sigma_{U_{A^*}}}$ so that the OCP can verify the signed user attributes using a single exponentiation operation using the CA verification key. This would also require a user client to include in the message a subset of her attributes A^* corresponding to the packed ones, *i.e.,* $P_{\sigma_{U_{A^*}}}$. Since a user client signs the message using the user's signing key, the user's verification key vk_U is also included in the message to let

---

[5] For instance, the user's date of birth might appear differently in an article, *i.e.,* in the form of her age as shown in Fig. 2. If this happens, the age could be compared with the difference of the user's date of birth and publication date of the article, if present. As we can see in the example, *30 years old* will be compared with *20.10.2014 - 29.07.1984.* Further tests for checking syntactic equivalence are conceivable, but are postponed to future work.

the OCP verify the message. For preventing replay attacks, a timestamp TS is also included in the message. The user client sends to the OCP (in Step 3) the message $M = (TS, \mathsf{vk}_U, A^*, P_{\sigma_{U_{A^*}}}, D)$ along with the signature σ_M.

Verifying Removal Request. Upon receiving a removal request, an OCP verifies it before issuing any ownership token. As a first step, the signature σ_M over the message M is verified. Next, the OCP checks the timestamp and verifies the packed version of the user attributes signed by the CA. Then, the OCP checks if all tagged attributes are valid. This step comprises the exact matching and/or synonym checking.

Face Recognition. Optionally, the face recognition algorithm could be run provided there is a user picture in the article. As we explained earlier in this section, faces are pre-identified by the user client, in order to ease the job of the OCP. The OCP compares the user-tagged face with one provided as a signed user attribute in the request (see Fig. 2). If the face recognition algorithm discovers similarity with a certain confidence, the user's picture in the article is considered matched with her profile picture.

Entity Disambiguation. When the given article contains text, the OCP can execute the disambiguation algorithm (*e.g.*, AIDA [18]) for ensuring the eligibility goal, *i.e.*, checking whether the article is about the user. The outcome of this algorithm is the relation between the user attributes, her name in particular, and the context of the text. The outcome, say satisfying the predefined threshold value, would help the OCP to mark the user as being affected by the data in the article. Figure 2 illustrates an example article about Alice Schmidt.

Issuing Ownership Token. On successful evaluations of all the steps performed by the OCP, the user is issued an ownership token. This is accomplished by the OCP by sending (in Step 4) an ownership token D_U to the user. It is important to note that the OCP verification protocol is non-interactive.

4.3 Reporting Phase

Once the user receives the ownership token, she can report to the indexing system. In this phase, a user reports by sending (in Step 5) the ownership token D_U (corresponding to D) to the indexing system. The indexing system verifies the token, fires the incident and sends (in Step 6) an acknowledgment Ack to the user. If the OCP is a third-party service, the ownership token is signed by the OCP and could be sent to multiple indexing systems simultaneously.

4.4 Efficient Cryptographic Realization

The cryptographic instantiation relies on RSA-full-domain hashing as the underlying signature scheme. We briefly recall the definition of this signature scheme. The scheme assumes a given collision-resistant family of hash functions $\mathcal{H}_k : \{0,1\}^* \rightarrow \{0,1\}^k$. In the following, we omit the security parameter k for readability. The key generation KeyGen computes a key pair (sk, vk) by first computing an RSA modulus $N = p \cdot q$, where p and q are two random primes, and then computing e and d such that $e \cdot d = 1 \mod (p-1)(q-1)$. The keys are $\mathsf{sk} = (d, \mathsf{vk})$ and $\mathsf{vk} = (e, N)$. The signing function $\mathsf{Sign}(\mathsf{sk}, M)$ computes $\sigma_M := \mathcal{H}(M)^d \mod N$. Finally, the verification function $\mathsf{Verify}(\mathsf{vk}, \sigma, M)$ outputs accept if $\mathcal{H}(M) = \sigma^e \mod N$ and reject otherwise.

Using this cryptographic primitive, we finally describe the construction that we propose for our framework to achieve goals defined in Sect. 3.2. The censorship-resistance and eligibility checking goals could be achieved using X.509 based schemes [19]; however, those schemes are not able to achieve goals including minimal disclosure (*i.e.*, disclosing only those attributes required for the ownership claim) and scalability (*i.e.*, reducing computational overhead on the OCP end). Using our construction, the user can provide a minimal set of her attributes required for the ownership claim, and we are able to delegate some computation to the user client so that the OCP could be offloaded. Our construction allows an OCP to verify all user attributes with just a single exponentiation.

Definition 1 (Data Ownership Scheme). *The data ownership scheme DATA-OWN is a tuple of algorithms ⟨Init, KeyGen, CA.SignA, U.SignM, OCP.VerifyM, U.PackA, OCP.VerifyA⟩. The definition of the algorithms can be found in Fig. 3.*

Init(k): The system is initialized by running RSA-Sig.Init(k), which returns $\mathcal{H}(.)$.	KeyGen(1^λ): It runs RSA-Sig.KeyGen(1^λ). For the certification authority CA, it returns ⟨sk_{CA}, vk_{CA}⟩. For each user U, it returns ⟨sk_U, vk_U⟩.
CA.SignA(sk_{CA}, vk_U, A): Given the CA's signing key sk_{CA}, the user's verification key vk_U and a list of user attributes $A = \{a_1, a_2, \ldots, a_n\}$, the certification authority CA returns the list of signed attributes $\sigma_{U_A} = \{\sigma_{U_{a_1}}, \sigma_{U_{a_2}}, \ldots, \sigma_{U_{a_n}}\}$, which represents a list of signed attributes that belong to the user U. For each attribute $a_i \in A$, it computes $\sigma_{U_{a_i}}$ by running RSA-Sig.Sign(sk_{CA}, $a_i \| \mathsf{vk}_U$), where $\|$ denotes concatenation.	U.SignM(sk_U, M): Given the user's signing key sk_U and the message M, it runs RSA-Sig.Sign(sk_U, M) and returns the signature $\sigma_M = \mathcal{M}(D)^{d_U}$.

OCP.VerifyM(vk_U, σ_M, M): Given the user's verification key vk_U, the signature σ_M and the message M, it runs RSA-Sig.Verify(vk_U, σ_M, M) and returns either accept or reject. |
| U.PackA(vk_{CA}, $\sigma_{U_{A^*}}$): Given the CA's verification key vk_{CA} and the list of signed attributes $\sigma_{U_{A^*}} \subseteq \sigma_{U_A}$, it returns the packed signature $P_{\sigma_{U_{A^*}}}$. It calculates: $$P_{\sigma_{U_{A^*}}} = \prod_{i=1}^{l} \sigma_{U_{a_i}} \mod N_{CA}$$ where $\sigma_{U_{a_i}} \in \sigma_{U_{A^*}}$ and $l = |\sigma_{U_{A^*}}|$. | OCP.VerifyA(vk_{CA}, vk_U, $P_{\sigma_{U_{A^*}}}$, A^*): Given the CA's verification key vk_{CA}, the user's verification key vk_U, the packed signature $P_{\sigma_{U_{A^*}}}$ and the list of attributes $A^* \subseteq A$, it returns either accept or reject. It checks if $$\prod_{i=1}^{l} \mathcal{H}(a_i \| \mathsf{vk}_U) \overset{?}{\equiv} (P_{\sigma_{U_{A^*}}})^{e_{CA}} \mod N_{CA}$$ where $a_i \in A^*$ and $l = |A^*|$. |

Fig. 3. Details on the algorithms of the data ownership scheme.

Lemma 1 (Correctness). *Informally speaking,* $OCP.VerifyA(\mathsf{vk}_{CA}, \mathsf{vk}_U,$ $P_{\sigma_{U_{A^*}}}, A^*)$ *will always return* accept *if the list of signed attributes that are packed by the user are the same as the list of attributes A^* provided by the user to the OCP. More formally,*

$$Pr[OCP.VerifyA(\mathsf{vk}_{CA}, \mathsf{vk}_U, P_{\sigma_{U_{A^*}}}, A^*) = \mathsf{accept}] = 1$$

The claim easily follows from the homomorphic property of exponentiation modulo N. We analyze the security properties of *Oblivion* in Appendix A.

5 Performance Analysis

In this section, we provide implementation details for all components that we newly developed for *Oblivion* and name libraries that this implementation relies on. We subsequently evaluate the performance overhead of this implementation for each involved component (CA, user client, and OCP).

5.1 Implementation Details and Evaluation Parameters

Components of the Implementation. The implementation prototype is written in Java. To reflect the different involved participants, the implementation consists of three components: a module for the CA (CA-module), a module for the OCP (OCP-module) and a module for the user client (user-module). For the sake of simplicity, the prototypical implementation assumes that the OCP and the indexing system are managed by the same organization; this avoids an additional trust level between these institutions and allows us to concentrate on the performance measurements. The size of each of these modules (without included libraries; see below) is below 5 KB.

Libraries Used. Our prototypical implementation relies on several existing open source libraries. First, we include the Stanford NER library [1] for identifying personal information in the textual article. The NER library is of size 3.2 MB and the NER classifier, for covering seven distinct classes of data, requires 16.6 MB. Second, we rely on OpenCV (Open Source Computer Vision Library), an open source computer vision and machine learning library [25], for face detection and recognition. Finally, we include the AIDA (Accurate Online Disambiguation of Named Entities) framework [18] to achieve ownership disambiguation. In our experiments, we used the AIDA framework itself and its corresponding web service, which works with entities registered in the DBpedia [3] or YAGO [30] knowledge base.

Evaluation Parameters. We have evaluated the performance of the implementation on a dataset of 150 news articles that we randomly crawled from the international news agency Reuters[6], using the Java-based web crawler *crawler4j* [10]. These articles cover different topics and range from 1 K to about 10 K words;

---

[6] http://www.reuters.com/.

the average length is 1.9 K words per article. The actual experiments were run on a standard notebook with 2.5 GHz dual-core processor and 8 GB RAM. The experimental results described below constitute the average over 100 independent executions. Network latency was not considered in the experiments.

5.2   Evaluating the CA-Module

Evaluating the performance of the CA-module consists of measuring the overhead of attribute certification.

Attribute Certification. Figure 4 illustrates the computational overhead for certifying user attributes. In our experiment, we generated up to 50 attributes and considered CA's signing keys of varying size, ranging from 512 to 4096 bits. As we expected, certification time grows linearly in the number of attributes. For the most complex cases under consideration — the CA signing 50 attributes, and thus far more than what a user would typically maintain, using a signing key of size 4096 bits — the attribute certification took 7.5 s. For smaller numbers of attributes, or for all

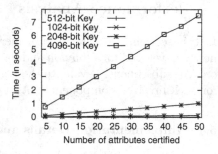

Fig. 4. Evaluation of the CA-module: Performance overhead for certifying user attributes.

smaller key sizes, this certification takes less than a second. Since attributes are typically certified only once per user, this computational overhead should be acceptable as a one-time upfront effort.

5.3   Evaluating the User-Module

Evaluating the user-module is performed in two steps: identifying suitable attributes in the given sample texts, and pre-processing these attributes for the subsequent ownership-proof phase.

Identifying Attributes. As explained in Sect. 3.3, the user-module pre-processes the article using NER techniques and appropriately selects all entities that are necessary for the identification process. We evaluate the performance of the user-module on the aforementioned 150 news articles from Reuters, and measure the time required to identify and extract all entities. The results are depicted in Fig. 5(a). The performance overhead varies from 77 to 814 millisecond (ms), with an average of 174 ms per article. The number of unique entities in the articles ranges from 43 to 590, where the average number of unique entities per article is 135.

Attribute Packing. After identifying all personal attributes in a given news article, the user-module pre-processes a set of signed attributes as required for the ownership proof. This pre-processing in particular reduces the number of

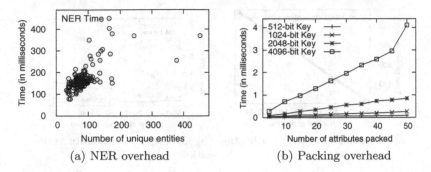

(a) NER overhead   (b) Packing overhead

Fig. 5. Evaluation of the user-module: Performance overhead of (a) identifying personal information and (b) for packing user attributes.

exponentiations that are required to verify the attributes for the OCP, and thereby avoids a potential bottleneck. In the performance measurement, we again considered up to 50 attributes and varying key sizes. As shown in Fig. 5(b), the time for this pre-processing increases linearly in the number of attributes, with an additional overhead for larger key sizes. For the maximum of 50 attributes, the pre-processing only took between 0.1 ms (for a 512-bit key) and 4.1 ms (for a 4096-bit key).

Message Signing. The user client signs the message using her signing key. For this experiment, we considered the aforementioned 150 news articles. Consider the overhead of signing a message with a signing key of size 1024 bits. Depending on the size of the article, the signing took between 2.8 and 3.8 ms, with an average of 2.9 ms per article.

5.4   Evaluating the OCP-Module

We split the performance evaluation of the OCP-module into two parts: First, we evaluate the time required to verify the validity of requests for varying parameters: for varying numbers of articles, for varying number of attributes, and for varying verification requests. Second, we evaluate the time required to decide whether the request is legitimate, *i.e.*, whether the document under consideration affects the user's data, either by means of entity disambiguation or face recognition.

Validating the User Request. Upon receiving a signed message from a user, the OCP verifies the validity of the signature using the user's verification key. This verification time (with a 1024-bit key) ranges from 2.9 to 4.3 ms with an average of 3.2 ms per article. Figure 6(a) illustrates the cumulative verification time to verify up to 150 articles. It grows linearly, so verifying message validity for 150 articles takes the OCP less than 0.72 s.

Similarly, Fig. 6(b) displays the time required to verify a certain number of signed user attributes. Recall that the user sends a packed version of her signed

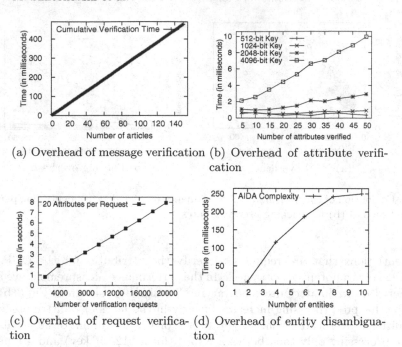

(a) Overhead of message verification (b) Overhead of attribute verification

(c) Overhead of request verification (d) Overhead of entity disambiguation

Fig. 6. Evaluation of the OCP-module: Performance overhead of (a) verifying the messages, (b) verifying user attributes signed by the CA, (c) verifying user requests and (d) running entity disambiguation.

attributes to ease the verification task of the OCP. Still, the OCP needs to calculate the hash of each individual attribute and multiply all hashes together before being able to verify the signature based on the packed version. Verifying 50 user attributes takes 0.37 ms (for a 512-bit key) and 10 ms (for a 4096-bit key), respectively. For l attributes, the packed version is at least $l - 2$ exponentiations faster than verifying each attribute individually.

Finally, Fig. 6(c) shows the performance overhead for verifying a certain number of user requests. In our experimentation, we assumed that every request requires the verification of 20 attributes, each one signed with a key of size 1024 bits. To measure the performance overhead, we gradually increased the number of user requests from 2000 to 20,000 and observed an (essentially linearly-growing) overhead from 0.824 to 7.96 s. Processing a single verification request with 20 attributes took less than 0.4 ms on average.

The overall computational overhead of the OCP-module is a combination of the message verification and the attribute request verification, each one incurring on average 3.2 ms and 0.4 ms, respectively. Therefore, our implementation manages to process a removal request within 3.6 ms. In summary, it allows the OCP to handle 278 requests per second (using the standard laptop that we based these experiments on).

Eligibility of the User Request. Identifying whether the requested article indeed contains personal data of the requesting user relies on appropriate entity disambiguation. Figure 6(d) illustrates the performance overhead for entity disambiguation with up to 10 entities.

Recall that we require the user client to run the face detection algorithm and select the appropriate face and send it the OCP along with the standard request. The performance overhead of the face recognition algorithm depends on multiple factors such as the picture resolution and the face position in the picture. In our experiments, we have chosen pictures with well-defined frontal faces. The resolution of the pictures is up to 3072×4608 pixels with an average size of 4 MB. Having all these predefined conditions, the runtime of the face recognition algorithm stays in the range of 150 to 300 ms.

The overall performance overhead, comprising both entity disambiguation and image recognition, currently constitutes the bottleneck for verifying the validity of removal requests in the OCP-module. Currently, we are exploring further optimization here.

6   Discussion

Deployability and Usability. In order to deploy our solution, *Oblivion* requires a national or local government-wide CA that issues credentials to citizens. We argue that this requirement does not limit practicality of our approach because the issuance of such credentials is already part of an EU standard [12], implemented by some member states and meant to be adopted by all the EU member states [13,32]. The European EID standards also enable the use of digital credentials for Internet communication (*e.g.*, for online shopping) [13] which also strengthens usability for *Oblivion*'s developers as well as end-users.

Scope of Eligibility. First, it is a hard problem to decide on the eligibility of an ownership claim if two persons have the same attributes, e.g., name. *Oblivion* addresses this issue by using attributes that in combination should be sufficiently unique for most people. Second, our framework cannot decide whether a piece of content is of public interest (such information falls into the category of freedom of the press) and outweighs the privacy interest of an individual. This decision is a legal assessment. This is outside of the scope of *Oblivion* and subject to ongoing research about the automation of legal assessments [4].

Privacy and Availability. The OCP could be a third-party service or managed by the search engine provider. From a privacy point of view, the latter setup may reveal personal information about citizens. However, we argue that a search engine provider does not learn more than what is already available in the article. This is because *Oblivion* follows a principle of least privilege, where only those particular attributes that are present in the article are sent to the OCP. The collection of information and verification makes the OCP a key component of *Oblivion*. The availability of the OCP becomes essential in the long-run success of *Oblivion*. Therefore, to prevent a single point of failure, we can consider deploying multiple instances of the OCP.

Robustness. *Oblivion* relies on NLP and image recognition techniques. The NLP technique we use in our framework is simple and sufficiently robust in practice. Concerning robustness of the image recognition technique, recent research has shown that automated face recognition is almost comparable to human face recognition accuracy [31]. Therefore, when the removal request includes a picture that uniquely identifies the user with a certain confidence (part of the deployed policy), our framework can easily approve the removal request.

7 Conclusion

In this work, we have introduced a universal framework, called *Oblivion*, providing the foundation to support the enforcement of the *right to be forgotten* in a scalable and automated manner both for users and indexing systems. The framework enables a user to automatically identify personal information in a given article and the indexing system to automatically verify the user's eligibility. The framework also achieves censorship-resistance, *i.e.*, users cannot blacklist a piece of data unless it affects them personally. This is accomplished using the government-issued digital credentials as well as applying the entity disambiguator technique. We have conducted comprehensive evaluations of *Oblivion* on existing articles, showing that the framework incurs only minimal overhead and is capable of handling 278 removal requests per second on a standard notebook (2.5 GHz dual core). In these evaluations, we have observed that the remaining performance bottleneck on the OCP is caused by the entity disambiguator (*i.e.*, AIDA) and the face recognition (*i.e.*, OpenCV) algorithms. We believe that optimized versions of both could help in significantly improving the performance.

For future work, we plan to improve *Oblivion's* accuracy and overall coverage for proving affectedness. Following the principle of reCAPTCHA digitizing books [33], improving the accuracy of NER by taking into account the user client tagging constitutes a promising approach. Another promising research direction is to analyze the assessment of lawfulness and automate the application of future guidelines for the *right to be forgotten*. Staying close to the precedent, this would also require semantically analyzing the article to determine if its content violates privacy rights, *e.g.*, by being outdated or by containing sensitive information for the entity requesting removal.

A   Security Analysis

The framework is supposed to achieve three security objectives: minimal disclosure, request unforgeability and censorship-resistance (cf. Sect. 3.2). In the following, we show that we achieved these goals.

Minimal Disclosure. Minimal disclosure in this context is the minimization of knowledge increase for the indexing system in order to verify eligibility of a request. In the case that OCP and IS are separate, this is given since the IS only receives a token from the OCP through the user. This token does not need to contain any information about the user. However, if the OCP and the IS collide, it has to receive the input to run OCP.VerifyA.

A user who wants to hide her verification key or credentials could potentially use interactive zero-knowledge proofs on top of our construction. This, however, would sacrifice efficiency and would not improve the disclosure of information. The reason is that the verification key is basically a pseudonym, *i.e.*, it is only linked to the attributes that we send. Thus, the only need to minimize is the sending of attributes. In *Oblivion*, we only send those attributes that are indeed necessary for proving that the user is affected, *i.e.*, that already occur in the link we report. We implement this by sending only subsets[7].

Request Unforgeability. For unforgeability we show that even the user cannot construct a message that verifies without having a signature on every single attribute. As a consequence, the user cannot show that she is affected by content concerning other users' attributes.

Theorem 1 (Request Unforgeability). *If OCP.VerifyA returns* accept *then the packed attributes correspond to the set* A^*. *More formally, every* $\mathcal{A}$ *that has access to a signing oracle* $\mathcal{S}$ *with public key* vk *can only generate* P *for subsets* A^* *of all signatures A requested from* $\mathcal{S}$.

Proof. Let A be the set of queried attributed signatures of the adversary $\mathcal{A}$ for a given execution. Assume there is a set $(B, P) \overset{\$}{\leftarrow} \mathcal{A}^{\mathcal{S}}(\text{vk}_u)$ such that OCP.VerifyA$(\text{vk}, \text{vk}_U, P, B) = \text{accept}$ and $B \not\subseteq A$. So there exists $b^* \in B$ such that $b^* \notin A$. Then there also exists an adversary $\mathcal{A}^*$ that queries $A \cup B \backslash \{b^*\}$, *i.e.*, b^* is the only unqueried attributed in B. Since OCP.VerifyA$(\text{vk}, \text{vk}_U, P, B) = \text{accept}$, it follows that $P^{e_{CA}} \equiv \prod_{b \in B} \mathcal{H}(b \| \text{vk}_U)$ by construction. Since we queried all b except b^* in B, we can compute $\sigma := P / \prod_{b \neq b^* \in B} \mathcal{H}(b_i \| \text{vk}_U)^{d_{CA}}$. For this σ, we have $\sigma^{e_{CA}} = \mathcal{H}(b^* \| \text{vk}_U)$. However, this contradicts the Chosen Message Attack (CMA) security of the underlying signature scheme. Thus, the adversary $\mathcal{A}$ cannot exist. ∎

Censorship-Resistance. Finally, we have to ensure that the overall system does not enable any user to censor, *i.e.*, to successfully report data that she is not affected by. There are two possible approaches. First, we could do a reduction proof to the CMA-security of the signature scheme as done for the request

---

[7] We stress again that we only show affectedness of the user. Arguing about the legal implications and whether this minimization of data is sufficient in order to apply them is beyond the scope of this (and all existing) work.

unforgeability[8]. Second, we can formulate the protocol in the applied π-calculus and automatically verify the properties of interest using tool support. The outcome can then be leveraged from the protocol to the implementation by using computational soundness which links symbolic execution traces to computational execution traces. Thus, we can use tools for symbolic verification and the outcome transfers to the implementation. In what follows, we pursue the second approach since the protocol is easy to express and verify using state-of-the-art verification tools.

The applied π-calculus defines a way of modeling processes (P,Q). Thereby, the calculus gives constructs for parallel execution of processes (P|Q), for repetition of processes (!P), for communication between processes (in(chan,msg),out(chan,x)) and for restricted computation. The restriction is that only symbolic constructors (let x=sig(sk,msg)) and destructors (let m=verify(vk,sig)) can be used to modify terms which consist of symbols. The difference is that constructors create symbolically larger symbols, *i.e.*, in the example x will be handled as the symbol sig(sk,msg) whereas destructors can give reduction rules to remove or replace constructors. Finally, for symbols, there are two classes, publicly known symbols and freshly introduced symbols (new N; P) which are unequal to all other symbols.

For the sake of exposition, we briefly describe the process for the indexing system. The system receives a message and verifies it with the corresponding key (computational soundness requires the key to be part of the signature). We then verify the first part of the signed message with the verification key of the OCP. This message must be the user's verification key and the requested data, *i.e.*, we check for equality before the IS is convinced that the signer is affected.

```
let IS = in(ch,x); let tmpkey = vkof(x);
    let (c,reportData) = verifySig(tmpKey, x) in
    let (sigKey, sigData) = verifySig(vkOCP, c) in
    if reqData==sigData then if tmpKey==sigKey then
    event affected(sigKey,reqData).
```

The end of the process is a so-called event. These events have no semantic meaning in the calculus, but can be used by the model checker to prove certain

---

[8] Such a proof would look like this: Assume censorship is possible. That means there is an execution that ends with a successful report at the indexing system without the user reporting the data. Therefore, there was a D_U sent to the IS that verifies with the key of the OCP. Either the OCP signed D_U or there is a contradiction to the signature scheme's CMA-property. Consequently, the OCP signed D_U and since we assume the OCP to be trustworthy, it means that the OCP received an M, σ_M from a user and verified it. Here, either the user's signature σ_M was forged (contradicting the CMA-property of the signature scheme) or the user forged a message M that verifies (contradicting the request unforgeability proven before). It follows that the user could not have generated such a request, proving censorship-resistance.

While this argumentation sounds plausible, it does not consider every possible interleaving or repetition of executions. In contrast, tool support offers a trustworthy guarantee that we did not overlook any execution generated by these processes.

properties of the protocol. In our example, the event symbolizes the belief of the IS that the user with verification key sigKey is affected by the data reqData. The model checker answers queries such as query ev:affected(k,d). which formalizes that the model checker can prove that this event can be reached in the protocol execution.

Censorship-resistance can be formulated as a sequence of events that has to occur whenever the IS thinks a user is affected, *i.e.*, whenever a request is considered to affect the requesting user, the OCP has verified that this data belongs to the user that sends the request. This can be done by two queries of the form query ev:affected(key,d) ==> ev:VerifiedOw(x,key,d). meaning that whenever the event affected occurs there has to be a corresponding event verifying the ownership beforehand. Analogously, we prove that the ownership verification is preceded by the attribute verification of the CA.

The complete formalization in the applied π-calculus can be found online at the project website[9]. The protocol verification takes 8 ms.

Other Security Goals. In order to prevent a replay attack, the user includes the timestamp in her request. One can argue that a replay attack is not an issue because it is a legitimate request by the authorized user. However, we consider that a replay attack could harm the credibility of the user if an adversary launches it to mount a Denial-of-Service (DoS) attack on the OCP.

References

1. Stanford Named Entity Recognizer (NER). http://nlp.stanford.edu/software/CRF-NER.shtml. Last Accessed: 11 October 2014
2. The web robots pages. http://www.robotstxt.org/. Last Accessed: 10 October 2014
3. Auer, S., Bizer, C., Kobilarov, G., Lehmann, J., Cyganiak, R., Ives, Z.G.: DBpedia: a nucleus for a web of open data. In: Aberer, K., et al. (eds.) ISWC/ASWC 2007. LNCS, vol. 4825, pp. 722–735. Springer, Heidelberg (2007)
4. Backes, M., Bendun, F., Hoffman, J., Marnau, N.: PriCL: Creating a Precedent. A Framework for Reasoning about Privacy Case Law (Extended Version) (2015). arxiv.org/abs/1501.03353
5. Backes, M., Gerling, S., Lorenz, S., Lukas, S.: X-pire 2.0 - a user-controlled expiration date and copy protection mechanism. In: Proceedings of the 29th ACM Symposium on Applied Computing (SAC 2014). ACM (2014)
6. Bandhakavi, S., Zhang, C.C., Winslett, M.: Super-sticky and declassifiable release policies for flexible information dissemination control. In: WPES, pp. 51–58 (2006)
7. Castelluccia, C., De Cristofaro, E., Francillon, A., Kaafar, M.A.: EphPub: toward robust ephemeral publishing. In: 2011 19th IEEE International Conference on Network Protocols (ICNP), pp. 165–175, October 2011
8. Chadwick, D.W., Lievens, S.F.: Enforcing "sticky" security policies throughout a distributed application. In: Middleware Security, pp. 1–6 (2008)
9. Court of Justice of the European Union: Judgment of the court (grand chamber). http://curia.europa.eu/juris/celex.jsf?celex=62012CJ0131. Last Accessed: 10 October 2014

---

[9] https://infsec.cs.uni-saarland.de/projects/oblivion/.

10. crawler4j: Open source web crawler for Java. https://code.google.com/p/crawler4j/. Last Accessed: 9 October 2014
11. Dierks, T.: The Transport Layer Security (TLS) protocol version 1.2 (2008)
12. European Parliament, Council of the European Union: Regulation (EU) No 910/2014 of the European Parliament and of the Council of 23 July 2014 on electronic identification and trust services for electronic transactions in the internal market and repealing Directive 1999/93/EC. http://eur-lex.europa.eu/legal-content/EN/TXT/?uri=CELEX:32014R0910. Last Accessed: 10 October 2014
13. Federal Ministry of the Interior: German national identity card. http://www.personalausweisportal.de/EN/Citizens/The-New-Identity-Card/The_New_Identity_Card_node.html. Last Accessed: 10 October 2014
14. Finkel, J.R., Grenager, T., Manning, C.D.: Incorporating non-local information into information extraction systems by gibbs sampling. In: Proceedings of the Conference on 43rd Annual Meeting of the Association for Computational Linguistics, ACL 2005, 25–30 June 2005. University of Michigan, USA (2005)
15. Geambasu, R., Kohno, T., Levy, A.A., Levy, H.M.: Vanish: increasing data privacy with self-destructing data. In: Proceedings of the 18th USENIX Security Symposium, Montreal, Canada, 10–14 August 2009, pp. 299–316 (2009)
16. Google: European privacy requests for search removals. https://www.google.com/transparencyreport/removals/europeprivacy/?hl=en. Last Accessed: 23 January 2015
17. Google Inc.: Search removal request under European Data Protection law. https://support.google.com/legal/contact/lr_eudpa?product=websearch. Last Accessed: 10 October 2014
18. Hoffart, J., Yosef, M.A., Bordino, I., Fürstenau, H., Pinkal, M., Spaniol, M., Taneva, B., Thater, S., Weikum, G.: Robust disambiguation of named entities in text. In: Proceedings of the 2011 Conference on Empirical Methods in Natural Language Processing, EMNLP 2011, John McIntyre Conference Centre, Edinburgh, UK, A meeting of SIGDAT, A Special Interest Group of the ACL, 27–31 July 2011, pp. 782–792 (2011)
19. Housley, R., Polk, W., Ford, W., Solo, D.: Internet X.509 Public Key Infrastructure Certificate and Certificate Revocation List (CRL) Profile. RFC 3280 (Proposed Standard), April 2002. http://www.ietf.org/rfc/rfc3280.txt. obsoleted by RFC 5280, updated by RFCs 4325, 4630
20. Microsoft: Request to block bing search results in europe. https://www.bing.com/webmaster/tools/eu-privacy-request. Last Accessed: 10 October 2014
21. Mont, M.C., Pearson, S., Bramhall, P.: Towards accountable management of identity and privacy: sticky policies and enforceable tracing services. In: DEXA Workshops, pp. 377–382 (2003)
22. Nair, S., Dashti, M., Crispo, B., Tanenbaum, A.: A hybrid PKI-IBC based ephemerizer system. In: Venter, H., Eloff, M., Labuschagne, L., Eloff, J., von Solms, R. (eds.) New Approaches for Security, Privacy and Trust in Complex Environments. IFIP, vol. 232, pp. 241–252. Springer, US (2007)
23. NLTK: WordNet Interface. http://www.nltk.org/howto/wordnet.html. Last Accessed: 29 September 2014
24. Olston, C., Najork, M.: Web crawling. Found. Trends Inf. Retrieval 4(3), 175–246 (2010)
25. OpenCV: Open source computer vision. http://opencv.org/. Last Accessed: 10 October 2014

26. Pearson, S., Mont, M.C.: Sticky policies: An approach for managing privacy across multiple parties. Computer **44**(9), 60–68 (2011)
27. Perlman, R.: The Ephemerizer: making data disappear. J. Inf. Syst. Secur. **1**, 51–68 (2005)
28. Reimann, S., Dürmuth, M.: Timed revocation of user data: long expiration times from existing infrastructure. In: WPES, pp. 65–74 (2012)
29. Rivest, R.L., Shamir, A., Adleman, L.: A method for obtaining digital signatures and public-key cryptosystems. Commun. ACM **21**(2), 120–126 (1978)
30. Suchanek, F.M., Kasneci, G., Weikum, G.: Yago: A core of semantic knowledge. In: Proceedings of the 16th International Conference on World Wide Web, WWW 2007, pp. 697–706 (2007)
31. Taigman, Y., Yang, M., Ranzato, M., Wolf, L.: Deepface: closing the gap to human-level performance in face verification. In: 2014 IEEE Conference on Computer Vision and Pattern Recognition, CVPR 2014, Columbus, OH, USA, 23–28 June 2014, pp. 1701–1708 (2014)
32. The Council of the European Union: Residence permits for third-country nationals. http://eur-lex.europa.eu/legal-content/en/TXT/?uri=CELEX:32008R0380. Last Accessed: 10 October 2014
33. Von Ahn, L., Maurer, B., McMillen, C., Abraham, D., Blum, M.: reCAPTCHA: Human-based character recognition via web security measures. Science **321**(5895), 1465–1468 (2008)
34. Yahoo: Requests to block search results in yahoo search: Resource for european residents. http://bit.ly/185Lije. Last Accessed: 20 January 2015

Authentication via Eye Tracking and Proofs of Proximity

Exploiting Eye Tracking for Smartphone Authentication

Dachuan Liu[1,2]($^\boxtimes$), Bo Dong[2], Xing Gao[1,2], and Haining Wang[1]

[1] University of Delaware, Newark, DE, USA
{dliu,xinggao}@cs.wm.edu, hnw@udel.edu
[2] College of William and Mary, Williamsburg, VA, USA
bdong@cs.wm.edu

Abstract. Traditional user authentication methods using passcode or finger movement on smartphones are vulnerable to shoulder surfing attack, smudge attack, and keylogger attack. These attacks are able to infer a passcode based on the information collection of user's finger movement or tapping input. As an alternative user authentication approach, eye tracking can reduce the risk of suffering those attacks effectively because no hand input is required. However, most existing eye tracking techniques are designed for large screen devices. Many of them depend on special hardware like high resolution eye tracker and special process like calibration, which are not readily available for smartphone users. In this paper, we propose a new eye tracking method for user authentication on a smartphone. It utilizes the smartphone's front camera to capture a user's eye movement trajectories which are used as the input of user authentication. No special hardware or calibration process is needed. We develop a prototype and evaluate its effectiveness on an Android smartphone. We recruit a group of volunteers to participate in the user study. Our evaluation results show that the proposed eye tracking technique achieves very high accuracy in user authentication.

Keywords: Authentication · Eye tracking · Privacy protection · Smartphone

1 Introduction

Two authentication methods, passcode-based and finger movement pattern-based, have been widely used by various smartphones for user authentication. However, previous research has revealed that both authentication methods are vulnerable to shoulder surfing attack [28], smudge attack [2], and keylogger attack [5,18,19,26]. For shoulder surfing attacks, an attacker could steal a password just by peeking over a user's shoulder when the user is entering its password. Recently, some researchers found that it is possible to steal a password even when a user is behind some obstacles [25]. Smudge attacks exploit the oily residues left on the screen for inferring a password. Keylogger attacks are launched from the inside of device. The malicious program running on the smartphone utilizes smartphone's sensors to record the vibrations during the authentication. Then attackers could

© Springer International Publishing Switzerland 2015
T. Malkin et al. (Eds.): ACNS 2015, LNCS 9092, pp. 457–477, 2015.
DOI: 10.1007/978-3-319-28166-7_22

figure out the password based on those information. All these attacks exploit the information from user's hand typing or finger moving activities.

The authentication methods leveraging eye tracking do not need hand input; therefore, they are resistant to those attacks above. So far, there are already some works applying eye tracking techniques in user authentication. These works can be classified into biometric-based [3,12–14] and pattern-based [7,9,10,15]. The biometric-based methods authenticate a user based on the biometric information extracted from the user's eyes or eye movement characteristics. Differently, the pattern-based methods require a user to issue commands via their eye movements. The pattern-based authentication can be further divided into two types. The first type [15] tracks a user's gaze point on the screen as the input. A calibration process is required for predicting the gaze point accurately. And users have to keep their heads fixed after the calibration. The other type [7,9,10] recognizes a user's eye movement trajectory that represents a specific command, and does not need calibration process. Most of these eye tracking applications are proposed for the devices with large screen. Many of them require special hardware like high resolution eye trackers.

However, it is impractical for smartphone users to either carry a high resolution eye tracker or conduct the calibration process. In this paper, we propose a new eye tracking authentication method for smartphone users. We leverage the eye movement trajectories as the input, which reflect eye moving direction but not the exact gaze point on the screen. Neither extra eye tracker nor calibration process is needed.

In our proposed scheme, there are multiple moving objects on the screen, one of which is the target. A user just tracks the moving target with her eyes. The authentication passes when the user's eye movement trajectories match the target's movement trajectories. The routes of all moving objects are *randomly* generated every time. Therefore, an attacker cannot infer the password by observing the user's eye movement during authentication. Each object should also move very differently from the others, and thus the user's eye tracking trajectory can easily match the target's trajectory. We develop a prototype based on Android 4.2.2 and deploy it on Google Nexus 4 smartphone. Then we invite 21 volunteers to take the user study. The evaluation results show that average authentication accuracy is as high as 91.6 %.

The major research contributions of this work are summarized as follows:

- To the best of our knowledge, this is the first smartphone authentication method applying the eye tracking technique that does not require extra eye tracker and calibration process.
- We design a movement pattern for the authentication. The randomness within the movement pattern reduces the risks of leaking a password. Besides, The movement pattern just requires four corresponding eye movement actions, which are basic and straightforward for users to perform, achieving high detection rate.
- We introduce and compare six metrics used for matching the eye movement trajectory and target movement trajectory. We identify the most effective

metric based on our experiments. Four of them are not used in previous works, and two newly introduced metrics lead to higher detection rate than those used in the previous works.
- We implement a prototype on Android OS, and conduct a user study to evaluate the effectiveness of this proposed user authentication scheme.

The remainder of the paper is organized as follows. In Sect. 2, we introduce threat models to the popular user authentication methods on smartphones. We present the new authentication method in Sect. 3. Then we evaluate its effectiveness in Sect. 4. The limitations of our work are discussed in Sect. 5. We survey related work in Sect. 6. Finally, we conclude this work in Sect. 7.

2   Threat Models

In this section we present the threat models in the existing authentication methods on smartphone. Two kinds of authentication methods are popular among most smartphone users. One is the passcode-based and the other is pattern-based. As a classic authentication method, the passcode-based methods need a user to type its passcode. Pattern-based methods require a user to move fingers following some pre-set patterns. Both authentication methods are vulnerable to shoulder surfing attack, smudge attack, and keylogger attack.

To launch a shoulder surfing attack, an attacker just peeks from a user's shoulder when the user is entering the password. Then the attacker can infer the password based on the keyboard layout and the user's typing actions. A recent research work [25] reveals that attackers could steal a password even if the user is behind some obstacles. A smudge attack [2] exploits the oily residues, called smudge, left on the touch screen to infer a user's password. Attackers just hold camera at special angle to the orientation of the touch screen, and put the device under special lighting source and lighting angle. Under the certain conditions, the password pattern could be exposed. Some other attacks utilizing the acoustic of the tapping are introduced in [4,29].

Keylogger attacks compromise a user's password from the inside of device. They leverage various sensors like the accelerometer and the gyroscope equipped on a smartphone to extract the behavior features of each individual. These information could result in the leakage of a password. In [5], it is observed that tappings on the different position of a screen cause different vibrations. Attackers can infer a password based on the vibration features. Xu et al. [26] proposed to collect the information from more sensors like the accelerometer, gyroscope, and orientation sensors. Using the collected information, they constructed the user pattern to calculate the user's action and input. TapPrints [18] estimates the tapping location by using machine learning to analyze the motion data. In [19], the authors can conjecture the input sequences using the data extracted from the accelerometer sensor.

3   A New Authentication Approach

Applying eye tracking techniques in user authentication can significantly reduce
the risks of suffering those attacks mentioned above. We design a new authentication approach based on eye movement pattern so that a smartphone user can
just use the device's front camera and skip the calibration before each authentication. Compared to the user patterns like EyePassShape and Eye gesture [7]
which require a user to draw some shape using eyes actively, tracking the moving object with eyes in a passive manner is much easier. Besides, users do not
need to remember the complex shapes but just the target object as a password.
Considering that humans' eyes move in fast and straight saccades and thus cannot perform any curves or other non-linear shapes [10], we make the objects
move in straight lines for eye tracking. In the following, we first introduce the
basic authentication process and the architecture of our eye tracking authentication system. Then we present how to measure the similarity between the eye
movement trajectory and the target movement trajectory.

3.1   Authentication Process

The basic authentication process is described as follows. There are four objects
in the center of the screen at the beginning. The layout is shown in Fig. 1a.
Each object is labeled with a number in the range of 1 to 4, and moves in a
straight line smoothly for five rounds. In each round, the four objects move to
different directions simultaneously. When the objects are moving, the user tracks
the target object using eyes. Figure 1b shows a snapshot when the objects are
moving. The target object represents the password in that round. When the
objects start to move, the user eye-tracks the target and could extend the vision
in that direction beyond the screen for providing a more clear eye movement

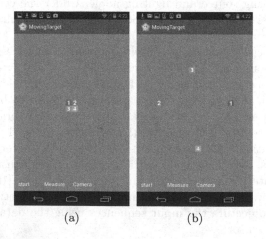

(a)   (b)

Fig. 1. (a) The layout of objects before they start to move (b) The four objects are
moving in four different directions (up, down, left and right) in a round.

trajectory. Once the movements stop at the end of each round, all objects return to the original positions. Meanwhile, there is a beep sound to notify the user to move eyes back to the center. Furthermore, before the next round starts, all the objects pause for one second to guarantee that the user moves eyes back to the center. The front camera of the smartphone captures the eye movements and delivers the frames to the analysis component, which extracts the eye points from each frames. Then a set of metrics will be calculated based on the eye points. These computed metrics are compared to those of the target's movement trajectory. If the metrics match, the authentication passes. Here is an example showing how our authentication scheme works.

- The user sets the password like 1-2-3-1-4. Each digit represents the target object in the corresponding movement round.
- When the user is ready, she just clicks the "start" button to initiate the authentication.
- All the objects are moving at the same time, the user uses her eyes to track the target object in that round.
- After the five rounds movement, the system outputs the match result.

3.2   System Architecture

The authentication system's architecture consists of two parts: the front-end and the back-end. The front-end includes pattern design, route generation, and moving control. The back-end mainly captures eye movement trajectory and matches it to the target movement trajectory. The architecture is illustrated in Fig. 2.

Front-End. We propose to secure the authentication by moving all the objects randomly each time. Since the authentication process does not need hand input, the smudge attack and keylogger attack cannot steal any information from the authentication process. For the shoulder surfing attack, even if attackers record the eye movement and figure out the eye movement trajectories, they cannot pass the authentication by replaying the same set of trajectories. This is because the target's routes for moving are random in each time. Moreover, attackers have to

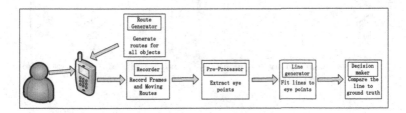

Fig. 2. Architecture of the system

deploy a camera close enough to the user's eyes to capture the eye movement trajectories, which makes it a challenging task without alerting the user.

With respect to the layout, all the objects are in the center of the screen at the beginning of each round. To make the user locate the target easily, the start positions of all objects should not be changed in each round. Pursuits [24] shows that the detection rate decreases when there are many objects on the screen. We also find that users may look towards some other moving objects when they are tracking the target. We call it distraction problem. It becomes serious when two moving objects are close to each other. If we leave the objects at one side of the screen or the corners of the screen at the beginning, the objects could move across one another. In addition, setting the start positions of the objects at different corners may exposure the password. In such a scenario, the user will look to a corner at the beginning of each round. Then, the attacker could figure out the start position of the target by only observing the gaze direction of the user. Thus, in our design, the objects move far away from each other while they are clustered together in the center of the screen at the beginning of a round.

The four objects move to four different directions: up, down, left, and right, which is shown in Fig. 3a. There are four reasons for such a design. (1) Since the screen of a smartphone is much smaller than a regular screen device, the number of the moving objects on the screen should be small to avoid the distraction problem. (2) For the purpose of not exposing the target, all the objects' movement directions are evenly distributed on the screen. Furthermore, the fewer objects, the larger the angle between two objects' movement directions. Consequently, it is easier to match the eye movement trajectory to the target movement trajectory. In other words, it is easier to distinguish the eye movement trajectory from the other objects' movement trajectories. (3) Although users can look at any direction theoretically, it is difficult for them to control eyes to move in an exact angle. Looking up, down, left, and right are the four most basic and simplest eye movement actions for users. (4) Since the eye movement just roughly follows the target movement, the problem appears when the eye movement trajectory is close to two different objects' movement trajectories. In such a case,

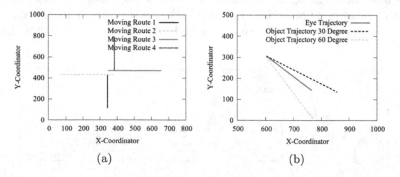

(a)   (b)

Fig. 3. (a) The trajectories of four objects in a round (b) It is hard to tell which object the user tracks with eyes when the trajectories of two objects are close to each other.

it is hard to tell which object the user eye-tracked. As shown in Fig. 3b, it is unclear which object the user is eye-tracking. In our design, the four directions are distinguishable from each other and help alleviate such problems.

Another disadvantage of a small screen is that the user's eye movement could be negligible if the user only looks inside of the screen boundary. Some users could be able to look any positions on the screen without obvious eye movements. In such a case, it is hard to tell the user's eye movement trajectory. To make the eye movement more clear to be detected, we allow the user to look beyond the screen area following the target's movement direction, and provide a beep sound to remind the user look back when the movement ends.

In our current design, we just set five movement rounds in the prototype and the corresponding key space is $4^5 = 1024$. The key space can be enlarged simply by allowing a user to choose different number of movement rounds for authentication. Specifically, a password could consist of arbitrary number of digits. The system first asks the user to input the number of movement rounds, then it provides corresponding object movements for authentication. More movement rounds make the authentication safer. Note that the authentication method can be applied in different scenarios, such as unlocking a phone and accessing an important file.

Back-End. We leverage the front camera to capture the eye movements. The record starts when the target begins to move. It ends when the target finishes its movement within one round. The eye tracking component will extract eye points from these continuous frames. After the 5th round eye tracking finishes, the Decision Maker starts to match the eye movement trajectory to the target's movement trajectory. Note that the Decision Maker only informs the user of the final match result after five rounds, and does not inform the user about the match result for each round. A mismatch notice could benefit the legitimate user because the user can start a new authentication early if the current eye-tracking round fails. However, it is insecure, because it also informs the attacker whether the guessed number in the current round is correct. Then, the attacker just needs to try at most four times to identify the target object in each round and 20 times to uncover the whole password.

There are two sets of eye points (left eye and right eye) whose corresponding trajectories could be different. It could be that both trajectories match the target's trajectory or only one of them matches that of the target. When the user is eye-tracking the target object, it is possible she peeks to another moving object because of the distraction problem. The problem could make one eye's movement trajectory deviate from the target's trajectory. However, it is very hard for the user to intentionally eye-track two different objects at the same time. So, we regard that the user eye-tracks the target when there is at least one eye's movement trajectory matching the target's movement trajectory.

We introduce six metrics to measure the similarity between the eye movement trajectory and an object's movement trajectory. If the eye movement trajectory is most similar to the target's movement trajectory, we regard it as a match. On the other hand, if the eye movement trajectory is most similar to a non-target object's movement trajectory, the authentication fails.

Measure the Similarity. After the pre-processor extracts eye points, the crucial task is how to effectively measure the similarity between the eye movement trajectory and the target's movement trajectory. Assume that the screen is a rectangular coordinate system, we can refine the problem as how to measure the similarity between two lines with directions. We expect that the user's eye movement trajectory should be similar to that of the moving target. The similarity is represented as that the two trajectories' direction should be close to each other.

In previous works [22, 24], correlation is used for matching. Principle Component Analysis (PCA) [3] is also used to estimate the direction. In this paper, we propose to fit a straight line into the eye points and compare the angle difference between this line and the target trajectory. We adopt RANdom SAmple Consensus (RANSAC) algorithm and introduce three error functions for line fitting. Simple Linear Regression (SLR) is another potential option for line fitting. We compare and evaluate them with the previous methods in the evaluation part.

In the following, we present the metrics used to measure the similarity. Correlation can measure the linear association between two variables X_a and X_b in statistics. It is defined as the covariance of the two variables divided by the product of the two variables' standard deviations. The formula is

$$\rho_{X_a, X_b} = \frac{E[(X_a - \mu_{X_a})(X_b - \mu_{X_b})]}{\sigma_{X_a} \sigma_{X_b}}$$

The coefficient is between $+1$ and -1, where $+1$ represents the total positive correlation, 0 means no correlation, and -1 stands for the total negative correlation. The formula can calculate the correlation between two variables. However, each eye point contains two variables X and Y coordinates. In such a case, the correlation between eye movement and object movement has to be calculated separately: one is for X and the other is for Y. In the previous works, the authors claimed that if X and Y of the eye movements change with those of the object movements, the user's eyes move following the objects. A threshold is set for determining whether the two trajectories match.

In this work, we propose to fit a straight line into the eye points whose angle should be close to the target's trajectory. Four methods are used to fit a line into the eye points. The first three are based on the RANSAC algorithm. RANSAC is designed for removing the noise and identifying the inliers in a set. As an iterative method, RANSAC cannot test all data points for the mathematic model exhaustively for a large set of data. However, the number of eye points is limited. Thus, we can try all possible combinations in a short time. The algorithm is described in Algorithm 1.

We leverage RANSAC's idea and introduce three error functions (Err1, Err2, Err3) in the algorithm. Err1 measures the number of points whose distance to the line is less than a threshold. Based on the observed data, we set the threshold to 3 pixels, implying that the line containing most points under this distance

Algorithm 1. RANSAC algorithm with error functions

1: Data: Eye movement points
2: Result: A line matches the points
3: BestModel, BestMode2, BestMode3
4: BestModelScore= 0
5: BestMode2Score = BestMode3Score = Infinity
6: Err1(line L): return the number of points whose distance to the line is smaller than a threshold
7: Err2(line L): return the sum of distance to the line of all points
8: Err3(line L): return the sum of squared distance of all points
9: **for** point p1 in the set **do**
10:    **for** another point p2 in the same set **do**
11:       generate a line L based on the two points p1 and p2
12:       **if** Err1(L) > BestModelScore **then**
13:          BestModel = L
14:       **end if**
15:       **if** Err2(L) < BestMode2Score **then**
16:          BestMode2 = L
17:       **end if**
18:       **if** Err3(L) < BestMode3Score **then**
19:          BestMode3 = L
20:       **end if**
21:    **end for**
22: **end for**
23: Return BestModel, BestMode2, BestMode3

---

bound is chosen as the best fitting. Err2 measures the sum of all points' distance to the line. Err2 chooses the line, which has the smallest sum, as the best fit. Err3 measures the sum of squared distance. The error functions 2 and 3 are similar, but their results could be different.

All of the three error functions choose the line that is calculated from two points in the eye point set. It is possible that a better-fit line would not pass any two points. Therefore, we introduce another function SLR to generate the line. The function SLR is used to fit a straight line through a set of points so that the sum of the squared residual of the mode is as small as possible. Suppose there are n eye points $(x_1, y_1), (x_2, y_2), \ldots, (x_n, y_n)$. SLR will fit a straight line $y = \alpha x + \beta$, which provides the minimum sum of squared residues (the vertical distance from a point to the line).

$$Find \min_{\alpha, \beta} Q(\alpha, \beta)$$

$$For Q(\alpha, \beta) = \sum_{i=1}^{n} \xi^2 = \sum_{i=1}^{n} (y_i - \alpha x_i - \beta)^2$$

The values of α and β that result in minimum Q can be computed by either using the calculus and the geometry of inner product spaces, or expanding to get quadratic in α and β:

$$\alpha = \frac{COV[x,y]}{Var[x]} = \frac{\sum_{i=1}^{n}(x_i - \bar{x})(y_i - \bar{y})}{\sum_{i=1}^{n}(x_i - \bar{x})}, \beta = y - \alpha x.$$

PCA is a statistical procedure which employs the orthogonal transformation to convert a set of observed possibly correlated data into a group of linear uncorrelated variables called principle components. In our case, PCA is used to estimate the direction of the set of eye points. Assume there are n eye points $(x_1, y_1), (x_2, y_2), \ldots, (x_n, y_n)$, the steps for PCA calculation are listed as follows:

- Calculate x' and y' as: $x_i' = x_i - \bar{x}, y_i' = y_i - \bar{y}$.
- Construct covariance matrix M

$$\begin{pmatrix} COV[x',x'] & COV[x',y'] \\ COV[y',x'] & COV[y',y'] \end{pmatrix}$$

- Calculate the eigenvalues and eigenvectors of the matrix. The eigenvector of the highest eigenvalue is the principle component of the data set.
- Assume the eigenvector is $\begin{pmatrix} x' \\ y' \end{pmatrix}$. The straight line's slope is the value of $\frac{y'}{x'}$.

To provide a detailed view of these metrices, we conduct some preliminary experiments to measure and compare them. We deploy a preliminary eye tracking prototype on Google Nexus 4 running Android 4.2.2. There is only one object moving on the screen. The object's moving distance is set as 300 pixels on the screen. The moving speed is 200 pixels per 1000 ms. The object moves on the screen with 45 degree. A volunteer eye-tracks the moving object for 10 times. The gaze point is used for eye tracking in the previous work. Considering the low resolution of front camera and the hand tremble during eye tracking, the gaze points could be unreliable for smartphone authentication. Therefore, we utilize eye points to identify the eye movement.

There are 10 movements corresponding to 10 sets of eye points. The average range of eye points' x coordinate is 19.4 ± 10.26 pixels; that of y coordinate is 7.9 ± 3.78 pixels. Figure 4a shows the straight lines which fit the eye points of one movement. The x-range is 11 and y-range is 5. It is clear that the lines generated by the five different methods can reflect the eye movement trajectory. Figure 4b shows the object movement trajectory and the lines generated by RANSAC Err2 using the 10 sets of eye points.

From this figure, we can see that the user's eye movement basically follows the object movement. In other words, the eye movement trajectory is similar to the object movement trajectory. However, we also observe that the user's eye movement cannot strictly follow the object movement. There are three possible reasons. First, the eye tracking technique cannot guarantee 100 % accuracy; second, distraction causes the user to move her eyes to a different direction; and third, the head and hand trembles impact the eye tracking. The average correlation of the 10 set data is 0.74 ± 0.1. The value is the sum of x-coordinate's and y-coordinate's correlation. Figure 5 depicts the angle difference between the eye movement and the object movement. The smaller the angle difference, the eye movement is more similar to the object movement.

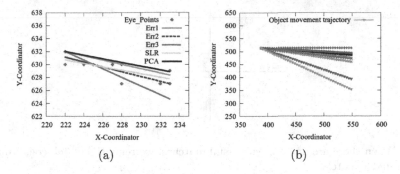

Fig. 4. (a) The lines generated by the five functions based on one set of eye points (b) The lines generated by one function (Err2) based on 10 sets of eye points

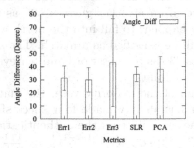

Fig. 5. The average angle difference between the trajectory of eye movement and that of object movement

3.3 Majority Vote

We regard that the eye movement trajectory matches the target movement trajectory if the angle difference between them is less than 45 degree. However, the user's eye movement trajectory could deviate more than 45 degree from the target movement trajectory in practice. The reasons could be eye tracking's error or the distraction problem. Moreover, a user cannot control her eyes to move in an exact straight line, which is just like that a user cannot draw an exact straight line.

To tolerate these errors, we introduce the majority vote to improve detection accuracy. The majority vote mechanism works as follows: as long as there are any 4 successful matches within 5 rounds, we relax the matching condition (i.e., the angle difference) from 45 degree to 90 degree for the deviated eye movement trajectory.

For example, assume that the object "1" in Fig. 6 is the target, the eye movement trajectories in red are regarded as successful matches, since their angle difference from the target movement trajectory is less than 45 degree; however, the eye movement trajectory in green, whose angle difference is larger than 45 degree but less than 90 degree, is still classified as a successful match under the relaxed matching condition. While the matching relaxation reduces

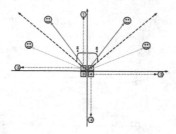

Fig. 6. When there are any four successful matches, we relax the match constraint for the remainder match.

the number of false rejections, it also increases the chance of false acceptance. Using the example above, if an attacker guesses "2" as the password and her eye movement trajectory happens to fall into the north-west quadrant with the probability of 50 %, it will be classified as a match. The similar situation exists when the attacker guesses "3" as the password and her eye movement trajectory falls into the north-east quadrant.

However, in the design of the majority vote, the matching relaxation happens only if the attacker has already made four successful matches. Thus, the probability that the attacker could pass the authentication by simply guessing a password is only $C_4^1 \cdot C_4^1 \cdot C_4^1 \cdot C_4^1 \cdot C_4^{(1+1/2+1/2)} = \frac{1+1/2+1/2}{4\times4\times4\times4\times4} = 0.2\,\%$.

4   Evaluation

We implement a prototype as an app based on Android 4.2.2. The prototype can be integrated as an option in Android's authentication setting. Currently, we use the beep sound to notify a user to look back to the screen center. In a noisy environment, we could replace the beep with vibration. We leverage the Snapdragon SDK from Qualcomm [1] to track the user's eye movement. The snapdragon can be deployed on many existing smartphones. It can extract the eye points in real time. To better evaluate and analyze the results, we record eye points and object routes into files. For future real world deployment, these functions can be easily integrated together and the data can be analyzed in real time without writing them into files.

To evaluate the effectiveness of the proposed authentication method, 21 volunteers are invited to participate our user study with age range from 24 to 33. Among them, 14 wear glasses. In the following, we first measure detection accuracy. Then we compare the performance of matching trajectories using different metrics. Finally, we assess the security of our scheme.

4.1   Experimental Setup

Our experiments consist of three parts: indoor, outdoor, and mimic attacks. The indoor experiments are conducted in a normal office environment with enough lights. It is common that people use smartphones indoors. Unlike outdoor lights, indoor lights remain stable as time goes on. So, indoors is the ideal environment for accuracy evaluation. All volunteers are involved with the indoor experiments, and each of them applies the correct password for 30 times. Users hold the smartphone in the front of their faces, and stay in a comfortable posture (either sitting or standing). They take a short break (at least 5 seconds) between two sets of experiments. After the indoor experiments are completed, we select five users to do the outdoor experiments. They perform the same operations as the indoor experiments. Two users do the outdoor experiments on a cloudy day. The other three use the smartphone under the tree shade on a sunny day. We do outdoor experiments under the tree shade because users feel uncomfortable when they look at the screen in the sun. It also results in inaccurate eye movement detection. Finally, five users are involved in the mimic attacks for security evaluation.

4.2 Detection Accuracy

Detection accuracy is the key performance indicator of an authentication method. A user could be unsatisfied if the authentication fails even when the correct password is applied. Our detection accuracy (i.e., true positive rate) is listed in Table 1.

While using the RANSAC Err2 metric for matching, the detection accuracy of indoor experiments is 77.1 % (486/630) and that of outdoor experiments is 79.3 % (119/150). We regard that such results are reasonable, considering that neither extra eye tracker nor calibration process is required. In the previous work [22] that utilizes the front camera for eye gesture detection, five users were enrolled in the user study with the smartphone fixed on the table. Its recognition rate is just about 60 %. In our evaluation, we further observe that many authentication failures only have one digit mismatch. After applying the majority vote, the detection accuracy of indoor experiments increases to 91.6 % (577/630) and that of outdoor experiments increases to 97.3 % (146/150).

Since we track the eye movement for authentication, users do not need to keep their heads fixed during the authentication. They can take a comfortable posture to conduct eye movements. Different postures like standing or sitting have little impact on detection accuracy. Our method can tolerate the slight head and hand tremble, because the eye point range is large enough for reflecting the eye movement trajectory. The eye point ranges are shown in Fig. 7a, b.

As stated before, a user's eye movement trajectory of left eye could be different from that of right eye. We choose the one which is closer to the target

Table 1. Accuracy of the authentication method

Users	Trials	Environment	Left eye	Right eye	Detection accuracy	Detection accuracy majority vote
21	630 (30 × 21)	Indoor	1584	1566	77.1 %	91.6 %
5	150 (30 × 5)	Outdoor	336	414	79.3 %	97.3 %

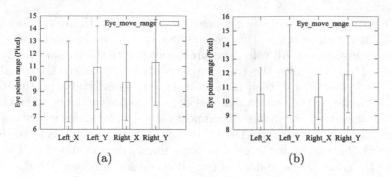

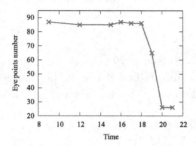

Fig. 7. The average range of eye points in indoor experiments (a) and that in outdoor experiments (b)

Fig. 8. The number of eye points captured at different time

movement trajectory for matching. There are 1584 left eye movement trajectories and 1566 right eye movement trajectories being used in the evaluation. Note that we use different eye movement data just for matching with higher accuracy. When left eye movement data is selected, it does not mean that the right eye movement data mismatches.

The accuracy of outdoor experiments during the daytime is close to that of indoor experiments. No matter it is sunny or cloudy, the accuracy does not change much. Our authentication method does not work well in weak light or dark. If there is adequate light, the number of captured eye points should be about 89. It means that we extract eye points from 16 frames in a second. The eye point number in weak light could be as low as 28, which corresponds to that 5 frames are handled in a second. It is clear that the eye point number in weak light is much less than that in normal light. This will negatively impact the line generation and match precision. Be aware that different people have different understanding of the weak light. Thus, we provide an approximation view on the connection between eye point number and light strength. Figure 8 shows the eye point number extracted at different time of a day. We can see that in most time when a user needs authentication, the light should be strong enough. We do not suggest to use this authentication method in weak light, which could cause

Table 2. Consecutive failures statistic

No majority vote	One time failure	Two failures	Three failures	Four and more failures
Number	83	36	21	4
Rate	13.2 %	5.7 %	3.3 %	0.6 %
Majority vote	One time failure	Two failures	Three failures	Four and more failures
Number	40	10	3	0
Rate	6.3 %	1.6 %	0.5 %	0 %

an authentication failure. In such a case, the user could choose an alternative option, for example the pattern-based authentication.

We further classify the failures into one time failure, two consecutive failures, three consecutive failures, four and more consecutive failures. When a legitimate user suffers a failure, she will expect to pass the authentication in the next trial. The consecutive failures will frustrate the users. Table 2 demonstrates the failure statistics. There are 84 one time failures, 18 two consecutive failures, 7 three consecutive failures, and only 1 four consecutive failures. The three and more consecutive failures happen in a low probability. When majority vote is applied, there are 42 one time failures, 5 two consecutive failures, and only 1 three consecutive failures.

4.3 Effectiveness Comparison

Correlation and PCA are used to estimate the eye movement direction in previous works. Besides these two metrics, we further consider four additional methods to fit a line into the eye points and compare the angle difference between the fitted line and the target movement trajectory. Thus, in total we use six metrics to measure the similarity between the eye movement trajectory and the target movement trajectory. Figure 9 shows the average successful match number among the 21 users.

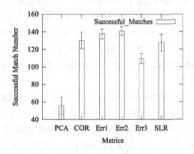

Fig. 9. Number of successful matches belonging to the 6 metrics

There are 150 (5 × 30) comparisons in 30 sets of experiments for one user. The correlation's average successful match number is 129.7, which corresponds

Table 3. Total match of all metrics

	PCA	Cor	Err1	Err2	Err3	SLR
Number	1200	2724	2890	2961	2304	2661
Rate	38.1 %	86.5 %	91.7 %	94 %	73.1 %	84.5 %

to the match rate of 86.5 %. RANSAC with error function 2 makes the largest number of successful matches (141), and the match rate is as high as 94 %. Among the 21 users, 20 user's RANSAC ERR2 successful match number exceeds that of other metrics, and only 1 user's SLR successful match number is higher than that of RANSAC ERR2. Table 3 lists the overall successful match number and the corresponding match rate for six metrics without applying the majority vote. We note that oscillation could happen during a user's eye movement. It means that users' eyes may move back, left, right, and then forward. Correlation is calculated by the eye point sequence. Such oscillation will impact the final correlation result. However, it brings little impact on fitting a line, since all these points are still distributed along the line. It could be a reason why fitting a line achieves higher match rate than correlation. Through the comparison, we identify that RANSAC ERR2 is the most effective and reliable metric for matching among the six metrics.

4.4 Security Evaluation

Since our authentication method requires no hand input, it is resistant to the smudge and keylogger attacks. We try to compromise it by mounting a shoulder surfing attack. When a user is authenticating, an "attacker" peeks the process from different angles around the user. However, the "attacker" cannot figure out the password no matter standing in the front of the user or facing the user's back. In such cases, the "attacker" can only see either the objects' movements on the screen or eye movement. We observe that the password could be stolen only if the "attacker" stands at a special position—the "attacker" stands very close to the user (less in a meter) and face to the user's one side so that the "attacker" can make slight turns to monitor both the user's eye movement and the objects' movements. But the user will notice the peek easily in such a special scenario. Thus, our authentication method can significantly reduce the vulnerability to shoulder surfing attacks.

To further evaluate the security of our proposed scheme, we ask 5 users to authenticate using incorrect passwords. Each user tries 15 incorrect passwords. These passwords are divided into 5 groups, one of which contains 3 passwords. Each password in the first group contains 0 correct digit. For example, if the correct password is "1-4-3-1-2", the incorrect passwords could be "2-3-1-3-1", "3-1-1-2-4", or "4-1-2-3-3". Each password in the second group contains 1 correct digit, each password in the third group contains 2 correct digits, and so forth. All incorrect passwords are generated randomly. In this set of experiments, all trails (75) fail as expected without matching relaxation. After matching relaxation is applied, there is still no false acceptance if the number of correct digits in a password is smaller than 4. The false acceptance could occur if an incorrect password contains 4 correct digits. However, as we discussed in Sect. 3.3, the false acceptance rate is merely 0.2 % given that matching relaxation is active.

5   Discussion

To provide a comprehensive view of this work, we discuss the limitations of this work and the potential future work in this section.

Like other applications leveraging face recognition and eye tracking techniques, our work depends on adequate light. It cannot accurately track a user's eyes in weak light or dark. We try to capture eye movements by leveraging the screen illumination in dark; however, the eye movements cannot be recorded. One possible solution is to use the infrared detector to capture the eye movements. Unfortunately, many current smartphones have not yet equipped with the infrared detector. We plan to explore this problem in the future.

Another limitation is that our method will cost longer time than passcode-based and pattern-based authentication. However, eye tracking authentication methods offer stronger security to resist those attacks discussed before. In addition, the time of conducting our authentication method for one time is about 9.6 seconds. It is shorter than the average time of existing works EyePIN (48.6 s) and EyePassShape (12.5 s) [7], which work with the assistance of desktop display.

When the eye points are clustered together, it is hard to tell the eye movement direction. A simple solution to this problem is that we just fail the authentication when either the x-range or y-range of eye points is less than a threshold. The threshold could vary from user to user.

This work is a first step towards applying the eye tracking technique in smartphone authentication. It may not be able to satisfy all because of individual difference. But it provides smartphone users a new authentication option for lowering the risks. With the development of hardware equipped on smartphone, e.g., higher resolution front camera, front infrared detector or front flash light, we believe that this authentication method can achieve higher accuracy within a shorter period.

6   Related Work

Biometric information, such as fingerprint, has been used in authentication. However, researchers have shown that a fingerprint-based authentication system could be defeated [17]. Moreover, an attacker may bypass the fingerprint-based authentication system using a carefully printed fingerprint image. Human behavioral biometrics have also been used for user authentication. Keystroke dynamics have been studied as a second-factor for user identification. Each individual shows unique rhythm during keypad tapping. Zahid et al. [27] extracted six features from a user's keystrokes for individual identification. In [6], neural network classifier is utilized to distinguish impostors from legitimate users when someone dials a phone number or types text.

An abundance of sensors equipped on a smartphone can provide much valuable information on a user's tapping behaviors. The sense data from multi-touch screen, accelerometer, orientation and compass is translated to a user's gesture in work [16]. The data is used to train a classifier which can decide whether a user is legitimate. Another work [8] collects touch pressure, size, X and Y coordinates, and time as the raw data, then uses Dynamic Time Warping (DTW) algorithm to decide whether the input data matches the legitimate user's pattern. GEAT [21] authenticates a user based on behavioral features, including finger velocity, device acceleration, and stroke time extracted from users' hand input. Zheng et al. [28] proposed an authentication method based on a four-feature combination (acceleration, pressure, size, and time). Their study indicates that the four-feature combination can effectively distinguish impostors from legitimate users. Different from other works, they used one-class classifier for user verification, which only needs the legitimate user's data in training. However, the work [20] reveals that it is feasible to highly increase the equal error rate of the classifiers, which could penetrate the second level authentication methods by utilizing the data from a general population of operation statistics.

Authentication based on eye tracking can be classified into two categories. The first authenticates a user using the biometric features of the user's eyes or eye movements. The second authenticates a user based on eye movement patterns.

The biometric authentication methods in the first category extract biometric features, e.g., the distance between two eyes, light reflection, and so on, to identify a user. These features belong to physical biometrics like fingerprint. Special hardware such as the eye tracker is needed for catching a user's biometric features. Usually, a calibration process will be launched before authentication, during which the user keeps head fixed in the front of the eye tracker and stays a certain distance from the device. Bednarik et al. [3] made the first step towards using eye movements as biometric identification. They found that the distance between eyes turns out to be the most discriminative and stable indicator. However, this feature does not truly reflect the behavioral properties of eyes. The best dynamic feature is the delta pupil size, which brings 60 % identification rate in this work. CUE [14] incorporates the individual and aggregated characteristics belonging to a scanpath. Using the combination of Oculomotor Plant Characteristics (OPC) and Complex Eye Movement (CEM) patterns, it can reduce the authentication error by 30 % comparing to using one of them. It can also achieve the highest False Rejection Rate (FRR) 18 % and False Acceptance Rate (FAR) 20 % at the same time. Holland and Komogortsev [12] evaluated the effects of stimulus types and eye tracking specifications on the accuracy of biometric verification based on CEM. The work [13] presents an objective evaluation of utilizing patterns identifiable in human eye movement to distinguish individuals. The authors hypothesized that the distribution of primitive features inherent in basic eye movements could be exploited to uniquely identify a given individual. However, these works are not applicable for portable devices because it is infeasible for a user to carry an eye tracker and conduct calibration in public places.

The methods in the second category leverages gaze points as the input. To use the authentication system proposed in [15], users input password by staring at corresponding buttons on the display. Researchers also proposed to use the trajectory of eye movement as password. Since recognizing a trajectory is much easier than identifying the gaze points, these methods do not need calibration process and high resolution eye tracker. De Luca et al. [9] evaluated three different eye gaze interaction methods. They also investigated an approach on gaze gestures and compared it to the well known gaze-interaction methods. The authors of work [10] introduced three types of password patterns-ShapePass, Eye Gesture and EyePass. ShapePass allows users to easily remember complex shapes, which consist of arbitrary combinations of eight basic strokes (eight directions). Eye gesture is constructed by different gaze tracks that represent different digits. EyePass is a combination of ShapePass and EyeGesture. They mentioned that the stroke perfectly fits human eye's biometric constraint because eyes move in fast and straight saccade, and thus cannot perform any curves or other non-linear shapes. EyePassShape [7] combines EyePin and PassShape. It requires a user to remember some shape and draw the shape via eye movement actively. Unfortunately, none of these works is applicable for smartphone users.

Some recent works reveal the feasibility of exploiting the eye tracking techniques for smartphone authentication. Drewes et al. [11] evaluated eye gaze interaction as a new input method on mobile phones with the assistance of eye tracker. They compared a dwell time based gaze interaction to the gaze gesture, and found that both methods are feasible on mobile phones. The work [22] presents the first prototype of eye gesture recognition system for portable devices. The system does not need any additional hardware. It incorporates techniques of image processing, computer vision, and pattern recognition to detect eye gestures in a video recorded by the device's front camera. Normalized correlation coefficient is used as the metric which brings about 60 % accuracy. Although eye gesture makes authentication robust, users cannot easily remember the complex eye gestures in practice. The work [23] introduces a novel set of shape features, which capture the characteristic shape of smooth pursuit movement over time. Each feature individually represents incomplete information about the smooth pursuit, but they can reflect the pursuit once combined. Pursuit [24] is proposed to recognize a user's eye movement when the user tracks a moving target on a big screen through eyes. It provides a general design guidance for pursuit applications.

7 Conclusion

In this paper, we propose an eye tracking authentication method for smartphone users. Unlike conventional user authentication on a smartphone, our scheme only needs a user to track a moving target on the screen through eyes. Thus, it is resistant to shoulder surfing attack, smudge attack, and many other attacks that infer a user's password based on the hand input information. In our design, the moving pattern consists of four basic strokes to reduce distraction as much as possible. Meanwhile, the object movement route is randomly changed to lower the risk of password leakage. We introduce six different metrics to measure the similarity between the eye movement trajectory and the target movement trajectory, and identify the most effective metric for development. To validate the efficacy of the proposed authentication approach, we implement a prototype on Android and conduct a user study with the help of 21 volunteers. The evaluation results show that our authentication method is able to achieve high accuracy.

References

1. https://developer.qualcomm.com/mobile-development/add-advanced-features/snapdragon-sdk-android
2. Aviv, A.J., Gibson, K., Mossop, E., Blaze, M., Smith, J.M.: Smudge attacks on smartphone touch screens. In: WOOT 2010, pp. 1–7. USENIX Association (2010)
3. Bednarik, R., Kinnunen, T., Mihaila, A., Fränti, P.: Eye-movements as a biometric. In: Kalviainen, H., Parkkinen, J., Kaarna, A. (eds.) SCIA 2005. LNCS, vol. 3540, pp. 780–789. Springer, Heidelberg (2005)
4. Berger, Y., Wool, A., Yeredor, A.: Dictionary attacks using keyboard acoustic emanations. In: ACM CCS 2006, pp. 245–254. ACM (2006)
5. Cai, L., Chen, H.: Touchlogger: Inferring keystrokes on touch screen from smartphone motion. In: Hot Topics in Security HotSec (2011)
6. Clarke, N.L., Furnell, S.M.: Authenticating mobile phone users using keystroke analysis. Int. J. Inf. Secur. $6(1)$, 1–14 (2006)
7. De Luca, A., Denzel, M., Hussmann, H.: Look into my eyes!: can you guess my password?. In: SOUPS 2009, pp. 7:1–7:12. ACM (2009)
8. De Luca, A., Hang, A., Brudy, F., Lindner, C., Hussmann, H.: Touch me once and I know it's you!: implicit authentication based on touch screen patterns. In: CHI 2012, pp. 987–996. ACM (2012)
9. De Luca, A., Weiss, R., Drewes, H.: Evaluation of eye-gaze interaction methods for security enhanced pin-entry. In: OZCHI 2007, pp. 199–202. ACM (2007)
10. De Luca, A., Weiss, R., Humann, H., An, X.: Eyepass-eye-stroke authentication for public terminals. In: Czerwinski, M., Lund, A.M., Tan, D.S. (eds.) CHI Extended Abstracts, pp. 3003–3008. ACM (2008)
11. Drewes, H., De Luca, A., Schmidt, A.: Eye-gaze interaction for mobile phones. In: Mobility 2007, pp. 364–371. ACM (2007)
12. Holland, C., Komogortsev, O.V.: Biometric verification via complex eye movements: the effects of environment and stimulus. In: Biometrics: Theory, Applications and Systems (BTAS), pp. 39–46, September 2012
13. Holland, C.D., Komogortsev, O.V.: Complex eye movement pattern biometrics: analyzing fixations and saccades. In: Proceedings of IAPR ICB (2013)
14. Komogortsev, O.V., Karpov, A., Holland, C.D.: Cue: counterfeit-resistant usable eye movement-based authentication via oculomotor plant characteristics and complex eye movement patterns, vol. 8371, pp. 83711X–83711X-9 (2012)
15. Kumar, M., Garfinkel, T., Boneh, D., Winograd, T.: Reducing shoulder-surfing by using gaze-based password entry. In: SOUPS 2007, pp. 13–19. ACM (2007)
16. Li, L., Zhao, X., Xue, G.: Unobservable re-authentication for smartphones. The Internet Society. In: NDSS (2013)

17. Matsumoto, T., Matsumoto, H., Yamada, K., Hoshino, S.: Impact of artificial "gummy" fingers on fingerprint systems, vol. 4677, pp. 275–289 (2002)
18. Miluzzo, E., Varshavsky, A., Balakrishnan, S., Choudhury, R.R.: Tapprints: your finger taps have fingerprints. In: MobiSys 2012, pp. 323–336. ACM (2012)
19. Owusu, E., Han, J., Das, S., Perrig, A., Zhang, J.: Accessory: password inference using accelerometers on smartphones. In: HotMobile 2012, pp. 9:1–9:6. ACM (2012)
20. Serwadda, A., Phoha, V.V.: When kids' toys breach mobile phone security. In: ACM CCS 2013, pp. 599–610. ACM (2013)
21. Shahzad, M., Liu, A.X., Samuel, A.: Secure unlocking of mobile touch screen devices by simple gestures: you can see it but you can not do it. In: MobiCom 2013, pp. 39–50. ACM (2013)
22. Vaitukaitis, V., Bulling, A.: Eye gesture recognition on portable devices. In: UbiComp 2012, pp. 711–714. ACM (2012)
23. Vidal, M., Bulling, A., Gellersen, H.: Detection of smooth pursuits using eye movement shape features. In: ETRA, pp. 177–180. ACM (2012)
24. Vidal, M., Bulling, A., Gellersen, H.: Pursuits: spontaneous interaction with displays based on smooth pursuit eye movement and moving targets. In: UbiComp 2013, pp. 439–448. ACM (2013)
25. Xu, Y., Heinly, J., White, A.M., Monrose, F., Frahm, J.: Seeing double: reconstructing obscured typed input from repeated compromising reflections. In: ACM CCS 2013, pp. 1063–1074. ACM (2013)
26. Xu, Z., Bai, K., Zhu, S.: Taplogger: inferring user inputs on smartphone touchscreens using on-board motion sensors. In: WISEC 2012, pp. 113–124. ACM (2012)
27. Zahid, S., Shahzad, M., Khayam, S.A., Farooq, M.: Keystroke-based user identification on smart phones. In: Kirda, E., Jha, S., Balzarotti, D. (eds.) RAID 2009. LNCS, vol. 5758, pp. 224–243. Springer, Heidelberg (2009)
28. Zheng, N., Bai, K., Huang, H., Wang, H.: You are how you touch: User verification on smartphones via tapping behaviors. In: IEEE ICNP (2014)
29. Zhuang, L., Zhou, F., Tygar, J.D.: Keyboard acoustic emanations revisited. ACM Trans. Inf. Syst. Secur. 13(1), 3:1–3:26 (2009)

Optimal Proximity Proofs Revisited

Handan Kılınç[✉] and Serge Vaudenay

EPFL, Lausanne, Switzerland
handan.kilinc@epfl.ch

Abstract. Distance bounding protocols become important since wireless technologies become more and more common. Therefore, the security of the distance bounding protocol should be carefully analyzed. However, most of the protocols are not secure or their security is proven informally. Recently, Boureanu and Vaudenay defined the common structure which is commonly followed by most of the distance bounding protocols: answers to challenges are accepted if they are correct and on time. They further analyzed the optimal security that we can achieve in this structure and proposed DBopt which reaches the optimal security bounds. In this paper, we define three new structures: when the prover registers the time of a challenge, when the verifier randomizes the sending time of the challenge, and the combined structure. Then, we show the optimal security bounds against distance fraud and mafia fraud which are lower than the bounds showed by Boureanu and Vaudenay for the common structure. Finally, we adapt the DBopt protocol according to our new structures and we get three new distance bounding protocols. All of them are proven formally. In the end, we compare the performance of the new protocols with DBopt and we see that we have a better efficiency. For instance, we can reduce the number of rounds in DB2 (one of the instances of DBopt) from 123 to 5 with the same security.

1 Introduction

Some important applications such as NFC-based payments, RFID access cards in our daily lives provide services according to the user's location. Relay attacks are serious threats against these applications. For instance, if someone makes a payment with a card on a malicious device then the device can relay to a fake card which is paying for something more expensive [13]. Similarly, a malicious person can open a car by relaying the communication between the wireless key and the car.

In [2], the fact that the speed of communication cannot be faster than the speed of light is used to detect relay attacks. Then, Brands and Chaum [7] introduced the notion of distance bounding (DB) protocols where a prover proves that he is close enough to a verifier. Simply, in distance bounding protocols, the verifier determines the proximity of the prover by computing the round

This work was partly sponsored by the ICT COST Action IC1403 Cryptacus in the EU Framework Horizon 2020.

© Springer International Publishing Switzerland 2015
T. Malkin et al. (Eds.): ACNS 2015, LNCS 9092, pp. 478–494, 2015.
DOI: 10.1007/978-3-319-28166-7_23

trip communication time in challenge/response rounds. The proximity proof is disincentive against relay attacks. The literature considers the following threat models:

- Distance Fraud (DF): A malicious prover far away from the verifier tries to convince him that he is close enough.
- Mafia Fraud (MF) [12]: A man-in-the-middle (MiM) adversary between a far away honest prover and a verifier relays or modifies the messages to make the verifier accept.
- Terrorist Fraud (TF) [12]: An adversary tries to make the verifier accept with the help of far away and malicious prover without gaining any advantage to later pass the protocol on his own.
- Impersonation fraud (IF) [1]: An adversary tries to impersonate the prover to the verifier.
- Distance Hijacking (DH) [11]: A far away prover takes advantage of some honest, active provers to make the verifier accept.

Some of the distance bounding protocols [7–9,15,18,20–22] have been broken since either their security were not proven formally or they do not have any security proofs. Amongst existing distance bounding protocols, only the SKI protocol [3–5], the Fischlin-Onete (FO) protocol [14,23] and the DBopt protocol [6] are formally proven to be secure against all above threats.

Boureanu and Vaudenay [6] formalize the threat models and propose a new distance bounding protocol DBopt which has three concrete instances DB1, DB2 and DB3. They give the definition of the "Common Structure" for the distance bounding protocols. A DB protocol in common structure consists of three phases: an initialization phase and a verification phase which do not depend on communication time, and a distance bounding phase between them. The distance bounding phase consists of number of rounds. In each round, the prover responds the challenge of the verifier. The verifier checks if the responses are on time and correct. DBopt follows the common structure and all instances have the security proofs against DF and MF. All but DB3 have a security proof for TF. The common structure is defined by four parameters: the number of rounds n, the minimal number of correct rounds τ, the cardinality num_c of the challenge set, and the cardinality num_r of the response set. The optimal security bounds for DB protocols that follow the common structure are given in [6]. All instances of DBopt have optimal security bounds against MF and all but DB2 have optimal security bounds against DF.

Random delays for the messages (challenges and responses) on both the verifier and the prover side in the distance bounding phase is used for location privacy as discussed in [17,19]. In this paper, we add random delays only on the verifier side and achieve better security bounds.

The contribution of this paper is as follows:

- We define three new structures for distance bounding protocols. Differently than the common structure [6], we suggest to add properties that the prover measures time like the verifier and the verifier sends challenge in a time that is randomly chosen.

- We show the optimal security bounds for each new structure. Compared to common structure [6], we obtain better security bounds.
- We modify DBopt protocol [6] according to the new structures and have new protocols DBoptSync, DBoptSyncRand and DBoptRand. We prove the security of them against DF, MF and IF (DH and TF resistance are unchanged compared to [6]). We reach the optimal security bounds for DF and MF for all of them in their respective structure.
- We analyse the performance of our new DB protocols and conclude that we have a better efficiency than previous works [3–6,14,23].

2 Definitions and Preliminaries

In this section, we recall the formal model of distance bounding protocols from [6].

Definition 1 (Distance Bounding Protocol). *A (symmetric) distance bounding protocol is a two party probabilistic polynomial time (PPT) protocol and consists of a tuple $(\mathcal{K}, P, V, B)$. Here, $\mathcal{K}$ is the key domain, P is the proving algorithm, V is the verifying algorithm where the inputs of P and V is from $\mathcal{K}$, and B is the distance bound. Given $x \in \mathcal{K}$, $P(x)$ and $V(x)$ interact with each other. At the end of the protocol, the verifier $V(x)$ sends a final message Out_V. If $\mathsf{Out}_V = 1$, then the verifier accepts. If $\mathsf{Out}_V = 0$, then the verifier rejects.*

In a DB protocol, apart from the prover and the verifier, there may exist other participants called adversaries. Each participant has instances and each instance has its own location. **P** denotes the set of instances of the prover, **V** denotes the set of the instances of the verifier and **A** denotes the set of the instances of the other participants.

Instances of an honest prover run the algorithm P denoted by $P(x)$. An instance of a malicious prover runs an arbitrary algorithm denoted by $P^*(x)$.

The verifier is always honest and its instances run the algorithm V denoted by $V(x)$.

The other participants are (without loss of generality) malicious. They may run any algorithm without no initialized key. $\mathcal{A}$ denotes a participant from **A**.

The locations of the participants are elements of a metric space.

Communication and Adversarial Model: The communication and adversarial model of a DB protocol [3] is the following:

DB protocols run in natural communication settings. There is a notion of time, e.g. time-unit, a notion of measurable distance and a location. Besides, timed communication follows the laws of physics, e.g., communication cannot be faster than speed of light.

An adversary can see all messages (whenever they reach him). He can change the destination of a message subject to constraints. Namely, a message sent by

U at time t to V can be corrupted by $\mathcal{A}$ at time t' if $t' + d(\mathcal{A}, V) \leq t + d(U, V)$ where d is a metric that shows the distance between its inputs. In addition, the adversary may have extra technology to correct the noise of the channel while honest participants cannot have it.

In fact, the adversary has very limited action because of the communication speed. For instance if the adversary relays the messages between the far away prover and the verifier, the responses arrive very late. Similarly if the adversary forces the far away prover for any online help, still he cannot succeed to respond correctly and on time. Basically, the adversary cannot break the laws of physics!

Definition 2 (DB Experiment). *An experiment* exp *for a distance bounding protocol with the tuple $(\mathcal{K}, P, V, B)$ is a setting $(\boldsymbol{P}, \boldsymbol{V}, \boldsymbol{A})$ with several PPT instances of participants, at some locations.*

We denote by $\mathsf{exp}(V)$ a distinguished experiment where we fix a verifier instance $\mathcal{V}$ called the distinguished verifier. Participants that are within a distance of at most B from $\mathcal{V}$ are called close-by participants. Others are called far-away participants.

Definition 3 (Common Structure [6]). *A DB protocol with the common structure based on parameters $(n, \tau, \mathsf{num}_c, \mathsf{num}_r)$ has some initialization and verification phases which do not depend on communication times. These phases are seperated by distance bounding phase which consists of n rounds of timed challenge/response exchanges. A* **response is called on time** *if the elapsed time between sending the challenge (by verifier) and receiving the response (by verifier) (See Fig. 1) is at most $2B$.* Provers do not measure the time. *Challenges and responses are in sets of cardinality num_c and num_r, respectively.*

When the protocol follows the specified algorithms but messages during the distance bounding phase can be corrupted during transmission, we say that the protocol is τ-complete if the verifier accepts if and only if at least τ rounds have a correct and on-time response.

In practice, the noise in the communication should be considered. We assume that there is probability of noise p_{noise} in one round of distance bounding phase. Therefore the probability that a number of τ responses are correct and on time in the case of a close-by prover is $\mathsf{Tail}(n, \tau, 1 - p_{\mathsf{noise}})$ where:

$$\mathsf{Tail}(n, \tau, \rho) = \sum_{i=\tau}^{n} \binom{n}{i} \rho^i (1 - \rho)^{n-i}$$

Accordingly, the probability to fail is negligible when $\frac{n}{\tau} < 1 - p_{\mathsf{noise}}$ due to the Chernoff-Hoeffding bound [10, 16].

We now give security definitions and theorems from [6] that show the optimal security bounds for the DB protocols following the common structure.

Definition 4. (α-resistance to Distance Fraud [6]). *The distance-bounding protocol α-resists to distance fraud if for any distinguished experiment $\mathsf{exp}(V)$ where there is no close participant to $\mathcal{V}$, the probability that $\mathcal{V}$ accepts is bounded by α.*

Theorem 1 ([6]). *A DB protocol following the common structure with parameters* $(n, \tau, \mathsf{num}_c, \mathsf{num}_r)$ *cannot* $\alpha-$*resists to distance fraud for* α *lower than* $\mathsf{Tail}(n, \tau, \max(\frac{1}{\mathsf{num}_c}, \frac{1}{\mathsf{num}_r}))$.

This is the optimal security bound that a DB protocol can reach against distance fraud. The DB1 and DB3 protocols from DBopt [6] reach this bound.

Definition 5 *(β-secure Distance Bounding Protocol [6])*. *We say that a distance-bounding protocol is β-secure if for any distinguished experiment* $\exp(V)$ *where the prover is honest, and the prover instances are all far away from* V *(the distance between the prover instances and* V *is more than B), the probability that* V *accepts is bounded by* β.

We recall that β-security captures the threat models MF, MiM and IF [6].

Theorem 2 ([6]). *A DB protocol following the common structure with parameters* $(n, \tau, \mathsf{num}_c, \mathsf{num}_r)$ *cannot be* $\beta-$*secure lower than* $\mathsf{Tail}(n, \tau, \max (\frac{1}{\mathsf{num}_c}, \frac{1}{\mathsf{num}_r}))$.

This is the optimal security bound that a DB protocol can reach against mafia fraud. All instances of DBopt protocols [6] reach this bound.

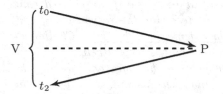
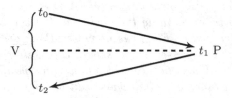

Fig. 1. The time check in the common structure is done by measuring the time difference between the curly parenthesis. t shows the time.

Fig. 2. The time check in the sync structure is done by measuring the time difference between the curly parentheses. t shows the time.

3   Optimal Distance Bounding Protocol with Almost Synchronized Parties

3.1   Definitions and Lemmas

Definition 6 *(Sync Structure)*. *A DB protocol with the sync structure based on parameters* $(n, \tau, \mathsf{num}_c, \mathsf{num}_r)$ *has some initialization and verification phase which do not depend on communication times. There is an n-round distance bounding phase between the initialization and verification phase. The* **challenge** *is on time if the elapsed time between sending the challenge (by verifier) and receiving the challenge (by prover) (Corresponds first part in Fig. 2) is at most*

B. *The **response is on time** if the elapsed time between sending the response (by prover) and receiving the response (by verifier) (Corresponds second part in Fig. 2) is at most B. Challenges and responses are in sets of cardinality* num_c *and* num_r*, respectively.*

*When the protocol follows the specified algorithms but messages during the distance bounding phase can be corrupted during transmission, we say that the protocol is τ-complete if the verifier accepts if and only if at least τ rounds have a correct and on-time **response and challenge**.*

The important difference between "Common Structure" and "Sync Structure" is that provers now need to measure time since the verifier needs to check if the challenge arrive on time to the prover.

Lemma 1. *Let* exp *be an experiment,* V *be a participant and t_0 be a time. We consider a simulation* exp_{t_0} *of the experiment in which each participant U stops just before time $t_0 + d(V, U)$. We denote by* $\mathsf{View}_t^{\mathsf{exp}}(U)$ *and* $\mathsf{View}_t^{\mathsf{exp}_{t_0}}(U)$ *the view of participant U at time t in* exp *and* exp_{t_0}*, respectively. For any $t < t_0 + d(V, U)$,*

$$\mathsf{View}_t^{\mathsf{exp}}(U) = \mathsf{View}_t^{\mathsf{exp}_{t_0}}(U).$$

Proof. We prove by induction on t that for all participant U such that $t < t_0 + d(V, U)$, $\mathsf{View}_t^{\mathsf{exp}}(U) = \mathsf{View}_t^{\mathsf{exp}_{t_0}}(U)$. Clearly this is the case at the beginning of the both experiments. If it is the case at any time less than or equal to $t - 1$, we can now prove it is the case at time t. Let participant U be such that $t < t_0 + d(V, U)$. We know that $\mathsf{View}_{t-1}^{\mathsf{exp}}(U) = \mathsf{View}_{t-1}^{\mathsf{exp}_{t_0}}(U)$. Any incoming message m at time t from a participant U' was sent at time $t' = t - d(U, U')$. We have $t' < t_0 + d(V, U) - d(U, U') \le t_0 + d(V, U')$. If U' is at a different location than U, we have $t' \le t - 1$ so we can apply the induction hypothesis. Therefore $\mathsf{View}_{t'}^{\mathsf{exp}}(U') = \mathsf{View}_{t'}^{\mathsf{exp}_{t_0}}(U')$ and so the message m is the same in exp and exp_{t_0}. This applies to all instances at the same location as U, since they locally compute the same messages for each other. Hence, $\mathsf{View}_t^{\mathsf{exp}}(U) = \mathsf{View}_t^{\mathsf{exp}_{t_0}}(U)$. □

Lemma 2. *Given an experiment, if a message c is randomly selected with fresh coins by a participant V at time t_0, any $\hat{c}$ received by a participant U at time $t_1 < t_0 + d(U, V)$ is statistically independent from c.*

Proof. We apply Lemma 1. c is not selected at all in exp_{t_0} because V stops just before t_0 in exp_{t_0}. Since $t_1 < t_0 + d(U, V)$, $\hat{c}$ is the same in exp and exp_{t_0}. c is randomly chosen with fresh coins, so $\hat{c}$ is statistically independent from c. □

Theorem 3. *Assuming the time when V sends his challenge can be predicted by the adversary, a $\tau-$complete DB protocol following the **sync structure** with parameters $(n, \tau, \mathsf{num}_c, \mathsf{num}_r)$ can not be β secure (Definition 5) for β lower than* $\mathsf{Tail}(n, \tau, \frac{1}{\mathsf{num}_c.\mathsf{num}_r})$*.*

Remark that this bound is an improvement compared to Theorem 2 in the common structure.

Proof. We consider $\mathcal{V}$, a far-away prover P and a MiM $\mathcal{A}$ with noiseless communication. $\mathcal{A}$ relays the messages between $\mathcal{V}$ and P in the initialization and verification phases which are time insensitive. During the challenge phase, $\mathcal{A}$ should arrange the response and the challenge time. Since P is far-away, he cannot just relay the messages. Therefore he should guess the challenge and the response before receiving them. We denote that the distance between $\mathcal{V}$ and $\mathcal{A}$ by d_1 and the distance between $\mathcal{A}$ and P by d_2. So it can do the following strategy:

No-ask Strategy: $\mathcal{A}$ can guess the response and the challenge and forward them before seeing them so that they arrive on time.

We assume that $\mathcal{A}$ knows the time t_0 that $\mathcal{V}$ sends the challenge c and he chooses a distance $d \leq B$. He guesses the challenge and sends it to P at time $t_0 + d - d_2$ so that P receives it at time t_1 where $t_1 = t_0 + d$. He guesses the response and sends $\mathcal{V}$ at time $t_0 + 2d - d_1$. $\mathcal{V}$ receives the response at time $t_2 = t_1 + d$. Since $t_1 - t_0 = d \leq B$ and $t_2 - t_1 = d \leq B$, the challenge and the response rounds are on time.

As a result, $\mathcal{A}$ can be successful on the verification of the challenge and the response time with no-ask strategy if he guesses both the challenge and response correctly. The probability that he passes the verification for one round is $\frac{1}{\text{num}_c \cdot \text{num}_r}$ and so the probability that the $\mathcal{V}$ accepts $\mathcal{A}$ is $\text{Tail}(n, \tau, \frac{1}{\text{num}_c \cdot \text{num}_r})$.

□

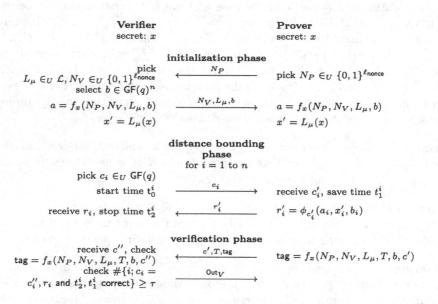

Fig. 3. The DBoptSync distance-bounding protocol

3.2 DBoptSync with Synchronized Parties

We propose a new distance bounding protocol DBoptSync described in Fig. 3 which uses the ideas in [6]. The assumption here is that the prover P and the verifier V have synchronized clocks.

DBoptSync is a symmetric distance bounding protocol in which P and V share a secret $x \in \mathbb{Z}_2^s$ where s is a security parameter. The notations are the folllowing: n is the number of rounds, ℓ_{tag} is the length of the tag, τ is a threshold, $\mathcal{T}$ is the set of all possible time values, q is a prime power.

As in DBopt, we use the function f_x which maps different codomains depending on the input. $f_x(N_P, N_V, L_\mu, b) \in GF(q)^n$ and $f_x(N_P, N_V, L_\mu, T, b, c) \in GF(q)^{\ell_{\text{tag}}}$. L_μ is a mapping defined from a vector $\mu \in \mathbb{Z}_2^s$ where $L_\mu(x) = (\mu(x), \mu(x), ..., \mu(x))$ and $\mu(x) = \text{map}(\mu.x)$ such that $\text{map} : \mathbb{Z}_2 \to GF(q)$ is an injection. Here $N_P, N_V \in \{0,1\}^{\ell_{\text{nonce}}}$, $L_\mu \in \mathcal{L}$ where $\mathcal{L}$ includes all possible L_μ mappings, $b, c \in GF(q)^n$ and $T \in \mathcal{T}^n$.

The *initialization phase* of the DBoptSync is the same as in the DBopt protocol [6]. The *distance bounding phase* is almost the same. The difference is that P saves the each time t_1^i that he receives the challenge c_i' from V at round i and V saves the times t_0^i and t_2^i that he sends the challenge c_i and he receives response r_i', respectively. In the *verification phase*, the prover sets $T = (t_1^1, t_1^2, ..., t_1^n)$ and $c' = (c_1', c_2', ..., c_n')$ and calculates the tag $f_x(N_P, N_V, L_\mu, T, b, c')$. Then he sends the tag and the verifier does the following:

– He checks if the tag and (c', T) are compatible which means the tag he received is equal to $f_x(N_P, N_V, L_\mu, T, b, c')$. If it is compatible, he does the next step. Otherwise he rejects P.
– V counts the number of correct rounds. A round is correct if $c_i' = c_i$ and $r_i' = r_i$. If the number of correct rounds are less then τ, he rejects P. Otherwise he continues with the next step.
– V checks the challenge and response time for each correct round i. The challenge and response time is correct if $t_0^i \leq t_1^i \leq t_2^i$, $t_1^i - t_0^i \leq B$ and $t_2^i - t_1^i \leq B$, respectively. If the number of timely and correct rounds is at least τ, then V accepts P. Otherwise, he rejects.

We note that the timely condition in DBoptSync implies $t_2^i - t_0^i \leq 2B$, which is the only verification done in DBopt [6]. Therefore, the DBoptSync's timely condition is more restrictive.

The responses are computed depending on the concrete instance of b and ϕ_{c_i}. There are three protocols defined in [6] whose instances are given in Table 1. Hence, DBoptSync has the same instances as well.

Theorem 4 (Security). *Assuming that V and P are synchronized, the DBopt-Sync protocol with the selection of b and ϕ as in Table 1 is $\beta-$secure,*

– *(DB1 and DB2)* $\beta = \text{Tail}(n, \tau, \frac{1}{q^2}) + \frac{r^2}{2} 2^{-\ell_{\text{nonce}}} + (r+1)\epsilon + r 2^{-\ell_{\text{tag}}}$ *when f is a (ϵ, K)-circular PRF (See Appendix A).*
– *(DB3)* $\beta = \text{Tail}(n, \tau, \frac{1}{q^2}) + \frac{r^2}{2} 2^{-\ell_{\text{nonce}}} + \epsilon + 2^{-\ell_{\text{tag}}}$ *when f is a (ϵ, K)-PRF.*

Here, r is the number of honest instances and K is a complexity bound on the experiment. β is negligible for $\frac{\tau}{n} \geq \frac{1}{q^2} + cte$ when r and K are polynomially bounded and ϵ is negligible.

Table 1. Classification of the protocols according the selection of b and ϕ in DBoptSync

Protocol	q	map	b	ϕ_{c_i}
DB1	$q > 2$	$\mathsf{map}(u) \neq 0$	no b used	$\phi_{c_i}(a, x_i', b_i) = a_i + c_i x_i'$
DB2	$q = 2$	$\mathsf{map}(u) = u$	Hamming weight $\frac{n}{2}$	$\phi_{c_i}(a, x_i', b_i) = a_i + c_i x_i' + c_i b_i$
DB3	$q \geq 2$	no map used	Hamming weight n	$\phi_{c_i}(a, x_i', b_i) = a_i + c_i b_i$

If ϵ, $2^{-\ell_{\mathsf{nonce}}}$ and $2^{-\ell_{\mathsf{tag}}}$ are negligible, DB1, DB2 and DB3 are **optimal** for the security according to Theorem 3.

Proof. The proof starts like in [6]. We consider a distinguished experiment $\exp(V)$ with no close-by participant and no adversary and V accepts with probability p. We consider a game Γ_0 where we simulate $\exp(V)$ and succeed if and only if V accepts P. So, the success probability of this game is p. We reduce Γ_1, Γ_2 and Γ_3 as in [6].

We reduce Γ_0 to Γ_1 whose success additionally requires that for every (N_P, N_V, L_μ) triplet there is no more than one instance $P(x)$ and one instance $V(x)$ using this triplet. Since $P(x)$ is honest and $P(x)$ and $V(x)$ are selecting N_P and N_V at random, respectively, so the success probability of Γ_1 is at least $p - \frac{r^2}{2} 2^{-\ell_{\mathsf{nonce}}}$.

Γ_2 is the reduction where Γ_1 and its success requires additionally that V does not accept forged tag. f_x satisfies the circular PRF assumptions (See Appendix A) as shown in [6]. It means that the tag can be forged with probability $\epsilon + 2^{-\ell_{\mathsf{tag}}}$. Therefore the success probability of Γ_2 is at least $p - \frac{r^2}{2} 2^{-\ell_{\mathsf{nonce}}} - r\epsilon - r2^{-\ell_{\mathsf{tag}}}$ (See [6] for the full proof of this step).

Now, in whole game Γ_2, we replace the oracle O_{x, f_x} by $O_{\tilde{x}, F}$ and obtain a simplified game Γ_3. Γ_3's requirements for the success is the same with Γ_2. So we have $\Pr_{\Gamma_3}[success] \geq p - \frac{r^2}{2} 2^{-\ell_{\mathsf{nonce}}} - (r+1)\epsilon - r2^{-\ell_{\mathsf{tag}}}$.

We now detail the analysis of Γ_3 which differs from [6]. In Γ_3, P and V never repeat the nonces and use a random function F to select a. So, the distinguished V has a single matching P and these two instances pick a at random. Furthermore, acceptance implies that both instances have seen the same L_μ, T, b, c. The acceptance message of V also depends on the correct and timely response and challenge. In the case that V accepts P, P has to receive the challenge c on time and V has to receive the corresponding response r on time for at least τ rounds. Let's denote t_0^i the time when V sends c_i, t_1^i the time when P receives c_i' and t_2^i is the time when V receives r_i. Thanks to Lemma 2, the challenge that $P(x)$ receives is independent from the challenge that is sent by $V(x)$, since the challenge c is randomly selected by $V(x)$, the message that $P(x)$ received matches with probability $\frac{1}{q}$.

Similarly, if we exchange the roles of P and V in Lemma 2 and replace t_0 with t_1^i and t_1 with t_2^i, we can conclude that r that $V(x)$ receives is independent from the response r_i' that is sent by $P(x)$ as well. The response functions on DB1, DB2 in each round i depends on challenge, a_i and x_i'. In Γ_3, a_i is random in $GF(q)^n$. Since $\phi_{c_i'}(a_i, x_i', b_i) = a_i + g(c_i', x_i', b_i)$ where g is a function (See Table 1 for the details of g) we can assume that a_i is randomly selected in $GF(q)$ just when r_i' is computed. Equivalently, r_i is uniformly selected in $GF(q)$ just before being sent. So, $r_i = r_i'$ with probability $\frac{1}{q}$.

To sum up, we have $p \leq \mathsf{Tail}(n, \tau, \frac{1}{q^2}) + \frac{r^2}{2}2^{-\ell_{\mathsf{nonce}}} + (r+1)\epsilon + r2^{-\ell_{\mathsf{tag}}}$.

If ϕ and b are as in $DB3$ [6], we lose $\frac{r^2}{2}2^{-\ell_{\mathsf{nonce}}}$ from Γ_0. In Γ_1, we apply full PRF reduction and lose ϵ to obtain Γ_2 with a random function. We lose $2^{-\ell_{\mathsf{tag}}}$ more to assume that tag is received by $\mathcal{V}$ was not forged in some Γ_3. Γ_3 succeeds with a probability bounded by $\mathsf{Tail}(n, \tau, \frac{1}{q^2})$ because of Lemma 1. In the end, we have $p \leq \mathsf{Tail}(n, \tau, \frac{1}{q^2}) + \frac{r^2}{2}2^{-\ell_{\mathsf{nonce}}} + \epsilon + 2^{-\ell_{\mathsf{tag}}}$ for DB3. $\square$

3.3   DBoptSync with Unsynchronized Verifier and Prover

DBoptSync assumes that the prover and the verifier have synchronized clocks. In this section, we discuss the problems of having unsynchronized clocks for P and $\mathcal{V}$ in the DBoptSync. Let's say that the time difference between the clocks of the verifier and prover is $|\delta|^1$. For example, $\mathcal{V}$ has time t on his local clock while P has time $T = t + \delta$ on his local clock. $\mathcal{V}$ sends the challenge at t_0 according to $\mathcal{V}$'s local clock and P receives it at $T_1 = t_0 + d_1 + \delta$ according to P's local clock. Then $\mathcal{V}$ receives the response at $t_2 \geq t_0 + 2d_1$. So $\mathcal{V}$ gets the following result in the verification of timing: $T_1 - t_0 = \delta + d_1$ and $t_2 - T_1 = d_1 - \delta$. If the prover is close, the inequality $|\delta| \leq B - d_1$ should be satisfied so that P passes the protocol.

In addition, unsynchronized honest prover and verifier give advantage to the adversary since he is able to do pre-ask (for $\delta > 0$) and post-ask (for $\delta < 0$). Indeed, if the honest prover is far at a distance up to $B + |\delta|$ and at least $\max(B, |\delta|)$, $\mathcal{A}$ passes the protocol with probability $\mathsf{Tail}(n, \tau, \max(\frac{1}{\mathsf{num}_c}, \frac{1}{\mathsf{num}_r}))$.

Note that $t_2^i - T_1^i \leq B$ and $T_1^i - t_0^i \leq B$ imply that $t_2^i - t_0^i \leq 2B$ which is what is described in DBopt [6]. So, the security result of [6] apply to our protocol even if the clocks are not synchronized.

Pre-ask: $\mathcal{A}$ guesses the challenge before it is released and asks for the response to P on time so that he can later on answer. If P and $\mathcal{V}$ are synchronized, this strategy never works because $\mathcal{A}$ relays the response from P to $\mathcal{V}$ where the distance between them is more than B. However the following happens if P and $\mathcal{V}$ are not synchronized and $\delta > 0$.

We consider $d_1 + d_2 \in [\max(B, |\delta|), B + |\delta|]$. $\mathcal{V}$ sends the challenge c at t_0. $\mathcal{A}$ guesses the challenge $\hat{c}$ and sends it to P at t_A to be determined which is before receiving the challenge from $\mathcal{V}$. P receives $\hat{c}$ at $T_1 = t_A + d_2 + \delta$ that is local time of P. P sends response r and $\mathcal{A}$ relays it and $\mathcal{V}$ receives r at $t_2 = t_A + 2d_2 + d_1$.

---

[1] If the difference between clocks is not constant it can be still considered as a constant during the protocol since the distance bounding phase takes very short time (order of nanoseconds).

$T_1 - t_0 = t_A + d_2 + \delta - t_0$. By selecting $t_A = t_0 + d_1 - 2\delta$, $T_1 - t_0 = d_1 + d_2 - \delta \in [0, B]$. So the challenge is considered on time.

$t_2 - T_1 = t_A + 2d_2 + d_1 - t_A - d_2 - \delta = d_1 + d_2 - \delta \in [0, B]$. So the response is considered on time.

Post-ask: $\mathcal{A}$ guesses the response at the same time he forwards the challenge to P. If P and $\mathcal{V}$ are synchronized, this strategy never works because $\mathcal{A}$ relays the challenge from $\mathcal{V}$ to P where the distance between them is more than B. However the following happens if P and $\mathcal{V}$ are not synchronized and $\delta < 0$.

We consider $d_1 + d_2 \in [-\delta, B - \delta]$. $\mathcal{V}$ sends the challenge c, then $\mathcal{A}$ relays c and P receives it at $T_1 = t_0 + d_1 + d_2 + \delta$. Without waiting the response from P, $\mathcal{A}$ guesses response and sends it at time t_A. So $\mathcal{V}$ receives it at $t_2 = t_A + d_1$.

$T_1 - t_0 = t_0 + d_1 + d_2 + \delta - t_0 = d_1 + d_2 + \delta \in [0, B]$. So the challenge is on time.

By selecting $t_A = t_0 + d_1 + 2d_2 + 2\delta$, we have $t_2 - T_1 = d_1 + d_2 + \delta \in [0, B]$. So the response is on time.

Therefore, there is an attack when the distance between P and $\mathcal{V}$ is in between $\max(B, |\delta|)$ and $B + |\delta|$.

As a result, we have the security bound of Theorem 4 if the distance between P and $\mathcal{V}$ is more than $B + |\delta|$ even though P and $\mathcal{V}$ are not synchronized. However if P is in the distance between B and $B + |\delta|$, we have the weaker security bound as in Theorem 2.

One of the important problems in DBoptSync with unsynchronized P and $\mathcal{V}$ is correctness, since the close-by P cannot pass the protocol, when $d(P, V) \leq B - |\delta|$. Therefore if the verification fails in DBoptSync, $\mathcal{V}$ can do the time verification of DBopt [6] which is checking if $t_2 - t_0 \leq 2B$, but in this case we have a weaker security which is as in DBopt. We stress that this does not require to restart the protocol. We rather obtain a variant of DBoptSync which Out_V can take 3 possible values: "reject", "DBopt accept", or "DBoptSync accept". Applications can decide if a "DBopt accept" is enough depending on the required security level.

4   Randomizing Sending Time of the Challenge

We think of a new modification to distance bounding protocols that are in either "Common Structure" or "Sync Structure". Before, we assumed that the sending time t_0^i of the challenge for each round i in distance bounding phase was known by the adversary. Now, we suggest a new modification where the verifier randomizes the sending time $t_0^i \in [T, T + \Delta]$ where T and Δ are public and t_0^i is uniformly distributed (as real numbers) so that the exact t_0^i cannot be accurately known by the adversary before seeing the challenge.

4.1   Definitions and Lemmas

Definition 7 (Rand Structure). *A DB protocol with the rand structure based on parameters $(n, \tau, \mathsf{num}_c, \mathsf{num}_r, \Delta)$ has the same properties with the <u>common</u>*

structure in Definition 3. Additionally, the verifier chooses randomly a sending time in the interval $[T, T + \Delta]$ for each challenge in the distance bounding phase.

Definition 8 (SyncRand Structure). *A DB protocol with the rand structure based on parameters* $(n, \tau, \mathsf{num}_c, \mathsf{num}_r, \Delta)$ *has the same properties with the sync structure in Definition 6. Additionally, the verifier chooses randomly a sending time in the interval* $[T, T + \Delta]$ *for each challenge in the distance bounding phase.*

Theorem 5. *A DB protocol following either the "Rand Structure" or the "SyncRand Structure" with parameters* $(n, \tau, \mathsf{num}_c, \mathsf{num}_r, \Delta)$ *cannot α-resists to distance fraud (DF) for α lower than* $\mathsf{Tail}(n, \tau, \max(\frac{1}{\mathsf{num}_c}, \frac{1}{\mathsf{num}_r}) \cdot \frac{2B}{\Delta})$.

Proof. We construct a DF following the early reply strategy: A malicious prover guesses the challenge c_i or the response r_i before it is emitted, and then already sends the response at time T_1^i (We use capital T since the prover does not have to be synchronized with the verifier). Therefore the prover has to guess proper time T_1^i to send the response because the verifier checks the inequalities $t_2^i - t_0^i \leq 2B$ for the "Rand Structure" and $T_1^i - t_0^i \leq B$ and $t_2^i - T_1^i \leq B$ for the "SyncRand Structure". t_2^i is the time that the verifier receives the response so it depends on the sending time T_1^i of response by the prover. It means that $0 \leq t_2^i - t_0^i = T_1^i + d - t_0^i \leq 2B$ where d is the distance between the prover and the verifier. So we can conclude that if $t_0^i \in [T_1^i + d - 2B, T_1^i + d]$ then P passes i^{th} verification. The probability that it happens is $\frac{2B}{\Delta}$. Once c is received, the prover can deduce t_0^i and use $t_1^i = \frac{t_0^i + t_2^i}{2}$ in the "SyncRand Structure" since verifier needs to know it to check if the response and challenge are on time. Therefore the probability that prover succeeds the round i is $\max(\frac{1}{\mathsf{num}_c}, \frac{1}{\mathsf{num}_r}) \cdot \frac{2B}{\Delta}$ since he also have to guess correctly c or r. We conclude that P succeeds at least τ rounds with probability at least $\mathsf{Tail}(n, \tau, \max(\frac{1}{\mathsf{num}_c}, \frac{1}{\mathsf{num}_r}) \cdot \frac{2B}{\Delta})$. $\square$

Note that in the "Rand Structure", there is no change on the optimal β which is given in Theorem 2. As for the "SyncRand Structure", the new bound is as follows.

Theorem 6. *A τ-complete DB protocol following the "SyncRand Structure" with parameters* $(n, \tau, \mathsf{num}_c, \mathsf{num}_r, \Delta)$ *cannot be β-secure for β lower than* $\mathsf{Tail}(n, \tau, \frac{1}{\mathsf{num}_c . \mathsf{num}_r} \cdot \frac{B}{\Delta})$.

Proof. We consider $\mathcal{V}$, a far away prover P and MiM $\mathcal{A}$ with noiseless communication. As showed in Theorem 3, $\mathcal{A}$ can use No-ask strategy to pass the protocol. Differently, he needs to guess proper time t_A^i to send guessed challenge to P. P receives the challenge from $\mathcal{A}$ at time t_1^i where $t_1^i = t_A^i + d_2$. If $\mathcal{A}$ passes i^{th} round, the following inequality $0 \leq t_1^i - t_0^i \leq B$ should be satisfied. It means that $0 \leq t_A + d_2 - t_0 \leq B$. If t_A satisfies this inequality then t_0 should be in the interval $[t_A + d_2 - B, t_A + d_2]$. The probability that it happens is $\frac{B}{\Delta}$. Therefore the probability that prover succeeds the round i is $\frac{1}{\mathsf{num}_c . \mathsf{num}_r} \cdot \frac{B}{\Delta}$ since he also have to guess correct c and r. We can conclude that P succeeds at least τ rounds with probability at least $\mathsf{Tail}(n, \tau, \frac{1}{\mathsf{num}_c . \mathsf{num}_r} \cdot \frac{B}{\Delta})$. $\square$

As a result of all the structures, "SyncRand Structure" gives the best optimal security bounds for both β-security and α-resistance. See Table 2 for the review of the optimal bounds for all of the structures.

Table 2. The review of optimal security bounds according to defined structures

Structure	DF	MF
Common	$\mathsf{Tail}(n, \tau, \max(\frac{1}{\mathsf{num}_c}, \frac{1}{\mathsf{num}_r}))$	$\mathsf{Tail}(n, \tau, \max(\frac{1}{\mathsf{num}_c}, \frac{1}{\mathsf{num}_r}))$
Sync	$\mathsf{Tail}(n, \tau, \max(\frac{1}{\mathsf{num}_c}, \frac{1}{\mathsf{num}_r}))$	$\mathsf{Tail}(n, \tau, \frac{1}{\mathsf{num}_c} \cdot \frac{1}{\mathsf{num}_r})$
Rand	$\mathsf{Tail}(n, \tau, \max(\frac{1}{\mathsf{num}_c}, \frac{1}{\mathsf{num}_r}) \cdot \frac{2B}{\Delta})$	$\mathsf{Tail}(n, \tau, \max(\frac{1}{\mathsf{num}_c}, \frac{1}{\mathsf{num}_r}))$
SyncRand	$\mathsf{Tail}(n, \tau, \max(\frac{1}{\mathsf{num}_c}, \frac{1}{\mathsf{num}_r}) \cdot \frac{2B}{\Delta})$	$\mathsf{Tail}(n, \tau, \frac{1}{\mathsf{num}_c} \cdot \frac{1}{\mathsf{num}_r} \frac{B}{\Delta})$

4.2 DBoptSyncRand and DBoptRand with Randomized Sending Time

We construct new distance bounding protocols DBoptSyncRand and DBoptRand. DBoptSyncRand follows the same steps as in DBoptSync and DBoptRand follows the same steps as in DBopt [6]. Differently in both of the protocols, the verifier randomizes the send time $t_0^i \in [T, T + \Delta]$ where T and Δ are public and t_0^i is uniformly distributed (as real numbers) for each round i in the distance bounding phase.

In Sect. 5, we consider $\Delta = 100B$. For instance, $\Delta = 1\mu s$ and $B = 10ns$ (this corresponds to $3\,\mathrm{m}$ according to speed of light). n rounds take n μs which is reasonable.

Theorem 7 *(Security).* *Assuming that $\mathcal{V}$ and P are synchronized, the sending time of the challenge is randomized and the time interval $[T, T + \Delta]$ to send the challenge is public. Then the DBoptSyncRand protocol is β−secure for*

- *(b and ϕ as in DB1 and DB2 [6])* $\beta = \mathsf{Tail}(n, \tau, \frac{1}{q^2} \cdot \frac{B}{\Delta}) + \frac{r^2}{2} 2^{-\ell_{\mathsf{nonce}}} + (r + 1)\epsilon + r 2^{-\ell_{\mathsf{tag}}}$ *when f is a (ϵ, K)-circular PRF [6].*
- *(b and ϕ as in DB3 [6])* $\beta = \mathsf{Tail}(n, \tau, \frac{1}{q^2} \cdot \frac{B}{\Delta}) + \frac{r^2}{2} 2^{-\ell_{\mathsf{nonce}}} + \epsilon + 2^{-\ell_{\mathsf{tag}}}$ *when f is a (ϵ, K)-PRF.*

Here, r is the number of honest instances of the prover and K is a complexity bound on the experiment and ϕ is response function. β is negligible for $\frac{\tau}{n} \geq \frac{1}{q^2} + cte$ and r and K polynomially bounded and ϵ is negligible.

If ϵ, $2^{-\ell_{\mathsf{nonce}}}$ and $2^{-\ell_{\mathsf{tag}}}$ are negligible, DB1, DB2 and DB3 are **optimal** for the security according to Theorem 6.

Proof. The proof is the same as Theorem 4 until game Γ_3. The success of Γ_3 depends on the correct and timely response and challenge. Lemma 2 shows that the challenge and the response have to be independent so that they arrive on time and these independent response and challenge can be correct with probability $\frac{1}{q^2}$ (See the proof of Theorem 4). Additionally, the independent challenge $\hat{c}$ is on time when the sending time is randomized, if $\hat{c}$ is sent on proper time. This proper time can be correct with probability $\frac{B}{\Delta}$ as showed in Theorem 6. Therefore the probability of one successful round is $\frac{1}{q^2} \cdot \frac{B}{\Delta}$.

Consequently, success probability Γ_0 is at least $\mathsf{Tail}(n, \tau, \frac{1}{q^2} \cdot \frac{B}{\Delta}) + \frac{r^2}{2} 2^{-\ell_{\text{nonce}}} + (r+1)\epsilon + r2^{-\ell_{\text{tag}}}$ for DB1 and DB2. For DB3, it is at least $\mathsf{Tail}(n, \tau, \frac{1}{q^2} \cdot \frac{B}{\Delta}) + \frac{r^2}{2} 2^{-\ell_{\text{nonce}}} + \epsilon + 2^{-\ell_{\text{tag}}}$. □

Theorem 8 *(DF-resistance). The DBoptSyncRand and DBoptRand protocols are $\alpha-$resistant to distance fraud for*

- *(DB1 and DB3)* $\alpha = \mathsf{Tail}(n, \tau, \frac{1}{q} \cdot \frac{2B}{\Delta})$.
- *(DB2)* $\alpha = \sum\limits_{\substack{i+j \geq \tau \\ i,j \leq n/2}}^{n} \binom{n/2}{i} (\frac{2B}{\Delta})^i (1 - \frac{2B}{\Delta})^{\frac{n}{2}-i} \binom{n/2}{j} (\frac{B}{\Delta})^j (1 - \frac{B}{\Delta})^{\frac{n}{2}-j}$.

DB1 and DB3 are **optimal** for the DF-resistance according to Theorem 5, while DB2 cannot reach the optimal bounds for DF.

Proof. We consider distinguished experiment $\exp(V)$ with no close-by participant. Due to the Fundamental Lemma in [6], the response r_i is independent (in the sense of Fundamental Lemma in [6]) from c_i. For DB1 and DB2, r_i is correct with probability $\frac{1}{q}$. Since r_i has to be arrived on time, the proper time has to be chosen. As stated in Theorem 5 the sending time is chosen correctly with probability $\frac{2B}{\Delta}$. So the probability of success in one round i is $\frac{1}{q} \cdot \frac{2B}{\Delta}$.

In DB2, half of the rounds where $x' = b_i$ are correct because of the hamming weight of b. Therefore, the only necessity in these rounds is sending the response in correct time which can be chosen well with probability $\frac{2B}{\Delta}$. For the remaining rounds ($\frac{n}{2}$ rounds), at least $\tau - \frac{n}{2}$ rounds should pass correctly. The correct response is chosen with the probability $\frac{1}{2}$ and correct time with the probability $\frac{2B}{\Delta}$. □

5 Performance

Three new protocols DBoptSync DBoptSyncRand and DBoptRand have different success probabilities for distance fraud and mafia fraud. DBoptSync and DBoptSyncRand have better bound against mafia fraud compared to DBopt while DBoptRand has the same security against mafia fraud with DBopt. In addition, DBoptRand and DBoptSyncRand have the same and better success probability for distance fraud compared to DBopt but DBoptSync is same with DBopt.

Assuming a noise level of $p_{\text{noise}} = 0.05$ and $\frac{B}{\Delta} = 0.01$, we get the results in Tables 3 and 4. We find τ in terms of rounds n such that $\mathsf{Tail}(n, \tau, 1 - p_{\text{noise}}) \approx 99\%$ for $\tau-$completeness. Table 3 shows the required number of rounds for distance fraud i.e. $\alpha \leq s$. Table 4 shows the number of rounds required for the security i.e. $\beta \leq s$. We used Theorems 4, 7 and 8 and theorems in [6] to compute the required number of rounds to achieve security level.

Table 3. Number of required rounds to be secure against distance fraud where s is the security level in DB protocols. The bold protocols improve DBopt

	$s = 2^{-10}$				$s = 2^{-20}$			
	DB1	DB1	DB2	DB3	DB1	DB1	DB2	DB3
	$(q = 3)$	$(q = 4)$			$(q = 3)$	$(q = 4)$		
DBoptSync	14	12	69	24	24	20	123	43
DBoptSyncRand	3	3	2	3	6	6	2	6
DBoptRand	3	3	2	3	6	6	2	6
DBopt	14	12	69	24	24	20	123	43

Table 4. Number of required rounds to be secure against mafia fraud where s is the security level in DB protocols. The bold protocols improve DBopt

	$s = 2^{-10}$			$s = 2^{-20}$		
	DB1	DB1	DB2-DB3	DB1	DB1	DB2-DB3
	$(q = 3)$	$(q = 4)$		$(q = 3)$	$(q = 4)$	
DBoptSync	7	6	12	12	8	20
DBoptSyncRand	3	1	3	5	5	5
DBoptRand	14	12	24	24	20	43
DBopt	14	12	24	24	20	43

As we can see in Tables 3 and 4, we can use DB2 with 5 rounds (instead of 123) in DBoptSyncRand and reach a pretty good security. If synchronized clocks are not realistic, we can see that we have a much better DF-security with DBoptRand with the same number of rounds.

6   Conclusion

We define new structures for DB protocols which are not used before. The first structure is the "Sync Structure" where the prover measures the time as well as the verifier. We modify the DBopt [6] according to sync structure and we get DBoptSync which has better security against mafia fraud. Then we add new modification which is randomizing the sending challenge time to both "Common Structure" and "Sync Structure" and get the second and third structures "Rand Structure" and "SyncRand Structure", respectively. Similarly, we modify the DBopt and DBoptSync protocols based on these structures and get better security bounds against distance fraud for the DBoptSyncRand and DBoptRand protocols and mafia fraud for DBoptSyncRand protocol. We give the optimal security bounds against distance fraud and mafia fraud for all DB protocols that follows the new structures.

A   Circular-Keying PRF

The notion of circular-keying in pseudorandom functions introduced in [4,5]. It is necessary to use circular-keying PRF in our protocols to prove security against MiM attacks. Circular-keying PRF has an extra assumption to the PRF $(f_x)_{x \in GF(q)^s}$ to handle reuse of a fixed x outside of a PRF instance f_x.

Definition 9 (Circular PRF [6]). *Let be s, n_1, n_2 and q some parameters. An oracle $O_{\tilde{x},F}$ is defined as $O_{\tilde{x},F}(y, L, A, B) = A \cdot L(\tilde{x}) + B \cdot F(y)$, using dot product over $GF(q)$, given $L : \{0,1\}^s \to GF(q)^{n_1}$ and $F : \{0,1\}^* \to GF(q)^{n_2}$. We assume that L is taken from a set of functions with polynomially bounded representation. Let $(f_x)_{x \in GF(q)^s}$ be a family of functions from $\{0,1\}^*$ to $\{0,1\}^{n_2}$. The family f is a (ϵ, K)-circular-PRF if for any distinguisher having K complexity, if the probability of distinguishing $O_{x,f_x}, x \in \{0,1\}^s$ from $O_{\tilde{x},F}$ is bounded by $\frac{1}{2} + \epsilon$. Additionally, we require two conditions on the list of queries:*

– for any pair of queries (y, L, A, B) and (y', L', A', B'), if $y = y'$, then $L = L'$.
– for any y, if (y, L, A_i, B_i), $i = 1, 2, ..., \ell$ is the list of queries using this value y, then $\forall \lambda_1, \lambda_2, ..., \lambda_\ell \in GF(q)$

$$\sum_{i=1}^{\ell} \lambda_i B_i \Rightarrow \sum_{i=1}^{\ell} \lambda_i A_i = 0$$

over the $GF(q)$-vector space $GF(q)^{n_2}$ and $GF(q)^{n_1}$.

References

1. Avoine, G., Tchamkerten, A.: An efficient distance bounding RFID authentication protocol: balancing false-acceptance rate and memory requirement. In: Samarati, P., Yung, M., Martinelli, F., Ardagna, C.A. (eds.) ISC 2009. LNCS, vol. 5735, pp. 250–261. Springer, Heidelberg (2009)
2. Beth, T., Desmedt, Y.: Identification tokens or: solving the chess grandmaster problem. In: Menezes, A.J., Vanstone, S.A. (eds.) Advances in Cryptology-CRYPTO 1990. LNCS, vol. 537, pp. 169–176. Springer, Heidelberg (1991)
3. Boureanu, I., Mitrokotsa, A., Vaudenay, S.: Secure and lightweight distance-bounding. In: Avoine, G., Kara, O. (eds.) LightSec 2013. LNCS, vol. 8162, pp. 97–113. Springer, Heidelberg (2013)
4. Boureanu, I., Mitrokotsa, A., Vaudenay, S.: Towards secure distance bounding. In: Moriai, S. (ed.) FSE 2013. LNCS, vol. 8424, pp. 55–68. Springer, Heidelberg (2014)
5. Boureanu, I., Mitrokotsa, A., Vaudenay, S.: Practical and Provably Secure Distance-Bounding. IOS Press, Amsterdam (2015)
6. Boureanu, I., Vaudenay, S.: Optimal proximity proofs. In: Lin, D., Yung, M., Zhou, J. (eds.) Inscrypt 2014. LNCS, vol. 8957, pp. 170–190. Springer, Heidelberg (2015)
7. Brands, S., Chaum, D.: Distance bounding protocols. In: Helleseth, T. (ed.) EUROCRYPT 1993. LNCS, vol. 765, pp. 344–359. Springer, Heidelberg (1994)
8. Bussard, L., Bagga, W.: Distance-bounding proof of knowledge to avoid real-time attacks. In: Sasaki, R., Qing, S., Okamoto, E., Yoshiura, H. (eds.) Security and Privacy in the Age of Ubiquitous Computing. IFIP AICT, vol. 181, pp. 223–238. Springer, Heidelberg (2005)

9. Capkun, S., Buttyan, L., Hubaux, J.-P.: Sector: secure tracking of node encounters in multi-hop wireless networks. In: ACM Workshop on Security of Ad Hoc and Sensor Networks (SASN), pp. 21–32 (2003)
10. Chernoff, H.: A measure of asymptotic efficiency for tests of a hypothesis based on the sum of observations. Ann. Math. Stat. **23**, 493–507 (1952)
11. Cremers, C., Rasmussen, K.B., Schmidt, B., Capkun, S.: Distance hijacking attacks on distance bounding protocols. In: 2012 IEEE Symposium on Security and Privacy (SP), pp. 113–127. IEEE (2012)
12. Desmedt, Y.: Major security problems with the unforgeable (Feige-) Fiat-Shamir proofs of identity and how to overcome them. In: Congress on Computer and Communication Security and Protection Securicom 1988, pp. 147–159. SEDEP, Paris (1988)
13. Drimer, S., Murdoch, S.J.: Keep your enemies close: distance bounding against smartcard relay attacks. In: USENIX Security (2007)
14. Fischlin, M., Onete, C.: Terrorism in distance bounding: modeling terrorist-fraud resistance. In: Jacobson, M., Locasto, M., Mohassel, P., Safavi-Naini, R. (eds.) ACNS 2013. LNCS, vol. 7954, pp. 414–431. Springer, Heidelberg (2013)
15. Hancke, G.P., Kuhn, M.G.: An RFID distance bounding protocol. In: First International Conference on Security and Privacy for Emerging Areas in Communications Networks, SecureComm 2005, pp. 67–73. IEEE (2005)
16. Hoeffding, W.: Probability inequalities for sums of bounded random variables. J. Am. Stat. Assoc. **58**(301), 13–30 (1963)
17. Mitrokotsa, A., Onete, C., Vaudenay, S.: Location leakage in distance bounding: why location privacy does not work. Comput. Secur. **45**, 199–209 (2014)
18. Munilla, J., Peinado, A.: Distance bounding protocols for RFID enhanced by using void-challenges and analysis in noisy channels. Wirel. Commun. Mob. Comput. **8**(9), 1227–1232 (2008)
19. Rasmussen, K.B., Čapkun, S.: Location privacy of distance bounding protocols. In: Proceedings of the 15th ACM Conference on Computer and Communications Security, pp. 149–160. ACM (2008)
20. Reid, J., Nieto, J.M.G., Tang, T., Senadji, B.: Detecting relay attacks with timing-based protocols. In: Proceedings of the 2nd ACM Symposium on Information, Computer and Communications Security, pp. 204–213. ACM (2007)
21. Singelée, D., Preneel, B.: Distance bounding in noisy environments. In: Stajano, F., Meadows, C., Capkun, S., Moore, T. (eds.) ESAS 2007. LNCS, vol. 4572, pp. 101–115. Springer, Heidelberg (2007)
22. Tu, Y.-J., Piramuthu, S.: RFID distance bounding protocols. In: First International EURASIP Workshop on RFID Technology, pp. 67–68 (2007)
23. Vaudenay, S.: On modeling terrorist frauds. In: Susilo, W., Reyhanitabar, R. (eds.) ProvSec 2013. LNCS, vol. 8209, pp. 1–20. Springer, Heidelberg (2013)

Malware Analysis and Side Channel Attacks

Replacement Attacks: Automatically Impeding Behavior-Based Malware Specifications

Jiang Ming[1]($\boxtimes$), Zhi Xin[2], Pengwei Lan[1], Dinghao Wu[1], Peng Liu[1], and Bing Mao[2]

[1] The Pennsylvania State University, University Park, State College, PA 16802, USA
{jum310,pul139,dwu,pliu}@ist.psu.edu
[2] Nanjing University, Nanjing 210093, China
{zxin,maobing}@nju.edu.cn

Abstract. As the underground market of malware flourishes, there is an exponential increase in the number and diversity of malware. A crucial question in malware analysis research is how to define malware specifications or signatures that faithfully describe similar malicious intent and clearly stand out from other programs. It is evident that the classical syntactic signatures are insufficient to defeat state-of-the art malware. Behavior-based specifications which capture real malicious characteristics during runtime, have become more prevalent in anti-malware tasks, such as malware detection and malware clustering. This kind of specification is typically extracted from system call dependence graphs that a malware sample invokes. In this paper we present *replacement attacks* to poison behavior-based specifications by concealing similar behaviors among malware variants. The essence of the attacks is to replace a behavior specification to its semantically equivalent one, so that similar malware variants within one family turn out to be different. As a result, malware analysts have to put more efforts to re-analyze similar samples. We distill general attacking strategies by mining more than 5,000 malware samples' behavior specifications and implement a compiler-level prototype to automate replacement attacks. Experiments on 960 real malware samples demonstrate effectiveness of our approach to impede multiple malware analyses based on behavior specifications, such as similarity comparison and malware clustering. In the end, we provide possible counter-measures to strengthen behavior-based malware analysis.

1 Introduction

Malware, or malicious software with harmful intent to compromise computer systems, is one of the major challenges to the Internet. Over the past years, the ecosystem of malware has evolved dramatically from "for-fun" activities to a profit-driven underground market [3], where malware developers sell their products and cyber-criminals can simply purchase access to tens of thousands of malware-infected hosts for nefarious purposes [1]. Normally malware developers do not write new code from scratch, but choose to update old code with new features or obfuscation methods [23]. With thousands of malware instances

© Springer International Publishing Switzerland 2015
T. Malkin et al. (Eds.): ACNS 2015, LNCS 9092, pp. 497–517, 2015.
DOI: 10.1007/978-3-319-28166-7_24

appearing every day, efficiently processing large quantity of malware samples which exhibit similar behavior, has become increasingly important. A key step to improve efficiency is to define discriminative specifications or signatures that faithfully describe intrinsic malicious intents, so that malware samples with similar functionalities tend to share common specifications. Malware analysts benefit from general specifications. For example, every time a suspicious program is found in the wild, malware analysts can quickly determine whether it belongs to a previous known family by matching its specification.

As malware keeps evolving to evade detection, the classical syntactic specifications are insufficient to defeat various obfuscation techniques, such as polymorphism [21], binary packing [31] and self-modifying code [12]. In contrast, behavior-based specifications, which are generated during malware execution, are more resilient to static obfuscation methods and able to disclose the natural behavior of malware, such as replication, download and execution and remote injection. The main means for malware to interact with an operating system is through system calls[1]. The dataflow dependencies among system calls are expressed as an acyclic graph, namely system calls dependency graph (SCDG), where nodes represent system calls executed and a directed edge indicates a data flow between two nodes. Typically, the dependencies derive from the return value or the arguments computed by previous system calls. When a data source is passed to one of its succeeding native APIs, a directed edge connecting these two nodes is created. Since data flow dependencies are hard to be reordered, SCDG has been broadly accepted as a reliable abstraction of malware behavior [15, 18], and widely employed in malware detection [6,20] and malware scalable clustering [7,28].

With quite a number of compelling applications, SCDG looks promising. However, it is not impossible to circumvent. In order to inspire more state-of-the-art malware analysis techniques, we exploit the limitations of the current approaches and present *replacement attacks* against malware behavior specifications. We show that *it is possible to automatically conceal similar behavior specifications among malware variants by replacing a SCDG to its semantically equivalent one, so that similar malware variants show large distances and therefore are assigned to different families.* Eventually, malware analysts have to re-analyze large number of malware samples exhibiting similar functionalities. To achieve this goal, we first mine two large data sets to identify popular system calls and OS objects dependencies. We summarize two general attacking strategies to replace SCDG: (1) mutate a sequence of dependent system calls (sub-SCDG) to its equivalent ones, and (2) insert redundant data flow dependent system calls. Our approach ensures that the new generating dependence relationships are so common that they cannot be easily recognized. After transformation, similar malware samples reveal large distance when they are measured with widely used similarity metrics, such as graph edit distance [13] or Jaccard Index [11]. As a result, subsequent analyses (e.g., malware detection and clustering) are misled.

---

[1] The systems call in Windows NT is called as native API.

To demonstrate the feasibility of replacement attacks, we have developed a compiler-level prototype, *API Replacer*, to automatically perform transformation on top of the LLVM framework [22] and Microsoft Visual Studio. Given a single malware source code, API Replacer is able to generate multiple malware binaries, and each one exhibits different behavior specifications. We evaluate our replacement attacks on a variety of real malware samples with different replacement ratio. Our experimental result shows that our approach successfully impede malware similarity comparison and state-of-the-art behavior-based malware clustering. The cost of transformation is low and the execution overhead after transformation is moderate.

In summary, we make the following contributions:

- We propose replacement attacks to camouflage similar behavior specifications among malware variants by replacing system call dependence graphs.
- We summarize the rules for equivalent replacements by mining large set of malware samples. The distilled attacking strategies tangle structure of system call dependency as well as behavior feature set without affecting semantics.
- We automate replacement attacks by developing a compiler-level prototype to perform source to binary transformation. The experimental results demonstrate our approach is effective.
- To the best of our knowledge, we are the first one to demonstrate the feasibility of automatically obfuscating behavior based malware clustering on real malware samples.

The rest of the paper is organized as follows. Section 2 introduces previous work on behavior based malware analysis. Section 3 describes in detail about how to generate replacement attacks rules with a case study. Section 4 highlights some of our implementation choices. We present the evaluation of our approach in Sect. 5. Possible counter-measures are discussed in Sect. 6 and we conclude the paper in Sect. 7.

2   Related Work

In this section we first present previous work on behavior based malware analysis, which is related to our work in that their methods rely on system call sequences or graphs that a malware sample invokes. Then, we introduce previous research on impeding malware dynamic analysis. In principle, our approach belongs to this category. At last we describe related work on system call API obfuscation, which is close in spirit to our approach.

Behavior Based Malware Analysis. Malware dynamic analysis techniques are characterized by analyzing the actual executing instructions of a program or the effects that this program brings to the operating system. Compared with static technique, dynamic analysis is less vulnerable to various code obfuscation [26]. Christodorescu et al. [15] introduce malware specifications on data-flow dependencies among system calls, which capture true relationships between system calls and are hard to be circumvented by random system call injection. Since then, such malware specifications based on SCDG have been widely used in malware analysis tasks, such as extracting malware discriminative feature by mining the difference between malware behavior and benign program behavior [18], determining malware family in which instances share common functionalities [6,7,28], and detecting malicious behavior [8,20,25]. However, none of the presented approaches is explicitly designed to be resilient to our replacement attacks.

Anti-malware Behavior Analysis. Some countermeasures have been proposed to evade behavior based malware analysis. Since malware behavior analysis is typically performed in a controlled sandbox environment, the lion's share of previous work focus on run time environment detection [14,27]. If a malware sample detects itself running in a sandbox rather than real physical machine, it will not carry out any malicious behaviors. To defeat environment-sensitive malware, Dinaburg et al. [17] build a transparent analysis platform, which remains invisible to such sandbox environment check. Another direction relies on contrasting different executions of a malware sample when running in multiple sandboxes. The control flow deviations may indicate evasion attempts [19]. Our method does not detect sandbox and is valid in any run time environment. Our replacement attacks shares similar idea to subvert malware clustering with recent work [9,10]. Our work is different from these previous works in that we attempt to obfuscate data flow dependencies between system calls, while the behavior features these works attack contain no data flow dependencies. As data relationships between behavior features are hard to be affected by random noise insertion, our attacking method is more challenging. Furthermore, these work evaluated their attacks by directly manipulating malware behavior feature set instead of malware code, which means their attacks may not be feasible in practice. In contrast, to demonstrate the feasibility of replacement attacks, we develop a compiler-level converter to transform malware source code to binary.

System Call Obfuscation. The original idea to obfuscate system call API can be traced to *mimicry attack* against intrusion detection [35]. *Illusion* [34] allows user-level malware to invoke kernel operations without calling the corresponding system calls. To launch the *Illusion* attack, the attacker has to install a malicious kernel module, which is not practical in many real attacking scenarios. Ma et al. [24] present *shadow attacks* by partitioning a malware sample into multiple shadow precesses and each shadow process presents no-recognizable malware behavior. But it's still an open question to launch a multi-process malware sample covertly. Our proposed attack is inspired by Xin et al. [37]'s approach to subvert behavior based software birthmark. However, their attacking method is restricted to replacing a dependency edge with a new vertex and two new edges. As shown in Sect. 5.2, this simple attacking method only has limited effect on reducing Jaccard Index. In contrast, our approach provides multiple attacking strategies. In addition, Xin et al. [37]'s attack code is pre-loaded as a dynamic library when the program starts running. The drawback is it's quite easy to detect such library interruption. Our *API Replacer* embeds newly added system calls into the native code transparently, so that our approach has better stealth.

3 Replacement Attacks Design

3.1 Overveiw

In spite of various metamorphic or polymorphic obfuscation, malware samples within the same family tend to reveal similar malicious behavior [23]. Our goal in this paper is to separate similar malware variants by replacing SCDG, the most prevalent expression to represent malware behavior specifications. Figure 1 shows an example of SCDG before/after replacement attacks. At the top of Fig. 1, we list pseudo code fragment written in MSVC for ease of understanding. In the original SCDG, the return value of "NtCreateFile" is a FileHandle ("hFile1"), denoting the new created file object. As hFile1 is passed to "NtClose", a data flow dependency connects "NtCreateFile → NtClose". Windows API "SetFile-Pointer" in the new code moves the file pointer and returns new position, which is quite similar to "lseek" system call in Unix. The return value of "SetFile-Pointer" is equal to moving distance plus the offset of starting point, which is 0 ("FILE_BEGIN") in this example. We exploit the fact that the data type of "hFile1" and the distance to move are both unsigned integers, and deliberately assign the distance to move with the same value of "hFile1" (line 2 in the new code). As a result, the return value of "SetFilePointer" ("dwFilePosition"), is equal to the "hFile1". Then "dwFilePosition" is passed to "NtClose" to close the file. When calling "SetFilePointer", native API "NtSetInformationFile" is invoked to change the position information of the file object represented by "hFile1". In this way, the new code still preserves the original data flow, while the SCDG changes significantly. Note that compared with the original code, the file object is updated with new position information. However, the file object is closed immediately, imposing no lasting side effect to the final state.

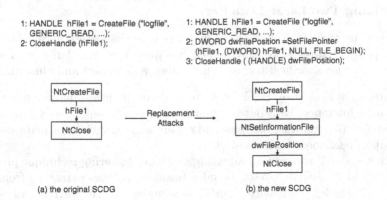

Fig. 1. An example of SCDG before and after replacement attacks

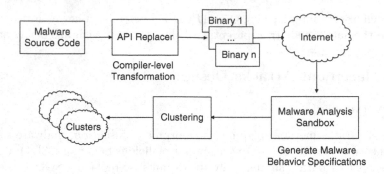

Fig. 2. Illustration of replacement attacks

A typical scenario to apply replacement attacks is illustrated in Fig. 2. Taking malware source code as input to API Replacer, our compiler-level transformation tool, malware authors generate multiple binary mutations of the initial version. Each mutation shares similar malicious functionalities, but exhibits different behavior specifications. Then cyber-criminals spread these malware samples to the Internet or plant them in the live vulnerable hosts. Suppose these transformed malware samples, with other suspicious binaries are finally collected by anti-malware companies. To process large number of malware samples, anti-malware companies utilize automated clustering tools to identify samples with similar behavior. These tools execute malware instances in a sandbox and collect run time information to generate behavior specifications, which will be normalized and then fed to clustering algorithm. As we mentioned in Sect. 2, current malware clustering tools are not designed to explicitly resist replacement attacks, therefore similar malware mutations after replacement attacks are probably assigned to different clusters. In that case, malware analysts have to waste excessive efforts to re-analyze these similar samples.

3.2 Mining Two Large Data Sets

Since there are various expressions of malware behavior based on SCDG, to find out the possible targets we may attack, we first mine two large data sets of malware behavior specifications used for malware detection and clustering.

- BRS-data [6] is used by Babić et al. to evaluate malware detection with tree automata inference. BRS-data contains system calls dependency graphs generated for 2631 malware samples and covers a large variety of malware, such as trojan, backdoor, worm, and virus.
- BCHKK-data [7] is used for evaluating malware clustering technique proposed by Bayer et al. BCHKK-data includes behavior profiles extracted from 2658 malware samples, and more than 75 % samples are the variants of Allaple worm. Note that SCDG is not amenable to scalable clustering techniques, which usually operate on numerical vectorial feature set. Bayer et al. converted

system call dependencies to a set of features in terms of operations (create, read, write, map, etc.) on OS objects (file, registry, process, section, thread, etc.) and dependencies between OS objects.

These two data sets reflect two typical applications of SCDG to represent malware specifications: (1) directly utilize rich structural information contained in SCDG [15,18,29], which is able to match behavioral patterns exactly but lacks of scalability; (2) extract higher level abstractions from SCDG to fit for efficient large-scale malware analysis [7,8,30] at the cost of precision. The similarity of BRS-data is normally measured by graph edit distance or graph isomorphism [13], while the similarity metrics of BCHKK-data is calculated by Jaccard Index [11].

Popular Dependencies. We calculate popular native API dependencies from BRS-data and OS operations and dependencies from BCHKK-data. Table 1 lists 11 popular native API dependencies out of BRS-data, which are mainly related to the operations on Windows registry, memory and file system. The second column is the medium data flow types passed between system calls. Most of the medium types are handles, which stands for various OS objects such as file, registry, section (memory-mapped file), process, etc. Table 2 presents popular OS object types, operations and dependencies from BCHKK-data. We believe as long as we diversify these popular dependencies and behavior features, the similarity among malware mutations can drop significantly.

Common Sub-SCDGs. Although extracted from different sources, these data reveal some common malicious functions, which are mapped to sub-SCDGs. The top 3 popular sub-SCDGs are corresponding to malware replication, registry modification for persistence and code remote injection. For example, the several frequent dependencies regarding "NtMapViewOfSection" and OS objects dependency between file and section, indicate malware writers commonly utilize memory mapped file to facilitate file manipulation. Malware often configure Windows registry for persistence in order to run automatically when machine starts, leading to frequent operations on Windows registry. "NtOpenProcess → NtWriteVirtualMemory" and "process → thread" are mainly introduced by creating a new thread in a remote process, the most common way to launch malware covertly in vulnerable hosts [33]. If we implement these common functions through different ways, the corresponding sub-SCDGs can be changed drastically as well.

3.3 Attacking Strategies

In this section we elaborate how to construct replacement attacks strategies. We propose 3 requirements that our attacking strategies have to meet:

1. (R1) Our replacement attacks should invalidate various malware behavior similarity metrics, such as graph edit distance and Jaccard Index.

Table 1. Popular windows native API dependencies

Dependencies	Data flow types	Ratio (%)
NtMapViewOfSection → NtProtectVirtualMemory	void *address	22.4
NtOpenKey → NtQueryValueKey	KeyHandle	19.4
NtCreateSection → NtMapViewOfSection	SectionHandle	9.6
NtMapViewOfSection → NtUnmapViewOfSection	void *address	8.9
NtOpenSection → NtMapViewOfSection	SectionHandle	6.3
NtCreateFile → NtReadFile	FileHandle	5.4
NtCreateSection → NtQuerySection	SectionHandle	4.8
NtOpenKey → NtQueryKey	KeyHandle	4.6
NtCreateFile → NtQueryInformationFile	FileHandle	4.2
NtOpenFile → NtSetInformationFile	FileHandle	4.1
NtOpenProcess → NtWriteVirtualMemory	ProcessHandle	3.8

Table 2. Popular OS object types, operations and dependencies

OS object type	OS operation
file	open, create, read, write, query_information, query_directory, set_information, query_file
registry	create, open, query_value, set_value
section	query, create, map, open, mem_read
process	create, open, query
thread	create, query, resume
OS object dependency	
file → file, registry → file, registry → registry, process → thread, section → file, file → section	

2. (R2) New system calls and dependencies impose no side effect to original data flow.
3. (R3) Transformed SCDG should be as common as possible.

We meet our design requirement R1 by two attacking methods. The first one is embedding redundant data flow dependent system calls to replace original popular dependencies. As a result, new vertices and dependencies are created (see example in Fig. 1). At the same time, we make sure data types and values of original dependencies are preserved (satisfy R2). Further more, we observe that malicious functionalities can be developed with different technical methods, making it possible for SCDG mutations without undermining the intended purpose. For example, malware replication can be implemented through either memory-mapped file or file I/O; multiple ways exist to modify registry for the purpose of persistence. Therefore our second attacking strategy is transforming a sub-SCDG to its semantically equivalent mutations (satisfy R2). As a result, the original dependencies probably do not exist anymore. A by-product of our mining result in Sect. 3.2 is that popular dependencies can also be served as possible candidates to be embedded in a SCDG, so that the new SCDG doesn't look unusual (satisfy R3). Note that these two attacking methods can seamlessly weave together to amplify each other's effect.

3.4 Replacement Attacks Arsenal

In this section we present the details of our replacement attacks arsenal. According to our attacking strategies, we classify them into 2 categories:

Inserting Redundant Dependencies. We summarize attacks belong to this category based on the medium data flow types listed in Table 1.

1. "NtSetInformationFile" attack. This attack can replace the dependencies with FileHandle as medium, which has been illustrated in Fig. 1.
2. "NtDuplicateObject" attack. "NtDuplicateObject" returns a duplicated object handle, which refers to the same object as the original handle.
3. "NtQuery*" attack. There are several windows native APIs for querying information of kernel objects, such as "NtQueryAttributesFile", "NtQueryKey", "NtQueryInformationProcess" and "NtQueryInformationFile". All of these query APIs take certain object handle as one of input argument and output object information. No any modification is introduced to the kernel objects. Hence "NtQuery*" native APIs are good candidates for our replacement attacks. For example, we could insert "NtQueryInformationFile" into a popular *NtCreateFile → NtSetInformationFile* dependency, where the output of "NtQueryInformationFile" ("FileInformation") is passed to "NtSetInformationFile". The two new dependencies also appear frequently.
4. The medium of "void *address" shown in Table 1 receives address of a mapped memory. To handle this medium, we can insert "NtQueryVirtualMemory" or "NtReadVirtualMemory", which do not affect the mapped memory address.

Sub-SCDG Mutations. We present multiple implementation ways to achieve 3 common malicious sub tasks we observed in Sect. 3.2, and what's more, we make sure that each implementation reveals different sub-SCDG with others.

1. Replication. When malware authors call Windows API "CopyFile" to replicate malware sample from source to target file, it is actually achieved through memory mapped file. When a process maps a file into its virtual address space, reading and writing to the file is simply manipulating the mapped memory region, which produces OS objects dependencies between file and section. First we can choose to map either source or destination file to memory section. Another implementation is only through file I/O operations. For example, we can copy a file by calling "NtReadFile" and "NtWriteFile" instead of using memory as medium.

2. Modify registry for persistence. Malware often add entries into the registry to remain active in the event of a reboot. There are multiple registry keys that can be configured to load malware at startup. The reference [4] lists 23 registry keys are accessed during system start. We leverage these multiple choices to randomly pick up available registry keys to update.

3. Code remote injection. Malicious code can be injected into another running process so that the process could execute the malware unwittingly. To achieve this functionality, we can either inject the malicious code directly into a remote process, or put the code into a DLL and force the remote process to load it [33].

3.5 Case Study

For a better understanding of our replacement attacks, we provide a real case to mutate the replication behavior of Worm.Win32.Hunatcha. Figure 3(a) shows a native API sequence fragment we collected from the initial version and the corresponding SCDG. The malware sample replicates the file "hunatcha.exe" to "ladygaga.mp3.exe" by first memory-mapping the source file and then writing the memory content to the destination file. Figure 4(a) presents the feature set abstracted from Fig. 3(a) , following the definition of BCHKK-data [7]. The first 3 lines are operations (open, create, write, etc.) on OS objects (file, section). The fourth line is an OS dependency from section to destination file.

Table 3. Similarity metrics of 3 mutations

	a vs. a	a vs. b	a vs. c	b vs. c
Graph edit distance	0.0	0.71	0.60	0.71
Jaccard Index	1.0	0.14	0.33	0.27

As shown in Fig. 3(b), we first mutate the generated SCDG by switching the file mapped to the memory, that is, we explicitly map the destination file (not source file) into the memory, so that file copying is achieved by reading content of source file to the mapped memory region. At the same time, we also insert redundant data flow dependent system calls to create new dependencies and decouple original dependencies. Therefore the structure of resulting SCDG and feature set (shown in Fig. 4(b)) are changed significantly. Figure 3(c) presents another round attack. Instead of utilizing memory mapped file, we directly copy file through file I/O. Therefore no memory section appears in SCDG and feature set. Table 3 shows the two similarity metrics for these 3 mutations. The calculation of these two metrics is introduced in Sect. 5.2. The graph edit distance value of 0.0 or Jaccard Index value of 1.0 indicates that two behaviors are identical. The large graph edit distance or small Jaccard Index value means that after our replacement attacks, the similarity of malware variants drops substantially.

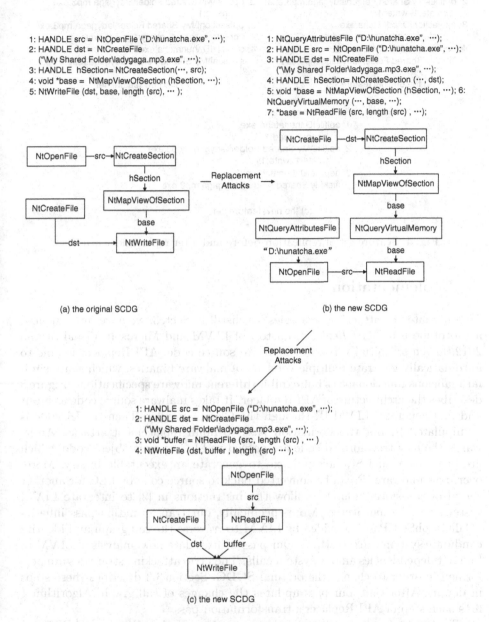

1: HANDLE src = NtOpenFile ("D:\hunatcha.exe", ⋯);
2: HANDLE dst = NtCreateFile
   ("\My Shared Folder\ladygaga.mp3.exe", ⋯);
3: HANDLE hSection= NtCreateSection(⋯, src);
4: void *base = NtMapViewOfSection (hSection, ⋯);
5: NtWriteFile (dst, base, length (src), ⋯);

1: NtQueryAttributesFile ("D:\hunatcha.exe", ⋯);
2: HANDLE src = NtOpenFile ("D:\hunatcha.exe", ⋯);
3: HANDLE dst = NtCreateFile
   ("\My Shared Folder\ladygaga.mp3.exe", ⋯);
4: HANDLE hSection= NtCreateSection (⋯, dst);
5: void *base = NtMapViewOfSection (hSection, ⋯); 6:
NtQueryVirtualMemory (⋯, base, ⋯);
7: *base = NtReadFile (src, length (src) , ⋯);

Replacement Attacks

(a) the original SCDG

(b) the new SCDG

Replacement Attacks

1: HANDLE src = NtOpenFile ("D:\hunatcha.exe", ⋯);
2: HANDLE dst = NtCreateFile
   ("\My Shared Folder\ladygaga.mp3.exe", ⋯);
3: void *buffer = NtReadFile (src, length (src) , ⋯)
4: NtWriteFile (dst, buffer , length (src) ⋯);

(c) the new SCDG

Fig. 3. System calls dependence graph (SCDG) of replication before and after replacement attacks

1: op|file|D:\hunatcha.exe
   open:1
2: op|file|\My Shared Folder\ladygaga.mp3.exe
   create:1, write: 1
3: op|section|D:\hunatcha.exe
   create:1, map:1, mem_read: 1
4: dep|section|D:\hunatcha.exe→
   file|\My Shared Folder\ladygaga.mp3.exe

(a) the original feature set

1: op|file|D:\hunatcha.exe
   open:1, query_file:1, read:1
2: op|file|\My Shared Folder\ladygaga.mp3.exe
   create:1
3: op|section|\My Shared Folder\ladygaga.mp3.exe
   create:1, map:1, query:1, mem_write: 1
4: dep|file|D:\hunatcha.exe →
   section|\My Shared Folder\ladygaga.mp3.exe

(b) the new feature set

1: op|file|D:\hunatcha.exe
   open:1, read:1
2: op|file|\My Shared Folder\ladygaga.mp3.exe
   create:1, write:1
3: dep|file|D:\hunatcha.exe →
   file|\My Shared Folder\ladygaga.mp3.exe

(c) the new feature set

Fig. 4. Feature set of replication before and after replacement attacks

4 Implementation

To automate the attacking strategies we distill in Sect. 3, we have implemented a prototype tool, *API Replacer*, on top of LLVM and Microsoft Visual Studio 2012. Given an initial version of malware source code, API Replacer is able to automatically generate multiple versions of malware binaries, which share similar malicious functionalities but exhibit different malware specifications. Figure 5 describes the architecture of API Replacer. It takes malware source code as input and first generates LLVM IR through the Clang compiler. Then the IR code is manipulated by our transformation pass to fulfill replacement attacks. Afterwards the new transformed code are passed to LLC to emit object code, which are given to Visual Studio's link.exe to generate an executable binary. Moreover, new malware IR can be converted back to source code by LLC for another round of transformation. We follow the instructions in [2] to integrate LLVM system with Visual Studio. More specifically, our transformation pass inherits "CallGraphSCCPass" provided by LLVM to traverse the call graph and identify candidate system calls to attack. Our pass utilizes data flow analysis of LLVM to find out dependencies among system calls. Then two attacking strategies are performed in order to change the original SCDG. Section 3.3 describes these steps in details. After that, our pass updates the changes of call graph. Algorithm 1 lists each step of API Replacer's transformation pass.

The major implementation choice we made is using Windows APIs as a proxy for Windows native APIs. The reason is Windows native APIs are not comprehensively documented, while Windows APIs is well described in MSDN[2].

---

[2] http://msdn.microsoft.com/.

According to the mapping between Windows APIs and native APIs [32], we are able to manipulate Windows APIs directly.

Algorithm 1. API Replacer's algorithm

1: Traverse call graph
2: Identify candidate system calls and their dependencies
3: Mutate a sequence of dependent system calls to their equivalent ones
4: Insert redundant data flow dependent system calls
5: Update new call graph

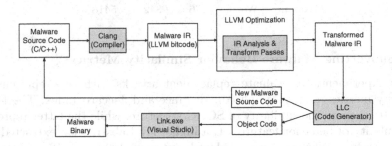

Fig. 5. The architecture of API Replacer

5   Evaluation

In this section, we apply API Replacer to transform real malware samples and evaluate the effectiveness of our approach to impede malware similarity metrics calculation and behavior-based malware clustering. We also test with 5 SPEC CPU2006 benchmarks to evaluate performance slowdown imposed by replacement attacks.

5.1   Experiment Setup

We transform malware source code collected from VX Heavens[3]. These malware samples are chosen for two reasons: (1) they do not contain any trigger-based behavior [36] or runtime environment checking condition [19]; (2) they have different malicious functionalities. In this way, we ensure that each sample fully exhibits its specific malicious intent during runtime execution and each sample presents different behavior specifications. Malware samples under experiment are executed in a malware dynamic analysis system, Cuckoo Sandbox[4], to collect windows native API calls traces. We first filter out isolated nodes which have no dependencies with others. Then we compute SCDG for each sample following the data flow dependencies between native APIs. Statistics for lines of code and SCDG are shown in Table 4.

---

[3] http://vxheaven.org/src.php.
[4] http://www.cuckoosandbox.org/.

Table 4. Test set statistics

Sample	Type	LoC #	SCDG	
			Node #	Edge #
BullMoose	Trojan	30	602	360
Clibo	Trojan	90	698	342
Branko	Worm	270	590	332
Hunatcha	Worm	340	756	408
WormLabs	Worm	420	895	506
KeyLogger	Trojan	460	811	439
Sasser	Worm	950	1860	1044
Mydoom	Worm	3276	9342	5418

5.2 Subverting Malware Behavior Similarity Metrics

In this experiment, we evaluate replacement attacks with two representative similarity metrics, namely graph edit distance and Jaccard Index. The former is used to measure the similarity of SCDG structure; while the latter represents the similarity of behavior feature set, a higher level abstraction extracted from SCDG. We first set the ratio of replaced system calls as 0 %, 10 %, 20 %, and 30 % and then generate 4 mutations respectively for each testing malware sample. Then we run these mutations in Cuckoo Sandbox to collect SCDGs in order to compute graph edit distance. After that, we convert SCDGs to feature sets to calculate their Jaccard Index.

Graph Edit Distance. We measure the similarity of SCDG G_1 and SCDG G_2 via graph edit distance [13], which is defined as

$$d(G_1, G_2) = 1 - \frac{|MCS(G_1, G_2)|}{max(|G_1|, |G_2|)}$$

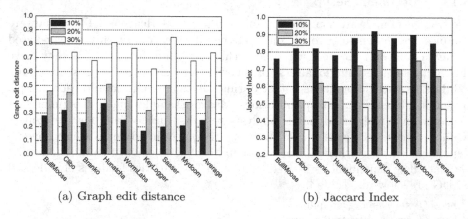

(a) Graph edit distance   (b) Jaccard Index

Fig. 6. Graph edit distance and Jaccard Index after replacement attacks

$MCS(G_1, G_2)$ is the maximal common subgraph and $|G|$ is the number of nodes in a graph. The value of the distance varies from 0.0 to 1.0. Distance value 0.0 denotes that two graphs are identical. Park et al. employed the graph edit distance for malware classification and clustering [28,29], where they set similarity threshold as 0.3. Graph distance above the threshold means two malware samples are different. Taken the sample with 0 % replacement ratio as the baseline, Fig. 6(a) shows the graph edit distance after replacement attacks. Basically the graph edit distance increases steadily as the amount of replaced system calls raises. Please note that when we only enforce 20 % replacement, all the distances are beyond the threshold of 0.3. This experiment demonstrates that our replacement attacks change the structure of SCDG significantly.

Jaccard Index. Assume behavior feature set of malware sample a and b are F_a and F_b, Jaccard Index is defined as

$$J(a,b) = \frac{|F_a \cap F_b|}{|F_a \cup F_b|}$$

Bayer et al. [7] identified two similar malware feature sets by checking whether their Jaccard Index is ≥ 0.7. Similar with the setting of Fig. 6(a), Fig. 6(b) presents the result of Jaccard Index after replacement attacks. We can draw a similar conclusion that Jaccard Index reduces as replacement ratio increases. However, the decline rate of Jaccard Index is not as large as the rising rate of graph edit distance. We attribute this to a better fault tolerance of large scale feature set. For example, Mydoom in our testing set has more the 1000 features. Consequently, small portion of system calls replacement imposes less effect on Jaccard Index. In spite of this, when the replacement ratio is increased to 30 %, all of the Jaccard Index value are below the similarity threshold of 0.7.

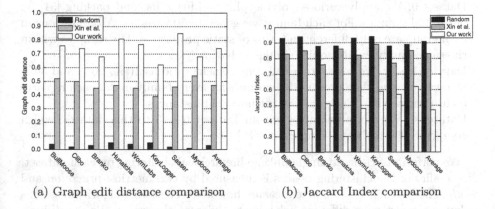

(a) Graph edit distance comparison   (b) Jaccard Index comparison

Fig. 7. Our attacks vs. other approaches

Our Attacks vs. Other Approaches. Furthermore, we compared our attacks with two other attacking approaches, that is system call random insertion ("Random" bar) and Xin et al.'s approach [37], which obfuscates SCDG by replacing a dependency edge with a new vertex and two new edges. The ratio of new system calls insertion, replaced edges and replaced system calls are all set as 30 %. The comparison results are presented in Fig. 7. The quite small graph edit distance and large Jaccard Index value show that SCDG is resilient to the attack of system call random insertion, which does not consider data flow dependencies. As shown in Fig. 7(a), although Xin et al.'s approach is able to subvert the structure of SCDG (the distance is >0.3), our attacks outperform their approach by a factor of 1.6x on average. Moreover, Fig. 7(b) indicates that Xin et al.'s attacking only has a marginal effect on the behavior feature set such as BCHKK-data [7]. The reason is Xin et al.'s approach neither introduces new OS objects nor brings new dependencies between OS objects.

5.3   Against Behavior-Based Clustering

In this section, we demonstrate that replacement attacks are able to impede behavior-based malware clustering approach. We choose the clustering approach proposed by Bayer et al. [7], which is a state-of-the-art clustering system for malware behavior. Bayer et al.'s approach contains two major steps: (1) employ locality sensitive hashing (LSH) to find approximate near-neighbors of feature sets; (2) perform single-linkage hierarchical clustering.

We use the LSH code from [5] in our experiment. To fairly evaluate the clustering approach, we stick to a similar setup. The Jaccard Index threshold and LSH parameters, are all exactly the same as in [7]. As mentioned in Sect. 5.1, malware samples in our initial dataset belong to 8 different families. To enlarge the dataset for our malware clustering evaluation, we generate 5 datasets:

- Dataset 0: We apply various polymorphism obfuscation and packing [31] on our initial samples. For each family, we generate 30 variants. All mutations in each group are only different in terms of static properties. The samples within the same family exhibit quite similar behavior.
- Dataset 1 ∼ 3: We set system call replacement ratio as 10 %, 20 % and 30 % respectively and then produce 30 variants for every family under each replacement ratio setting. Each dataset includes 240 instances.
- Dataset 4: We mix all samples within Dataset 0 ∼ 3 to this dataset, which comprises 960 malware samples in total.

We perform LSH-based single-linkage hierarchical clustering on each dataset. The quality of the clustering results is measured by two metrics: *precision* and *recall*. The goal of *precision* is to measure how well a clustering algorithm assigns malware samples with different behavior to different clusters, while *recall* indicates how well a clustering algorithm puts malware with the same behavior into the same cluster. The naive clustering method that creates only one cluster comprising all samples has the highest recall (1.0), but the worst precision. On the contrary, the method sets up a clustering for each sample achieves the highest precision (1.0) but with low recall number. An optimal clustering method should provide both high precision and recall at the same time. Please refer to [7] for detailed information.

Table 5. Quality of the clustering

Dataset	0	1	2	3	4
Samples #	240	240	240	240	960
Cluster #	8	12	35	110	208
Precision	1.000	0.981	0.978	0.965	0.973
Recall	0.975	0.933	0.483	0.121	0.529

Table 5 summarizes our results. Since the samples in Dataset 0 are only different in terms of static features, the clustering result has the optimal precision and recall. Because 6 samples crashed after applying virtualization obfuscators [16], the recall value is slightly smaller than 1.0. The results of Dataset 1 ∼ 3 show the trend that the recall value falls as system call replacement ratio raises. For example, under the replacement ratio of 30 %, on average only about 2 samples are clustered into each family. A small recall value implies that more clusters are created than expected. Dataset 4 simulates a real scenario we mentioned in Sect. 3.1: malware samples after replacement attacks, mixed with other suspicious binaries, are finally collected for clustering. The low recall value demonstrates that our approach is effective in practice.

5.4 Performance

Since switching between kernel and user mode is inherently expensive, the redundant system calls introduced by replacement attacks will no doubt impact runtime performance. We measure runtime performance after applying replacement attacks on 5 SPEC CPU 2006 benchmarks, including `bzip2`, `libquantum`, `omnetpp`, `astar` and `xalancbmk`. Our testbed is a laptop with a 2.30 GHz Intel(R) Core i5 CPU and 8 GB of memory, running on the operating system of Windows 7. On average, testing programs have a slowdown of 1.33 times (normalized to the runtime without transformation) when the system call replacement ratio is 30 %. Considering the significant effect under this replacement ratio, the performance tradeoff is worthy.

6 Discussion

Limitations. Currently the compatibility with Visual Studio and LLVM tool chain is not perfect. For example, C++ standard library and Windows Platform

SDK are not fully supported by clang, which prevent us from testing more complicated malware. The attacking strategies we summarized in Sect. 3.3, especially the sub-SCDG mutation rules are limited. Implementing the same functionality through diverse ways need comprehensive domain knowledge. We plan to extend our replacement attacks arsenal in future work.

Possible Ways to Defeat. We suggest possible ways to defend against replacement attacks. As one of our attacking strategies is to insert redundant dependencies, the size of SCDG could be enlarged. An analyzer is able to detect such change by comparing new SCDG with the original one. However, without more close investigation (usually involving tedious work), analyzer cannot easily differentiate whether the size change of SCDG comes from incremental updates or our attacks. Another countermeasure is to normalize the behavior graph mutations. For example, the multiple semantically equivalent graph patterns of malware replication can be unified as a canonical form before clustering. The effort in this direction is Martignoni et al.'s work [25]. They designed a layered architecture to detect alternative events that deliver the same high-level functionality. However, admitted by the authors, the layered hierarchy is generated manually and tested only with 7 malware samples. A general and automated behavior graph normalization is still missing. Moreover, high-level malware behavior abstractions may overlook subtle distinctions among malware samples. Therefore, the higher-level of behavior abstractions are probably valid in distinguishing malware from benign program, but are incompetent to differentiate malware variants. Another way is to perform more fine-grained data flow analysis. For example, If the data passed in two sequential dependencies are not changed, the medium system call is probably a redundant native API such as *NtSetInformationFile* and *NtDuplicateObject*. However, this approach cannot defeat sub-SCDG mutations, which may completely change the structure of sub-SCDG.

7   Conclusion

Behavior-based malware specifications have been broadly employed in malware detection and clustering. In this paper we study the vulnerability of current behavior based malware analysis and propose replacement attacks to impede malware behavior specifications. We distill general attacking strategies by mining large malware behavior data sets and develop a compiler level prototype to demonstrate their feasibilities. Our evaluation on real malware samples shows that the transformed malware could evade malware similarity comparison and impede behavior-based clustering. We expect our study can cultivate further research to improve resistance to this potential threat.

Acknowledgements. We are very grateful to Paolo Milani Comparetti and Christopher Kruegel for providing access to the BCHKK-data dataset. This research was supported in part by the NSF Grant CNS-1223710, CCF-1320605 and ARO W911NF-13-1-0421 (MURI).

References

1. Cybercriminals sell access to tens of thousands of malware-infected Russian hosts. http://www.webroot.com/blog/2013/09/23/. Accessed 03 October 2014
2. Getting started with the llvm system using Microsoft Visual Studio. http://llvm.org/docs/GettingStartedVS.html. Accessed 03 October 2014
3. Malicious software and its underground economy. https://www.coursera.org/course/malsoftware. Accessed 03 October 2014
4. Windows registry persistence, part 2: The run keys and search-order. http://blog.cylance.com. Accessed 03 October 2014
5. Andoni, A., Indyk, P.: Near-optimal hashing algorithms for approximate nearest neighbor in high dimensions. Commun. ACM **51**(1), 117–122 (2008)
6. Babić, D., Reynaud, D., Song, D.: Malware analysis with tree automata inference. In: Gopalakrishnan, G., Qadeer, S. (eds.) CAV 2011. LNCS, vol. 6806, pp. 116–131. Springer, Heidelberg (2011)
7. Bayer, U., Comparetti, P. M., Hlauschek, C., Kruegel, C., Kirda, E.: Scalable, behavior based malware clustering. In: Proceedings of the Network and Distributed System Security Symposium (NDSS) (2009)
8. Bayer, U., Kirda, E., Kruegel, C.: Improving the efficiency of dynamic malware analysis. In: Proceedings of the 2010 ACM Symposium on Applied Computing (SAC) (2010)
9. Biggio, B., Pillai, I., Rota Bulò, S., Ariu, D., Pelillo, M., Roli, F.: Is data clustering in adversarial settings secure? In: Proceedings of the 6th ACM Workshop on Artificial Intelligence and Security (AISec) (2013)
10. Biggio, B., Rieck, K., Ariu, D., Wressnegger, C., Corona, I., Giacinto, G., Rol, F.: Poisoning behavioral malware clustering. In: Proceedings of the 7th ACM Workshop on Artificial Intelligence and Security (AISec) (2014)
11. Broder, A.Z., Glassman, S.C., Manasse, M.S., Zweig, G.: Syntactic clustering of the web. In: Proceedings of the Sixth International Conference on World Wide Web (1997)
12. Bruschi, D., Martignoni, L., Monga, M.: Detecting self-mutating malware using control-flow graph matching. In: Buschkes, R., Laskov, P. (eds.) DIMVA 2006. LNCS, vol. 4064, pp. 129–143. Springer, Heidelberg (2006)
13. Bunke, H., Shearer, K.: A graph distance metric based on the maximal common subgraph. Pattern Recogn. Lett. **19**(3–4), 255–259 (1998)
14. Chen, X., Andersen, J., Mao, Z., Bailey, M., Nazario, J.: Towards an understanding of anti-virtualization and anti-debugging behavior in modern malware. In: Proceedings of the International Conference on Dependable Systems and Networks (DSN) (2008)
15. Christodorescu, M., Jha, S., Kruegel, C.: Mining specifications of malicious behavior. In: ESEC-FSE 2007 Proceedings of the the the 6th Joint Meeting of the European Software Engineering Conference and the ACM SIGSOFT Symposium on the Foundations of Software Engineering (2007)
16. Coogan, K., Lu, G., Debray, S.: Deobfuscation of virtualization-obfuscated software. In: Proceedings of the 18th ACM Conference on Computer and Communications Security (CCS) (2011)
17. Dinaburg, A., Royal, P., Sharif, M., Lee, W.: Ether: malware analysis via hardware virtualization extensions. In: Proceedings of the ACM Conference on Computer and Communications Security (CCS) (2008)

18. Fredrikson, M., Jha, S., Christodorescu, M., Sailer, R., Yan, X.: Synthesizing near-optimal malware specifications from suspicious behaviors. In: Proceedings of the 2010 IEEE Symposium on Security and Privacy (2010)
19. Kang, M.G., Yin, H., Hanna, S., McCamant, S., Song, D.: Emulating emulation-resistant malware. In: Proceedings of the Workshop on Virtual Machine Security (VMSec) (2009)
20. Kolbitsch, C., Comparetti, P.M., Kruegel, C., Kirda, E., Zho, X., Wang, X.: Effective and efficient malware detection at the end host. In: Proceedings of the 18th USENIX Security Symposium (2009)
21. Kruegel, C., Kirda, E., Mutz, D., Robertson, W., Vigna, G.: Polymorphic worm detection using structural information of executables. In: Valdes, A., Zamboni, D. (eds.) RAID 2005. LNCS, vol. 3858, pp. 207–226. Springer, Heidelberg (2006)
22. Lattner, C., Adve, V.: LLVM: a compilation framework for lifelong program analysis and transformation. In: Proceedings of the International Symposium on Code Generation and Optimization (CGO) (2004)
23. Lindorfer, M., Di Federico, A., Maggi, F., Comparetti, P.M., Zanero, S.: Lines of malicious code: insights into the malicious software industry. In: Proceedings of the 28th Annual Computer Security Applications Conference (ACSAC) (2012)
24. Ma, W., Duan, P., Liu, S., Gu, G., Liu, J.-C.: Shadow attacks: automatically evading system-call-behavior based malware detection. Comput. Virol. 8(1–2), 1–13 (2012)
25. Martignoni, L., Stinson, E., Fredrikson, M., Jha, S., Mitchell, J.C.: A layered architecture for detecting malicious behaviors. In: Lippmann, R., Kirda, E., Trachtenberg, A. (eds.) RAID 2008. LNCS, vol. 5230, pp. 78–97. Springer, Heidelberg (2008)
26. Moser, A., Kruegel, C., Kirda, E.: Limits of static analysis for malware detection. In: Proceedings of the 23th Annual Computer Security Applications Conference (ACSA), December 2007
27. Paleari, R., Martignoni, L., Roglia, G.F., Bruschi, D.: A fistful of red-pills: how to automatically generate procedures to detect cpu emulators. In: Proceedings of the USENIX Workshop on Offensive Technologies (WOOT) (2009)
28. Park, Y., Reeves, D.: Deriving common malware behavior through graph clustering. In: Proceedings of the 6th ACM Symposium on Information, Computer and Communications Security (ASIACCS) (2011)
29. Park, Y., Reeves, D., Mulukutla, V., Sundaravel, B.: Fast malware classification by automated behavioral graph matching. In: Proceedings of the 6th Annual Workshop on Cyber Security and Information Intelligence Research (2010)
30. Rieck, K., Trinius, P., Willems, C., Holz, T.: Automatic analysis of malware behavior using machine learning. J. Comput. Secur. 19(4), 639–668 (2011)
31. Roundy, K.A., Miller, B.P.: Binary-code obfuscations in prevalent packer tools. ACM Comput. Surv. 46(1), 4 (2013)
32. Russinovich, M.: Inside the native API. http://netcode.cz/img/83/nativeapi.html. Accessed 03 October 2014
33. Sikorski, M., Honig, A.: Practical Malware Analysis: The Hands-On Guide to Dissecting Malicious Software. No Starch Press, San Francisco (2012)
34. Srivastava, A., Lanzi, A., Giffin, J., Balzarotti, D.: Operating system interface obfuscation and the revealing of hidden operations. In: Holz, T., Bos, H. (eds.) DIMVA 2011. LNCS, vol. 6739, pp. 214–233. Springer, Heidelberg (2011)
35. Wagner, D., Soto, P.: Mimicry attacks on host-based intrusion detection systems. In: Proceedings of the 9th ACM Conference on Computer and Communications Security (CCS) (2002)

36. Wang, Z., Ming, J., Jia, C., Gao, D.: Linear obfuscation to combat symbolic execution. In: Atluri, V., Diaz, C. (eds.) ESORICS 2011. LNCS, vol. 6879, pp. 210–226. Springer, Heidelberg (2011)
37. Xin, Z., Chen, H., Wang, X., Liu, P., Zhu, S., Mao, B., Xie, L.: Replacement attacks on behavior based software birthmark. In: Lai, X., Zhou, J., Li, H. (eds.) ISC 2011. LNCS, vol. 7001, pp. 1–16. Springer, Heidelberg (2011)

Partial Key Exposure Attacks on CRT-RSA: Better Cryptanalysis to Full Size Encryption Exponents

Atsushi Takayasu$^{(\boxtimes)}$ and Noboru Kunihiro

The University of Tokyo, Chiba, Japan
a-takayasu@it.k.u-tokyo.ac.jp, kunihiro@k.u-tokyo.ac.jp

Abstract. There have been several papers which studied the security of CRT-RSA when some bits of CRT-exponents d_p and d_q are known to attackers. At first, Blömer and May (Crypto 2003) proposed attacks which used the most or the least significant bits of either d_p or d_q. Next, Sarkar and Maitra (ACNS 2009) generalized the scenario and proposed an attack which used the most significant bits of both d_p and d_q. Recently, Lu et al. (ACNS 2014) proposed improved attacks for the same scenario as Blömer and May. These works showed that public RSA modulus can be factored when $e < N^{3/8}$, or sizes of unknown bits are less than $N^{1/4}$. In this paper, we propose improved attacks when attackers know the most/least significant bits of d_p or/and d_q. Unlike previous works, our attacks work in the same conditions regardless of positions of known bits; either the most or the least significant bits are not the matter. In addition, using our attacks, public RSA modulus can be factored even when an encryption exponent is full size or sizes of unknown bits are less than $N^{1/3}$.

Keywords: CRT-RSA · Cryptanalysis · Partial key exposure · Coppersmith's method · Lattices

1 Introduction

1.1 Background

CRT-RSA. RSA [RSA78] is one of the most famous cryptosystems and is widely used. Let $N = pq$ be a public RSA modulus where prime factors p and q are the same bit size. An encryption exponent e and a decryption exponent d satisfy $ed = 1 \mod (p-1)(q-1)$. For encryption/verifying (resp. decryption/signing), we should calculate the heavy modular exponentiation. To speed up the calculation, a simple solution is to use a smaller encryption (resp. decryption) exponent. However, public RSA modulus can be factored in polynomial time when too small decryption exponent is used. At first, Wiener [Wie90] proposed a polynomial time attack which works when $d < N^{0.25}$. Boneh and Durfee [BD00] revisited the attack and improved the bound to $d < N^{0.292}$ using the Coppersmith method [Cop96a].

© Springer International Publishing Switzerland 2015
T. Malkin et al. (Eds.): ACNS 2015, LNCS 9092, pp. 518–537, 2015.
DOI: 10.1007/978-3-319-28166-7_25

To thwart the attack and achieve a faster calculation for decryption/signing, Chinese Remainder Theorem (CRT) is often used as described by Quisquater and Couvreur [QC82]. Instead of the original decryption exponent d, we use CRT-exponents d_p and d_q which satisfy

$$ed_p = 1 \mod (p-1) \quad \text{and} \quad ed_q = 1 \mod (q-1).$$

However, when too small CRT-exponents are used, analogous attacks to [BD00] have been proposed [May02, GHM05, BM06, JM07, HM10]. Jochemsz and May [JM07] revealed that public RSA modulus N can be factored in polynomial time when an encryption exponent is full size, and d_p and $d_q < N^{0.073}$. In addition, CRT-RSA is more vulnerable than standard RSA against fault injection attacks [BDL97]. To use RSA efficiently and securely, we should analyze the security in detail.

Partial Key Exposure Attacks on RSA. It is widely known that factorization and RSA problems become easy when certain amount of secret information is known to attackers. When we know the most significant bits of primes factors, we can factor public RSA modulus N [RS86, Cop95, Cop96b]. Coppersmith [Cop96b] showed that the half most significant bits of a prime factor suffices to factor N.

RSA becomes vulnerable also with partial bits of decryption exponent d. Boneh et al. [BDF98] showed that the most or the least significant bits of a decryption exponent d enable us to factor public RSA modulus N. Later, several papers revisited the attack [BM03, EJMW05, Aon09, SGM10, JL12, TK14], and Ernst et al. [EJMW05] revealed that RSA is vulnerable even for a full size encryption/decryption exponent against the attack.

Partial Key Exposure Attacks on CRT-RSA. As with standard RSA, several attacks which use partial information of d_p and d_q have also been considered [BM03, SM09, LZL14]. Blömer and May [BM03] proposed attacks when the most or the least significant bits of either d_p or d_q are known to attackers. The attacks work when encryption exponent is small, $e < N^{1/4}$ when the most significant bits are known and $e = poly(\log N)$ when the least significant bits are known. In addition, the attacks can recover unknown bits which are less than $N^{1/4}$. Recently, Lu et al. [LZL14] revisited Blömer and May's attack [BM03]. When the most significant bits are known and d_p and $d_q \approx N^{1/2}$, they cannot improve Blömer and May's attack. However, for smaller d_p and d_q, they improved the previous attack. When the least significant bits are known, they improved Blömer and May's result and their attack works when $e < N^{3/8}$.

Sarkar and Maitra [SM09] generalized partial key exposure attacks on CRT-RSA. Unlike other previous works [BM03, LZL14], they proposed an attack when the most significant bits of both d_p and d_q are known to attackers[1]. However, the

---

[1] In their paper [SM09], they also used the most significant bits of a prime factor p. However, we do not consider the additional information in this paper.

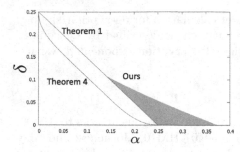

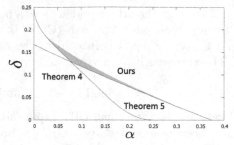

Fig. 1. Recoverable conditions for partial key exposure attacks on CRT-RSA when the most significant bits of either d_p or d_q are known to attackers.

Fig. 2. Recoverable conditions for partial key exposure attacks on CRT-RSA when the least significant bits of either d_p or d_q are known to attackers.

attack is weaker than other attacks [BM03, LZL14] in the sense that the attack does not work when d_p and $d_q \approx N^{1/2}$ though they used more information than [BM03, LZL14]. The attack works only for smaller d_p and d_q.

1.2 Our Contributions

Our Results. In this paper, we study partial key exposure attacks on CRT-RSA. We propose improved attacks when the most/least significant bits of d_p or/and d_q are known. Unlike previous works, the conditions when our attacks work do not depend on the position of known bits, that is, either the most or the least significant bits are not the matter.

When we know the most/least significant bits of d_p or d_q, we improve Blömer and May's results [BM03] and Lu et al.'s results [LZL14] for a large encryption exponent e. As we claimed, our attack works in the same condition regardless of positions of known bits. Therefore, this is the first result to attack CRT-RSA when $1/4 \le e < N^{3/8}$ and the most siginificant bits of either d_p or d_q are known. Figures 1 and 2 compares the recoverable ranges by each algorithm when d_p and $d_q \approx N^{1/2}$. Horizontal axis α represents a size of encryption exponent, $\alpha = \log_N e$. Vertical axis δ represents a size of unknown bits. We obtain improvements in gray areas. Our improved algorithms can recover larger δ for large α. Note that we do not compare the bound of Theorem 2 by Blömer and May [BM03], since the algorithm works only for an extremely small encryption exponent $e = poly(\log N)$.

When we know the most significant bits of both d_p and d_q, we improve Sarkar and Maitra's result [SM09]. In addition, we also propose an analogous attack when the least significant bits of d_p and d_q are known. Our algorithm works even when an encryption exponent e is full size and sizes of unknown bits are less than $N^{1/3}$. Figure 3 shows the recoverable ranges by our algorithm when d_p and $d_q \approx N^{1/2}$. We again stress that Sarkar and Maitra's algorithm does not work when d_p and $d_q \approx N^{1/2}$. Their algorithm works only for smaller d_p and d_q.

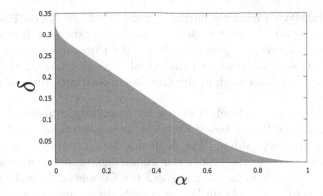

Fig. 3. Recoverable conditions for partial key exposure attacks on CRT-RSA when the most/least significant bits of both d_p and d_q are known to attackers.

Technical Overview. At Eurocrypt 1996, Coppersmith introduced two lattice-based methods, (1) to find small roots of modular univariate polynomials [Cop96a] and (2) to find small roots of bivariate polynomials over the integers [Cop96b]. The methods can be generalized to find small roots with more variables under heuristic argument. So far, several RSA vulnerabilities have been revealed by using the methods. See [Cop97, Cop01, NS01, May03, May10] for more information.

Recoverable sizes of roots using the Coppersmith methods depend on two factors, Newton polygon and a size of a modulus of a polynomial[2]. The simpler Newton polygon of a polynomial is, and the larger the size of the modulus is, we can recover larger roots. To the best of our knowledge, there are no exact criteria to decide which methods (1) or (2) enable us to recover larger roots. Therefore, we should use the appropriate method for each problem.

Blömer and May [BM03] and Lu et al. [LZL14] used the method (1). Though Lu et al.'s first attack (Theorem 4) works under the same condition regardless of positions of known bits, Blömer and May's attack (Theorem 1) and Lu et al.'s second attack (Theorem 5) work for only the case when the most or the least significant bits are known, respectively. Blömer and May's attack makes use of the most significant bits of d_p or d_q and exploits a modular polynomial with a simple Newton polygon. Lu et al.'s attack makes use of the least significant bits of d_p or d_q and exploits a modular polynomial with a large modulus. Therefore, these attacks cannot simply be generalized to the other cases when the least or the most significant bits known, respectively.

In this paper, we use the Coppersmith method (2) for partial key exposure attacks on CRT-RSA. For the attacks, we can consider polynomials with the same Newton polygon regardless of positions of known bits. Note that the Newton polygons of these polynomials are the same as that of the polynomials

---

[2] Note that when we use the Coppersmith method (2), we set a suitable modulus and solve a modular equation. The size of the modulus depends on a size of the polynomial.

Ernst et al. [EJMW05] used for partial key exposure attacks on RSA. In addition, Ernst et al.'s attacks work under the same condition regardless of positions of known bits, since sizes of polynomials are the same and we can use moduli for the same sizes. Analogous to Ernst et al.'s results, our partial key exposure attacks on CRT-RSA work in the same conditions regardless of positions of known bits.

To achieve better bounds when we use the Coppersmith method, it is crucial to select appropriate lattice bases. Our lattice constructions are based on the Jochemsz-May strategy [JM06]. The Jochemsz-May strategy is very simple to understand. Moreover, to the best of our knowledge, there are no results known which achieve better bounds when we use the Coppersmith method (2). The finer analyses enable us to obtain better bounds than previous results including Sarkar and Maitra's results [SM09] which also use the Coppersmith method (2).

1.3   Organization

In Sect. 2, we introduce tools for the Coppersmith method to find small roots of multivariate polynomials over the integers, Howgrave-Graham's Lemma and the LLL algorithm. Afterward, we explain the Jochemsz-May lattice construction strategy. In Sect. 3, we define the situations of partial key exposure attacks on CRT-RSA and summarize previous results [BM03, SM09, LZL14]. In Sect. 4, we propose our attacks when the most/least significant bits of either d_p or d_q are known. In Sect. 5, we propose our attacks when the most/least significant bits of both d_p and d_q are known.

2   Preliminaries

In this section, we summarize the Coppersmith method to find small roots of polynomials over the integers [Cop96b] and the Jochemsz-May strategy for lattice constructions [JM06]. So far, simpler reformulations of the method have been proposed by Coron [Cor04, Cor07]. In this paper, we introduce Coron's reformulation in [Cor04]. Though the method needs larger dimensional lattice than the other methods [Cop96b, Cor07], is much easier to understand.

For a k-variate polynomial over the integers $h(x_1, \ldots, x_k) = \sum h_{i_1, \ldots, i_k} x_1^{i_1} \cdots x_k^{i_k}$, we define a norm of a polynomial $\|h(x_1, \ldots, x_k)\| = \sqrt{\sum h_{i_1, \ldots, i_k}^2}$ and $\|h(x_1, \ldots, x_k)\|_\infty = \max_{i_1, \ldots, i_k} |h_{i_1, \ldots, i_k}|$. To find roots of a polynomial $h(x_1, \ldots, x_k)$, it suffices to find new $k - 1$ polynomials which have the same roots over the integers. We use l_j to denote the largest exponent of x_j in the polynomial $h(x_1, \ldots, x_k)$. We set a integer m and $W \leq \|h(x_1, \ldots, x_k)\|_\infty$. Based on the Jochemsz-May strategy [JM06], we set a integer $R := W \prod_{j=1}^{k} X_j^{l_j(m-1)}$ and consider a modular equation $h(x_1, \ldots, x_k) = 0 \mod R$. To derive new polynomials from the modular equation, we introduce Howgrave-Graham's Lemma [How97].

Lemma 1 (Howgrave-Graham's Lemma [How97]). *Let* $h(x_1, \ldots, x_k) \in \mathbb{Z}[x_1, \ldots, x_k]$ *be a polynomial over the integers, which consists of at most* n

monomials. Let $R, X_1, \ldots, X_k$ be positive integers. Consider the case that the polynomial $h(x_1, \ldots, x_k)$ satisfies
1. $h(\tilde{x}_1, \ldots, \tilde{x}_k) = 0 \pmod{R}$, where $|\tilde{x}_1| < X_1, \ldots, |\tilde{x}_k| < X_k$,
2. $\|h(x_1 X_1, \ldots, x_k X_k)\| < R/\sqrt{n}$.
Then $h(\tilde{x}_1, \ldots, \tilde{x}_k) = 0$ holds over the integers.

To find new polynomials which have the same roots as the original polynomial, we should find $k - 1$ new polynomials which have the same roots modulo R and whose norms are small enough to satisfy Howgrave-Graham's Lemma.

To find such small polynomials, we use the LLL Algorithm. Let $\mathbf{b}_1, \ldots, \mathbf{b}_n \in \mathbb{Z}^d$ be linearly independent d-dimensional vectors. All vectors are row representations. The lattice $L(\mathbf{b}_1, \ldots, \mathbf{b}_n)$ spanned by the basis vectors $\mathbf{b}_1, \ldots, \mathbf{b}_n$ is defined as $L(\mathbf{b}_1, \ldots, \mathbf{b}_n) = \{\sum_{j=1}^{n} c_j \mathbf{b}_j : c_j \in \mathbb{Z}\}$. We also use matrix representations for lattice bases. A basis matrix B is defined as the $n \times d$ matrix that has basis vectors $\mathbf{b}_1, \ldots, \mathbf{b}_n$ in each row. In this representation, a lattice spanned by the basis matrix B is defined as $L(B) = \{\mathbf{c}B : \mathbf{c} \in \mathbb{Z}^n\}$. We call n a rank of the lattice, and d a dimension of the lattice. We call the lattice full-rank when $n = d$. In this paper, we only use full-rank lattices. We define a determinant of a lattice $\det(L(B))$ as $\det(L(B)) = \sqrt{\det(BB^T)}$ where B^T is a transpose of B. A determinant of a full-rank lattice can be computed as $\det(L) = |\det(B)|$.

For a cryptanalysis, to find short lattice vectors is a very important problem. In 1982, Lenstra et al. [LLL82] proposed a polynomial time algorithm to find short lattice vectors.

Proposition 1 (LLL algorithm [May03]). *Given a lattice L spanned by a basis matrix $B \in \mathbb{Z}^{n \times n}$, the LLL algorithm finds new reduced bases $\mathbf{b}'_1, \ldots, \mathbf{b}'_n$ for the same lattice that satisfy*

$$\|\mathbf{b}'_j\| \le 2^{n(n-1)/4(n-j+1)}(\det(L(B)))^{1/(n-j+1)},$$

for all $j = 1, 2, \ldots, n$. These norms are all Euclidean norms. The running time of the LLL algorithm is polynomial time in n and input length.

Based on the Jochemsz-May strategy [JM06], we define a set of shift-polynomials g and g' as

$$g : x_1^{i_1} \cdots x_k^{i_k} \cdot h(x_1, \ldots, x_k) \prod_{j=1}^{n} X_j^{l_j(m-1)-i_j} \quad \text{for } x_1^{i_1} \cdots x_k^{i_k} \in S,$$

$$g' : x_1^{i_1} \cdots x_k^{i_k} \cdot R \quad \text{for } x_1^{i_1} \cdots x_k^{i_k} \in M \backslash S,$$

for

$$S := \{x_1^{i_1} \cdots x_k^{i_k} | x_1^{i_1} \cdots x_k^{i_k} \text{ is a monomial of } h(x_1, \ldots, x_k)^{m-1}\},$$
$$M := \{\text{monomials of } x_1^{i_1} \cdots x_k^{i_k} \cdot h(x_1, \ldots, x_k) \text{ for } x_1^{i_1} \cdots x_k^{i_k} \in S\}.$$

All these shift-polynomials g and g' modulo R have the same roots as h $(x_1, \ldots, x_k)$. We construct a lattice with coefficient vectors of $g(x_1 X_1, \ldots, x_k X_k)$

and $g'(x_1 X_1, \ldots, x_k X_k)$ as the bases. Polynomials whose coefficients correspond to any lattice vectors modulo R also have the same roots as the original roots. By omitting a small term and Jochemsz and May showed that new $k-1$ polynomials obtained by vectors output by the LLL algorithm satisfy Howgrave-Graham's Lemma when

$$\prod_{j=1}^{k} X_j^{s_j} < W^{|S|} \text{ for } s_j = \sum_{x_1^{i_1} \cdots x_k^{i_k} \in S} i_j.$$

When the condition holds, we can find all small roots.

The above lattice construction is based on the Jochemsz-May *basic* strategy. In the *extended* strategy, we add extra shifts for some variables. We omit the detail in this section though we use the strategy in the following sections. See [JM06] for more detailed information.

We should note that the method needs heuristic argument. There are no assurance if new polynomials obtained by vectors output by the LLL algorithm are algebraically independent though Coron [Cor04] proved that the original polynomial and each new polynomial is algebraically independent. In this paper, we assume that these polynomials are always algebraically independent and resultants of polynomials will not vanish since there have been few negative reports which contradict the assumption.

3   Previous Works

3.1   Definitions of Partial Key Exposure Attacks on CRT-RSA

We use α, β to represent the sizes of encryption/CRT exponents, that is, $e \approx N^{\alpha}$ and $d_p, d_q \approx N^{\beta}$. When attackers know some bits of either d_p or d_q, we call an attack a *single* partial key exposure attack on CRT-RSA. Similarly, when attackers know some bits of both d_p and d_q, we call an attack a *double* partial key exposure attack on CRT-RSA. Without loss of generality, we assume that attackers know some bits of d_p for single cases.

Next, we formulate exposed bits. When attackers know the most significant bits (MSBs) of d_p and d_q, we write d_{p_0} and d_{q_0} as partial information. Therefore, we can rewrite

$$d_p = d_{p_0} M + d_{p_1} \quad \text{and} \quad d_q = d_{q_0} M + d_{q_1}$$

with some positive integer $M \approx N^{\delta}$. Attackers do not know the least significant bits d_{p_1} and $d_{q_1} < N^{\delta}$. Similarly, when attackers know the least significant bits (LSBs) of d_p and d_q, we write d_{p_0} and d_{q_0} as partial information. Therefore, we can rewrite

$$d_p = d_{p_1} M + d_{p_0} \quad \text{and} \quad d_q = d_{q_1} M + d_{q_0}$$

with some positive integer $M \approx N^{\beta-\delta}$. Attackers do not know the most significant bits d_{p_1} and $d_{q_1} < N^{\delta}$.

3.2   Previous Results

Next, we summarize the previous results for single/double MSBs/LSBs partial key exposure attacks on CRT-RSA which work in polynomial time in $\log N$.

Theorem 1 (Single MSBs [BM03]). *Let* $0 < \alpha \leq 1/4$. *For a single MSBs partial key exposure attacks on CRT-RSA, when*

$$\delta < \frac{1}{4} - \alpha,$$

then public RSA modulus N *can be factored in polynomial time.*

The algorithm is the best when α is small and β is large.

Theorem 2 (Single LSBs [BM03]). *Let* $e = poly\,(\log N)$. *For a single LSBs partial key exposure attacks on CRT-RSA, when*

$$\delta < \beta - \frac{1}{4},$$

then public RSA modulus N *can be factored in polynomial time.*

In this paper, we do not compare our results with the above result, since the algorithm works only for an extremely small encryption exponent.

Theorem 3 (Double MSBs Adapted from [SM09]). *Let* $1/2 - \beta < \alpha < 5/4 - 5\beta/2$. *For a double MSBs partial key exposure attacks on CRT-RSA, when*

$$\delta < \frac{(18 - 36\beta - 12\alpha)\tau^2 + (20 - 40\beta - 16\alpha)\tau + 5 - 10\beta - 4\alpha}{24\tau^3 + 30\tau^2 + 16\tau + 4}$$

holds for some $\tau \geq 0$, *then public RSA modulus* N *can be factored in polynomial time.*

Theorem 4 (Single MSBs/LSBs [LZL14]). *Let* $1/2 < \alpha + \beta < 3/4$. *For a single MSBs/LSBs partial key exposure attacks on CRT-RSA, when*

$$\left(\alpha + \beta - \frac{1}{2}\right)\left(\frac{3}{2} - \delta - 2\sqrt{\alpha + \beta - \delta - \frac{1}{2}}\right) < \frac{1}{8} \quad for \quad 1 - \frac{\sqrt{2}}{4} \leq \alpha + \beta < \frac{3}{4},$$

$$\alpha + \beta + \delta < \frac{1}{\sqrt{2}},$$

$$\delta\left(2 - \alpha - \beta - 2\sqrt{\delta - \alpha - \beta + \frac{1}{2}}\right) < \frac{1}{8} \quad for \quad \frac{1}{2} < \alpha + \beta \leq \frac{3\sqrt{2}}{4} - \frac{1}{2},$$

then public RSA modulus N *can be factored in polynomial time.*

The algorithm is the best for the single LSBs attack for small α. Note that the second condition is valid when $1/2 < \alpha + \beta \leq 1/\sqrt{2}$ and better than the other conditions when $3\sqrt{2}/4 - 1/2 < \alpha + \beta < 1 - \sqrt{2}/4$.

Theorem 5 (Single LSBs Adapted from [LZL14]). *Let* $1/2 < \alpha + \beta \leq 7/8$. *For a single LSBs partial key exposure attacks on CRT-RSA, when*

$$\delta < \frac{5 - 2\sqrt{1 + 6(\alpha + \beta)}}{6},$$

then public RSA modulus N *can be factored in polynomial time.*

The algorithm is the best for large α and the first algorithm which works when $1/4 < \alpha \leq 3/8$. Note that the condition of Theorem 5 is slightly worse than that was written in [LZL14]. Though we omit the detail, thier condition is not valid, since their analysis implicitly has a restriction for the parameter $\sigma \leq \tau$ in their notation and the result does not satisfy the restriction.

4   Single Partial Key Exposure Attacks on CRT-RSA

For single MSBs/LSBs partial key exposure attacks on CRT-RSA, we obtain the following result.

Theorem 6 (Single MSBs/LSBs). *Let* $1/2 < \alpha + \beta \leq 7/8$. *For single MSBs/LSBs partial key exposure attacks on CRT-RSA, when*

$$-5 + 8(\alpha + \beta) + 8\delta - 12\delta^2 - 2(1 - 4\delta)\sqrt{1 - 4\delta} < 0,$$

then public RSA modulus N *can be factored in polynomial time.*

In this section, we focus on the MSBs case.

Based on the Jochemsz-May Basic Strategy. At first, we start from the Jochemsz-May basic strategy. It is interesting that the lattice construction yields the second condition of Theorem 4.

For a single MSBs partial key exposure attack on CRT-RSA, looking at CRT-RSA key generation,

$$e(d_{p_0} M + d_{p_1}) = 1 + \ell(p - 1),$$

with some integer $\ell \approx N^{\alpha + \beta - 1/2}$. We consider a polynomial over the integers

$$f_{sMSBs}(x, y, z_1) := c_{sMSBs} + ex + y(z_1 - 1)$$

where $c_{sMSBs} = 1 - ed_{p_0} M$ whose roots are $(x, y, z_1) = (-d_{p_1}, \ell, p)$. If we can find two polynomials which have the same roots over the integers as f_{sMSBs}, we can recover the roots. We also use an additional variable $z_2 = q$ and the Durfee-Nguyen technique [DN00] $z_1 z_2 = N$ which Bleichenbacher and May [BM06] and Lu et al. [LZL14] used to attack CRT-RSA. Sizes of the solutions are bounded by $X := N^\delta, Y := N^{\alpha + \beta - 1/2}, Z_1 := N^{1/2}, Z_2 := N^{1/2}$.

We set an integer $W_{sMSBs} := N^{\alpha + \beta}$ since $\|f_{sMSBs}(x, y, z_1)\|_\infty \geq |c_{sMSBs}| \approx N^{\alpha + \beta}$. Next, we set an integer $R_{s1} := W_{sMSBs}(XY)^{m-1} Z_1^{m-1-k} Z_2^k$ with some integer m and $k = \eta m$ with a restriction $0 \le \eta \le 1$ such that $\gcd(c_{sMSBs}, R_{s1}) = 1$. We compute $a_{sMSBs1} = c_{sMSBs}^{-1} \bmod R_{s1}$ and $f'_{sMSBs1}(x, y, z_1) := a_{sMSBs1} \cdot f_{sMSBs}(x, y, z_1) \bmod R_{s1}$. We define a set of shift-polynomials g_{sMSBs1}, g_{sMSBs2} and g'_{sMSBs1}, g'_{sMSBs2} as

$$g_{sMSBs1} : x^{i_x} y^{i_y} z_1^{i_{z_1}-k} \cdot f'_{sMSBs1}(x, y, z_1) X^{m-1-i_x} Y^{m-1-i_y} Z_1^{m-1-i_{z_1}} Z_2^k$$

$$\text{for } x^{i_x} y^{i_y} z_1^{i_{z_1}} \in S_{s1},$$

$$g_{sMSBs2} : x^{i_x} y^{i_y} z_2^{k-i_{z_1}} \cdot f'_{sMSBs1}(x, y, z_1) X^{m-1-i_x} Y^{m-1-i_y} Z_1^{m-1-k} Z_2^{i_{z_1}}$$

$$\text{for } x^{i_x} y^{i_y} z_1^{i_{z_1}} \in S_{s2},$$

$$g'_{sMSBs1} : x^{i_x} y^{i_y} z_1^{i_{z_1}-k} \cdot R_{s1} \quad \text{for } x^{i_x} y^{i_y} z_1^{i_{z_1}} \in M_{s1} \backslash (S_{s1} \cup S_{s2}),$$

$$g'_{sMSBs2} : x^{i_x} y^{i_y} z_2^{k-i_{z_1}} \cdot R_{s1} \quad \text{for } x^{i_x} y^{i_y} z_1^{i_{z_1}} \in M_{s2} \backslash (S_{s1} \cup S_{s2}),$$

for

$$S_1 := \{ x^{i_x} y^{i_y} z_1^{i_{z_1}} | x^{i_x} y^{i_y} z_1^{i_{z_1}} \text{ is a monomial of } f'_{sMSBs1}(x, y, z_1)^{m-1} \text{ and } i_{z_1} \ge k \},$$

$$S_2 := \{ x^{i_x} y^{i_y} z_1^{i_{z_1}} | x^{i_x} y^{i_y} z_1^{i_{z_1}} \text{ is a monomial of } f'_{sMSBs1}(x, y, z_1)^{m-1} \text{ and } i_{z_1} < k \},$$

$$M_1 := \{ x^{i_x} y^{i_y} z_1^{i_{z_1}} | \text{monomials of } x^{i'_x} y^{i'_y} z_1^{i'_{z_1}} \cdot f'_{sMSBs1}(x, y, z_1)$$

$$\text{for } x^{i'_x} y^{i'_y} z_1^{i'_{z_1}} \in S_{s1} \cup S_{s2} \text{ and } i_{z_1} \ge k \},$$

$$M_2 := \{ x^{i_x} y^{i_y} z_1^{i_{z_1}} | \text{monomials of } x^{i'_x} y^{i'_y} z_1^{i'_{z_1}} \cdot f'_{sMSBs1}(x, y, z_1)$$

$$\text{for } x^{i'_x} y^{i'_y} z_1^{i'_{z_1}} \in S_{s1} \cup S_{s2} \text{ and } i_{z_1} < k \}.$$

For shift-polynomials g_{sMSBs2}, we eliminate the term $z_1 z_2$ by using the Durfee-Nguyen technique $z_1 z_2 = N$. By definition, the index sets become

$$S_{s1} \Leftrightarrow i_x = 0, 1, \ldots, m-1-k; i_y = k, k+1, \ldots, m-1-i_x;$$

$$i_{z_1} = k, k+1, \ldots, m-1-i_x,$$

$$S_{s2} \Leftrightarrow i_x = 0, 1, \ldots, m-1; i_y = 0, 1, \ldots, m-1-i_x;$$

$$i_{z_1} = 0, 1, \ldots, \min\{k-1, m-1-i_x\},$$

$$M_{s1} \Leftrightarrow i_x = 0, 1, \ldots, m-k; i_y = k, k+1, \ldots, m-i_x; i_{z_1} = k, k+1, \ldots, m-i_x,$$

$$M_{s2} \Leftrightarrow i_x = 0, 1, \ldots, m; i_y = 0, 1, \ldots, m-i_x; i_{z_1} = 0, 1, \ldots, \min\{k-1, m-i_x\}.$$

All these shift-polynomials g_{sMSBs1}, g_{sMSBs2} and g'_{sMSBs1}, g'_{sMSBs2} modulo R_{s1} have the roots $(x, y, z_1, z_2) = (-d_{p_1}, \ell, p, q)$ which are the same as $f_{sMSBs}(x, y, z_1)$ and the definition of z_2. We construct a lattice with coefficient vectors of $g_{sMSBs1}(xX, yY, z_1 Z_1, z_2 Z_2), g_{sMSBs2}(xX, yY, z_1 Z_1, z_2 Z_2)$ and $g'_{sMSBs1}(xX, yY, z_1 Z_1, z_2 Z_2), g'_{sMSBs2}(xX, yY, z_1 Z_1, z_2 Z_2)$ as the bases. Based on the Jochemsz-May strategy [JM06], LLL outputs two short lattice vectors which satisfy Howgrave-Graham's Lemma when

$$X^{\frac{m^3}{6}+o(m^3)} Y^{\frac{m^3}{3}+o(m^3)} Z_1^{\frac{(1-\eta)^3}{6} m^3+o(m^3)} Z_2^{\left(\frac{\eta^2}{2}-\frac{\eta^3}{6}\right)m^3+o(m^3)} < W_{sMSBs}^{\frac{m^3}{6}+o(m^3)}.$$

Ignoring low order terms of m, and the condition becomes

$$\delta \cdot \frac{1}{6} + \left(\alpha + \beta - \frac{1}{2}\right) \cdot \frac{1}{3} + \frac{1}{2} \cdot \left(\frac{(1-\eta)^3}{6} + \frac{\eta^2}{2} - \frac{\eta^3}{6}\right) < (\alpha + \beta) \cdot \frac{1}{6}.$$

The detailed calculation is discussed later. We optimize the parameter $\eta = 1 - 1/\sqrt{2}$ which satisfy $0 \le \eta \le 1$ and obtain the condition,

$$\alpha + \beta + \delta < \frac{1}{\sqrt{2}}.$$

The condition corresponds to the second condition of Theorem 4.

Based on the Jochemsz-May Extended Strategy. Next, we show our lattice construction based on the Jochemsz-May extended strategy. The lattice construction enables us to solve the equation $f_{sMSBs}(x, y, z_1) = 0$ for larger $\alpha + \beta$ and yields the condition of Theorem 6.

We set an integer $R_{s2} := W_{sMSBs}(XY)^{m-1}Z_1^{m-1-k+t}Z_2^k$ with some integers $m, k = \eta m$ and $t = \tau m$ with restrictions $0 \le \tau \le \eta \le 1$ such that $\gcd(c_{sMSBs}, R_{s2}) = 1$. We compute a_{sMSBs2} and $f'_{sMSBs2}(x, y, z_1)$ as in the basic strategy and define a set of shift-polynomials g_{sMSBs3}, g_{sMSBs4} and g'_{sMSBs3}, g'_{sMSBs4} as

$$g_{sMSBs3} : x^{i_x} y^{i_y} z_1^{i_{z_1}-k} \cdot f'_{sMSBs2}(x, y, z_1) X^{m-1-i_x} Y^{m-1-i_y} Z_1^{m-1+t-i_{z_1}} Z_2^k$$

$$\text{for } x^{i_x} y^{i_y} z_1^{i_{z_1}} \in S_{s3},$$

$$g_{sMSBs4} : x^{i_x} y^{i_y} z_2^{k-i_{z_1}} \cdot f'_{sMSBs2}(x, y, z_1) X^{m-1-i_x} Y^{m-1-i_y} Z_1^{m-1-k+t} Z_2^{i_{z_1}}$$

$$\text{for } x^{i_x} y^{i_y} z_1^{i_{z_1}} \in S_{s4},$$

$$g'_{sMSBs3} : x^{i_x} y^{i_y} z_1^{i_{z_1}-k} \cdot R_{s2} \quad \text{for } x^{i_x} y^{i_y} z_1^{i_{z_1}} \in M_{s3} \backslash (S_{s3} \cup S_{s4}),$$

$$g'_{sMSBs4} : x^{i_x} y^{i_y} z_2^{k-i_{z_1}} \cdot R_{s2} \quad \text{for } x^{i_x} y^{i_y} z_1^{i_{z_1}} \in M_{s4} \backslash (S_{s3} \cup S_{s4}),$$

for

$$S_{s3} := \bigcup_{0 \le j \le t} \{x^{i_x} y^{i_y} z_1^{i_{z_1}+j} | x^{i_x} y^{i_y} z_1^{i_{z_1}} \text{ is a monomial of } f'_{sMSBs2}(x, y, z_1)^{m-1}$$

$$\text{and } i_{z_1} \ge k\},$$

$$S_{s4} := \bigcup_{0 \le j \le t} \{x^{i_x} y^{i_y} z_1^{i_{z_1}+j} | x^{i_x} y^{i_y} z_1^{i_{z_1}} \text{ is a monomial of } f'_{sMSBs2}(x, y, z_1)^{m-1}$$

$$\text{and } i_{z_1} < k\},$$

$$M_{s3} := \{x^{i_x} y^{i_y} z_1^{i_{z_1}} | \text{monomials of } x^{i'_x} y^{i'_y} z_1^{i'_{z_1}} \cdot f'_{sMSBs2}(x, y, z_1)$$

$$\text{for } x^{i'_x} y^{i'_y} z_1^{i'_{z_1}} \in S_{s3} \cup S_{s4} \text{ and } i_{z_1} \ge k\},$$

$$M_{s4} := \{x^{i_x} y^{i_y} z_1^{i_{z_1}} | \text{monomials of } x^{i'_x} y^{i'_y} z_1^{i'_{z_1}} \cdot f'_{sMSBs2}(x, y, z_1)$$

$$\text{for } x^{i'_x} y^{i'_y} z_1^{i'_{z_1}} \in S_{s3} \cup S_{s4} \text{ and } i_{z_1} < k\}.$$

For shift-polynomials g_{sMSBs4}, we eliminate the term z_1z_2 by using the Durfee-Nguyen technique $z_1z_2 = N$. By definition, the index sets become

$$S_{s3} \Leftrightarrow i_x = 0, 1, \ldots, m - 1 - k + t; i_y = k - t, k - t + 1, \ldots, m - 1 - i_x;$$
$$i_{z_1} = k, k + 1, \ldots, m - 1 + t - i_x,$$
$$S_{s4} \Leftrightarrow i_x = 0, 1, \ldots, m - 1; i_y = 0, 1, \ldots, m - 1 - i_x;$$
$$i_{z_1} = 0, 1, \ldots, \min\{k - 1, m - 1 + t - i_x\},$$
$$M_{s3} \Leftrightarrow i_x = 0, 1, \ldots, m - k + t; i_y = k - t, k - t + 1, \ldots, m - i_x;$$
$$i_{z_1} = k, k + 1, \ldots, m + t - i_x,$$
$$M_{s4} \Leftrightarrow i_x = 0, 1, \ldots, m; i_y = 0, 1, \ldots, m - i_x;$$
$$i_{z_1} = 0, 1, \ldots, \min\{k - 1, m + t - i_x\}.$$

All these shift-polynomials g_{sMSBs3}, g_{sMSBs4} and g'_{sMSBs3}, g'_{sMSBs4} modulo R_{s2} have the roots $(x, y, z_1, z_2) = (-d_{p_1}, \ell, p, q)$ which are the same as $f_{sMSBs}(x, y, z_1)$ and the definition of z_2. We construct a lattice with coefficient vectors of $g_{sMSBs3}(xX, yY, z_1Z_1, z_2Z_2), g_{sMSBs4}(xX, yY, z_1Z_1, z_2Z_2)$ and $g'_{sMSBs3}(xX, yY, z_1Z_1, z_2Z_2), g'_{sMSBs4}(xX, yY, z_1Z_1, z_2Z_2)$ as the bases. Based on the Jochemsz-May strategy [JM06], LLL outputs two short lattice vectors which satisfy Howgrave-Graham's Lemma when $X^{s_X} Y^{s_Y} Z_1^{s_{Z_1}} Z_2^{s_{Z_2}} < W_{sMSBs}^{|S|}$ where

$$s_X = \sum_{i=0}^{m} \sum_{j=0}^{m-i} (m - i - j) + \sum_{i=0}^{m} \sum_{j=1}^{t} (m - i) = \left(\frac{1}{6} + \frac{\tau}{2}\right) m^3 + o(m^3),$$

$$s_Y = \sum_{i=0}^{m} \sum_{j=0}^{m-i} (i + j) + \sum_{i=0}^{m} \sum_{j=1}^{t} i = \left(\frac{1}{3} + \frac{\tau}{2}\right) m^3 + o(m^3),$$

$$s_{Z_1} = \sum_{i=s}^{m} \sum_{j=0}^{m-i} (i - s) + \sum_{i=s-t}^{m} \sum_{j=s-t-i}^{t} (i + j - s) = \frac{(1 + \tau - \eta)^3}{6} m^3 + o(m^3),$$

$$s_{Z_2} = \sum_{i=0}^{s} \sum_{j=0}^{m-i} (s - i) + \sum_{i=0}^{s} \sum_{j=1}^{\min\{t,s-i\}} (s - i - j) = \left(\frac{\eta^2}{2} - \frac{(\eta - \tau)^3}{6}\right) m^3 + o(m^3),$$

$$|S| = \sum_{i_x=0}^{m-1} \sum_{i_y=0}^{m-1-i_x} \sum_{i_{z_1}=0}^{m-1+t-i_x} 1 = \left(\frac{1}{6} + \frac{\tau}{2}\right) m^3 + o(m^3).$$

Ignoring low order terms of m, the condition becomes

$$\delta \cdot \left(\frac{1}{6} + \frac{\tau}{2}\right) + \left(\alpha + \beta - \frac{1}{2}\right) \cdot \left(\frac{1}{3} + \frac{\tau}{2}\right) + \frac{1}{2} \cdot \left(\frac{(1 + \tau - \eta)^3}{6} + \frac{\eta^2}{2} - \frac{(\eta - \tau)^3}{6}\right)$$
$$< (\alpha + \beta) \cdot \left(\frac{1}{6} + \frac{\tau}{2}\right).$$

Let $\tau = 0$ and we can obtain the condition based on the Jochemsz-May basic strategy. We optimize the parameter $\eta = (1 - 2\delta)/2, \tau = \left(\sqrt{1 - 4\delta} - 2\delta\right)/2$ and obtain the condition,

$$-5 + 8(\alpha + \beta) + 8\delta - 12\delta^2 - 2(1 - 4\delta)\sqrt{1 - 4\delta} < 0.$$

Note that the restriction $\tau \leq \eta \leq 1$ always holds. The restriction $0 \leq \tau$ holds only when $\delta \leq 1/\sqrt{2} - 1/2$. However, the condition always holds for $\alpha + \beta > 1/2$, which is the smallest choice of $\alpha + \beta$ for CRT-RSA.

Single LSBs Partial Key Exposure Attack on CRT-RSA. For a single LSBs partial key exposure attack on CRT-RSA, looking at CRT-RSA key generation,

$$e(d_1 M + d_0) = 1 + \ell(p - 1),$$

with some integer $\ell \approx N^{\alpha + \beta - 1/2}$. We consider a polynomial over the integers

$$f_{sLSBs}(x, y, z_1) := c_{sLSBs} + eMx + y(z_1 - 1)$$

where $c_{sLSBs} = 1 - ed_0$ whose roots are $(x, y, z_1) = (-d_0, \ell, p)$. We also use an additional variable $z_2 = q$. Sizes of the solutions are bounded by $X := N^\delta, Y := N^{\alpha + \beta - 1/2}, Z_1 := N^{1/2}, Z_2 := N^{1/2}$.

We set an integer $W_{sLSBs} := N^{\alpha + \beta}$ since $\|f_{sLSBs}(x, y, z_1)\|_\infty \geq |eMx| \approx N^{\alpha + \beta}$. The polynomial $f_{sLSBs}(x, y, z_1)$ has the same Newton polygon as $f_{sMSBs}(x, y, z_1)$, and the integers W_{sMSBs} and W_{sLSBs} are the same sizes. Therefore, we use the same lattice construction as above and obtain the condition of Theorem 6.

5   Double Partial Key Exposure Attacks on CRT-RSA

For double MSBs/LSBs partial key exposure attacks on CRT-RSA, we obtain the following result.

Theorem 7 (Double MSBs/LSBs). *Let $1/2 < \alpha + \beta \leq 3/2$. For double MSBs/LSBs partial key exposure attacks on CRT-RSA, when*

$$\delta < \frac{(18 - 12(\alpha+\beta))\tau^2 + (20 - 16(\alpha+\beta))\tau + 5 - 4(\alpha+\beta)}{24\tau^3 + 54\tau^2 + 40\tau + 10} \quad for \ \frac{15}{16} < \alpha + \beta < \frac{3}{2},$$

$$\delta < \frac{5 - 4(\alpha + \beta)}{10},$$

$$\delta < \frac{(12 - 24(\alpha+\beta))\tau^3 + (27 - 30(\alpha+\beta))\tau^2 + (20 - 16(\alpha+\beta))\tau + 5 - 4(\alpha+\beta)}{36\tau^2 + 40\tau + 10}$$

$$for \ \frac{1}{2} < \alpha + \beta < \frac{15}{26},$$

hold for some $\tau > 0$, then public RSA modulus N can be factored in polynomial time.

Note that the second condition is valid when $1/2 \leq \alpha + \beta \leq 5/4$ and better than the other conditions when $15/26 \leq \alpha + \beta \leq 15/16$.

In this section, we focus on the MSBs case.

Based on the Jochemsz-May Basic Strategy. As in a previous section, we start from the Jochemsz-May basic strategy. The lattice construction yields the second condition of Theorem 7.

Looking at CRT-RSA key generation,

$$ed_p = 1 + \ell_p(p-1) \quad \text{and} \quad ed_q = 1 + \ell_q(q-1),$$

with some integers $\ell_p, \ell_q \approx N^{\alpha+\beta-1/2}$. We multiply following two equations

$$ed_p - 1 + \ell_p = \ell_p p \quad \text{and} \quad ed_q - 1 + \ell_q = \ell_q q,$$

and obtain

$$e^2 d_p d_q + ed_p(\ell_q - 1) + ed_q(\ell_p - 1) - (N-1)\ell_p \ell_q - (\ell_p + \ell_q - 1) = 0.$$

For a double MSBs partial key exposure attack on CRT-RSA, we obtain

$$e^2(d_{p_0}M + d_{p_1})(d_{q_0}M + d_{q_1}) + e(d_{p_0}M + d_{p_1})(\ell_q - 1)$$
$$+ e(d_{q_0}M + d_{q_1})(\ell_p - 1) - (N-1)\ell_p \ell_q - (\ell_p + \ell_q - 1) = 0.$$

We consider a polynomial over the integers,

$$\begin{aligned}
f_{dMSBs}(x_1, x_2, y_1, y_2) = {} & e^2 x_1 x_2 + (e^2 d_{q_0}M - e)x_1 + (e^2 d_{p_0}M - e)x_2 \\
& + e x_1 y_2 + e x_2 y_1 + (ed_{q_0}M - 1)y_1 + (ed_{p_0}M - 1)y_2 \\
& - (N-1)y_1 y_2 + c_{dMSBs},
\end{aligned}$$

where $c_{dMSBs} = e^2 d_{p_0} d_{q_0} M^2 - ed_{p_0}M - ed_{q_0}M + 1$ whose roots are $(x_1, x_2, y_1, y_2) = (d_{p_1}, d_{q_1}, \ell_p, \ell_q)$. Sizes of the roots are bounded by $X_1 := N^\delta, X_2 := N^\delta, Y_1 := N^{\alpha+\beta-1/2}, Y_2 := N^{\alpha+\beta-1/2}$.

We set an integer $W_{dMSBs} := N^{2(\alpha+\beta)}$ since $\|f_{dMSBs}(x_1, x_2, y_1, y_2)\|_\infty \geq |(N-1)y_1 y_2| \approx N^{2(\alpha+\beta)}$. Note that $f_{dMSBs}(x_1, x_2, y_1, y_2)$ has the same monomials as the polynomial which Jochemsz and May considered in [JM07]. Therefore, we use the same lattice construction as [JM07]. We set an integer $R_{d1} := W_{dMSBs}(X_1 X_2 Y_1 Y_2)^{m-1}$ with some integer m such that $\gcd(c_{dMSBs}, R_{d1}) = 1$. We compute $a_{dMSBs1} = c_{dMSBs}^{-1} \bmod R_{d1}$ and $f'_{dMSBs1}(x_1, x_2, y_1, y_2) := a_{dMSBs1} \cdot f_{dMSBs}(x_1, x_2, y_1, y_2) \bmod R_{d1}$. We define a set of shift-polynomials g_{dMSBs1} and g'_{dMSBs1} as

$$g_{dMSBs1} : x_1^{i_{x_1}} x_2^{i_{x_2}} y_1^{i_{y_1}} y_2^{i_{y_2}}$$
$$\cdot f'_{dMSBs1}(x_1, x_2, y_1, y_2) X_1^{m-1-i_{x_1}} X_2^{m-1-i_{x_2}} Y_1^{m-1-i_{y_1}} Y_2^{m-1-i_{y_2}}$$
$$\text{for } x_1^{i_{x_1}} x_2^{i_{x_2}} y_1^{i_{y_1}} y_2^{i_{y_2}} \in S_{d1},$$

$$g'_{dMSBs1} : x_1^{i_{x_1}} x_2^{i_{x_2}} y_1^{i_{y_1}} y_2^{i_{y_2}} \cdot R_{d1} \quad \text{for } x_1^{i_{x_1}} x_2^{i_{x_2}} y_1^{i_{y_1}} y_2^{i_{y_2}} \in M_{d1} \setminus S_{d1},$$

for

$$S_{d1} := \{ x_1^{i_{x_1}} x_2^{i_{x_2}} y_1^{i_{y_1}} y_2^{i_{y_2}} \mid x_1^{i_{x_1}} x_2^{i_{x_2}} y_1^{i_{y_1}} y_2^{i_{y_2}} \text{ is a monomial of}$$
$$f'_{dMSBs1}(x_1, x_2, y_1, y_2)^{m-1} \},$$
$$M_{d1} := \{ \text{monomials of } x_1^{i_{x_1}} x_2^{i_{x_2}} y_1^{i_{y_1}} y_2^{i_{y_2}} \cdot f'_{dMSBs1}(x_1, x_2, y_1, y_2) \mid$$
$$x_1^{i_{x_1}} x_2^{i_{x_2}} y_1^{i_{y_1}} y_2^{i_{y_2}} \in S_{d1} \}.$$

By definition, the index sets become

$$S_{d1} \Leftrightarrow i_{x_1} = 0, 1, \ldots, m - 1 - i_{y_1}; i_{x_2} =; 0, 1, \ldots, m - 1 - i_{y_2};$$
$$i_{y_1} = 0, 1, \ldots, m - 1; i_{y_2} = 0, 1, \ldots, m - 1,$$
$$M_{d1} \Leftrightarrow i_{x_1} = 0, 1, \ldots, m - i_{y_1}; i_{x_2} =; 0, 1, \ldots, m - i_{y_2}; i_{y_1} = 0, 1, \ldots, m;$$
$$i_{y_2} = 0, 1, \ldots, m.$$

Shift-polynomials g_{dMSBs1} and g'_{dMSBs1} modulo R_{d1} have the roots $(x_1, x_2, y_1, y_2) = (d_{p_1}, d_{q_1}, \ell_p, \ell_q)$ which are the same as $f_{dMSBs}(x_1, x_2, y_1, y_2)$. We construct a lattice with coefficient vectors of $g_{dMSBs1}(x_1 X_1, x_2 X_2, y_1 Y_1, y_2 Y_2)$ and $g'_{dMSBs1}(x_1 X_1, x_2 X_2, y_1 Y_1, y_2 Y_2)$ as the bases. Based on the Jochemsz-May strategy [JM06], LLL outputs three short lattice vectors which satisfy Howgrave-Graham's Lemma when

$$(X_1 X_2)^{\frac{5}{12} m^4 + o(m^4)} (Y_1 Y_2)^{\frac{5}{12} m^4 + o(m^4)} < W_{dMSBs}^{\frac{1}{4} m^4 + o(m^4)}.$$

Ignoring low order terms of m, the condition becomes

$$\delta \cdot 2 \cdot \frac{5}{12} + \left(\alpha + \beta - \frac{1}{2} \right) \cdot 2 \cdot \frac{5}{12} < 2(\alpha + \beta) \cdot \frac{1}{4},$$

that is,

$$\delta < \frac{5 - 4(\alpha + \beta)}{10}.$$

The detailed calculation is discussed later.

Based on the Jochemsz-May Extended Strategy. Next, we show our lattice construction based on the Jochemsz-May extended strategy. The lattice construction enables us to solve the equation $f_{dMSBs}(x_1, x_2, y_1, y_2) = 0$ for larger $\alpha + \beta$ and yields the first and the third condition of Theorem 7. At first, we show the lattice construction for the first condition of Theorem 7.

We set an integer $R_{d2} := W_{dMSBs}(X_1 X_2)^{m-1+t}(Y_1 Y_2)^{m-1}$ with some integers m and $t = \tau m$ such that $\gcd(c_{dMSBs}, R_{d2}) = 1$. We compute $a_{dMSBs2} = c_{dMSBs}^{-1} \bmod R_{d2}$ and $f'_{dMSBs2}(x_1, x_2, y_1, y_2)$ as in the basic strategy. We define a set of shift-polynomials g_{dMSBs2} and g'_{dMSBs2} as

$$g_{dMSBs2} : x_1^{i_{x_1}} x_2^{i_{x_2}} y_1^{i_{y_1}} y_2^{i_{y_2}}$$
$$\cdot f'_{dMSBs2}(x_1, x_2, y_1, y_2) X_1^{m-1+t-i_{x_1}} X_2^{m-1+t-i_{x_2}} Y_1^{m-1-i_{y_1}} Y_2^{m-1-i_{y_2}}$$
$$\text{for } x_1^{i_{x_1}} x_2^{i_{x_2}} y_1^{i_{y_1}} y_2^{i_{y_2}} \in S_{d2},$$
$$g'_{dMSBs2} : x_1^{i_{x_1}} x_2^{i_{x_2}} y_1^{i_{y_1}} y_2^{i_{y_2}} \cdot R_{d2} \quad \text{for } x_1^{i_{x_1}} x_2^{i_{x_2}} y_1^{i_{y_1}} y_2^{i_{y_2}} \in M_{d2} \backslash S_{d2},$$

for

$$S_{d2} := \bigcup_{0 \leq j_1, j_2 \leq t} \{x_1^{i_{x_1}+j_1} x_2^{i_{x_2}+j_2} y_1^{i_{y_1}} y_2^{i_{y_2}} \mid x_1^{i_{x_1}} x_2^{i_{x_2}} y_1^{i_{y_1}} y_2^{i_{y_2}} \text{ is a monomial of}$$

$$f'_{dMSBs2}(x_1, x_2, y_1, y_2)^{m-1}\},$$

$$M_{d2} := \{\text{monomials of } x_1^{i_{x_1}} x_2^{i_{x_2}} y_1^{i_{y_1}} y_2^{i_{y_2}} \cdot f'_{dMSBs2}(x_1, x_2, y_1, y_2) \mid$$

$$x_1^{i_{x_1}} x_2^{i_{x_2}} y_1^{i_{y_1}} y_2^{i_{y_2}} \in S_{d2}\}.$$

By definition, the index sets become

$$S_{d2} \Leftrightarrow i_{x_1} = 0, 1, \ldots, m-1+t-i_{y_1}; i_{x_2} =; 0, 1, \ldots, m-1+t-i_{y_2};$$
$$i_{y_1} = 0, 1, \ldots, m-1; i_{y_2} = 0, 1, \ldots, m-1,$$
$$M_{d2} \Leftrightarrow i_{x_1} = 0, 1, \ldots, m+t-i_{y_1}; i_{x_2} =; 0, 1, \ldots, m+t-i_{y_2}; i_{y_1} = 0, 1, \ldots, m;$$
$$i_{y_2} = 0, 1, \ldots, m.$$

Shift-polynomials g_{dMSBs2} and g'_{dMSBs2} modulo R_{d2} have the roots $(x_1, x_2, y_1, y_2) = (d_{p_1}, d_{q_1}, \ell_p, \ell_q)$ which are the same as $f_{dMSBs}(x_1, x_2, y_1, y_2)$. We construct a lattice with coefficient vectors of $g_{dMSBs2}(x_1 X_1, x_2 X_2, y_1 Y_1, y_2 Y_2)$ and $g'_{dMSBs2}(x_1 X_1, x_2 X_2, y_1 Y_1, y_2 Y_2)$ as the bases. Based on the Jochemsz-May strategy [JM06], LLL outputs three short lattice vectors which satisfy Howgrave-Graham's Lemma when[3]

$$(X_1 X_2)^{(\tau^2 + \frac{9}{4}\tau^2 + \frac{5}{3}\tau + \frac{5}{12})m^4 + o(m^4)} (Y_1 Y_2)^{(\frac{3}{2}\tau^2 + \frac{5}{3}\tau + \frac{5}{12})m^4 + o(m^4)}$$
$$< W_{dMSBs}^{(\tau^2 + \tau + \frac{1}{4})m^4 + o(m^4)}.$$

Ignoring low order terms of m, the condition becomes

$$\delta \cdot 2 \cdot \left(\tau^2 + \frac{9}{4}\tau^2 + \frac{5}{3}\tau + \frac{5}{12}\right) + \left(\alpha + \beta - \frac{1}{2}\right) \cdot 2 \cdot \left(\frac{3}{2}\tau^2 + \frac{5}{3}\tau + \frac{5}{12}\right)$$
$$< 2(\alpha + \beta) \cdot \left(\tau^2 + \tau + \frac{1}{4}\right),$$

that is,

$$\delta < \frac{(18 - 12(\alpha + \beta))\tau^2 + (20 - 16(\alpha + \beta))\tau + 5 - 4(\alpha + \beta)}{24\tau^3 + 54\tau^2 + 40\tau + 10}.$$

The condition becomes the first condition of Theorem 7.

Next, we briefly summarize the lattice construction to yield the third condition of Theorem 7. This is the almost the same as the lattice construction described above except we add extra-shifts to y_1 and y_2 instead of x_1 and x_2.

To solve the equation $f_{dMSBs}(x_1, x_2, y_1, y_2) = 0$, we set an integer $R_{d3} := W_{dMSBs}(X_1 X_2)^{m-1}(Y_1 Y_2)^{m-1+t}$ with some integer m and $t = \tau m$ such

---

[3] In this paper, we omit the calculation since that is the same as [JM07]. See the paper for detailed calculation.

that $\gcd(c_{dMSBs}, R_{d3}) = 1$. We compute $a_{dMSBs3} = c_{dMSBs}^{-1} \mod R_{d3}$ and $f'_{dMSBs3}(x_1, x_2, y_1, y_2) := a_{dMSBs3}f_{dMSBs}(x_1, x_2, y_1, y_2) \mod R_{d3}$. We define a set of shift-polynomials g_{dMSBs3} and g'_{dMSBs3} as

$$g_{dMSBs3} : x_1^{i_{x_1}} x_2^{i_{x_2}} y_1^{i_{y_1}} y_2^{i_{y_2}}$$
$$\cdot f'_{dMSBs3}(x_1, x_2, y_1, y_2) X_1^{m-1-i_{x_1}} X_2^{m-1-i_{x_2}} Y_1^{m-1+t-i_{y_1}} Y_2^{m-1+t-i_{y_2}}$$
$$\text{for } x_1^{i_{x_1}} x_2^{i_{x_2}} y_1^{i_{y_1}} y_2^{i_{y_2}} \in S_{d3},$$
$$g'_{dMSBs3} : x_1^{i_{x_1}} x_2^{i_{x_2}} y_1^{i_{y_1}} y_2^{i_{y_2}} \cdot R_{d3} \quad \text{for } x_1^{i_{x_1}} x_2^{i_{x_2}} y_1^{i_{y_1}} y_2^{i_{y_2}} \in M_{d3} \backslash S_{d3},$$

for

$$S_{d3} := \bigcup_{0 \le j_1, j_2 \le t} \{x_1^{i_{x_1}} x_2^{i_{x_2}} y_1^{i_{y_1}+j_1} y_2^{i_{y_2}+j_2} \mid x_1^{i_{x_1}} x_2^{i_{x_2}} y_1^{i_{y_1}} y_2^{i_{y_2}} \text{ is a monomial of}$$
$$f'_{dMSBs3}(x_1, x_2, y_1, y_2)^{m-1}\},$$
$$M_{d3} := \{\text{monomials of } x_1^{i_{x_1}} x_2^{i_{x_2}} y_1^{i_{y_1}} y_2^{i_{y_2}} \cdot f'_{dMSBs3}(x_1, x_2, y_1, y_2) \mid$$
$$x_1^{i_{x_1}} x_2^{i_{x_2}} y_1^{i_{y_1}} y_2^{i_{y_2}} \in S_{d3}\}.$$

By definition, the index sets become

$$S_{d3} \Leftrightarrow i_{x_1} = 0, 1, \ldots, m-1-i_{y_1}; i_{x_2} =; 0, 1, \ldots, m-1-i_{y_2};$$
$$i_{y_1} = 0, 1, \ldots, m-1+t; i_{y_2} = 0, 1, \ldots, m-1+t,$$
$$M_{d3} \Leftrightarrow i_{x_1} = 0, 1, \ldots, m-i_{y_1}; i_{x_2} =; 0, 1, \ldots, m-i_{y_2}; i_{y_1} = 0, 1, \ldots, m+t;$$
$$i_{y_2} = 0, 1, \ldots, m+t.$$

Shift-polynomials g_{dMSBs3} and g'_{dMSBs3} modulo R_{d3} have the roots $(x_1, x_2, y_1, y_2) = (d_{p_1}, d_{q_1}, \ell_p, \ell_q)$ which are the same as $f_{dMSBs}(x_1, x_2, y_1, y_2)$. We construct a lattice with coefficient vectors of $g_{dMSBs3}(x_1 X_1, x_2 X_2, y_1 Y_1, y_2 Y_2)$ and $g'_{dMSBs3}(x_1 X_1, x_2 X_2, y_1 Y_1, y_2 Y_2)$ as the bases. Based on the Jochemsz-May strategy [JM06], LLL outputs three short lattice vectors which satisfy Howgrave-Graham's Lemma when

$$(X_1 X_2)^{(\frac{3}{2}\tau^2 + \frac{5}{3}\tau + \frac{5}{12})m^4 + o(m^4)} (Y_1 Y_2)^{(\tau^2 + \frac{9}{4}\tau^2 + \frac{5}{3}\tau + \frac{5}{12})m^4 + o(m^4)}$$
$$< W_{dMSBs}^{(\tau^2 + \tau + \frac{1}{4})m^4 + o(m^4)}.$$

Ignoring low order terms of m, the condition becomes

$$\delta \cdot 2 \cdot \left(\frac{3}{2}\tau^2 + \frac{5}{3}\tau + \frac{5}{12}\right) + \left(\alpha + \beta - \frac{1}{2}\right) \cdot 2 \cdot \left(\tau^2 + \frac{9}{4}\tau^2 + \frac{5}{3}\tau + \frac{5}{12}\right)$$
$$< 2(\alpha + \beta) \cdot \left(\tau^2 + \tau + \frac{1}{4}\right),$$

that is,

$$\delta < \frac{(12 - 24(\alpha+\beta))\tau^3 + (27 - 30(\alpha+\beta))\tau^2 + (20 - 16(\alpha+\beta))\tau + 5 - 4(\alpha+\beta)}{36\tau^2 + 40\tau + 10}.$$

The condition becomes the third condition of Theorem 7.

Double LSBs Partial Key Exposure Attack on CRT-RSA. As above, we can obtain the following equation

$$e^2 d_p d_q + e d_p(\ell_q - 1) + e d_q(\ell_p - 1) - (N-1)\ell_p \ell_q - (\ell_p + \ell_q - 1) = 0,$$

from CRT-RSA key generations. For a double LSBs partial key exposure attack on CRT-RSA, we obtain

$$e^2(d_{p_1} M + d_{p_0})(d_{q_1} M + d_{q_0}) + e(d_{p_1} M + d_{p_0})(\ell_q - 1)$$
$$+ e(d_{q_1} M + d_{q_0})(\ell_p - 1) - (N-1)\ell_p \ell_q - (\ell_p + \ell_q - 1) = 0.$$

We consider a polynomial over the integers,

$$f_{dLSBs}(x_1, x_2, y_1, y_2) = e^2 M^2 x_1 x_2 + (e^2 d_{q_0} - e)M x_1 + (e^2 d_{p_0} - e)M x_2$$
$$+ eM x_1 y_2 + eM x_2 y_1 + (e d_{q_0} - 1)y_1 + (e d_{p_0} - 1)y_2$$
$$- (N-1)y_1 y_2 + c_{dLSBs},$$

where $c_{dLSBs} = e^2 d_{p_0} d_{q_0} - e d_{p_0} - e d_{q_0} + 1$ whose roots are $(x_1, x_2, y_1, y_2) = (d_{p_1}, d_{q_1}, \ell_p, \ell_q)$. Sizes of the roots are bounded by $X_1 := N^\delta, X_2 := N^\delta, Y_1 := N^{\alpha+\beta-1/2}, Y_2 := N^{\alpha+\beta-1/2}$.

We set an integer $W_{dLSBs} := N^{2(\alpha+\beta)}$ since $\|f_{dLSBs}(x_1, x_2, y_1, y_2)\|_\infty \geq |e^2 M^2 x_1 x_2| \approx N^{2(\alpha+\beta)}$. The polynomial $f_{dLSBs}(x_1, x_2, y_1, y_2)$ has the same Newton polygon as $f_{dMSBs}(x_1, x_2, y_1, y_2)$, and the integers W_{dMSBs} and W_{dLSBs} are the same sizes. Therefore, we use the same lattice construction as above and obtain the condition of Theorem 7.

Acknowledgement. We would like to thank members of the study group "Shin-Akarui-Angou-Benkyou-Kai" for their helpful comments. The first author is supported by a JSPS Fellowship for Young Scientists. This research was supported by CREST, JST and JSPS KAKENHI Grant Number 25280001.

References

[Aon09] Aono, Y.: A new lattice construction for partial key exposure attack for RSA. In: Jarecki, S., Tsudik, G. (eds.) PKC 2009. LNCS, vol. 5443, pp. 34–53. Springer, Heidelberg (2009)

[BM06] Bleichenbacher, D., May, A.: New attacks on RSA with small secret CRT-exponents. In: Yung, M., Dodis, Y., Kiayias, A., Malkin, T. (eds.) PKC 2006. LNCS, vol. 3958, pp. 1–13. Springer, Heidelberg (2006)

[BM03] Blömer, J., May, A.: New partial key exposure attacks on RSA. In: Boneh, D. (ed.) CRYPTO 2003. LNCS, vol. 2729, pp. 27–43. Springer, Heidelberg (2003)

[BDL97] Boneh, D., DeMillo, R.A., Lipton, R.J.: On the importance of checking cryptographic protocols for faults. J. Cryptol. **10**(4), 233–260 (1997)

[BD00] Boneh, D., Durfee, G.: Cryptanalysis of RSA with private key d less than $N^{0.292}$. IEEE Trans. Inf. Theory **46**(4), 1339–1349 (2000)

[BDF98] Boneh, D., Durfee, G., Frankel, Y.: An attack on RSA given a small fraction of the private key bits. In: Ohta, K., Pei, D. (eds.) ASIACRYPT 1998. LNCS, vol. 1514, pp. 25–34. Springer, Heidelberg (1998)

[Cop95] Coppersmith, D.: Factoring with a hint. IBM Research Report RC 19905 (1995)

[Cop96a] Coppersmith, D.: Finding a small root of a univariate modular equation. In: Maurer, U.M. (ed.) EUROCRYPT 1996. LNCS, vol. 1070, pp. 155–165. Springer, Heidelberg (1996)

[Cop96b] Coppersmith, D.: Finding a small root of a bivariate integer equation; factoring with high bits known. In: Maurer, U.M. (ed.) EUROCRYPT 1996. LNCS, vol. 1070, pp. 178–189. Springer, Heidelberg (1996)

[Cop97] Coppersmith, D.: Small solutions to polynomial equations, and low exponent RSA vulnerabilities. J. Cryptol. $10(4)$, 233–260 (1997)

[Cop01] Coppersmith, D.: Finding small solutions to small degree polynomials. In: Silverman, J.H. (ed.) CaLC 2001. LNCS, vol. 2146, pp. 20–31. Springer, Heidelberg (2001)

[Cor04] Coron, J.-S.: Finding small roots of bivariate integer polynomial equations revisited. In: Cachin, C., Camenisch, J.L. (eds.) EUROCRYPT 2004. LNCS, vol. 3027, pp. 492–505. Springer, Heidelberg (2004)

[Cor07] Coron, J.-S.: Finding small roots of bivariate integer polynomial equations: a direct approach. In: Menezes, A. (ed.) CRYPTO 2007. LNCS, vol. 4622, pp. 379–394. Springer, Heidelberg (2007)

[DN00] Durfee, G., Nguyên, P.Q.: Cryptanalysis of the RSA schemes with short secret exponent from Asiacrypt 1999. In: Okamoto, T. (ed.) ASIACRYPT 2000. LNCS, vol. 1976, pp. 14–29. Springer, Heidelberg (2000)

[EJMW05] Ernst, M., Jochemsz, E., May, A., de Weger, B.: Partial key exposure attacks on RSA up to full size exponents. In: Cramer, R. (ed.) EURO-CRYPT 2005. LNCS, vol. 3494, pp. 371–386. Springer, Heidelberg (2005)

[GHM05] Galbraith, S.D., Heneghan, C., McKee, J.F.: Tunable balancing of RSA. In: Boyd, C., González Nieto, J.M. (eds.) ACISP 2005. LNCS, vol. 3574, pp. 280–292. Springer, Heidelberg (2005)

[HM10] Herrmann, M., May, A.: Maximizing small root bounds by linearization and applications to small secret exponent RSA. In: Nguyen, P.Q., Pointcheval, D. (eds.) PKC 2010. LNCS, vol. 6056, pp. 53–69. Springer, Heidelberg (2010)

[How97] Howgrave-Graham, N.: Finding small roots of univariate modular equations revisited. In: Darnell, M.J. (ed.) Cryptography and Coding 1997. LNCS, vol. 1355, pp. 131–142. Springer, Heidelberg (1997)

[JM06] Jochemsz, E., May, A.: A strategy for finding roots of multivariate polynomials with new applications in attacking RSA variants. In: Lai, X., Chen, K. (eds.) ASIACRYPT 2006. LNCS, vol. 4284, pp. 267–282. Springer, Heidelberg (2006)

[JM07] Jochemsz, E., May, A.: A polynomial time attack on RSA with private CRT-exponents smaller than $N^{0.073}$. In: Menezes, A. (ed.) CRYPTO 2007. LNCS, vol. 4622, pp. 395–411. Springer, Heidelberg (2007)

[JL12] Joye, M., Lepoint, T.: Partial key exposure on RSA with private exponents larger than N. In: Ryan, M.D., Smyth, B., Wang, G. (eds.) ISPEC 2012. LNCS, vol. 7232, pp. 369–380. Springer, Heidelberg (2012)

[LLL82] Lenstra, A.K. Lenstra Jr., H.W., Lovász, L.: Factoring polynomials with rational coefficients. Math. Ann. **261**, 515–534 (1982)

[LZL14] Lu, Y., Zhang, R., Lin, D.: New partial key exposure attacks on CRT-RSA with large public exponents. In: Boureanu, I., Owesarski, P., Vaudenay, S. (eds.) ACNS 2014. LNCS, vol. 8479, pp. 151–162. Springer, Heidelberg (2014)

[May02] May, A.: Cryptanalysis of unbalanced RSA with small CRT-exponent. In: Yung, M. (ed.) CRYPTO 2002. LNCS, vol. 2442, pp. 242–256. Springer, Heidelberg (2002)

[May03] May, A.: New RSA vulnerabilities using lattice reduction methods. Ph.D. thesis, University of Paderborn (2003)

[May10] May, A.: Using LLL-reduction for solving RSA and factorization problems: a survey. http://www.cits.rub.de/permonen/may.html (2010)

[NS01] Nguyên, P.Q., Stern, J.: The two faces of lattices in cryptology. In: Silverman, J.H. (ed.) CaLC 2001. LNCS, vol. 2146, pp. 146–180. Springer, Heidelberg (2001)

[QC82] Quisquater, J.J., Couvreur, C.: Fast decipherment algorithm for RSA public-key cryptosystems. Electron. Lett. **18**, 905–907 (1982)

[RS86] Rivest, R.L., Shamir, A.: Efficient factoring based on partial information. In: Pichler, F. (ed.) EUROCRYPT 1985. LNCS, vol. 219, pp. 31–34. Springer, Heidelberg (1986)

[RSA78] Rivest, R.L., Shamir, A., Adleman, L.M.: A method for obtaining digital signatures and public-key cryptosystems. Commun. ACM **21**(2), 120–126 (1978)

[SGM10] Sarkar, S., Sen Gupta, S., Maitra, S.: Partial key exposure attack on RSA – improvements for limited lattice dimensions. In: Gong, G., Gupta, K.C. (eds.) INDOCRYPT 2010. LNCS, vol. 6498, pp. 2–16. Springer, Heidelberg (2010)

[SM09] Sarkar, S., Maitra, S.: Partial key exposure attack on CRT-RSA. In: Abdalla, M., Pointcheval, D., Fouque, P.-A., Vergnaud, D. (eds.) ACNS 2009. LNCS, vol. 5536, pp. 473–484. Springer, Heidelberg (2009)

[TK14] Takayasu, A., Kunihiro, N.: Partial key exposure attacks on RSA: achieving the Boneh-Durfee bound. In: Joux, A., Youssef, A. (eds.) SAC 2014. LNCS, vol. 8781, pp. 345–362. Springer, Heidelberg (2014)

[Wie90] Wiener, M.J.: Cryptanalysis of short RSA secret exponents. IEEE Trans. Inf. Theory **36**(3), 553–558 (1990)

Differential Power Analysis
of a McEliece Cryptosystem

Cong Chen[1], Thomas Eisenbarth[1(✉)], Ingo von Maurich[2],
and Rainer Steinwandt[3]

[1] Worcester Polytechnic Institute, Worcester, MA, USA
{cchen3,teisenbarth}@wpi.edu
[2] Ruhr-Universität Bochum, Bochum, Germany
ingo.vonmaurich@rub.de
[3] Florida Atlantic University, Boca Raton, USA
rsteinwa@fau.edu

Abstract. This work presents the first differential power analysis of an implementation of the McEliece cryptosystem. Target of this side-channel attack is a state-of-the-art FPGA implementation of the efficient QC-MDPC McEliece decryption operation as presented at DATE 2014. The presented cryptanalysis succeeds to recover the complete secret key after a few observed decryptions. It consists of a combination of a differential leakage analysis during the syndrome computation followed by an algebraic step that exploits the relation between the public and private key.

Keywords: Differential power analysis · McEliece cryptosystem · QC-MDPC Codes · FPGA

1 Introduction and Motivation

The basic idea of the McEliece public-key encryption scheme can be traced back more than 35 years [19]. Having passed the test of time, today it is considered one of the most promising alternatives to public-key encryption schemes whose underling hardness assumptions are invalidated by known quantum algorithms [23]. A critical point of McEliece-based constructions is the large key size, and to tackle this problem it is tempting to impose additional structure on the code involved. For some proposals in this line of work, including constructions building on Goppa codes, cryptanalytic strategies to exploit the additional structure have been put forward [5–7]. Lacking obvious algebraic code structure that can be exploited by an adversary, *quasi-cyclic moderate-density parity-check (QC-MDPC)* codes currently receive considerable attention as an implementation choice [3,9,17,18]. In this paper we take a closer look at a lightweight state-of-the-art FPGA implementation of this scheme as presented in [17].

Our Contribution. In this paper we are not concerned with the security of the specific parameters in [17] against the underlying theoretical problem, and

© Springer International Publishing Switzerland 2015
T. Malkin et al. (Eds.): ACNS 2015, LNCS 9092, pp. 538–556, 2015.
DOI: 10.1007/978-3-319-28166-7_26

instead focus on *side-channel attacks*. Even in a post-quantum world, i.e., when scalable quantum computers are available, implementation-specific information leakage will remain a serious issue, but so far no differential power analysis (DPA) has been documented on implementations of McEliece. In fact, [10] concluded that a classical DPA attack is not possible for their target implementations. In this paper we demonstrate that DPA can be a realistic threat for a state-of-the-art FPGA implementation of McEliece. Besides showing that significant parts of the private key can be recovered by DPA, we show that knowledge of the public key can be utilized to recover missing key information or to correct remaining errors in hypothesized key bits.

On the conceptual side it deserves to be noted that our cryptanalysis targets the decoding algorithm, and thus is not restricted to a basic McEliece as presented in [17]. If the basic scheme is augmented with a padding to establish stronger provable guarantees, then this does not prevent our side-channel attack as long as the decryption algorithm is applied to the ciphertext directly, possibly followed by some plausibility checks. This type of padding is common in combination with the McEliece cryptosystem [13, 22].

Related Work. Using QC-MDPC codes in the McEliece cryptosystem was first proposed by [20] and later published with small changes in the parameter set in [21]. These codes have no obvious algebraic structure and still allow small key sizes, which gained high interest in the research community. First implementations of this scheme for AVR microcontrollers and Xilinx FPGAs were proposed in [9]. Their FPGA implementation aimed for a high throughput at the cost of a high resource consumption while their microcontroller implementation for the first time showed that it is possible to implement McEliece without external memory to store the keys. A recent lightweight FPGA implementation showed the full potential of this promising scheme [17]. Occupying less than 230 slices and 4 Block RAMs on Xilinx's smallest Spartan-6 FPGA (XC6SLX4) for a combined encryption/decryption unit, their implementation still provides a reasonable performance of 3.4 ms and 23 ms for en-/decryption, respectively.

Side-channel leakages of McEliece have first been studied in [26]. This work, as well as two follow-up studies focused on analyzing timing behavior of different parts of PC implementations of McEliece [24, 25]. Subsequently, [1] improved over prior results, presented countermeasures and pointed out leakages in the preprocessing steps of McEliece encryption. Heyse et al. [10] performed power analysis on software implementations of classic McEliece implementations. Their work relies on simple power analysis (SPA)-based approaches, which usually do not translate well to hardware implementations, due to the increased parallel processing of data and the much smaller side-channel leakage. They also show that side-channel analysis is impeded by the large key sizes of McEliece. In a recent work, AVR/ARM microcontroller implementations of QC-MDPC McEliece were shown to be susceptible to SPA attacks [18]. The found weaknesses rely on secret dependent branches, which allow to recover the encrypted message as well as to recover the secret key.

2 Background

McEliece based on (QC-)MDPC codes is fully described in [21]. To provide the necessary context for our attack, this section gives a brief summary of (QC-) MDPC codes and their instantiation in the McEliece cryptosystem.

2.1 Quasi-Cyclic Moderate-Density Parity-Check Codes

A *binary linear* $[n, k]$ *error-correcting code* C of length n is a k-dimensional vector subspace of $\mathbb{F}_2^n$. We write $r = n - k$ for the co-dimension of C. The code C can be specified by providing a *generator matrix* $G \in \mathbb{F}_2^{k \times n}$, i.e., a matrix whose rows form a basis of C. Alternatively, one can provide a *parity-check matrix* $H \in \mathbb{F}_2^{r \times n}$ which characterizes the linear code as $C = \{c \in \mathbb{F}_2^n \mid cH^T = 0^r\}$. Given a parity-check matrix and a vector $x \in \mathbb{F}_2^n$, we refer to $s = Hx^T \in \mathbb{F}_2^r$ as *syndrome* of x. In particular, a vector from $\mathbb{F}_2^n$ is contained in C if and only if its syndrome is 0^r.

If a code C is closed under cyclic shifts of its codewords by n_0 positions for some integer $n_0 \geq 1$, we refer to C as *quasi-cyclic* (QC). If $n = n_0 \cdot p$ for some integer p, both generator and parity-check matrix can be chosen to be composed of $p \times p$ circulant blocks. This has the advantage that only one row (usually the first) of each circulant block needs to be stored to completely describe the matrices. For a *moderate-density parity-check* (MDPC) code, we choose the weight of each row to have the same density $w = O(\sqrt{n \log(n)})$. For short, we refer to a binary linear $[n, k]$ error-correcting code defined by a parity-check matrix with constant row weight w and co-dimension r as an (n, r, w)-MDPC code. If such a code is in addition quasi-cyclic with $n = n_0 r$, we speak of an (n, r, w)-QC-MDPC code.

2.2 The QC-MDPC McEliece Public-Key Encryption Scheme

The QC-MDPC McEliece public-key encryption scheme uses t-error correcting (n, r, w)-QC-MDPC codes, i.e., up to t "flipped bits" in any codeword $c \in C$ can be corrected. Specifically, using such a code, key generation, encryption, and decryption operations can be described as follows.

Key-Generation. The secret key is comprised of the first rows $h_0, \ldots, h_{n_0-1} \in \mathbb{F}_2^r$ of the n_0 parity-check matrix blocks $H_0, \ldots, H_{n_0-1}$. These rows are chosen at random and it has to be ensured that their weights—the number of non-zero entries—sum up to w: $\sum_{i=0}^{n_0-1} \text{wt}(h_i) = w$, where wt() denotes the Hamming weight computation function. Iterated cyclic rotation of the h_i yields the parity-check matrix blocks $H_0, \ldots, H_{n_0-1} \in \mathbb{F}_2^{r \times r}$ and thereby the secret parity-check matrix $H = (H_0 | \ldots | H_{n_0-1})$ of an (n, r, w)-QC-MDPC code with $n = n_0 r$. Assuming the last block H_{n_0-1} to be non-singular, the public key is obtained as generator matrix $G = [I_k | Q]$ in standard form, simply concatenating the identity matrix $I_k \in \mathbb{F}_2^{k \times k}$ with

$$Q = \begin{pmatrix} (H_{n_0-1}^{-1} \cdot H_0)^T \\ (H_{n_0-1}^{-1} \cdot H_1)^T \\ \cdots \\ (H_{n_0-1}^{-1} \cdot H_{n_0-2})^T \end{pmatrix}.$$

Similarly as for the secret key, the public matrix G is determined through its first row. For a textbook version of McEliece the systematic form of G is problematic, but in combination with a conversion to protect against chosen-ciphertext attacks (cf. [13,22]) having the generator matrix G in systematic form is accepted practice.

Encryption. To encrypt a message $m \in \mathbb{F}_2^k$, an error vector $e \in \mathbb{F}_2^n$ of weight $\mathrm{wt}(e) \leq t$ is chosen at random. With this, the ciphertext evaluates to $x = (m \cdot G \oplus e) \in \mathbb{F}_2^n$.

Decryption. To decrypt a ciphertext $x \in \mathbb{F}_2^n$, a t-error correcting (QC-)MDPC decoder Ψ_H is applied to x, recovering $mG \leftarrow \Psi_H(x)$. Since G is in systematic form, the message m can simply be read off from the first k positions of mG.

Parameters. For the implementation investigated in this paper, we used parameters, which in [21] have been considered for an 80-bit security level: $n_0 = 2, n = 9602, r = 4801, w = 90, t = 84$. With these parameters a 4801-bit plaintext block results in a 9602-bit codeword to which $t = 84$ errors are added. The parity-check matrix H has constant row weight $w = 90$ and is obtained as juxtaposition of $n_0 = 2$ circulant blocks. The Q-part of the public generator matrix G consists of a single circulant block.

2.3   Decoding (QC-)MDPC Codes

Several decoders have been proposed to actually decode (QC-)MDPC codes [2,8,9,11,21]. The implementation investigated in this paper employs the decoder from [9], an optimized version of the *bit-flipping decoder* by [8]. The precomputed thresholds are derived from the code parameters as proposed by [8]. To decode a received ciphertext $x \in \mathbb{F}_2^n$, four main steps are involved:

1. Compute the syndrome $s = Hx^T$.
2. Count the number of unsatisfied parity checks for every ciphertext bit.
3. If the number of unsatisfied parity checks for a ciphertext bit exceeds a precomputed threshold, flip the ciphertext bit and update the syndrome.
4. If $s = 0^r$, the codeword was decoded successfully. If $s \neq 0^r$, go to Step 2 or abort after a defined maximum of iterations with a decoding error.

2.4   Target Implementation

The target under investigation is a lightweight implementation of QC-MDPC McEliece for reconfigurable devices by [17]. The resource requirements are 64 slices and 1 block RAM (BRAM) to implement encryption and 159 slices and 3 BRAMs to implement decryption on a Xilinx Spartan-6 XC6SLX4 FPGA. This lightweight implementation is possible mainly for two reasons. First, QC-MDPC codes allow smaller keys compared to (optimized) binary Goppa codes. Second, the implementation stores inputs, outputs and most intermediate values during encryption and decryption in block memories. Since our attack focuses on secret-key recovery, we limit the description of the details of the implementation to the decryption, especially to the part in which the syndrome is computed.

Decryption uses three BRAMs, one BRAM stores the $2 \cdot 4801$-bit secret key, one BRAM stores the $2 \cdot 4801$-bit ciphertext, and one BRAM stores the 4801-bit syndrome. Each BRAM is dual-ported, offers 18/36 kBit, and allows to read/write two 32-bit values at different addresses in one clock cycle. To compute the syndrome, set bits in the ciphertext select rows of the parity-check matrix blocks that are accumulated. Since only one row of each block is stored in the BRAM, they need to be rotated by one bit to generate the next rows. To generate all rows of H, the rotation is repeated 4801 times.

Rotating the two parts of the secret key is implemented in parallel, which means that the 4801-bit rows of the first and the second part of the parity-check matrix are rotated at the same time. Efficient rotation is realized using the READ_FIRST mode of Xilinx's BRAMs which allows to read the content of a 32-bit memory cell and then to overwrite it with a new value, all within one clock cycle.

The key rotation is implemented as follows: in the first clock cycle, the least significant bit (LSB) is loaded from the last memory cell. The first 32-bit of the row to be rotated are loaded next. In all following clock cycles, the succeeding 32-bit blocks of the row are read and overwritten by the rotated preceding 32-bit block. The LSB of each 32-bit block is delayed by a flip-flop and becomes the most significant bit (MSB) of the following block. An abstraction of this implementation is depicted in Fig. 1. In addition to a rotation of the rows, this introduces a rotation of the memory cells. After one 4801-bit rotation, the most significant 32 bits of a parity-check matrix row do not reside in memory cell 0 but in memory cell 1.

The syndrome s is computed by processing the ciphertext x in a bitwise fashion. If the j-th bit is set, i.e., $x_j = 1$, then the j-th row of H is added to the syndrome s. The implementation adds two 32-bit words in parallel: one word of the rotated h_0 and one word of h_1 are processed in each clock cycle.

3   Attack Description

Usually DPA attacks exploit an intermediate state $y = f(x, k)$ that is a function of both a known data item x and a subkey k. The subkey space $\mathcal{K}$ should be small enough so that a hypothesis y can be checked for all candidates $k \in \mathcal{K}$. Some works that elaborate on this model are [14,16,27]. McEliece does not offer itself for this approach, as also noted in [10]. One would expect the syndrome s to serve as a potential predictable intermediate state y. However, the bits in

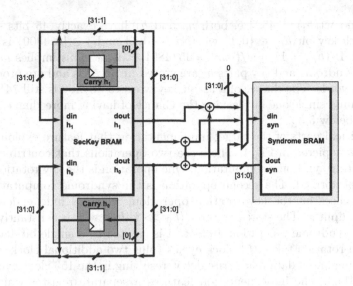

Fig. 1. Abstract block diagram of the syndrome computation circuit including key rotation as implemented in [17].

the ciphertext x only determine which rows of the parity check matrix H are added to s, where H is the secret key to be recovered. Predicting (parts of) the syndrome s requires an additional key bit hypothesis for each variation of each bit of s, i.e., each bit of s depends on l key bits after l variations, supporting the infeasibility claim of [10]. One of the strengths of QC-MDPC, its small private key size, comes from the fact that secret information is highly redundant: each row of H contains the same information—namely $\langle h_0 \ggg z || h_1 \ggg z \rangle$—only rotated by one bit per row, $z \in \{0, 4800\}$. This redundancy allows for an efficient recovery of key information. More important, it enables a *differential* analysis approach which greatly enhances the visibility of even faint leakages.

We exploit this leakage of the key rotation operation during syndrome computation. Our analysis recovers a static key leakage that is completely independent of the known or chosen ciphertext input x. Since the exploited leakage occurs several times during one syndrome computation, our attack combines these leakage events, as commonly done in horizontal side channel attacks.

3.1   Leakage Behavior of the Target Implementation

The described attack recovers the key during the syndrome computation step of the decryption algorithm. The key for QC-MDPC consists of a single line of the parity check matrix H, namely $h_0 || h_1$. As described in Sect. 2.4, only this line of H, or one of its rotated versions $\langle h_0 \ggg z || h_1 \ggg z \rangle$, is stored in BRAM. The key has some noteworthy features that influence the derived DPA attacks. First, the private key is of *low weight*: both parts of the secret key h_0 and h_1 are of low Hamming weight such that, $\mathrm{wt}(h_0 || h_1) = w$. For the target implementation,

$w = 90$ and $\mathrm{wt}(h_i) = 45$, i.e. both h_0 and h_1 have exactly 45 bits set. This means, each key bit $h_{i,j} \in \{0,1\}$ where $i \in \{0,1\}$ and $j \in \{0,4800\}$ is set with probability $\Pr(h_{i,j} = 1) = w/(n_0 r) = 45/4801 \approx .94\%$. This implies *low-weight leakages*: Syndrome and key parts h_i are stored in BRAMs and are processed as 151 32-bit words. The chance of a 32-bit key word to be all-0 is still 74%, about 22% contain a single one bit, leaving the chance of having more than one bit set in a word below 5%.

The critical parts of the target implementation that feature exploitable key leakage are depicted in Fig. 1. There are two operations that contribute to the leakage during syndrome computation. One operation is the key rotation, which is always performed. The second operation is the syndrome computation. Our analysis focuses on the key rotation operation, which is independent of the ciphertext input x. The stored key row $\langle h_0 \ggg z || h_1 \ggg z \rangle$ is constantly rotated during the syndrome generation. In fact, it is rotated by a single bit 4801 times, where each rotation takes 151 clock cycles (plus two additional clock cycles for preprocessing and a data read-write delay, resulting in the 153 clock cycles mentioned in [17]). The implementation features a separate register which stores the carry bit during rotations. In each of these clock cycles, one bit $h_{i,j}$—the LSB of the last accessed word—is written to the carry register, causing leakage $\lambda_{\mathrm{carry}}(i,j)$. In the following clock cycle, that bit is overwritten with the LSB of the next word, $h_{i,j+32}$. Assuming a Hamming distance leakage function, this register leaks first

$$\lambda_{\mathrm{carry}}(i,j) = w_1 \cdot \mathrm{wt}(h_{i,j-32} \oplus h_{i,j}), \qquad (1)$$

then, in the subsequent clock cycle, leaks $\lambda_{\mathrm{carry}}(i,j+32) = w_1 \cdot \mathrm{wt}(h_{i,j} \oplus h_{i,j+32})$, where $w_1 \in \mathbb{R}$ is an appropriate weight. Assuming that $h_{i,j} = 1$ and further $h_{i,j\pm32} = 0$, $\lambda_{\mathrm{carry}}(i,j)$ gives a clearly distinguishable leakage from the case where $h_{i,j} = 0$. This leakage is the target of the described attack.

In addition to the leakage of the carry register $\lambda_{\mathrm{carry}}(i,j)$ described in Eq. (1), there are related leakages happening in the same clock cycles. In fact, when $h_{i,j}$ is written to the carry register, the implementation also reads the word $\langle h_{i,j+1} \ldots h_{i,j+32} \rangle$ from the block memory at one address and then stores the word $\langle h_{i,j-32} \ldots h_{i,j-1} \rangle$ into the block memory at the same address. Both reading and storing operations will cause leakages at different levels. Assuming a Hamming weight leakage function here, reading data and storing data words leaks as

$$\lambda_{\mathrm{read}}(i,j) = w_2 \cdot \mathrm{wt}(\langle h_{i,j+1} \ldots h_{i,j+32} \rangle) \text{ and}$$
$$\lambda_{\mathrm{store}}(i,j) = w_3 \cdot \mathrm{wt}(\langle h_{i,j-32} \ldots h_{i,j-1} \rangle),$$

respectively. Here, $w_2 \in \mathbb{R}$ and $w_3 \in \mathbb{R}$ are appropriate weights for the different types of operations. The overall observed leakage is approximated as:

$$\mathcal{L}_i(j) = \lambda_{\mathrm{carry}}(i,j) + \lambda_{\mathrm{read}}(i,j) + \lambda_{\mathrm{store}}(i,j) + \mathcal{N}$$

where $\mathcal{L}_i$ is the overall leakage at the clock cycle where $h_{i,j}$ is written into the carry register and $\mathcal{N}$ is noise, which is assumed to be Gaussian. Please note that the target implementation processes h_0 and h_1 in parallel. This means that the leakage functions $\mathcal{L}_0$ and $\mathcal{L}_1$ for h_0 and h_1 overlap. There are two carry registers (cf. Fig. 1), one stores $h_{0,j}$ when the other stores $h_{1,j}$. While these leakages slightly differ, we will not attempt to distinguish them. Instead we recover the combined leakages. That is, we predict the combined leakage $h_\Sigma = h_0 + h_1$, which is still sparse. Note that the addition here is *not* in $\mathbb{F}_2$, i.e., we can distinguish the case where $h_{0,j} = h_{1,j} = 1$ from the case $h_{0,j} = h_{1,j} = 0$, although this case is very rare (and will be ignored in the further description). While the model is not perfect, it describes the observed leakages well enough to base a decent key recovery on it.

As in the classical DPA by Kocher et al. [15], we can now hypothesize the value of each key bit $h_{i,j}$ separately. We further know at which clock cycle the leakage of the carry registers (for the key rotation) occurs. Based on this knowledge, one can build the following attack.

3.2 DPA of Key Rotation

As mentioned above, we do not distinguish $h_{0,j}$ and $h_{1,j}$. Instead, we predict the combined leakage $h_{\Sigma,j} = h_{0,j} + h_{1,j}$. Our key recovery works well for this combined leakage, as explained in Sect. 5. Note that we know for each key bit $h_{i,j}$ at which clock cycle it is processed (if not, several hypotheses can be checked in parallel by analyzing neighboring clock cycles). In fact, knowing the implementation, it is predictable which key bit $h_{i,j}$ enters the carry register in which clock cycle for the key rotation. We use this information to build a differential power analysis attack. In spite of the independence of the input x we claim the analysis method to be differential leakage analysis, since differential leakage traces can be computed—similar to the approach originally proposed in [15].

Our algorithm identifies all clock cycles where $h_{i,j}$ is written to or overwritten in the carry register in each trace L and extracts that leakage from L. Per processed ciphertext bit, only 150 words are rotated. The additional bit is stored in the carry register. Hence, all rotations together result in a total of $4801 \cdot 150$ carry register overwrites for each h_i. Since there are 4801 bits in h_i, each bit is written to the carry register 150 times. The corresponding clock cycles l are then identified and their corresponding leakage $\mathcal{L}_i(j, l)$ is combined, as done in horizontal SCA. The result is a differential leakage trace Δ_{carry} with only one bin per key bit. In other words, the *difference* between a key bit being zero and a key bit being one can be observed by comparing points of the leakage trace Δ_{carry} horizontally. Since the key is sparse, there are only very few bins that correspond to a bit $h_{i,j} = 1$, while most bins correspond to a bit $h_{i,j} = 0$. The implicit assumption of all bits leaking the same way is perfectly justified: each bit $h_{i,j}$ takes each column position exactly once, in a specific row. That means due to the rotation, each key bit leaks in every position exactly once, averaging out any position-specific leakages.

In order to detect whether a key bit is set, i.e., $h_{i,j} = 1$, we average over all clock cycles where $h_{i,j}$ is written to the carry register.

$$\Delta_{\text{carry}}(j) = \frac{1}{150} \sum_{l=1}^{150} (\mathcal{L}_0(j,l) + \mathcal{L}_1(j,l))$$

$$= \text{avg} \left(\lambda_{\text{carry}}(0,j) + \lambda_{\text{read}}(0,j) + \lambda_{\text{store}}(0,j) \right.$$

$$\left. + \lambda_{\text{carry}}(1,j) + \lambda_{\text{read}}(1,j) + \lambda_{\text{store}}(1,j) \right)$$

Since $h_{i,j-32} = 0$ with very high probability, $\Delta_{\text{carry}}(j)$ depends directly on the key bit. Further, $h_{i,j} = 1$ has an even stronger influence on $\Delta_{\text{carry}}(j \pm 32)$, since it leaks through $\lambda_{\text{carry}}(i,j)$ and either $\lambda_{\text{read}}(i,j)$ or $\lambda_{\text{store}}(i,j)$. The dependence of $\Delta_{\text{carry}}(j)$ on neighboring key bits $h_{i,j \pm \delta}$, with $\delta \leq 32$, implies that each set key bit not only results in an increased leakage signal for its own position (i.e., index j), but also in the neighboring positions. Note that due to the differing weights, each set key bit imprints a characteristic shape onto the leakage trace. These shapes can (and actually will) overlap if several key bits in the same region are set. Figure 2 shows the comparison of the simulated leakage trace (red(gray) line) using the power model and the real leakage trace (blue/black line). The characteristic shape is highlighted in Fig. 3, which is a magnification of a single set bit of the key, surrounded by zeroes.

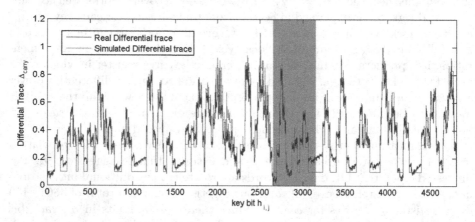

Fig. 2. Differential leakage trace for key rotation. The plot shows the normalized leakage (vertical axis) of both key parts $h_{\Sigma,j} = h_0 + h_1$ over the key bit index (horizontal axis). The red(gray) line is the simulated leakage while the blue/black line is the observed leakage from the target implementation (Color figure online).

In summary, the key rotation analysis allows us to detect joint leakages of h_0 and h_1. This is due to the target implementation that processes both in parallel. The key rotation leakage features a characteristic shape with easily detectable bounds. This allows for a precise location of set key bits. Furthermore, the analysis of the key rotation is mostly input-independent, as will be discussed in Sect. 4. More importantly, each bit features 150 leakage observations per trace L, resulting in a very strong leakage.

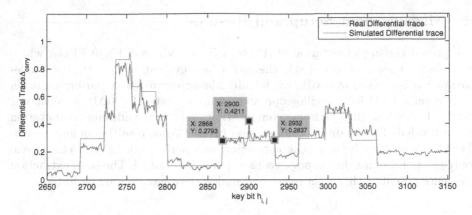

Fig. 3. A magnified version of Fig. 2 that highlights the characteristic shape of a single set bit (center) as well as the overlap of two (right) and three (left) "adjacent" set bits.

3.3 Key Bit Recovery

The key rotation causes leakages which can be analyzed in the presented differential leakage traces where characteristic shapes caused by set key bits can be detected and used to recover the set key bits. In the same way, the traces can be used to detect key bits that are not set. Since the analyzed implementation processes h_0 and h_1 in parallel during the key rotation, resulting in an overlap of the leakages, the differential leakage trace actually recovers the key bits of $h_\Sigma = h_0 + h_1$.

In order to recover key bits, the characteristic shapes need to be detected. We propose a generic shape detection algorithm that works as follows:

1. **Shape Definition.** From the differential leakage trace, one singular characteristic shape can be identified and used as a template for set bits. The template is used to generate a shape threshold as shown in Fig. 3. The threshold is defined by the value of features in this shape such as edges, slopes and pulses.
2. **Shape Detection.** For each key bit in the differential leakage trace, we check if this key bit together with the neighboring key bits can form a characteristic shape. This is done by checking if there are features that are beyond the threshold. If more than two features exist, it is highly probable that this key bit is set. If no feature exists, then it is highly probable that this key bit is 0. Otherwise, we mark this key bit as an undetermined bit.

Note that the shapes will overlap if two set key bits are close to each other. Furthermore, the leakage traces are noisy, hence we can only recover parts of the key bits, leaving the other key bits as undetermined. By choosing the thresholds for shape detection carefully, the number of detected bits can be maximized while keeping the number of false positive errors as low as needed.

4   Measurement Setup and Results

We ported the implementation of [17] to a Xilinx Virtex-5 LX50 FPGA which is mounted on a Sasebo-GII side-channel attack evaluation board[1]. The implementation is clocked at 3 MHz by default. Measurements were performed using a Tektronix DPO 5104 oscilloscope at a sampling rate of 100 MS/s. Since our attack focuses on the syndrome computation, only the syndrome computation was recorded. The syndrome computation takes 245 ms, resulting in long traces. For the ease of analysis, a peak extraction was performed. In each clock cycle only the point of maximum power consumption is retained. The peak extraction prevents potential alignment issues and makes data handling much faster.

4.1   DPA Results of the Key Rotation

Since the key rotation is independent of the ciphertext, the choice of the ciphertext could be arbitrary. However, key rotation and syndrome computation run in parallel, leading to a mixed leakage. To determine the influence of the syndrome computation, two different ciphertext scenarios are studied. One is the all-0 ciphertext to minimize the influence of the syndrome computation. In this scenario the syndrome remains all-0 throughout the entire computation. The other scenario assumes random ciphertexts for each decryption, where each bit in x is set with a 50 % probability. For each scenario we took 256 measurements.

Next, we averaged over all considered traces in both scenarios. From the resulting average trace, $4801 \cdot 150$ peaks are extracted and used to construct the differential leakage traces Δ_{carry} as explained in Sect. 3.2. Note that averaging explicitly before the computation of Δ_{carry} or implicitly during the computation of Δ_{carry} does not influence the result. Figure 4 shows the differential leakage traces for the key rotation, showing the key bit position (horizontal axis) vs. the bit leakage (vertical axis) for all key bits. The blue (black) line indicates the result for the all-0 ciphertext scenario while the green (gray) line indicates the results for the random ciphertext. The latter one is slightly noisier, but nevertheless provides a well-exploitable leakage for a low number of observations. Figure 3 shows magnifications of the differential leakage trace to highlight the characteristic shapes, particularly the one generated by setting the key bit $h_{i,2900}$ as 1 and the neighboring key bits as 0.

The other shapes in Fig. 3 result from the overlapping of characteristic shapes that occur when set key bits of h are close to each other. We noticed that set key bits for h_0 result in a slightly different shape than those of h_1. Since this difference cannot be distinguished as easily, we did not further try to exploit this information.

Key Extraction. To extract keys from Δ_{carry}, we used the algorithm described in Sect. 3.3. The first step is to define the characteristic shape. Distinguishable

---

[1] The VHDL code of the QC-MDPC McEliece implementation of [17] is available at http://www.sha.rub.de/research/projects/code/.

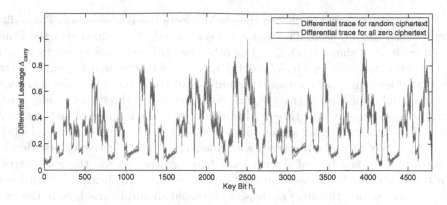

Fig. 4. Normalized differential leakage trace Δ_{carry} for the key rotation for the bits of $h_{\Sigma,j} = h_0 + h_1$. Whether the ciphertext is known (green(gray) line) or all-0 (blue(black) line) has only marginal influence on the observed leakage (Color figure online).

features such as the rising edge, the pulse in the center and the falling edge are clearly visible in Fig. 3 and are used to detect the shape. These features are quantified using a threshold vector. Then, for each key bit $h_{i,j}$ in Δ_{carry}, we check if there is a pulse at $h_{i,j}$, a rising edge at $h_{i,j-32}$ and a falling edge at $h_{i,j+32}$. If more than one feature exists for $h_{i,j}$, we take $h_{i,j}$ as 1. If no feature exists, $h_{i,j}$ is taken as 0. If only one feature exists, $h_{i,j}$ is left as undetermined key bit. Depending on the number of traces used for generating Δ_{carry}, it can be noisy and there will be false positive errors in recovered key bits. Errors can also be introduced by unfavorable overlapping of shapes.

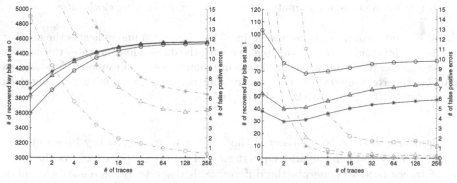

5.1: Recovered 0 bits vs. false positives   5.2: Recovered 1 bits vs. false positives

Fig. 5. Key bit recovery rates for a range of detection thresholds for recovering 0 key bits (left) and 1 key bits (right). Solid line indicates the number of recovered bits (out of 90 ones and 4711 zeroes, scale on left), the dashed line indicates the number of false positives (scale on right). Markers ○, then △, and then * indicate the increasing values for the threshold.

Figure 5 shows how the chosen threshold affects the key recovery. Three different thresholds are used. The first one (o) is exactly the value extracted from the characteristic shape in Δ_{carry}. The other two ($\triangle$ and then $*$) are increased based on the first one. In Fig. 5.1, as the number of traces used to generate the differential leakage trace increases, the number of recovered 0 key bits increases and the number of false positive errors decreases for all three thresholds. However, the less aggressive the threshold is, the lower is the number of false positive errors. In contrast, Fig. 5.2 shows that with the least aggressive threshold (o), more key bits of 1 can be recovered with a few more false positive errors. Hence, to recover more key bits of 0 with least false positive errors, the less aggressive threshold should be used. In contrast, to recover key bits of 1 with least false positive errors, the more aggressive threshold should be used. Note that we repeated our experiments for five different randomly generated keys to ensure the result is not key dependent. The figures show the average result for those experiments.

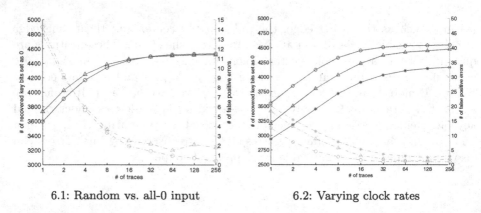

6.1: Random vs. all-0 input   6.2: Varying clock rates

Fig. 6. Key bit recovery rates for recovering 0 key bits. Solid line indicates the number of recovered bits (out of 4711 zeroes, scale on left), the dashed line indicates the number of false positives (scale on right). The left figure compares *known* random (o) vs. *chosen* all-0 ($\triangle$) ciphertext inputs. The right figure compares the experiments for varying clock rates: o for 3 MHz, $\triangle$ for 8 MHz, and $*$ for 16 MHz.

Figure 6.1 shows a comparison of the number of recovered key bits and false positive errors between the all-0 ciphertext and random ciphertext. As the number of traces used to generate the differential leakage trace increases, the number of recovered key bits of 0 increases and the number of false positive errors decreases for both cases. However, with the all-0 ciphertext, there are less positive errors. In conclusion, the all-0 ciphertext is more advantageous to the DPA of key rotation. Hence, we use the traces with the all-0 ciphertext in the other experiments.

Modern electronic devices run faster than 3 MHz which is the default clock rate for the SASEBO board and widely used in power analysis experiments. In order to validate our attack on faster platforms, the performance of the attack was measured for the same design clocked at 8 MHz and 16 MHz. The sampling rate was accordingly increased to 200 MS/s and 250 MS/s, respectively. For each case, 256 traces were obtained using the all-0 ciphertext, followed by peak extraction. Figure 6.2 shows the degradation of the leakage over the increasing clock rate by comparing the number of recovered 0 key bits and false positive errors. In all three cases, the number of recovered 0 key bits increases and the number of false positive errors decreases, as the number of analyzed traces increases. However, the lower the clock rate is, the better the key bits extraction works. With a 3 MHz clock rate (○), almost 4500 of the 0 key bits can be recovered with about 1 false positive error when using all 256 traces while 4000 of the 0 bits are recovered with about 3 false positive errors at a clock rate of 16 MHz (∗).

Overall, it can be seen that with as little as 10 measurements, more than half the key bits can be recovered with a remaining number of errors that is small enough to allow for efficient error correction. With 100 measurements and a careful choice of thresholds, the determined bits are entirely error-free at lower clock rates. This strong leakage is partially due to the fact that 150 leakages are extracted from each measurement, strongly amplifying the amount of leakage gained from each individual trace.

5   Full Key Recovery

Next we analyze how to recover the full key of QC-MDPC McEliece if the adversary has knowledge of several 1 bits of the key as well as several 0 bits of the key, possibly with few errors. We show that the structure of the key can be used to recover the remaining uncertain bits efficiently, or to detect remaining errors.

5.1   Exploiting a Connection Between Secret Key and Public Key

As described in Sect. 2.2, the secret key consists of two related parts, h_0 and h_1. Due to the relation between the secret h_0, h_1 and the public matrix Q, we can express h_0 as:

$$h_0 = h_1 \cdot Q^T \tag{2}$$

Likewise, given h_0, one can compute h_1, since Q is invertible. This means that once the first half of the secret key is recovered, the second half can be computed using the public key. More interestingly, this relationship can be used for *error detection* for each h_i independently: since Q is of high weight (each bit has approximately a 50 % chance of being 1), even a single bit error in h_i^* will result in a high weight of a consequently derived $h_{\bar{i}}^*$, i.e., $\mathrm{wt}(h_{\bar{i}}^*) \approx r/2$. A correct h_i, however, will result in an $h_{\bar{i}}$ of low weight, in our case $\mathrm{wt}(h_{\bar{i}}) = 45$. We are currently not aware how slightly faulty or noisy information of h_0 and h_1 can be combined more efficiently without a trial and error approach using the above mentioned relationship.

If the adversary observes a combined leakage of h_0 and h_1 as described above, this is not a problem, since knowledge of $h_0 \oplus h_1$ can also enable key recovery. Adding h_1 on both sides of Eq. (2) we obtain

$$h_0 \oplus h_1 = h_1 \cdot (Q^T \oplus I_{4801}). \tag{3}$$

If side-channel leakage allows us to obtain the combined leakage $h_0 \oplus h_1$ and the rank of $Q^T \oplus I_{4801}$ is high, we can solve this linear system of equations for h_1 with a computer algebra system like Magma [4]—and then derive h_0 from Eq. (2). In our experiments, the rank observed for $Q^T \oplus I_{4801}$ was 4800, resulting in two candidate solutions with only one of them having the correct Hamming weight. So in cases where all ones can be correctly identified, Eqs. (2) and (3) enable a practical key recovery.

Due to noise and leakage overlapping, there are probably false positive errors in the recovered bits and hence error correction would be essential to correct positions that are slightly off. Guessing error positions becomes infeasible quickly, even with small improvements over an exhaustive search of $\binom{4801}{l}$ possibilities for l errors. We did not try to devise elaborate error-correction strategies, as a different attack strategy which relies on exploiting detected zeroes turned out to be quite effective. We explain this strategy next.

5.2 Efficient Key Recovery from Partial Information

After having identified several 1 bits and 0 bits of the secret key correctly, we aim at an efficient way to recover remaining unknown or uncertain key bits. For this, we define B_0, B_1 and B_u as index sets indicating the locations of definite zeroes, definite ones and positions of undetermined bits in $h_0 \oplus h_1$ such that

$$B_0 \mathbin{\dot\cup} B_1 \mathbin{\dot\cup} B_u = \{0, 1, \dots, 4800\}. \tag{4}$$

Positions in B_0 indicate that both h_0 and h_1 are zero in that position, while positions in B_1 will mean a one in either h_0 or h_1.[2] Hence, the uncertain positions for h_1 are $B_u^1 = B_1 \mathbin{\dot\cup} B_u$, and with Iverson's convention [12] we can summarize our knowledge of $h_0 \oplus h_1$ and h_1 as $h_0 \oplus h_1 = \langle 1 \cdot [i \in B_1] + u \cdot [i \in B_u] \rangle_{0 \le i \le 4800}$ and $h_1 = \langle u \cdot [i \in B_u^1] \rangle_{0 \le i \le 4800}$, where u indicates unknown bits ("erasures"). So Eq. (3) yields

$$\langle 1 \cdot [i \in B_1] + u \cdot [i \in B_u] \rangle_{0 \le i \le 4800} = \langle u \cdot [i \in B_u^1] \rangle_{0 \le i \le 4800} \cdot (Q^T \oplus I_{4801}).$$

As the indices in B_0 indicate definite zeroes in $h_0 \oplus h_1$ and h_1, the corresponding *rows* in the matrix $Q^T \oplus I_{4801}$ will always be multiplied with a zero coefficient. We remove these $|B_0|$ rows and the corresponding known 0-entries in h_1, obtaining an updated equation system

$$\langle 1 \cdot [i \in B_1] + u \cdot [i \in B_u] \rangle_{0 \le i \le 4800} = \langle u \cdot [i \in B_u^1] \rangle_{i \notin B_0} \cdot Q'. \tag{5}$$

---

[2] The (rare) case of h_0 and h_1 having a one in the same position is not considered here, as this situation is quite apparent from the side-channel leakage.

with a (smaller) matrix $Q' \in \mathbb{F}_2^{(4801-|B_0|)\times 4801}$. There are $4801 - |B_0| - |B_1|$ unknown bits on the left- and $4801 - |B_0|$ unknown bits on the right-hand side of Eq. (5). As we are only interested in finding h_1, we can try to eliminate unknown values in $h_0 \oplus h_1$ by dropping *columns* from Q'. One may hope that $|B_u|$ columns can be eliminated without Q' dropping in rank, so that we end up with a linear system of equations

$$\langle 1 \cdot [i \in B_1] \rangle_{i \notin B_u} = \langle u \cdot [i \in B_u^1] \rangle_{i \notin B_0} \cdot Q'' \tag{6}$$

in $4801 - |B_0|$ unknowns and a matrix $Q'' \in \mathbb{F}_2^{(4801-|B_0|)\times(4801-|B_u|)}$. If $|B_u| \leq |B_0|$ one may hope that this linear system of equations can be solved and yields a unique candidate for h_1.

To check the practical feasibility of this approach, we ran several experiments in Magma [4], solving the equation system given in (6) for several different vectors B_0 and B_1. We were particularly interested in the situation where knowledge of 1-positions in $h_0 \oplus h_1$ is ignored (i.e., $B_1 = \emptyset$), because in our measurements the 0-detection was more reliable. With $B_1 = \emptyset$, the resulting system of equations is homogeneous and thus in addition to h_1 also has the trivial solution. From Eq. (4) we see that the condition $|B_u| \leq |B_0|$ now implies that $|B_0| \geq \lceil 4801/2 \rceil$. Staying above this threshold, in our experiments we obtained no more than 8 candidates for h_1, and the weight condition identified the correct secret key uniquely.

For $|B_0| < 2400$, the kernel of the matrix Q'' in Eq. (6) gets larger quickly and we obtain additional candidates for h_1, but finding the correct h_1 may still be feasible by looking at the Hamming weight of the candidates as long as the number of candidates is not overwhelming. The results in Sect. 4 show that for the target implementation the attacker can expect to recover more information from the side-channel than necessary for recovering the secret key. Having $|B_0|$ comfortably above the threshold of 2400, a few false positives in B_0 can be dealt with efficiently: Instead of using all of these bit positions, one can select subsets of size 2401 at random. Assuming a hypergeometric distribution, with f false positive errors among the $|B_0|$ indices, the probability of guessing 2401 error-free positions is $\binom{|B_0|-f}{2401}/\binom{|B_0|}{2401}$. E.g., with $|B_0| = 3281$ and $f = 4$, this probability is still $\approx 2^{-7.6}$. In summary, as long as more than half the bits of the key can be recovered with a low error rate, the remaining key bits can be determined using the above-described algebraic methods. Knowledge of additional bits of $h_0 \oplus h_1$ facilitates the handling of possibly remaining errors. Not being able to recover more than half the number of key bits can make the search infeasible, although—due to the highly biased key—guessing a few additional zeroes may still be an option.

6   Preventing the Attack

The described attack is somewhat specific to the implementation choices of the target, but can be adjusted to other implementation parameters as well. For example, an implementation that does not process h_0 and h_1 in parallel would simplify the attack and amplify the leakage. Implementations that use a different word size (the targeted implementation processes 32-bit words due to the BRAM structure of the FPGAs) will influence the described attack as well. The smaller the word size, the more leakages per target bit, most likely facilitating the attack further. However, a massively parallelized implementation such as the one described in [9] could impede the described attack, since all bits would always be leaking in parallel. One might still be able to exploit resource-specific leakages, e.g., leakage from a carry register. Furthermore, such an implementation is very resource-consuming and might not find widespread use.

A more reliable way to prevent this attack is provided by side-channel countermeasures. A good overview of standard DPA countermeasures is available in [16]. Countermeasures are typically classified as *masking* or *hiding* countermeasures. Both classes can be applied to an implementation of (QC-)MDPC McEliece and, if done correctly, should prevent the above-mentioned attack.

7   Conclusion

This work presents the first successful differential power analysis of a state-of-the-art McEliece implementation based on quasi-cyclic MDPC codes. The analysis is not affected by a potentially present padding as commonly used to achieve CCA security. The analysis exploits the leakages of a key rotation operation which occurs during the syndrome computation step of the decryption and recovers a combined leakage of h_0 and h_1. The leakage model provides precise and strong leakage. The resulting attack is independent of the ciphertext and succeeds with tens of traces. A significant part of the key recovery stems from the relation between the private key and public key, which can be exploited to ease key recovery. In fact, recovering only half the bits of the (highly biased) secret key with a low error rate is sufficient for full key recovery.

Acknowledgments. This work is supported by the National Science Foundation under Grant CNS-1261399 and Grant CNS-1314770. IvM is supported by the European Union H2020 PQCrypto project (Grant no. 645622) and the German Research Foundation (DFG). RS is supported by NATO's Public Diplomacy Division in the framework of "Science for Peace", Project MD.SFPP 984520.

References

1. Avanzi, R., Hoerder, S., Page, D., Tunstall, M.: Side-channel attacks on the McEliece and Niederreiter public-key cryptosystems. J. Cryptographic Eng. **1**(4), 271–281 (2011)
2. Berlekamp, E.R., McEliece, R.J., van Tilborg, H.C.: On the inherent intractability of certain coding problems (Corresp.). IEEE Trans. Inf. Theory **24**(3), 384–386 (1978)

3. Biasi, F.P., Barreto, P.S.L.M., Misoczki, R., Ruggiero, W.V.: Scaling efficient code-based cryptosystems for embedded platforms. J. Cryptographic Eng. **4**(2), 123–134 (2014). http://dx.doi.org/10.1007/s13389-014-0070-1
4. Bosma, W., Cannon, J., Playoust, C.: The Magma algebra system. I. The user language. J. Symbolic Comput. **24**, 235–265 (1997)
5. Faugère, J.C., Otmani, A., Perret, L., de Portzamparc, F., Tillich, J.P.: Folding Alternant and Goppa Codes with Non-Trivial Automorphism Groups. Cryptology ePrint Archive: Report 2014/353, May 2014. http://eprint.iacr.org/2014/353
6. Faugère, J.C., Otmani, A., Perret, L., de Portzamparc, F., Tillich, J.P.: Structural Cryptanalysis of McEliece Schemes with Compact Keys. Cryptology ePrint Archive: Report 2014/210, March 2014. http://eprint.iacr.org/2014/210
7. Faugère, J.-C., Otmani, A., Perret, L., Tillich, J.-P.: Algebraic cryptanalysis of McEliece variants with compact keys. In: Gilbert, H. (ed.) EUROCRYPT 2010. LNCS, vol. 6110, pp. 279–298. Springer, Heidelberg (2010)
8. Gallager, R.: Low-density parity-check codes. IRE Trans. Inf. Theory **8**(1), 21–28 (1962)
9. Heyse, S., von Maurich, I., Güneysu, T.: Smaller keys for code-based cryptography: QC-MDPC McEliece implementations on embedded devices. In: Bertoni, G., Coron, J.-S. (eds.) CHES 2013. LNCS, vol. 8086, pp. 273–292. Springer, Heidelberg (2013)
10. Heyse, S., Moradi, A., Paar, C.: Practical power analysis attacks on software implementations of McEliece. In: Sendrier, N. (ed.) PQCrypto 2010. LNCS, vol. 6061, pp. 108–125. Springer, Heidelberg (2010)
11. Huffman, W.C., Pless, V.: Fundamentals of Error-Correcting Codes. Cambridge University Press, Cambridge (2010)
12. Knuth, D.E.: Two notes on notation. Am. Math. Mon. **99**(5), 403–422 (1992)
13. Kobara, K., Imai, H.: Semantically secure McEliece public-key cryptosystems - conversions for McEliece PKC-. In: Kim, K. (ed.) PKC 2001. LNCS, vol. 1992, pp. 19–35. Springer, Berlin Heidelberg (2001)
14. Kocher, P., Jaffe, J., Jun, B., Rohatgi, P.: Introduction to differential power analysis. J. Cryptographic Eng. **1**(1), 5–27 (2011)
15. Kocher, P.C., Jaffe, J., Jun, B.: Differential power analysis. In: Wiener, M. (ed.) CRYPTO 1999. LNCS, vol. 1666, pp. 388–397. Springer, Heidelberg (1999)
16. Mangard, S., Oswald, E., Popp, T.: Power Analysis Attacks: Revealing the Secrets of Smartcards. Springer, New York (2007)
17. von Maurich, I., Güneysu, T.: Lightweight code-based cryptography: QC-MDPC McEliece encryption on reconfigurable devices. In: Design, Automation and Test in Europe - DATE 2014, pp. 1–6. IEEE (2014)
18. von Maurich, I., Güneysu, T.: Towards side-channel resistant implementations of QC-MDPC McEliece encryption on constrained devices. In: Mosca, M. (ed.) PQCrypto 2014. LNCS, vol. 8772, pp. 266–282. Springer, Heidelberg (2014). http://dx.doi.org/10.1007/978-3-319-11659-4_16
19. McEliece, R.J.: A public-key cryptosystem based on algebraic coding theory. Deep Space Netw. Prog. Rep. **44**, 114–116 (1978)
20. Misoczki, R., Tillich, J.P., Sendrier, N., Barreto, P.S.L.M.: MDPC-McEliece: New McEliece Variants from Moderate Density Parity-Check Codes. Cryptology ePrint Archive, report 2012/409 (2012). http://eprint.iacr.org/2012/409
21. Misoczki, R., Tillich, J.P., Sendrier, N., Barreto, P.S.L.M.: MDPC-McEliece: new McEliece variants from moderate density parity-check codes. In: Proceedings of the 2013 IEEE International Symposium on Information Theory (ISIT), pp. 2069–2073. IEEE (2013)

22. Nojima, R., Imai, H., Kobara, K., Morozov, K.: Semantic security for the McEliece cryptosystem without random oracles. Des. Codes Crypt. **49**(1–3), 289–305 (2008)
23. Shor, P.W.: Polynomial-time algorithms for prime factorization and discrete logarithms on a quantum computer. SIAM J. Comput. **26**(5), 1484–1509 (1997)
24. Shoufan, A., Strenzke, F., Molter, H.G., Stöttinger, M.: A timing attack against patterson algorithm in the McEliece PKC. In: Lee, D., Hong, S. (eds.) ICISC 2009. LNCS, vol. 5984, pp. 161–175. Springer, Heidelberg (2010)
25. Strenzke, F.: A timing attack against the secret permutation in the McEliece PKC. In: Sendrier, N. (ed.) PQCrypto 2010. LNCS, vol. 6061, pp. 95–107. Springer, Heidelberg (2010)
26. Strenzke, F., Tews, E., Molter, H.G., Overbeck, R., Shoufan, A.: Side channels in the McEliece PKC. In: Buchmann, J., Ding, J. (eds.) PQCrypto 2008. LNCS, vol. 5299, pp. 216–229. Springer, Heidelberg (2008)
27. Whitnall, C., Oswald, E., Standaert, F.-X.: The myth of generic DPA...and the Magic of Learning. In: Benaloh, J. (ed.) CT-RSA 2014. LNCS, vol. 8366, pp. 183–205. Springer, Heidelberg (2014)

Side Channel Countermeasures and Tamper Resistance/PUFs

Arithmetic Addition over Boolean Masking
Towards First- and Second-Order Resistance in Hardware

Tobias Schneider$^{(\boxtimes)}$, Amir Moradi, and Tim Güneysu

Horst Görtz Institute for IT Security, Ruhr-Universität Bochum, Bochum, Germany
{tobias.schneider-a7a,amir.moradi,tim.gueneysu}@rub.de

Abstract. A common countermeasure to thwart side-channel analysis attacks is algorithmic masking. For this, algorithms that mix Boolean and arithmetic operations need to either apply two different masking schemes with secure conversions or use dedicated arithmetic units that can process Boolean masked values. Several proposals have been published that can realize these approaches securely and efficiently in software. But to the best of our knowledge, no hardware design exists that fulfills relevant properties such as efficiency and security at the same time.

In this paper, we present two design strategies to realize a secure and efficient arithmetic adder for Boolean-masked values. First, we introduce an architecture based on the ripple-carry adder that targets low-cost applications. The second architecture is based on a pipelined Kogge-Stone adder and targets high-performance applications. In particular, all our implementations adopt the *threshold implementation* approach to improve their resistance against SCA attacks even in the presence of glitches. We evaluated the security of our designs practically against SCA using a non-specific statistical t-test. Based on our analysis, we show that our constructions not only achieve resistance against first- and (univariate) second-order attacks but also require fewer random bits per operation compared to any existing software-based approach.

Keywords: Side-channel analysis · Threshold implementation · Boolean masking · Arithmetic modular addition

1 Introduction

Side-channel analysis (SCA) poses a serious threat to any cryptographic implementation. If no dedicated countermeasure is applied, the secret of the underlying device can be easily extracted by SCA. A popular approach to increase the security of a cryptographic implementation is the use of *masking*. It is achieved by blinding the processed values by means of random masks [21] so that it should become impossible for an attacker to predict intermediate values.

To date there exist several types of masking schemes that differ in the level of abstraction and the target operation. In this work we focus on the techniques developed to be applied at algorithmic level, e.g., Boolean and arithmetic

© Springer International Publishing Switzerland 2015
T. Malkin et al. (Eds.): ACNS 2015, LNCS 9092, pp. 559–578, 2015.
DOI: 10.1007/978-3-319-28166-7_27

masking, which need to be adjusted according to the underlying cryptographic algorithm [21]. Note that nearly all proposed ciphers employ both logical and arithmetic operations.

As an example, ARX-based designs consist of three operations: integer addition, rotation, and XOR. Such constructions are the foundation for block ciphers (like FEAL [23] or Threefish [13]), stream ciphers (Salsa20 [5], ChaCha [4], HC-128 [35]) and hash functions (BLAKE [2], Skein [13]). There are further examples that also include a mixture of Boolean and arithmetic operations like the TEA family of block ciphers [34] and SHA-2 [30]. To realize a masked implementation of these constructions, one option is to employ both Boolean and arithmetic masking schemes. Rotation and XOR operations can be protected by Boolean masking, while arithmetic masking is advantageous for the addition operations. However, the required conversions between both operations can also be the target of an SCA attacker and hence need to be implemented in a secure way. In particular, many existing results discussing this method identified the conversion between arithmetic and Boolean masking as a major hurdle [3,9,14].

Related Works. We now briefly highlight several works on the conversion between Boolean and arithmetic masking. The conversion techniques can be categorized into those which use *precomputation* [12] and those *without precomputation* [17]; however most of them were designed specifically for software platforms. Unfortunately, these constructions cannot be easily mapped to a dedicated hardware module without violating their claims on security. Roughly speaking, this is mainly due to critical glitches that occur inside masked circuits [22]. To avoid this problem, every step would need to be separated by a register stage which would be detrimental to the performance.

We like to remark that a hardware design for such conversions has been proposed in [15], but since both the mask and masked data are involved in the processes of the proposed techniques, such constructions are expected to still have first-order leakages (see [25]). Another problem is the transformation of conversion algorithms to higher orders. It has been shown in [10] how to secure the conversions against higher-order attacks, but this feature comes with a prohibitive overhead for any cryptographic implementation.

Along the same lines, in order to avoid the conversions a technique to securely perform modular arithmetic addition on Boolean masked operands has been introduced in [18]. However, this scheme has been developed to be used in software applications and cannot be easily applied on a hardware platform where performance is a key factor.

Recently, an approach was developed in [11] which uses the Kogge-Stone adder as a basis. But the conversion and masked addition requires more random bits compared to the solutions from [17,18] and are only faster for larger bit sizes (i.e., 64 bits). Still their focus lies on software applications which makes them inefficient in hardware.

Contributions. The target of this work is to design efficient hardware modules for modular addition of Boolean masked operands. More precisely, our goal is to develop a similar technique such as [18] for a hardware platform.

Since masked hardware designs face severe challenges due to glitches, we apply the concept of threshold implementations (TI) [29] that can satisfy the security requirements even in the presence of glitches. TI combines the ideas of Boolean secret sharing and multiparty computation. It has previously been applied to realize the secure hardware design of symmetric ciphers [6,26,31]. Although it has initially been developed with respect to first-order security, its extension to higher orders has been recently introduced [7].

In this paper we consider two factors to design the aforementioned module: (a) *throughput* and (b) *SCA security order*. With respect to performance (i.e., throughput) we consider two designs to implement a 32-bit arithmetic adder that is required by many cryptographic algorithms:

1. Ripple-Carry Adder (RCA) that requires 32 clock cycles to perform a complete addition, and
2. Kogge-Stone Adder (KSA) with 6 clock cycles latency and a fully pipelined architecture.

We present the first-order and (univariate) second-order secure threshold implementation of the two above mentioned designs. We show that our designs not only outperform the inefficient approaches of [10] but also reduce the number of fresh random mask bits required for each addition. We also present practical SCA evaluations performed on a Spartan-6 FPGA to confirm the claimed security levels. To the best of our knowledge, our four proposed architectures are the only available hardware-dedicated solutions that are supported by security proofs as well as by practical investigations.

2   Background

In this section, we introduce the used notations and present the basic ideas behind our designs.

2.1   Notations

In the following all equations are bit-level operations. An n-bit integer operand a is represented as $(a_{n-1}a_{n-2}\ldots a_1a_0)$ where a_0 is the least significant bit. These integers are split up into shares of which the j-th share of a bit $a_{i\in\{0,\ldots,n-1\}}$ is denoted by a_i^j. Inside the equations two Boolean operators are used: $\oplus$ denotes the logical XOR and $\wedge$ the logical AND. AND operators are always evaluated before any XOR operators.

2.2   Ripple-Carry Adder

In [18] the authors presented a way to securely add two Boolean masked values. Instead of three conventional steps (conversion, addition, reconversion), the addition can be implemented in just one step. Depending on the application, this can signficantly increase the performance over the classical approach. The algorithm introduced in [18] is based on a ripple-carry adder (RCA). This adder has been rewritten into a sequence of Boolean operations that take the Boolean masks into consideration. The algorithm is word-oriented for efficiency in software but not in hardware.

Similarly, our design is based on the basic algorithm described in [18]. The underlying algorithm builds on the fact that one bit of sum s can be computed as

$$s_i = a_i \oplus b_i \oplus c_i. \tag{1}$$

Therefore, the addition is replaced by a simple XOR of the two operands a and b and the carry c. The only unknown part in such an equation is the carry bit which can be computed using a recursive formula

$$c_{i+1} = a_i \wedge b_i \oplus a_i \wedge c_i \oplus b_i \wedge c_i, \tag{2}$$

where $c_0 = 0$. The costly part of the RCA is the recursive carry computation. Its function has to be evaluated iteratively which leads to a high circuit depth in case of a fully combinatorial design.

2.3   Kogge-Stone Adder

Another addition circuit with a lower depth is given by the Kogge-Stone adder (KSA) [19] that splits the carry generation into generate (g) and propagate (p) functions. Instead of evaluating the carry function recursively, the KSA benefits from a tree-like structure and achieves a logarithmic complexity. For a hardware design, a KSA can significantly increase the overall performance.

The basic structure of KSA for $n = 4$-bit operands is shown in Fig. 1. For operands a and b it computes the carry bits in three steps. During preprocessing the initial g_i and p_i values are generated as

$$g_i = a_i \wedge b_i, \quad p_i = a_i \oplus b_i. \tag{3}$$

In the following stages a function is used to combine the g and p values of different bit positions. This function receives 4 bits as input and returns 2 output bits. For $i > j$ the output values are computed as

$$g_{i:j} = g_i \oplus g_j \wedge p_i, \quad p_{i:j} = p_i \wedge p_j. \tag{4}$$

After $\log_2(n = 4) = 2$ stages, the computation is finished and all carry bits can be derived as

$$c_{i \in \{2...n\}} = g_{i-1:0}, \quad c_1 = g_0, \quad c_0 = 0.$$

Finally the sum s can be obtained according to Eq. (1).

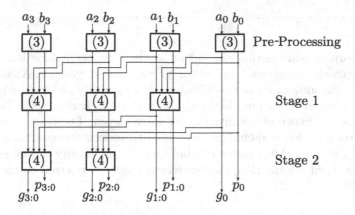

Fig. 1. The structure of the carry generation for 4-bit operands using the KSA

2.4 Threshold Implementations

In order to realize secure masked implementations and avoid the leakage caused by glitches (e.g., [22,25]), the threshold implementation (TI) scheme has been introduced and developed in [7,27–29]. Based on the algebraic degree t of the targeted non-linear function (Sbox) as well as the desired order[1] of security d, the minimum number of input shares s_{in} and the minimum number of output shares s_{out} are defined as

$$s_{in} = t \times d + 1, \quad s_{out} = \binom{s_{in}}{t}.$$

The input x of the e.g., Sbox is represented by $(x^1, \ldots, x^{s_{in}})$ in such a way that $x = \bigoplus_{i=1}^{s_{in}} x^i$. The output of the TI of the corresponding Sbox $(y^1, \ldots, y^{s_{out}})$ should be also a shared representation of $y = S(x) = \bigoplus_{j=1}^{s_{out}} y^j$ while each y^j is provided by a component function $f^j(\ldots)$ over a subset of input shares $(x^1, \ldots, x^{s_{in}})$. This property is known as *correctness* while *non-completeness* is referred to the fact that any d (security order) selection of component functions $f^1(\ldots), \ldots, f^{s_{out}}(\ldots)$ is independent of at least one input share. These two properties are relatively easy to achieve, but the third property *uniformity* is challenging. As the security of masking schemes is based on the uniform distribution of the masks, the output of a TI Sbox must be uniform as it is used as input in further parts of the implementation.

Suppose that for a certain input x all possible sharings $\left\{ (_1x^1, \ldots, _1x^{s_{in}}), (_2x^1, \ldots, _2x^{s_{in}}), \ldots, (_px^1, \ldots, _px^{s_{in}}) \right\}$ are given to the TI Sbox. The tuple $(f^1(\ldots), \ldots, f^{s_{out}}(\ldots))$ should be drawn uniformly from the set $\left\{ (_1y^1, \ldots, \right.$

---

[1] With respect to [32] only univariate security at order $d > 1$ can be achieved.

$_1y^{s_{out}}), (_2y^1, \ldots, _2y^{s_{out}}), \ldots, (_qy^1, \ldots, _qy^{s_{out}})\}$ as all possible sharings of $y = S(\mathrm{x})$.

An important point is that the output of the component functions must be stored in dedicated registers to avoid the propagation of glitches. Another issue is related to the uniformity of the TI functions of security order $d > 1$. In such a case, the number of output shares s_{out} is usually higher than the number of input shares s_{in}; hence uniformity cannot be achieved. Therefore, some of the registered output shares should be combined to reduce the number of output shares to s_{in} at most. After such a combination the uniformity can be examined. For more detailed information, the interested reader is referred to the original works [7,29].

3   Implementation

We present two designs of a modulo 2^{32} adder that provides resistance against first- and second-order SCA. This is a quite common type of addition used in many cryptographic algorithms (e.g., Salsa20, HC-128, SHA-2), but our architectures can be also easily adapted to other bit lengths.

3.1   Ripple-Carry Adder (First-Order SCA-Resistant)

Based on the scheme presented in Sect. 2.2 we build a first-order SCA-resistant adder. To achieve this, Eqs. (1) and (2) should be transformed to meet the three required TI properties.

Given that Eq. (2) is of degree 2, at least 3 shares (for input as well as for output) are necessary. It is supposed that each processed value, e.g., a_i, is split into 3 shares as (a_i^1, a_i^2, a_i^3). In case of Eq. (1), due to its linearity the shares are easily combined via XOR as

$$s_i^1 = a_i^1 \oplus b_i^1 \oplus c_i^1, \quad s_i^2 = a_i^2 \oplus b_i^2 \oplus c_i^2, \quad s_i^3 = a_i^3 \oplus b_i^3 \oplus c_i^3. \tag{5}$$

As mentioned before, Eq. (2) is non-linear and has algebraic degree of 2. Following *direct sharing* approach represented in [8], we can construct a correct and uniform shared implementation of such a function. The shares of the carry bit can be computed as

$$c_{i+1}^1 = a_i^2 \wedge b_i^2 \oplus a_i^2 \wedge b_i^3 \oplus a_i^3 \wedge b_i^2 \oplus a_i^2 \wedge c_i^2 \oplus a_i^2 \wedge c_i^3 \oplus a_i^3 \wedge c_i^2 \oplus b_i^2 \wedge c_i^2 \oplus b_i^2 \wedge c_i^3 \oplus b_i^3 \wedge c_i^2 \tag{6}$$

$$c_{i+1}^2 = a_i^3 \wedge b_i^3 \oplus a_i^3 \wedge b_i^1 \oplus a_i^1 \wedge b_i^3 \oplus a_i^3 \wedge c_i^3 \oplus a_i^3 \wedge c_i^1 \oplus a_i^1 \wedge c_i^3 \oplus b_i^3 \wedge c_i^3 \oplus b_i^3 \wedge c_i^1 \oplus b_i^1 \wedge c_i^3 \tag{7}$$

$$c_{i+1}^3 = a_i^1 \wedge b_i^1 \oplus a_i^1 \wedge b_i^2 \oplus a_i^2 \wedge b_i^1 \oplus a_i^1 \wedge c_i^1 \oplus a_i^1 \wedge c_i^2 \oplus a_i^2 \wedge c_i^1 \oplus b_i^1 \wedge c_i^1 \oplus b_i^1 \wedge c_i^2 \oplus b_i^2 \wedge c_i^1 \tag{8}$$

Here we should note that Eqs. (1) and (2) can be seen as a function $f : (a_i, b_i, c_i) \mapsto (s_i, c_{i+1})$. At a first glance one may think of examining the uniformity of the (s_i, c_{i+1}) tuple[2]. However, such a tuple is never supplied to

---

[2] If sharing of x and y are uniform, the tuple of sharing of (x, y) is not necessarily uniform if x and y are not independent.

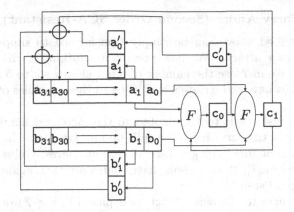

Fig. 2. Structure of the first-order secure adder based on RCA

any function within the RCA algorithm. Note that s_i is an output bit and is not propagated while c_{i+1} is given to the next stage where it is combined with a_{i+1} and b_{i+1} which are independent of c_{i+1}. Hence the uniformity of c_{i+1} suffices to fulfill the corresponding property.

During the implementation of such a design we encountered an issue that has never been reported before. The output of the shared carry computation function (Eqs. (6) to (8)) cannot be directly used as feedback signal since the output of a function from a previous cycle is used as input in the next clock cycle.

As a remedy we constructed a two-stage design as depicted in Fig. 2. The three shares of the two operands a and b are stored in shift registers. The RCA algorithm and the deployment of shift registers supports an efficient scanning of operand bits. Two instances of the shared carry computation function are implemented whose outputs are stored in carry registers c_0 and c_1. The carry registers are enabled alternately while the other intermediate registers (c_0', a_0', a_1', b_0' and b_1') are enabled every second clock cycle synchronized with that of c_1. The operand registers are also shifted two bits every other second clock cycle. The additional registers, i.e., c_0', a_0', a_1', b_0', and b_1' synchronize the computation of the sum bits, which need to be performed one clock cycle after that of the carry bits. Note that we use the shift register of operand a to save the result of the addition.

Another issue is related to the first stage, i.e., when $i = 0$. In our designs we suppose that input carry $c_0 = 0$ so that (c_0^1, c_0^2, c_0^3) should be a shared representation of 0. Therefore, both carry registers have to be initialized with a random set representing 0. In other words, our design requires four fresh mask bits $fm_1, \ldots, fm_4$ only at the start of the addition to initialize c_0 and c_1 with $(fm_1, fm_2, fm_1 \oplus fm_2)$ and $(fm_3, fm_4, fm_3 \oplus fm_4)$ respectively. Note that all other stages of our design do not require fresh random bits leading to an efficient design with respect to the number of required fresh mask bits. For instance, our design is considerably more efficient than the solutions proposed in [10, 11, 18].

3.2   Ripple-Carry Adder (Second-Order SCA-Resistant)

The design described above can be simply transformed to support resistance against higher-order attacks. We now present a solution for the second-order resistant design. We increase the number of input shares s_{in} to 5 and all corresponding functions have to be chosen according to the principles of higher-order TI [7].

Equation (5) just needs to be adapted to the increased number of shares. The computation of the carry has to be split up into two steps. In the first step, $s_{out} = 10$ component functions generate 10 output shares. Following the same concept presented in [7], these intermediate shares are then again reduced to 5 shares in the second step.

No major changes to the basic structure depicted in Fig. 2 are necessary for implementation. Just the registers have to be adjusted to the increased number of shares and the F block is split by an additional register stage. All uniform equations for the F function, obtained by direct sharing, are described in detail in the appendix of this work.

As a consequence, the amount of utilized resources increases and the number of clock cycles needed for the carry computation doubles. Just as before, the carry registers need fresh randomness during the initialization. Therefore, the number of required fresh random masks increases to 8 bits.

3.3   Kogge-Stone Adder (First-Order SCA-Resistant)

The design based on the RCA has low requirements for space and randomness. However, the number of clock cycles for one addition grows linearly with the bit length of the operands. For increased performance we therefore implemented a design that uses a KSA as foundation and which is still secure against first-order attacks.

Equations (3) and (4) need to be split into shares. Since all the corresponding formulas are of degree two, similar to that of the RCA, at least 3 shares are required to realize a functional TI.

The two outputs of the preprocessing step are both given to the next stages; thus, the uniformity of each tuple (g_i, p_i) must be taken into account. One part of Eq. (3) needs to be implemented by the AND of the two operands for which no uniform TI with 3 shares exists [29]. For this, fresh mask bits have to be used to make it uniform (see remasking in [8,26]). In our design, we adopted the solution from [8] with only a single virtual share. One fresh random bit m_i is required for every invocation of the function in the preprocessing step:

$$g_i^1 = a_i^2 \wedge b_i^2 \oplus a_i^2 \wedge b_i^3 \oplus a_i^3 \wedge b_i^2 \oplus m_i \tag{9}$$

$$g_i^2 = a_i^3 \wedge b_i^3 \oplus a_i^1 \wedge b_i^3 \oplus a_i^3 \wedge b_i^1 \oplus a_i^1 \wedge m_i \oplus b_i^1 \wedge m_i \tag{10}$$

$$g_i^3 = a_i^1 \wedge b_i^1 \oplus a_i^1 \wedge b_i^2 \oplus a_i^2 \wedge b_i^1 \oplus a_i^1 \wedge m_i \oplus b_i^1 \wedge m_i \oplus m_i. \tag{11}$$

Further, preprocessing involves another linear XOR-function. We implement this part similar to Eq. (5). Both functions as well as their joint output (g_i, p_i) fulfill the three TI properties.

The preprocessing step is followed by stages in which the g and p values are updated according to Eq. (4). These two functions can be considered as a 4-bit to 2-bit mapping. Similar to the preprocessing step, the tuple of the 2-bit output has to be considered for the uniformity check. For the computation of the g part of Eq. (4) (as an AND/XOR operation), we followed the *direct sharing* approach [8] and achieved:

$$g_{i:j}^1 = g_i^2 \oplus g_j^2 \wedge p_i^2 \oplus g_j^2 \wedge p_i^3 \oplus g_j^3 \wedge p_i^2 \tag{12}$$

$$g_{i:j}^2 = g_i^3 \oplus g_j^3 \wedge p_i^3 \oplus g_j^1 \wedge p_i^3 \oplus g_j^3 \wedge p_i^1 \tag{13}$$

$$g_{i:j}^3 = g_i^1 \oplus g_j^1 \wedge p_i^1 \oplus g_j^1 \wedge p_i^2 \oplus g_j^2 \wedge p_i^1. \tag{14}$$

The other part (computation of p) of Eq. (4) can be implemented similar to Eq. (9). To reduce the amount of required fresh random bits, we replaced m_i with g_j^1. This bit is not used in this equation and can take the role of a mask. Although our construction does not closely follow the assumptions in [8] considering the construction of virtual shares, we can demonstrate that this has no impact on security. Our simulation results show not only the uniformity of shared $p_{i:j}$ but also the uniformity of the shared tuple $(p_{i:j}, g_{i:j})$. We need to emphasize that due to the specific architecture of the KSA algorithm, g_j^1 is only used once as a mask to introduce uniformity into the computation of a p. In other words, the mask bit g_j^1 is never reused again what could potentially violate the uniformity in later stages.

Our design is optimized for maximum throughput by using a fully pipelined architecture. Figure 3 depicts the basic structure of our design. Since only the preprocessing step requires fresh random bits and – as stated above – all other stages are computed without additional mask, the total number of required fresh mask bits is $n = 32$. Compared to the other solutions like [10, 11, 18] this is still reasonable.

3.4   Kogge-Stone Adder (Second-Order SCA-Resistant)

Similar as for the RCA, the design based on the KSA is also easily extensible to higher orders. We outline the exemplary procedure for second-order security. In this case, the number of input shares is again set to 5. The four aforementioned equations are adjusted to meet the requirements of the second-order TI.

The XOR part of Eq. (3) is implemented as before but adapted to the higher number of shares. The AND part to compute g_i of Eq. (3) is split into two steps. As before, the first step results in 10 output shares and the second step merges the last 6 shares into a total number of 5 shares again. Furthermore, we have to use fresh masks to assure the uniformity. In this case, four fresh random bits are necessary. The two functions of the following stages are also split into two steps. For the computation of $g_{i:j}$ of Eq. (4) we use the second-order TI representation of the AND/XOR function given in [7]. For the $p_{i:j}$ part (the AND operation) we use the same construction of g_i of the preprocessing step. Instead of four fresh mask bits, we used 4 shares of g_j as fresh masks to reduce the required

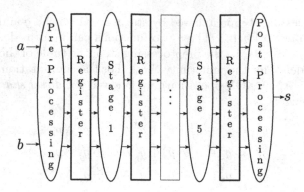

Fig. 3. Block diagram of the first-order secure adder based on KSA

randomness. Details of the underlying uniform equations can be found in the appendix.

The basic structure as shown in Fig. 3 is also the template for the architecture of most other parts. It has mainly to be adapted to 5 shares and the functions need to be split into two steps with a register in between. Hence the number of clock cycles for one addition is doubled. In terms of randomness the demand of our implementation quadruples, because each invocation of the AND operation in the preprocessing step requires 4 random bits.

3.5   Comparison

We now compare our designs in terms of size and performance that are implemented on a Spartan-6 FPGA with other solutions. All our findings are summarized in Table 1. In terms of size, the RCA-based variant is clearly superior to other solutions due to the iterative structure. On the contrary, the designs based on the KSA provide low latency and high-performance applications.

Due to the different implementation platforms, we cannot fairly compare our hardware designs with software-based solutions [10,11,18]. Therefore, Table 1 restricts the comparison to the number of required fresh random bits.

We can conclude that the RCA-based design is most efficient regarding the number of required random bits. The requirement of $4 \cdot d$ random bits outperforms all other proposals and is also independent of the operands bit length n. The approach based on KSA requires a higher number of random bits which also depends on n. Nevertheless, the first-order secure design uses the same amount of fresh masks as the solution of [18] and less than [11]. For higher orders it even outperforms the design of [10]. It is noteworthy that the number of fresh masks for d-order KSA with $d \geq 2$ can be decreased even further. For $d = 1$ we can use the trick presented in [8] that requires only one fresh mask bit for an AND operation. Such a construction – with one virtual variable – might be also found for higher-order TI of the AND operation thereby reducing the number of required fresh mask bits.

Table 1. Results and comparison of our hardware architectures

Design	LUTs	FFs	Latency (CLK)	Frequency (MHz)	Throughput (Mbit/s)	Randomness (bit)
RCA 1st order	227	223	32	101	101	4
RCA 2nd order	388	387	65	107	52	$8 = 4 \cdot d$
KSA 1st order	937	1330	6	62	330	32
KSA 2nd order	4223	5509	12	63	168	$128 = 2 \cdot d \cdot n$
[18] (1st order)	-	-	-	-	-	n
[10] (d order)	-	-	-	-	-	$(2 \cdot d^2 + d) \cdot n$
[11] (1st order)	-	-	-	-	-	$3 \cdot n$

4 Analysis

For the practical SCA evaluations we employed a SAKURA-G platform [1] populated with a Spartan-6 FPGA as target. All SCA traces have been collected by a digital oscilloscope while measuring the voltage drop over a $1\,\Omega$ resistor in Vdd path. In order to obtain clean signals and reduce the electrical noise, we used the embedded amplifier of the SAKURA-G and restricted the bandwidth of the oscilloscope to $20\,\text{MHz}$.

As evaluation metric we applied a *non-specific* statistical t-test [16]. The feature of this test is to indicate the existence of any leakage at a defined order in the power traces. Following the concept of non-specific t-test, power traces corresponding to fixed and randomly selected inputs are collected. Hence this scheme is also denoted as fixed vs. random t-test. During the measurements the fixed and random inputs need to be randomly interleaved. Then, the traces T are categorized into two groups G_1 and G_2 with respect to the fixed and random inputs, respectively. In the following explanation, we consider only one point of the collected traces for the sake of simplicity:

Recall that Welch's (two-tailed) t-test is computed as

$$t = \frac{\mu(T \in G_1) - \mu(T \in G_2)}{\sqrt{\frac{\delta^2(T \in G_1)}{|G_1|} + \frac{\delta^2(T \in G_2)}{|G_2|}}},$$

where μ and δ^2 denote the sample mean and sample variance respectively, and $|.|$ represents the cardinality. The t-test indeed examines the validity of the *null hypothesis* as the samples in both groups were drawn from the same population. If the null hypothesis is correct, it can be concluded with a high level of confidence that the device under test does not have any first-order leakage, given the recorded traces.

For such a conclusion the Student's t-distribution function (in addition to the degree of freedom) is applied to determine the probability of rejecting the aforementioned hypothesis (cf. [7,16]). For typical evaluations, a threshold for $|t|$ as > 4.5 is defined to reject the null hypothesis and indicate that a first-order attack is feasible. This process is repeated at each sample point independently to obtain a curve of t value.

The aforementioned scheme can be easily extended to higher orders by pre-processing the traces as, for example, centered square (for the second-order), standardized cube (for the third order), etc. It is noteworthy that the same evaluation scheme has been applied in [7,20] to investigate the existence of first- and higher-order leakages. For detailed information on how to conduct the tests at higher orders the interested reader is referred to [33].

4.1   Ripple-Carry Adder

Now we analyze the security of our first-order SCA-resistant RCA design. A sample trace of such a design is shown in Fig. 4(a). In order to have a reference for the existing leakage in our platform as well as an evidence for the suitability of the applied evaluation scheme, we first turned the PRNG off that provides the randomness for initial sharing and fresh masks. Hence all outputs of the PRNG are set to zero and the underlying design receives unshared inputs as $(a, 0, 0)$ and $(b, 0, 0)$. With such a setting we collected 100 000 traces corresponding to a mixture of fixed and random inputs. Therefore, we expect the t-test to report clearly exploitable first-order leakages, which is confirmed by the corresponding result shown in Fig. 4(b). It can be seen that the t value exceeds 400 during the cryptographic operation exceeding the defined threshold by far.

As the next step we activated the PRNG so that the adder circuit receives randomly shared inputs and fresh random masks. Hence the design is expected to provide first-order security. In order to examine this we collected 100 000 000 traces and performed the t-test up to third order. The corresponding results shown in Fig. 4 indicate the resistance of the design to first-order attacks and – as expected – its vulnerability to second- and third-order attacks.

We continued our evaluation with the second-order-SCA-resistant RCA design with an active PRNG. Due to the high amount of randomness, i.e., fourth-order Boolean masking (five shares), exploiting a leakage from such a design needs a large number of traces. Therefore, following the above-explained procedure we collected 300 000 000 traces and ran the t-test evaluations. The results shown in Fig. 5 confirm the resistance of our design to first- and second-order attacks. Similar to the results of [7], the third-order leakage still cannot be detected, but we observe fourth- and fifth-order leakages as the design with five shares is expected to be vulnerable to a fifth-order attack.

4.2   Kogge-Stone Adder

Both analyses on the first- and second-order RCA were repeated on the first- and second-order SCA-resistant KSA designs. We even collected the same number of traces, i.e., 100 000 000 traces to evaluate the 1st-order KSA and 300 000 000 traces for the second-order KSA. The results which confirm the resistance of our constructions are shown in Figs. 6 and 7, respectively.

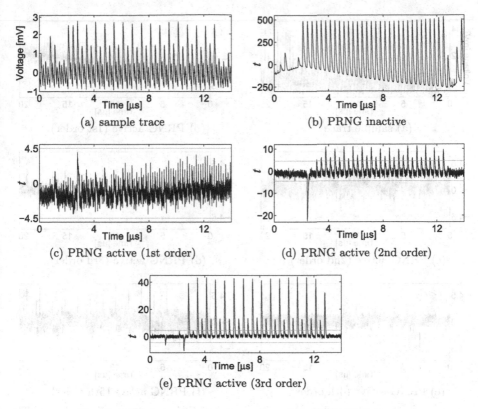

Fig. 4. RCA 1st order, t-test results using 100 000 000 traces

4.3 Higher-Order Security

Recently, Reparaz published a note [32] on the security of higher-order threshold implementations. It states that when different intermediates values, i.e., shares, from different clock cycles are combined, a second-order TI might be vulnerable to the corresponding second-order attack. Although confirming this statement in general, we like to emphasize that this is not addressed in [7]. The idea behind higher-order TI is to resist against *univariate* higher-order attacks where the leakage of different points (of different clock cycles) are not combined. Hence, in the model of univariate higher-order attacks, all lemmas and proofs as given in [7] remain valid. Furthermore, this is backed by our practical investigations as shown above. Still we need to highlight that the second-order TI designs we presented in this work are designed to resist against univariate second-order attacks.

In this context, it has been previously shown in [24] that multivariate leakages can be easily summed up and be represented in a univariate form. The suggested approaches for such a combination include (a) running the target device at a relatively high frequency, e.g., 24 MHz–48 MHz, and (b) making use of a DC blocker and/or certain amplifiers in the measurement setup. Both techniques

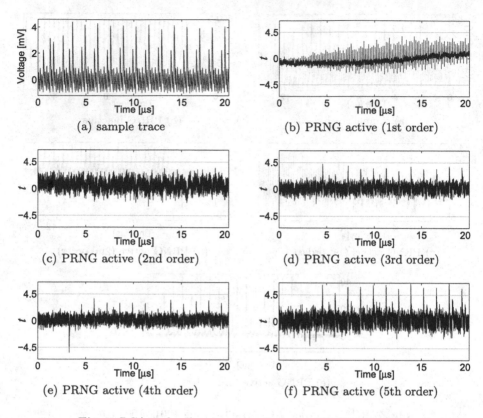

Fig. 5. RCA 2nd order, t-test results using 300 000 000 traces

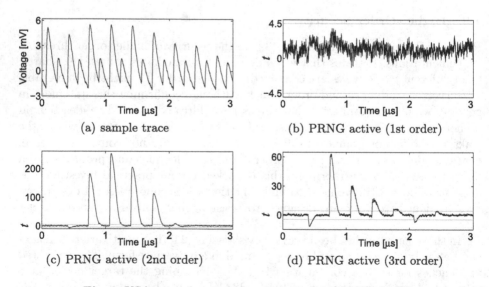

Fig. 6. KSA 1st order, t-test results using 100 000 000 traces

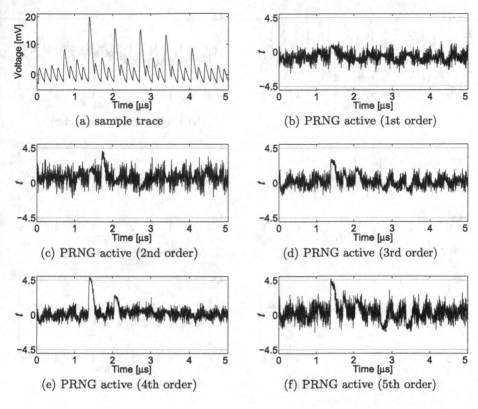

(a) sample trace

(b) PRNG active (1st order)

(c) PRNG active (2nd order)

(d) PRNG active (3rd order)

(e) PRNG active (4th order)

(f) PRNG active (5th order)

Fig. 7. KSA 2nd order, t-test results using 300 000 000 traces

cause overlapping the power peaks of adjacent clock cycles, and hence the leakage associated to consecutive clock cycles are somehow added together. In [24] it has been shown that employing any of the aforementioned techniques causes an implementation of a univariate second-order resistant design to be vulnerable to a univariate second-order attack.

In order to examine the effect of such an issue on our second-order TI designs, we considered the second aforementioned technique. In other words, we employed a DC blocker (BLK-89-S+ from Mini-Circuits) and two serially conected AC amplifiers (ZFL-1000LN+ from Mini-Circuits) in the measurement setup. By means of this setup we repeated the same measurements and evaluations of our developed second-order Kogge-Stone Adder using the same number of 300 000 000 traces. We kept the measurement settings, e.g., sampling rate, bandwidth, and the target frequency of operation, the same as the last experiments. The results shown in Fig. 8 indeed practically confirm the note given in [32]. The second-order TI design demonstrates second-order leakages when the power peak of consecutive clock cycles are combined (by the measurement setup). Interestingly, by such a measurement setup the 4th-order and 5th-order analyses (in contrary to the previous experiment of Fig. 7) do not show a detectable

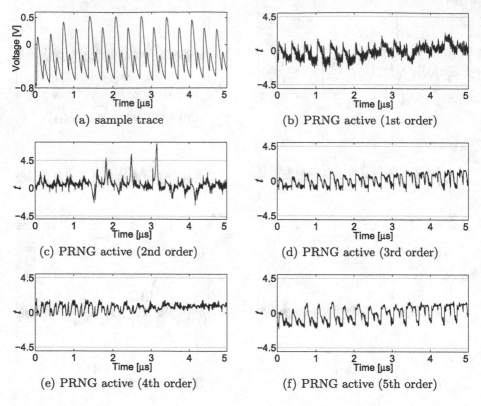

(a) sample trace

(b) PRNG active (1st order)

(c) PRNG active (2nd order)

(d) PRNG active (3rd order)

(e) PRNG active (4th order)

(f) PRNG active (5th order)

Fig. 8. (modified measurement setup) KSA 2nd order, t-test results using 300 000 000 traces

leakage. We believe that it is due to the noise introduced by the measurement setup, i.e., overlapping the adjacent power peaks, which can certainly affect the feasibility of higher-order attacks.

5   Conclusion

In this paper, we presented two ways of performing addition on Boolean masked values that are secure against SCA attacks on a hardware platform. Compared to the KSA-based approach, the RCA-based solution is slower but requires less space and the least amount of random bits. In terms of performance, the design based on the KSA provides a suitable choice due to its pipelined architecture. In comparison to other already published algorithms, our approaches are able to match and even reduce the randomness requirements especially for higher orders. The resistance of both approaches has been verified by practical evaluations showing the security of our constructions. Our proposed designs enable an efficient and secure implementation of ARX-based designs in hardware which have not been fully investigated yet.

Acknowledgment. The authors would like to thank Begül Bilgin from Katholieke Universiteit Leuven, Dept. ESAT/SCD-COSIC and Iminds (Belgium) for her helpful discussions and comments. The research in this work was supported in part by the DFG Research Training Group GRK 1817/1.

A Second-Order RCA

A.1 Carry (1. Step)

$$\tilde{c}_{i+1}^1 = a_i^2 \wedge b_i^2 \oplus a_i^1 \wedge b_i^2 \oplus a_i^2 \wedge b_i^1 \oplus a_i^2 \wedge c_i^2 \oplus a_i^1 \wedge c_i^2 \oplus a_i^2 \wedge c_i^1 \oplus c_i^2 \wedge b_i^2 \oplus c_i^1 \wedge b_i^2 \oplus c_i^2 \wedge b_i^1 \quad (15)$$

$$\tilde{c}_{i+1}^2 = a_i^3 \wedge b_i^3 \oplus a_i^1 \wedge b_i^3 \oplus a_i^3 \wedge b_i^1 \oplus a_i^3 \wedge c_i^3 \oplus a_i^1 \wedge c_i^3 \oplus a_i^3 \wedge c_i^1 \oplus c_i^3 \wedge b_i^3 \oplus c_i^1 \wedge b_i^3 \oplus c_i^3 \wedge b_i^1 \quad (16)$$

$$\tilde{c}_{i+1}^3 = a_i^4 \wedge b_i^4 \oplus a_i^1 \wedge b_i^4 \oplus a_i^4 \wedge b_i^1 \oplus a_i^4 \wedge c_i^4 \oplus a_i^1 \wedge c_i^4 \oplus a_i^4 \wedge c_i^1 \oplus c_i^4 \wedge b_i^4 \oplus c_i^1 \wedge b_i^4 \oplus c_i^4 \wedge b_i^1 \quad (17)$$

$$\tilde{c}_{i+1}^4 = a_i^1 \wedge b_i^1 \oplus a_i^1 \wedge b_i^5 \oplus a_i^5 \wedge b_i^1 \oplus a_i^1 \wedge c_i^1 \oplus a_i^1 \wedge c_i^5 \oplus a_i^5 \wedge c_i^1 \oplus c_i^1 \wedge b_i^1 \oplus c_i^1 \wedge b_i^5 \oplus c_i^5 \wedge b_i^1 \quad (18)$$

$$\tilde{c}_{i+1}^5 = a_i^2 \wedge b_i^3 \oplus a_i^3 \wedge b_i^2 \oplus a_i^2 \wedge c_i^3 \oplus a_i^3 \wedge c_i^2 \oplus c_i^2 \wedge b_i^3 \oplus c_i^3 \wedge b_i^2 \quad (19)$$

$$\tilde{c}_{i+1}^6 = a_i^2 \wedge b_i^4 \oplus a_i^4 \wedge b_i^2 \oplus a_i^2 \wedge c_i^4 \oplus a_i^4 \wedge c_i^2 \oplus c_i^2 \wedge b_i^4 \oplus c_i^4 \wedge b_i^2 \quad (20)$$

$$\tilde{c}_{i+1}^7 = a_i^5 \wedge b_i^5 \oplus a_i^2 \wedge b_i^5 \oplus a_i^5 \wedge b_i^2 \oplus a_i^5 \wedge c_i^5 \oplus a_i^2 \wedge c_i^5 \oplus a_i^5 \wedge c_i^2 \oplus c_i^5 \wedge b_i^5 \oplus c_i^2 \wedge b_i^5 \oplus c_i^5 \wedge b_i^2 \quad (21)$$

$$\tilde{c}_{i+1}^8 = a_i^3 \wedge b_i^4 \oplus a_i^4 \wedge b_i^3 \oplus a_i^3 \wedge c_i^4 \oplus a_i^4 \wedge c_i^3 \oplus c_i^3 \wedge b_i^4 \oplus c_i^4 \wedge b_i^3 \quad (22)$$

$$\tilde{c}_{i+1}^9 = a_i^3 \wedge b_i^5 \oplus a_i^5 \wedge b_i^3 \oplus a_i^3 \wedge c_i^5 \oplus a_i^5 \wedge c_i^3 \oplus c_i^3 \wedge b_i^5 \oplus c_i^5 \wedge b_i^3 \quad (23)$$

$$\tilde{c}_{i+1}^{10} = a_i^4 \wedge b_i^5 \oplus a_i^5 \wedge b_i^4 \oplus a_i^4 \wedge c_i^5 \oplus a_i^5 \wedge c_i^4 \oplus c_i^4 \wedge b_i^5 \oplus c_i^5 \wedge b_i^4 \quad (24)$$

A.2 Carry (2. Step)

$$c_{i+1}^1 = \tilde{c}_{i+1}^1 \tag{25}$$

$$c_{i+1}^2 = \tilde{c}_{i+1}^2 \tag{26}$$

$$c_{i+1}^3 = \tilde{c}_{i+1}^3 \tag{27}$$

$$c_{i+1}^4 = \tilde{c}_{i+1}^4 \tag{28}$$

$$c_{i+1}^5 = \tilde{c}_{i+1}^5 \oplus \tilde{c}_{i+1}^6 \oplus \tilde{c}_{i+1}^7 \oplus \tilde{c}_{i+1}^8 \oplus \tilde{c}_{i+1}^9 \oplus \tilde{c}_{i+1}^{10} \tag{29}$$

B Second-Order KSA

B.1 AND (1. Step)

$$\tilde{g}_i^1 = a_i^2 \wedge b_i^2 \oplus a_i^1 \wedge b_i^2 \oplus a_i^2 \wedge b_i^1 \oplus m_i^1 \tag{30}$$

$$\tilde{g}_i^2 = a_i^3 \wedge b_i^3 \oplus a_i^1 \wedge b_i^3 \oplus a_i^3 \wedge b_i^1 \oplus m_i^2 \tag{31}$$

$$\widetilde{g}_i^3 = a_i^4 \wedge b_i^4 \oplus a_i^1 \wedge b_i^4 \oplus a_i^4 \wedge b_i^1 \oplus m_i^3 \tag{32}$$

$$\widetilde{g}_i^4 = a_i^1 \wedge b_i^1 \oplus a_i^1 \wedge b_i^5 \oplus a_i^5 \wedge b_i^1 \oplus m_i^4 \tag{33}$$

$$\widetilde{g}_i^5 = a_i^2 \wedge b_i^3 \oplus a_i^3 \wedge b_i^2 \tag{34}$$

$$\widetilde{g}_i^6 = a_i^2 \wedge b_i^4 \oplus a_i^4 \wedge b_i^2 \oplus m_i^1 \tag{35}$$

$$\widetilde{g}_i^7 = a_i^5 \wedge b_i^5 \oplus a_i^2 \wedge b_i^5 \oplus a_i^5 \wedge b_i^2 \tag{36}$$

$$\widetilde{g}_i^8 = a_i^3 \wedge b_i^4 \oplus a_i^4 \wedge b_i^3 \oplus m_i^2 \tag{37}$$

$$\widetilde{g}_i^9 = a_i^3 \wedge b_i^5 \oplus a_i^5 \wedge b_i^3 \oplus m_i^3 \tag{38}$$

$$\widetilde{g}_i^{10} = a_i^4 \wedge b_i^5 \oplus a_i^5 \wedge b_i^4 \oplus m_i^4 \tag{39}$$

B.2 AND/XOR (1. Step)

$$\widetilde{g}_{i:j}^1 = g_i^2 \oplus g_j^2 \wedge p_i^2 \oplus g_j^1 \wedge p_i^2 \oplus g_j^2 \wedge p_i^1 \tag{40}$$

$$\widetilde{g}_{i:j}^2 = g_i^3 \oplus g_j^3 \wedge p_i^3 \oplus g_j^1 \wedge p_i^3 \oplus g_j^3 \wedge p_i^1 \tag{41}$$

$$\widetilde{g}_{i:j}^3 = g_i^4 \oplus g_j^4 \wedge p_i^4 \oplus g_j^1 \wedge p_i^4 \oplus g_j^4 \wedge p_i^1 \tag{42}$$

$$\widetilde{g}_{i:j}^4 = g_i^1 \oplus g_j^1 \wedge p_i^1 \oplus g_j^1 \wedge p_i^5 \oplus g_j^5 \wedge p_i^1 \tag{43}$$

$$\widetilde{g}_{i:j}^5 = g_j^2 \wedge p_i^3 \oplus g_j^3 \wedge p_i^2 \tag{44}$$

$$\widetilde{g}_{i:j}^6 = g_j^2 \wedge p_i^4 \oplus g_j^4 \wedge p_i^2 \tag{45}$$

$$\widetilde{g}_{i:j}^7 = g_i^5 \oplus g_j^5 \wedge p_i^5 \oplus g_j^2 \wedge p_i^5 \oplus g_j^5 \wedge p_i^2 \tag{46}$$

$$\widetilde{g}_{i:j}^8 = g_j^3 \wedge p_i^4 \oplus g_j^4 \wedge p_i^3 \tag{47}$$

$$\widetilde{g}_{i:j}^9 = g_j^3 \wedge p_i^5 \oplus g_j^5 \wedge p_i^3 \tag{48}$$

$$\widetilde{g}_{i:j}^{10} = g_j^4 \wedge p_i^5 \oplus g_j^5 \wedge p_i^4 \tag{49}$$

References

1. Side-channel AttacK User Reference Architecture. http://satoh.cs.uec.ac.jp/SAKURA/index.html
2. Aumasson, J.-P., Henzen, L., Meier, W., Phan, R.C.-W.: SHA-3 proposal BLAKE. Submission to NIST (2008)
3. Benoît, O., Peyrin, T.: Side-channel analysis of six SHA-3 candidates. In: Mangard, S., Standaert, F.-X. (eds.) CHES 2010. LNCS, vol. 6225, pp. 140–157. Springer, Heidelberg (2010)
4. Bernstein, D.J.: ChaCha, a variant of Salsa20. In: Workshop Record of SASC, vol. 8 (2008)
5. Bernstein, D.J.: The Salsa20 family of stream ciphers. In: Robshaw, M., Billet, O. (eds.) New Stream Cipher Designs. LNCS, vol. 4986, pp. 84–97. Springer, Heidelberg (2008)

6. Bilgin, B., Gierlichs, B., Nikova, S., Nikov, V., Rijmen, V.: A more efficient AES threshold implementation. In: Pointcheval, D., Vergnaud, D. (eds.) AFRICACRYPT 2014. LNCS, vol. 8469, pp. 267–284. Springer, Heidelberg (2014)
7. Bilgin, B., Gierlichs, B., Nikova, S., Nikov, V., Rijmen, V.: Higher-order threshold implementations. In: Sarkar, P., Iwata, T. (eds.) ASIACRYPT 2014, Part II. LNCS, vol. 8874, pp. 326–343. Springer, Heidelberg (2014)
8. Bilgin, B., Nikova, S., Nikov, V., Rijmen, V., Stütz, G.: Threshold implementations of all 3×3 and 4×4 S-boxes. In: Prouff, E., Schaumont, P. (eds.) CHES 2012. LNCS, vol. 7428, pp. 76–91. Springer, Heidelberg (2012)
9. Boura, C., Lévêque, S., Vigilant, D.: Side-channel analysis of Grøstl and Skein. In: Symposium on Security and Privacy Workshops 2012, pp. 16–26. IEEE Computer Society (2012)
10. Coron, J.-S., Großschädl, J., Vadnala, P.K.: Secure conversion between boolean and arithmetic masking of any order. In: Batina, L., Robshaw, M. (eds.) CHES 2014. LNCS, vol. 8731, pp. 188–205. Springer, Heidelberg (2014)
11. Coron, J., Großschädl, J., Vadnala, P.K., Tibouchi, M.: Conversion from arithmetic to boolean masking with logarithmic complexity. Cryptology ePrint Archive, Report 2014/891 (2014). http://eprint.iacr.org/
12. Debraize, B.: Efficient and provably secure methods for switching from arithmetic to boolean masking. In: Prouff, E., Schaumont, P. (eds.) CHES 2012. LNCS, vol. 7428, pp. 107–121. Springer, Heidelberg (2012)
13. Ferguson, N., Lucks, S., Schneier, B., Whiting, D., Bellare, M., Kohno, T., Callas, J., Walker, J.: The Skein Hash Function Family. http://www.skein-hash.info/sites/default/files/skein1.3.pdf (2010)
14. Gierlichs, B., Batina, L., Clavier, C., Eisenbarth, T., Gouget, A., Handschuh, H., Kasper, T., Lemke-Rust, K., Mangard, S., Moradi, A., Oswald, E.: Susceptibility of eSTREAM candidates towards side-channel analysis. In: Proceedings of SASC, pp. 123–150 (2008)
15. Golic, J.D.: Techniques for random masking in hardware. IEEE Trans. Circ. Syst. 54–I(2), 291–300 (2007)
16. Goodwill, G., Jun, B., Jaffe, J., Rohatgi, P.: A testing methodology for side channel resistance validation. In: NIST non-invasive attack testing workshop (2011). http://csrc.nist.gov/news_events/non-invasive-attack-testing-workshop/papers/08_Goodwill.pdf
17. Goubin, L.: A sound method for switching between boolean and arithmetic masking. In: Koç, Ç.K., Naccache, D., Paar, C. (eds.) CHES 2001. LNCS, vol. 2162, pp. 3–15. Springer, Heidelberg (2001)
18. Karroumi, M., Richard, B., Joye, M.: Addition with blinded operands. In: Prouff, E. (ed.) COSADE 2014. LNCS, vol. 8622, pp. 41–55. Springer, Heidelberg (2014)
19. Kogge, P.M., Stone, H.S.: A parallel algorithm for the efficient solution of a general class of recurrence equations. IEEE Trans. Comput. 22(8), 786–793 (1973)
20. Leiserson, A.J., Marson, M.E., Wachs, M.A.: Gate-level masking under a path-based leakage metric. In: Batina, L., Robshaw, M. (eds.) CHES 2014. LNCS, vol. 8731, pp. 580–597. Springer, Heidelberg (2014)
21. Mangard, S., Oswald, E., Popp, T.: Power Analysis Attacks - Revealing the Secrets of Smart Cards. Springer, Berlin (2007)
22. Mangard, S., Pramstaller, N., Oswald, E.: Successfully attacking masked AES hardware implementations. In: Rao, J.R., Sunar, B. (eds.) CHES 2005. LNCS, vol. 3659, pp. 157–171. Springer, Heidelberg (2005)
23. Miyaguchi, S.: The FEAL cipher family. In: Menezes, A., Vanstone, S.A. (eds.) CRYPTO 1990. LNCS, vol. 537, pp. 627–638. Springer, Heidelberg (1991)

24. Moradi, A., Mischke, O.: On the simplicity of converting leakages from multivariate to univariate. In: Bertoni, G., Coron, J.-S. (eds.) CHES 2013. LNCS, vol. 8086, pp. 1–20. Springer, Heidelberg (2013)
25. Moradi, A., Mischke, O., Eisenbarth, T.: Correlation-enhanced power analysis collision attack. In: Mangard, S., Standaert, F.-X. (eds.) CHES 2010. LNCS, vol. 6225, pp. 125–139. Springer, Heidelberg (2010)
26. Moradi, A., Poschmann, A., Ling, S., Paar, C., Wang, H.: Pushing the limits: a very compact and a threshold implementation of AES. In: Paterson, K.G. (ed.) EUROCRYPT 2011. LNCS, vol. 6632, pp. 69–88. Springer, Heidelberg (2011)
27. Nikova, S., Rechberger, C., Rijmen, V.: Threshold implementations against side-channel attacks and glitches. In: Ning, P., Qing, S., Li, N. (eds.) ICICS 2006. LNCS, vol. 4307, pp. 529–545. Springer, Heidelberg (2006)
28. Nikova, S., Rijmen, V., Schläffer, M.: Secure hardware implementation of non-linear functions in the presence of glitches. In: Lee, P.J., Cheon, J.H. (eds.) ICISC 2008. LNCS, vol. 5461, pp. 218–234. Springer, Heidelberg (2009)
29. Nikova, S., Rijmen, V., Schläffer, M.: Secure hardware implementation of nonlinear functions in the presence of glitches. J. Cryptology 24(2), 292–321 (2011)
30. NIST. Secure Hash Standard (SHS) (FIPS PUB 180–4) (2012)
31. Poschmann, A., Moradi, A., Khoo, K., Lim, C., Wang, H., Ling, S.: Side-channel resistant crypto for less than 2,300 GE. J. Cryptology 24(2), 322–345 (2011)
32. Reparaz, O.: A note on the security of higher-order threshold implementations. Cryptology ePrint Archive, Report 2015/001 (2015). http://eprint.iacr.org/
33. Schneider, T., Moradi, A.: Leakage assessment methodology - a clear roadmap for side-channel evaluations. Cryptology ePrint Archive, Report 2015/207 (2015). http://eprint.iacr.org/
34. Wheeler, D.J., Needham, R.M.: TEA, a tiny encryption algorithm. In: Preneel, B. (ed.) FSE 1994. LNCS, vol. 1008, pp. 363–366. Springer, Heidelberg (1995)
35. Wu, H.: The stream cipher HC-128. In: Robshaw, M., Billet, O. (eds.) New Stream Cipher Designs. LNCS, vol. 4986, pp. 39–47. Springer, Heidelberg (2008)

Foundations of Reconfigurable PUFs

Jonas Schneider[✉] and Dominique Schröder

Saarland University, Saarbrücken, Germany
s9joscne@stud.uni-saarland.de

Abstract. A Physically Unclonable Function (PUF) can be seen as
a source of randomness that can be challenged with a stimulus and
responds in a way that is to some extent unpredictable. PUFs can be used
to provide efficient solutions for common cryptographic primitives such
as identification/authentication schemes, key storage, and hardware-
entangled cryptography. Moreover, Brzuska et al. have recently shown,
that PUFs can be used to construct UC secure protocols (CRYPTO
2011). Most PUF instantiations, however, only provide a static chal-
lenge/response space which limits their usefulness for practical instantiations. To overcome this limitation, Katzenbeisser et al. (CHES 2011)
introduced Logically Reconfigurable PUFs (LR-PUFs), with the idea to
introduce an "update" mechanism that changes the challenge/response
behaviour without physically replacing or modifying the hardware.

In this work, we revisit LR-PUFs. We propose several new ways to
characterize the unpredictability of LR-PUFs covering a broader class of
realistic attacks and examine their relationship to each other. In addition,
we reconcile existing constructions with these new characterizations and
show that they can withstand stronger adversaries than originally shown.
Since previous constructions are insecure with respect to our strongest
unpredictability notion, we propose a secure construction which relies on
the same assumptions and is almost as efficient as previous solutions.

Keywords: Physically unclonable functions · Logically reconfigurable ·
Tamper-resistance

1 Introduction

Physically Unclonable Function (PUFs) are non-programmable hardware tokens
that can be challenged with a stimulus and output responses that are unpredictable. The unpredictable output of the PUFs results from the manufac-
tory process and cannot be controlled even by the producer itself. PUFs are
extremely useful to build cryptographic applications, such as e.g., identifica-
tion/authentication schemes, key storage, and hardware-entangled cryptography,
and also to obtain protocols that are secure in Canetti's UC framework as shown
by Brzuska et al. [4]. Most PUF instantiations, however, only provide a static
challenge/response space which limits their usefulness for practical instantiations. To overcome this limitation, Katzenbeisser et al. [8] introduced Logically

© Springer International Publishing Switzerland 2015
T. Malkin et al. (Eds.): ACNS 2015, LNCS 9092, pp. 579–594, 2015.
DOI: 10.1007/978-3-319-28166-7_28

Reconfigurable PUFs (LR-PUFs), with the idea to introduce an "update" mechanism that allows to change the input/output behaviour of a PUF. In this work, we revisit LR-PUFs presenting several ways to characterize the unpredictability, we examine their relationship to each other, and we show that previous constructions can withstand stronger adversaries than originally shown.

1.1   Background and Related Work

Physically Unclonable Functions were proposed as *Physical One-Way Functions* [13]. They consist of a physical device which can be challenged with a stimulus and responds in a way that is to some extent unpredictable.

- The PUF provides unpredictable, but robust responses. This means the response for a given challenge does not vary beyond a typically low bound, but it should be not be possible to predict the response for a stimulus that has not yet been applied.
- The PUF is not clonable, i.e., one cannot produce a device which exhibits the same response behavior. This goes even as far as not being able to recreate the same behavior if one has physical access to the device itself and not just a list of challenge-response pairs.

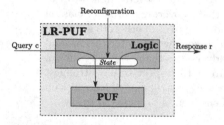

Fig. 1. Schematic of a generic Logically Reconfigurable PUF construction.

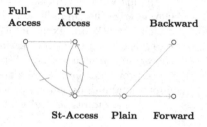

Fig. 2. The relations between the unpredictability notions we introduce.

A third property that is usually cited is tamper-evidence, which is closely related to unclonability. These properties are derived from imprecisions in the manufacturing process of some other object, such as differing gate delays in an integrated circuit. For a survey on the multitude of different PUF constructions, we refer the reader to [11]. A formal description of these properties has been the subject of many research efforts. An in-depth treatment to the definition of these properties that proposes a game-based framework for the description of PUF properties and even PUF creation is given in [2]. Brzuska et al. propose an entropy based characterization of the unpredictability property and examine how PUFs can be integrated into the UC-security framework in [4]. We use their formalization of PUFs as families of distributions.

The tamper-evidence property forbids most PUF designs to have a stimulus-response behavior which is anything but static. In applications where PUFs serve as physical tokens for e.g., access control this can be a disadvantage. Consider for example that the PUF-token should be transferable to a different person. The traditional PUF designs do not allow this, unless the new owner of the PUF should be allowed to carry the same credentials as the previous owner. Thus, there have been efforts to construct reconfigurable PUFs, the first being Controlled Physical Random Functions [6], and a more recent one being Reconfigurable PUFs, short rPUFs [10].

Both of these approaches have their own limitations. Controlled PUFs effectively limit the PUF response space a single user can draw from, thereby lessening security. Physically reconfigurable rPUFs require a potentially costly physical reconfiguration process, and there are no guarantees regarding the effectiveness of that process.

A solution which aims to sidestep these limitations are Logically Reconfigurable PUFs (LR-PUFs) [8]. In this approach, reconfiguration leaves the physical device untouched and is instead performed on a piece of state, which is stored together with the PUF. The stimulus mechanism of the PUF is encapsulated in a query algorithm, which processes challenges by entangling them in some way with the current state of the device. See Fig. 1 for a visual representation of the LR-PUF concept. The idea is a combination of the state and the challenge to perform a *logical* reconfiguration, in which a new state is chosen instead of altering the actual physical device. This preserves the original input/output characteristics of the PUF, but does not require physical manipulation of the device.

1.2   Applications

PUFs have a wide range of applications such as key extraction and authentication [9,16–18], remote attestation [16], and tamper-proof and fault injection resilient implementations of cryptographic primitives [1,3,15]. Most of these applications assume that the PUFs are somewhat ideal in the sense that they support large challenge and/or response spaces. Since most of the known PUF instantiations do not fulfil these properties, LR-PUFs seem to be better suited. Another application of LR-PUFs are electronic fare systems for public transport as suggested in [8]. In this setting, an access token is equipped with an LR-PUF, that serves to authenticate the passenger at the entry points to the transport system and can be used to secure a credit stored on the token. The reconfiguration capability of the device enables the easy reuse of tokens, as reconfiguration of the LR-PUF is (ideally) equivalent to physically replacing the device without causing the cost of a new device.

Another interesting application of LR-PUF technology is presented in [5]. Here, the LR-PUF is used to provide secure key storage and helps to prevent cloning and downgrading of embedded software authenticated using the stored keys. In this application, software is bound to an embedded device by encrypting it with a device-specific key. This key is generated by querying a PUF that is part of the device, making the key dependent on the unique properties of the PUF in each device. This prevents cloning of the software to a new device, as the key on a cloned device will be generated differently. The reconfigurability is used in the event of a software update, to prevent downgrading to an older version of the software. In this event, a new key to encrypt the updated software is derived, and the old software version will no longer be useful, because the old key can no longer be retrieved from the LR-PUF.

1.3   Contribution

We revisit the LR-PUFs as introduced in [8] and present several ways to charaterize the unpredictability notion. We reconsider existing constructions with respect to these new measures, and we propose a novel construction that is secure w.r.t. our strongest notion of unpredictability. In the following, we discuss each contribution more in detail.

Definitions. We introduce four different notions of unpredictability. The first one is called **Plain**-unpredictability and it is a natural extension of backward/forward-unpredictability of [8]. The basic idea of this definition is to allow the adversary to reconfigure the PUF several times. The second notion, called **St-Access**-unpredictability, removes the assumption that the state is stored in a tamper-evident manner and allows the adversary to directly write the state. The third notion, called **PUF-Access**-unpredictability, models the case where the adversary manages to bypass the query and reconfiguration logic and where it gains direct access to the PUF. The fourth notion, called **Full-Access**-unpredictability, combines **PUF-Access**-unpredictability and **St-Access** unpredictability in the sense that the adversary has direct access to the PUF and is allowed to set the state maliciously. Perhaps surprisingly there is an obstacle when trying to compare the power of state-setting adversaries to PUF-access adversaries. The issue is that a PUF-access adversary might be able to completely precompute the behavior of an LR-PUF given the current state, which makes both notions incomparable. A visual representation of these relations is given in Fig. 2, where an arrow A → B denotes, that notion A implies notion B and an arrow A ↛ B means that notion A does not imply notion B.

Analysis. In Appendix C we give a comprehensive security analysis of the "speed-optimized" and the "area-optimized-construction" from [8] w.r.t. our unpredictability notions. The former employs a collision resistant hash function both to combine state information and query and to generate a new state frome the old one. The latter uses an identical reconfiguration algorithm, but is geared towards PUFs with small area, i.e., small input range by providing a query mechanism that involves iteratively constructing a response from smaller subqueries. (For full definitions, please refer to Fig. 8). Our analysis shows that both constructions are **St-Access**-unpredictable. Previously, it was only known that both constructions are backward (resp. forward) unpredictable. The practical consequences of this result is that the scheme remains secure, even if the state is *not* stored in a tamper-evident manner. On the negative side we show that both constructions are not secure against adversaries that have direct access to the PUF. In fact, our result here is more general, showing that any LR-PUF cannot satisfy this notion where access to the underlying PUF makes the query and reconfiguration algorithms completely predictable to the adversary.

Construction. We propose a simple LR-PUF construction that is **Full-Access-**unpredictable. Our scheme can be seen as a randomized variant of the "speed-optimized" construction from [8] with the difference being that our reconfiguration algorithm samples a fresh state st upon reconfiguration and it evaluates the underlying PUF on $w \leftarrow \mathsf{Hash}(\mathsf{st} \| c)$. This construction relies on the same computational assumptions as the scheme of [8], it is almost as efficient, but it satisfies both **Full-Access-** and **St-Access-**unpredictability.

1.4 Outline

In Sect. 2 we give some background by reviewing a formalization of Physically Unclonable Functions and present our formalization of LR-PUFs. Section 3 introduces the new unpredictability notions we propose and the relations among them. Section 4 contains the specification of a construction which achieves the strongest of our unpredictability notions.

2 Logically Reconfigurable PUFs

2.1 Physically Unclonable Functions

A Physically Unclonable Function (PUF) is a noisy function that is realized through a physical object [13]. The PUF can be queried with a challenge c and answers with a response r. The output of the PUF is noisy meaning that querying the PUF twice with the same challenge yields most likely two different but closely related responses. In the following we recall the definition of PUFs and their main security property given in [4].

Definition 1 (Physically Unclonable Functions). *Let ρ be the dimension of the range of the PUF responses of the PUF family, and let d_{noise} be a bound on the PUF's noise. A pair $\mathcal{P} = (\mathsf{S}, \mathsf{E})$ is a family of (ρ, d_{noise})-PUFs if it satisfies the following properties:*

Index Sampling. *Let $\mathcal{I}_\lambda$ be an index set. The sampling algorithm S outputs, on input the security parameter 1^λ, an index $\mathsf{id} \in \mathcal{I}_\lambda$. We do not require that the index sampling can be done efficiently. Each index $\mathsf{id} \in \mathcal{I}_\lambda$ corresponds to a set $\mathcal{D}_{\mathsf{id}}$ of distributions. For each challenge $c \in \{0,1\}^\lambda$, $\mathcal{D}_{\mathsf{id}}$ contains a distribution $\mathcal{D}_{\mathsf{id}}(c)$ on $\{0,1\}^{\rho(c)}$. We do not require that $\mathcal{D}_{\mathsf{id}}$ has a short description or an efficient sampling algorithm.*

Evaluation. *The evaluation algorithm E gets as input a tuple $(1^\lambda, \mathsf{id}, c)$, where $c \in \{0,1\}^\lambda$. It outputs a response $r \in \{0,1\}^{\rho(\lambda)}$ according to distribution $\mathcal{D}_{\mathsf{id}}$. It is not required that E is a PPT algorithm.*

Bounded Noise. *For all indices $\mathsf{id} \in \mathcal{I}$, for all challenges $c \in \{0,1\}^\lambda$, we have that when running $\mathsf{E}(1^\lambda, \mathsf{id}, c)$ twice, then for any two outputs r_1, r_2 that are produced the Hamming distance $\mathsf{dis}(r_1, r_2)$ is smaller than $d_{noise}(\lambda)$.*

Unpredictability of PUFs. Loosely speaking, a PUF is unpredictable if it is difficult to predict the response of the PUF to a given, previously unknown challenge. This intuition is formalized in an experiment where the adversary can adaptively query the PUF on challenges of its choice and wins if it can predict the response to a fresh challenge of its choice, within the bound d_{noise}. Fresh means that the adversary did not query the PUF on this challenge.

Definition 2 (PUF-Unpredictability). *A family of PUFs $\mathcal{P} = (\mathsf{S}, \mathsf{E})$ is unpredictable if for any PPT algorithm $\mathcal{A}$ the probability that the experiment $\mathrm{PRE}_{\mathcal{A}}^{\mathcal{P}}(\lambda)$ evaluates to 1 is negligible (in the security parameter λ), where*

Experiment $\mathrm{PRE}_{\mathcal{A}}^{\mathcal{P}}(\lambda)$
  $\mathrm{id} \leftarrow \mathsf{S}(1^\lambda)$
  $(c^*, r^*) \leftarrow \mathcal{A}^{\mathsf{E}}(\mathrm{id})$
  $r \leftarrow \mathsf{E}(c^*)$
Return 1 iff $\mathsf{dis}(r, r^*) \leq d_{noise}$ *and* c^* *is fresh.*

For the sake of simplicity we use this game based definition of unpredictability. A formulation with respect to entropy contained in the PUF responses is given in [4]. A comprehensive and more in-depth game-based formulation of PUF properties is found in [2].

2.2   Definition of Logically Reconfigurable PUFs

In practice, many PUF instances have only a restricted challenge and response space, such that after a certain number of queries they cannot be used anymore. The basic idea of Logically Reconfigurable PUF (LR-PUFs) is to extend the PUF by a control logic that allows to change the challenge and response behavior of the system. Our definition is similar to the one of [8].

Definition 3 (Logically Reconfigurable PUFs). *Let $\mathcal{P} = (\mathsf{S}, \mathsf{E})$ be a family of (ρ, d_{noise})-PUFs. A logically reconfigurable PUF (LR-PUF) with black-box access to $\mathcal{P}$ is a tuple of efficient algorithms $\mathcal{L} = (\mathsf{Setup}^{\mathsf{S},\mathsf{E}}, \mathsf{Query}^{\mathsf{E}}, \mathsf{Rcnf}^{\mathsf{E}})$, which satisfies the following properties*

Setup. *The Setup algorithm takes as input the security parameter 1^λ. It outputs an index $\mathrm{id} \in \mathcal{I}$, determining the underlying PUF from $\mathcal{P}$ and an initial state $\mathrm{st} \in \{0,1\}^{\ell(\lambda)}$ of the LR-PUF. We require that $\ell(\lambda) \geq \lambda$.*
Query mechanism. *The $\mathsf{Query}_{\mathrm{st}}$ algorithm takes as input a challenge $c \in \{0,1\}^\lambda$ and outputs a response $r \in \rho(\lambda)$.*
Reconfiguration. *The $\mathsf{Rcnf}_{\mathrm{st}}$ algorithm updates the state of the LR-PUF to a new state $\mathrm{st}' \in \{0,1\}^{\ell(\lambda)}$ which is (possibly probabilistically) computed from the old state st. The new state is also output.*

The three algorithms may interact with the underlying PUF family via the oracles E and S. We will often omit giving the oracle access explicitly. Additionally, we assume that the noise of the LR-PUF responses is bounded in the same way as the noise of the underlying PUF's responses.

Remark 1. The setup algorithm of almost all constructions in this paper is the same and consists of the following steps. $\mathsf{Setup}(1^\lambda)$ generates the underlying PUF id $\leftarrow_\$ S(1^\lambda)$, chooses a string st $\leftarrow_\$ \{0,1\}^{\ell(\lambda)}$ uniformly at random, and outputs (id, st). In the following, unless stated otherwise, all constructions will use this standard setup algorithm.

Unpredictability of LR-PUFs. Ideally, an LR-PUF in one specific state should be as unpredictable as its underlying physical PUF, so the internal state of the LR-PUF can be seen as a mapping from LR-PUF queries to PUF queries that is ideally a permutation. Reconfiguration then constitutes a "shuffling" of this mapping, such that a completely new permutation is reached. To formalize this, the authors of [8] propose two complimentary notions of unpredictability:

Forward-unpredictability: The reconfiguration changes the mapping in such a way, that knowledge about the previous state does not enable an adversary to predict the challenge-response behavior for the reconfigured LR-PUF.

Backward-unpredictability: The reconfiguration reveals no additional information about the old internal state, i.e., after reconfiguration an adversary should not be able to predict the challenge-response behavior for the old state.

We provide a formal characterization of these properties as derivatives of our plain unpredictability notion (see Definition 4).

3   New Notions of Unpredictability

In this section we extend the original unpredictability notion by considering strengthened adversaries. We show how the new notions relate to each other and in which scenarios their consideration might be beneficial.

3.1   Multiple Reconfigurations

In [8], the unpredictability experiments revolve around a single reconfiguration process. However, an adversary might witness several reconfigurations and thereby deduce some information about the influence of the state on the LR-PUFs behavior. This motivates our first unpredictability definition, which is an extension of the backward/forward-unpredictability properties to multiple reconfigurations of the LR-PUF. To this end, we provide the adversary access to a reconfiguration oracle, which invokes the reconfiguration algorithm.

Let Rcnf denote the reconfiguration oracle for an LR-PUF $\mathcal{L}$ with current state st. The oracle Rcnf accepts two kinds of inputs: $\perp$, upon which Rcnf_{st} is invoked, and st' upon which the internal state of $\mathcal{L}$ is set to st'. The latter input functionality allows the adversary to program the state and is only available to state-setting adversaries (see Appendix C.2). Let $\mathcal{S}$ denote the list of states the adversary obtains over the course of an experiment, be it through Setup or the oracle Rcnf. Further, let Query denote the query oracle, which takes as input a state st and a challenge c and returns $\mathsf{Query}_{st}(c)$ to the adversary. The adversary can only invoke the query oracle with states stored in $\mathcal{S}$.

Definition 4 (Plain-Unpredictability). *An LR-PUF* $\mathcal{L} = $ (Setup, Query$_{st}$, Rcnf$_{st}$) *is* unpredictable *if for any PPT adversary* $\mathcal{A}$ *the probability that the experiment* PLAIN$_{\mathcal{A}}^{\mathcal{L}}(\lambda)$ *evaluates to 1 is negligible (in the security parameter* λ), *where the game is defined in* Fig. 3.

Remark 2. We can obtain the backward- and forward-unpredictability notions described in [8] by considering restricted adversaries that invoke Rcnf($\perp$) only once, setting and obtaining the new state st', in the following only query Query(st', $\cdot$).

Corollary 1. *Let* $\mathcal{L}$ *be a* **Plain**-*unpredictable LR-PUF, then* $\mathcal{L}$ *is also backward- and forward-unpredictable.*

Separation of Plain- and Backward/Forward-Unpredictability. In what follows we show that **Plain**-unpredictability is strictly stronger than the previous notions. Let **Backward**$_{\mathcal{A}}^{\mathcal{L}}(\lambda)$ (resp. **Forward**$_{\mathcal{A}}^{\mathcal{L}}(\lambda)$) denote $\Pr\left[\text{PLAIN}_{\mathcal{A}}^{\mathcal{L}}(\lambda) = 1\right]$ where $\mathcal{A}$ is a backward-unpredictability adversary (resp. forward-unpredictability adversary) as described above. We separate the security notions with the following two propositions.

Proposition 1. *If collision-resistant hash functions relative to a PUF exist (cf. Appendix A), then there exist backward-unpredictable LR-PUFs, which are not* **Plain**-*unpredictable.*

The basic idea of our counterexample is to let the adversary learn a prediction by calling the reconfiguration oracle. This prediction, however, only helps him in combination with the evaluation oracle, that outputs the evaluation on a point

Experiment PLAIN$_{\mathcal{A}}^{\mathcal{L}}(\lambda)$
  (id, st) $\leftarrow$ Setup(1^{λ})
  (st*, c^*, r^*) $\leftarrow$ $\mathcal{A}^{\text{Query,Rcnf}(\perp)}(1^{\lambda}, \text{st})$
  $r \leftarrow$ Query$_{\text{st}^*}(c^*)$
  Output 1 iff dis(r, r^*) $\leq d_{noise}$ and c^*
    was not queried to Query(st*, $\cdot$)
    and st$^* \in \mathcal{S}$.

Fig. 3. Security of plain unpredictability.

Experiment ST-ACCESS$_{\mathcal{A}}^{\mathcal{L}}(\lambda)$
  (id, st) $\leftarrow$ Setup(1^{λ})
  (st*, c^*, r^*) $\leftarrow$ $\mathcal{A}^{\text{Query,Rcnf}}(1^{\lambda}, \text{st})$
  $r \leftarrow$ Query$_{\text{st}^*}(c^*)$
  Output 1 iff dis(r, r^*) $\leq d_{noise}$ and
    c^* was not queried to Query(st*, $\cdot$)
    and st$^* \in \mathcal{S}$.

Fig. 4. Security of state-setting unpredictability.

Experiment PUF-ACCESS$_{\mathcal{A}}^{\mathcal{L}}(\lambda)$
  (id, st) $\leftarrow$ Setup(1^{λ})
  (st*, c^*, r^*) $\leftarrow$ $\mathcal{A}^{\text{Rcnf}(\perp),\text{E}}(1^{\lambda}, \text{st})$
  Set LR-PUF state to st* using Rcnf(st*)
  st' $\leftarrow$ Rcnf$_{\text{st}^*}$
  $r \leftarrow$ Query$_{\text{st}'}(c^*)$
  Output 1 iff dis(r, r^*) $\leq d_{noise}$.

Fig. 5. Security of direct access unpredictability.

Experiment FULL-ACCESS$_{\mathcal{A}}^{\mathcal{L}}(\lambda)$
  (id, st) $\leftarrow$ Setup$^{\text{S,E}}(1^{\lambda})$
  (st*, c^*, r^*) $\leftarrow$ $\mathcal{A}^{\text{Rcnf,E}}(1^{\lambda}, \text{st})$
  Set LR-PUF state to st* using Rcnf(st*)
  st' $\leftarrow$ Rcnf$_{\text{st}^*}$
  $r \leftarrow$ Query$_{\text{st}'}(c^*)$
  Output 1 iff dis(r, r^*) $\leq d_{noise}$.

Fig. 6. Security of full access unpredictability.

different from the challenge, if the query contains a specific prediction. More precisely, we store a pair (u, v) in the state. Then we modify the query algorithm, whose input is a challenge c, such that it evaluates the PUF on $(1^\lambda \oplus c \| \mathsf{st}')$ if $c = \mathsf{E}(u)$. Clearly, in our construction the attacker can never invoke the query oracle on u and thus, cannot exploit this part directly. However, whenever the attacker queries the reconfiguration oracle, it obtains this answer through the state.

A more detailed proof appears in the full version of this paper.

Proposition 2. *If collision-resistant hash functions relative to a PUF (cf. Appendix A) exist, then there exist forward-unpredictable LR-PUFs, which are not* **Plain**-*unpredictable.*

The proof is analogous to the one of Proposition 1, as the same construction describe there is also forward-unpredictable and is thus omitted.

3.2 State-Setting Adversaries

The authors of [8] assume that the state is stored in a tamper-evident manner and therefore an attacker cannot set the state of the LR-PUF to arbitrary values. We believe that there are many plausible scenarios where tamper-evident storage of the state is too expensive and where the adversary might be able to change the state, even though the internal physical PUF is tamper-evident. Therefore, we propose the following unpredictability notion, in which an adversary can set the internal state of the LR-PUF. As mentioned above, this is formalized via the type of inputs to the reconfiguration oracle Rcnf which are arbitrary states that are to be set as the new state of the LR-PUF.

Definition 5 (St-Access-Unpredictability). *An LR-PUF* $\mathcal{L}$ = (Setup, Query$_{\mathsf{st}}$, Rcnf$_{\mathsf{st}}$) *is* unpredictable *for a state-setting adversary if for any PPT adversary* $\mathcal{A}$ *the probability that the experiment* ST-ACCESS$_{\mathcal{A}}^{\mathcal{L}}(\lambda)$ *evaluates to 1 is negligible (in the security parameter* λ), *where the game is defined in Fig. 4.*

The state-setting adversary can be thought of as bypassing the reconfiguration algorithm, thus security against state-setting adversaries should be considered a property of the Query mechanism.

Remark 3. It is easy to see that an LR-PUF construction satisfying this notion of unpredictability must also be **Plain**-unpredictable (Definition 4). Any adversary against **Plain**-unpredictability is also a valid adversary in the ST-ACCESS-unpredictability experiment, which simply does not invoke the reconfiguration oracle on an input other than $\perp$.

Corollary 2. *Let* $\mathcal{L}$ = (Setup, Query$_{\mathsf{st}}$, Rcnf$_{\mathsf{st}}$) *be* **St**-**Access**-*unpredictable. Then* $\mathcal{L}$ *is also* **Plain**-*unpredictable.*

The inverse relationship does, however, not hold.

Proposition 3. *There exist* **Plain**-*unpredictable LR-PUF constructions, which are not* **St-Access**-*unpredictable.*

To show the separation, we consider a construction which has a "vulnerable" state, i.e., a state which does not support a secure reconfiguration. A state-setting adversary can then prepare the LR-PUF to have that state and get an advantage through the defective reconfiguration algorithm. An adversary without state-setting capabilities, however, would have to wait for that state to occur in a chain of honest reconfigurations to get any advantage, as long as the reconfiguration is working correctly for any other state. For more details, please refer to the full version of this paper.

3.3   Direct Access Adversaries

Another assumption made in [8] is that the attacker cannot bypass the Query mechanism and thus, does not have direct access to the embedded PUF. In the real world, however, it might be that case that the attacker finds a way to stimulate the physical PUF directly, circumventing the control logic of the LR-PUF. In what follows, we remove this assumption by giving the adversary direct access to the embedded PUF as well.

Definition 6 (PUF-Access-Unpredictability). *An LR-PUF* $\mathcal{L} =$ (Setup, Query_{st}, Rcnf_{st}) *is* unpredictable for an adversary with direct PUF access *if for any PPT adversary* $\mathcal{A}$ *the probability that the experiment* $\mathsf{PUF\text{-}ACCESS}_{\mathcal{A}}^{\mathcal{L}}(\lambda)$ *evaluates to 1 is negligible (in the security parameter* λ*), where the game is defined in* Fig. 5.

Because an LR-PUF construction might rely solely upon the PUF itself to perform reconfiguration and querying, an adversary that has access to the PUF may be able, given the current state of the PUF, to compute challenge-response pairs for all the following states the LR-PUF will have.

Proposition 4. *If collision-resistant hash functions relative to a PUF exist, then there exists a* **Plain**-*unpredictable LR-PUF construction, which is not* **PUF-Access**-*unpredictable.*

The proof relies on the fact that an adversary can in some construction simulate the Rcnf and Query oracles himself. The full proof can be found in the full version of this paper.

Perhaps surprisingly there is an obstacle when trying to compare the power of state-setting adversaries to PUF-access adversaries. As described above, a PUF-access adversary might be able to completely precompute the behavior of an LR-PUF given the current state. Thus the definition of **PUF-Access**-unpredictability demands the adversary predict a challenge response pair not for the state, which it finally outputs, but for the state which results from the reconfiguration based on that state. This excludes bypassing the Rcnf oracle and enables the definition to capture the unpredictability gain provided by the Rcnf algorithm.

Proposition 5. *Unpredictability against state-setting adversaries is not comparable to unpredictability against PUF-access adversaries, i.e.,*

*(i) There exists an LR-PUF which is **PUF**-Access-unpredictable but not **St**-Access-unpredictable.*

*(ii) If collision-resistant hash functions w.r.t. PUFs exist, there exist LR-PUFs, which are **St**-Access-unpredictable but not **PUF**-Access-unpredictable.*

The proof of this proposition appears in the full version of this paper.

3.4 Full Access Adversaries

A combination of the previous scenarios provides the PUF access adversary with the possibility to set the internal state. This is intuitively the strongest notion, as it provides the adversary with essentially complete control over the LR-PUF during the query phase of the experiment.

Definition 7 (Full-Access-Unpredictability). *An LR-PUF $\mathcal{L}$ = (Setup, Query$_{st}$, Rcnf$_{st}$) is unpredictable for a state-setting adversary with PUF access if for any PPT adversary $\mathcal{A}$ the probability that the experiment FULL-ACCESS$_{\mathcal{A}}^{\mathcal{L}}(\lambda)$ evaluates to 1 is negligible (in the security parameter λ), where the game is defined in Fig. 6.*

As **Full-Access**-unpredictability is an immediate extension of **PUF-Access**-unpredictability, it is easy to see that any **Full-Access**-unpredictable $\mathcal{L}$ is also **PUF-Access**-unpredictable. However, the **PUF-Access**-unpredictability adversary is strictly weaker than the state-setting **Full-Access**-unpredictability adversary.

Proposition 6. *There are LR-PUF constructions which are **PUF-Access**-unpredictable, but not **Full-Access**-unpredictable.*

For the full proof, please refer to the full version of this paper.

Since **Full-Access**-unpredictability implies **PUF-Access**-unpredictability and we because have seen that **St-Access**- and **PUF-Access**-unpredictability do not imply each other (see Proposition 5), **Full-Access**-unpredictability can also not follow from **St-Access**-unpredictability.

Corollary 3. *There exists a **St**-Access-unpredictable LR-PUF construction, which is not secure w.r.t. **Full**-Access-unpredictability.*

4 Construction

In this section we present our construction that fulfills the **Full-Access** notion of unpredictability we defined in Sect. 3. Our scheme can be seen as a randomized version of the speed-optimized construction from [8] with the difference that the reconfiguration algorithm chooses a fresh state uniformly at random (instead of computing it as the hash of the old state). Afterwards, we show that the reconfiguration algorithm must be randomized in order to achieve our strongest notion of unpredictability.

590   J. Schneider and D. Schröder

$$\begin{array}{ll}
\text{Query}_{st}(c) & \text{Rcnf}_{st} \\
\quad w \leftarrow \text{Hash}(st \parallel c) & \quad st \leftarrow_\$ \{0,1\}^{\ell(\lambda)} \\
\quad y \leftarrow \text{E}(w) & \quad \textbf{Return } st \\
\quad \textbf{Return } y &
\end{array}$$

Fig. 7. The full LR-PUF construction.

Theorem 1. *The* full *construction (*Fig. 7*) is* **Full-Access**-*unpredictable.*

As the reconfiguration algorithm chooses a new state uniformly at random, the probability that the adversary correctly predicts the new state is negligible. The probability that the output prediction made by the adversary is valid for a different state as well can be bounded by the probability of predicting the outputs of the underlying physical PUF, which was assumed to be negligible. The full proof of this theorem appears in the full version of this paper.

Proposition 7. *The* full *construction is* **St-Access**-*unpredictable.*

As the construction's Query algorithm is the same as the speed-construction's (see Fig. 8), and the Rcnf-algorithm cannot be used in any advantageous way by an adversary, the construction is **St-Access**-unpredictable as long as the speed-construction is **St-Access**-unpredictable. This is shown in Proposition 9. The proof of this theorem appears in the full version of this paper.

5   Conclusion

In this paper, we have reconsidered the concept of Logically Reconfigurable PUFs, an extension of the PUF primitive with applications in embedded devices for access control or object tracking. We have given a formal definition of LR-PUFs and presented several new notions of unpredictability, which help to classify constructions according to the scenarios they could be employed in. An evaluation of two previously given construction has shown these constructions to withstand stronger adversaries than initially shown. Finally, we have given a new construction that can handle the strongest adversaries defined in this work and we have seen that these notions create an interesting separation between such constructions that rely on deterministic reconfiguration algorithms and such that randomize reconfiguration.

Acknowledgements. Dominique Schröder was supported by the German Federal Ministry of Education and Research (BMBF) through funding for the Center for IT-Security, Privacy and Accountability (CISPA www.cispa-security.org) and also by an Intel Early Career Faculty Honor Program Award. Finally, we thank the reviewers for their valuable comments.

A   PUFs and Collision-Resistant Hash Functions

As some of the LR-PUF constructions we will discuss use collision resistant hash functions, we will first have to define this primitive.

Definition 8 (Hash Function). *Let $\ell : \mathbb{N} \to \mathbb{N}$ be a polynomial. A pair of PPT algorithms* (Gen, Hash) *is called a hash function if:*

Gen. *Takes as input a security parameter 1^λ and returns an index* id *from some index set $\mathcal{I}_\lambda$.*

Hash. *Takes as input an index* id *and a bit string $x \in \{0,1\}^*$. It returns an output string* $\mathsf{Hash}(\mathsf{id}, x) \in \{0,1\}^{\ell(\lambda)}$. *We set* $\mathsf{Hash}(x) := \mathsf{Hash}(\mathsf{id}, x)$.

What follows is the usual definition of collision resistance against a PPT adversary [7], modified to account for possible advantages an adversary might have through PUF Access. For a discussion of the possible complexity theoretic implications of PUF access, please refer to [4,12].

Definition 9 (Collision Resistance w.r.t. PUFs). *Let $\mathcal{P} = (\mathsf{S}, \mathsf{E})$ be a PUF family. A hash function is called collision-resistant with respect to $\mathcal{P}$, if for all PPT algorithms $\mathcal{A}$ that have black-box access to $\mathcal{P}$ the probability that the experiment* $\mathsf{COLL}_{\mathcal{A}}^{\mathcal{P}}$ *evaluates to 1 is negligible, where*

$$\textbf{\textit{Experiment}} \ \mathsf{COLL}_{\mathcal{A}}^{\mathcal{P}}(\lambda)$$
$$\mathsf{id} \leftarrow \mathsf{Gen}(1^\lambda)$$
$$(x, x') \leftarrow \mathcal{A}^{\mathsf{S},\mathsf{E}}(\mathsf{id})$$
$$\textit{Return 1 iff } \mathsf{Hash}(x) = \mathsf{Hash}(x') \textit{ and } x \neq x'.$$

A.1   PUFs and Asymptotic Security

From a practitioners perspective, the asymptotic formulation of unpredictability presented in this paper can seem problematic, as it does not quantify exactly how much security a given construction provides. In [14] there is also an argument made against asymptotic security claims about PUFs which suggests that such claims are not meaningful. The core of the argument is that PUFs are finite functions and an adversary could just have a hard-coded table of challenge response pairs for a given PUF. We believe this criticism is not applicable in our case, as we define PUFs as families of functions from which one is sampled in the unpredictability experiment. As the probability is also taken over the randomness of this sampling process, it is unlikely that the adversary will have the lookup table *for this specific PUF* hard-coded.

B   Deterministic Reconfiguration Algorithms

As seen before, the PUF-access variants of unpredictability exclude LR-PUF constructions where access to the underlying PUF makes the Query and Rcnf algorithms completely predictable to the adversary. We will now show that an LR-PUF construction, which is, in this sense, deterministic cannot achieve PUF-access unpredictability.

$\text{Query}_{st}(c)$	Rcnf_{st}	$\text{Query}_{st}(c)$	Rcnf_{st}
$w \leftarrow \text{Hash}(st \| c)$	$st \leftarrow \text{Hash}(st)$	**FOR** $j = 0$ to n	$st \leftarrow \text{Hash}(st)$
$y \leftarrow E(w)$	**Return st**	$\quad w_j \leftarrow \text{Hash}(st \| c \| j)$	**Return st**
Return y		$\quad y_j \leftarrow E(w_j)$	
		Return $(y_0 \| \ldots \| y_n)$	

Fig. 8. The speed-optimized construction speed and the area-optimized construction area from [8].

Proposition 8. *A LR-PUF construction* $\mathcal{L} = (\text{Setup}, \text{Query}_{st}, \text{Rcnf}_{st})$, *where* Rcnf_{st} *is deterministic cannot achieve* **PUF-Access**-*unpredictability.*

The proof appears in the full version of this paper.

As **PUF-Access**-unpredictability is implied by **Full-Access**-unpredictability, the following corollary follows immediately.

Corollary 4. *An LR-PUF construction* $\mathcal{L} = (\text{Setup}, \text{Query}_{st}, \text{Rcnf}_{st})$, *where* Rcnf_{st} *is deterministic cannot achieve* **Full-Access**-*unpredictability.*

Of course, these claims exclude LR-PUF constructions which involve more than one PUF, as the **PUF-Access**- and **Full-Access**-unpredictability experiments only provide access to a single underlying PUF. It is, however, straightforward to extend the definition to multiple PUFs. This can also be intuitively motivated, as a multi-PUF construction, which does not secure access to one of the employed PUFs is unlikely to secure access to the other PUFs.

Remark 4. As generation of proper randomness on an highly embedded system such as a public transport access token seems impractical, this result establishes that the **Full-Access**-unpredictability notion might not be achievable for all application scenarios. However, in scenarios, where reconfigurations occur infrequently the negative effect of randomness that comes from a weak source is likely to be tolerable. Additionally, if the degree of sophistication of the device is high enough, there could already be a circuit in the device implementing a hash function such as SHA-2, which may be used to extract some randomness in a heuristic fashion.

C   Revisiting Earlier Constructions

Based on the newly proposed unpredictability notions it is worthwhile to revisit the original LR-PUF constructions given in [8]. We show that they provide unpredictability in more adverse settings than originally demonstrated.

C.1   Speed-Optimized-Construction

Let us first consider the *speed-optimized* implementation of LR-PUFs given in [8]. The basic idea of the construction is to use a collision-resistant hash function to compound the state and the LR-PUF challenge into one PUF stimulus. The formal description of the algorithms is shown in the left part of Fig. 8. As the reconfiguration algorithm is deterministic, this construction cannot achieve **PUF-Access-** or **Full-Access-**unpredictability (see Sect. 4), however, we can show that it is **St-Access-**unpredictable, which is an improvement on the unpredictability result given in [8].

Proposition 9. *The* speed *construction is* **St-Access-***unpredictable.*

The proof can be found in the full version of this paper.

C.2   Area-Optimized-Construction

Beside the speed-optimized construction, [8] also propose an area-optimized construction, in which a small-range PUF is stimulated repeatedly on different sub-challenges derived from the original challenge. The sub-challenge responses are then assembled to one larger response to the original challenge. The formal description is given in the right part of Fig. 8. We will now see that the construction *can* be **St-Access-**unpredictable, but the degree of unpredictability depends on the choice of underlying PUF and the iteration count n. Note, that a noise bound d_{noise} on the full response means that the underlying PUF should not produce responses that are noisier than $\frac{d_{noise}}{n}$.

Proposition 10. *If there exist collision-resistant hash functions with respect to PUFs, and the underlying PUF is unpredictable, then the* area-construction *is* **St-Access-***secure.*

For the proof of this statement, please refer to the full version of this paper.

References

1. Akdemir, K.D., Wang, Z., Karpovsky, M., Sunar, B.: Design of cryptographic devices resilient to fault injection attacks using nonlinear robust codes. In: Joye, M., Tunstall, M. (eds.) Fault Analysis in Cryptography. Information Security and Cryptography, pp. 171–199. Springer, Berlin Heidelberg (2012)
2. Armknecht, F., Maes, R., Sadeghi, A.-R., Standaert, F.-X., Wachsmann, C.: A formalization of the security features of physical functions. In: 2011 IEEE Symposium on Security and Privacy, pp. 397–412, Berkeley, California, USA. IEEE Computer Society Press, 22–25 May 2011
3. Armknecht, F., Maes, R., Sadeghi, A.-R., Sunar, B., Tuyls, P.: Memory leakage-resilient encryption based on physically unclonable functions. In: Matsui, M. (ed.) ASIACRYPT 2009. LNCS, vol. 5912, pp. 685–702. Springer, Heidelberg (2009)
4. Brzuska, C., Fischlin, M., Schröder, H., Katzenbeisser, S.: Physically uncloneable functions in the universal composition framework. In: Rogaway, P. (ed.) CRYPTO 2011. LNCS, vol. 6841, pp. 51–70. Springer, Heidelberg (2011)
5. Eichhorn, I., Koeberl, P., van der Leest, V.: Logically reconfigurable pufs: memory-based secure key storage. In: Proceedings of the Sixth ACM Workshop on Scalable Trusted Computing, pp. 59–64. ACM (2011)

6. Gassend, B., Clarke, D., van Dijk, M., Devadas, S.: Controlled physical random functions. In: Proceedings of the 18th Annual Computer Security Conference (2002)
7. Katz, J., Lindell, Y.: Introduction to Modern Cryptography. CRC Press, Boca Raton (2008)
8. Katzenbeisser, S., Koçabas, Ü., van der Leest, V., Sadeghi, A.-R., Schrijen, G.-J., Schröder, H., Wachsmann, C.: Recyclable PUFs: logically reconfigurable PUFs. In: Preneel, B., Takagi, T. (eds.) CHES 2011. LNCS, vol. 6917, pp. 374–389. Springer, heidelberg (2011)
9. Škorić, B., Tuyls, P., Ophey, W.: Robust key extraction from physical uncloneable functions. In: Ioannidis, J., Keromytis, A.D., Yung, M. (eds.) ACNS 2005. LNCS, vol. 3531, pp. 407–422. Springer, Heidelberg (2005)
10. Kursawe, K., Sadeghi, A., Schellekens, D., Skoric, B., Tuyls, P.: Reconfigurable physical unclonable functions - enabling technology for tamper-resistant storage. In: IEEE International Workshop on Hardware-Oriented Security and Trust, HOST 2009, pp. 22–29 (2009)
11. Maes, R., Verbauwhede, I.: Physically unclonable functions: a study on the state of the art and future research directions. In: Sadeghi, A.-R., Naccache, D. (eds.) Towards Hardware-Intrinsic Security. Information Security and Cryptography, pp. 3–37. Springer, Berlin Heidelberg (2010)
12. Ostrovsky, R., Scafuro, A., Visconti, I., Wadia, A.: Universally composable secure computation with (malicious) physically uncloneable functions. In: Johansson, T., Nguyen, P.Q. (eds.) EUROCRYPT 2013. LNCS, vol. 7881, pp. 702–718. Springer, Heidelberg (2013)
13. Pappu, R.S.: Physical one-way functions. PhD thesis (2001)
14. Rührmair, U., Sölter, J., Sehnke, F.: On the foundations of physical unclonable functions. Cryptology ePrint Archive, Report 2009/277 (2009). http://eprint.iacr.org/
15. Sadeghi, A.-R., Visconti, I., Wachsmann, C.: PUF-enhanced RFID security and privacy. In: Secure Component and System Identification (SECSI), Cologne, Germany, April 2010
16. Schulz, S., Sadeghi, A.-R., Wachsmann, C.: Short paper: lightweight remote attestation using physical functions. In: Proceedings of the Fourth ACM Conference on Wireless Network Security, WiSec 2011, pp. 109–114. ACM, New York, NY, USA (2011)
17. Suh, G.E., Devadas, S.: Physical unclonable functions for device authentication and secret key generation. In: Proceedings of the 44th Annual Design Automation Conference, DAC 2007, pp. 9–14. ACM, New York, NY, USA (2007)
18. Tuyls, P., Batina, L.: RFID-tags for anti-counterfeiting. In: Pointcheval, D. (ed.) CT-RSA 2006. LNCS, vol. 3860, pp. 115–131. Springer, Heidelberg (2006)

mrPUF: A Novel Memristive Device Based Physical Unclonable Function

Yansong Gao[1,2](✉), Damith C. Ranasinghe[2], Said F. Al-Sarawi[1], Omid Kavehei[3], and Derek Abbott[1]

[1] School of Electrical and Electronic Engineering,
The University of Adelaide, Adelaide, SA 5005, Australia
{yansong.gao,said.alsarawi,derek.abbott}@adelaide.edu.au
[2] Auto-ID Labs, School of Computer Science,
The University of Adelaide, Adelaide, SA 5005, Australia
damith.ranasinghe@adelaide.edu.au
[3] Functional Materials and Microsystems Research Group,
School of Electrical and Computer Engineering, Royal Melbourne Institute
of Technology, Melbourne, VIC 3001, Australia
omid.kavehei@rmit.edu.au

Abstract. Physical unclonable functions (PUFs) exploit the intrinsic complexity and irreproducibility of physical systems to generate secret information. They been proposed to provide higher level security as a hardware security primitive. Notably PUFs are an emerging and promising solution for establishing trust in an embedded system with low overhead with respect to energy and area. Most current PUF designs traditionally focus on exploiting process variations in CMOS (Complementary Metal Oxide Semiconductor) technology. In recent years, progress in nanoelectronic devices such as memristors has demonstrated the prevalence of process variations in scaling electronics down to the nano region. In this paper we exploit the extremely large information density available in the nanocrossbar architecture and the large resistance variations of memristors to develop on-chip memristive device based PUF (mrPUF). Our proposed architecture demonstrates good uniqueness, reliability and improved number of challenge-response pairs (CRPs). The proposed mrPUF is validated using nanodevices characteristics obtained from experimental data and extensive simulations. In addition, the performance of our mrPUF is compared with existing memristor based PUF architectures. Furthermore, we analyze and demonstrate the improved security with respect to model building attacks by expounding upon the inherent nature of nanocrossbar arrays where we use the independence between nanocrossbar columns to generate responses to challenges.

Keywords: Physical unclonable function · PUFs · Hardware security · Memristor · Nanocrossbar · Model building attack

© Springer International Publishing Switzerland 2015
T. Malkin et al. (Eds.): ACNS 2015, LNCS 9092, pp. 595–615, 2015.
DOI: 10.1007/978-3-319-28166-7_29

1   Introduction

Modern security systems establish the authenticity of products or identity of users based on the principle of protecting 'keys' required for securing systems and allowing secret key to be obtained solely by authorized participants. However, developments in invasive and non-invasive physical tampering methods such as micro-probing, laser cutting, and power analysis and monitoring have made it possible to extract digitalized secret information from integrated circuits (ICs), and consequently compromising conditional access systems by using illegal copies of the secret information. Tamper proofing techniques used in smartcards to protect the secret keys such as cutting power or tripping tamper-sensitive circuitry that leaks the secret information have shown to be vulnerable to physical attacks [1]. For instance, an adversary can remove a smartcard package and reconstruct the layout of the circuit using chemical and optical methods. Even the data in some types of non-volatile memories, such as electrically erasable programmable read-only memory (EPROM) can be revealed by sophisticated tampering methods. To protect secret information, the emerging area of physical unclonable functions (PUFs) promise a reliable and highly-secure approach and is receiving increasing attention. Note that PUFs express inherent and unclonable instance-specific features of physical systems and provide an alternative to storing keys on insecure hardware devices [2,3]. A PUF produces an output signal (response) to an external physical excitation signal (challenge). The response is a function of the physical properties of the system such as signal delay variations across identical integrated circuits and the applied challenge. A significant advantage in using PUFs is that the key is not digitally stored in the memory of a device (such as smart cards) but is extracted from device specific characteristics in response to an external stimulus. Besides the aforementioned device authentication and identification, PUFs can be used for cryptographic key generation and more complicated cryptographic protocols such as oblivious transfer (OT), bit commitment (BC), key exchange (KE) [4–8].

Conventional PUFs such as Ring Oscillator PUF, Arbiter PUF, SRAM (static random access memory) PUF exploit uncontrollable process variations in conventional CMOS fabrication technology. Although technological developments in CMOS devices such as FinFET enhanced device operations in ultra deep submicron technologies, such developments are expected to confront the physical limitation imposed by the continuing trend towards smaller feature sizes [46]. Consequently, CMOS based PUF designs will also face a roadblock in terms of providing secure physical unclonable functions in the future.

Recent developments in nanoelectronics demonstrated a potentially low-cost and high-performa nce nonionic nonvolatile resistive memory device called the memristor (in literatures, memristor and memristive device is used interchangeably) [9–11]. Memristors have inherent randomness due to fabrication process variations (i.e., thickness, cross-sectional area). This inherent randomness provides opportunities for building up physical unclonable functions with high performance. Furthermore, these nanodevices are easy to fabricate and are compatible with CMOS fabrication processes offering a potentially low cost security primitive.

The proposed mrPUF architecture, which combines nano-crossbars and current mirror controlled ring oscillators, and the proposed authentication mechanism are unique and have not been considered in the past to the best of our knowledge. Our architecture allows the extraction of secret information by exploiting the abundant variations in nanodevices and nanofabrication. A summary of our contributions in this paper are:

1. We propose a novel PUF architecture that exploits the fabrication variations inherent in nano-electronic devices. In particular we exploit the significant variations in the resistance values on a nanocrossbar structure based resistive memory to build mrPUF.
2. We conduct extensive studies to evaluate mrPUF and demonstrate its superior performance with respect to key performance metrics: diffuseness; uniqueness; and reliability.
3. We show that mrPUF is resistant to model building attacks by exploiting characteristics inherent to nanocrossbar arrays, in particular the independence of information in individual columns, to develop a challenge selection strategy for a direct authentication mechanism using a mrPUF. We also demonstrate the significantly large number of challenge response pairs possible with our proposed architecture when compared to existing memristor based PUF designs.

The rest of this paper is organized as follows: Sect. 2 presents related work; The mrPUF architecture is presented in Sect. 3; Sect. 4 evaluates mrPUF's performance metrics and compares it with other PUF structures in the literature; Sect. 5 presents two applications of mrPUF with respect to key generation and challenge response pairs based authentication protocol, and analyses their security; Sect. 6 compares mrPUF with other memristor based PUFs and Sect. 7 concludes this paper.

2 Related Work

Over the years, a number of PUF structures have been proposed, built and analyzed. These include *time delay based* PUFs such as the Arbiter PUF [2, 12] (APUF), Feed-Forward APUF [13], An arbiter based PUF built on current starved inverters [14], Ring-Oscillator PUF [15] (RO-PUF), and Glitch PUF [16]; *Memory-based* PUFs leveraging device mismatch such as SRAM PUF [17,18], Latch PUF [19], Flip-flop PUF [20,21], Butterfly PUF [22]. A comprehensive review of different PUF architectures can be found in [23,24].

Here we introduce the RO-PUF as our mrPUF will integrate it. In addition, we provide a brief review of nanocrossbar arrays and memristive devices which our PUF architecture utilizes. Furthermore, we briefly review previous memristor based PUF architectures.

2.1 RO-PUF

The RO-PUF is one of the leading microelectronic PUF designs because of its relatively high reliability. A typical RO-PUF circuit consists of k ring-oscillators, two k-to-1 multiplexers that select a pair of ring-oscillators, RO_i and RO_j, two counters and a comparator, as shown in Fig. 1. All the ring-oscillators in this structure are identical. Ideally, the frequency of each oscillator is unique, however, because the oscillating frequency is a function of the physical device parameters, which are subject to device process variation, the oscillation frequencies of each oscillator are not all identical. Therefore, the oscillation frequencies of each pair is compared by counting this frequency using a digital counter. If $f_i < f_j$ (where f_i and f_j are the oscillating frequencies of RO_i and RO_j, respectively) the digital comparator output will be '0', otherwise '1'. The pairing of oscillators is controlled using two digital multiplexers, each use a subset of the input challenge bits to select an oscillator.

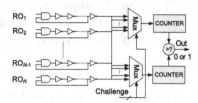

Fig. 1. A conventional ring-oscillator PUF (RO-PUF)

In order to avoid an extremely large number of bits in counters, it is important to design relatively slow oscillators with an oscillation frequency of the order of hundreds of MHz. Therefore, depending on the technology, 50–100 inverters are needed for one RO to produce a frequency in this range [23,25]. This design constraint will increase costly area and power overhead. In contrast, we propose an ring oscillator design that slows the oscillating frequency by using only a fraction of the number of inverters used in a RO-PUF.

2.2 Nanocrossbar Arrays and Memristive Devices

Crossbar arrays of metal-oxide based devices have attracted much attention in recent decades because of their high information density, compatibility with current CMOS technology, and simple implementation. The nanocrossbar array consists of parallel horizontal wires on top and perpendicular vertical wires at the bottom. At each junction, a two terminal device with or without a nonlinear selector element is formed and acts as a switch.

A nanocrossbar array structure is shown in Fig. 2(a) where each nanodevice is located at the crosspoint of the top and bottom wires. When reading a targeted memristive device, reading voltage is applied to the selected word line and the current of the selected bit line is sensed to determine the state of the memristive

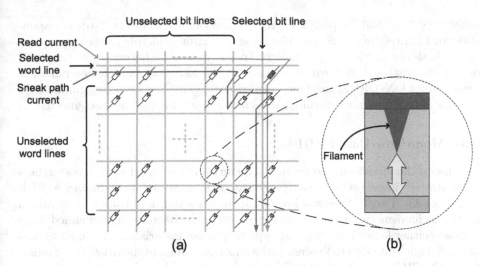

Fig. 2. (a) Nanocrossbar array of nanoionic memristive devices. (b) Illustrates the operation principles of a memristive device. The top electrode contains active ionic which stands for low resistance, while the bottom electrode is poor ionic region. Gray arrow indicates the ionic motion. The memristive device switches from OFF to ON with a positive potential difference between the top electrode and bottom electrode corresponding to 'SET' operation as one or more conductive filaments grow or form, while switches from ON to OFF with a negative potential difference between the top electrode and bottom electrode as the filaments disrupt (Color figure online).

device. For other unselected word lines and bit lines, they can be connected to ground or floating. Floating is preferred since it consumes much less power. During reading it is important to note that there also exists many sneak path currents (red line) besides the desired read current (blue line).

Recently, a number of nanoscale electronic device implementations have emerged that include resistive switching and memristive devices. Realization of a solid-state memristive device [9–11], namely the memristor, shown in Fig. 2(b), presents a new opportunity for realizing ultra high density memory arrays together with nanocrossbar structures [31]. The unique properties of such devices are the non-volatile memory and nanoscale dimensions.

In redox (reduction-oxidation) based resistive switching devices there are two major types of devices available: (i) electrochemical metalization (ECM) memory; and (ii) valence change memory (VCM) [48]. Both are examples of memristive device realizations. The memristor is a solid-state device consisting of a thin-film semiconductor sandwiched between two metal contacts. Inside a memristive element there is a built-in concentration gradient of anions (VCM systems) or cations (ECM systems) together with a temperature gradient which is a direct result of current passing through the conductive channel (conductive filament) and is known as Joule-heating. The ionic gradient consists of rich and poor ionic regions. The rich ionic region (top region in Fig. 2(b)) gives rise to low resistance, R_{ON}, and the poor ionic region (bottom region in Fig. 2(b)) is responsible for high resistance, R_{OFF}. The basic operating principle of the memristive device is shown in Fig. 2(b). A positive/negative voltage between two terminals of the memristive device will form/disrupt the filaments, and hence push the device in its ON/OFF state. Once memristive device has been programmed its memristance will remain unchanged even if its power supply is disconnected.

2.3 Memristor-Based PUFs

Because of the interesting properties of memristors discussed earlier, researchers have started investigating the feasibility of memristors for building a PUF [30,35,43,45]. Two of these studies [35,45] employ a time and voltage constrained write mechanism (weak-write) to force each memristor to an undefined logic region (neither logic '1' or '0'). Subsequently, these memristors attain an unpredictable logic state due to process variations that influence memristance. Similar to SRAM PUF, a memristor PUF [35,45] is only capable of producing a limited number of CRPs. More significantly, the PUF in [35,45] requires a calibration procedure to determine the weak-write parameters (time and voltage) to force memristors into the undefined logic region.

In [44] the author leveraged sneak path currents inherent in memristor-based nanocrossbars and bidirectional features to build up a nano Public Physical Unclonable Functions (PPUF). Unlike PUFs, security of the PPUF no longer relies on the secrecy of its physical parameters that define its uncontrollable variations and the model of a PPUF that exactly matches the PPUF hardware behavior is publicly known to every one. The security of a PPUF is based on the time difference (several orders of magnitude) between fast execution time on PPUF hardware to acquire correct response and the much longer time required to compute the response correctly using the PPUF model. In fact, PUFs and PPUFs are hardware primitives with different requirements for authentication and other security services. Moreover, the nano PPUF always needs accurate measurements of its physical parameters to obtain through an accurate model of the nano PPUF that is inconvenient and expensive. Although the PPUF provides an alternative to securely storing challenge response pairs, the poor reliability of the nano PPUF designs still need to be addressed. We refer readers to [41] for a more comprehensive overview.

Our preliminary design of mrPUF was first outlined in [30] where we illustrated the possibility to use the significantly increased variations in high state and low state of memristor resistance in a nanocrossbar array together with an RO-PUF. In this paper we build on our initial concept outline. It should be noted that in this paper, we only exploit abundant resistance variations in R_{ON} state in individual memristors to achieve a more reliable PUF architecture. In addition, we evaluate key PUF performance metrics of mrPUF and analyze the security of the PUF based applications: key generation, and device authentication, which are not investigated in our previous work.

3   mrPUF

3.1   Concept

It has been shown that the memristor can be used to store digital states by utilizing the two distinct resistance values of the memristor, namely ON and OFF resistances, referred to as R_{ON} and R_{OFF}. These resistances are random variables with log-normal distribution values [10]. Figure 3 illustrates the distribution of these resistances after an initial programming step of randomly selected binary values in a nanocrossbar array. As mentioned in Sect. 2.2, variations in memristors is prevalent when their dimensions approach the nano-scale region. These inherent variations can be effectively utilized to design a novel PUF architecture, as we will demonstrate in this article.

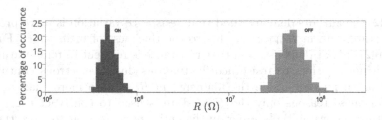

Fig. 3. Experimental resistance variation extracted from a 40×40 nanocrossbar array (1600 memristors) from the experimental data [10].

A memristor-based nanocrossbar architecture has the ability to combine large number of memristive devices in a compact area, and hence, has the ability to store a very large amount of information within a small physical size. When reading a targeted memristor resistance value, in addition to the current through the targeted memristor, there exist a number of other current paths that are commonly referred to as *sneak path* currents that result in an inaccurate reading of the targeted memristor device value (see Fig. 2). To suppress sneak path currents, a number of techniques are proposed [10]. Three of the leading techniques at the center of attention in today's industry and academic research community to suppress sneak path currents are; (i) an intrinsic current-rectifying behavior [10,50] which is translated into an extremely high current-voltage nonlinearity as shown in Fig. 4; (ii) having a highly nonlinear series element with a transistor-like or a diode-like behavior; and (iii) Complementary resistive switches (CRS) [38]. Presently, the first solution appears more promising than the two latter approaches due to its ability to maintain competing memory features such as small area and the highly nonlinear self-rectifying feature in these solid-state devices. As for CRS, the read operation is destructive and multilevel capability of the memristive device can not be used. In fact, sneak path current in nanocrossbar arrays mitigates the effect of process variations in individual memristors during readout. So intrinsic diode characteristic of the memristor helps maintain the process variations influence on resistance of memristor during readout; this is desirable for a PUF design aiming to exploit process variation.

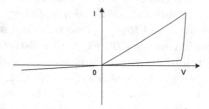

Fig. 4. Memristor with intrinsic diode characteristic.

In [42] the authors demonstrated that resistance variation is more prevalent in R_{ON} state than in R_{OFF} state due to the thickness of memristors. Furthermore, in [27] it was demonstrated that resistance is resilient to temperature and telegraph noise (refers to resistance fluctuations due to electrons captured or released again near or inside the filament) in R_{ON} state more than in R_{OFF} state. For these reasons only the R_{ON} state is used to construct the mrPUF architecture (i.e. we initially program the entire nanocrossbar to store the logic value '1') to reduce susceptibility to both temperature increases and telegraph noise and consequently increase the reliability of the PUF architecture. The sources of variations exploited in our mrPUF are listed below:

1. Memristor manufacturing variations: These variations are prevalent in the nanoscale region, and can be due to variation in device layer thicknesses, dimensions, or doping.
2. Programing variations: In the first programing operation (i.e., programming the state to '0' or '1'), it will introduce variations because the filament location and width in memristor are random.
3. CMOS device manufacturing variations: CMOS device properties due to inherent CMOS process variations, although CMOS process variations in CMOS components such as decoder, ring oscillators is very small compared with the first two listed sources.

3.2   mrPUF Architecture

The proposed mrPUF architecture shown in Fig. 5(a) comprises two key components: a $M \times N$ nanocrossbar array and two current mirror-controlled ring oscillators (CM-ROs), shown in Fig. 5(b). Individual memristor variations in the nanocrossbar array is the source of mrPUF's secrecy. While the CM-RO that has i (in this work, $i = 5$) inverters translates the analog resistance variations of a individual memristor into frequency for digitizing the analog variations to facilitate measurements.

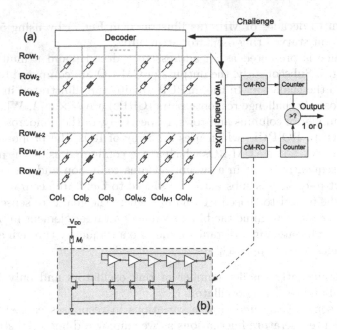

Fig. 5. Memristor-based nanocrossbar PUF architecture, mrPUF. (a) All memristors are in the ON state, the red color (or dark) marked memristors are selected memristors in the nanocrossbar array. (b) Current controlled RO (CM-RO). One current mirror configures all the inverters in a RO structure, M_i is the selected memristor in nanocrossbar array, Although variations in the oscillation frequency of each RO is slightly influenced by the threshold voltage variations in the CMOS transistor composing the starved inverter and current mirror structures, the overall variation in the oscillation frequency is primarily determined by the variations in memresistance of M_i if the supply voltage, V_{DD}, is kept constant (Color figure online).

Challenge bits are used to provide the address bits for both the analog multiplexer and the decoder. The decoder is used to select one column of the nanocrossbar array. Two analog $M \times 1$ multiplexers select two rows acting as bit lines. For example, we can select the red marked memristors (one memristor between Row_2 and Col_2 and the other memristor between Row_{M-1} and Col_2) after applying a single challenge. It should be noted that in this reading scheme the two randomly selected memristors have to be from the same column.

Each selected memristor is then used to control the current in the current mirror structure used to starve the current in each inverter in the ring oscillator loop, resulting in a *current starved ring oscillator* structure. So, the oscillation frequency is a direct function of this current which in turn is a direct function of the value of the memristor. The oscillation frequency of each oscillator is measured using a counter (as in RO-PUF). The outputs from the two counting circuits are compared and a response bit is generated accordingly. The reason only 5 inverters are used in one CM-RO is that the oscillation frequency is already down to decades of MHz (as illustrated in Fig. 7) by using 5 inverters due to a current starved ring oscillator structure.

A challenge is presented as an address to a decoder and a multiplexer as shown in Fig. 5. Subsequently, the outputs of CM-RO are compared to generate a response to the challenge. In the mrPUF architecture illustrated in Fig. 5 the number of possible challenge response pairs (CRPs) are $N \times \binom{M}{2}$. Where N and M are the number of columns and rows, respectively, in the nanocrossbar array.

In contrast to RO-PUF, which uses an array of ROs, the proposed mrPUF efficiently uses two 5-stage CM-ROs which are re-configured using the nanocrossbar and consequently result in a significant area reduction and ease of reading as the output frequency is substantially reduced to facilitate accurate counting. Also unlike the memristor-based PUF in [35] where the goal is to sense the value of the resistance to determine the binary value of a target element in nanocrossbar array, we translate a memristance value into a frequency through a CM-RO. The advantages of this approach are:

1. Use of significantly smaller number of ring oscillators and only 5 inverter stages to build each ring oscillator.
2. Mitigate some of the undesirable variations in responses caused by power supply and temperature fluctuations as we employ a differential structure to generate a response bit.
3. Unlike in [35] we do not need complex circuitry to readout a memory cell and we do not directly expose full physical information (binary value in memory) at each junction of a nanocrossbar array.

4   mrPUF Evaluation

4.1   Simulation Environment and Settings

We conduct extensive experiments to evaluate our mrPUF architecture. The simulation was carried out using Cadence tools. In these simulations the mrPUF was built using a 40×40 nanocrossbar array with $1.25\,\Omega$ segment resistance for nano-wires and two 5-stage CM-ROs as shown in Fig. 5. Each memristor is programmed to R_{ON} where the value of R_{ON} is selected from the log-normal distribution shown in Fig. 3. It should be noted here that the log-normal distribution values are extracted from the fabricated experimental data in [10]. Readout is achieved using a $1\,V$ supply voltage. Our selected voltage ensures that we are operating below the memristor's threshold voltage and ensures the device memristance does not alter with respect to time. In these simulations we use the GPDK 90 nm standard CMOS technology in Cadence with a $1.0\,V$ supply voltage. The memristor model is adapted from [36,49] and written in Verilog-A language. The simulated results of our memristor model shown in Fig. 6 agrees well with experimental results published in [10].

We simulated a 40×40 nanocrossbar array architecture shown in Fig. 5 and obtained 31,200 CRPs using 15 bit length challenges.

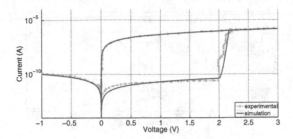

Fig. 6. Memristor with intrinsic diode characteristics. Red dash line is obtained from experimental data [10,32] and the dot line depicts the accuracy of the simulated results produced by our memristor model written by Verilog-A language and used in generating the simulation results in our study (Color figure online).

4.2 Performance

There are a number of performance measures proposed in the literature for evaluating PUFs. We have selected fundamental metrics to demonstrate the performance of mrPUF using uniqueness, uniformity, diffuseness and reliability as proposed in [40] and [29]. Detailed definitions and explanations of these metrics for evaluating PUF architecture can be found therein. In addition to PUF performance we firstly investigate the frequency distribution of CM-RO to ensure that the frequency is indeed, mainly, a function of the resistance of the selected individual memristor.

Frequency Distribution. To test whether the frequency is determined by the variations from the resistance distribution of memristors in the nanocrossbar array, we readout all of the frequencies in one mrPUF instance from CM-RO configured by challenge bits, which select a target memristor in the nanocrossbar. The number of frequencies are equal to the number of memristors in nanocrossbar array (i.e. 1600). The frequency distribution is shown in Fig. 7. It can be

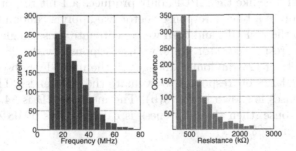

Fig. 7. The plot on the left shows the frequency distribution and the plot on the right shows the resistance distribution in a 40×40 nanocrossbar array. As expected, the frequency distribution agrees well with the resistance distribution.

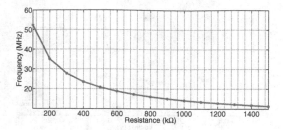

Fig. 8. The relationship between CM-RO's frequency and memristor's resistance. The circuit is shown in Fig. 5(b).

seen that, as expected, the frequency distribution follows a log-normal distribution. For comparison, we show the resistance distribution in the nanocrossbar array in Fig. 7 as well. The close alignment of the frequency distribution and the resistance distribution plots illustrates that the dominant variation determining the mrPUF response is from the inherent random variations of individual memristors in the nanocrossbar array (which is more prevalent in the nano-region) instead of the CMOS technology variations in the peripheral CMOS circuitry. Detailed relationship between CM-RO's frequency and memristor's resistance is shown in Fig. 8 where we can see how the frequency of a CM-RO is determined by the resistance of a memristor.

Uniformity. Randomness or uniformity is an indicator of the balance of '0' and '1' in the response vector. An ideal PUF should show that a '0' or '1' response is equiprobable. For mrPUF our results show that the probability of a '0' or '1' response is very close to 50 % (probability of '1' is 50.34 % as shown in Fig. 9(a)).

Diffuseness measures the difference between responses for different challenges applied to the same PUF. Diffuseness quantifies the information content that can be extracted from a PUF. Diffuseness is measured by calculating the mean of Hamming Distance (HD) for all the possible responses generated by the PUF. Diffuseness for an ideal PUF is 50 %.

Note the mrPUF, like the APUF, only produces a 1 bit response for a given challenge. To obtain a binary response vector, we apply a randomly selected set of challenges to the mrPUF, and then we concatenate these single response bits to a multiple bit response vector. Here, we use responses with 128 bits, therefore we apply 100 sets of 128 random challenges to the mrPUF. Subsequentially, we gain one hundred 128 bit responses to evaluate the diffuseness. The HD among these 100 responses is shown in Fig. 9(b). The mean of HD is 64.10 bits out of the 128 bit response, then the diffuseness is calculated as 50.08 % close to the expected value of 50 %.

Uniqueness. When applying the same challenge set to different PUFs, the responses from different PUFs are expected to be different due to intrinsic variations of each PUF. This is a highly desirable characteristic that be capable

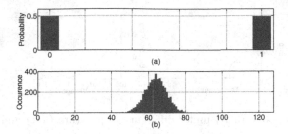

Fig. 9. (a) Uniformity or randomness of mrPUF: probability of output logic '1' and '0' are close to 50%, which are 50.34% and 49.66% for logic '1' and logic '0' respectively. (b) Diffuseness of the mrPUF: mean of HD among 100 randomly generated responses is 64.10 bits out of 128 bits (50.08%)

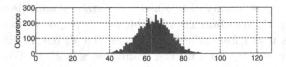

Fig. 10. Uniqueness evaluation: mean of inter HD among 100 responses generated from 100 PUF instances for the same given challenge is 64.22 bits out of 128 bits (50.17%).

of distinguish one PUF from a large population. Uniqueness is the inter-device performance that can be measured by inter-HD. The mean of hamming distance is uniqueness expected to be 50% as an ideal value.

We use 100 different mrPUF instances to evaluate the uniqueness and the result is shown in Fig. 10. It can be observed that the mean of inter HD for the mrPUF is 64.22 bits out of the 128 bit response and this value agrees with that expected from an ideal PUF (i.e. 64 bits). The uniqueness is 50.17%.

Reliability. Reliability or steadiness indicates stability of the PUF output bits, i.e. the ability to consistently generate the same response to a corresponding challenge. Reliability of an ideal PUF should be strong (100%). However, because noise (environmental variations, instabilities in circuit, aging) are unavoidable, there are always uncertain factors affecting the response. Reliability is measured by intra-chip HD among different samples of PUF response bits to the same challenge set applied to the same PUF instance.

A reference response Ref_i is recorded at normal operating condition (27°C and 1.0 V supply voltage for our simulation), then a response Ref_i' is extracted at a different operating condition but using the same set of challenges as before. After samples of Ref_i' are collected, the HD between Ref_i and Ref_i' is calculated. An ideal PUF's intra HD between Ref_i and Ref_i' should be 0 bits. Reliability can also be described by Bit Error Rate (BER), which is the percentage of flipped (error) bits (also called measurement noise) out of response bits due to noise.

Under simulation settings, we would always obtain the same responses for the same challenges if the temperature and voltage conditions do not change.

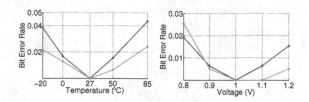

Fig. 11. Bit error rate (BER) under different temperature (left) and voltage (right) deviations.

In other words, the BER caused by measurement noise can not be evaluated. However, it is feasible to evaluate reliability under different temperature and supply voltages as discussed below.

We evaluate the reliability of two mrPUF instances and the results obtained are shown in Fig. 11. We obtained a 500 bit length response by repeatedly challenging mrPUFs under four different voltages: 0.8 V; 0.9 V; 1.1 V; and 1.2 V. The temperature settings used for the evaluation was 27°C. Worst-case BER is 2.6 % under ±20 % deviation and 0.65 % under ±10 % deviation from nominal power supply voltage of 1.0 V.

The resistance temperature coefficient of memristive devices in ON state is similar to a metallic resistor [26,37]. Therefore, we used metallic resistor temperature coefficient to conduct reliability evaluation under different temperature conditions. Reliability tests were repeated for four different ambient temperatures (−20°C, 0°C, 50°C, 85°C). The supply voltage used in these tests was 1.0 V. Worst BER of the two mrPUFs is 4.4 % when the temperature is 85°C.

5   Applications and Security Analysis

5.1   Cryptographic Key Generation

It is impractical to use raw responses of a PUF as cryptographic keys directly because the BER is higher than the industrial standard of BER that is in the order of 10^{-6} (the industrial standard of BER for cryptographic key generation) [6]. As illustrate in [28], a fuzzy extractor can be used to correct the raw response and hash the corrected response to build a cryptographic key.

For example, to obtain 63 secret bits with a BER rate lower than 10^{-6}, the BCH(255,63,61) code can be used to correct raw PUF responses. Our mrPUF is expected to generate 11 unreliable bits out of a 255 bit response considering the worst-case BER of 4.4 %. The BCH(255,63,61) code can correct up to 61/2 errors out of 255 bits. Therefore, a BER of 3.9×10^{-7}, lower than the desired 10^{-6}, can be obtained by using the BCH code. However, the syndrome generated from the BCH code can reveal at most 192 (255 − 63) bits of information and therefore there are 63 secret bits that can be used from the 255 bits response. Hence an attacker has to guess at least 63 bits to find the correct PUF response. In general, as proposed in [15], the regenerated response can be hashed to obtain a fixed size key or serve as a seed for a key generation algorithm.

5.2 Authentication

Our PUF can also be directly used for device authentication using a simple challenge-response based authentication protocol. The authentication protocol follows 5 steps [15,33,34]:

First: A trusted party applies randomly chosen challenges to obtain responses and saves these CRPs in a database for future authentication (characterization of the PUF) before the PUF (as part of an integrated circuit) is sent to end-users. This is called the provision phase.

Second: Whenever an end-user needs to authenticate the authenticity of the product to which the PUF has been integrated, the user requests an authentication from the trusted party.

Third: The trusted party randomly selects a challenge from those stored securely in a database and sends it securely to the end-user. Subsequently, the end-user applies the challenge to their PUF and obtains a response.

Fourth: The user securely sends the obtained response to the trusted party.

Fifth: The trusted party compares the received response with the response stored. If they are close to each other, within an expected BER, authenticity of the product integrated with a PUF is established.

In order to prevent a replay attack by a passive attacker, a single CRP is only used once. This is possible because of the large number of CRPs that can be generated from a mrPUF.

To evaluate PUF security there are two analysis approaches: (i) evaluate the internal entropy of the PUF; and (ii) evaluate the number of independent CRPs produced by the PUF, or in other words, the number of CRPs needed by an adversary to build a model of the physical PUF with a high prediction accuracy. In terms of the first approach, it has been demonstrated that the internal entropy of the PUF does not provide the attacker information to break a PUF, even if the entropy is very low. In addition, it is not clear that the internal entropy is a good indicator of a PUF's security as highlighted in [47]. While the second approach is a better way to evaluate the security of a PUF [47]. So we use the second approach to evaluate the security of mrPUF.

PUFs such as APUF and RO-PUF have shown that after exposing a specific number of CRPs an attacker gains enough knowledge to build a model to predict responses for a given unused challenge [13,39,47]. This model building attack can threaten our mrPUF. In this section, we are going to illustrate how to avoid such a model building attack by leveraging properties inherent to our mrPUF architecture and a challenge selection strategy.

We assume the attacker does not have authority to physically access the mrPUF. The CRPs they can acquire is only from eavesdropping. Consider the mrPUF shown in Fig. 5 with N columns and M rows. Each challenge will select one column and two rows. In other words, each challenge selects two memristors in the same column but from different rows, then the resistance of these two memristors are translated into frequencies by two CM-ROs to generate a single response bit. Now, if we only consider memristors in one column within the

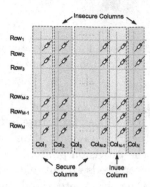

Fig. 12. mrPUF access mechanism resilient to model building attacks by using information from independent columns: firstly, we use CRPs generated from one randomly selected *Secure Column*, after N_{CRP} (number of CRPs required to train the attacker's model to acquire needed prediction accuracy) CRPs are used, this column becomes an *Insecure Column*. Secondly, we move to another randomly selected *Secure Column*. The column currently in use while its number of CPRs exposed is below N_{CRP} is labeled *Inuse Column*.

nanocrossbar array, we can model a mrPUF instance as a k ring oscillators PUF. From [47] we can obtain an estimate of the number of CRPs needed to train a machine learning based model to achieve an error rate of ϵ as

$$N_{\mathrm{CRP}} \approx \frac{k(k-1)(1-2\epsilon)}{2+\epsilon(k-1)} \tag{1}$$

where N_{CRP} is the number of CRPs needed to train a machine learning classifier and k is the number of RO in RO-PUF. The total number of CRPs in RO-PUF is NT_{CRP}, which is equal to $k \times (k-1)/2$. If an attacker wants to impersonate the PUF through building a predictive model, the error rate of the predictions of the model should be less than ϵ, or the trusted party can still distinguish the impersonated PUF from the original PUF. Based on Eq. 1, to achieve a prediction accuracy of 1-ϵ, an adversary needs N_{CRP} CRPs to train a machine learning classifier.

It is noticeable that each challenge applied to mrPUF only selects two memristors in the same column, therefore information exposed in one column does not leak any information related to other columns. This property can be exploited to avoid machine learning based model building attacks through careful challenge selection.

In this paper, we propose a challenge selection strategy outlined in Fig. 12 to avoid model building attacks. The nanocrossbar columns are separated into three categories. If CRPs produced from one column have never been used, then this column is a *Secure Column*, since there is no information exposed to an adversary thus far. Under the condition that we only use CRPs from one column, the adversary needs N_{CRP} CRPs to train their machine learning classifier and build a model of the memristor related delays for a given column. Thus if N_{CRP}

CRPs generated (obtained using Eq. 1) from the *Inuse Column* has been used then this column becomes an *Insecure Column* because an adversary may have gathered enough CPRs to build a model and can potentially predict the response to future challenges with high accuracy. If the number of used CRPs generated from the column is still less than N_{CRP}, the column is an *Inuse Column*.

In our mrPUF, each column can be used to generate N_{CRP} secure CRPs because the attacker cannot predict the response with a high enough accuracy (1– ϵ) unless N_{CRP} CRPs are exposed. After more than N_{CRP} CRPs generated from the *Inuse Column* are exposed, the *Inuse Column* becomes an *Insecure Column*. We do not use CRPs generated from this *Insecure Column* again. Since each column is independent, the attacker is unable to use their existing knowledges to construct a model of the subsequent *Secure Columns*. This process can continue until all *Secure Columns* have been exhausted.

By using our proposed challenge selection mechanism in Fig. 12, we can make mrPUF more resilient to model building attacks. To increase security using our proposed mechanism above, it is better to set $N > M$. In this way, we are able to obtain more independent columns.

6 Comparison

Here we compare mrPUF with other memristor based PUFs. However, Comparison with nano PPUF is not presented because the nano PPUF has been developed to meet the requirements for a public PUF, where the need to build a model of a nano PPUF requires highly accurate measurements of each individual memristor in the nanocrossbar array in the provisioning phase. Furthermore, since the performance evaluations of RO-PUF, APUF and SRAM PUFs are acquired from experimental data, it is unfair to compare these with our simulated result. So here, we compare our mrPUF with existing memristor based PUFs where their results are also from simulation based studies.

Table 1. Comparison with memristor based PUFs

	[35]	[45]	mrPUF
Uniqueness	$\approx 50\%$	$\approx 50\%$	50.17%
Uniformity	—	$\approx 50\%$	49.66%
Crossbar	used	No	used
CRP number	$M \times N$	M	$N \times \binom{M}{2}$

Since all the PUFs in Table 1 are based on large uncontrollable variations in nanofabrication and nanodevices, the uniqueness and uniformity are all close to the ideal value of 50%. We do not compare reliability performance because there is no such information presented in other memristor based PUFs. In Table 1, whether a nanocrossbar is used or not determines the circuit density. In terms of the CRP number, M and N denote the number of rows and columns, respectively, in a nanocrossbar array. In particular, for the PUF presented in [45],

M denotes the number of memristors used in the PUF architecture. The number of CRPs of the other two memristor based PUFs is equal to the number of memristors. As for our mrPUF, it can be seen that it is capable of yielding a significantly larger number of CRPs.

In summary, we have evaluated the uniqueness, randomness performance of mrPUF. In addition, we also investigate the reliability under different temperature and voltage conditions. Such evaluation is missing in the currently published memristor based PUFs. Moreover, we have also analyzed the security of our mrPUF for two potential applications and proposed a challenge selection strategy to avoid model building attacks when mrPUF is used directly for authentication applications.

7   Conclusion

In this paper, we present a novel PUF architecture named mrPUF. Our approach exploits the robustness of RO-PUFs and exploits the large variations in nanodevices as well as the high information density available in nanocrossbar structures to create a novel PUF. Our architecture not only achieves sound reliability, uniqueness, diffuseness, but also improves the number of available CRPs in comparison with other recent memristor based PUF architectures. In particular, we show that mrPUF achieves higher levels of security due to the inherent features of nanocrossbar arrays that the information in one column is independent from other columns. We also demonstrate a mechanism using mrPUF in an authentication protocol that is resistant to model building attacks by the proposed challenge selection strategy.

A limitation of our work is that our experiments are conducted based on device simulations, albeit using de-facto industry standard modelling tools and experimentally verified process variations, rather than physical realizations, Addressing this limitation forms the subject of our future work. Furthermore, in our future work we will investigate the possibility of building a re-configurable and strong memeristive device based PUF architecture [51] by exploiting the variations induced during re-programming and increasing the number of CRPs significantly.

Acknowledgment. This research was supported by a grant from the Australian Research Council (DP140103448). The authors also appreciate sponsorship from the China Scholarship Council, and the support from the Department of Further Education, Employment, Science and Technology (DFEEST) under the Collaboration Pathways Program, Government of South Australia.

References

1. Kömmerling, O., Kuhn, M.G.: Design principles for tamper-resistant smartcard processors. In: Proceedings of the USENIX Workshop on Smartcard Technology, pp. 9–20. USENIX Association (1999)

2. Lee, J.W., Lim, D., Gassend, B., Suh, G.E., Van Dijk, M., Devadas, S.: A technique to build a secret key in integrated circuits for identification and authentication applications. In: Proceedings of the IEEE Symposium on VLSI Circuits, pp. 176–179 (2004)
3. Ranasinghe, D.C., Cole, P.H.: Networked RFID Systems and Lightweight Cryptography. Springer, Berlin (2008)
4. Maes, R., Van Herrewege, A., Verbauwhede, I.: PUFKY: a fully functional PUF-based cryptographic key generator. In: Prouff, E., Schaumont, P. (eds.) CHES 2012. LNCS, vol. 7428, pp. 302–319. Springer, Heidelberg (2012)
5. van Dijk, M., Rührmair, U.: Physical unclonable functions in cryptographic protocols: security proofs and impossibility results. IACR Cryptology ePrint Archive 2012: 228 (2012)
6. Zhang, L., Kong, Z.H., Chang, C.-H.: PCKGen: a phase change memory based cryptographic key generator. In: Proceedings of the IEEE International Symposium on Circuits and Systems (ISCAS), pp. 1444–1447 (2013)
7. Ruhrmair, U., van Dijk, M.: PUFs in security protocols: attack models and security evaluations. In: IEEE Symposium on Security and Privacy (SP), pp. 286–300 (2013)
8. Kang, H., Hori, Y., Katashita, T., Hagiwara, M., Iwamura, K.: Cryptographie key generation from PUF data using efficient fuzzy extractors. In: Proceedings of the IEEE 16th International Conference on Advanced Communication Technology (ICACT), pp. 23–26 (2014)
9. Strukov, D.B., Snider, G.S., Stewart, D.R., Williams, R.S.: The missing memristor found. Nature 453(7191), 80–83 (2008)
10. Kim, K.-H., Gaba, S., Wheeler, D., Cruz-Albrecht, J.M., Hussain, T., Srinivasa, N., Lu, W.: A functional hybrid memristor crossbar-array/CMOS system for data storage and neuromorphic applications. Nano Lett. 12(1), 389–395 (2011)
11. Kavehei, O., Al-Sarawi, S., Cho, K.-R., Eshraghian, K., Abbott, D.: An analytical approach for memristive nanoarchitectures. IEEE Trans. Nanotechnol. 11(2), 374–385 (2012)
12. Gassend, B., Lim, D., Clarke, D., Van Dijk, M., Devadas, S.: Identification and authentication of integrated circuits. Concurrency Comput. Pract. Experience 16(11), 1077–1098 (2004)
13. Lim, D., Lee, J.W., Gassend, B., Suh, G.E., Van Dijk, M., Devadas, S.: Extracting secret keys from integrated circuits. IEEE Trans. Very Large Scale Integr. VLSI Syst. 13(10), 1200–1205 (2005)
14. Kumar, R., Patil, V. C., Kundu, S.: Design of unique and reliable physically unclonable functions based on current starved inverter chain. In: Proceedings of the IEEE Computer Society Annual Symposium on VLSI (ISVLSI), pp. 224–229 (2011)
15. Suh, G.E., Devadas, S.: Physical unclonable functions for device authentication and secret key generation. In: Proceedings of the 44th Annual Design Automation Conference, pp. 9–14 (2007)
16. Suzuki, D., Shimizu, K.: The glitch PUF: a new delay-PUF architecture exploiting glitch shapes. In: Mangard, S., Standaert, F.-X. (eds.) CHES 2010. LNCS, vol. 6225, pp. 366–382. Springer, Heidelberg (2010)
17. Holcomb, D.E., Burleson, W.P., Fu, K.: Initial SRAM state as a fingerprint and source of true random numbers for RFID tags. In Proceedings of the Conference on RFID Security, vol. 7 (2007)
18. Holcomb, D.E., Burleson, W.P., Fu, K.: Power-up SRAM state as an identifying fingerprint and source of true random numbers. IEEE Trans. Comput. 58(9), 1198–1210 (2009)

614   Y. Gao et al.

19. Su, Y., Holleman, J., Otis, B.P.: A digital 1.6 pJ/bit chip identification circuit using process variations. IEEE J. Solid-State Circuits **43**(1), 69–77 (2008)
20. Maes, R., Tuyls, P., Verbauwhede, I.: Intrinsic PUFs from flip-flops on reconfigurable devices. In: 3rd Benelux Workshop on Information and System Security (WISSec 2008), vol. 17 (2008)
21. van der Leest, V., Schrijen, G.-J., Handschuh, H., Tuyls, P.: Hardware intrinsic security from D flip-flops. In: Proceedings of the Fifth ACM Workshop on Scalable Trusted Computing, pp. 53–62. ACM (2010)
22. Kumar, S.S., Guajardo, J., Maes, R., Schrijen, G.-J., Tuyls, P.: The butterfly PUF protecting IP on every FPGA. In: IEEE International Workshop on Hardware-Oriented Security and Trust, 2008, HOST 2008, pp. 67–70 (2008)
23. Roel, M.: Physically unclonable functions: constructions, properties and applications. Ph.D. thesis, Dissertation, University of KU Leuven (2012)
24. Herder, C., Yu, M.D., Koushanfar, F., Devadas, S.: Physical unclonable functions and applications: a tutorial. Proc. IEEE **102**(8), 1126–1141 (2014)
25. Maiti, A., Casarona, J., McHale, L., Schaumont, P.: A large scale characterization of RO-PUF. In: IEEE International Symposium on Hardware-Oriented Security and Trust (HOST), pp. 94–99 (2010)
26. Borghetti, J., Strukov, D.B., Pickett, M.D., Yang, J.J., Stewart, D.R., Williams, R.S.: Electrical transport and thermometry of electroformed titanium dioxide memristive switches. J. Appl. Phys. **106**(12), 124504 (2009)
27. Choi, S., Yang, Y., Lu, W.: Random telegraph noise and resistance switching analysis of oxide based resistive memory. Nanoscale **6**(1), 400–404 (2014)
28. Dodis, Y., Reyzin, L., Smith, A.: Fuzzy extractors: how to generate strong keys from biometrics and other noisy data. In: Cachin, C., Camenisch, J.L. (eds.) EUROCRYPT 2004. LNCS, vol. 3027, pp. 523–540. Springer, Heidelberg (2004)
29. Hori, Y., Yoshida, T., Katashita, T., Satoh, A.: Quantitative and statistical performance evaluation of arbiter physical unclonable functions on FPGAs. In: International Conference on Reconfigurable Computing and FPGAs (ReConFig), pp. 298–303. IEEE (2010)
30. Kavehei, O., Hosung, C., Ranasinghe, D.C., Skafidas, S.: mrPUF: a memristive device based physical unclonable function. arXiv preprint arXiv:1302.2191 (2013)
31. Kavehei, O., Linn, E., Nielen, L., Tappertzhofen, S., Skafidas, E., Valov, I., Waser, R.: An associative capacitive network based on nanoscale complementary resistive switches for memory-intensive computing. Nanoscale **5**(11), 5119–5128 (2013)
32. Kim, K.-H., Jo, S.H., Gaba, S., Lu, W.: Nanoscale resistive memory with intrinsic diode characteristics and long endurance. Appl. Phys. Lett. **96**(5), 053106 (2010)
33. Ranasinghe, D.C., Engels, D.W., Cole, P.H.: Security and privacy solutions for low-cost rfid systems. In: Proceedings of the IEEE Inelligent Sensors, Sensor Networks and Information Processing Conference, pp. 337–342 (2004)
34. Ranasinghe, D.C., Cole, P.H.: Confronting security and privacy threats in modern RFID systems. In: Proceedings of the IEEE Fortieth Asilomar Conference on Signals, Systems and Computers, pp. 2058–2064 (2004)
35. Koeberl, P., Kocabaş, Ü., Sadeghi, A.-R.: Memristor PUFs: a new generation of memory-based physically unclonable functions. In: Proceedings of the Conference on Design, Automation and Test in Europe, pp. 428–431. EDA Consortium (2013)
36. Kvatinsky, S., Talisveyberg, K., Fliter, D., Friedman, E.G., Kolodny, A., Weiser, U.C.: Verilog-A for memristor models. Technical report, Citeseer (2011)
37. Kwon, D.-H., Kim, K.M., Jang, J.H., Jeon, J.M., Lee, M.H., Kim, G.H., Li, X.-S., Park, G.-S., Lee, B., Han, S., et al.: Atomic structure of conducting nanofilaments in TiO_2 resistive switching memory. Nature Nanotechnology **5**(2), 148–153 (2010)

38. Linn, E., Rosezin, R., Kügeler, C., Waser, R.: Complementary resistive switches for passive nanocrossbar memories. Nat. Mater. **9**(5), 403–406 (2010)
39. Mahmoud, A., Rührmair, U., Majzoobi, M., Koushanfar, F.: Combined modeling and side channel attacks on strong PUFs. IACR Cryptology ePrint Archive 2013:632 (2013)
40. Maiti, A., Gunreddy, V., Schaumont, P.: A systematic method to evaluate and compare the performance of physical unclonable functions. In: Athanas, P., Pnevmatikatos, D., Sklavos, N. (eds.) Embedded Systems Design with FPGAs, pp. 245–267. Springer, New York (2013)
41. Potkonjak, M., Goudar, V.: Public physical unclonable functions. Proc. IEEE **102**(8), 1142–1156 (2014)
42. Rajendran, J., Karri, R., Rose, G.S.: Improving tolerance to variations in memristor-based applications using parallel memristors. IEEE Trans. Comput. **64**(3), 733–746 (2015)
43. Rajendran, J., Karri, R., Wendt, J.B., Potkonjak, M., McDonald, N.R., Rose, G.S., Wysocki, B.T.: Nanoelectronic solutions for hardware security. IACR Cryptology ePrint Archive 2012:575 (2012)
44. Rajendran, J., Rose, G.S., Karri, R., Potkonjak, M.: Nano-PPUF: a memristor-based security primitive. In: 2012 IEEE Computer Society Annual Symposium on VLSI (ISVLSI), pp. 84–87 (2012)
45. Rose, G.S., McDonald, N., Yan, L.-K., Wysocki, B.: A write-time based memristive PUF for hardware security applications. In: IEEE/ACM International Conference on Computer-Aided Design (ICCAD), pp. 830–833 (2013)
46. Rostami, M., Wendt, J.B., Potkonjak, M., Koushanfar, F.: Quo vadis, PUF?: trends and challenges of emerging physical-disorder based security. In: Proceedings of the Conference on Design, Automation & Test in Europe, p. 352. European Design and Automation Association (2014)
47. Rührmair, U., Sehnke, F., Sölter, J., Dror, G., Devadas, S., Schmidhuber, J.: Modeling attacks on physical unclonable functions. In: Proceedings of the 17th ACM Conference on Computer and Communications Security, pp. 237–249. ACM (2010)
48. Valov, I., Waser, R., Jameson, J.R., Kozicki, M.N.: Electrochemical metallization memoriesfundamentals, applications, prospects. Nanotechnology **22**(25), 254003 (2011)
49. Vourkas, I., Batsos, A., Sirakoulis, G.C.: SPICE modeling of nonlinear memristive behavior. Int. J. Circuit Theory and Appl. **43**(5), 553–565 (2013)
50. Wu, S., Ren, L., Qing, J., Yu, F., Yang, K., Yang, M., Wang, Y., Meng, M., Zhou, W., Zhou, X., Li, S.: Bipolar resistance switching in transparent $ITO/LaAlO_3/SrTiO_3$ memristors. ACS Appl. Mater. Interfaces **6**(11), 8575–8579 (2014)
51. Gao, Y., Ranasinghe, D.C., Al-Sarawi, S.F., Kavehei, O., Abbott, D.: Memristive crypto primitive for building highly secure physical unclonable functions. Sci. Rep. **5** (2015). Article Number 12785

Leakage Resilience
and Pseudorandomness

On the XOR of Multiple Random Permutations

Bart Mennink[(✉)] and Bart Preneel

Department of Electrical Engineering, ESAT/COSIC,
KU Leuven, and iMinds, Leuven, Belgium
{bart.mennink,bart.preneel}@esat.kuleuven.be

Abstract. A straightforward way of constructing an n-bit pseudorandom function is to XOR two or more pseudorandom permutations: $p_1 \oplus \ldots \oplus p_k$. This XOR construction has gained broad attention over the last two decades. In this work, we revisit the security of this well-established construction. We consider the case where the underlying permutations are considered secret, as well as the case where these permutations are publicly available to the adversary. In the secret permutation setting, we present a simple reduction showing that the XOR construction achieves optimal 2^n security for all $k \geq 2$, therewith improving a recent result of Cogliati et al. (FSE 2014). Regarding the public permutation setting, Mandal et al. (INDOCRYPT 2010) proved $2^{2n/3}$ security for the case $k = 2$, but we point out the existence of a non-trivial flaw in the proof. We re-establish and generalize the claimed security bound for general $k \geq 2$ using a different proof approach.

Keywords: XOR of permutations · Indifferentiability · Beyond birthday bound · H-coefficient technique

1   Introduction

A fundamental research question in cryptography is how to construct a pseudorandom function (PRF) from a pseudorandom permutation (PRP). The first to formally consider this problem were Bellare et al. [21]. They named the problem "Luby-Rackoff backwards", referring to the celebrated result by Luby and Rackoff who showed how to construct a PRP from a PRF [31]. Their PRF construction consisted of two sequential block cipher calls, where the output of the first call is the key input to the second one: $f(k, x) = E(E(k, x), x)$. This construction only achieves security up to the birthday bound on the output size.

Various methods to construct a PRF from a PRP have been presented that achieve security beyond the $2^{n/2}$ birthday bound, the most notable approach being the XOR of multiple n-bit permutations. In more detail, let $p_1, \ldots, p_k$ be $k \geq 1$ n-bit permutations, and define the following function:

$$f_k = p_1 \oplus \cdots \oplus p_k. \tag{1}$$

For $k = 1$, the security of f_1 is commonly known as the PRP-PRF switch, and primary analysis on this function has, among others, been performed by

© Springer International Publishing Switzerland 2015
T. Malkin et al. (Eds.): ACNS 2015, LNCS 9092, pp. 619–634, 2015.
DOI: 10.1007/978-3-319-28166-7_30

Impagliazzo and Rudich [25], Black et al. [19], Hall et al. [29], and Bellare and Rogaway [4]. For general $k \geq 1$, Lucks [9] proved that this function is a secure PRF up to about $2^{\frac{k}{k+1}n}$ queries. For $k = 2$, Bellare and Impagliazzo [18] proved security up to approximately $2^n/n^{2/3}$, and Patarin [30] improved this bound to approximately 2^n. The latter result is proven using the H-coefficient technique [10], a proof technique that has recently been revisited by Chen and Steinberger [27] and found adoption (among others) in the security of key alternating ciphers [27], cascade encryption [1], and MACs [5,24]. Using the same techniques, Cogliati et al. [28] recently improved the security bounds of f_k for $k \geq 3$, proving that it behaves like a PRF up to approximately $2^{\frac{2k+1}{2k+2}n}$ queries. The authors also mention that the bound could be improved to 2^n, via methods similar to the iterative method employed by Patarin [30], but no proof is given. The state of the art is summarized in Table 1.

All of above-mentioned results are in the secret permutation setting. In more detail, one considers an adversary that is given access to either f_k (using secret permutations), or a random function $\mathcal{R}$, and its goal is to *distinguish* both worlds. While to a certain degree it is possible to view the permutations as secret – one can consider them being instantiated as block ciphers with fixed and secret keys – a novel trend in cryptography is to view permutations as standalone and publicly available objects. For instance, various permutation-based hash functions have appeared over the last years [6,7,16,20,22,23] and the recently started CAESAR competition [11] received various permutation-based submissions, and all of these constructions have been analyzed in the public permutation model. If we wish to consider f_k in the case where the underlying permutations are publicly available, the indistinguishability model is deficient. An improved notion is the *indifferentiability* framework, introduced by Maurer et al. [15]. Informally, it gives a sufficient condition under which an ideal functionality $\mathcal{R}$ can be replaced by f_k using ideal, publicly available, primitives $p = (p_1, \ldots, p_k)$. Indifferentiability proofs consider the existence of a simulator $\mathcal{S}$ with access to $\mathcal{R}$ such that (f_k, p) on the one hand and $(\mathcal{R}, \mathcal{S})$ on the other hand are indistinguishable. In this indifferentiability model, Mandal et al. [2] proved that f_2 achieves $\mathcal{O}(2^{2n/3})$ security. The authors conjecture that their simulator allows to achieve optimal $\mathcal{O}(2^n)$ indifferentiability. An additional open problem is to generalize this result to $k > 2$ permutations. Table 1 also summarizes the state of the art for the public permutation setting.

A related result is the construction of a permutation XORed with its inverse, $p \oplus p^{-1}$, as introduced by Dodis et al. [12]. However, this construction is only proven to achieve indifferentiability security up to the birthday bound.

Our Contributions

We revisit the state of the art in both the secret permutation setting and the public permutation setting.

Starting with security in the secret permutation setting, we present an alternative and short proof showing that f_k indeed achieves 2^n indistinguishability

Table 1. State of the art for indistinguishability (first) and indifferentiability (second). Results in **bold** are derived in this work

	k	bound	reference	remark
indistinguishability (p_i secret)	≥ 1	$2^{\frac{k}{k+1}n}$	[9]	
	2	$2^n/n^{2/3}$	[18]	
	2	2^n	[30]	
	≥ 3	$2^{\frac{2k+1}{2k+2}n}$	[28]	conjectured 2^n
	≥ 3	**2^n**	**Sect. 3**	
indifferentiability (p_i public)	2	$2^{n/2}$	[2]	
	2	$2^{2n/3}$	[2]	**flawed (Sect. 4.3)**
	≥ 2	**$2^{2n/3}$**	**Sect. 4**	

security for all $k \geq 3$. The proof is fairly straightforward, consisting of a reduction of the security of f_{k+1} to f_k for all $k \geq 2$, and using Patarin's proof of 2^n security of f_2 [30]. The proof is simpler than the one suggested by Cogliati et al. to achieve 2^n security [28], but the price to pay is a slightly worse security bound. (The difference lies in the security exponent. Informally, this is a value c such that the security bound behaves like $(q/2^n)^c$. A larger c means a sharper curve for the security advantage, or in other words that the threshold value q_0 such that $(q_0/2^n)^c = 1/2$, is higher. The approach suggested in [28] is expected to result in a larger security exponent.)

Regarding security in the public permutation setting, we revisit the work of Mandal et al. [2] and note that the proof contains a subtle but non-negligible flaw. The bug appears in the technical part of the proof, it is not straightforwardly fixable, and thus invalidates the security result, leaving the indifferentiability of f_2 *beyond* $2^{n/2}$ as an open problem. Nevertheless, the mistake does not have a direct influence on the proposed simulator. For a generalization of their simulator to $k \geq 2$ rounds, we next restore the claimed security bound. In more detail, we re-confirm that f_k achieves at least $2^{2n/3}$ indifferentiability security. The security result is obtained by following a different proof approach and avoiding the flawed part all the way. The new proof particularly relies on a result from the area of Fourier theory proven by Babai [3], Steinberger [13], and Chen et al. [14], that (informally) bounds the number of solutions to $a \oplus b = c$ for $(a, b, c) \in A \times B \times C$, where C is a set of random elements and A and B are two arbitrarily chosen sets of size $|C|$ (details follow in Sect. 4.4). This problem found earlier adoption in the area of permutation-based hashing [23], digital signatures [17], and the security of Even-Mansour [14].

The new results are also included in Table 1.

Outline

We introduce some mathematical preliminaries and discuss the indistinguishability and indifferentiability models in Sect. 2. We present our short and alternative proof for the indistinguishability of f_k in Sect. 3. A new indifferentiability proof for $k \geq 2$, using a generalization of the simulator of Mandal et al. [2], is given in Sect. 4. The work is concluded in Sect. 5. In this section, we also elaborate on possible improvements of our result to 2^n security.

2   Preliminaries

Let $n \geq 1$ be an integer. By $\mathsf{Func}(n)$ we denote the set of all functions from $\{0,1\}^n$ to $\{0,1\}^n$ and by $\mathsf{Perm}(n)$ the set of all permutations on $\{0,1\}^n$. For a set $\mathcal{X}$, we denote by $x \xleftarrow{\$} \mathcal{X}$ the uniformly random sampling of an element from $\mathcal{X}$. If x and y are two bitstrings of the same size, $x \oplus y$ denotes their bitwise XOR.

Throughout, a distinguisher $\mathcal{D}$ is a computationally unbounded probabilistic algorithm that has oracle access to one or more oracles $\mathcal{O}$. The distinguisher can make a certain amount of oracle queries to $\mathcal{O}$, and after this interaction $\mathcal{D}^{\mathcal{O}}$ outputs a 0 or a 1.

Definition 1 (Indistinguishability). *For an integer $k \geq 1$, consider f_k of (1) based on $p = (p_1, \ldots, p_k) \xleftarrow{\$} \mathsf{Perm}(n)^k$. Let $\mathcal{R} \xleftarrow{\$} \mathsf{Func}(n)$. The distinguishing advantage of $\mathcal{D}$ against f_k is defined as*

$$\mathsf{Adv}^{\mathrm{dist}}_{f_k}(\mathcal{D}) = \left| \mathbf{P}\left(\mathcal{D}^{f_k} = 1 \right) - \mathbf{P}\left(\mathcal{D}^{\mathcal{R}} = 1 \right) \right|,$$

where the probabilities are taken over the randomness of p, $\mathcal{R}$, and $\mathcal{D}$.

Maurer et al. [15] introduced indifferentiability as an extension of indistinguishability, more suitable for the case the underlying primitives are publicly available. Indifferentiability of a function f_k from a random function $\mathcal{R}$, intuitively, means that f_k shows no structural design flaws and that it can replace $\mathcal{R}$ in any construction, up to the indifferentiability security bound of f_k. We employ the adaptation and simplification by Coron et al. [26], rewritten in our own terminology.

Definition 2 (Indifferentiability). *For an integer $k \geq 1$, consider f_k of (1) based on $p = (p_1, \ldots, p_k) \xleftarrow{\$} \mathsf{Perm}(n)^k$. Let $\mathcal{R} \xleftarrow{\$} \mathsf{Func}(n)$. Let $\mathcal{S}$ be a simulator with the same interface as p and with oracle access to $\mathcal{R}$. The differentiating advantage of $\mathcal{D}$ against f_k for simulator $\mathcal{S}$ is defined as*

$$\mathsf{Adv}^{\mathrm{diff}}_{f_k, \mathcal{S}}(\mathcal{D}) = \left| \mathbf{P}\left(\mathcal{D}^{f_k, p} = 1 \right) - \mathbf{P}\left(\mathcal{D}^{\mathcal{R}, \mathcal{S}} = 1 \right) \right|,$$

where the probabilities are taken over the randomness of p, $\mathcal{R}$, $\mathcal{S}$, and $\mathcal{D}$.

The indistinguishability and indifferentiability definitions are depicted in Fig. 1.

3   Indistinguishability of f_k

We present a short proof for the indistinguishability of f_k from a random function $\mathcal{R}$ from $\mathsf{Func}(n)$, in accordance with Definition 1. We start with a security reduction of f_{k+1} to f_k for all $k \geq 2$.

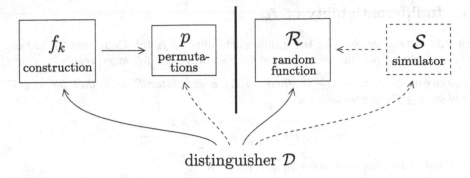

Fig. 1. Indistinguishability (without dashed elements) and indifferentiability (with dashed elements)

Theorem 1. *For all* $k \geq 2$, *for any distinguisher* $\mathcal{D}$, *we have* $\mathsf{Adv}^{\mathrm{dist}}_{f_{k+1}}(\mathcal{D}) \leq \mathsf{Adv}^{\mathrm{dist}}_{f_k}(\mathcal{D})$.

Proof. We consider a distinguisher $\mathcal{D}^{\mathcal{O}}$ that has access to an oracle $\mathcal{O}$, either f_{k+1} or $\mathcal{R} \xleftarrow{\$} \mathsf{Func}(n)$, and makes q queries to this oracle. If $\mathcal{D}^{\mathcal{O},\mathcal{O}'}$ is given access to an additional oracle $\mathcal{O}'$ with the same domain as $\mathcal{O}$, this means that for every query $\mathcal{D}$ makes to $\mathcal{O}$, it gets the same query to $\mathcal{O}'$ for free. In other words, if $\mathcal{D}^{\mathcal{O},\mathcal{O}'}$ queries x to its oracle $\mathcal{O}$, it gets as response the values $\mathcal{O}(x)$ *and* $\mathcal{O}'(x)$.

For brevity, we denote $\mathbf{P}\left(\mathcal{D}^{\mathcal{O}} = 1\right) = \mathbf{P}\left(\mathcal{O}\right)$ and $\mathbf{P}\left(\mathcal{D}^{\mathcal{O},\mathcal{O}'} = 1\right) = \mathbf{P}\left(\mathcal{O},\mathcal{O}'\right)$. Recall that $f_{k+1} = p_1 \oplus \cdots \oplus p_{k+1}$. By construction:

$$\mathsf{Adv}^{\mathrm{dist}}_{f_{k+1}}(\mathcal{D}) = |\mathbf{P}\left(p_1 \oplus \cdots \oplus p_{k+1}\right) - \mathbf{P}\left(\mathcal{R}\right)|$$

$$\overset{(a)}{\leq} |\mathbf{P}\left(p_1 \oplus \cdots \oplus p_{k+1}, p_{k+1}\right) - \mathbf{P}\left(\mathcal{R}, p_{k+1}\right)|$$

$$\overset{(b)}{=} |\mathbf{P}\left(p_1 \oplus \cdots \oplus p_k, p_{k+1}\right) - \mathbf{P}\left(\mathcal{R}, p_{k+1}\right)|$$

$$\overset{(c)}{=} |\mathbf{P}\left(p_1 \oplus \cdots \oplus p_k\right) - \mathbf{P}\left(\mathcal{R}\right)| = \mathsf{Adv}^{\mathrm{dist}}_{f_k}(\mathcal{D}),$$

where (a) holds as extra access may only increase the advantage, (b) holds as $(p_1 \oplus \cdots \oplus p_k, p_{k+1})$ can be computed from $(p_1 \oplus \cdots \oplus p_{k+1}, p_{k+1})$ and vice versa, and (c) holds as p_{k+1} is an independent permutation. $\qquad\square$

Next, we recall the result of Patarin [30] on the indistinguishability of f_2.

Lemma 1 (Patarin [30]). *For any* $\mathcal{D}$ *making* q *oracle queries, we have* $\mathsf{Adv}^{\mathrm{dist}}_{f_2}(\mathcal{D}) = \mathcal{O}(q/2^n)$.

From Theorem 1 and Lemma 1, the following corollary immediately follows, showing that f_k is indistinguishable up to about 2^n queries, for all $k \geq 2$.

Corollary 1. *For all* $k \geq 2$, *for any* $\mathcal{D}$ *making* q *oracle queries, we have* $\mathsf{Adv}^{\mathrm{dist}}_{f_k}(\mathcal{D}) = \mathcal{O}(q/2^n)$.

4   Indifferentiability of f_k

In this section we consider the indifferentiability of f_k (cf. Definition 2), in case the underlying permutations are public. We prove the following result.

Theorem 2. *For all $k \geq 2$, there exists a simulator $\mathcal{S}$ such that for any $\mathcal{D}$ making $q \geq 9n$ oracle queries,*

$$\mathsf{Adv}_{f_k,\mathcal{S}}^{\mathrm{diff}}(\mathcal{D}) \leq \frac{4q^3}{2^{2n}} + \frac{3n^{1/2}q^{3/2}}{2^n} + \frac{2}{2^n}.$$

The simulator makes at most $2q$ queries to $\mathcal{R}$.

While the theorem is stated for general k, the bound is independent of k. This is caused by the fact that we consider a direct generalization of the simulator of Mandal et al. [2], but the core problems that determine the bound find their roots in the basic case of $k = 2$. We refer to Sect. 5 for a more detailed discussion.

The remainder of the section is organized as follows. Firstly, we describe a generalization of the simulator $\mathcal{S}$ introduced by Mandal et al. [2] to $k \geq 2$ (in Sect. 4.1). Secondly, we present Patarin's H-coefficient technique upon which the proof is based, along with some preliminary observations (in Sect. 4.2). These follow [2] with the difference that we use the re-formalization of Patarin's technique by Chen and Steinberger [27]. Thirdly, we discuss the original indifferentiability proof of [2] (in Sect. 4.3). Fourthly, we present our new proof (in Sect. 4.4).

4.1   Simulator

We describe the simulator used in our work. It is a direct generalization of the simulator $\mathcal{S}$ of Mandal et al. [2] to a general number of $k \geq 2$ permutations.

The goal of the simulator $\mathcal{S}$ is to mimic the permutations $p = (p_1, \ldots, p_k)$ in such a way that (f_k, p) and $(\mathcal{R}, \mathcal{S})$ look indistinguishable. $\mathcal{S}$ therefore has the same interface as p, and we write $\mathcal{S} = (\mathcal{S}_1, \ldots, \mathcal{S}_k)$. The distinguisher can make forward and inverse queries to each of these functionalities, which means that it can query $\mathcal{S}$ in $2k$ ways. However, the simulator should look like $\mathcal{R} = \mathcal{S}_1 \oplus \cdots \oplus \mathcal{S}_k$, and if a distinguisher would, for instance, query $\mathcal{S}_1(x)$, it very likely also wishes to know $\mathcal{S}_2(x), \ldots, \mathcal{S}_k(x)$. To suit the analysis, we model the simulator in such a way that on a forward query x, the distinguisher is given all values $\mathcal{S}(x) = (\mathcal{S}_1(x), \ldots, \mathcal{S}_k(x))$. This simplification essentially corresponds to giving the distinguisher $k - 1$ "free" queries. It also means that $\mathcal{S}$ has only one interface for forward queries.

A similar issue arises for inverse queries. If the distinguisher makes a query to $\mathcal{S}_\ell^{-1}$ for $\ell \in \{1, \ldots, k\}$, the simulator will not only output a preimage x, but also the corresponding range values $\mathcal{S}_1(x), \ldots, \mathcal{S}_{\ell-1}(x), \mathcal{S}_{\ell+1}(x), \ldots, \mathcal{S}_k(x)$. Also here, the distinguisher essentially gets $k - 1$ queries for free.

The simulator maintains a sequence of responses $\{(x_i, y_i^1, \ldots, y_i^k)\}_{i=1}^q$, where q denotes the number of queries to $\mathcal{S}$. These tuples correspond to the evaluations

$$\mathcal{S}(x_i) = (\mathcal{S}_1(x_i), \ldots, \mathcal{S}_k(x_i)) = (y_i^1, \ldots, y_i^k),$$

for $i = 1, \ldots, q$. Note that every forward query as well as every inverse query to $\mathcal{S}$ results in exactly one such tuple. Here and throughout, we assume $\mathcal{D}$ never repeats an old query, e.g., in a forward query $\mathcal{S}(x_i)$, we have $x_i \notin \{x_1, \ldots, x_{i-1}\}$.

The simulator $\mathcal{S}$ is defined as follows. We consider its description for the ith query, for $i \in \{1, \ldots, q\}$. We describe the simulator for forward queries $\mathcal{S}(x_i)$, and for inverse queries $\mathcal{S}_\ell^{-1}(y_i^\ell)$ for $\ell \in \{1, \ldots, k\}$.

Forward Query $\mathcal{S}(x_i)$. For $\ell = 3, \ldots, k$, the simulator draws y_i^ℓ uniformly randomly from $\{0,1\}^n \backslash \{y_1^\ell, \ldots, y_{i-1}^\ell\}$. Then, it queries x_i to $\mathcal{R}$ and generates y_i^1 uniformly randomly from

$$\{0,1\}^n \backslash \{y_1^1, \ldots, y_{i-1}^1, \bar{y}_i \oplus y_1^2, \ldots, \bar{y}_i \oplus y_{i-1}^2\} \tag{2}$$

where we define $\bar{y}_i = \mathcal{R}(x_i) \oplus y_i^3 \oplus \ldots \oplus y_i^k$. Finally, it sets $y_i^2 = \bar{y}_i \oplus y_i^1$.

Informally, $\mathcal{S}(x_i)$ selects random y_i^ℓ for $\ell = 3, \ldots, k$, and uses y_i^1 and y_i^2 to make sure that $\mathcal{R}(x_i) = y_i^1 \oplus \ldots \oplus y_i^k$. Note that, due to the drawing of y_i^1 from (2), we have $y_i^2 \notin \{y_1^2, \ldots, y_{i-1}^2\}$.

Inverse Query $\mathcal{S}_\ell^{-1}(y_i^\ell)$. The simulator generates its response as follows.

(1) Draw $y_i^{\ell'}$ uniformly randomly from $\{0,1\}^n \backslash \{y_1^{\ell'}, \ldots, y_{i-1}^{\ell'}\}$ for $\ell' \in \{\ell + 1, \ldots, \ell + k - 2\}$;[1]
(2) Draw x_i uniformly randomly from $\{0,1\}^n \backslash \{x_1, \ldots, x_{i-1}\}$ and query x_i to $\mathcal{R}$;
(3) Set $y_i^{\ell-1} = \mathcal{R}(x_i) \oplus y_i^\ell \oplus \ldots \oplus y_i^{\ell+k-2}$. If $y_i^{\ell-1} \in \{y_1^{\ell-1}, \ldots, y_{i-1}^{\ell-1}\}$, return to (2).

We call a drawing x_i such that the resulting value $y_i^{\ell-1}$ in step (3) is not new a "failed guess". As in [2], in the proof we will limit the simulator to make at most 2 attempts (and thus at most 1 failed guess) per query. The simulator will abort once it exceeds this bound for some query.

4.2 Patarin's Technique

Fix any distinguisher $\mathcal{D}$ making q queries. As it is computationally unbounded, without loss of generality we can assume it is deterministic. We summarize the interaction of $\mathcal{D}$ with its oracles by a transcript τ, which consists of all query-response tuples $\mathcal{D}$ sees during its interaction with its oracles. We assume $\mathcal{D}$ never makes duplicate queries. The set of all possible transcripts is denoted by $\mathcal{T}$. Denote by X (resp. Y) the probability distribution of transcripts in the ideal (resp. simulated) world, for the fixed deterministic distinguisher $\mathcal{D}$.

Patarin's H-coefficient technique [27,30] states the following.[2]

---

[1] Here and throughout, all indices are taken modulo k and in the range $\{1, \ldots, k\}$.
[2] The H-coefficient technique in fact applies to indistinguishability in general, but to suit the presentation, we introduce it in the context of the indifferentiability of f_k.

Lemma 2 (H-coefficient Technique [27,30]). *Consider a fixed deterministic distinguisher $\mathcal{D}$. Let $\mathcal{T} = \mathcal{T}_{\text{good}} \cup \mathcal{T}_{\text{bad}}$ be a partition of the set of transcripts. Let ε be such that for all $\tau \in \mathcal{T}_{\text{good}}$,*

$$\mathbf{P}\left(Y = \tau\right) \geq \mathbf{P}\left(X = \tau\right) \cdot \left(1 - \varepsilon\right). \tag{3}$$

Then, $\mathsf{Adv}^{\text{diff}}_{f_k,\mathcal{S}}(\mathcal{D}) \leq \varepsilon + \mathbf{P}\left(X \in \mathcal{T}_{\text{bad}}\right).$

Proof. The proof is fairly straightforward, and we include it for completeness. We refer to [27] for a more detailed discussion.

We consider a deterministic distinguisher $\mathcal{D}$, and as such, its differentiating advantage equals the statistical distance between the distributions of transcripts in the ideal and simulated world:

$$\mathsf{Adv}^{\text{diff}}_{f_k,\mathcal{S}}(\mathcal{D}) = \frac{1}{2} \sum_{\tau \in \mathcal{T}} \left| \mathbf{P}\left(X = \tau\right) - \mathbf{P}\left(Y = \tau\right) \right|$$

$$\overset{(a)}{=} \sum_{\tau \in \mathcal{T} : \mathbf{P}(X=\tau) > \mathbf{P}(Y=\tau)} \left(\mathbf{P}\left(X = \tau\right) - \mathbf{P}\left(Y = \tau\right) \right)$$

$$\overset{(b)}{=} \sum_{\tau \in \mathcal{T} : \mathbf{P}(X=\tau) > \mathbf{P}(Y=\tau)} \mathbf{P}\left(X = \tau\right) \left(1 - \frac{\mathbf{P}\left(Y = \tau\right)}{\mathbf{P}\left(X = \tau\right)} \right)$$

$$\overset{(c)}{\leq} \sum_{\tau \in \mathcal{T}_{\text{good}}} \mathbf{P}\left(X = \tau\right) \varepsilon + \sum_{\tau \in \mathcal{T}_{\text{bad}}} \mathbf{P}\left(X = \tau\right)$$

$$\leq \varepsilon + \mathbf{P}\left(X \in \mathcal{T}_{\text{bad}}\right),$$

where (a) holds by symmetry, (b) as $\mathbf{P}\left(X = \tau\right) > 0$ by construction, and (c) holds by (3). $\qquad\square$

The main idea of the technique is exposed in the last step: for almost all transcripts (the good ones), the ratio of (3) will be rather close to one and for these transcripts we can take ε close to 0. For the few bad transcripts, ε may become large (even close to 1). Additionally, the technique allows us to focus on fixed transcripts and compute the probability of such a transcript to occur.

We build the following distinguisher $\mathcal{D}'$ on top of $\mathcal{D}$. Distinguisher $\mathcal{D}'$ operates as $\mathcal{D}$, and particularly outputs the same decision. However, at the end $\mathcal{D}'$ will make an additional amount of q_1 primitive queries to $p/\mathcal{S}$ as follows: for each of the queries to $f_k/\mathcal{R}$ it has made, $\mathcal{D}'$ makes the same query to $p/\mathcal{S}$, except if this would imply a duplicate primitive query in which case $\mathcal{D}'$ may replace it with a random non-repeating query. Clearly, $\mathcal{D}$ and $\mathcal{D}'$ always output the same decision, and hence $\mathsf{Adv}^{\text{diff}}_{f_k,\mathcal{S}}(\mathcal{D}) = \mathsf{Adv}^{\text{diff}}_{f_k,\mathcal{S}}(\mathcal{D}')$. Also, if $\mathcal{D}$ makes q_1 queries to its construction oracle and q_2 queries to its primitive, then $\mathcal{D}'$ makes exactly q_1 additional queries to its primitive. Note that, particularly, $\mathcal{D}'$ makes q queries to the primitive. In a transcript of $\mathcal{D}'$, all queries to the construction oracle (f_k or $\mathcal{R}$) are encapsulated in the queries to the primitive oracle (p or $\mathcal{S}$). Therefore, this approach reduces our problem to the problem of comparing $(p_1, \ldots, p_k)$ with $(\mathcal{S}_1, \ldots, \mathcal{S}_k)$, the former called the ideal and the latter the simulated world.

Finally, recall that the simulator may abort. This is formalized by including in the transcript a dedicated symbol $b \in \{\top, \bot\}$. In the ideal world, we always have $b = \top$, and in the simulated world, $b = \top$ *unless* the simulator aborted. Note that if $b = \bot$, the distinguisher succeeds with probability 1. In fact, in this case the transcript will be considered a bad transcript, and due to Lemma 2, the technical part of the work centers around good transcripts.

Let $\tau = (\{(x_i, y_i^1, \ldots, y_i^k)\}_{i=1}^q, b) \in \mathcal{T}$ be any transcript that can be seen by distinguisher $\mathcal{D}'$. Note that, as $\mathcal{D}'$ makes no duplicate queries, we have $x_i \neq x_{i'}$ and $y_i^\ell \neq y_{i'}^\ell$ for all i, i', ℓ. For arbitrary $z \in \{0,1\}^n$, we define

$$N(z) = \{(j, j') \in \{1, \ldots, q\}^2 \mid y_j^1 \oplus y_{j'}^2 = z\}. \tag{4}$$

4.3   Intermezzo: Proof of Mandal et al. [2]

The skeleton of our proof is similar to the one of [2]. Differences arise at the definition of the bad event, and the remainder of the proof. Before proceeding with our proof, we revisit the one of [2] at a high level (in our terminology), point out the presence of a flaw, and briefly discuss to what extent our proposed fix differs. Recall that the proof of [2] is for $k = 2$.

In the original proof, a transcript[3] $\tau = \{(x_i, y_i^1, y_i^2)\}_{i=1}^q$ is called "bad" if $N(z) > \frac{24q^2}{2^n - q}$ for some $z \in \{0,1\}^n$. In [2, Theorem 5], it is then proven that

$$\mathbf{P}\left(X \in \mathcal{T}_{\text{bad}}\right) = \mathbf{P}\left(\exists z \in \{0,1\}^n : N(z) > \frac{24q^2}{2^n - q}\right) \leq 1/2^{11n}.$$

The proof assumes randomness of $\{(y_i^1, y_i^2)\}_{i=1}^q$, but if an adversary makes an inverse query to one of its primitive oracles, it can freely choose y_i^1 or y_i^2. Inspired by this, we can consider an adversary that operates as follows (define $q' = q/2$):

- Choose $z \in \{0,1\}^n$;
- Query $y_i^1 \xrightarrow{p_1^{-1}} x_i, y_i^2$ for $i = 1, \ldots, q'$, all distinct values;
- Query $y_i^2 = y_{i-q'}^1 \oplus z \xrightarrow{p_2^{-1}} x_i, y_i^1$ for $i = q'+1, \ldots, 2q' = q$, all distinct values.

Then, we have $y_i^1 \oplus y_{i+q'}^2 = z$ for all $i = 1, \ldots, q'$. In other words, $N(z) \geq q/2$ after q queries, invalidating the claim for any $2 \leq q \leq 2^n/49$. (In a personal communication, the authors of [2] have confirmed the presence of this flaw.)

We note that a straightforward fix of the proof of [2], consisting of imposing $N(z) \leq \text{const} \cdot q$ for good transcripts, does not work: it only results in $\mathcal{O}(2^{n/2})$ security of the construction. This issue is resolved in our proof by using a structurally different bad event, and relying on existing results from the area of Fourier theory [3, 13, 14]. Naturally, the employment of a different bad event also leaves its traces in the analysis of good transcripts, as becomes clear from the proof.

---

[3] The abortion bit b is absent in the original proof.

4.4 Proof of Theorem 2

The proof of Theorem 2 roughly consists of four steps: (i) we define what type of transcripts we consider "bad", (ii) we bound the probability a bad transcript occurs, (iii) we derive a bound on the ratio a good transcript is seen in the real and ideal world, and (iv) the pieces are connected and the proof of Theorem 2 is completed.

The proof differs from the one of [2] in the definition of bad transcripts and the probability analysis thereof, and in the analysis of forward queries for good transcripts.

Bad Transcripts

Let $\tau = \left(\{(x_i, y_i^1, , \ldots, y_i^k)\}_{i=1}^q, b \right) \in \mathcal{T}$ be any attainable transcript. Recall the definition of $N(z)$ for arbitrary $z \in \{0,1\}^n$, Eq. (4). Transcript τ is called *bad* if $b = \perp$, or if

$$\sum_{i=1}^q |N(y_i^1 \oplus y_i^2)| > C \qquad (5)$$

for some to-be-determined $C > 0$. Next, we upper bound the probability a bad transcript is obtained in the ideal world, $\mathbf{P}(X \in \mathcal{T}_{\text{bad}})$, and lower bound the ratio $\mathbf{P}(Y = \tau) / \mathbf{P}(X = \tau)$ for $\tau \in \mathcal{T}_{\text{good}}$.

Upper Bounding $\mathbf{P}(X \in \mathcal{T}_{\text{bad}})$

The ideal world never aborts, hence $b = \top$ by construction. Consequently, the badness of transcripts is solely defined based on the values (y_i^1, y_i^2). We isolate the problem, and consider an adversary whose sole objective is to maximize $\sum_{i=1}^q |N(y_i^1 \oplus y_i^2)|$.

In a forward query, the adversary chooses x_i and receives randomly drawn y_i^1 and y_i^2. In an inverse query, it may choose either of the y_i-values and receives a randomly drawn opposite. Therefore, the adversary will be most successful if it only makes inverse queries to p_ℓ^{-1} for $\ell \in \{1,2\}$. In light of this, we consider an adversary engaged in the following game. For $i = 1, \ldots, q$, either choose a y_i^1 to receive $y_i^2 = p_2 \circ p_1^{-1}(y_i^1)$, or choose a y_i^2 to receive $y_i^1 = (p_2 \circ p_1^{-1})^{-1}(y_i^2)$. Define $z_i = y_i^1 \oplus y_i^2$. The adversary's goal is to maximize

$$\sum_{i=1}^q |N(y_i^1 \oplus y_i^2)| = \sum_{i=1}^q |N(z_i)| = \left| \{(j, j', i) \in \{1, \ldots, q\}^3 \mid y_j^1 \oplus y_{j'}^2 = z_i\} \right|.$$

Note that, as $p_1, p_2 \xleftarrow{\$} \text{Perm}(n)$, also $\pi = p_2 \circ p_1^{-1}$ behaves like a random permutation. We generalize the game as follows. Let $\pi \xleftarrow{\$} \text{Perm}(n)$. The adversary can query π adaptively and in both directions to obtain two lists $Y^1 = \{y_1^1, \ldots, y_q^1\}$ and $Y^2 = \{y_1^2, \ldots, y_q^2\}$ such that $y_i^2 = p_2 \circ p_1^{-1}(y_i^1)$ for $i = 1, \ldots, q$. Write

$Z = \{z_1, \ldots, z_q\}$, with the z_i's as before. Then, its goal is now to find two lists U and V of q elements that maximize

$$\lambda(U, V, Z) = \left| \{ (u, v, z) \in U \times V \times Z \mid u \oplus v = z \} \right|.$$

Note that, by construction,

$$\sum_{i=1}^{q} |N(y_i^1 \oplus y_i^2)| = \lambda(Y^1, Y^2, Z) \le \max_{U, V : |U| = |V| = q} \lambda(U, V, Z) =: \mu(Z).$$

We therefore obtain:

$$\mathbf{P}\left(X \in \mathcal{T}_{\text{bad}} \right) \le \mathbf{P}\left(\sum_{i=1}^{q} |N(y_i^1 \oplus y_i^2)| > C \right) \le \mathbf{P}\left(\mu(Z) > C \right).$$

The problem of bounding $\mu(Z)$ appeared before in works on permutation-based hashing by Mennink and Preneel [23], on digital signatures by Kiltz et al. [17], and on the security of Even-Mansour by Chen et al. [14]. It is also known as the "sum-capture problem". We follow Chen et al. [14, Theorem 1], which in turn builds upon Babai [3] and Steinberger [13]:

Lemma 3 (Sum-Capture Problem [14]). *Let $\pi \xleftarrow{\$} \text{Perm}(n)$ be a random permutation. Let $\mathcal{A}$ be some adversary that makes q two-sided adaptive queries to π, resulting in transcript $\{(y_1^1, y_1^2), \ldots, (y_q^1, y_q^2)\}$. Write $Z = \{z_1, \ldots, z_q\}$, where $z_i = y_i^1 \oplus y_i^2$ for $i = 1, \ldots, q$. Then, assuming $9n \le q \le 2^n/2$,*

$$\mathbf{P}\left(\mu(Z) > 3q^3/2^n + 3n^{1/2}q^{3/2} \right) \le \frac{2}{2^n}.$$

We, logically, define $C = 3q^3/2^n + 3n^{1/2}q^{3/2}$.

Lower Bounding Ratio $\mathbf{P}\left(Y = \tau \right) / \mathbf{P}\left(X = \tau \right)$

Let $\tau = \left(\{ (x_i, y_i^1, \ldots, y_i^k) \}_{i=1}^{q}, b \right) \in \mathcal{T}_{\text{good}}$ be a good transcript. This particularly implies that $b = \top$ and that the simulator never aborts, and we omit this symbol in the remaining analysis. Note that in the ideal world $p_1, \ldots, p_k$ are ideal permutations, and $\mathbf{P}\left(X = \tau \right) = \prod_{i=1}^{q} 1/\left(2^n - (i-1) \right)^k$. In the remainder, we will compute $\mathbf{P}\left(Y = \tau \right)$. For $\ell = 1, \ldots, q$, we denote by e_ℓ the event that the failed guess in the ℓth query (if any) does not equal any $x_1, \ldots, x_q$ and has not occurred before (the same condition was posed by Mandal et al. [2]). We write $E_\ell = e_1 \wedge \cdots \wedge e_\ell$. Clearly,

$$\mathbf{P}\left(Y = \tau \right) \ge \mathbf{P}\left(Y = \tau \wedge E_q \right), \tag{6}$$

and we focus on the latter probability. Denote $\tau_i = (x_i, y_i^1, \ldots, y_i^k)$ for $i = 1, \ldots, q$. Similarly for random variable Y, denote by Y_i the random variable corresponding to the ith tuple. We have

$$\mathbf{P}\left(Y = \tau \wedge E_q \right) = \prod_{i=1}^{q} \underbrace{\mathbf{P}\left(Y_i = \tau_i \wedge E_i \mid \vee_{j=1}^{i-1} Y_j = \tau_j \wedge E_{i-1} \right)}_{\mathbf{P}_i}. \tag{7}$$

We proceed with the analysis of $\mathbf{P}_i$ for $i \in \{1, \ldots, q\}$.

Forward Query $\mathcal{S}(x_i)$. Due to attainability of the transcript, x_i is distinct of $x_1, \ldots, x_{i-1}$. Additionally, E_{i-1} implies that x_i has not been queried to $\mathcal{R}$ before. Therefore, the response value $\mathcal{R}(x_i) = y_i^1 \oplus \cdots \oplus y_i^k$ is randomly drawn from a set of size 2^n. The values $y_i^3, \ldots, y_i^k$ are all drawn from a set of size $2^n - (i-1)$. Finally, y_i^1 is uniformly randomly drawn from the set (2) which is of size at most $2^n - 2(i-1) + |N(\bar{y}_i)|$, where $\bar{y}_i = \mathcal{R}(x_i) \oplus y_i^3 \oplus \ldots \oplus y_i^k$. Indeed, the sets

$$\{y_1^1, \ldots, y_{i-1}^1\} \qquad \text{and} \qquad \{\bar{y}_i \oplus y_1^2, \ldots, \bar{y}_i \oplus y_{i-1}^2\}$$

have an overlap of at most $|N(\bar{y}_i)|$. For forward queries we thus have

$$\mathbf{P}_i \geq \frac{1}{\left(2^n - (i-1)\right)^{k-2}} \cdot \frac{1}{2^n} \cdot \frac{1}{2^n - 2(i-1) + |N(\bar{y}_i)|}$$

$$\geq \frac{1}{\left(2^n - (i-1)\right)^k} \cdot \left(1 - \frac{|N(\bar{y}_i)|}{2^n}\right),$$

which follows from the fact that (writing $B = |N(\bar{y}_i)|$)

$$\frac{1}{2^n} \cdot \frac{1}{2^n - 2(i-1) + B} = \frac{1}{\left(2^n - (i-1)\right)^2} \cdot \frac{(2^n - (i-1))^2}{2^n(2^n - 2(i-1) + B)}$$

$$= \frac{1}{\left(2^n - (i-1)\right)^2} \cdot \left(1 - \frac{B}{2^n} \cdot \frac{2^n - (i-1)^2/B}{2^n - 2(i-1) + B}\right)$$

$$\geq \frac{1}{\left(2^n - (i-1)\right)^2} \cdot \left(1 - \frac{B}{2^n}\right),$$

where in the last step we use that $2^n - (i-1)^2/B \leq 2^n - 2(i-1) + B$ as $(i-1)^2/B - 2(i-1) + B = (i-1-B)^2/B \geq 0$.

Finally, as $\bar{y}_i = y_i^1 \oplus y_i^2$ by construction, we have $B = |N(\bar{y}_i)| = |N(y_i^1 \oplus y_i^2)|$.

Inverse Query $\mathcal{S}_\ell^{-1}(y_i^\ell)(\ell \in \{1, \ldots, k\})$. Regarding x_i, the simulator may make 2 trials in order to find a successful x_ℓ. For $\beta = 1, 2$, denote by $\mathsf{succ}(\beta)$ the event that attempts $1, \ldots, \beta - 1$ failed but attempt β succeeds. Then,

$$\mathbf{P}_i \geq \sum_{\beta=1}^{2} \underbrace{\mathbf{P}\left(Y_i = \tau_i \wedge \mathsf{E}_i \wedge \mathsf{succ}(\beta) \mid \forall_{j=1}^{i-1} Y_j = \tau_j \wedge \mathsf{E}_{i-1}\right)}_{\mathbf{P}_{i,\beta}}. \tag{8}$$

Now, $\mathbf{P}_{i,\beta}$ covers the case that (i) the drawings $y_i^{\ell+1}, \ldots, y_i^{\ell+k-2}$ are all correct, (ii) the first guess fails (if $\beta = 2$), and (iii) the βth succeeds. Firstly, $y_i^{\ell+1}, \ldots, y_i^{\ell+k-2}$ are all randomly drawn from a set of size $2^n - (i-1)$. Secondly (if $\beta = 2$), the first guess fails with probability at least

$$\left(1 - \frac{(q - (i-1)) + (i-1)}{2^n - (i-1)}\right) \cdot \frac{i-1}{2^n},$$

where the first fraction comes from the number of invalid guesses x_i (which would violate the conditions in e_i), and the second fraction is because every guess corresponds to a random draw from $\{0,1\}^n$ (by $\mathcal{R}$) and it fails if $\mathcal{R}(x_i) \in \{\bar{y}_i \oplus y_1^{\ell-1}, \ldots, \bar{y}_i \oplus y_{i-1}^{\ell-1}\}$, for $\bar{y}_i = y_i^\ell \oplus \cdots \oplus y_i^{\ell+k-2}$. The βth attempt succeeds with probability $\dfrac{1}{2^n - (i-1)} \cdot \dfrac{1}{2^n}$, where x_i is again taken from a set of size $2^n - (i-1)$ and $y_i^{\ell-1}$ is defined as the outcome of $\mathcal{R}$. Therefore, from (8):

$$
\begin{aligned}
\mathsf{P}_i &\geq \frac{1}{\left(2^n - (i-1)\right)^{k-1}} \cdot \frac{1}{2^n} \cdot \left(\underbrace{1}_{\beta=1} + \underbrace{\frac{2^n - q - (i-1)}{2^n - (i-1)} \cdot \frac{i-1}{2^n}}_{\beta=2} \right) \\
&= \frac{1}{\left(2^n - (i-1)\right)^k} \cdot \frac{2^n(2^n - (i-1)) + (2^n - q - (i-1))(i-1)}{2^{2n}} \\
&= \frac{1}{\left(2^n - (i-1)\right)^k} \cdot \left(1 - \frac{(q + (i-1))(i-1)}{2^{2n}} \right) \\
&\geq \frac{1}{\left(2^n - (i-1)\right)^k} \cdot \left(1 - \frac{2(i-1)q}{2^{2n}} \right).
\end{aligned}
$$

Combination. Combining forward and inverse queries, we find that

$$
\mathsf{P}_i \geq \frac{1}{\left(2^n - (i-1)\right)^k} \cdot \left(1 - \frac{|N(y_i^1 \oplus y_i^2)|}{2^n} - \frac{2(i-1)q}{2^{2n}} \right),
$$

and thus, via (6–7):

$$
\begin{aligned}
\mathbf{P}\left(Y = \tau \right) &\geq \mathbf{P}\left(X = \tau \right) \cdot \prod_{i=1}^{q} \left(1 - \frac{|N(y_i^1 \oplus y_i^2)|}{2^n} - \frac{2(i-1)q}{2^{2n}} \right) \\
&\geq \mathbf{P}\left(X = \tau \right) \cdot \left(1 - \sum_{i=1}^{q} \frac{|N(y_i^1 \oplus y_i^2)|}{2^n} - \sum_{i=1}^{q} \frac{2(i-1)q}{2^{2n}} \right) \\
&\geq \mathbf{P}\left(X = \tau \right) \cdot \left(1 - \sum_{i=1}^{q} \frac{|N(y_i^1 \oplus y_i^2)|}{2^n} - \frac{q^3}{2^{2n}} \right).
\end{aligned}
$$

As τ is a good transcript, we know that $\sum_{i=1}^{q} |N(y_i^1 \oplus y_i^2)| \leq C = 3q^3/2^n + 3n^{1/2}q^{3/2}$, and hence we obtain,

$$
\varepsilon = \frac{4q^3}{2^{2n}} + \frac{3n^{1/2}q^{3/2}}{2^n}. \tag{9}
$$

Conclusion of Proof

Using Lemma 2, the value ε of (9) and Lemma 3 for a bound on the probability of a bad transcript combine to

$$
\mathsf{Adv}_{f_k,S}^{\mathrm{diff}}(\mathcal{D}) = \mathsf{Adv}_{f_k,S}^{\mathrm{diff}}(\mathcal{D}') \leq \frac{4q^3}{2^{2n}} + \frac{3n^{1/2}q^{3/2}}{2^n} + \frac{2}{2^n}.
$$

This completes the proof of Theorem 2.

5 Conclusions

Since their first appearance in [18], XOR constructions have received broad attention in the cryptographic community [2,9,10,18,28,30]. As a matter of fact, the security of the XOR construction in the secret permutation setting is well-studied, as reflected in Table 1, and our proof of Corollary 1 closes the case. On the other hand, for the more relevant case of security in the public permutation setting, the only result in this direction [2] claimed $2^{2n/3}$ security. We pointed out a bug in their analysis, and also our proof only guarantees security as long as the number of queries does not exceed this bound.

The original simulator of [2], and more generally the simulator of Sect. 4.1 for $k \geq 2$ is conjectured to allow for security up to $q \ll 2^n$ queries. We expect this to be a highly non-trivial exercise. Our generalized proof clearly shows the bottleneck (in the proof of Mandal [2] this was a bit less clear): while the analysis of the ratio $\mathbf{P}\left(Y = \tau\right)/\mathbf{P}\left(X = \tau\right)$ and the description of bad transcripts as imposed by our analysis leaves little room for tightening, the lossiness of the bound seems to originate from the analysis of $\mathbf{P}\left(X \in \mathcal{T}_{\mathrm{bad}}\right)$, or in more detail that the quantity of (5) is bounded by $\mathcal{O}(q^3/2^n)$. The bound we derive on this probability, however, relies on various well-established results from Fourier theory [3,13,14].

A possible alternative improvement lies in the description of the simulator. Indeed, the presented simulator is constructed to effectively use two out of k of its responses to comply with $\mathcal{R}$. It may be possible to generate its responses so as to minimize the quantity of (5) or a generalized variant thereof. This, however, leads to a simulator that is significantly harder to analyze, and it may additionally influence the ratio for good transcripts. We recall that, already for the case $k = 2$, optimal security is conjectured.

Acknowledgments. The authors would like to thank Elena Andreeva, Rodolphe Lampe, Atul Luykx, Avradip Mandal, and Jacques Patarin for their comments. This work was supported in part by the Research Fund KU Leuven, OT/13/071, and in part by the Research Council KU Leuven: GOA TENSE (GOA/11/007). Bart Mennink is a Postdoctoral Fellow of the Research Foundation – Flanders (FWO).

References

1. Assche, G., Andreeva, E., Mennink, B., Daemen, J.: Security of keyed sponge constructions using a modular proof approach. In: Leander, G. (ed.) FSE 2015. LNCS, vol. 9054, pp. 364–384. Springer, Heidelberg (2015)
2. Babai, L.: The Fourier Transform and Equations over Finite Abelian Groups (Lecture Notes, version 1.3) (2002). http://people.cs.uchicago.edu/laci/reu02/fourier.pdf
3. Bellare, M., Impagliazzo, R.: A tool for obtaining tighter security analyses of pseudorandom function based constructions, with applications to PRP to PRF Conversion. Cryptology ePrint Archive, Report 1999/024 (1999)
4. Bellare, M., Kilian, J., Rogaway, P.: The security of cipher block chaining. In: Desmedt, Y.G. (ed.) CRYPTO 1994. LNCS, vol. 839, pp. 341–358. Springer, Heidelberg (1994)

5. Bellare, M., Krovetz, T., Rogaway, P.: Luby-Rackoff backwards: increasing security by making block ciphers non-invertible. In: Nyberg, K. (ed.) EUROCRYPT 1998. LNCS, vol. 1403, pp. 266–280. Springer, Heidelberg (1998)
6. Bellare, M., Rogaway, P.: The security of triple encryption and a framework for code-based game-playing proofs. In: Vaudenay, S. (ed.) EUROCRYPT 2006. LNCS, vol. 4004, pp. 409–426. Springer, Heidelberg (2006)
7. Bertoni, G., Daemen, J., Peeters, M., Van Assche, G.: Sponge functions. In: ECRYPT Hash Function Workshop (2007). http://sponge.noekeon.org/SpongeFunctions.pdf
8. Bertoni, G., Daemen, J., Peeters, M., Van Assche, G.: On the security of the keyed sponge construction. In: Symmetric Key Encryption Workshop (2011)
9. CAESAR: Competition for Authenticated Encryption: Security, Applicability, and Robustness (2014). http://competitions.cr.yp.to/caesar.html
10. Chen, S., Lampe, R., Lee, J., Seurin, Y., Steinberger, J.: Minimizing the two-round even-mansour cipher. In: Garay, J.A., Gennaro, R. (eds.) CRYPTO 2014, Part I. LNCS, vol. 8616, pp. 39–56. Springer, Heidelberg (2014)
11. Chen, S., Steinberger, J.: Tight security bounds for key-alternating ciphers. In: Nguyen, P.Q., Oswald, E. (eds.) EUROCRYPT 2014. LNCS, vol. 8441, pp. 327–350. Springer, Heidelberg (2014)
12. Cogliati, B., Lampe, R., Patarin, J.: The indistinguishability of the XOR of k permutations. In: Cid, C., Rechberger, C. (eds.) FSE 2014. LNCS, vol. 8540, pp. 285–302. Springer, Heidelberg (2015)
13. Coron, J.-S., Dodis, Y., Malinaud, C., Puniya, P.: Merkle-Damgård revisited: how to construct a hash function. In: Shoup, V. (ed.) CRYPTO 2005. LNCS, vol. 3621, pp. 430–448. Springer, Heidelberg (2005)
14. Dai, Y., Lee, J., Mennink, B., Steinberger, J.P.: The security of multiple encryption in the ideal cipher model. In: Garay and Gennaro [31], pp. 20–38
15. Dodis, Y., Pietrzak, K., Puniya, P.: A new mode of operation for block ciphers and length-preserving MACs. In: Smart, N.P. (ed.) EUROCRYPT 2008. LNCS, vol. 4965, pp. 198–219. Springer, Heidelberg (2008)
16. Garay, J.A., Gennaro, R. (eds.): CRYPTO 2014, Part I. LNCS, vol. 8616. Springer, Heidelberg (2014)
17. Gauravaram, P., Knudsen, L.R., Matusiewicz, K., Mendel, F., Rechberger, C., Schläffer, M., Thomsen, S.: Grøstl - a SHA-3 candidate (2009). Submission to NIST's SHA-3 competition
18. Hall, C., Wagner, D., Kelsey, J., Schneier, B.: Building PRFs from PRPs. In: Krawczyk, H. (ed.) CRYPTO 1998. LNCS, vol. 1462, pp. 370–389. Springer, Heidelberg (1998)
19. Impagliazzo, R., Rudich, S.: Limits on the provable consequences of one-way permutations. In: Goldwasser, S. (ed.) CRYPTO 1988. LNCS, vol. 403, pp. 8–26. Springer, Heidelberg (1990)
20. Kiltz, E., Pietrzak, K., Szegedy, M.: Digital signatures with minimal overhead from indifferentiable random invertible functions. In: Canetti, R., Garay, J.A. (eds.) CRYPTO 2013, Part I. LNCS, vol. 8042, pp. 571–588. Springer, Heidelberg (2013)
21. Luby, M., Rackoff, C.: How to construct pseudorandom permutations from pseudorandom functions. SIAM J. Comput. **17**, 373–386 (1988)
22. Lucks, S.: The sum of PRPs is a secure PRF. In: Preneel, B. (ed.) EUROCRYPT 2000. LNCS, vol. 1807, pp. 470–484. Springer, Heidelberg (2000)
23. Mandal, A., Nachef, V., Patarin, J.: Indifferentiability beyond the birthday bound for the XOR of two public random permutations. In: Gong, G., Gupta, K.C. (eds.) INDOCRYPT 2010. LNCS, vol. 6498, pp. 69–81. Springer, Heidelberg (2010)

24. Maurer, U.M., Renner, R.S., Holenstein, C.: Indifferentiability, impossibility results on reductions, and applications to the random oracle methodology. In: Naor, M. (ed.) TCC 2004. LNCS, vol. 2951, pp. 21–39. Springer, Heidelberg (2004)

25. Mennink, B., Preneel, B.: Hash functions based on three permutations: a generic security analysis. In: Safavi-Naini, R., Canetti, R. (eds.) CRYPTO 2012. LNCS, vol. 7417, pp. 330–347. Springer, Heidelberg (2012)

26. Mouha, N., Mennink, B., Van Herrewege, A., Watanabe, D., Preneel, B., Verbauwhede, I.: Chaskey: an efficient MAC algorithm for 32-bit microcontrollers. In: Joux, A., Youssef, A. (eds.) SAC 2014. LNCS, vol. 8781, pp. 306–323. Springer, Heidelberg (2014)

27. Patarin, J.: A proof of security in $O(2^n)$ for the XOR of two random permutations. In: Safavi-Naini, R. (ed.) ICITS 2008. LNCS, vol. 5155, pp. 232–248. Springer, Heidelberg (2008)

28. Patarin, J.: The "Coefficients H" technique. In: Avanzi, R.M., Keliher, L., Sica, F. (eds.) SAC 2008. LNCS, vol. 5381, pp. 328–345. Springer, Heidelberg (2009)

29. Steinberger, J.P., Rogaway, P.: Constructing cryptographic hash functions from fixed-key blockciphers. In: Wagner, D. (ed.) CRYPTO 2008. LNCS, vol. 5157, pp. 433–450. Springer, Heidelberg (2008)

30. Steinberger, J.: The Sum-Capture Problem for Abelian Groups (2014). arxiv.org/abs/1309.5582

31. Wu, H.: The Hash Function JH (2009). Submission to NIST's SHA-3 Competition

Robust Pseudo-Random Number Generators with Input Secure Against Side-Channel Attacks

Michel Abdalla[1], Sonia Belaïd[1,2], David Pointcheval[1],
Sylvain Ruhault[1,3(✉)], and Damien Vergnaud[1]

[1] Ecole Normale Supérieure, CNRS, INRIA, and PSL, Paris, France
{michel.abdalla,sonia.belaid,david.pointcheval,
sylvain.ruhault,damien.vergnaud}@ens.fr
[2] Thales Communications and Security, Gennevilliers, France
[3] Oppida, Montigny-le-Bretonneux, France

Abstract. A pseudo-random number generator (PRNG) is a deterministic algorithm that produces numbers whose distribution is indistinguishable from uniform. In this paper, we extend the formal model of PRNG with input defined by Dodis *et al.* at CCS 2013 to deal with partial leakage of sensitive information. The resulting security notion, termed *leakage-resilient robust PRNG with input*, encompasses all the previous notions, but also allows the adversary to continuously get some leakage on the manipulated data. Dodis *et al.* also proposed an efficient construction, based on simple operations in a finite field and a classical deterministic pseudo-random generator **G**. Here, we analyze this construction with respect to our new stronger security model, and prove that with a stronger **G**, it also resists leakage. We show that this stronger **G** can be obtained by tweaking some existing constructions based on AES. We also propose a new instantiation which may be better in specific cases. Eventually, we show that the resulting scheme remains quite efficient in spite of its new security properties. It can thus be recommended in contexts where side-channel resistance is required.

Keywords: Randomness · Entropy · Side-channel countermeasures · Security models

1 Introduction

While most cryptosystems require access to a perfect source of randomness for their security, such sources are extremely difficult to obtain in practice. For this reason, concrete implementations of cryptographic schemes often use a pseudo-random number generator (PRNG). The latter allows to generate a sequence of bits whose distribution is computationally indistinguishable from the uniform distribution, when given as input a secret short random value, called *seed*.

To get around the need for a truly random seed, Barak and Halevi [6] proposed a tweaked primitive, called PRNG with inputs, which still generates pseudo-random values but now remains secure even in presence of a potentially biased random source. Moreover, they also proposed a new security notion, called

© Springer International Publishing Switzerland 2015
T. Malkin et al. (Eds.): ACNS 2015, LNCS 9092, pp. 635–654, 2015.
DOI: 10.1007/978-3-319-28166-7_31

robustness, which states that a PRNG with inputs should meet three security properties: *resilience, forward security*, and *backward security*. While resilience models the inability of an adversary to predict future PRNG outputs even when manipulating the entropy source, forward and backward security ensures that an adversary cannot predict past or future outputs of the PRNG even when compromising its internal state. More recently, Dodis *et al.* [10] extended the work of Barak and Halevi to integrate the process of accumulation of entropy into the internal state. For this purpose, they refined the notion of robustness and proposed a very practical scheme satisfying it. Under the robustness security notion, an adversary can observe the inputs and outputs of a PRNG, manipulate its entropy source, and compromise its internal state.

Side-Channel Resistance for PRNGs. While the notion of robustness seems reasonably strong for practical purposes, it still does not fully consider the reality of embedded devices, which may be subject to *side-channel attacks*. In these attacks, an attacker can exploit the physical leakage of a device by several means such as power consumption, execution time or electromagnetic radiation. In order to consider such attacks, a first and important step was made by Micali and Reyzin [18] who proposed the framework of *physically observable cryptography*. In particular, they formally defined a classical assumption according to which *only computation leaks information*. Later, Dziembowski and Pietrzak went a step further by defining the *leakage-resilient cryptography model* [13]. In the latter, every computation leaks a limited amount of information whose size is bounded by some parameter λ. It benefits from capturing most of the known side-channel attacks and was consequently used to build many recent primitives [14,15,19]. In a different direction, we should mention a recent and important work which was proposed by Prouff and Rivain [20] and then extended by Duc et al. [12] to formally prove the security of masking implementations. In the latter works, the sensitive variables are split into different share and the adversary needs to recover all of them to reconstruct the secret.

In the specific context of PRNGs and stream ciphers, several constructions have been proposed so far and proved secure in the leakage-resilient cryptography model (e,g., [22,24,25]). The work of Yu *et al.* [24], for instance, proposes a very efficient construction of a leakage-resilient PRNG. Likewise, the work of Standaert *et al.* [22] shows how to obtain very efficient constructions of leakage-resilient PRNGs by relying on empirically verifiable assumptions. None of these works, however, consider potentially biased random sources, which is our main goal here.

Our Contributions. In this paper, we aim to build a practical and robust PRNG with input that can resist side-channel attacks. Since the construction proposed by Dodis et al. [10] seems to be a good candidate, we use it as the basis of our work. In doing so, we extend its security model to include the leakage-resilient security and we prove the whole construction secure under stronger requirements for the underlying deterministic pseudo-random generator[1]. Since

---

[1] A recent work by Dodis *et al.* in [11] also extends the robustness model to address the *premature next attack* where the internal state has insufficient entropy and an output is generated. Our work is a different complement.

it is not obvious how to instantiate the construction to meet our stronger needs, we propose three solutions based on AES in counter mode that are only slightly less efficient than the original instantiation proposed in [10]. Two of them are tweaked existing constructions and the third one is a new proposal which may be better in specific cases. All three instantiations only require that the implementation of AES in counter mode is secure against Simple Power Analysis attacks since very few calls are made with the same secret key.

Organization. From a theoretical side, we propose in Sect. 3 a new formal security model for PRNGs with input, which, in addition to encompassing all previous security notions [10], also guarantees security in the *leakage-resilient cryptography* model. In Sect. 4, we analyze the robust construction based on polynomial hash functions given in [10] showing why its instantiation may be vulnerable to side-channel attacks. We then prove that, under non-restrictive conditions on the underlying deterministic pseudo-random generator, the generic construction actually meets our stronger security property. Finally, in Sect. 5, we discuss the instantiations of this construction.

2 Preliminaries

2.1 Notations and Definitions

Probabilities. When X is a distribution, or a random variable following this distribution, we denote $x \xleftarrow{\$} X$ when x is sampled according to X. For a variable X and a set S, the notation $X \xleftarrow{\$} S$ denotes both assigning X a value uniformly chosen from S and letting X be a uniform random variable over S. The uniform distribution over n bits is denoted $\mathcal{U}_n$.

Indistinguishability. Two distributions X and Y are said (t,ε)-*computationally indistinguishable* (and we denote this property by $\mathbf{CD}_t(X,Y)$), if for any distinguisher $\mathcal{A}$ running within time t, its advantage in distinguishing a random variable following X from a random variable following Y, denoted $|\Pr[\mathcal{A}(X) = 1] - \Pr[\mathcal{A}(Y) = 1]|$ is bounded by ε. When $t = \infty$, meaning $\mathcal{A}$ is unbounded, we say that X and Y are ε-*close*.

Pseudo-Random Generators. A function $\mathbf{G} : \{0,1\}^m \to \{0,1\}^n$ is a (deterministic) (t,ε)-pseudo-random generator (PRG) if $\mathbf{CD}_t(\mathbf{G}(\mathcal{U}_m),\mathcal{U}_n) \leqslant \varepsilon$.

Pseudo-Random Functions. A keyed family of functions $\mathbf{F} : \{0,1\}^\mu \times \{0,1\}^\mu \to \{0,1\}^\mu$ is a (t,q,ε)-pseudo-random function (PRF) if no adversary can have an advantage greater than ε, within time t, in distinguishing, for a random key $K \xleftarrow{\$} \{0,1\}^\mu$, q answers $F_K(x_i)$ for adaptively chosen inputs (x_i), from q random answers $y_i \xleftarrow{\$} \{0,1\}^\mu$, for $i = 1, \ldots, q$.

Entropy. For a discrete distribution X, we denote its *min-entropy* by $\mathbf{H}_\infty(X) = \min_{x \in X}\{-\log \Pr[X = x]\}$.

Extractors. Let $\mathcal{H} = \{h_X : \{0,1\}^n \to \{0,1\}^m\}_{X \in \{0,1\}^d}$ be a hash function family. We say that $\mathcal{H}$ is a (k,ε)-*extractor* if for any random variable I over $\{0,1\}^n$ with $\mathbf{H}_\infty(I) \geqslant k$, the distributions $(X, h_X(I))$ and (X, U) are ε-close where X is uniformly random over $\{0,1\}^d$ and U is uniformly random over $\{0,1\}^m$. We say that $\mathcal{H}$ is ρ-universal if for any inputs $I \neq I' \in \{0,1\}^n$ we have $\Pr_{X \xleftarrow{\$} \{0,1\}^d}[h_X(I) = h_X(I')] \leqslant \rho$.

Lemma 1 (Leftover-Hash Lemma). *[21, Theorem 8.37] Assume that $\mathcal{H}$ is ρ-universal where $\rho = (1+\alpha)2^{-m}$ for some $\alpha > 0$. Then, for any $k > 0$, it is also a (k, ε)-extractor for $\varepsilon = \frac{1}{2}\sqrt{2^{m-k} + \alpha}$.*

2.2 Basic Security Model

In this section, we recall notations and the security notion of a PRNG with input and of distribution sampler, introduced in [10]. In Sect. 3, we will propose a stronger security model that takes into account possible leakage of information in the context of side-channel attacks.

Definition 1 (PRNG with Input). *A PRNG with input is a triple of algorithms $\mathcal{G} = (\mathsf{setup}, \mathsf{refresh}, \mathsf{next})$, with n the state length, ℓ the output length, and p the input length:*

- setup *is a probabilistic algorithm that outputs some public parameters* seed;
- $\mathsf{refresh}$ *is a deterministic algorithm that, given* seed, *a state $S \in \{0,1\}^n$ and an additional input $I \in \{0,1\}^p$, outputs a new state $S' = \mathsf{refresh}(S, I; \mathsf{seed}) \in \{0,1\}^n$;*
- next *is a deterministic algorithm that, given* seed *and a state $S \in \{0,1\}^n$, outputs a pair $(S', R) = \mathsf{next}(S; \mathsf{seed})$ where $S' \in \{0,1\}^n$ is the new state and $R \in \{0,1\}^\ell$ is the output randomness.*

The parameter seed is public and fixed in the system once for all. For the sake of clarity, we drop it in the notations and we write $S' = \mathsf{refresh}(S, I)$ instead of $\mathsf{refresh}(S, I; \mathsf{seed})$ and $(S', R) = \mathsf{next}(S)$ instead of $\mathsf{next}(S; \mathsf{seed})$. When a specific part of the seed will be required, we will explicitly add it as input.

In practice, the global internal state contains all the PRNG features and some structured and redundant information, such as counters, in addition to a random pool of length n. When the adversary will have access to the state, this will be to all this information, with both reading (get-state) and writing (set-state) capabilities. However, when we denote S in this paper, for the sake of simplicity, we refer to the randomness pool, that we expect to be truly random, or with as much entropy as possible.

Adversary. We consider an attacker divided in two parts: a distribution sampler $\mathcal{D}$ and a classical attacker $\mathcal{A}$. The former generates seed-independent inputs that will be used by the PRNG to improve the quality of its entropy with the refresh algorithm. These inputs, potentially biased under *partial* adversarial control, are generated in practice from the device activities (e.g., system interrupts) and cannot consequently depend on the parameter seed. Note that as explained in [10] and in [11], seed-independence is necessary to achieve security of the scheme.

Definition 2 (Distribution Sampler). *A distribution sampler $\mathcal{D}$ is a stateful and probabilistic algorithm which, given the current state σ, outputs a tuple (σ', I, γ, z) where σ' is the new state for $\mathcal{D}$, $I \in \{0, 1\}^p$ will be the next input for the refresh algorithm, γ is some entropy estimation of I, z is the possible leakage about I given to the adversary $\mathcal{A}$[2].*

If q denotes an upper bound on the number of executions of $\mathcal{D}$, such a distribution sampler is said *legitimate* if the min-entropy of every input I_j is not smaller than the entropy estimate γ_j, even given all the additional information: $\mathbf{H}_\infty(I_j \mid I_1, \ldots, I_{j-1}, I_{j+1}, \ldots, I_q, z_1, \ldots, z_q, \gamma_1, \ldots, \gamma_q) \geqslant \gamma_j$, for all $j \in \{1, \ldots, q\}$ where $(\sigma_i, I_i, \gamma_i, z_i) = \mathcal{D}(\sigma_{i-1})$ for $i \in \{1, \ldots, q\}$ and $\sigma_0 = 0$.

Robustness. We now recall the security game $\mathsf{ROB}(\gamma^*)$, from [10], that defines the main security notion for a PRNG with input, the *robustness*. We have slightly modified the initial definition, but in an equivalent way (see Fig. 1, without the leaking procedures nor the leakage function f as input to the initialize procedure). In the security game,

- the parameter γ^* defines the minimal entropy that is required in the internal state of the PRNG so that the output looks random. Under this threshold, the PRNG has not accumulated enough entropy in its internal state, and then is not considered safe for generating random-looking outputs;
- the variable c is an estimation of the actual entropy collected in the internal state of the PRNG. It does not make use of any entropy estimator, but just considers the lower-bound provided by the distribution sampler on the entropy of the input. In case of a legitimate distribution sampler, this lower-bound is correct;
- the flag/function compromised is a Boolean variable that is true if the actual entropy (the parameter c) is under the threshold γ^*. In such a case, the PRNG is with an unsafe status, and thus the adversary may have some control on it;
- the challenge b is a bit that will be used to challenge the adversary, whose goal is to guess it.

The game $\mathsf{ROB}(\gamma^*)$ starts with an initialize procedure, applies procedures to answer to oracle queries from the adversary $\mathcal{A}$, and ends with a finalize procedure. The procedure initialize sets the parameter seed with a call to algorithm setup, the internal state S of the PRNG, as well as c and b. After all oracle queries, the adversary $\mathcal{A}$ outputs a bit b^*, given as input to the procedure finalize, which compares the response of $\mathcal{A}$ to the challenge bit b. The procedures used to answer to oracle queries are the following:

- the procedures get-state/set-state allow the adversary $\mathcal{A}$ to learn or to fix the whole internal state of the PRNG, including the structured part. However, as mentioned above, we just model the impact on the random pool in this analysis;

---

[2] This leakage is not related to side-channel attacks but represents the partial knowledge the adversary has on the inputs because of its control on the distribution.

- the procedure next-ror is used to challenge the adversary $\mathcal{A}$ on its capability to distinguish the output of the PRNG from a truly random output. In the safe case (when $c \geqslant \gamma^*$), the new estimated entropy of the internal state, in the variable c, is then set to the state length, that is n. In the unsafe case, as explained in [10], the real value for R, which might reveal non-trivial information about the weak internal state, is first output and then the new estimated entropy of the internal state, in the variable c, is reset to 0^3.
- the procedure $\mathcal{D}$-refresh allows the adversary $\mathcal{A}$ to call the distribution sampler $\mathcal{D}$ to get a new input and to run the refresh algorithm with this specific input to improve the quality of the internal state. In addition to the input I for the PRNG, the distribution sampler $\mathcal{D}$ also outputs the leakage z on input I that is given to $\mathcal{A}$ and an estimate γ of the entropy of the input (with respect to all the other inputs and the leakage information z). We use a more conservative definition, by considering that it really accumulates more entropy only if c was below γ^*, otherwise, it stays unchanged. The new estimated entropy of the internal state, in the variable c, is thus set to $c + \gamma$ if c was below γ^*, but of course with a maximum of n.

Note that we dropped the get-next procedure from [10], but as noted by [4,8], multiple calls to next-ror are enough to capture a similar security level.

Definition 3 (Robustness of PRNG with Input). *A pseudo-random number generator with input* $\mathcal{G} = (\mathsf{setup}, \mathsf{refresh}, \mathsf{next})$ *is called* $(t, q_r, q_n, q_s, \gamma^*, \varepsilon)$-*robust, if for any adversary $\mathcal{A}$ running within time t, that first generates a legitimate distribution sampler $\mathcal{D}$ (for the $\mathcal{D}$-refresh procedure), that thereafter makes at most q_r calls to $\mathcal{D}$-refresh, q_n calls to next-ror, and q_s calls to* get-state/set-state, *the advantage of $\mathcal{A}$ in game* $\mathsf{ROB}(\gamma^*)$ *is at most ε.*

2.3 Model for Information Leakage

In this paper, we aim to protect the construction of Dodis et al. against side-channel attacks. In this purpose, we describe hereafter the leakage model.

Only Computation Leaks. From the axiom "Only Computation Leaks" of Micali and Reyzin [18], we assume that only the data being manipulated in a computation can leak during this computation. This assumption actually well fits the reality of practical observations. As a consequence, we can split our cryptographic primitives into small blocks that independently leak functions of their inputs. We also authorize the adversary to choose different leakage functions for each block.

Bounded Leakage Per Iteration. Since it is more suited for a PRNG [7], we follow the model of leakage-resilient cryptography, with the strong requirement to preserve reasonable performances. We let the adversary the choice of the polynomial time leakage functions with a bound λ on their output length.

---

[3] We could have strengthened this definition, by only reducing c by ℓ bits in this case, but we kept the conservative notion.

proc. initialize($\mathcal{D}, f$)		proc. finalize(b^*)	proc. compromised
seed $\xleftarrow{\$}$ setup		IF $b = b^*$	OUTPUT $(c < \gamma^*)$
$\sigma \leftarrow 0$; $S \leftarrow 0$; $c \leftarrow 0$; $b \xleftarrow{\$} \{0,1\}$		RETURN 1	
OUTPUT seed		ELSE	
		RETURN 0	

proc. $\mathcal{D}$-refresh	proc. next-ror	proc. get-state	proc. leak-refresh	proc. leak-next
$(\sigma, I, \gamma, z) \xleftarrow{\$} \mathcal{D}(\sigma)$	$(S, R_0) \leftarrow \text{next}(S)$	$c \leftarrow 0$	$(\sigma, I, \gamma, z) \xleftarrow{\$} \mathcal{D}(\sigma)$	$\left\{ \begin{array}{l} L \leftarrow f(S, \text{seed}) \\ (S, R) \leftarrow \text{next}(S; \text{seed}) \end{array} \right\}$
$S \leftarrow \text{refresh}(S, I)$	$R_1 \xleftarrow{\$} \{0,1\}^{\ell}$	OUTPUT S	$\left\{ \begin{array}{l} L \leftarrow f(S, I, \text{seed}) \\ S \leftarrow \text{refresh}(S, I; \text{seed}) \end{array} \right\}$	IF compromised
IF compromised	IF compromised		$c \leftarrow \max\{0, c - \lambda\}$	$c \leftarrow 0$
$c \leftarrow \min(c+\gamma, n)$	$c \leftarrow 0$	proc. set-state(S^*)	IF compromised	ELSE
OUTPUT (γ, z)	OUTPUT R_0	$c \leftarrow 0$	$c \leftarrow 0$	$c \leftarrow \alpha$
	ELSE	$S \leftarrow S^*$	OUTPUT (L, γ, z)	OUTPUT (L, R)
	$c \leftarrow n$			
	OUTPUT R_b			

Fig. 1. Procedures in the leakage-resilient robustness security game $\mathsf{LROB}(\gamma^*, \lambda)$

This parameter is closely related to the security parameter of the underlying cryptographic primitives and will be part of global scheme's security bound.

Non-adaptive Leakage. The choice of leakage functions left to the adversary reveals the desire to consider every possible component whatever its way of leaking. However, we based our work on the practical observation whereby leakage functions completely depend on the inherent device. On the contrary, a few works (e.g., [13,19]) give the adversary the possibility to modify its leakage functions according to its current knowledge. Even if this model aims to be more general, it leads to unrealistic scenarios since the adversary is then able to predict further steps of the algorithm through impossible leakage functions. For these reasons, this work, as many others before [2,15,24,25], only consider non-adaptive leakage functions.

3   Leakage-Resilient Robustness of a PRNG with Input

In the security model of [10], recalled in the previous section, the distribution sampler $\mathcal{D}$ generates the external inputs used to refresh the PRNG and already gives the adversary $\mathcal{A}$ some information about how the environment of the PRNG behaves when it generates these inputs. This information is modeled by z. In order to model information leakage during the executions of the PRNG algorithms refresh and next, we give the adversary the choice of the leakage functions, that we globally name f, associated to each algorithm, or even each small block. Since we restrict our model to non-adaptive leakage, we ask the adversary to choose them beforehand. So they are provided as input to the initialize procedure by the adversary (see Fig. 1). Then, each leakage function will be implicitly used by our two new procedures named leak-refresh and leak-next that, in addition to the usual outputs, also provide some leakage L about the manipulated data, as described in Sect. 2.3. We thus have a new parameter λ, that bounds the output length of the leakage function. Our new *Leakage-Resilient Robustness* security game $\mathsf{LROB}(\gamma^*, \lambda)$ makes use of the procedures described in Fig. 1 and is described in details below:

- the parameter γ^*, the variable c, and the Boolean flag/function compromised are the same as in Sect. 2.2 for the basic robustness;
- the new parameter λ fixes the maximal information leakage which can be collected during the execution of operations refresh and next. Namely, for each operation (refresh or next), the leakage functions globally output at most λ bits. Such a leakage will be available when querying the leaking procedures leak-refresh and leak-next below;
- the new parameter α is an integer that models the minimal expected entropy of S after a leak-next (next with leakage) call, in a safe case (compromised is false), that is when the entropy of the internal state was assumed greater than γ^*. This captures both the creation of computational entropy during a next execution and the smaller loss of entropy caused by the leakage. We could expect $\alpha = n - \lambda$, but it may depend on the explicit construction;
- the procedures initialize($\mathcal{D}, f$)/finalize(b^*) initiate the security game with the additional leakage function f, check whether the adversary has won the game and output 1 in this case or 0 otherwise. Contrary to the choice made in [10] (which is also valid), the initial state S is here set to zero (as well as the entropy counter) so that no assumption needs to be made on its initialization;
- the procedures get-state/set-state, $\mathcal{D}$-refresh, and next-ror are the same as for the basic robustness;
- the procedure leak-refresh runs the refresh algorithm but additionally provides some information leakage L on the input (S, I) and seed, as above. As for the next-ror-queries, the leakage can reveal non-trivial information about a weak internal state even before the effectiveness of the refresh, and then we reduce c by λ bits. And if it drops below the threshold γ^*, it is reset to 0. Again, we could have strengthened this definition, but we preferred to keep a conservative notion. Furthermore, this strict notion is important w.r.t. our new definitions of recovering and preserving security with leakage. Note that if the $\mathcal{D}$-refresh algorithm is complex, several leakage functions can be defined at every step, but the global leakage is limited to λ, hence the notation $\{\ldots\}$, since they can be interleaved.
- the procedure leak-next runs the next algorithm but additionally provides some information leakage L on the input S and seed, according to the leakage function f provided to the initialize procedure. If the status was safe, then the new entropy estimate c is set to α, otherwise, it is reset to 0 (as for the next-ror). As above, if the next algorithm is complex, several leakage functions can be defined at each step, but the global leakage is limited to λ.

As in [10], attackers have two parts: a distribution sampler and a classical attacker with the former only used to generate seed-independent inputs (potentially *partially* biased) from device activities. Examples of the entropy's traces for the procedures defined in [10] and in our new model are provided in Fig. 2. The threshold γ^* has to be slightly higher in our new model, because for a similar next algorithm, we need to accumulate a bit more of entropy to maintain security even in presence of leakage. Typically, it has to be increased by λ. Now we detailed the new security game, we can define the notion of leakage-resilient robustness of a PRNG with input.

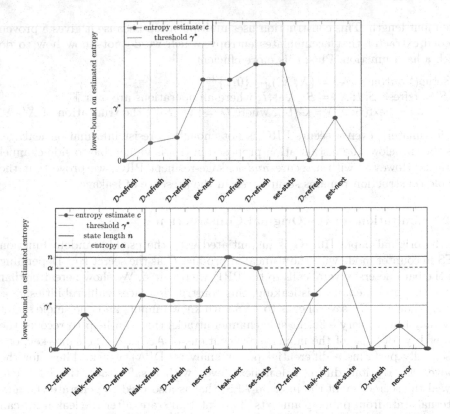

Fig. 2. Traces of entropy estimates in the model [10] (up) and in our new model (down)

Definition 4 (Leakage-Resilient Robustness of PRNG with Input). *A pseudo-random number generator with input* $\mathcal{G} =$ (setup, refresh, next) *is called* $(t, q_r, q_n, q_s, \gamma^*, \lambda, \varepsilon)$-*leakage-resilient robust, if for any adversary* $\mathcal{A}$ *running in time* t*, that first generates a legitimate distribution sampler* $\mathcal{D}$ *(for the* $\mathcal{D}$-refresh/ leak-refresh *procedure), that after makes at most* q_r *calls to* $\mathcal{D}$-refresh/leak-refresh, q_n *calls to* next-ror/leak-next, *and* q_s *calls to* get-state/set-state *with a leakage bounded by* λ*, the advantage of* $\mathcal{A}$ *in game* LROB(γ^*, λ) *is at most* ε.

4   New Construction

In this section, we show how to modify the original construction of [10] to achieve the robustness together with the resistance against side-channel attacks.

4.1   Original Construction

We first recall the *robust* PRNG construction of [10], named $\mathcal{G}$. It makes use of a (t, ε)-secure pseudo-random generator (PRG) $\mathbf{G} : \{0,1\}^m \rightarrow \{0,1\}^{n+\ell}$. The seed is a pair (X, X'), n is the state length, ℓ is the output length, and $p = n$ is the input length. This construction uses multiplication because it gives a proven seeded extractor that accumulates entropy, which we do not know how to do with a hash function. Plus, it is more efficient:

- setup() outputs seed $= (X, X') \leftarrow \{0,1\}^{2n}$;
- $S' = \mathsf{refresh}(S, I; X) = S \cdot X + I$, where all operations are over $\mathbb{F}_{2^n}$;
- $(S', R) = \mathsf{next}(S; X') = \mathbf{G}(U)$, where $U = [X' \cdot S]_1^m$, the truncation of $X' \cdot S$.

Unfortunately, even a secure PRG is not enough to resist information leakage. As shown below, the instantiation proposed in [10] is vulnerable to side-channel attacks. However, with a secure *and* leakage-resilient PRG, we prove that the whole construction remains secure even in the presence of leakage.

4.2   Limitations of the Original Construction

In the original paper [10], $\mathbf{G}$ is instantiated with the pseudo-random function AES in counter mode with the truncated product U as the secret key. Depending on the parameters, several calls to the PRF are required. We show hereafter that when the implementation is leaking, this construction faces vulnerabilities.

As shown in [7], several calls to AES with known inputs and one single secret key may lead to very efficient side-channel attacks that can help to recover the secret key. Because of the numerous executions of AES with the same key, one essentially performs a differential power analysis (DPA) attack. Then, for the above construction, during a leak-next, even with a safe state, the DPA can reveal the secret key of the internal AES, that is also used to generate the new internal state from public plaintexts. This internal state, after the leak-next, can thus be recovered, whereas it is considered as safe in the security game. A next-ror challenge can then be easily broken.

Furthermore, even if we only make a few calls with the same key, with a counter as input, the adversary can predict future randomness. This vulnerability applies to AES with predictable inputs. As determined by the security games, the adversary chooses a leakage function f to further collect the leakage during the product and the truncation between the internal state S and the public seed X'. Assume that this function is $f(S, X') =$

$$\left[\mathsf{AES}_{\left(\left[X' \cdot \left(\mathsf{AES}_{[X' \cdot S]_1^m}(C_0) || ... || \mathsf{AES}_{[X' \cdot S]_1^m}(C_0 + \lceil \frac{n}{m} \rceil - 1) \right) \right]_1^m \right)} \left(C_0 + \lceil \frac{n+\ell}{m} \rceil \right) \right]_1^\lambda$$

with C_0 an integer arbitrarily chosen by the attacker. With this leakage function set, the adversary can make a set-state-call and fix the counter C to C_0. Indeed, this counter is a part of the global internal state which can be compromised by the adversary. Following this compromission, sufficient calls to $\mathcal{D}$-refresh are made to refresh S so that its entropy increases above the threshold γ^*. Then, the attacker can ask a leak-next-query and gets back the leakage $f(S, X')$ described above. Eventually, the attacker asks a challenge next-ror-query, and either gets the real output or a random one. The λ bits it got from the leakage are exactly the first λ bits of the real output. The attacker has consequently a significant advantage in the next-ror challenge.

4.3   New Assumption

We slightly modify the requirements of [10] on the PRG **G**, to keep the PRNG secure even in the presence of leakage: The PRG **G** : $\{0,1\}^m \rightarrow \{0,1\}^{n+\ell}$ instantiated with the truncated product $U = [X' \cdot S]_1^m$ is now required to be a (α, λ)-leakage-resilient and (t, ε)-secure PRG according to Definition 5. In that definition, λ denotes the leakage during one execution of **G**, and α is the expected entropy of the output, even given the leakage.

Definition 5. *A PRG* **G** : $\{0,1\}^m \rightarrow \{0,1\}^N$ *is* (α, λ)-*leakage-resilient and* (t, ε)-*secure if it is first a* (t, ε)-*secure PRG, but in addition, for any adversary* $\mathcal{A}$, *running within time* t, *that first outputs a leakage* f *with* λ-*bit outputs, there exists a source* S *that outputs couples* $(L, T) \in \{0,1\}^\lambda \times \{0,1\}^N$, *so that the entropy of* T, *conditioned on* L *being greater than* α, *and the advantage with which* $\mathcal{A}$ *can distinguish* $(f(\mathcal{U}_m), \mathbf{G}(\mathcal{U}_m))$ *from* (L, T) *is bounded by* ε. *Note that* $f(\mathcal{U}_m)$ *denotes the information leakage generated by* f *during this execution of* **G** *(on the inputs at the various atomic steps of the computation, that includes* $\mathcal{U}_m$ *and possibly some internal values).*

This definition ensures that for one execution of **G**, its output is indistinguishable from a source of min-entropy α, with a leakage of size λ on the input of **G**.

4.4   Security Analysis

Theorem 1 shows that the PRNG $\mathcal{G}$ is leakage-resilient robust.

Theorem 1. *Let* m, n, α, *and* γ^* *be integers, such that* $n > m$ *and* $\alpha > \gamma^*$, *and* **G** : $\{0,1\}^m \rightarrow \{0,1\}^{n+\ell}$ *an* $(\alpha + \ell, \lambda)$-*leakage-resilient and* $(t, \varepsilon_{\mathbf{G}})$-*secure PRG. Then, the PRNG* $\mathcal{G}$ *previously defined and instantiated with* **G** *is* $(t', q_r, q_n, q_s, \gamma^*, \lambda, \varepsilon)$-*leakage-resilient robust where* $t' \approx t$, *after at most* $q = q_r + q_n + q_s$ *queries, where* q_r *is the number of* $\mathcal{D}$-refresh/ leak-refresh-*queries,* q_n *the number of* next-ror/leak-next-*queries, and* q_s *the number of* get-state/set-state-*queries, where* $\varepsilon \leq qq_n \cdot ((q_r^2 + 1) \cdot \varepsilon_{ext} + 3\varepsilon_{\mathbf{G}})$ *and* $\varepsilon_{ext} = \sqrt{2^{m+1-\delta}}$ *for* $\delta = \min\{n - \log q_r, \gamma^* - \lambda\}$.

To prove Theorem 1, we need to adapt the notions of *recovering* and *preserving* introduced in [10] to also capture information leakage. We then prove an intermediate result which states that the combination of recovering and preserving, both with leakage, imply leakage-resilient robustness. Finally, we show that the PRNG $\mathcal{G}$ satisfies both the recovering security with leakage and the preserving security with leakage. Full details of the proof are given in the full version [3].

5   Instantiations of the PRG G

In the previous section, we explained that the original instantiation in [10] was vulnerable to side-channel attacks, and needs a stronger PRG **G**, namely a leakage-resilient PRG which takes as input a perfectly random m-bit string

U, and generates an $(n + \ell)$-bit output $T = (S, R)$ that looks random. Even in case of leakage, S should have enough entropy. In this section, we first discuss the use of existing primitives for such a leakage-resilient PRG $\mathbf{G}$. Then, we propose a new concrete instantiation that may achieve better performances in specific scenarios by taking advantage of the PRNG design. Eventually, we provide a security analysis of our solution and we implement it to give some benchmarks.

5.1 Existing Constructions

To instantiate the PRG $\mathbf{G}$, we need a leakage-resilient construction which can get use of a bounded part of the internal state. We recall here two leakage-resilient constructions which can be tweaked to fit these requirements at a reasonable cost. The first one is a binary tree PRF introduced by Faust, Pietzrak and Schipper at CHES 2012 [15] and the second one is a sequential PRNG with minimum public randomness proposed by Yu and Standaert at CT-RSA 2013 [25]. We voluntarily ignore the chronological order and start the description with the second instantiation since it will be used to complete the first one.

Sequential PRNG from [25]. The PRNG of Yu and Standaert comes with an internal state made of two randomly chosen values : a secret key $K_0 \in \{0,1\}^\mu$ and a public seed $s \in \{0,1\}^\mu$. The construction is made of two stages. In the upper stage, a (non leakage-resilient) generator $\mathbf{F}'$ is processed in counter mode to expand the seed s into uniformly random values $p_0, p_1, \dots$. In the lower stage, a (non leakage-resilient) PRF $\mathbf{F}$ generates outputs with public values p_i and updates the secret so it is never used more than twice. The parameter s can be included in our PRNG seed (under the notation X'') since it shares the same properties than X and X'. However, the current counter is varying and thus need to be stored in the deterministic part of the internal state. In the proof of [25], the counter is implicitly required to be different at each use since the public values p_i need to be independent. But in our model of leakage-resilient robustness, the deterministic part of the internal state can be definitively compromised. Attacker could, in this case, set the counter to a previous value, making the public p_i not independent anymore. To thwart this issue, we suggest to extend the internal state so that the truncated part of full entropy can contain both the secret key K_0 and a uniformly random counter used only for a single execution of next. Hence, no parameter can be compromised and we are back to the context of the original proof. The only difference in the security comes from the probability of collisions when using a uniformly random counter at each call.

This two-stage instantiation is illustrated in Fig. 3. One can note that the input U is split in two slices, to initiate the secret key K_0 and the counter C, each of size μ. In order to relate these parameters with the parameters of our PRNG from Sect. 4 that provides an m-bit random string U as input to the PRG $\mathbf{G}$, and wants to receive back an N-bit string, where $N = n + \ell$, that is $\kappa = N/\mu$ blocks generated with κ keys. The κ blocks of output and new internal state are all generated using $2\kappa - 1$ calls to $\mathbf{F}'$ and $2\kappa - 1$ calls to $\mathbf{F}$.

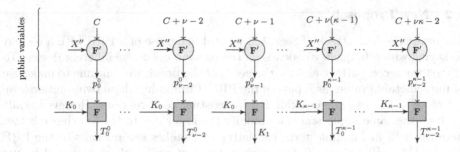

Fig. 3. Instantiation of generator $\mathbf{G}$ from [25] with random input $U = (C, K_0)$

Tweaked Binary Tree PRF from [15]. The second solution was proposed by Faust et al. at CHES 2012 [15]. Thanks to its structure of binary tree, it requires less calls to $\mathbf{F}$ and consequently overtakes the performances of the first solution. However, the original construction does not provide sources for the required randomness. That is why we suggest to use the same upper stage than [25] recommended in and proven secure in [2,25]. Plus, with the advantageous reuse of the two same random values at each layer, the number of calls to $\mathbf{F}'$ is limited to $2\log_2(\kappa)$ which is less than the number of $\mathbf{F}$ calls. Eventually, for the reasons depicted above, we also need to use a uniformly random counter, updated at each call to next. The tweaked construction is depicted in Fig. 4.

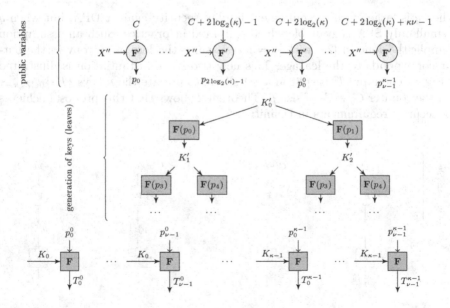

Fig. 4. Instantiation of generator $\mathbf{G}$ from [15] with random input $U = (C, K_0')$

5.2   New Proposal

To thwart the first attack of Sect. 4.2, we still make use of a PRF with a regular re-keying whose frequency depends on the parameters of the inherent device. To thwart the second attack and for the needs of the proof, we continue to make use of unpredictable values as inputs of the PRF. Combining these two solutions, we get close to the two stages exhibited by existing constructions. However, while we keep the same upper stage, we modify the lower one to try to achieve better performances in function next. The latter still makes several calls to the PRF $\mathbf{F} : \{0,1\}^\mu \times \{0,1\}^\mu \to \{0,1\}^\mu$, with public but uniformly distributed inputs and κ distinct secret keys (as in the second existing construction). However, the secret keys are all directly extracted from the input value $U = [X' \cdot S]_1^m$ together with the counter C. In this way, there is no need to derive the next keys in function next but the internal state is much more larger: the extracted value U is of length $(\kappa + 1)\mu$ instead of 2μ in previous constructions. The precise security requirements are formalized in Definition 6 and the performances comparison with existing solutions is given in Table 1, Sect. 5.3.

Definition 6 (Leakage-Resilient PRF). *A PRF* $\mathbf{F} : \{0,1\}^\mu \times \{0,1\}^\mu \to \{0,1\}^\mu$ *is* (α, λ)-*leakage-resilient and* (t, q, ε)-*secure if it is a* (t, q, ε)-*PRF and if, for any adversary* $\mathcal{A}$, *running within time* t, *that first outputs a leakage* f *with* λ-*bit outputs, there exists a source* $\mathcal{S}$ *that outputs* $(L_i, P_i, T_i)_i \in (\{0,1\}^\lambda \times \{0,1\}^\mu \times \{0,1\}^\mu)^q$, *with a uniform distribution for the* P's, *so that the entropy of* $(T_i)_i$, *conditioned to* $(L_i, P_i)_i$, *is greater than* α, *and the advantage with which* $\mathcal{A}$ *can distinguish the tuple* $(f(K_i, P_i), P_i, \mathbf{F}_K(P_i))_i$ *from* $(L_i, P_i, T_i)_i$ *is bounded by* ε.

When q is large, such a requirement implies security against DPA, but when q is small only SPA is available which is limited in practice. Such an assumption is implicitly done in [25] with $\alpha = \mu - \lambda$, since the loss of entropy in the output corresponds to the leakage. This new two-stage instantiation is illustrated in Fig. 5. The input U is split in $\kappa + 1$ slices, to initiate the κ keys $\{K_i\}_{0 \leqslant i \leqslant \kappa - 1}$ and the counter C, each of size μ. Theorem 2 shows that this proposal achieves the security requirements in Definition 5.

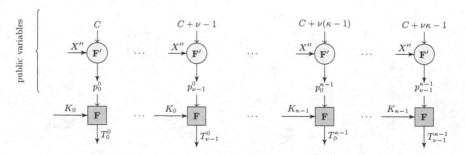

Fig. 5. New instantiation of generator $\mathbf{G}$ with random input $U = (C, K_0, \ldots, K_{\kappa-1})$

Theorem 2. *Let μ and κ be paramaters such that $\nu\kappa\mu = N$. Let $\mathbf{F} : \{0,1\}^\mu \times \{0,1\}^\mu \to \{0,1\}^\mu$ be a $(\alpha/\kappa, \lambda)$-leakage-resilient and $(t, \nu, \varepsilon_{\mathbf{F}})$-secure PRF and $\mathbf{F'} : \{0,1\}^\mu \times \{0,1\}^\mu \to \{0,1\}^\mu$ be a $(t, q\nu\kappa, \varepsilon_{\mathbf{F'}})$-secure PRF, where q is a bound on the global number of executions of $\mathbf{G}$. The instantiation proposed for $\mathbf{G}$ in Sect. 5.2 with $\mathbf{F}$ and $\mathbf{F'}$ provides an (α, λ)-leakage-resilient and $(t, \varepsilon_{\mathbf{G}})$-secure PRG where $\varepsilon_{\mathbf{G}} \le \kappa \cdot \varepsilon_{\mathbf{F}} + \varepsilon_{\mathbf{F'}} + q^2\nu\kappa/2^\mu$.*

In the proposal, each call to $\mathbf{G}$ makes $\nu\kappa$ calls to the PRF $\mathbf{F}$: κ keys are used at most ν times. The inputs of $\mathbf{F}$ are generated by $\mathbf{F'}$ with the key X'' (randomly set in seed) on a counter C randomly initialized, and then incremented for each $\mathbf{F'}$ call in an execution of $\mathbf{G}$. The details of the proof which uses a similar argument as [25] in the minicrypt world [16], can be found in the full version [3]. However, for the global security, we need all the intermediate values (p_j^i) to be distinct and unpredictable to avoid the aforementioned attack. We thus require $\mathbf{F'}$ to be secure after $q_n\nu\kappa$ queries and the inputs to be all distinct: by setting the $\log(\nu\kappa)$ least significant bits of C to zero, we just have to avoid collisions on the $\mu - \log(\nu\kappa)$ most significant bits for the q_n queries. The probability of collision is thus less than $q_n{}^2\nu\kappa/2^\mu$ and can appear once and for all in the global security:

Corollary 1. *Let us consider parameters n, m, and ℓ in the construction of the PRNG with input $\mathcal{G}$ from Sect. 4.1, using the generator $\mathbf{G}$ as described in this section. Let μ and κ be paramaters such that $\nu\kappa\mu = n + \ell$, and $\alpha > \gamma^*$. Let $\mathbf{F} : \{0,1\}^\mu \times \{0,1\}^\mu \to \{0,1\}^\mu$ be a $(\alpha/\kappa, \lambda)$-leakage-resilient and $(t, \nu, \varepsilon_{\mathbf{F}})$-secure PRF, and $\mathbf{F'} : \{0,1\}^\mu \times \{0,1\}^\mu \to \{0,1\}^\mu$ be a $(t, q_n\nu\kappa, \varepsilon_{\mathbf{F'}})$-secure PRF. Then, $\mathcal{G}$ is $(t, q_r, q_n, q_s, \gamma^*, \lambda, \varepsilon)$-leakage-resilient robust after at most $q = q_r + q_n + q_s$ queries, where q_r is the number of $\mathcal{D}$-refresh/leak-refresh-queries, q_n the number of next-ror/leak-next-queries, and q_s the number of get-state/set-state-queries, where $\varepsilon \le qq_n \cdot \left((q_r{}^2 + 1) \cdot \sqrt{2^{m+1-\delta}} + 3(\kappa \cdot \varepsilon_{\mathbf{F}} + \varepsilon_{\mathbf{F'}}) \right) + q_n{}^2\nu\kappa/2^\mu$, for $\delta = \min\{n - \log q_r, \gamma^* - \lambda\}$.*

It seems reasonable to have (α, λ)-leakage resilience with $\alpha = n + \ell - \nu\kappa\lambda$: with a large γ^*, ε can be made small.

5.3 Practical Analysis: Implementation and Benchmarks

We present some benchmarks of the construction of [10] and the three instantiations. Since our leakage-resilient construction is based on [10], we use the latter as a reference when measuring efficiency. Thus, we simply implemented them on an Intel Core i7 processor to show that the new property does not significantly impact the performances. This is mainly due to the use of SPA-resistant AES implementations instead of DPA-resistant (*e.g.*, masked) ones. We used the same public cryptographic libraries that in [10] and to achieve a similar security level as the construction of [10], our experiments show that the tweaked binary tree construction is only less than 4 times slower.

General Benchmarks. We recall that our construction is based on the construction of [10]: $\mathsf{refresh}(S, I) = S \cdot X + I \in \mathbb{F}_{2^n}$ and $\mathsf{next}(S) = \mathbf{G}(U)$, with $U = [X' \cdot S]_1^m$. In [10], the PRG $\mathbf{G}$ is defined by $\mathbf{G}(U) = \mathsf{AES}_U(0) \| \ldots \| \mathsf{AES}_U(\nu - 1)$, where ν is the number of calls to AES with a 128-bit key U, and thus $m = 128$. For a security parameter $k = 40$, the security analysis leads to $n = 489$, $\gamma^* = 449$, and $\nu = 5$. To achieve leakage-resilience, we need additional security requirements for the PRG $\mathbf{G}$. The three instantiations split $\mathbf{G}$ between two PRFs $\mathbf{F}$ and $\mathbf{F}'$, where $\mathbf{F}$ is used with public uniformly distributed inputs and κ different secret keys. In the existing constructions, a first key is extracted from the truncated product U and the other ones are derived through a re-keying process. In the new instantiation, all the secret keys are extracted from U. The public inputs of $\mathbf{F}$ are generated by the PRF $\mathbf{F}'$ in counter mode, with a secret initial value for the counter also extracted from U: $m = 2 \cdot 128$ for the existing constructions or $m = 128(\kappa + 1)$ for the new instantiation if both $\mathbf{F} = \mathbf{F}' = \mathsf{AES}$ with 128-bit keys. To provide the security bounds of the three constructions, we need to fix the security bounds of functions $\mathbf{F}$ and $\mathbf{F}'$. As far as we know, the best key recovery attacks on AES without leakage [9] require a complexity of $2^{162.1}$ with 2^{88} data. However, our functions being executed at most twice (resp. 6 times) with the same secret keys for 2^{-40} security (resp. for 2^{-64} security), such a complexity is unreachable. As for the leakage, we give the adversary λ bits of useful information by leaking query. Nevertheless, until now it remains unclear how these λ bits of information in a single trace may reduce the security bound of the AES. In [23] for instance, the authors show that a single trace on the AES might give the adversary all the required knowledge to recover the secret key, namely, when a sufficient number of noisy Hamming Weight values are available. But summing the useful information of these noisy Hamming Weight values would give a very large λ for which we cannot guarantee anything. However, we can expect either a larger amount of noise, a desynchronization of the traces or a low leaking from the inherent component which would result in a reasonable value for λ. In this case, we can fix $\varepsilon_{\mathbf{F}} = \varepsilon_{\mathbf{F}'} \approx 2^{-127}$. The resulting security bounds are given in Table 1 with the size n of the internal state, the number of 128 or 256-bit keys and the number of AES calls in function next, for 2^{-40} and 2^{-64} security.

Table 1. Security bounds and complexity of the three instantiations

Refs	Security bound ϵ_G	2^{-40} security			2^{-64} security		
		n	keys (128)	AES calls	n	keys (256)	AES calls
[25]	$\kappa \epsilon_F + \epsilon_F' + q^2(\nu\kappa - 1)/2^\mu$	768	7	26	1152	5	30
[15]	$2\kappa \epsilon_F + \epsilon_F' + q^2(\nu\kappa + 2\log_2(\kappa))/2^\mu$	896	4	20	1408	4	24
New	$\kappa \varepsilon_{\mathbf{F}} + \varepsilon_{\mathbf{F}'} + q^2\nu\kappa/2^\mu$	1408	6	24	1792	5	30

The best instantiation in terms of complexity is the construction from [15]. This is not surprising considering the advantageous binary shape of this function. However, if we relax the security assumptions on the AES with $\varepsilon_F = \varepsilon'_F = 2^{-126}$, the conditions of the security proof are not met and therefore we cannot guarantee its security based on Corollary 1. In these specific cases, our construction seems to be the best one to use since it guarantees that the conditions of the security proof are met. Note that for 2^{-64} security, as explained in Sect. 5.3, we cannot get a provable security with 128-bits input blocks, and we need ε_F and $\varepsilon_{F'}$ to be smaller than 2^{-200}, and then use AES with 256-bit keys. Since the implementation built from [15] appears to be the best one in the general case, we implement it to compare it with the instantiation of [10]. As in [10], we use fb_mul_lodah and fb_add from RELIC open source library [5], extended with the necessary fields ($\mathbb{F}_{2^{489}}$, defined with $X^{489} + X^{83} + 1$ and $\mathbb{F}_{2^{896}}$, defined with $X^{896} + X^7 + X^5 + X^3 + 1$). We use public functions aes_setkey_enc and aes_crypt_ctr from PolarSSL open source library [1]. As in [10], we measure the number of CPU cycles for a recovering process and a key generation process. The CPU cycles count is done using ASM instruction RDTSC, our C code is optimized with O2 flag. We simulate a full recovery of the PRNG for [15] and [10] implementations, with an input containing one bit of entropy per byte. Then, 8 inputs of size 489 bits are necessary to recover from a compromise for [10], whereas, for [15], 8 inputs of size 896 bits are necessary. Then we simulate the generation of 2048-bit keys that each requires 16 calls to next, as every call outputs 128 bits. Figure 6 gives the numbers of CPU cycles for 100 complete recovering experiments (left) and 100 key generations (right) for [10] and [15]. Both processes require on average 4 times less CPU cycles to perform for [15] implementation than for [10] implementation.

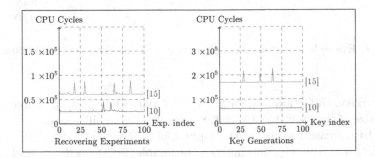

Fig. 6. Benchmarks between [15] and [10]

The Tweaked Binary Tree Instantiation. We first recall the constraints (similar to Corollary 1): the quality of the pseudo-random number generator is measured by $\varepsilon \leq qq_n \cdot \left((q_r{}^2 + 1) \cdot \sqrt{2^{m+1-\delta}} + 3(2\kappa \cdot \varepsilon_{\mathbf{F}} + \varepsilon_{\mathbf{F}'}) \right) + q_n{}^2(2\log_2(\kappa) + \nu\kappa)/2^\mu$, for $\delta = \min\{n - \log q_r, \gamma^* - \lambda\}$. With $q_r = q_n = q_s = 2^k$, we get:

$$\varepsilon \leq 3 \cdot 2^{2k} \cdot \left((2^{2k} + 1) \cdot \sqrt{2^{m+1-\delta}} + 3(2\kappa \cdot \varepsilon_{\mathbf{F}} + \varepsilon_{\mathbf{F}'}) \right) + (2\log_2(\kappa) + \nu\kappa) \cdot 2^{2k}/2^\mu$$
$$\leq \varepsilon_1 + \varepsilon_2 + \varepsilon_3 + \varepsilon_4$$

with $\varepsilon_1 = 2^{4k+2+(m+1-\delta)/2}$, $\varepsilon_2 = 18\kappa \cdot 2^{2k} \cdot \varepsilon_{\mathbf{F}}$, $\varepsilon_3 = 9 \cdot 2^{2k} \cdot \varepsilon_{\mathbf{F}'}$ and $\varepsilon_4 = 2^{2k-\mu} \cdot (2\log_2(\kappa) + \nu\kappa)$.

2^{-v} Security. With $m = 256$, $\mu = 128$, $\varepsilon_{\mathbf{F}} = \varepsilon_{\mathbf{F}'} \approx 2^{-127}$: $\varepsilon_1 < 2^{-v}$, as soon as $8k + 2v + 5 + m < \delta$, which is verified for $n > 9k + 2v + 5 + m$ and $\gamma^* > n + \lambda - k$; $\varepsilon_2 < 2^{-v}$, as soon as $2k + v < 127 - \log_2(18\kappa)$; $\varepsilon_3 < 2^{-v}$, as soon as $2k + v < 127 - \log_2(9) < 123$; $\varepsilon_4 < 2^{-v}$, as soon as $2k + v < 128 - \log_2(2\log_2(\kappa) + \nu\kappa)$.

2^{-40} Security. For $k = v = 40$, the constraint on ε_3 is satisfied. The constraints on ε_1 are satisfied as soon as $n > 701$ and $\gamma^* > n + \lambda - 40$. With $\nu = 2$, we need $n = 256\kappa - 128 > 701$ and thus $\kappa = 4$, which ensures that the constraints on ε_2 and ε_4 are satisfied . Finally, $n = 896$ and $\gamma^* = 858$ for $\lambda \approx 2$.

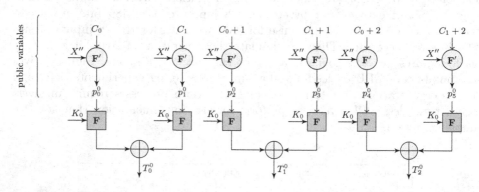

Fig. 7. Example of instantiation of generator **G** for higher security bounds

2^{-64} Security. Unfortunately, for $k = v = 64$, one cannot get a provable security with the size of the input block $\mu = 128$, because of the collisions on the counters. In order to increase the size of the input blocks, one can XOR PRPs to get a PRF on larger inputs [17]. This makes ε_4 negligible: $2^{2k-2\mu} = 2^{-128}$, and thus the factor $\nu\kappa$ will not affect it. On the other hand, to make ε_2 and ε_3 small enough, we need $\varepsilon_{\mathbf{F}}$ and $\varepsilon_{\mathbf{F}'}$ to be smaller than 2^{-200}, and then use AES with 256-bit keys. But then we have to use the same key 6 times in order to extract 384 bits (see a 3-block extraction in Fig. 7), where κ keys are used $\nu = 6$ times, and two counters C_0 and C_1 are extracted: $m = 3 \cdot 128 = 384$, $n = 3 \times 128 \times \kappa - 128 = 384\kappa - 128$. As for the constraint on ε_1, we need $384\kappa > 1221$. We can take $\kappa = 4$. Then, $n = 1408$ and $\gamma^* = 1346$.

6   Conclusion

We have put forward a new property for PRNGs with input, that captures security in a setting where partial sensitive information may leak. Then, we have tweaked the PRNG with input proposed by Dodis *et al.* to meet our new property of leakage-resilient robustness. Finally, we have proposed three secure instantiations of the new PRNG with input including a new one which provide the same level of security as the construction of [10] for a limited additional cost in efficiency and size.

As further work, the security bounds could be made tighter if the construction was proven robust with leakage without going through the preserving-with-leakage and recovering-with-leakage steps. Another interesting future work would be to implement the construction on constrained devices.

Acknowledgments. This research was supported in part by the French ANR-12-JS02-0004 ROMAnTIC Project and the French ANR-10-SEGI-015 PRINCE Project.

References

1. PolarSSL is an open source and commercial SSL library licensed by Offspark B.V. https://polarssl.org
2. Abdalla, M., Belaïd, S., Fouque, P.-A.: Leakage-resilient symmetric encryption via re-keying. In: Bertoni, G., Coron, J.-S. (eds.) CHES 2013. LNCS, vol. 8086, pp. 471–488. Springer, Heidelberg (2013)
3. Abdalla, M., Belaïd, S., Pointcheval, D., Ruhault, S., Vergnaud, D.: Robust pseudo-random number generators with input secure against side-channel attacks - full version. Cryptology ePrint Archive (2015)
4. Abdalla, M., Fouque, P.-A., Pointcheval, D.: Password-based authenticated key exchange in the three-party setting. In: Vaudenay, S. (ed.) PKC 2005. LNCS, vol. 3386, pp. 65–84. Springer, Heidelberg (2005)
5. Aranha, D.F., Gouvêa, C.P.L.: RELIC is an Efficient LIbrary for Cryptography. http://code.google.com/p/relic-toolkit/
6. Barak, B., Halevi, S.: A model and architecture for pseudo-random generation with applications to /dev/random. In: Atluri, V., Meadows, C., Juels, A. (eds.) ACM CCS 05, pp. 203–212. ACM Press, November 2005
7. Belaïd, S., Grosso, V., Standaert, F.-X.: Masking and leakage-resilient primitives: one, the other(s) or both? Crypt. Commun. 7(1), 163–184 (2015)
8. Bellare, M., Desai, A., Jokipii, E., Rogaway, P.: A concrete security treatment of symmetric encryption. In: 38th FOCS, pp. 394–403. IEEE Computer Society Press, October 1997
9. Bogdanov, A., Khovratovich, D., Rechberger, C.: Biclique cryptanalysis of the full AES. In: Lee, D.H., Wang, X. (eds.) ASIACRYPT 2011. LNCS, vol. 7073, pp. 344–371. Springer, Heidelberg (2011)
10. Dodis, Y., Pointcheval, D., Ruhault, S., Vergnaud, D., Wichs, D.: Security analysis of pseudo-random number generators with input: /dev/random is not robust. In: Sadeghi, A.-R., Gligor, V.D., Yung, M. (eds.) ACM CCS 13, pp. 647–658. ACM Press, November 2013

11. Dodis, Y., Shamir, A., Stephens-Davidowitz, N., Wichs, D.: How to eat your entropy and have it too – optimal recovery strategies for compromised RNGs. In: Garay, J.A., Gennaro, R. (eds.) CRYPTO 2014, Part II. LNCS, vol. 8617, pp. 37–54. Springer, Heidelberg (2014)
12. Duc, A., Dziembowski, S., Faust, S.: Unifying leakage models: from probing attacks to noisy leakage. In: Nguyen, P.Q., Oswald, E. (eds.) EUROCRYPT 2014. LNCS, vol. 8441, pp. 423–440. Springer, Heidelberg (2014)
13. Dziembowski, S., Pietrzak, K.: Leakage-resilient cryptography. In: 49th FOCS, pp. 293–302. IEEE Computer Society Press, October 2008
14. Faust, S., Kiltz, E., Pietrzak, K., Rothblum, G.N.: Leakage-resilient signatures. In: Micciancio, D. (ed.) TCC 2010. LNCS, vol. 5978, pp. 343–360. Springer, Heidelberg (2010)
15. Faust, S., Pietrzak, K., Schipper, J.: Practical leakage-resilient symmetric cryptography. In: Prouff, E., Schaumont, P. (eds.) CHES 2012. LNCS, vol. 7428, pp. 213–232. Springer, Heidelberg (2012)
16. Impagliazzo, R.: A personal view of average-case complexity. In: Structure in Complexity Theory Conference, pp. 134–147 (1995)
17. Lucks, S.: The sum of PRPs Is a secure PRF. In: Preneel, B. (ed.) EUROCRYPT 2000. LNCS, vol. 1807, pp. 470–484. Springer, Heidelberg (2000)
18. Micali, S., Reyzin, L.: Physically observable cryptography. In: Naor, M. (ed.) TCC 2004. LNCS, vol. 2951, pp. 278–296. Springer, Heidelberg (2004)
19. Pietrzak, K.: A leakage-resilient mode of operation. In: Joux, A. (ed.) EUROCRYPT 2009. LNCS, vol. 5479, pp. 462–482. Springer, Heidelberg (2009)
20. Prouff, E., Rivain, M.: Masking against side-channel attacks: a formal security proof. In: Johansson, T., Nguyen, P.Q. (eds.) EUROCRYPT 2013. LNCS, vol. 7881, pp. 142–159. Springer, Heidelberg (2013)
21. Shoup, V.: A Computational Introduction to Number Theory and Algebra. Cambridge University Press, New York (2006)
22. Standaert, F.-X., Pereira, O., Yu, Y.: Leakage-resilient symmetric cryptography under empirically verifiable assumptions. In: Canetti, R., Garay, J.A. (eds.) CRYPTO 2013, Part I. LNCS, vol. 8042, pp. 335–352. Springer, Heidelberg (2013)
23. Veyrat-Charvillon, N., Gérard, B., Standaert, F.-X.: Soft analytical side-channel attacks. In: Sarkar, P., Iwata, T. (eds.) ASIACRYPT 2014. LNCS, vol. 8873, pp. 282–296. Springer, Heidelberg (2014)
24. Yu, Y., Standaert, F.-X., Pereira, O., Yung, M.: Practical leakage-resilient pseudorandom generators. In: Al-Shaer, E., Keromytis, A.D., Shmatikov, V. (eds.) ACM CCS 10, pp. 141–151. ACM Press, October 2010
25. Yu, Y., Standaert, F.-X.: Practical leakage-resilient pseudorandom objects with minimum public randomness. In: Dawson, E. (ed.) CT-RSA 2013. LNCS, vol. 7779, pp. 223–238. Springer, Heidelberg (2013)

Leakage-Resilient Cryptography over Large Finite Fields: Theory and Practice

Marcin Andrychowicz[1], Daniel Masny[2], and Edoardo Persichetti[3]($\boxtimes$)

[1] University of Warsaw, Warsaw, Poland
[2] HGI, Ruhr-Universität Bochum, Bochum, Germany
[3] Dakota State University, Madison, USA
edoardo.persichetti@dsu.edu

Abstract. Information leakage is a major concern in modern day IT-security. In fact, a malicious user is often able to extract information about private values from the computation performed on the devices. In specific settings, such as RFID, where a low computational complexity is required, it is hard to apply standard techniques to achieve resilience against this kind of attacks. In this paper, we present a framework to make cryptographic primitives based on large finite fields robust against information leakage with a bounded computational cost. The approach makes use of the inner product extractor and guarantees security in the presence of leakage in a widely accepted model. Furthermore, we show how to apply the proposed techniques to the authentication protocol Lapin, and we compare it to existing solutions.

1 Introduction

A major concern for the implementation of secure cryptographic protocols is resistance to *side-channel attacks* (SCA). This class of attacks makes use of information obtained by the observation of physical phenomena that may occur in the device used to implement the scheme. These include measurements of timings, power consumption level, running machine's sound or an electromagnetic radiation (cf. for instance [ISW03, MR04, DP08, FKPR10, GR10, DHLAW10, BKKV10, DF11, DF12, GR12, GST13]).

The technique called *masking* is a very efficient way to protect sensitive data. The idea behind masking is to split the sensitive values into d (the *masking order*) random shares and to compute every intermediate value of the algorithm on these shares. The security requirement is that each subset of $d - 1$ shares is independent from the original value. In this way, in fact, an adversary would need to combine leakage samples obtained by several separate shares in order to

Marcin Andrychowicz and Edoardo Persichetti were supported by the WELCOME/2010-4/2 grant founded within the framework of the EU Innovative Economy (National Cohesion Strategy) Operational Programme. At the time when this research was carried out Edoardo Persichetti was a post-doc at the University of Warsaw.

© Springer International Publishing Switzerland 2015
T. Malkin et al. (Eds.): ACNS 2015, LNCS 9092, pp. 655–674, 2015.
DOI: 10.1007/978-3-319-28166-7_32

recover useful information about the sensitive data. Multiple candidates for d-th order masking schemes have been proposed, such as *Boolean* masking [RP10] and *polynomial* masking [PR11].

Recently, an efficient way to mask the LPN-based authentication protocol Lapin [HKL+12] with Boolean masking was proposed by Gaspar et al. [GLS14]. The proposal takes advantage of the linearity of the Learning Parity with Noise (LPN) assumption, on which Lapin is based. This makes it easy and therefore very efficient to apply Boolean masking to Lapin. While Boolean masking decreases the efficiency of AES quadratically in the number of shares, it decreases the efficiency only linearly in case of Lapin.

The above mentioned masking schemes, however, lack a strong formal security proof. A way to deal with this issue from a theoretical point of view was suggested by Ishai et al. [ISW03], who proposed to use a *leakage resilient circuit compiler* based on Boolean masking. Such a compiler takes as input a certain circuit Γ and returns a modified circuit $\hat{\Gamma}$ that computes the same functionality but is designed to be resilient against a restricted class of leakage attacks. This was subsequently extended to a broader class of attacks in [FRR+10]. Solutions based on more complicated algebraic frameworks have been also proposed, for example Juma and Vahlis [JV10] and Goldwasser and Rothblum [GR10]. These solutions achieve leakage resilience against *polynomial-time computable* functions, but require a very heavy and inefficient machinery that involves public-key encryption to protect the shares.

In two independent works by Dziembowski and Faust [DF12] and again Goldwasser and Rothblum [GR12], it was shown how to achieve the same results without relying on secure encryption schemes. Both papers describe leakage-resilient compilers, which encode values on the internal wires using an inner product. The leakage resilience follows from the extractor property of the inner product as a strong extractor which builds a strong theoretical security basis. The framework has been adjusted and optimized in terms of efficiency for AES in a work by Balasch et al. [BFGV12], along with a sample implementation and an analysis of performance results. Unfortunately, the authors lose the strong theoretical security basis in favor of efficiency by using the inner product as a masking scheme but not as an extractor. Furthermore, Prouff et al. [PRR14] showed that some of their proposed algorithms to compute operations in finite fields can be attacked in theory. It is unclear yet, if these attacks can be exploited by real world SCAs.

Our Contribution. We use inner product extractor based techniques to gain leakage resilience while preserving the efficiency such that our techniques are applicable in practice. Compared to the algorithms proposed by [DF12, BFGV12, GR12] in order to perform operations on the encoded values we use non-interactive algorithms which do not use any refresh subroutine, thus improving the efficiency. Furthermore, the security of these procedures is easy to verify and does not need any leakage-free components or oracles. The drawback is that the size of the secret state will grow when using our proposed algorithms. To overcome this issue, we propose a procedure to shrink down the secret internal state. This is an interactive algorithm which uses a refresh algorithm as a sub-routine. We emphasize that this shrinking procedure is optional and in many applications not necessary. A refreshing algorithm is required when a computed value is retrieved from the encodings.

The generation of leak-free randomness is a serious issue in many concrete scenarios. While [DF12,BFGV12] access leakage-free components in almost all procedures to perform operations in a finite field, we only access leakage-free components to retrieve a final value and, depending on the application, to shrink down the internal state. We also give a complete security analysis for every proposed algorithm, while, in particular for low dimension encodings together with large finite fields, the security of some of the algorithms given by [DF12, BFGV12] is not clear.

We emphasize that an inner product extractor based leakage-resilient storage is very attractive when using a finite field of an exponential size. Since even encodings with a low dimension preserve strong statistical extractor properties of the inner product. This is shown by the analyses of inner product based leakage-resilient storage of [DDV10,DF11]. Further, we improve the analysis of the inner product based leakage-resilient storage to get even stronger results.

A suitable application of our techniques are LPN- or LWE-based protocols over large fields. We will show how to perform a leakage-resilient computation of the LPN-based protocol Lapin and give implementation results. The results show that our implementation is efficient enough such that it can be considered for applications in practice.

2 Preliminaries

We write $[n]$ to indicate the set $\{1, \ldots, n\}$. We denote with $\mathbb{F}$ the finite field $\mathbb{Z}_2[x]/(g(x))$, where $g(x)$ is a degree m polynomial irreducible over $\mathbb{Z}_2[x]$ and $\mathbb{F}^* := \mathbb{F} \setminus \{0\}$. Let $A = (A_1, \ldots, A_n)$ and $B = (B_1, \ldots, B_n)$ be two vectors with elements in $\mathbb{F}$. The notation $A\|B$ indicates the concatenation of the two vectors. Moreover, we denote with $A \otimes B$ the following vector of length n^2:

$$A \otimes B := (A_1B_1, \ldots, A_1B_n, A_2B_1, \ldots, A_2B_n, \ldots, A_nB_1, \ldots, A_nB_n).$$

The inner product between A and B is defined in the usual way as

$$\langle A, B \rangle := \sum_{i=1}^{n} A_i \cdot B_i.$$

If an algorithm A has oracle access to a distribution $\mathcal{D}$, we write $A^{\mathcal{D}}$. A probabilistic polynomial time algorithm is called PPT.

The *statistical distance* between two random variables A and B with values in a finite set $\mathcal{X}$ is defined as $\Delta(A, B) = \frac{1}{2}\sum_{x \in \mathcal{X}} \left| \Pr[A = x] - \Pr[B = x] \right|$. If this distance is negligible, we say that the two variables are *statistically indistinguishable*. The *min-entropy* of a random variable A is defined as $H_\infty(A) = -\log(\max_{x \in \mathcal{X}} \Pr[A = x])$.

Two-source extractors. Two-source extractors, introduced in 1988 by Chor and Goldreich [CG88], are an important and powerful tool in cryptography.

Definition 2.1. Let $\mathcal{L}$, $\mathcal{R}$ and $\mathcal{C}$ be finite sets, and let U be the uniform distribution over $\mathcal{C}$. A function $\mathsf{ext} : \mathcal{L} \times \mathcal{R} \to \mathcal{C}$ is a *weak* (m, ϵ) *two-source extractor* if for all distributions of independent random variables $L \in \mathcal{L}$ and $R \in \mathcal{R}$ such that $H_\infty(L) \geq m$ and $H_\infty(R) \geq m$ we have $\Delta(\mathsf{ext}(L, R), U) \leq \epsilon$.

If we change the condition on the min-entropy to $H_\infty(L) + H_\infty(R) \geq k$, the extractor is called *flexible*. Note that if $k = 2m$ this requirement is weaker than the original, hence flexibility is a stronger notion.

The fact that the inner product is a strong extractor is well known in the literature ([Vaz85], [CG88]). The security results in this work are based on the following lemma regarding the inner product extractor over finite fields.

Lemma 2.1 *(Proof of Theorem 3.1 [Rao07]). The inner product function* $\langle .,. \rangle$: $\mathbb{F}^n \times \mathbb{F}^n \to \mathbb{F}$ *is a weak flexible* (k, ϵ) *two-source extractor for* $\epsilon \leq 2^{((n+1) \log |\mathbb{F}| - k)/2}$.

Limited adversaries and leakage-resilient storage. There have been several proposals to model SCA in theory [DF11, DF12, GR12]. In the so-called *split-state model*, we assume that the memory of a physical device can be split in two distinct parts, called respectively P_L and P_R. These could be, for instance, two separate processors, or also a single processor operating at distinct and separate times.

All the computation carried out on the device (for computing, for example, a cryptographic primitive or an algorithm) is performed as a two-party protocol Π between the two parties P_L and P_R. More precisely, each of the two parties has an internal state (initially just some input) and at each step communicates with the other party by sending some messages. These messages depend on the initial state, the local randomness, and the messages received earlier in the protocol. At the end of the execution of Π, each party outputs a new state.

The main reason to adopt this setting is that we assume that the two parties operate independently, and hence are subject to completely independent leakage. In our model, we consider an adversary A that is able to interact with both memory parts. After each execution of Π, the adversary is allowed to query a *leakage oracle* $\Omega(\mathsf{view}_L, \mathsf{view}_R)$, where $(\mathsf{view}_L, \mathsf{view}_R)$ are the respective *views* of the players. The view of a player consists of all the information that was available to him during the execution of the protocol, i.e. his initial state, his local randomness and all the messages sent and/or received. The adversary submits functions f_L and f_R and after submission, he gets back $f_L(\mathsf{view}_L)$ and $f_R(\mathsf{view}_R)$. The only restriction is that the total amount of bits output by the function f_L during *one execution of the protocol* is limited to a certain constant λ, and the same holds for f_R. An adversary is called λ-*limited* with respect to the limited amount of leakage during a single execution, but an arbitrary amount of leakage over all executions of the protocol. A more formal description of the model may be found in [DF12] or [GR12].

An important primitive used to achieve leakage resilience in this model is a *leakage-resilient storage* (LRS) [DDV10, DF11, DF12]. An LRS for a set of values $\mathbb{S}$ consists of two PPT algorithms $\mathsf{LRS} := (\mathsf{Encode}, \mathsf{Decode}, \mathsf{Refresh})$:

- $\mathsf{Encode}(1^\kappa, S) \to (L, R)$: Outputs an encoding (L, R) of a value $S \in \mathbb{S}$.
- $\mathsf{Decode}(L, R) = S$: Outputs the private value S corresponding to the encoding (L, R).

For *correctness* it is required that $\mathsf{Decode}(\mathsf{Encode}(S)) = S$ for all $S \in \mathbb{S}$.

Definition 2.2. We say an LRS is (λ, ϵ)-*secure* if for every private value S and any λ-limited adversary $\mathsf{A}^{\Omega(L,R)}$ querying the functions $f_L(L)$ to P_L and $f_R(R)$ to P_R we have

$$\Delta([f_L(L), f_R(R) \mid \mathsf{Decode}(L, R) = S], [f_L(L'), f_R(R')]) \leq \epsilon$$

where (L', R') is an encoding of a uniformly chosen value.

With this security notion, a λ-limited adversary cannot distinguish whether the leakage is obtained from a specific value S or a uniformly sampled value S'.

The protocol Π computes operations on encoded values and outputs encodings of the final values. These can be later retrieved with a dedicated procedure.

Remark 2.1. In our leakage model, the total amount of leakage obtained from each memory part in a single round is bounded by λ. However, after a few observations, an adversary could recover the shares completely, and trivially break the security of the scheme. The first procedure we need to define, then, is a *refreshing* procedure that allows to inject new randomness in the protocol. Namely the procedure $\mathsf{Refresh}$ takes as input an encoding (L, R) of a value S and outputs a new encoding (L', R') for S. Due to space limitations, we will leave the details and issues of the $\mathsf{Refresh}$ procedure to the appendix. We will mention, however, that all known provably-secure refreshing algorithms for two parties need a leakage-free sampling of the randomness[1]. We will discuss leakage-free oracles in Sect. 5.

3 A Leakage-Resilient Storage Based on the Inner Product

An LRS based on the inner product was first proposed by [DDV10]. Given a field $\mathbb{F}$ and an integer n (the dimension of the encodings), the LRS Φ^n based on the inner product for values in $\mathbb{F}$ is given by:

- $\mathsf{Encode}(1^\kappa, S) \to (L, R)$: Sample values $(L_1, \ldots, L_n, R_1, \ldots, R_{n-1}) \xleftarrow{\$} (\mathbb{F}^*)^{2n-1}$ and set $R_n = L_n^{-1}(S - \langle L_1\| \ldots \|L_{n-1}, R_1\| \ldots \|R_{n-1}\rangle)$. If $R_n = 0$, resample. Finally, output $(L := L_1\| \ldots \|L_n, R := R_1\| \ldots \|R_n)$.

---

[1] The construction of a compiler from [GR12] implies a refreshing procedure, which does not need any leak-free gates. However, it assumes that a number of parties executing the protocol is much bigger than 2 and is rather unefficient.

- Decode$(L, R) = S$: Output $S = \langle L, R \rangle$.

Correctness and security were proved in [DF11]. However, we manage to improve the bounds for which security holds. We will present our result in the next theorem.

Theorem 3.1. *For separated P_L and P_R and a finite field $\mathbb{F}$, Φ^n is a (λ, ϵ)-secure LRS for*

$$\epsilon \leq 2^{-\frac{2n \log |\mathbb{F}^*| - (n+3) \log |\mathbb{F}| - 2\lambda}{2}}$$

Proof. Let A be a λ-limited adversary with access to oracle $\Omega(\text{view}_L, \text{view}_R)$. He is allowed to query $f_L(\text{view}_L)$ and $f_R(\text{view}_R)$ since P_L and P_R are separated. The functions f_L and f_R have joint output size 2λ. These functions define a mapping f from $(\mathbb{F}^*)^{2n}$ to $\{0,1\}^{2\lambda}$. For simplicity we will write $f(L, R)$ instead of $f_L(\text{view}_L)$ and $f_R(\text{view}_R)$. Let $\mathbb{P}_x$ be the set of all preimages of $x \in \{0,1\}^{2\lambda}$. Then the min-entropy of L and R given a certain leakage $x \in \{0,1\}^{2\lambda}$ is $\forall f : (\mathbb{F}^*)^{2n} \to \{0,1\}^{2\lambda}$:

$$H_{\infty,x}((L, R) \mid f(L, R) = x)$$

$$= -\log \left(\max_{(L',R') \in (\mathbb{F}^*)^{2n}} \left(\Pr_{(L,R) \xleftarrow{\$} (\mathbb{F}^*)^{2n}} [(L, R) = (L', R') \mid f(L, R) = x] \right) \right)$$

$$= -\log \left(\max_{(L',R') \in \mathbb{P}_x} \left(\Pr_{(L,R) \xleftarrow{\$} \mathbb{P}_x} [(L, R) = (L', R')] \right) \right) = \log |\mathbb{P}_x|$$

Since $f_L(\text{view}_L)$ depends only on L and $f_R(\text{view}_R)$ only on R, L and R are independent given f. Hence Lemma 2.1 implies the following bounds on the statistical distances for the elements of $\{0,1\}^{2\lambda}$:

$$\epsilon_x = \Delta_x([\langle L, R \rangle \mid f(L, R) = x], \langle L', R' \rangle) \leq \sqrt{|\mathbb{F}|^{n+1}}\sqrt{|\mathbb{P}_x|^{-1}}$$

for a uniform $\langle L', R' \rangle \in \mathbb{F}$. Notice that the statistical distance ϵ_x is not necessarily negligible. For instance an adversary could choose a function f such that the function is 1 if all entries of L and R are $1 \in \mathbb{F}$ and otherwise 0. In this case if a leakage $f(L, R) = x = 1$ appears, L and R are statistically fixed and $\epsilon_x = \epsilon_1 = 1$. Even if an adversary will choose such a function f, a $x = 1$ will appear only with a negligible probability then. A straight forward but a lossy technique to prove the Theorem would be: Either x appears with negligible probability or ϵ_x is negligible. We are not using this approach which is also a reason why we get better bounds.

We get the Theorem by bounding the final advantage of A: For all $S \in \mathbb{F}$

$$\epsilon = \Delta([f(L, R) \mid \langle L, R \rangle = S], f(L', R'))$$

$$= \frac{1}{2} \sum_{x \in \{0,1\}^{2\lambda}} |\Pr[f(L, R) = x \mid \langle L, R \rangle = S] - \Pr[f(L', R') = x]|$$

$$= \frac{1}{2} \sum_{x \in \{0,1\}^{2\lambda}} \left| \frac{\Pr[\langle L, R \rangle = S \mid f(L, R) = x] \cdot \Pr[f(L', R') = x]}{\Pr[\langle L, R \rangle = S]} - \Pr[f(L', R') = x] \right|$$

$$\leq \frac{1}{2}|\mathbb{F}| \sum_{x\in\{0,1\}^{2\lambda}} \Pr[f(L',R')=x] \left|\Pr[\langle L,R\rangle = S \mid f(L,R)=x] - \frac{1}{|\mathbb{F}|}\right|$$

$$\leq |\mathbb{F}| \sum_{x\in\{0,1\}^{2\lambda}} \Pr[f(L',R')=x] \left(\frac{1}{2}\sum_{S'\in\mathbb{F}} |\Pr[\langle L,R\rangle = S' \mid f(L,R)=x] - \Pr[\langle L',R'\rangle = S']|\right)$$

$$= |\mathbb{F}| \sum_{x\in\{0,1\}^{2\lambda}} \Pr[f(L',R')=x] \left(\Delta_x([\langle L,R\rangle \mid f(L,R)=x],\langle L',R'\rangle)\right)$$

$$\leq \frac{|\mathbb{F}|\sqrt{|\mathbb{F}|^{n+1}}}{|\mathbb{F}^*|^{2n}} \sum_{x\in\{0,1\}^{2\lambda}} \sqrt{|\mathbb{P}_x|} \leq \frac{\sqrt{|\mathbb{F}|^{n+3}\cdot 2^\lambda}}{|\mathbb{F}^*|^n} = 2^{-\frac{2n\log|\mathbb{F}^*|-(n+3)\log|\mathbb{F}|-2\lambda}{2}}$$

The first steps are straight forward. Then for the first inequality, we use a probably lossy bound. In the second last line, we sum over the probability, that a leakage x appears multiplied with the statistical distance ϵ_x implied by x. Finally we plugin the probabilities and apply the bounds on ϵ_x for all $x \in \{0,1\}^{2\lambda}$ and use Jensen's Inequality.   □

Flexibility and graceful degradation. The LRS Φ^n satisfies two additional, very useful properties. It is *flexible*, since an adversary could query 2λ bits on a single party instead of querying λ bits on each of them, without decreasing the statistical distance. More generally, an adversary is allowed to arbitrary split the amount of leakage among the two parties, as long as the sum is equal to the total amount of tolerated leakage.

Even more interesting is the *graceful degradation* achieved by an LRS in general. If an adversary queries $2\lambda + 2k$ bits instead of 2λ bits, the security will not entirely break down. In case of Φ^n, it will only increase the statistical distance from uniform by a factor of 2^k. If the statistical distance is 2^κ for security parameter κ, then the security parameter will be decreased to $\kappa' = \kappa - k$.

Remark 3.1. For seeing the improvement compared to previous results, we use the parameters of Lemma 1 in [DF11] which is also used in [DF12]. We set $m = 1$ and the given leakage and statistical distance is $\lambda = (1/2 - \delta)n\log|\mathbb{F}| - \log\gamma^{-1}$ and $\epsilon' = 2(|\mathbb{F}|^{3/2-n\delta} + |\mathbb{F}|\gamma)$ for $\gamma > 0$ and $1/2 > \delta > 0$. If we plug in λ in Theorem 3.1, our bound yields $\epsilon = |\mathbb{F}^*|^{-n}|\mathbb{F}|^{n+3/2-n\delta}\gamma \approx |\mathbb{F}|^{3/2-n\delta}\gamma$ for large fields. Hence $\epsilon' > \epsilon$.

Remark 3.2. Further, for a total leakage 2λ of $1/2$ of the bits of the encodings or more, security is not guaranteed anymore. This follows from the fact that $(n+3)\log|\mathbb{F}|$ is larger than $n\log|\mathbb{F}^*|$ which is the entropy of one of the encodings.

4 Computation and Retrieving Computed Values

To begin, we show how to perform non-interactive operations on the encoded values. Non-interactivity guarantees that the computation doesn't contradict the split-state model's assumptions, thus ensuring to achieve security. After describing the non-interactive operations, we give a more formal description of a set of leakage-resilient operations based on the LRS Φ^n.

Addition of a constant and an encoded value. Let $X = \langle L, R \rangle$ be the input secret value and $c \in \mathbb{F}$ be a constant. To compute $c + X$, we set $L' = L \| c$ and $R' = R \| 1$. Then

$$\langle L', R' \rangle = \sum_{i=1}^{n} (L_i \cdot R_i) + c = X + c.$$

Addition of two encoded values. Let $X = \langle L, R \rangle$ and $Y = \langle K, Q \rangle$ be the input secret values, and (L', R') the encoding for $Z = X + Y$. The simplest addition procedure is to set $L' = L \| K$ and $R' = R \| Q$. It is trivial to verify that

$$\langle L', R' \rangle = \sum_{i=1}^{n} (L_i \cdot R_i + K_i \cdot Q_i) = \sum_{i=1}^{n} (L_i \cdot R_i) + \sum_{i=1}^{n} (K_i \cdot Q_i) = \langle L, R \rangle + \langle K, Q \rangle.$$

Multiplication of an encoded value by a constant. Let c be a public constant and let $X = \langle L, R \rangle$ be the input secret value. We would like to obtain shares (L', R') for $c \cdot X$. It is then enough to set $L' = L$ and $R'_i = c \cdot R_i$ for $i \in [n]$. It is immediate to verify that

$$\langle L', R' \rangle = \sum_{i=1}^{n} (L_i \cdot c \cdot R_i) = c \cdot \langle L, R \rangle = c \cdot X.$$

Multiplication of two encoded values. Let $X = \langle L, R \rangle$ and $Y = \langle K, Q \rangle$ be the input secret values and (L', R') the encoding for $Z = X \cdot Y$. The simplest multiplication procedure is to set $L' = L \otimes K$ and $R' = R \otimes Q$. It is now easy to verify that

$$\langle L', R' \rangle = \sum_{i=1}^{n} \sum_{j=1}^{n} (L_i \cdot K_j \cdot R_i \cdot Q_j) = \sum_{i=1}^{n} (L_i \cdot R_i) \cdot \sum_{i=1}^{n} (R_i \cdot Q_i) = \langle L, R \rangle \cdot \langle K, Q \rangle.$$

We emphasize that this operation is too costly for large dimensions. If a multiplication between two encoded values is necessary, using the algorithm given by [DF12] should be considered.

A set of leakage-resilient operations. To describe the set of leakage-resilient operations, we use again the algorithms of Φ^n. More precisely, the set of leakage-resilient operations Ψ^n consists of nine PPT algorithms for two parties P_L and P_R:

- Initialize($S_1, \ldots, S_s$): For all $i \in [s]$ compute Encode$_{\Phi^n}(1^\kappa, S_i) \to (L_i, R_i)$. Start P_L with input $L_1, \ldots L_s$ and P_R with input $R_1, \ldots, R_s$.
- Refresh(i): P_L and P_R replace (L_i, R_i) by $(L'_i, R'_i) \leftarrow$ Refresh(L_i, R_i).
- cAdd(i, j, c): P_L sets $L_i := L_j \| c$ and P_R sets $R_i := R_j \| 1$.
- Add(i, j, k): P_L sets $L_i := L_j \| L_k$ and P_R sets $R_i := R_j \| R_k$.
- cMult(i, j, c): P_L sets $L_i := (cL_{j,1} \| cL_{j,2} \| \ldots)$ for $L_j = (L_{j,1} \| L_{j,2} \| \ldots)$ and P_R sets $R_i := R_j$.
- Mult(i, j, k): P_L sets $L_i := L_j \otimes L_k$ and P_R sets $R_i := R_j \otimes R_k$.

- RetrieveValue(i) → (L', R'): Invoke Refresh(i), P_L outputs L_i and P_R outputs R_i.
- ShrinkDown(i): Shrinks down L_i and R_i to dimension $n + 1$. For more details and the security analysis, we refer to Appendix B.

Remark 4.1. Note that, apart from cMult, the length of the encodings increases in all the other operations. This can influence the performance of the following operations. Thus, we have designed a Shrink procedure that allows to reduce an arbitrary length of encodings down to $n + 1$ field elements.

It turns out that, in the protocols we considered, using this operation does not improve the overall efficiency. This is because it requires a call to the Refresh procedure, which is quite costly. For completeness, we present the Shrink operation in Appendix B. We remark that this operation is still useful in many situations, because it does improve the performance for more complicated patterns of operations (indeed, even for just two consecutive multiplications on encoded values).

The main property of Ψ^n is that functions computable by two parties P_L and P_R with the operations described above can be made leakage resilient in a straightforward way. The procedure Initialize, which receives as input all sensitive values, is called at the beginning of the computation. This process has to be free of leakage. Once encodings for the sensitive values are created and shared among P_L and P_R, arbitrary functions can be computed and retrieved and the leakage during the computation will not leak any information about the sensitive values, even if the computed function may reveal them.

After the computation, P_L and P_R can refresh their encodings by using Refresh to compute another function without leaking information about the sensitive values during the computation. If Refresh is used, the amount of tolerated leakage is as large as during the first computation. This follows directly from the property of Refresh. We prove the general statement about Ψ^n in the next theorem.

Theorem 4.1. *Let F be an arbitrary function computable by two parties P_L, P_R using Ψ^n. Let the encodings used by P_L, P_R for computing a value be fresh and independent. Let $S_1, \ldots, S_s \in \mathbb{F}$ be a set of input values for F among additional inputs that may be chosen uniformly or by an adversary. Then for any λ-limited adversary A and any $q \in \mathbb{N}$:*

$$\Delta(\mathsf{A}^{\Omega(\mathbb{P}_L, \mathbb{P}_R)}(x_1, \ldots x_q), \mathsf{A}^{\Omega(\mathbb{P}_U, \mathbb{P}_U)}(x_1, \ldots x_q)) \leq q 2^{-\frac{2n \log |\mathbb{F}^*| - (n+3) \log |\mathbb{F}| - 2\lambda}{2}}$$

where x_i is an output of F on input $S_1, \ldots, S_s$. Furthermore, for every $i \in [q]$, $\Omega(\mathbb{P}_L, \mathbb{P}_R)$ gives access to λ bits of leakage on each of the views of P_L and P_R during the computation of x_i, whereas $\Omega(\mathbb{P}_U, \mathbb{P}_U)$ indicates leakage obtained from the computation of x_i for uniform $S'_1, \ldots, S'_s \in \mathbb{F}$.

Proof. We start with $q = 1$. Without loss of generality we set $x_1 = \{S_1, \ldots S_s\}$ and assume that A sends queries $f_{L,1}(L_{S_1,1}), \ldots, f_{L,s}(L_{S_s,1})$ to P_L and

$f_{R,1}(R_{S_1,1}), \ldots, f_{R,s}(R_{S_s,1})$ to P_R with a total ouput size of 2λ bits. Let λ_i be the output size of $f_{L,1}(L_{S_i,1})$ and $f_{R,1}(R_{S_i,1})$ for $i \in [s]$. Then according to Theorem 3.1:

$$\epsilon = \Delta(\mathsf{A}^{\Omega(\mathbb{P}_L, \mathbb{P}_R)}(x_1), \mathsf{A}^{\Omega(\mathbb{P}_U, \mathbb{P}_U)}(x_1))$$

$$= \Delta(\mathsf{A}^{\Omega(\mathbb{P}_L, \mathbb{P}_R)}(S_1, \ldots, S_s), \mathsf{A}^{\Omega(\mathbb{P}_U, \mathbb{P}_U)}(S_1, \ldots, S_s))$$

$$\leq \sum_{i=1}^{s} 2^{-\frac{2n \log |\mathbb{F}^*| - (n+3) \log |\mathbb{F}| - \lambda_i}{2}}$$

$$= 2^{-\frac{2n \log |\mathbb{F}^*| - (n+3) \log |\mathbb{F}|}{2}} \sum_{i=1}^{s} 2^{\frac{\lambda_i}{2}}$$

$$\leq 2^{-\frac{2n \log |\mathbb{F}^*| - (n+3) \log |\mathbb{F}| - 2\lambda}{2}}$$

This is because Theorem 3.1 holds for any private value $S \in \mathbb{F}$, which is harder to achieve than if S is known or even chosen by A. To extend the result to q outputs of F, we use a simple hybrid argument. For x_1, we showed that A can not distinguish if the leakage is received from encodings of $S_1, \ldots S_s$ or from some uniform $S'_1, \ldots S'_s$ with probability more than ϵ. Since we use fresh and independent encodings of $S_1, \ldots S_s$ for the computation of x_2 to x_q, we can apply Theorem 3.1 again. So for every single x_i, A will notice with at most probability ϵ, if the leakage is based on $S'_1, \ldots S'_s$ instead of $S_1, \ldots S_s$. Summing up over q we get:

$$\Delta(\mathsf{A}^{\Omega(\mathbb{P}_L, \mathbb{P}_R)}(x_1, \ldots x_q), \mathsf{A}^{\Omega(\mathbb{P}_U, \mathbb{P}_U)}(x_1, \ldots x_q)) \leq q\epsilon.$$

$\square$

Note that Theorem 4.1 provides leakage resilience for any function F with private values $\mathbb{S}$ and computable by two parties P_L, P_R using Ψ^n. More precisely, given q outputs of F and leakage retrieved during the computation of F, an adversary cannot distinguish if the leakage comes from the computation of F on input $\mathbb{S}$ or a uniformly sampled input in $\mathbb{F}$.

Corollary 4.1. *Let F be a function with private input $\mathbb{S}$ and additional input that may be chosen at uniform or by an adversary. Suppose that, for any PPT algorithm, q outputs of F are distinguishable from uniform with probability at most ϵ. Then q outputs of F computed by two parties P_L, P_R using Ψ^n are distinguishable from uniform with probability at most ϵ' by any PPT λ-limited adversary, where*

$$\epsilon' \leq \epsilon + q2^{-\frac{2n \log |\mathbb{F}^*| - (n+3) \log |\mathbb{F}| - 2\lambda}{2}}.$$

5   Leakage-Resilient Computation Of Lapin

Even though the techniques presented above can be easily applied to other primitives or protocols (for example [LM13]), we set our focus on Lapin. The instantiation of Lapin with a large field fits perfectly the proposed techniques. We use the parameters given in [HKL+12]. The authors propose to use the field $\mathbb{F} = \mathbb{F}_2[X]/(X^{532} + X + 1)$, which results in a size $|\mathbb{F}| = 2^{532}$. Lapin uses two private key elements $s_1, s_2 \in \mathbb{F}$ and for every protocol execution, a sensitive noise term e is sampled from the distribution $\mathcal{B}_\tau^{\mathbb{F}}$, i.e. the distribution over the polynomials of $\mathbb{F}$ where each of the coefficients is chosen from the binary Bernoulli distribution. While s_1 and s_2 could be stored in encoded form on two separated parts P_L and P_R on the device, e has to be resampled after every computation and not just refreshed. During the protocol a term $z = r(cs_1 + s_2) + e$ for uniform field elements r, c is computed. Due to space constraintments, we refer for details to [HKL+12]. A leakage-resilient computation of z would imply a leakage-resilient variant of Lapin.

On leak-free oracles. For sampling and encoding e, we use a *leak-free* oracle $\mathcal{O}_e$. The reason for using $\mathcal{O}_e$ to generate an encoding for e is that it is fundamental to securely sample the randomness. In fact, even leaking a single bit of the sampled noise is enough to undermine security, since revealing the noise from a LPN sample provides a linear equation from which the secret can be recovered. Hence we assume that an encoding of the random noise is computed in a leak-free way. This may be not reasonable to assume in some situations. On the other side, the $\mathcal{O}_e$ oracle does not have any input, and the noise e is independent from any interaction between the parties of the authentication protocol, this makes it harder to attack such an oracle with a SCA.

One strategy to deal with this issue (that also concerns refreshing procedures), is to sample the vectors L_e and R_e in advance, i.e. even before the challenge c is known. One can therefore compute a number of pairs (L_{e_1}, R_{e_1}), $(L_{e_2}, R_{e_2}), \ldots$ and pick one of them (possibly at random) whenever a fresh pair is needed. Storing these pairs on the Tag even for a long time is completely safe under the assumption that only computation leaks information. Even if an adversary got access to a stored pair, the scheme would still be secure as long as the adversary did not learn more than what he could have learned via leakage queries during a single execution of the protocol. Whenever a Tag is running out of (L_e, R_e) pairs, it could sample a few new pairs from $\mathcal{O}_e$ and store them in the memory or sample a new pair after every protocol execution. Even if the oracle $\mathcal{O}_e$ was not completely leakage-free, it would still be hard to attack the system, since the (L_e, R_e) pairs are sampled in a different moment from the actual execution of the protocol and it is probably not easy for an adversary to figure out which pair is used next time.[2]

Describing the leakage-resilient computation. At the core of Lapin, there is the function $F(r, c, s_1, s_2, e) = z = r(s_1c + s_2) + e = rcs_1 + rs_2 + e$. In Fig. 1 we give the details of its implementation using the set of leakage-resilient operations Ψ^n from Sect. 4.

---

[2] Because the pair to be used can be picked at random from the set of available pairs.

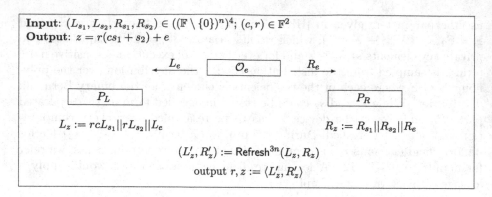

Fig. 1. Leakage resilient computation for a lapin tag. To see which instructions of Ψ^n are used, see Sect. 4. For the encodings hold $\langle L_{s_1}, R_{s_1} \rangle = s_1$, $\langle L_{s_1}, R_{s_1} \rangle = s_2$ and $\langle L_e, R_e \rangle = e$. Before perfoming the next computation, the encodings of s_1 and s_2 need to be refreshed.

The encodings $L_{s_1}, L_{s_2}, R_{s_1}, R_{s_2}$ for s_1 and s_2 are stored on the device and e is obtained from $\mathcal{O}_e$. The two parties P_L and P_R perform non-interactive additions of shares and multiplications by constants to create an encoding of the response z. The retrieving procedure is used to get an encoding of z in a secure way. Finally, z itself can be obtained by computing the inner product of the encodings. Before starting the next protocol execution, the encodings of s_1 and s_2 need to be refreshed using the refreshing operation of Ψ^n.

The security of the scheme and robustness against leakage can be easily obtained from Corollary 4.1. Let ϵ_L be the winning probability against Lapin. This is essentially the probability of distinguishing, for q outputs, the function $F(r, c, s_1, s_2, e) = z$ from uniform, where r is uniform and c is chosen by an adversary. The values s_1, s_2 and e are the sensitive values and hence they are encoded. The winning probability ϵ_p against the proposed leakage-resilient protocol for q executions is $\epsilon_p = \epsilon_L + \epsilon_{\Psi^n}$, where ϵ_{Ψ^n} is the distinguishing probability stated in Theorem 4.1.

Sampling the randomness and refreshing. As we already mentioned, it is necessary that both the on-chip randomness sampling and the refreshing procedure be secure against continual leakage. In particular, if the refreshing procedure accesses a sensitive value in order to generate new encodings for it, the overall security of the protocol could be critically harmed. The sensitive value could in fact be easily retrieved during refresh executions. In Appendix A we describe two existing refreshing algorithms for inner product shares. Neither of them directly accesses a sensitive value so both perform much better, in the presence of leakage, than simply executing an Decode operation followed by a new Encode operation. While the weaker refreshing algorithm is not provably secure in a theoretical sense, the stronger, leakage-resilient refreshing procedure comes at a cost of a less efficient computation and requires a larger amount of randomness. Note that even the leakage-resilient refreshing requires that the randomness is drawn from a leakage-free oracle.

Efficiency. The efficiency of the scheme is calculated in terms of inversions and multiplications over $\mathbb{F}$. In Table 1 we report our efficiency analysis of Lapin when instantiated with the stronger (second row) and the weaker (third row) refreshing procedures. In our analysis, we do not include the computation of a refreshing procedure between two protocol executions.

Table 1. Efficiency of the Framework and Robustness Against Leakage. In the table above, n is the dimension of the encodings, ϵ_L is the winning probability against Lapin and ϵ_p is the winning probability against the leakage-resilient protocol with λ bits of leakage on each of the two parties per protocol execution. The refresh procedure in between two protocol executions is not covered in the presented computational costs. The 8 bit AVR implementation for multiplication and division is a straight forward implementation of the algorithms given in [HVM04] and for Lapin a uniform challenge c in $\mathbb{F}$ is used instead of a sparse element in $\mathbb{F}$.

Protocol	Refresh	n	Efficiency		Security	
			Multiplications & Invertions	8 bit AVR	λ	ϵ_p
Lapin	-	-	2 &0	0.3 mio cycles	0	ϵ_L
Lapin	Leakage-Resilient	4	$19n$ &$6n+1$	43 mio cycles	141	$\epsilon_L + 2^{-81}$
Lapin	Leakage-Free	4	$11n + 1$ &1	9 mio cycles	141	$\epsilon_L + 2^{-81}$

Even though the protocol is quite simple, the computation is perhaps more expensive than one would expect, due to the expensive refreshing operation (which we describe in Appendix A). Compared to standard Lapin, the efficiency decreases by at least a factor of 30. Lapin performs better over a ring with a reducible multiplication, but in order to apply the proposed techniques, the extractor properties of a field are necessary. Furthermore, Lapin takes advantage of a multiplication with sparse field elements. In our framework, only a few field elements are sparse and hence the optimization does not have a big effect on the overall efficiency.

The 8 bit AVR implementation is based on a shift and add based division and multiplication. Even the most costly implementation with 43 million cycles has a running time of 1.34 seconds on a 32 Mhz architecture. The cycle amount would drastically decrease on an implementation on a 32 bit architecture, since shifts and additions can be carried out four times faster. We emphasize, that the cost of sampling the randomness is not covered here.

Leakage resilience. Our proposal accomplishes leakage resilience in a model which allows continuous and arbitrarily chosen leakage functions as long as leakage-free components are not addressed. A choice of $n = 4$ results in a leakage-resilient protocol for chosen leakage functions of 141 bits output size per round for each of the two parties. To get these results, we first set the statistical distance gained by the inner product to 2^{-81}. For meaningful results, Theorem 4.1 requires $n \geq 4$. Finally we set the amount of protocol executions to be at most $q = 2^{40}$.

6   Conclusions and Future Work

This work provides techniques to perform leakage-resilient operations which perfectly fits cryptographic primitives or protocols running over large finite fields. It achieves strong provable security results thanks to the improved results for the underlying LRS based on the inner product extractor and the large size of the field. This framework could be very helpful to make other primitives leakage-resilient without using heavy machinery. Since the known refresh algorithms are still costly, more efficient alternatives would greatly increase the overall efficiency.

An issue from which our techniques suffer is the generation of on-chip randomness. Furthermore, it is required to use leakage-free oracles to sample randomness without leaking information.

Applying the proposed techniques to Lapin, we obtain a very high level of leakage resilience. In terms of efficiency, it is still very expensive, decreasing the efficiency compared to standard Lapin by at least a factor of 30. This is also a drawback for leakage resilience, since additional computation will cause additional leakage. Therefore, in settings in which performance is very important and leakage resilience plays a minor role, the Boolean masking of Lapin seems to be a better choice. On the other hand, in applications in which a high leakage resilience is necessary, the proposed techniques applied to Lapin provides an interesting option while still having reasonable responding times during a protocol interaction.

Acknowledgements. The authors would like to thank Krzysztof Pietrzak and Eike Kiltz for the helpful discussions on the leakage resilience of LPN and Tim Güneysu, Thomas Pöppelmann and Ingo von Maurich for helping with the implementation on the avr microcontroller.

A   Refreshing Procedures for the Inner Product LRS

As a first security requirement, a refreshing procedure needs to be *rerandomizing*.

Definition A.1 (Rerandomizing). *The refreshed encodings are uniformly distributed over the set of encodings of the encoded value.*

Dziembowski and Faust in [DF11] describe two possible refreshing procedures, starting from an intuitive, but flawed, one, and then providing a secure one. The latter makes use of a leak-free component $\mathcal{O}_R$ that samples uniformly random pairs of orthogonal vectors, and has a complexity of $O(n^2)$ field operations. An improved version appears in [DF12]. The procedure was then revisited and adapted to the AES case in [BFGV12]. We report it in Fig. 2.

This formulation of a refreshing procedure is very simple but, as the authors incidentally mention, security is based on the (rather unrealistic) assumption that the whole procedure is leakage-free. The reason for this is that, during the interaction between P_L and P_R, one of the parties might learn additional information about the secret state of the other one. While leakage on input

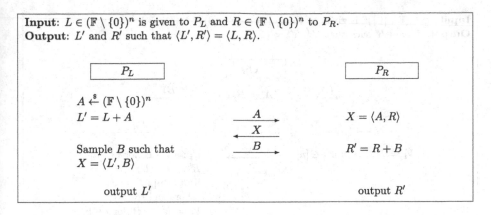

Input: $L \in (\mathbb{F} \setminus \{0\})^n$ is given to P_L and $R \in (\mathbb{F} \setminus \{0\})^n$ to P_R.
Output: L' and R' such that $\langle L', R' \rangle = \langle L, R \rangle$.

Fig. 2. Refreshing Procedure. The refreshing procedure proposed in [BFGV12].

and output does not cause any problem, an adversary could use this additional knowledge of one of the parties during the procedure to query a leakage function which depends partially on both the encodings. This might reveal information about the inner product of the encodings and hence of the encoded value. Even though in practice, it is not known yet, how to exploit this by a SCA.

To deal with this issue, a property called *reconstructability* was introduced in [FRR+10]. Let Op be a masked operation with input (L, R), and output (L', R'). We call *reconstructor* a simulator algorithm Rec that is able to recreate the views that both parties would have after executing Op, without actually executing it. More specifically, Rec takes as input (L, R) and (L', R'), and returns $(\text{view}_L, \text{view}_R)$. In addition, it is important that the execution of Rec does not require any interaction between the parties after they are given the input.[3]

Definition A.2 (Reconstructability). *A masked operation* Op *is said to be ϵ-reconstructable if there exists a reconstructor* Rec *such that, for every $X \in \mathbb{F}$, it holds that*

$$\Delta((L', R', \text{view}_L, \text{view}_R), (L', R', \text{view}'_L, \text{view}'_R)) \leq \epsilon,$$

where $(L, R) = \text{Encode}(X)$, view_L and view_R are the views of the two parties after the execution of $\text{Op}(L, R) = (L', R')$ and $(\text{view}'_L, \text{view}'_R) = \text{Rec}((L, R), (L', R'))$.

This property guarantees that leaking from the internal states during the operation on the encodings does not reveal more than just leaking from the input and output of the operation.

A reconstructable refreshing procedure was suggested by Andrychowicz in [And12] and we present it in Figure 3.

As opposed to previous proposals, this procedure is more efficient, having a complexity of $O(n)$ operations: it requires $2n$ inversions, $4n$ multiplications and

---

[3] Therefore, the parties can jointly draw some common randomness in advance. This will be referred to as *offline sampling* later in this paper.

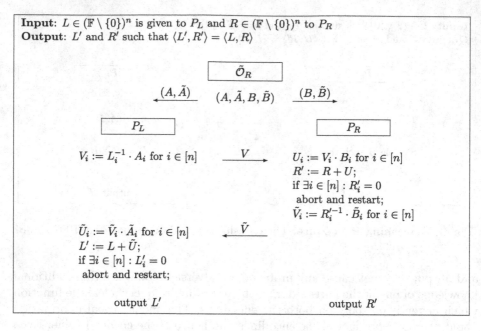

Input: $L \in (\mathbb{F} \setminus \{0\})^n$ is given to P_L and $R \in (\mathbb{F} \setminus \{0\})^n$ to P_R
Output: L' and R' such that $\langle L', R' \rangle = \langle L, R \rangle$

Fig. 3. Refreshing Procedure. The procedure $\mathsf{Refresh}^n$ is used to refresh the shares of a secret. The values $A, \tilde{A}, B, \tilde{B}$ are such that $\langle A, B \rangle = -\langle \tilde{A}, \tilde{B} \rangle$ and $A_i \neq 0$ and $\tilde{B}_i \neq 0$ for $1 \leq i \leq n$.

$2n$ additions in the finite field. The procedure makes use of a modified leak-free component $\tilde{\mathcal{O}}_R$ that generates quadruples of vectors $(A, \tilde{A}, B, \tilde{B})$ such that $\langle A, B \rangle = -\langle \tilde{A}, \tilde{B} \rangle$ and for $1 \leq i \leq n$ it holds that $A_i \neq 0$ and $\tilde{B}_i \neq 0$. It is easy to see that this oracle can be simulated by players in possession of $\mathcal{O}_R$.

Note that his refreshing algorithm assumes that the shares have all non-zero coordinates. In practice, we will use very big fields (at least $|\mathbb{F}| \geq 2^{256}$), so a random vector would have all non-zero coordinates with overwhelming probability.

It is easy to verify that the procedure $\mathsf{Refresh}^n$ of Figure 3 verifies the rerandomizing property. First of all, it is evident that the two shares output by $\mathsf{Refresh}^n$ are indeed a correct masking for the input secret, since

$$
\begin{aligned}
\langle L', R' \rangle &= \\
&= \langle L, R' \rangle + \langle \tilde{U}, R' \rangle = \langle L, R' \rangle + \textstyle\sum_{i=0}^{n} \tilde{U}_i \cdot R'_i = \\
&= \langle L, R' \rangle + \textstyle\sum_{i=0}^{n} \tilde{A}_i \cdot \tilde{B}_i \cdot (R')_i^{-1} \cdot R'_i = \langle L, R' \rangle + \langle \tilde{A}, \tilde{B} \rangle = \\
&= \langle L, R \rangle + \langle L, U \rangle + \langle \tilde{A}, \tilde{B} \rangle = \langle L, R \rangle + \textstyle\sum_{i=0}^{n} L_i \cdot U_i + \langle \tilde{A}, \tilde{B} \rangle = \\
&= \langle L, R \rangle + \textstyle\sum_{i=0}^{n} L_i \cdot L_i^{-1} \cdot A_i \cdot B_i + \langle \tilde{A}, \tilde{B} \rangle = \langle L, R \rangle + \langle A, B \rangle + \langle \tilde{A}, \tilde{B} \rangle = \\
&= \langle L, R \rangle.
\end{aligned}
$$

To see that L' are R' are independent from the input, we set $U = R' - R$ and $\tilde{U} = L' - L$. From the condition $\langle L, R \rangle = \langle L', R' \rangle$ follows $\langle L, U \rangle = -\langle \tilde{U}, R' \rangle$

which is the constraint of $\mathcal{O}_R$. Therefore $\mathcal{O}_R$ outputs samples of the correct distribution to make L', R' independent of L, R.

A reconstructor for $\mathsf{Refresh}^n$ was given in [And12]. We present it in Figure 4.

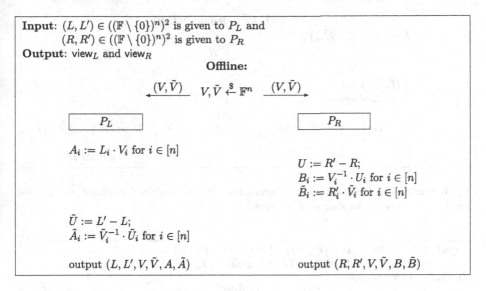

Input: $(L, L') \in ((\mathbb{F} \setminus \{0\})^n)^2$ is given to P_L and
$(R, R') \in ((\mathbb{F} \setminus \{0\})^n)^2$ is given to P_R
Output: view_L and view_R

Offline:

$\overset{(V, \tilde{V})}{\longleftarrow}$ $V, \tilde{V} \overset{\$}{\leftarrow} \mathbb{F}^n$ $\overset{(V, \tilde{V})}{\longrightarrow}$

P_L P_R

$A_i := L_i \cdot V_i$ for $i \in [n]$

$U := R' - R;$
$B_i := V_i^{-1} \cdot U_i$ for $i \in [n]$
$\tilde{B}_i := R_i' \cdot \tilde{V}_i$ for $i \in [n]$

$\tilde{U} := L' - L;$
$\tilde{A}_i := \tilde{V}_i^{-1} \cdot \tilde{U}_i$ for $i \in [n]$

output $(L, L', V, \tilde{V}, A, \tilde{A})$ output $(R, R', V, \tilde{V}, B, \tilde{B})$

Fig. 4. Reconstructor. The above algorithm describes a reconstructor for the procedure $\mathsf{Refresh}^n$. The only communication between the parties is the sampling of random vectors V and $\tilde{V}$, which can be done offline.

The author provides a proof that the above procedure is an ϵ-reconstructor for $\mathsf{Refresh}^n$ with $\epsilon = 0$.

B   A Shrinking Procedure for the Inner Product LRS

The Shrink operation is presented in Fig. 5. It transforms an encoding of length m into an encoding of length $n+1$. It is based on the implicit shrinking procedure used in the multiplication gadget in [DF12].

The algorithm Shrink is interactive, so we need to analyze its security carefully. The reason for this is that for example P_L learns during the execution the value of $\hat{R}$, which reveals some partial information about the secret state of P_R. An adversary can use this fact and query a leakage function, which depends partially on both of the encodings, and thus break the security of LRS.

We already introduced reconstruct ability in Appendix A. Reconstructability implies that the interaction between two parties does not contradict the leakage resilience. Since the views of P_L and P_R during a reconstructable procedure can be simulated by a non-interactive reconstructor. This reconstructor only uses Oracles which sample randomness which is independent of sensitive values and he does not require any interaction between P_L and P_R.

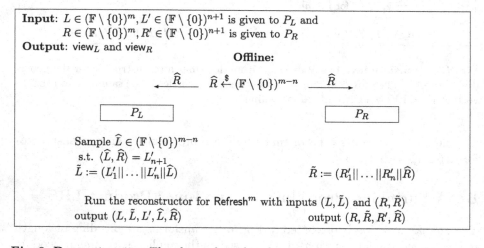

Input: $L \in (\mathbb{F} \setminus \{0\})^m$ is given to P_L and $R \in (\mathbb{F} \setminus \{0\})^m$ to P_R
Output: $L' \in (\mathbb{F} \setminus \{0\})^{n+1}$ and $R' \in (\mathbb{F} \setminus \{0\})^{n+1}$ such that $\langle L', R' \rangle = \langle L, R \rangle$

P_L $\qquad\qquad\qquad\qquad\qquad\qquad\qquad$ P_R

$(\tilde{L}, \tilde{R}) := \mathsf{Refresh}^m(L, R)$

$\hat{L} := (\tilde{L}_{n+1} \| \dots \| \tilde{L}_m)$

$\xleftarrow{\hat{R}}$ $\qquad\qquad$ $\hat{R} := (\tilde{R}_{n+1} \| \dots \| \tilde{R}_m)$

if $\langle \hat{L}, \hat{R} \rangle = 0$
  abort and restart;

$L' := (\tilde{L}_1 \| \dots \| \tilde{L}_n \| \langle \hat{L}, \hat{R} \rangle)$ $\qquad\qquad$ $R' := (\tilde{R}_1 \| \dots \| \tilde{R}_n \| 1)$

$\qquad$ output L' $\qquad\qquad\qquad\qquad\qquad$ output R'

Fig. 5. Shrinking Procedure. The procedure Shrink described in this figure is used to reduce the size of the shares of a secret.

Input: $L \in (\mathbb{F} \setminus \{0\})^m, L' \in (\mathbb{F} \setminus \{0\})^{n+1}$ is given to P_L and
  $R \in (\mathbb{F} \setminus \{0\})^m, R' \in (\mathbb{F} \setminus \{0\})^{n+1}$ is given to P_R
Output: view_L and view_R

Offline:

$\xleftarrow{\hat{R}}$ $\quad \hat{R} \xleftarrow{\$} (\mathbb{F} \setminus \{0\})^{m-n} \quad \xrightarrow{\hat{R}}$

P_L $\qquad\qquad\qquad\qquad\qquad\qquad\qquad$ P_R

Sample $\hat{L} \in (\mathbb{F} \setminus \{0\})^{m-n}$
s.t. $\langle \hat{L}, \hat{R} \rangle = L'_{n+1}$
$\tilde{L} := (L'_1 \| \dots \| L'_n \| \hat{L})$ $\qquad\qquad$ $\tilde{R} := (R'_1 \| \dots \| R'_n \| \hat{R})$

Run the reconstructor for $\mathsf{Refresh}^m$ with inputs $(L, \tilde{L})$ and $(R, \tilde{R})$
output $(L, \tilde{L}, L', \hat{L}, \hat{R})$ $\qquad\qquad$ output $(R, \tilde{R}, R', \hat{R})$

Fig. 6. Reconstructor. The above algorithm describes a reconstructor for the procedure Shrink. The views created by the reconstructor for Refresh are treated as part of the output.

Theorem B.1. Shrink *is 0-reconstructable.*

Proof. The reconstructor for the Shrink operation is presented on Fig. 6. We need to show that reconstructed views $(L, \tilde{L}, L', \hat{L}, \hat{R})$ and $(R, \tilde{R}, R', \hat{R})$ have the same distribution as in the shrink down procedure. This is already clear for L, R and L', R' since the input is identical. In the shrink procedure $\hat{L}$ and $\hat{R}$ are uniform elements in $(\mathbb{F} \setminus \{0\})^{m-n}$ and their inner product is $\langle \hat{L}, \hat{R} \rangle = \tilde{L}_{n+1}$. The presented reconstructor samples $\hat{L}$ such that this is the case. The correct distribution of $\tilde{L}$, $\tilde{R}$ follows from the correct distribution of L', R' and $\hat{L}$, $\hat{R}$: The first n field elements of $\tilde{L}$, $\tilde{R}$ are identical to the first n field elements of L', R' and the last $m - n$ field elements are identical to $\hat{L}$, $\hat{R}$. The reconstructability of the view during the refresh procedure follows from the reconstructability of the refresh procedure.   □

References

[And12] Andrychowicz, M.: Efficient refreshing protocol for leakage-resilient storage based on the inner-product extractor. CoRR, abs/1209.4820 (2012)

[BFGV12] Balasch, J., Faust, S., Gierlichs, B., Verbauwhede, I.: Theory and practice of a leakage resilient masking scheme. In: Wang, X., Sako, K. (eds.) ASIACRYPT 2012. LNCS, vol. 7658, pp. 758–775. Springer, Heidelberg (2012)

[BKKV10] Brakerski, Z., Kalai, Y.T., Katz, J., Vaikuntanathan, V.: Overcoming the hole in the bucket: public-key cryptography resilient to continual memory leakage. In: FOCS, pp. 501–510. IEEE Computer Society (2010)

[CG88] Chor, B., Goldreich, O.: Unbiased bits from sources of weak randomness and probabilistic communication complexity. SIAM J. Comput. **17**(2), 230–261 (1988)

[DBL12] 53rd Annual IEEE Symposium on Foundations of Computer Science, FOCS 2012, New Brunswick, NJ, USA, 20–23 October 2012. IEEE Computer Society (2012)

[DDV10] Davì, F., Dziembowski, S., Venturi, D.: Leakage-resilient storage. In: Garay, J.A., De Prisco, R. (eds.) SCN 2010. LNCS, vol. 6280, pp. 121–137. Springer, Heidelberg (2010)

[DF11] Dziembowski, S., Faust, S.: Leakage-resilient cryptography from the inner-product extractor. In: Lee, D.H., Wang, X. (eds.) ASIACRYPT 2011. LNCS, vol. 7073, pp. 702–721. Springer, Heidelberg (2011)

[DF12] Dziembowski, S., Faust, S.: Leakage-resilient circuits without computational assumptions. In: Cramer, R. (ed.) TCC 2012. LNCS, vol. 7194, pp. 230–247. Springer, Heidelberg (2012)

[DHLAW10] Dodis, Y., Haralambiev, K., López-Alt, A., Wichs, D.: Cryptography against continuous memory attacks. In: FOCS, pp. 511–520. IEEE Computer Society (2010)

[DP08] Dziembowski, S., Pietrzak, K.: Leakage-resilient cryptography. In: FOCS 2008: Proceedings of the 49th Annual IEEE Symposium on Foundations of Computer Science, Washington, DC, USA. IEEE Computer Society (2008)

[FKPR10] Faust, S., Kiltz, E., Pietrzak, K., Rothblum, G.N.: Leakage-resilient signatures. In: Micciancio, D. (ed.) TCC 2010. LNCS, vol. 5978, pp. 343–360. Springer, Heidelberg (2010)

[FRR+10] Faust, S., Rabin, T., Reyzin, L., Tromer, E., Vaikuntanathan, V.: Protecting circuits from leakage: the computationally-bounded and noisy cases. In: Gilbert, H. (ed.) EUROCRYPT 2010. LNCS, vol. 6110, pp. 135–156. Springer, Heidelberg (2010)

[GLS14] Gaspar, L., Leurent, G., Standaert, F.-X.: Hardware implementation and side-channel analysis of lapin. In: Benaloh, J. (ed.) CT-RSA 2014. LNCS, vol. 8366, pp. 206–226. Springer, Heidelberg (2014)

[GR10] Goldwasser, S., Rothblum, G.N.: Securing computation against continuous leakage. In: Rabin, T. (ed.) CRYPTO 2010. LNCS, vol. 6223, pp. 59–79. Springer, Heidelberg (2010)

[GR12] Goldwasser, S., Rothblum, G.N.: How to compute in the presence of leakage. In: 53rd Annual IEEE Symposium on Foundations of Computer Science, FOCS 2012, New Brunswick, NJ, USA, 20–23 October 2012. IEEE Computer Society, pp. 31–40 (2012)

[GST13] Genkin, D., Shamir, A., Tromer, E.: Rsa key extraction via low-bandwidth acoustic cryptanalysis. Cryptology ePrint Archive, Report 2013/857 (2013). http://eprint.iacr.org/

[HKL+12] Heyse, S., Kiltz, E., Lyubashevsky, V., Paar, C., Pietrzak, K.: Lapin: an efficient authentication protocol based on ring-LPN. In: Canteaut, A. (ed.) FSE 2012. LNCS, vol. 7549, pp. 346–365. Springer, Heidelberg (2012)

[HVM04] Hankerson, D., Vanstone, S., Menezes, A.J.: Guide to Elliptic Curve Cryptography. Springer, New York (2004)

[ISW03] Ishai, Y., Sahai, A., Wagner, D.: Private circuits: securing hardware against probing attacks. In: Boneh, D. (ed.) CRYPTO 2003. LNCS, vol. 2729, pp. 463–481. Springer, Heidelberg (2003)

[JV10] Juma, A., Vahlis, Y.: Protecting cryptographic keys against continual leakage. In: Rabin, T. (ed.) CRYPTO 2010. LNCS, vol. 6223, pp. 116–137. Springer, Heidelberg (2010)

[LM13] Lyubashevsky, V., Masny, D.: Man-in-the-middle secure authentication schemes from LPN and weak PRFs. In: Canetti, R., Garay, J.A. (eds.) CRYPTO 2013, Part II. LNCS, vol. 8043, pp. 308–325. Springer, Heidelberg (2013)

[MR04] Micali, S., Reyzin, L.: Physically observable cryptography. In: Naor, M. (ed.) TCC 2004. LNCS, vol. 2951, pp. 278–296. Springer, Heidelberg (2004)

[PR11] Prouff, E., Roche, T.: Higher-order glitches free implementation of the AES using secure multi-party computation protocols. In: Preneel, B., Takagi, T. (eds.) CHES 2011. LNCS, vol. 6917, pp. 63–78. Springer, Heidelberg (2011)

[PRR14] Prouff, E., Rivain, M., Roche, T.: On the practical security of a leakage resilient masking scheme. In: Benaloh, J. (ed.) CT-RSA 2014. LNCS, vol. 8366, pp. 169–182. Springer, Heidelberg (2014)

[Rab10] Rabin, Tal (ed.) CRYPTO 2010. LNCS, vol. 6223, pp. 116–137. Springer, Heidelberg (2010)

[Rao07] Rao, A.: An exposition of bourgains 2-source extractor. In: Electronic Colloquium on Computational Complexity (ECCC), vol. 14 (2007)

[RP10] Rivain, M., Prouff, E.: Provably secure higher-order masking of AES. In: Mangard, S., Standaert, F.-X. (eds.) CHES 2010. LNCS, vol. 6225, pp. 413–427. Springer, Heidelberg (2010)

[Vaz85] Vazirani, U.V.: Towards a strong communication complexity theory or generating quasi-random sequences from two communicating slightly-random sources. In: Proceedings of the Seventeenth Annual ACM Symposium on Theory of Computing, pp. 366–378. ACM (1985)

Secrecy Without Perfect Randomness: Cryptography with (Bounded) Weak Sources

Michael Backes, Aniket Kate, Sebastian Meiser$^{(\boxtimes)}$, and Tim Ruffing

CISPA, Saarland University, Saarbrücken, Germany
{backes,meiser}@cs.uni-saarland.de,
{aniket,tim.ruffing}@mmci.uni-saarland.de

Abstract. Cryptographic protocols are commonly designed and their security proven under the assumption that the protocol parties have access to perfect (uniform) randomness. Physical randomness sources deployed in practical implementations of these protocols often fall short in meeting this assumption, but instead provide only a steady stream of bits with certain high entropy. Trying to ground cryptographic protocols on such imperfect, weaker sources of randomness has thus far mostly given rise to a multitude of impossibility results, including the impossibility to construct provably secure encryption, commitments, secret sharing, and zero-knowledge proofs based solely on a weak source. More generally, indistinguishability-based properties break down for such weak sources. In this paper, we show that the loss of security induced by using a weak source can be meaningfully quantified if the source is *bounded*, e.g., for the well-studied Santha-Vazirani (SV) sources. The quantification relies on a novel relaxation of indistinguishability by a quantitative parameter. We call the resulting notion *differential indistinguishability* in order to reflect its structural similarity to differential privacy. More concretely, we prove that indistinguishability with uniform randomness implies differential indistinguishability with weak randomness. We show that if the amount of weak randomness is limited (e.g., by using it only to seed a PRG), all cryptographic primitives and protocols still achieve differential indistinguishability.

Keywords: Indistinguishability · Randomness · Weak sources · Differential privacy · Pseudorandom generators · Santha-Vazirani sources

1 Introduction

Cryptographic protocols are commonly designed and their security proven under the assumption that the protocol parties have access to perfect, i.e., uniform, randomness. Actual physical randomness sources that cryptographic implementations rely on, however, rarely meet this assumption: instead of providing uniform randomness, they provide only a stream of bits with a certain high amount of entropy. Moreover, these so-called *weak sources*, such as the Santha-Vazirani

© Springer International Publishing Switzerland 2015
T. Malkin et al. (Eds.): ACNS 2015, LNCS 9092, pp. 675–695, 2015.
DOI: 10.1007/978-3-319-28166-7_33

(SV) sources [32], are often non-extractable [15,32], i.e., it is computationally infeasible to extract more than a super-logarithmic amount of (almost) uniform randomness from them.

There have been several attempts to bridge this gap, i.e., to ground the security guarantees of cryptographic systems on such weak sources. As soon as indistinguishability-based secrecy properties are being desired, however, this line of research has mostly given rise to a multitude of impossibility results [7,15,29], only complemented by a few constructive results if additional assumptions are being imposed. For instance, encryption can be realized using weak sources, if one imposes strong assumptions on the entropy of encrypted messages [5], or if the weak source is restricted to the key generation algorithm and a perfect source is available for the actual encryption algorithm [18]. The plurality of impossibility results in this area, as well as the absence of comprehensive constructive results, indicates that traditional indistinguishability-based secrecy notions fall short in capturing the impact of weak randomness on cryptography. This constitutes an unsatisfactory situation, with several open questions looking for an answer:

- Is it possible to quantify the secrecy loss of cryptographic operations and primitives, if a weak source (such as an SV source) is being used?
- Imagine that today a cryptographic protocol (e.g., an e-voting system) is executed and tomorrow it turns out that the employed randomness was weak. Given that there are strong impossibility results [7,15,29] for indistinguishability, is all lost or can we still give quantitative guarantees about the secrecy of the system?
- Given that these quantitative guarantees will necessarily be weaker than traditional cryptographic guarantees, under which assumptions do they still provide reasonable practical security guarantees?

In this paper we address all of these questions.

1.1   Our Contributions

Relaxing Indistinguishability to Quantify the Secrecy Loss. We derive quantitative guarantees for all indistinguishability-based cryptographic constructions that are used with arbitrary weak sources that are additionally *bounded* in the following sense: in addition to imposing an upper bound on the probability of each individual bitstring (i.e., requiring a sufficiently high min-entropy), one additionally imposes a lower bound on these probabilities. These *bounded weak sources* include SV sources [32] and resemble balanced sources [23].

To quantify the secrecy loss that weak randomness imposes on cryptography, we define *differential indistinguishability*, a quantitative relaxation of cryptographic indistinguishability in the spirit of differential privacy [19,30] and pseudodensity [31]. The necessity of a new, relaxed notion arises from the impossibility result of Dodis et al. [15] who showed that whenever only weak sources of randomness are available, traditional indistinguishability is provably impossible for cryptographic primitives that have a secrecy requirement, e.g., encryption, commitments, and zero-knowledge proofs. More concretely, one cannot ensure that the advantage in distinguishing two challenger machines X_0 and X_1 is negligible for every probabilistic polynomial-time adversary. However, it might still be the case that no adversary has a non-negligible advantage in performing a practical attack that breaks the security *entirely*, e.g., by reaching a state in which it is *certain* whether it interacts with X_0 or X_1. The notion of differential indistinguishability consequently aims at quantifying the resulting loss of secrecy without overestimating the adversary's power to break the scheme entirely: Two games, i.e., interactions with two machines X_0 and X_1, are (ε, δ)-differentially indistinguishable if for all interactive distinguisher machines A, the output probabilities for all outputs x are related by

$$\Pr\left[\langle A|X_0\rangle = x\right] \leq 2^\varepsilon \cdot \Pr\left[\langle A|X_1\rangle = x\right] + \delta,$$

where x is a possible output of A.[1] Here $\varepsilon \geq 0$ is a reasonably small constant or a decreasing function such as $1/p(\cdot)$ for a polynomial p. We allow only a negligible function for δ, which corresponds to a negligible probability to break the security of the scheme entirely. Differential indistinguishability thus offers quantitative parameters to reason about the loss of secrecy incurred by the use of imperfect randomness.

Guarantees for Cryptographic Primitives Using Weak Sources. As our main contribution we show that traditional indistinguishability (given a uniform randomness source) suffices to guarantee differential indistinguishability if the uniform source is replaced by an arbitrary bounded weak source. This result immediately entails meaningful quantitative lower security bounds in cases where indistinguishability-based definitions are provably impossible to achieve [15].

In particular, our methodology can be applied in hindsight and produces meaningful quantitative guarantees for all cryptographic primitives and protocols, provided that the amount of used imperfect randomness is bounded; there is no need for new cryptographic constructions for any of the existing primitives whose security is defined and proven by means of indistinguishability, including simulator-based notions.

Moreover, we show that if the bounded weak randomness is used only to seed a secure PRG, differential indistinguishability suffers only a negligible quantitative (additional) security loss under composition – just as traditional indistinguishability.

Intuitively, is not surprising that the provided secrecy does not degrade substantially if the quality of the randomness degrades within certain small bounds, because otherwise virtually all practical implementations of cryptography would be insecure due to the inherent imperfection of physical sources. Our work confirms this intuition and provides a framework to analyze the resulting loss of secrecy quantitatively.

---

[1] In contrast to differential privacy and pseudodensity, we use 2 instead of e as a base for the exponential function, because the base 2 fits standard definitions of entropy better.

Technically, Theorem 1 states that the interactions with two machines X_0 and X_1 are differentially indistinguishable for bounded weak distributions if they are indistinguishable for the uniform distribution. These machines X_0 and X_1 can then be instantiated by arbitrary challenger machines to immediately derive results for cryptographic notions. Theorem 1 comprises arbitrary classes of adversaries and thus covers information-theoretical and computational indistinguishability. To derive quantitative guarantees, the theorem only imposes the requirement that the entropy of the bounded weak randomness used by the primitive or protocol is bounded in terms of the security parameter. Thus all existing primitives that use a bounded amount of randomness can immediately be analyzed and their secrecy loss quantified by an additional multiplicative factor that only depends on the quality of the random source.

Connection to Differential Privacy. We analyze the relation between differential indistinguishability and the well-studied notion of differential privacy [19,30], especially in terms of composition. Similar to the privacy loss in differential privacy when the privacy of several users is analyzed, differential indistinguishability suffers from a commensurate loss of entropy, which consequently leads to a secrecy loss in cases where several users use weak, potentially even dependent randomness. This relation is of particular interest in scenarios in which the users are not aware of using imperfect randomness and thus fail to deploy existing methods [12,24,26] to improve their randomness using multiple sources.

Organization. The rest of the paper is organized as follows: We recall important concepts and introduce our notation in Sect. 2. We define differential indistinguishability and present our main results in Sect. 3. We then demonstrate the utility of differential indistinguishability to public-key encryption and study composability of differentially indistinguishable primitives in Sect. 4. We interpret and analyze differential indistinguishability in Sect. 5, including a comparison between differential indistinguishability with differential privacy. Finally, we discuss related work in Sect. 6 and possible future directions in Sect. 7. To improve readability, we have shifted several proofs to the appendix.

2   Preliminaries and Notation

We denote sampling an element r from a distribution D by $r \leftarrow D$. The probability of the event $F(r)$, where r is sampled from the distribution D, is denoted by $\Pr[F(r)|r \leftarrow D]$ or more compactly by $\Pr[F(D)]$. To keep the notation simple, we write f_k for the value of a function $f(\cdot)$ applied to k, where k is typically the security parameter. We drop the explicit dependence of parameters and security bounds $(\alpha, \beta, \varepsilon, \gamma)$ on k whenever it is clear from the context. We denote by $\{D_k\}_{k \in \mathbb{N}}$ a family of distributions such that for each $k \in \mathbb{N}$ the distribution D_k samples elements from $\{0,1\}^k$. In particular, $\{U_k\}_{k \in \mathbb{N}}$ is the family of uniform distributions, where U_k is the uniform distribution over $\{0,1\}^k$.

Throughout the paper we consider (possibly interactive) Turing machines X that always have implicitly access to a *random tape with an infinite sequence of uniformly distributed random bits*, even if the machines get an additional input drawn from some random source. Unless we mention that they run in proba- bilistic polynomial time (ppt) in the length of their first input, those machines are *not bounded*. The distribution on the outputs of X when run on input x is denoted by $X(x)$. Similarly, we write $\langle X(x)|Y(y)\rangle$ to denote the distribution on the output of the machine X on input x in an interaction with the machine Y on input y. We write $\log := \log_2$ for the logarithm to base 2.

Randomness Sources. In addition to the commonly used min-entropy, we make use of a symmetrically defined counterpart, coined *max-entropy* by Haitner et. al. [23]: whereas min-entropy bounds the maximum likelihood event, max-entropy bounds the minimum likelihood event (and consequently requires probability distributions with full support).[2]

Definition 1. *Let D be a distribution over the set S. The* min-entropy *of D is $H_{min}(D) := \min_{x \in S}(-\log \Pr[D = x])$; the* max-entropy *of D is $H_{max}(D) := \max_{x \in S}(-\log \Pr[D = x])$.*

These entropy measures allow us to define *bounded weak* sources, which must additionally provide a certain amount of max-entropy in comparison to weak sources.

Definition 2. *A family of distributions $\{D_n\}_{n \in \mathbb{N}}$, each over the set $\{0,1\}^n$ of bitstrings of length n, is a (α, β) -bounded weak source, if every D_n satisfies the following entropy requirements:*

(i) D_n has min-entropy at least $n - \alpha$, and
(ii) D_n has max-entropy at most $n + \beta$.

If a family of distributions $\{D_n\}_{n \in \mathbb{N}}$ satisfies only requirement (i), but not requirement (ii), we call it an α -weak source (or a min-entropy source) instead.

The following generalization of Santha-Vazirani (SV) sources [32] to block sources [11,15] is a special case of (α, β)-bounded weak sources. Block sources are well-suited to describe both physical random sources as well as certain random sources that have been "tampered with" by an adversary [1].

Definition 3. (SV Block Source). *A tuple of distributions $D = (D^1, \ldots, D^t)$, each over the set $\{0,1\}^n$ of bitstrings of length n, is (n, γ) -Santha-Vazirani (SV) (for $0 < \gamma < 1$) if for all $0 \le i \le t$ and for all $x_1, \ldots, x_i \in \{0,1\}^n$,*

$$(1 - \gamma) \cdot 2^{-n} \le \Pr\left[D^i = x_i \mid x_1 \leftarrow D^1, \ldots, x_{i-1} \leftarrow D^{i-1}\right] \le (1 + \gamma) \cdot 2^{-n}.$$

The original SV sources are a special case of Definition 3 that arises for $n = 1$. Every (n, γ)-SV block source over $\{0,1\}^{tn}$ is an (α, β)-bounded weak source where $\alpha = t \cdot \log(1 + \gamma)$ and $\beta = -t \cdot \log(1 - \gamma)$.

---

[2] This notion of *max-entropy* is not to be confused with *Hartley entropy*, which is also sometimes called max-entropy.

Remark 1. Our complete analysis is also possible for sources that are only *statistically close* to (α, β)-bounded weak sources such as sources in [23] that have a limited number of outliers. We refer to the full version [3] for both definitions and results for such sources.

3 Differential Indistinguishability

In this section we present our main results, which can be applied to a variety of cryptographic notions. Traditional cryptography defines two machines X_0 and X_1 to be *indistinguishable* for a certain class of distinguishers $\mathcal{A}$ if no distinguisher $A \in \mathcal{A}$ in this class is able to notice a difference between an interaction with X_0 and an interaction with X_1. Formally, the concept of "noticing a difference" is captured by requiring that any possible view of a distinguisher is (almost) equally likely for both X_0 and X_1, i.e., the difference between the probability that A outputs any given view in the interaction with X_0 and the probability that A outputs the same view in the interaction with X_1 is negligible. We consider a variant of indistinguishability that allows these probabilities to be also related by a multiplicative factor $2^\varepsilon > 1$, similar to the concept of mutual pseudodensity [31] and differential privacy [19,30].

Definition 4 (Differential Indistinguishability). *Two probabilistic machines X_0 and X_1 are (ε, δ)-differentially indistinguishable for a distribution $\{D_\ell\}_{\ell \in \mathbb{N}}$ over $\{0,1\}^\ell$ for a positive polynomial ℓ and a class $\mathcal{A}$ of adversaries (probabilistic machines) if for all $A \in \mathcal{A}$, for all sufficiently large k, for all possible outputs x of A, and for all $b \in \{0,1\}$,*

$$\Pr\left[\langle A(1^k)|X_b(1^k, D_\ell)\rangle = x\right] \leq 2^\varepsilon \Pr\left[\langle A(1^k)|X_{1-b}(1^k, D_\ell)\rangle = x\right] + \delta_k.$$

This definition allows to express many of the traditional cryptographic indistinguishability notions [21,27]. We discuss the impact of the multiplicative factor, that can (and must) be interpreted carefully, in Sect. 5. For the traditional case of $\varepsilon = 0$ we speak of δ-indistinguishability. The definition covers interactive and non-interactive notions, as well as simulation-based notions. For perfect (information-theoretic) indistinguishability, the class of adversaries is the class $\mathcal{A}_\infty$ of all probabilistic (possibly unbounded) machines and we have $\delta = 0$.[3] Statistical indistinguishability can be expressed with the same class of adversaries for $\delta > 0$. Cryptographic (computational) indistinguishability can be achieved with the class $\mathcal{A}_{ppt}$ of ppt machines with δ being a negligible function.[4]

3.1 Main Result

Traditional indistinguishability for uniform randomness directly implies differential indistinguishability for (α, β)-bounded weak sources. This is captured by the

---

[3] We additionally drop the formulation "for sufficiently large k" in the case of information-theoretic security.

[4] Note that this is equivalent to requiring a negligible function for every adversary [4].

following theorem. It allows us to easily give guarantees for cryptographic primitives whenever their security notions can be expressed in terms of Definition 4.

Theorem 1. *If two probabilistic machines* X_0 *and* X_1 *are* δ-*indistinguishable for a class of probabilistic machines* $\mathcal{A}$ *and the family of uniform sources* $\{U_n\}_{n\in\mathbb{N}}$ *over* $\{0,1\}^n$, *then* X_0 *and* X_1 *are also* $(\alpha+\beta, 2^{\alpha}\cdot\delta)$-*differentially indistinguishable for* $\mathcal{A}$ *and any* (α,β)-*bounded weak source over* $\{0,1\}^n$.

Proof. We show the theorem by first proving a technical lemma about bounded weak distributions: Even though an (α,β)-bounded weak distribution is not negligibly close to a uniform distribution, the parameters α and β give a bound on the discrepancy between the uniform distribution and the bounded weak distribution.

Lemma 1. *Let* $\{D_n\}_{n\in\mathbb{N}}$ *be an* (α,β)-*bounded weak source over* $\{0,1\}^n$ *and let* $\{U_n\}_{n\in\mathbb{N}}$ *be a family of uniform sources over* $\{0,1\}^n$. *For all probabilistic machines* A, *for all* $k\in\mathbb{N}$ *and for all possible outputs* x *of* A,

$$\Pr\left[\mathsf{A}(1^k, D_n) = x\right] \leq 2^{\alpha}\Pr\left[\mathsf{A}(1^k, U_n) = x\right] \qquad (a)$$

and $\quad\Pr\left[\mathsf{A}(1^k, U_n) = x\right] \leq 2^{\beta}\Pr\left[\mathsf{A}(1^k, D_n) = x\right].\qquad (b)$

Proof. Let $\{D_n\}_{n\in\mathbb{N}}$ be an (α,β)-bounded weak distribution over $\{0,1\}^n$. By Definition 2, D_n has min-entropy at least $n-\alpha$ and max-entropy at most $n+\beta$. We start with (a). For all values $r_0 \in \{0,1\}^n$,

$$\log\left(\frac{\Pr[D_n = r_0]}{\Pr[U_n = r_0]}\right) = \log\left(\Pr[D_n = r_0]\right) - \log\left(2^{-n}\right)$$

$$\leq -\min_{y\in\{0,1\}^n}\left(-\log\left(\Pr[D_n = y]\right)\right) - \log\left(2^{-n}\right)$$

$$\leq -(n-\alpha) + n = \alpha.$$

Using this inequality we can show (a) as follows. For all possible outputs x of A,

$$\Pr\left[\mathsf{A}(1^k, D_n) = x\right] = \sum_{r_0\in\{0,1\}^n}\Pr\left[\mathsf{A}(1^k, r_0) = x\right]\Pr[D_n = r_0]$$

$$\leq \sum_{r_0\in\{0,1\}^n}\Pr\left[\mathsf{A}(1^k, r_0) = x\right]\cdot 2^{\alpha}\cdot\Pr[U_n = r_0]$$

$$\leq 2^{\alpha}\Pr\left[\mathsf{A}(1^k, U_n) = x\right].$$

This shows (a). For (b), note that for all values $r_0 \in \{0,1\}^n$, the probability $\Pr[D_n = r_0]$ is strictly larger than zero because $\beta < \infty$. For all values $r_0 \in \{0,1\}^n$,

$$\log\left(\frac{\Pr[U_n = r_0]}{\Pr[D_n = r_0]}\right) = \log\left(2^{-n}\right) - \log\left(\Pr[D_n = r_0]\right)$$

$$\leq \log\left(2^{-n}\right) + \max_{y\in\{0,1\}^n}\left(-\log\left(\Pr[D_n = y]\right)\right)$$

$$\leq -n + (n+\beta) = \beta.$$

Using this equation we can show (b) as follows. For all possible outputs x of A,

$$\Pr\left[\mathsf{A}(1^k, U_n) = x\right] = \sum_{r_0 \in \{0,1\}^n} \Pr\left[\mathsf{A}(1^k, r_0) = x\right] \Pr\left[U_n = r_0\right]$$

$$\leq \sum_{r_0 \in \{0,1\}^n} \Pr\left[\mathsf{A}(1^k, r_0) = x\right] \cdot 2^\beta \cdot \Pr\left[D_n = r_0\right]$$

$$\leq 2^\beta \Pr\left[\mathsf{A}(1^k, D_n) = x\right].$$

This completes the proof of Lemma 1.   □

Now we use the lemma to prove our main theorem. Let $\{D_n\}_{n \in \mathbb{N}}$ be an (α, β)-bounded weak source, and $\{U_n\}_{n \in \mathbb{N}}$ be the uniform source, both over $\{0,1\}^n$. Furthermore, let X_0, X_1 be probabilistic (not necessarily polynomially bounded) machines, and let $\mathsf{A} \in \mathcal{A}$ be an adversary machine such that for a function δ,

$$\Pr\left[\langle\mathsf{A}(1^k)|\mathsf{X}_0(1^k, U_n)\rangle = x\right] \leq \Pr\left[\langle\mathsf{A}(1^k)|\mathsf{X}_1(1^k, U_n)\rangle = x\right] + \delta.$$

Using Lemma 1, we show that A behaves similarly on D_n, as otherwise a machine that simulates $\langle\mathsf{A}(1^k)|\mathsf{X}_0(1^k, r)\rangle$ (or $\langle\mathsf{A}(1^k)|\mathsf{X}_1(1^k, r)\rangle$) could distinguish $\{D_n\}_{n \in \mathbb{N}}$ and $\{U_n\}_{n \in \mathbb{N}}$.

$$\Pr\left[\langle\mathsf{A}(1^k)|\mathsf{X}_0(1^k, D_n)\rangle = x\right] \leq 2^\alpha \Pr\left[\langle\mathsf{A}(1^k)|\mathsf{X}_0(1^k, U_n)\rangle = x\right] \tag{1}$$

$$\leq 2^\alpha \Pr\left[\langle\mathsf{A}(1^k)|\mathsf{X}_1(1^k, U_n)\rangle = x\right] + 2^\alpha \cdot \delta \tag{2}$$

$$\leq 2^{\alpha+\beta} \Pr\left[\langle\mathsf{A}(1^k)|\mathsf{X}_1(1^k, D_n)\rangle = x\right] + 2^\alpha \cdot \delta \tag{3}$$

Here, inequalities (1) and (3) follow from inequalities (a) and (b) in Lemma 1, respectively. The remaining inequality (2) holds by assumption.   □

Recall that every (n, γ)-SV block source over $\{0,1\}^{tn}$ (Definition 3) is an (α, β)-bounded weak source where $\alpha = t \cdot \log(1 + \gamma)$ and $\beta = -t \cdot \log(1 - \gamma)$. With $\gamma < 1/2$, it holds that $\beta \leq 2t\gamma$ and $\alpha \leq 2t\gamma$. Thus, we can instantiate Theorem 1 for SV block sources as follows:

Corollary 1. *If two probabilistic machines X_0 and X_1 are δ-indistinguishable for a class of probabilistic machines $\mathcal{A}$ and the family of uniform sources $\{U_{nt}\}_{nt \in \mathbb{N}}$ over $\{0,1\}^{nt}$, then X_0 and X_1 are also $(\varepsilon, 2^\varepsilon \delta)$-differentially indistinguishable for $\mathcal{A}$ and any family of (n, γ)-SV block sources $\{D_{nt}\}_{nt \in \mathbb{N}}$ over $\{0,1\}^{tn}$ with $\gamma \leq \frac{1}{2}$, where $\varepsilon = \gamma \cdot 4t$.*

Remark 2. Lemma 1 can also be interesting for sources with unbounded max-entropy. In this case, β is infinitely large and consequently, inequality (b) does not yield interesting guarantees anymore. However, for restricting undesirable events that are not based on indistinguishability, inequality (a) suffices, which is in line with the results of Dodis and Yu [18]. We refer to Appendix B for a discussion.

3.2   Computational Differential Indistinguishability Guarantees

In the computational setting where adversaries are ppt machines, we can achieve a stronger result: If we rely on a pseudorandom generator (PRG), we can expand a short seed from a randomness source to polynomially many bits of pseudorandomness. This well-known property is especially interesting here, as it allows us to apply Theorem 1 in a much broader form: Virtually every classically secure protocol is differentially secure when only a short random seed has been drawn from a bounded weak source and then expanded via a PRG, as this puts a limit on the entropy loss imposed by the actual bounded weak source. We formalize this observation in the following corollary, which is central to our work.

Corollary 2. *If two probabilistic machines* X_0 *and* X_1 *are computationally indistinguishable for a class of ppt machines* $\mathcal{A}$ *and uniform randomness, then* X_0 *and* X_1 *are also* $(\alpha + \beta, 2^\alpha \cdot \delta)$-*differentially indistinguishable for* $\mathcal{A}$ *and for a negligible function* δ, *if they draw their randomness from a PRG that is seeded with a* (α, β)-*bounded weak source.*

The corollary also gives guarantees for protocols and security proofs in which the amount of necessary randomness can be influenced by the adversary, e.g., by sending requests to the machine.

4   Application to Cryptography

We apply differential indistinguishability to a common secrecy definition, namely indistinguishability under chosen ciphertext attacks for public-key encryption. This definition serves as example for how to instantiate the notion and how to apply our main results to quantify the secrecy loss under imperfect randomness.

Moreover, we analyze differential indistinguishability under composition. We obtain a general composability result for differential indistinguishability that comes, similar to the composability of differential privacy, with a loss of secrecy. We refer to the full version [3] for a discussion about additional examples (commitment schemes and zero-knowledge proofs).

4.1   Public-Key Encryption

For PKE, standard security definitions, e.g., *indistinguishability under adaptive chosen ciphertext attack* (IND-CCA) [21] can naturally be relaxed to use differential indistinguishability instead of traditional indistinguishability.

Definition 5. $((\varepsilon, \delta)$-DIF-IND-CCA). *A pair* A $=$ (A_0, A_1) *of ppt oracle machines is an* IND-CCA *adversary if* A_0 *outputs two messages* x_0, x_1 *of the same length together with a state* s, A_1 *outputs a bit, and both* A_0 *and* A_1 *have access to decryption oracles as defined below. A PKE scheme* $\mathcal{E} = (\mathsf{Gen}, \mathsf{Enc}, \mathsf{Dec})$ *has* (ε, δ) -*differentially indistinguishable encryptions under adaptive chosen ciphertext attack for a randomness source* $\{D_n\}_{n \in \mathbb{N}}$ *if for all* IND-CCA *adversaries* *and for all sufficiently large k and bitstrings z of polynomial length in k, it holds that* $\Pr\left[\mathsf{P}_{k,z}^{(0)} = 1\right] \leq 2^{\varepsilon} \Pr\left[\mathsf{P}_{k,z}^{(1)} = 1\right] + \delta$, *where $P_{k,z}^{(i)}$ is defined as:*

$$\mathsf{P}_{k,z}^{(i)} := (e,d) \leftarrow \mathsf{Gen}(1^k); \quad ((x_0, x_1),) \leftarrow \mathsf{A}_0^{\mathsf{Dec}(d,\cdot)}(1^k, e, z)$$
$$c \leftarrow \mathsf{Enc}(e, x_i; D_n); \quad \text{output } \mathsf{A}_1^{\mathsf{Dec}_c(d,\cdot)}(1^k, , c)$$

Here, $\mathsf{Dec}_c(d, \cdot)$ *denotes a decryption oracle that answers on all ciphertexts except for c, where it returns an error symbol $\bot$. The randomness used by the encryption algorithm* Enc *is drawn from D_n.*

Note that $(0, \delta)$-DIF-IND-CCA security is equivalent to traditional δ-IND-CCA security.

Encryption with Imperfect Randomness. Both the encryption algorithm and the key generation algorithm require randomness. Dodis and Yu [18] show that even if weak sources are used for the key generation of IND-CCA secure encryption schemes, the security is preserved. However, this result does not apply when imperfect randomness is used by the *encryption algorithm*. The next theorem, an application of Theorem 1, quantifies the secrecy loss whenever the encryption algorithm has only access to an (α, β)-bounded weak source.

Theorem 2. *Let $\mathcal{E} = (\mathsf{Gen}, \mathsf{Enc}, \mathsf{Dec})$ be any PKE scheme that is δ-IND-CCA secure under the assumption that Enc consumes at most n bits of uniform randomness. Then $\mathcal{E}$ is $(\alpha + \beta, 2^{\alpha}\delta)$-DIF-IND-CCA secure if Enc uses an (α, β)-bounded weak source $\{D_n\}_{n \in \mathbb{N}}$ instead of a uniform source.*

We refer to Appendix A.1 for a proof.

Discussion. Theorem 2 enables us to provide meaningful guarantees if an IND-CCA secure encryption scheme relies on imperfect randomness, as long as the randomness used to encrypt the ciphertext in question is drawn from a bounded weak source. If an encryption scheme is (ε, δ)-DIF-IND-CCA secure, the adversary may learn that the probability that a ciphertext contains a particular message m_0 is 2^{ε} times higher than the probability that it contains another message m_1. However, if ε is reasonably small, e.g., $\varepsilon = 0.001$ (and thus $2^{\varepsilon} \approx 1.001$), both m_0 and m_1 are a plausible content of the ciphertext. In particular, the adversary cannot reasonably believe or even convince a third party that m_0 is the value that has been encrypted. Moreover, the encryptor retains (a weak form of) deniability: She could indeed have encrypted any message.

Imperfect Randomness in Both Key Generation and Encryption. Our results also enable us to give a differential indistinguishability guarantee in the case when both the key generation algorithm Gen and the encryption algorithm Enc make use of a bounded weak source. If a PRG was used, seeded by a bounded weak random source, then we can immediately apply Corollary 2 to derive a differential indistinguishability guarantee. In contrast to the result of Dodis and Yu that requires the encryption scheme to be simulatable as defined by [18], which excludes, e.g., stateful schemes, we do not require any such structural property of the scheme.[5] If, for some reason, no PRG was used, one can still apply Theorem 1, but this will naturally yield weaker guarantees, as the combined randomness of Gen and Enc needs to be taken into account (and moreover the security loss under composition is significant, as discussed below).

Multiple Encryptions. Theorem 2 states a guarantee only for a single encryption (namely the encryption of one challenge message). However, it can be extended to the encryption of a message vector. In particular, if a PRG is used (and thus the amount of bounded weak randomness is limited to the seed of the PRG), Corollary 2 yields immediately a differential indistinguishability guarantee with ε being independent of the number of encrypted messages. If however, the encryption algorithm Enc is run several times with (fresh) imperfect randomness, the entropy loss of the randomness can increase linearly in the number of messages in the vector for SV block sources, and consequently, ε increases significantly.

Other Security Definitions. Although we focus on IND-CCA security for PKE in this section, the broad applicability of Theorem 1 allows to handle other security definitions such as *indistinguishability under chosen plaintext attack* (IND-CPA) similarly.

4.2 Composability

Traditional indistinguishability with a negligible function δ and $\varepsilon = 0$ allows for polynomially many compositions, because a polynomial factor for the advantage of an adversary, which might come from seeing multiple samples, does not help the adversary substantially (the advantage remains negligible). This is not true for differential indistinguishability in general, because the (non-negligible) multiplicative factors can, under certain conditions, be accumulated as well.

For individual users we have shown that sequential composition of one or more primitives is possible without an (additional) loss of secrecy if a PRG is used (Corollary 2). If, however, several users within a protocol use imperfect randomness, the secrecy can degrade. Interestingly, we can give a bound on the loss of secrecy that is similar to the composition that occurs for differential privacy. We formulate a general composition lemma that we can instantiate to cope with several situations.

Lemma 2. *Let $\mathcal{A}$ be a class of adversaries. If X_0 and X_1 are (ε, δ)-differentially indistinguishable for $\mathcal{A}$, and X_1 and X_2 are (ε', δ')-differentially indistinguishable for $\mathcal{A}$, then X_0 and X_2 are $(\varepsilon'', \delta'')$-differentially indistinguishable for $\mathcal{A}$ where $\varepsilon'' = \varepsilon + \varepsilon'$ and $\delta'' = 2^{\varepsilon'}\delta + 2^{\varepsilon}\delta'$.*

We refer to Appendix A.2 for a proof.

A direct application of the lemma is the above described scenario in which multiple users (sequentially or concurrently) contribute to a protocol and use

---

[5] We discuss simulatability as well as the relation between our result and the result by Dodis and Yu [18] in Sect. 5.2.

bad randomness. In this case, the machine X_1 can express an intermediate scenario that is used in a straightforward hybrid argument, where for two users X_1 is the only hybrid. Moreover, the lemma is applicable to scenarios where an individual user draws from a random source several times (for several primitives or protocols) instead of using a PRG, and also to compositions of differential indistinguishability guarantees in information-theoretical settings, where a PRG cannot be employed in the first place.

5   Interpretation and Analysis

In this section, we analyze and interpret the security guarantees provided by differential indistinguishability. In particular, we study the impact of a multiplication factor, and the influence of min- and max-entropy on differential indistinguishability. Furthermore, we discuss the relation between differential indistinguishability and differential privacy.

5.1   Impact of a Multiplicative Factor

Similar to differential privacy, differential indistinguishability adds a multiplicative factor to the inequality used in the traditional indistinguishability notion. We observe that a multiplicative bound may express properties that are inexpressible by an additive bound. While every multiplicative bound of the form $\Pr[A] \le 2^\varepsilon \Pr[B] + \delta$ implies a purely additive bound $\Pr[A] \le \Pr[B] + \delta + 2^\varepsilon - 1 \approx \Pr[B] + \delta + \varepsilon$, the converse does not hold in general. No matter which additive bound can be shown between two probabilistic events, there does not necessarily exist a multiplicative bound. In particular, there are machines that are δ-indistinguishable for some δ but not (ε, δ')-indistinguishable for any ε such that $\delta' < \delta$. We refer to Appendix A.3 for a formal counterexample.

For secrecy properties, traditional indistinguishability intuitively states that no adversary can learn any information about the secret, except with negligible probability. The multiplicative factor generalizes indistinguishability to additionally allow the adversary to learn information about the secret with more than a negligible probability, as long as the loss of secrecy is bounded; e.g., if ε is a small constant, then differential indistinguishability ensures that the owner of the secret retains deniability by introducing doubt for the adversary.

Besides differential privacy, a multiplicative factor has also been used to achieve a specialized relaxation of semantic security in the presence of efficient adversaries that may tamper with an SV source [1, App B.4], and additionally for a security analysis of anonymous communication protocols [2].

Example. Let us assume that Alice participates in an e-voting protocol based on, e.g., a commitment scheme. If the random source that she uses to seed her PRG turns out to be an (α, β)-bounded weak source, the commitments are still ε -*differentially hiding* (see the full version [3] for a formal definition), where $\varepsilon = \alpha + \beta$ is a small constant. Assume that Alice can vote for one of two popular candidates, say, Bob and Charlie, and she chooses to vote for Bob. In the traditional indistinguishability case, a non-negligible additive difference in the guarantee could result from a non-negligible probability of leaking the vote, which is highly unsatisfactory. The multiplicative factor 2^ε, however, allows us to guarantee that both cases will still maintain non-zero probability and no distinguisher can be sure whether Alice voted for Bob or for Charlie. Consider a distinguisher that only outputs, say '1' if it is certain that the vote was cast for Bob, and '0' in all other cases. Such a distinguisher is affected by the multiplicative bound as the output '1' is almost equally probable in all cases. Moreover, if the probability of outputting '1' is zero when the vote was cast for Charlie, then differential indistinguishability implies that the probability of outputting '1' is zero when the vote was cast for Bob.

Notice that the same analysis applies if a negligible additive value $\delta \neq 0$ is present. In this case, there might be a negligible chance for the adversary to be certain about the vote, but in all other cases, deniability is preserved.

5.2   Influence of Min- and Max-Entropy

The literature on imperfect randomness has focused on "weak (entropy) sources" (called α-weak sources in this paper), because a non-trivial amount of min-entropy suffices for many applications. It is known to be sufficient to achieve unpredictability-based definitions, i.e., security notions in which the adversary has to guess a whole bitstring, e.g., the *binding* property of commitments and *unforgeability* of signatures and message authentication codes [13,15,28] (see also Appendix B).

Recently, Dodis and Yu [18] have extended this result significantly by showing that if such an unpredictability game can be considered a part of an indistinguishability game (e.g., for an encryption scheme with a weakly generated key) and if a *simulatability* condition proposed by the authors holds, then min-entropy also suffices for the indistinguishability game. In particular, they consider a primitive that can be divided into a setup phase (generating setup elements such as a key pair) and a simulatable (i.e., stateless and repeatable) indistinguishability game phase. They show that indistinguishability for such a primitive that can be preserved despite the setup phase (but not the game phase!) employing an α-weak source instead of uniform randomness. Here, the security notion under consideration is indeed divided. The setup phase has some, usually not explicitly specified, unpredictability notion (e.g., no adversary must be able to guess a correct key), and a corresponding game. Nevertheless, due to the impossibility result by Dodis et al. [15], whenever only min-entropy is ensured, a secrecy guarantee cannot be achieved in general, but only for certain schemes and under certain conditions. We discuss this in detail for public-key encryption in Sect. 4.1.

If, however, the randomness source has additionally a bounded max-entropy (and thus, among other properties, a full support), generic results are possible. In particular, a differential secrecy guarantee is still possible for a secrecy notion that is not simulatable (as defined by Dodis and Yu [18]), when an (α, β)-bounded weak source is used for generating the key. More importantly, such a differential guarantee is achievable when bounded weak randomness is used by the encryption algorithm itself.

Interestingly, max-entropy on its own is not sufficient for giving meaningful guarantees. If only the max-entropy of a source is bounded, the source could still output one individual element with a very high probability such that the probability over the other elements is evenly distributed. Therefore, we require both min-entropy and max-entropy measures for giving reasonable quantitative guarantees in all cases for which none of the specialized (e.g., unpredictability-based) solutions is applicable.

5.3   Relation to Differential Privacy and Sensitivity

Differential privacy [19] quantifies the privacy provided by database query mechanisms: Intuitively, differential privacy requires that the output of a query mechanism should not allow to distinguish similar databases better than with a small multiplicative factor. Both in terms of the definition and in terms of the small but usually non-negligible multiplicative factor, differential privacy and differential indistinguishability are closely related. We find this relation to be helpful for interpreting the guarantees and for understanding the drawbacks of differential indistinguishability. Differential privacy is influenced by the *sensitivity* of a statistical query, i.e., the amount of influence individual database records can have on the output of the query. Typical differential private mechanisms sanitize their output by adding random noise to guarantee a certain ε-level of privacy; the amount of added noise directly depends on the sensitivity.

Although there are neither databases nor the concept of utility (in the same sense as in differential privacy) in our setting, the fact that a bounded weak source is differentially indistinguishable from a uniform source is analogous to the differential privacy of a query mechanism. From this point of view, the missing entropy of the weak source corresponds to the sensitivity in differential privacy.

This relation between sensitivity and entropy is interesting for sources that can be analyzed in a block-by-block manner, e.g., (n, γ)-SV sources. For such a source the entropy loss and thus the "sensitivity" is directly associated with the parameter γ and the amount of blocks that are drawn from this source. The higher the sensitivity, i.e., the more randomness is drawn by honest parties, the smaller γ must be to allow for guaranteeing ε-differential indistinguishability for a given value of ε. Clearly, the bias and thus the entropy loss in a $(1, \gamma)$-SV source can be arbitrarily increased, e.g., by drawing more random bits and taking the majority vote over them. Although this amplification does not make a difference for uniform randomness, it may increase the bias of the bits for SV sources. Therefore, for SV sources, the amount of randomness is a necessary parameter that influences the security.

6   Related Work

The effect of imperfect randomness on traditional cryptography is well-studied. On the negative side, several papers demonstrate the inherent limitations of indistinguishability-based cryptographic guarantees with imperfect randomness [1,7,15,16]. Remarkably, Dodis et al. [15] show that traditional indistinguishability required for encryption, commitments, secret sharing, and zero-knowledge cannot be realized if a bounded weak source is used, which constitutes the main motivation for our work. More precisely, they prove that no protocol for any of these primitives can be secure against certain block sources, which include bounded weak sources. These sources sample blocks (i.e., several bits at once) that are $1/poly(k)$ close to the uniform distribution [11,15,32] for an arbitrary polynomial, where k is the security parameter.

This impossibility result has been refined and generalized over the last few years. Bosley and Dodis [7] show that information-theoretically secure encryption of more than $\log(n)$ bits is possible only if more than $\log(n)$ almost-uniform bits can be extracted from the source in the first place. In the universal composability (UC) setting [9], Canetti, Pass, and Shelat [10] show that even for (sampleable) sources for which a deterministic extractor exists, UC-secure commitments are not possible. Austrin et. al. [1] refined the impossibility result by Dodis et. al. [15] to show that it holds even when the adversary that tampers with the SV source is required to be efficient. Recently, Dodis and Yao [17] proposed a novel classification of random sources that groups them into "separable" and "expressive" sources. They apply their notions to rule out even one-bit encryption, commitment, and zero-knowledge proofs for many weak sources.

On the positive side, one line of research examines the extraction of (almost) perfect randomness from several kinds of imperfect randomness sources [6,11, 12,26,33,34]. However, extraction generally requires the source to have a certain degree of independence, whereas the only main requirement for bounded weak sources is to provide some entropy.

Aiming at particular applications, it has been shown that a few primitives can be securely instantiated even if only imperfect randomness is available [1,14,25], e.g., signatures [15] and Byzantine agreement [22].

Dodis et al. [14] prove that differential privacy of statistical queries can be preserved even when the noise is generated using an imperfect random source. In particular, they ask whether differential privacy is possible if no uniform randomness is available, and give a positive answer for SV sources by presenting a γ-differentially private algorithm that works on these sources. Relevant to our observations, they note that traditional indistinguishability-based privacy is a stronger notion as compared to, e.g., unforgeability.

A multiplicative factor as in this work has also been used to achieve a specialized relaxation of semantic security in the presence of efficient adversaries that may tamper with an SV source [1, App. B.4]. Moreover, such a factor has proven useful for a security analysis of anonymous communication protocols [2].

Most closely related to our work, Dodis and Yu [18] show that for all unpredictability-based primitives as well as for a class of restricted indistinguishability-based primitives, randomness sources with high min-entropy suffice to guarantee security whenever a uniform random source already guarantees security. While this is related to our result for unpredictability-based primitives (Corollary 3), Dodis and Yu establish a traditional indistinguishability guarantee (i.e., $\varepsilon = 0$) for a restricted class of indistinguishability-based primitives under weaker assumptions on the randomness source, clearly surpassing our results in these cases. However, the imposed gray-box requirements on indistinguishability games rule out many common and interesting cases. In particular, their analysis applies only to scenarios in which imperfect randomness is used at the beginning of a game, i.e., typically as input to a key generation algorithm. This leads to the observation that, e.g., for encryption, their result is restricted to imperfectly generated keys, and does not take care of the case where the *encryption algorithm* has access only to imperfect randomness.[6] In contrast, while our method provides only a differential guarantee, it is capable of obliviously analyzing essentially all indistinguishability games that make use of imperfect randomness, without imposing restrictions on the usage of this imperfect randomness. We refer to Sect. 5.2 for a more thorough analysis of our requirements on randomness and the possible results.

Kamara and Katz [25] propose a notion of security for symmetric-key encryption that is able to cope with imperfect randomness. However, their notion applies only if the challenge messages are encrypted using uniform randomness. While we consider their approach orthogonal to ours, it turns out that a combination with our approach is possible. In the public-key setting, Bellare et al. [5] define and realize the notion of hedged public-key encryption, which provides secrecy guarantees even in the case of randomness failures, as long as the encrypted *message* has enough entropy.

7   Future Directions

Our work presents a novel view on the relation between weak randomness and indistinguishability, and it naturally leads to many more interesting questions.

From a theoretical point of view, we can ask whether it can be used in more scenarios such as for leakage-resilient cryptography [8,20]. In particular, is it possible to give differential guarantees in cases where the adversary learns more than allowed by existing leakage-resilient schemes?

On the practical side, a natural next step is to apply our results to real applications and to random sources that are used in practice: Can we use entropy measurements of real randomness generators (both hardware generators and software generators) together with differential indistinguishability to give cryptographic guarantees?

Acknowledgments. We would like to thank Jalaj Upadhyay for insightful discussions about randomness sources and differential privacy. This work was supported by the German Ministry for Education and Research (BMBF) through funding for the Center

---

[6] We note that this restriction cannot be circumvented by storing enough imperfect randomness at the beginning of the game in order to use it later during encryption. This approach would require the challenger to remember what parts of the stored randomness have already been used, which is implicitly excluded in [18]. We refer to Sect. 4.1 for a discussion.

for IT-Security, Privacy and Accountability (CISPA) and the German Universities Excellence Initiative.

A   Postponed Proofs

A.1   Proof of Theorem 2 (Public-Key Encryption)

Proof. Let $\mathcal{E} = (\mathsf{Gen}, \mathsf{Enc}, \mathsf{Dec})$ be a public-key encryption scheme, let $\mathcal{A}_{ppt}$ be the class of ppt machines, and let $\{D_n\}_{n \in \mathbb{N}}$ be an (α, β)-bounded weak source. To simplify the notation we write $P_{k,z}^{(b,r)}$ for simulating $P_{k,z}^{(b)}$ and using $r \in \{0,1\}^n$ as the randomness for Enc. Let $\mathsf{X}_0(1^k, r) := P_{k,z}^{(0,r)}$ and $\mathsf{X}_1 := P_{k,z}^{(1,r)}$ with the modification that X_0 and X_1 additionally provide a decryption oracle (as defined in Definition 5) to the adversary. Observe that by our definition of X_0 and X_1, the following two statements hold:

(i) $\mathsf{X}_0(1^k, U_n)$ and $\mathsf{X}_1(1^k, U_n)$ are indistinguishable for the class $\mathcal{A}_{ppt}$ of adversaries if and only if $\mathcal{E}$ is IND-CCA.
(ii) $\mathsf{X}_0(1^k, D_n)$ and $\mathsf{X}_1(1^k, D_n)$ are (ε, δ)-differential indistinguishability for the class $\mathcal{A}_{ppt}$ of adversaries if and only if $\mathcal{E}$ is (ε, δ)-DIF-IND-CCA for $\{D_n\}_{n \in \mathbb{N}}$.

Thus, the claim follows immediately from Theorem 1.   □

A.2   Proof of Lemma 2 (General Composition)

Proof. Given any adversary $\mathsf{A} \in \mathcal{A}$, for sufficiently large k and every possible output x of A, applying the definition of differential indistinguishability for X_0 and X_1 as well as X_1 and X_2 yields

$$\begin{aligned}
\Pr\left[\langle\mathsf{A}(1^k)|\mathsf{X}_0(1^k)\rangle = x\right] &\leq 2^\varepsilon \Pr\left[\langle\mathsf{A}(1^k)|\mathsf{X}_1(1^k)\rangle = x\right] + \delta \\
&\leq 2^\varepsilon(2^{\varepsilon'} \Pr\left[\langle\mathsf{A}(1^k|\mathsf{X}_2(1^k)\rangle = x\right] + \delta') + \delta \\
&\leq 2^{\varepsilon+\varepsilon'} \Pr\left[\langle\mathsf{A}(1^k)|\mathsf{X}_2(1^k)\rangle = x\right] + 2^\varepsilon\delta + 2^\varepsilon\delta'.
\end{aligned}$$

Symmetrically, we obtain the opposite bound

$$\Pr\left[\langle\mathsf{A}(1^k)|\mathsf{X}_2(1^k)\rangle = x\right] \leq 2^{\varepsilon'+\varepsilon} \Pr\left[\langle\mathsf{A}(1^k)|\mathsf{X}_0(1^k)\rangle = x\right] + 2^\varepsilon\delta' + 2^{\varepsilon'}\delta. \quad □$$

A.3   On Additive and Multiplicative Bounds (Sect. 5.1)

Given any arbitrary function δ with $1 \geq \delta_k > 0$, we construct a commitment scheme $\mathcal{C}$ such that for every adversary there is an additive bound of δ ($\mathcal{C}$ is δ-hiding), but there is no pair (ε, δ') with $\delta'_k < \delta_k$ (for sufficiently large k) such that $\mathcal{C}$ is (ε, δ')-differentially hiding. No matter which additive bound can be shown between two probabilistic events, there does not necessarily exist a non-trivial multiplicative bound, i.e., a multiplicative bound that could be used to improve on the additive bound.

Proof. Let $\mathcal{C}_{IT}$ be an information-theoretically hiding commitment scheme. We construct $\mathcal{C} = (\mathsf{S}, \mathsf{R})$ from $\mathcal{C}_{IT}$ as follows. For security parameter k, $\mathcal{C}$ behaves like $\mathcal{C}_{IT}$ but with probability δ_k, the algorithm S additionally leaks the message. Clearly the scheme is δ-hiding. Consider the distinguisher A that sends two messages m_0, m_1 to the challenger for the hiding game. Only if S leaks m_0, A outputs 0. In all other cases, A outputs 1. Let $\varepsilon \geq 0$ and δ be functions with $\delta'_k < \delta_k$ for sufficiently large k. For such k,

$$\Pr\left[\langle \mathsf{A}(1^k)|\mathsf{S}(1^k, m_0)\rangle = 0\right] = \delta > \delta' = 2^\varepsilon 0 + \delta'$$
$$= 2^\varepsilon \Pr\left[\langle \mathsf{A}(1^k)|\mathsf{S}(1^k, m_1)\rangle = 0\right] + \delta'.$$

Consequently, $\mathcal{C}$ is not (ε, δ')-differentially hiding. □

B   Unpredictability

So far we only considered the effect of (bounded) weak randomness on cryptographic indistinguishability notions. The security games for notions such as the *binding* property of commitments, *unforgeability* of signatures and message authentication codes, or guessing the key of an encryption scheme do not require indistinguishability. Instead, the adversary typically has to predict a particular bitstring, which should only be possible with negligible probability. It is well-known that such unpredictability (or unbreakability) notions are achievable even if an α-weak source is employed [13,15,18,28].

We further analyze how imperfect randomness influences the probability for guessing a whole bitstring, e.g., for breaking the binding property of a commitment. The corresponding security definitions typically require that no adversary has more than a negligible chance to reach a certain bad event. We generalize the intuition of *breaking a scheme* by dividing a game Z into two parts. The "normal game" Z_0 and a judge Z_1 that decides whether or not a given string constitutes a break of the scheme. Technically, the output of an adversary A in interaction with Z_0 is fed into Z_1, which finally outputs a bit $b \in \{0,1\}$ indicating whether the adversary has won.

Definition 6 (Unpredictability). *Let $\mathsf{Z} = (\mathsf{Z}_0, \mathsf{Z}_1)$ be a probabilistic machine that may keep state. We say that Z is δ-unpredictable for a class $\mathcal{A}$ of adversaries and for a distribution $\{D_n\}_{n\in\mathbb{N}}$, if for all $\mathsf{A} \in \mathcal{A}$ and for sufficiently large k,*

$$\Pr\left[\mathsf{Z}_1\left(\langle \mathsf{A}(1^k)|\mathsf{Z}_0(1^k, D_n)\rangle\right) = 1\right] \leq \delta.$$

We show that for all games that can be described as a unpredictability game and for which the probability to win is negligible under uniform randomness, the probability is still negligible if an α-weak source is used. Similar to our comments in Remark 2, we notice that min-entropy suffices for this result.

Corollary 3. *If a probabilistic machine $\mathsf{Z} = (\mathsf{Z}_0, \mathsf{Z}_1)$ that may keep state is δ-unpredictable for a class of probabilistic machines $\mathcal{A}$ and consumes at most n bits of uniform randomness, then Z is $(2^\alpha \delta)$-unpredictable for $\mathcal{A}$ for any α-weak source $\{D_n\}_{n\in\mathbb{N}}$.*

Proof. We reduce this corollary to Lemma 1 as follows: Let $Z = (Z_0, Z_1)$ be a probabilistic (not necessarily polynomially bounded) machine that may keep state. Given any adversary $A \in \mathcal{A}$, we construct a probabilistic machine B on input $r \in \{0,1\}^n$ as follows. B simulates the interaction between A and $Z_0(1^k, r)$, yields an output a and simulates Z_1 on a. If Z_0 keeps state for Z_1, B also simulates this behavior. It holds that

$$\Pr\left[Z_1(a) = 1 \mid a \leftarrow \langle A(1^k)|Z_0(1^k, D_n)\rangle\right] \tag{B.1}$$

$$= \Pr\left[B(1^k, D_n) = 1\right] \leq 2^\alpha \Pr\left[B(1^k, U_n) = 1\right] \tag{B.2}$$

$$= 2^\alpha \Pr\left[Z_1(a) = 1 \mid a \leftarrow \langle A(1^k)|Z_0(1^k, U_n)\rangle\right] \leq 2^\alpha \delta. \tag{B.3}$$

Inequality (B.2) follows from Lemma 1 and inequality (B.3) holds by assumption. $\square$

References

1. Austrin, P., Chung, K.-M., Mahmoody, M., Pass, R., Seth, K.: On the impossibility of cryptography with tamperable randomness. In: Garay, J.A., Gennaro, R. (eds.) CRYPTO 2014, Part I. LNCS, vol. 8616, pp. 462–479. Springer, Heidelberg (2014)
2. M. Backes, A. Kate, P. Manoharan, S. Meiser, and E. Mohammadi. AnoA: A framework for analyzing anonymous communication protocols. In Proc. of the 26th Computer Security Foundations Symposium (CSF'13), pages 163–178. IEEE, 2013
3. Backes, M., Kate, A., Meiser, S., Ruffing, T.: Secrecy without perfect randomness: Cryptography with (bounded) weak sources. IACR Cryptology ePrint Archive, Report (2015). 2013/808. Technical report (full version of this paper)
4. Bellare, M.: A note on negligible functions. J. Cryptology **15**(4), 271 (2002)
5. Bellare, M., Brakerski, Z., Naor, M., Ristenpart, T., Segev, G., Shacham, H., Yilek, S.: Hedged public-key encryption: how to protect against bad randomness. In: Matsui, M. (ed.) ASIACRYPT 2009. LNCS, vol. 5912, pp. 232–249. Springer, Heidelberg (2009)
6. Bennett, C.H., Brassard, G., Robert, J.-M.: Privacy amplification by public discussion. SIAM J. Comput. **17**(2), 210–229 (1988)
7. Bosley, C., Dodis, Y.: Does privacy require true randomness? In: Vadhan, S.P. (ed.) TCC 2007. LNCS, vol. 4392, pp. 1–20. Springer, Heidelberg (2007)
8. Brakerski, Z., Kalai, Y.T., Katz, J., Vaikuntanathan, V.: Overcoming the hole in the bucket: Public-key cryptography resilient to continual memory leakage. In: Proceedings of the 51st Symposium on Foundations of Computer Science (FOCS 2010), pp. 501–510. IEEE (2010)
9. Canetti, R.: Universally composable security: A new paradigm for cryptographic protocols. In:1 Proceedings of the 42nd Symposium on Foundations of Computer Science (FOCS 2001), pp. 36–145. IEEE (2001)
10. R. Canetti, R. Pass, and A. Shelat. Cryptography from sunspots: How to use an imperfect reference string. In Proc. of the 48th Symposium on Foundations of Computer Science (FOCS'07), pages 249–259. IEEE, 2007
11. Chor, B., Goldreich O.: UN Based bits from sources of weak randomness and probabilistic communication complexity. In: Proceedings of the 26th Symposium on Foundations of Computer Science (FOCS1985), pp. 429–442. IEEE (1985)

12. Dodis, Y., Elbaz, A., Oliveira, R., Raz, R.: Improved randomness extraction from two independent sources. In: Jansen, K., Khanna, S., Rolim, J.D.P., Ron, D. (eds.) RANDOM 2004 and APPROX 2004. LNCS, vol. 3122, pp. 334–344. Springer, Heidelberg (2004)

13. Dodis, Y., Katz, J., Reyzin, L., Smith, A.: Robust fuzzy extractors and authenticated key agreement from close secrets. In: Dwork, C. (ed.) CRYPTO 2006. LNCS, vol. 4117, pp. 232–250. Springer, Heidelberg (2006)

14. Dodis, Y., López-Alt, A., Mironov, I., Vadhan, S.: Differential privacy with imperfect randomness. In: Safavi-Naini, R., Canetti, R. (eds.) CRYPTO 2012. LNCS, vol. 7417, pp. 497–516. Springer, Heidelberg (2012)

15. Dodis, Y., Ong, S.J., Prabhakaran, M., Sahai, A.: On the (im)possibility of cryptography with imperfect randomness. In: Proceedings of the 45th Symposium on Foundations of Computer Science (FOCS 2004), pp. 196–205. IEEE (2004)

16. Dodis, Y., Pietrzak, K., Przydatek, B.: Separating sources for encryption and secret sharing. In: Halevi, S., Rabin, T. (eds.) TCC 2006. LNCS, vol. 3876, pp. 601–616. Springer, Heidelberg (2006)

17. Dodis, Y., Yao, Y.: Privacy and imperfect randomness. IACR Cryptology ePrint Archive, Report (2014). 2014/623

18. Dodis, Y., Yu, Y.: Overcoming weak expectations. In: Sahai, A. (ed.) TCC 2013. LNCS, vol. 7785, pp. 1–22. Springer, Heidelberg (2013)

19. Dwork, C., McSherry, F., Nissim, K., Smith, A.: Calibrating noise to sensitivity in private data analysis. In: Halevi, S., Rabin, T. (eds.) TCC 2006. LNCS, vol. 3876, pp. 265–284. Springer, Heidelberg (2006)

20. Dziembowski, S. Pietrzak, K.: Leakage-resilient cryptography. In: Proceedings of the 48th Symposium on Foundations of Computer Science (FOCS 2007), pp. 293–302. IEEE (2008)

21. Goldreich, O.: Foundations of Cryptography: Basic Tools. Foundations of Cryptography, vol. 1. Cambridge University Press, New York (2001)

22. Goldwasser, S., Sudan, M., Vaikuntanathan, V.: Distributed computing with imperfect randomness. In: Fraigniaud, P. (ed.) DISC 2005. LNCS, vol. 3724, pp. 288–302. Springer, Heidelberg (2005)

23. Haitner, I., Horvitz, O., Katz, J., Koo, C.-Y., Morselli, R., Shaltiel, R.: Reducing complexity assumptions for statistically-hiding commitment. In: Cramer, R. (ed.) EUROCRYPT 2005. LNCS, vol. 3494, pp. 58–77. Springer, Heidelberg (2005)

24. Kalai, Y.T., Li, X., Rao, A., Zuckerman, D.: Network extractor protocols. In: Proceedings of the 49th Symposium on Foundations of Computer Science (FOCS 2008), pp. 654–663. IEEE (2008)

25. Kamara, S., Katz, J.: How to encrypt with a malicious random number generator. In: Nyberg, K. (ed.) FSE 2008. LNCS, vol. 5086, pp. 303–315. Springer, Heidelberg (2008)

26. Kamp, J., Zuckerman, D.: Deterministic extractors for bit-fixing sources and exposure-resilient cryptography. In: Proceedings of the 44th Symposium on Foundations of Computer Science (FOCS 2003), pp. 92–101. IEEE (2003)

27. Katz, J., Lindell, Y.: Introduction to Modern Cryptography. CRC Press, Boca Raton (2007)

28. Maurer, U.M., Wolf, S.: Privacy amplification secure against active adversaries. In: Kaliski Jr, B.S. (ed.) CRYPTO 1997. LNCS, vol. 1294, pp. 307–321. Springer, Heidelberg (1997)

29. McInnes, J.L., Pinkas, B.: On the impossibility of private key cryptography with weakly random keys. In: Menezes, A., Vanstone, S.A. (eds.) CRYPTO 1990. LNCS, vol. 537, pp. 421–435. Springer, Heidelberg (1991)

30. Mironov, I., Pandey, O., Reingold, O., Vadhan, S.: Computational differential privacy. In: Halevi, S. (ed.) CRYPTO 2009. LNCS, vol. 5677, pp. 126–142. Springer, Heidelberg (2009)
31. Reingold, O., Trevisan, L.,Tulsiani, M., Vadhan, S.: Dense subsets of pseudorandom sets. In: Proceedings of the 49th Symposium on Foundations of Computer Science (FOCS'08), pp. 76–85. IEEE (2008)
32. Santha, M., Vazirani, U.V.: Generating quasi-random sequences from slightly-random sources. In: Proceedings of the 25th Symposium on Foundations of Computer Science (FOCS 1984), po. 434–440. IEE (1984)
33. Trevisan, L., Vadhan, S.: Extracting randomness from samplable distributions. In: Procedings of the 41st Symposium on Foundations of Computer Science (FOCS 2000), pp. 32–42. IEEE (2000)
34. Von Neumann, J.: Various techniques used in connection with random digits. Nat. Bur. Stand. Appl. Math. Ser. **12**, 36–38 (1951)

Author Index

Printed in the United States
by Bookmasters

Printed in the United States
By Bookmasters